The Many Worlds
of Literature

STUART HIRSCHBERG

RUTGERS: THE STATE UNIVERSITY
OF NEW JERSEY, NEWARK

Editor: Eben W. Ludlow
Production Supervisors: Ann-Marie WongSam and France Burke
Production Manager: Francesca Drago
Text and Cover Designer: Robert Freese
Cover photographs: Background—Courtesy of NASA; Clockwise from
upper left—© R. & S. Michaud/Woodfin Camp & Associates, Inc.; © Jose
Azel/Contact Press Images; © Catherine Karnow/Woodfin Camp &
Associates, Inc.; © Lindsay Hebberd/Woodfin Camp & Associates, Inc.;
© Lindsay Hebberd/Woodfin Camp & Associates, Inc.; Spine—© J.B.
Diederich/Contact Press Images
Map: Maryland Cartographics

This book was set in Palatino by Digitype, Inc.
and was printed and bound by Rand McNally.
The cover was printed by New England Book Components, Inc.

Macmillan Publishing Company
866 Third Avenue, New York, New York 10022

Macmillan Publishing Company is part of
the Maxwell Communication Group of Companies.

Maxwell Macmillan Canada, Inc.
1200 Eglinton Avenue East
Suite 200
Don Mills, Ontario M3C 3N1

Library of Congress Cataloging–in–Publication Data

Hirschberg, Stuart.
    The many worlds of literature/Stuart Hirschberg.
        p. cm.
    Includes index.
    ISBN 0-02-355082-1 (pbk.)
    1. Literature—Collections. 2. College readers. I. Title.
PN6014.H5125   1994
808—dc20   93-7886
                                                    CIP

Printing: 1 2 3 4 5 6 7   Year: 4 5 6 7 8 9 0

Acknowledgments appear on pages 1065–1073, which constitute a
continuation of the copyright page.

For my cousins, Ruth and Arnold

Preface

The Many Worlds of Literature is a global, contemporary anthology whose international and multicultural selections offer a new direction for freshman composition, introduction to literature, and contemporary world literature courses. Writers from over sixty countries are represented by 127 works of fiction, nonfiction, poetry, and drama. Approximately half the selections are by women writers. Ninety percent of these works have been published since 1965 and acquaint readers with stories, poems, essays, and plays representing a wide variety of cultural and ethnic backgrounds.

The Themes of the Chapters

The seven thematically organized chapters move outward from the most personal sphere to encompass social and spiritual dimensions. Readers are encouraged to relate the selections to their own personal experiences and to see commonalities between their own lives and those of others in radically different cultural circumstances. Compelling and provocative writings by authors from the Caribbean, Africa, Asia, South America, and Central America reflect the cultural and ethnic heritage of increasing numbers of student-readers.

Chapter 1, "Family and Cultural Heritage," features selections by writers who show us the common and unique elements that define family life in many countries around the world. These works also show how our identity is shaped by all those attitudes, traditions, and customs that make up the ethnic and cultural heritage we often take for granted.

Chapter 2, "Coming of Age," offers insights into the need people have in growing up to assert their own sense of individuality—often by defining themselves in opposition to the values held by their parents and society.

Chapter 3, "Gender," presents contemporary works by writers around the world that illuminate the complexities of the interactions between the sexes.

Chapter 4, "Class," takes up the crucial and often unrecognized relationships involving race, sense of identity, and class, through stories, essays, poems, and plays exploring positions of power and powerlessness.

Chapter 5, "The Individual and the State," reflects the ordeals faced by ordinary citizens trying to survive in repressive military and political regimes.

Chapter 6, "Exile," investigates the condition of exiles, whether refugees, immigrants, or travelers, who are caught between two cultures, at home in neither. Works in this chapter address the need of those who have left home to make sense of their lives in a new place.

Chapter 7, "The Spiritual Dimension," shows how people in many different cultures throughout the world look at themselves in relationship to the absolute, the eternal, the cosmic, or the supernatural.

The Editorial Apparatus

The editorial apparatus is designed to highlight both the themes of the selections and important elements in the study of literature. An introductory chapter, "Reading in the Different Genres," shows students how to approach all four genres represented in the anthology.

Chapter introductions discuss the theme of each chapter as it relates to the individual selections. Biographical sketches preceding each selection give background information on the writer's life and identify the cultural, historical, and personal contexts in which the selection was written.

The "Questions for Discussion and Writing" following each of the selections encourage readers to discover relationships between personal experiences and the ideas in the text, and to evaluate the authors' handling of specific literary elements. The literary terms in these questions are printed in small capital letters (for example, SPEAKER, SETTING, CHARACTER, PLOT) and are keyed to the end-of-chapter discussions of important elements in literature as well as to the glossary of literary terms at the end of the book.

The writing suggestions for each selection afford opportunities for personal and expressive writing as well as for expository and persuasive writing. These assignments draw on the thematic organization of the text and ask readers to enter empathetically into viewpoints of the writer and to bring their own experiences into relationship with those of writers around the world.

"Writing about Literature" discussions at the end of each chapter introduce important elements for analyzing and appreciating the formal aspects of literature. Those discussions not only emphasize the traditional elements of character, setting, point of view, conflict and plot structure, and myth and symbol, but reflect recent developments in literary theory. For example, the discussion of reader expectations at the end of Chapter 4 takes up developments in reader response theory. The discussion at the end of Chapter 3 explores the connections between language use and gender roles. The discussion of social, political, and literary contexts at the end of Chapter 6 acquaints readers with recent perspectives in cultural criticism.

Questions following each chapter, "Connections," encourage readers to consider relationships among selections within the chapter and to compare how short story writers, essayists, poets, and playwrights adapt techniques within a particular genre and treat the same theme.

Instructor's Manual

The *Instructor's Manual* provides guidelines for using the text, supplemental bibliographies of books and periodicals, suggested answers to questions in the text, and a filmography for instructors who wish to use films and videos connected to particular selections.

Acknowledgments

No expression of thanks can adequately convey my gratitude to all those teachers of composition and literature who offered thoughtful comments and gave this book the benefit of their scholarship and teaching experience. I would especially like to thank the instructors who reviewed the various stages of the manuscript, including Nancy K. Barry, Luther College; Stephen C. Behrendt, University of Nebraska, Lincoln; Charmazel Dudt, West Texas State University; Susan Dean Jacobs, DePaul University; George Otte, Baruch College, The City University of New York; William E. Sheidley, University of Connecticut; and Carol Wershoven, Palm Beach Community College, South Campus.

For their dedication and skill, I owe much to the able staff at Macmillan, especially to Meredith Blume, Robert Freese, Fran Drago, and M. V. Callcott. I am most grateful to France Burke and Ann-Marie WongSam for their outstanding work as Production Supervisors. To Eben W. Ludlow I owe all the things that one owes to an extraordinarily gifted editor. Ultimately, to Terry, I owe more than words can say.

Contents

2   Coming of Age   179

3 Gender 328

6   **Exile**   **784**

7   The Spiritual Dimension   936

Reading in the Different Genres

Reading Fiction

Works of literature communicate intense, complex, deeply felt responses to human experiences that speak to the heart, mind, body, and imagination.

Although the range of situations that stories can offer is limitless, what makes any particular story enjoyable is the writer's capacity to present an interesting plot, believable characters, and convincing dialogue. The nature of the original events matters less than the writer's ability to make us feel the impact of this experience intellectually, physically, and emotionally. The writer who uses language in skillful and precise ways allows us to share the perceptions and feelings of people different from ourselves. Works of fiction not only can take us to parts of the world we never have the opportunity to visit, but can deepen our emotional capacity to understand what life is like for others in conditions very different from our own. We become more conscious of ourselves as individual human beings when our imaginations and emotions are fully involved. We value a story when, through it, we touch the aspirations, motives, and feelings of other people in diverse personal and cultural situations.

Works of fiction, as distinct from biographies and historical accounts, are imaginative works that tell a story. Fiction writers use language to re-create the emotional flavor of experiences and are free to restructure their accounts in ways that will create suspense and even build conflict. They can add to, or take away from, the known facts, expand or compress time, invent additional imaginative details, or even invent new characters or a narrator through whose eyes the story is told.

The oldest works of fiction took the form of myths and legends that described the exploits of heroes and heroines, gods and goddesses, and supernatural beings. Other ancient forms of literature included FABLES (stating explicit lessons using animal characters) and PARABLES (using analogies to suggest rather than state moral points or complex philosophical concepts) of the kind related by Jesus in the New Testament.

1

The modern short story differs from earlier narrative forms in emphasizing life as most people know it. The short story originated in the nineteenth century as a brief fictional prose narrative that was designed to be read in a single sitting. In a short story all the literary elements of plot, character, setting, and the author's distinctive use of language work together to create a single effect. Short stories usually describe the experiences of one or two characters over the course of a series of related events. REALISTIC stories present sharply etched pictures of characters in real settings reacting to kinds of crises with which readers can identify. The emotions, reactions, perceptions, and motivations of the characters are explored in great detail. We can see these realistic elements in short stories ranging from Kate Chopin's "Désireé's Baby" (1899) through a recent story by Louise Erdrich, "The Bingo Van" (1990).

Contemporary writers offer many different kinds of representations of reality. These may take the form of fact-based accounts of everyday life, as in Mahasweta Devi's "Giribala" (1982), or may reflect a courtroom drama, as in Elena Poniatowska's "The Night Visitor" (1986). Stories can present realistic portraits of cultural conflict of the kind seen in works of Arun Mukherjee ("Visiting Places," 1990), Sembene Ousmane ("Her Three Days," 1974), and Sheila Roberts ("The Weekenders," 1981). We can enjoy realistic comedies of social manners in works by Dal Stivens ("Warrigal," 1981) and Fernando Sorrentino ("The Life of the Party," 1983). Some writers address themselves to momentous historical events in the twentieth century as in Sahni's treatment of the 1947 partition of India in "We Have Arrived in Amritsar" (1989) and the representation of the Cultural Revolution in China by P'an Jen-mu in "A Pair of Socks with Love" (1985). Other writers, reacting against the prevailing conventions of realistic fiction, create a kind of story in which everyday reality is not presented directly but is filtered through the perceptions, associations, and emotions of the main character. In these nonrealistic stories the normal chronology of events is displaced by a psychological narrative that reflects the ebb and flow of the characters' feelings and associations. NONREALISTIC stories may include fantastic, bizarre, or supernatural elements as well. We can see this alternative tradition illustrated in stories ranging from Machado de Assis's "A Canary's Ideas" (1895) to Julio Cortázar's "Letter to a Young Lady in Paris" (1974).

The Many Worlds of Literature is designed to express the range and diversity of contemporary fiction. Unlike anthologies whose works reflect the Eurocentric tradition, *The Many Worlds of Literature* offers works drawn from many cultural contexts reflecting diverse styles and perspectives. Fiction produced in the second half of the twentieth century differs in a number of important ways from that produced before World War II. Writers in this postmodern period avoid seeing events as having only one meaning and produce works that represent reality in unique, complex, and highly individual ways. Whereas writers in the first half of the century saw artistic works of fiction as self-contained worlds governed by a central theme, idea, or principle, postmodernist fiction presents a decentered network of relationships and intertextual connections. Postmodernist writers produce works that actively involve the reader in the interpretation of the text.

Suspicious of claims of a set reality, postmodernist fiction offers works that suggest that reality is not capable of being reduced to a single approved meaning. Stories can take the form of a confusing or ambiguous reality as in Julio Cortázar's "Letter to a Young Lady in Paris" (1974). Or they may appear as hallucinatory episodes, as in François Barcelo's "The Man Who Stopped Trains" (1983) and Jean-Yves Soucy's "The Red Boots" (1981). In other stories, history and fantasy merge so that magical or impossible scenes occur in the middle of apparently realistic narratives, as in Dino Buzzati's "The Falling Girl" (1983), Naguib Mahfouz's "Half a Day" (1989), and Carmen Naranjo's "And We Sold the Rain" (1988). Other works offer oblique descriptions, ambiguously related events, gaps, and frustratingly spare dialogue that call on the reader to interpret events. We can see these features in Keri Hulme's "Unnamed Islands in the Unknown Sea" (1985), Clarice Lispector's "A Special Friendship" (1986), and Peter Carey's "The Last Days of a Famous Mime" (1974).

Although the objectives and methods of writers in the second half of the twentieth century vary widely, what identifies these works as postmodernist is a shift toward the concept of identity as being continuously redefined and reconstructed through interactions in different social and cultural contexts. Not only are postmodernist works different in kind, but they encourage the reader to participate in ways that traditional stories do not. Whereas traditional works tended to guide, manipulate, and control the reader's response, putting the audience into a passive role, postmodernist writers create open works that encourage the reader to participate in interpreting the text. For example, Sheila Roberts, in "The Weekenders" (1981), replaces the traditional omniscient narrator with a series of narrators whose cumulative effect is to avoid creating any sense of completeness or central reference point. In another case, Viktoria Tokareva, in "Nothing Special" (1986), offers a picture of personal growth that never quite reaches completion. Characters in postmodernist fiction must be understood in terms of specific situations, through interactions that are capable of being understood in different ways by different readers. For example, in Albert Camus's "The Guest" (1957), the protagonist's identity is constantly redefined through interactions that depend on the moment-by-moment circumstances described in the story.

Postmodernists often reject defined characters and disrupt traditional narrative points of view through flashbacks (traditional authors used flashbacks to bring out a consistent psychological characterization) that emphasize how reality shifts as the observer's position changes from moment to moment. This is illustrated in Jerzy Kosinski's

"The Miller's Tale" (1964) and in Inés Arredondo's "The Shunammite" (1986).

Contemporary writers have a great deal to say about the forces that shape ethnic, sexual, and racial identity in different cultural contexts. Unlike traditional works that presented social dilemmas in order to resolve them, postmodernist works underscore the difficulty of integrating competing ethnic, sexual, and racial identities within a single culture. This is especially apparent in Chinua Achebe's "Things Fall Apart" (1958), Arun Mukherjee's "Visiting Places" (1990), and Kim Chi-Wŏn's "A Certain Beginning" (1974). Other writers address themselves to how different cultures define gender roles and class relationships in terms of power and powerlessness. These issues are explored in Talat Abbasi's "Facing the Light" (1989), Shirley Saad's "Amina" (1985), and Henri Lopes's "The Esteemed Representative" (1971).

The Many Worlds of Literature is designed to reflect the pluralism of twentieth-century society by presenting a full spectrum of works whose diversity corresponds to the heterogeneous diversity of a new geopolitical age.

Reading Essays

As a literary genre the essay harks back to the form invented four hundred years ago by the French writer Michel Montaigne who called his writings *essais* (attempts) because they were intended less as accounts of objective truth than as personal disclosures of a mind exploring its own attitudes, values, and assumptions on a diverse range of subjects. The essayist speaks his or her mind directly without the mediation of imagined characters and events.

Essayists invite us to share the dramatic excitement of an observant and sensitive mind struggling to understand and clarify an issue that is of great importance to the writer. It is this quality of struggle that makes essays both interesting to read and the intellectual equivalent of a clash of opposing characters in fiction and drama. We feel the writer trying to reconcile opposing impulses to evolve a personal viewpoint that takes into account known facts as well as personal values.

We can see how an essayist brings these various elements into play and works through her reactions in "The Mutilated Half," by Nawal El-Saadawi. El-Saadawi offers a personal account of the genital mutilation she experienced in her childhood. She tells how this event permanently changed her relationship with her parents, and describes the hostility she encountered as a physician in Egypt when she investigated the reasons for this practice and documented its harmful emotional and physical effects on women. She uses a broad range of rhetorical means as she works through her personal reactions and tries to find out what cultural sanctions permit this practice to continue into the present. The horrifying nature of this practice is compelling because

El-Saadawi's descriptions are precise, detailed, and realistic. The reader shares her astonishment and anger as she tries to sort through various explanations for this practice and to uncover the reasons why even other female physicians accept this practice as necessary. Her essay looks at the subject in many ways: She draws on incidents from her own life to illustrate ideas, she relates incidents and stories that bear on the subject, she observes her own reactions and those of others, she cites case histories of the destructive emotional and physical consequences of this operation, and ultimately draws her own conclusion. Her essay tries to influence readers to view the practice of female circumcision as she does. She has worked through her reactions to the subject and has attained an intellectual and emotional perspective on it.

All of the ten essayists in this book embark on a voyage of self-discovery as they reflect on topics including African-American hairstyles, what schoolchildren in Germany learn about the Holocaust, female circumcision, food shortages in Croatia, the obligations of a Native American poet, surviving in Argentina under fascism, political persecution of the Quiché Indians in Guatemala, the difference between black attitudes in the United States and South Africa, fiestas in Mexico, and traditions of story-telling among the Laguna-Pueblo in the Southwest.

Reading Poetry

Poetry differs from other genres in that it achieves its effects with fewer words, compressing details into carefully organized forms in which sound, word, and images work together to create a single intense experience. Poetry uses language in ways that communicate experience rather than simply giving information. The difference between prose and poetry emerges quite clearly when you compare a stanza from Grace Caroline Bridges's poem "Lisa's Ritual, Age 10" with the same words punctuated as a sentence in prose:

> The wall is steady while she falls away: first the hands lost arms dissolving feet gone the legs disjointed body cracking down the center like a fault she falls inside slides down like dust like kitchen dirt slips off the dustpan into noplace a place where nothing happens, nothing ever happened.

Notice how in a stanza from the poem the arrangement of the words and lines creates an entirely different relationship:

> The wall is steady
>
> while she falls   away:
>
>   first the hands   lost
>
> arms dissolving   feet gone

<pre>
 5   the legs   dis-   jointed

              body cracking down

          the center like a fault

              she falls inside

                            slides down like

10   dust   like kitchen dirt

                       slips off

       the dustpan into

                            noplace

        a place where

15   nothing happens,

       nothing ever happened.
</pre>

The way the words are arranged communicates the experience of the child's detachment, alienation, and sense of shock while the same words in prose merely describe it. Each detail, coupled with the way the words are arranged on the page, stands for feelings and ideas too complex for direct statement.

Because it communicates an extraordinarily compressed moment of thought, feeling, or experience, poetry relies on figurative language, connotation, imagery, sound, and rhythm. Poetry evokes emotional associations through images whose importance is underscored by a rhythmic beat or pulse.

Patterns of sounds and images emphasize and underscore distinct thoughts and emotions, appealing simultaneously to the heart, mind, and imagination. The rhythmic beat provides the sensuous element coupled with imagery that appeals to the senses and touches the heart. At the same time, the imagination is stimulated through the unexpected combinations and perceptions through figurative language (similes, metaphors, personification) that allow the reader to see things in new ways. Because these effects work simultaneously, the experience of a poem is concentrated and intense.

Like fiction, poems may have a narrator (called a speaker), a particular point of view, and a distinctive tone and style. Every poem is a projection of a single human voice with unifying properties that make a poem a poem.

The speaker's relationship with the events and scenes described in the poem may be of several kinds. In LYRIC or REFLECTIVE POETRY we seem to overhear the thoughts of the speaker. This poetry is subjective, psychological, and intensely personal and usually takes the form of a brief intense expression of the speaker's mood. The personality of the speaker is created through the music of the verse, its diction and imagery. For example, in Anna Ahkmatova's five poems, "Cinque," we experience directly and intimately the extremes of ecstasy and despair that she experiences. This focus on feelings and perception from the inside is characteristic of lyric poetry. Although most lyric poems relate crises of a very personal nature, in some poems the voice we hear speaks for a group rather than for an individual. For instance, Sandra Esteves's poem "Weaver" acts as a ritual, through chants and incantations, to transcend the merely personal and, through the imagination, to bring about an identification with a spirit beyond oneself. In another poem, by Chenjerai Hove, "You Will Forget," the speaker pronounces a curse on those who have foresaken their tribal roots. Whether the voice we hear represents an individual or a whole community, we get a very precise sense of the speaker's personality, mood, and reactions.

Narrative poems tend to be objective, centering around important events, and tell a story about an event that has changed the speaker's perspective or relationship with others. Narrative poems preserve a certain emotional detachment by relating events that have occurred in the past. For example, Cathy Song's poem "The Youngest Daughter" is shaped as an account of a long-brewing crisis in the life of the speaker as to whether she should continue caring for her mother or seek independence. In another case, Judith Ortez Cofer in "The Woman Who Was Left at the Altar" relates the lifelong consequences to a woman whose love and trust were betrayed. Narrative poems hark back to the older forms of epics, romances, and ballads. For example, we can see features of the ballad in the repeated refrains, varied repetition, and tag-lines of Yambo Ouologuem's poem "When Black Men's Teeth Speak Out." Typically, the narrative structures of these poems enable us to understand how the events described in them have changed the lives of the characters.

The descriptive elements of poetry become dominant in poems where the speaker describes things in terms of what the eye sees, such as colors, shapes, and other descriptive details. The intensity and depth with which the scene is described suggest that the physical, sensuous elements of the environment and the faculty of seeing things as exactly as possible is a virtue in itself. In these poems it is the speaker's response to the setting or the aspect of the speaker's sensibility that emerges through the description that is most important. In "Red Azalea on the Cliff" by Xu Gang, the speaker responds with awe to the sight of a delicate red azalea surviving on a wind-whipped mountainside. In "Greek Carters" by Yannis Ritsos, the image of workmen washing off the dirt and dust from their horses and themselves at the end of a long day suggests the enduring purity of the ancient Greek world admidst the commercialism of the twentieth century. The effects of descriptive poetry range from simple visual images stated directly, as in Ritsos's poem, to the complex descriptive effects of a poem by Garrett Hongo, "Who Among You Knows the Essence of Garlic," that depend on transposing sense impressions achieved by presenting an appeal to one sense in terms of another.

Whereas lyric poetry focuses on personal reflections, narrative poetry tells a story through actions and events, and descriptive poetry sees the external world in realistic terms, dramatic poetry takes the form of confrontations between characters that are "staged" in ways that suggest events are happening at the moment. We get the sense that we have suddenly begun to eavesdrop in the middle of a dramatic situation. For example, in Damas's poem "Hiccup" we hear two voices arguing in a moment of dramatic conflict that highlights the mother's expectations and the son's lapses of manners and etiquette.

Dramatic poems are constructed to lead up to a dramatic climax by building up suspense as Etheridge Knight does in "Hard Rock Returns to Prison from the Hospital for the Criminal Insane." Dramatic poems create an illusion of reality that presents living figures who move, converse, and affect one another (inmates in a prison discussing the fate of Hard Rock, in Knight's poem), engaging the reader's sympathy more effectively than would a narrative account of the same situation.

Learning to enjoy what poetry has to offer requires the reader to pay close attention to specific linguistic details of sound and rhythm, connotations of words, and the sensations, feelings, memories, and associations that these words evoke. After reading a poem, preferably aloud, try to determine who the speaker is. What situation does the poem describe? How might the title provide insight into the speaker's predicament? What attitude does the poet project toward the events described in the poem? Observe the language used by the speaker. What emotional state of mind is depicted? You might look for recurrent references to a particular subject and see whether these references illuminate some psychological truth.

Although it has a public use, poetry mainly unfolds private joys, tragedies, and challenges common to all people, such as the power of friendship, value of self-discovery, bondage of outworn traditions, delight in nature's beauty, devastation of war, achievement of self-respect, and despair over failed dreams. The universal elements in poetry bridge gaps in time and space and tie people together in expressing emotions shared by all people in different times, places, and cultures.

Reading Drama

Drama, unlike fiction and poetry, is meant to be performed on a stage. The text of a play includes dialogue (conversation between two or more characters)—or a monologue (lines spoken by a single character to the audience)—and the playwright's stage directions.

Although the dramatist makes use of plot, characters, setting, and language, the nature of drama limits the playwright to presenting the events from an objective point of view. There are other important differences between fiction and drama as well. The dramatist must restrict the action in the play to what can be shown on the stage in two or three hours. Since plays must hold the attention of an audience, playwrights prefer obvious rather than subtle conflicts, clearly defined sequences of action, and fast-paced exposition that is not weighed down by long descriptive or narrative passages. Everything in drama has to be shown directly, concretely, through vivid images of human behavior.

The structure of most plays begins with an EXPOSITION or INTRODUCTION that introduces the characters, shows their relationship to one another, and provides background information necessary for the audience or reader to understand the main conflict of the play. The essence of drama is conflict. Conflict is produced when an individual pursuing an objective meets with resistance either from another person, from society, from nature, or from an internal aspect of his or her own personality. In the most effective plays, the audience can see the central conflict through the eyes of each character in the play. As the play proceeds, **complications** make the problem more difficult to solve and increase suspense as to whether the protagonist, or main character, or the opposing force (referred to as the antagonist) will triumph. In the **climax** of the play the conflict reaches the height of emotional intensity and one side achieves a decisive advantage over the other. This is often the moment of truth when characters see themselves and the situation clearly for the first time. The end of the play, or conclusion, explores the implications of the nature of the truth that has been realized and what the consequences will be.

The kind of conflicts embodied in plays varies from age to age and reveals underlying societal values. Greek tragedies dramatize conflicts between human beings and the gods and led to the recognition of the role Fate played in preserving an underlying order to the universe. For example, an audience watching *Oedipus, the King* would see how the workings of destiny combined with the protagonist's flawed judgment and excessive pride (**tragic flaw**) precipitate his downfall. The action of Greek tragedies for the most part was confined to one location and a time span that rarely exceeded a day.

By contrast, the action in a Shakespeare play can span years and can encompass places at great distances from each other. The emphasis in Shakespeare's tragedies is less on the inexorable workings of Fate than on the tragic weaknesses within human beings that destroy not only them but those they love. Othello's jealousy and Hamlet's excessive intellectualizing are familiar examples of Shakespeare's depiction of human beings at war with themselves. Shakespeare saw the conflict as being between good and evil rather than between human beings and Fate. These plays are compelling because we experience the predicament and emotions of the protagonist and at the same time gain an objective understanding of the situation as it appears to the other characters.

The focus of theater on the French and English stage in the 1800s emphasizes the conflict between individuals and prevailing social norms and customs. Plays by Molière (*The Misanthrope*) and Richard Brinsley Sheridan (*School for Scandal*) satirize people whose eccentricities and personality flaws make them unable to fit into established society. The characters in these works are dramatized as social beings with humorous rather than tragic flaws. The conflicts in these plays assure the audience of a happy ending in which quarreling factions are reconciled and the values of society are reaffirmed.

Modern drama began as a reaction to the stilted conventions and superficial tone of nineteenth-century plays. Henrik Ibsen and George Bernard Shaw created realistic plays set in recognizable everyday environments that explored conflicts in the lives of ordinary people struggling with social institutions. In *A Doll's House* (1879), *Ghosts* (1881), and *Hedda Gabler* (1890), Ibsen showed women protagonists oppressed by the male-dominated societies in which they lived. In *Major Barbara* (1905), *Saint Joan* (1924), and *Arms and the Man* (1894), Shaw explored conflicts between individuals, usually women, and legal, political, economic, and military authorities of that era. The German playwright Bertolt Brecht continued to explore the conflict between individuals and the less than ideal world by assailing the economic and political causes and consequences of totalitarianism, war, and poverty in such well-known works as *The Three Penny Opera* (1928), *Mother Courage and Her Children* (1939), and *The Caucasian Chalk Circle* (1944). Unlike Ibsen and Shaw, Brecht sought to make the audience aware of the representational nature of what they were watching on the stage. In Russia, Anton Chekhov created dramas that explored the psychological conflicts people experienced as they yearned to make real their personal visions of happiness. Later, American playwrights including Eugene O'Neill, Thornton Wilder, Tennessee Williams, Lorraine Hansberry, Arthur Miller, and recently John Guare, Wendy Wasserstein, and Irene Maria Fornes, continued to explore the conflicts between personal dreams and reality.

Reading a script of a play or the screenplay for a film is a very different kind of experience from seeing these works performed on the stage or screen. When watching a play or movie you are part of an audience whose collective reactions, whether tears or laughter, enhance your experience. Reading a play engages your imagination by requiring you to visualize what characters look like, how they move or speak, their facial expressions, intonations, and gestures as well as the details of the setting that are laid out before an audience in a theatrical production. In effect, you become all the actors as well as the director, set designer, and even playwright.

From a script containing dialogue and brief descriptions you must visualize what the characters look like and sound like, imagine how they relate to one another, and predict how an audience might react to them. For example, try to imagine the following scene from *The Donkey Market* by the Egyptian playwright Tewfik al-Hakim. In the preceding scene, an unemployed laborer, Mr. Hassawi, has convinced a gullible farmer that he, the laborer, is actually the donkey the farmer has just bought at the market. The humor of the scene would be enhanced for an Egyptian audience since "Hassawi" is a well-known breed of riding donkey.

SCENE TWO

Inside the farmer's house his WIFE is occupied with various household jobs. She hears knocking at the door.

WIFE: Who is it?

FARMER (*from outside*):   Me, woman. Open up.

WIFE (*Opens the door and her husband enters*):   You were all this time at the market?

FARMER: I've only just got back.

WIFE: You bought the donkey?

FARMER: I bought . . .

WIFE: You put it into the fold?

FARMER: What fold are you talking about, woman? Come along in, Mr Hassawi.

WIFE: You've got a guest with you?

FARMER: Not a guest. He's what you might . . . I'll tell you later.

WIFE: Please come in.

FARMER: Off you go and make me a glass of tea.

The WIFE goes off.

How do you stage this scene in your mind? What do the farmer, his wife, and Mr. Hassawi look like? Do you imagine the laborer stooping over or walking upright? What reaction passes across the wife's face when the farmer hesitates in telling her about the donkey? What do you imagine the intonation of their voices sound like? What is everyone wearing? How do you see or envision the interior of the farmer's house? By imagining each aspect of the scene, you bring it to life, becoming, in effect, the actors, the producer, director, set designer, and the playwright.

The screenplay and nine plays presented in this book will challenge you to enter the lives of people in societies as diverse as those of Japan, Egypt, Argentina, Nigeria, Italy, Vietnam, the Czech and Slovak republics, China, Cuba, and the United States.

1

Family and Cultural Heritage

"Some people are your relatives but others are your ancestors, and you choose the ones you want to have as ancestors. You create yourself out of those values."

— *Ralph Ellison*

Shared practices, ceremonies, customs, beliefs, and values together make up a cultural heritage and provide an invaluable connection between the present and the traditions of the past. A cultural heritage serves as a collective memory that provides a link to one's forebears. The folktales, art, music, institutions, rituals, and traditions shared by a group are a social, rather than biological, inheritance that guides people within a culture by providing common assumptions about the world that are passed on from generation to generation.

This chapter explores the extent to which our identity is shaped by all those attitudes, traditions, and customs that make up the ethnic and cultural heritage we often take for granted. The works of fiction and nonfiction presented here dramatize a wide range of cultural attitudes. We learn of the role traditions play in Australia, Botswana, Costa Rica, Egypt, Syria, the Republic of Mali, Scotland, Japan, and, in the United States, in the African-American community and among the Chippewa Indians.

Many stories dramatize the tension between continuing allegiance to traditional values and ambivalence toward those traditions as something antiquated to be transcended. Each of the stories projects this tension on different objects and settings that represent either the old ways or new possibilities. Louise Erdrich presents the lure of the new in "The Bingo Van." In Dal Stivens's "Warrigal," relinquishing a pet dingo symbolizes this conflict. In both Bessie Head's "Looking for a Rain God" and Carmen Naranjo's "And We Sold the Rain," invoking and preserving a country's most precious resource makes people

12

do shocking things. Alasdair Gray's "The Crank That Made the Revolution" satirically shows how so-called progress twists traditional cultural values into unrecognizable forms.

Contrasting views toward traditional Mideastern culture are portrayed in three stories set in Egypt, Syria, and Mali. Nabil Gorgy in "Cairo Is a Small City" shows how ancient Bedouin traditions balance the scales of justice in modern-day Cairo. By contrast, long-held practices are seen as timeworn and oppressive in "Seventy Years Later" by Ulfa Idelbi and in Sembene Ousmane's poignant story "Her Three Days," depicting the plight of a third wife waiting for her husband's infrequent three-day visit. In the United States, an award-winning black journalist, Itabari Njeri, describes, in "Hair Piece," the cultural obstacles she encounters when trying to find a hairstylist.

A variety of responses toward one's cultural heritage are presented by the poems in this chapter. Joseph Brodsky (Russia), in "A Halt in the Desert," reveals how poetry itself is a means of transmitting collective memory. Chenjerai Hove (Zimbabwe) sums up the consequences of losing contact with one's roots in "You Will Forget." The displacement of tribal culture by civilization is the subject of "Sunset" by Mbuyiseni Oswald Mtshali (South Africa). Yambo Ouologuem (Mali), in "When Black Men's Teeth Speak Out," frames a witty defense of a vegetarian accused of eating tourists. Garrett Hongo (Hawaii), in "Who Among You Knows the Essence of Garlic," explores the interrelationship between particular foods and one's cultural heritage. Sandra María Esteves (Puerto Rico), in "Weaver," invokes a multicultural tapestry as an ideal for a poet. Insight into the traditions and values of the Mennonite community is offered by the American poet, Julia Kasdorf, in her "Mennonites."

One of the most penetrating and original works of the Japanese theater, *Friends* by Kōbō Abe, explores the question as to whether individual freedom can coexist with family life in modern Japan.

Last, the Arab world's leading playwright, Tewfik al-Hakim, adapts a centuries-old folktale in his hilarious play *The Donkey Market*, to satirize the lack of progressive reform in modern Egyptian society.

Louise Erdrich

The Bingo Van

Louise Erdrich is of Chippewa Indian and German heritage. Born in 1954 in Little Falls, Minnesota, Erdrich grew up as part of the Turtle Mountain band of Chippewa in Wahpeton, North Dakota, where her grandfather was tribal chair of the reservation. While attending Dartmouth College, she received several awards for her poetry and fiction, including the American Academy of Poets Prize. After graduating she returned to North Dakota to teach in the Poetry in the Schools Program. Her poetry has been published in Jacklight *(1984). Her first novel,* Love Medicine, *won the 1984 National Book Critics Circle Award for Fiction and is part of an ongoing series of novels exploring Native American life in North Dakota. Recent novels continuing the saga of the Chippewa clan are* Beet Queen *(1986) and* Tracks *(1988). She is married to Michael Dorris, a professor of Native American Studies at Dartmouth and author of* The Broken Cord: A Family's Ongoing Struggle with Fetal Alcohol Syndrome *(1989). Together they collaborated on a novel called* The Crown of Columbus *(1991). Erdrich's work has been praised for the sensitivity and psychological depth of her depiction of the lives of contemporary Native Americans. In "The Bingo Van" Erdrich conveys with unflinching humor the bittersweet experiences of Lipsha Morrisey, a character who first appeared in* Love Medicine. *This story originally appeared in* The New Yorker, *February 1990.*

1   When I walked into bingo that night in early spring, I didn't have a girlfriend, a home or an apartment, a piece of land or a car, and I wasn't tattooed yet, either. Now look at me. I'm walking the reservation road in borrowed pants, toward a place that isn't mine, downhearted because I'm left by a woman. All I have of my temporary riches is this black pony running across the back of my hand—a tattoo I had Lewey's Tattoo Den put there on account of a waking dream. I'm still not paid up. I still owe for the little horse. But if Lewey wants to repossess it, then he'll have to catch me first.

2   Here's how it is on coming to the bingo hall. It's a long, low quonset barn. Inside, there used to be a pall of smoke, but now the smoke-eater fans in the ceiling take care of that. So upon first entering you can pick out your friends. On that night in early spring, I saw Eber, Clay, and Robert Morrissey sitting about halfway up toward the curtained stage with their grandmother Lulu. By another marriage, she was my grandma, too. She had five tickets spread in front of her. The boys each had only one. When the numbers rolled, she picked up a dabber in each hand. It was the Earlybird game, a one-hundred-dollar prize, and nobody had got too wound up yet or serious.

14

"Lipsha, go get us a Coke," said Lulu when someone else bingoed. 3
"Yourself, too."

I went to the concession with Eber, who had finished high school 4
with me. Clay and Robert were younger. We got our soft drinks and
came back, set them down, pulled up to the table, and laid out a new
set of tickets before us. Like I say, my grandmother, she played five at
once, which is how you get the big money. In the long run, much more
than breaking even, she was one of those rare Chippewas who actually
profited by bingo. But, then again, it was her only way of gambling. No
pull-tabs, no blackjack, no slot machines for her. She never went into
the back room. She banked all the cash she won. I thought I should
learn from Lulu Lamartine, whose other grandsons had stiff new boots
while mine were worn down into the soft shape of moccasins. I
watched her.

Concentration. Before the numbers even started, she set her mouth, 5
snapped her purse shut. She shook her dabbers so that the foam-rubber
tips were thoroughly inked. She looked at the time on her watch. The
Coke, she took a drink of that, but no more than a sip. She was a
narrow-eyed woman with a round jaw, curled hair. Her eyeglasses,
blue plastic, hung from her neck by a gleaming chain. She raised the
ovals to her eyes as the caller took the stand. She held her dabbers
poised while he plucked the ball from the chute. He read it out: B-7.
Then she was absorbed, scanning, dabbing, into the game. She didn't
mutter. She had no lucky piece to touch in front of her. And afterward,
even if she lost a blackout game by one square, she never sighed or
complained.

All business, that was Lulu. And all business paid. 6

I think I would have been all business too, like her, if it hadn't been 7
for what lay behind the stage curtain to be revealed. I didn't know it,
but that was what would change the order of my life. Because of the
van, I'd have to get stupid first, then wise. You see, I had been floundering since high school, trying to catch my bearings in the world. It all
lay ahead of me, spread out in the sun like a giveaway at a naming ceremony. Only thing was, I could not choose a prize. Something always
stopped my hand before it reached.

"Lipsha Morrisey, you got to go for a vocation." That's what I told 8
myself, in a state of nervous worry. I was getting by on almost no
money, relying on my job as night watchman in a bar. That earned me a
place to sleep, twenty dollars per week, and as much beef jerky, Beer
Nuts, and spicy sausage sticks as I could eat.

I was now composed of these three false substances. No food in a 9
bar has a shelf life of less than forty months. If you are what you eat, I
would live forever, I thought.

And then they pulled aside the curtain, and I saw that I wouldn't 10
live as long as I had coming unless I owned that van. It had every option you could believe—blue plush on the steering wheel, diamond

side windows, and complete carpeted interior. The seats were easy chairs, with little headphones, and it was wired all through the walls. You could walk up close during intermission and touch the sides. The paint was cream, except for the design picked out in blue, which was a Sioux Drum border. In the back there was a small refrigerator and a carpeted platform for sleeping. It was a home, a portable den with front-wheel drive. I could see myself in it right off. I could see I *was* it.

11   On TV, they say you are what you drive. Let's put it this way: I wanted to be that van.

12   Now, I know that what I felt was a symptom of the national decline. You'll scoff at me, scorn me, say, What right does that waste Lipsha Morrissey, who makes his living guarding beer, have to comment outside of his own tribal boundary? But I was able to investigate the larger picture, thanks to Grandma Lulu, from whom I learned to be one-minded in my pursuit of a material object.

13   I went night after night to the bingo. Every hour I spent there, I grew more certain I was close. There was only one game per night at which the van was offered, a blackout game, where you had to fill every slot. The more tickets you bought, the more your chances increased. I tried to play five tickets, like Grandma Lulu did, but they cost five bucks each. To get my van, I had to shake hands with greed. I got unprincipled.

14   You see, my one talent in this life is a healing power I got passed down through the Pillager branch of my background. It's in my hands. I snap my fingers together so hard they almost spark. Then I blank out my mind, and I put on the touch. I had a reputation up to then for curing sore joints and veins. I could relieve ailments caused in an old person by a half century of grinding stoop-over work. I had a power in myself that flowed out, resistless. I had a richness in my dreams and waking thoughts. But I never realized I would have to give up my healing source once I started charging for my service.

15   You know how it is about charging. People suddenly think you are worth something. Used to be, I'd go anyplace I was called, take any price or take nothing. Once I let it get around that I charged a twenty for my basic work, however, the phone at the bar rang off the hook.

16   "Where's that medicine boy?" they asked. "Where's Lipsha?"

17   I took their money. And it's not like beneath the pressure of a twenty I didn't try, for I did try, even harder than before. I skipped my palms together, snapped my fingers, positioned them where the touch inhabiting them should flow. But when it came to blanking out my mind I consistently failed. For each time, in the center of the cloud that came down into my brain, the van was now parked, in perfect focus.

18   I suppose I longed for it like for a woman, except I wasn't that bad yet, and, anyway, then I did meet a woman, which set me back in my quest.

19   Instead of going for the van with everything, saving up to buy as

many cards as I could play when they got to the special game, for a few nights I went short term, for variety, with U-Pickem cards, the kind where you have to choose the numbers for yourself.

First off, I wrote in the shoe and pants sizes of those Morrissey boys. 20 No luck. So much for them. Next I took my birth date and a double of it—still no go. I wrote down the numbers of my grandma's address and her anniversary dates. Nothing. Then one night I realized if my U-Pickem was going to win it would be more like *revealed*, rather than a forced kind of thing. So I shut my eyes, right there in the middle of the long bingo table, and I let my mind blank out, white and fizzing like the screen of a television, until something formed. The van, as always. But on its tail this time a license plate was officially fixed and numbered. I used that number, wrote it down in the boxes, and then I bingoed.

I got two hundred dollars from that imaginary license. The money 21 was in my pocket when I left. The next morning, I had fifty cents. But it's not like you think with Serena, and I'll explain that. She didn't want something from me; she didn't care if I had money, and she didn't ask for it. She was seventeen and had a two-year-old boy. That tells you about her life. Her last name was American Horse, an old Sioux name she was proud of even though it was strange to Chippewa country. At her older sister's house Serena's little boy blended in with the younger children, and Serena herself was just one of the teen-agers. She was still in high school, a year behind the year she should have been in, and she had ambitions. Her idea was to go into business and sell her clothing designs, of which she had six books.

I don't know how I got a girl so decided in her future to go with me, 22 even that night. Except I told myself, "Lipsha, you're a nice-looking guy. You're a winner." And for the moment I was. I went right up to her at the Coin-Op and said, "Care to dance?," which was a joke—there wasn't anyplace to dance. Yet she liked me. We had a sandwich and then she wanted to take a drive, so we tagged along with some others in the back of their car. They went straight south, toward Hoopdance, off the reservation, where action was taking place.

"Lipsha," she whispered on the way, "I always liked you from a dis- 23 tance."

"Serena," I said, "I liked you from a distance, too." 24

So then we moved close together on the car seat. My hand was on 25 my knee, and I thought of a couple of different ways I could gesture, casually pretend to let it fall on hers, how maybe if I talked fast she wouldn't notice, in the heat of the moment, her hand in my hand, us holding hands, our lips drawn to one another. But then I decided to boldly take courage, to take her hand as, at the same time, I looked into her eyes. I did this. In the front, the others talked among themselves. Yet we just sat there. After a while she said, "You want to kiss me?"

But I answered, not planning how the words would come out, "Our 26 first kiss has to be a magic moment only we can share."

27   Her eyes went wide as a deer's, and her big smile bloomed. Her skin was dark, her long hair a burnt-brown color. She wore no jewelry, no rings, just the clothing she had sewed from her designs—a suit jacket and pair of pants that were the tan of eggshells, with symbols picked out in blue thread on the borders, the cuffs, and the hem. I took her in, admiring, for some time on that drive before I realized that the reason Serena's cute outfit nagged me so was on account of she was dressed up to match my bingo van. I could hardly tell her this surprising coincidence, but it did convince me that the time was perfect, the time was right.

28   They let us off at a certain place just over the reservation line, and we got out, hardly breaking our gaze from each other. You want to know what this place was? I'll tell you. O.K. So it was a motel—a long, low double row of rooms, painted white on the outside, with brown wooden doors. There was a beautiful sign set up, featuring a lake with some fish jumping out of it. We stood beside the painted water.

29   "I haven't done this since Jason," she said. That was the name of her two-year-old son. "I have to call up my sister first."

30   There was a phone near the office, inside a plastic shell. She went over there.

31   "He's sleeping," she said when she returned.

32   I went into the office, stood before the metal counter. There was a number floating in my mind.

33   "Is Room 22 available?" I asked.

34   I suppose, looking at me, I look too much like an Indian. The owner, a big sandy-haired woman in a shiny black blouse, noticed that. You get so you see it cross their face the way wind blows a disturbance on water. There was a period of contemplation, a struggle in this woman's thinking. Behind her the television whispered. Her mouth opened, but I spoke first.

35   "This here is Andrew Jackson," I said, tenderizing the bill. "Known for setting up our Southern relatives for the Trail of Tears. And to keep him company we got two Mr. Hamiltons."

36   The woman turned shrewd, and took the bills.

37   "No parties." She held out a key attached to a square of orange plastic.

38   "Just sex." I could not help but reassure her. But that was talk, big talk from a person with hardly any experience and nothing that resembled a birth-control device. I wasn't one of those so-called studs who couldn't open up their wallets without dropping a foil-wrapped square. No, Lipsha Morrissey was deep at heart a romantic, a wild-minded kind of guy, I told myself, a fool with no letup. I went out to Serena, and took her hand in mine. I was shaking inside but my voice was steady and my hands were cool.

39   "Let's go in." I showed the key. "Let's not think about tomorrow."

40   "That's how I got Jason," said Serena.

41   So we stood there.

"I'll go in," she said at last. "Down two blocks, there's an all-night   42
gas station. They sell 'em."

I went. O.K. Life in this day and age might be less romantic in some   43
ways. It seemed so in the hard twenty-four-hour fluorescent light, as I
tried to choose what I needed from the rack by the counter. It was quite
a display; there were dazzling choices—textures, shapes. I saw I was
being watched, and I suddenly grabbed what was near my hand—two
boxes, economy size.

"Heavy date?"   44

I suppose the guy on the late shift was bored, could not resist. His   45
T-shirt said "Big Sky Country." He was grinning in an ugly way. So I
answered.

"Not really. Fixing up a bunch of my white buddies from Montana.   46
Trying to keep down the sheep population."

His grin stayed fixed. Maybe he had heard a lot of jokes about   47
Montana blondes, or maybe he was from somewhere else. I looked at
the boxes in my hand, put one back.

"Let me help you out," the guy said. "What you need is a bag of   48
these."

He took down a plastic sack of little oblong party balloons, Day-Glo   49
pinks and oranges and blues.

"Too bright," I said. "My girlfriend's a designer. She hates clashing   50
colors." I was breathing hard suddenly, and so was he. Our eyes met
and narrowed.

"What does she design?" he said. "Bedsheets?"   51

"What does yours design?" I said. "Wool sweaters?"   52

I put money between us. "For your information, my girlfriend's not   53
only beautiful but she and I are the same species."

"Which is?"   54

"Take the money," I said. "Hand over my change and I'll be out of   55
here. Don't make me do something I'd regret."

"I'd be real threatened." The guy turned from me, ringing up   56
my sale. "I'd be shaking, except I know you Indian guys are chicken
shit."

I took my package, took my change.   57

"Baaaaa," I said, and beat it out of there. It's strange how a bashful   58
kind of person like me gets talkative in some of our less pleasant bor-
der-town situations.

I took a roundabout way back to Room 22 and tapped on the door.   59
There was a little window right beside it. Serena peeked through, and
let me in.

"Well," I said then, in that awkward interval, "guess we're set."   60

She took the bag from my hand and didn't say a word, just put it on   61
the little table beside the bed. There were two chairs. Each of us took
one. Then we sat down and turned on the television. The romance
wasn't in us now for some reason, but there was something invisible
that made me hopeful about the room.

62   It was just a small place, a modest kind of place, clean. You could smell the faint chemical of bug spray the moment you stepped inside. You could look at the television hung on the wall, or examine the picture of golden trees and a waterfall. You could take a shower for a long time in the cement shower stall, standing on your personal shower mat for safety. There was a little tin desk. You could sit down there and write a letter on a sheet of plain paper from the drawer. The lampshade was made of reeds, pressed and laced tight together. The spread on the double mattress was reddish, a rusty cotton material. There was an air-conditioner, with a fan we turned on.

63   "I don't know why we're here," I said at last. "I'm sorry."

64   Serena took a small brush from her purse.

65   "Comb my hair?"

66   I took the brush and sat on the bed, just behind her. I began at the ends, very careful, but there were hardly any tangles to begin with. Her hair was a quiet brown without variation. My hand followed the brush, smoothing after each stroke, until the fall of her hair was a hypnotizing silk. I could lift my hand away from her head and the hair would follow, electric to my touch, in soft strands that hung suspended until I returned to the brushing. She never moved, except to switch off the light and then the television. She sat down again in the total dark and said, "Please, keep on," so I did. The air got thick. Her hair got lighter, full of blue static, charged so that I was held in place by the attraction. A golden spark jumped on the carpet. Serena turned toward me. Her hair floated down around her at that moment like a tent of energy.

67   Well, the money part is not related to that. I gave it all to Serena, that's true. Her intention was to buy material and put together the creations that she drew in her notebooks. It was fashion with a Chippewa flair, as she explained it, and sure to win prizes at the state home-ec. contest. She promised to pay me interest when she opened her own shop. The next day, after we had parted, after I had checked out the bar I was supposed to night-watch, I went off to the woods to sit and think. Not about the money, which was Serena's—and good luck to her—but about her and me.

68   She was two years younger than me, yet she had direction and a child, while I was aimless, lost in hyperspace, using up my talent, which was already fading from my hands. I wondered what our future could hold. One thing was sure: I never knew a man to support his family by playing bingo, and the medicine calls for Lipsha were getting fewer by the week, and fewer, as my touch failed to heal people, fled from me, and lay concealed.

69   I sat on ground where, years ago, my greats and my great-greats, the Pillagers, had walked. The trees around me were the dense birch and oak of old woods. The lake drifted in, gray waves, white foam in a bobbing lace. Thin gulls lined themselves up on a sandbar. The sky

went dark. I closed my eyes, and that is when the little black pony galloped into my mind. It sped across the choppy waves like a skipping
stone, its mane a banner, its tail a flag, and vanished on the other side of
the shore.

It was luck. Serena's animal. American Horse. 70

"This is the last night I'm going to try for the van," I told myself. I 71
always kept three twenties stuffed inside the edging of my blanket in
back of the bar. Once that stash was gone I'd make a real decision. I'd
open the yellow pages at random, and where my finger pointed I
would take that kind of job.

Of course, I never counted on winning the van. 72

I was playing for it on the shaded side of a blackout ticket, which is 73
always hard to get. As usual, I sat with Lulu and her boys. Her vigi-
lance helped me. She let me use her extra dabber and she sat and
smoked a filter cigarette, observing the quiet frenzy that was taking
place around her. Even though that van had sat on the stage for five
months, even though nobody had yet won it and everyone said it was a
scam, when it came to playing for it most people bought a couple of
tickets. That night, I went all out and purchased eight.

A girl read out the numbers from the hopper. Her voice was clear 74
and light on the microphone. I didn't even notice what was happening—Lulu pointed out one place I had missed on the winning ticket.
Then I had just two squares left to make a bingo and I suddenly
sweated, I broke out into a chill, I went cold and hot at once. After all
my pursuit, after all my plans, I was N-6 and G-60. I had narrowed myself, shrunk into the spaces on the ticket. Each time the girl read a number and it wasn't that 6 or 60 I sickened, recovered, forgot to breathe.

She must have read twenty numbers out before N-6. Then, right af- 75
ter that, G-60 rolled off her lips.

I screamed. I am ashamed to say how loud I yelled. That girl came 76
over, got the manager, and then he checked out my numbers slow and
careful while everyone hushed.

He didn't say a word. He checked them over twice. Then he pursed 77
his lips together and wished he didn't have to say it.

"It's a bingo," he finally told the crowd. 78

Noise buzzed to the ceiling—talk of how close some others had 79
come, green talk—and every eye was turned and cast on me, which
was uncomfortable. I never was the center of looks before, not Lipsha,
who everybody took for granted around here. Not all those looks were
for the good, either. Some were plain envious and ready to believe the
first bad thing a sour tongue could pin on me. It made sense in a way.
Of all those who'd stalked that bingo van over the long months, I was
now the only one who had not lost money on the hope.

O.K., so what kind of man does it make Lipsha Morrissey that the 80
keys did not tarnish his hands one slight degree, and that he beat it out

that very night in the van, completing only the basic paperwork? I didn't go after Serena, and I can't tell you why. Yet I was hardly ever happier. In that van, I rode high, but that's the thing. Looking down on others, even if it's only from the seat of a van that a person never really earned, does something to the human mentality. It's hard to say. I changed. After just one evening riding the reservation roads, passing with a swish of my tires, I started smiling at the homemade hot rods, at the clunkers below me, at the old-lady cars nosing carefully up and down the gravel hills.

81   I started saying to myself that I should visit Serena, and a few nights later I finally did go over there. I pulled into her sister's driveway with a flourish I could not help, as the van slipped into a pothole and I roared the engine. For a moment, I sat in the dark, letting my head-lamps blaze alongside the door until Serena's brother-in-law leaned out.

82   "Cut the lights!" he yelled. "We got a sick child."

83   I rolled down my window, and asked for Serena.

84   "It's her boy. She's in here with him." He waited. I did, too, in the dark. A dim light was on behind him and I saw some shadows, a small girl in those pajamas with the feet tacked on, someone pacing back and forth.

85   "You want to come in?" he called.

86   But here's the gist of it: I just said to tell Serena hi for me, and then I backed out of there, down the drive, and left her to fend for herself. I could have stayed there. I could have drawn my touch back from wher-ever it had gone to. I could have offered my van to take Jason to the I.H.S. I could have sat there in silence as a dog guards its mate, its own blood. I could have done something different from what I did, which was to hit the road for Hoopdance and look for a better time.

87   I cruised until I saw where the party house was located that night. I drove the van over the low curb, into the yard, and I parked there. I watched until I recognized a couple of cars and saw the outlines of Indians and mixed, so I knew that walking in would not involve me in what the newspapers term an episode. The door was white, stained and raked by a dog, with a tiny fan-shaped window. I went through and stood inside. There was movement, a kind of low-key swirl of bright hair and dark hair tossing alongside each other. There were about as many Indians as there weren't. This party was what we call around here a Hairy Buffalo, and most people were grouped around a big brown plastic garbage can that served as the punch bowl for the all-purpose stuff, which was anything that anyone brought, dumped in along with pink Hawaiian Punch. I grew up around a lot of the people, and others I knew by sight. Among those last, there was a young familiar-looking guy.

88   It bothered me. I recognized him, but I didn't know him. I hadn't been to school with him, or played him in any sport, because I did not

play sports. I couldn't think where I'd seen him until later, when the heat went up and he took off his bomber jacket. Then "Big Sky Country" showed, plain letters on a bright-blue background.

I edged around the corner of the room, into the hall, and stood there to argue with myself. Would he recognize me, or was I just another face, a customer? He probably wasn't really from Montana, so he might not even have been insulted by our little conversation, or remember it anymore. I reasoned that he had probably picked up the shirt vacationing, though who would want to go across that border, over to where the world got meaner? I told myself that I should calm my nerves, go back into the room, have fun. What kept me from doing that was the sudden thought of Serena, of our night together and what I had bought and used.

Once I remembered, I was lost to the present moment. One part of me caught up with the other. I realized that I had left Serena to face her crisis, alone, while I took off in my brand-new van.

I have a hard time getting drunk. It's just the way I am. I start thinking and forget to fill the cup, or recall something I have got to do, and just end up walking from a party. I have put down a full can of beer before and walked out to weed my grandma's rhubarb patch, or work on a cousin's car. Now I was putting myself in Serena's place, feeling her feelings.

What would he want to do that to me for?

I hear her voice say this out loud, just behind me, where there was nothing but wall. I edged along until I came to a door, and then I went through, into a tiny bedroom full of coats, and so far nobody either making out or unconscious upon the floor. I sat on a pile of parkas and jean jackets in this little room, an alcove in the rising buzz of the party outside. I saw a phone, and I dialled Serena's number. Her sister answered.

"Thanks a lot," she said when I said it was me. "You woke up Jason."

"What's wrong with him?" I asked.

There was a silence, then Serena's voice got on the line. "I'm going to hang up."

"Don't."

"He's crying. His ears hurt so bad he can't stand it."

"I'm coming over there."

"Forget it. Forget you."

She said the money I had loaned her would be in the mail. She reminded me it was a long time since the last time I had called. And then the phone went dead. I held the droning receiver in my hand, and tried to clear my mind. The only thing I saw in it, clear as usual, was the van. I decided this was a sign for me to get in behind the wheel. I should drive straight to Serena's house, put on the touch, help her son out. So I set my drink on the windowsill. Then I slipped out the door and I walked down the porch steps, only to find them waiting.

102   I guess he had recognized me after all, and I guess he was from Montana. He had friends, too. They stood around the van, and their heads were level with the roof, for they were tall.

103   "Let's go for a ride," said the one from the all-night gas pump.

104   He knocked on the window of my van with his knuckles. When I told him no thanks, he started karate-kicking the door. He wore black cowboy boots, pointy-toed, with hard-edged new heels. They left ugly dents every time he landed a blow.

105   "Thanks anyhow," I repeated. "But the party's not over." I tried to get back into the house, but, like in a bad dream, the door was stuck, or locked. I hollered, pounded, kicked at the very marks that desperate dog had left, but the music rose and nobody heard. So I ended up in the van. They acted very gracious. They urged me to drive. They were so polite that I tried to tell myself they weren't all that bad. And sure enough, after we had drove for a while, these Montana guys said they had chipped in together to buy me a present.

106   "What is it?" I asked. "Don't keep me in suspense."

107   "Keep driving," said the pump jockey.

108   "I don't really go for surprises," I said. "What's your name, anyhow?"

109   "Marty."

110   "I got a cousin named Marty," I said.

111   "Forget it."

112   The guys in the back exchanged a grumbling kind of laughter, a knowing set of groans. Marty grinned, turned toward me from the passenger seat.

113   "If you really want to know what we're going to give you, I'll tell. It's a map. A map of Montana."

114   Their laughter got wild and went on for too long.

115   "I always liked the state," I said in a serious voice.

116   "No shit," said Marty. "Then I hope you like sitting on it." He signalled where I should turn, and all of a sudden I realized that Lewey's lay ahead. Lewey ran his Tattoo Den from the basement of his house, kept his equipment set up and ready for the weekend.

117   "Whoa," I said. I stopped the van. "You can't tattoo a person against his will. It's illegal."

118   "Get your lawyer on it tomorrow." Marty leaned in close for me to see his eyes. I put the van back in gear but just chugged along, desperately thinking. Lewey was a strange kind of guy, an old Dutch sailor who got beached here, about as far as you can get from salt water. I decided that I'd ask Marty, in a polite kind of way, to beat me up instead. If that failed, I would tell him that there were many states I would not mind so much—smaller, rounder ones.

119   "Are any of you guys from any other state?" I asked, anxious to trade.

"Kansas."   120

"South Dakota."   121

It wasn't that I really had a thing against those places, understand;   122
it's just that the straight-edged shape is not a Chippewa preference.
You look around you, and everything you see is round, everything in
nature. There are no perfect boundaries, no borders. Only human-made
things tend toward cubes and squares—the van, for instance. That was
an example. Suddenly I realized that I was driving a wheeled version of
the state of North Dakota.

"Just beat me up, you guys. Let's get this over with. I'll stop."   123

But they laughed, and then we were at Lewey's.   124

The sign on his basement door said "COME IN." I was shoved from   125
behind and strapped together by five pairs of heavy, football-tough-
ened hands. I was the first to see Lewey, I think, the first to notice that
he was not just a piece of all the trash and accumulated junk that
washed through the concrete-floored cellar but a person, sitting still as
any statue, in a corner, on a chair that creaked and sang when he rose
and walked over.

He even looked like a statue—not the type you see in history books,   126
I don't mean those, but the kind you see for sale as you drive along the
highway. He was a Paul Bunyan, carved with a chain saw. He was
rough-looking, finished in big strokes.

"Please," I said, "I don't want . . ."   127

Marty squeezed me around the throat and tousled up my hair, like   128
friendly.

"He's just got cold feet. Now remember, Lewey, map of Montana.   129
You know where. And put in a lot of detail."

I tried to scream.   130

"Like I was thinking," Marty went on, "of those maps we did in   131
grade school showing products from each region. Cows' heads, oil
wells, those little sheaves of wheat, and so on."

"Tie him up," said Lewey. His voice was thick, with a commanding   132
formal accent. "Then leave."

They did. They took my pants and the keys to the van. I heard the   133
engine roar and die away, and I rolled from side to side in my strict
bindings. I felt Lewey's hand on my shoulder.

"Be still." His voice had changed, now that the others were gone, to   134
a low sound that went with his appearance and did not seem at all unkind. I looked up at him. A broke-down God is who he looked like
from my worm's-eye view. His beard was pure white, long and patchy,
and his big eyes frozen blue. His head was half bald, shining underneath the brilliant fluorescent tubes in the ceiling. You never know
where you're going to find your twin in the world, your double. I don't
mean in terms of looks—I'm talking about mind-set. You never know
where you're going to find the same thoughts in another brain, but
when it happens you know it right off, just like the two of you were

connected by a small electrical wire that suddenly glows red-hot and sparks. That's what happened when I met Lewey Koep.

135   "I don't have a pattern for Montana," he told me. He untied my ropes with a few quick jerks, sneering at the clumsiness of the knots. Then he sat in his desk chair again, and watched me get my bear-

136   ings.

        "I don't want anything tattooed on me, Mr. Koep," I said. "It's a

137   kind of revenge plot."

        He sat in silence, in a waiting quiet, hands folded and face composed. By now I knew I was safe, but I had nowhere to go, and so I sat down on a pile of magazines. He asked, "What revenge?" and I told him the story, the whole thing right from the beginning, when I walked into the bingo hall. I left out the personal details about Serena and me, but he got the picture. I told him about the van.

138   "That's an unusual piece of good fortune."

139   "Have you ever had any? Good fortune?"

140   "All the time. Those guys paid plenty, for instance, though I suppose they'll want it back. You pick out a design. You can owe me."

141   He opened a book he had on the table, a notebook with plastic pages that clipped in and out, and handed it over to me. I didn't want a tattoo, but I didn't want to disappoint this man, either. I leafed through the dragons and the hearts, thinking how to refuse, and then suddenly I saw the horse. It was the same picture that had come into my head as I sat in the woods. Now here it was. The pony skimmed, legs outstretched, reaching for the edge of the page. I got a thought in my head, clear and vital, that this little horse would convince Serena I was serious about her.

142   "This one."

143   Lewey nodded, and heated his tools.

144   That's why I got it put on, that little horse, and suffered pain. Now my hand won't let me rest. It throbs and aches as if it was coming alive again after a hard frost had made it numb. I know I'm going somewhere, taking this hand to Serena. Even walking down the road in a pair of big-waisted green pants belonging to Lewey Koep, toward the So Long Bar, where I keep everything I own in life, I'm going forward. My hand is a ball of pins, but when I look down I see the little black horse running hard, fast, and serious.

145   I'm ready for what will come next. That's why I don't fall on the ground, and I don't yell, when I come across the van in a field. At first, I think it is the dream van, the way I always see it in my vision. Then I look, and it's the real vehicle. Totalled.

146   My bingo van is smashed on the sides, kicked and scratched, and the insides are scattered. Stereo wires, glass, and ripped pieces of carpet are spread here and there among the new sprouts of wheat. I force open a door that is bent inward. I wedge myself behind the wheel, which is

tipped over at a crazy angle, and I look out. The windshield is shattered in a sunlight burst, through which the world is cut to bits.

I've been up all night, and the day stretches long before me, so I decide to sleep where I am. Part of the seat is still wonderfully upholstered, thick and plush, and it reclines now—permanently, but so what? I relax into the small comfort, my body as warm as an animal, my thoughts drifting. I know I'll wake to nothing, but at this moment I feel rich. Sinking away, I feel like everything worth having is within my grasp. All I have to do is put my hand into the emptiness.

147

Questions for Discussion and Writing

1. What does Lipsha reveal about himself that makes him seem endearing despite his very real errors in judgment? How effective do you find this method of CHARACTERIZATION?
2. What connections does Erdrich suggest between Lipsha's desire for the bingo van and his waning healing powers? What values does the van represent to Lipsha?
3. What is at stake in Lipsha's relationship with Serena? Why is it significant that Serena's outfit and the van are described in similar terms? To what extent is Lipsha's choice between the van and Serena a reflection of his ambivalence toward his Chippewa heritage?
4. How do Erdrich's descriptions of SETTINGS and artifacts (such as the van, motel room, and lake) underscore the conflict Lipsha experiences between his Chippewa heritage and the modern world?
5. How might the destruction of the van and Lipsha's treatment by the young white men he has antagonized be seen as an appropriate punishment for his treatment of Serena and betrayal of his heritage?
6. Under what circumstances does Lipsha acquire the tattoo of the small black pony? How is its significance foreshadowed earlier in the story?
7. In your opinion, have Lipsha's experiences changed him sufficiently to allow his healing gifts to return?
8. Describe in detail, using as many different senses as possible, a real place that you regard as special (as Lipsha does with the lake).
9. What do the names of surrounding lakes, mountains, parks, or towns in your environment mean or refer to? Are any of them of Indian origin?
10. Describe the first time you ever won a prize, contest, or lottery. Discuss the circumstances and what you did with your winnings. If you have never won a prize, then describe what you would do with your winnings if you did.

Dal Stivens

Warrigal

Born in 1911, in Blayney, Australia, Dal Stivens has been one of his country's best-known short story writers since the 1930s. He is also a painter whose work has been exhibited in many galleries and institutions including James Cook University and John Curtin House. He has been a Commonwealth Literature Fund Lecturer at the University of Adelaide, 1963; a member of the New South Wales Australian Broadcasting Commission; and the founder in 1962 of the Australian Society of Authors (P.E.N.), serving as its president from 1962 to 1973. While much of his writing takes the form of fables that have no regional setting, some of his best known works are set in recognizable Australian terrain. A prolific writer, Stivens has published collections of short stories including The Unicorn and Other Tales *(1976) and* The Demon Bowler and Other Cricket Stories *(1981). He received the Miles Franklin Award for the best Australian novel, 1970, for* A Horse of Air. *He has also been a contributor to natural history periodicals including* Wildlife, Pacific Discovery, *and* Animal Kingdom. *"Warrigal" (1976) is the amusing tale of the deteriorating relationship between the narrator and his neighbors who fail to appreciate the virtues of his pet dingo, a wolflike wild dog native to Australia.*

1   "You'll have to get rid of that dingo before long," my neighbour Swinburne said to me across the fence. "Why, he's an Asiatic wolf—"

2   "No one of any authority says that the dingo is an Asiatic wolf," I said. "The Curator of Mammals at the Australian Museum classifies the dingo as *Canis familiaris* variety *dingo*—that is, a variety of the common dog. Another eminent authority says it's most unlikely that the dingo is descended from the northern wolf—"

3   "I know a wolf when I see it," this classic pyknic said. "I don't care what some long-haired professors say. I was brought up in the bush."

4   As my wife Martha says, I can be insufferable at times—particularly when I'm provoked. I said: "So much for your fears of this animal attacking you—it's most unlikely as long as he continues to look on you as the *gamma* animal. Of course, you need to act like a *gamma* animal at all times."

5   I thought for a moment he was going to climb over the paling fence that divided our properties and throw a punch at me.

6   "You be careful who you call an animal!" he said. His big red face and neck were swelling like a frog's. It was pure Lorenz and Heidigger I was throwing at him. This was during my animal behaviour period.

7   "I'm not calling you an animal," I said. "I'm just explaining how the dingo sees you. He sees me as the *alpha* animal—*alpha* is Greek for A.

28

I'm the pack leader in his eyes. He sees my wife, Martha, as the *beta* animal. *Beta* is B and *gamma* is C. He probably sees you and your wife and kids as *gamma* or *delta* animals. *Delta* is D. While you behave like *gamma* or *delta* animals, you'll be O.K. He'll defer to you."

He seemed a little assured—or confused, anyway. 8

"This *gamma* stuff," he began uncertainly. "You're sure of it, now?" 9

"I'll lend you a book," I said. 10

"All the same, he's got pretty powerful jaws," he said, pointing to 11
Red, who was crouching at my feet, his eyes not leaving me. The jaws were, as he said, powerful, and the white shining canine teeth rather large. The head was a little too large, the prick ears a bit too thick at the roots for Red to be a really handsome dog, but there was a compact power in his strong tawny chest and limbs.

"No more than a German shepherd's," I said. There were two of 12
them in Mansion Road—that wasn't the name but it will do.

"I suppose so," he said doubtfully. 13

"If I hadn't told you Red was a dingo you wouldn't be worrying," I 14
said. "I could have told you Red was a mongrel."

"Are you trying to tell me I wouldn't know a dingo?" he started in 15
belligerently.

Before I could answer, his own dog, a Dobermann Pinscher and a 16
real North Shore status job, came out and began challenging Red. Both dogs raced up and down on their sides of the fence, the Pinscher growling and barking and Red just growling. (Dingoes don't bark in the wilds. When domesticated some learn to do so but Red hadn't.)

Red ran on his toes, his reddish-brown coat gleaming and white- 17
tipped bushy tail waving erect. His gait was exciting to watch: it was smooth, effortless and one he could maintain for hours.

"This is what I mean," he said. "Your Asiatic wolf could savage my 18
dog to death."

"Yours is making the most noise," I said. The Pinscher was as ag- 19
gressive as his master.

"Noise isn't everything," he said. "Look at that wolf-like crouch- 20
ing."

"Innate behaviour," I said. "Dingoes have acquired that over thou- 21
sands of years of attacking emus and kangaroos. They crouch to avoid the kicks."

"So your wolf is getting ready to attack, is he?" 22

"Not necessarily," I said. "No more than yours is. Of course, if one 23
dog were to invade the other's territory, then there would be a fight. But they won't invade."

"Yours could jump the fence," he said. "I've seen him. He could kill 24
my dog and clean up my fowls."

"Not into your place," I said. I was beginning to lose my temper. 25
"He wouldn't. He knows it isn't his."

"So he's moral, is he?" he shouted. "This wild dog—" 26

27   "They're all moral although the term is anthropomorphic. Wild dogs or domestic dogs usually won't invade another's territory."

28   "So you say," he said. His face was purpling. "I warn you now yours had better not. If he does I'll shoot him. The law's on my side."

29   I was so angry I went inside and got a hammer. I started knocking palings out of the fence.

30   "Hey!" he shouted. "That's my fence. And I meant what I said about shooting that Asiatic mongrel."

31   "Pure-bred dingo," I grunted. I was out of condition and the nails were tough. "Our fence."

32   I got four palings out and, as I knew would happen, the dogs kept racing past the gap and ignoring the chance to enter and attack. I was dishing out pure Lorenz.

33   "It's just bluff," I said. "You can see it for yourself. They talk big. After they've said their bit, they'll knock off."

34   "Perhaps," he said, doubtfully.

35   "Call your dog out into the street," I said. "I'll call mine. They'll meet in the middle and sniff each other's anal quarters but they won't fight. There's nothing to fight about—none lays claim to the centre of the road. Of course, the footpath is different."

36   "I won't risk it," he said and he called the Pinscher and started off. "You may be right and your dingo ought to be at home in your garden."

37   It might have sounded conciliatory to you. But there was a crack in it. This was during my Australian native flora period. When I bought this block I had the house built well down the hillside and left all the trees and shrubs. I wanted a native bushland garden and I had left what the other people in Mansion Road called "that rubbish" in its near-natural state. I had planted some more natives—waratahs like great red Roman torches, delicately starred wax flowers and native roses, piquantly scented boronias, flannel flowers, and subtly curving spider flowers. This was in keeping with my newly acquired feeling for *furyu*, which is often used to describe things Japanese. It can be translated as "tasteful," but the Japanese characters convey a fuller meaning of "flowing with the wind"—the acceptance of nature, of the material itself, and of the patterns it imposes. Transferring the concept to Australia, I was accepting nature and learning to appreciate the muted beauty of Australian shrubs and flowers.

38   The neighbours didn't approve. They all had lots of lawns and terraces and beds of perennials and annuals. They'd chopped down most of the native trees and planted exotics. They thought my garden lowered the tone of the street. And they thought the same about our unobtrusive low-line house, blending with the slim eucalypts and the sandstone outcrops. They preferred double-fronted mod. bungs.

39   We'd have got on a lot better if we had lived in Mansion Street

during my azalea and camellia period. At our last house Martha and I had gone in for landscaping—vistas, focus points, and the rest. And we'd used azaleas and camellias for much of the mass planting. I'd got myself wised up on azaleas, particularly, and I knew as much as most about Wilson's fifty Kurumes; I once engaged in some learned discussion in a specialist journal as to whether or not some experts were correct in thinking Pink Pearl (*Azuma Kagami*) was, indeed, the progenitor of all the pink-flowered forms.

That was some time ago, and although I still like azaleas, the love affair was then over. Not everyone appreciates Australian natives. We went away for a week once and when we came back someone had dumped two tons of rubbish into our place. We had no fence at the street level and someone had thought it was a virgin block. The house is well down the slope and hard to see from the street. Of course, he should have noticed the rather heavy concentration of native flora. He had tipped the rusting tins, galvanized iron, mattresses, and so on, onto a stand of native roses, too.

We didn't really fit into Mansion Road for a number of reasons. First, there was my profession as a journalist and writer. And moreover, Martha and I were in our Chagall period; our earlier Rembrandt love affair might have been accepted.

And there was the car business. They all had one or two cars but we didn't see the need when there was a good taxi and hire car service. When they finally got the idea that we could afford a car but wouldn't have one, it struck them as un-Australian or something.

The dingo business was merely another straw, though Swinburne seemed to be trying to push it a bit further.

"Why get yourself angry?" Martha reproached me when I went inside.

"A conformist ass!?" I said.

"You can't educate him," she said.

"I know," I said. "I was having a bit of fun."

"Whatever you call it, we'll probably have to get rid of Red," she said.

"Where?" I said.

That was the question. I wasn't giving him to the Zoo, as some in Mansion Road had hinted I should. Dingoes are far-ranging, lively, intelligent creatures and it would be cruelty to confine him. And I couldn't release him in the bush now that he was a year old and had had no training in hunting for himself. Normally, he would have acquired this from his mother, but I'd got Red as a pup. A zoologist friend had brought him to Sydney and then found his wife wouldn't let him keep a dingo.

I didn't see Swinburne again until the next week-end. He called me over the fence.

52   "What you say about that dingo might be true at present but he'll revert to type," he said. "The hunting instinct is too strong. It will be someone's chicken run eventually even if it's not mine."

53   "He hasn't been taught to hunt fowls—or anything else," I said. "So why should he? He's well fed."

54   "Primitive instincts are strong," said Swinburne.

55   "We don't know what his primeval instincts are," I said.

56   "He's a wild dog."

57   I said, insufferably: "Professor Konrad Lorenz, who is one of the world's greatest authorities on dogs, says that the dingo is a descendant of a domesticated dog brought here by the Aborigines. He points out that a pure-blooded dingo often has white stockings or stars and nearly always a white tip to its tail. He adds that these points are quite irregularly distributed. This, as everyone knows, is a feature never seen in wild animals but it occurs frequently in all domestic animals."

58   "Has this foreign professor ever seen a dingo in the wilds?" he asked.

59   I couldn't see what his question had to do with the paraphrase I had given him, but I told him that while Lorenz had not been to Australia so far as I knew, he had bred and studied dingoes.

60   He changed the subject abruptly.

61   "You seem to know all about animals and birds," he said. "Perhaps you have a cure for a crowing rooster? Mine is upsetting some of the neighbours by crowing during the night. He answers other roosters across the valley." (There were farms there.) "In a street like Mansion Road, you have to fit in."

62   He was getting at me but I ignored it.

63   "I think so," I said.

64   "I'd like to hear it," he said, too sweetly.

65   "You have to get on with people, as you say," I said, also too sweetly. "But roosters can be stopped from crowing in a very simple fashion. A rooster, as you know, has to stretch its neck to crow. I'd suggest tacking a piece of hessian over the perch, a couple of inches above his head. When he goes to stretch his neck, he'll bump the hessian and won't be able to crow."

66   He took it in after a few questions and said he'd try it. It took him and his fifteen-year-old son most of the afternoon. I must say they were thorough. It took them ten minutes to catch that White Leghorn and then they held him with his feet on the ground and measured the distance to a couple of inches over his head. They measured the hessian meticulously and then they had a conference during which they kept looking towards me. I was sowing some flannel flower seeds. I'd gone to the near-by bushland reserve several times to observe the soil and aspect of flannel flowers so that I could plant the seeds in the right place in my garden.

67   Swinburne came over to the fence finally. "I'm sorry to trouble

you," he said. This was a change. "But there are several perches in the hen house."

"The top one," I said. "He's the *alpha* animal." 68

They fixed it there and Swinburne asked me to come and have a 69 beer at his place. But he hadn't changed his mind much about the dingo because he and his wife started telling me about the merits of budgerigars as pets.

"Now, budgerigars make marvellous pets," he said. "Our Joey is a 70 wonderful talker."

The bird, a male pied blue, was perched on his hand, and while Mrs 71 Swinburne smiled dotingly, it displayed and then, with wings downdragging, it tried to copulate with Swinburne's big red hand.

"Isn't he quaint?" asked Mrs Swinburne. "He does that by the 72 hour."

Poor bloody bird, I thought. 73

"No wonder," I said aloud. 74

"What do you mean?" 75

"Nothing," I said. "I mean it's wonderful." 76

"And they tell me budgerigars don't talk in the wilds," said Mrs 77 Swinburne.

"No," I said. "Only when they're caged." I refrained from saying 78 anything about mimicry being due to starved sexuality, to banked-up energy.

I couldn't see Mansion Road letting up on Red—Swinburne was 79 just the official spokesman as it were, one of the *alpha* members in the street, the managing director of a shoe factory. I knew the others were saying the same things among themselves.

They said them to me a few nights later. Mrs Fitter called. If 80 Swinburne was an *alpha* male, she was *the alpha* female. Her father had been a drapery knight and had built the big house in which the Fitters lived with a feature window and two cars.

"I've come on behalf of the mothers of Mansion Road," she started 81 in. She was a large dark woman with a hint of a moustache. "They're very frightened that ravening wild dingo will attack their children. They have to pass it on their way to school and it crouches in the gutter."

She was laying it on. Most of the children were driven to school. 82

"It won't attack them," I said. "He lies in the gutter because that's 83 his territorial boundary. Like ourselves animals are land owners."

"And what's more he barks at them," she said, going too far. 84

"Dingoes don't bark," I said, gently, but I was getting angry. Martha 85 was making signs.

"And at cars, too," she said. "I had to swerve to miss him. And he 86 slavers at the lips."

"He has well-developed salivary glands," I said. "I assure you he 87 won't attack anyone, but in any case the solution is simple. Your

Schnauzer owns your footpath, Mrs Fitter—or thinks he does. I respect his property right and don't walk on his footpath and we get on very well."

88   It wasn't tactful but I didn't want to be.

89   After Mrs Fitter had left, Martha said, "Red has been going out after cars the last couple of days."

90   "But not barking?" I asked.

91   "No," she said.

92   Three nights later a young policeman called. Mrs Fitter had complained that Red had killed one of her fowls.

93   "Did she see him?" I asked.

94   "No, but she is convinced it could only have been the dingo," he said.

95   "Well, constable, you know the legal position as well as I do," I said. I didn't like it but I had to tack a bit. "Every dog is allowed one bite— but not two. I don't admit that Red did kill the fowl. It could have been any one of the dogs in the street. And, further, Red is not necessarily a dingo. He could be a mongrel. I don't know his parentage. He was found in the outback by a friend and brought to Sydney."

96   He went away but was back the next night.

97   "Mrs Fitter says that you have admitted that the animal is a dingo," he said.

98   "I admit nothing," I said tacking again. "I have called the dog a dingo without any accurate knowledge and purely out of a spirit of fantasy. I wanted to indulge in a little fancy. It has been fun to think of Red as a dingo."

99   He was a bit shaken and I went on, "I'm no expert on dingoes, nor is anyone else in this street. Have you ever seen a pure-bred dingo?"

100   "I think so—at the Zoo—" he said, uncertainly.

101   "Exactly," I said. "And how do you know it was a pure one and even if it was, would you be able to point to any dog with certainty and say that is a dingo or that another was a Dobermann Pinscher—"

102   "A Doberman what, sir?"

103   "Mr Swinburne's dog is a Dobermann Pinscher. Mrs Fitter, on the other hand, has a Schnauzer. Of course, the two have points in common, according to the experts. I am told that a Manchester Terrier is even closer in appearance to a Dobermann Pinscher and that only the well informed can pick one from the other. Now when you come to mongrels, the question of identification is much more complicated—"

104   There was a bit more of it. He fled in some confusion and Martha and I rolled around the floor, helpless with laughter, and went to bed earlier. But it was getting serious. If I didn't cure Red of going out on the road, Mrs Fitter, or someone else, wasn't going to swerve next time.

105   What I did was undiluted Lorenz.

106   If you want to stop a dog chasing cars you have to fire a small stone

at him from behind from a catapult when he is in the middle of chasing. When you do it this way the dog is taken by surprise. He doesn't see you do it and it seems to him like the hand of God. That is anthropomorphic, but you know what I'm getting at; it's a memorable experience for the dog and usually cures him completely.

I stayed home the next day. It took me an hour to make a catapult that worked properly and I had to practise for twenty minutes. Then I was ready. I cured Red that morning with two hits, which were, I hope, not too painful. The gutter and the street were abandoned by him. Encouraged, I decided to cure him of establishing himself on the footpath. I achieved that, too. 107

I knew it only won a respite for the dingo. I had to return him to the wilds. The alternatives of giving him to the Zoo, or having him put away, I'd already rejected. Swinburne came home early that day. 108

"I see you're still insisting on keeping that Asiatic wolf," he said. 109

"*Canis familiaris* variety *dingo*," I corrected. "But you're wrong about keeping him. I'm returning him to the wilds." 110

"But they're sheep killers." 111

"Not where there are no sheep." 112

"There are sheep everywhere," he said stubbornly. 113

"Australia's a big place," I said. "There ought to be a place somewhere where he can live his own life. But he'll have to be taught to hunt before I can release him." 114

"You mean on wild animals?" 115

"What else?" I said. 116

"You'll soon have the fauna protection people after you," he said. 117

"Rabbits aren't protected," I said. 118

"They're vermin—and so are dingoes!" he said. 119

They didn't give me time to put my plan into operation. I had thought it just possible that they might give Red a bait. But I couldn't believe they hated him so much. Besides it's an offence to lay baits and they were most law-abiding in Mansion Road. They didn't poison Red. What happened was that Red went wandering off one day through the bushland reserve and a poultry farmer on the other side of the valley shot the dingo, as he was legally entitled to do. 120

"Sorry to hear about that dog of yours," said Swinburne later. 121

"But why should he go off?" I asked. 122

"I know a bit about dingoes," he said and his eyes were gleaming. "Most likely he followed a bitch on heat. It's a question of studying animal behaviour." 123

I knew then that he'd done it with a farmer in on the job. They were legal in Mansion Road. But I wouldn't be able to prove anything. 124

"It's better to keep budgerigars as pets," I said blazing inside. "You keep them sex-starved and they'll try to mate with your hand." Only I used a blunter word. "It's all nice and jolly and they'll talk, too." 125

I was sorry afterwards for losing my temper. Swinburne wrung 126 the budgerigar's neck the next time it displayed on his wife's hand.

127   We sold out soon afterwards. I was coming to the end of my Australian native flora period, anyway.

Questions for Discussion and Writing

1. What kind of a person does the NARRATOR seem to be? How does his allegiance to an authentic Australian heritage put him into conflict with his suburban neighbors?
2. In what way is Swinburne presented as a flat or one-dimensional character in contrast to the narrator? What methods of CHARACTERIZATION does Stivens use to make the narrator seem to be a fully developed character?
3. How do the descriptions of the way the narrator landscaped his home express the same attachment to an authentic Australian tradition as his choice of the dingo (warrigal is an old Australian name for dingo) as a pet? How does Stivens use SETTINGS to underscore the conflict between the narrator and his neighbors?
4. How does the narrator's behavior begin to change when the police pay him a visit? What efforts does he make to tame the dingo so that it will fit in? After the dingo is shot, does the narrator's reaction suggest he is no longer willing to oppose the values of modern suburbia?
5. Is there a particular animal or insect abundant in your area? What is it and how do people deal with it?
6. What could your pet say about you that no human knows?
7. How do pets allow people to project their real feelings and interact with each other indirectly through the pet? Has your pet ever brought you into conflict with a neighbor?
8. Describe the plants and animals in a place using accurate zoological and botanical terms.

Bessie Head

Looking for a Rain God

Bessie Head (1937–1986) was born in Pietermaritzburg, South Africa, the daughter of a black father and a white mother. She suffered the childhood trauma of being "reclassified"; she was taken from her mother at birth and brought up by foster parents as a Coloured. Her mother was treated as insane because of her relationship with a black man. Head was raised by her foster parents until she was thirteen, when she was placed in a mission orphanage. The emotional scars of her childhood are powerfully recorded in the widely acclaimed A Question of Power (1973), a fictional study of madness produced by the violence of the apartheid system. After completing her education, she taught grammar school and wrote fiction for a local newspaper. In 1963, Head moved to a farm commune in Serowe, Botswana, with her son. She lived there, working as a teacher and a gardener in a local village until her death.

Head's writing grows directly out of her experience of village life. Her first novel, When Rain Clouds Gather (1968), presents the epic struggle of a village trying to survive a devastating drought. Her next two novels, Maru (1971) and A Question of Power (1973), depict women struggling to overcome oppression in their societies and earned her the distinction of being one of Africa's major female writers. As a chronicler of village life, Head wrote two histories, Serowe: Village of the Rain Wind (1981) and A Bewitched Crossroad (1985). "Looking for a Rain God," from The Collector of Treasures and Other Botswana Village Tales (1977), is based on a shocking local incident revealing how an ancient tribal ritual resurfaced after years of drought in modern-day Botswana.

It is lonely at the lands where the people go to plough. These lands are vast clearings in the bush, and the wild bush is lonely too. Nearly all the lands are within walking distance from the village. In some parts of the bush where the underground water is very near the surface, people made little rest camps for themselves and dug shallow wells to quench their thirst while on their journey to their own lands. They experienced all kinds of things once they left the village. They could rest at shady watering places full of lush, tangled trees with delicate pale-gold and purple wildflowers springing up between soft green moss and the children could hunt around for wild figs and any berries that might be in season. But from 1958, a seven-year drought fell upon the land and even the watering places began to look as dismal as the dry open thorn-bush country; the leaves of the trees curled up and withered; the moss became dry and hard and, under the shade of the tangled trees, the ground turned a powdery black and white, because there was no rain. People said rather humorously that if you tried to catch the rain in a cup it would only fill a teaspoon. Toward the beginning of the seventh year of drought, the summer had become an anguish to live through. The air was so dry and moisture-free that it burned the skin. No one knew what to do to escape the heat and tragedy was in the air. At the beginning of that summer, a number of men just went out of their homes and hung themselves to death from trees. The majority of the people had lived off crops, but for two years past they had all returned from the lands with only their rolled-up skin blankets and cooking utensils. Only the charlatans, incanters, and witch doctors made a pile of money during this time because people were always turning to them in desperation for little talismans and herbs to rub on the plough for the crops to grow and the rain to fall.

2   The rains were late that year. They came in early November, with a promise of good rain. It wasn't the full, steady downpour of the years of good rain but thin, scanty, misty rain. It softened the earth and a rich growth of green things sprang up everywhere for the animals to eat. People were called to the center of the village to hear the proclamation of the beginning of the ploughing season; they stirred themselves and whole families began to move off to the lands to plough.

3   The family of the old man, Mokgobja, were among those who left early for the lands. They had a donkey cart and piled everything onto it, Mokgobja—who was over seventy years old; two girls, Neo and Boseyong; their mother Tiro and an unmarried sister, Nesta; and the father and supporter of the family, Ramadi, who drove the donkey cart. In the rush of the first hope of rain, the man, Ramadi, and the two women, cleared the land of thornbush and then hedged their vast ploughing area with this same thornbush to protect the future crop from the goats they had brought along for milk. They cleared out and deepened the old well with its pool of muddy water and still in this light, misty rain, Ramadi inspanned two oxen and turned the earth over with a hand plough.

4   The land was ready and ploughed, waiting for the crops. At night, the earth was alive with insects singing and rustling about in search of food. But suddenly, by mid-November, the rain flew away; the rain clouds fled away and left the sky bare. The sun danced dizzily in the skin, with a strange cruelty. Each day the land was covered in a haze of mist as the sun sucked up the last drop of moisture out of the earth. The family sat down in despair, waiting and waiting. Their hopes had run so high; the goats had started producing milk, which they had eagerly poured on their porridge, now they ate plain porridge with no milk. It was impossible to plant the corn, maize, pumpkin, and watermelon seeds in the dry earth. They sat the whole day in the shadow of the huts and even stopped thinking, for the rain had fled away. Only the children, Neo and Boseyong, were quite happy in their little-girl world. They carried on with their game of making house like their mother and chattered to each other in light, soft tones. They made children from

sticks around which they tied rags, and scolded them severely in an exact imitation of their own mother. Their voices could be heard scolding the day long: "You stupid thing, when I send you to draw water, why do you spill half of it out of the bucket!" "You stupid thing! Can't you mind the porridge pot without letting the porridge burn!" And then they would beat the rag dolls on their bottoms with severe expressions.

The adults paid no attention to this; they did not even hear the 5 funny chatter; they sat waiting for rain; their nerves were stretched to breaking-point willing the rain to fall out of the sky. Nothing was important, beyond that. All their animals had been sold during the bad years to purchase food, and of all their herd only two goats were left. It was the women of the family who finally broke down under the strain of waiting for rain. It was really the two women who caused the death of the little girls. Each night they started a weird, high-pitched wailing that began on a low, mournful note and whipped up to a frenzy. Then they would stamp their feet and shout as though they had lost their heads. The men sat quiet and self-controlled; it was important for men to maintain their self control at all times but their nerve was breaking too. They knew the women were haunted by the starvation of the coming year.

Finally, an ancient memory stirred in the old man, Mokgobja. When 6 he was very young and the customs of the ancestors still ruled the land, he had been witness to a rain-making ceremony. And he came alive a little, struggling to recall the details which had been buried by years and years of prayer in a Christian church. As soon as the mists cleared a little, he began consulting in whispers with his youngest son, Ramadi. There was, he said, a certain rain god who accepted only the sacrifice of the bodies of children. Then the rain would fall; then the crops would grow, he said. He explained the ritual and as he talked, his memory became a conviction and he began to talk with unshakable authority. Ramadi's nerves were smashed by the nightly wailing of the women and soon the two men began whispering with the two women. The children continued their game: "You stupid thing! How could you have lost the money on the way to the shop! You must have been playing again!"

After it was all over and the bodies of the two little girls had been 7 spread across the land, the rain did not fall. Instead, there was a deathly silence at night and the devouring heat of the sun by day. A terror, extreme and deep, overwhelmed the whole family. They packed, rolling up their skin blankets and pots, and fled back to the village.

People in the village soon noted the absence of the two little girls. 8 They had died at the lands and were buried there, the family said. But people noted their ashen, terror-stricken faces and a murmur arose. What had killed the children, they wanted to know? And the family replied that they had just died. And people said amongst themselves that it was strange that the two deaths had occurred at the same time.

And there was a feeling of great unease at the unnatural looks of the family. Soon the police came around. The family told them the same story of death and burial at the lands. They did not know what the children had died of. So the police asked to see the graves. At this, the mother of the children broke down and told everything.

9   Throughout that terrible summer the story of the children hung like a dark cloud of sorrow over the village, and the sorrow was not assuaged when the old man and Ramadi were sentenced to death for ritual murder. All they had on the statute books was that ritual murder was against the law and must be stamped out with the death penalty. The subtle story of strain and starvation and breakdown was inadmissible evidence at court; but all the people who lived off crops knew in their hearts that only a hair's breadth had saved them from sharing a fate similar to that of the Mokgobja family. They could have killed something to make the rain fall.

Questions for Discussion and Writing

1. Why doesn't Head withhold knowledge of the ending in telling this story? How does knowing what happened shift the focus of the story and make us want to understand what motivated the CHARACTERS to do what they did?
2. Why is it important to know that the events described in this story occurred after a seven-year drought?
3. What details foreshadow the eventual fate of Neo and Boseyong? In a culture where every morsel of food and every drop of water is precious how would the adults look upon the behavior of the two girls? How do the games Neo and Boseyong play reflect how they are already being treated?
4. How does SETTING enter the story as a major force shaping the events that take place? How do Head's detailed descriptions of the blistering heat and dessicated landscape enable the reader to better understand why the idea of ritual sacrifice takes root?
5. The story concludes with the statement that the other villagers "could have killed something to make the rain fall." Explain what you think Head meant by this.
6. Is there a secret in your town that only the people who live there know? Does it involve a crime once committed there?
7. In your opinion, what actions or reactions would serve as a sign that someone was guilty of a crime and not simply nervous?
8. Analyze this story in terms of the elements of crime, motive, clues, suspects, victim, detective, alibi, solution, and confession associated with the mystery genre.

Carmen Naranjo

And We Sold the Rain

Born in Cartago, Costa Rica, in 1931, Carmen Naranjo has been an outstanding figure in Costa Rican cultural and political life, having served as ambassador to Israel. She is a prolific writer whose works include six novels, the most recent of which, Sobrepunto, was published in 1985, three volumes of short stories, and several volumes of poetry, plays, and essays. She has twice received Costa Rica's National Prize for Literature and was awarded the Magon Prize, the highest honor conferred by the government on an individual, in recognition of her work on the behalf of culture. Naranjo served as secretary of culture and directs the most important publishing organization in Central America, the Editorial Universitaria Centro America. Naranjo's fiction blends realism with fantasy as a way of exploring important social issues through innovative narrative perspectives. "And We Sold the Rain," translated by Jo Anne Engelbert (1988), is a funny, yet grim satire of the economic agonies of a small Third World country in Central America that decides to raise cash by selling their most precious natural resource, rain, to the Saudi Arabians.

"This is a royal fuck-up," was all the treasury minister could say a few days ago as he got out of the jeep after seventy kilometers of jouncing over dusty rutted roads and muddy trails. His advisor agreed: there wasn't a cent in the treasury, the line for foreign exchange wound four times around the capital, and the IMF was stubbornly insisting that the country could expect no more loans until the interest had been paid up, public spending curtailed, salaries frozen, domestic production increased, imports reduced, and social programs cut.

The poor were complaining, "We can't even buy beans—they've got us living on radish tops, bananas and garbage; they raise our water bills but don't give us any water even though it rains every day, and on top of that they add on a charge for excess consumption for last year, even though there wasn't any water in the pipes then either."

"Doesn't anyone in this whole goddamned country have an idea that could get us out of this?" asked the president of the republic, who shortly before the elections, surrounded by a toothily smiling, impeccably tailored meritocracy, had boasted that by virtue of his university-trained mind (Ph.D. in developmental economics) he was the best candidate. Someone proposed to him that he pray to La Negrita; he did and nothing happened. Somebody else suggested that he reinstate the Virgin of Ujarrás. But after so many years of neglect, the pretty little virgin had gone deaf and ignored the pleas for help, even though the entire cabinet implored her, at the top of their lungs, to light the way to a better future and a happier tomorrow.

41

4   The hunger and poverty could no longer be concealed: the home-less, pockets empty, were squatting in the Parque Central, the Parque Nacional, and the Plaza de la Cultura. They were camping along Central and Second Avenues and in a shantytown springing up on the plains outside the city. Gangs were threatening to invade the national theater, the Banco Central, and all nationalized banking headquarters. The Public Welfare Agency was rationing rice and beans as if they were medicine. In the marketplace, robberies increased to one per second, and homes were burgled at the rate of one per half hour. Business and government were sinking in sleaze; drug lords operated uncontrolled, and gambling was institutionalized in order to launder dollars and at-tract tourists. Strangely enough, the prices of a few items went down: whiskey, caviar and other such articles of conspicuous consumption.

5   The sea of poverty that was engulfing cities and villages contrasted with the growing number of Mercedes Benzes, BMWs and a whole al-phabet of trade names of gleaming new cars.

6   The minister announced to the press that the country was on the verge of bankruptcy. The airlines were no longer issuing tickets because so much money was owed them, and travel became impossible; even official junkets were eliminated. There was untold suffering of civil ser-vants suddenly unable to travel even once a month to the great cities of the world! A special budget might be the solution, but tax revenues were nowhere to be found, unless a compliant public were to go along with the president's brilliant idea of levying a tax on air—a minimal tax, to be sure, but, after all, the air was a part of the government's pat-rimony. Ten *colones* per breath would be a small price to pay.

7   July arrived, and one afternoon a minister without portfolio and without umbrella, noticing that it had started to rain, stood watching people run for cover. "Yes," he thought, "here it rains like it rains in Comala, like it rains in Macondo. It rains day and night, rain after rain, like a theater with the same movie, sheets of water. Poor people with-out umbrellas, without a change of clothes, they get drenched, people living in leaky houses, without a change of shoes for when they're ship-wrecked. And here, all my poor colleagues with colds, all the poor deputies with laryngitis, the president with that worrisome cough, all this on top of the catastrophe itself. No TV station is broadcasting; all of them are flooded, along with the newspaper plants and the radio sta-tions. A people without news is a lost people, because they don't know that everywhere else, or almost everywhere else, things are even worse. If we could only export the rain," thought the minister.

8   Meanwhile, the people, depressed by the heavy rains, the damp-ness, the lack of news, the cold, and their hunger and despair without their sitcoms and soap operas, began to rain inside and to increase the baby population—that is, to try to increase the odds that one of their progeny might survive. A mass of hungry, naked babies began to cry in concert every time it rained.

When one of the radio transmitters was finally repaired, the president was able to broadcast a message: He had inherited a country so deeply in debt that it could no longer obtain credit and could no longer afford to pay either the interest or the amortization on loans. He had to dismiss civil servants, suspend public works, cut off services, close offices, and spread his legs somewhat to transnationals. Now even these lean cows were dying; the fat ones were on the way, encouraged by the International Monetary Fund, the AID and the IDB, not to mention the EEC. The great danger was that the fat cows had to cross over the neighboring country on their way, and it was possible that they would be eaten up—even though they came by air, at nine thousand feet above the ground, in a first class stable in a pressurized, air-conditioned cabin. Those neighbors were simply not to be trusted.

The fact was that the government had faded in the people's memory. By now no one remembered the names of the president or his ministers; people remembered them as "the one with glasses who thinks he's Tarzan's mother," or "the one who looks like the baby hog someone gave me when times were good, maybe a little uglier."

The solution came from the most unexpected source. The country had organized the Third World contest to choose "Miss Underdeveloped," to be elected, naturally, from the multitudes of skinny, dusky, round-shouldered, short-legged, half-bald girls with cavity-pocked smiles, girls suffering from parasites and God knows what else. The prosperous Emirate of the Emirs sent its designée, who in sheer amazement at how it rained and rained, widened her enormous eyes— fabulous eyes of harem and Koran delights—and was unanimously elected reigning Queen of Underdevelopment. Lacking neither eyeteeth nor molars, she was indeed the fairest of the fair. She returned in a rush to the Emirate of the Emirs, for she had acquired, with unusual speed, a number of fungal colonies that were taking over the territory under her toenails and fingernails, behind her ears, and on her left cheek.

"Oh, Father Sultan, my lord, lord of the moons and of the suns, if your Arabian highness could see how it rains and rains in that country, you would not believe it. It rains day and night. Everything is green, even the people; they are green people, innocent and trusting, who probably have never even thought about selling their most important resource, the rain. The poor fools think about coffee, rice, sugar, vegetables, and lumber, and they hold Ali Baba's treasure in their hands without even knowing it. What we would give to have such abundance!"

Sultan Abun dal Tol let her speak and made her repeat the part about the rain from dawn to dusk, dusk to dawn, for months on end. He wanted to hear over and over about that greenness that was forever turning greener. He loved to think of it raining and raining, of singing in the rain, of showers bringing forth flowers . . .

A long distance phone call was made to the office of the export minister from the Emirate of the Emirs, but the minister wasn't in. The trade minister grew radiant when Sultan Abun dal Tol, warming to his subject, instructed him to buy up rain and construct an aqueduct between their countries to fertilize the desert. Another call. Hello, am I speaking with the country of rain, not the rain of marijuana or cocaine, not that of laundered dollars, but the rain that falls naturally from the sky and makes the sandy desert green? Yes, yes, you are speaking with the export minister, and we are willing to sell you our rain. Of course, its production costs us nothing; it is a resource as natural to us as your petroleum. We will make you a fair and just agreement.

15   The news filled five columns during the dry season, when obstacles like floods and dampness could be overcome. The president himself made the announcement: We will sell rain at ten dollars per cc. The price will be reviewed every ten years. Sales will be unlimited. With the earnings we will regain our independence and our self-respect.

16   The people smiled. A little less rain would be agreeable to everyone, and the best part was not having to deal with the six fat cows, who were more than a little oppressive. The IMF, the World Bank, the AID, the Embassy, the International Development Bank and perhaps the EEC would stop pushing the cows on them, given the danger that they might be stolen in the neighboring country, air-conditioned cabin, first class stable and all. Moreover, one couldn't count on those cows really being fat, since accepting them meant increasing all kinds of taxes, especially those on consumer goods, lifting import restrictions, spreading one's legs completely open to the transnationals, paying the interest, which was now a little higher, and amortizing the debt that was increasing at a rate only comparable to the spread of an epidemic. And as if this were not enough, it would be necessary to structure the cabinet a certain way, as some ministers were viewed by some legislators as potentially dangerous, as extremists.

17   The president added with demented glee, his face garlanded in sappy smiles, that French technicians, those guardians of European meritocracy, would build the rain funnels and the aqueduct, a guarantee of honesty, efficiency and effective transfer of technology.

18   By then we had already sold, to our great disadvantage, the tuna, the dolphins, and the thermal dome, along with the forests and all Indian artifacts. Also our talent, dignity, sovereignty, and the right to traffic in anything and everything illicit.

19   The first funnel was located on the Atlantic coast, which in a few months looked worse than the dry Pacific. The first payment from the emir arrived—in dollars!—and the country celebrated with a week's vacation. A little more effort was needed. Another funnel was added in the north and one more in the south. Both zones immediately dried up like raisins. The checks did not arrive. What happened? The IMF garnished them for interest payments. Another effort: a funnel was installed in the center of the country; where formerly it had rained and

rained. It now stopped raining forever, which paralyzed brains, altered behavior, changed the climate, defoliated the corn, destroyed the coffee, poisoned aromas, devastated canefields, dessicated palm trees, ruined orchards, razed truck gardens, and narrowed faces, making people look and act like rats, ants, and cockroaches, the only animals left alive in large numbers.

To remember what we once had been, people circulated photo- 20
graphs of an enormous oasis with great plantations, parks, and animal sanctuaries full of butterflies and flocks of birds, at the bottom of which was printed, "Come and visit us. The Emirate of Emirs is a paradise."

The first one to attempt it was a good swimmer who took the pre- 21
caution of carrying food and medicine. Then a whole family left, then whole villages, large and small. The population dropped considerably. One fine day there was nobody left, with the exception of the president and his cabinet. Everyone else, even the deputies, followed the rest by opening the cover of the aqueduct and floating all the way to the cover at the other end, doorway to the Emirate of the Emirs.

In that country we were second-class citizens, something we were 22
already accustomed to. We lived in a ghetto. We got work because we knew about coffee, sugar cane, cotton, fruit trees, and truck gardens. In a short time we were happy and felt as if these things too were ours, or at the very least, that the rain still belonged to us.

A few years passed; the price of oil began to plunge and plunge. The 23
emir asked for a loan, then another, then many; eventually he had to beg and beg for money to service the loans. The story sounds all too fa-miliar. Now the IMF has taken possession of the aqueducts. They have cut off the water because of a default in payments and because the sul-tan had the bright idea of receiving as a guest of honor a representative of that country that is a neighbor of ours.

Questions for Discussion and Writing

1. What details most effectively dramatize the desperate circumstances beset-ting the country that led them to resort to selling their most precious re-source? How was the plan implemented and with what effects? What mea-sures had the country taken in the past to raise currency?
2. How are government officials CHARACTERIZED in terms of how responsible they are for safeguarding or squandering their country's natural resources?
3. How would you characterize the attitude of the NARRATOR toward the events in the story? What details suggest the narrator may serve as a PERSONA or al-ter ego for Naranjo herself?
4. How do the detailed descriptions of sights, sounds, and SETTINGS lend credi-bility to the bizarre events in the story?
5. What current governmental policies impacting on natural resources seem worthy of being treated in a satire similar to this one? You might wish to cre-ate your own satire.

6. In a paragraph or two, describe a world, including its unique geography, flora and fauna, and inhabitants that is entirely different from the one we know. Is there a resource that is plentiful on our Earth that is scarce and much sought after in this world?
7. Does the area you live in grow something or possess a natural resource that distinguishes it? What effect does this have on the people who live there?

Nabil Gorgy

Cairo Is a Small City

Nabil Gorgy was born in Cairo in 1944 and studied civil engineering at Cairo University. After working as an engineer in New York City, he returned to Cairo where he now runs his own art gallery and writes. His interests in mysticism, Egyptology, and Sufi traditions are reflected in his latest novel, The Door (1981). In "Cairo Is a Small City," translated by Denys Johnson-Davies (1983), an upper-class Egyptian engineer falls victim to an age-old Bedouin tradition.

On the balcony of his luxury flat Engineer Adil Salim stood watching some workmen putting up a new building across the wide street along the centre of which was a spacious garden. The building was at the foundations stage, only the concrete foundations and some of the first-floor columns having been completed. A young ironworker with long hair was engaged on bending iron rods of various dimensions. Adil noticed that the young man had carefully leant his Jawa motorcycle against a giant crane that crouched at rest awaiting its future tasks. "How the scene has changed!" Adil could still remember the picture of old-time master craftsmen, and of the workers who used to carry large bowls of mixed cement on their calloused shoulders.

The sun was about to set and the concrete columns of a number of new constructions showed up as dark frameworks against the light in this quiet district at the end of Heliopolis.

As on every day at this time there came down into the garden dividing the street a flock of sheep and goats that grazed on its grass, and behind them two bedouin women, one of whom rode a donkey, while the younger one walked beside her. As was his habit each day, Adil fixed his gaze on the woman walking in her black gown that not so much hid as emphasized the attractions of her body, her waist being tied round with a red band. It could be seen that she wore green plastic slippers on her feet. He wished that she would catch sight of him on the balcony of his luxurious flat; even if she did so, Adil was thinking, those bedouin had a special code of behaviour that differed greatly from what he was used to and rendered it difficult to make contact with them. What, then, was the reason, the motive, for wanting to think up some way of talking to her? It was thus that he was thinking, following her with his gaze as she occasionally chased after a lamb that was going to be run over by a car or a goat left far behind the flock.

Adil, who was experienced in attracting society women, was aware of his spirit being enthralled: days would pass with him on the balcony,

47

sunset after sunset, as he watched her without her even knowing of his existence.

5   Had it not been for that day on which he had been buying some fruit and vegetables from one of the shopkeepers on Metro Street, and had not the shopkeeper seen another bedouin woman walking behind another flock, and had he not called out to her by name, and had she not come, and had he not thrown her a huge bundle of waste from the shop, after having flirted with her and fondled her body—had it not been for that day, Adil's mind would not have given birth to the plan he was determined, whatever the cost, to put through, because of that woman who had bewitched his heart.

6   As every man, according to Adil's philosophy of life, had within him a devil, it was sometimes better to follow this devil in order to placate him and avoid his tyranny. Therefore Engineer Adil Salim finally decided to embark upon the terrible, the unthinkable. He remembered from his personal history during the past forty years that such a temporary alliance with this devil of his had gained him a courage that had set him apart from the rest of his colleagues, and through it he had succeeded in attaining this social position that had enabled him to become the owner of this flat whose value had reached a figure which he avoided mentioning even in front of his family lest they might be upset or feel envy.

7   Thus, from his balcony on the second floor in Tirmidhi Street, Engineer Adil Salim called out in a loud voice "Hey, girl!" as he summoned the one who was walking at the rear of the convoy. When the flock continued on its way without paying any attention, he shouted again: "Hey, girl—you who sell sheep," and before the girl moved far away he repeated the word "sheep." Adil paid no attention to the astonishment of the doorman, who had risen from the place where he had been sitting at the entrance, thinking that he was being called. In fact he quietly told him to run after the two bedouin women and to let them know that he had some bread left over which he wanted to give them for their sheep.

8   From the balcony Adil listened to the doorman calling to the two women in his authoritative Upper Egyptian accent, at which they came to a stop and the one who was riding the donkey looked back at him. Very quickly Adil was able to make out her face as she looked towards him, seeking to discover what the matter was. As for the young girl, she continued on behind the flock. The woman was no longer young and had a corpulent body and a commanding look which she did not seek to hide from him. Turning her donkey round, she crossed the street separating the garden from his building and waited in front of the gate for some new development. Adil collected up all the bread in the house and hurried down with it on a brass tray. Having descended to the street, he went straight up to the woman and looked at her. When she opened a saddlebag close by her leg, he emptied all the bread into it.

"Thanks," said the woman as she made off without turning towards 9
him. He, though, raising his voice so that she would hear, called out,
"And tomorrow too."

During a period that extended to a month Adil began to buy bread 10
which he did not eat. Even on those days when he had to travel away
or to spend the whole day far from the house, he would leave a large
paper parcel with the doorman for him to give to the bedouin woman
who rode the donkey and behind whom walked she for whom the engineer's heart craved.

Because Adil had a special sense of the expected and the probable, 11
and after the passing of one lunar month, and in his place in front of the
building, with the bread on the brass tray, there occurred that which he
had been wishing would happen, for the woman riding the donkey had
continued on her way and he saw the other, looking around her carefully before crossing the road, ahead of him, walking towards him. She
was the most beautiful thing he had set eyes on. The speed of his pulse
almost brought his heart to a stop. How was it that such beauty was to
be found without it feeling embarrassed at ugliness, for after it any and
every thing must needs be so described? When she was directly in front
of him, and her kohl-painted eyes were scrutinizing him, he sensed a
danger which he attributed to her age, which was no more than twenty.
How was it that she was so tall, her waist so slim, her breasts so full,
and how was it that her buttocks swayed so enticingly as she turned
away and went off with the bread, having thanked him? His imagination became frozen even though she was still close to him: her pretty
face with the high cheekbones, the fine nose and delicate lips, the silver,
crescent-shaped earrings, and the necklace that graced her bosom?
Because such beauty was "beyond the permissible," Adil went on
thinking about Salma—for he had got to know her name, her mother
having called her by it in order to hurry her back lest the meeting between the lovers be prolonged.

Adil no longer troubled about the whistles of the workers who had 12
now risen floor by floor in the building opposite him, being in a state of
infatuation, his heart captured by this moonlike creature. After the affair, in relation to himself, having been one of boldness, to end in seeing
or greeting her, it now became a matter of necessity that she turn up before sunset at the house so that he might not be deprived of the chance
of seeing her. So it was that Engineer Adil Salim fell in love with the
beautiful bedouin girl Salma. And just as history is written by historians, so it was that Adil and his engineering work determined the history of this passion in the form of a building each of whose columns
represented a day and each of whose floors was a month. He noted
that, at the completion of twenty-eight days and exactly at full moon,
Salma would come to him in place of her mother to take the bread. And

so, being a structural engineer, he began to observe the moon, his yearning increasing when it was in eclipse and his spirits sparkling as its fullness drew near till, at full moon, the happiness of the lover was completed by seeing the beloved's face.

13   During seven months he saw her seven times, each time seeing in her the same look she had given him the first time: his heart would melt, all resolution would be squeezed out of him and that fear for which he knew no reason would be awakened. She alone was now capable of granting him his antidote. After the seventh month Salma, without any preamble, had talked to him at length, informing him that she lived with her parents around a spring at a distance of an hour's walk to the north of the airport, and that it consisted of a brackish spring alongside which was a sweet one, so that she would bathe in the first and rinse herself clean in the other, and that there were date palms around the two springs, also grass and pasturage. Her father, the owner of the springs and the land around them, had decided to invite him and so tomorrow "he'll pass by you and invite you to our place, for tomorrow we attend to the shearing of the sheep."

14   Adil gave the lie to what he was hearing, for it was more than any stretch of the imagination could conceive might happen.

15   The following day Adil arrived at a number of beautifully made tents where a vast area of sand was spread out below date palms that stretched to the edge of a spring. Around the spring was gathered a large herd of camels, sheep and goats that spoke of the great wealth of the father. It was difficult to believe that such a place existed so close to the city of Cairo. If Adil's astonishment was great when Salma's father passed by him driving a new Peugeot, he was yet further amazed at the beauty of the area surrounding this spring. "It's the land of the future," thought Adil to himself. If he were able to buy a few *feddans* now he'd become a millionaire in a flash, for this was the Cairo of the future. "This is the deal of a lifetime," he told himself.

16   On the way the father asked a lot of questions about Adil's work and where he had previously lived and about his knowledge of the desert and its people. Though Adil noticed in the father's tone something more than curiosity, he attributed this to the nature of the bedouin and their traditions.

17   As the car approached the tents Adil noticed that a number of men were gathered under a tent whose sides were open, and as the father and his guest got out of the car the men turned round, seated in the form of a horse-shoe. With the father sitting down and seating Engineer Adil Salim alongside him, one of the sides of the horse-shoe was completed. In front of them sat three men on whose faces could be seen the marks of time in the form of interlaced wrinkles.

18   The situation so held Adil's attention that he was unaware of Salma except when she passed from one tent to another in the direction he was looking and he caught sight of her gazing towards him.

The man who was sitting in a squatting position among the three 19
others spoke. Adil heard him talking about the desert, water and sheep,
about the roads that went between the oases and the *wadi*, the towns
and the springs of water, about the bedouin tribes and blood ties; he
heard him talking about the importance of protecting these roads and
springs, and the palm trees and the dates, the goats and the milk upon
which the suckling child would be fed; he also heard him talk about
how small the *wadi* was in comparison to this desert that stretched out
endlessly.

In the same way as Adil had previously built the seven-storey build- 20
ing that represented the seven months, each month containing twenty-
eight days, till he would see Salma's face whenever it was full moon, he
likewise sensed that this was the tribunal which had been set up to
make an enquiry with him into the killing of the man whom he had one
day come across on the tracks between the oases of Kharga and
Farshout. It had been shortly after sunset when he and a friend, having
visited the iron ore mines in the oases of Kharga had, instead of taking
the asphalt road to Assiout, proceeded along a rough track that took
them down towards Farshout near to Kena, as his friend had to make a
report about the possibility of repairing the road and of extending the
railway line to the oases. Going down from the high land towards the
wadi, the land at a distance showing up green, two armed men had appeared before them. Adil remembered how, in a spasm of fear and astonishment, of belief and disbelief, and with a speed that at the time he
thought was imposed upon him, a shot had been fired as he pressed his
finger on the trigger of the revolver which he was using for the first
time. A man had fallen to the ground in front of him and, as happens in
films, the other had fled. As for him and his friend, they had rushed off
to their car in order to put an end to the memory of the incident by
reaching the *wadi*. It was perhaps because Adil had once killed a man
that he had found the courage to accept Salma's father's invitation.

"That day," Adil heard the man address him, "with a friend in a car, 21
you killed Mubarak bin Rabia when he went out to you, Ziyad al-
Mihrab being with him."

This was the manner in which Engineer Adil Salim was executed in 22
the desert north-west of the city of Cairo: one of the men held back his
head across a marble-like piece of stone, then another man plunged the
point of a tapered dagger into the spot that lies at the bottom of the
neck between the two bones of the clavicle.

Questions for Discussion and Writing

1. How is the engineer, Adil Salim, CHARACTERIZED? What incidents reveal these
   character traits most clearly? How does he see himself? To what does he attribute his success and affluence?

2. Under what circumstances does the engineer first meet the bedouin girl? What is his attitude toward her?
3. How do the engineering projects Adil designs after meeting the bedouin girl reflect the period of his growing infatuation?
4. How do Gorgy's descriptions of modern urban Cairo and the bedouin encampment underscore the conflicting sets of values this story explores? How would you characterize these opposing values as they are revealed in the respective descriptions of each SETTING?
5. After reading the story, discuss the significance of the title, especially as it sheds light on the surprising consequences for the engineer. To what extent does the title suggest that the Cairo of the bedouins and of the engineer, although seemingly very different, are basically the same?
6. In a short essay, discuss Gorgy's attitude toward ancient cultural traditions as they emerge in the story.
7. Adil's actions and reactions indicate that he is in love. What actions and reactions of your own or of someone you know serve as sure-fire signs of being in love?
8. Analyze this story in terms of the elements of crime, motive, clues, suspects, victim, detective, alibi, and solution associated with the mystery genre.

Ulfa Idelbi

Seventy Years Later

Ulfa Idelbi was born in Damascus, Syria, in 1912, the only daughter in a fam-ily with four brothers. Her father encouraged her to read all the Arab classics as well as the works of Shakespeare, Chekhov, and de Maupassant. At seventeen she was married before she could get her baccalaureate. In response to a BBC-organized competition for short stories in the Arab world, Idelbi sent in a story that won a prize. She is the author of four volumes of short stories, including Damascene Stories *(1960) and* Goodbye, Damascus *(1963), three collec-tions of literary articles, and a novel,* Damascus, Smile of Sorrow *(1981). "Seventy Years Later," translated by Simone Fattal, is from the collection* When the Devil Laughs *(1970). Like most of her fiction, this story presents Syrian society in transition from the perspective of an upper-class, older woman.*

That charity organisation held a ball as a fund raising event for its activ- 1
ities at the beginning of each year. It was customary that a "surprise" be
announced at the ball to attract people to support the organisation.

That year the surprise was exquisite and entertaining. Twenty 2
young girls were asked to wear a dress that had belonged to their
grandmothers at their age. This was not too difficult a demand as a
great number of older women kept their favourite dresses as a souvenir. A committee from among the guests was elected to choose the
most beautiful garment worn by the most beautiful girl to whom the organisation would give a precious prize.

When the moment for the competition came, the twenty young girls 3
paraded their antique dresses to the guests. There was laughter and
merriment. Some young men joked and even made fun of the dresses,
which had faded or had been damaged by time. One of the young girls
was wearing a robe which looked as if it had never been worn before. It
was so perfectly intact that the audience was filled with admiration. It
was a superb dress in the style worn by nineteenth century European
princesses. It was of a precious silvery velvet embroidered with glowing golden flowers. The embroidery was magnificent. It was a ceremonial dress which left the lovely neck and the round shoulders bare. The
sleeves narrowed to the wrists, making the shape of the arms beautiful
and smooth. The dress showed off the graceful waist under a large
golden belt. It flew out in front barely touching the floor, and at the
back it spread into a long embroidered tail like that of a peacock. All of
this gave its wearer the air of a princess promenading in a vast palace.
As soon as the committee was formed, the wearer was given the first
prize and the audience applauded enthusiastically.

4   The mother of the winner was sitting with her friends at one of the tables, looking at her daughter with a tenderness and pride that seemed to be mixed with sorrow and grief. One of her friends asked, "Why are you sitting silent and sorry as if you were not the winner's mother? Why are your eyes so close to tears? No doubt, they are tears of joy?" The mother of the prize-winner smiled and replied, "It is joy that provokes my tears. Yet, the dress has awakened a very painful memory. I recall my mother, its owner. I wish that she were alive to see this cherished, forbidden garment of hers come out in the open at last to be admired above all the other dresses at an important social event like this. It remained hidden in her chest for seventy years. And now my daughter, her favourite and most beloved granddaughter, is wearing it."

5   One of the friends said, "This dress must have a strange story. Do tell us."

6   The mother replied, "It is a very sad story, but I will tell it to you so you will know how much our grandmothers and our poor mothers were prisoners of customs and habits unbelievable to us today.

7   "My mother was an only child of parents who showered her with love and care. At fourteen she was married to my father and moved from her father's house and her happy life there, to the house of her husband. It was the custom then for a young bride to live with her in-laws. Her husband's family was large. Besides his parents, he lived with his three unmarried sisters and four brothers with their own wives and many children. Her mother-in-law, who was my grandmother, was in charge of everything pertaining to the household. She took care of problems with great experience and ability. She was determined to be just and wise and to be fair in an absolute sense toward her daughters, her daughters-in-law, and her grandchildren. At the beginning of every summer and every winter, she provided each member of the family, and her daughters-in-law, with a wardrobe. The young women had to accept her choice whether they liked it or not. She also assigned to each young woman a day to be in charge of the cleaning and good order of the house. The sons worked in their father's business. He alone had the right to dispose of the family fortune. He was responsible for the whole family, as was the rule in Damascus in those days.

8   "The family affairs went as smoothly as possible under such circumstances. Of course, there was no lack of problems and difficulties, as when jealousies erupted between the young women. They were soon ironed out, however, when the mother-in-law applied her authority, experience and care. Another custom of those days was for the daughter-in-law never to leave the house unless accompanied by her mother-in-law, and this only to weddings and funerals. Additionally, she could take her children to visit her own family once a month for three full days, a welcome relief from life with her in-laws.

9   "However, my poor mother was deprived of that pleasure when two years after her marriage, her parents left for Istanbul where her fa-

ther was transferred. My mother could write and read perfectly, rare among women of her time. She wrote letters to her parents expressing her sadness at being parted from them and the bitterness of her solitude. She described all the things she had to put up with, all her joys and all her sorrows.

"One day she wrote to them telling them that the oldest of her husband's sisters was engaged and that a great wedding was being prepared. Her parents, whose hearts were forever grieving over their separation from their only child, wondered, 'What can we send her that will bring her joy and lighten her loneliness?' 10

"They gave it considerable thought and finally their choice fell upon the dress you see tonight. It must have been the most precious and the most beautiful dress in all of Istanbul, then the capital of elegance and refinement throughout the Orient. My mother's father paid fifty golden pounds for it. He was not a rich man and had to borrow money to fulfil his wish to honour his daughter. He thought her dignity would be enhanced when her dress became the talk of all the women in town. 11

"My mother used to describe to us the joy that filled her heart when she received this lavish and unexpected gift. She called all the inhabitants of the house to show it to them. She started to worry, however, when she detected signs of displeasure on her mother-in-law's face. 12

"A few moments later, her mother-in-law summoned her to her private room and said, 'My daughter, in no way can you wear this dress in our house. We are not able to provide the likes of it to my other daughters and daughters-in-law. You very well know that it is our custom that none of you is to be set above the others.' 13

"My mother was stunned and said in awe, 'How can it be possible for me not to wear it? It is a gift from my father, and I have none more beautiful! . . . .' 14

"The other answered, "Have I not given you a beautiful dress made of golden threads for the wedding night? Isn't it the most expensive material available in Damascus this year? Don't you want to be like the other women of the family?' 15

"For the first time my mother dared to rebel against her and said firmly, 'I swear by God that I will not wear any other dress no matter what you say . . . And where do you want me to wear it if I don't wear it the night of the wedding . . .' 16

"She answered, 'You can wear it in your private chamber and in front of your husband only.' 17

"My mother said, 'But it is embroidered, and made for balls and grand occasions. My father did not send it for me to wear it in my room which is too small to even contain its train.' 18

"Thereupon her mother-in-law left her. She was very angry indeed. It was the first time she had met with rebellion in one of her daughters-in-law. She paced up and down the floor of the courtyard, waiting for her son to return from work to tell him about the problem before he 19 could see his wife. She thought if he saw her and the gift she had received from her parents, he might be won over to his wife's side. As soon as he came home, she called him to her room and disclosed the problem, saying, 'Would you like your wife to show that we are of a lesser station than her parents? Would you like, my son, to hear people criticise us saying that your wife's dress was more expensive than that of your sister on her wedding day? Would you accept, my son, would you countenance that your wife provoke the jealousy of your sisters-in-law and make the lives of your brothers more difficult?'

20   "'I have advised her to wear it in your private quarters only and for your benefit alone, so that we are spared problems we don't need, but she refuses to listen to my advice, and be persuaded by me, her mother-in-law and the eldest in the family! She swears she is going to wear it for the wedding because it is a gift from her parents . . . She is arrogant and stubborn. God help you with her! But you can handle the matter, I have brought you up to be a man . . .'

21   "My father had never refused anything to his mother before as he feared to arouse her wrath, for fear of God. He rose promptly full of anger against his wife and entered her room, as she was hastily putting on the magnificent dress in order to surprise him. Without even a look at the dress and cutting short any discussion he said, 'I will declare you divorced three times if you ever wear this dress. I will never anger my mother for the sake of a dress given to you by your parents.'

22   "My mother was seized with fear and nearly lost her mind under the blow but she said nothing. What could she do in the face of a divorce without recourse?

23   "So the young woman of sixteen years threw herself on the splendid dress, crying and kissing it passionately until midnight came. Then she arose, forced to admit defeat. She folded the dress and threw it at the bottom of a chest and sat in front of it, crying and wailing as she would have done had she been sitting before the coffin of a loved one . . .

24   "All her life she wished she could have worn it at least once. She also used to say to me when recounting the story, 'How many times did I wish to shred it to pieces but a devilish thought stopped me. I used to tell myself: I will keep this dress in a safe, unreachable place and if, one day, this man, your father becomes unbearable to me, I will have an easy recourse. All I shall need to do is to wear this dress and I will be divorced in an instant.' "

25   One of the friends said, "If the story you tell had happened to me, I would have worn the dress immediately."

26   The story-teller answered, "My mother lived peacefully with my father for seventy years and never had to confront him by wearing the dress. But, we often saw her take the dress out of the chest and gaze at it for a long time. She would take great care of it, exposing it to the sun and the air so that the moths wouldn't eat it. She would also tell its story with pain and passion to anyone around her as if it had happened

only the day before. She would have liked one of us, her three daughters, to wear it but none of us fulfilled her wish. It was out of fashion when we grew up and there were no events like this in our time.

"That is why I feel sad and weep. I wish she was alive to see at least   27
her beloved dress getting the appreciation it deserved in a grand ballroom and winning a first prize after having been buried in the depths of her chest for seventy years . . ."

Questions for Discussion and Writing

1. How is the NARRATOR of the story, that is, the mother of the girl who is wearing the dress, CHARACTERIZED? What is her attitude toward the events she describes?
2. How do the circumstances under which the dress was acquired offer insight into the relationships between the grandmother and her own family and with her in-laws?
3. What circumstances led to the dress being worn after seventy years? How does the dress come to stand for the possibilities available to women in Syrian society that could not manifest themselves at the turn of the century?
4. How do Idelbi's descriptions of time, SETTINGS, and social environment provide a historical and cultural context reflecting basic changes in attitudes toward women in Syria over the last three generations?
5. Why did the grandmother keep a dress she could never wear in public?
6. Write about one of your grandparents or parents as seen through an object you connect with him or her. Under what circumstances did you first come across this object? What associations connect this object with your parent or grandparent?
7. Interview an older member of your family to discover how customs when they were growing up differ from current practices in regard to dating, courtship, marriage, child-rearing, medicine, cures, food preparation, or celebrations.
8. Describe a wedding gown (accompanied by a sketch, if you wish) and a dream wedding you would plan for yourself or a friend—the setting, guests, music, food, and so on.

Sembene Ousmane

Her Three Days

Sembene Ousmane was born in Senegal, North Africa, in 1923. Essentially self-educated, he became a fisherman like his father, then moved to Dakar until the outbreak of World War II when he was drafted into the French Army and saw action in Italy and Germany. After the war, he went to Marseille where he worked as a docker, joined the French Communist party, and became a union organizer. After his fourth novel, Ousmane studied at the Moscow Film School and wrote and directed several films including The Money Order, *which won a prize at the Venice Film Festival.* Zala, *based on his 1973 novel, went on to become one of a series of successful films that established his reputation as a director. Ousmane's latest novel, a massive two-volume work,* Le Dernier de l'empire, *was published in 1981. "Her Three Days," translated by Len Ortzen, is taken from Ousmane's 1974 collection of short stories,* Tribal Scars. *In this compassionate and realistic account of the plight of a third wife waiting for her husband to return, Ousmane dramatizes the rules governing Muslim life in Mali under which, according to the Koran, "every wife of a Muslim is entitled to three days of her husband's company each month."*

1   She raised her haggard face, and her far-away look ranged beyond the muddle of roofs, some tiled, others of thatch or galvanized-iron; the wide fronds of the twin coconut-palms were swaying slowly in the breeze, and in her mind she could hear their faint rustling. Noumbe was thinking of "her three days." Three days for her alone, when she would have her husband Mustapha to herself . . . It was a long time since she had felt such emotion. To have Mustapha! The thought comforted her. She had heart trouble and still felt some pain, but she had been dosing herself for the past two days, taking more medicine than was prescribed. It was a nice syrup that just slipped down, and she felt the beneficial effects at once. She blinked; her eyes were like two worn buttonholes, with lashes that were like frayed thread, in little clusters of fives and threes; the whites were the colour of old ivory.

2   "What's the matter, Noumbe?" asked Aida, her next-door neighbour, who was sitting at the door of her room.

3   "Nothing," she answered, and went on cutting up the slice of raw meat, helped by her youngest daughter.

4   "Ah, it's your three days," exclaimed Aida, whose words held a meaning that she could not elaborate on while the little girl was present. She went on: "You're looking fine enough to prevent a holy man from saying his prayers properly!"

5   "Aida, be careful what you say," she protested, a little annoyed.

6   But it was true; Noumbe had plaited her hair and put henna on her

58

hands and feet. And that morning she had got the children up early to give her room a thorough clean. She was not old, but one pregnancy after another—and she had five children—and her heart trouble had aged her before her time.

"Go and ask Laity to give you five francs' worth of salt and twenty francs' worth of oil," Noumbe said to the girl. "Tell him I sent you. I'll pay for them as soon as your father is here, at midday." She looked disapprovingly at the cut-up meat in the bottom of the bowl.

The child went off with the empty bottle and Noumbe got to her feet. She was thin and of average height. She went into her one-room shack, which was sparsely furnished; there was a bed with a white cover, and in one corner stood a table with pieces of china on display. The walls were covered with enlargements and photos of friends and strangers framed in passe-partout.

When she came out again she took the Moorish stove and set about lighting it.

Her daughter had returned from her errand.

"He gave them to you?" asked Noumbe.

"Yes, mother."

A woman came across the compound to her. "Noumbe, I can see that you're preparing a delicious dish."

"Yes," she replied. "It's my three days. I want to revive the feasts of the old days, so that his palate will retain the taste of the dish for many moons, and he'll forget the cooking of his other wives."

"Ah-ha! So that his palate is eager for dishes to come," said the woman, who was having a good look at the ingredients.

"I'm feeling in good form," said Noumbe, with some pride in her voice. She grasped the woman's hand and passed it over her loins.

"*Thieh, souya dome!* I hope you can say the same tomorrow morning . . ."

The woman clapped her hands; as if it were a signal or an invitation, other women came across, one with a metal jar, another with a saucepan, which they beat while the woman sang:

Sope dousa rafetail,
Sopa nala dousa rafetail
Sa yahi n'diguela.
(Worship of you is not for your beauty,
I worship you not for your beauty
But for your backbone.)

In a few moments, they improvised a wild dance to this chorus. At the end, panting and perspiring, they burst out laughing. Then one of them stepped into Noumbe's room and called the others.

"Let's take away the bed! Because tonight they'll wreck it!"

"She's right. Tomorrow this room will be . . ."

Each woman contributed an earthy comment which set them all

laughing hilariously. Then they remembered they had work to do, and brought their amusement to an end; each went back to her family occupations.

23 Noumbe had joined in the laughter; she knew this boisterous "ragging" was the custom in the compound. No one escaped it. Besides, she was an exceptional case, as they all knew. She had a heart condition and her husband had quite openly neglected her. Mustapha had not been to see her for a fortnight. All this time she had been hoping that he would come, if only for a moment. When she went to the clinic for mothers and children she compelled her youngest daughter to stay at home, so that—thus did her mind work—if her husband turned up the child could detain him until she returned. She ought to have gone to the clinic again this day, but she had spent what little money she possessed on preparing for Mustapha. She did not want her husband to esteem her less than his other wives, or to think her meaner. She did not neglect her duty as a mother, but her wifely duty came first—at certain times.

24 She imagined what the next three days would be like; already her "three days" filled her whole horizon. She forgot her illness and her baby's ailments. She had thought about these three days in a thousand different ways. Mustapha would not leave before the Monday morning. In her mind she could see Mustapha and his henchmen crowding into her room, and could hear their suggestive jokes. "If she had been a perfect wife . . ." She laughed to herself. "Why shouldn't it always be like that for every woman—to have a husband of one's own?" She wondered why not.

25 The morning passed at its usual pace, the shadows of the coconut-palms and the people growing steadily shorter. As midday approached, the housewives busied themselves with the meal. In the compound each one stood near her door, ready to welcome her man. The kids were playing around, and their mothers' calls to them crossed in the air. Noumbe gave her children a quick meal and sent them out again. She sat waiting for Mustapha to arrive at any moment . . . he wouldn't be much longer now.

26 An hour passed, and the men began going back to work. Soon the compound was empty of the male element; the women, after a long siesta, joined one another under the coconut-palms and the sounds of their gossiping gradually increased.

27 Noumbe, weary of waiting, had finally given up keeping a lookout. Dressed in her mauve velvet, she had been on the watch since before midday. She had eaten no solid food, consoling herself with the thought that Mustapha would appear at any moment. Now she fought back the pangs of hunger by telling herself that in the past Mustapha had a habit of arriving late. In those days, this lateness was pleasant. Without admitting it to herself, those moments (which had hung terribly heavy) had been very sweet; they prolonged the sensual pleasure of

anticipation. Although those minutes had been sometimes shot through with doubts and fears (often, very often, the thought of her coming disgrace had assailed her; for Mustapha, who had taken two wives before her, had just married another), they had not been too hard to bear. She realized that those demanding minutes were the price she had to pay for Mustapha's presence. Then she began to reckon up the score, in small ways, against the *veudieux*, the other wives. One washed his *boubous* when it was another wife's turn, or kept him long into the night; another sometimes held him in her embrace a whole day, knowing quite well that she was preventing Mustapha from carrying out his marital duty elsewhere.

She sulked as she waited; Mustapha had not been near her for a   28
fortnight. All these bitter thoughts brought her up against reality: four months ago Mustapha had married a younger woman. This sudden realization of the facts sent a pain to her heart, a pain of anguish. The additional pain did not prevent her heart from functioning normally, rather was it like a sick person whose sleep banishes pain but who once awake again finds his suffering is as bad as ever, and pays for the relief by a redoubling of pain.

She took three spoonfuls of her medicine instead of the two pre-   29
scribed, and felt a little better in herself.

She called her youngest daughter. "Tell Mactar I want him."   30
The girl ran off and soon returned with her eldest brother.   31
"Go and fetch your father," Noumbe told him.   32
"Where, mother?"   33
"Where? Oh, on the main square or at one of your other mothers'."   34
"But I've been to the main square already, and he wasn't there."   35
"Well, go and have another look. Perhaps he's there now."   36
The boy looked up at his mother, then dropped his head again and   37
reluctantly turned to go.

"When your father has finished eating, I'll give you what's left. It's   38
meat. Now be quick, Mactar."

It was scorching hot and the clouds were riding high. Mactar was   39
back after an hour. He had not found his father. Noumbe went and joined the group of women. They were chattering about this and that; one of them asked (just for the sake of asking), "Noumbe, has your uncle (darling) arrived?" "Not yet," she replied, then hastened to add, "Oh, he won't be long now. He knows it's my three days." She deliberately changed the conversation in order to avoid a long discussion about the other three wives. But all the time she was longing to go and find Mustapha. She was being robbed of her three days. And the other wives knew it. Her hours alone with Mustapha were being snatched from her. The thought of his being with one of the other wives, who was feeding him and opening his waistcloth when she ought to be doing all that, who was enjoying those hours which were hers by right, so numbed Noumbe that it was impossible for her to react. The idea that

Mustapha might have been admitted to hospital or taken to a police station never entered her head.

40 She knew how to make tasty little dishes for Mustapha which cost him nothing. She never asked him for money. Indeed, hadn't she got herself into debt so that he would be more comfortable and have better meals at her place? And in the past, when Mustapha sometimes arrived unexpectedly—this was soon after he had married her—hadn't she hastened to make succulent dishes for him? All her friends knew this.

41 A comforting thought coursed through her and sent these aggressive and vindictive reflections to sleep. She told herself that Mustapha was bound to come to her this evening. The certainty of his presence stripped her mind of the too cruel thought that the time of her disfavour was approaching; this thought had been as much a burden to her as a heavy weight dragging a drowning man to the bottom. When all the bad, unfavourable thoughts besetting her had been dispersed, like piles of rubbish on waste land swept by a flood, the future seemed brighter, and she joined in the conversation of the women with childish enthusiasm, unable to hide her pleasure and her hopes. It was like something in a parcel; questioning eyes wondered what was inside, but she alone knew and enjoyed the secret, drawing an agreeable strength from it. She took an active part in the talking and brought her wit into play. All this vivacity sprang from the joyful conviction that Mustapha would arrive this evening very hungry and be hers alone.

42 In the far distance, high above the tree-tops, a long trail of dark-grey clouds tinged with red was hiding the sun. The time for the *tacousane*, the afternoon prayer, was drawing near. One by one, the women withdrew to their rooms, and the shadows of the trees grew longer, wider and darker.

43 Night fell; a dark, starry night.

44 Noumbe cooked some rice for the children. They clamoured in vain for some of the meat. Noumbe was stern and unyielding: "The meat is for your father. He didn't eat at midday." When she had fed the children, she washed herself again to get rid of the smell of cooking and touched up her toilette, rubbing oil on her hands, feet and legs to make the henna more brilliant. She intended to remain by her door, and sat down on the bench; the incense smelt strongly, filling the whole room. She was facing the entrance to the compound and could see the other women's husbands coming in.

45 But for her there was no one.

46 She began to feel tired again. Her heart was troubling her, and she had a fit of coughing. Her inside seemed to be on fire. Knowing that she would not be going to the dispensary during her "three days," in order to economize, she went and got some wood-ash which she mixed with water and drank. It did not taste very nice, but it would make the medicine last longer, and the drink checked and soothed the burning within her for a while. She was tormenting herself with the thoughts

passing through her mind. Where can he be? With the first wife? No, she's quite old. The second then? Everyone knew that she was out of favour with Mustapha. The third wife was herself. So he must be with the fourth. There were puckers of uncertainty and doubt in the answers she gave herself. She kept putting back the time to go to bed, like a lover who does not give up waiting when the time of the rendezvous is long past, but with an absurd and stupid hope waits still longer, self-torture and the heavy minutes chaining him to the spot. At each step Noumbe took, she stopped and mentally explored the town, prying into each house inhabited by one of the other wives. Eventually she went indoors.

So that she would not be caught unawares by Mustapha nor lose the advantages which her make-up and good clothes gave her, she lay down on the bed fully dressed and alert. She had turned down the lamp as far as possible, so the room was dimly lit. But she fell asleep despite exerting great strength of mind to remain awake and saying repeatedly to herself, "I shall wait for him." To make sure that she would be standing there expectantly when he crossed the threshold, she had bolted the door. Thus she would be the devoted wife, always ready to serve her husband, having got up at once and appearing as elegant as if it were broad daylight. She had even thought of making a gesture as she stood there, of passing her hands casually over her hips so that Mustapha would hear the clinking of the beads she had strung round her waist and be incited to look at her from head to foot. 47

Morning came, but there was no Mustapha. 48

When the children awoke they asked if their father had come. The oldest of them, Mactar, a promising lad, was quick to spot that his mother had not made the bed, that the bowl containing the stew was still in the same place, by a dish of rice, and the loaf of bread on the table was untouched. The children got a taste of their mother's anger. The youngest, Amadou, took a long time over dressing. Noumbe hurried them up and sent the youngest girl to Laity's to buy five francs' worth of ground coffee. The children's breakfast was warmed-up rice with a meagre sprinkling of gravy from the previous day's stew. Then she gave them their wings, as the saying goes, letting them all out except the youngest daughter. Noumbe inspected the bottle of medicine and saw that she had taken a lot of it; there were only three spoonfuls left. She gave herself half a spoonful and made up for the rest with her mixture of ashes and water. After that she felt calmer. 49

"Why, Noumbe, you must have got up bright and early this morning, to be so dressed up. Are you going off on a long journey?" 50

It was Aida, her next-door neighbour, who was surprised to see her dressed in such a manner, especially for a woman who was having "her three days." Then Aida realized what had happened and tried to rectify her mistake. 51

"Oh, I see he hasn't come yet. They're all the same, these men!" 52

53   "He'll be here this morning, Aida." Noumbe bridled, ready to defend her man. But it was rather her own worth she was defending, wanting to conceal what an awful time she had spent. It had been a broken night's sleep, listening to harmless sounds which she had taken for Mustapha's footsteps, and this had left its mark on her already haggard face.

54   "I'm sure he will! I'm sure he will!" exclaimed Aida, well aware of this comedy that all the women played in turn.

55   "Mustapha is such a kind man, and so noble in his attitude," added another woman, rubbing it in.

56   "If he weren't, he wouldn't be my master," said Noumbe, feeling flattered by this description of Mustapha.

57   The news soon spread round the compound that Mustapha had slept elsewhere during Noumbe's three days. The other women pitied her. It was against all the rules for Mustapha to spend a night elsewhere. Polygamy had its laws, which should be respected. A sense of decency and common dignity restrained a wife from keeping the husband day and night when his whole person and everything connected with him belonged to another wife during "her three days." The game, however, was not without its underhand tricks that one wife played on another; for instance, to wear out the man and hand him over when he was incapable of performing his conjugal duties. When women criticized the practice of polygamy they always found that the wives were to blame, especially those who openly dared to play a dirty trick. The man was whitewashed. He was a weakling who always ended by falling into the enticing traps set for him by woman. Satisfied with this conclusion, Noumbe's neighbours made common cause with her and turned to abusing Mustapha's fourth wife.

58   Noumbe made some coffee—she never had any herself, because of her heart. She consoled herself with the thought that Mustapha would find more things at her place. The bread had gone stale; she would buy some more when he arrived.

59   The hours dragged by again, long hours of waiting which became harder to bear as the day progressed. She wished she knew where he was . . . The thought obsessed her, and her eyes became glazed and searching. Every time she heard a man's voice she straightened up quickly. Her heart was paining her more and more, but the physical pain was separate from the mental one; they never came together, alternating in a way that reminded her of the acrobatic feat of a man riding two speeding horses.

60   At about four o'clock Noumbe was surprised to see Mustapha's second wife appear at the door. She had come to see if Mustapha was there, knowing that it was Noumbe's three days. She did not tell Noumbe the reason for her wishing to see Mustapha, despite being pressed. So Noumbe concluded that it was largely due to jealousy, and was pleased that the other wife could see how clean and tidy her room

was, and what a display of fine things she had, all of which could hardly fail to make the other think that Mustapha had been (and still was) very generous to her, Noumbe. During the rambling conversation her heart thumped ominously, but she bore up and held off taking any medicine.

Noumbe remembered only too well that when she was newly married she had usurped the second wife's three days. At that time she had been the youngest wife. Mustapha had not let a day pass without coming to see her. Although not completely certain, she believed she had conceived her third child during this wife's three days. The latter's presence now and remarks that she let drop made Noumbe realize that she was no longer the favourite. This revelation, and the polite, amiable tone and her visitor's eagerness to inquire after her children's health and her own, to praise her superior choice of household utensils, her taste in clothes, the cleanliness of the room and the lingering fragrance of the incense, all this was like a stab in cold blood, a cruel reminder of the perfidy of words and the hypocrisy of rivals; and all part of the world of women. This observation did not get her anywhere, except to arouse a desire to escape from the circle of polygamy and to cause her to ask herself—it was a moment of mental aberration really—"Why do we allow ourselves to be men's playthings?"

The other wife complimented her and insisted that Noumbe's children should go and spend a few days with her own children (in this she was sincere). By accepting in principle, Noumbe was weaving her own waist-cloth of hypocrisy. It was all to make the most of herself, to set tongues wagging so that she would lose none of her respectability and rank. The other wife casually added—before she forgot, as she said— that she wanted to see Mustapha, and if mischief-makers told Noumbe that "their" husband had been to see her during Noumbe's three days, Noumbe shouldn't think ill of her, and she would rather have seen him here to tell him what she had to say. To save face, Noumbe dared not ask her when she had last seen Mustapha. The other would have replied with a smile, "The last morning of my three days, of course. I've only come here because it's urgent." And Noumbe would have looked embarrassed and put on an air of innocence. "No, that isn't what I meant. I just wondered if you had happened to meet him by chance."

Neither of them would have lost face. It was all that remained to them. They were not lying, to their way of thinking. Each had been desired and spoilt for a time; then the man, like a gorged vulture, had left them on one side and the venom of chagrin at having been mere playthings had entered their hearts. They quite understood, it was all quite clear to them, that they could sink no lower; so they clung to what was left to them, that is to say, to saving what dignity remained to them by false words and gaining advantages at the expense of the other. They did not indulge in this game for the sake of it. This falseness contained all that remained of the flame of dignity. No one was taken in, certainly not themselves. Each knew that the other was lying, but neither could bring herself to further humiliation, for it would be the final crushing blow.

64   The other wife left. Noumbe almost propelled her to the door, then stood there thoughtful for a few moments. Noumbe understood the reason for the other's visit. She had come to get her own back. Noumbe felt absolutely sure that Mustapha was with his latest wife. The visit meant in fact: "You stole those days from me because I am older than you. Now a younger woman than you is avenging me. Try as you might to make everything nice and pleasant for him, you have to toe the line with the rest of us now, you old carcass. He's slept with someone else—and he will again."

65   The second day passed like the first, but was more dreadful. She ate no proper food, just enough to stave off the pangs of hunger.

66   It was Sunday morning and all the men were at home; they nosed about in one room and another, some of them cradling their youngest in their arms, others playing with the older children. The draught-players had gathered in one place, the card-players in another. There was a friendly atmosphere in the compound, with bursts of happy laughter and sounds of guttural voices, while the women busied themselves with the housework.

67   Aida went to see Noumbe to console her, and said without much conviction, "He'll probably come today. Men always seem to have something to do at the last minute. It's Sunday today, so he'll be here."

68   "Aida, Mustapha doesn't work," Noumbe pointed out, hard-eyed. She gave a cough. "I've been waiting for him now for two days and nights! When it's my three days I think the least he could do is to be here—at night, anyway. I might die . . ."

69   "Do you want me to go and look for him?"

70   "No."

71   She had thought "yes." It was the way in which Aida had made the offer that embarrassed her. Of course she would like her to! Last night, when everyone had gone to bed, she had started out and covered quite some distance before turning back. The flame of her dignity had been fanned on the way. She did not want to abase herself still further by going to claim a man who seemed to have no desire to see her. She had lain awake until dawn, thinking it all over and telling herself that her marriage to Mustapha was at an end, that she would divorce him. But this morning there was a tiny flicker of hope in her heart: "Mustapha will come, all the same. This is my last night."

72   She borrowed a thousand francs from Aida, who readily lent her the money. And she followed the advice to send the children off again, to Mustapha's fourth wife.

73   "Tell him that I must see him at once, I'm not well!"

74   She hurried off to the little market near by and bought a chicken and

several other things. Her eyes were feverishly, joyfully bright as she carefully added seasoning to the dish she prepared. The appetizing smell of her cooking was wafted out to the compound and its Sunday atmosphere. She swept the room again, shut the door and windows, but the heady scent of the incense escaped through the cracks between the planks.

The children returned from their errand. 75

"Is he ill?" she asked them. 76

"No, mother. He's going to come. We found him with some of his 77 friends at Voulimata's (the fourth wife). He asked about you."

"And that's all he said?" 78

"Yes, mother." 79

"Don't come indoors. Here's ten francs. Go and play somewhere 80 else."

A delicious warm feeling spread over her. "He was going to come." 81 Ever since Friday she had been harbouring spiteful words to throw in his face. He would beat her, of course . . . But never mind. Now she found it would be useless to utter those words. Instead she would do everything possible to make up for the lost days. She was happy, much too happy to bear a grudge against him, now that she knew he was coming—he might even be on the way with his henchmen. The only means of getting her own back was to cook a big meal . . . then he would stay in bed.

She finished preparing the meal, had a bath and went on to the rest 82 of her toilette. She did her hair again, put antimony on her lower lip, eyebrows and lashes, then dressed in a white starched blouse and a hand-woven waist-cloth, and inspected her hands and feet. She was quite satisfied with her appearance.

But the waiting became prolonged. 83

No one in the compound spoke to her for fear of hurting her feel- 84 ings. She had sat down outside the door, facing the entrance to the compound, and the other inhabitants avoided meeting her sorrowful gaze. Her tears overflowed the brim of her eyes like a swollen river its banks; she tried to hold them back, but in vain. She was eating her heart out.

The sound of a distant tom-tom was being carried on the wind. 85 Time passed over her, like the seasons over monuments. Twilight came and darkness fell.

On the table were three plates in a row, one for each day. 86

"I've come to keep you company," declared Aida as she entered the 87 room. Noumbe was sitting on the foot of the bed—she had fled from the silence of the others. "You mustn't get worked up about it," went on Aida. "Every woman goes through it. Of course it's not nice! But I don't think he'll be long now."

Noumbe raised a moist face and bit her lips nervously. Aida saw 88 that she had made up her mind not to say anything.

Everything was shrouded in darkness; no light came from her room. After supper, the children had refrained from playing their noisy games.

89   Just when adults were beginning to feel sleepy and going to bed, into the compound walked Mustapha, escorted by two of his lieutenants. He was clad entirely in white. He greeted the people still about in an oily manner, then invited his companions into Noumbe's hut.

90   She had not stirred.

91   "Wife, where's the lamp?"

92   "Where you left it this morning when you went out."

93   "How are you?" inquired Mustapha when he had lit the lamp. He went and sat down on the bed, and motioned to the two men to take the bench.

94   "God be praised," Noumbe replied to his polite inquiry. Her thin face seemed relaxed and the angry lines had disappeared.

95   "And the children?"

96   "They're well, praise be to God."

97   "Our wife isn't very talkative this evening," put in one of the men.

98   "I'm quite well, though."

99   "Your heart isn't playing you up now?" asked Mustapha, not unkindly.

100   "No, it's quite steady," she answered.

101   "God be praised! Mustapha, we'll be off," said the man, uncomfortable at Noumbe's cold manner.

102   "Wait," said Mustapha, and turned to Noumbe. "Wife, are we eating tonight or tomorrow?"

103   "Did you leave me something when you went out this morning?"

104   "What? That's not the way to answer."

105   "No, uncle (darling). I'm just asking . . . Isn't it right?"

106   Mustapha realized that Noumbe was mocking him and trying to humiliate him in front of his men.

107   "You do like your little joke. Don't you know it's your three days?"

108   "Oh, uncle, I'm sorry, I'd quite forgotten. What an unworthy wife I am!" she exclaimed, looking straight at Mustapha.

109   "You're making fun of me!"

110   "Oh, uncle, I shouldn't dare! What, I? And who would help me into Paradise, if not my worthy husband? Oh, I would never poke fun at you, neither in this world nor the next."

111   "Anyone would think so."

112   "Who?" she asked.

113   "You might have stood up when I came in, to begin with . . ."

114   "Oh, uncle, forgive me. I'm out of my mind with joy at seeing you again. But whose fault is that, uncle?"

115   "And just what are these three plates for?" said Mustapha with annoyance.

116   "These three plates?" She looked at him, a malicious smile on her

lips. "Nothing. Or rather, my three days. Nothing that would interest you. Is there anything here that interests you . . . uncle?"

As if moved by a common impulse, the three men stood up. 117

Noumbe deliberately knocked over one of the plates. "Oh, uncle, 118 forgive me . . ." Then she broke the other two plates. Her eyes had gone red; suddenly a pain stabbed at her heart, she bent double, and as she fell to the floor gave a loud groan which roused the whole compound.

Some women came hurrying in. "What's the matter with her?" 119

"Nothing . . . only her heart. Look what she's done, the silly 120 woman. One of these days her jealousy will suffocate her. I haven't been to see her—only two days, and she cries her eyes out. Give her some ash and she'll be all right," gabbled Mustapha, and went off.

"Now these hussies have got their associations, they think they're 121 going to run the country," said one of his men.

"Have you heard that at Bamako they passed a resolution condemn- 122 ing polygamy?" added the other. "Heaven preserve us from having only one wife."

"They can go out to work then," pronounced Mustapha as he left 123 the compound.

Aida and some of the women lifted Noumbe on to the bed. She 124 was groaning. They got her to take some of her mixture of ash and water . . .

Questions for Discussion and Writing

1. How is the story shaped as an exploration of the importance that having "her three days" with her husband has for Noumbe?
2. How do the preparations Noumbe makes provide important insights into her CHARACTER that explain her relationships with Mustapha, his other wives, and her friends and neighbors?
3. In what sense does Noumbe's heart condition reflect or symbolize her predicament?
4. How do the descriptions both of the way Noumbe prepares herself and of the SETTING, including the living quarters and the supper she makes, add a dimension of pathos?
5. How do Noumbe's memories of how she behaved when she was the new wife add an ironic dimension to the story? How does it make you feel about her?
6. What changes can you observe in Noumbe's character between the beginning of the story through its conclusion? What does she do or say at the end of the story that implies she will never be the same person she was at the beginning of the story?
7. In a short essay, discuss the author's attitude toward polygamy and its effect on the relationship between men and women as it emerges in this story.
8. Describe a daydream you remember that made you feel happy or anxious.
9. Describe someone who initially had very little self-esteem but who gained self-confidence.

Itabari Njeri

Hair Piece

Itabari Njeri graduated from Boston University and the Columbia University Graduate School of Journalism. She has worked as a reporter and producer for National Public Radio in Boston, as an arts critic and essayist for the Miami Herald, and is currently a reporter for the Los Angeles Times. She has received numerous fellowships and awards including the Associated Press Award for Feature Writing and the National Association for Black Journalists Award. Njeri won the 1990 American Book Award for Every Goodbye Ain't Gone, from which "Hair Piece" is taken. This engaging and witty account of the difficulties black women face in finding hairdressers poignantly evokes the panorama of obstacles that have been put in the way of black women for the past four hundred years.

1   The king of curls in Opa-Locka, Florida, has no first name. He's just Mr. Vance. My hairdresser in Atlanta has no last name. He's just Kamal. In Miami, it's Raul. In New York, it's Mr. Joseph. This new breed of haute coiffeur was driving me mad.

2   "Hello, Mr. Vance, I'm a friend of Sujay's. I think she mentioned I'd be calling."

3   Silence.

4   "I'd like to make an appointment for a cold wave. Could you see me sometime next—"

5   "You'll have to come in for a consultation first," said a preoccupied voice.

6   "I see. Well, when can I have an appointment for a consultation?"

7   "I can do nothing until we consult."

8   "But you don't understand. I have a very busy schedule. If I have to take time off to get my hair done, I need to plan in advance, so—"

9   "You'll have to come in for a consultation."

10   The *b*'s in "bu-but" were exploding on my lips when he hung up.

11   "That's why I do my own hair," said Norma, standing over me laughing. There was a bald spot in the middle of her pageboy. "You had a call from the city manager's office while you were on the phone. And I have a doctor from the National Institute of Drug Abuse on hold for you now."

12   "Thanks. Let me call the city manager. Take a message from the NIDA guy, please."

13   I made the call, then walked to Norma's desk. On the way, I looked around the newsroom. I didn't see a single hairstyle that I liked on a black woman. Pageboys in 1981. Miami, what a backwater.

"What did the guy from NIDA want?"   14

"You can interview him the end of the week in Washington for your   15
cocaine story."

"Great," I growled, one hand on my hip, the other trying to sculpt   16
the hair at the back of my head into place.

"Your hair looks fine to me," Norma said. I was standing over her   17
now. I had a direct view of the few wisps of hair covering a shiny, two-
by-three-inch patch of scalp.

"I resent having to search from here to East Jablip for a competent   18
hairdresser. You should, too. Don't you remember what black beauty
salons were like twenty years ago?"

"No."   19

"How old are you?"   20

"Twenty-six," she said. "And you ain't much older."   21

"I'm trying to place this in some historical and cultural perspective   22
for you."

"Really?" she said, her lips pursed, her eyebrows raised.   23

"Never mind," I said, and walked back to my desk. But I remem-   24
bered.

They were where my grandmother bet a quarter every day on the   25
numbers, sometimes more when she'd had a dream. "Here's a dollar, I
dreamt seven-four-two last night. Play a combination." They were
where *Let's Make a Deal* took on new meaning: hot goods peddled at
record speeds to the music of police sirens. I once got a Borgana jacket,
a pair of real leather gloves and a rabbit hat for twenty-five dollars.
Had I been flush that day at Frankie's Harlem salon, I could have had a
color TV and stereo for a hundred dollars.

But I liked my first beautician best. Her name was Mrs. Lane. She   26
was our landlady, too, and ran a discreet salon on the ground floor of
her Brooklyn row house. If hot goods were peddled there, it was done
with the greatest subtlety. Or maybe my head was just in the shampoo
bowl when they came. After my wash, Mrs. Lane would put me under
the dryer, press my hair, then send me upstairs to our apartment for
dinner. That gave her time to work on another head. When I heard a
knock on the kitchen pipes, I'd go back down for a curl. I miss that.

"Mr. Vance? This is Itabari Njeri. I spoke to you a few weeks ago."   27

"Yes, I thought you would have been in by now."   28

"Well, it's my schedule. It's difficult for me to take time off for a   29
consultation without some guarantee that you'll see me. At least give
me an appointment that can be broken."

"As I explained to you, we can do nothing until we consult."   30

"If I come in for a consultation and you decide to do my hair, will   31
you confer with my previous hairdresser?"

"That's not necessary."   32

"It's taken many trials and much error for hairdressers to find what   33 works on my hair. My previous hairdresser knows all this. He can save us both a lot of grief."

34   "Then go back to your hairdresser if you like him so much."

35   "But he's in Atlanta."

36   "Then you have a problem."

37   I felt a migraine coming on.

38   Anne, the reporter next to me, leaned over the top of her video display terminal. "Itabari, why are you putting yourself through all these changes over a hairdresser?"

39   I looked at her freckled face and blond hair for a moment in silence. Then slowly I said, "Most white hairdressers don't know how to handle black hair unless they chemically straighten it first. I don't want my hair straightened. And a lot of black hairdressers, who use all sorts of chemicals for a variety of hairstyles, don't really know what they are doing. But the ones who do all seem to be a pain in the ass."

40   "Oh," she said, her head cocked like a dog's. I dropped it.

41   But even among the talented bastards, it was hard to know whom to trust. One stylist's concoctions left me almost bald, and I swore the next time that happened I'd sue.

42   But there was not going to be a next time, I told myself. Myself told me there was. I was having trouble sleeping at night. I began dreaming about baldness. There I was in a wig, on a date. My passionate companion clasped the back of my neck with his left hand and kissed me full on the mouth. The fingers of his right hand stroked my temple. And as he kissed me harder and pulled at my tongue with his teeth, his hand slipped under the wig's elastic band and his fingers became enmeshed in the netting.

43   Sujay swore by Mr. Vance. He had saved her troubled curls; maybe he could help me. After all, he had more than a salon. His business card said: "The Famous Mr. Vance's Professional Unisex Hair *Clinic* Salon. The hair clinic that embraces science, technology and you."

44   "How do you do, Mr. Vance. I'm Itabari Njeri. As you may recall, I'm the woman you gave such a hard way to go on the telephone yesterday."

45   "Oh," he said, surprised by the sight of me. I had dressed for the occasion. I wore a sun-yellow tunic made of Indian cotton with matching jodhpur pants. The tunic was cinched at the waist by a cummerbund cut from the same cloth. The sash gathered the starched tunic's skirt and caused it to puff and stay like an air-filled shell. The wide sleeves billowed when I moved. Any moment, I could be airborne. I was a brilliant butterfly. "Please have a seat," he said.

46   I patiently sat reading the signs in his small but attractive salon: NO CHECK, NO CREDIT, NO KIDS. THERE ARE TWO SIDES TO EVERY STORY. BUT I DON'T HAVE TIME TO HEAR YOURS.

47   This is the salon that embraces you?

"Now, tell me about some of the concerns you mentioned on the phone." 48

Butter wouldn't melt in his mouth. I relaxed, too. 49

I told him my troubles with past beauticians. "I'm determined to be more careful this time," I said. 50

"I feel sorry for you," he said. "You are a very unhappy woman. You don't trust people. No wonder your hair fell out." 51

"Look, I don't need a dime-store shrink. Are you trying to tell me it was my fault? It was the hairdresser's fault." 52

"That is speculation. We deal in facts here." 53

"Oh yeah? Well, when I went to the hairdresser, I had a full head of hair. A week later, my hair was in the sink." 54

"I wish you were as concerned about the other things I see wrong with you as you are about your hair," he said, staring at the enlarged pores on my nose and the pimple on my chin. 55

I wanted to deck him. 56

"Have you tried vitamins?" he asked. 57

"Look," I said, my voice spiraling toward hysteria, "I just worked a seventy-hour week at the paper, I can't find a decent apartment because people won't let me in the door once they see my black face, I got an editor who thinks that Jews and Italians are a separate race of people, and I can't get a bottle of my regular shampoo because the company doesn't ship as far south as Miami. You bet I look bad." 58

He smiled beatifically. "You are very attractive. You seem to be an intelligent woman. I want you to be satisfied." 59

He gave me a special shampoo and conditioner to use for a week before he did my hair. 60

"Mr. Vance, this is Itabari Njeri. That stuff you gave me left my hair bone dry and it's breaking." 61

"Yes. That'll be fine." 62

"What do you mean that'll be fine?" 63

"You must trust me. You have such a lovely voice." 64

"Thanks. But my hair is so dry it's breaking off." 65

"Yes, that's just the way I want it." 66

I wanted to cry. These pretentious shaft artists had forgotten their roots. Then I thought about Kamal. His shop was one of the few high-fashion salons that retained the warmth I remembered as a child. But he was in Atlanta. 67

I remembered Raul. A black woman had mentioned him to me before she left the paper and Miami. "In a pinch," she told me, "try Raul." 68

He was courtly and courteous. Unlike Mr. Vance, he consulted with Kamal by telephone and gave him his credentials. Things seemed to be going well. Raul handed me the phone. 69

"Don't let that man touch your hair," Kamal screamed. "I'm coming down there on the first thing smoking. He wants to put sodium hydrox- 70 ide on your hair—lye. He wants to relax your hair, then put in a cold wave. You don't need that. Your hair will fall out again. I won't be responsible if you let anyone touch your hair. I'm coming down there this weekend to do it myself."

71 "That's not practical," I said. "It'll cost three hundred dollars just to fly you here and back and another sixty bucks to get my hair done. I can't afford that."

72 Besides, Kamal could mean trouble. The last time his fingers massaged my scalp it was a clandestine affair, carried out about midnight at the house of my girlfriend. He had just been sprung from jail for nonsupport of three kids and two ex-wives, one of whom he had married twice.

73 "No, Kamal, you'll have a horde of women thinking there's something going on between us."

74 "Noooooo, Itabareeeee, I'm straight now. I need a short trip to cool out anyway."

75 "Why do I feel you don't do this for everybody?" I told him I'd think about it.

76 I looked in the mirror. Nothing was wrong with my hair, I reasoned. I looked at *Essence*. I looked at the model on the cover. I looked in the mirror. I picked up the phone.

77 I called every kinky-headed, curly-haired Hispanic and African-American in the newsroom. I knew I wasn't the only woman who couldn't get the cut or curl she wanted from any hairdresser in town.

78 Within an hour, it was agreed. Five of us would fly him in and pay sixty dollars apiece.

79 Saturday night, nine-ten P.M., I went to pick up Kamal at the airport.

80 Nine-thirty P.M. No Kamal. How could I forget about old undependable? This is the man who would arrive three hours late for my appointment after I'd driven 144 miles from Greenville, South Carolina, to Atlanta just to have him do my hair.

81 Nine forty-five P.M. I call Atlanta.

82 "Itabareeeee, I'll be there. I tried to call you."

83 "You didn't try to call me, you jive so-and-so. 'Cause I've been home all afternoon, cleaning, cooking, preparing for you. You've got two cold waves; one Afro cut; one wash, shape and trim and a potential permanent stirring restlessly in my living room."

84 "I'll be there, Itabari."

85 "Yeah, well you can call me from the airport when your feet touch Miami soil. Then I'll come and get you."

86 I went home and played my stress-reduction tape.

87 At eight-fifteen the next morning, the phone rang.

88 "I'm here." The voice was full of gravel.

89 "Who is this?"

90 "Kamal."

91 "I don't believe it."

"I told you you could count on me." 92

One of the other desperate heads, who lived close to the airport, 93
went to get him while I whipped up the quiches and spiked the juices.
The *Miami Herald* photographer arrived. My problem had become a sociological epic: the hairy plight of the black woman.

By day's end, our coifs were cover girl perfect. 94

Two months later we did it again; Kamal was two days late that 95
time. During the fourth episode, Kamal called three days late to say he
was "on his way." He didn't show. Not even vanity could compel me
to maintain this shuttle beauty service. I called his Atlanta shop. I
learned he was in a drug treatment program for cocaine addiction.

The long waits. The sudden disappearances from his salon. All 96
Kamal's erratic behavior over the years became clear.

What was I going to do about my hair now? 97

A braider named Mashariki, who'd read the article about my search 98
for a beautician, called me. She was considered one of the best African-
hair sculptors in the country, she said. Perhaps I'd like to do a story
about her, she said. I told her I'd be glad to stop by her salon one day.

"Have you read *Four Hundred Years Without a Comb*?" she asked the 99
day I visited her shop.

"No. I'm not familiar with that one." 100

"Well, I thought you might like a copy after reading about all the 101
problems you've had with your hair. Black people have a terrible preoccupation with hair because of our four hundred years without a
comb," she explained.

"I'm not sure I understand." 102

"We didn't have a comb. We couldn't comb our hair with European 103
combs so we were poorly groomed and self-conscious about our hair.
That's why we resorted to all sorts of things to make us look better.
Bacon fat to make it lie down—we didn't have anything else. Rags to
cover it up. All because we didn't have a comb."

"You mean an Afro pick?" 104

"Yes," she said. 105

"Well, we've got the comb now." 106

"But we haven't changed our behavior. As a braider, I'm trying to 107
get black women to give up these harsh chemicals and go back to natural hairstyles," she said.

I like braids, I told her. For the past thirteen years, when my hair 108
wasn't in an Afro, it had been cornrowed. But I got tired of both styles.
Besides, I told her, "the cornrows were tight. They either gave me a
headache or made my head itch."

"Ohhhh," she cooed, "then you'd love the individual braids. No 109
tension on the scalp. Great styling versatility."

"How much is it?" I asked. 110

"Four hundred dollars." 111

"What!" 112

113   "Oh, it takes a great deal of skill and time. It's an art. I take credit cards. And if you don't have cash, I'm not locked into this capitalist system. We can barter. Or, you can give me something as collateral. Do you have any jewelry or African art?"

114   "Well," I said, watching her braid as we talked—she did do beautiful work, "I have some Makonde statues I brought back from Tanzania."

115   "I'd love to see those," she said.

116   I noticed she had several pieces of beautiful African art in the shop already. I wondered if one ever got one's "collateral" back from her.

117   "No," I said, musing, "I wouldn't want to put up my African art as collateral."

118   "What else do you have?"

119   "I've got that famous photograph of Billie Holiday at her last recording session, shot by Milt Hinton."

120   "I'd love to see that," she said eagerly.

121   I gave in eventually, but I never put up any of my art as collateral.

122   The price of a good braider has dropped since then. The one I have in Los Angeles now is reliable and reasonably priced. She works out of her home—I like that. And when we take breaks—braiding is an all-day affair—we make an indoor picnic out of it. It reminds me a little of the old days and Mrs. Lane.

123   You can't get hot goods at my braider's house, but she makes up for it with great stories. Like the one about her friend who checks insurance claims. One claim was for a lady who'd been rushed to the emergency room to have a potato removed. The woman told the doctor she'd been in her garden that night digging up potatoes and fell on one. The potatoectomy—from the woman's most intimate bodily orifice—went unchallenged by the insurance company. Even though the raw tuber was completely peeled when retrieved.

124   I never heard anything that good in Mrs. Lane's shop.

Questions for Discussion and Writing

1. How would you characterize the NARRATOR, her personality, her job, and what kind of image she would like to project? Why is having a satisfactory hairdresser so important to her?
2. Compare and contrast the kinds of relationships the narrator has had with two of her past hairdressers, Kamal and Mr. Vance.
3. Describe the narrator's relationship with the African hair sculptor Mashariki.
4. To what extent do the difficulties the narrator faces in getting someone who can satisfactorily do her hair reflect the challenge she and, by implication, all black women face in coming to terms with a cultural heritage that is not mainstream?
5. How do the different hair styles the narrator goes through show a movement towards an authentic affirmation of her African-American heritage?

6. Do you see any significance in the fact that the narrator's first hairdresser was a woman (Mrs. Lane), her hairdressers along the way were all men, and that she is now happy with a woman hairdresser once again, in modern-day circumstances quite reminiscent of those in Mrs. Lane's house. What does this tell you about the narrator?

7. Discuss the significance of the essay's title and all its possible ramifications. Why would hair be such an accurate image to reflect the progress made by an entire generation and the change in society's attitudes? How would you characterize these changes?

8. Describe a person in the context of where you met them that makes it clear why you will always associate this person with this particular place, as Njeri does with Mrs. Lane's.

9. Describe an accident you know of that people still laugh about.

Alasdair Gray

The Crank That Made the Revolution

Alasdair Gray was born in Glasgow, Scotland, in 1934. He graduated from the Glasgow Art School in 1957, worked as an art teacher and a theatrical scene painter, and was Writer in Residence at the University of Glasgow from 1977 to 1979. After more than twenty years as a painter and as a scriptwriter for radio and television, he rose to literary prominence with the publication of several books in the 1980s. Gray's first novel, Lanark: A Life in Four Books *(1981), was critically acclaimed as a classic in the literature of adolescence. His second novel,* 1982 Janine *(1984), introduced audiences in the United States to Gray's protagonist, Jock McLeish, a disappointed, middle-aged, Scottish businessman, during a long night of heavy drinking. Gray's third novel,* The Fall of Kelvin Walker *(1987), is shorter and less surrealistic than his previous novels and shows the author fully in command of his technique as a stylist and storyteller. The title character, inspired by Gray's personal experience, is a young Scotsman who arrives in London with few assets but considerable self-confidence and a glib tongue that win him a national following as an interviewer on a television show. These novels provide a mixture of realistic social commentary and vivid fantasy augmented by the author's own arresting illustrations. Gray's short story collections,* Unlikely Stories, Mostly *(1983), from which "The Crank That Made the Revolution" is taken, and* Lean Tales *(1985) have been widely praised for their imaginativeness and dark satiric undercurrent. Here, Gray's sardonic parable about the Industrial Revolution describes how a single-minded Glasgow inventor comes up with a world-shaking scheme to improve the efficiency of his Granny's knitting.*

1   Nowadays Cessnock is a heavily built-upon part of industrial Glasgow, but two hundred and seventy-three years ago you would have seen something very different. You would have seen a swamp with a duck-pond in the middle and a few wretched hovels round the edge. The inmates of these hovels earned a living by knitting caps and mufflers for the inhabitants of Glasgow who, even then, wore almost nothing else. The money got from this back-breaking industry was pitifully inadequate. Old Cessnock was neither beautiful nor healthy. The only folk living there were too old or twisted by rheumatism to move out. Yet this dismal and uninteresting hamlet saw the beginning of that movement which historians call The Industrial Revolution; for here, in seventeen hundred and seven, was born Vague McMenamy, inventor of the crankshaft which made the Revolution possible.

2   There are no records to suggest that Vague McMenamy had parents. From his earliest days he seems to have lived with his Granny upon a diet of duck-eggs and the proceeds of the old lady's knitting. A German

biographer has suggested that McMenamy's first name (Vague) was a nickname. The idea, of course, is laughable. No harder-headed, clearer-sighted individual than McMenamy ever existed, as his crankshaft proves. The learned Herr Professor is plainly ignorant of the fact that Vague is the Gaelic for Alexander. Yet it must be confessed that Vague was an introvert. While other boys were chasing the lassies or stoning each other he would stand for long hours on the edge of the duck-pond wondering how to improve his Granny's ducks.

Now, considered mechanically, a duck is not an efficient machine, for it has been designed to perform three wholly different and contradictory tasks, and consequently it does none of them outstandingly well. It flies, but not as expertly as the swallow, vulture or aeroplane. It swims, but not like a porpoise. It walks about, but not like you or me, for its legs are too short. Imagine a household appliance devised to shampoo carpets, mash potatoes and darn holes in socks whenever it feels like it. A duck is in a similar situation, and this made ducks offensive to McMenamy's dourly practical mind. He thought that since ducks spend most of their days in water they should be made to do it efficiently. With the aid of a friendly carpenter he made a boat-shaped container into which a duck was inserted. There was a hole at one end through which the head stuck out, allowing the animal to breathe, see and even eat; nonetheless it protested against the confinement by struggling to get out and in doing so its wings and legs drove the cranks which conveyed motion to a paddle-wheel on each side. On its maiden voyage the duck zig-zagged around the pond at a speed of thirty knots, which was three times faster than the maximum speed which the boats and ducks of the day had yet attained. McMenamy had converted a havering all-rounder into an efficient specialist. He was not yet thirteen years of age.

He did not stop there. If this crankshaft allowed one duck to drive a vessel three times faster than normal, how much faster would two, three or ten ducks drive it? McMenamy decided to carry the experiment as far as he could take it. He constructed a craft to be driven by every one of his Granny's seventeen ducks. It differed from the first vessel in other ways. The first had been a conventional boat shape propelled by paddles and constructed from wood. The second was cigar-shaped with a screw propeller at the rear, and McMenamy did not order it from the carpenter, but from the blacksmith. It was made of sheet iron. Without the seventeen heads and necks sticking up through holes in the hull one would have mistaken it for a modern submarine. This is a fact worth pondering. A hundred years elapsed before the *Charlotte Dundas*, the world's first paddle steamer, clanked along the Forth and Clyde canal from Bowling. Fifty years after that the first ironclad screw-driven warship fired its first shot in the American Civil War. In two years the imagination of a humble cottage lad had covered ground which the world's foremost engineers took two generations to traverse in the following century. Vague was fifteen years old when he launched his second vessel. Quacking hysterically, it crossed the pond with such velocity that it struck the opposite bank at the moment of departure from the near one. Had it struck soil it would have embedded itself. Unluckily, it hit the root of a tree, rebounded to the centre of the pond, overturned and sank. Every single duck was drowned.

5   In terms of human achievement, McMenamy's duckboat ranks with Leonardo Da Vinci's helicopter which was designed four hundred years before the engine which could have made it fly. Economically it was disastrous. Deprived of her ducks, McMenamy's Granny was compelled to knit faster than ever. She sat in her rocking-chair, knitting and rocking and rocking and knitting and McMenamy sat opposite, brooding upon what he could do to help. He noticed that the muscular energy his Granny used to handle the needles was no greater than the energy she used to rock the chair. His Granny, in fact, was two sources of energy, one above the waist and one below, and only the upper source brought in money. If the power of her *legs and feet* could be channelled into the knitting she would work twice as fast, and his crankshaft made this possible. And so McMenamy built the world's first knitting frame, later nicknamed "McMenamy's Knitting Granny." Two needles, each a yard long, were slung from the kitchen ceiling so that the tips crossed at the correct angle. The motion was conveyed through crankshafts hinged to the rockers of a cast-iron rocking-chair mounted on rails below. McMenamy's Granny, furiously rocking it, had nothing to do with her hands but steer the woollen coils through the intricacies of purl and plain. When the McMenamys came to display their stock of caps and mufflers on a barrow in Glasgow's Barrowland that year, the strongest knitters in the West of Scotland, brawny big-muscled men of thirty and thirty-five, were astonished to see that old Mrs. McMenamy had manufactured twice as much as they had.

6   Vague, however, was modest enough to know that his appliance was improvable. The power generated by a rocking-chair is limited, for it swings through a very flattened arc. His second knitting frame was powered by a see-saw. His Granny was installed on one end with the needles mounted in front of her. Hitherto, Vague had avoided operating his inventions himself, but now he courageously vaulted into the other end and set the mighty beam swinging up and down, up and down, with a velocity enabling his Granny to turn out no less than eight hundred and ninety caps and mufflers a week. At the next Glasgow Fair she brought to market as much produce as the other knitters put together, and was able to sell at half the normal price and still make a handsome profit. The other inhabitants of Cessnock were unable to sell their goods at all. With the desperation of starving men, they set fire to the McMenamy cottage and the machinery inside it. Vague and his Granny were forced to flee across the swamp, leaving

their hard-earned gold to melt among the flames. They fled to the Burgh of Paisley, and placed themselves under the protection of the Provost, and from that moment their troubles were at an end.

In 1727 Paisley was fortunate in having, as Provost, an unusually   7
enlighted philanthropist, Sir Hector Coats. (No relation to the famous thread manufacturers of the following century.) He was moved by McMenamy's story and impressed by his dedication. He arranged for Vague to superintend the construction of a large knitting mill containing no less than twenty beam-balance knitting frames. Not only that, he employed Vague and his Granny to work one of them. For the next ten years Vague spent fourteen hours a day, six days a week, swinging up and down the opposite end of the beam from the woman who had nourished and inspired him. It is unfortunate that he had no time to devote to scientific invention, but his only holidays were on a Sunday and Sir Hector was a good Christian who took stern measures against workmen who broke the Sabbath. At the age of thirty Vague McMenamy, overcome by vertigo, fell off the see-saw never to rise again. Strangely enough his Granny survived him by twenty-two years, toiling to the last at the machine which had been named after her. Her early days in the rocking-chair had no doubt prepared her for just such an end, but she must have been a remarkable old lady.

Thirty is not an advanced age and Vague's achievement was   8
crowded into seven years between the ages of twelve and nineteen. In that time he invented the paddle boat and the ironclad, dealt a deathblow to the cottage knitting industry, and laid the foundations of the Scottish Textile Trade. When Arkwright, Cartwright, Wainright and Watt completed their own machines, McMenamy's crankshaft was in every one of them. Truly, he was the crank that made the Revolution possible.

Questions for Discussion and Writing

1. How does the way the NARRATOR presents Vague McMenamy make him appear as a one-dimensional (rather than fully fleshed out) CHARACTER who is defined in a very narrow way? In your opinion, what is his single defining character trait?
2. How do the different connotations of the word *crank* add to the humor of the story?
3. How does Vague's treatment of his Granny and her ducks spoof the principles of the Industrial Revolution and raise the question of how human beings fare in an age of industrialization?
4. How do Gray's detailed descriptions of SETTING make the seemingly implausible experiences of the characters more credible?
5. How does the manner of Vague's demise serve as an ironic commentary on the value of Vague's enterprise?

6. In your opinion, what is the object of Gray's satire—the Industrial Revolution, or qualities of thrift, efficiency, and engineering brilliance traditionally linked with the Scots (as symbolized by the character, Scotty in the "Star Trek" series)?
7. In a short essay, describe an invention that you believe would make the world a better place even if it defies the laws of reality.
8. Describe an accident or inadvertent discovery that changed history.

Joseph Brodsky

A Halt in the Desert

Joseph Alexandrovich Brodsky was born in Leningrad (now, again, Saint Petersburg) on May 24, 1940. He attended schools there until he was sixteen, when his formal education came to an end. On his own, he learned both Polish and English so that he could read the works of contemporary writers he admired, such as Zbigniew Herbert, Czeslaw Milosz, William Faulkner, T. S. Eliot, W. H. Auden, and William Butler Yeats. He was close friends with Anna Akhmatova, who singled him out as the most gifted lyric poet of his generation. He was repeatedly reprimanded by the Soviet authorities on charges of "social parasitism" and served twenty months of a five-year sentence at hard labor in the harsh regions of northern Russia. He immigrated to the United States in 1972 and became a naturalized citizen in 1977. He has held positions as poet in residence and as a professor at the University of Michigan, Columbia University, and Queens College. A prolific and diverse writer, Brodsky has recently published a volume of essays, Less Than One *(1986),* Marbles: A Play in Three Acts *(1989), and* Watermark *(1992), an account of his travels. Recognition of his poetry has come in the form of a MacArthur Fellowship, election to the American Academy of Arts and Sciences, and the Nobel Prize for literature in 1991. "A Halt in the Desert," taken from* Selected Poems, *translated by George L. Kline (1973), was written in 1966 during the period when Brodsky increasingly turned to poetry as a means of surviving persecution and imprisonment.*

So few Greeks live in Leningrad today
that we have razed a Greek church, to make space
for a new concert hall, built in today's
grim and unhappy style.[1] And yet a concert hall with more than fifteen hundred seats[2]   5
is not so grim a thing. And who's to blame
if virtuosity has more appeal
than the worn banners of an ancient faith?
Still, it is sad that from this distance now
we see, not the familiar onion domes,   10
but a grotesquely flattened silhouette.
Yet men are not so heavily in debt
to the grim ugliness of balanced forms
as to the balanced forms of ugliness.

I well remember how the church succumbed.   15
I was then making frequent springtime calls
at the home of a Tartar family

who lived nearby. From their front window one
could clearly see the outline of the church.
20   It started in the midst of Tartar talk,
but soon the racket forced its rumbling way
into our conversation, mingling with,
then drowning out, our steady human speech.
A huge power shovel clanked up to the church,
25   an iron ball dangling from its boom, and soon
the walls began to give way peaceably.
Not to give way would be ridiculous
for a mere wall in face of such a foe.
Moreover, the power shovel may have thought
30   the wall a dead and soulless thing and thus,
to a degree, like its own self. And in
the universe of dead and soulless things
resistance is regarded as bad form.
Next came the dump trucks, then the bulldozers . . .
35   So, in the end, I sat—late that same night—
among fresh ruins in the church's apse.
Night yawned behind the altar's gaping holes.
And through these open altar wounds I watched
retreating streetcars as they slowly swam
40   past phalanxes of deathly pale streetlamps.
I saw now through the prism of that church
a swarm of things that churches do not show.

Some day, when we who now live are no more,
or rather after we have been, there will
45   spring up in what was once our space
a thing of such a kind as will bring fear,
a panic fear, to those who knew us best.
But those who knew us will be very few.
The dogs, moved by old memory, still lift
50   their hindlegs at a once familiar spot.
The church's walls have long since been torn down,
but these dogs see the church walls in their dreams—
dog-dreams have cancelled out reality.
Perhaps the earth still holds that ancient smell:
55   asphalt can't cover up what a dog sniffs.
What can this building be to such as dogs!
For them the church still stands; they see it plain.
And what to people is a patent fact
leaves them entirely cold. This quality
60   is sometimes called "a dog's fidelity."
And, if I were to speak in earnest of
the "relay race of human history,"

I'd swear by nothing but this relay race—
this race of all the generations who
have sniffed, and who will sniff, the ancient smells.   65

So few Greeks live in Leningrad today,
outside of Greece, in general, so few—
too few to save the buildings of the faith.
And to have faith in buildings—none asks that.
It is one thing to bring a folk to Christ;   70
to bear His cross is something else again.[3]
Their duty was a single thing and clear,
but they lacked strength to live that duty whole.
Their unploughed fields grew thick with vagrant weeds.
"Thou who doest sow, keep thy sharp plough at hand   75
and we shall tell thee when thy grain is ripe."
They failed to keep their sharp ploughs close at hand.

Tonight I stare out through the black window
and think about that point to which we've come,
and then I ask myself: from which are we   80
now more remote—the world of ancient Greece,
or Orthodoxy? Which is closer now?
What lies ahead? Does a new epoch wait
for us? And, if it does, what duty do we owe?—
What sacrifices must we make for it?   85

1. During the mid-1960s a Greek Orthodox church was torn down and a large steel-and-glass structure—the "October" Concert Hall—erected in its place in a section of Leningrad not far from where Brodsky then lived.
2. Literally, "over a thousand seats"; in fact, the October Concert Hall seats more than four thousand.
3. An untranslatable play on words: *natsiyu krestit,* literally, "to baptize a nation," and *krest nesti,* literally, "to bear a cross."

Questions for Discussion and Writing

1. How would you characterize the SPEAKER's attitude toward the tearing down of the Greek Orthodox Church to make way for a concert hall? How do the speaker's descriptions of the different SETTINGS, that is, the Church and the concert hall, reveal what he considers valuable?
2. How does the speaker's CHARACTERIZATION of the "Tartar" family emphasize his sensitivity to the destruction of ethnic heritages?
3. How does the speaker use the sounds and sights of heavy construction equipment to represent the destructive forces that are destroying any connection with the past?
4. According to the speaker, what role will instinct play in preserving an

awareness of the past once all visible signs are gone? How does this relate to the role the poet can play?

5. If you can locate a photograph of a place that no longer exists, describe the clues that tell you the picture was taken a long time ago, for example, how the people are dressed. What in the picture would require an explanation?

6. Describe a person in the context of where you met them that makes it clear why you will always associate this person with this particular place as Brodsky does with the Tartar family.

7. If, in the space across the street from where you are sitting, a building were to be demolished and replaced, describe the kind of building you would design to put in its place—its function, appearance, uses for the people who would inhabit it, the materials, structure, and so on. You have an unlimited budget.

Chenjerai Hove

You Will Forget

Chenjerai Hove, born in Zimbabwe in 1956, is currently a cultural journalist based in Harare, Zimbabwe, whose poetry is part of an emerging tradition in recent African poetry. He has sought to make his novels and poems a vehicle to celebrate the cultural heritage of a continent that has suffered centuries of colonial oppression. Hove differs from other African writers (most notably Ngũgĩ wa Thiong'o, the Kenyan novelist) who feel the continued use of European languages—English, French, Portuguese—perpetuates a colonial dependency. Hove chooses to use English to express an alternative vision of the African world. His recent novel Bones *(1988) won the 1988 Zimbabwean Publishers/Writers Literary Award as well as the 1989 Noma Award. His volume of poetry* Up in Arms *(1982) received joint special commendation in the 1983 Noma Award for publishing in Africa, and another volume,* Red Hills of Home *(1985), received special mention in the 1986 Noma Awards. Hove is also the author of* Poems Inspired by the Struggle in Zimbabwe *(1985). "You Will Forget" (1990) describes the psychological costs of losing touch with one's cultural heritage.*

If you stay in comfort too long
you will not know
the weight of a water pot
on the bald head of the village woman

5   You will forget
the weight of three bundles of thatch grass
on the sinewy neck of the woman

whose baby cries on her back
for a blade of grass in its eyes

Sure, if you stay in comfort too long   10
you will not know the pain
of child birth without a nurse in white

You will forget
the thirst, the cracked dusty lips
of the woman in the valley   15
on her way to the headman who isn't there

You will forget
the pouring pain of a thorn prick
with a load on the head.
If you stay in comfort too long   20

You will forget
the wailing in the valley
of women losing a husband in the mines

You will forget
the rough handshake of coarse palms   25
full of teary sorrow at the funeral.

If you stay in comfort too long
You will not hear
the shrieky voice of old warriors sing
the songs of fresh stored battlefields.   30

You will forget
the unfeeling bare feet
gripping the warm soil turned by the plough

You will forget
the voice of the season talking to the oxen.   35

Questions for Discussion and Writing

1. What elements in the poem suggest that the voice that we hear speaks for collective rather than simply personal values? What are the values the SPEAKER claims are most in danger of being lost as a consequence of staying "in comfort too long"?
2. How does the speaker's description of the kinds of things that would be forgotten evoke the SETTING of tribal life? Why is this catalogue or inventory more effective than a single extended description?
3. If you were in danger of losing touch with your own cultural heritage, inventory those aspects you would most miss.

4. Describe a place where you lived as a child that you left and visited later on. What did you discover about it that you weren't aware of as a child?

Mbuyiseni Oswald Mtshali

Sunset

Mbuyiseni Oswald Mtshali was born in 1940 in Netal, South Africa. His first book of poems, Sounds of a Cowhide Drum *(1971), made a profound impression as one of the first manifestations of the new angry and energetic generation of black South African poets. He has lived in Johannesburg for many years, and has often been placed under house arrest for his outspoken opposition to apartheid. Mtshali's poetry blends urban and tribal images. In "Sunset" (1971) he juxtaposes the purples, reds, blues, and oranges that tint the sky with the intrusive urban sprawl of twentieth-century civilization, reflected in the metaphor of a "tossed coin" dropping into a slot.*

The sun spun like
a tossed coin.
It whirled on the azure sky,
it clattered into the horizon.
5 it clicked in the slot,
and neon-lights popped
and blinked "Time expired,"
as on a parking meter.

Questions for Discussion and Writing

1. What can you infer about the personality of the SPEAKER from his description of the sunset? Is the sunset a less awe-inspiring experience for the speaker because he sees it in terms of an expired parking meter?
2. What associations are suggested by likening the sun to a "tossed coin"? What does the phrase "time expired" suggest?
3. To what senses does the speaker draw on most effectively in describing the SETTING? How do words conveying actions contribute to the effect of the poem?
4. Did you ever have a favorite location that was once beautiful but that has been commercialized? Describe the transformation and your changed feelings.
5. Describe the associations you have with a particular natural phenomenon.

Yambo Ouologuem

When Black Men's Teeth Speak Out

Yambo Ouologuem, novelist and poet, was born in Bandiagara in the region of Mopti in the Republic of Mali, North Africa, in 1940. He is the son of a civil servant and a member of the traditional Dogon ruling-class family. Ouologuem was educated in the African language, Bamako, in Mali and holds advanced degrees in literature, English, and philosophy from the Sorbonne in Paris. He is fluent in several African and European languages. His first novel, Bound to Violence *(1968), was awarded the Prix Renaudot in France and has been translated into many languages. Drawing on the village story-telling traditions of the* griot, *this novel presents a searing indictment of the effect of colonialism in African history. Ouologuem followed this novel with a collection of satirical letters and pamphlets exposing African and European political hypocrisy. He became infamous for his trenchant satirical pamphlet addressed to General de Gaulle titled* Lettre Ouverte à la France Negre *(1968). "When Black Men's Teeth Speak Out," translated by Norman Shapiro, assails racial stereotypes in a fanciful and sardonic exposé.*

People think I'm a cannibal
But you know how people talk

People see that I have red gums but then who has
White ones
Hurrah for tomatoes   5

People say that there aren't as many tourists coming
Nowadays
But you know
We aren't in America and nobody
Has much cash   10

People think it's all my fault and that they're afraid of my teeth
But look
My teeth are white not red
I've never eaten anybody

People are pretty nasty and they say I gobble up   15
Tourists boiled alive
Or maybe grilled
So I said which is it grilled or boiled
Then they shut up and took an uneasy look at my gums
Hurrah for tomatoes   20

Everyone knows that they grow things in a farming country
Hurrah for vegetables

Everyone says that no farmer
Can live off his vegetables
25   And that I'm a pretty husky guy for someone so under-developed
A no good lowlife who lives on tourists
Down with my teeth

So all of a sudden I was surrounded
Tied up
30   Thrown to the ground
At the feet of justice

Cannibal or not a cannibal
Yes or no
Ha ha you think you're pretty clever
35   Playing high and mighty

Well we'll see about that I'll settle your hash
You're sentenced to death poor thing
What are your last words

I yelled hurrah for tomatoes

40   People are no good and women are a pretty inquisitive bunch
There happened to be one in the curious crowd
Who yapped
With a voice like a leper's rattle and the gurgle
Of a leaky pot
45   Open his stomach
I'm sure that daddy is still inside

With no knives around
Which is understandable for vegetarians
Of the Western world
50   Somebody grabbed a Gillette blade
And very patiently
Slishhh
Slashhh
Plonkkk
55   They opened my belly

And there they found a tomato field in bloom
Washed by streams flowing with palm-tree wine
Hurrah for tomatoes

Questions for Discussion and Writing

1. What does the SPEAKER reveal about the past causes of the crime of which he is accused? How is the way he presents his case designed to appeal to the reader's sympathy?
2. Why would the nature of the crime of which the speaker is accused be so threatening to those countrymen who are anxious to attract tourists?
3. How does the description of the "tomato field in bloom" discovered when the speaker is dissected contrast ironically with how he has been perceived? What does this interior SETTING suggest about the speaker's true CHARACTER?
4. How do elements of repeated refrains and tag lines give this poem the quality of a folk ballad?
5. In what way is this poem a protest against stereotyped perception? Have you ever been misperceived because of what you represented to other people? Describe your experiences.
6. Imagine that you have a landscape inside you that corresponds to what kind of person you are and describe it.

Garrett Hongo

Who Among You Knows the Essence of Garlic?

Garrett Hongo was born in 1951 in Volcano, Hawaii. His family moved to the San Fernando Valley in California where he and his brother were the only Japanese in the school. The family finally moved to Gardena, a Japanese-American community in south Los Angeles. He graduated from Claremont College, traveled to Japan on a Thomas J. Watson Fellowship, and returned to do graduate work at the University of Michigan. He received an M.F.A. from the University of California, Irvine, then taught at the universities of Washington and Southern California before taking on his present post at the University of Missouri at Columbia where he is poetry editor of the Missouri Review. *Hongo studied with poets Donald Hall and Philip Levine, among others, but was most influenced by the writing of Frank Chin, the first Asian-American playwright, and Lawson Inada, a pioneer Japanese-American poet. In 1976 Hongo founded, and until 1978 directed, a theater group in Seattle, The Asian Exclusion Act, which staged Frank Chin's* The Year of the Dragon *and premiered Wakako Yamachi's* And the Soul Shall Dance. *Hongo has received numerous awards, including the Hopwood Prize for Poetry, the Pushcart Prize, and the Wesleyan University Press Poetry Competition award. Hongo's poetry has been motivated by his quest for authentic roots of cultural identity in Japanese, Hawaiian, and southern Californian contexts. His collected books of poetry include* The Buddha Bandits Down Highway 99, *with Lawson Inada and Alan Lau (1978),* Yellow Light *(1982), and* The River of Heaven *(1988). He is currently writing poems for his fourth collection, tentatively titled* Volcano Journal. *"Who Among You Knows the Essence of Garlic" (1982) pursues Hongo's exploration of ethnic roots and cultural identity through the associations evoked by specific foods.*

Can your foreigner's nose smell mullets
roasting in a glaze of brown bean paste
and sprinkled with novas of sea salt?

Can you hear my grandmother
5   chant the mushroom's sutra?

Can you hear the papayas crying
as they bleed in porcelain plates?

I'm telling you that the bamboo
slips the long pliant shoots
10   of its myriad soft tongues
into your mouth that is full of oranges.

I'm saying that the silver waterfalls
of bean threads will burst in hot oil
and stain your lips like zinc.

15   The marbled skin of the blue mackerel
works good for men. The purple oils
from its flesh perfume the tongues of women.

If you swallow them whole, the rice cakes
soaking in a broth of coconut milk and brown sugar
20   will never leave the bottom of your stomach.

Flukes of giant black mushrooms
leap from their murky tubs
and strangle the toes of young carrots.

Broiling chickens ooze grease,
25   yellow tears of fat collect
and spatter in the smoking pot.

Soft ripe pears, blushing
on the kitchen window sill,
kneel like plump women
30   taking a long luxurious shampoo,
and invite you to bite their hips.

Why not grab basketfuls of steaming noodles,
lush and slick as the hair of a fine lady,
and squeeze?

The shrimps, big as Portuguese thumbs, 35
stew among cut guavas, red onions,
ginger root, and rosemary in lemon juice,
the palm oil bubbling to the top,
breaking through layers and layers
of shredded coconut and sliced cashews. 40

Who among you knows the essence
of garlic and black lotus root,
of red and green peppers sizzling
among squads of oysters in the skillet,
of crushed ginger, fresh green onions, 45
and pale-blue rice wine simmering
in the stomach of a big red fish?

Questions for Discussion and Writing

1. What associations are triggered in the SPEAKER's memory in the process of describing the sensuous features of foods with specific ethnic and cultural qualities? How are those qualities used to suggest a richness and diversity of which Anglo culture is unaware?
2. How do the complex descriptive effects of the poem depend on transposing sense impressions—that is, presenting an appeal to one sense in terms of another? Where can you see this operating?
3. How does the title of the poem and the way in which the speaker presents his sense perceptions suggest someone who is witty, knowledgeable, and extraordinarily sensitive?
4. Is there some dish in your own ethnic heritage that you could describe in ways that would suggest not only its specific taste and qualities, but the importance it has for you?
5. Can you remember the first "foreign" food you ever ate? Describe your experience.
6. Write a sensory description of a place whose mood is inextricably connected with the odors you smell. You may, as Hongo does, transpose sense impressions so that your descriptions of taste and smell include the other senses as well.

Sandra María Esteves

Weaver

Sandra María Esteves, a Latina of Puerto Rican background, writing in English, is a poet, essayist, and director/producer. She was born in 1948 in the South Bronx where she was raised and still lives today. To date, Esteves has published three volumes of poetry: Yerba Buena *(selected as one of the most notable works for 1981 by the* Library Journal*),* Tropical Rains: A Bilingual Downpour *(1984), and* Bluestown Mockingbird Mamba *(1990). In 1985 she was the recipient of a poetry fellowship from the New York Foundation for the Arts. In recent years, as executive director/producer of the African Caribbean Poetry Theater, a Bronx-based arts organization, she has produced eight seasons of poetry readings and staged theater productions. She was honored in 1990 by New York University for outstanding achievement in the Latino community. Her poetry is written from the perspective of a world citizen who seeks to understand the conditions that surround her. Her vision of the future, expressed in "Weaver" from* Yerba Buena, Chapbook #47 *(1980) and from* Puerto Rican Writers at Home in the U.S.A. *(1991), is uncompromisingly optimistic and is celebrated in a poem whose language is clear, direct, and musical.*

for Phil George

Weave us a song of many threads

Weave us a red of fire and blood
that tastes of sweet plum
fishing around the memories of the dead
5   following a scent wounded
our spines bleeding with pain

Weave us a red of passion
that beats wings against a smoky cloud
and forces motion into our lungs

10   Weave us a song
of yellow and gold and life itself
a wildgrowth
into the great magnetic center
topaz canyons
15   floral sweatseeds
in continuous universal suspension

94

Weave us a song of red and yellow and brown
that holds the sea and sky in its skin
the bird and mountain in its voice
that builds upon our graves a home   20
with fortifications
strength, unity and direction

And weave us a white song to hold us
when the wind blows so cold to make our children wail
submerged in furious ice   25
a song pure and raw
that burns paper
and attacks the colorless venom stalking hidden
in the petal softness of the black night

Weave us a rich round black that lives   30
in the eyes of our warrior child
and feeds our mouths with moon breezes
with rivers interflowing
through ALL spaces of existence

Weave us a song for our bodies to sing   35
a song of many threads
that will dance with the colors of our people
and cover us with the warmth of peace.

Questions for Discussion and Writing

1. How does the poem enact its own meaning? What features link it with prayers and incantations? How do these chantlike elements communicate the mood, tone, and spirit of the situation the speaker seeks to evoke?
2. How does the SPEAKER draw equivalences between the different colors into which humankind is divided and the colored threads the weaver uses to create a tapestry?
3. How is the poem designed to act as a kind of ritual to bring the speaker and listener together into an alliance encompassing all races?
4. How do the specific images of sight, taste, touch, and sound contribute to creating the overall tapestry the speaker describes?
5. In a short essay, discuss whether the value Esteves seems to place on poetry is realistic or unrealistic.
6. Have you ever constructed a family tree? Describe your experiences and the methods you used to turn up and corroborate information.

Julia Kasdorf

Mennonites

Julia Kasdorf grew up in a Mennonite community in Pennsylvania and is now a community activist working with local immigrant associations in Brooklyn. Her poetry has appeared in many periodicals, including The Journal. *"Mennonites" first appeared in* West Branch, *#24 in 1988. Kasdorf provides insight into the self-sufficient religious community whose adherence to values drawn from their own distinct cultural heritage often puts them at odds with the rest of the modern world.*

We keep our quilts in closets and do not dance.
We hoe thistles along fence rows for fear
we may not be perfect as our Heavenly Father.
We clean up his disasters. No one has to
5   call; we just show up in the wake of tornadoes
with hammers, after floods with buckets.
Like Jesus, the servant, we wash each other's feet
twice a year and eat the Lord's Supper,
afraid of sins hidden so deep in our organs
10   they could damn us unawares,
swallowing this bread, his body, this juice.
Growing up, we love the engravings in *Martyr's Mirror:*
men drowned like cats in burlap sacks,
the Catholic inquisitors,
15   the woman who handed a pear to her son,
her tongue screwed to the roof of her mouth
to keep her from singing hymns while she burned.
We love Catherine the Great and the rich tracts
she gave us in the Ukraine, bright green winter wheat,
20   the Cossacks who torched it, and Stalin
who starved our cousins while wheat rotted
in granaries. We must love our enemies.
We must forgive as our sins are forgiven,
our great uncle tells us, showing the chain
25   and ball in a cage whittled from one block of wood
while he was in prison for refusing to shoulder
a gun. He shows the clipping from 1916:
"Mennonites are German milksops, too yellow to fight."
We love those Nazi soldiers, who, like Moses,
30   led the last cattle cars rocking out of the Ukraine,
crammed with parents—children then—

learning the names of Kansas, Saskatchewan, Paraguay.
This is why we cannot leave the beliefs
or what else would we be? Why we eat
til we're drunk on shoo-fly and moon pies and borscht.
We do not drink; we sing. Unaccompanied on Sundays,
those hymns in four parts, our voices lift with such force
that we lift, as chaff lifts, toward God.

35

Questions for Discussion and Writing

1. What picture does this poem give you of Mennonite life, customs, and beliefs? What details show the extent to which the Mennonite community is self-sufficient and does not look to the outside world for help?
2. What elements in the poem create a sense that we have suddenly begun to eavesdrop in the middle of a dramatic situation in which we are directly hearing the inner voice of the community?
3. How has the Mennonites' willingness to forgive enemies, one of their most important doctrines, ironically resulted in their becoming martyrs?
4. How does the description of the different SETTINGS in which Mennonites have had to live help you understand the difficulties they have experienced in pursuing their religious freedom? How does the image of the "harvest" develop the theme of the Mennonites' single-minded devotion to God?
5. What insight did this poem give you into Mennonite life and what stereotyped impressions did it correct?
6. If you are part of a community with its own traditional ways, explain the history of this community and the importance of its values from the perspective of people inside the community.
7. Who were the first settlers in your area and why did they choose this place?
8. Were you ever invited by someone from another cultural background to participate in or witness a ceremony or ritual that was important to them? Describe your experiences.

Kōbō Abe

Friends

Kōbō Abe (1924–1993), the dramatist, short story writer, and novelist, was born in Tokyo but grew up in Mukden, Manchuria, then a possession of Japan. He returned to Tokyo to prepare to become a doctor, like his father, but by 1948, when he graduated from the medical school of Tokyo University, his father had died and Abe had already decided upon a career in literature rather than medicine. He is best known for his ironic, meticulously detailed avant-garde novels that include The Woman in the Dunes *(1964),* The Face of Another *(1966),* The Ruined Map *(1969), and* The Box Man *(1974). All of these works deal with the themes of isolation and urban alienation. Much of Abe's energy has been devoted to writing for stage and screen: notably, adapting* The Woman in the Dunes *and later novels for the brilliant films directed by Teshigahara Hiroshi. In recent years, Abe founded an acting company and produced and directed a number of innovative plays including* Friends, *which was first presented in 1967 in Tokyo. This play, a tragicomedy, translated into English by Donald Keene, combines elements of the bizarre with realistic details to satirize the precarious state of the individual in contemporary Japanese society.*

CAST

MIDDLE DAUGHTER, *twenty-four years old; a trim-looking, sweet girl who gives the impression of being a crystallization of good will*

GRANDMOTHER, *eighty years old*

FATHER, *a gentleman who at first glance might be taken for a clergyman; he wears a worn but quite respectable suit and carries a briefcase*

MOTHER, *her old-fashioned hat and glasses become her*

YOUNGER SON, *he once won a prize as an amateur boxer; he carries a guitar under one arm and a suitcase in the other*

ELDER SON, *clever, but frail-looking and rather gloomy; formerly a private detective; he carries suitcases in both hands when he enters*

ELDEST DAUGHTER, *thirty years old; a prospective old maid who still preserves her dreams of being raped by some man*

MAN, *thirty-one years old; section head in a commercial firm*

YOUNGEST DAUGHTER, *a little devil, though she doesn't look it*

MIDDLE-AGED POLICEMAN

YOUNG POLICEMAN

BUILDING SUPERINTENDENT, *a woman*

FIANCÉE, *she works in the same office as* MAN; *looks like a city girl*

REPORTER, *formerly on the staff of a weekly magazine*

. . . SCENE ONE

The curtain rises to the sweetly seductive melody of "The Broken Necklace" (music by Inomata Takeshi).

> Night time in the big city—
> Now that the string is broken, the beads of the necklace
> Scatter here and scatter there
> In every direction.
> Poor broken necklace, where is the breast that warmed you once?
> When did you leave it, where has it gone?
> Little lost beads, little lost beads.

Two large, partitionlike walls meet in a "V" at the middle of the stage. Shadows of human figures, four each from left and right, appear on the walls and, to the rhythm of the music, gradually grow larger, until in the end they seem to loom like giants over the audience.

As the music comes to an end, the owners of the shadows reveal themselves from the wings on both sides. The composition of this family of eight could hardly be more average, but one senses something peculiar about its members. They move mechanically, nobody as yet showing any expression on his face.

MIDDLE DAUGHTER *steps forth from the group and advances to the center of the stage. The music should continue, but without words.*

MIDDLE DAUGHTER (*taking up the words of the song that has been heard, her voice pleading and romantic*):   But we can't just leave them to their fate. We'll gather up those poor little beads. Yes, we'll gather them up and run a new string through them. (*She turns to GRANDMOTHER.*) We can do it, Grandma, can't we?

GRANDMOTHER (*in a completely matter-of-fact tone*):   Of course we can. That's our job, isn't it?

MIDDLE DAUGHTER (*turning back to audience and continuing her previous remarks*):   It's wrong for there to be lost children and lonely people. It's all wrong. But you can't make a necklace without running a string through the beads. (*She turns to FATHER.*) We'll be the string for the necklace. Won't we, Father?

FATHER (*with a look of having heard this before*):   Don't you think I know it already, that being a string is our job?

MIDDLE DAUGHTER (*singing to the music*):

> Where is the breast that warmed you once?
> When did you leave it, where has it gone?
> Little lost beads, little lost beads.

YOUNGEST DAUGHTER *suddenly gives a loud sneeze that stops the music.*

MOTHER: My poor darling. (*To the others, reproachfully.*) If we don't settle down somewhere soon, it'll be ten o'clock before we know it.

YOUNGER SON: That's right. (*He yawns ostentatiously.*) I for one have had enough of this gabbing.

ELDER SON (*sharply*): Don't talk like a fool. It's our job, isn't it?

ELDEST DAUGHTER (*without expression*): That's right. It's our job.

The music begins again.

MIDDLE DAUGHTER (*resuming her exalted tone*): And that's why we must go on. We must search out all the lonely people and offer them our love and friendship. We are the messengers of love who can heal their loneliness. We must sniff out the faint wisps of sadness that escape like drops of starlight from the windows of the city, and go there with our gift of joy. (*She spreads her arms open as if introducing the family to the audience.*) Yes, we are the angels of broken necklaces.

Each member of the family simultaneously shines a flashlight from below on his face and smiles timidly. The contrast with the mood of what has preceded should be as strong as possible.

Blackout.

. . . SCENE TWO

The partitions are drawn aside to reveal Man's room. The furniture and household accessories should all be of one color, either a reddish brown or gray.

A door leads to the kitchen at stage-right front. At stage-left rear a door leads to another room. The entrance door to the apartment is at stage-left front. Next to the door, in the hall, is a rather elaborate coat rack. (This rack will later be used as a cage; it must therefore have suitable vertical and horizontal supports.) All the furnishings, including the doors, should be simplified and abbreviated as much as possible.

MAN sits at the desk. He wears a jacket and jiggles his leg as he telephones. The telephone is the only real object in the room.

MAN: Well, that's about all for now. I'll call you later on to say good night . . . What? It has yellow spots? Sounds like an alley cat, doesn't it? . . . No, I'm sorry. I assure you, I have absolute confidence in your taste . . . Oh, just a second. (*He removes the receiver from his ear and listens.*) No, it wasn't anything. I can't imagine anyone coming to see me now, at this hour of the night . . . Yes, isn't that what I've been saying all along? Next payday I'd like you to move in here for good. You should have your things packed and ready by then.

The eight members of the family approach slowly and hesitantly, walking on tiptoe.

It sounds like rain? Yes, maybe it is raining. It couldn't be foot steps—It'd take too many people for that. You know, the insurance agent in the apartment below mine is a nut for poker . . . Of course the noise has nothing to do with me.

The footsteps suddenly grow louder. MAN *cocks his head and listens. The family enters from stage right and crosses stage front in a single line.* YOUNGER SON, *who has in the meantime passed his guitar to* ELDER SON, *goes past the entrance to Man's apartment, then turns back; at which all the others stop in their tracks.* FATHER *and* YOUNGER SON *stand on either side of the entrance.* FATHER *takes out a notebook and, after thumbing through the pages, compares what he finds with the name on the door. He nods and gives the signal to* MIDDLE DAUGHTER, *who is standing behind him. She comes forward and stands at the door, then knocks gently.*

MAN: Say, it's at my door! (*He glances hurriedly at his watch.*) Must be a telegram, at this hour of the night. (MIDDLE DAUGHTER *knocks again and he calls to other side of the door.*) I'll be with you in a minute! (*The family is visibly relieved. He speaks into the telephone.*) I'll go out and have a look. I'll call you later. Here's a kiss. (*He makes a noise with his lips and puts down the telephone.*)

. . . SCENE THREE

GRANDMOTHER, *having slipped around from behind* MIDDLE DAUGHTER, *peeps through the keyhole. She sees* MAN *coming to the door.*

GRANDMOTHER: Goodness—what a handsome man!
FATHER: Shhh! (*He takes* GRANDMOTHER *by her sleeve and pulls her back.*)
MAN: Who is it? Who's there?
MIDDLE DAUGHTER (*in a girlish voice*): Excuse me, please. I'm sorry to bother you so late.
MAN: Who is it, please? (*He is disarmed to discover the visitor is a young woman, but is all the more suspicious.*)
MIDDLE DAUGHTER: I'm so sorry. I intended to come earlier.

MAN *shakes his head doubtfully, but eventually yields to curiosity and opens the door a little. Instantly* YOUNGER SON *inserts his foot into the opening.* FATHER *takes the doorknob and pulls the door open. The family, moving into action, assembles before the door.* MAN, *dumfounded, stands rooted.*

MIDDLE DAUGHTER: Oh, that's a relief! You hadn't gone to bed yet, had you?

FATHER (*in the tone of an old friend*):   Of course not! The young folks
these days are night owls, all of them.

MOTHER (*pushing* GRANDMOTHER *from behind*):   Shall we go inside,
Grandma? The night air is bad for you.

MAN (*his voice choked*):   Who are you, anyway?

GRANDMOTHER (*ignoring* MAN *and starting to go in*):   Oh, dear, it's pretty
bare, isn't it?

ELDEST DAUGHTER (*exhibiting strong curiosity*):   What do you expect? It's
a bachelor apartment, after all.

MIDDLE DAUGHTER: That's right. And that's why it's so important
somebody come and help him.

MAN (*baffled*):   Just a minute, please. I wonder if you haven't got the
wrong party.

ELDER SON (*with a melancholy smile*):   I used to work for a detective
agency, you know.

MAN: But still—

YOUNGEST DAUGHTER: I'm cold.

MOTHER: Poor darling. You'll take an aspirin and get to bed early.

MOTHER, *her arms around* YOUNGEST DAUGHTER, *propels* GRANDMOTHER
into the apartment. MAN *tries to prevent her, but* YOUNGER SON *sees an opening and darts inside.*

MAN: What do you mean, breaking in, without even taking off your
shoes?

YOUNGER SON: Oh—sorry. (*He removes his shoes.*)

*The family takes advantage of Man's distraction to surge into the apartment in
one wave.* FATHER, *the last in, shuts the door behind him and turns the key.*
MAN, *in face of the concerted action of the eight of them, is powerless to resist.
The members of the family scatter around the room with a kind of professional
competence, neatly surrounding* MAN. *They flash at him their usual bashful
smiles. They seem to have got the better of him.*

MAN: What's the big idea? It's enough to give a man the creeps.

FATHER (*unruffled*):   Please, I beg you, don't get so upset.

MAN: If you've got some business with me, how about explaining
exactly what it is?

FATHER: It puts us in an awkward position if you're going to turn on
us that way . . . (*He looks around from one to another of the family
as if enlisting their support.*)

MAN (*excitedly*):   Puts you in an awkward position! You break in, without warning, on a total stranger, and you say it puts you in an
awkward position! I'm the one who has something to complain
about.

ELDER SON (*taps on the wall*):   Pretty good! The walls have been sound-
proofed.

ELDEST DAUGHTER: It's freezing in here. Doesn't he have an electric heater, I wonder.

MAN (*unable to take any more*): Stop loitering around my apartment! All of you, get out of here! Now!

YOUNGER SON (*coolly*): Why, I feel as if we weren't wanted.

MAN: That's not surprising, is it? Of all the crassness!

YOUNGEST DAUGHTER *peeps into the back room.*

YOUNGEST DAUGHTER: Look, there's another room here.

GRANDMOTHER: It won't be easy dividing the space with only two rooms for nine people. (*She goes up beside* YOUNGEST DAUGHTER *and examines the other room with her.*)

MIDDLE DAUGHTER: We can't be fussy, you know. We didn't come here for our amusement.

MAN *stands at the door to the back room, blocking it. He is bewildered and uneasy.*

MAN: Out with all of you, and right now! If you refuse to go, I'll charge you with trespassing.

YOUNGEST DAUGHTER (*with an exaggerated show of terror*): Oh, he scares me!

MOTHER (*admonishingly*): There's nothing for you to be afraid of. He's really a very nice man. There, just look at this face. He's just pretending to frighten you, that's all.

GRANDMOTHER: That's right. He's what I'd call a handsome man. If I were only ten years younger . . .

MAN: I've had all I can stand! (*He starts to lift the telephone.*)

FATHER (*quietly restraining him*): Now calm yourself. You seem to be under some terrible misapprehension. You're making such a fuss anybody might think we intended to do you some harm.

MAN: What *do* you intend, if not to harm me?

FATHER: Why should you say such a thing?

MAN: You're in a stranger's home here.

FATHER (*with an expression of dismay*): A stranger's home?

ELDER SON (*contemptuously*): A stranger's home! He certainly takes a very narrow view of things.

MAN: But, as a matter of fact, we are strangers, aren't we?

FATHER (*soothing him*): You mustn't get so worked up over each little thing. Have you never heard the saying that being brothers marks the first step on the way to being strangers? That means, if you trace strangers back far enough you'll find they were once brothers. What difference does it make if we're strangers? A little thing like that shouldn't upset you.

MOTHER: Yes, when you get to know us better you'll see we're just so relaxed and easygoing it's positively funny. (*She laughs.*)

MAN: Don't act silly. Whatever you may think, the fact is, this is my apartment.

ELDEST DAUGHTER: That's obvious, isn't it? If it weren't your apartment, you wouldn't be here.

YOUNGER SON: And if it weren't your apartment do you suppose we'd have listened in silence all this time to your bellyaching?

MIDDLE DAUGHTER: I thought I told you to lay off him.

YOUNGER SON: I apologize. The fact is, I have a wee bit of a hangover. Damn it!

YOUNGER SON *shadowboxes briefly to cover his confusion.* MIDDLE DAUGHTER, *acting as if she has suddenly noticed it, puts out her hand to remove a bit of wool fluff from Man's jacket.* ELDEST DAUGHTER *tries to beat her to it. But* MAN *shrinks back from both of them, and neither is successful.* YOUNGEST DAUGHTER *chooses this moment to disappear into the kitchen.*

ELDEST DAUGHTER: I'm going to take off my coat, if you don't mind.

FATHER: Yes, we can't go on standing around this way indefinitely. Why don't we sit down and discuss things in a more relaxed mood?

They all remove their coats and hats. YOUNGER SON *also removes his jacket. Eldest Daughter's dress rather emphasizes her physique.*

MAN *steps forward resolutely, pushes* FATHER *aside, and picks up the telephone and dials with an air of determination.*

MAN: One, one, zero. (*He pauses, his finger inserted in the zero.*) Leave at once! Otherwise, I have only to release my finger and I'll be connected.

YOUNGER SON: To the police?

ELDEST DAUGHTER: Aren't you carrying things a bit too far?

FATHER (*perplexed*):   It's a misunderstanding . . . a complete misunderstanding.

MAN: I have no time to bandy words with you. I'll give you until I count ten, that's all. I advise you to start getting ready. (*He starts to count slowly.*)

YOUNGER SON *stands menacingly before* MAN. *He looks at the family to see whether they want him to go ahead.*

FATHER (*sharply*):   Stop! I forbid you to use violence.

MOTHER: Yes, we don't want people saying bad things about us. Stop it!

ELDER SON: How about, as a last resort, abiding by the will of the majority?

Man's attention is caught by the words "will of the majority." *He slows down the speed of his counting.*

ELDEST DAUGHTER: Even if we win a majority decision, it'd still be picking on someone weaker than us, wouldn't it?

ELDER SON: Don't be an idiot. The will of the majority means . . .

FATHER: Let's drop the whole matter. We know which side is going to win anyway. There aren't any thrills in this game.

GRANDMOTHER: Where might is master, justice is servant.

MIDDLE DAUGHTER (*somewhat uneasy*):   What do you intend to do, anyway?

MAN: That's what I'd like to know. When I count one more, that'll make ten.

FATHER: It can't be helped. If you think it's absolutely necessary, do whatever you think best. It won't be very pleasant, but who knows?—it may prove more effective in bringing you to your senses than repeating the same old arguments.

MAN: Don't try to intimidate me! You're prepared, I take it? I'm really phoning the police.

FATHER: Go right ahead.

MAN (*releasing his finger from the dial emphatically*):   Don't say I didn't warn you!

MOTHER (*sighs*):   It's true, just as they say, a child never knows its parent's love.

MIDDLE DAUGHTER (*sighs*):   This is the test run.

. . . SCENE FOUR

The telephone rings at the other end, then stops as the call is put through. The members of the family betray their tension in their expressions as they stand around the telephone. YOUNGER SON *puts a cigarette in his mouth.* GRANDMOTHER, *with an obsequious smile, tries to snatch away the cigarette, but* YOUNGER SON *brusquely pushes his hand aside and lights the cigarette.* MAN *is worked up, but he keeps himself on guard against the family.*

MAN: I'm sorry to bother you, but I've been intruded on by a crazy outfit . . . No, it's not exactly a burglary . . . But there are eight of them. I've tried in every way I know to persuade them to leave, but they absolutely refuse to listen . . . No, it's not a vendetta or anything like that. They're total strangers . . . Yes, forced entry would be about right. I suppose you could call it a kind of burglary in that sense . . . That's right, eight of them . . . I? I'm all alone . . . Will you? Sorry to bother you. The place—it's a little hard to explain. Would you mind telephoning 467–0436 and asking the superintendent for directions? That's her number. My name is Homma and I'm in Apartment 12 . . . No, I don't think there's any im-

mediate danger of violence, but there's no telling under the circumstances . . . Yes, I'd appreciate that. I'll be waiting for you
. . . (*He heaves a sigh and puts down the telephone.*)

ELDER SON, YOUNGER SON, *and* ELDEST DAUGHTER *smile to themselves, each
with obvious satisfaction.*

FATHER (*admonishingly*):   There's nothing to smile about! I'm sure he
was quite in earnest in doing what he did.

ELDER SON: But how can I help smiling? Burglary, he called it!
Burglary! If a cat denounced a mouse as a burglar you couldn't keep
the mouse from smiling just by telling him he shouldn't.

ELDEST DAUGHTER: I realize of course he doesn't mean any harm.

YOUNGER SON (*imitating Man's voice*):   Yes, sir. There are eight of them,
but I am all alone.

The members of the family start giggling again.

MAN (*challenging them*):   Don't be so stubborn. You still have a few
minutes left before the patrol car comes. I advise you not to waste
your last chance.

YOUNGEST DAUGHTER *sticks her head out from the kitchen. Her face is
smeared around the mouth with something she has been eating.* GRAND-
MOTHER *quickly surmises what has happened.*

GRANDMOTHER: Look at that! She's been nibbling something in the
kitchen.

YOUNGEST DAUGHTER (*wiping her mouth and singing out*):   The menu for
tonight is two bottles of milk, six eggs, a loaf of bread, one bag of
popcorn, one slice of mackerel, a pickle and some relish, two slices
of frozen whalemeat, salad oil, and the usual spices.

YOUNGER SON: Quite a sweet tooth, hasn't he? Is there nothing in the
way of liquor?

YOUNGEST DAUGHTER: Now that you mention it, there were two bottles
of beer. That's all, I think.

YOUNGER SON: That's fine. I wanted a hair of the dog that bit me.
(*He claps his hands in anticipation.*)

MOTHER: You can't drink it alone. We've got to save it to drink a toast
to our new friendship.

ELDER SON: It's certainly not much of a menu in any case. You could
find a better selection at a roadside diner.

MIDDLE DAUGHTER: Leave worrying about dinner to me. Those ingredients are more than enough for me to make quite a decent soup.
(*She goes to the kitchen.*)

MAN: At last you've shown yourselves in your true colors. Out-and-out robbery is what I'd call it. The police will be here any minute. How do you plan to explain yourselves?

FATHER (*calmly*): You'll find out soon enough, when the time comes.

MAN: What will I find out?

ELDEST DAUGHTER: There's nothing for us to explain, is there? We're not doing anything we feel especially ashamed of.

MAN: Well, can you beat that? You talk as if you have the right to install yourselves in here. On what grounds can you justify—

MOTHER *pauses in her unpacking of her suitcase.*

MOTHER: But you're all alone here, aren't you?

MIDDLE DAUGHTER (*through the kitchen door*): It's terrible being alone. It's the worst thing that can happen to anybody.

ELDEST DAUGHTER: Yes, loneliness is bad for a person. In the first place, it makes you lose all resilience.

MAN: Supposing that's true, what business is it of yours?

FATHER: We're your friends. We can't abandon you, can we?

MAN: My friends?

FATHER: Of course we are. There are millions, even tens of millions of people in this city. And all of them are total strangers . . . Everywhere you look you see nothing but strangers . . . Don't you think that's frightening? There's no getting around it, we all need friends. Friends to help us, friends to encourage us.

GRANDMOTHER: In traveling, a companion; in life, sympathy. A wonderful thing, isn't it?

YOUNGER SON (*to* FATHER): Can't I have just one bottle of beer?

MAN (*nearly screaming*): I've had enough! I'm quite happy being alone. I'll thank you to stop your uncalled-for meddling. I don't want your sympathy. I'm enjoying my life just the way it is.

FATHER (*hesitantly*): But in general it's true, isn't it, that lunatics claim that they alone are sane?

MAN: Lunatics?

FATHER: Forgive me. I was using the word entirely by way of a simile.

MAN: As long as you're on the subject of lunatics, the description suits you all very well.

FATHER: Of course, it's difficult to define what we mean by a lunatic.

MOTHER *sits before the mirror and begins to apply vanishing cream.*

MOTHER: Nobody actually knows himself as well as he *thinks* he does.

ELDEST DAUGHTER (*suddenly clapping her hands*): That's right! I just remembered, I know a shop where they sell neckties that would look marvelous on you. I'll take you there the next time I go.

MOTHER (*reproving*): Instead of talking about such things you'd do better if you started helping in the kitchen. My stomach is beginning to tell me I need something to eat.

ELDEST DAUGHTER (*sulking*): Lend me your nail-polish remover, will you?

GRANDMOTHER: I'm in charge of dividing up the jam!

MAN: Who the hell *are* you all anyway?

YOUNGER SON (*with an air of arrogant assurance*): I'll tell you this once and for all—the most important thing for anybody to learn is how to get along with other people. A man who can get along with other people will stay out of trouble.

ELDER SON: It has been proven statistically that most criminals are antisocial.

FATHER: Be that as it may, please trust in us, and feel secure in your trust as a passenger on a great ocean liner. I'm certain that one day you'll need us and be grateful to us.

MAN: I've had all I can stand of your high-pressure salesmanship. Of all the colossal nerve!

FATHER: But we have no choice. You consider yourself to be a human being, don't you? It stands to reason, then, that it is your privilege, and also your duty, to live in a manner worthy of a human being.

YOUNGER SON *begins to strum the melody of "The Broken Necklace" on his guitar.*

MIDDLE DAUGHTER *emerges from the kitchen and begins to sing the song, still peeling a carrot. The peel hangs down to the floor in a long, unbroken coil.*

MIDDLE DAUGHTER:

> Night time in the big city—
> Now that the string is broken, the beads of the necklace
> Scatter here and scatter there
> In every direction.
> Poor broken necklace, where is the breast that warmed you once?
> When did you leave it, where has it gone?
> Little lost beads, little lost beads.

. . . SCENE FIVE

Two policemen are led to the door of the apartment by the SUPERINTENDENT, *who is a woman. The policemen have apparently been dropped some sort of hint by the* SUPERINTENDENT; *at any rate, they seem uncommonly lax in their demeanor.*

It may be that the SUPERINTENDENT *has been on bad terms with the* MAN, *or that she may already have been bought over by the family; or it simply may be that she is pretending to be neutral for fear of getting involved—this is not clear.*

The SUPERINTENDENT *points out the door of the Man's apartment and starts to make a hurried exit, but the* MIDDLE-AGED POLICEMAN, *with a wry smile, plucks her back by the sleeve, his gesture suggesting a man catching a bug. The* YOUNG POLICEMAN *puts his ear to the door and listens to the sounds emanating from within, consulting his wristwatch as he does so. Then, with great deliberation, he presses the bell next to the door.*

MAN *rushes to the door in response to the bell, all but knocking down the members of the family nearest to him (probably* GRANDMOTHER *and* MIDDLE DAUGHTER), *and pushes the door open. This action barely misses causing the* YOUNG POLICEMAN *to fall on his ear.*

MAN (*flurried, but with great eagerness*):   Oh, I'm sorry. Well, this will give you an idea of the situation. Come in, please, and have a look for yourself. The culprits are still holding out. I'm glad you got here in time. Oh, there are two of you? (*He notices* SUPERINTENDENT.) It's good to have you along too, to back me up. Please step right in. Don't mind about me.

The policemen and SUPERINTENDENT, *at his urging, go inside. The* MIDDLE-AGED POLICEMAN, *standing at center, runs his eyes professionally over the family. They betray no noticeable agitation. With absolute self-possession, they all stop whatever they were doing and return the policeman's suspicious stare with smiles and nods that all but overflow with a sincerity that could only come from the heart.*

MAN (*excitedly*):   They're eight of them altogether. The other one's in the kitchen.

YOUNGEST DAUGHTER *enters from the kitchen, wiping her mouth. She obviously has been nibbling again.* GRANDMOTHER *gives the girl a severe look and starts to scold, but* FATHER *and* ELDER SON *restrain her casually.*

YOUNGEST DAUGHTER: Here I am.
MOTHER: Say hello to the gentlemen.
YOUNGEST DAUGHTER (*in a childish, bashful manner*):   Good evening.
MIDDLE-AGED POLICEMAN (*confused*):   Hmmm. Well then, what's the offense?
MAN (*failing to catch the words*):   Excuse me?
YOUNG POLICEMAN: Their offense—what specific injury have you suffered?
MAN (*indignant*):   I don't have to specify, do I? You've caught them red-handed in the act.

The members of the family continue to smile, quite unperturbed. Their smiles are confident and beyond all suspicion. MAN, *however, has become so upset by the passive attitude of the policemen that he is flustered and does not seem to have become aware of the performance the family is putting on.* MIDDLE-AGED POLICEMAN *looks as if the smile tactics of the family have got the better of him. He lowers his eyes to his notebook and reads as he speaks.*

MIDDLE-AGED POLICEMAN: According to the complaint, illegal entry has occurred on these premises.

MAN: That's it precisely!

MIDDLE-AGED POLICEMAN: In other words, even though you, the injured party, have plainly indicated to the parties responsible for the injury your wish that they not intrude into your apartment . . .

MAN: Naturally I've indicated it.

MIDDLE-AGED POLICEMAN: . . . the offenders have brutally ignored or resisted the wishes of the injured party . . .

MAN: Ignored is a mild word for it.

MIDDLE-AGED POLICEMAN: Have you got any proof?

MAN: Proof?

YOUNG POLICEMAN: Have you any evidence of violence a doctor might be able to put in a medical certificate—broken bones or bruises?

MAN (*losing his temper*):   I don't need any such evidence. All you have to do is look. They're eight against one.

MIDDLE-AGED POLICEMAN (*considers this seriously*):   Eight against one and not a single bone broken? That makes it a little harder to prove violence, doesn't it?

MAN *does not speak and the* YOUNG POLICEMAN *lets his glance run over the smiling faces of the members of the family.*

YOUNG POLICEMAN (*to* MIDDLE-AGED POLICEMAN):   The question would seem to arise, rather, why the complainant should have conceived such hostility toward these people—his motives, I mean.

MAN (*dumfounded*):   Do you suspect *me*?

MIDDLE-AGED POLICEMAN: It's not that we *suspect* you. But complaints lodged over private, family matters often create a lot of trouble for us.

MAN (*in earnest*):   This is preposterous. These people are complete strangers!

The members of the family, exchanging glances, smile sadly; one or two rub their chins as much as to say, "There he goes again!" and others wink at the policemen, enlisting their support. All remain silent as before.

MIDDLE-AGED POLICEMAN (*to* YOUNG POLICEMAN):   What are we to do about this, anyway?

YOUNG POLICEMAN (*to* MAN):   I'd be glad to offer my services in helping to patch up the difficulties amicably.

MAN (*almost writhing with impatience*):   Why can't you accept what I
say? I tell you I have absolutely no connection with these people. It
doesn't make sense to talk of patching up our difficulties amicably.

YOUNG POLICEMAN: That's a little hard to believe.

MIDDLE-AGED POLICEMAN: Have you any positive evidence that these
people are strangers, as you claim?

MAN: Why don't you ask them?

*The members of the family maintain their smiles intact. They even contrive to
mingle a subtle suggestion of embarrassment in their smiles, exactly as if they
were sympathizing with the policemen's predicament, or feeling embarrassment themselves over the deranged behavior of one of their own family.*

MIDDLE-AGED POLICEMAN: That won't be necessary. I think I've got a
pretty good idea of the essential points. It's my conclusion that there
has been no injury to speak of.

MAN (*so enraged he stammers*):   I'm disgusted. What more can I say to
convince you? . . . And if you go on insisting that there has been
no injury, even after what's happened, well, there's nothing left for
me to say.

MIDDLE-AGED POLICEMAN: Excuse me for mentioning it, but you
wouldn't be suffering from a persecution complex, would you?

MAN (*to* SUPERINTENDENT):   You can tell them, ma'am, can't you? You
know I'm the one who's always paid the rent. And the name—the
apartment is registered in my name, and letters are delivered regularly here to me, under my name. That's right, isn't it? This is my
apartment. There's no doubt about it. I'm the only one with any
rights here. That's correct, isn't it? You can surely vouch for me,
can't you?

SUPERINTENDENT (*irritated*):   Well, I can't say for sure.

MAN: You can't say for sure?

SUPERINTENDENT: I've always made it my practice, as long as a tenant
pays the rent promptly each month, never to butt into his private
life.

MAN: But at least I can ask you to vouch for the fact that I am the
tenant.

SUPERINTENDENT: I'd rather not go into such things, but you know, in a
place like this the person living in an apartment isn't always the
same as the person who pays the rent.

MIDDLE-AGED POLICEMAN: I can imagine.

SUPERINTENDENT: Take the case of a young, unmarried woman, living
alone . . .

At once FATHER *and* YOUNGER SON *react, but they restrain each other and instantly revert to the virtuous smiles they have displayed up to now.* GRANDMOTHER *begins to search the desk drawer.*

MIDDLE-AGED POLICEMAN: Hmmm. I see.

SUPERINTENDENT: In extreme cases we may be sent money orders without even the sender's name.

MAN (*furious*): But I . . . I signed and sealed the contract, didn't I?

MIDDLE-AGED POLICEMAN: Come, now. You mustn't get so excited. Of course I understand your problem, but if there's no injury worth reporting at this stage . . .

MAN: But it's illegal entry, isn't it? It's trespassing, isn't it?

YOUNG POLICEMAN: We always ask the concerned parties in such private disputes to try to settle them among themselves. The police have their hands full as it is, what with the shortage of men.

MAN: I've told you, haven't I, these people are total strangers.

MIDDLE-AGED POLICEMAN: Well, in the event you suffer any specific injuries, please don't hesitate to get in touch with us again. (*He winks to the family, as much as to say that he has sized up the situation perfectly.*) It doesn't look as if I can write a charge—it won't make a case. I'm sorry to have bothered you all.

MOTHER (*as if the thought has suddenly struck her*): Oh, are you leaving so soon? And to think I haven't even offered you so much as a cup of tea.

MIDDLE-AGED POLICEMAN: Please don't bother.

MAN (*utterly bewildered*): But . . . just a second . . . what do you mean by . . . I've never heard of such a damned stupid . . . What am I going to . . . It's crazy. No matter how you look at it.

The SUPERINTENDENT *and the policemen ignore* MAN, *who runs after them as if to implore their help. They go out very quickly and shut the door behind them. Once outside, they exchange sarcastic grimaces and exit at once.*

. . . SCENE SIX

YOUNGER SON *strikes a chord on his guitar, as if by way of a signal. The smiles that seemed to have been imprinted on the eight faces of the family are instantly replaced by their normal expressions.*

FATHER (*consolingly*): That, my friend, is what people mean when they talk of good, common sense.

ELDER SON: Good, common sense, and at the same time, accomplished fact.

GRANDMOTHER: The proof of the pudding is in the eating.

ELDEST DAUGHTER: It seems to come as quite a shock to him. He's still standing there in a daze.

MOTHER: It'll do him good to have such an experience once.

YOUNGEST DAUGHTER: I don't understand him. Why, even a child knows how lonely it is to be without friends.

YOUNGER SON: His whole outlook's warped. He's bluffing, that's all.

MIDDLE DAUGHTER: I wish it wouldn't take him so long to understand what a miserable thing loneliness is, and how lucky he is to have us . . . (*She seems to be addressing herself to* MAN *only. She wraps the long peel from the carrot around her neck.*)

MAN (*suddenly turning on her*): I've had all I can stand of your meddling.

FATHER (*as if reasoning with himself*): It's certainly irritating, but this is no time to lose my temper. Patient care is the only way to treat the sick.

MIDDLE DAUGHTER: Would you like a glass of water?

MAN (*unmoved*): Stop bothering me! I swear, I'll get rid of you, if it's the last thing I do. You can make up your minds to that! I tell you I won't stand being humiliated this way!

MIDDLE DAUGHTER (*unwrapping the carrot peel around her neck*): If we don't do something about it, the broken necklace will never be the same again. Isn't there anything we can do to convince him of our sincerity?

ELDEST DAUGHTER: Humpf. Such exquisite sensitivity!

MIDDLE DAUGHTER (*with an abrupt shift of mood*): Don't act so sour!

FATHER: Now, now—don't forget, anybody who creates dissension or starts a quarrel must pay a fine.

GRANDMOTHER (*still rummaging through the desk, but her tone is magnanimous*): It's a long lane that has no turning . . . There's nothing worth making a fuss over.

MIDDLE DAUGHTER (*to* YOUNGEST DAUGHTER): Come on, help me in the kitchen.

GRANDMOTHER (*sharply*): This time don't do any nibbling on the sly. It's disgraceful.

YOUNGEST DAUGHTER *sticks out her tongue, then exits with* MIDDLE DAUGHTER.

MAN (*suddenly becoming aware of Grandmother's suspicious activities*): It's all very well for you to talk, but what are you doing there, anyway?

GRANDMOTHER: I was just looking for a cigarette.

MAN: Cut it out! Stop acting like a sneak thief!

GRANDMOTHER (*with exaggerated dismay*): Oh—I'm a sneak thief, am I?

FATHER: Of course you're not a sneak thief. I ask you all to refrain from making remarks that might cast aspersions on anyone else's character.

ELDER SON: How about setting a fine of a hundred yen on any remark which is decided by majority vote to be offensive?

FATHER: An excellent suggestion. Yes, that appeals to me. There's no

such thing as being too discreet when it concerns a person's character, is there?

GRANDMOTHER (*more engrossed than ever in her search for cigarettes*):
Imagine calling me a sneak thief! A cigarette only turns to smoke, no
matter who smokes it.

MAN: Stop rummaging that way through my desk!

MAN, *thinking he will stop* GRANDMOTHER, *steps forward automatically, only
for* ELDER SON *to stick out his foot and trip him.* MAN *flops down magnificently.*

ELDER SON: Oops—excuse me!

The family at once rushes over to MAN *in a body and surrounds him, lifting
him to his feet, massaging his back, brushing the dust from his suit, and otherwise showering him with extreme attentions.*

ELDEST DAUGHTER: Are you sure you're all right?

MOTHER: You haven't hurt yourself?

YOUNGER SON: Can you stand okay?

GRANDMOTHER: No pain anywhere?

FATHER: No broken bones?

MAN (*freeing himself*):   Lay off, for God's sake!

ELDER SON (*apologetically*):   I'm sorry. I was just worried you might get
so carried away by your feelings you would resort to violence.

MAN: Wouldn't you describe what you did as violence?

ELDER SON: Not in the least. It was a precaution against violence.

YOUNGER SON (*cheerfully*):   We won't let you get away with that!
Allowing yourself to get involved in a quarrel is just the same as
starting one. You'll have to pay a fine. Or would you rather make
amends in kind?

ELDER SON (*dejectedly*):   I don't have to tell you how hard up I am for
money.

ELDEST DAUGHTER: But even if he prefers to make amends in kind, it
won't be easy. How can anybody trip himself?

YOUNGER SON: Can't you think of anything better to do than butt
into other people's business? Do you plan to go on removing nail
polish forever? It's just a matter of time before you dissolve your
finger-tips. (*To* MAN.) I wonder if you'd mind tripping my brother
back?

MAN (*angrily*):   Don't be an idiot!

YOUNGER SON: It can't be helped, then. I'll take over as your substitute.

As soon as YOUNGER SON *finishes speaking he gets up and deftly trips* ELDER
SON, *who tumbles over with a loud groan.* YOUNGER SON *at once drags* ELDER
SON *to his feet, only to trip him again, without allowing him an instant's*

respite. He repeats this a third time, and is about to trip him a fourth time when MAN, *unable to endure any more, cries out.*

MAN: That's enough, for God's sake!

MOTHER (*relieved*): At last, he's forgiven you.

ELDER SON (*grimacing with pain and rubbing the small of his back*): Thanks.

YOUNGER SON: Well, what do you know? Perspiring seems to have relieved my hangover a little.

GRANDMOTHER (*suddenly*): I've found them! (*She clutches a package of cigarettes.*)

MAN *takes a step in her direction only to remember immediately what happened to him the last time. He stops in his tracks.* FATHER *can't quite allow* GRANDMOTHER *to get away with it and takes away the cigarettes.*

FATHER: That's going too far, Mother.

MAN: Sneaking around my desk like a cat. She's a regular cat burglar! (*He puts out his hand, expecting to get back his cigarettes as a matter of course.*)

FATHER (*withdrawing his hand, sounding surprised*): What did you just say?

MAN *does not speak.*

GRANDMOTHER: He called me a cat burglar!

FATHER: A cat burglar!

ELDER SON (*calmly*): That calls for a fine. Number one, right?

FATHER (*his voice is strained*): I see . . . Without warning, it's come to this . . . I may seem a little too much of a stickler for the rules, but if we hope to live together amicably . . .

ELDER SON: Yes, a rule's a rule . . .

ELDEST DAUGHTER (*massaging her face*): Just a minute. There's nothing to get so upset about.

GRANDMOTHER (*getting angry*): You're always trying to be different from everyone else.

ELDEST DAUGHTER (*ignoring her*): I think cats are sweet. I adore them. They're the most aristocratic of all animals.

ELDER SON: But there's a big difference cats and cat burglars, isn't there?

ELDEST DAUGHTER: And there's also a big difference between burglars and cat burglars.

GRANDMOTHER (*excited*): Then you say I'm a cat?

ELDEST DAUGHTER: Don't be conceited, Grandmother!

GRANDMOTHER: But that's what he said . . . He plainly called me a cat burglar.

ELDEST DAUGHTER: I'm sure he meant it as a compliment.

FATHER: Now wait, please. The meaning is quite different, depending on whether the emphasis was on burglar or on cat. In other words, did he mean a cat that resembled a burglar, or a burglar that resembled a cat?

GRANDMOTHER: I don't care what he said, I'm not a cat.

YOUNGER SON: That's so, I guess. If you were a cat, Grandma, that'd make us all half-breed cats.

FATHER: Therefore the logical meaning must be a catlike burglar.

ELDER SON: That rates a fine, doesn't it?

ELDEST DAUGHTER (*persisting*): Why should it? He didn't say she was a burglar plain and simple, but a catlike burglar.

ELDER SON: But a burglar's a burglar. The only difference is whether or not the word has an adjective before it.

GRANDMOTHER (*moaning*): I'm not a burglar!

ELDEST DAUGHTER: Do you mean to say that applying a different adjective doesn't change the meaning of a word? Well, that's the first I've ever heard of *that* argument! If a big fish and a little fish, a sunny day and a cloudy day, a decrepit old man and a snotty-faced kid, a brand-new car and an old buggy, a smiling face and a crying face all amount to the same thing, then there's no distinction either between a burglar man and a burglarized man. I've never heard such a funny story.

YOUNGER SON: It looks as if you've lost the first round, Brother. Eh?

ELDER SON: A woman's superficial cleverness, that's all it is.

ELDEST DAUGHTER (*assertively*): A cat is a superb animal.

MOTHER (*indifferently*): I don't like cats.

ELDEST DAUGHTER (*her tone is extremely objective*): They say that a dislike of cats is the mark of an egoist.

YOUNGEST DAUGHTER (*sticking her head in from the kitchen*): But people who don't like cats often like them.

YOUNGER SON: You don't say! That's not bad, you know.

MOTHER (*to* YOUNGEST DAUGHTER): Children should be seen and not heard.

YOUNGEST DAUGHTER: Hurry up and help us in the kitchen.

ELDEST DAUGHTER: I have more important things to do. We're having a serious discussion.

GRANDMOTHER: Anyway, I'm not a cat.

ELDEST DAUGHTER (*her tone becoming hysterical*): Stop it, won't you? I can't stand you speaking so sneeringly about cats.

MAN (*finally having had all he can take*): Won't you drop the whole thing, for pity's sake? I can settle this by paying a hundred yen—right? It's too ridiculous. (*He starts to look in his pockets for his wallet.*)

ELDEST DAUGHTER (*coquettishly*): Oh? But that's cheating . . . After I went to all the trouble of taking your side . . .

FATHER (*recovering himself*): That's right. You don't leave us much to say if you're going to talk in such extremes . . . We still haven't reached any conclusion, after all . . . The situation has become unexpectedly complicated.

MAN: What's so complicated? (*He continues to search his pockets.*)

FATHER: I meant merely that our opinions continue to be opposed.

ELDEST DAUGHTER: Yes. You must remember you aren't alone any more. There's someone on your side. Anyway, cats are absolutely marvelous animals.

MOTHER: But I don't like them.

GRANDMOTHER: I told you I wasn't a cat!

FATHER: There you have the problem.

MAN: What difference does it make? The long and short of it is that I have to pay a fine. Right?

FATHER: But the basic principle of communal living is respect for the opinions of each person.

MAN (*his voice dropping sarcastically*): Is that so? I'm delighted to hear it. I'll be sure to remember that. (*He is still unable to find his wallet, and begins to look rather worried. He takes his coat from its hook on the wall and starts to search the pockets.*)

FATHER (*to the others*): What do you say, all of you? Wouldn't this be a good point to try to put some order into the discussion? Now, if you'll permit me to express my opinion, the question, it seems to me, is whether the animal known as the cat—when, for example, it is compared with the dog . . .

ELDEST DAUGHTER: There's no comparison!

YOUNGER SON: Still, nobody ever talks of a dog burglar.

ELDEST DAUGHTER: That's because dogs are stupid.

ELDER SON: That's a lie.

ELDEST DAUGHTER: What do you know about it?

ELDER SON: There are police dogs, but I've never heard of police cats.

ELDEST DAUGHTER: Of course not. Cats have a higher social status.

MOTHER: But, it seems to me, cats are lazy.

YOUNGER SON: Wait a second. Hard workers don't necessarily get very far.

ELDEST DAUGHTER: That's precisely it.

YOUNGER SON: But if you'll permit me to express my own preferences, I like dogs better.

ELDEST DAUGHTER: They certainly suit you. Let sleeping dogs lie. Go to the dogs. Lead a dog's life . . .

YOUNGER SON: Don't be too sure of yourself with cats, you caterwauling, cat-calling, caterpillar . . .

ELDEST DAUGHTER: Every dog has his day.

YOUNGEST SON: Catnip is to a cat as cash to a whore in a cathouse.

ELDEST DAUGHTER: Dog eat dog. Die like a dog. Dog in the manger.

ELDER SON: You see—friends and foes are all confused. A majority decision is the only way, Father.

MAN: I wish you'd drop the whole thing. A majority decision! (*He is still searching frantically.*)

ELDER SON: At this rate we'll never get to eat dinner.

MIDDLE DAUGHTER (*emerging from the kitchen with a frying pan in her hand*):   Sorry to keep you waiting. Dinner will be ready in just a few minutes. Sis, please help me dish out the food.

MAN (*pauses in his search, with vehemence*):   Dinner—of all the crazy nonsense! What crass nerve, here, in my house! Listen, I warn you, I intend to use every means at my disposal to obstruct anything you do. (*To* MIDDLE DAUGHTER.) Get rid of that mess. Throw it in the garbage can, now!

MIDDLE DAUGHTER (*recoiling*):   But that would be a terrible waste!

FATHER (*looks into the frying pan*):   Mmm. It certainly smells good.

ELDER SON: I'm convinced that food is meant to be eaten with lots of company. Nothing is drearier than shoveling in a quick meal. I can tell you that from my own personal experience.

MAN: Unfortunately, there are some people whose temperament is such that they prefer to live alone.

ELDER SON: Well, I can see that once you've argued yourself into a point of view you'd want to stick to it.

While they are talking MIDDLE DAUGHTER *exits.*

ELDEST DAUGHTER: My sister used to take a course in cooking. (*At last she gets up and starts toward the kitchen.*)

GRANDMOTHER (*to* ELDEST DAUGHTER):   I'm in charge of dividing up the jam.

ELDEST DAUGHTER: It's quite something to have been able to make a curry with the ingredients she had. (*She exits.*)

YOUNGER SON (*stifling a yawn*):   I feel more like sleeping than eating now . . . My hangover is beginning to take its toll.

GRANDMOTHER: I'm no good without my food. I can't get to sleep without first putting my tapeworm to bed.

MAN (*strangely self-possessed*):   In that case, you should stay awake all the time. Stay awake for years, or maybe dozens of years, as long as you like. I warned you, didn't I, that I intend to do everything in my power to obstruct you? That wasn't an empty threat. I assure you I intend to carry it out. I'll make sure you don't get to eat even a slice of bread.

GRANDMOTHER: Why won't we?

ELDER SON (*with a faint smile*):   He talks exactly as if he's turned into a magician or something, doesn't he?

MAN (*walking toward the kitchen*):   You're going to laugh on the wrong side of your faces!

MOTHER (*to the people in the kitchen, in a casual voice*):   You've put away everything harmful, haven't you?

MIDDLE DAUGHTER (*from the kitchen*): Of course we have. I've hidden everything—the tile cleanser, the rat poison, the cockroach spray. They're in a safe place.

YOUNGER SON (*in a loud voice*): It might be a good idea, while you're at it, to stow away the detergents and soap powder too.

MIDDLE DAUGHTER: Right.

MAN *stops in his tracks in dumb confusion at the kitchen door.*

ELDER SON: You see! He intended to use one of them.

YOUNGER SON (*to* MAN): You planned to use a spray to squirt foam over the dinner, didn't you?

FATHER (*a consoling expression on his face*): For good or for evil, everybody tends to think, more or less, along the same lines.

YOUNGER SON: Foam—that reminds me—beer! (*As if appealing for sympathy he looks up at ceiling.*)

While the preceding conversation has been going on, MOTHER *has at last finished removing her makeup. She puts away her beauty aids and, rising to her feet, turns to face the others. All of a sudden she takes hold of her hair and pulls up, to reveal she is wearing a wig. She blows into the wig, fans it with her hand, and after shaking it out thoroughly, puts it back on her head.*

MOTHER (*to* MAN, *with an artificial laugh*): You don't mind, do you? You're not a stranger any more, after all. (*Abruptly changing her tone.*) By the way, what ever happened to the fine we were talking about?

FATHER (*perplexed*): We didn't seem to be able to reach any conclusion in our discussion of cats, and the person in question doesn't seem very enthusiastic about a majority decision.

MAN (*searching frantically through all his pockets, and even in the cuffs of his trousers, with an intense display of determination*): I'll pay, I tell you. You don't suppose I want to be in your debt for a mere hundred yen! I'm paying, not because I recognize I was at fault, but simply because I don't feel like arguing over anything so extremely stupid.

The attention of the entire family is at last attracted by his distraught actions, and they observe him carefully. MAN *suddenly stops searching, as if he found what he was looking for.*

MAN: Damn it! That's funny . . .

MOTHER: Was it your wallet? Or do you carry your money loose?

MAN: I carried it in a wallet with my monthly pass . . . I can't imagine . . .

The glances of the others converge at the same moment in accord on ELDER SON. *He returns their gaze. There is a moment of silence.*

ELDER SON: What's the matter with you all? Have I done something wrong?

YOUNGER SON (*crooking his index finger to suggest a robber with a gun*): Did you do it, Brother?

ELDER SON (*with feigned innocence*):   What are you talking about, anyway?

FATHER (*uneasily*):   It's not true, is it? I'm sure you wouldn't stoop to that sort of thing . . . At a critical moment like this we must, above all, show the greatest respect for the integrity of the individual.

YOUNGER SON: But he's got a criminal record, you know.

ELDER SON: Stop it! You're ruining my reputation!

At this juncture the people in the kitchen begin to stick out their heads and observe what is going on.

YOUNGER SON: Everybody of course has committed youthful indiscretions.

ELDER SON: Haven't I told you I've completely given up all that?

MOTHER: Please. Look into Mother's eyes. Yes, look straight into my eyes.

ELDER SON: I've come back to you, haven't I? You can see that I have . . . I learned, so well it hurt me, how wonderful it is when people can trust one another and what a blessing it is when people who trust one another can live together. So I came back to you, from that horrible world where every man is a stranger . . . Do you think I'd betray you all? No, stop it, please . . . As far as I'm concerned, the one thing that makes life worth living is being together, hand in hand.

GRANDMOTHER (*apparently unimpressed*):   You aren't trying to make us cry, are you?

ELDER SON: I'm serious, I assure you.

YOUNGER SON: I'll bet if ever I tried to lie seriously I could really warm up to it.

ELDER SON (*uncertain how he should react to this comment, betraying his confusion momentarily*):   I understand the situation perfectly . . . And I'm glad . . . I don't feel in the least offended. I'm flattered you should retain such a high opinion of my former skill.

MOTHER (*brooding*):   Then, you mean . . .

ELDER SON: I leave it to your imagination.

FATHER (*embarrassed*):   That won't do . . . You, better than anyone else, are in the position to put the matter straight. How can you speak of leaving it to our imagination? I thought we had promised not to recognize private prerogatives when it came to money.

ELDEST DAUGHTER: Yes, he himself was the first to propose that.

YOUNGER SON (*as if reading aloud*):   As previously agreed, in cases where suspicions have been aroused with respect to monetary matters, no one, whosoever he may be, for whatever reason, may refuse a request for a body search.

GRANDMOTHER: Love flies out the window when poverty comes in at the door.

FATHER: I can't understand it. You have the best brains of the lot of us, there's no getting around it. And you're amenable to reason. We all depend on you. It's intolerable that we should have to treat you like a defendant in court.

ELDER SON (*laughs*): You have nothing to worry about.

FATHER (*relieved*): Then you're innocent?

MOTHER: You should have set our minds at rest sooner.

ELDER SON: I mean, I haven't done anything that warrants a physical examination.

ELDER SON *suddenly raises his hand and reveals that he is holding Man's wallet. The following dialogue by members of the family occurs almost simultaneously.*

MOTHER: You took it, then!

ELDEST DAUGHTER: You've got to keep your eye on him every minute.

YOUNGEST DAUGHTER: Take me on as your apprentice, won't you?

YOUNGER SON: Now I know why you're never short of cigarette money.

MOTHER (*firmly*): Hand it over, here!

As MOTHER *steps forward,* MAN *springs to his feet with an incomprehensible cry and makes a grab for Elder Son's hand. The wallet instantly disappears.*

MAN (*carried away, searching Elder Son's pockets*): What've you done with it? Give it back!

ELDER SON: Oh, you're tickling me! (*He holds up his hands, as before a gunman, and twists himself free.*)

MOTHER (*severely*): You know the rules, don't you? I take charge of the safe.

ELDER SON (*to* MAN): I surrender! If you would kindly look in the righthand pocket of your pants . . .

MAN *doubtfully puts his hand into his pocket and with an incredulous expression he produces the wallet.*

MAN: This is it, all right.

YOUNGEST DAUGHTER (*clapping her hands*): He's a regular wizard!

MIDDLE DAUGHTER (*reproving*): You mustn't say that! You're not to admire him.

MOTHER (*to* ELDER SON, *angrily*): Haven't you done quite enough? Surely you can't have forgotten all about your own family.

MAN (*turning wallet upside down and shaking it*): Not a thing. There's not a penny in it . . . (*He stands there glaring at* ELDER SON, *grinding his teeth, for the moment unable to find even words of protest.*)

ELDER SON (*apparently enjoying it*): A pro who couldn't do that much wouldn't be worthy of the name.

MOTHER: I won't allow it—sneaking off with other people's money.

GRANDMOTHER: Like a cat burglar?

MOTHER (*to* MAN): How much was in it?

MAN: How should I know?

MOTHER (*to* FATHER): Don't just stand there, without saying anything. Don't you think it'll set a bad example if we shut our eyes to this sort of thing?

FATHER: That's right, a very bad example . . . Still, I don't understand it . . . I thought we'd thrashed the whole thing out, only to find you're still keeping secrets from us. Why do you do it? It's not like you.

MOTHER: I beg you, don't make your mother any unhappier than she already is.

ELDER SON (*blandly*): That's what you say, Mother, but were you really so confident you could fleece this guy out of his money entirely by persuasive tactics?

MOTHER: Fleece him out of his money? I was going to take custody of it!

ELDER SON (*to* MAN): Are you willing to let my mother take custody of your property?

MAN: Take custody of my property? She could ask till she was blue in the face and I'd still refuse!

FATHER: There's no getting around it. Money troubles are the worst cause of disharmony among friends.

MAN (*his anger returning*): Can it! You've got no reason to call me one of your friends . . . And as for taking custody of my property . . . I'm getting nauseous. You give me cold chills.

ELDER SON (*to the others*): Now you have a pretty good idea of the situation. You couldn't call him exceptionally cooperative. And he's just as attached to his money as the next man. He wants to have his cake and eat it. You'll find he's a hard customer to deal with. Supposing I hadn't used my special talents . . . I can't help being rather skeptical about whether that money would've ended up, as we hoped, in Mother's safe.

FATHER: That doesn't mean you have the right to grab it for yourself.

ELDEST DAUGHTER: That's right. Stealing a march on the rest of us is unfair.

MOTHER: I wonder if a person who always tries to get the lion's share for himself hasn't got something twisted inside him? It makes me unhappy.

YOUNGER SON (*whispering into his brother's ear*): I'll go to your defense, if you like, for a service charge of twenty percent.

ELDER SON: Don't underestimate me.

MIDDLE DAUGHTER (*hesitantly*): What do you intend to do about dinner?

GRANDMOTHER: I'm in charge of dividing up the jam.

MAN (*suddenly bursting into a rage*): Are you still yattering on about such things? To talk about dinner, in the midst of this crazy farce! Listen to me. I'm the original victim. Nobody else has a claim on my money, and I want it back. What possible difference does it make whether he takes sole possession of the money or two of you take it? It's illegal either way. The fact is, it's mine, and I'm the only one qualified to investigate what's happened to it. (*Suddenly he has an idea.*) That's right! The situation has assumed a completely new aspect. My friend, you've pulled a real blunder. You have enabled me to file a formal complaint. A flagrant act of pickpocketing has occurred. This time there's no doubt about it. Even the members of your family will testify. Well, are you going to give back my money? Or will I have to bother the police again?

FATHER: There's something in what he says . . . As things stand, your old tricks have boiled down to nothing more than theft, plain and simple.

MOTHER (*sighs*): You've really done a dreadful thing.

FATHER: You've ruined everything. In order to carry out our mission of spreading love for our neighbors, we ourselves must be models of neighborly love.

MIDDLE DAUGHTER steps forward, seemingly unable to bear what is happening.

MIDDLE DAUGHTER (*to* ELDER SON): Why don't you say something? You must've had some reason, surely? Say something. Don't just grin that way.

YOUNGER SON: There are some things about which all you can do is grin. Wouldn't you agree, Brother?

MAN: It looks as if the wolves have finally shed their sheep's clothing. The salesmen for Neighborly Love, Incorporated!

ELDEST DAUGHTER (*fiercely*): I'm sick of it. After all we've gone through, I don't want the bother of moving again. (*To* ELDER BROTHER.) I suppose you think you're the only one with the privilege of doing exactly what you please?

YOUNGEST DAUGHTER (*in a low voice*): There's a cold wind blowing outside.

GRANDMOTHER: I don't understand it. What devil got into him that he should have done such a thing?

ELDER SON (*his expression becomes severe*):   Your own shortcomings don't seem to bother you.

FATHER (*soothing him*):   Believe me, I understand what you've been going through . . . I understand perfectly . . . I'm sure you need more pocket money . . . You'd like to lead a more cheerful life . . . But you must recognize the eternal law that happiness which is for yourself alone is certainly not true happiness . . .

ELDER SON: I am gradually losing my amiability.

MOTHER: The brazen nerve of the thief!

ELDER SON: But, Mother, haven't I been following the ideal of neighborly love? Anything I have is yours, and anything you have is mine . . . Aren't you overdoing it a bit when you treat me like a pickpocket or a thief?

FATHER: I understand . . . I understand perfectly.

ELDEST DAUGHTER: It doesn't help much, no matter how well you understand him. We're the ones who suffer in the end.

ELDER SON: You wouldn't be jaundiced because you can't do as much yourself?

ELDEST DAUGHTER *flares up;* FATHER *quiets her with a gesture.*

FATHER: Depending on the end, a certain leeway is permitted in the means. But the fundamental thing, of course, is the end. Neighborly love is a splendid ideal, but if it is only an ideal, it's a little too abstract, isn't it? Why don't we think it through together? What is the common end we all share?

ELDER SON: I wonder if any of you know how many times altogether I have been insulted in the course of this argument?

FATHER: "Insulted" is an exaggeration. It distresses me to have you take it that way. My only hope was that I might rouse you somehow from your errors.

ELDER SON: Would you like to know? Don't be too surprised—fifty-three times!

YOUNGER SON: Fifty-three times? That's a little too precise!

ELDER SON: I assure you, there's been no padding. I made a careful count.

ELDEST DAUGHTER: Isn't that silly? He has nothing better to do with his time, it would seem.

ELDER SON: There! That makes fifty-four times.

MOTHER: When someone of your age tramples the peace of the family underfoot, it's not surprising that he should be insulted a hundred times, or even a thousand times.

ELDER SON: Fifty-five times.

YOUNGER SON *apparently has a glimmering of what his brother has in mind.*

YOUNGER SON: Ah-hah. I'm beginning to see . . .

ELDER SON: Now it's my turn to ask you a question. What are these ends you keep talking about that seem to justify everything?

MOTHER: The family safe is one of them. (*She holds up an unusually large purse that she takes from her suitcase.*)

ELDER SON: What's this? (*He pretends to peep inside.*) Mother . . . there's quite a bulge in the pocket of that purse.

MOTHER (*surprised, looking inside the purse*):   Dear me, why it's . . . (*Bewildered, she takes out a handful of bills and change.*) Oh . . . how shocking! (*She gives a forced laugh.*)

The next instant the faces of everybody present except MAN *change completely in expression. Now they are all smiling.*

YOUNGER SON: I was completely taken in, I must say.

ELDEST DAUGHTER: You certainly more than live up to your reputation.

FATHER: I have to apologize . . .

MIDDLE DAUGHTER: Oh, I'm so glad. (*She looks around the family.*) We're all good people, aren't we?

YOUNGEST DAUGHTER: I wonder if I should start practicing too. (*She flexes her fingers.*)

MOTHER: Really, it's enough to take a person aback. He was always a mischievous child, but I never expected . . . (*She removes her glasses and starts to count the money with an air of efficiency.*)

MAN: Hey! Stop it! That's my money! You can deduct the hundred yen for the fine.

ELDER SON *blocks* MAN, *who starts to make a rush for the money.*

ELDER SON: You're wasting your time. I don't suppose you noted down the numbers of the bills or marked them?

At the same time FATHER, YOUNGER SON, ELDEST DAUGHTER, YOUNGEST DAUGHTER, *and even* GRANDMOTHER *form a kind of defensive setup around* MOTHER. *It might be effective for* YOUNGEST DAUGHTER *to brandish a cleaver.*

YOUNGER SON: You see how easy it is for trouble to arise over money.

YOUNGEST DAUGHTER: A clever burglar absolutely refuses to touch anything except cash.

MAN (*to* ELDER SON):   Your own words prove that you yourself admit that you've picked my pocket.

ELDER SON (*playing the innocent*):   I picked your pocket? (*He turns to family.*) Did I say anything like that?

MAN: You weren't the only one. The whole lot of you, without exception, all admitted it.

ELDEST DAUGHTER: I don't know anything about it.

GRANDMOTHER: Do you think any grandchild of mine would ever do such a wicked thing? I wouldn't let him, even if he tried to.

MAN: You're all in cahoots to cover up for him, aren't you? And just a minute ago you were denouncing him so!

MOTHER (*paying no attention to the arguments around her; to* MAN): Tell me, how much did you have?

MAN: I have no idea.

ELDEST DAUGHTER: Pretty careless of him not to know how much he has in his own wallet.

MIDDLE DAUGHTER: A little carelessness makes a man more attractive.

ELDEST DAUGHTER (*darting a sidelong glance at her*): Doing your best to make a hit with him, aren't you?

FATHER (*looking onto Mother's hands*): Well, how much is there, anyway?

MOTHER (*complaining*): Not much, 5,600 yen. That's all.

FATHER (*frowns*): 5,600 yen . . .

ELDER SON: I suppose it's just before his payday.

MOTHER (*sarcastically*): I see. I'm sure that explanation suits your convenience.

ELDER SON: There's something disturbing about your tone.

MAN (*not missing the chance*): You see! You're admitting to one another that you swiped the money from me.

FATHER: Young man, if you're going to jump to such conclusions, you'll make it hard for all of us. People often conduct discussions on a purely hypothetical basis.

MAN: Stop quibbling!

FATHER: Well then, shall I concede a point and admit that the money was yours? But you don't even seem to know the amount of this valuable commodity. Don't you realize that the world is swarming with sinister people who have their eye on other people's wallets? The thought of it makes me shudder.

MAN: Wouldn't you yourselves qualify without any trouble for membership in that gang of sinister people?

FATHER: Don't be absurd! We've acted entirely out of good will. We felt it our duty to protect your money by taking custody of it.

MAN (*excitedly*): What right have you anyway . . . without even asking me . . .

FATHER (*emphatically*): It's a duty, a *duty*. I have no intention of insisting on any rights.

MIDDLE DAUGHTER (*heatedly*): Yes. It's true even of companies—they're all making mergers and amalgamations, aren't they? And the same thing applies to human beings too, I'm sure. Two is better than one,

three is better than two. The more people put their strength together, the more . . .

GRANDMOTHER: Little drops of water, little grains of sand, make the
mighty ocean . . .

MOTHER (*still looking suspiciously at* ELDER SON): But there's only 5,600
yen altogether. That won't last for two days, feeding nine people.

ELDER SON (*angrily*): You talk just as if it were my fault.

MOTHER: I didn't mean it that way.

ELDER SON: After I tried to be smart, and save you some trouble . . .
(*In a self-mocking tone.*) This is what they mean when they talk of a
man who's fallen so low in the world his artistic accomplishments
learned in happier days are his only support.

FATHER (*trying to save the situation*): What do you mean? Haven't we
all been praising your skill, without uttering so much as a word of
complaint?

ELDER SON (*going up to* MOTHER): If that's the case, I wish you'd stop giving me that look.

MOTHER (*turning aside and wiping her glasses*): It's a lot harder than you
suppose, trying to make ends meet for a family of nine . . .

ELDER SON (*sits beside* MOTHER): I *do* understand, Ma. But I wanted
you, if nobody else, to believe in me. In the course of less than ten
minutes I was insulted fifty-five times . . . and that by the people I
trusted most in the whole world, my own family . . . It was
painful, I tell you.

MOTHER (*hesitantly*): Talking that way won't do any good . . .

ELDER SON (*ignoring her; to* MAN): Payday in your company must
come the day after tomorrow or the next day, doesn't it?

MAN *is taken by surprise. He is unable either to affirm or deny this.*

ELDER SON (*standing abruptly; speaking as he goes away from* MOTHER): So
you see, Ma, there's no need for you to worry over such a paltry
sum of money, is there? If people can't live a little more expan-
sively . . .

MOTHER (*with an expression that suggests she hasn't grasped the situation
very well*): I know, but no matter how much money you have, it always seems to sprout wings and fly away. (*Suddenly noticing
something.*) Ohh . . . it's gone!

FATHER: What's gone?

MOTHER (*to* ELDER SON): You've done it again, haven't you? (*As she
stands a 100 yen coin drops from her lap.*)

ELDER SON, *flashing the bills ostentatiously, folds them and puts them in his
pocket.*

ELDER SON: Received with thanks the sum of 5,500 yen, representing fines collected from all of you for those fifty-five insults. Look, Ma, the missing hundred yen coin dropped on the floor. That's his share of the fine (*points at* MAN). It's wonderful how exactly the accounts have balanced.

They all stand motionless, too dumfounded to say a word. A fairly long pause.

MOTHER (*her voice is like a moan*):   Dreadful, dreadful . . .

ELDER SON (*perfectly self-possessed*):   Words, like chickens, come home to roost. (*Turns back to* MAN.) I hope it's been a good lesson for you too. Now you know how severe the penalty is for betraying another person's trust . . . But of course, I owe this extra income all to you. It's too late today, but I'll treat you to a drink, tomorrow if you like. There's nothing to feel squeamish about. I got the money completely legally . . . You see, nobody can say a word against it . . . Yes, it really serves as an object lesson.

MAN (*suddenly shouting*):   Get out of here! I'll give you the money, only get out of here, now! If it's not money you want, I'll give you anything else, only go!

YOUNGEST DAUGHTER (*playfully*):   Do you really mean it?

GRANDMOTHER (*hurrying to the kitchen*):   The jam is for me. You promised from the start.

MAN: Go ahead. Take anything you like. Only go.

They begin to take their pick of the things in the room excitedly. But nobody as yet does anything positive.

YOUNGER SON: He's certainly become a lot more generous, hasn't he?

ELDEST DAUGHTER: Do you mind if I look in the other room?

MAN: Go right ahead. Don't mind me. If you'd like the rats in the ceiling, you can have them too. But all this is on one condition—you leave at once. I'll give you five—no, ten minutes, that's the limit. I won't make allowances for even one minute beyond the deadline.

FATHER (*timidly*):   I appreciate your kind intentions, but I wonder if two different questions aren't involved?

MAN: Two different questions?

FATHER: Your offer to turn over all your possessions to us, without holding anything back, is more than we dared hope for. That is precisely the way that true communal living is to be brought about . . . But when you tell us that in return we must leave you, aren't you guilty of something like a logical contradiction?

MIDDLE DAUGHTER: That's right. Living together is what gives meaning to the act of sharing.

YOUNGER SON: What's yours is mine, what's mine is yours.

ELDEST DAUGHTER: You smell of liquor!

YOUNGER SON: That's why I've been pleading with you to let me have a quick pick-me-up.

MAN (*turning on* FATHER):   You can't have forgotten it was you yourself who claimed you respect the wishes of the individual.

FATHER: Of course I respect them. But you're not the only individual, are you?

MOTHER (*to nobody in particular*):   If you ask me, there's nothing here anybody'd want. The place lacks the bare necessities. It'd take a bit of doing even to make it habitable.

MAN: This is *my* apartment!

ELDER SON (*coldly*):   This is the apartment *we've* chosen.

YOUNGER SON (*trying on Man's shoes, which have been left at the entrance*):   Well, what do you know? These shoes fit me perfectly!

MAN *suddenly kneels on the floor. His voice, completely altered, sounds pathetic.*

MAN: Please, I beg you. Please don't torture me any more . . . Of course I understand it's all a joke—it is one, isn't it—but I'm exhausted . . . I just don't feel like joking . . . Maybe something I've said has offended you, but please, I beg you, leave me here alone.

MAN, *continuing to kneel, bows his head, like a victim awaiting his sentence.*

The members of the family, struck speechless, exchange glances. But their expressions are not merely of surprise—heartfelt sympathy and pity seem to have shaken them.

FATHER: Stand up please, young man. (*He places his hand on Man's elbow and helps him to his feet, then dusts his knees.*) It's embarrassing for us if you're going to act that way. Our only wish is to promote your happiness in whatever way we can, to serve you somehow . . . That's what first led us to come here.

ELDER SON: Or, it occurs to me, you may have subjectively interpreted our actions as being in some way opposed to your wishes—clearly, a misunderstanding . . . In other words, there may exist a difference of opinion concerning means.

MIDDLE DAUGHTER (*enthusiastically*):   But hasn't it become warm in here, just because we're all together this way? It feels just like spring, even without having our soup.

ELDEST DAUGHTER: Spring? It feels more like summer. Oh, it's hot! (*She removes her jacket and exposes her bare throat and arms.*)

MAN (*weakly*):   But I like being alone . . .

MIDDLE DAUGHTER: Why must you say such cruel things?

YOUNGER SON (*sounds at the end of his patience*): It can't be helped. Everybody's sick until his sickness gets better.

So saying, YOUNGER SON *begins to strum his guitar. The following dialogue is declaimed to the rhythm of the guitar.*

MIDDLE DAUGHTER:
The streets are full of people,
So full of people, they're ready to burst.

YOUNGER SON:
But everywhere you go,
There're nothing but strangers.

MIDDLE DAUGHTER:
I'm still not discouraged,
I go on searching—
My friends, where are you now,
My loved ones, where are you now?

ELDER SON:
They've gone to the pinball parlor.

FATHER:
They've gone to a bar.

MOTHER:
To the beauty parlor or the department store.

GRANDMOTHER:
They're eating eels and rice.

YOUNGEST DAUGHTER:
They're riding escalators,
They're going to an amusement park.

ELDEST DAUGHTER (*meditatively; if necessary, can be sung to music*): And I have dreams. I dream of a streetcar on tracks that stretch far, far away. A streetcar packed with people goes running away over the tracks. Under the weight of all those strangers packed inside, it shoots off sparks. And in the sparks thrown off by all those innumerable strangers, I am burnt to a crisp, like a little fish forgotten in the oven.

YOUNGER SON (*in a soft voice*): Like a dried sardine, with only little bones.

MIDDLE DAUGHTER:
>I'm still not discouraged,
>I go on searching.
>My shining sun, where have you gone?
>Come back and melt away my loneliness!

FATHER (*whispering confidentially to* MAN):   That's why we've come all the way here. We heard your voice crying for help and we searched till we found you through the long dark tunnel they call other people. We wanted to bring you, if not the sun, at least the light from a glowing lump of coal.

MAN (*driven into a corner*):   I never cried for help. I . . . . It refreshes me to be alone.

ELDER SON: That's conceit! Why, in prison the thing that hits you hardest is solitary confinement. (*An expression of recollection crosses his face.*)

ELDEST DAUGHTER: I'm *completely* hopeless when I'm alone. Even when I'm left to look after the house, as soon as I'm by myself I feel as if I'll go out of my mind.

GRANDMOTHER: It's all written down in Mother Goose. Let me see, how did it go again? (*To* MOTHER.) You remember, don't you?

MAN: I don't interfere with other people and I don't want to be interfered with myself.

YOUNGER SON *begins to play with feeling "The Broken Necklace."* MIDDLE DAUGHTER *sings to the tune. When they reach the second verse the telephone rings suddenly. For a moment they are all startled into attitudes of* tableaux vivants.

ELDEST DAUGHTER: Shall I answer?

MAN (*confused*):   It's all right. I'll go. (*He runs to the telephone and grabs it, but he does not lift the receiver at once.*) Will you do me a favor? At least while I'm talking on the phone, will you please keep quiet?

YOUNGER SON: At least while you're talking on the phone? Have we been making so much noise?

FATHER: Shhh. (*He puts his hand to his lips and silences* YOUNGER SON.) Go right ahead. Don't worry about us. (*He looks to the side. At the same time the other members of the family strike poses of ostentatious indifference.*)

After another brief hesitation, MAN *resolutely lifts the receiver. But he is still worried about the family, and his voice is extremely tentative.*

MAN: Hello, yes, it's me. (*Pause.*) No, nothing special. No, I mean it, it's nothing . . . All right, then, good night . . . The day after tomorrow? It's not necessary, I tell you. There's nothing I need your help on at this stage . . . Well, good night. You're going to bed, aren't you? No, it's not that. We can talk when I see you again tomorrow.

Suddenly YOUNGEST DAUGHTER *emits a protracted strange noise in the process of stifling a great sneeze.* MAN, *alarmed, covers the mouthpiece and glares at* YOUNGEST DAUGHTER.

FATHER: Shh!

MOTHER: Do be quiet!

YOUNGER SON: Stupid, isn't she? (*He picks up his guitar without thinking, and the guitar, bumping against something, resounds.*)

ELDER SON: You're the one that should be more careful.

YOUNGER SON: You're making more noise scolding me . . .

MAN: I beg you, stop it please!

GRANDMOTHER: I don't understand. Why do you have to act so secret? We're not hiding from the police, after all.

ELDER SON: It's from his girl.

ELDEST DAUGHTER (*reacting sharply*): His girl?

ELDER SON: I've surveyed the whole situation.

ELDEST DAUGHTER: But isn't that strange? It's a complete contradiction. After all his insisting that he prefers to be alone . . .

MAN (*desperately*): I beg you, keep quiet, please! (*Into the telephone.*) I'm terribly sorry. There was a funny noise in the kitchen . . . What? Of course I'm alone . . . A sneeze? A woman's sneeze? Don't be silly.

ELDER SON: I've never heard anything so disgraceful. Stumbling all over the place.

FATHER (*simultaneously*): Shhh!

MAN (*instantly covering the mouthpiece*): I thought I told you to please shut up.

ELDEST DAUGHTER: It may be your girlfriend, or I don't care who, but why must you keep our being here a secret? It's insulting.

MAN (*into the telephone*): Just a second, please. There's that funny noise again in the kitchen. (*He covers the mouthpiece.*) Think a minute and you'll see why. How can I possibly explain such a thing so that an outsider could understand? It's crazy . . . It'll only make things more complicated if I make a mess of explaining.

YOUNGER SON: Would you like us to explain for you?

FATHER: A good suggestion. We'll have to make it clear, sooner or later, whether we're to ask her to join us or to break with him.

ELDER SON: Making things clear is my specialty.

ELDEST DAUGHTER: It's easier for a woman to talk to another woman.

MAN (*protecting the telephone from* ELDER SON *and* ELDEST DAUGHTER, *both of whom come forward at the same time*): I give up. I surrender. But won't you please let me deal with her? In return, yes, I agree to let you stay here for tonight only. That's fair enough, isn't it? You can use any and all of my apartment, as you please . . . I promise not to interfere in any way with your meals . . . All I ask is that you keep quiet while I'm making this call.

FATHER (*looking around at the others*): He hasn't made any conditions that present special difficulties, has he?

ELDER SON *and* ELDEST DAUGHTER (*simultaneously moving back*): I suppose not.

MAN (*hastily returning to the telephone*): It wasn't anything. It must have been the wind . . . Hello . . . Hello . . . (*He realizes that the other party has hung up on him and dazedly puts down the telephone.*)

ELDEST DAUGHTER: Did she hang up on you?

MIDDLE DAUGHTER: That wasn't nice of her, was it?

MAN, *unable to say a word, crouches beside the telephone, his head in his hands.*

YOUNGEST DAUGHTER: He must really be in love with her.

MOTHER: Don't butt into grownups' affairs.

FATHER (*to* MAN): You know her phone number, don't you?

ELDER SON: I know it.

FATHER: Should we call and apologize?

MAN (*moaning*): I beg you, please leave things as they are.

MIDDLE DAUGHTER: Why don't you get to bed?

MOTHER: That's right. It must be about time.

MAN: I don't want you worrying about me. You don't suppose, in the first place, I could get to sleep with all the noise going on here.

FATHER: Of course we intend to retire to the other room. Come on, everybody, get ready!

Hardly has he spoken than the members of the family throw themselves into furious activity. ELDER SON *and* YOUNGER SON *take a hammock from their suitcase and suspend it.* MOTHER *and* YOUNGEST DAUGHTER *bring blankets in from the next room.* GRANDMOTHER *inflates an air pillow.* ELDEST DAUGHTER *and* MIDDLE DAUGHTER *swiftly remove Man's outer clothes. Then the whole family lifts* MAN *willy-nilly onto the hammock.* MAN *shows some resistance, but in the end proves no match for their organized activity. By the time* MAN *sits up in the hammock the family has already withdrawn to the next room. They peep in and throw* MAN *their radiant smiles.*

FAMILY (*whispering in unison*): Good night!

MIDDLE DAUGHTER *sticks out her hand and switches off the light in Man's room. The stage becomes dark with only a spotlight on* MAN. YOUNGER SON *enters on tiptoe and crosses the room on his way to the kitchen.*

YOUNGER SON (*in a low voice*): Beer!

Slow curtain.

. . . SCENE SEVEN (*INTERMISSION*)

The music of "The Broken Necklace" is played in the lobby during the intermission. Presently, the actress who has appeared as SUPERINTENDENT, *still dressed in the costume for the part, makes her way among the spectators, both in the lobby and in the auditorium, distributing the following leaflet.*

AN APPEAL . . .

Some people, it would seem, have been critical of my attitude toward the tenant in Apartment 12. Unpleasant rumors are being spread that I was bought over by the visitors or (what's worse) that I reached some sort of understanding with one or the other of the two brothers and gave him a passkey to the apartment.

I realize, having had the misfortune to lose my husband only a few years ago, there is nothing I can do about it if people, meaning to be sympathetic, say, "She must've needed money," or "She must've been lonely." But I will take an oath that I am speaking the absolute truth when I say that the first time I ever laid eyes on those people was when I saw them in Apartment 12. But in my business you get to be a pretty good judge of character, and I could see at once that there was nothing particularly suspicious about those people. The tenants in this building are all my valued guests, and the guests of my guests, you might say, are also my guests. That's why, as I'm sure you'll understand, I couldn't very well make uncalled-for remarks simply because there's been some sort of misunderstanding.

I wish also to take advantage of this occasion to confide a secret, in all candor. To the tell the truth, situations of this kind are not in the least unusual. When you're in my business you see this kind of thing happening all the time. I wonder if all the commotion hasn't simply proved the gentleman doesn't know much about people? I beg you, ladies and gentlemen, not to be deceived by any false rumors or to let your confidence be shaken in our apartment house.

THE SUPERINTENDENT

. . . SCENE EIGHT

The curtain rises to disclose the benches in a public park somewhere. Sounds of cars and people passing make it clear that the park is in the city. The sounds, however, are filtered and the buildings surrounding the park are concealed by trees (or something suggesting trees); the spot is somehow isolated from the outside world. The woman sitting on a bench who seems to be waiting for someone is the person with whom MAN *was talking on the telephone, his*

FIANCÉE. *She glances at her wristwatch, then looks left and right. Her expression suggests she is immersed in thought.*

YOUNGEST DAUGHTER *enters from stage right, skipping along in a way that suggests she is kicking a stone. She strolls past* FIANCÉE. *When she reaches far stage left she gestures as if looking off to the other side of the trees. She strikes a peculiar pose and exits, still maintaining the pose.*

As she leaves, ELDER SON *enters from stage left. Evidently Youngest Daughter's pose was a signal to him.* ELDER SON *struts up to* FIANCÉE.

ELDER SON (*with a slight bow of the head*): Excuse me. (*He starts to seat himself beside* FIANCÉE, *indifferent to her reactions.*)

FIANCÉE: I'm sorry, but I'm waiting for somebody.

ELDER SON: Oh, I see. (*He decides not to sit, but shows no sign of going away. He continues to stare boldly at the woman.*) I was impressed even by your picture, but you're far more charming in the flesh. Oh, you've changed the way you do your hair, haven't you? A natural effect looks better on you than fancy styling. That only goes to show how good the foundations are.

FIANCÉE: I don't think we've met . . . (*Her expression reveals mingled caution and curiosity.*)

ELDER SON: But I know all about you . . . Of course, you make such an impression that nobody who ever saw you once could forget you the second time. It's only natural, I suppose.

FIANCÉE: I wonder where I've had the pleasure . . . ?

ELDER SON: Last night, in the drawer of your fiancé's desk.

FIANCÉE (*at last catching on*): Then it was you last night . . .

ELDER SON (*nods*): Yes, it was. Against my own inclinations I interrupted you in the midst of your telephone call.

FIANCÉE (*sharply*): Have you come as his stand-in?

ELDER SON: Heaven forbid! I wouldn't do such a thing even if he asked me. To tell the truth, he and I have had a slight difference of opinion concerning what happened last night.

FIANCÉE: And you've come to tell on him?

ELDER SON: How severe you are! I wonder what he could've told you about us? I gather from your tone he hasn't been too friendly. I suppose he's trying to clean up the mess left behind by shifting the blame onto us for that telephone call.

FIANCÉE: What happened anyway?

ELDER SON: How can I answer unless I know the nature of his explanation?

FIANCÉE (*finally induced to discuss the matter on his terms*): I couldn't make the least sense out of him. He was so vague that I . . .

ELDER SON (*with a suppressed laugh that does not seem malicious*): I can well imagine . . . I wonder if the problem is that he's timid, or clumsy at expressing himself, or can never get to the point, or that he's too earnest or too good-natured or too inflexible, or that he's stubborn or an introvert or self-centered . . .

FIANCÉE (*mustering her courage*):   Were there also women present?

ELDER SON: Yes, four—no, five.

FIANCÉE: Five!

ELDER SON: But there were men there, too—three of us, besides him.

FIANCÉE: What were you all doing, so many of you?

ELDER SON: It's a little hard to explain.

FIANCÉE (*rather irritated*):   But generally speaking, when people have gathered together for a purpose there's some sort of name for their activity. Would you describe it as a meeting, or a card game, or a drinking party? Is there anything that can't be given a name?

ELDER SON: That's the crux of the problem. (*He takes out a comb and smooths his hair.*) I'd really be most interested to hear how *he* would answer that question. (*He puts away the comb.*) But I've been making a great nuisance of myself, when you've more important things on your mind. (*He bows and starts to leave.*)

FIANCÉE (*standing before she realizes*):   Wait a moment! What is it you came to tell, anyway? You and he make a good pair—one's just as vague as the other. I don't suppose you could have come for the express purpose of mystifying me.

ELDER SON (*sanctimoniously, his eyes lowered*):   Of course not. But when I meet you face to face this way I suddenly lose my courage.

FIANCÉE: Go ahead. You're not bothering me.

ELDER SON (*lighting a cigarette; slowly*):   To be perfectly honest, I don't really understand his feelings . . . Correct me if I'm wrong, but I gather he's engaged to you and has been planning to hold the wedding in the near future.

FIANCÉE: Yes, he only recently managed at last to rent that apartment. It's more than he could afford, but we needed it to get married.

ELDER SON: In other words, he and you are already as good as married. Right? Why, then, should he have had to keep things a secret from you, of all people, in such a furtive way? If I may cite a rather vulgar example, you often see in the advice to the lovelorn column how a man is extremely reluctant to introduce the girl he's interested in to his parents or his family . . . In such cases is it not fair to assume in general that the man's sincerity is to be doubted?

FIANCÉE: You mean you and your family are in that relationship with him?

ELDER SON: Of course, I don't know how he would answer you.

FIANCÉE (*reduced to supplication*):   For heaven's sake, please tell me! Who are you all and what is your connection with him?

ELDER SON (*avoiding the issue*):   Oh, yes. I've just remembered. It was something he let slip in the course of the conversation last night, but I wonder if it doesn't give us a clue to his intentions. He seems to hold extremely prejudiced views against any form of communal living, and even with respect to family life he seems to be feeling something close to dread.

FIANCÉE: I can't believe that.

ELDER SON: He went so far as to say that it actually refreshed him to be all alone in a crowd of total strangers.

FIANCÉE: But he's even made arrangements with the movers to have my furniture taken to his place at the end of the month.

ELDER SON: I'd like to believe that he got carried away by his own words. Or maybe he was just bluffing . . . After all, with such a pretty girl as you . . .

FIANCÉE: You still haven't answered my question.

ELDER SON: Oh—you mean our relationship with him? I wonder if it wouldn't be better, though, for you to get him to verify it with his own mouth. I wouldn't want my words to have the effect of implanting any preconceptions . . . It's not that I'm trying to pretend to be more of a gentleman than I am, but I just wouldn't want to make a sneak attack, or anything like that . . . I realize that it must be hard for you to understand, but basically speaking, we're closer to him than blood relations.

FIANCÉE: You must have known him a long time, then?

ELDER SON (calmly): We don't set too much store by the past. The same holds true of a marriage, doesn't it? The real problems are always in the future.

FIANCÉE (again withdrawing into her shell): Then was it something like a political meeting?

ELDER SON (looking at his watch): I'm sure he has no intention of trying to strengthen his position by lying to you . . . He may in fact be planning to use this opportunity to reveal to you his true feelings. Anyway, I advise you to sound him out. Maybe we'll meet again, depending on how your interview turns out.

FIANCÉE (looking stage left): Oh, there he is now.

ELDER SON (showing no special embarrassment): I hope and pray that all goes well. But I suppose I'm also half-hoping that things don't go well. In that case I'll get to see you again. (Suddenly, as if he had remembered something urgent.) Excuse me, but would you mind sitting there again? Just the way you were before . . . Hurry!

FIANCÉE, overcome by his urgency, sits as requested.

ELDER SON (with a conspiratorial smile): That's right. Now I can see the dimples in your knees . . . Aren't they sweet? I could eat them up, those dimples.

FIANCÉE, flustered, brings together the hems of her coat. At the same moment MAN hurriedly enters from stage left. He catches sight of ELDER SON, and stops in his tracks with an expression of amazement.

. . . SCENE NINE

FIANCÉE, *noticing* MAN *approach, stands and turns toward him as he speaks. In other words, her actions should be simultaneous with the beginning of Man's dialogue.*

MAN (*to* ELDER SON, *sharply*): What are *you* doing here?

ELDER SON *turns to* MAN *as if having become aware of his presence only then. Far from showing any embarrassment, he smiles broadly, as if greeting an old friend.*

ELDER SON: Late, aren't you? This will never do!

MAN *looks from* FIANCÉE *to* ELDER SON *and back, then steps forward aggressively.*

MAN: What's the meaning of this, anyway?

FIANCÉE (*unable to hide her guilty conscience*): It was a complete coincidence.

ELDER SON: But as far as I'm concerned, an accidental meeting that only a marvelous necessity could have brought about.

MAN (*angrily*): I don't know what mischief you've been up to, but you're to get the hell out of here, right now.

ELDER SON (*still smiling*): Don't be uncouth. Well, I'll be saying good-by. (*He winks secretly at* FIANCÉE.) Go to it now, the both of you. (*He makes a clownish gesture with his hand, then saunters off to stage left.*)

The couple stands for a time in silence, still looking off in the direction ELDER SON *has gone. They slowly turn and exchange glances, only to avert their eyes.* FIANCÉE *sits down on the bench, and* MAN *then also sits. Each occupies an end of the bench.*)

MAN (*gloomily*): What was he filling your ear with?

FIANCÉE (*looking at* MAN *reproachfully*): Before we go into that, it seems to me you have a lot of explaining to do.

MAN: Explaining? There's nothing worth explaining. It's just as I told you on the phone this morning. I'm the victim. I'm sorry I worried you with that call last night. But even that was their fault, if you get right down to it.

FIANCÉE: So it would seem. It's pretty hard to keep someone from guessing, even over the phone, when you have eight people in the room with you. But tell me, why was it necessary for you to act so secretly, as if you were playing hide-and-seek with me?

MAN: I thought I'd told you. I couldn't think of any way of explaining in an intelligible manner who those people were or what they were doing.

FIANCÉE: And you're going to explain now, is that it?

MAN: Unfortunately, I still don't know what happened, even now.

FIANCÉE (*a little defiantly*): But I thought you asked me here in order to explain.

MAN (*bearing up under the confusion*): Yes, that's so . . . But my real purpose was not so much to explain as to get you to understand how difficult it is to make an explanation. Maybe I won't succeed in making you understand . . . How could you understand an outfit like that? I suppose that if it happened that I had been on the receiving end of this story, I wouldn't have been able to believe it either . . . I don't know where to start. The only way to describe what happened is to say it was plain crazy.

FIANCÉE (*losing her temper*): That certainly doesn't seem to be an explanation of anything.

MAN: But have you ever heard anything like it—a bunch of complete strangers suddenly march in on me without warning, and install themselves in my apartment, exactly as if it were their natural right?

FIANCÉE (*coldly*): It *is* a little unusual.

MAN: It certainly is. As a matter of fact, even the policemen who came after I called refused to take it seriously. (*His voice becomes more emphatic.*) But I assure you, it happened. This impossible thing has befallen me.

FIANCÉE: That man who was just here also thought it was strange. He couldn't figure out what your motive was in keeping their presence such a secret.

MAN: A secret? It's simply that I couldn't think how to explain, don't you see? So he encouraged you to act suspicious. But you're carrying your foolishness too far. Tell me, what possible advantage could there be in it for me to cover up for that bunch of parasites?

FIANCÉE: For a parasite, that man just now certainly acted like a gentleman. Unlike you, he didn't say one harsh thing. Why, he didn't even try to justify himself.

MAN: Yes, that's their technique.

FIANCÉE: I understand, by the way, that five of them are women.

MAN: Five of them? (*He bursts into derisive laughter. His voice takes on a triumphant note.*) Five women? That's a good one. Gradually I'm beginning to catch on to their tactics.

FIANCÉE: Was he lying, then?

MAN: No, it wasn't a lie. The five women include a seventy-year-old grandmother, a housewife of fifty, and a junior-high-school student.

FIANCÉE (*beginning to lose her confidence*): They certainly make an odd group of people.

MAN: No, there's nothing odd about them. Didn't tell you? They're all one family—five children, the parents, and the grandmother, a family of eight. Five women . . . that's good. You couldn't call it a lie, and it was effective as a trick. You must've been imagining I was involved with some sort of secret society.

FIANCÉE: You were the one who first gave me that impression.

MAN (*with an expression of relief*):   When you've seen what the facts really are, they don't amount to much, do they?

FIANCÉE: You can't blame me. You exaggerated so much.

MAN (*resuming his subdued tone*):   It would've been easier to explain if they had actually been a secret society or a gang. But when they look so absurdly and indisputably like a family, it makes it impossible to complain to anybody.

FIANCÉE (*dubious again*):   But are you sure these people have no relationship to you at all?

MAN: Absolutely none.

FIANCÉE: I can't understand it. Are you sure there wasn't some reason behind it, however slight? It's hard to imagine otherwise that they'd move in on you like that.

MAN: They say that I'm lonely and that they intend to envelop and warm me in their neighborly love.

FIANCÉE: They've ignored me completely, then?

MAN: No, I'm sure that, as long as you were willing, they'd be delighted to have you join them.

FIANCÉE (*with intensity*):   This is no laughing matter.

MAN (*holding his head between his hands*):   That's why I told you they were monstrous parasites.

FIANCÉE: Why don't you tell them to leave?

MAN: I have, of course.

FIANCÉE: Firmly? And clearly?

MAN: In a voice so loud it hurt my throat. (*Weakly.*) But it still didn't do any good. It made no impression on them. They have the nerve to say that occupying our apartment is not merely their privilege but their duty.

FIANCÉE (*after a pause, uncertainly*):   Is that really all? Is that all there is to it?

MAN: As far as I know.

FIANCÉE: You've explained three of the five women, but what about the other two?

MAN: Stop it! If you'd only seen how I struggled with them.

FIANCÉE: It's funny . . . my engagement ring doesn't seem to fit my finger any more . . . I wonder if I should take it off.

MAN (*bewildered*):   What do you mean?

FIANCÉE: I want you to be frank with me. If you've been putting on a show in order to get rid of me, you needn't go to all the trouble.

MAN: There you go again, tormenting me with your groundless accusations.

FIANCÉE: But what else can I do, as long as you're unable to take back our apartment from those people?

MAN: Insult added to injury! If I'm to be deserted even by you, I'll lose the will to fight altogether.

FIANCÉE (*suddenly sharp*): Then I can really trust what you say?

MAN: Of course! Haven't I been begging you over and over, till I'm hoarse, to do just that?

FIANCÉE: Then how would it be if I visited the apartment tomorrow with a friend?

MAN: A friend?

FIANCÉE: A man who used to be a feature writer for a weekly magazine. Exposés were always his strong suit, so I'm sure he's one person who'll be able to tell what's going on.

MAN: Are you trying to spite me?

FIANCÉE: Let the chips fall where they may. I'm only after the guilty party. If things are the way you've described them, I'm sure the family will be the ones to suffer. You understand, don't you? I desperately want to believe you.

MAN: In that case, I have no objections. There's nothing more I want than to have you believe me.

FIANCÉE: I do want to believe you.

MAN: And I want to be believed.

Suddenly YOUNGEST DAUGHTER *pops up from behind the bench and starts tiptoeing off to stage right.* MAN, *sensing somebody is there, turns around, and, with a shout, grabs her arm.*

MAN: Wait!

YOUNGEST DAUGHTER (*letting out a scream*): Murder!

MAN, *surprised, releases her arm.* YOUNGEST DAUGHTER *sticks out her tongue and runs off.*

FIANCÉE: Who was that?

MAN: One of the five women in the case.

The stage darkens.

. . . SCENE TEN

A strangely shaped male head emerges from the darkness. The left and right sides of the face do not seem to match, giving an impression of madness. This is the REPORTER *who has come at Fiancée's request. (By changing the lighting, however, it is possible to make the expression change to one of extreme gentleness.)*

REPORTER (*abruptly, all but shouting*):   Marvelous, isn't it? I mean it, it's really marvelous. This is what I've dreamt of for years, the model of what family life should be, solid and generous as the earth itself.

In another corner of the stage the faces of the members of the family are revealed, forming a group. They begin to sing a chorus of "The Broken Necklace" to the accompaniment of Younger Son's guitar. The chorus gives way to a solo by MIDDLE DAUGHTER *and the stage gradually becomes lighter.* FIANCÉE *stands in another part of the stage, looking utterly baffled.* REPORTER *goes up to* MIDDLE DAUGHTER, *applauding.*

REPORTER: I'm impressed. Yes, impressed. That one word "impressed" sums up my feelings. Tell me, young lady, what is your philosophy of life? (*He takes out a notebook and holds his pencil poised.*)
MIDDLE DAUGHTER: My philosophy?
REPORTER: I mean, what you believe in . . .
MIDDLE DAUGHTER: Let me see . . . Maybe it is to forget myself.
REPORTER: Marvelous! Not to believe in your own existence is infinitely more of a strain on rationalism than believing in something that doesn't exist. (*To* FIANCÉE.) Thank you. Thank you for having introduced me to such wonderful people. I'm grateful to you from the bottom of my heart.

REPORTER, *overcome by emotion, spreads open his arms and all but embraces* FIANCÉE. *She steps back in confusion.*

FIANCÉE: But it isn't as if we'd especially asked them to stay here.
REPORTER: Well, ask them now. They're not the kind of people to insist on formalities. (*To family.*) That's right, isn't it?
FATHER: Go right ahead.
FIANCÉE: But I don't think it's necessary any more.

ELDER SON *has been combing his hair and winking at* FIANCÉE. *Now, seeing his chance, he steps forward with a theatrical gesture.*

ELDER SON: Young lady, why do you disappoint us by saying such things? Your adorable lips were never meant to pronounce such uncouth words as "necessary" or "unnecessary."
YOUNGER SON (*singing to the accompaniment of his guitar*):   Chase him, chase him, but still he trots after you, that pooch is really sweet . . . (*He suddenly gets down on all fours at Fiancée's feet.*) Lady, I'm your pooch!

FIANCÉE *is driven into a corner of the stage, but ends up by bursting into giggles.*

REPORTER (*suddenly cries out*): No! This'll never do! I mustn't go on procrastinating any more. (*To* FATHER.) I've definitely made up my mind. I'm going to join you. I'd like you to include me in your group. Where are the headquarters? Where should I apply for membership? What are the prerequisites? The entrance fees? The conditions?

The members of the family exchange meaningful glances.

FATHER: It's hard, after having been praised so enthusiastically, to know how to answer.

REPORTER: Please believe me! I'll keep it an absolute secret.

MOTHER: A secret? We haven't any secrets, have we?

GRANDMOTHER: We're honest people, we are.

REPORTER: I don't mean to suggest I suspect you of anything. But surely your family couldn't be the only people carrying on this great movement?

FATHER: Well, of course . . . The world is not such a hopeless place.

REPORTER (*greatly in earnest*): I understand. You're saying that it's presumptuous for anyone like myself to hope to be admitted to your ranks.

ELDER SON: Somehow I think you're overestimating us a little . . .

REPORTER: Such modesty!

FATHER: What we've been doing is just plain, ordinary . . . Let's put it this way. All we're doing is what anybody with the least grain of normal human decency couldn't help but do.

MOTHER: You might say we're knitting a fabric, not out of yarn but out of people.

REPORTER: Such humility! That fabric will spread as it is knitted, from village to village, from town to town, until soon it grows into an enormous jacket covering and warming the country and the entire people. This is magnificent! Such magnificence, and such humility! I will become your disciple. Yes, I will sit at your feet. But at least you can tell me where I can find the headquarters of your knitting club.

FATHER: If you'll forgive me for saying so, you should act more spontaneously, as the voices within you command.

REPORTER: Then it's all right if I go right ahead as I please, without any license or authorization?

FATHER: Why should you hesitate? When what you want to do is right, you should throw yourself into it, with full confidence.

REPORTER: Thank you!

FATHER: As long as you perform your services with sincerity and devotion, one of these days you're sure to receive word from headquarters recognizing your work.

REPORTER: Then there is a headquarters?

ELDEST DAUGHTER: I wonder.

FATHER: I'm sure there must be one. It stands to reason . . .

ELDEST DAUGHTER: But we've never once received word from headquarters, have we?

REPORTER (*surprised*): Not even you?

FATHER: Society is demanding. But that's no reason to doubt the existence of a headquarters—it doesn't get you anywhere. If you want to believe in a headquarters, why, there's no harm in that.

REPORTER: I see . . .

ELDEST DAUGHTER: I don't mean to deny it myself. Either way, it doesn't affect my beliefs.

REPORTER: Ah? Your beliefs? (*He gets his notebook ready.*) I wonder if I might trouble you to tell me a little about them.

ELDEST DAUGHTER (*emphasizing the importance of her words*): Ask not, but give . . . That sums them up in a nutshell.

REPORTER: Ask not, but give . . . That's quite something . . . Ask not, but give . . . Isn't that splendid? How can any man be so obstinate, even after you've said *that* to him? It beats me. A feast is set before him and he refuses to eat! What a disgrace! Something must have happened to his head!

Suddenly MAN, *who has been lying in the hammock, sits up.*

MAN: Give? Don't make me laugh! What have they ever given me? The dirty swine!

REPORTER: Who's that?

FATHER: You might call him a kind of blotting paper, I suppose.

REPORTER: Blotting paper?

ELDEST DAUGHTER (*going up to* MAN): That's right. I've never seen anyone so unresponsive.

REPORTER: Repulsive, isn't he?

The stage becomes dark again, leaving light only on MAN *and* ELDEST DAUGHTER. *She produces a small bottle of whisky from the pocket of her dressing gown and takes a swig.*

ELDEST DAUGHTER: Come on down, Mr. Blotting Paper.

MAN: At your service, Miss Parasite.

ELDEST DAUGHTER: Do you know why I've never married?

MAN: Today I made the most terrible blunder. I absent-mindedly sent the carpool manager some papers that were supposed to be delivered to the chief of the planning department.

ELDEST DAUGHTER: Speaking of your company, that reminds me—you took your time coming home from work today. Did you stop off somewhere?

MAN: Are you kidding? You and your family took away my pay check, envelope and all. There's no chance of my stopping off anywhere.

ELDEST DAUGHTER: Don't try to fool me. I know all about it. You stopped off to see—what was his name?—the lawyer, didn't you?

MAN *does not respond.*

ELDEST DAUGHTER: He telephoned us immediately afterwards. And we all had a good laugh. (*She giggles.*) Why, even the lawyer . . . (*She hurriedly changes her tone.*) But you mustn't be offended. We're . . . how shall I say it . . . we're considerate. That's why, even after we had our big laugh, we decided not to tell you.

MAN: Then, there's nothing more to say, is there?

ELDEST DAUGHTER: I suppose not. Of course we should have said something, if only to induce you to reconsider your attitude, but we refrained.

MAN: You keep saying you haven't told me, but aren't you telling me now?

ELDEST DAUGHTER: I must be drunk!

MAN: You're running around like a broken-down neon sign.

ELDEST DAUGHTER: What a thing to say!

MAN: Damn him! And he calls himself a lawyer!

ELDEST DAUGHTER (*to herself*): I mustn't be over-eager.

MAN: Anyway, it isn't easy talking to you. There's no getting around it, you're one of the family.

ELDEST DAUGHTER (*in a syrupy voice*): Then, you have some feeling for me?

MAN: Heaven forbid!

ELDEST DAUGHTER: If you're still interested in that girl, I'm sorry for you, but you'd better forget her. My brother's talents as a thief aren't restricted to the contents of people's pockets.

MAN: I can't believe in anything any more.

ELDEST DAUGHTER: Doubt is the door to progress . . . Talking about doors, I can't help feeling all the time as if I'm a door that's been left permanently ajar . . . Please, come down from there. Hurry!

MAN: You know, the lawyer was in tears . . .

ELDEST DAUGHTER (*suddenly laughs*): I gather he was wearing a bandage on his head?

MAN: It's a wonder he can still stay in business!

ELDEST DAUGHTER: It's just a matter of getting used to it. Nowadays it's not all that unusual for a man to be visited by friends like us.

MAN: But the bandage clearly shows there's been violence.

ELDEST DAUGHTER: Even love has its whips, hasn't it?

MAN: The lawyer said eleven parasites had descended on him!

ELDEST DAUGHTER: He must be an even better quality of blotting paper than you.

MAN: What the devil's the matter with this hammock?

ELDEST DAUGHTER: Excuse me, but I'm taking off my clothes. I feel unbearably hot. I suppose it must be the whisky . . . (*She is wearing under her dressing gown only net tights and a short negligee.*)

MAN: If such a thing as hot ice existed—there may be, for all I know, in fact I'm sure there is—a snowstorm in midsummer, sun stroke in midwinter . . .

ELDEST DAUGHTER: The bottle will be empty if you don't hurry.

MAN (*writhing*):   That's funny. What's happened to this hammock?

ELDEST DAUGHTER (*as if she has made a surprising discovery*):   Just feel me . . . I really seem to be hot and cold at the same time. I wonder why.

MAN: But what the hell's wrong with this hammock?

. . . SCENE ELEVEN

Lights are suddenly turned on in the room. ELDEST DAUGHTER *wheels around in astonishment.* MIDDLE DAUGHTER *stands in pajamas by the wall, near the door of the adjoining room. Her hand is still on the wall switch.*

ELDEST DAUGHTER (*angrily*):   So you were listening!

MIDDLE DAUGHTER (*quietly and calmly*):   Yes, I heard everything.

ELDEST DAUGHTER (*retrieving her gown and putting it back on*):   What a way to talk? Not a scrap of respect for other people's feelings . . . I've never known anyone less lovable than you.

MIDDLE DAUGHTER: But it's something important.

ELDEST DAUGHTER: I don't care how important it is. Who ever heard of leaving the lights burning indefinitely? Why even he looks as if the light's too strong for him.

MAN (*seems rather dazed*):   Yes, it'll soon be morning.

MIDDLE DAUGHTER (*ignoring him; to* ELDEST DAUGHTER):   Are you drunk?

ELDEST DAUGHTER (*losing her temper*):   I tell you, I'm going to give you a piece of my mind if you keep tormenting me with such stupid tricks. I don't care how important you think it is, eavesdropping is still eavesdropping. You didn't listen because it was important. You listened and then you found out something that happened to be important. Why don't you at least pretend to be a little embarrassed? (*To* MAN, *still fiddling with the hammock, unable to get out.*) I'm sorry, really I am . . .

MIDDLE DAUGHTER: Hmmm. Isn't what you really have to apologize for something quite different?

ELDEST DAUGHTER (*worsted in the argument, she adjusts the front of her gown*): I don't know what you're talking about, but there's something weird about you. (*She goes toward the door.*) Anyway, with your permission, I'd like to get a little sleep.

MIDDLE DAUGHTER (*showing her first emotional reaction*): No, you can't! Stay right where you are! You're an important witness. (*She calls through the door to the next room.*) Father, Brother . . . would you come here a minute?

ELDEST DAUGHTER (*agitated*): What are you up to, anyway?

YOUNGER SON (*calling from offstage*): Which brother do you want?

MIDDLE DAUGHTER: Both of you! Hurry! It's extremely important.

Noises from the next room—sleepy murmurs, fits of coughing, and the like— suggest people getting out of bed reluctantly.

MAN (*becoming uneasy*): Isn't there some sort of misunderstanding? Well, misunderstandings get cleared up sooner or later. There's nothing to be so excited about . . . But what the devil's happened to this hammock?

ELDEST DAUGHTER (*glaring at* MIDDLE DAUGHTER): After all this uproar I'm sure we'll discover that the mountain labored to bring forth a mouse. You're not going to get away with paying a hundred yen fine this time . . . I trust you've got a good stock of pin money.

MIDDLE DAUGHTER (*quietly*): It hurts me to tell you, but this is no mouse. You mean to say you haven't caught on yet?

ELDER SON, FATHER, *and* YOUNGER SON, *in that order, appear from the next room. All look groggy, as if they just got out of bed. Each is muttering to himself.*

YOUNGER SON: Damn it! I've got another corker of a hangover.

ELDEST DAUGHTER *starts to make a sneering remark, but* MIDDLE DAUGHTER *interrupts at once.*

MIDDLE DAUGHTER: He was planning an escape!

FATHER (*at once wide awake*): Escape?

They all show reactions of astonishment.

MIDDLE DAUGHTER (*slowly goes up to Man's hammock*): He was just about to try running away.

FATHER (*turning to the sons*): Running away! Things have taken a serious turn.

ELDER SON (*extremely confused*): I can see that everything has not been arranged exactly as he might have wished, but still.

MAN (*apprehensive*): That's an exaggeration. The fact is, I'm here now. Right? Run away? Fat chance I'd have, when I'm wrapped up in this crazy hammock like a tent caterpillar. (*With an unnatural, forced laugh.*) Run away . . . why I can't even get out to take a leak. I'm suffering, I tell you!

MIDDLE DAUGHTER *takes the cord at one end of the hammock and jerks it loose. The hammock at once opens out, and in the recoil* MAN *drops to the floor.* MAN *makes feeble sounds of laughter, but none of the others so much as smile.*

MIDDLE DAUGHTER (*helping* MAN *to his feet*): I'm sorry. Did you hurt yourself?

ELDEST DAUGHTER (*aggressively*): So, it was your handiwork, was it?

MIDDLE DAUGHTER: I didn't want to mention it, but you've been flirting with him for the past three days, haven't you?

ELDEST DAUGHTER: Don't say anything you'll regret! For the past three days? Go ahead, be as jealous as you like—that's your privilege— but if you get carried away to any such wild conclusions, the rest of us will be the ones to suffer.

MIDDLE DAUGHTER (*cool; to* FATHER *and the others*): I had a feeling tonight would be the crisis. So, just to be on the safe side, I tied up the hammock after he went to sleep.

ELDEST DAUGHTER: That's a lie! An out-and-out lie! Ask him to his face. He'll say which of us is telling the truth. (*To* MAN, *seeking his assent.*) That's right, isn't it?

MAN (*hesitates before answering*): It's true she's kindly come here every evening for the last three days to keep me company, but . . .

ELDEST DAUGHTER (*unabashed*): I've no intention of hiding anything. I've been trying my best to advertise myself, hoping he'd respond to my overtures. But to hear you talk, I was inducing him to run away! That's going too far, even for a false accusation.

MIDDLE DAUGHTER (*spitefully*): It's quite possible tonight was the first time you resorted to open inducement. But how about hints?

ELDEST DAUGHTER: Mystification doesn't become you.

GRANDMOTHER (*imitating Eldest Daughter's manner of speech*): "There's nothing to be worried about. This place and time exist just for the two of us . . . If you pretend that nobody else is here, why it's just the same as if nobody were actually here. Think of the others as being insubstantial as the air . . ."

ELDEST DAUGHTER (*bursts into laughter*): How disgusting! Aren't those the usual clichés every woman uses when seducing a man? Didn't you even know that?

FATHER: What was this direct incitement she resorted to tonight?

MIDDLE DAUGHTER (*again imitating* ELDEST DAUGHTER; *with passion*): "You must give up all hope of getting rid of them. You'll just exhaust yourself with useless efforts. Yes, it'd be better to run away than try to chase them out. We'll run far, far away to some distant place where nobody knows us."

ELDEST DAUGHTER: That's enough!

FATHER: Mm. That was pretty direct.

YOUNGER SON: Even with my hangover I can't help being impressed.

ELDER SON: And what was his reaction to her incitement?

MIDDLE DAUGHTER (*severely*): I felt it was certainly a good thing I had tied the hammock so he couldn't get out.

ELDER SON: What a mess!

MAN (*in confused tone*): But don't you think it's unfair to base your judgments on such a one-sided . . .

FATHER (*reassuringly*): It's all right. It's all right. Please don't worry about it any more.

ELDER SON (*to* ELDEST DAUGHTER): But were you serious in trying to tempt him into such a thing?

ELDEST DAUGHTER (*sulkily*): What makes you think I was serious? Don't insult me. It doesn't take much common sense to see that there's absolutely no likelihood of his running away. This is the most disgusting thing I've ever heard of, making such a fuss, so early in the morning.

MIDDLE DAUGHTER: What makes you so sure he can't run away?

ELDEST DAUGHTER: You don't see?

MIDDLE DAUGHTER: I certainly don't.

ELDEST DAUGHTER: He's the acting department head. His fortune's assured—he's a rising star. He knows better than anyone else, I should think, how important his work is to him. He can talk all he wants about how he likes to be alone, or how he longs for freedom, but one thing he can never in the world do is to give up his job.

ELDER SON: That sounds logical, all right.

ELDEST DAUGHTER: Supposing he ran away from here without giving up his job. He'd have to find somewhere else to stay, and it'd be simple enough for us to find out where he went.

ELDER SON: Yes, that'd be no problem.

ELDEST DAUGHTER: And once we found him we surely wouldn't spare ourselves the trouble of moving in with him, would we? We'd go to help him again, as our natural duty, wouldn't we?

FATHER: Of course. We couldn't neglect our duty. That would be out of the question.

ELDEST DAUGHTER (*her self-confidence quite recovered*): And even he must be fully convinced, after living with us for almost two weeks, how strong our sense of duty is. (*To* MAN.) Am I wrong?

MAN: No, I am deeply aware of it.

ELDEST DAUGHTER (*triumphantly*): Well, there you have it, ladies and gentlemen.

They all strike various attitudes which suggest they are ruminating on the above. ELDEST DAUGHTER *throws* MIDDLE DAUGHTER *an unconcealed smile of derision.*

FATHER: In that case, the incident is not as serious as we had imagined.

YOUNGER SON: Then, I hope you'll pardon me if I go back to bed before the rest of you. I may vomit at any minute.

MIDDLE DAUGHTER: I can't help being worried, all the same.

ELDEST DAUGHTER: The more you talk, the more shame you bring on yourself. Pretending to be an innocent little girl is all very well, but it's exhausting for the rest of us to play your game.

MIDDLE DAUGHTER: But when I heard him say, "All right, let's run away!" I was so frightened I shuddered with fear. I wonder if a man can talk in that tone of voice if he doesn't mean it.

ELDEST DAUGHTER: A mere impression, even from someone as bright as you, is not sufficient evidence.

ELDER SON: Yes, if it was nothing more than impression.

YOUNGER SON: O.K. That settles it. (*He exits, staggering, to the next room.*) It's probably my liver.

FATHER (*cautiously, observing* MAN):   Finally, just as a formality, I'd like to ask the subject of our discussion his opinion. Then I'll adjourn the meeting.

MAN (*gradually regaining his self-confidence*):   My opinion? After all we've gone through? (*He laughs.*) That's no longer of any importance, is it? How shall I put it? To tell the truth, it's as if some devil got into me tonight . . . Or rather, as if I'd been bewitched by a goddess . . . I felt when I was talking as if I were singing the words of a song . . . (*To* ELDEST DAUGHTER.) I'm not the kind to flatter people, but I really felt as if I were swimming in a pool of whisky . . . When I proposed that we run away I wonder if I wasn't expressing, in spite of myself, the reverse of what I actually felt—my desire to hold fast to you. (*To* FATHER.) People sometimes say precisely the opposite of what they're thinking.

In the course of the above dialogue GRANDMOTHER, MOTHER, *and* YOUNGEST DAUGHTER, *in that order, stick their heads in from the next room. They observe what is happening with expressions of intense curiosity.*

FATHER (*reflectively*):   I see . . . Well, now we seem to have heard the opinions of everyone. (*He looks from* MIDDLE DAUGHTER *to* ELDEST DAUGHTER.) How about it—will you agree to leave the final judgment to me?

ELDEST DAUGHTER (*in good spirits, now that* MAN *has flattered her*):   That's fine with me.

MIDDLE DAUGHTER: I don't suppose I have much choice.

FATHER (*abruptly gives order to* ELDER SON):   Prepare the cage!

They all look astonished. But ELDER SON *instantly moves into action. The other members of the family follow him, displaying remarkable teamwork: one arranges the coat rack in the hall, another produces a lock, another overpowers* MAN, *still another throws a blanket over him. Finally,* MAN, *wrapped in the blanket, is shut up inside the coat rack, which has been converted into a cage. A large lock is hung on the outside.*

MAN *at length manages to stick his head out from inside the blanket.*

MAN: What're you doing? Didn't I promise you I wouldn't run away? This is inhuman! There's no excuse for it. It's inhuman!

ELDEST DAUGHTER (*with an expression of inability to understand it herself*): Yes, really, what's happened? After he assured us so positively he had no intention of running away . . .

MAN: That's right. You tell them . . . There must be some mistake!

FATHER: The thing is, you insisted a little too emphatically that you wouldn't run away.

MAN: It's natural for a man to be emphatic when he's speaking from the heart.

FATHER: You yourself were just expressing the view that sometimes people say the opposite of what they feel.

MAN: That's a false accusation!

GRANDMOTHER: The blind man envies the one-eyed man.

FATHER: In a matter of this gravity there's no such thing as taking too many precautions.

YOUNGEST DAUGHTER *looks into the cage as if she were watching a monkey at the zoo.* MAN *spits at youngest daughter.*

MAN: Get the hell away!

YOUNGEST DAUGHTER: Isn't he awful? Even a chimpanzee wouldn't be so rude.

MOTHER: Don't get too close to him. He's still overexcited.

MAN: Damn it! All your clever talk about neighborly love and the rest was a lot of bunk . . . Not even a slave would endure such treatment.

MIDDLE DAUGHTER (*severely*):   There's been a misunderstanding. A terrible misunderstanding. You've taken everything in the wrong spirit.

MAN: Shut up! I don't even want to see your face!

FATHER: Yes, the misunderstanding was definitely on your side. And you still don't seem to understand that these measures have been taken because we earnestly desire your safety and security.

MAN: Understand! You don't suppose there's any chance I would understand that!

MIDDLE DAUGHTER: But running away means disappearing. And that's a much more frightening thing than you seem to suppose. You don't think we could expose you to such a danger, knowing how frightening it is to disappear.

ELDEST DAUGHTER (*still not satisfied*):   I think you're overrating him.

ELDER SON: It seems to be our fate always to have our efforts rewarded by enmity.

MOTHER: In short, the world's fallen on evil days.

MAN (*gasping*):   But if I can't go to the office, you'll be the ones to suffer. I wonder if you've thought about that.

FATHER: We don't intend to keep you in there forever. Just as soon as your frame of mind improves, of course we'll let you out.

MAN: Isn't that nice? You expect my frame of mind to improve? You amaze me. Don't you think it's a lot more likely to boomerang on you? Don't you realize I'll get to hate this place more and more?

FATHER: Please, just leaves things to me. While you're meditating over your solitude in there, the pleasures of your ordinary everyday life, how you used to go to the office each morning, will come back and the happy memories will gush forth inside you like a fountain.

MOTHER: That's right. Happy memories are generally of quite ordinary things. They leave the deepest impression.

FATHER: And then your desire to escape will drop from you like the scab from a wound that has healed.

MIDDLE DAUGHTER: And your peace of mind will come back again.

FATHER: Now for the blankets.

The instant after FATHER *speaks several blankets are draped over the cage. The stage darkens at once.*

. . . SCENE TWELVE

The stage blacks out completely for a moment, but almost immediately afterwards the inside of the cage is illuminated. MAN *sits, his knees cradled in his arms, and his face pressed against his knees.*

He suddenly raises his head and looks uneasily around him. He listens attentively. Then he lies down on his side in a fetal posture. The next moment he gets on all fours like a dog. He starts to imitate a dog's howling, at which the howling of a real dog is heard from a loudspeaker. MAN *again lies on his side in a fetal posture.*

. . . SCENE THIRTEEN

Now light and dark are reversed: inside the cage is dark and outside is light. It is daytime. MIDDLE DAUGHTER *enters from the kitchen carrying a breakfast tray.*

MIDDLE DAUGHTER (*standing before cage*):   Are you awake? I've brought your breakfast.

MAN (*dispiritedly*):   Thanks.

She puts the tray on the floor for the moment, removes the blanket covering the cage, then slips the tray into the cage from the end.

MIDDLE DAUGHTER: How do you feel?

MAN: How do you expect? (*He stares at the food, then begins to eat little by little, but without enjoyment.*)

MIDDLE DAUGHTER: You don't seem to have much of an appetite . . . If you don't go out and get some exercise soon—

MAN: What's the weather like today?

MIDDLE DAUGHTER: It seems to be clearing gradually.

MAN: The place is strangely silent. Is nobody here?

MIDDLE DAUGHTER (*sitting down and staring at* MAN *through the bars of the cage*):   Father has gone to the miniature golf links. My older sister's at the beauty parlor and the younger one at school. The rest are out shopping, I suppose.

MAN (*entreatingly*):   Couldn't you let me have a look at the newspaper, even if it's only the headlines?

MIDDLE DAUGHTER: Nothing doing. We must keep you quiet while you're convalescing.

MAN: You're certainly a hard girl to figure out. Sometimes I think you're kind, only for you to act just as much of a stickler for the rules as the others. Sometimes you seem affectionate, but then you're just as stubborn as the others.

MIDDLE DAUGHTER (*smiling*):   That's because you only think about yourself.

MAN (*laughing faintly*):   I know, that's what you say. But surely not even you pretend that shutting me up this way is for my own good.

MIDDLE DAUGHTER: But it's the truth.

MAN: I don't believe it.

MIDDLE DAUGHTER: It's strange, isn't it? My head is so full of you that I've never even given a thought to anything else.

MAN (*taken aback*):   If that's the case, how can you fail so completely to understand my feelings? I have you and your family to thank for the opportunity to study to my heart's content the blessings of neighborly love.

MIDDLE DAUGHTER (*suddenly dejected*):   I do understand. I understand much better than you suppose.

MAN: What do you understand?

MIDDLE DAUGHTER (*speaking hesitantly*):   Well, for example . . .

MAN: For example?

MIDDLE DAUGHTER: The fact that your sickness has not in the least improved.

MAN (*his interest aroused*):   I see . . . You may be right.

MIDDLE DAUGHTER: If I listen very carefully I can hear it, the sound of your heart flying far, far away.

MAN: Just like a bird.

MIDDLE DAUGHTER: And the commuter's train, your time card, the desk with your nameplate on it, the street corner with your company's building—they're all gradually melting away like sculpture carved of ice.

MAN: You do understand.

MIDDLE DAUGHTER (*changing her tone*):   Oh, that's right. I was forgetting something important. Here. (*She takes a little packet wrapped in paper from her pocket.*) My brother asked me to give this to you.

MAN (*unwrapping the packet*):   From your brother, is it? I see.

MIDDLE DAUGHTER: That's an engagement ring, isn't it?

MAN: It's a kind of metal object. It used to be an engagement ring once.

MIDDLE DAUGHTER (*staring at* MAN *with great earnestness*):   Oh, I'm so worried.

MAN: About what?

MIDDLE DAUGHTER: You seem already to have gone farther away than I had thought.

MAN (*laughing cynically*):   How sentimental we've become!

MIDDLE DAUGHTER: Sentimental? That's not it at all. I meant to say you're a traitor!

MAN: A traitor!

MIDDLE DAUGHTER: How about a glass of milk?

MAN: Yes, I'd like one. The food today was a little too salty.

MIDDLE DAUGHTER *hurries into the kitchen and returns immediately with a glass of milk. She watches affectionately as* MAN, *with a word of thanks, drains the glass with one gulp.*

MIDDLE DAUGHTER (*holding out her fist; she has something in it*):   If I give you the key to this lock, will you promise not to scold me even if I tell you I love you? (*She opens her hand. The key glitters in her palm.*)

MAN (*at a loss for words before this too-sudden realization of his wishes*):   That's the easiest thing in the world. Why, if you hadn't been a member of your family, I'm sure I would have spoken first, and told you I was in love with you . . . I'm not saying this just to please you . . . I'm sure I would have. (*He starts to shake.*)

MIDDLE DAUGHTER: Are you cold?

MAN: It must be an excess of joy. And now, for the key . . .

MAN *tries to take the key, but his shaking has become so violent that he cannot manage to grasp it. Suddenly Man's face is shot with fear.*

MIDDLE DAUGHTER: If only you hadn't turned against us, we would have been no more than company for you . . .

Man's shaking suddenly stops. He lies motionless. MIDDLE DAUGHTER *tenderly drapes a blanket over the cage and, kneeling beside him, quietly sobs.*

MIDDLE DAUGHTER: There's no need any more to run away . . . Nobody will bother you now . . . It's quiet, isn't it? You look so well . . . Your sickness must be better.

YOUNGER SON *appears without warning from the next room.*

YOUNGER SON (*putting on his shirt*): Hey, what're you bawling about?
MIDDLE DAUGHTER: Oh, were you there all the time?
YOUNGER SON (*having sized up the situation from Middle Daughter's appearance*): So, you've done it again.
MIDDLE DAUGHTER: What else could I do?
YOUNGER SON: You're hopeless . . . But there's no use crying over spilt milk . . . Well, we're going to be busy again, what with one thing and another.
MIDDLE DAUGHTER: He was such a nice man. Really sweet. And so sensitive. At the slightest touch his heart would start to pound.
YOUNGER SON (*brushing the dandruff from his head*): We borrowed in advance on his retirement pay. We've got nothing to complain about as far as our balance sheet is concerned.
MIDDLE DAUGHTER: Show a little more tact in what you say. What I lost and what you lost are not the same things.
YOUNGER SON (*looking around the room; to no one in particular*): It's funny with belongings. I don't know why it is, but every time we move we seem to have more and more of them.
MIDDLE DAUGHTER (*throwing her arms around the cage and caressing it*): If only you hadn't turned against us, we would have been no more than company for you.

The melody of "The Broken Necklace" begins to sound, this time in a melancholy key. The members of the family return in full strength and arrange themselves in a line. They are already dressed for travel. They all take out handkerchiefs and press them to their eyes.

FATHER: The deceased was always a good friend to us. Friend, why were you destined for such a fate? Probably you yourself do not know. Naturally, we do not know either. (*He opens the newspaper.*) Here is the newspaper you were waiting for. Please listen as I read, without the least anxiety. (*He begins to read snatches from the main news items of that day's newspaper, ranging from international events to advertisements.*) Yes, the world is a big place. A big place and a complicated one. (*To* MIDDLE DAUGHTER.) Come, be more cheerful. (*He lifts her to her feet.*) They're all waiting for us. (*To* MAN.) Good-by.

They all wave their handkerchiefs and put them back into their pockets.

FATHER: Nobody's forgotten anything?

They begin to march off. The curtain falls slowly. Halfway off the lighting is extinguished, and all that can be recognized is the laughter of the family.

Questions for Discussion and Writing

1. From the family's point of view what justifies the family in usurping the apartment, possessions, and life of the CHARACTER identified as "Man"? How does the song "The Broken Necklace" express their mission?
2. From the description of the SETTING and the conversation we overhear, what can we infer about the life of "Man" before the family enters his apartment?
3. Why is it significant that no one the protagonist turns to for help, including the superintendent, police, reporter, or even his fiancée, takes his side over that of the family?
4. How are members of the family defined as characters solely in terms of the roles they play in society?
5. How does the middle daughter's sympathy for the protagonist bring her into conflict with the other members of the family?
6. What means does the family use to justify its appropriation of "Man's" money?
7. To what extent does "Man's" reaction to the family contribute to his fate? Are there points in the play where he seems to be genuinely wavering?
8. How does your response to individual scenes in this play reflect your own cultural assumptions? Which scene did you find the most shocking and why?
9. What attitudes toward modern Japanese society does Abe express in this play? How does he present the conflict between polite appearance and underlying brutality. How does he present the conflict between the rights of the collective versus those of the individual?
10. In a short essay, discuss how you would have responded if you found yourself in the same predicament as the protagonist. What would you have done if you were in his situation?

Tewfik al-Hakim
The Donkey Market

Widely recognized as the Arab world's leading playwright, Tewfik al-Hakim was born in Alexandria, Egypt, in 1902. He studied law at the University of Cairo and at the Sorbonne in Paris. After serving as a public prosecutor in Alexandria, he held a variety of positions with the Egyptian government. He was appointed director general of the Egyptian National Library and served as Egyptian representative to UNESCO, based in Paris, in 1959–1960. He was awarded the State Literature Prize in 1961. Al-Hakim has made major pioneering contributions to the development of modern literary Arabic in his over one hundred plays, several novels, essays, and memoirs. His unique ability to seamlessly blend the theater of the absurd with satire and social criticism can be seen in plays such as Food for the Millions *(1963),* The Tree Climber *(1966), and* Fate of a Cockroch and Other Plays *(1973). In* The Donkey Market *(1975), translated by Denys Johnson-Davies, al-Hakim adapts a well-known story about the wise fool that has been part of Egyptian folklore for centuries. Desperate for food and longing for a place to sleep, two unemployed laborers hatch an ingenious scheme to delude a gullible farmer into believing that his newly purchased donkey has been transformed into a human being. Under its hilarious surface, this play grapples with the centuries-old cultural intransigence that makes it difficult to introduce constructive social changes into contemporary Egyptian society.*

CAST

Two Unemployed Men
Farmer
Farmer's Wife

SCENE ONE

Near the donkey market. From afar is heard the braying of donkeys. Outside the market sit two men whose ragged clothes and filthy appearance indicate that they are out-of-work loafers.

First Unemployed (*To his companion*):   Are you able to tell me what the difference is between us and donkeys?
Second Unemployed: You can hear the difference with your own ears.
First Unemployed: The braying?
Second Unemployed: Just so, the braying.
First Unemployed: Couldn't this braying be donkey talk?
Second Unemployed: That's what it must be.

FIRST UNEMPLOYED: So they're talking now.

SECOND UNEMPLOYED: Maybe they're also shouting.

FIRST UNEMPLOYED: I wonder what they're saying?

SECOND UNEMPLOYED: You'd have to be a donkey to know that.

FIRST UNEMPLOYED: They talk to each other so loudly.

SECOND UNEMPLOYED: Naturally, don't they have to hear each other?

FIRST UNEMPLOYED: I thought donkeys whispered together.

SECOND UNEMPLOYED: Why? Why should they?

FIRST UNEMPLOYED: Just like us.

SECOND UNEMPLOYED: Don't worry . . . donkeys aren't like us.

FIRST UNEMPLOYED: You're quite right, donkeys are a civilised species.

SECOND UNEMPLOYED: What are you saying? Civilised?

FIRST UNEMPLOYED: Have you ever seen wild donkeys? There are wild horses and wild buffaloes and wild pigeons and wild cats, but ever since donkeys have been going around amongst us they've been working peacefully and talking freely.

SECOND UNEMPLOYED: Freely?

FIRST UNEMPLOYED: I mean aloud.

SECOND UNEMPLOYED: Talking about aloud, can you tell me why we aren't able to live decently, your goodself and my goodself?

FIRST UNEMPLOYED: Because your goodself and my goodself are broke.

SECOND UNEMPLOYED: And why are we broke?

FIRST UNEMPLOYED: Because no one gives a damn about us. If only we had a market like this donkey market, someone would buy us.

SECOND UNEMPLOYED: And why doesn't anybody buy us?

FIRST UNEMPLOYED: Because we're local merchandise.

SECOND UNEMPLOYED: What's wrong with that?

FIRST UNEMPLOYED: There's only money for foreign merchandise.

SECOND UNEMPLOYED: Why don't we go off and advertise ourselves?

FIRST UNEMPLOYED: How?

SECOND UNEMPLOYED: With our voices.

FIRST UNEMPLOYED: They wouldn't come out loud enough.

SECOND UNEMPLOYED: How is it that a donkey's voice comes out all right?

FIRST UNEMPLOYED: Because, as I told you, they're a civilised species.

SECOND UNEMPLOYED: You've got me interested. Oh, if only I were a donkey, like this one coming along? Look over there . . . the donkey being led along by the man who's taking it out from the market. I wonder how much he paid for it! Look how proud and cock-a-hoop he is as he takes it away!

FIRST UNEMPLOYED: I've had an idea.

SECOND UNEMPLOYED: What is it?

FIRST UNEMPLOYED: Would you like to become a donkey?

SECOND UNEMPLOYED: Me? How?

FIRST UNEMPLOYED: Don't ask questions. Would you like to or wouldn't you?

SECOND UNEMPLOYED: I'd like to, but how?

FIRST UNEMPLOYED: I'll tell you. You see the donkey that's coming towards us, being led by the man who bought it. Well, I'll go up to the man and distract him by chatting him up. At the same time you undo the rope round the donkey's neck without its owner noticing and tie it round your own neck.

SECOND UNEMPLOYED: That's all? And then what?

FIRST UNEMPLOYED: And then he'll lead you off and I'll lead off the donkey.

SECOND UNEMPLOYED: And where will he lead me off to?

FIRST UNEMPLOYED: I wouldn't be knowing, that's in the lap of the gods.

SECOND UNEMPLOYED: Are you talking seriously?

FIRST UNEMPLOYED: Isn't it you who want it this way?

SECOND UNEMPLOYED: I tie a rope round my neck and he leads me away?

FIRST UNEMPLOYED: And what's wrong with that? At least you'll have found yourself someone to guarantee that you get a bite to eat.

SECOND UNEMPLOYED: It won't be what you call a bite . . . more like a munch.

FIRST UNEMPLOYED: It's all the same . . . just something to eat.

SECOND UNEMPLOYED: As you say, it'll be a change from being hungry and without a roof over one's head. But how am I going to put myself over to the man?

FIRST UNEMPLOYED: That depends on how smart you are.

SECOND UNEMPLOYED: We'll have a go.

FIRST UNEMPLOYED: Hide yourself . . . the man mustn't catch sight of us together.

The two men part and the stage is empty. A man—he looks like a farmer— appears. He holds a rope with which he is leading a donkey. The FIRST UNEMPLOYED *approaches him.*

FIRST UNEMPLOYED: Peace be upon you!

FARMER: And upon you be peace!

FIRST UNEMPLOYED: Good God, man, is it that you don't know me or what?

FARMER: You . . . who would you be?

FIRST UNEMPLOYED: Who would I be? Didn't we break bread together?

FARMER: I don't understand. You mean to say we once broke bread together?

FIRST UNEMPLOYED: You mean you've forgotten all that quickly? No one but a bastard forgets a good turn.

FARMER: Are you calling me a bastard?

FIRST UNEMPLOYED: May God strike dead anyone who said such a thing about you. What I meant was that anyone who forgets his friends . . . but then, thank God, you're really decent and civil person, it's merely that it's just slipped your mind what I look like. The point is that we met at night, over dinner, and it just happened the moon wasn't out that night.

FARMER: The moon? When? Where?

FIRST UNEMPLOYED: I'll remind you. Just be patient till the knot's untied.

He looks furtively at his companion who has slipped by unnoticed and is engrossed in undoing the knot of the rope.

FARMER: What's untied?

FIRST UNEMPLOYED: I'm tongue-tied. You've embarrassed me, you've made me forget what I was saying. Give me some help. (*Stealing a glance at his companion and urging him to hurry up*) Get the knot untied and do me the favour of getting me out of this.

FARMER: I can't understand a thing you're saying.

FIRST UNEMPLOYED: You'll understand soon enough . . . once the knot's untied, which it must be . . . things have gone on for a long time . . . far too long. Man, get it untied quickly.

FARMER: But what shall I untie?

FIRST UNEMPLOYED (*Seeing that his companion has finished undoing the rope and has tied it round his neck and let the donkey loose*):   Well, it's finally got untied all right. It's the Almighty God Himself who unties and solves things. Everything is untied and solved in its own good time. Everything has its time, and seeing as how you don't remember me now I'll leave you time in which to think it over at your leisure. God willing, we'll be meeting up soon and you'll remember me and you'll give me a real warm welcome. Peace be upon you.

He leaves the FARMER *in a state of confusion. He goes behind the donkey, takes it and moves off without being noticed.*

FARMER (*To himself*):   Where did I meet him? Where did we have dinner? The moon wasn't out? Could be . . . these days one's mind wanders a bit.

He pulls at the donkey's halter so as to lead it away, not knowing that the SECOND UNEMPLOYED *has taken the donkey's place.*

FARMER (*Calling out*):   C'mon, donkey.

The SECOND UNEMPLOYED *imitates the braying of a donkey.*

FARMER (*Looking round and being startled*):   Hey, what's this? Who are you?

SECOND UNEMPLOYED: I'm the donkey.

FARMER: Donkey?

SECOND UNEMPLOYED: Yes, the donkey you've just bought at the market.

FARMER: It's impossible!

SECOND UNEMPLOYED: Why are you so surprised? Didn't you just buy me at the market?

FARMER: Yes, but . . .

SECOND UNEMPLOYED: But what?

FARMER: In the name of God the Merciful, the Compassionate!

SECOND UNEMPLOYED: Don't be frightened, I'm your donkey all right.

FARMER: How? . . . you're human.

SECOND UNEMPLOYED: It's your destiny, your good luck.

FARMER: Are you really human or are you . . . ?

SECOND UNEMPLOYED: Yes, human, not a genie. Don't worry, it can all be explained. Just calm down a bit.

FARMER: I . . . I've calmed down.

SECOND UNEMPLOYED: Listen, then, my dear sir . . . the explanation is that my father . . . a nice fellow like your goodself . . . was, however, real stubborn and got it into his head to marry me off to a girl I'd never seen and who'd never seen me. I refused but he still insisted. I suggested to him that we talk it over and come to some sort of understanding, that it had to be discussed in a spirit of freedom. He got angry and said, "I won't have sons of mine arguing with me." I said to him, "I refuse to accept what you're saying." So he said to me, "You're an ass." I said to him "I'm not an ass." He said, "I said you're an ass and you've got to be an ass," and he called upon God to turn me into an ass. It seems that at that moment the doors of Heaven were open and the prayer was answered and I was actually turned into a donkey. My father died and they found me in the livestock fold, having become part of his estate. They sold me at the market and you came along and bought me.

FARMER: Extraordinary! Then you are the donkey I bought?

SECOND UNEMPLOYED: The very same.

FARMER: And how is that you're now back again as a human being?

SECOND UNEMPLOYED: I told you, it's your destiny, your good luck. It seems you're one of those godly people and the good Lord, may He be praised and exalted, decided to honour you . . .

FARMER: Really! But what's to be done now?

SECOND UNEMPLOYED: What's happened?

FARMER: What's happened is that you . . . is that I . . . I don't know how to go about things. What I mean to say is that I've lost my money, I'm ruined.

SECOND UNEMPLOYED: You haven't lost a thing.

FARMER: How's that?

SECOND UNEMPLOYED: Didn't you buy yourself a donkey? The donkey's right here.

FARMER: Where is he?

SECOND UNEMPLOYED: And where have I gone to?

FARMER: You?

SECOND UNEMPLOYED: Yes, me.

FARMER: You want to tell me that you're . . .

SECOND UNEMPLOYED: Wholly your property. You bought me with
your money on the understanding I'm a donkey. The deal was concluded. Let's suppose that after that I turn into something else,
that's no fault of yours. You've made a purchase and that's the end
of it.

FARMER: Yes, I bought . . .

SECOND UNEMPLOYED: That's it . . . relax.

FARMER: You mean to say you're my property now?

SECOND UNEMPLOYED: In accordance with the law. I'm yours by right.
Right's right . . . and yours is guaranteed.

FARMER: Fair enough. Good, so let's get going.

SECOND UNEMPLOYED: At your disposal.

FARMER: Turn here, O . . . Hey, what shall I call you?

SECOND UNEMPLOYED: Call me by any name. For instance, there's . . .
there's Hassawi.[1] What d'you think of that for a name? Hassawi
. . . come, Hassawi . . . go Hassawi!

FARMER: Hassawi?

SECOND UNEMPLOYED: It's relevant!

FARMER: May it have God's blessings. Let's go then . . . Mr Hassawi!
Wait a moment, I think this business of the rope round your neck
isn't really necessary.

SECOND UNEMPLOYED: As you think best.

FARMER: Better do without the rope . . . after all where would you
go to? Wait while I undo it from round your neck.

SECOND UNEMPLOYED (*Undoing the rope himself*):   Allow me. Allow me
. . . if you'd be so good.

FARMER: Yes, that's right. Come along, let's go home, Mr . . .
Hassawi.

SCENE TWO

Inside the farmer's house his WIFE *is occupied with various household jobs.*
She hears knocking at the door.

WIFE: Who is it?

FARMER (*From outside*):   Me, woman. Open up.

WIFE (*Opens the door and her husband enters*):   You were all this time at
the market?

FARMER: I've only just got back.

WIFE: You bought the donkey?

---

[1]Hassawi is a well-known breed of riding donkey in Egypt.

FARMER: I bought . . .

WIFE: You put it into the fold?

FARMER: What fold are you talking about, woman? Come along in, Mr Hassawi.

WIFE: You've got a guest with you?

FARMER: Not a guest. He's what you might . . . I'll tell you later.

WIFE: Please come in.

FARMER: Off you go and make me a glass of tea.

The WIFE *goes off.*

HASSAWI (*Looking around him*): It seems I . . .

FARMER: And what shall I say to my wife?

HASSAWI: Tell her the truth.

FARMER: The truth?

HASSAWI: Exactly . . . not a word more and not a word less. There's nothing better than plain-speaking.

FARMER: And where will you be sleeping in that case?

HASSAWI: In the fold.

FARMER: What do you mean "the fold"? Do you think that's right?

HASSAWI: That's where I belong. Don't change the order of things. The only thing is that if you've a mattress and a pillow you could put them down for me there.

FARMER: Fine, but what about food? It's not reasonable for you to eat straw, clover and beans.

HASSAWI: I'll eat beans . . . just as long as they're broad beans.

FARMER: With a little oil over them?

HASSAWI: And a slice of lemon.

FARMER: And you'll go on eating beans forever?

HASSAWI: It's all a blessing from God!

FARMER: Just as you say. Donkeys have just the one food. They don't know the difference between breakfast, lunch and dinner. It's straw and clover and beans and that's all.

HASSAWI: I know that.

FARMER: Fine, we've settled your sleeping and your food. Tell me now, what work are you going to do?

HASSAWI: All work donkeys do . . . except being ridden.

FARMER: Ridden?

HASSAWI: You can't ride me because you'd only fall off.

FARMER: And carrying things? For example I was intending taking a load of radishes and leeks on the donkey to the vegetable merchant.

HASSAWI: I'll do that job.

FARMER: You'll carry the vegetables on your shoulders?

HASSAWI: That's my business. I'll manage. I may be a donkey but I've got a brain.

FARMER: Brain? I was forgetting this question of a brain.

HASSAWI: Don't worry, this brain of mine's at your service. You can always rely on me. Just give me confidence and the right to talk things over with you freely.

FARMER: Meaning you can go on your own to the merchant with the produce?

HASSAWI: And agree for you the best price with him.

FARMER: We'll see.

WIFE (*From outside*):   Tea!

HASSAWI: If you'll excuse me.

FARMER: Where are you going?

HASSAWI: I'm going to inspect the fold I'm sleeping in.

FARMER: You'll find it on your right as you go out.

HASSAWI *goes out. The* WIFE *enters with the glass of tea.*

WIFE (*Giving the tea to her husband*):   Your guest has gone out?

FARMER: He's not a guest, woman. He's . . .

WIFE: What?

FARMER: He'd be a . . . a . . .

WIFE: Be a what?

FARMER: He's a . . . a . . .

WIFE: Who is he?

FARMER: You won't believe it.

WIFE: What won't I believe?

FARMER: What I'll tell you now.

WIFE: All right then, just tell me.

FARMER: He's . . . the donkey I bought.

WIFE: The donkey?

FARMER: Yes, didn't I go to the donkey market today to buy a donkey? He's the donkey I bought at the market.

WIFE: Man, do you want to make an utter fool of me?

FARMER: Didn't I tell you that you wouldn't believe me?

WIFE: But what shall I believe . . . that the market's selling human donkeys?

FARMER: He wasn't a human at the time I bought him . . . he was a donkey like the rest . . . and he was braying.

WIFE: He brays as well?

FARMER: Yes, by God, I swear by the Holy Book he was braying.

WIFE: And then?

FARMER: And then on the way home . . . I was leading him by the rope . . . I turned round and found that he'd changed into a human.

WIFE: God save us! . . . an afreet!

FARMER: No, woman, he's no *afreet* . . . he was transformed. Originally he was a human being, the son of decent folk like ourselves. He was then transformed into a donkey and they sold him off at the market. I bought him and God, may He be praised and exalted, decided to honour me so He turned him back into a human.

WIFE: Your omnipotence, O Lord!

FARMER: Well, that's what happened.

WIFE: But after all . . .

FARMER: What? What do you want to say?

WIFE: Nothing.

FARMER: No, there's something you want to say.

WIFE: I want to say . . . what I mean is . . . is . . . what are we going to do with him now, with him being a . . . a human being?

FARMER: Do what with him? Exactly as with any other donkey . . . and in addition to that he's got a brain as well.

WIFE: I suppose we won't be able to ride him?

FARMER: Let's forget about the question of riding for the moment.

WIFE: And we'll talk to him as with other human beings?

FARMER: Yes, talk to him and call him by his name.

WIFE: He's got a name?

FARMER: Of course, what do you think? His name's Hassawi. We'll call him and say to him, "Come here, Hassawi; go there, Hassawi."

WIFE: And where will he sleep?

FARMER: In the fold. You can put a mattress out for him there.

WIFE: And what will he eat?

FARMER: Beans . . . but with oil.

WIFE: With oil?

FARMER: And lemon.

WIFE: And he drinks tea?

FARMER: Let's not get him used to that.

WIFE: How lovely! . . . we've got a human donkey!

FARMER: Be careful, woman not to say such things to the neighbours or they'll be saying we've gone off our heads!

WIFE: And what shall I say to them?

FARMER: Say . . . say for example that he's a relative of ours from far away who's come to help us with the work during these few days just as we're coming into the month of Ramadan.

A knock at the door.

WIFE: Who is it?

HASSAWI (*From outside*): Me . . . Hassawi.

WIFE (*To her husband*): It's him!

FARMER: Open the door for him.

WIFE (*Opens the door*): Come in . . . and wipe your feet on the doorstep.

HASSAW (*Entering*): I've cleaned myself a corner in the fold and spread it out with straw.

FARMER: There you are, my dear lady, he cleans up and makes his own bed . . . yet another advantage.

WIFE: Yes, let him get used to doing that.

HASSAWI: I was coming about an important matter.

FARMER: To do with what?

HASSAWI: To do with the vegetable merchant.

FARMER: The vegetable merchant? What about him?

HASSAWI: A man came on his behalf . . . I just met him at the door and he said the merchant was in a hurry to take delivery. I got him talking and understood that the prices of radishes and leeks would go up in Ramadan. I told him that you were still giving the matter your consideration because there's a new buyer who's offered you a better price. The man was shaken and immediately said that he was prepared to raise the price he was offering.

FARMER: He said so?

HASSAWI (*Producing some money*):   I took a higher price from him. Here you are!

FARMER: God bless you!

HASSAWI: But I have a request to make of you.

FARMER: What is it?

HASSAWI: Would you allow me, before you decide definitely about something, to talk the matter over with you freely and frankly?

FARMER: I'm listening.

HASSAWI: Were you intending to hand over the whole crop to the merchant?

FARMER: Yes, the whole of it.

HASSAWI: Why?

FARMER: Because we need the money.

HASSAWI: Is it absolutely necessary at the present time?

FARMER: Yes it is. We're in dire need of money as we come up to Ramadan. Have you forgotten the dried fruits, the mixed nuts and the dried apricot paste we need to buy?

HASSAWI: I've had an idea.

FARMER: Let's have it.

HASSAWI: We set apart a portion of the crop and have it for seed for the new sowing instead of buying seed at a high price during the sowing season.

FARMER: It's a long long time until the new sowing.

WIFE: The Lord will look after the new sowing . . . we're living in today.

HASSAWI: As you say. In any event I've given you my opinion . . . I'm just afraid the time for the new sowing will come and you won't have the money to pay for the seeds and you'll have to borrow at interest or go off to a money-lender, and perhaps you'll be forced to sell me in the market.

FARMER: Let God look after such things.

WIFE: What's he talk so much for?

FARMER (*To* HASSAWI): Have you got anything else to say?

HASSAWI: Yes, I'm frightened . . .

FARMER: What are you frightened about? Tell us and let happen what may!

HASSAWI: Yes, I must say what I have in my mind and clear my conscience. As I was passing by your field just now I noticed that the feddans sown under radishes and leeks had at least ten kerats lying fallow because the irrigation water isn't reaching there.

FARMER: And what can we do about that?

HASSAWI: It needs one or two shadoofs.

FARMER: We thought about it.

HASSAWI: And what stopped you?

FARMER: Money . . . where's the money?

HASSAWI (*Looking at the* WIFE's *wrist*): Just one of the lady's bracelets . . .

WIFE (*Shouting*): Ruination!

HASSAWI: By putting ten kerats under irrigation you'll get the price of the bracelet back from the first sowing.

FARMER: You think so?

WIFE (*Beating her chest*): What disaster! Man, are you thinking of listening to what that animal has to say? Are you seriously thinking of selling my bracelets?

FARMER: We haven't yet bought or sold anything . . . we're just talking things over.

WIFE: Talking things over with your donkey, you sheep of a man?

FARMER: What's wrong with that? Let me hear what he has to say . . . you too.

WIFE: Me listen? Listen to that? Listen to that nonsensical talk that gives you an ache in the belly? He's been nothing but an ache in the belly from the moment he came.

FARMER: He's entitled to his opinion.

WIFE: His opinion? What opinion would that be? That thing has an opinion? Are we to be dictated to by the opinion of a donkey in the fold?

FARMER: He's not like other donkeys.

WIFE: So what! I swear by Him who created and fashioned you that if that donkey of yours doesn't take himself off and keep his hands away from my bracelets I'll not stay on under this roof!

FARMER: Be sensible and calm down. After all, have we agreed to go along with his opinion?

WIFE: That was all that was missing . . . for you to go along with his opinion! All your life you've been master in your own house and your word has been law. Then off you go to the market and come back dragging along behind you your dear friend Mr Hassawi, whose every opinion you listen to.

FARMER: His opinions and help have gained for us an increase in price from the merchant.

WIFE: An increase? He won't allow us to enjoy it. He wants to waste it all on his crazy ideas, just as we're about to have all the expenses of Ramadan . . . and then don't forget there's the Feast directly after Ramadan and for which we'll need cake . . .

FARMER: And after the cake for the Feast we'll have to face up to the Big Feast for which we'll need a sheep.

WIFE: Knowing this as you do, why do you listen to his talk?

FARMER: Listening doesn't do any harm.

WIFE: Who said so? A lot of buzzing in the ears is worse than magic.

FARMER: What you're saying is that we should tell him to keep his mouth shut?

WIFE: With lock and bolt . . . and put a sock in it! He's a donkey and must remain a donkey and you're the master of the house and must remain master of the house. You're not some tassel on a saddlebag at this time of life. Have some pride man . . . you, with your grey hairs!

FARMER: So I'm a tassel on a saddlebag?

WIFE: You're getting that way, I swear it. Your dear friend Hassawi is almost all-powerful here.

FARMER: How all-powerful, woman? I still have the reins in my hand.

HASSAWI (*To himself*):   The reins?

WIFE: All right, what are you waiting for? Why don't you put the bridle on him as from now?

FARMER: And what does it matter if we let him ramble on as he wants?

HASSAWI (*To himself*):   Ramble on?

WIFE: I'm frightened of all this rambling and rumbling of his.

FARMER: What are you frightened of?

WIFE: That he'll try to fool you and you'll believe him.

FARMER: Believe him? Why should I? Who said I was a donkey?

WIFE: The donkey's there in front of you and he's had his say.

FARMER: Talking's one thing and action's another.

WIFE: What action are you talking about . . . you've let the rope go.

FARMER: You're saying I should tie him by the neck?

WIFE: Like every other donkey.

FARMER: But he's human, woman.

WIFE: Originally he was a donkey. When you bought him from the donkey market, when you paid good money for him, he was a donkey, and so his place is out there in the fold and he mustn't enter the house or have a say in things. That's how it should be. If you don't like it I'll go out and call upon the neighbours to bear witness. I'll say to them: "Come to my rescue, folk . . . my man's gone crazy in the head and has bought a donkey from the market which he's made into a human and whose opinions he's listening to."

FARMER: Don't be mad, woman!

WIFE: By the Prophet, I'll do it . . .

FARMER: All right, keep quiet . . . that's it!

WIFE: What d'you mean, "That's it?" Explain!

FARMER: We'll go back to how we were and relax. Hey, you, Hassawi, listen here!

HASSAWI: Sir!

FARMER: See, this business of my asking your opinion and your asking mine doesn't work. I'm the man with the say-so round here, and all you've got to do is obey. What I mean is that that mouth of yours mustn't utter a word . . . understand? Go off to the fold while I arrange about your work.

HASSAWI: Certainly, but would you just allow me to say something . . . one last word?

WIFE: What cheek! He's told you that you shouldn't talk, that you should keep your mouth closed and shut up. You really are a cheeky fellow!

HASSAWI: That's it then . . . I've closed my mouth and shut up. With your permission. (*He goes out*)

SCENE THREE

Outside the door of the FARMER's *house* HASSAWI *suddenly sees his companion, the* FIRST UNEMPLOYED, *approaching and leading the original donkey. The two friends embrace.*

HASSAWI (*To his companion*): Tell me . . . what did you do?

FIRST UNEMPLOYED: And you? How did you get on?

HASSAWI: I'll tell you right now. How, though, did you know I was here?

FIRST UNEMPLOYED: I walked along far behind you without your noticing. Tell me . . . what happened with our friend the owner of the donkey?

HASSAWI: You're well rid of him. He's an idiotic man who doesn't know where his own good lies. And why have you now come back with the donkey?

FIRST UNEMPLOYED: We don't need it. Things are settled . . . the good Lord's settled them.

HASSAWI: How's that?

FIRST UNEMPLOYED: We've found work.

HASSAWI: You've found work?

FIRST UNEMPLOYED: For you and me.

HASSAWI: Where? Tell me quickly!

FIRST UNEMPLOYED: After I left you and went off, I and the donkey, I found a large field where there were people sowing. I said them: "Have you got any work?" "Lots," they said . . . "for you and ten like you." I said to them: "I've got someone with me." "You're welcome," they said to me, "Go and bring him along immediately and start working." So I came to you right away.

HASSAWI: Extraordinary! There we were absolutely dying to get work, remember? People used to look at us and say "Off with you, you down-and-out tramps, off with the two of you . . . we've got no work for down-and-outs!"

FIRST UNEMPLOYED: It seems that having the donkey alongside me improved my reputation!

HASSAWI: You're right. Don't people always say "He works like a donkey"? A donkey means work just as a horse means honour. Don't people say that the riding of horses brings honour, that dogs are good guards, and that cats are thieves?

FIRST UNEMPLOYED: Yes, by God, that's right. They saw me with the donkey and said to themselves, "He can't be a down-and-out tramp . . . he must be one for hard work," so they took me on my face value and you sight unseen . . . on the basis of my recommendation!

HASSAWI: Your recommendation or the donkey's?

FIRST UNEMPLOYED: The donkey's. It actually got the work for both you and me. Isn't it only fair that we should return it to its owner?

HASSAWI: That's only fair.

FIRST UNEMPLOYED: What shall we say to him?

HASSAWI: We'll tell him to take back his donkey.

FIRST UNEMPLOYED: And you . . . didn't you pretend to be his donkey and tie the halter round your neck?

HASSAWI: He'll now prefer the real donkey.

FIRST UNEMPLOYED: Look, instead of handing over the donkey to him and getting into all sorts of arguments, with him asking us where the donkey was and where we were, we'll tie the donkey up for him in front of his house and clear off. What d'you think?

HASSAWI: Much the best idea . . . let's get going.

They tie the donkey to the door of the house, then knock at the door and disappear from view. The door opens and the FARMER appears.

FARMER (*Sees the donkey and is astonished and shouts*):   Come along, woman!

WIFE (*Appearing at the door*):   What's up?

FARMER: Look and see!

WIFE: What?

FARMER: He's been transformed again . . . Hassawi's become a donkey like he was at the market. He's exactly the same as he was when I bought him.

WIFE: Thanks be to God . . . how generous you are, O Lord!

FARMER: Yes, but . . .

WIFE: But what? What else do you want to say?

FARMER: But we're the cause.

WIFE: Why, though? What did we do to him?

FARMER: We did the same as his father did to him . . . he silenced him and turned him into a donkey!

WIFE: And what's wrong with him being a donkey? At least we can ride him.

FARMER: You're right. When he was a human with a brain he was useless for riding.

WIFE: And what did we need his brain for? What we want is something to ride, something that's going to bear our weight and take us from one place to another. Give thanks to the Lord, man, for returning your useful donkey to you.

FARMER (*Gently stroking the donkey's head*): Don't hold it against us, Hassawi! Fate's like that. I hope you're not annoyed. For us, though, you're still as you were . . . Mr Hassawi.

WIFE: Are you still at it, man? Are you still murmuring sweet nothings to that donkey? Mind . . . he'll go back to speaking again!

The FARMER *leads his donkey away in silence towards the fold, while the* WIFE *lets out shrill cries of joy.*

Questions for Discussion and Writing

1. How does the conversation between the two unemployed laborers create sympathy for their plight and set up the premise of the play—if only they were donkeys they would have better lives than they do as human beings?

2. How do descriptions of the two CHARACTERS and the variety of sound effects communicate the time, SETTING, and social circumstances necessary to understand the action of the play?

3. How would you characterize the farmer on whom they play their trick? What persuades him to accept the "donkey's" story?

4. How do the wife's reactions to the "donkey" in human form offer insight into her character?

5. How do the "donkey's" suggestions (that are initially so well received) for improving their lives bring him into conflict with the farmer and his wife?

6. To what extent do you think al-Hakim is expressing criticism of the inertia and time-worn traditions of Egyptian society when the farmer and his wife no longer view the human "donkey" as a blessing and wish he were a real donkey instead?

7. What features of this play suggest al-Hakim adapted it from a well-known Egyptian folktale?

8. Names may have a special significance. Describe the origin of your first, middle, or last name. To what extent does it express your cultural heritage, religious tradition, or forebears? Do you have a nickname that offers an interesting contrast to the name given to you at birth?

WRITING ABOUT CHARACTERIZATION AND SETTING

Characterization and Setting in Short Fiction

The study of CHARACTER in fiction, drama, and poetry involves discovering clues the author has provided to understand the forces shaping character, a term that not only refers to individuals in a fictional work but to a whole matrix of characteristics that an individual possesses, and discovering how these character traits reveal themselves through specific consequences. Writers use a variety of means to create and develop fictional characters.

An author can use direct methods of revealing character through statements made by an OMNISCIENT NARRATOR. The author's attitude toward the character may express itself directly through editorial comments or by directly describing the character's personality, as does Alasdair Gray in describing the protagonist in "The Crank That Made the Revolution" ("No harder-headed, clearer-sighted individual than McMenamy ever existed, as his crankshaft proves").

More typically, authors use indirect methods to reveal character. These include descriptions of physical appearance, dress and mannerisms, names that have metaphorical or associative significance, as well as the character's relationships with other people, places, and things, and the dialogue. A character's thoughts and feelings (especially those thoughts as overheard by the reader or commented on by the author) and the opinions and judgments of other people regarding the character (bearing in mind that these are not direct comments by the author) also offer important indirect clues to understanding the forces shaping crucial personality traits. For example, Louise Erdrich in "The Bingo Van" offers important clues about the protagonist Lipsha through his comments on how working as a night watchman in a bar not only gives him a place to sleep and $20 a week, but as much "beef jerky, beer nuts, and spicy sausage sticks" as he could eat. Lipsha thinks "no food in a bar has a shelf life of less than 40 months. If you are what you eat I would live forever." Erdrich does not directly tell the reader what kind of person Lipsha is, but supplies more than enough information to give the reader insight into Lipsha's ironic, self-deprecatory frame of mind.

Characters presented in the same way throughout are referred to as ONE-DIMENSIONAL, or STOCK, or STEREOTYPED CHARACTERS. For example, the neighbor Swinburne in "Warrigal" is presented as continually incensed over the narrator's owning a wild pet dingo ("you'll have to get rid of that dingo before long," my neighbour Swinburne said to me across the fence. "Why he's an Asiatic wolf—"). Other characters are

172

presented less as types and more as individuals capable of complex motivations and reactions who change in response to a crisis or conflict in ways that make them seem like real people. For example, when we first encounter the long-suffering Noumbe in "Her Three Days," she is anxiously waiting for her husband ("three days for her alone, when she would have her husband Mustapha to herself . . . it was a long time since she had felt such emotion"). But as the hours stretch into days her mood goes through many stages. First she rationalizes his late arrival, until finally a fleeting thought—"why do we allow ourselves to be men's playthings"—begins to lodge itself in her mind. Then when Mustapha and his friends finally do arrive, his cruel indifference leads her to purposely knock over the plates of food she has so carefully prepared. She also purposely humiliates him in front of his friends, an action that would have been unthinkable at the start of the story. In response to her crisis, Noumbe has changed in ways that lead her to insights about her life; she decides to do something about it and reveals a capacity for resisting the oppression of polygamy that earlier she did not appear to possess. Fully developed characters such as Noumbe surprise the reader by their reactions in ways one-dimensional characters never do.

By understanding the exact nature of the character's change in status, attitude, or relationships, we can create a plausible interpretation based on important events as to what significance is implied by this character's change between the beginning and the end of the story, poem, or play.

A student essay that analyzes character in a work of fiction can begin by identifying the character to be analyzed, then define the character's leading traits, habits, or characteristics, discuss key incidents that reveal the character's personality, and describe any changes or developments that occur in the character between the beginning and the end of the story. The essay might consider what changes take place in the thinking of the character over the span of the story. It might examine whether the evidence of the change is external (through action, dialogue, behavior) and/or internal (through self-revelation). Is the change consistent with what we know about the character? Is it believable?

In organizing the essay, the introduction should define central character traits; the body should pinpoint key incidents that reveal these character traits, especially those moments that suggest a character has clearly changed in the course of the story, poem, or play. The conclusion should clarify or elaborate the significance of the character's change as it relates to an important idea in the work. Most frequently, the title embodies the crisis or conflict that brings about the change in the life of the protagonist, as the bingo van does for Lipsha and the three days does for Noumbe.

Often, it helps to ask how characters represent opposing points of view or differences in attitude toward values. For example, the owner of the dingo is defined in contrast to the neighbor Swinburne in "Warrigal." Lipsha's willingness to relinquish tribal values contrasts with Serena's holding onto them in "The Bingo Van." In "Cairo Is a Small City," the engineer's live-for-the-moment attitude is defined in contrast with the Bedouins' methodical long-term planning in exacting their revenge.

The time and place in which a work is set, as well as the sights, sounds, and details of the location, collectively make up the SETTING. Setting serves to anchor the work, imbues it with a specific reality, and lends credibility to the experiences of the characters. Setting can play a role in creating a specific mood or emotional tone. For example, Njeri's nostalgia in "Hair Piece" for Mrs. Lane's is inseparable from her description of the congenial nature of the salon.

Setting can symbolize the values, ideals, attitudes, and emotional states of the characters and can reveal much about the social and cultural forces that shape their lives. For example, in "Her Three Days," Ousmane's description of Noumbe's house, the food she cooks, and the clothes she wears, not only reveal her mood of hopeful expectation but introduce the important theme of the injustice of polygamy.

Setting can enter the story as an active force and almost play the part of a character as it does in "Looking for a Rain God," where the persistent drought makes a family resort to taking measures they would normally not even consider. The descriptions of the blistering heat and dessicated landscape symbolize the corrosion of the family's physical strength and moral values. The importance of setting can be measured by the fact that no story would remain the same if its action and events occurred in an entirely different location.

An essay on setting might analyze how a character's response to the setting reveals important things about him or her. The introduction should identify where the action takes place and offer examples that illustrate the dominant impression the author creates. Try to pinpoint key phrases that evoke the look, sound, touch, and feel of the environment. The body of the essay should discuss the methods of description the writer uses, whether precise details, comparisons, allusions, or sensory images. The discussion should illuminate the role setting plays in enabling the reader to better understand the action of the story and the emotions of the characters. If appropriate, the discussion might address the extent to which the environment becomes an active force in the story, changing the action and determining the fate of the characters.

Characterization and Setting in Poetry

In poetry, we use the word SPEAKER to identify the character whose voice we hear speaking in the poem. The speaker is not necessarily the same person as the poet. She or he may represent one facet, or PERSONA, of the poet's personality or may be a wholly imaginary character.

The point of view the poet chooses to adopt colors our perception of the events in the poem. LYRIC poems are intensely personal expressions of a speaker's mood and are most likely to be perceived as expressing feelings identical to the poet's. For example, the "I" who speaks in Brodsky's poem "A Halt in the Desert" reflects on a past event in ways that seem indistinguishable from the poet. The speaker in NARRATIVE poems is distanced emotionally from the past events the poem describes, as in Ouologuem's in "When Black Men's Teeth Speak Out." In DESCRIPTIVE poems, such as those by Mtshali and Hongo, the sensibility of the speaker is revealed through the way the sense perceptions are presented. We know, for example, the speaker's attitude toward commercialization in "Sunset." In DRAMATIC poetry such as that of Kasdorf ("Mennonites") the poem is presented as if directly from the mind and heart of the speaker.

The major difference in characterization between a short story and a poem is that the greater part of characterization in a poem springs from the way a character speaks as opposed to the way he or she acts. Speakers reveal themselves—their emotions, beliefs, attitudes, values, and desires—in the process of articulating their response to a particular emotional conflict, crisis, or situation. An essay on character in poetry should analyze how the kind of voice you hear—ironic, amused, incensed—suggests a certain kind of person.

As with short stories, setting in poems can function literally or symbolically (for example, the "tomato field in bloom" discovered in the belly of the speaker in Ouologuem's "When Black Men's Teeth Speak Out" symbolizes his inner nonviolent, vegetarian nature).

Writing about setting in poetry entails discovering how descriptive images of sense, sight, sound, motion, taste, and touch are used to reveal the speaker's inner state. How does the description of setting help to establish the situation in which the speaker finds himself or herself? How do changes in setting relate to the development of thought in the organization of the poem? In a longer poem, you might investigate how change of setting from stanza to stanza brings out important facets of the speaker's personality.

Characterization and Setting in Drama

Characters in drama define themselves through what they say and what they do as well as through their appearance and gestures. Unlike fiction, we must infer what characters are thinking without direct access to their minds. Playwrights reveal the personality of characters through methods of characterization adapted to the limitations of the dramatic form. Dramas must compress action into what can be shown on the stage in two to three hours. Therefore, every moment in the play must communicate something important about the person speaking and make it possible for the audience to determine why the characters act as they do. Every speech and every action must divulge something about the characters, their backgrounds, intentions, and desires as they relate to other characters in the play. Consider what we can tell about the protagonist, "Man," in Abe's *Friends* in the following speech:

MAN (*nearly screaming*): I've had enough! I'm quite happy being alone. I'll thank you to stop your uncalled for meddling. I don't want your sympathy. I'm enjoying my life just the way it is.

"Man" reveals himself to be in a state of near hysteria, defensive, and somewhat incredulous that he should have to defend his right to live alone without having to share his apartment and provisions with eight strangers. The playwright's suggestion as to what tone of voice and gestures should accompany the speech provides invaluable information in enabling the audience to analyze the protagonist's character.

From the audience's point of view nothing is more important than that the characters be believable, and nothing creates credibility more quickly than consistency from scene to scene. When the audience can infer a motivation that explains behavior, then characters are believable. Playwrights must keep portrayals of characters simple, consistent, clear-cut, and plausible to allow an audience to grasp essential character traits over the course of a two- or three-hour performance.

Each of the characters in *Friends*, for example, is defined in terms of an easily grasped personality trait. The younger son is always aggressive, somewhat threatening, and intimidating; "Man" is outraged and increasingly frustrated over his inability to get anyone to understand his predicament; the middle daughter is flirtatious and sympathetic to the man's plight. Abe gives each of the characters one or two easily recognizable personality traits that remain consistent over the course of the play.

The essence of drama is CONFLICT. For this reason, the playwright's methods of characterization must bring to light unmistakable differences between one character and another. In al-Hakim's *The Donkey Market*, the unemployed laborer's desire to remain with the farmer and his wife brings him into direct conflict with the farmer's wife. She is unwilling to sell her few pieces of jewelry to provide the money to finance improvements to their irrigation system and tells her husband to get rid of the "donkey." Her actions reveal the kind of person she is. Thus, words and actions in combination with appearance, gestures, and tone of voice are the means by which playwrights reveal character.

Writing about character in drama requires you to focus on a significant figure, formulate a THESIS that discusses the most important aspect of that character's role in the play, and refer to points in the play that illustrate and clarify your thesis. For example, if you thought Abe was critical of a prevailing cultural value in modern Japan that placed society above the individual, you might explore how in different scenes every outside person to whom the "Man" goes for help (policeman, building superintendent, reporter, and even financée) side with the family rather than with him.

In deciding what can actually be shown on the stage, the playwright, in contrast to poets and short story writers, is limited to tangible props, materials, sets, and costumes. For example, al-Hakim cannot literally place a donkey market or thousands of unemployed laborers on the stage. For the audience, the sound of braying donkeys and the sight of two men with "ragged clothes and filthy appearance" must serve to symbolize what cannot be shown.

What the audience sees must allow it to grasp enough about the time, place, and social and historical circumstances in which the action takes place to understand the main connections between the setting and the world beyond. For example, a Japanese audience watching Abe's play would instantly be aware of how unusual it was for an individual to have a large apartment in Tokyo all to oneself.

Props, costumes, and scenery all help to establish the prevailing values as well as the actual time and place in which the events of the play occur. More important, the setting creates a framework that constitutes the starting point for the action in the play. The setting with which the play opens represents the status quo of things as they are and provides the audience with a sense of what is normal and usual as a frame of reference against which to perceive the emerging conflict as a disruption of the status quo.

The student approaching an essay on setting should pay close attention to the opening descriptions of scenes and any subsequent stage directions. How much detail do the stage directions give in describing the setting? If the stage directions are sparse, to what extent can the setting be reconstructed from the dialogue? To what extent is the setting literal and realistic or symbolic and representational? If it is symbolic, what do objects in the play represent?

Connections

1. To what extent do Lipsha's loss of his inherited gift of healing in "The Bingo Van" and the loss of the rain as a natural resource in "And We Sold the Rain" illustrate the theme of exploiting a traditional God-given resource for money?

2. How do the authors of "Warrigal," "You Will Forget," and "Mennonites" use descriptions to express startlingly similar attitudes toward the struggle to retain their cultural heritage when other forces are at work to encourage assimilation and rejection of this heritage? What difficulties do the protagonists in each of these works undergo in order to retain contact with their respective heritages?

3. How do both "Cairo Is a Small City" and "Looking for a Rain God" develop the theme of reliance on primitive tribal rituals? How does the treatment of this subject imply very different attitudes toward it on the part of Bessie Head and Nabil Gorgy?

4. How do both "Seventy Years Later" and "Cairo is a Small City" express

contrasting views on the role tradition plays in protecting or restricting women within these Islamic societies?

5. In both "Cairo Is a Small City" and "The Crank That Made the Revolution," the engineer protagonists are characterized in unflattering ways. How, for both writers, does being an engineer symbolize being insensitive and even antagonistic to nature and tradition? How does the fate of each engineer in these two very different stories, one set in Glasgow and one in Cairo, reveal each of the authors' attitudes toward the events portrayed in the stories?

6. What are the different aspects of Egyptian culture that you see in "Cairo Is a Small City" and in *The Donkey Market* and, more important, how is al-Hakim's attitude toward time-honored ways and traditions very different from that of Nabil Gorgy?

7. How do the authors of "Her Three Days" and "Seventy Years Later" express similar criticisms of the traditional restrictions placed on women in Mali and Syria, respectively, and to what extent do the protagonists in these two stories rebel against the status quo?

8. How do "The Crank That Made the Revolution" and "And We Sold the Rain" use similar descriptive techniques by extending the literal to fantastic extremes to satirize the exploitation of the natural by turning it into a salable commodity? To what extent do these stories satirize the urge to mechanize, or the impulse to specialize, and the destructive uses of human ingenuity? In what sense does the exploitation of the natural destroy it in both works? How do both satires express the authors' condemnation of this process?

9. How is Brodsky's attitude in "A Halt in the Desert" (toward preservation of an endangered cultural tradition) expressed in images surprisingly similar to those expressed by the author of "Cairo Is a Small City"?

10. How is the encroachment of modernization explored in Brodsky's poem and in Mtshali's "Sunset," and how do specific descriptions of setting express the attitude of each author toward this process?

11. How do the authors of "When Black Men's Teeth Speak Out" and "Who Among You Knows the Essence of Garlic" use imagery drawn from a particular culture's associations with specific foods to symbolize the spiritual nourishment provided by one's cultural heritage?

12. How does sacrificial, ritualized murder play an important part in the imagery of "When Black Men's Teeth Speak Out" and the plot of "Cairo Is a Small City"? How does each work develop as an uncovering of a substratum that is always present, but hidden, just out of sight of the contemporary world in Mali and in Egypt?

13. To what extent do the plays by Abe and al-Hakim criticize anachronistic attitudes that are perceived as dominant values—the value of the group over the individual in Japan and the value of tradition over innovation in Egypt?

14. How do both Hongo and Esteves in their respective poems express that the richness of a culture depends on diversity?

15. How do Njeri in "Hair Piece" and Hongo in his poem dramatize the importance of features of a cultural heritage of which the outside world remains unaware?

2

Coming of Age

"The old believe everything. The middle aged suspect everything. The young know everything."

— *Oscar Wilde*

In everyone's life there are moments of psychological insight, moments of self-knowledge, and self-definition when you see yourself as being a certain kind of person. Sometimes these moments correspond with doing away with a false image of yourself. Sometimes it is the moment when you see yourself, not as you would wish, but as you actually appear to others. Frequently, the experiences you have while in college are decisive in this psychological turning point, this moment of an emerging sense of your real self. It is a moment when you actually define yourself apart from your family and reconcile often-conflicting roles you may have been playing in trying on different identities. A sense of self develops by establishing a connection among who you are now, who you were in the past, and who you would like to be in the future. These moments of insight may be private psychological turning points or they may occur in the context of ceremonies that initiate the individual into adulthood within a community.

These crucial moments in which individuals move from childhood innocence to adult awareness often involve learning a particular society's rules governing values, knowledge, what should or should not be done under different circumstances, and expectations as to how the individual should present himself or herself in a wide variety of situations. Because this chapter is rich in a wide variety of perspectives, it invites you to make discoveries about turning points in your own life.

This chapter features stories that provide insight into the need people have in growing up to assert their own sense of individuality—often by defining themselves in opposition to the values held by the societies in which they live. An essay by the German writer Sabine Reichel, "Learning What Was Never Taught," tells of the difficulties she faced in finding out about the Holocaust from her teachers. The lure of sophistication to a naive nineteen-year-old girl in Italy is explored in Dino Buzzati's surrealistic tale "The Falling Girl." Set in Poland during World War II, Jerzy Kosinski's tale describes a young boy's first experience with the consequences of jealousy and revenge.

179

Unexpectedly acquired high intelligence transforms the outlook of a mentally disadvantaged young man in a story from the United States by Daniel Keyes. A child in Lebanon discovers the truth behind her mother's divorce in Hanan al-Shaykh's "The Persian Carpet."

You belong to a family but often choose your friends as a way of discovering your own identity. Two teenage boys in Brazil discover that friendship is an unusually fragile commodity in Clarice Lispector's "A Sincere Friendship." In "China" by the African-American writer Charles Johnson, when a middle-aged mailman takes up kung-fu, his relationship with his wife and friends alters irrevocably.

Poetry is one of the most powerful ways in which people come to know themselves, externalizing thoughts, memories, and associations. The works of poetry in this chapter are intended to offer insight into the role poetry can play in developing self-awareness. England's poet laureate, Ted Hughes, creates a compelling portrait of the struggle to live in "Examination at the Womb-Door." In "I Found It," Fadwa Tuqan, one of the Arab world's best-known poets, draws on imagery from the Sufi tradition to express her sense of self-realization. Maurice Kenny, a Mohawk Indian, in "Sometimes . . . Injustice" depicts the quixotic circumstances that shaped his destiny. From the United States, Grace Caroline Bridges in "Lisa's Ritual, Age 10" creates an indelible portrait of the traumatic psychological effects of sexual abuse on a young girl. Eavan Boland, in "Anorexic," speaks of the difficulties of coming of age for women in Ireland through the metaphor of self-starvation. From China, Xu Gang, in "Red Azalea on the Cliff," describes how what is most worth having is often hardest to achieve. The struggle simply to survive to adulthood in Newark is the subject of the African-American poet Imamu Amiri Baraka (LeRoi Jones) in "An Agony. As Now." The psychological costs of independence are confronted in "The Youngest Daughter," by the Chinese-American writer Cathy Song. From Mexico, Octavio Paz, in "The Street," enters an eerie twilight land where pursuer and pursued are different aspects of the speaker's own personality.

Lastly, Leonard Schrader's screenplay adapted from the Argentinian writer Manuel Puig's novel, *Kiss of the Spider Woman*, shows how two men sharing a jail cell, one a political prisoner and the other a homosexual window-dresser, start with nothing in common but are transformed through their relationship to help each other survive. This powerful work shows how, for both, identity is formed at the boundary between fantasy and reality.

Sabine Reichel

Learning What Was Never Taught

Sabine Reichel was born in Hamburg, Germany, in 1946, to a German actor and a Lithuanian artist. She grew up in West Germany (now Germany) and since 1965 has had a varied career as clothing designer, free-lance journalist, contributor of film criticism, lecturer, filmmaker, and social worker active in projects caring for homeless children. She immigrated to the United States in 1976. Dissatisfied with the silence she and others of her generation encountered concerning the systematic slaughter of European Jews by Hitler and the Nazis, Reichel spent six months interviewing soldiers and teachers whose lives seemed to her to represent Germany's amnesia. The autobiographical essay that resulted was published under the title What Did You Do in the War, Daddy? *(1989). In this chapter from that book, Reichel describes the moral complacency of those of her parents' generation who refuse to acknowledge the realities of the Nazi era and its lingering effects in contemporary Germany.*

I remember Herr Stock and Fräulein Lange without much affection. 1
Partly because they weren't extraordinary people, partly because they failed their profession. They were my history teachers, ordinary civil servants, singled out to bring the tumultuous events of European history into perspective for a classroom of bored German schoolkids.

As it happened, Hitler and the Third Reich were the subjects under 2
discussion when we were about fourteen years old, which is not to say that we discussed anything at all. I always thought that the decision to study the subject then was the result of a carefully calculated estimate by the school officials—as if German students were emotionally and intellectually ready to comprehend and digest the facts about Nazi Germany at exactly the age of 14.3. I learned much later that it had nothing to do with calculation; it was a matter of sequence. German history is taught chronologically, and Hitler was there when we were fourteen, whether we were ready or not.

Teaching this particular period was a thankless, though unavoid- 3
able, task. It was accompanied by sudden speech impediments, hoarse voices, uncontrollable coughs, and sweaty upper lips. A shift of mood would creep into the expansive lectures about kings and conquerors from the old ages, and once the Weimar Republic came to an end our teachers lost their proud diction.

We knew what it meant. We could feel the impending disaster. Only 4
a few more pages in the history book, one last nervous swallowing, and then in a casual but controlled voice, maybe a touch too loud, Fräulein Lange would ask, "We are now getting to a dark chapter in German history. I'm sure you all know what I mean?"

5   We did, because each of us had already skimmed through the whole book countless times in search of exotic material and, naturally, had come across the man with the mustache. We knew that she was referring to the terrible time between 1933 and 1945 when Germany fell prey to a devil in brown disguise. There were fifteen pages devoted to the Third Reich, and they were filled with incredible stories about a mass movement called National Socialism which started out splendidly and ended in a catastrophe for the whole world.

6   And then there was an extra chapter, about three-quarters of a page long. It was titled "The Extermination of the Jews," and I had read it in my room at home many times. I always locked the door because I didn't want anybody to know what I was reading. Six million Jews were killed in concentration camps, and as I read about Auschwitz and the gas chambers a wave of feelings—fearful fascination mingled with disgust—rushed over me. But I kept quiet. What monsters must have existed then. I was glad it had all happened in the past and that the cruel Germans were gone, because, as the book pointed out, the ones responsible were punished. I couldn't help feeling alarmed by something I couldn't put my finger on. How could so many innocent people be murdered?

7   There was no explanation for my unspoken questions, no answers in Fräulein Lange's helpless face. She seemed embarrassed and distraught, biting her lip and looking down at her orthopedic shoes while trying to summarize the Third Reich in fifty minutes. That worked out to one minute for every one million people killed in World War II . . . and twenty-six lines for six million Jews, printed on cheap, yellowish paper in a German history book published in 1960. An efficient time-saver, the German way.

8   We never read that particular chapter aloud with our teacher as we did with so many other ones. It was the untouchable subject, isolated and open to everyone's personal interpretation. There was a subtle, unspoken agreement between teacher and student not to dig into something that would cause discomfort on all sides. Besides, wanting to have known more about concentration camps as a student would have been looked upon as sick.

9   All things must come to an end, however, and once the Third Reich crumbled in our classroom to the sound of hastily turning pages, the suffocating silence was lifted. Everybody seemed relieved, especially Fräulein Lange, who became her jolly old self again. She had survived two world wars, she would survive a bunch of unappreciative teenagers.

10   In her late fifties in 1960, Fräulein Lange was a tiny, wrinkled woman who matched my idea of the institutional matron right down to her baggy skirt, steel-gray bun at the nape of her neck, and seamed stockings. She also had a trying predilection for Gutenberg, the inventer of movable type, whom we got to know more intimately than Hitler.

But she did her duty, more or less. German teachers had to teach history whether they liked it or not.

The teachers of my time had all been citizens of the Third Reich and therefore participants in an epoch that only a few years after its bitter collapse had to be discussed in a neutral fashion. But what could they possibly have said about this undigested, shameful subject to a partly shocked, partly bored class of adolescents? They had to preserve their authority in order to appear credible as teachers. Yet they were never put to the test. A critical imagination and unreasonable curiosity were unwelcome traits in all the classrooms of my twelve years in school. There was no danger that a precocious student would ever corner a teacher and demand more facts about the Nazis; they could walk away unscathed. We didn't ask our parents at home about the Nazis; nor did we behave differently in school.

The truth was that teachers were not allowed to indulge in private views of the Nazi past. There were nationwide guidelines for handling this topic, including one basic rule: The Third Reich and Adolf Hitler should be condemned unequivocally, without any specific criticism or praise. In reality, however, there were basically three ways to deal with the German past: (1) to go through the chapter as fast as possible, thereby avoiding any questions and answers; (2) to condemn the past passionately in order to deflate any suspicion about personal involvement; (3) to subtly legitimate the Third Reich by pointing out that it wasn't really as bad as it seemed; after all, there were the *Autobahnen.*

But no matter what the style of prevarication, the German past was always presented as an isolated, fatal accident, and so the possibility of investigating the cause of such a disaster was, of course, eliminated. Investigating crimes reinforces guilt. If something is programmatically depicted as black and bad, one doesn't look for different shades and angles. The Third Reich was out of reach for us; it couldn't be cut down to size.

I wonder now what could have been accomplished by a teacher who had taken part in the war—as a soldier, or a Nazi, or an anti-Nazi—and who talked candidly about his personal experience. But that never happened. Instead we were showered with numbers and dates. A few million dead bodies are impossible to relate to; raw numbers don't evoke emotions. Understanding is always personal. Only stories that humanized the numbers might have reached us. Had we been allowed to draw a connection between ourselves and the lives of other people, we might have been able to identify and feel compassion. But we were not aware of how blatantly insufficiently the past was handled in school because we resented the subject as much as the teacher who was somewhat entangled in it. Teenagers generally have little interest in history lessons; we learned facts and dates in order to pass a test or get a good grade and weren't convinced that comprehension of the warp and woof of historical events made any difference to the world or anybody in particular.

15   Another history teacher in a new school I attended in 1962 took an activist approach, mixing pathos and drama into a highly entertaining theatrical performance. To introduce highlights of the Third Reich there was no finer actor than Herr Stock. His voice was angry, his brows furrowed, and his fist was raised when he talked about the Führer's ferocious reign. Some of the more outgoing male teachers might even mimic parts of a Hitler speech. Yet when it came time to discuss the war itself, everything went downhill. His hands stopped moving, his voice became reproachful—no more victories to report. His saddest expression was reserved for the tragic end of "Germany under National Socialist dictatorship." It was time for the untouchable chapter again, the chapter that made Herr Stock nervously run his hands over his bald head, clear his throat, and mumble something about "six million Jews." It was the chapter that made him close the book with a clap, turn his back to the class, and announce with a palpable sigh of relief, "Recess."

16   In our next history lesson that chapter was usually forgotten, and nobody followed up with any questions. Happy to have escaped interrogation, Herr Stock turned the pages quickly, ignoring "unpleasantries" like capitulation, denazification, and the humiliating aftermath of a defeated nation. The dark clouds were gone, the past had been left behind, and he turned jocular and voluble again.

17   But Herr Stock wasn't really talking to us, he was rather trying to convince us of something, assuming the stance of a prosecutor. For him, the scandal wasn't the casualties of World War II, but the resulting partition of Germany and the malevolence of the Russians. Rage, anger, and disappointment over the lost war, always repressed or directed at others, could be openly displayed now, disguised as righteousness. "They" had stolen parts of Germany—no word of what we stole from other countries. The Russians were war criminals; the Germans were victims.

18   If I had been unexpectedly curious about Nazi Germany, I would have received little help from my history books. The conclusions to be drawn from a twelve-year catastrophe packed with enough dramatic material to fill a library were reduced to a few cryptic phrases: "The Germans showed very little insight" and "No real feelings of contrition were expressed." Teachers and history books were their own best examples of how to eviscerate the Nazi terror without ever really trying to come to terms with it.

19   But a new chapter, a new era, and a magic word—*Wirtschaftswunder*—soon revived our classroom and inspired another patriotic performance by Herr Stock. The undisputed star of German history education in the sixties was the remarkable reconstruction of postwar Germany. Now here was something an old schoolteacher could sink his teeth into. Gone were stutters and coughs. A nation of survivors had

rolled up its sleeves, and Herr Stock had certainly been one of them. Here was a chance to rehabilitate Germany and put some gloss over its rotten core. Postwar Germany was a genuine communal construction, a well-made product, mass-manufactured by and for the tastes of the former citizens of the Reich. Every German with two functioning hands had taken part in rebuilding Germany, and history teachers all over the country waxed nostalgic about the united strength, the grim determination, and the close camaraderie that had helped build up Germany brick by brick.

We schoolchildren couldn't have cared less about these achievements. We were all born under occupation; the postwar years were ours too and the memories of ruins and poverty were just as indelible—if not as traumatic—as they had been for our parents. But in his enthusiasm he overlooked the fact that his words were falling on deaf ears: we didn't like Herr Stock; nor did we trust or admire him. In all this excitement about the "economic miracle," another, even greater miracle was conveniently left unexplained. On page 219 of my history book, Germany was described as a nation living happily under National Socialism and a seemingly accepted Führer without any visible crisis of conscience. Yet only fourteen pages later the same *Volk* is depicted in the midst of an entirely different world, miraculously denazified and retrained, its murderous past neatly tucked away behind a tattered but nevertheless impenetrable veil of forgetfulness. [20]

How did they do it? The existing Federal Republic of Germany is only one state away from the Nazi Reich. Where did they unload the brown ballast? The role change from obedient Nazi citizen to obedient *Bundes* citizen went too smoothly from "*Sieg Heil!*" to democracy, and from marching brown uniforms to marching gray flannel suits. Where was the genuine substance which had initially constituted the basic foundation and ideology of the Third Reich? Could it still be there, hidden, repressed, put on ice? [21]

Such questions were never asked, or encouraged. The schoolteachers that I encountered were a uniformly intimidating group of people (with one glorious exception): older men and women who demanded respect, order, and obedience. They were always curbing my curiosity with the clobbering logic of people who get paid for controlling outbursts of independent thinking. Their assessment of my character in report cards read: "She talks too much and could accomplish more if she would be more diligent." [22]

Even though prohibited when I went to school, corporal punishment in many forms was still practiced with parental support, and my own classroom recollections are thick with thin-lipped, hawk-eyed, bespectacled men and women with mercilessly firm hands ready to take up the switch. [23]

I always felt powerless toward teachers, and all of these emotions crystallized in 1983, when I was preparing to interview one of them. I [24] couldn't help feeling a little triumphant. I was asking the questions now because I had discovered a slight spot on their white vests, something I couldn't see clearly when I was young and under their control. Now I had the power to make them nervous. My victory over German authority seemed complete. A schoolgirl's revenge?

25   But that wasn't all. I had a genuine interest in finding out how teachers in Germany feel today about their past failures. Had they found new ways to justify their damaging elisions, euphemisms, and omissions? More than any other age group, my generation was in desperate need not only of historical education but also of some form of emotional assistance from the adults who were linked to that not so distant yet unspeakable past.

26   In a way, I was looking for Herr Stock. But teachers as mediocre as he and Fräulein Lange had little to contribute to the kind of discussion I had in mind: I wanted the perspective of a teacher who had at least attempted to come to grips with his past. I was lucky to find one in Cäsar Hagener, a seventy-six-year-old former teacher and history professor. Hagener lives with his wife in a cozy, old-fashioned house with a garden in a suburb of Hamburg, in a quiet, safe neighborhood with lots of trees, many dachshunds, and little activity. He owns the type of one-family house, surrounded by a fence, that was commonly built in the thirties. A German house must have a fence. A house without a fence is disorderly, like a coat with a missing button.

27   Cäsar Hagener exuded integrity and an appealing friendliness—yet I found it impossible to forget that he had also been a teacher in the Third Reich. Hitler had envisioned a training program that would make every German youth "resilient as leather, fast as a weasel, and hard as Krupp steel." He believed that "too much education spoils the youth." (Not surprisingly, after a few years of dictatorship 30 percent of the university professors, including Jews, had left the country.)

28   In 1933, Cäsar Hagener was a teacher of pedagogy and history at a liberal school in Hamburg, and when he heard that Hitler was appointed Reichs Chancellor he happened to be studying Das Kapital together with some left-wing colleagues. "My friend said to me, 'It'll be over in no time. When you and I write a history book in twenty years, the Nazis will only be a footnote.'"

29   Even a skillful dictator like Hitler couldn't turn a country upside down overnight, and school life changed slowly under the Nazis. "But after 1934, the Nazis began to investigate the teachers' adaptation to the new order. Some were fired, and some were retrained in special camps. We had, of course, some 'overnight' Nazis who were strutting around in uniform, which didn't impress the students, who were quite critical. Later, in 1937, the young teachers were told to join the Nazi Party or else, so I joined the Party. Still, the first years of National Socialism were almost bearable."

30   However, at least once a week, teachers and students had to muster

for the raising of the swastika flag and the singing of the "Horst-Wessel-Lied" or other Nazi songs. The Führer's speeches were required listening on the popular *Volksempfänger* for teachers and older students, while the nazified text in the new schoolbooks read like this: "If a mental patient costs 4 Reichsmarks a day in maintenance, a cripple 5.50, and a criminal 3.50, and about 50,000 of these people are in our institutions, how much does it cost our state at a daily rate of 4 Reichsmarks—and how many marriage loans of 1,000 Reichsmarks per couple could have been given out instead?"

The new features of Nazi education like race hygiene and heredity theory were given different degrees of importance in different schools. Hagener prepared himself: "I made sure to get a class with school beginners because children of that age weren't taught history or any of that Nazi nonsense. Besides, as a teacher, you were pretty much independent in your classroom and could make your own decision about what to say and what to skip. There were ways of getting around the obnoxious Nazi ideology." 31

The first public action by the Nazis right after January 1933 was to purge public and school libraries of "Jewish and un-German elements," leaving empty spaces on the shelves, since new "literature" wasn't written yet and new schoolbooks, adapted to the Nazis' standards, weren't printed until 1936. That same year they initiated compulsory membership in the Hitler Youth, starting at the age of ten with boys organized into Jungvolk and Hitler Jungen and girls and young women into the Bund Deutscher Mädel (League of German Girls). What the Reich of the future needed were fearless, proud men of steel and yielding, fertile women—preferably blond—not effete intellectuals. 32

"The children can't be blamed for having been enthusiastic members of the Hitler Youth," Cäsar Hagener points out. "They grew up with that ideology and couldn't be expected to protect themselves from National Socialism; to do so, children would have had to be unaffected by all outside influences. It was their world, and the Hitler Youth programs were very attractive, with sports, contests, and decorations. It was possible for the son of a Communist or a Social Democrat to become a highly decorated Hitler Youth leader. I accuse the teachers who didn't perceive what was going on, and who taught Nazi ideology and glorified war, of having failed their profession." 33

In the last years of the war there was not much academic activity in Germany. The Nazi state was concerned with other problems besides education. Many schools were destroyed by bombs and virtually all Germans between fifteen and sixty years of age—Cäsar Hagener was drafted in 1940—were mobilized for the *Endkampf* (the final struggle) by the end of 1944. Hunger, death, and the will to survive prevailed over culture and education. Who needs to know algebra when the world is falling apart? 34

In 1945 denazification fever broke out in the defeated nation and 35 reversed the roles of master and servant. For over a decade the country had been straining to purge itself of "un-German elements," and now the occupying powers were trying to purge it of all Nazi elements. Yet their efforts only exposed the unfeasibility of such a gargantuan task, since it involved much more than just the Nazi Party and the SS. Twelve years under the swastika had produced all kinds of "literature," art, music, film—indeed, a whole society had to be taken apart and its guiding principles destroyed. Naturally, reforming the educational system was a high priority, and millions of schoolbooks were thrown out, but some had to be preserved. The specially assigned Allied education officers decided which schoolbooks could still be used (after tearing out a Nazi-contaminated page or censoring a suspicious chapter or two). The approved books were stamped, and were circulated until new ones could be printed, which wasn't until the early fifties.

36   "The British, our occupiers, did everything wrong, because nothing could be worked out intellectually. They came over here with certain expectations and this incredibly bad image of the enemy, and they were very surprised to find their task not as easy as they had thought. They tried to control the situation by being very strict."

37   Reforming the faculty was even more problematic, since many teachers had been forced to join the Nazi Party and it wasn't always easy to tell who was a "real" Nazi and who wasn't. As a rule of thumb, those who appeared to have cooperated unwillingly were permitted to continue teaching, younger teachers who had been educated under the Nazi regime were retrained in special seminars, while those who had been active supporters were barred from teaching for as long as two years.

38   Cäsar Hagener still gets angry over how easily former colleagues were rehired. "After 1945, nobody seemed to remember what a Nazi was, and people who I knew were definitely Nazis by nature landed on top again. I was one of a group of young teachers who protested violently against this tendency—and I felt like a McCarthy witch-hunter. I saw these people as criminals who did a lot of harm to us teachers."

39   Still, the main consideration was that teachers were badly needed. The war had wiped out a whole generation of young men, and keeping professionals from their profession in Germany after 1945 was as uneconomical as it was impractical: what was left was what Germany's children got. It's safe to say that by 1950 almost all teachers were back in schools and universities regardless of their past.

40   In the years immediately following the war, the few schools that were not badly damaged were overcrowded with children of all ages and several grades gathered together in one room. There was cardboard in place of windows, and opening umbrellas inside the school on rainy days was as natural as being sent home for a "cold-weather holiday" because there was no heat. The teacher had to be a good-humored ringmaster, innovative and full of stories; because of the book shortage,

he had to know his lessons by heart. The students also needed good memories, because there wasn't any paper. Arithmetic and grammar assignments were often written down on the margins of newspapers.

It might have been the only time in Germany when school lessons were extemporaneous, personal, and an accurate reflection of real life. School was suddenly a popular place where humanity prevailed over theory. Teachers were not merely authority figures but people who had been harmed by the war just like the students and their families, and much of the time was spent discussing how to steal potatoes and coal and other survival tactics, which were more pressing than Pythagoras. 41

How did a teacher in those years explain history while it was happening? The change from "Nazis are good" to "Nazis are bad" must have been a confusing experience for the uprooted, disillusioned children of the Third Reich. Children weren't denazified. They had to adapt to "democracy" without shedding a brown skin. All the values they had learned to defend so passionately crumbled before their eyes and the reality they once trusted was rearranged silently, without their consent. The glorious, thunderous Third Reich was a gyp. The Jews weren't "*Volks* enemy number one" anymore. And as for the Führer, he wasn't a superhuman hero, but a vicious little coward, a maniac who wanted to exterminate a whole people and almost succeeded. What irreparable mistrust must have become lodged in the minds of all these young Germans whose youth was trampled flat by goose-stepping jackboots. 42

But teachers didn't explain history at all. "I'm afraid to say that it didn't occur to the students to bring up Adolf in any form. We had all survived and dealt mostly with the effects of the war in a practical sense. I tried to do nice, positive things with the children, who had it bad enough as it was," Cäsar Hagener explains, and adds, almost surprised, "It is amazing how extremely apolitical we were. Any reflection was impossible under the circumstances, because everything was defined in terms of the struggle of daily life, which had a dynamic all by itself." 43

He also knows why the adolescents of the fifties and sixties were as uninquisitive as their teachers and parents were silent. "There was strong resentment toward the grown-ups. The teenagers had a fine sense for the things that didn't quite fit together with the Nazis. I didn't have any luck with my own three sons; they frustrated my desire to talk about the past by calling it lecturing, so I ended up talking about it mostly in foreign countries, where the people seemed to be more interested in it." 44

Things have changed radically during the last twenty years. There has been a small revolution in the German classroom. While teachers after the war were much younger and more outspoken than their predecessors, students became rebellious and undisciplined. 45

Cäsar Hagener remembers his school days. "My own generation 46 and my students lived in a very strict and conformist structure which existed much earlier than 1933. Sure, there were provocative and rebellious personalities, but this phenomenon of developing an independent mind is new. Today it wouldn't be possible to stand in front of a class in uniform and in all seriousness talk about racial theory. The students would die laughing."

47   German students today often know more facts about the Third Reich than both their parents and the immediate postwar generation, and are not afraid to ask questions. Yet their interest in Nazism is strictly intellectual, and they generally succeed in remaining emotionally detached. They don't know yet that they can't escape the past. Tragically, almost all of Cäsar Hagener's contemporaries have managed to escape their Nazi past. In his opinion: "You can't put a whole nation on the couch. I find my own contemporaries just plain terrible and I don't have much contact with many old friends anymore. In their eyes I'm too critical, a guy who fouls his own nest and who can't see the good sides of the Nazi era—which infuriates and bores me at the same time. They reject the radical examination of the past. But it's necessary, since we know better than most that terrible things can and did happen."

Questions for Discussion and Writing

1. What features of this essay allow the reader to share the struggle of a sensitive mind trying to clarify an issue that is of great importance to the writer? Where do you feel she is evolving a viewpoint that takes into account personal values and known facts?
2. How did her search for a satisfactory explanation about the way information concerning the Holocaust was taught change her relationships with her family and school authorities?
3. From the narrator's perspective, what was odd about the way in which the Holocaust was taught and the attitude of her teachers toward the events? In what way did accounts in history books of the postwar reconstruction not correspond with her own memories as a child during this period?
4. How is the way this essay is constructed designed to raise expectations as to the kinds of answers she would ultimately receive?
5. How does her interview with Herr Hagener provide insights into the kinds of pressures to which teachers were subjected and give her some of the answers for which she has been searching?
6. Has the way in which any historical event was taught to you raised questions comparable to Reichel's, where you wanted to get more information? Describe your experiences.
7. Speculate about why a member of your family or a relative acts the way he or she does. What clues from the past do you think account for this person's present behavior?
8. Based on interviews with parents and grandparents, compare schooling as it was in their day with what it is now.

Dino Buzzati

The Falling Girl

Dino Buzzati (1906–1972) spent most of his working life in Milan as an editor and correspondent for the Corriere della Sera, *one of Italy's largest daily newspapers. As both painter and writer, he used fantasy and allegory to circumvent the censorship of the arts under fascism in Italy. A prolific writer, Buzzati uses satire and paradox to combine fantasy with reality in order to assail the materialistic values of contemporary society. He is the author of poems, librettos, a children's book, hundreds of short stories in collections such as* Catastrophe and Other Stories *(1982) and* The Siren *(1984), and novels, including* Barnabo of the Mountains *(1933) and the internationally acclaimed* The Tartar Steppe *(1952). His innovative play* A Clinical Case *(1955) was translated into French by Albert Camus and performed on stages throughout the world. "The Falling Girl," translated by Lawrence Venuti, from his short story collection* Restless Nights *(1983), is a typical Buzzatian mixture of surrealism, journalistic coverage of a human interest story, and social commentary on the effects of the economic boom in post–World War II Italy.*

Marta was nineteen. She looked out over the roof of the skyscraper, and seeing the city below shining in the dusk, she was overcome with dizziness. 1

The skyscraper was silver, supreme and fortunate in that most beautiful and pure evening, as here and there the wind stirred a few fine filaments of cloud against an absolutely incredible blue background. It was in fact the hour when the city is seized by inspiration and whoever is not blind is swept away by it. From that airy height the girl saw the streets and the masses of buildings writhing in the long spasm of sunset, and at the point where the white of the houses ended, the blue of the sea began. Seen from above, the sea looked as if it were rising. And since the veils of the night were advancing from the east, the city became a sweet abyss burning with pulsating lights. Within it were powerful men, and women who were even more powerful, furs and violins, cars glossy as onyx, the neon signs of nightclubs, the entrance halls of darkened mansions, fountains, diamonds, old silent gardens, parties, desires, affairs, and, above all, that consuming sorcery of the evening which provokes dreams of greatness and glory. 2

Seeing these things, Marta hopelessly leaned out over the railing and let herself go. She felt as if she were hovering in the air, but she was falling. Given the extraordinary height of the skyscraper, the streets and squares down at the bottom were very far away. Who knows how long it would take her to get there. Yet the girl was falling. 3

At that hour the terraces and balconies of the top floors were filled 4 with rich and elegant people who were having cocktails and making silly conversation. They were scattered in crowds, and their talk muffled the music. Marta passed before them and several people looked out to watch her.

5   Flights of that kind (mostly by girls, in fact) were not rare in the skyscraper and they constituted an interesting diversion for the tenants; this was also the reason why the price of those apartments was very high.

6   The sun had not yet completely set and it did its best to illuminate Marta's simple clothing. She wore a modest, inexpensive spring dress bought off the rack. Yet the lyrical light of the sunset exalted it somewhat, making it chic.

7   From the millionaires' balconies, gallant hands were stretched out toward her, offering flowers and cocktails. "Miss, would you like a drink? . . . Gentle butterfly, why not stop a minute with us?"

8   She laughed, hovering, happy (but meanwhile she was falling): "No, thanks, friends. I can't. I'm in a hurry."

9   "Where are you headed?" they asked her.

10   "Ah, don't make me say," Marta answered, waving her hands in a friendly good-bye.

11   A young man, tall, dark, very distinguished, extended an arm to snatch her. She liked him. And yet Marta quickly defended herself: "How dare you, sir?" and she had time to give him a little tap on the nose.

12   The beautiful people, then, were interested in her and that filled her with satisfaction. She felt fascinating, stylish. On the flower-filled terraces, amid the bustle of waiters in white and the bursts of exotic songs, there was talk for a few minutes, perhaps less, of the young woman who was passing by (from top to bottom, on a vertical course). Some thought her pretty, others thought her so-so, everyone found her interesting.

13   "You have your entire life before you," they told her, "why are you in such a hurry? You still have time to rush around and busy yourself. Stop with us for a little while, it's only a modest little party among friends, really, you'll have a good time."

14   She made an attempt to answer but the force of gravity had already quickly carried her to the floor below, then two, three, four floors below; in fact, exactly as you gaily rush around when you are just nineteen years old.

15   Of course, the distance that separated her from the bottom, that is, from street level, was immense. It is true that she began falling just a little while ago, but the street always seemed very far away.

16   In the meantime, however, the sun had plunged into the sea; one could see it disappear, transformed into a shimmering reddish mushroom. As a result, it no longer emitted its vivifying rays to light up the

girl's dress and make her a seductive comet. It was a good thing that the windows and terraces of the skyscraper were almost all illuminated and the bright reflections completely gilded her as she gradually passed by.

Now Marta no longer saw just groups of carefree people inside the apartments; at times there were even some businesses where the employees, in black or blue aprons, were sitting at desks in long rows. Several of them were young people as old as or older than she, and weary of the day by now, every once in a while they raised their eyes from their duties and from typewriters. In this way they too saw her, and a few ran to the windows. "Where are you going? Why so fast? Who are you?" they shouted to her. One could divine something akin to envy in their words. [17]

"They're waiting for me down there," she answered. "I can't stop. Forgive me." And again she laughed, wavering on her headlong fall, but it wasn't like her previous laughter anymore. The night had craftily fallen and Marta started to feel cold. [18]

Meanwhile, looking downward, she saw a bright halo of lights at the entrance of a building. Here long black cars were stopping (from the great distance they looked as small as ants), and men and women were getting out, anxious to go inside. She seemed to make out the sparkling of jewels in that swarm. Above the entrance flags were flying. [19] [20]

They were obviously giving a large party, exactly the kind that Marta dreamed of ever since she was a child. Heaven help her if she missed it. Down there opportunity was waiting for her, fate, romance, the true inauguration of her life. Would she arrive in time?

She spitefully noticed that another girl was falling about thirty meters above her. She was decidedly prettier than Marta and she wore a rather classy evening gown. For some unknown reason she came down much faster than Marta, so that in a few moments she passed by her and disappeared below, even though Marta was calling her. Without doubt she would get to the party before Marta; perhaps she had a plan all worked out to supplant her. [21]

Then she realized that they weren't alone. Along the sides of the skyscraper many other young women were plunging downward, their faces taut with the excitement of the flight, their hands cheerfully waving as if to say: look at us, here we are, entertain us, is not the world ours? [22]

It was a contest, then. And she only had a shabby little dress while those other girls were dressed smartly like high-fashion models and some even wrapped luxurious mink stoles tightly around their bare shoulders. So self-assured when she began the leap, Marta now felt a tremor growing inside her; perhaps it was just the cold; but it may have been fear too, the fear of having made an error without remedy. [23]

It seemed to be late at night now. The windows were darkened one [24] after another, the echoes of music became more rare, the offices were empty, young men no longer leaned out from the windowsills extending their hands. What time was it? At the entrance to the building down below—which in the meantime had grown larger, and one could now distinguish all the architectural details—the lights were still burning, but the bustle of cars had stopped. Every now and then, in fact, small groups of people came out of the main floor wearily drawing away. Then the lights of the entrance were also turned off.

25   Marta felt her heart tightening. Alas, she wouldn't reach the ball in time. Glancing upwards, she saw the pinnacle of the skyscraper in all its cruel power. It was almost completely dark. On the top floors a few windows here and there were still lit. And above the top the first glimmer of dawn was spreading.

26   In a dining recess on the twenty-eighth floor a man about forty years old was having his morning coffee and reading his newspaper while his wife tidied up the room. A clock on the sideboard indicated 8:45. A shadow suddenly passed before the window.

27   "Alberto!" the wife shouted. "Did you see that? A woman passed by."

28   "Who was it?" he said without raising his eyes from the newspaper.

29   "An old woman," the wife answered. "A decrepit old woman. She looked frightened."

30   "It's always like that," the man muttered. "At these low floors only falling old women pass by. You can see beautiful girls from the hundred-and-fiftieth floor up. Those apartments don't cost so much for nothing."

31   "At least down here there's the advantage," observed the wife, "that you can hear the thud when they touch the ground."

32   "This time not even that," he said, shaking his head, after he stood listening for a few minutes. Then he had another sip of coffee.

Questions for Discussion and Writing

1. Why is it an advantage for Buzzati to tell Marta's story from the POINT OF VIEW of an OMNISCIENT NARRATOR who can describe both what Marta thinks and feels and how others feel about her?
2. How does the story chart the movement of Marta from naivete to self-awareness? To what extent does her journey correct the false image she has of herself?
3. How does Buzzati transform the figurative concept of "falling" (as in "falling in love") into the literal premise of the story? Describe the change that takes place in Marta as she falls. Do you find evidence that her initial optimism and idealism give way to envy, fear, competition, and even despair?
4. The name Marta suggests "martyr." What details might confirm that she is sacrificing herself to a dream?
5. To what extent does the phrase "flights of that kind" suggest Marta's story is

characteristic of nineteen-year-olds? What assumptions and qualities does Marta exhibit that are typical of this age in terms of energy, idealism, and a belief that choices will always be available?

6. What do you make of the fact that the couple at the bottom of the skyscraper fails to hear a "thud"? Do you interpret the lack of this sound as having positive or negative significance? Does this mean Marta has landed lightly and simply walked away, that she has not made an "impact" on society, or that she continues to fall? Explain your interpretation.

7. In an essay, discuss the way this story might be viewed as a parable. What issues are involved?

8. How do you see this story, as a parable of youth and old-age, social striving, an idealist who has a martyr complex, or simply the experience of what it is like to be nineteen?

Jerzy Kosinski

The Miller's Tale

Jerzy Kosinski (1933–1991) was born in Lodz, Poland. When the Nazis occu-
pied Poland in 1939 he was sent by his parents to live in the countryside, where
his nightmarish experiences later formed the basis for his classic of Holocaust
fiction, The Painted Bird *(1965). After receiving degrees in sociology and his-*
tory, he immigrated to the United States in 1957 and published two nonfiction
books, The Future Is Ours Comrade *(1960) and* No Third Path *(1962), un-*
der the pseudonym Joseph Novak. In 1973, he was elected the president of the
American Center for P.E.N., the international writer's association, and served
two terms, working effectively for the release of imprisoned writers throughout
the world. A prolific writer, Kosinski's second novel, Steps *(1968), received the*
National Book Award. In 1970 he received the American Academy of Arts and
Letters Award for Literature. His other novels include The Devil Tree *(1973),*
Cockpit *(1975),* Blind Date *(1977),* Passion Play *(1979),* Pinball *(1982),*
and The Hermit of 69th Street *(1988). His 1971 novel* Being There, *a satire*
on American politics and the impact of television, was made into the Academy
Award–winning 1979 film (starring Peter Sellers) for which Kosinski wrote
the screenplay. Burdened by an increasingly serious heart condition, Kosinski
committed suicide in May 1991. The protagonists in his fiction are always in
recoil against outside forces that they must confront and manipulate in order to
survive. It is characteristic of Kosinski's art that every word is there for a rea-
son. His stories are unique in their ability to engage the reader and bring about
genuine self-awareness. "The Miller's Tale," drawn from The Painted Bird,
describes an episode in the life of a young boy who, like Kosinski himself, was
left to survive as best he could among peasants in Eastern Europe during
World War II. The protagonist, a seven-year-old boy known only as "the
gypsy," learns firsthand of the effects of jealousy and revenge.

1   I was now living at the miller's, whom the villagers had nicknamed
Jealous. He was more taciturn than was usual in the area. Even when
neighbors came to pay him a visit, he would just sit, taking an occasional sip of vodka, and drawling out a word once in a while, lost in
thought or staring at a dried-up fly stuck to the wall.

2   He abandoned his reverie only when his wife entered the room.
Equally quiet and reticent, she would always sit down behind her husband, modestly dropping her gaze when men entered the room and
furtively glanced at her.

3   I slept in the attic directly above their bedroom. At night I was
awakened by their quarrels. The miller suspected his wife of flirting
and lasciviously displaying her body in the fields and in the mill before
a young plowboy. His wife did not deny this, but sat passive and still.
Sometimes the quarrel did not end. The enraged miller lit candles in the

room, put on his boots, and beat his wife. I would cling to a crack in the floorboards and watch the miller lashing his naked wife with a horsewhip. The woman cowered behind a feather quilt tugged off the bed, but the man pulled it away, flung it on the floor, and standing over her with his legs spread wide continued to lash her plump body with the whip. After every stroke, red blood-swollen lines would appear on her tender skin.

The miller was merciless. With a grand sweep of the arm he looped the leather thong of the whip over her buttocks and thighs, slashed her breasts and neck, scourged her shoulders and shins. The woman weakened and lay whining like a puppy. Then she crawled toward her husband's legs, begging forgiveness. 4

Finally the miller threw down the whip and, after blowing out the candle, went to bed. The woman remained groaning. The following day she would cover her wounds, move with difficulty, and wipe away her tears with bruised, cut palms. 5

There was another inhabitant of the hut: a well-fed tabby cat. One day she was seized by a frenzy. Instead of mewing she emitted half-smothered squeals. She slid along the walls as sinuously as a snake, swung her pulsating flanks, and clawed at the skirts of the miller's wife. She growled in a strange voice and moaned, her raucous shrieks making everyone restless. At dusk the tabby whined insanely, her tail beating her flanks, her nose thrusting. 6

The miller locked the inflamed female in the cellar and went to his mill, telling his wife that he would bring the plowboy home for supper. Without a word the woman set about preparing the food and table. 7

The plowboy was an orphan. It was his first season of work at the miller's farm. He was a tall, placid youth with flaxen hair which he habitually pushed back from his sweating brow. The miller knew that the villagers gossiped about his wife and the boy. It was said that she changed when she gazed into the boy's blue eyes. Heedless of the risk of being noticed by her husband, she impulsively hiked her skirt high above her knees with one hand, and with the other pushed down the bodice of her dress to display her breasts, all the time staring into the boy's eyes. 8

The miller returned with the young man, carrying in a sack slung over his shoulder, a tomcat borrowed from a neighbor. The tomcat had a head as large as a turnip and a long, strong tail. The tabby was howling lustingly in the cellar. When the miller released her, she sprang to the center of the room. The two cats began to circle one another mistrustfully, panting, coming nearer and nearer. 9

The miller's wife served supper. They ate silently. The miller sat at the middle of the table, his wife on one side and the plowboy on the other. I ate my portion squatting by the oven. I admired the appetites of the two men: huge chunks of meat and bread, washed down with gulps of vodka, disappeared in their throats like hazelnuts. 10

11   The woman was the only one who chewed her food slowly. When she bowed her head low over the bowl the plowboy would dart a glance faster than lightning at her bulging bodice.

12   In the center of the room the tabby suddenly arched her body, bared her teeth and claws, and pounced on the tomcat. He halted, stretched his back, and sputtered saliva straight into her inflamed eyes. The female circled him, leaped toward him, recoiled, and then struck him in the muzzle. Now the tomcat stalked around her cautiously, sniffing her intoxicating odor. He arched his tail and tried to come at her from the rear. But the female would not let him; she flattened her body on the floor and turned like a millstone, striking his nose with her stiff, outstretched paws.

13   Fascinated, the miller and the other two stared silently while eating. The woman sat with a flushed face; even her neck was reddening. The plowboy raised his eyes, only to drop them at once. Sweat ran down through his short hair and he continually pushed it away from his hot brow. Only the miller sat calmly eating, watching the cats, and glancing casually at his wife and guest.

14   The tomcat suddenly came to a decision. His movements became lighter. He advanced. She moved playfully as if to draw back, but the male leapt high and flopped onto her with all fours. He sank his teeth in her neck and intently, tautly, plunged directly into her without any squirming. When satiated and exhausted, he relaxed. The tabby, nailed to the floor, screamed shrilly and sprang out from under him. She jumped onto the cooled oven and tossed about on it like a fish, looping her paws over her neck, rubbing her head against the warm wall.

15   The miller's wife and the plowboy ceased eating. They stared at each other, gaping over their food-filled mouths. The woman breathed heavily, placed her hands under her breasts and squeezed them, clearly unaware of herself. The plowboy looked alternately at the cats and at her, licked his dry lips, and got down his food with difficulty.

16   The miller swallowed the last of his meal, leaned his head back, and abruptly gulped down his glass of vodka. Though drunk, he got up, and grasping his iron spoon and tapping it, he approached the plowboy. The youth sat bewildered. The woman hitched up her skirt and began puttering at the fire.

17   The miller bent over the plowboy and whispered something in his reddened ear. The youth jumped up as if pricked with a knife and began to deny something. The miller asked loudly now whether the boy lusted after his wife. The plowboy blushed but did not answer. The miller's wife turned away and continued to clean the pots.

18   The miller pointed at the strolling tomcat and again whispered something to the youth. The latter, with an effort, rose from the table, intending to leave the room. The miller came forward overturning his stool and, before the youth realized it, suddenly pushed him against the wall, pressed one arm against his throat, and drove a knee into his

stomach. The boy could not move. Terror stricken, panting loudly, he babbled something.

The woman dashed toward her husband, imploring and wailing. The awakened tabby cat lying on the oven looked down on the spectacle, while the frightened tomcat leapt onto the table.   19

With a single kick the miller got the woman out of his way. And with a rapid movement such as women use to gouge out the rotten spots while peeling potatoes, he plunged the spoon into one of the boy's eyes and twisted it.   20

The eye sprang out of his face like a yolk from a broken egg and rolled down the miller's hand onto the floor. The plowboy howled and shrieked, but the miller's hold kept him pinned against the wall. Then the blood-covered spoon plunged into the other eye, which sprang out even faster. For a moment the eye rested on the boy's cheek as if uncertain what to do next; then it finally tumbled down his shirt onto the floor.   21

It all had happened in a moment. I could not believe what I had seen. Something like a glimmer of hope crossed my mind that the gouged eyes could be put back where they belonged. The miller's wife was screaming wildly. She rushed to the adjoining room and woke up her children, who also started crying in terror. The plowboy screamed and then grew silent covering his face with his hands. Rivulets of blood seeped through his fingers down his arms, dripping slowly on his shirt and trousers.   22

The miller, still enraged, pushed him toward the window as though unaware that the youth was blind. The boy stumbled, cried out, and nearly knocked over a table. The miller grabbed him by the shoulders, opened the door with his foot, and kicked him out. The boy yelled again, stumbled through the doorway, and fell down in the yard. The dogs started barking, though they did not know what had happened.   23

The eyeballs lay on the floor. I walked around them, catching their steady stare. The cats timidly moved out into the middle of the room and began to play with the eyes as if they were balls of thread. Their own pupils narrowed to slits from the light of the oil lamp. The cats rolled the eyes around, sniffed them, licked them, and passed them to one another gently with their padded paws. Now it seemed that the eyes were staring at me from every corner of the room, as though they had acquired a new life and motion of their own.   24

I watched them with fascination. If the miller had not been there I myself would have taken them. Surely they could still see. I would keep them in my pocket and take them out when needed, placing them over my own. Then I would see twice as much, maybe even more. Perhaps I could attach them to the back of my head and they would tell me, though I was not quite certain how, what went on behind me. Better still, I could leave the eyes somewhere and they would tell me later what happened during my absence.   25

26   Maybe the eyes had no intention of serving anyone. They could easily escape from the cats and roll out of the door. They could wander over the fields, lakes, and woods, viewing everything about them, free as birds released from a trap. They would no longer die, since they were free, and being small they could easily hide in various places and watch people in secret. Excited, I decided to close the door quietly and capture the eyes.

27   The miller, evidently annoyed by the cats' play, kicked the animals away and squashed the eyeballs with his heavy boots. Something popped under his thick sole. A marvelous mirror, which could reflect the whole world, was broken. There remained on the floor only a crushed bit of jelly. I felt a terrible sense of loss.

28   The miller, paying no attention to me, seated himself on the bench and swayed slowly as he fell asleep. I stood up cautiously, lifted the bloodied spoon from the floor and began to gather the dishes. It was my duty to keep the room neat and the floor swept. As I cleaned I kept away from the crushed eyes, uncertain what to do with them. Finally I looked away and quickly swept the ooze into the pail and threw it in the oven.

29   In the morning I awoke early. Underneath me I heard the miller and his wife snoring. Carefully I packed a sack of food, loaded the comet with hot embers and, bribing the dog in the yard with a piece of sausage, fled from the hut.

30   At the mill wall, next to the barn, lay the plowboy. At first I meant to pass him by quickly, but I stopped when I realized that he was sightless. He was still stunned. He covered his face with his hands, he moaned and sobbed. There was caked blood on his face, hands, and shirt. I wanted to say something, but I was afraid that he would ask me about his eyes and then I would have to tell him to forget about them, since the miller had stamped them into pulp. I was terribly sorry for him.

31   I wondered whether the loss of one's sight would deprive a person also of the memory of everything that he had seen before. If so, the man would no longer be able to see even in his dreams. If not, if only the eyeless could still see through their memory, it would not be too bad. The world seemed to be pretty much the same everywhere, and even though people differed from one another, just as animals and trees did, one should know fairly well what they looked like after seeing them for years. I had lived only seven years, but I remembered a lot of things. When I closed my eyes, many details came back still more vividly. Who knows, perhaps without his eyes the plowboy would start seeing an entirely new, more fascinating world.

32   I heard some sound from the village. Afraid that the miller might wake up, I went on my way, touching my eyes from time to time. I walked more cautiously now, for I knew that eyeballs did not have strong roots. When one bent down they hung like apples from a tree

and could easily drop out. I resolved to jump across fences with my head held up; but on my first try I stumbled and fell down. I lifted my fingers fearfully to my eyes to see whether they were still there. After carefully checking that they opened and closed properly, I noticed with delight the partridges and thrushes in flight. They flew very fast but my sight could follow them and even overtake them as they soared under the clouds, becoming smaller than raindrops. I made a promise to myself to remember everything I saw; if someone should pluck out my eyes, then I would retain the memory of all that I had seen for as long as I lived.

Questions for Discussion and Writing

1. How does the youth and innocence of the NARRATOR affect how events are described? Cite examples where the boy's FIRST-PERSON POINT OF VIEW reveals these naive assumptions about what is taking place.
2. In what circumstances does the young boy find himself? How do the miller and his wife appear from his perspective?
3. What does the miller wish to discover by bringing the tomcat home when both his wife and the plowboy will be there? What happens?
4. In what way does seeing the detached eyes of the plowboy lead the narrator to conclude that the ability to remember events and experiences is all-important?
5. How does this insight signal a turning point in his transformation from innocence to growing self-awareness?
6. How would the same events appear from the POINT OF VIEW of one of the other characters?
7. Describe a real or imagined person who could provoke you to committing a violent act against them.

Daniel Keyes

Flowers for Algernon

Daniel Keyes was born in Brooklyn, New York, in 1927, and was educated at Brooklyn College. He has been a high school teacher of English, an instructor of English at Wayne State University, and, since 1966, a professor of English at Ohio University, Athens. Two of Keyes's books, The Fifth Sally *(1980) and* The Minds of Billy Milligan *(1981), deal with the subject of multiple personalities and are dramatic reproductions of actual cases. In* The Fifth Sally, *a novel, the title character, Sally Porter, is based on the case of a woman who harbored four personalities that embodied her various emotional states. The nonfiction work,* The Minds of Billy Milligan, *is based on the case of Billy Milligan, who was arrested on rape charges in Ohio in 1977 and was the first person in United States history to be acquitted of a major felony by reason of multiple personality. At the time of his arrest, Milligan was found to possess no fewer than twenty-four personalities. Keyes was contacted to write Milligan's story after several of Milligan's selves read Keyes's best-known work, his novel* Flowers for Algernon *(1966). This moving story describes the growing awareness of a mentally retarded man who is temporarily transformed by psychosurgery into a genius with an I.Q. of 185, only, eventually, to regress. Keyes brilliantly uses this work to explore a whole range of emotional and moral issues. Keyes received the Hugo Award for science fiction (1959), the Nebula Award for science fiction (1966), and, in a recent poll, leading science fiction writers voted* Flowers for Algernon *the best science fiction story of the last half-century. Adaptations of this story include the film* Charly *(1968), for which Cliff Robertson won the Academy Award for the title role, and dramatic productions in France, Ireland, Australia, Poland, and Japan.*

progris riport 1—martch 5 1965

1 Mr. Strauss says I shud rite down what I think and evrey thing that happins to me from now on. I don't know why but he says its importint so they will see if they will use me. I hope they use me. Miss Kinnian says maybe they can make me smart. I want to be smart. My name is Charlie Gordon. I am 37 years old and 2 weeks ago was my brithday. I have nuthing more to rite now so I will close for today.

progris riport 2—martch 6

2 I had a test today. I think I faled it. and I think that maybe now they wont use me. What happind is a nice young man was in the room and he had some white cards with ink spillied all over them. He sed Charlie what do you see on this card. I was very skared even tho I had my rabits foot in my pockit because when I was a kid I always faled tests in school and I spillled ink to.

I told him I saw a inkblot. He said yes and it made me feel good. I thot that was all but when I got up to go he stopped me. He said now sit down Charlie we are not thru yet. Then I dont remember so good but he wantid me to say what was in the ink. I dint see nuthing in the ink but he said there was picturs there other pepul saw some picturs. I coudnt see any picturs. I reely tryed to see. I held the card close up and then far away. Then I said if I had my glases I coud see better I usally only ware my glases in the movies or TV but I said they are in the closit in the hall. I got them. Then I said let me see that card agen I bet Ill find it now.

I tryed hard but I still coudnt find the picturs I only saw the ink. I told him maybe I need new glases. He rote somthing down on a paper and I got skared of faling the test. I told him it was a very nice inkblot with littel points all around the eges. He looked very sad so that wasnt it. I said please let me try agen. Ill get it in a few minits becaus Im not so fast somtimes. Im a slow reeder too in Miss Kinnians class for slow adults but I'm trying very hard.

He gave me a chance with another card that had 2 kinds of ink spilled on it red and blue.

He was very nice and talked slow like Miss Kinnian does and he ex-planed it to me that it was a *raw shok*. He said pepul see things in the ink. I said show me where. He said think. I told him I think a inkblot but that wasnt rite eather. He said what does it remind you—pretend something. I closd my eyes for a long time to pretend. I told him I pre-tend a fowntan pen with ink leeking all over a table cloth. Then he got up and went out.

I dont think I passd the *raw shok* test.

progris report 3—martch 7

Dr Strauss and Dr Nemur say it dont matter about the inkblots. I told them I dint spill the ink on the cards and I coudnt see anything in the ink. They said that maybe they will still use me. I said Miss Kinnian never gave me tests like that one only spelling and reading. They said Miss Kinnian told that I was her bestist pupil in the adult nite scool be-caus I tryed the hardist and I reely wantid to lern. They said how come you went to the adult nite scool all by yourself Charlie. How did you find it. I said I askd pepul and sumbody told me where I shud go to lern to read and spell good. They said why did you want to. I told them becaus all my life I wantid to be smart and not dumb. But its very hard to be smart. They said you know it will probly be tempirery. I said yes. Miss Kinnian told me. I dont care if it herts.

Later I had more crazy tests today. The nice lady who gave it me told me the name and I asked her how do you spellit so I can rite it in my progris riport. THEMATIC APPERCEPTION TEST. I dont know the frist 2 words but I know what *test* means. You got to pass it or you get bad marks. This test lookd easy becaus I coud see the picturs. Only this time she dint want me to tell her the picturs. That mixd me up. I said the man yesterday said I shoud tell him what I saw in the ink she said that dont make no difrence. She said make up storys about the pepul in the picturs.

10   I told her how can you tell storys about pepul you never met. I said why shud I make up lies. I never tell lies any more becaus I always get caut.

11   She told me this test and the other one the raw-shok was for getting personalty. I laffed so hard. I said how can you get that thing from inkblots and fotos. She got sore and put her picturs away. I dont care. It was sily. I gess I faled that test too.

12   Later some men in white coats took me to a difernt part of the hospitil and gave me a game to play. It was like a race with a white mouse. They called the mouse Algernon. Algernon was in a box with a lot of twists and turns like all kinds of walls and they gave me a pencil and a paper with lines and lots of boxes. On one side it said START and on the other end it said FINISH. They said it was *amazed* and that Algernon and me had the same *amazed* to do. I dint see how we could have the same *amazed* if Algernon had a box and I had a paper but I dint say nothing. Anyway there wasnt time because the race started.

13   One of the men had a watch he was trying to hide so I woudnt see it so I tryed not to look and that made me nervus.

14   Anyway that test made me feel worser than all the others because they did it over 10 times with difernt *amazeds* and Algernon won every time. I dint know that mice were so smart. Maybe thats because Algernon is a white mouse. Maybe white mice are smarter then other mice.

progris riport 4—Mar 8

15   Their going to use me! Im so exited I can hardly write. Dr Nemur and Dr Strauss had a argament about it first. Dr Nemur was in the office when Dr Strauss brot me in. Dr Nemur was worryed about using me but Dr Strauss told him Miss Kinnian rekemmended me the best from all the people who she was teaching. I like Miss Kinnian becaus shes a very smart teacher. And she said Charlie your going to have a second chance. If you volenteer for this experament you mite get smart. They dont know if it will be perminint but theirs a chance. Thats why I said ok even when I was scared because she said it was an operashun. She said dont be scared Charlie you done so much with so little I think you deserv it most of all.

16   So I got scaird when Dr Nemur and Dr Strauss argud about it. Dr Strauss said I had something that was very good. He said I had a good *motor-vation*. I never even knew I had that. I felt proud when he said that not every body with an eye-q of 68 had that thing. I dont know what it is or where I got it but he said Algernon had it too. Algernons

motor-vation is the cheese they put in his box. But it cant be that because I didnt eat any cheese this week.

Then he told Dr Nemur something I dint understand so while they were talking I wrote down some of the words. 17

He said Dr Nemur I know Charlie is not what you had in mind as the first of your new brede of intelek** (coudnt get the word) superman. But most people of his low ment** are host** and uncoop** they are usualy dull apath** and hard to reach. He has a good natcher hes intristed and eager to please. 18

Dr Nemur said remember he will be the first human beeng ever to have his intelijence trippled by surgicle meens. 19

Dr Strauss said exakly. Look at how well hes lerned to read and write for his low mentel age its as grate an acheve** as you and I lerning einstines therey of **vity without help. That shows the intenss motor-vation. Its comparat** a tremen** achev** I say we use Charlie. 20

I dint get all the words and they were talking to fast but it sounded like Dr Strauss was on my side and like the other one wasnt. 21

Then Dr Nemur nodded he said all right maybe your right. We will use Charlie. When he said that I got so exited I jumped up and shook his hand for being so good to me. I told him thank you doc you wont be sorry for giving me a second chance. And I mean it like I told him. After the operashun Im gonna try to be smart. Im gonna try awful hard. 22

progris ript 5—Mar 10

Im skared. Lots of people who work here and the nurses and the people who gave me the tests came to bring me candy and wish me luck. I hope I have luck. I got my rabits foot and my lucky penny and my horse shoe. Only a black cat crossed me when I was comming to the hospitil. Dr Strauss says dont be supersitis Charlie this is sience. Anyway Im keeping my rabits foot with me. 23

I asked Dr Strauss if Ill beat Algernon in the race after the operashun and he said maybe. If the operashun works Ill show that mouse I can be as smart as he is. Maybe smarter. Then Ill be abel to read better and spell the words good and know lots of things and be like other people. I want to be smart like other people. If it works perminint they will make everybody smart all over the wurld. 24

They dint give me anything to eat this morning. I dont know what that eating has to do with getting smart. Im very hungry and Dr Nemur took away my box of candy. That Dr Nemur is a grouch. Dr Strauss says I can have it back after the operashun. You cant eat befor a operashun . . . 25

progress report 6—Mar 15

The operashun dint hurt. He did it while I was sleeping. They took off the bandijis from my eyes and my head today so I can make a PROGRESS REPORT. Dr Nemur who looked at some of my other ones says I spell 26

PROGRESS wrong and he told me how to spell it and REPORT too. I got to try and remember that.

27   I have a very bad memary for spelling. Dr Strauss says its ok to tell about all the things that happin to me but he says I shoud tell more about what I feel and what I think. When I told him I dont know how to think he said try. All the time when the bandijis were on my eyes I tryed to think. Nothing happened. I dont know what to think about. Maybe if I ask him he will tell me how I can think now that Im suppose to get smart. What do smart people think about. Fancy things I suppose. I wish I knew some fancy things alredy.

progress report 7—mar 19

28 Nothing is happining. I had lots of tests and different kinds of races with Algernon. I hate that mouse. He always beats me. Dr Strauss said I got to play those games. And he said some time I got to take those tests over again. Thse inkblots are stupid. And those pictures are stupid too. I like to draw a picture of a man and a woman but I wont make up lies about people.

29   I got a headache from trying to think so much. I thot Dr Strauss was my frend but he dont help me. He dont tell me what to think or when Ill get smart. Miss Kinnian dint come to see me. I think writing these progress reports are stupid too.

progress report 8—Mar 23

30 Im going back to work at the factery. They said it was better I shud go back to work but I cant tell anyone what the operashun was for and I have to come to the hospitil for an hour evry night after work. They are gonna pay me mony every month for lerning to be smart.

31   Im glad Im going back to work because I miss my job and all my frends and all the fun we have there.

32   Dr Strauss says I shud keep writing things down but I dont have to do it every day just when I think of something or something speshul happins. He says dont get discoridged because it takes time and it happins slow. He says it took a long time with Algernon before he got 3 times smarter then he was before. Thats why Algernon beats me all the time because he had that operashun too. That makes me feel better. I coud probly do that *amazed* faster than a reglar mouse. Maybe some day Ill beat Algernon. Boy that would be something. So far Algernon looks like he mite be smart perminent.

33 *Mar 25* (I dont have to write PROGRESS REPORT on top any more just when I hand it in once a week for Dr Nemur to read. I just have to put the date on. That saves time)

34   We had a lot of fun at the factery today. Joe Carp said hey look where Charlie had his operashun what did they do Charlie put some brains in. I was going to tell him but I remembered Dr Strauss said no.

Then Frank Reilly said what did you do Charlie forget your key and open your door the hard way. That made me laff. Their really my friends and they like me.

Sometimes somebody will say hey look at Joe or Frank or George he really pulled a Charlie Gordon. I dont know why they say that but they always laff. This morning Amos Borg who is the 4 man at Donnegans used my name when he shouted at Ernie the office boy. Ernie lost a packige. He said Ernie for godsake what are you trying to be a Charlie Gordon. I dont understand why he said that. I never lost any packiges.

Mar 28 Dr Strauss came to my room tonight to see why I dint come in like I was suppose to. I told him I dont like to race with Algernon any more. He said I dont have to for a while but I shud come in. He had a present for me only it wasnt a present but just for lend. I thot it was a little television but it wasnt. He said I got to turn it on when I go to sleep. I said your kidding why shud I turn it on when Im going to sleep. Who ever herd of a thing like that. But he said if I want to get smart I got to do what he says. I told him I dint think I was going to get smart and he put his hand on my sholder and said Charlie you dont know it yet but your getting smarter all the time. You wont notice for a while. I think he was just being nice to make me feel good because I dont look any smarter.

Oh yes I almost forgot. I asked him when I can go back to the class at Miss Kinnians school. He said I wont go their. He said that soon Miss Kinnian will come to the hospitil to start and teach me speshul. I was mad at her for not comming to see me when I got the operashun but I like her so maybe we will be frends again.

Mar 29 That crazy TV kept me up all night. How can I sleep with something yelling crazy things all night in my ears. And the nutty pictures. Wow. I dont know what it says when Im up so how am I going to know when Im sleeping.

Dr Strauss says its ok. He says my brains are lerning when I sleep and that will help me when Miss Kinnian starts my lessons in the hospitl (only I found out it isnt a hospitil its a labatory). I think its all crazy. If you can get smart when your sleeping why do people go to school. That thing I dont think will work. I use to watch the late show and the late late show on TV all the time and it never made me smart. Maybe you have to sleep while you watch it.

PROGRESS REPORT 9—April 3

Dr Strauss showed me how to keep the TV turned low so now I can sleep. I dont hear a thing. And I still dont understand what it says. A few times I play it over in the morning to find out what I lerned when I was sleeping and I dont think so. Miss Kinnian says Maybe its another langwidge or something. But most times it sounds American. It talks so fast faster than even Miss Gold who was my teacher in 6 grade and I remember she talked so fast I coudnt understand her.

41   I told Dr Strauss what good is it to get smart in my sleep. I want to be smart when Im awake. He says its the same thing and I have two minds. Theres the *subconscious* and the *conscious* (thats how you spell it). And one dont tell the other one what its doing. They dont even talk to each other. Thats why I dream. And boy have I been having crazy dreams. Wow. Ever since that night TV. The late late late late late show.

42   I forgot to ask him if it was only me or if everybody had those two minds.

43   (I just looked up the word in the dictionary Dr Strauss gave me. The word is *subconscious. adj. Of the nature of mental operations yet not present in consciousness; as, subconscious conflict of desires.*) Theres more but I still don't know what it means. This isnt a very good dictionary for dumb people like me.

44   Anyway the headache is from the party. My frends from the factery Joe Carp and Frank Reilly invited me to go with them to Muggsys Saloon for some drinks. I dont like to drink but they said we will have lots of fun. I had a good time.

45   Joe Carp said I shoud show the girls how I mop out the toilet in the factory and he got me a mop. I showed them and everyone laffed when I told that Mr Donnegan said I was the best janiter he ever had because I like my job and do it good and never come late or miss a day except for my operashun.

46   I said Miss Kinnian always said Charlie be proud of your job because you do it good.

47   Everybody laffed and we had a good time and they gave me lots of drinks and Joe said Charlie is a card when hes potted. I dont know what that means but everybody likes me and we have fun. I cant wait to be smart like my best frends Joe Carp and Frank Reilly.

48   I dont remember how the party was over but I think I went out to buy a newspaper and coffe for Joe and Frank and when I came back there was no one their. I looked for them all over till late. Then I dont remember so good but I think I got sleepy or sick. A nice cop brot me back home. Thats what my landlady Mrs Flynn says.

49   But I got a headache and a big lump on my head and black and blue all over. I think maybe I fell but Joe Carp says it was the cop they beat up drunks some times. I don't think so. Miss Kinnian says cops are to help people. Anyway I got a bad headache and Im sick and hurt all over. I dont think Ill drink anymore.

50   *April 6* I beat Algernon! I dint even know I beat him until Burt the tester told me. Then the second time I lost because I got so exited I fell off the chair before I finished. But after that I beat him 8 more times. I must be getting smart to beat a smart mouse like Algernon. But I dont *feel* smarter.

I wanted to race Algernon some more but Burt said thats enough for 51
one day. They let me hold him for a minit. Hes not so bad. Hes soft like
a ball of cotton. He blinks and when he opens his eyes their black and
pink on the eges.

I said can I feed him because I felt bad to beat him and I wanted to 52
be nice and make frends. Burt said no Algernon is a very specshul
mouse with an operashun like mine, and he was the first of all the animals to stay smart so long. He told me Algernon is so smart that every
day he has to solve a test to get his food. Its a thing like a lock on a door
that changes every time Algernon goes in to eat so he has to lern something new to get his food. That made me sad because if he coudnt lern
he would be hungry.

I dont think its right to make you pass a test to eat. How woud Dr 53
Nemur like it to have to pass a test every time he wants to eat. I think Ill
be frends with Algernon.

April 9 Tonight after work Miss Kinnian was at the laboratory. She 54
looked like she was glad to see me but scared. I told her dont worry
Miss Kinnian Im not smart yet and she laffed. She said I have confidence in you Charlie the way you struggled so hard to read and right
better than all the others. At werst you will have it for a littel wile and
your doing somthing for sience.

We are reading a very hard book. I never read such a hard book be- 55
fore. Its called *Robinson Crusoe* about a man who gets merooned on a
dessert Iland. Hes smart and figers out all kinds of things so he can
have a house and food and hes a good swimmer. Only I feel sorry because hes all alone and has no frends. But I think their must be somebody else on the iland because theres a picture with his funny umbrella
looking at footprints. I hope he gets a frend and not be lonly.

April 10 Miss Kinnian teaches me to spell better. She says look at a 56
word and close your eyes and say it over and over until you remember.
I have lots of truble with *through* that you say *threw* and *enough* and
tough that you dont say *enew* and *tew*. You got to say *enuff* and *tuff*.
Thats how I use to write it before I started to get smart. Im confused but
Miss Kinnian says theres no reason in spelling.

Apr 14 Finished *Robinson Crusoe*. I want to find out more about what 57
happens to him but Miss Kinnian says thats all there is. *Why*

Apr 15 Miss Kinnian says Im lerning fast. She read some of the 58
Progress Reports and she looked at me kind of funny. She says Im a
fine person and Ill show them all. I asked her why. She said never mind
but I shoudnt feel bad if I find out that everybody isnt nice like I think.
She said for a person who god gave so little to you done more then a lot
of people with brains they never even used. I said all my frends are

smart people but there good. They like me and they never did anything
that wasnt nice. Then she got something in her eye and she had to run
out to the ladys room.

59 *Apr 16*   Today, I lerned, the *comma*, this is a comma (,) a period, with a
tail, Miss Kinnian, says its importent, because, it makes writing, better,
she said, somebody, coud lose, a lot of money, if a comma, isnt, in the,
right place, I dont have, any money, and I dont see, how a comma,
keeps you, from losing it,

60   But she says, everybody, uses commas, so Ill use, them too,

61 *Apr 17*   I used the comma wrong. Its punctuation. Miss Kinnian told
me to look up long words in the dictionary to lern to spell them. I said
whats the difference if you can read it anyway. She said its part of your
education so now on Ill look up all the words Im not sure how to spell.
It takes a long time to write that way but I think Im remembering. I
only have to look up once and after that I get it right. Anyway thats
how come I got the word *punctuation* right. (Its that way in the dictionary). Miss Kinnian says a period is punctuation too, and there are lots
of other marks to lern. I told her I thot all the periods had to have tails
but she said no.

62   You got to mix them up, she showed? me'' how. to mix! them(up,.
and now; I can! mix up all kinds'' of punctuation, in! my writing?
There, are lots! of rules? to lern; but Im gettin'g them in my head.

63   One thing I? like about, Dear Miss Kinnian: (thats the way it goes in
a business letter if I ever go into business) is she, always gives me' a
reason'' when—I ask. She's a gen'ius! I wish! I cou'd be smart'' like,
her;

64   (Punctuation, is; fun!)

65 *April 18*   What a dope I am! I didn't even understand what she was
talking about. I read the grammar book last night and it explanes the
whole thing. Then I saw it was the same way as Miss Kinnian was trying to tell me, but I didn't get it. I got up in the middle of the night, and
the whole thing straightened out in my mind.

66   Miss Kinnian said that the TV working in my sleep helped out. She
said I reached a plateau. Thats like the flat top of a hill.

67   After I figgered out how punctuation worked, I read over all my old
Progress Reports from the beginning. Boy, did I have crazy spelling
and punctuation! I told Miss Kinnian I ought to go over the pages and
fix all the mistakes but she said, "No, Charlie, Dr. Nemur wants them
just as they are. That's why he let you keep them after they were photo-
stated, to see your own progress. You're coming along fast, Charlie."

68   That made me feel good. After the lesson I went down and played
with Algernon. We don't race any more.

April 20 I feel sick inside. Not sick like for a doctor, but inside my chest it feels empty like getting punched and a heartburn at the same time. 69

I wasn't going to write about it, but I guess I got to, because it's important. Today was the first time I ever stayed home from work. 70

Last night Joe Carp and Frank Reilly invited me to a party. There were lots of girls and some men from the factory. I remembered how sick I got last time I drank too much, so I told Joe I didn't want anything to drink. He gave me a plain Coke instead. It tasted funny, but I thought it was just a bad taste in my mouth. 71

We had a lot of fun for a while. Joe said I should dance with Ellen and she would teach me the steps. I fell a few times and I couldn't understand why because no one else was dancing besides Ellen and me. And all the time I was tripping because somebody's foot was always sticking out. 72

Then when I got up I saw the look on Joe's face and it gave me a funny feeling in my stomack. "He's a scream," one of the girls said. Everybody was laughing. 73

Frank said, "I ain't laughed so much since we sent him off for the newspaper that night at Muggsy's and ditched him." 74

"Look at him. His face is red." 75

"He's blushing. Charlie is blushing." 76

"Hey, Ellen, what'd you do to Charlie? I never saw him act like that before." 77

I didn't know what to do or where to turn. Everyone was looking at me and laughing and I felt naked. I wanted to hide myself. I ran out into the street and I threw up. Then I walked home. It's a funny thing I never knew that Joe and Frank and the others liked to have me around all the time to make fun of me. 78

Now I know what it means when they say "to pull a Charlie Gordon." 79

I'm ashamed. 80

PROGRESS REPORT 11

April 21 Still didn't go into the factory. I told Mrs. Flynn my landlady to call and tell Mr. Donnegan I was sick. Mrs. Flynn looks at me very funny lately like she's scared of me. 81

I think it's a good thing about finding out how everybody laughs at me. I thought about it a lot. It's because I'm so dumb and I don't even know when I'm doing something dumb. People think it's funny when a dumb person can't do things the same way they can. 82

Anyway, now I know I'm getting smarter every day. I know punctuation and I can spell good. I like to look up all the hard words in the dictionary and I remember them. I'm reading a lot now, and Miss Kinnian says I read very fast. Sometimes I even understand what I'm 83 reading about, and it stays in my mind. There are times when I can close my eyes and think of a page and it all comes back like a picture.

84   Besides history, geography, and arithmetic, Miss Kinnian said I should start to learn a few foreign languages. Dr. Strauss gave me some more tapes to play while I sleep. I still don't understand how that conscious and unconscious mind works, but Dr. Strauss says not to worry yet. He asked me to promise that when I start learning college subjects next week I wouldn't read any books on psychology—that is, until he gives me permission.

85   I feel a lot better today, but I guess I'm still a little angry that all the time people were laughing and making fun of me because I wasn't so smart. When I become intelligent like Dr. Strauss says, with three times my I.Q. of 68, then maybe I'll be like everyone else and people will like me and be friendly.

86   I'm not sure what an I.Q. is. Dr. Nemur said it was something that measured how intelligent you were—like a scale in the drugstore weighs pounds. But Dr. Strauss had a big argument with him and said an I.Q. didn't weigh intelligence at all. He said an I.Q. showed how much intelligence you could get, like the numbers on the outside of a measuring cup. You still had to fill the cup up with stuff.

87   Then when I asked Burt, who gives me my intelligence tests and works with Algernon, he said that both of them were wrong (only I had to promise not to tell them he said so). Burt says that the I.Q. measures a lot of different things including some of the things you learned already, and it really isn't any good at all.

88   So I still don't know what I.Q. is except that mine is going to be over 200 soon. I didn't want to say anything, but I don't see how if they don't know *what* it is, or *where* it is—I don't see how they know *how much* of it you've got.

89   Dr. Nemur says I have to take a *Rorshach Test* tomorrow. I wonder what *that* is.

90   *April 22*   I found out what a *Rorshach* is. It's the test I took before the operation—the one with the inkblots on the pieces of cardboard. The man who gave me the test was the same one.

91   I was scared to death of those inkblots. I knew he was going to ask me to find the pictures and I knew I wouldn't be able to. I was thinking to myself, if only there was some way of knowing what kind of pictures were hidden there. Maybe there weren't any pictures at all. Maybe it was just a trick to see if I was dumb enough to look for something that wasn't there. Just thinking about that made me sore at him.

92   "All right, Charlie," he said, "you've seen these cards before, remember?"

93   "Of course I remember."

94   The way I said it, he knew I was angry, and he looked surprised. "Yes, of course. Now I want you to look at this one. What might this

be? What do you see on this card? People see all sorts of things in these inkblots. Tell me what it might be for you—what it makes you think of."

I was shocked. That wasn't what I had expected him to say at all. 95 "You mean there are no pictures hidden in those inkblots?"

He frowned and took off his glasses. "What?" 96

"Pictures. Hidden in the inkblots. Last time you told me that every- 97 one could see them and you wanted me to find them too."

He explained to me that the last time he had used almost the exact 98 same words he was using now. I didn't believe it, and I still have the suspicion that he misled me at the time just for the fun of it. Unless—I don't know any more—could I have been *that* feeble-minded?

We went through the cards slowly. One of them looked like a pair of 99 bats tugging at something. Another one looked like two men fencing with swords. I imagined all sorts of things. I guess I got carried away. But I didn't trust him any more, and I kept turning them around and even looking on the back to see if there was anything there I was sup- posed to catch. While he was making his notes, I peeked out of the cor- ner of my eye to read it. But it was all in code that looked like this:

WF + A DdF-Ad orig. WF-A SF + obj

The test still doesn't make sense to me. It seems to me that anyone 100 could make up lies about things that they didn't really see. How could he know I wasn't making a fool of him by mentioning things that I didn't really imagine? Maybe I'll understand it when Dr. Strauss lets me read up on psychology.

April 25 I figured out a new way to line up the machines in the fac- 101 tory, and Mr. Donnegan says it will save him ten thousand dollars a year in labor and increased production. He gave me a twenty-five-dol- lar bonus.

I wanted to take Joe Carp and Frank Reilly out to lunch to celebrate, 102 but Joe said he had to buy some things for his wife, and Frank said he was meeting his cousin for lunch. I guess it'll take a little time for them to get used to the changes in me. Everybody seems to be frightened of me. When I went over to Amos Borg and tapped him on the shoulder, he jumped up in the air.

People don't talk to me much any more or kid around the way they 103 used to. It makes the job kind of lonely.

April 27 I got up the nerve today to ask Miss Kinnian to have dinner 104 with me tomorrow night to celebrate my bonus.

At first she wasn't sure it was right, but I asked Dr. Strauss and he 105 said it was okay. Dr. Strauss and Dr. Nemur don't seem to be getting along so well. They're arguing all the time. This evening when I came in to ask Dr. Strauss about having dinner with Miss Kinnian, I heard them shouting. Dr. Nemur was saying that it was *his* experiment and *his* research, and Dr. Strauss was shouting back that he contributed just as much, because he found me through Miss Kinnian and he performed the operation. Dr. Strauss said that someday thousands of neurosurgeons might be using his technique all over the world.

106   Dr. Nemur wanted to publish the results of the experiment at the end of this month. Dr. Strauss wanted to wait a while longer to be sure. Dr. Strauss said that Dr. Nemur was more interested in the Chair of Psychology at Princeton than he was in the experiment. Dr. Nemur said that Dr. Strauss was nothing but an opportunist who was trying to ride to glory on *his* coattails.

107   When I left afterwards, I found myself trembling. I don't know why for sure, but it was as if I'd seen both men clearly for the first time. I remember hearing Burt say that Dr. Nemur had a shrew of a wife who was pushing him all the time to get things published so that he could become famous. Burt said that the dream of her life was to have a big-shot husband.

108   Was Dr. Strauss really trying to ride on his coattails?

109   *April 28*   I don't understand why I never noticed how beautiful Miss Kinnian really is. She has brown eyes and feathery brown hair that comes to the top of her neck. She's only thirty-four! I think from the beginning I had the feeling that she was an unreachable genius—and very, very old. Now, every time I see her she grows younger and more lovely.

110   We had dinner and a long talk. When she said that I was coming along so fast that soon I'd be leaving her behind, I laughed.

111   "It's true, Charlie. You're already a better reader than I am. You can read a whole page at a glance while I can take in only a few lines at a time. And you remember every single thing you read. I'm lucky if I can recall the main thoughts and the general meaning."

112   "I don't feel intelligent. There are so many things I don't understand."

113   She took out a cigarette and I lit it for her. "You've got to be a *little* patient. You're accomplishing in days and weeks what it takes normal people to do in half a lifetime. That's what makes it so amazing. You're like a giant sponge now, soaking things in. Facts, figures, general knowledge. And soon you'll begin to connect them, too. You'll see how the different branches of learning are related. There are many levels, Charlie, like steps on a giant ladder that take you up higher and higher to see more and more of the world around you.

114   "I can see only a little bit of that, Charlie, and I won't go much higher than I am now, but you'll keep climbing up and up, and see more and more, and each step will open new worlds that you never even knew existed." She frowned. "I hope . . . I just hope to God—"

"What?" 115

"Never mind, Charles. I just hope I wasn't wrong to advise you to 116
go into this in the first place."

I laughed. "How could that be? It worked, didn't it? Even Algernon 117
is still smart."

We sat there silently for a while and I knew what she was thinking 118
about as she watched me toying with the chain of my rabbit's foot and
my keys. I didn't want to think of that possibility any more than elderly
people want to think of death. I *knew* that this was only the beginning. I
knew what she meant about levels because I'd seen some of them already. The thought of leaving her behind made me sad.

I'm in love with Miss Kinnian. 119

PROGRESS REPORT 12

April 30   I've quit my job with Donnegan's Plastic Box Company. Mr. 120
Donnegan insisted that it would be better for all concerned if I left.
What did I do to make them hate me so?

The first I knew of it was when Mr. Donnegan showed me the peti- 121
tion. Eight hundred and forty names, everyone connected with the factory, except Fanny Girden. Scanning the list quickly, I saw at once that
hers was the only missing name. All the rest demanded that I be fired.

Joe Carp and Frank Reilly wouldn't talk to me about it. No one else 122
would either, except Fanny. She was one of the few people I'd known
who set her mind to something and believed it no matter what the rest
of the world proved, said, or did—and Fanny did not believe that I
should have been fired. She had been against the petition on principle
and despite the pressure and threats she'd held out.

"Which don't mean to say," she remarked, "that I don't think 123
there's something mighty strange about you, Charlie. Them changes, I
don't know. You used to be a good, dependable, ordinary man—not
too bright maybe, but honest. Who knows what you done to yourself to
get so smart all of a sudden. Like everybody around here's been saying,
Charlie, it's not right."

"But how can you say that, Fanny? What's wrong with a man be- 124
coming intelligent and wanting to acquire knowledge and understanding of the world around him?"

She stared down at her work and I turned to leave. Without looking 125
at me, she said: "It was evil when Eve listened to the snake and ate
from the tree of knowledge. It was evil when she saw that she was
naked. If not for that none of us would ever have to grow old and sick,
and die."

Once again now I have the feeling of shame burning inside me. This 126
intelligence has driven a wedge between me and all the people I once
knew and loved. Before, they laughed at me and despised me for my

ignorance and dullness; now, they hate me for my knowledge and understanding. What in God's name do they want of me?

127   They've driven me out of the factory. Now I'm more alone than ever before . . .

128   *May 15* Dr. Strauss is very angry at me for not having written any progress reports in two weeks. He's justified because the lab is now paying me a regular salary. I told him I was too busy thinking and reading. When I pointed out that writing was such a slow process that it made me impatient with my poor handwriting, he suggested that I learn to type. It's much easier to write now because I can type nearly seventy-five words a minute. Dr. Strauss continually reminds me of the need to speak and write simply so that people will be able to understand me.

129   I'll try to review all the things that happened to me during the last two weeks. Algernon and I were presented to the American Psychological Association sitting in convention with the World Psychological Association last Tuesday. We created quite a sensation. Dr. Nemur and Dr. Strauss were proud of us.

130   I suspect that Dr. Nemur, who is sixty—ten years older than Dr. Strauss—finds it necessary to see tangible results of his work. Undoubtedly the result of pressure by Mrs. Nemur.

131   Contrary to my earlier impressions of him, I realize that Dr. Nemur is not at all a genius. He has a very good mind, but it struggles under the spectre of self-doubt. He wants people to take him for a genius. Therefore, it is important for him to feel that his work is accepted by the world. I believe that Dr. Nemur was afraid of further delay because he worried that someone else might make a discovery along these lines and take the credit from him.

132   Dr. Strauss on the other hand might be called a genius, although I feel that his areas of knowledge are too limited. He was educated in the tradition of narrow specialization; the broader aspects of background were neglected far more than necessary—even for a neurosurgeon.

133   I was shocked to learn that the only ancient languages he could read were Latin, Greek, and Hebrew, and that he knows almost nothing of mathematics beyond the elementary levels of the calculus of variations. When he admitted this to me, I found myself almost annoyed. It was as if he'd hidden this part of himself in order to deceive me, pretending—as do many people I've discovered—to be what he is not. No one I've ever known is what he appears to be on the surface.

134   Dr. Nemur appears to be uncomfortable around me. Sometimes when I try to talk to him, he just looks at me strangely and turns away. I was angry at first when Dr. Strauss told me I was giving Dr. Nemur an inferiority complex. I thought he was mocking me and I'm oversensitive at being made fun of.

135   How was I to know that a highly respected psychoexperimentalist

like Nemur was unacquainted with Hindustani and Chinese? It's absurd when you consider the work that is being done in India and China today in the very field of his study.

I asked Dr. Strauss how Nemur could refute Rahajamati's attack on his method and results if Nemur couldn't even read them in the first place. That strange look on Dr. Strauss' face can mean only one of two things. Either he doesn't want to tell Nemur what they're saying in India, or else—and this worries me—Dr. Strauss doesn't know either. I must be careful to speak and write clearly and simply so that people won't laugh. 136

May 18 I am very disturbed. I saw Miss Kinnian last night for the first time in over a week. I tried to avoid all discussions of intellectual concepts and to keep the conversation on a simple, everyday level, but she just stared at me blankly and asked me what I meant about the mathematical variance equivalent in Dorbermann's *Fifth Concerto*. 137

When I tried to explain she stopped me and laughed. I guess I got angry, but I suspect I'm approaching her on the wrong level. No matter what I try to discuss with her, I am unable to communicate. I must review Vrostadt's equations on *Levels of Semantic Progression*. I find that I don't communicate with people much any more. Thank God for books and music and things I can think about. I am alone in my apartment at Mrs. Flynn's boardinghouse most of the time and seldom speak to anyone. 138

May 20 I would not have noticed the new dishwasher, a boy of about sixteen, at the corner diner where I take my evening meals if not for the incident of the broken dishes. 139

They crashed to the floor, shattering and sending bits of white china under the tables. The boy stood there, dazed and frightened, holding the empty tray in his hand. The whistles and catcalls from the customers (the cries of "hey, there go the profits!" . . . "Mazeltov!" . . . and "well, *he* didn't work here very long . . ." which invariably seems to follow the breaking of glass or dishware in a public restaurant) all seemed to confuse him. 140

When the owner came to see what the excitement was about, the boy cowered as if he expected to be struck and threw up his arms as if to ward off the blow. 141

"All right! All right, you dope," shouted the owner, "don't just stand there! Get the broom and sweep that mess up. A broom . . . broom, you idiot! It's in the kitchen. Sweep up all the pieces." 142

The boy saw that he was not going to be punished. His frightened expression disappeared and he smiled and hummed as he came back with the broom to sweep the floor. A few of the rowdier customers kept up the remarks, amusing themselves at his expense. 143

"Here, sonny, over here there's a nice piece behind you . . ." 144

145   "C'mon, do it again . . ."

146   "He's not so dumb. It's easier to break 'em than to wash 'em . . ."

147   As his vacant eyes moved across the crowd of amused onlookers, he slowly mirrored their smiles and finally broke into an uncertain grin at the joke which he obviously did not understand.

148   I felt sick inside as I looked at his dull, vacuous smile, the wide, bright eyes of a child, uncertain but eager to please. They were laughing at him because he was mentally retarded.

149   And I had been laughing at him too.

150   Suddenly, I was furious at myself and all those who were smirking at him. I jumped up and shouted, "Shut up! Leave him alone! It's not his fault he can't understand! He can't help what he is! But for God's sake . . . he's still a human being!"

151   The room grew silent. I cursed myself for losing control and creating a scene. I tried not to look at the boy as I paid my check and walked out without touching my food. I felt ashamed for both of us.

152   How strange it is that people of honest feelings and sensibility, who would not take advantage of a man born without arms or legs or eyes—how such people think nothing of abusing a man born with low intelligence. It infuriated me to think that not too long ago I, like this boy, had foolishly played the clown.

153   And I had almost forgotten.

154   I'd hidden the picture of the old Charlie Gordon from myself because now that I was intelligent it was something that had to be pushed out of my mind. But today in looking at that boy, for the first time I saw what I had been. *I was just like him!*

155   Only a short time ago, I learned that people laughed at me. Now I can see that unknowingly I joined with them in laughing at myself. That hurts most of all.

156   I have often reread my progress reports and seen the illiteracy, the childish naïveté, the mind of low intelligence peering from a dark room, through the keyhole, at the dazzling light outside. I see that even in my dullness I knew that I was inferior, and that other people had something I lacked—something denied me. In my mental blindness, I thought that it was somehow connected with the ability to read and write, and I was sure that if I could get those skills I would automatically have intelligence too.

157   Even a feeble-minded man wants to be like other men.

158   A child may not know how to feed itself, or what to eat, yet it knows of hunger.

159   This then is what I was like, I never knew. Even with my gift of intellectual awareness, I never really knew.

160   This day was good for me. Seeing the past more clearly, I have decided to use my knowledge and skills to work in the field of increasing human intelligence levels. Who is better equipped for this work? Who else has lived in both worlds? These are my people. Let me use my gift to do something for them.

Tomorrow, I will discuss with Dr. Strauss the manner in which I can work in this area. I may be able to help him work out the problems of widespread use of the technique which was used on me. I have several good ideas of my own.

161

There is so much that might be done with this technique. If I could be made into a genius, what about thousands of others like myself? What fantastic levels might be achieved by using this technique on normal people? On *geniuses*?

162

There are so many doors to open. I am impatient to begin.

163

PROGRESS REPORT 13

May 23 It happened today. Algernon bit me. I visited the lab to see him as I do occasionally, and when I took him out of his cage, he snapped at my hand. I put him back and watched him for a while. He was unusually disturbed and vicious.

164

May 24 Burt, who is in charge of the experimental animals, tells me that Algernon is changing. He is less co-operative; he refuses to run the maze any more; general motivation has decreased. And he hasn't been eating. Everyone is upset about what this may mean.

165

May 25 They've been feeding Algernon, who now refuses to work the shifting-lock problem. Everyone identifies me with Algernon. In a way we're both the first of our kind. They're all pretending that Algernon's behavior is not necessarily significant for me. But it's hard to hide the fact that some of the other animals who were used in this experiment are showing strange behavior.

166

Dr. Strauss and Dr. Nemur have asked me not to come to the lab any more. I know what they're thinking but I can't accept it. I am going ahead with my plans to carry their research forward. With all due respect to both of these fine scientists, I am well aware of their limitations. If there is an answer, I'll have to find it out for myself. Suddenly, time has become very important to me.

167

May 29 I have been given a lab of my own and permission to go ahead with the research. I'm on to something. Working day and night. I've had a cot moved into the lab. Most of my writing time is spent on the notes which I keep in a separate folder, but from time to time I feel it necessary to put down my moods and my thoughts out of sheer habit.

168

I find the *calculus of intelligence* to be a fascinating study. Here is the place for the application of all the knowledge I have acquired. In a sense it's the problem I've been concerned with all my life.

169

May 31 Dr. Strauss thinks I'm working too hard. Dr. Nemur says I'm trying to cram a lifetime of research and thought into a few weeks. I

170

know I should rest, but I'm driven on by something inside that won't let me stop. I've got to find the reason for the sharp regression in Algernon. I've got to know *if* and *when* it will happen to me.

171   *June 4*

LETTER TO DR. STRAUSS (*copy*)

Dear Dr. Strauss:

172   Under separate cover I am sending you a copy of my report entitled, "The Algernon-Gordon Effect: A Study of Structure and Function of Increased Intelligence," which I would like to have you read and have published.

173   As you see, my experiments are completed. I have included in my report all of my formulae, as well as mathematical analysis in the appendix. Of course, these should be verified.

174   Because of its importance to both you and Dr. Nemur (and need I say to myself, too?) I have checked and rechecked my results a dozen times in the hope of finding an error. I am sorry to say the results must stand. Yet for the sake of science, I am grateful for the little bit that I here add to the knowledge of the function of the human mind and of the laws governing the artificial increase of human intelligence.

175   I recall your once saying to me that an experimental *failure* or the *disproving* of a theory was as important to the advancement of learning as a success would be. I know now that this is true. I am sorry, however, that my own contribution to the field must rest upon the ashes of the work of two men I regard so highly.

Yours truly,

Charles Gordon

encl.: rept.

176   *June 5*   I must not become emotional. The facts and the results of my experiments are clear, and the more sensational aspects of my own rapid climb cannot obscure the fact that the tripling of intelligence by the surgical technique developed by Drs. Strauss and Nemur must be viewed as having little or no practical applicability (at the present time) to the increase of human intelligence.

177   As I review the records and data on Algernon, I see that although he is still in his physical infancy, he has regressed mentally. Motor activity is impaired; there is a general reduction of glandular activity; there is an accelerated loss of co-ordination.

178   There are also strong indications of progressive amnesia.

179   As will be seen by my report, these and other physical and mental deterioration syndromes can be predicted with statistically significant results by the application of my formula.

180   The surgical stimulus to which we were both subjected has resulted

in an intensification and acceleration of all mental processes. The unforeseen development, which I have taken the liberty of calling the *Algernon-Gordon Effect*, is the logical extension of the entire intelligence speed-up. The hypothesis here proven may be described simply in the following terms: Artifically increased intelligence deteriorates at a rate of time directly proportional to the quantity of the increase.

I feel that this, in itself, is an important discovery. 181

As long as I am able to write, I will continue to record my thoughts 182 in these progress reports. It is one of my few pleasures. However, by all indications, my own mental deterioration will be very rapid.

I have already begun to notice signs of emotional instability and for- 183 getfulness, the first symptoms of the burnout.

June 10   Deterioration progressing. I have become absent-minded. 184 Algernon died two days ago. Dissection shows my predictions were right. His brain had decreased in weight and there was a general smoothing out of cerebral convolutions as well as a deepening and broadening of brain fissures.

I guess the same thing is or will soon be happening to me. Now that 185 it's definite, I don't want it to happen.

I put Algernon's body in a cheese box and buried him in the back 186 yard. I cried.

June 15   Dr. Strauss came to see me again. I wouldn't open the door 187 and I told him to go away. I want to be left to myself. I have become touchy and irritable. I feel the darkness closing in. It's hard to throw off thoughts of suicide. I keep telling myself how important this introspective journal will be.

It's a strange sensation to pick up a book that you've read and en- 188 joyed just a few months ago and discover that you don't remember it. I remembered how great I thought John Milton was, but when I picked up *Paradise Lost* I couldn't understand it at all. I got so angry I threw the book across the room.

I've got to try to hold on to some of it. Some of the things I've 189 learned. Oh, God, please don't take it all away.

June 19   Sometimes, at night, I go out for a walk. Last night I couldn't 190 remember where I lived. A policeman took me home. I have the strange feeling that this has all happened to me before—a long time ago. I keep telling myself I'm the only person in the world who can describe what's happening to me.

June 21   Why can't I remember? I've got to fight. I lie in bed for days 191 and I don't know who or where I am. Then it all comes back to me in a flash. Fugues of amnesia. Symptoms of senility—second childhood. I can watch them coming on. It's so cruelly logical. I learned so much and so fast. Now my mind is deteriorating rapidly. I won't let it happen. I'll fight it. I can't help thinking of the boy in the restaurant, the blank expression, the silly smile, the people laughing at him. No—please—not that again . . .

192   *June 22* I'm forgetting things that I learned recently. It seems to be following the classic pattern—the last things learned are the first things forgotten. Or is that the pattern? I'd better look it up again. . . .

193   I reread my paper on the *Algernon-Gordon Effect* and I get the strange feeling that it was written by someone else. There are parts I don't even understand.

194   Motor activity impaired. I keep tripping over things, and it becomes increasingly difficult to type.

195   *June 23* I've given up using the typewriter completely. My co-ordination is bad. I feel that I'm moving slower and slower. Had a terrible shock today. I picked up a copy of an article I used in my research, Krueger's *Uber psychische Ganzheit*, to see if it would help me understand what I had done. First I thought there was something wrong with my eyes. Then I realized I could no longer read German. I tested myself in other languages. All gone.

196   *June 30* A week since I dared to write again. It's slipping away like sand through my fingers. Most of the books I have are too hard for me now. I get angry with them because I know that I read and understood them just a few weeks ago.

197   I keep telling myself I must keep writing these reports so that somebody will know what is happening to me. But it gets harder to form the words and remember spellings. I have to look up even simple words in the dictionary now and it makes me impatient with myself.

198   Dr. Strauss comes around almost every day, but I told him I wouldn't see or speak to anybody. He feels guilty. They all do. But I don't blame anyone. I knew what might happen. But how it hurts.

199   *July 7* I don't know where the week went. Todays Sunday I know because I can see through my window people going to church. I think I stayed in bed all week but I remember Mrs. Flynn bringing food to me a few times. I keep saying over and over Ive got to do something but then I forget or maybe its just easier not to do what I say Im going to do.

200   I think of my mother and father a lot these days. I found a picture of them with me taken at a beach. My father has a big ball under his arm and my mother is holding me by the hand. I dont remember them the way they are in the picture. All I remember is my father drunk most of the time and arguing with mom about money.

201   He never shaved much and he used to scratch my face when he

hugged me. My mother said he died but Cousin Miltie said he heard his mom and dad say that my father ran away with another woman. When I asked my mother she slapped my face and said my father was dead. I dont think I ever found out which was true but I don't care much. (He said he was going to take me to see cows on a farm once but he never did. He never kept his promises . . .)

July 10 My landlady Mrs Flynn is very worried about me. She says the way I lay around all day and dont do anything I remind her of her son before she threw him out of the house. She said she doesn't like loafers. If Im sick its one thing, but if Im a loafer thats another thing and she wont have it. I told her I think Im sick.

    I try to read a little bit every day, mostly stories, but sometimes I have to read the same thing over and over again because I dont know what it means. And its hard to write. I know I should look up all the words in the dictionary but its so hard and Im so tired all the time.

    Then I got the idea that I would only use the easy words instead of the long hard ones. That saves time. I put flowers on Algernons grave about once a week. Mrs Flynn thinks Im crazy to put flowers on a mouses grave but I told her that Algernon was special.

July 14 Its sunday again. I dont have anything to do to keep me busy now because my television set is broke and I dont have any money to get it fixed. (I think I lost this months check from the lab. I dont remember)

    I get awful headaches and asperin doesnt help me much. Mrs Flynn knows Im really sick and she feels very sorry for me. Shes a wonderful woman whenever someone is sick.

July 22 Mrs Flynn called a strange doctor to see me. She was afraid I was going to die. I told the doctor I wasnt too sick and that I only forget sometimes. He asked me did I have any friends or relatives and I said no I dont have any. I told him I had a friend called Algernon once but he was a mouse and we used to run races together. He looked at me kind of funny like he thought I was crazy.

    He smiled when I told him I used to be a genius. He talked to me like I was a baby and he winked at Mrs Flynn. I got mad and chased him out because he was making fun of me the way they all used to.

July 24 I have no more money and Mrs Flynn says I got to go to work somewhere and pay the rent because I havent paid for over two months. I dont know any work but the job I used to have at Donnegans Plastic Box Company. I dont want to go back there because they all knew me when I was smart and maybe theyll laugh at me. But I dont know what else to do to get money.

210   *July 25*   I was looking at some of my old progress reports and its very funny but I cant read what I wrote. I can make out some of the words but they dont make sense.

211   Miss Kinnian came to the door but I said go away I dont want to see you. She cried and I cried too but I wouldnt let her in because I didnt want her to laugh at me. I told her I didn't like her any more. I told her I didnt want to be smart any more. Thats not true. I still love her and I still want to be smart but I had to say that so shed go away. She gave Mrs Flynn money to pay the rent. I dont want that. I got to get a job.

212   Please . . . please let me not forget how to read and write . . .

213   *July 27*   Mr Donnegan was very nice when I came back and asked him for my old job of janitor. First he was very suspicious but I told him what happened to me then he looked very sad and put his hand on my shoulder and said Charlie Gordon you got guts.

214   Everybody looked at me when I came downstairs and started working in the toilet sweeping it out like I used to. I told myself Charlie if they make fun of you dont get sore because you remember their not so smart as you once thot they were. And besides they were once your friends and if they laughed at you that doesnt mean anything because they liked you too.

215   One of the new men who came to work there after I went away made a nasty crack he said hey Charlie I hear your a very smart fella a real quiz kid. Say something intelligent. I felt bad but Joe Carp came over and grabbed him by the shirt and said leave him alone you lousy cracker or Ill break your neck. I didnt expect Joe to take my part so I guess hes really my friend.

216   Later Frank Reilly came over and said Charlie if anybody bothers you or trys to take advantage you call me or Joe and we will set em straight. I said thanks Frank and I got choked up so I had to turn around and go into the supply room so he wouldnt see me cry. Its good to have friends.

217   *July 28*   I did a dumb thing today I forgot I wasnt in Miss Kinnians class at the adult center any more like I use to be. I went in and sat down in my old seat in the back of the room and she looked at me funny and she said Charles. I dint remember she ever called me that before only Charlie so I said hello Miss Kinnian Im redy for my lesin today only I lost my reader that we was using. She startid to cry and run out of the room and everybody looked at me and I saw they wasnt the same pepul who used to be in my class.

218   Then all of a suddin I remembered some things about the operashun and me getting smart and I said holy smoke I reely pulled a Charlie Gordon that time. I went away before she come back to the room.

219   Thats why Im going away from New York for good. I dont want to do nothing like that agen. I dont want Miss Kinnian to feel sorry for me.

Evry body feels sorry at the factery and I dont want that eather so Im going someplace where nobody knows that Charlie Gordon was once a genus and now he cant even reed a book or rite good.

Im taking a cuple of books along and even if I cant reed them Ill 220 practise hard and maybe I wont forget every thing I lerned. If I try reel hard maybe Ill be a littel bit smarter then I was before the operashun. I got my rabits foot and my luky penny and maybe they will help me.

If you ever reed this Miss Kinnian dont be sorry for me Im glad I got 221 a second chanse to be smart becaus I lerned a lot of things that I never even new were in this world and Im grateful that I saw it all for a littel bit. I dont know why Im dumb agen or what I did wrong maybe its becaus I dint try hard enuff. But if I try and practis very hard maybe Ill get a littl smarter and know what all the words are. I remember a littel bit how nice I had a feeling with the blue book that has the torn cover when I red it. Thats why Im gonna keep trying to get smart so I can have that feeling agen. Its a good feeling to know things and be smart. I wish I had it rite now if I did I would sit down and reed all the time. Anyway I bet Im the first dumb person in the world who ever found out somthing importent for sience. I remember I did somthing but I dont remember what. So I gess its like I did it for all the dumb pepul like me.

Good-by Miss Kinnian and Dr Strauss and evreybody. And P.S. 222 please tell Dr Nemur not to be such a grouch when pepul laff at him and he woud have more frends. Its easy to make frends if you let pepul laff at you. Im going to have lots of frends where I go.
P.P.S. Please if you get a chanse put some flowrs on Algernons grave in the bak yard . . .

Questions for Discussion and Writing

1. What was the advantage for Keyes in having Charlie tell the story from a FIRST-PERSON POINT OF VIEW? How does this create a strong sense of empathy and involvement? How does this vantage point make it possible for readers to evaluate how the changes in Charlie's intelligence determine his ability to understand the world around him?
2. What do you know about Charlie from his "progress reports" before the experiment begins? How does the fact that he cannot see "pictures" in the Rorschach or make up stories on the TAT give you an insight of what it would be like to have an I.Q. of 68? What is the significance of the fact that he cannot make up lies about the people in the pictures of the TAT?
3. How do changes in the style and content of Charlie's journal entries beginning with report number 7 reflect his increasing intelligence and important changes in his personality? What is Charlie able to do that he could not do before? How do details such as his uncharacteristic anger, his desire to save time and not write the words "progress report" over and over again, suggest he is becoming more intelligent?
4. How does the difference in Charlie's reaction to the Rorschach test before

and after the operation reveal the qualitative nature of intelligence? How do his reactions show an increase in self-awareness and the ability to generalize and remember?

5. How does Charlie's enhanced intelligence change his relationship with his landlady, co-workers, the doctors, Algernon, and Miss Kinnian?

6. What details in the story underscore the connections between Algernon and Charlie? How is Algernon used as an index of Charlie's increasing self-awareness? What is the significance of the title "Flowers for Algernon" as it relates to Charlie's transformation?

7. As Charlie develops, he reacts to the same events in very different ways, uses language that reflects his new intelligence—and what he writes about and how he arranges the information reveals his growing awareness. It is as if his former self and his new self are two different people and have entirely different things to say about the same experiences. Is there some situation, experience, or person that you now understand in an entirely different way than you did originally?

Hanan al-Shaykh
The Persian Carpet

Hanan al-Shaykh was born in 1945 in Lebanon and was raised in a traditional Shiite Moslem family. She began her studies at the American College for Girls in Cairo in 1963 and four years later returned to Beirut where she worked as a journalist and began writing short stories and novels. Originally written in Arabic, al-Shaykh's works have been published in Lebanon and have been ac- claimed for her capacity to realistically create situations in which her protago- nists, often women, gain a new perspective despite the cultural pressures forced upon them. Two of her novels, The Story of Zahra *(1986) and* Women of Sand and Myrrh *(1989), have been translated into English. "The Persian Carpet," translated by Denys Johnson-Davies (1983) from* Arabic Short Stories, *closely observes the behavior and emotions of a girl who is forced to re- alize that the circumstances leading to her parents getting divorced were very different from what she had believed as a child.*

When Maryam had finished plaiting my hair into two pigtails, she put 1
her finger to her mouth and licked it, then passed it over my eyebrows, moaning: "Ah, what eyebrows you have—they're all over the place!" She turned quickly to my sister and said: "Go and see if your father's still praying." Before I knew it my sister had returned and was whis- pering "He's still at it," and she stretched out her hands and raised them skywards in imitation of him. I didn't laugh as usual, nor did Maryam; instead, she took up the scarf from the chair, put it over her hair and tied it hurriedly at the neck. Then, opening the wardrobe care- fully, she took out her handbag, placed it under her arm and stretched out her hands to us. I grasped one and my sister the other. We under- stood that we should, like her, proceed on tiptoe, holding our breath as we made our way out through the open front door. As we went down the steps, we turned back towards the door, then towards the window. Reaching the last step, we began to run, only stopping when the lane had disappeared out of sight and we had crossed the road and Maryam had stopped a taxi.

Our behaviour was induced by fear, for today we would be seeing 2
my mother for the first time since her separation by divorce from my father. He had sworn he would not let her see us, for, only hours after the divorce, the news had spread that she was going to marry a man she had been in love with before her family had forced her into marry- ing my father.

My heart was pounding. This was not from fear or from running 3
but was due to anxiety and a feeling of embarrassment about the meet-

227

ing that lay ahead. Though in control of myself and my shyness, I knew that I would be incapable—however much I tried—of showing my emotions, even to my mother; I would be unable to throw myself into her arms and smother her with kisses and clasp her head as my sister would do with such spontaneity. I had thought long and hard about this ever since Maryam had whispered in my ear—and in my sister's— that my mother had come from the south and that we were to visit her secretly the following day. I began to imagine that I would make myself act exactly as my sister did, that I would stand behind her and imitate her blindly. Yet I know myself: I have committed myself to myself by heart. However much I tried to force myself, however much I thought in advance about what I should and shouldn't do, once I was actually faced by the situation and was standing looking down at the floor, my forehead puckered into an even deeper frown, I would find I had forgotten what I had resolved to do. Even then, though, I would not give up hope but would implore my mouth to break into a smile; it would none the less be to no avail.

4   When the taxi came to a stop at the entrance to a house, where two lions stood on columns of red sandstone, I was filled with delight and immediately forgot my apprehension. I was overcome with happiness at the thought that my mother was living in a house where two lions stood at the entrance. I heard my sister imitate the roar of a lion and I turned to her in envy. I saw her stretching up her hands in an attempt to clutch the lions. I thought to myself: She's always uncomplicated and jolly, her gaiety never leaves her, even at the most critical moments— and here she was, not a bit worried about this meeting.

5   But when my mother opened the door and I saw her, I found myself unable to wait and rushed forward in front of my sister and threw myself into her arms. I had closed my eyes and all the joints of my body had grown numb after having been unable to be at rest for so long. I took in the unchanged smell of her hair, and I discovered for the first time how much I had missed her and wished that she would come back and live with us, despite the tender care shown to us by my father and Maryam. I couldn't rid my mind of that smile of hers when my father agreed to divorce her, after the religious sheikh had intervened following her threats to pour kerosene over her body and set fire to herself if my father wouldn't divorce her. All my senses were numbed by that smell of her, so well preserved in my memory. I realized how much I had missed her, despite the fact that after she'd hurried off behind her brother to get into the car, having kissed us and started to cry, we had continued with the games we were playing in the lane outside our house. As night came, and for the first time in a long while we did not hear her squabbling with my father, peace and quiet descended upon the house—except that is for the weeping of Maryam, who was related to my father and had been living with us in the house ever since I was born.

Smiling, my mother moved me away from her so that she could hug   6
and kiss my sister, and hug Maryam again, who had begun to cry. I
heard my mother, who was in tears, say to her "Thank you," and she
wiped her tears with her sleeve and looked me and my sister up and
down, saying: "God keep them safe, how they've sprung up!" She put
both arms round me, while my sister buried her head in my mother's
waist, and we all began to laugh when we found that it was difficult for
us to walk like that. Reaching the inner room, I was convinced her new
husband was inside because my mother said, smiling: "Mahmoud loves
you very much and he would like it if your father would give you to
me so that you can live with us and become his children too." My sister
laughed and answered: "Like that we'd have two fathers." I was still in
a benumbed state, my hand placed over my mother's arm, proud at the
way I was behaving, at having been able without any effort to be liberated from myself, from my shackled hands, from the prison of my shyness, as I recalled to mind the picture of my meeting with my mother,
how I had spontaneously thrown myself at her, something I had
thought wholly impossible, and my kissing her so hard I had closed my
eyes.

Her husband was not there. As I stared down at the floor I froze. In   7
confusion I looked at the Persian carpet spread on the floor, then gave
my mother a long look. Not understanding the significance of my look,
she turned and opened a cupboard from which she threw me an embroidered blouse, and moving across to a drawer in the dressing-table,
she took out an ivory comb with red hearts painted on it and gave it to
my sister. I stared down at the Persian carpet, trembling with burning
rage. Again I looked at my mother and she interpreted my gaze as being one of tender longing, so she put her arms round me, saying: "You
must come every other day, you must spend the whole of Friday at my
place." I remained motionless, wishing that I could remove her arms
from around me and sink my teeth into that white forearm. I wished
that the moment of meeting could be undone and re-enacted, that she
could again open the door and I could stand there—as I should have
done—with my eyes staring down at the floor and my forehead in a
frown.

The lines and colours of the Persian carpet were imprinted on my   8
memory. I used to lie on it as I did my lessons; I'd be so close to it that
I'd gaze at its pattern and find it looking like slices of red water-melon
repeated over and over again. But when I sat down on the couch, I
would see that each slice of melon had changed into a comb with thin
teeth. The clusters of flowers surrounding its four sides were purple-
coloured. At the beginning of summer my mother would put mothballs
on it and on the other ordinary carpets and would roll them up and
place them on top of the cupboard. The room would look stark and depressing until autumn came, when she would take them up to the roof
and spread them out. She would gather up the mothballs, most of

which had dissolved from the summer's heat and humidity, then, having brushed them with a small broom, she'd leave them there. In the evening she'd bring them down and lay them out where they belonged. I would be filled with happiness as their bright colours once again brought the room back to life. This particular carpet, though, had disappeared several months before my mother was divorced. It had been spread out on the roof in the sun and in the afternoon my mother had gone up to get it and hadn't found it. She had called my father and for the first time I had seen his face flushed with anger. When they came down from the roof, my mother was in a state of fury and bewilderment. She got in touch with the neighbours, all of whom swore they hadn't seen it. Suddenly my mother exclaimed: "Ilya!" Everyone stood speechless: not a word from my father or from my sister or from our neighbours Umm Fouad and Abu Salman. I found myself crying out: "Ilya? Don't say such a thing, it's not possible."

9   Ilya was an almost blind man who used to go round the houses of the quarter repairing cane chairs. When it came to our turn, I would see him, on my arrival back from school, seated on the stone bench outside the house with piles of straw in front of him and his red hair glinting in the sunlight. He would deftly take up the strands of straw and, like fishes, they'd slip through the mesh. I would watch him as he coiled them round with great dexterity, then bring them out again until he had formed a circle of straw for the seat of the chair, just like the one that had been there before. Everything was so even and precise: it was as though his hands were a machine and I would be amazed at the speed and nimbleness of his fingers. Sitting as he did with his head lowered, it looked as though he were using his eyes. I once doubted that he could see more than vague shapes in front of him, so I squatted down and looked into his rosy-red face and was able to see his half-closed eyes behind his glasses. They had in them a white line that pricked at my heart and sent me hurrying off to the kitchen, where I found a bag of dates on the table, and I heaped some on a plate and gave them to Ilya.

10   I continued to stare at the carpet as the picture of Ilya, red of face and hair, appeared to me. I was made aware of his hand as he walked up the stairs on his own; of him sitting on his chair, of his bargaining over the price for his work, of how he ate and knew that he had finished everything on the plate, of his drinking from the pitcher, with the water flowing easily down his throat. Once at midday, having been taught by my father that before entering a Muslim house he should say "Allah" before knocking at the door and entering, as a warning to my mother in case she were unveiled, my mother rushed at him and asked him about the carpet. He made no reply, merely making a sort of sobbing noise. As he walked off, he almost bumped into the table and, for the first time, tripped. I went up to him and took him by the hand. He knew me by the touch of my hand, because he said to me in a half-

whisper: "Never mind, child." Then he turned round to leave. As he bent over to put on his shoes, I thought I saw tears on his cheeks. My father didn't let him leave before saying to him: "Ilya, God will forgive you if you tell the truth." But Ilya walked off, steadying himself against the railings. He took an unusually long time as he felt his way down the stairs. Then he disappeared from sight and we never saw him again.

Questions for Discussion and Writing

1. How is the girl whose voice we hear characterized?
2. What circumstances have made it necessary for her and her sister to visit their mother in secret?
3. What details suggest how much it means to her to see her mother again? Why is her reaction on first seeing her mother especially poignant and ironic in view of what she discovers subsequently?
4. How does seeing the situation before, during, and after the discovery from the girl's POINT OF VIEW make the story more dramatic than if it were related by an OMNISCIENT NARRATOR?
5. Why does seeing the Persian carpet cause the young girl to experience such a dramatic change in attitude toward her mother? How does seeing what Ilya, the blind man, meant to her enable the reader to understand her feelings of anger?
6. Did you ever experience a moment of disillusionment with an adult member of your family that represented a turning-point in your relationship? Describe your experience.
7. Write about one of your grandparents or parents as seen through an object you connect with him or her. Under what circumstances did you first come across this object? What associations connect this object with your parent or grandparent?
8. Analyze this story in terms of the elements of crime: motive, clues, suspects, victim, detective, alibi, and solution associated with the mystery genre.

Clarice Lispector

A Sincere Friendship

Clarice Lispector (1925–1977) was born in the Ukraine and was barely two months old when her family emigrated to Brazil. She was raised in Recife, but moved to Rio de Janeiro where she lived for most of her life. She graduated in law before turning to journalism and writing full-time. She was married to a Brazilian diplomat and lived abroad for several years. Considered one of Brazil's innovative and influential novelists and short story writers, her work is like that of Borges and Cortazar in its use of narrative to explore psychological and philosophical truths about the human condition. She is best known for her exploration of inner psychological states, especially of women protagonists who suddenly become aware of the extent to which they are trapped, shaping their lives in accordance with society's expectations. She gained widespread acclaim for Family Ties, *a collection of short stories (1960), and for* The Apple in the Dark *(1961), a complex and philosophical journey into human consciousness. Her best-known work,* The Hour of the Star *(1978), later made into an award-winning film, is a haunting and moving account of a girl surviving in the lower depths of São Paulo. Lispector's style is unique and has been widely praised for its composure and depth. These qualities underlie "A Sincere Friendship," which first appeared in* The Foreign Legion *(1964), a collection of short stories, and was translated into English. In this story, Lispector probes the fragile basis of a friendship between two adolescents. She uses an internal monologue to subtly convey the speaker's ambivalence toward a friendship that was all-important.*

1   We had not been friends for very long. We had only started to know each other well during our last year at school. From that moment onwards we were never apart. For a long time, we had both needed a friend in whom we could confide. Our friendship reached the point where we could not keep a thought to ourselves: the one would telephone the other immediately, arranging to meet without a moment's delay. After talking to each other, we felt as pleased as if we just had introduced ourselves. This continuous communication reached such a pitch of exaltation that on those days when we had nothing to confide, we anxiously searched for some topic of conversation. But the topic had to be serious, because any old topic could never accommodate the vehemence of this sincerity we were experiencing for the first time.

2   Already at this stage, the first signs of tension between us began to appear. Sometimes one of us would telephone the other, we would meet, and then have nothing to say to each other. We were very young and we did not know how to remain silent. From the outset, when we could find no topic of conversation, we tried to discuss other people.

But we were both well aware that we were debasing the nucleus of our friendship. To attempt to discuss our mutual girlfriends was also out of the question, for a fellow did not talk about his love affairs. We tried to remain silent—but became uneasy the moment we separated.

Upon returning from similar encounters, my solitude was immense and arid. I started to read books just to be able to discuss them. But a sincere friendship demanded the most pure sincerity. In my search for such sincerity, I felt nothing but emptiness. Our encounters became ever more unsatisfactory. My sincere poverty gradually became manifest. I knew that my friend had also reached an impasse.   3

About this time, my family moved to São Paulo. My friend was living alone for his family had settled in Piauí. So I invited him to move into our apartment, where I had been left in charge. We felt so excited! We eagerly arranged our books and records, and planned the ideal setting for friendship. When everything was ready—here we were in our home, somehow at a loss, silent, full only of friendship.   4

We were so anxious to save each other. Friendship is a question of salvation.   5

But all the problems had already been touched on, all the possibilities examined. All we possessed was this thing which we had eagerly sought from the beginning and found at last: sincere friendship. The only way we knew, and how bitterly we knew, to escape the solitude every spirit carries in its body.   6

But how artificial we discovered friendship to be. As if we were trying to expand a truism into a lengthy discourse which could be exhausted with one word. Our friendship was as inextricable as the sum of two numbers: it was useless to attempt to elaborate for more than a second on the fact that two and three make five.   7

We tried to organize some wild parties in the apartment, but it was not only the neighbours who protested, so that was no use.   8

If only we could at least do each other favours. But there was never the opportunity, nor did we believe in giving proof of a friendship that needed no proof. The most we could hope to do was what we were already doing: simply to know that we were friends. Yet this was not enough to fill our days, especially the long summer holidays.   9

The start of our real troubles dates from those long summer holidays.   10

The friend to whom I could offer nothing except my sincerity, turned out to be an accusation of my poverty. Moreover, our solitude at each other's side while listening to music or reading was much greater than when we found ourselves alone. Not only much greater, but also disturbing. There was no longer any peace. When we finally retired to our respective rooms, we felt so relieved that we could not bring ourselves to look at each other.   11

It is true that there was a pause in the course of these developments, a truce which gave us more hope than the reality of our situation justi-   12 fied. This occurred when my friend ran into some trouble with the Authorities. It was nothing serious, but we treated it as such in order to exploit the situation. For by that time we were already showing our readiness to do each other favours. I went eagerly from the office of one family friend to another, mustering support for my friend. And when the time came to start rubber-stamping the documents, I went all over the city—I can say in all conscience that there was not a single authorized signature which I had not been instrumental in securing.

13   During this crisis, we spent our evenings at home, worn out and animated: we related the day's achievements and planned our next move. We did not probe very deeply into what was happening, it was sufficient that all this activity should have the seal of friendship. I thought I could now understand why bride and groom pledge themselves to each other; why the husband insists upon providing for his bride, while she solicitously prepares his meals, and why a mother fusses over her children. It was, moreover, during this crisis, that at some cost I gave a small gold brooch to the woman who was to become my wife. It was only much later that I came to realize that just to be there is also a form of giving.

14   Having settled the problem with the Authorities—let it be said in passing, with a successful outcome for us—we remained close friends, without finding that word which would surrender our soul. Surrender our soul? but after all, who wanted to surrender their soul? Whatever next?

15   But what did we want after all? Nothing. We were worn out and disillusioned.

16   On the pretext of spending a holiday with my family, we separated. Besides, my friend was off to Piauí. With an emotional handshake we said goodbye at the airport. We knew that we would never see each other again, unless by accident. More than this: that we did not wish to see each other again. And we also knew that we were friends. Sincere friends.

Questions for Discussion and Writing

1. What can you infer about the narrator's personality, thought processes, education, and level of sophistication from the way in which he expresses himself?
2. How is the reader's knowledge of the friendship restricted by the FIRST-PERSON POINT OF VIEW through which it is told? At what points would you have wanted to know how the same events appeared from the friend's perspective?
3. What effect did the friendship described in the story have on the narrator? Under what circumstances was the friendship formed? In your opinion, what caused it to break up?
4. What features of the text initially led you to believe the relationship might have been between two men, two women, or a man and a woman?

5. In a short essay, describe how the relationship might have appeared from the friend's perspective.
6. Were you ever involved in a friendship where you felt as much was at stake in maintaining the friendship as did your friend? What happened?
7. Describe a time when you had to say goodbye to a friend. Include what you both said, what you felt, and the circumstances. Then describe how you first met and the high points of your relationship, including any problems you shared and overcame.

Charles Johnson

China

Born in 1948 in Evanston, Illinois, Charles Johnson graduated from Southern Illinois University and studied with the late author John Gardner, under whose direction he wrote Faith and the Good Thing *(1974), a modern folktale. Johnson's second novel,* Oxherding Tale *(1982), an entertaining story of the coming of age of a young mulatto slave in the pre–Civil War south, was praised for its ability to blend pathos, nostalgia, and comedy. His novel,* Middle Passage *(1990), won the National Book Award. Johnson was ranked as one of the ten best short story writers in America in a 1990 survey conducted by the University of Southern California. He has served as director of the creative writing program at the University of Washington in Seattle and currently is a fiction editor of* The Seattle Review. *He received the Writer's Guild Award for his PBS drama,* Booker *(1989). In addition to numerous essays and short stories, he is the author of a work of aesthetics and criticism,* Being and Race: Black Writing Since 1970 *(1988). As a writer, Johnson is committed to the development of work that explores metaphysical questions in the context of black American life. He has been a martial artist since he was nineteen and a practicing Buddhist since 1980. His deep interest in blending Asian philosophy with new perceptions of the distinctive black experience can be seen in "China," taken from his collection of short stories,* The Sorcerer's Apprentice *(1986), which explores the effect on a couple's relationship when a retired black middle-aged mailman takes up kung fu.*

> *If one man conquer in battle a thousand men, and if another conquers himself, he is the greatest of conquerors.*
>
> — *The Dharmapada*

1   Evelyn's problems with her husband, Rudolph, began one evening in early March—a dreary winter evening in Seattle—when he complained after a heavy meal of pig's feet and mashed potatoes of shortness of breath, an allergy to something she put in his food perhaps, or brought on by the first signs of wild flowers around them. She suggested they get out of the house for the evening, go to a movie. He was fifty-four, a postman for thirty-three years now, with high blood pressure, emphysema, flat feet, and, as Evelyn told her friend Shelberdine Lewis, the lingering fear that he had cancer. Getting old, he was also getting hard to live with. He told her never to salt his dinners, to keep their Lincoln Continental at a crawl, and never run her fingers along his inner thigh when they sat in Reverend William Merrill's church, because anything, even sex, or laughing too loud—Rudolph was serious—might bring on heart failure.

236

So she chose for their Saturday night outing a peaceful movie, a ² mildly funny comedy a *Seattle Times* reviewer said was fit only for tit- ters and nasal snorts, a low-key satire that made Rudolph's eyelids droop as he shoveled down unbuttered popcorn in the darkened, half- empty theater. Sticky fluids cemented Evelyn's feet to the floor. A man in the last row laughed at all the wrong places. She kept the popcorn on her lap, though she hated the unsalted stuff and wouldn't touch it, sighing as Rudolph pawed across her to shove his fingers inside the cup.

She followed the film as best she could, but occasionally her eyes ³ frosted over, flashed white. She went blind like this now and then. The fibers of her eyes were failing; her retinas were tearing like soft tissue. At these times the world was a canvas with whiteout spilling from the far left corner toward the center; it was the sudden shock of an empty frame in a series of slides. Someday, she knew, the snow on her eyes would stay. Winter eternally: her eyes split like her walking stick. She groped along the fractured surface, waiting for her sight to thaw, listen- ing to the film she couldn't see. Her only comfort was knowing that, de- spite her infirmity, her Rudolph was in even worse health.

He slid back and forth from sleep during the film (she elbowed him ⁴ occasionally, or pinched his leg), then came full awake, sitting up sud- denly when the movie ended and a "Coming Attractions" trailer began. It was some sort of gladiator movie, Evelyn thought, blinking, and it was pretty trashy stuff at that. The plot's revenge theme was a poor ex- cuse for Chinese actors or Japanese (she couldn't tell those people apart) to flail the air with their hands and feet, take on fifty costumed extras at once, and leap twenty feet through the air in perfect defiance of gravity. Rudolph's mouth hung open.

"Can people really do that?" He did not take his eyes off the screen, ⁵ but talked at her from the right side of his mouth. "Leap that high?"

"It's a *movie*," sighed Evelyn. "A *bad* movie." ⁶

He nodded, then asked again, "But can they?" ⁷

"Oh, Rudolph, for God's sake!" She stood up to leave, her seat slap- ⁸ ping back loudly. "They're on *trampolines*! You can see them in the cor- ner—there!—if you open your eyes!"

He did see them, once Evelyn twisted his head to the lower left cor- ⁹ ner of the screen, and it seemed to her that her husband looked disap- pointed—looked, in fact, the way he did the afternoon Dr. Guylee told Rudolph he'd developed an extrasystolic reaction, a faint, moaning sound from his heart whenever it relaxed. He said no more and, after the trailer finished, stood—there was chewing gum stuck to his trouser seat—dragged on his heavy coat with her help, and followed Evelyn up the long, carpeted aisle, through the exit of the Coronet Theater, and to their car. He said nothing as she chattered on the way home, remind- ing him that he could not stay up all night puttering in his basement shop because the next evening they were to attend the church's revival meeting.

10   Rudolph, however, did not attend the revival. He complained after lunch of a light, dancing pain in his chest, which he had conveniently whenever Mount Zion Baptist Church held revivals, and she went alone, sitting with her friend Shelberdine, a beautician. She was forty-one; Evelyn, fifty-two. That evening Evelyn wore spotless white gloves, tan therapeutic stockings for the swelling in her ankles, and a white dress that brought out nicely the brown color of her skin, the most beautiful cedar brown, Rudolph said when they were courting thirty-five years ago in South Carolina. But then Evelyn had worn a matching checkered skirt and coat to meeting. With her jet-black hair pinned be-hind her neck by a simple wooden comb, she looked as if she might have been Andrew Wyeth's starkly beautiful model for *Day of the Fair*. Rudolph, she remembered, wore black business suits, black ties, black wing tips, but he also wore white gloves because he was a senior usher—this was how she first noticed him. He was one of four young men dressed like deacons (or blackbirds), their left hands tucked into the hollow of their backs, their right carrying silver plates for the offer-ing as they marched in almost military fashion down each aisle: Christian soldiers, she'd thought, the cream of black manhood, and to get his attention she placed not her white envelope or coins in Rudolph's plate but instead a note that said: "You have a beautiful smile." It was, for all her innocence, a daring thing to do, according to Evelyn's mother—flirting with a randy young man like Rudolph Lee Jackson, but he did have nice, tigerish teeth. A killer smile, people called it, like all the boys in the Jackson family: a killer smile and good hair that needed no more than one stroke of his palm to bring out Quo Vadis rows pomaded sweetly with the scent of Murray's.

11   And, of course, Rudolph was no dummy. Not a total dummy, at least. He pretended nothing extraordinary had happened as the congre-gation left the little whitewashed church. He stood, the youngest son, between his father and mother, and let old Deacon Adcock remark, "Oh, how strong he's looking now," which was a lie. Rudolph was the weakest of the Jackson boys, the pale, bookish, spiritual child born when his parents were well past forty. His brothers played football, they went into the navy; Rudolph lived in Scripture, was labeled 4-F, and hoped to attend Moody Bible Institute in Chicago, if he could ever find the money. Evelyn could tell Rudolph knew exactly where she was in the crowd, that he could feel her as she and her sister, Debbie, waited for their father to bring his DeSoto—the family prize—closer to the front steps. When the crowd thinned, he shambled over in his slow, ministerial walk, introduced himself, and unfolded her note.

12   "You write this?" he asked. "It's not right to play with the Lord's money, you know."

13   "I like to play," she said.

14   "You do, huh?" He never looked directly at people. Women, she guessed, terrified him. Or, to be exact, the powerful emotions they

caused in him terrified Rudolph. He was a pud puller if she ever saw one. He kept his eyes on a spot left of her face. "You're Joe Montgomery's daughter, aren't you?"

"Maybe," teased Evelyn.   15

He trousered the note and stood marking the ground with his toe.   16
"And just what you expect to get, Miss Playful, by fooling with people during collection time?"

She waited, let him look away, and, when the back-and-forth swing   17
of his gaze crossed her again, said in her most melic, soft-breathing voice: "*You*."

Up front, portly Reverend Merrill concluded his sermon. Evelyn   18
tipped her head slightly, smiling into memory; her hand reached left to pat Rudolph's leg gently; then she remembered it was Shelberdine beside her, and lifted her hand to the seat in front of her. She said a prayer for Rudolph's health, but mainly it was for herself, a hedge against her fear that their childless years had slipped by like wind, that she might return home one day and find him—as she had found her father—on the floor, bellied up, one arm twisted behind him where he fell, alone, his fingers locked against his chest. Rudolph had begun to run down, Evelyn decided, the minute he was turned down by Moody Bible Institute. They moved to Seattle in 1956—his brother Eli was stationed nearby and said Boeing was hiring black men. But they didn't hire Rudolph. He had kidney trouble on and off before he landed the job at the Post Office. Whenever he bent forward, he felt dizzy. Liver, heart, and lungs—they'd worn down gradually as his belly grew, but none of this was as bad as what he called "the Problem." His pecker shrank to no bigger than a pencil eraser each time he saw her undress. Or when Evelyn, as was her habit when talking, touched his arm. Was she the cause of this? Well, she knew she wasn't much to look at anymore. She'd seen the bottom of a few too many candy wrappers. Evelyn was nothing to make a man pant and jump her bones, pulling her fully clothed onto the davenport, as Rudolph had done years before, but wasn't sex something else you surrendered with age? It never seemed all that good to her anyway. And besides, he'd wanted oral sex, which Evelyn—if she knew nothing else—thought was a nasty, unsanitary thing to do with your mouth. She glanced up from under her spring hat past the pulpit, past the choir of black and brown faces to the agonized beauty of a bearded white carpenter impaled on a rood, and in this timeless image she felt comforted that suffering was inescapable, the loss of vitality inevitable, even a good thing maybe, and that she had to steel herself—yes—for someday opening her bedroom door and finding her Rudolph facedown in his breakfast oatmeal. He would die before her, she knew that in her bones.

And so, after service, Sanka, and a slice of meat pie with Shel-   19
berdine downstairs in the brightly lit church basement, Evelyn returned home to tell her husband how lovely the Griffin girls had sung that

day, that their neighbor Rod Kenner had been saved, and to listen, if necessary, to Rudolph's fear that the lump on his shoulder was an early-warning sign of something evil. As it turned out, Evelyn found that except for their cat, Mr. Miller, the little A-frame house was empty. She looked in his bedroom. No Rudolph. The unnaturally still house made Evelyn uneasy, and she took the excruciatingly painful twenty stairs into the basement to peer into a workroom littered with power tools, planks of wood, and the blueprints her husband used to make bookshelves and cabinets. No Rudolph. Frightened, Evelyn called the eight hospitals in Seattle, but no one had a Rudolph Lee Jackson on his books. After her last call the starburst clock in the living room read twelve-thirty. Putting down the wall phone, she felt a familiar pain in her abdomen. Another attack of Hershey squirts, probably from the meat pie. She hurried into the bathroom, lifted her skirt, and lowered her underwear around her ankles, but kept the door wide open, something impossible to do if Rudolph was home. Actually, it felt good not to have him underfoot, a little like he was dead already. But the last thing Evelyn wanted was that or, as she lay down against her lumpy backrest, to fall asleep, though she did, nodding off and dreaming until something shifted down her weight on the side of her bed away from the wall.

20 "Evelyn," said Rudolph, "look at this." She blinked back sleep and squinted at the cover of a magazine called *Inside Kung-Fu*, which Rudolph waved under her nose. On the cover a man stood bowlegged, one hand cocked under his armpit, the other corkscrewing straight at Evelyn's nose.

21 "Rudolph!" She batted the magazine aside, then swung her eyes toward the cluttered nightstand, focusing on the electric clock beside her water glass from McDonald's, Preparation H suppositories, and Harlequin romances. "It's morning!" Now she was mad. At least working at it. "Where have you been?"

22 Her husband inhaled, a wheezing, whistlelike breath. He rolled the magazine into a cylinder and, as he spoke, struck his left palm with it. "That movie we saw advertised? You remember—it was called *The Five Fingers of Death*. I just saw that and one called *Deep Thrust*."

23 "Wonderful." Evelyn screwed up her lips. "I'm calling hospitals and you're at a Hong Kong double feature."

24 "Listen," said Rudolph. "You don't understand." He seemed at that moment as if he did not understand either. "It was a Seattle movie premiere. The Northwest is crawling with fighters. It has something to do with all the Asians out here. Before they showed the movie, four students from a kwoon in Chinatown went onstage—"

25 "A what?" asked Evelyn.

26 "A kwoon—it's a place to study fighting, a meditation hall." He looked at her but was really watching, Evelyn realized, something exciting she had missed. "They did a demonstration to drum up their

membership. They broke boards and bricks, Evelyn. They went through what's called kata and kumite and . . ." He stopped again to breathe. "I've never seen anything so beautiful. The reason I'm late is because I wanted to talk with them after the movie."

Evelyn, suspicious, took a Valium and waited.   27

"I signed up for lessons," he said.   28

She gave a glacial look at Rudolph, then at his magazine, and said in   29
the voice she had used five years ago when he wanted to take a vacation to Upper Volta or, before that, invest in a British car she knew they
couldn't afford:

"You're fifty-*four* years old, Rudolph."   30

"I know that."   31

"You're no Muhammad Ali."   32

"I know that," he said.   33

"You're no Bruce Lee. Do you want to be Bruce Lee? Do you know   34
where he is now, Rudolph? He's dead—dead here in a Seattle cemetery
and buried up on Capitol Hill."

His shoulders slumped a little. Silently Rudolph began undressing,   35
his beefy backside turned toward her, slipping his pajama bottoms on
before taking off his shirt so his scrawny lower body would not be fully
exposed. He picked up his magazine, said, "I'm sorry if I worried you,"
and huffed upstairs to his bedroom. Evelyn clicked off the mushroom-
shaped lamp on her nightstand. She lay on her side, listening to his
slow footsteps strike the stairs, then heard his mattress creak above
her—his bedroom was directly above hers—but she did not hear him
click off his own light. From time to time she heard his shifting weight
squeak the mattress springs. He was reading that foolish magazine, she
guessed; then she grew tired and gave this impossible man up to God.
With a copy of *The Thorn Birds* open on her lap, Evelyn fell heavily
asleep again.

At breakfast the next morning any mention of the lessons gave   36
Rudolph lockjaw. He kissed her forehead, as always, before going to
work, and simply said he might be home late. Climbing the stairs to his
bedroom was painful for Evelyn, but she hauled herself up, pausing at
each step to huff, then sat on his bed and looked over his copy of *Inside
Kung-Fu*. There were articles on empty-hand combat, soft-focus photos
of ferocious-looking men in funny suits, parables about legendary Zen
masters, an interview with someone named Bernie Bernheim, who began to study karate at age fifty-seven and became a black belt at age
sixty-one, and page after page of advertisements for exotic Asian
weapons: nunchaku, shuriken, sai swords, tonfa, bo staffs, training
bags of all sorts, a wooden dummy shaped like a man and called a
Mook Jong, and weights. Rudolph had circled them all. He had torn the
order form from the last page of the magazine. The total cost of the
things he'd circled—Evelyn added them furiously, rounding off the figures—was $800.

37   Two minutes later she was on the telephone to Shelberdine.

38   "Let him tire of it," said her friend. "Didn't you tell me Rudolph had Lower Lombard Strain?"

39   Evelyn's nose clogged with tears.

40   "Why is he doing this? Is it me, do you think?"

41   "It's the Problem," said Shelberdine. "He wants his manhood back. Before he died, Arthur did the same. Someone at the plant told him he could get it back if he did twenty-yard sprints. He went into convulsions while running around the lake."

42   Evelyn felt something turn in her chest. "You don't think he'll hurt himself, do you?"

43   "Of course not."

44   "Do you think he'll hurt *me*?"

45   Her friend reassured Evelyn that Mid-Life Crisis brought out these shenanigans in men. Evelyn replied that she thought Mid-Life Crisis started around age forty, to which Shelberdine said, "Honey, I don't mean no harm, but Rudolph always was a little on the slow side," and Evelyn agreed. She would wait until he worked this thing out of his system, until Nature defeated him and he surrendered, as any right-thinking person would, to the breakdown of the body, the brutal fact of decay, which could only be blunted, it seemed to her, by decaying *with* someone, the comfort every Negro couple felt when, aging, they knew enough to let things wind down.

46   Her patience was rewarded in the beginning. Rudolph crawled home from his first lesson, hunched over, hardly able to stand, afraid he had permanently ruptured something. He collapsed facedown on the living room sofa, his feet on the floor. She helped him change into his pajamas and fingered Ben-Gay into his back muscles. Evelyn had never seen her husband so close to tears.

47   "I can't *do* push-ups," he moaned. "Or sit-ups. I'm so stiff—I don't know my body." He lifted his head, looking up pitifully, his eyes pleading. "Call Dr. Guylee. Make an appointment for Thursday, okay?"

48   "Yes, dear." Evelyn hid her smile with one hand. "You shouldn't push yourself so hard."

49   At that, he sat up, bare-chested, his stomach bubbling over his pajama bottoms. "That's what it means. *Gung-fu* means 'hard work' in Chinese. Evelyn"—he lowered his voice—"I don't think I've ever really done hard work in my life. Not like this, something that asks me to give *every*thing, body and soul, spirit and flesh. I've always felt . . ." He looked down, his dark hands dangling between his thighs. "I've never been able to give *every*thing to *any*thing. The world never let me. It won't let me put all of myself into play. Do you know what I'm saying? Every job I've ever had, everything I've ever done, it only demanded part of me. It was like there was so much *more* of me that went unused after the job was over. I get that feeling in church sometimes." He lay

back down, talking now into the sofa cushion. "Sometimes I get that feeling with you."

Her hand stopped on his shoulder. She wasn't sure she'd heard him right, his voice was so muffled. "That I've never used all of you?"

Rudolph nodded, rubbing his right knuckle where, at the kwoon, he'd lost a stretch of skin on a speed bag. "There's still part of me left over. You never tried to touch all of me, to take everything. Maybe you can't. Maybe no one can. But sometimes I get the feeling that the unused part—the unlived life—*spoils*, that you get cancer because it sits like fruit on the ground and rots." Rudolph shook his head; he'd said too much and knew it, perhaps had not even put it the way he felt inside. Stiffly, he got to his feet. "Don't ask me to stop training." His eyebrows spread inward. "If I stop, I'll die."

Evelyn twisted the cap back onto the Ben-Gay. She held out her hand, which Rudolph took. Veins on the back of his hand burgeoned abnormally like dough. Once when she was shopping at the Public Market she'd seen monstrous plastic gloves shaped like hands in a magic store window. His hand looked like that. It belonged on Lon Chaney. Her voice shook a little, panicky. "I'll call Dr. Guylee in the morning."

Evelyn knew—or thought she knew—his trouble. He'd never come to terms with the disagreeableness of things. Rudolph had always been too serious for some people, even in South Carolina. It was the thing, strange to say, that drew her to him, this crimped-browed tendency in Rudolph to listen with every atom of his life when their minister in Hodges, quoting Marcus Aurelius to give his sermon flash, said "Live with the gods," or later in Seattle, the habit of working himself up over Reverend Merrill's reading from Ecclesiastes 9:10: "Whatsoever thy hand findeth to do, do it with thy might." Now, he didn't *really* mean that, Evelyn knew. Nothing in the world could be taken that seriously; that's *why* this was the world. And, as all Mount Zion knew, Reverend Merrill had a weakness for high-yellow choir girls and gin, and was forever complaining that his salary was too small for his family. People made compromises, nodded at spiritual commonplaces—the high seriousness of Biblical verses that demanded nearly superhuman duty and self-denial—and laughed off their lapses into sloth, envy, and the other deadly sins. It was what made living so enjoyably *human*: this built-in inability of man to square his performance with perfection. People were naturally soft on themselves. But not her Rudolph.

Of course, he seldom complained. It was not in his nature to complain when, looking for "gods," he found only ruin and wreckage. What did he expect? Evelyn wondered. Man was evil—she'd told him that a thousand times—or, if not evil, hopelessly flawed. Everything failed; it was some sort of law. But at least there was laughter, and lovers clinging to one another against the cliff; there were novels—

wonderful tales of how things should be—and perfection promised in the afterworld. He'd sit and listen, her Rudolph, when she put things this way, nodding because he knew that in his persistent hunger for perfection in the here and now he was, at best, in the minority. He kept his dissatisfaction to himself, but occasionally Evelyn would glimpse in his eyes that look, that distant, pained expression that asked: *Is this all?* She saw it after her first miscarriage, then her second; saw it when he stopped searching the want ads and settled on the Post Office as the fulfillment of his potential in the marketplace. It was always there, that look, after he turned forty, and no new, lavishly praised novel from the Book-of-the-Month Club, no feature-length movie, prayer meeting, or meal she fixed for him wiped it from Rudolph's eyes. He was, at least, this sort of man before he saw that martial-arts B movie. It was a dark vision, Evelyn decided, a dangerous vision, and in it she whiffed something that might destroy her. What that was she couldn't say, but she knew her Rudolph better than he knew himself. He would see the error—the waste of time—in his new hobby, and she was sure he would mend his ways.

55   In the weeks, then months, that followed, Evelyn waited, watching her husband for a flag of surrender. There was no such sign. He became worse than before. He cooked his own meals, called her heavy soul-food dishes "too acidic," lived on raw vegetables, seaweed, nuts, and fruit to make his body "more alkaline," and fasted on Sundays. He ordered books on something called Shaolin fighting and meditation from a store in California, and when his equipment arrived UPS from Dolan's Sports in New Jersey, he ordered more—in consternation, Evelyn read the list—leg stretchers, makiwara boards, air shields, hand grips, bokken, focus mitts, a full-length mirror (for Heaven's sake) so he could correct his form, and protective equipment. For proper use of his headgear and gloves, however, he said he needed a sparring partner—an opponent—he said, to help him instinctively understand "combat strategy," how to "flow" and "close the Gap" between himself and an adversary, how to create by his movements a negative space in which the other would be neutralized.

56   "Well," crabbed Evelyn, "if you need a punching bag, don't look at *me.*"

57   He sat across the kitchen table from her, doing dynamic-tension exercises as she read a new magazine called *Self*. "Did I ever tell you what a black belt means?" he asked.

58   "You told me."

59   "Sifu Chan doesn't use belts for ranking. They were introduced seventy years ago because Westerners were impatient, you know, needed signposts and all that."

60   "You told me," said Evelyn.

61   "Originally, all you got was a white belt. It symbolized innocence. Virginity." His face was immensely serious, like a preacher's. "As you

worked, it got darker, dirtier, and turned brown. Then black. You were a master then. With even more work, the belt became frayed, the threads came loose, you see, and the belt showed white again."

"Rudolph, I've heard this before!" Evelyn picked up her magazine and took it into her bedroom. From there, with her legs drawn up under the blankets, she shouted: "I *won't* be your punching bag!" 62

So he brought friends from his kwoon, friends she wanted nothing to do with. There was something unsettling about them. Some were street fighters. Young. They wore tank-top shirts and motorcycle jackets. After drinking racks of Rainier beer on the front porch, they tossed their crumpled empties next door into Rod Kenner's yard. Together, two of Rudolph's new friends—Truck and Tuco—weighed a quarter of a ton. Evelyn kept a rolling pin under her pillow when they came, but she knew they could eat that along with her. But some of his new friends were students at the University of Washington. Truck, a Vietnamese only two years in America, planned to apply to the Police Academy once his training ended; and Tuco, who was Puerto Rican, had been fighting since he could make a fist; but a delicate young man named Andrea, a blue sash, was an actor in the drama department at the university. His kwoon training, he said, was less for self-defense than helping him understand his movements onstage—how, for example, to convincingly explode across a room in anger. Her husband liked them, Evelyn realized in horror. And they liked him. They were separated by money, background, and religion, but something she could not identify made them seem, those nights on the porch after his class, like a single body. They called Rudolph "Older Brother" or, less politely, "Pop." 63

His sifu, a short, smooth-figured boy named Douglas Chan, who, Evelyn figured, couldn't be over eighteen, sat like the Dalai Lama in their tiny kitchen as if he owned it, sipping her tea, which Rudolph laced with Korean ginseng. Her husband lit Chan's cigarettes as if he were President Carter come to visit the common man. He recommended that Rudolph study T'ai Chi, "soft" fighting systems, ki, and something called Tao. He told him to study, as well, Newton's three laws of physics and apply them to his own body during kumite. What she remembered most about Chan were his wrist braces, ornamental weapons that had three straps and, along the black leather, highly polished studs like those worn by Steve Reeves in a movie she'd seen about Hercules. In a voice she thought girlish, he spoke of eye gouges and groin tearing techniques, exercises called the Delayed Touch of Death and Din Mak, with the casualness she and Shelberdine talked about bargains at Thriftway. And then they suited up, the boyish Sifu, who looked like Maharaj-ji's rougher brother, and her clumsy husband; they went out back, pushed aside the aluminum lawn furniture, and pommeled each other for half an hour. More precisely, her Rudolph was on the receiving end of hook kicks, spinning back fists faster than 64 thought, and foot sweeps that left his body purpled for weeks. A sensible man would have known enough to drive to Swedish Hospital pronto. Rudolph, never known as a profound thinker, pushed on after Sifu Chan left, practicing his flying kicks by leaping to ground level from a four-foot hole he'd dug by their cyclone fence.

65   Evelyn, nibbling a Van de Kamp's pastry from Safeway—she was always nibbling, these days—watched from the kitchen window until twilight, then brought out the Ben-Gay, a cold beer, and rubbing alcohol on a tray. She figured he needed it. Instead, Rudolph, stretching under the far-reaching cedar in the backyard, politely refused, pushed the tray aside, and rubbed himself with Dit-Da-Jow, "iron-hitting wine," which smelled like the open door of an opium factory on a hot summer day. Yet this ancient potion not only instantly healed his wounds (said Rudolph) but prevented arthritis as well. She was tempted to see if it healed brain damage by pouring it into Rudolph's ears, but apparently he was doing something right. Dr. Guylee's examination had been glowing; he said Rudolph's muscle tone, whatever that was, was better. His cardiovascular system was healthier. His erections were outstanding—or upstanding—though lately he seemed to have no interest in sex. Evelyn, even she, saw in the crepuscular light changes in Rudolph's upper body as he stretched: Muscles like globes of light rippled along his shoulders; larval currents moved on his belly. The language of his new, developing body eluded her. He was not always like this. After a cold shower and sleep his muscles shrank back a little. It was only after his workouts, his weight lifting, that his body expanded like baking bread, filling out in a way that obliterated the soft Rudolph-body she knew. This new flesh had the contours of the silhouetted figures on medical charts: the body as it must be in the mind of God. Glistening with perspiration, his muscles took on the properties of the free weights he pumped relentlessly. They were profoundly tragic, too, because their beauty was earthbound. It would vanish with the world. You are ugly, his new muscles said to Evelyn; old and ugly. His self-punishment made her feel sick. She was afraid of his hard, cold weights. She hated them. Yet she wanted them, too. They had a certain monastic beauty. She thought: He's doing this to hurt me. She wondered: What was it like to be powerful? Was clever cynicism—even comedy—the byproduct of bulging bellies, weak nerves, bad posture? Her only defense against the dumbbells that stood between them—she meant both his weights and his friends—was, as always, her acid Southern tongue:

66   "They're all fairies, right?"

67   Rudolph looked dreamily her way. These post-workout periods made him feel, he said, as if there were no interval between himself and what he saw. His face was vacant, his eyes—like smoke. In this afterglow (he said) he saw without judging. Without judgment, there were no distinctions. Without distinctions, there was no desire. Without desire . . .

He smiled sideways at her. "Who?" 68

"The people in your kwoon." Evelyn crossed her arms. "I read 69
somewhere that most body builders are homosexual."

He refused to answer her. 70

"If they're not gay, then maybe I should take lessons. It's been good 71
for you, right?" Her voice grew sharp. "I mean, isn't that what you're
saying? That you and your friends are better'n everybody else?"

Rudolph's head dropped; he drew a long breath. Lately his re- 72
sponses to her took the form of quietly clearing his lungs.

"You should do what you *have* to, Evelyn. You don't have to do 73
what anybody else does." He stood up, touched his toes, then brought
his forehead straight down against his unbent knees, which was physically impossible, Evelyn would have said—and faintly obscene.

It was a nightmare to watch him each evening after dinner. He 74
walked around the house in his Everlast leg weights, tried push-ups on
his fingertips and wrists, and, as she sat trying to watch "The
Jeffersons," stood in a ready stance before the flickering screen, throwing punches each time the scene, or shot, changed to improve his timing. It took the fun out of watching TV, him doing that—she preferred
him falling asleep in his chair beside her, as he used to. But what truly
frightened Evelyn was his "doing nothing." Sitting in meditation,
planted cross-legged in a full lotus on their front porch, with Mr. Miller
blissfully curled on his lap, a bodhisattva in the middle of houseplants
she set out for the sun. Looking at him, you'd have thought he was
dead. The whole thing smelled like self-hypnosis. He breathed too
slowly, in Evelyn's view—only three breaths per minute, he claimed.
He wore his gi, splotchy with dried blood and sweat, his calloused
hands on his knees, the forefingers on each tipped against his thumbs,
his eyes screwed shut.

During his eighth month at the kwoon, she stood watching him as 75
he sat, wondering over the vivid changes in his body, the grim firmness
where before there was jolly fat, the disquieting steadiness of his posture, where before Rudolph could not sit still in church for five minutes
without fidgeting. Now he sat in zazen for forty-five minutes a day, fifteen when he awoke, fifteen (he said) at work in the mailroom during
his lunch break, fifteen before going to bed. He called this withdrawal
(how she hated his fancy language) similar to the necessary silences in
music, "a stillness that prepared him for busyness and sound." He'd
never breathed before, he told her. Not once. Not clear to the floor of
himself. Never breathed and emptied himself as he did now, picturing
himself sitting on the bottom of Lake Washington: himself, Rudolph
Lee Jackson, at the center of the universe; for if the universe was infinite, any point where he stood would be at its center—it would shift
and move with him. (That saying, Evelyn knew, was minted in Douglas
Chan's mind. No Negro preacher worth the name would speak that
way.) He told her that in zazen, at the bottom of the lake, he worked to
discipline his mind and maintain one point of concentration; each

thought, each feeling that overcame him he saw as a fragile bubble, which he could inspect passionlessly from all sides; then he let it float gently to the surface, and soon—as he slipped deeper into the vortices of himself, into the Void—even the image of himself on the lake floor vanished.

76   Evelyn stifled a scream.

77   Was she one of Rudolph's bubbles, something to detach himself from? On the porch Evelyn watched him narrowly, sitting in a rain-whitened chair, her chin on her left fist. She snapped the fingers on her right hand under his nose. Nothing. She knocked her knuckles lightly on his forehead. Nothing. (Faker, she thought.) For another five minutes he sat and breathed, sat and breathed, then opened his eyes slowly as if he'd slept as long as Rip Van Winkle. "It's dark," he said, stunned. When he began, it was twilight. Evelyn realized something new: he was not living time as she was, not even that anymore. Things, she saw, were slower for him; to him she must seem like a woman stuck in fast-forward. She asked:

78   "What do you see when you go in there?"

79   Rudolph rubbed his eyes. "Nothing."

80   "Then *why* do you do it? The world's out here!"

81   He seemed unable to say, as if the question were senseless. His eyes angled up, like a child's, toward her face. "Nothing is peaceful some-times. The emptiness is full. I'm not afraid of it now."

82   "You empty yourself?" she asked. "Of me, too?"

83   "Yes."

84   Evelyn's hand shot up to cover her face. She let fly with a whimper. Rudolph rose instantly—he sent Mr. Miller flying—then fell back hard on his buttocks; the lotus cut off blood to his lower body—which pro-vided more to his brain, he claimed—and it always took him a few sec-onds before he could stand again. He reached up, pulled her hand down, and stroked it.

85   "What've I done?"

86   "That's it," sobbed Evelyn. "I don't know what you're doing." She lifted the end of her bathrobe, blew her nose, then looked at him through streaming, unseeing eyes. "And you don't either. I wish you'd never seen that movie. I'm sick of all your weights and workouts—sick of them, do you hear? Rudolph, I want you back the way you were: *sick*." No sooner than she said this Evelyn was sorry. But she'd done no harm. Rudolph, she saw, didn't want anything; everything, Evelyn in-cluded, delighted him, but as far as Rudolph was concerned, it was all shadows in a phantom history. He was humbler now, more patient, but he'd lost touch with everything she knew was normal in people: weak-ness, fear, guilt, self-doubt, the very things that gave the world thick-ness and made people do things. She *did* want him to desire her. No, she didn't. Not if it meant oral sex. Evelyn didn't know, really, what she wanted anymore. She felt, suddenly, as if she might dissolve before

his eyes. "Rudolph, if you're 'empty,' like you say, you don't know who—or what—is talking to you. If you said you were praying, I'd understand. It would be God talking to you. But this way . . ." She pounded her fist four, five times on her thigh. "It could be *evil* spirits, you know! There *are* evil spirits, Rudolph. It could be the Devil."

Rudolph thought for a second. His chest lowered after another long breath. "Evelyn, this is going to sound funny, but I don't believe in the Devil." 87

Evelyn swallowed. It had come to that. 88

"Or God—unless we are gods." 89

She could tell he was at pains to pick his words carefully, afraid he might offend. Since joining the kwoon and studying ways to kill, he seemed particularly careful to avoid her own most effective weapon: the wry, cutting remark, the put-down, the direct, ego-deflating slash. Oh, he was becoming a real saint. At times it made her want to hit him. 90

"Whatever is just *is*," he said. "That's all I know. Instead of worrying about whether it's good or bad, God or the Devil, I just want to be quiet, work on myself, and interfere with things as little as possible. Evelyn," he asked suddenly, "how can there be *two* things?" His brow wrinkled; he chewed his lip. "You think what I'm saying is evil, don't you?" 91

"I think it's strange! Rudolph, you didn't grow up in China," she said. "They can't breathe in China! I saw that today on the news. They burn soft coal, which gets into the air and turns into acid rain. They wear face masks over there, like the ones we bought when Mount St. Helens blew up. They all ride bicycles, for Christ's sake! They want what we have." Evelyn heard Rod Kenner step onto his screened porch, perhaps to listen from his rocker. She dropped her voice a little. "You grew up in Hodges, South Carolina, same as me, in a right and proper colored church. If you'd *been* to China, maybe I'd understand." 92

"I can only be what I've been?" This he asked softly, but his voice trembled. "Only what I was in Hodges?" 93

"You can't be Chinese." 94

"I don't want to be Chinese!" The thought made Rudolph smile and shake his head. Because she did not understand, and because he was tired of talking, Rudolph stepped back a few feet from her, stretching again, always stretching. "I only want to be what I *can* be, which isn't the greatest fighter in the world, only the fighter *I* can be. Lord knows, I'll probably get creamed in the tournament this Saturday." He added, before she could reply, "Doug asked me if I'd like to compete this weekend in full-contact matches with some people from the kwoon. I have to." He opened the screen door. "I will." 95

"You'll be killed—you know that, Rudolph." She dug her fingernails into her bathrobe, and dug this into him: "You know, you never were very strong. Six months ago you couldn't open a pickle jar for me." 96

He did not seem to hear her. "I bought a ticket for you." He held the 97 screen door open, waiting for her to come inside. "I'll fight better if you're there."

98   She spent the better part of that week at Shelberdine's mornings and Reverend Merrill's church evenings, rinsing her mouth with prayer, sitting most often alone in the front row so she would not have to hear Rudolph talking to himself from the musty basement as he pounded out bench presses, skipped rope for thirty minutes in the backyard, or shadowboxed in preparation for a fight made inevitable by his new muscles. She had married a fool, that was clear, and if he expected her to sit on a bench at the Kingdome while some equally stupid brute spilled the rest of his brains—probably not enough left now to fill a teaspoon—then he was wrong. How could he see the world as "perfect"? That was his claim. There were poverty, unemployment, twenty-one children dying every minute, every day, every year from hunger and malnutrition, more than twenty murdered in Atlanta; there were sixty thousand nuclear weapons in the world, which was dreadful, what with Seattle so close to Boeing; there were far-right Republicans in the White House: *good* reasons, Evelyn thought, to be "negative and life-denying," as Rudolph would put it. It was almost sin to see harmony in an earthly hell, and in a fit of spleen she prayed God would dislocate his shoulder, do some minor damage to humble him, bring him home, and remind him that the body was vanity, a violation of every verse in the Bible. But Evelyn could not sustain her thoughts as long as he could. Not for more than a few seconds. Her mind never settled, never rested, and finally on Saturday morning, when she awoke on Shelberdine's sofa, it would not stay away from the image of her Rudolph dead before hundreds of indifferent spectators, paramedics pounding on his chest, bursting his rib cage in an effort to keep him alive.

99   From Shelberdine's house she called a taxi and, in the steady rain that northwesterners love, arrived at the Kingdome by noon. It's over already, Evelyn thought, walking the circular stairs to her seat, clamping shut her wet umbrella. She heard cheers, booing, an Asian voice with an accent over a microphone. The tournament began at ten, which was enough time for her white belt husband to be in the emergency ward at Harborview Hospital by now, but she had to see. At first, as she stepped down to her seat through the crowd, she could only hear— her mind grappled for the word, then remembered—kiais, or "spirit shouts," from the great floor of the stadium, many shouts, for contests were progressing in three rings simultaneously. It felt like a circus. It smelled like a locker room. Here two children stood toe to toe until one landed a front kick that sent the other child flying fifteen feet. There two lean-muscled female black belts were interlocked in a delicate ballet, like dance or a chess game, of continual motion. They had a kind of sense, these women—she noticed it immediately—a feel for space and their place in it. (Evelyn hated them immediately.) And in the farthest

circle she saw, or rather felt, Rudolph, the oldest thing on the deck, who, sparring in the adult division, was squared off with another white belt, not a boy who might hurt him—the other man was middle-aged, graying, maybe only a few years younger than Rudolph—but they were sparring just the same.

Yet it was not truly him that Evelyn, sitting down, saw. Acoustics in the Kingdome whirlpooled the noise of the crowd, a rivering of voices that affected her, suddenly, like the pitch and roll of voices during service. It affected the way she watched Rudolph. She wondered: who are these people? She caught her breath when, miscalculating his distance from his opponent, her husband stepped sideways into a roundhouse kick with lots of snap—she heard the cloth of his opponent's gi crack like a gunshot when he threw the technique. She leaned forward, gripping the huge purse on her lap when Rudolph recovered and retreated from the killing to the neutral zone, and then, in a wide stance, rethought strategy. This was not the man she'd slept with for twenty years. Not her hypochondriac Rudolph who had to rest and run cold water on his wrists after walking from the front stairs to the fence to pick up the *Seattle Times*. She did not know him, perhaps had never known him, and now she never would, for the man on the floor, the man splashed with sweat, rising on the ball of his rear foot for a flying kick—was he so foolish he still thought he could fly?—would outlive her; he'd stand healthy and strong and think of her in a bubble, one hand on her headstone, and it was all right, she thought, weeping uncontrollably, it was all right that Rudolph would return home after visiting her wet grave, clean out her bedroom, the pillboxes and paperback books, and throw open her windows to let her sour, rotting smell escape, then move a younger woman's things onto the floor space darkened by her color television, her porcelain chamber pot, her antique sewing machine. And then Evelyn was on her feet, unsure why, but the crowd had stood suddenly to clap, and Evelyn clapped, too, though for an instant she pounded her gloved hands together instinctively until her vision cleared, the momentary flash of retinal blindness giving way to a frame of her husband, the postman, twenty feet off the ground in a perfect flying kick that floored his opponent and made a Japanese judge who looked like Oddjob shout "ippon"—one point—and the fighting in the farthest ring, in herself, perhaps in all the world, was over.

100

Questions for Discussion and Writing

1. How would you characterize the relationship between Evelyn and Rudolph before he decides to take up kung fu? From Evelyn's POINT OF VIEW what attitude should one have toward physical infirmities and encroaching old age?
2. In what way does Rudolph change as he progresses in kung fu? How do his new philosophy and new friends bring him into conflict with Evelyn?
3. How does the use of a LIMITED OMNISCIENT POINT OF VIEW allow the reader to

see the changes taking up kung fu produces on Rudolph from the perspective of his wife, Evelyn? Keeping in mind evidence in the story that Evelyn may be losing her eyesight, how would you interpret the final paragraph in the story? Is it possible that Rudolph was really making a twenty-foot leap?

4. In your view, what are the most important turning points in Rudolph's new sense of himself? Discuss one or two of these moments.

5. If you know anyone who has taken up one of the martial arts, discuss the extent to which their experience was similar to Rudolph's.

6. Describe how any eastern form of exercise such as t'ai chi chu'an or Yoga differs in form and purpose from western exercise such as aerobics, push-ups, jumping-jacks, or sit-ups. What objectives do the eastern kinds of exercise have that transcend their western counterparts?

Ted Hughes

Examination at the Womb-Door

Who owns these scrawny little feet?   *Death.*
Who owns this bristly scorched-looking face?   *Death.*
Who owns these still-working lungs?   *Death.*
Who owns this utility coat of muscles?   *Death.*
Who owns these unspeakable guts?   *Death.*   5
Who owns these questionable brains?   *Death.*
All this messy blood?   *Death.*
These minimum-efficiency eyes?   *Death.*
This wicked little tongue?   *Death.*
This occasional wakefulness?   *Death.*   10

Given, stolen, or held pending trial?
Held.

Who owns the whole rainy, stony earth?   *Death.*
Who owns all of space?   *Death.*

Who is stronger than hope?   *Death.*   15
Who is stronger than the will?   *Death.*

Stronger than love?   *Death.*
Stronger than life?   *Death.*
But who is stronger than death?
                                    Me, evidently.
20   Pass, Crow.

Questions for Discussion and Writing

1. How is the situation of Crow akin to that of a prisoner on trial for his life?
2. What details underscore the fragility of life when compared to the seemingly overwhelming power of death?
3. How does the poem use the back and forth movement of question and answer to carry the dramatic confrontation forward?
4. How does Hughes raise the stakes by linking Crow's survival to the broader issue of continued human existence?
5. How do the different meanings of the word *pass* add an equivocal, ironic touch to the fact that Crow will be allowed to enter life?
6. In a short essay, discuss the qualities that Crow possesses that allow him to "pass." What must Crow recognize in order to live?
7. Crow is a device that is used to see the world from a nonhuman POINT OF VIEW, to get a new perspective on a familiar environment. Can you achieve the same result by creating a riddle, without telling the reader what the answer is? Your subject may be a creature or thing that is usually silent. Your description should employ active verbs to help your readers imagine the answer to the riddle.
8. Imagine what you would hear and see if you were suddenly shrunk to the size of a pencil eraser and traveled through your own body. Describe your experiences.
9. Describe a new species of animal, including its physical appearance, habitat, unusual qualities, type of food, and mating habits. Give this new species a name.

Fadwa Tuqan

I Found It

Fadwa Tuqan, one of ten children, was born in 1917 to an influential land-owning family in Nablus, which is now the west bank of the Jordan where she still lives. Her brother was the nationalist poet, Ibrahim Tuqan, whose work influenced her greatly. Born into a very conservative society where women were kept in isolation and away from opportunities for intellectual endeavor, Tuqan succeeded despite extraordinary difficulties and today is one of the most widely recognized poets in the Arab world. She has met with world leaders, including

President Jamal Abd al-Nasser of Egypt and Moshe Dayan of Israel. Tuqan has been publishing her poetry since 1952, including the highly acclaimed collections In Front of the Locked Door *(1973) and* Give Us Love *(1979). Her poetry is characterized by an unusual candor about her emotional life, as in "I Found It" from her autobiography,* A Mountainous Journey, *translated by Naomi Shihab Nye and Salma Khadra Jayyusi (1990). "I Found It" conveys the excitement of bringing one's talent and individuality to flower against incredible cultural odds. The joyful voice of this poem made it a rallying cry for many Arabic women authors.*

I found it on a radiant day
after a long drifting.
It was green and blossoming
as the sun over palm trees
scattered golden bouquets;   5
April was generous that season
with loving and sun.

I found it
after a long wandering.
It was a tender evergreen bough   10
where birds took shelter,
a bough bending gently under storms
which later was straight again,
rich with sap,
never snapping in the wind's hand.   15
It stayed supple
as if there were no bad weather,
echoing the brightness of stars,
the gentle breeze,
the dew and the clouds.   20

I found it
on a vivid summer day
after a long straying,
a tedious search.
It was a quiet lake   25
where thirsty human wolves
and swirling winds could only briefly
disturb the waters.
then they would clear again like crystal
to be the moon's mirror,   30
swimming place of light and blue,
bathing pool for the guardian stars.

I found it!
And now when the storms wail

35 and the face of the sun is masked in clouds,
when my shining fate revolves to dark,
my light will never be extinguished!
Everything that shadowed my life
wrapping it with night after night
40 has disappeared, laid down
in memory's grave,
since the day
my soul found
my soul.

Questions for Discussion and Writing

1. How are descriptions of different SETTINGS used to represent the SPEAKER'S inner psychological journey to find inner peace?
2. How does the POINT OF VIEW from which the speaker's efforts to obtain inner peace is presented allow the reader to understand how important this quest was to her?
3. How does each of the stanzas describing a different environment represent a stage in the psychological journey? What details suggest that the "it" the speaker finds is a point of equilibrium within herself?
4. How would attaining this inner peace and equilibrium provide the speaker with the strength to cope with the turbulent environment depicted in the last stanza?
5. Is there one particular natural environment that you associate with your "real" self? Describe it and its effect on you.
6. Describe an object, animal, natural force, or psychological state, using metaphors or similes, but in the form of a riddle, without telling the reader what the answer is. Your description should use active verbs to help your readers imagine the answer to the riddle.

Maurice Kenny

Sometimes . . . Injustice

Born in 1929 near the Saint Lawrence River in upstate New York, in the traditional lands of the "People of the Flint," his Mohawk Indian ancestors, Kenny was later taken south to Bayonne, New Jersey, to live with his mother. A year later, when he was in danger of being sent to reform school, his father came to New York to retrieve him and took him back to live with him in Watertown, New York. After high school, Kenny returned to Manhattan, worked in a bookstore, and studied with Louise Bogan, the distinguished American poet. He spent two years in Mexico and then opened a nightclub in Puerto Rico. In 1967, he settled in Brooklyn where he continues to live. A near fatal heart attack in 1974 renewed his desire to focus on his Native American roots, and in the years immediately following some of his best-known works were published. By the 1980s his work brought him into such prominence that he was invited to teach, first accepting an appointment at the University of Oklahoma and later at North Country Community College in Saranac Lake, New York. Twenty-four of his books have been published and his poems have been translated into a dozen languages. He has been influential in shaping the course of Native American writing. He has coedited the poetry journal Contact/II, *is publisher of* Strawberry Press, *and through his associations with A. K. Wesasne Notes (named for the location of the Mohawk nation) and Studies in American Indian Literature, he has encouraged young Native American poets. Kenny has been nominated twice for the Pulitzer Prize. His novel* Black Robe: Isaac Jogues *(1987) was given the National Public Radio for Broadcasting Award and has been translated into French and Russian. Collections of his works include* Is Summer This Bare *(1985),* Rain and Other Fictions *(1985),* Greyhounding This America *(1987), and* Roman Nose and Other Essays *(1987). Kenny received the American Book Award in 1984 for* The Mama Poems *in which "Sometimes . . . Injustice" first appeared. As with other poems in this volume, Kenny projects a voice that, despite being dispossessed, finds strength in claiming his heritage against all odds.*

The day I was born my father bought me a 22.
A year later my mother traded it for a violin.
Ten years later my big sister traded that
for a guitar, and gave it to her boy-friend . . .
who sold it.   5

Now you know why I never learned to hunt,
or learned how to play a musical instrument,
or became a Wall St. broker.

Questions for Discussion and Writing

1. Explain how the SPEAKER's destiny was determined by actions taken by members of his family.
2. How does the POINT OF VIEW from which events in the poem are related suggest that the speaker is now willing to confront these past events?
3. Do you feel the speaker has transcended any bitterness he might have felt because of these past events?
4. Speculate on the story behind each of the events the speaker describes. What can you infer about his relationship with each of the members of the family he mentions?
5. To what extent was your family active in deciding what hobbies or career you should pursue? How did you react to their suggestions and/or interventions?
6. Describe a situation where you thought that something (a material object, a

trip, an event, a grade, a relationship, or anything else) was a sure thing, but then it did not materialize, or it disappeared even after you "had it in your hands."

7. Try your hand at writing an imitation of Kenny's poem, either as a straight adaptation using details from your own life or as a parody that captures the tone of the original and exaggerates the ending.

8. Create a poem made up of a list of images of, or phrases or sentences concerning things that drive you crazy.

Grace Caroline Bridges

Lisa's Ritual, Age 10

Grace Caroline Bridges is a psychotherapist working in Minneapolis. Her poems have appeared in the Evergreen Chronicles, The Northland Review, *and* Great River Review. *"Lisa's Ritual, Age 10" was published in* Looking for Home: Women Writing about Exile *(1990). The distinctive effects of Bridges's poetry are due to her ability to communicate a child's experience of violation through words and images that re-create the shock of this experience rather than merely describing it.*

Afterwards when he is finished with her
lots of mouthwash helps
to get rid of her father's cigarette taste.
She runs a hot bath
5   to soak away the pain
                    like red dye leaking from her
                              school dress in the washtub.
She doesn't cry.
When the bathwater cools she adds more hot.
10   She brushes her teeth for a long time.

Then she finds the corner of her room,
curls against it. There the wall is
hard and smooth
as teacher's new chalk, white
15   as a clean bedsheet. Smells
fresh. Isn't sweaty, hairy, doesn't stick
to skin. Doesn't hurt much
when she presses her small backbone
into it. The wall is steady

while she falls   away: 20
   first the hands   lost
arms dissolving   feet gone
   the legs   dis-   jointed
     body cracking down
      the center like a fault   25
       she falls inside
          slides down like
dust   like kitchen dirt
        slips off
   the dustpan into   30
              noplace

  a place where
nothing happens,
nothing ever happened.

When she feels the cool   35
wall against her cheek
she doesn't want to
come back. Doesn't want to
think about it.
The wall is quiet, waiting.   40
It is tall like a promise
only better.

Questions for Discussion and Writing

1. How does the visual appearance of the words and the way they are arranged help communicate Lisa's emotional shock and withdrawal as a result of the trauma she has experienced? Do you find this an effective POINT OF VIEW from which to describe the events?
2. To what extent might the title refer not only to the physical ritual of cleansing but the psychological ritual of distancing herself from the memories?
3. Which images in the poem do you find particularly effective in intensifying the contrast between what is innocent and what is sullied?
4. As a psychotherapist, the poet would be familiar with the clinical symptoms of children who have been sexually abused. What features of the poem indicate that children who experience this kind of abuse may become schizophrenic as a way of dealing with the trauma?
5. How is the meaning of the poem expressed in its form as well as in ideas, images, and actual words?

Eavan Boland

Anorexic

Eavan Boland, the youngest of five children, was born in 1944 in Dublin. Her father was a medievalist in law and the classics at Trinity College in Dublin and a diplomat who served in London and the United Nations. Her mother was a painter. When Boland was six years old, her family moved to London where she attended a convent school and encountered anti-Irish hostility that strongly influenced her perception of her homeland. In 1956, her family moved to New York City where she attended another Catholic school. After several years, she returned to Dublin to attend the Holy Child Convent. After graduating, she worked as a housekeeper and began writing poetry. Since then she has taught at Trinity College and the School of Irish Studies in Dublin, written poetry, and is a frequent contributor to The Irish Times. *Her first collection,* The War Horse *(1980), examines the theme of entrapment, a central motif in Boland's works, and addresses political turmoil in northern Ireland. The collection that followed,* In Her Own Image *(1980), angrily addresses the victimization of women in poems such as "Mastectomy," "Menses," and "Anorexic," reprinted here. These poems are confessional and force the reader into an intimacy that may be disquieting. In subsequent collections of poems, including* Night Feed *(1982), which focuses on motherhood,* The Journey *(1983), based on Boland's childhood relationship with her mother, and* Selected Poems *(1990), as well as in related essays such as "The Woman Poet in National Tradition" (published in the Irish journal* Studies, *Summer 1987), Boland moves the image of woman in Irish poetry from the margin to the center. In "Anorexic," hunger is used as a metaphor for the difficulties of gaining visibility and recognition in a culture that relegates women to an emblematic and passive role.*

Flesh is heretic.
My body is a witch.
I am burning it.

Yes I am torching
5   her curves and paps and wiles.
They scorch in my self denials.

How she meshed my head
in the half-truths
of her fevers

10   till I renounced
milk and honey
and the taste of lunch.

260

I vomited
her hungers.
Now the bitch is burning. 15

I am starved and curveless.
I am skin and bone.
She has learned her lesson.

Thin as a rib
I turn in sleep.
My dreams probe 20

a claustrophobia
a sensuous enclosure.
How warm it was and wide

once by a warm drum, 25
once by the song of his breath
and in his sleeping side.

Only a little more,
only a few more days
sinless, foodless, 30

I will slip
back into him again
as if I had never been away.

Caged so
I will grow 35
angular and holy

past pain,
keeping his heart
such company

as will make me forget 40
in a small space
the fall

into forked dark,
into python needs
heaving to hips and breasts 45
and lips and heat
and sweat and fat and greed.

Questions for Discussion and Writing

1. How does "Anorexic" draw on the framework of the emergence of Eve from Adam's rib in the Garden of Eden, as described in the Bible, as a source of irony? What does the SPEAKER wish to do?
2. How does the speaker's POINT OF VIEW shift from the beginning to the end of the poem? How does the shift underscore an important idea in the poem?
3. What images in the poem suggest that the SPEAKER is not merely dieting to become thin, but wishes to throw off her physical identity as a woman?
4. Discuss societal pressures on women to be thin and to merge their identities with those of men in ways that are self-destructive.
5. Have you ever gone without food or water for religious or spiritual reasons? In a short narrative, tell how you felt before, during, and after your fast.
6. Which parts of your body are you happy with and which are you dissatisfied with? To what extent do you feel your views are influenced by societal expectations promoted through advertising?

Xu Gang

Red Azalea on the Cliff

Xu Gang was born in 1945 in Shanghai, and was drafted into the Army in 1962. He began publishing poetry in 1963, and initially became well known for his poems that supported the objectives of the Cultural Revolution. Disillusioned by the bloodshed it produced, Gang experienced the frustration and alienation felt by many intellectuals after the Revolution, a mood that is expressed in "Red Azalea on the Cliff." In 1974, he graduated from Beijing University and worked for The People's Daily, *China's most important newspaper, until 1987. Published collections of his poetry include* The Great River of Full Tide, The Flower of Rain, Dedicated to October, Songs for the Far Away, *and* One Hundred Lyrics. *He has received the National Prize for Poetry, the October Magazine Award, the Yu Hua Prize, and other awards. Since 1989 he has lived in Guangdong Province and in Paris. Lyrical and symbolic in the way that they invest common objects with metaphorical meanings, Xu Gang's poems characteristically infuse landscapes with sentiments and emotions as in "Red Azalea on the Cliff," translated by Fang Dai, Dennis Ding, and Edward Morin (1982).*

Red azalea, smiling
From the cliffside at me,
You make my heart shudder with fear!

A body could smash and bones splinter in the canyon—
Beauty, always looking on at disaster.   5

But red azalea on the cliff,
That you comb your twigs even in a mountain gale
Calms me down a bit.
Of course you're not wilfully courting danger,
Nor are you at ease with whatever happens to you.   10
You're merely telling me: beauty is nature.

Would anyone like to pick a flower
To give to his love
Or pin to his own lapel?
On the cliff there is no road   15
And no azalea grows where there is a road.
If someone actually reached that azalea,
Then an azalea would surely bloom in his heart.

Red azalea on the cliff,
You smile like the Yellow Mountains,   20
Whose sweetness encloses slyness,
Whose intimacy embraces distance.
You remind us all of our first love.
Sometimes the past years look
Just like the azalea on the cliff.   25

MAY 1982
Yellow Mountain
Revised at Hangzhou

Questions for Discussion and Writing

1. What does the red azalea seem to represent to the SPEAKER? What associations are touched off in his memory when he sees it?
2. How does the POINT OF VIEW or angle from which the red azalea is seen magnify the speaker's sense of danger if he were to attempt to climb the steep cliff to obtain the beautiful flower?
3. How would being able to do something like that change the way he would see himself forever?
4. How does the red azalea come to stand for a whole set of qualities that are hard to obtain? Why is it important to the speaker that, although the flower is so fragile, it can survive in such a harsh environment unaffected by the swirling mountain winds?
5. Describe the associations you have with a particular flower.
6. Describe the time you achieved a goal after overcoming considerable difficulties.

Imamu Amiri Baraka

An Agony. As Now.

Baraka was born Everett Leroy Jones in Newark, New Jersey, in 1934. After attending Rutgers and Howard universities, he served in the Air Force and worked as a jazz critic before beginning his career as a poet, playwright, and social activist (writing initially under the name LeRoi Jones). In the 1960s he lived in Greenwich Village in New York City, edited avant-garde literary journals, and, with the production of his play Dutchman *(1964), which won an Obie Award, became a central figure of the 1960s black arts movement. After the assassination of Malcolm X, Baraka organized the Black Arts Repertory Theatre-School in Harlem, and returned to Newark where he founded the Spirit House Theater in 1966 and became a leading figure in the black liberation movement. He has continued to provide inspiration and guidance for generations of black artists in the United States, England, the Caribbean, and Africa. A prolific writer, Baraka has written thirteen volumes of poetry, beginning with his critically acclaimed* Preface to a Twenty Volume Suicide Note *(1961), twenty plays, three jazz operas, a novel, a collection of stories, and seven nonfiction works. He has taught at San Francisco State University and is now director of the African Studies Program at the State University of New York at Stony Brook. The key features of Baraka's poetry are its sense of intensity, of rebellion and reconstruction, in both the sound and form. "An Agony. As Now," from* The Dead Lecturer *(1964), speaks of the pressures that can reshape identity in response to the pain, isolation, and psychic impact of being black in a white society.*

I am inside someone
who hates me. I look
out from his eyes. Smell
what fouled tunes come in
5   to his breath. Love his
wretched women.

Slits in the metal, for sun. Where
my eyes sit turning, at the cool air
the glance of light, or hard flesh
10   rubbed against me, a woman, a man,
without shadow, or voice, or meaning.

This is the enclosure (flesh,
where innocence is a weapon. An
abstraction. Touch. (Not mine,
15   Or yours, if you are the soul I had

and abandoned when I was blind and had
my enemies carry me as a dead man
(if he is beautiful, or pitied.

It can be pain. (As now, as all his
flesh hurts me.) It can be that. Or   20
pain. As when she ran from me into
that forest.
         Or pain, the mind
silver spiraled whirled against the
sun, higher than even old men thought   25
God would be. Or pain. And the other. The
yes. (Inside his books, his fingers. They
are withered yellow flowers and were never
beautiful.) The yes. You will, lost soul, say
"beauty." Beauty, practiced, as the tree. The   30
slow river. A white sun in its wet sentences.

Or, the cold men in their gale. Ecstasy. Flesh
or soul. The yes. (Their robes blown. Their bowls
empty. They chant at my heels, not at yours.) Flesh
or soul, as corrupt. Where the answer moves too quickly.   35
Where the God is a self, after all.)

Cold air blown through narrow blind eyes. Flesh,
white hot metal. Glows as the day with its sun.
It is a human love, I live inside. A bony skeleton
you recognize as words or simple feeling.   40

But it has no feeling. As the metal, is hot, it is not,
given to love.

It burns the thing
inside it. And that thing
screams.   45

Questions for Discussion and Writing

1. How would you characterize the personality of the SPEAKER in this poem? What details in the poem suggest that the SPEAKER is an alter ego or PERSONA the poet has created specifically to express these feelings?
2. What details suggest that the barrier the SPEAKER created to protect himself also limits his humanity? What situation has arisen that now makes the SPEAKER keenly aware of his "agony"?
3. What aspects of the poem create an impression that you are overhearing the private, innermost thoughts of a soul in torment?

4. What specific feelings, thoughts, descriptive details, or actions create a picture of an imprisoned self? How does the poet use opposing sets of images (for example, intense heat and intense cold, fullness and emptiness, hard metal and soft skin) to create the enormous sense of alienation the SPEAKER feels?

5. How does the shift in POINT OF VIEW at the end of the poem enable the reader to share the SPEAKER's feelings of how he sees himself?

6. Have you ever known anyone who built a barrier between himself or herself and others to avoid pain and rejection, only to discover this made them more vulnerable to any kind of human contact?

7. The speaker in this poem has closed himself off from others. Have you ever literally or figuratively closed yourself off or locked others out of your life emotionally—or, conversely, have you ever been ostracized or befriended someone who was? Discuss the circumstances.

8. Describe a situation where someone (teacher, salesperson) did not see the real you and reacted instead to some attribute such as gender, race, ethnicity, or appearance.

Cathy Song

The Youngest Daughter

_____

Born in 1955 in Honolulu, Hawaii, of Chinese and Korean ancestry, Cathy Song was educated at Wellesley and at Boston University. Song currently teaches at the University of Hawaii at Manoa. Her first book of poems, Picture Bride *(1983), won the Yale Younger Poets Award and was nominated for the National Book Critics Circle Award. It tells the story of Song's Korean grandmother who was sent for as a mail-order bride in Hawaii on the basis of her photograph. Much of Song's poetry is autobiographical and treats family relationships often from a first-person female point of view. Her poetry has been praised often for its quiet strength, candor, and immediacy conveyed through images from everyday life. Her second collection,* Frameless Windows, Squares of Light *(1988), is also autobiographical and is based on her experiences in Denver and as the mother of a young boy and girl. "The Youngest Daughter" (from* Picture Bride*) depicts a crucial moment in which the speaker must decide between her own need to be independent and the need of her elderly mother for continued care.*

The sky has been dark
for many years.
My skin has become as damp
and pale as rice paper
5   and feels the way

mother's used to before the drying sun
parched it out there in the fields.

Lately, when I touch my eyelids,
my hands react as if
I had just touched something
hot enough to burn.   10
My skin, aspirin colored,
tingles with migraine. Mother
has been massaging the left side of my face
especially in the evenings
when the pain flares up.   15

This morning
her breathing was graveled,
her voice gruff with affection
when I wheeled her into the bath.   20
She was in a good humor,
making jokes about her great breasts,
floating in the milky water
like two walruses,
flaccid and whiskered around the nipples.   25
I scrubbed them with a sour taste
in my mouth, thinking:
six children and an old man
have sucked from those brown nipples.

I was almost tender   30
when I came to the blue bruises
that freckle her body,
places where she had been injecting insulin
for thirty years. I soaped her slowly,
she sighed deeply, her eyes closed.   35
It seems it has always
been like this: the two of us
in this sunless room,
the splashing of the bathwater.

In the afternoons   40
when she has rested,
she prepares our ritual of tea and rice,
garnished with a shred of gingered fish,
a slice of pickled turnip,
a token for my white body.   45
We eat in the familiar silence.
She knows I am not to be trusted,

even now planning my escape.
As I toast to her health
50   with the tea she has poured,
a thousand cranes curtain the window,
fly up in a sudden breeze.

Questions for Discussion and Writing

1. How is this poem shaped as an account of a long-brewing crisis between the SPEAKER and her mother that has finally reached the moment of decision?
2. How does the fact that the poem is related from the point of view of the youngest daughter help explain the nature of the emotional conflict she is experiencing?
3. How do details related to the SPEAKER'S brothers and sister give you insight into her dilemma? In your opinion, how aware is her mother of the crisis the daughter is experiencing?
4. In a short essay, discuss whether you think the daughter should stay with her mother or go out on her own.
5. If you or anyone you know has been faced with a similar choice, what did they do?
6. Describe the experience you had the first time you lived away from home.

Octavio Paz

The Street

Born in Mexico City in 1914, Octavio Paz has spent a good deal of his life traveling throughout the world. He lived in Spain during the Spanish Civil War and was influenced by the poetry of Quevedo and Gongora. In 1940, he resided in the United States when he received a Guggenheim Fellowship and came into contact with the poetry of Eliot, Pound, and Cummings. From 1946 to 1951 he lived in Paris, participated in the Surrealist movement and drew upon ancient Mexican mythology to produce Sun Stone, *a masterpiece of this period. From 1962 until 1968 he was Mexico's ambassador to India, whose culture, art, and philosophy influenced his writing. The concepts of detachment from the outside world, the illusory nature of reality, the illusion of the ego, and transcendence through the senses appear as themes in his poetry written during this period. Paz resigned as ambassador to protest the Mexican government's repressive actions taken against students before the 1968 Olympic games. He has held distinguished teaching positions at Cambridge University, the University of Texas at Austin, and Harvard. Paz's influence on contemporary Mexican writing has been extraordinary because of his ability to encompass the main intellectual currents of modern times in a bewildering number of fields, including*

art, aesthetics, philosophy, Oriental religion, anthropology, psychology, and political ideology, themes that appear in his twenty volumes of essays, short fiction, and poetry. His monumental achievement was recognized in 1990 when
he was awarded the Nobel Prize for Literature. Most of his poetry has appeared
in English in the Collected Poems, 1957–1987 (1987). Volumes of his poetry
include Piedra de Sol (1957) and Configurations 1958–69 (1973), and
among his celebrated prose works are Labyrinth of Solitude (1961),
Convergences (1987), and Eagle or Sun (1990). In "The Street," translated
by Willis Knapp Jones (1963), Paz presents an eerie dream world from the perspective of a speaker who is both pursuer and pursued. In this work, Paz blends
surrealism with symbolism to depict a fragmented consciousness searching for
lost unity.

The street is very long and filled with silence.
I walk in shadow and I trip and fall,
And then get up and walk with unseeing feet
Over the silent stones and the dry leaves,
And someone close behind, tramples them, too. 5
If I slow down and stop, he also stops.
If I run, so does he. I look. No one!
The whole street seems so dark, with no way out.
And though I turn and turn, I can't escape.
I always find myself on the same street 10
Where no one waits for me and none pursues.
Where I pursue, a man who trips and falls
Gets up and seeing me, keeps saying: "No one!"

Questions for Discussion and Writing

1. In your own words tell the story contained in the poem. How does the
   SPEAKER find himself in a situation very different from the one he expected?
2. What features in this poem link it with the strange reality we often encounter
   in dreams?
3. What does the speaker realize at the end of the poem that he did not acknowledge at the beginning?
4. How does the shift in POINT OF VIEW in the last lines contrast ironically with
   the preceding events?
5. How do you see the speaker in this poem—as one destined to repeat his
   mistakes, as a paranoid personality, or as someone who is experiencing
   déja vu?
6. Describe a dream in which you were being chased. Include a description of
   any surrealistic elements in your dream.
7. Describe a dream you would like to have and describe a nightmare you
   would be afraid to have.
8. Describe the people, actions, and atmosphere of the most interesting street
   corner you have ever seen.

Manuel Puig

Kiss of the Spider Woman

Manuel Puig (1932–1990) was born in a remote town in the Argentine pampas. He gained an early command of English and a lifelong love of films by watching Hollywood movies of the 1930s and 1940s. Puig studied philosophy at the University of Buenos Aires and in 1956 received a scholarship to study film at the Cinecitta in Rome. He finished his first novel, Betrayed by Rita Hayworth, *in 1968. His second novel was titled* Heartbreak Tango *(1969), and in 1973* Buenos Aires Affair *was published. The work for which he is best known,* Kiss of the Spider Woman *(1976), explores the relationship between two cellmates, one, Molina, an aging homosexual immersed in fantasies from his favorite films, and a young Marxist, Valentin, who has been tortured and imprisoned for his political activities. As the relationship between Molina and Valentin becomes more complex we gain insights into the forces that shape political, sexual, and basic human identity. The story of how each is transformed through their relationship led to various adaptations, including a play and a 1987 Academy Award–winning film, directed by the Argentine director Hector Babenco, starring William Hurt and Raul Julia. The screenplay, adapted by Leonard Schrader from Puig's novel as translated by Thomas Colchie, faithfully follows the original. In the novel, Puig used a variety of dramatic techniques, including dialogue between characters, internal monologues, excerpts from news and police reports, and descriptions of films, interwoven to tell the story of Molina and Valentin. Writing a screenplay from this novel required Schrader not only to construct dialogue and actions for the characters in order to show us scenes that are only narrated in the novel, but also to indicate the camera work that determines how we view the scene.*

A SCREENPLAY BY

Leonard Schrader

BASED ON THE NOVEL BY

Manuel Puig

Kiss of the Spider Woman

INTRODUCTION
BY DAVID WEISMAN

I welcome this opportunity to introduce a screenplay that changed my life. Although screenwriter Leonard Schrader and I come from radically different backgrounds, we both arrived in Hollywood in the early seventies after extensive journeys abroad during the sixties. When we met we soon found that we shared similar views on independent filmmaking, and deep affinities for the cultures of Japan and South America.

Leonard left the intense Dutch-Calvinist life of Grand Rapids, Michigan, by accepting a teaching post at Kyoto University. He wound up living five years in Japan, and in some senses still does. Personal experiences there led to the writing of Sidney Pollock's film *The Yakuza*, and his younger brother Paul Schrader's film *Mishima*. Additionally, Len has written several strictly Japanese movies, including the prize-winning *Taiyo Nusunde Otoko* (*The Man Who Stole the Sun*). Before becoming immersed in Japan, Leonard did graduate studies in modern Latin American Literature at the Iowa Writers' Workshop. And by coincidence, while Len was in the midwest learning his craft under Jose Danosa and Borges himself, I was wandering South America on my own Candide-like adventure before discovering *my* second homeland—Brazil.

Leonard and I met making a film in Japan that unexpectedly became a blockbuster in that market. Encouraged by our first collaboration, we struggled to find a new project we could both believe in. About this time we saw several Brazilian films that were playing the arthouse circuit: Carlos Diegues' *Bye Bye Brasil, Dona Flor* (which introduced Sonia Braga to the world), and Hector Babenco's *Pixote*, among others. Clearly, something exciting was happening below the equator, so I decided to return to Brazil for the first time in thirteen years to investigate the possibilities. I arrived in Rio de Janeiro on Christmas day, 1981—my Portuguese rusty, but still fluent. I had been given some subtle hints by Fabiano Canosa (of the Public Theater in New York, who championed Brazilian cinema in the United States) and by New Year's Day I managed to meet the Brazilian directors whose work Len and I had

271

seen—a small but remarkably sophisticated circle of filmmakers, most of whom had emerged from the underground *cinema novo* movement of the sixties. I sensed that I had found my destiny. I would make the first really international Brazilian movie. My twenty-year-long familiarity with the language, culture, and sensibilities of Brazil was clearly the only asset I needed to build the bridge. Then, just as I began to look for the right project, Hector Babenco introduced me to the movie-obsessed world of author Manuel Puig and his exquisite novel *Kiss of the Spider Woman*. A stage play of Puig's cult bestseller was popular in Rio/São Paulo at the time, and Babenco sensed that it would make a wonderful film, if only he could persuade the reclusive novelist to grant the rights. Hector was in despair. Puig was disgusted by versions of his earlier works done by Latin American filmmakers, and staunchly refused to sell Babenco the rights—both were Argentines living in Brazil, and if Puig was skeptical about regional directors, another Argentine was out of the question.

As I listened to Hector bemoan his plight, I began to think out another approach. When Puig and I met, he immediately began to explain his concerns; gradually it became clear that all Manuel really wanted was reliable assurances of a quality screen adaptation—in English—a kind of "international passport" for his most cherished creation. He shrewdly understood that this was the way to attract two really fine international actors for Molina and Valentin. When he saw that I understood this as well, Manuel began to view the proposal in a whole new light. Eventually he gave his blessings and generous support to the film.

In retrospect I realize that the direction established during the process of acquiring the Puig rights was the first of three fundamental turning points in making *Kiss of the Spider Woman* a unique film. Unwittingly, I had taken the first step in evolving a hybrid form of independent production. This would be the first time a South American film was made in English with American stars for the international market. And inevitably, the issue at the heart of each crucial juncture was the script.

When I returned to Los Angeles I asked Leonard Schrader to read Puig's novel. He was struck by its avant-garde mix of cool style and hot content. He considered Molina as rich a character as Falstaff or Hamlet. I was pleased that he shared my enthusiasm; it seemed as if we'd found the project we were looking for—the one we could believe in despite evidence that our beliefs would take us on a long road of sacrifice and humility.

In the beginning is the word; or, as Len puts it, black marks on white paper. Until you have a good script, nothing of substance can ever happen on a production. And if you have a script that is *really* good, other good things will happen.

The second critical juncture in the project's evolution was casting

Molina and Valentin. Early on, Burt Lancaster had read Puig's novel and expressed a strong desire to play Molina—at the time, a mammoth risk for a star of his stature and age. Moreover, he was so taken with the challenge that he himself suggested he would go to Brazil and work for nothing, if necessary, to get the film made. With Lancaster's enthusiasm as an inspiration, Len worked a year for almost no money to write a script he was proud of, one he felt would convey the power and emotion of Puig's story on the screen. Leonard is not the kind of writer who dashes out a script haphazardly; in fact, he generally will not write the first sentence until he pretty much has the last one in his mind.

Waiting for Leonard to complete his draft drove poor Hector mad. He never believed we would find financing in the United States—no South American production ever had before. All Babenco really wanted to achieve in America was to nail down the participation of Burt Lancaster, an actor he deeply admired and who had often worked with foreign directors. Waiting a year for a writer to perfect a script was not part of Babenco's spontaneous and emotion-charged style. Moreover, he was extremely insecure about making a film in English, a language he had not yet mastered. Luckily, this factor plus his anxieties about Latino integrity caused us to gravitate to Raul Julia as the ideal Valentin to Burt Lancaster's Molina. But even that charismatic cast and a proposed budget under $3 million could not persuade a single studio or independent to finance the film. One after another, the reactions were the same: "A fascinating and brilliant script; we're sure it will make a great film—but unfortunately it's not for us. Good luck and if you do get it made please let us be the first to see it."

What we had in the eyes of any potential money source was a marketing nightmare. Typical Marketing Analysis one-liner: "A QUEER AND A COMMIE TRAPPED IN A PRISON CELL DISCUSS OLD MOVIES AND LEARN TO LOVE." Only Los Angeles attorney Peter Dekom shared my dogged determination to pursue each financing lead to the end, but nothing could overcome the perception of marketing nightmare—except the quality of the script, when it was finished the way Leonard wanted it.

In mid-March of 1983, shortly after Raul Julia's agent Jeff Hunter confirmed that Raul would do Valentin, I got a strange call from another agent in the same office, Gene Parseghian, who praised the script as one of the best he'd read in years and asked if I had ever considered William Hurt.

I was baffled by the question, assuming he meant William Hurt for the role of Valentin, to which his agency had just committed Raul Julia. Sensing my confusion, Parseghian clarified that he was suggesting Hurt for the role of Molina. I must admit I was even more baffled, because the icon of Burt Lancaster as Molina had dominated my mind for over a year. Parseghian understood and gently requested that if for any reason

Lancaster did not do the part, would we please consider William Hurt. I agreed.

For me, it was a remarkable experience to have a script that had such a powerful effect on virtually all who read it—except the money people. But perhaps the ultimate irony was that Burt Lancaster, who we had hoped so much would like the script, never really felt comfortable with it. Then, in late May, '83, we learned he was to undergo major heart surgery. Now, for health reasons, he could no longer contemplate the strain of making a movie in Brazil that year.

With Lancaster out of the picture, Babenco was once again in despair. He was determined to make his movie before the Puig rights-option expired, and had long since abandoned any hope of finding money in the States. He returned to São Paulo with his page-by-page Portuguese translation of Len's script to raise the *cruzeiros* to make the film with Brazilian actors.

The following week, I called Gene Parseghian in New York and asked if he was still serious about William Hurt. He responded affirmatively and immediately pouched the script to Hurt in London, where he'd just completed *Gorky Park*. Three days later, Parseghian called and quietly said, "David, William Hurt loves Leonard Schrader's script and will do *Kiss of the Spider Woman* subject to a meeting with Hector Babenco and a screening of his previous film."

The power of black marks on white paper.

It was understandably difficult for a director like Babenco to assimilate the notion of William Hurt as Molina. Virtually since the project was born, Burt Lancaster had been Hector's fantasy of Molina. Now, before he could forget his dream of Lancaster, he was informed that the script had had a profound effect on William Hurt, an artist whose work Hector scarcely knew, but whose craft and power as a screen actor were undeniable. Len and I were thrilled, and our optimism persuaded Hector to fly north once more to see what would happen.

In early July we all met in New York and decided to make the film together: Bill, Raul, Hector, Len, and myself. We all worked without compensation; our salaries became "deferred equity" investments in the film. The cash needed for production (including the "Nazi Movie" insert film) in Brazil and post-production in Los Angeles was raised from a group of investors in São Paulo and my friends Jane Holzer and Michael Maiello in New York, plus a small advance against Brazilian rights from Embrafilme in Rio de Janeiro. We had no completion bond, nor any real guarantee that the film would ever be finished or distributed. Those who invested agreed to recoup simultaneously with the deferred equity participants, the deal language reciting the mutual risks and sacrifice required to make the film without compromise to anyone but ourselves.

On the plane, Hector ran into Sonia Braga and spontaneously invited her to play the cameo role of Marta, Valentin's girlfriend. By

September, when we began rehearsals, Len had completed the final shooting script, including modifications of the Molina character for William Hurt and certain structural adjustments, such as the decision to make the "Nazi Movie" the only complete movie tale Molina would tell. The novel contains five movie tales; in one preliminary shooting script Molina told portions of both the "Nazi Movie" and the original *Cat People*, while another draft opened with the conclusion of a Mexican melodrama. Sonia was also cast as diva Leni La Maison, the chanteuse in the Nazi propaganda film-within-the-film, and the enigmatic Spider Woman, linking the three women characters in the story. Manuel Puig came to São Paulo from Rio often during pre-production, generously providing details for the "Nazi Movie."

We shot for a total of ninety-seven days, from October '83 through February '84. As grueling as it may have seemed, the real heartache was yet to come. Post-production was done in Los Angeles on a shoestring that kept getting longer and longer. Leonard had left São Paulo shortly after shooting began to join his brother Paul in the making of *Mishima* in Tokyo. Hector and I had big problems in the editing room. In his eyes, the film was finished at a length and pace I found unbearable. Through the Los Angeles summer we remained deadlocked until Len resurfaced, exhausted from the ordeal of the *Mishima* shoot, but nonetheless with a vital fresh eye. Hector then returned to Brazil to supervise the musical score while Len and I began to hone down the picture. In São Paulo, Hector discovered he had lymphoma cancer. This tragedy had a profound effect on the completion of the film. Len and I had to supervise the balance of post-production, involving continual refining of the picture cut and extensive ADR (voice-dubbing) of the actors, while Bob Dawson created the complex main titles and color desaturation for the "Nazi Movie." Hector was able to be with us during the first mix at Sound One Studio in New York during November '84, but not for the final re-cut mix at Fantasy Studios in Berkeley the following April.

Leonard's return from Tokyo in mid-July was the film's final turning point. He saw the film in his mind's eye, as only the screenwriter can. Despite physical exhaustion, he could instantly analyze the problems of pacing and cutting by a very blunt standard: "Slow doesn't mean profound, and art is never boring—because if it's boring, it's not art." The script design required holding audience attention for an inordinate span before sinking the plot hook—to achieve this, performances and pacing were crucial.

From the independent production worldview that Leonard Schrader and I shared before my visit to Brazil in 1981, four Academy Award nominations—Best Picture, Best Actor, Best Director, Best Screenplay Adaptation—and a Best Actor Oscar were beyond the realm of possibility. Starting with William Hurt's triumph at the 1985 Cannes Film Festival, through the record-breaking openings of *Kiss of the Spider Woman* that summer, critics' lists, Golden Globes, right up to the "Big Night" itself on March 24th, 1986—it was a dream voyage that began with Len's black marks on white paper.

Kiss of the Spider Woman

The screen is BLACK. *We hear a "woman's"* VOICE.

VOICE OF MOLINA: She, uh. Well, something a little strange, that's what you notice that she's not a woman like all the others.
(*pause*)
She seems all wrapped up in herself. Lost in a world she carries deep inside her. But surrounded by a world of luxury.
(FADE TO:)

INT. PRISON CELL—NIGHT

We PAN *a stark cell and discover a woman's touch—glamor magazines, earrings, clothesline, pin-ups of Lana Turner and Rita Hayworth.*

VOICE OF MOLINA: A sumptuous boudoir. Her bed all quilted satin. Chiffon drapes. From her window you can see the Eiffel Tower.
(*pause*)
Suddenly her maid brings in a gift-wrapped box, a token from an admirer. She's a cabaret star, of the highest rank. She opens the box, it's a diamond bracelet, but she sends it back.
(*pause*)
Men are really at her feet. She's known a few; but not the one she's been waiting for all her life—a real man.
(*The camera finds the* PRISONER *who is speaking.*
He is LUIS MOLINA, 41, *his red-tinted hair no longer hiding the gray. He has the seasoned face of a man who has seen it all, and been hurt by most of it.*)
MOLINA: Her maid has prepared her a foam bath. The star takes a towel and wraps it around her hair like a turban. Her fingernails painted a rosy peach, she unfastens her taffeta night gown and lets it slide smoothly down her thighs to the tile floor.
(*Molina, playing the role, wraps a red towel around his head and sashays toward the other bunk.*)
MOLINA: Her skin glistens, her petite ankle slips into the perfumed wa-

ter, then her sensuous legs, until finally her whole body is caressed with foam.

(*The* CELL-MATE *glances over his shoulder. He is* VALENTIN ARREGUI, 34, *his arms marked by torture. He has the intense look of a man who has been hurt in more ways than one.*)

VALENTIN: I told you.—No erotic descriptions.

(*Molina hides his delight at having evoked a response.*)

MOLINA: Whatever, but she's a ravishing woman, do you know what I mean? I mean the most ravishing woman in the world.

VALENTIN: Yeah, sure.

MOLINA: She really is—perfect figure, classical features, but with these big green eyes.

(*We drift into the* MOVIE *he describes. A glamorous* STAR *in a lavish bathtub caresses her skin with foam. Valentin's voice wrenches us back to the cell.*)

VALENTIN: They're black.

MOLINA: I'm the one who saw the movie, but if that's what you want—big black eyes.

(*resumes*)

Kind eyes, tender eyes, but beware. They can see everything.

(*pause*)

There's nothing you can hide from them.

(*Another* MOVIE *flash. The Star steps from the foamy water and gazes into a mirror with big sad eyes.*)

MOLINA: No matter how lonely she may be, she keeps men at a distance.

VALENTIN (*laughs*):   She's probably got bad breath or something.

MOLINA: If you're going to crack jokes about a film I happen to be fond of, there's no reason to go on.

(*Molina glares at him. Valentin turns away, too weak to care one way or the other.*)

VALENTIN: Alright, alright. Go ahead.

MOLINA: Suddenly we're in Paris! Troops are marching right underneath the Arc de Triomphe. Really handsome soldiers, and the French girls are applauding as they pass by.

(*pause*)

Then we're on this typical Parisian back-street, dead end, sort of looking up a hill.

(*Another flash.* TWO FRENCHMEN *with yarmulkes unload a truck in the dark. The images resemble a slapdash Nazi propaganda film.*)

MOLINA: And these really weird-looking Frenchmen, not the typical ones with the berets, are unloading a truck. It's wartime, of course, and the boxes contain contraband delicacies. Like canned meat . . . the best cheeses . . . peaches in syrup—

VALENTIN (*sitting up*):   Don't talk about food.

MOLINA: Not to mention the hams, and the pates—

VALENTIN: I'm serious. No food and no naked women.
    (*Valentin struggles to the shit-bucket in the corner and, exhausted, leans against the wall as he urinates.*)
MOLINA: You still feeling dizzy?
VALENTIN: It's my back.
MOLINA: You've been bleeding again. Look at your shirt, it's all wet.
VALENTIN: It's just sweat. I had another fever break.
MOLINA: What do you think so far?
    (*pause*)
    Isn't it fabulous?
VALENTIN: It helps pass the time.
    (*Valentin hobbles toward his bunk. His shirtback is streaked with old bloodstains.*)
MOLINA: Does that mean you like it?
VALENTIN: Doesn't help any great cause, but I guess it's alright.
MOLINA: Blessed Mary, is that all you can talk about? You must've studied Political Philosophies in school.
VALENTIN: The phrase is Political *Science*, and the answer is no, I studied Journalism.
MOLINA: Ah! So you *can* appreciate a good story.
VALENTIN: And easily spot a cheap one.
MOLINA: Well, I know it's nothing terribly intellectual like you must be used to. It's just a romance, but it's so beautiful.
    (*pause*)
    Now. Suddenly this military convoy rushes forward.
    (CUT TO:)

EXT. PARIS BACK-STREET—NIGHT (NAZI MOVIE)

Spotlights hit the Frenchmen unloading the truck. German TROOPS *grab them. A handsome* LIEUTENANT *shoves one against the truck.*

VOICE OF MOLINA: Marvelous German soldiers catch those weird smugglers in the act and arrest them all.
    (*A small truck lurks in the shadows.*)
VOICE OF MOLINA: But watching nearby is this small truck, with these two French thugs from the Resistance who are spying on the Germans.—This hulking Clubfoot and his half-deaf Flunky.
    (CUT TO:)

INT. CELL—NIGHT

Valentin sits up on his bunk.

VALENTIN: Wait a minute. Those weird guys the Germans arrested?
MOLINA: Yes?
VALENTIN: What do you mean, they didn't look French?
MOLINA: They didn't look French. They looked, uh, Turkish. I'm not

sure, they had like these caps on their heads—like these, like these,
uh . . . Turkish. Like fezzes.

VALENTIN: Those caps are yarmulkes. Can't you see this is a fucking
anti-Semitic film?

MOLINA: Oh, come on!

VALENTIN: Wait. This must've been a German movie, right?

MOLINA: I don't know, it was from years ago.—Look. I don't explain
my movies. It just ruins the emotion.

VALENTIN: This must've been a Nazi propaganda film done during the
war.

MOLINA: I don't know, that's just the background. This is where the
important part begins, the part about the lovers. It's divine.
(CUT TO:)

INT. PARIS CABARET—NIGHT (NAZI MOVIE)

Deco doors swing open. Elegant waiters move along dimly-lit tables.

VOICE OF MOLINA: Every night the chic set flocks to this exclusive
club—with lovers at every table, spies in every corner. And the top
officers of the German High Command.
(*pause*)
One of them is Werner. Werner, so distant, so divine. And the Chief
of Counter-Intelligence for all France.
(*pause*)
And Michelle with her angel face, the cigarette girl who really is
working for the— well, you'll see.
(*Michelle leaves the table of the handsome blond Werner. Musical* FAN-
FARE. *Dancing couples sit and applaud.*)

VOICE OF MOLINA: And then, the moment they're all waiting for.
(CUT TO:)

INT. CELL—NIGHT

*Molina opens his clothesline towels like a stage curtain and strikes a grandiose
pose.*

MOLINA: Stepping into the spotlight is that legendary star, that ravishing chanteuse—Leni La Maison!
(CUT TO:)

INT. CABARET—NIGHT (NAZI MOVIE)

LENI *turns to the crowd in a deco pose and, singing, glides and swirls among
the hushed tables. Werner can't take his eyes off her. Michelle hurries backstage and picks up the phone.*

MICHELLE: Yes?

CLUBFOOT (*on phone*):   Did you get the map?

MICHELLE: No, there was no time.

CLUBFOOT (*hanging up*): Just get it. Nothing else matters. Vive La
France.

(*Leni, still singing, passes Werner's table with a haughty glance and concludes with a flourish, then sees him gazing at her. Wild applause.*)

VOICE OF MOLINA: Werner's eyes begin to burn into her soul. Eyes like
the claws of an eagle—inescapable.

(*Leni clutches her pounding heart and dashes away from his piercing eyes.*)

(CUT TO:)

INT. CELL—NIGHT

*Valentin muffles his scornful laughter. Molina, miffed, plunks down on his
bunk.*

MOLINA: What are you laughing at?

(*more laughter*)

Well, it must be something.

(*Valentin stares straight at Molina.*)

VALENTIN: At you.

(*looks away*)

And me.

(*Molina blows out his candle. The two men sit in silence on opposite ends
of the dark cell.*)

(CUT TO:)

EXT. PRISON CORRIDOR—NIGHT

TWO GUARDS *drag an old* HOODED PRISONER *into a cell across the courtyard.
His shirt is covered with bloodstains.*

(CUT TO:)

INT. CELL—NIGHT

*Valentin watches through the food slot in the door. Molina wakes up and rubs
his eyes.*

MOLINA: What's going on?

VALENTIN (*tense whisper*):   Quiet! They're bringing in someone new.

MOLINA: What time is it anyway?

VALENTIN: He's really bleeding.

MOLINA: Is it a political prisoner?

VALENTIN: They don't treat you like that for stealing bananas.

MOLINA: You know him?

(*Valentin, deeply disturbed, says nothing.*)

(CUT TO:)

INT. PRISON CORRIDOR—DAWN

GUARDS *conduct the morning bedcheck. Prisoners bark out their names.*

VALENTIN: Valentin Arregui!

MOLINA: Luis Molina!

(*Valentin strains to see the hooded prisoner across the courtyard. The guard shoves him in his cell.*)

(CUT TO:)

INT. CELL—DAY

Molina finishes shaving and offers the razor.

MOLINA: Do you want to shave?

VALENTIN (*turns away*):   Shit.

MOLINA: Well, I didn't mean your legs.

(*Valentin looks out the crack in the metal wall plates.*)

MOLINA: *What* is the matter?

VALENTIN: I don't understand why they stopped my interrogation. It's been almost a week.

MOLINA: Why couldn't they give me that handsome leading blond man to keep me company—instead of you.

VALENTIN: What the hell are you talking about?

MOLINA: Afraid to talk about sex?

VALENTIN: You really wanna know, Molina? I find you boring.

MOLINA: Darling, you don't know page one. You know I'm a faggot? Well, congratulations. You know I corrupted a minor? Well, that's even on TV, film at eleven.

VALENTIN: You really like those Nazi blonds, don't you?

MOLINA: Well, no, you see I detest politics but I'm *mad* about the leading man. He's so romantic.

(*pause*)

Should I be shot for that?

VALENTIN: Your Nazis are about as romantic as the fucking warden and his torture room.

MOLINA: I can imagine.

VALENTIN (*hard*):   No. You can't.

(*Valentin stares into his eyes. Molina, chagrined, looks away.*)

(CUT TO:)

INT. CELL—NIGHT

Valentin, unable to sleep, climbs up to the barred window and stares at the city lights in the dark. Molina, drowsy, sits up on his bunk.

MOLINA: You can't sleep?

(*pause*)
Mind if I tell my picture?
(*Valentin stares out the window.*)
MOLINA: After the show, Leni changes into a satin evening-gown that makes her look heavenly. Firm breasts. Thin waist. Smooth hips.
VALENTIN: Is this propaganda or porno?
MOLINA: Just listen, you'll see.
(CUT TO:)

INT. CABARET DRESSING ROOM—NIGHT (NAZI MOVIE)

KNOCK *on the door. Michelle, upset, enters Leni's ornate dressing room.*

MICHELLE: Excuse me. Leni
LENI: What is it, Michelle?
MICHELLE (*near tears*):   Leni, I'm a traitor. A traitor to France.
LENI: What do you mean?
MICHELLE: I'm going to have a baby. But the father is a young Lieutenant of the Occupation Army.
LENI: Is that so? My poor Michelle.
MICHELLE: But he loves me. And wants to get married as soon as he can get permission.
LENI: I really can't understand. How could you fall in love with an enemy of our France?
MICHELLE: Love has no country, Leni.
(*pause*)
But there's something else you don't know. I'm working for the Resist—
(*Another* KNOCK. *Michelle gasps.*)
LENI: Come in!
(*A* MESSENGER *enters with a bouquet of flowers. The two women sigh with relief.*)
MESSENGER: For you, Madame.
(CUT TO:)

INT. CELL—NIGHT

Valentin shakes his head in disgust.

VALENTIN: How can you remember all this crap? You must be making it up.
MOLINA: No, I'm not, I swear. Well, I embroider a little, so you can see it the way I did.
VALENTIN: God help me.
MOLINA: You atheists never stop talking about God.

VALENTIN: And you gays never face facts. Fantasies are no escape.

MOLINA: If you've got the keys to that door, I will gladly follow. Otherwise I'll escape in my own way, thank you.

VALENTIN: Then your life is as trivial as your movies.—I'm going to sleep.

MOLINA: Tell the truth, Valentin. Who do you identify with the most —the Clubfoot patriot or the handsome Werner?

VALENTIN: Who do *you* identify with?

MOLINA: Oh, the singer. She's the star. I'm always the heroine.
(CUT TO:)

INT. CELL—DAY

Sunlight streams through the bars. Molina slices an avocado and offers it to Valentin.

MOLINA: Have some, it's delicious.

VALENTIN: No thanks.

MOLINA: What's wrong, you don't like it?

VALENTIN: Sure I like it, but no thanks.

MOLINA: Well, then go ahead and have some. It's a long time till lunch.

VALENTIN: Can't afford to get spoiled.

MOLINA: Do you really think eating this avocado will make you spoiled and weak? Enjoy what life offers you.

VALENTIN: What life "offers" me is the struggle. When you're dedicated to that, pleasure becomes secondary.

MOLINA: Does your girlfriend think the same thing?

VALENTIN (*suspicious*): How do you know I have a girl?

MOLINA (*shrugs*): It's the normal thing. Does she avoid pleasure too?

VALENTIN: She knows what really counts. That the most important thing is serving a cause that is noble.

MOLINA: What kind of cause is that, one that doesn't let you eat an avocado?

VALENTIN (*turns away*): Molina, you would never understand.

MOLINA: Well, I understand one thing. I offer you half of my precious avocado and you throw it back in my face!

VALENTIN: Don't act like that. You sound just like a—

MOLINA: Like a what? Say it. Like a woman, you mean.
(*Valentin shrugs yes.*)

MOLINA: What's wrong with being like a woman? Why do only women get to be sensitive? Why not a man, a dog, or a faggot? If more men acted like women, there wouldn't be so much violence.— Like that!
(*Molina points at the welts on Valentin's face.*)
(CUT TO:)

EXT. PRISON CORRIDOR—DAY

A GUARD *walks down the corridor and unlocks their door.*

VALENTIN (O.S.):   Maybe you have a point, a flimsy one but still—
MOLINA (O.S.):   Oh nice! Maybe I have a point!
  (CUT TO:)

INT. CELL—DAY

The fat guard steps into their cell.

GUARD: Molina, today's yer lucky day. The Warden wanna talk to ya.
  (*Molina is led away.*)
  (CUT TO:)

INT. CELL—NIGHT

Molina mends a shirt with needle and thread. Valentin cleans his teeth with a damp rag.

VALENTIN: Why did the Warden want to see you?
MOLINA: My lawyer called. Parole seems out of the question.
  (*sighs*)
  For a while, at least.
VALENTIN: How'd he treat you, the Warden?
MOLINA: Like a faggot, same as always.
  (*lights out*)
  Oh, no. Shit.
  (*Curfew* BUZZER. *Molina lights a candle and places it near the photo of his mother.*)
MOLINA: He told me something else. My mother's not doing too well. She has high blood-pressure, and her heart is kind of weak.
VALENTIN: People can go on forever like that.
MOLINA (*melancholy*):   Sure, but not if you upset them. Can you imagine the shame of having a son in prison?
  (*pause*)
  And the reason.
VALENTIN: Go to sleep, you'll feel better.
MOLINA: No, only one thing can help.
VALENTIN (*grudgingly*):   Sure, man. Go ahead.
MOLINA: Man! Is there a man in here? Don't let him go!
  (*looks under bed*)
  Did he get away?
VALENTIN (*exasperated smile*):   Okay, cut the crap and tell your movie.
  (*Molina, beaming, spins his web of romantic intrigue.*)
MOLINA: And now, waiting in the moonlight behind the cabaret is Werner's limousine.
  (CUT TO:)

EXT. CABARET BACK DOOR—NIGHT (NAZI MOVIE)

Werner watches Leni say goodbye to Michelle.

VOICE OF MOLINA: Werner's eyes are locked on the backstage exit. "La sortie des artistes." He signals his chauffeur to open the door for her. Maybe because Leni sees a chance to help Michelle, or maybe because Leni wants to know what kind of a man is hidden inside this enemy invader—she decides to join him for the evening.
(Leni descends the stairs. Werner offers his hand.)
WERNER: Madame.
(With a haughty glance, she enters his limousine.)
(CUT TO:)

INT. NIGHTCLUB—NIGHT (NAZI MOVIE)

Leni and Werner lift champagne glasses. Their eyes meet.

WERNER (*clicks glasses*):   To a great artiste.
(CUT TO:)

EXT. PARIS STREET—NIGHT (NAZI MOVIE)

Michelle walks along a dark neighborhood street.

VOICE OF MOLINA: Michelle hurries to meet her secret love. But dark forces have already decided the fate of this sweet girl. This girl from the French Resistance in love with a German Lieutenant. Because . . .
(The Clubfoot and his Flunky watch her hurry past their parked truck.)
CLUBFOOT: Her time is up.
FLUNKY (*grips hearing aid*):   What?
(Michelle approaches an elegant apartment building.)
VOICE OF MOLINA: Because . . . love is a luxury a spy cannot afford.
(She calls up to the balcony.)
MICHELLE: Hanschen!
*(The German Lieutenant appears on the balcony, smiles and tosses down his key. It lands in the street.
Michelle stoops down to pick it up. Suddenly the truck hurtles toward her at full speed. Turning in horror, she sees the Clubfoot at the wheel.
The truck races into the night, leaving Michelle sprawled across the dark pavement.)*
(CUT TO:)

INT. CELL—NIGHT

Valentin is deep in thought. Molina approaches and snaps his fingers.

MOLINA: Valentin, are you listening?

(pause)

How can you leave me chattering to myself like some silly parrot?

VALENTIN: Strange. When Michelle was killed, I—it was chilling.

(Molina, touched by the compliment, sits on the floor beside his bunk.)

MOLINA: It's just a movie, Valentin. One of Mother's many stories.

VALENTIN: Yeah, but I keep thinking about—someone I know.

MOLINA: Your girlfriend. Tell me about her. My lips are sealed.

VALENTIN: It's just that I'm so helpless in here, with no way to protect her.

MOLINA: So you have a heart after all.

VALENTIN: Mm.

MOLINA: Write to her. Tell her to stop taking chances.

(Valentin snaps out of his reverie.)

VALENTIN: If you think like that, you'll never change anything in this world.

MOLINA *(amused)*:   Now look who's living a fantasy.

(Valentin angrily lifts his shirt, displaying the torture welts on his torso.)

VALENTIN: You call this a fantasy?

MOLINA: —I'm so sorry.

VALENTIN: Some day the struggle will be won.

MOLINA: Don't worry, Valentin. You'll have your day, I'm sure.

(CUT TO:)

EXT. PRISON CORRIDOR—DAY

Both men stand outside their door for morning bed-check.

VALENTIN: Valentin Arregui.

MOLINA: Luis Molina.

(CUT TO:)

INT. CELL—DAY

Molina leans on his bunk, humming Leni's song. Valentin paces for exercise. Two tin plates are pushed through the food slot in the door.

VALENTIN: Great. I'm starving.—Here.

MOLINA: No, you take this one. It has twice as much.

VALENTIN: Sure, because those bastards want us to fight over it. Take it.

MOLINA: No, you need it more than I do. Please, please, to build your strength.

VALENTIN: Don't argue. Take it.

(Molina reluctantly accepts the larger portion.)

MOLINA *(snide)*:   May I have a spoon?

(Valentin obliges.)

Thanks.

(*Valentin sits on his bunk and eats the black beans, then notices Molina toying with his food.*)

VALENTIN: What's the matter? Afraid of getting fat?

MOLINA: No.

VALENTIN: This glue is not so bad today.

(*Molina hesitantly swallows another spoonful.*)

MOLINA: Valentin.

(*pause*)

When I said you should write your girlfriend, I also meant you should tell her you love her. It's so nice to get a letter from someone you love.

VALENTIN: Are you crazy? A letter would be like denouncing her to them. The only reason I'm still alive is because they want information from me. And if anyone tries to save me, they'd hide my arrest by killing me on the spot.

MOLINA (*upset*):   Valentin, please don't say things like that.

VALENTIN: The same thing could be happening to her. Right now.

MOLINA (*melancholy*):   You love her very much, don't you. Love should always come first.

VALENTIN: That's great.

(*turns away*)

Now I'd like to eat in peace.

MOLINA: Don't worry, I won't disturb you.

(*Molina bursts into muffled sobs.*)

VALENTIN (*annoyed*):   What is it now?

MOLINA (*weepy moans*):   It's my mother. She must really be in bad shape or she'd come visit me with groceries. This happened once before.

VALENTIN (*cold*):   Sorry to hear that.

(*Molina moans more. Valentin keeps eating and tries to ignore him. Molina moans louder, then says:*)

MOLINA: Yeah, well, I told you she was sick, but of course you weren't paying any attention.

(*pause*)

But that's not what I'm crying about.

VALENTIN (*very annoyed*):   So what is it, for Chrissake?

MOLINA (*wipes tears*):   Because it's so beautiful when lovers are together for a lifetime. Why is it so impossible?

VALENTIN: You gotta be crazy, crying about something like that.

MOLINA: I will cry about whatever I want to.

(*stops crying*)

Valentin, do you think you're the only one who's suffered? You think it's easy to find a real man? One who's humble, and yet has dignity?

(*pause*)

How many years have I been searching? How many nights? How
many faces filled with scorn and deceit?
(CUT TO:)

EXT. STORE WINDOW—DAY (FLASHBACK)

*The window contains two mannequins dressed as bride and groom. Molina
meticulously adjusts the fluffy bridal gown.*

VOICE OF MOLINA: You know, working as a window dresser, enjoyable
    as it is, sometimes at the end of the day you wonder what it's all
    about. And you feel kind of empty inside.
    (*pause*)
    Then, one night. . . .
    (CUT TO:)

INT. RESTAURANT—NIGHT (FLASHBACK)

*Molina takes a table with two effeminate friends. One is black. The other is
GRETA, 31, babbling with chit-chat.*

GRETA: It's something new she just invented herself. She calls it La
    Chika-Chaka and she goes chika-chaka, chika-chaka. And she's an
    overnight sensation, the next day she's in *all* the newspapers, and
    her husband becomes so jealous because he thinks—
    (*Molina's eyes are riveted on* GABRIEL, *34, a handsome waiter in a white
    tunic.*)
GABRIEL: Good evening, gentlemen. Would you care for the daily spe-
    cial? Or would you like to order a la carte?
MOLINA: I haven't decided yet.
    (*Gabriel offers a menu and leaves.*)
VOICE OF MOLINA: My heart was pounding . . . so afraid that I would
    be hurt once again.
    (CUT TO:)

INT. RESTAURANT—NIGHT (FLASHBACK)

Molina sits alone, impeccably dressed, immaculately groomed.

GABRIEL: Are you ready for me, sir?
MOLINA: What do you suggest?
GABRIEL: Perhaps the lasagna and antipasto.
MOLINA: Don't you think the lasagna might be fattening?
GABRIEL: Then perhaps the steak and onion soup.
MOLINA (*returning the menu*):   Sounds wonderful.
    (*Gabriel goes to place the order. Molina can't take his eyes off him.*)
VOICE OF MOLINA: His white tunic, the way he moved, his sad smile.
    Everything seemed so perfect, like in the movies.
    (CUT TO:)

INT. RESTAURANT—NIGHT (FLASHBACK)

The restaurant is closed. Gabriel mops the floor. The only customer is Molina, still in his chair, waiting.

VOICE OF MOLINA: You have no idea how much trouble I went through, month after month, just to get him to go for a walk. But little by little I made him see I respected him.
(CUT TO:)

INT. CELL—NIGHT

Molina sits on the floor, hugging his knees.

MOLINA: Anyway, after more than a year, we finally became friends.
VALENTIN: Jesus, did it take another year to get him in the sack?
MOLINA: Are you out of your mind? Nothing at all happened. Ever!
VALENTIN: You gotta be kidding.
MOLINA: Don't you know anything at all? He's straight. He's married. I said to him, let's do it just once. But he never wanted to.
VALENTIN: I don't believe this. Here I am, staying up all night, thinking about your boyfriend.
(*pause*)
Sounds like a real bind, Molina. All you can do is take it like a man.
MOLINA: I take it like a woman. Always. That's why I want a husband who's the boss.
(*Molina stretches across the floor toward Valentin's bunk. Valentin awkwardly changes the subject.*)
VALENTIN: Uh, did you ever meet his wife?
MOLINA: No, but when they were on the verge of splitting up—God, such illusions I had.
VALENTIN: Like what?
MOLINA: That he might come home to live with me, with my mother and me. And I would take care of him and help him lose that sadness of his forever.
(CUT TO:)

EXT. BAR DISTRICT—NIGHT (FLASHBACK)

Molina and Gabriel stroll up the narrow street. Most of the garish bars are dark. Male and female HOOKERS stand in shadowy doorways.

GABRIEL (*shrugs*): That's life, Molina.
MOLINA: No, it's a shame. With your looks and charm, you should work in a chic restaurant in a luxury hotel. Making three times what you get in that stinkhole.
GABRIEL: It's not so easy.
MOLINA: I know someone who works in a big hotel on the Coast. He could talk to the manager and presto, a new life.

GABRIEL: And be what, a busboy in a snob joint? I'd make less money than now.

MOLINA: I could help you with a loan. With your poise, you'd be a waiter in six months.

GABRIEL: I don't know.

MOLINA: Of course you do. And in a year, a maitre d'. In a tuxedo! You could pay me back in no time.

GABRIEL: Maybe. Anyway, I appreciate your offer. I'll think about it.
(*leaving*)
I gotta get my bus, I'm gonna be late. See you tomorrow, Molina.

MOLINA: Goodnight, Gabriel. Kiss the children for me.
(*Molina watches the bus leave, then heads back down the dark street toward the male hookers. A teenage* BOY *asks for a light. Molina responds and they walk off together.*)

VOICE OF MOLINA: And then it's over . . . again . . . my dreams disappear . . . into the darkness. And I wake up alone.
(CUT TO:)

INT. CELL—NIGHT

Molina, stretched out on the floor, looks up at Valentin.

MOLINA: Waiting as always. Waiting and waiting. Waiting and waiting and waiting.

VALENTIN: Waiting for what?

MOLINA: A man. A real man. But that can't happen because a real man, what he wants is a real woman.

VALENTIN (*stands up*):   Can I ask you a question? What is a real man in your terms?

MOLINA: Well, to be marvelous looking and strong. Without making any fuss about it. And walking very tall. Like my waiter.

VALENTIN: He just gives you that impression, but inside it's another story. In this society, without power behind you, no one walks tall.

MOLINA: Don't be jealous.

VALENTIN: Don't be stupid.

MOLINA: You see how you react? There's just no talking about a guy with another guy without getting into a fuss.

VALENTIN (*hard*):   Look, just keep it on a certain level, okay? Or let's not talk at all.

MOLINA: Okay, you tell me what a real man is.

VALENTIN (*caught off guard*):   I don't know.

MOLINA: Sure you do. Go ahead, tell me.

VALENTIN: Well, not taking any crap from anyone, not even the powers-that-be. That's not the most important thing; what really makes a man has to do with not humiliating anybody. It's not letting the people around you feel degraded.

MOLINA: That sounds like a saint.

VALENTIN: Forget it.

(*Molina suddenly grabs his stomach and doubles over, groaning in pain.*)

VALENTIN: What's wrong?

MOLINA (*drops to floor*):   —My stomach.

VALENTIN: Maybe it's your appendix?

MOLINA: No, I had mine out.

(*grimacing*)

God, it hurts, it hurts!

VALENTIN: You feel like throwing up?

MOLINA: No, it's below there. It's in my guts.

(*Valentin pulls Molina to his feet and helps him hobble to his bunk.*)

VALENTIN: The food didn't do anything to me.

MOLINA (*lies down*):   I don't know, maybe it's my ulcer.

(*writhing in pain*)

I—I don't like this!

VALENTIN: Why don't you go on with your movie?

MOLINA: God, I never felt a pain like this.

VALENTIN: Go ahead and tell it.

(CUT TO:)

EXT. LENI'S APARTMENT—NIGHT (NAZI MOVIE)

Leni stands at her window, waving goodbye to Werner in his limousine.

VOICE OF MOLINA: Leni lingers at the window, so sad, so alone, so afraid that she will fall in love.

(*Suddenly a hand reaches from the shadows and muffles her scream. It's the half-deaf Flunky.*)

(CUT TO:)

INT. LENI'S APARTMENT—NIGHT (NAZI MOVIE)

The Flunky flings Leni onto a sofa. She sees the Clubfoot in her armchair.

CLUBFOOT: Tonight the invaders murdered your friend Michelle.

LENI (*shocked*):   No.

CLUBFOOT: You must complete her mission and find the secret map to the German arsenal. The Chief of Counter-Intelligence is in love with you.

LENI: I could never get involved with such a thing.

CLUBFOOT (*approaching*):   Nonsense, nothing could be safer. Do you love France?

LENI: Of course I do.

CLUBFOOT: That Kraut can't keep his hands off you. Next time he touches you like this—

(*fondling her*)

—and like this, think of your country. And get the map.

(*Leni has grasped a statuette of "Justice." She hammers his skull and dashes out the door. The Clubfoot tumbles to the carpet and shouts at his Flunky.*)
CLUBFOOT: Stop her, you idiot!
(CUT TO:)

EXT. PARIS STREET—NIGHT (NAZI MOVIE)

Leni runs across dark cobblestones, turns a corner and sees a taxi in the distance.

LENI: Taxi! Taxi!
(*The bleeding Clubfoot lumbers around the corner.*)
VOICE OF MOLINA: Leni, desperate, runs along this dark empty street. The furious Clubfoot hobbles after her, when suddenly—
(CUT TO:)

INT. CELL—NIGHT

Molina, hunched over the edge of his bed, clutches his stomach and whispers:

MOLINA: —this girl is finished.
VALENTIN: What girl?
MOLINA: Me, stupid.
(*Molina, passing out, slumps onto the floor. Valentin pounds the cell door.*)
VALENTIN: Guard! *Guard!*
(CUT TO:)

INT. PRISON INFIRMARY—NIGHT

Molina sleeps on an infirmary cot.

(CUT TO:)

INT. CELL—NIGHT

Valentin looks under Molina's bunk and finds his crucifix neck-chain. He places the gold chain on Molina's pillow.

(CUT TO:)

INT. PRISON INFIRMARY—DAY

Molina, in bed, reaches for his missing crucifix and looks up at the prison DOCTOR.

DOCTOR: You're strong enough to go back to your cell. Your diarrhea will stop tomorrow. Till then, no food. Only water. Clean water. If you can find it.

MOLINA: Doctor, I need to see the Warden. Right away.

DOCTOR (*leaving*):   That's what they all say.

(CUT TO:)

INT. CELL—NIGHT

Valentin does pushups on the floor. Molina pages through glamor magazines on his bunk.

VALENTIN: I don't understand how you can pass out from an ulcer.

MOLINA: I'm no spring chicken, darling. I'm getting dizzy just looking at these pictures.

(*Molina sighs for attention. Valentin says nothing.*)

MOLINA: God, wouldn't it be wonderful if you told me a movie for a change. One that I haven't seen.

VALENTIN: I don't remember any.

MOLINA: Don't be like that. Come on, tell me one.

(*pause*)

Please.

VALENTIN: Don't be such a cry-baby.

MOLINA: Valentin. Have you ever loved someone you didn't *want* to love?

VALENTIN (*wary*):   What do you mean?

MOLINA: Leni didn't want to fall in love with Werner, but what could she do? She steps through his doorway like a goddess. Her slim graceful figure trembles at the sight of Werner descending the marble staircase. Their eyes meet. Leni says—

(CUT TO:)

INT. CHATEAU—NIGHT (NAZI MOVIE)

Werner descends his marble stairs. Leni stands beside the BUTLER *in the vestibule.*

LENI: My best friend has been killed. I need a place to stay.

WERNER (*to Butler*):   Prepare the guest room.

LENI: This music is magical. I feel like I'm floating on air.

(*Wagnerian music fills the baroque chateau. Werner leads Leni inside.*)

VOICE OF MOLINA: But her heart is saying. Oh Werner, you seem like a god, but your tears—

(CUT TO:)

INT. CELL—NIGHT

Molina savors his sad reverie.

MOLINA: —your tears are proof you have the feelings of a man.

VALENTIN: Quiet! I can't hear.

(*Valentin peers through the wall plate and* SEES *two Guards returning the Hooded Prisoner in blood-stained underpants. His skin is covered with welts and burns.*

Valentin bangs the door with his metal cup.)

VALENTIN: Murderers! Fascist murderers. Fascist murderers!

(*More prisoners join the protest. The guards use clubs to crush the outbreak.*

Valentin sees a guard's shoes facing his cell. Suddenly a stream of urine splashes onto Valentin. SOUND *of guards laughing.*)

VALENTIN: Motherfucker. Motherfucker!

MOLINA: I'll clean it up.

(*Valentin, furious, spins around and hurls his metal cup at Molina's head. Molina ducks. Valentin stalks forward.*)

VALENTIN: You son of a bitch! They're killing one of my brothers and what am I doing? Listening to your fucking Nazi movie!

(*Molina clutches his ragdoll to his chest.*)

VALENTIN: Don't you know what the Nazis did to people—Jews, Marxists, Catholics? Homosexuals!

MOLINA: Of course I know. What do you take me for, an even dumber broad than I am?

(*Valentin grabs Molina and hurls him headfirst across the cell, then fires the doll at his face. Molina cowers on the floor.*

Valentin clenches his fist and approaches.)

VALENTIN: You don't know shit. You wouldn't know reality if it was stuck up your ass.

MOLINA (*terrified*):   Why should I think about reality in a stinkhole like this? Why should I get more depressed than I already am?

(*Molina shrinks back into the corner. Valentin, seething, kneels down and rips off Molina's earrings.*)

VALENTIN: You're worse than I thought. You just use these movies to jerk yourself off.

MOLINA (*bursts into tears*):   If you don't stop, I will never speak to you again.

VALENTIN: Stop crying! You sound just like an old woman.

MOLINA (*sobbing*):   That's what I am, that's what I am.

(*Molina looks down, whimpering. Valentin violently wrenches apart Molina's knees.*)

VALENTIN: What's this between your legs? Huh? Tell me, "lady"!

MOLINA: It's an accident. If I had the courage, I'd cut it off.

(*Molina struggles to regain his dignity. Valentin moves in for the kill.*)

VALENTIN: You'd still be a man! A man in prison, just like the faggots the Nazis shoved in the ovens.

MOLINA (*pleading*):   Don't. Don't look at me like that.

(*Molina, sobbing, looks up at the barred window.*)

(CUT TO:)

INT. COURTROOM—DAY (FLASHBACK)

Molina stands beside his LAWYER, *facing the massive oak desk. The* JUDGE *glowers down at him.*

JUDGE: . . . Luis Alberto Molina. You shall endure the full weight of the law and not one day less. You will be confined without chance of parole for a period of not less than eight years.
(*Molina turns from the Judge to gaze forlornly at his* MOTHER. *She pulls a handkerchief from her purse. As their eyes meet, she smiles warmly through her tears.*)

VOICE OF MOLINA: Poor Mama. Her eyes full of tears as if someone had died. A life full of humiliation and then the humiliation of a son steeped in vice, but she never gave me that black look. Her heart broken by too much suffering, too much forgiving. Because of me she could die.
(CUT TO:)

INT. CELL—DAY

Molina's red eyes are stark and determined.

MOLINA: If he ever says one unkind word about her, I'll strangle the son of a bitch. Him and his filthy words and his piss-ass revolution.
(*Lightning flashes through the barred window.*)
(CUT TO:)

INT. CELL—NIGHT

Two plates are shoved through the food slot. Molina, still angry, plops one on Valentin's bunk and goes to eat by the window. Lightning flashes.
     Suddenly Valentin clutches his stomach and groans in pain. Molina rushes to his side.

VALENTIN: My stomach. It's like a bomb exploding.
MOLINA: The same thing I had.
VALENTIN (*grimacing*): I think it's the food.
MOLINA: You gotta go to the Infirmary right now.—Guard!
(*Molina hurries to the door. Valentin lunges forward and grabs him.*)
VALENTIN: No! Wait. Stop.
MOLINA: Why?
VALENTIN: I'm a political prisoner.
MOLINA: Don't be ridiculous. This is no time for your damn discipline.
VALENTIN: Get away from the door.
MOLINA: They gave me a shot, and I'm better already.
VALENTIN: Are you crazy? That's just what they want. They get me hooked on those shots, and I'll tell them everything.

MOLINA: What else can we do?
  (*Valentin, groaning, returns to his bunk and mutters:*)
VALENTIN: Leave me alone.
  (*Molina thinks, then gets a scarf and says:*)
MOLINA: What about my movie? It might help you forget the pain.
  (CUT TO:)

EXT. CHATEAU—NIGHT (NAZI MOVIE)

Leni and Werner slowly waltz among billowing white curtains.
VOICE OF MOLINA: Later that night, on the moonlit veranda, Leni feels
  so safe, so secure in Werner's arms.
  (*music stops*)
  Even when the phonograph stops, they continue dancing . . .
  dancing.
  (CUT TO:)

INT. CELL—NIGHT

Molina dances with the scarf as if his empty arms held Werner.

MOLINA: To the music of the evening breezes, whooh, whoooh.
  (*Molina sees Valentin shivering in his sleep, drenched with sweat. He
  kneels down and wipes Valentin's fevered forehead with the scarf.*)
VALENTIN (*asleep*):   Marta . . . Marta.
  (*opens eyes*)
  . . . who are you?
MOLINA: It's okay. Try to rest.
  (*Valentin closes his weary eyes. Molina tenderly adjusts the blanket.*)

INT. CELL—NIGHT

Both men are eating. Molina watches Valentin reading a letter.

MOLINA: You shouldn't eat this garbage while you're sick.
VALENTIN (*keeps eating*):   I have to get my strength back.
MOLINA: It'll only make you worse.
VALENTIN: Tastes like dog piss.
MOLINA (*shakes his head*):   My poor little Valentina.
VALENTIN: Don't call me Valentina. I'm not a woman.
MOLINA (*leans forward*):   Well, I've never seen proof to the contrary.
VALENTIN: And you never will.
MOLINA: Now, the Clubfoot told—
  (*Valentin grimaces in disgust.*)
MOLINA: You'll like this part, wait and see.
  (CUT TO:)

INT. WERNER'S BEDROOM—DAY (NAZI MOVIE)

*Leni wakes in a lavish antique bed, reaches for Werner and discovers he is
gone.*

VOICE OF MOLINA: The Clubfoot told Leni that her sweet lover was ordering the execution of her countrymen everyday. But she refused to believe it. She only wanted to live this love, to feel his touch, to hear his voice.
(The phone rings. Leni eavesdrops on Werner.)
WERNER'S VOICE: It's a difficult decision.
CALLER'S VOICE: Ja, Herr Commandant.
(CUT TO:)

INT. WERNER'S STUDY—DAY (NAZI MOVIE)

Werner, in uniform, stands at a desk piled with documents.

CALLER'S VOICE: We captured ten of them. They're all French, but their activities prove they are enemies of the people.
WERNER: They call themselves patriots, but in fact they are common criminals.
(CUT TO:)

INT. WERNER'S BEDROOM—DAY (NAZI MOVIE)

Leni sits up in shock.

WERNER'S VOICE: Let the execution take place at dawn.
(CUT TO:)

INT. CELL—NIGHT

Molina looks at his fingers.

MOLINA: Her fingers tremble with the agony of betraying the man she loves.
(Valentin suddenly curls up with pain.)
VALENTIN: It's like a nail in my gut.
(pause)
That's better. Do me a favor and stop all this crap about beautiful women in tears.
(Molina goes to the corner for coconut shells and returns, clutching them to his chest under his robe.)
MOLINA: Leni's heart was beating so fast that her swelling breasts leapt out of her low-cut gown. Like luscious hors d'oeuvres on a silver platter.
(Valentin chokes with laughter.)
VALENTIN: Don't make me laugh. It hurts.
(Molina opens his robe, revealing the coconut-shell breasts.)
MOLINA: Here, have a nice juicy tit. Have another. The best places serve them in pairs.
(Valentin laughs out loud. Suddenly, his eyes snap open in pain. Trying to sit up, he clutches his pants and points to the shit-bucket.)

VALENTIN: The bucket! Quick!

(*Molina dashes to the bucket. Valentin struggles to his feet and tugs his zipper. Diarrhea fills his trousers. Valentin collapses on the floor, covering his face in shame.*)

VALENTIN: Oh, no.

MOLINA: Christ, what a smell.

VALENTIN (*groaning*):   I'm sorry. You don't know how much it hurts.

MOLINA: Let it all out. It can't smell any worse than it already does.

VALENTIN: God, I can't stand this.

(*Valentin trembles on the floor. Molina pulls the sheet from his own bed and grabs some rags.*)

MOLINA: You've been through worse. Much worse.

VALENTIN: I'm so ashamed.

MOLINA: Aren't you the one always saying take it like a man? So what's this business about being embarrassed?

VALENTIN: I can't stand it. I can't stand myself like this.

(*Valentin lifts his hand to hide his tears. Molina kneels down with maternal concern.*)

MOLINA: Take off your pants. Cover yourself with this. Why do you always have to pick on yourself so much?

(*Molina tosses the soiled trousers and underpants beside the bucket, then grabs the rags.*)

MOLINA: Wipe yourself off.

VALENTIN: No, it's yours.

MOLINA: No, it's ours. Wipe yourself. There's a little more here, and here.

(*Valentin struggles to remove the glop from his buttocks. Molina wipes the brown liquid from his ankles.*

   Despondent, Valentin gives up. Molina, taking over, cleans his thighs and buttocks like a mother cleaning a child.)

VALENTIN (*turning away*):   Jesus, aren't you disgusted?

MOLINA: No, it breaks my heart to see you like this. There, almost finished. Good. Now take off your shirt.

VALENTIN: No, it's alright.

MOLINA: The shirt-tails are soiled. Please.

(*Valentin removes his shirt. Tossing it, Molina feels a letter in the pocket and keeps it.*)

MOLINA: Okay, now try and stand up.

(*Molina, tenderly insistent, helps him to his feet and puts the bedsheet around his shoulders.*)

VALENTIN: No, it'll stink.

MOLINA: My weekly shower is tomorrow. I'll have it all clean by noon. There we go. All wrapped up like a little papoose.

(*Molina wraps the bedsheet around him like a toga and helps him crawl back in bed.*)

VALENTIN: It doesn't disgust you?

MOLINA: Lie down. Don't want you to catch a chill. What a shame I have no talcum left. Are you comfortable now?

VALENTIN: Yes, but I'm so cold.

MOLINA: I'll make you a nice hot cup of tea.

(*Valentin, deeply touched, watches him pour a cup.*)

MOLINA: This will work wonders.

(*hands cup*)

It's hot, you'll burn yourself.

(*Valentin takes a sip.*)

VALENTIN: You're very kind, honestly, I don't know what to say.

MOLINA: Don't burn yourself.

(*Molina finishes cleaning the floor, then pulls out the hidden letter.*)

MOLINA: Oh, uh, this fell out of your shirt.

VALENTIN: Go ahead, read it. I know you've been curious.

MOLINA: No, I only read love letters. I don't want to know anything about your politics.

VALENTIN: It's from my girlfriend. Her name is Lydia.

MOLINA: —What about Marta?

VALENTIN (*bolts upright*): How do you know about Marta?

MOLINA: You mumbled her name in your sleep.

VALENTIN (*worried*): What else did I mumble?

MOLINA: Nothing.

VALENTIN: The letter's from Lydia. She's my girlfriend in the movement.

(*Molina opens the pages and scans the letter.*)

MOLINA: Her handwriting is like a child's.

VALENTIN: —She hasn't had much of an education.

(*Valentin lays back down with a sigh.*)

VALENTIN: I'm going to tell you the truth. During torture, whenever I felt close to death, it was Marta I would think about, and she would save me. My whole body ached to hold her.

MOLINA: What's she like?

VALENTIN: She's upper-class. Pure bourgeoisie. She's got everything. Money, looks, education, freedom. I'm such a hypocrite. Just like all those class-conscious pigs.

(*pause*)

I must admit it was convenient, a safe place to stay when I was forced to hide. Until one day I had to tell her about my other life.

(CUT TO:)

INT. HIGH-RISE APARTMENT—DAY (FLASHBACK)

MARTA, 29, *puts out a cigarette and listens.*

VOICE OF VALENTIN: She just listened in silence like she knew already. Then she asked me to leave the movement. But how could I do nothing when my friends were disappearing every day? I sensed that she was right but I had no choice. So once again I didn't know what to say.

(*Marta steps onto the balcony and looks at the city. Her strong eyes brim with tears. Valentin approaches.*)

VALENTIN: Things are what they are. I'll be back in a few days. Same as always.

MARTA: I can't take it any more. Always waiting, watching the phone. Always alone.

(*Valentin brushes back her long black hair and kisses her cheek. She makes no response. He turns to leave.*)

MARTA (*fights back tears*):   Valentin. If you leave, don't come back. Please, don't come back.

(*Valentin hesitates, then leaves.*)

(CUT TO:)

INT. TRAIN—DAY (FLASHBACK)

Valentin, deep in thought, stares out the train window at the passing slums.

VOICE OF VALENTIN: I no longer believed in violence, but I had to do something. As a journalist, I was always hearing about the illegal arrests and secret torture, then leaking this information abroad.

(CUT TO:)

EXT. TRAIN STATION—DAY (FLASHBACK)

The train pulls into a station. Valentin steps onto the platform.

VOICE OF VALENTIN: My assignment was to meet one of the last surviving members of the original movement. His code name was Americo. He needed my passport to leave the country.

(*Valentin approaches an old man.* AMERICO, 62, *walks with a cane toward a railing. Valentin stops beside him.*)

VALENTIN: Are you all right?

AMERICO: A little tired.

VALENTIN: You should have left long ago, Doctor Americo.

AMERICO (*points down*):   This is where I'm needed.

VALENTIN: I keep wondering if it's all worth it—when nothing really changes.

(*Valentin tugs the passport from his pocket and slides it along the railing.*)

VALENTIN: Well, good luck. Here's your passport. Take care of yourself.

AMERICO: Thank you.

(*Americo walks away. Valentin stays at the railing.*)

VOICE OF VALENTIN: He had accomplished almost nothing, but I was glad I could help him.

(CUT TO:)

EXT. STATION ENTRANCE—DAY (FLASHBACK)

Reaching street level, Valentin steps off the escalator and enters the turnstyle. Suddenly THREE PLAIN-CLOTHES AGENTS *surround him with guns.*

Their burly leader, PEDRO, *44, black, spins Valentin around and jams an automatic pistol in the back of his head.*

PEDRO: Freeze! Stop!
  (*frisks him*)
  Open your legs.
  (*handcuffs him*)
  Move!
  (*Pedro shoves Valentin toward a black car.*)
VOICE OF MOLINA: What happened to Marta?
  (CUT TO:)

INT. CELL—NIGHT

Valentin, tormented, lays on his bunk in the sheet. Molina sits at the foot of the bed.

VALENTIN: I don't know anything for sure. Except that I'll never see her again.
MOLINA: Don't say that.
VALENTIN (*writhing*): I don't deserve to die in this cell. I only confessed some code names they already knew. I can't stand being a martyr, it infuriates me. I don't *want* to be a martyr.
  (*deeply depressed*)
  My whole life . . . a mistake.
MOLINA: No.
  (*Valentin, fighting despair, extends his hand.*)
VALENTIN: Give me your hand.
  (*Molina grips his hand tightly. Valentin whispers:*)
VALENTIN: I don't want to die, Molina. I don't want to die. Don't let me die.
MOLINA (*grips tighter*): Of course not.
  (CUT TO:)

INT. WARDEN'S OFFICE—DAY

The WARDEN, *60, gray-haired in a business suit, leans forward at his large desk.*

WARDEN: You look thin, Molina, what's the matter?
MOLINA: It's nothing, sir. I was sick, but I'm better now.
WARDEN: So stop trembling. There's nothing to be afraid of.
  (*pause*)
  Arregui doesn't suspect anything, does he?

MOLINA: No, sir.

WARDEN: What has he told you?

MOLINA: Uhh. Nothing yet. He, uh, I feel I should proceed very cautiously.

(Stepping from the adjoining bathroom is Pedro, the Secret Agent who arrested Valentin. Wearing a three-piece suit, he adjusts his tie and measures Molina with ice-cold eyes.)

PEDRO: Molina, you are lying. What are you hiding?

MOLINA: Nothing.

(to Warden)

How can you accuse me when I almost died for you? He insisted I eat the bowl with the poison.

(The Warden pushes back from his desk and rolls around front in a wheelchair.)

WARDEN: Why? You made a mistake there.

MOLINA: One plate had twice as much as the other one, so he insisted I eat the larger portion. Sir, you told me the poisoned food would be in a new tin plate, but they loaded it up so much I had no choice. I had to eat it myself, or he would've become suspicious.

WARDEN: Poor Molina. I'm sorry for the mix-up. I commend you. Sit down here. Please.

(Molina takes a seat. The Warden wheels closer, treating him like a child.)

WARDEN: Your mother's feeling much better since she learned you may be paroled.

MOLINA: Really?

WARDEN: Of course. So stop crying. You should be pleased.

MOLINA: It's from happiness, sir.

(Pedro takes the chair beside Molina and says curtly:)

PEDRO: What did Valentin say about his cadre?

MOLINA *(puzzled)*: His what?

PEDRO: His group—who they are, where they meet.

MOLINA: Nothing, sir. He is very sick. If he has any more poison, I don't know *what* will happen.

PEDRO: His girlfriend, what'd he say about her?

MOLINA: He says personal things are secondary to revolution, he thinks everything else is trash, so I think he's warming up to talking about it.

(The Warden hands him a cup of coffee.)

MOLINA: For me? Thank you.

PEDRO: What did he say about the new prisoner? The one across the hall.

MOLINA: The one who's all messed up? He said that no crime justifies that kind of punishment.

(takes a sip)

This coffee really hits the spot.

PEDRO: Did he tell you his name?

MOLINA (*puzzled*):   Of course, sir. It's Valentin Arregui.

PEDRO: No, you idiot! The name of the new prisoner.

MOLINA (*frightened*):   Of course not. He's always wearing a hood.

   (*Pedro, furious, glances at the Warden.*)

PEDRO: Who put a hood on him?

WARDEN (*worried*):   It's routine. He's political.

PEDRO: How do you expect him to talk if he can't even see the bastard's face?

WARDEN: It won't happen again.

   (*Pedro looks at his "female" prisoner. He's not sure if this "actress" is really naive—or just pretending.*)

PEDRO: Molina, we gotta know everything they're planning.

   (*pause*)

   As soon as he sees that new prisoner's face, he'll spill his guts. Remember every damn word he says.

MOLINA: Yes, sir.

PEDRO: The quicker he talks, the quicker you get out. Now get back to work.

   (*Molina stands up to leave, then hesitates.*)

MOLINA: Uh, Warden, one more thing. He heard the guard say my mother was coming. And I told him that, uh, she always brings me a bag full of groceries. I don't want him to get suspicious.

WARDEN: Okay, dictate what she brings.

MOLINA: To you, sir?

WARDEN: Yes, to me! And make it quick. I'm busy.

MOLINA: Um. Two roast chickens in butter, egg salad, canned peaches, condensed milk. Two boxes of tea—one regular, one camomile. A jar of pickled herring, four bars of toilet soap. What else?

   (*Pedro, disgusted, watches the Warden write it down. Molina nervously taps his teeth, watching from the corner of his eye, pushing them to the limit.*)

MOLINA: Blessed Mary, my mind's a blank. Let me think. Rye bread. Sugar, I need. Uhh.

   (*The Warden, exasperated, eyes the ceiling.*)

   (CUT TO:)

INT. CELL—DAY

Valentin struggles to sit up in bed. Molina, victorious, unpacks two bags of groceries.

MOLINA: Roast chickens! Canned peaches! Cheddar cheese! Rye bread!

VALENTIN: What happened?

MOLINA: Look at this. Two roast chickens, *two*! How about that. Just watch how fast you get better now.

VALENTIN: Your mother came.

MOLINA: Yes! Tea, sugar, and—
(*proud chuckle*)
cigarettes.

VALENTIN: That's great. How is she?

MOLINA: Oh, she's much better, thank you. And look at all she brought me. I mean *us*.

VALENTIN: Well, really that's all meant for you.

MOLINA: No, you have to stop eating that damn prison chow, and you'll feel better in no time.

VALENTIN: You think so?

MOLINA: You're damn right I do. Starting today a new life begins. Oh, I took a chance and left the sheets out to dry, and no one walked away with them. So tonight we both have clean sheets.
(*He tosses the sheets. Valentin catches them and smiles.*)

VALENTIN: Nice going.

MOLINA (*lights the burner*): Let met get this started and presto, in a few minutes you'll be licking your fingers. I expect you to eat all of those chickens, *both* of them.

VALENTIN: But what about you? I'm not gonna let you just sit around and drool.

MOLINA: No, I've gotta keep an eye on my girlish figure. At least what's left of it.
(*Valentin reaches for the peaches. Molina slaps his hand.*)

MOLINA: Not yet, that's for dessert.

TIME CUT:

Spread across the floor is a picnic blanket of leftovers. Valentin relaxes with a cigarette. Molina stretches.

MOLINA: Would you like some more peaches?

VALENTIN: No thanks. I'm stuffed.
(*rubs stomach*)
Good food, good cigarette. I don't remember when I felt so good. There's only one thing missing.

MOLINA: Christ! And I thought I was supposed to be the one who's the degenerate around here.

VALENTIN (*laughs*): No, I mean a good movie.

MOLINA: Of course! Jeez, why didn't I think of that?

VALENTIN: Your Nazi movie, how does it end?

MOLINA: I thought you hated it.

VALENTIN: Yeah, but I'm curious to see how it turns out.

MOLINA (*stands up*): Well, let's see.
(CUT TO:)

INT. WERNER'S DINING ROOM—NIGHT (NAZI MOVIE)

Leni and Werner sit at a magnificent table.

VOICE OF MOLINA: They are dining at the majestic table in Werner's chateau. As Werner begins to notice Leni's cold distance, she suddenly—
(Leni stands up with a crystal goblet. INSERT: In the cell, Molina flings his tin cup at the wall. In the chateau, his tin cup turns into her crystal goblet.)
VOICE OF MOLINA: —Impulsively, hurls her wine glass across the room and says—
LENI: I refuse to love a man who is the butcher of my country.
WERNER (*stands up*): Oh, my love. Come with me and you'll understand.
(CUT TO:)

INT. CELL—DAY

Molina and Valentin sit side-by-side against the wall. In the fading daylight, Molina spins his delicate web.

MOLINA: Werner takes her to his government archive, filled with photos and documents about famine throughout the world.
(CUT TO:)

INT. PROJECTION ROOM—DAY (NAZI MOVIE)

Slides show the tragedy of famine. Leni wipes a teardrop.

VOICE OF MOLINA: He shows her how the elite create false shortages to enslave the masses. Leni is deeply moved and begins to see things through Werner's eyes.
(CUT TO:)

EXT. GOVERNMENT ARCHIVE—DAY (NAZI MOVIE)

Leni and Werner walk arm-in-arm along a corridor of columns.

VOICE OF MOLINA: From that moment on, Leni understood Werner's mission. To liberate humanity from injustice and domination. As they leave the baroque archive, Leni feels the anguish in her heart being transformed back to her previous admiration, but this time with the depth of a love reborn.
(Leni stops on the balustrade and looks into his eyes.)
LENI: My love, how could I ever have doubted you.
(CUT TO:)

INT. CELL—NIGHT

In the darkened cell Molina quietly says:

MOLINA: She begs him to forgive her and promises to help ensnare his enemies.
(CUT TO:)

INT. CAR—NIGHT (NAZI MOVIE)

The Flunky drives an old sedan with Leni in the backseat.

VOICE OF MOLINA: She arranges this secret meeting with the head of the Resistance by telling him that she will give the map—remember the map? —only to him.
(CUT TO:)

EXT. CASTLE—NIGHT (NAZI MOVIE)

The sedan stops beside a dark castle. Leni runs up the stone steps and enters an underground tunnel. The Flunky waits at the entrance.

(CUT TO:)

INT. CASTLE—NIGHT (NAZI MOVIE)

Leni enters an underground chamber and sees the Resistance LEADER *in the shadows.*

LENI (*offers map*):   I believe this is what you want.
LEADER: Yes, well done. So often I was tempted to steal it from him myself. But some things are best done by a woman. A woman who betrays the man she loves.
(*The Leader steps from the shadows with a lecherous grin.*)
LEADER: And there is something else I have wanted almost as much as the map.
LENI: What?
(*Taking the map, the Leader backs Leni against the wall and nuzzles her neck.*)
LEADER: You know very well. I've prepared a lavish banquet for two.
LENI: I'm not hungry.
LEADER: I am. For you.
(*He paws her. Leni, struggling, spots a steak knife on the banquet table. Pretending to submit, she maneuvers him sideways and grabs the knife.*
   Kissing him, she plunges the blade into his back. The Leader moans and topples to the floor.
   Leni grabs the map and dashes into the dark tunnel.)
(CUT TO:)

EXT. CASTLE—NIGHT (NAZI MOVIE)

*Rushing outside, Leni is grabbed by the Flunky. She elbows his throat and
starts down the stone stairs.*

*He pulls a handgun and aims at her but, suddenly, is shot in the chest and
drops to the ground.*

*Werner stands at the foot of the stairway with a smoking pistol. Leni, smil-
ing, rushes into his embrace and kisses him.*

*The dying Flunky raises his gun and fires. Leni slumps back and dies in
Werner's arms.*

VOICE OF MOLINA: Werner hears her sing. She sings like never before.
She sings of her eternal love for him and—
(CUT TO:)

INT. CELL—NIGHT

*They sit side-by-side in the dark. Valentin is wrapped in his blanket. Molina is
rapt in his web.*

MOLINA: —begs him not to cry, because her sacrifice was not in vain.
(*sighs*)
The End.
(*pause*)
What did you think?
VALENTIN (*shrugs*):   You told it well. Next time tell one I like.
MOLINA: Come off it, the love story was divine. Forget about the rest.
It's so perfect when Leni—
(*corridor noise*)
What's going on?
(*Valentin jumps up*)
What is it?
(*Valentin peers through the wall plate and* SEES *two guards dragging the
Hooded Prisoner to his cell. He has no hood.*)
VALENTIN (*stunned*):   That guy is Americo.
MOLINA: Who?
VALENTIN: The man with my passport.
(*looks down*)
They don't know he's here.
MOLINA: Who doesn't know?
(*Valentin, depressed, turns to the wall.*)
MOLINA: Please, Valentin. Maybe I can help.
(*Valentin says nothing.*)
(CUT TO:)

EXT. PRISON COURTYARD—DAY

A prison WORK CREW *cleans out Americo's empty cell. They toss his bloody
shirt in a trash can.*

(CUT TO:)

INT. CELL—DAY

Molina watches through the wall plate, then hears Valentin waking up.

MOLINA: Good morning. Did you sleep well?
VALENTIN (*glances down*):   Turn the other way, will you?
MOLINA: Why?
VALENTIN: Because you'll laugh.
MOLINA: At what?
VALENTIN: Something on any healthy man, that's all.
MOLINA: A hard-on. Well, that *is* healthy.
   (*turns away*)
   Should I close my eyes too?
   (*Valentin grins and wraps a towel around his waist.*)
VALENTIN: Hey, I missed breakfast. Why didn't you wake me?
MOLINA: I told the guard not to bring anything as long as our food
   holds out.
VALENTIN: Dammit, Molina, stop running my life for me.
   (*Molina nods an apology. Valentin moves toward the crack in the wall
   plate.*)
MOLINA: They already took him away. I didn't want to wake you. The
   water's almost hot if you want some tea.
   (*Valentin stares at dead Americo's cell. Molina unwraps some baked
   goods.*)
MOLINA: Have some cake.
VALENTIN: You eat it.
MOLINA (*offers cake*):   Come on, let me spoil you a little bit.
VALENTIN (*turns, glares*):   Back off, Molina.
MOLINA: It's not my fault they killed your friend.
VALENTIN: Shut up!
   (*slaps cake*)
   You damn faggot!
   (CUT TO:)

EXT. PRISON CORRIDOR—DAY

*Two guards escort Molina across the courtyard and open his cell door. He car-
ries two new bags of groceries.*

   (CUT TO:)

INT. CELL—DAY

Molina puts down the bags and pulls out a red heart-shaped box of candy.

MOLINA: Look at the wonderful things Mama brought me. And there's
   a special treat. Assorted bonbons.
   (*Valentin watches in silence from his bunk, his hands folded around his
   knee. Molina sits near him with the candy box.*)

MOLINA: What's the matter? You don't like candy?

VALENTIN: About this morning . . . about my temper, I'm really sorry.

MOLINA: Oh, nonsense.

VALENTIN: It wasn't even you I was mad at.
> (*pause*)
>
> But I've been thinking. Maybe I *am* mad at you.

MOLINA: Why?

VALENTIN: Because you're so kind. I don't want to feel obligated to treat you the same way.

MOLINA (*sing-song*):   "Unable to take, unable to give."
> (*Molina opens the candy box and slides it toward Valentin.*)

VOICE OF MOLINA: Every day he opens up more and more with me.
> (NOTE: *We leave and return to the candy in the cell as Molina recalls his latest meeting with the Warden and Pedro.*)
> (CUT TO:)

EXT. PRISON ROOFTOP—DAY

Molina faces them on the prison roof.

MOLINA (*continues*):   Just give me a few more days. I'm sure he'll talk.

PEDRO: If he don't, he'll be interrogated again. And thoroughly this time.

MOLINA: But he's too weak to be tortured. If he drops dead, we all lose out.
> (CUT TO:)

INT. CELL—DUSK

Valentin sits on the floor beside the half-empty candy box.

VALENTIN: I can't take someone being nice to me without asking anything in return.

MOLINA: Well, if I'm nice to you, it's because I want your friendship and, why not say it? . . . . your affection.
> (*offers cigarette*)
>
> The same way I try to be nice to my mother who's never harmed anyone, and who accepts me for what I am and loves me. It's like a gift from heaven, and the only thing that keeps me going, the only thing.
> (*lights cigarette*)
>
> And you too are a very good person.
> (*Valentin, embarrassed, moves to the wall and smokes the cigarette.*)

MOLINA: Very selfless and devoted, risking your life for your ideals, ready to die even in here for what you believe in. Am I embarrassing you?

VALENTIN (*shrugs*):   No.
> (CUT TO:)

EXT. PRISON ROOFTOP—DAY

Molina turns to the Warden.

MOLINA: Well, sir, there might be a way to speed this up. I'm not sure but I'm—it's just a hunch.

WARDEN (*exasperated*): Say it straight, Molina.

MOLINA: You know inmates, sir. When a cell-mate leaves, they feel all sentimental and helpless. Well, he's gotten a bit attached to me, so if he thought that I was being released, he's bound to open up and talk. Get a few things off his chest.

WARDEN (*to Pedro*): What do you think?
    (CUT TO:)

INT. CELL—NIGHT

Valentin still leans against the wall with his cigarette. Molina watches from the bunk.

MOLINA: So that's why I respect you and like you, and hope that you feel the same way about me. So I want us always to be friends.

VALENTIN: Sure.

MOLINA: The reason I wanted to get this in the open is because I may be leaving, since I just heard from the Warden that I may be paroled soon.

VALENTIN: —When?
    (CUT TO:)

EXT. PRISON ROOFTOP—DAY

Pedro removes his suitcoat, revealing a shoulder holster.

PEDRO: Tell him you're up for parole, that we're gonna move you to another cell in 24 hours.

MOLINA: Yes, sir.

WARDEN: And this is your last chance, so get going. You got 24 hours.

MOLINA: One thing, sir. You can't catch a fish without bait. I need more food. This time, sir, I prepared a list.
    (*Molina hands him a long list.*)
    (CUT TO:)

INT. CELL—NIGHT

Molina still sits on Valentin's bunk.

MOLINA: They'll probably move me to another cell in 24 hours. My lawyer says that's the procedure.
    (*Valentin turns away. Molina walks back to his own bunk.*)

MOLINA: I don't want to get my hopes up too high. Do you want an apple?

VALENTIN: No, thanks. I guess I should be happy for you, but uh—I don't know.

MOLINA: Yes, all I wanted in life was to get out of here and take care of my mother. Nothing else mattered, but now that my wish might be—

VALENTIN: Be happy, dammit. I'd give anything to get out.

MOLINA: But is it fair?

VALENTIN: What?

MOLINA: That I always end up with nothing. That I don't have anything truly my own in life.

VALENTIN: You've got your mother.

MOLINA: Yes, but listen though. She's had a life and lived it. She had a husband and a son, but I'm still waiting.

VALENTIN: At least she's still alive.

MOLINA: But so am I. When is my life supposed to begin?
(*pause*)
When do I strike it lucky and have something for my own?

VALENTIN (*approaches*): Right now. You just *got* lucky. Take advantage of it. You're getting out.

MOLINA: And do what? Hang out with my friends, a bunch of silly old queens like me? Tell a few jokes until I can't stand the sight of them, because they're a bunch of mirrors that send me running for my life? My life of waiting for nothing.

VALENTIN: Tell a movie. You'll feel better.
(*Curfew* BUZZER. *The dim light bulb goes out. Valentin moves to his bunk.*
Alone in the dark, Molina turns to the moonlit window and spins another web.)

MOLINA: Once upon a time, on a tropical island far away, there lived a strange woman.
(*pause*)
She wore a long gown of black lamé that fit her like a glove. But the poor thing, she was caught in a giant spider web that grew from her own body.
(CUT TO:)

EXT. TROPICAL BEACH—NIGHT (SPIDER MOVIE)

The masked SPIDER WOMAN *stands silhouetted against the moonlit ocean, waiting and waiting inside a huge silvery spider web.*

Gliding from the web, she moves across the sandy beach and slowly approaches the body of a MAN *washed onto her island shore.*

VOICE OF MOLINA: One day a shipwrecked man drifted onto the beach.
(*She kneels in the sand beside him.* INSERT: *Valentin leans against the cell wall, listening in the candlelight.*)

VOICE OF MOLINA: She fed him and cared for his wounds. She nourished him with love and brought him back to life.
   (*The Shipwrecked Man opens his eyes.*)
VOICE OF MOLINA: When he awoke, he gazed up at the Spider Woman and saw a perfect tear-drop slide from under her mask.
   (CUT TO:)

INT. CELL—NIGHT

Misty-eyed, Molina steps into the candlelight and approaches Valentin. INSERT: *The Shipwrecked Man lifts his head for a closer look at the Spider Woman.*

VOICE OF VALENTIN: Why is she crying?
   (*Molina answers with a lump in his throat.*)
MOLINA: I don't know. Why do you always need explanations?
   (*sad sigh*)
   Valentin, I'm tired. Tired of suffering. You're not the only one they've hurt. You don't know, I hurt so much inside.
VALENTIN: Where does it hurt you?
MOLINA: In my neck and shoulders. Why does the sadness always jam up in the same spot?
   (*Valentin places a sympathetic hand on his shoulder. Molina tightens up and pulls away.*)
MOLINA: Please. Don't touch me.
VALENTIN: Can't a friend even pat your back?
MOLINA (*sits on bunk*):   It only makes it worse.
VALENTIN: Why?
   (*Molina, dropping his many masks, speaks with stark vulnerability.*)
MOLINA: Because I've fallen in love with you.
   (*pause*)
   I'm sorry, Valentin, I wish it hadn't happened.
VALENTIN (*looks away*):   I understand.
   (*looks back*)
   Don't be ashamed.
   (*Valentin moves to Molina's bunk and tentatively sits down. Molina, motionless, keeps looking away. Valentin clears his throat and says:*)
VALENTIN: Can I touch you?
MOLINA (*looking away*):   If it doesn't disgust you.
   (*pause*)
   I'd like you to.
   (*Valentin wraps a friendly arm around his shoulders. Molina shudders, then turns and looks apprehensively into his eyes.*)
MOLINA: Can I touch your scar?
VALENTIN (*shrugs*):   Sure.
   (*Molina gently caresses the scar near Valentin's eyebrow, then rests his head on Valentin's chest and whispers:*)
MOLINA: Do what you want with me, because that's what I want.

(*pause*)

If it doesn't disgust you.

VALENTIN (*hesitant*):   Okay.

(*Molina trembles. Valentin holds him against his chest like a father comforting a child. Molina looks up and says:*)

MOLINA: You are so kind to me.

VALENTIN: No. You're the one who's kind.

(*Valentin straightens up and removes his shirt, then leans forward and blows out the candle.*

The cell is dark. The camera lingers on the candle-spark amid wisps of smoke.)

MOLINA (O.S.):   Wait. I'm squeezed against the wall. That's better.

(*pause*)

No, wait. Let me lift my legs.

(*The spark fades. The screen is* BLACK.)

(CUT TO:)

INT. CELL—DAY

Molina, radiant, looks at the morning sunlight.

MOLINA: You know when I woke up, I put my hand to my eyebrow, to feel my scar like—

VALENTIN: You don't have one.

MOLINA: —like I wasn't me anymore. As if somehow I was you.

(*pause*)

Look, let's not talk about this. Let's not talk about anything at all. Just for this morning I'm asking. Aren't you going to ask me why?

VALENTIN: Why?

MOLINA: Because I'm happy, I'm really happy, and I don't want to spoil it.

(*sad smile*)

The nicest thing about feeling happy is that you think you'll never feel unhappy again.

(CUT TO:)

INT. WARDEN'S OFFICE—DAY

Pedro, seething, leans into Molina's face.

PEDRO: You shit-face motherfuck. Talk!

(*Molina looks down in fear. The Warden wheels forward and motions Pedro away.*)

WARDEN: Let me handle this.

(*wheels closer*)

Look at me, Molina. What's the matter? You're afraid his group will kill you, is that it?

MOLINA: No sir. I *want* to help.

WARDEN: So what did he say?

MOLINA: Nothing. Wouldn't it be worse if I told you something that wasn't true?

WARDEN: I'll have to move you to another cell, Molina.

MOLINA: No sir, please. Don't do that. As long as I'm with him, there's still a chance that he might talk.

(*Pedro leans around the Warden into Molina's face.*)

PEDRO: You faggot piece of shit! You fell in love with that bastard.

WARDEN: Okay, Molina. You can go.

(*Molina stands up. The Warden reaches in his pocket.*)

WARDEN: Get your things ready. You're leaving today.

(*hands document*)

Here, the Ministry approved your parole.

(*Molina kisses the Warden's hand.*)

MOLINA: Thank you, sir.

WARDEN: And no more hanky-panky with the little boys.

MOLINA: Oh no, sir. I swear.

(*Molina leaves.*)

(CUT TO:)

INT. CELL—DAY

Molina pulls his mother's photo from the wall and packs his suitcase. Valentin stoops beside him.

VALENTIN: They, they would never suspect you. I mean really, there's no risk at all.

MOLINA: Sorry, I can't do it. I, uh, I'm just too afraid.

VALENTIN: All you have to do is give them a message. From any public phone.

MOLINA: No. No names, no phone numbers, nothing. I'm terrified of the police.

VALENTIN: Okay. I guess I shouldn't drag you into this.

(*Valentin moves to the far corner. Molina watches him.*)

MOLINA: I swear, Valentin. My only desire is to stay here with you.

VALENTIN: Take care of yourself.

MOLINA: Valentin, I've only loved two people in my life. My mother and you.

VALENTIN: I'm gonna miss you, Molina.

MOLINA: At least the movies.

VALENTIN (*smiles*):   Yeah, whenever I go to sleep, I'll probably be thinking of you and your crazy movies.

MOLINA: And whenever I see bonbons, I'll be thinking of you.

(*pause*)

Valentin, there's something I'd like to ask you, although we've done much more.

(*pause*)

A kiss.

VALENTIN: Okay. But first promise me something.

MOLINA: I told you, I can't. I'm so sorry.

VALENTIN: No, no, no.

(*approaches*)

Promise you'll never let anybody humiliate you again, that you'll make them respect you. Promise me you'll never let anybody exploit you again. Nobody has the right to do that to anybody.

MOLINA (*deeply moved*):

I promise. Thank you.

(*pause*)

Valentin?

VALENTIN: What? The kiss?

MOLINA: No. The uhh. The phone number.

(*Valentin, overwhelmed, hugs him. Molina, surprised, returns the embrace.*)

VALENTIN: Wait a few days. Dial two times and hang up. The third time . . .

(*Valentin whispers in his ear. Molina nods twice. Their eyes meet. Valentin grips his shoulders and kisses him on the mouth. The Guard unlocks the door, then steps inside and says:*)

GUARD: Molina, let's go.

(*Molina picks up his suitcase and moves toward the door.*)

VALENTIN: Wait.

(VALENTIN *holds out the heart-shaped box.* MOLINA, *touched, takes it and looks deep into his eyes.*)

VALENTIN: Good luck, Molina.

(*Molina nods with a sad smile. The Guard pushes him outside.*)

GUARD: Come on.

(*The door is slammed shut on Valentin.*)

(CUT TO:)

EXT. PRISON COURTYARD—DAY

The Guard escorts Molina across the courtyard to the gate.

(CUT TO:)

INT. CELL—DAY

Valentin, alone, paces the empty cell, then sits down and stares at Molina's bunk.

(CUT TO:)

EXT. PRISON GATE—DAY

Molina crosses the busy street to a bus stop, then turns to the nearby counter of an open cafe.

MOLINA: A beer.

(The waiter uncaps a beer bottle.)
(CUT TO:)

INT. WARDEN'S OFFICE—DAY

Pedro opens the venetian blinds and watches Molina sipping beer at the bus stop. We HEAR him typing a Secret Police report.

VOICE OF PEDRO: Subject was granted a special parole by the Minister of Justice, on orders from the Department of Political Surveillance. The Department believes he will lead our agents to the cadre of Valentin Arregui.
(The bus arrives. Molina tosses his bottle in a trash can and climbs on board.)
(CUT TO:)

INT. BUS—DAY

Molina watches the passing city with sad and empty eyes.

(CUT TO:)

INT. MOLINA'S APARTMENT—DAY

Molina opens the door, moves quietly down the hallway and sees her at the sewing machine, unspooling thread with the quiet precision of a spider.

MOLINA: —Mama.
MOTHER *(surprised)*:   Ahhh.
(She hurries into his waiting arms. He wraps her in a warm embrace.)
(CUT TO:)

INT. CABARET—NIGHT

Molina, wearing a leopard pullover, crosses a smoke-filled cabaret to a table of MIDDLE-AGED HOMOSEXUALS. *They flatter him with campy flair.*

GROUP VOICES: —Luisa! So nice to see you!—You look great! Ten years younger, darling. Doesn't she—The return of the Leopard Woman.
(Molina's transvestite friend Greta finishes a song on the small stage and approaches the microphone.)
GRETA *(rowdy applause)*:   Oh shut up, you bunch of faggots.
(indicates Molina)
I'd like to welcome home a cherished sister who sacrificed Lord-knows-how-many precious nights to pay a stupid debt to a hypo-critical society.
(throws a kiss)
This is for you, lovely Luisa.
(He sings in a feminine voice. Molina, touched, nods.)
(CUT TO:)

INT. MOLINA'S APARTMENT—NIGHT

Molina, motionless, sits in the bay window. His stark sad eyes gaze across the city lights at the prison on the dark horizon.

(CUT TO:)

EXT. MOLINA'S APARTMENT—NIGHT

Pedro waits in a car parked in the shadows. His piercing eyes are fixed on Molina in the bay window. We HEAR *him file a police report.*

VOICE OF PEDRO: Surveillance reveals subject has not returned to work and almost never leaves home. He spends his evenings staring out the window for no apparent reason.
(CUT TO:)

INT. RESTAURANT—DAY

Molina sips coffee alone at a table. Gabriel approaches.

GABRIEL: You sure you won't eat something?
MOLINA: Just coffee.
GABRIEL: You wanna talk, Molina? Is something wrong?
MOLINA: No, I'm just not gonna see you for awhile. I'm going away.
GABRIEL: With another boy?
    (*sad smile*)
    That's good. Don't get arrested again. You're too old for it.
    (CUT TO:)

INT. MOLINA'S APARTMENT—NIGHT

Molina sits with his arm around his frail mother. They are bathed in the blue radiance of a late movie on TV.

(CUT TO:)

INT. MOLINA'S BEDROOM—NIGHT

Molina slumps in bed in the robe he wore in prison. A red lamp illumines his poster of Rita Hayworth.

His sad eyes stare at the red box in his lap. His fingers trace the heart-shaped edges.

(CUT TO:)

INT. BAY WINDOW—NIGHT

Molina sits in the bay window with his head in his hands, then lifts his head and gazes across the rooftops at the distant prison.

Wearing a yellow satin jacket, he is dressed to go out but remains seated. Finally he sighs and moves to the door.

(CUT TO:)

INT. SUBWAY STATION—NIGHT

Molina enters an empty subway station, glances around and approaches a row of futuristic phones.
He dials twice and hangs up, then dials a third time and nervously brushes back his red-tinted hair.

MOLINA: I have a message from Valentin Arregui.
   (*short pause*)
   Yes, a pay phone.
   (*short pause*)
   Excuse me, is that really necessary?
   (*long pause*)
   Alright. I'll be wearing a red scarf.
   (CUT TO:)

INT. BANK—DAY

The BANK TELLER *hands Molina a thick wad of money.*

TELLER: You don't have to close your account. There's no penalty if
   you maintain a minimum balance of—
MOLINA: Thank you. Do you have an envelope please?
   (*Molina slips the money in the envelope and leaves.*)
   (CUT TO:)

EXT. PARK—DAY

Molina sits on a park bench with Greta and hands him the envelope.

MOLINA: This is for Mama. To take care of her while I'm gone. Please.
GRETA: All right, I'll handle it.
   (*pause*)
   Wherever you're going, it's probably for the best.
   (CUT TO:)

INT. MOTHER'S BEDROOM—NIGHT

Molina tiptoes into his mother's bedroom and whispers:

MOLINA: Mama, you look so beautiful.
   (*She is asleep. He gently kneels beside her.*)
MOLINA: You remember, Mama, when I was little and you used to
   come into my room to kiss me goodnight. I always pretended to be
   asleep, but I was always waiting for your kiss.
   (*pause*)
   Although you're sleeping now, I know you understand me. It's time
   for me to take care of my own life. You understand, don't you,
   Mama?
   (*pause*)

Don't be sad.
(*He kisses her forehead.*)
(CUT TO:)

INT. MOLINA'S BEDROOM—DAY

Molina steps to his bedroom mirror and, expressionless, ties a red scarf around his neck. Rita Hayworth watches over his shoulder.

(CUT TO:)

EXT. CITY STREETS—DAY

Molina, tense, jockeys his way through a street jammed with pedestrians. Glancing up, he spots Pedro and three Secret Agents on an overpass.

Frightened, Molina plunges into the crowd. Pedro sprints down the overpass and barges through the crowd, his Agents right behind him. Molina turns a corner into a shopping arcade and, hurrying, glances back. He sees Pedro round the corner and stares into his eyes.

Molina desperately elbows through the shoppers. Pedro keeps a safe distance.

Struggling, Molina weaves his way inside a dense cluster of pedestrians, then darts down a narrow alley.

Pedro scans the four alleys. Molina is gone.

PEDRO: Go that way. Hurry.
(*The Agents split into two groups and go the wrong way.*)
(CUT TO:)

EXT. CATHEDRAL SQUARE—DAY

Molina steps from an alley into an open square. Fingering his red scarf, he searches the crowd for Secret Police.

Relieved, he crosses the square to the cathedral and stops beside a BEGGAR *playing an accordion. Pretending to listen, he scrutinizes the street and nervously taps his teeth.*

A white taxi slowly approaches the cathedral steps. The YOUNG WOMAN *beside the driver nervously eyes Molina.*

He hesitantly stoops down and sees a pistol half-hidden by a newspaper on her lap. She leans out the window.

LYDIA: —Who are you?
MOLINA: I have a message from Valentin. Are you Lydia?
LYDIA: Yes, get in. Quick.
(*Molina reaches for the door handle.*)
PEDRO: Get 'em!
(*Suddenly an Agent slams Molina aside and thrusts a revolver in the window. Lydia rapid-fires two shots and blasts the Agent to the pavement.*
The taxi roars away. Molina runs. Pedro and two Agents bolt forward, firing at the taxi careening through the terrified crowd. Turning, Pedro

*sprints after Molina disappearing into a dark alley. The two Agents follow
at top speed, firing warning shots in the air.)*
(CUT TO:)

EXT. PLAZA—DAY

*Molina, gasping, races along the dark alley toward the sunlit plaza across a
busy avenue.*
    *Pedro barrels around the corner with his automatic pistol and charges
down the alley. Bystanders run for cover.*

PEDRO: Molina! Stop!
    *(Molina rushes toward the plaza when, suddenly, the white taxi skids to a
stop on the avenue directly ahead. Lydia rapid-fires three shots out the window.*
        *Molina, twisted sideways, grabs his bleeding chest. The taxi screeches
away. Molina lurches across the avenue into the plaza. Bystanders scream
and scatter. Pedro reaches the corner and fires at the fleeing taxi, then aims
at Molina and strides into the plaza. Molina, clutching his blood-stained
shirt, staggers into a flock of pigeons. Agents surround him with aimed
handguns. Molina turns and faces them, then drops to his knees.*
        The pigeons scatter. Pedro motions to an Agent.)

PEDRO: Get the car. Move, hurry.
    *(The Agent runs. Pedro steps forward and slowly circles behind Molina,
then jams the automatic against the back of his head and frisks him.*
        The car pulls up. Pedro jerks Molina to his feet.)
PEDRO: Get up. Move! Get in the car.
    *(Pedro hurls Molina into the backseat, climbs in and slams the door. The
car speeds away.)*
    (CUT TO:)

INT. PEDRO'S CAR—DAY

*Molina lies stretched out on the backseat. Pedro straddles his waist and sticks
the automatic in his face.*

PEDRO: The number. Tell me the phone number and you go to the hos-
    pital.
    (Molina spits up foamy blood, then calmly gazes at Pedro.)
PEDRO: Talk! You fucking fag!
    (Molina's eyes slowly close. His head slumps sideways.)
    (CUT TO:)

EXT. SLUM—DAY

*The car turns off a busy street into a shanty-town slum and stops beside a pile
of garbage.*
    Pedro drags Molina's body from the backseat and dumps it on the garbage.

VOICE OF PEDRO: Subject was shot to death by the extremists. His recent activities, such as closing his bank account, suggest that he
planned to escape with them. Also, the way he was shot seems to indicate he had agreed, if necessary, to be eliminated by them.
(*pause*)
In any case, it appears he was more deeply involved than we suspected.
(CUT TO:)

INT. PRISON INFIRMARY—DAY

*Valentin, dying, lies on a cot. His face is swollen with bloody bruises. His
chest is disfigured by electric burns.*

A prison INTERN *takes out a hypodermic needle.*

INTERN: This is morphine. So you can get some rest, okay?
(*Valentin nods feebly. The Intern injects the needle.*)
INTERN: My God, the way they worked you over.
(*removes needle*)
Just don't tell about this or I'll lose my job. Count to forty and you'll
be asleep.
(*Valentin takes two deep breaths and falls sound asleep. A woman's dream-
like hand slowly reaches out and touches his wrist.*
VOICE OF VALENTIN: . . . Marta . . .
(*Valentin turns in his sleep and sees the beaming smile of his love. Marta,
vibrant in a pure white dress, caresses his battered head and tenderly tugs
him to his feet.*)
MARTA: Come, Valentin, come with me. Don't be afraid. You won't
wake up in the cell.
(CUT TO:)

EXT. PRISON COURTYARD—DAY (DREAM)

*Running hand-in-hand, Marta leads Valentin across the dark courtyard to-
ward the gate. The guards and prisoners cannot see them. Valentin, bleeding,
stops and looks back.*

VOICE OF VALENTIN: —What about Molina?
VOICE OF MARTA: Come, my love. Only he knows if he died happy or
sad.
(*She takes his hand and opens the prison gate, revealing a burst of
sunlight.*)
(CUT TO:)

EXT. TROPICAL ISLAND—DAY (DREAM)

*Smiling in the sunshine, they run toward the ocean across a sandy beach—the
same beach in Molina's movie about the Spider Woman.*

Valentin, radiant, has no scars or wounds. Stopping at the shoreline, he brushes back her hair and looks into her eyes.

VOICE OF VALENTIN: I love you so much. That's the one thing I never said, because I was afraid of losing you forever.
(*They kiss warmly. Marta caresses his healed face and looks into his loving eyes.*)
VOICE OF MARTA: That can never happen now. This dream is short, but this dream is happy.
(*Holding hands, they wade into the water and climb into a wooden rowboat. Taking the oars, Valentin rows farther and farther toward the sparkling horizon.*)

Questions for Discussion and Writing

1. In what way are Valentin and Molina defined by their contrast to each other? How do these differences emerge through their very different reactions to the film that Molina is narrating?
2. What circumstances have led each to be incarcerated?
3. What details make it possible for the audience to understand Valentin's profound ambivalence toward the ultimate value of political activism? How is this ambivalence dramatized in his memories of Marta and Lydia?
4. How does the developing relationship between Valentin and Molina account for the dramatic changes that occur in each of them? What are these changes?
5. What details allow the audience to understand how keenly Molina is torn between saving his mother and his feelings for Valentin?
6. What features of the highly stylized movie narrated by Molina allow the audience to understand that it serves as an imaginative escape from the daily reality of prison life?
7. In which sequence of separate scenes can you most clearly see how meaning in any particular scene is created by the juxtaposition of individual scenes? For example, how is your reaction to the scene in which we see Molina alone wearing his prison robe staring at the red candy box conditioned by its juxtaposition with the previous scene in which Molina sits watching television with his arm around his frail mother? Because of the context, what emotion do you infer Molina is experiencing? What other examples can you cite of MONTAGE in the SCREENPLAY where meaning is created not by the content of the individual scenes but through the juxtaposition or contextual relationship of the scenes to each other?
8. What is the relationship between the meaning of the Spider Woman movie Molina tells Valentin and the "real" events that take place? How does the Spider Woman story serve as a metaphor for the relationship between Molina and Valentin? In your opinion, which one is the Spider Woman?
9. In a short essay, discuss what makes Molina actually jeopardize his hard-won freedom to carry out Valentin's last wish.
10. In your opinion, which of the two is the real hero? Explain your answer.
11. Think of any painting or photo as a single frame from a film. Describe events as they lead up to this picture, painting, or photograph, and describe what happens afterward.

WRITING ABOUT POINT OF VIEW

The vantage point from which the author chooses to tell about the events that take place in a story determines its POINT OF VIEW. Although readers tend to identify the voice they hear telling the events as that of the writer, we must remember the narrator is another character created to tell the story. The point of view of the story depends on who this narrator is and how he or she is related to the characters and events being described.

There are four basic vantage points from which the narrator can tell the story: omniscient, limited omniscient, first person, and objective, or dramatic.

In OMNISCIENT narration, the most traditional form of telling a story, the author creates an all-knowing storyteller who knows everything there is to know about every character and event in the story. The omniscient narrator is free is to divulge anything that goes on in the minds of the characters, and can easily move from the consciousness of one character to another, giving the reader insight into each character's innermost thoughts and feelings. The advantages of knowing more than we could ever possibly know through mere observation are offset by the fact that we are distanced from the characters and cannot share their feelings except through the narrator's judgments and speculations. For example, Dino Buzzati in "The Falling Girl" describes both what Marta, the protagonist, and onlookers feel and think ("she felt fascinating, stylish . . . some thought her pretty, others thought her so so, everyone found her interesting").

The point of view that writers prefer in twentieth-century fiction is the LIMITED OMNISCIENT, in which the author uses a third-person narrator and limits our perceptions to a single character's view of events. In limited omniscience, the narrator cannot reveal what is going on in the minds of all the characters, but rather focuses our attention on one character, encouraging the reader to identify with that character and discover things with the character as the story progresses. This creates an extremely strong sense of empathy and involvement. By restricting our perspective to a single character's consciousness, the story seems more coherent and attains a sense of unity without the distraction of shifting into the minds of other characters. This character may be the protagonist, a minor character, or an outside observer. Charles Johnson in "China" uses the third-person perspective to allow us to share the feelings, thoughts, and gamut of emotions of Evelyn, who observes the changes in her husband, Rudolph, following his decision to take up kung fu. Johnson provides insight into Evelyn's thoughts as she watches his vigorous training sessions ("his self-punishment made her feel sick. She was afraid of his hard cold weights. She hated them. Yet she wanted them too. They had a certain monastic beauty") and his surprising sudden commitment to kung fu.

In the FIRST-PERSON POINT OF VIEW (grammatically signaled by the use of "I") the author further limits what we can know by eliminating the narrator and having one of the characters tell the story. The events in these stories are filtered through the consciousness of a narrator who may be a protagonist, as in stories by Keyes and Lispector, a minor character, as in al-Shaykh's story, or an outside observer, as in Kosinski's work. In all these stories we are restricted to the report, commentary, and opinion of one character, however incorrect, naive, or biased their view might be.

Like the limited omniscient vantage point, first-person point of view provides a single, unified view of events that encourages the reader to accept that the events reported actually happened. At the same time, the use of a first-person narrator who is so deeply involved in the events may cause the reader to question the reliability of the narrator's perceptions. Unlike limited omniscience, the first-person narrator remains the reader's sole source of information. Think, for example, how differently the events the narrator describes in "A Sincere Friendship" might look from his friend's point of view. Is the narrator's report of the events and commentary on them to be taken as trustworthy and reliable in Lispector's story or as a self-serving rationalization of why the friendship dissolved? Often the advantages of increased empathy are offset by suspicions or a prejudiced viewpoint and unreliable conclusions on the part of the narrator.

The fourth point of view the author can adopt is the so-called OBJECTIVE or DRAMATIC VANTAGE POINT. We view the characters as we would in a play. Because the author shows us events without commenting on them or filtering them through the personality of a particular character, we must form our opinions based solely on what the characters do and say and how they interact with others. The dramatic point of view produces an immediacy and illusion of reality that places the reader in the position of spectator.

In writing about point of view, the first question to ask yourself is through whose consciousness or from whose vantage point are the events of the story experienced. If the point of view is omniscient, does the author clearly distinguish his or her perspective from that of the characters? If the point of view is limited omniscient, is the character allowed to know only what someone in that position could know? If the point of view is first person, what internal clues suggest that the narrator's view of things is reliable and to be trusted? Are there clues to the contrary? The most interesting essays on point of view investigate how the author's choice affects the reader's perception of the characters and plot. Has the writer chosen the most effective point of view for the story he or she wants to tell? What other points of view might work as well? You might even choose to rewrite one of the stories as it might appear from another point of view.

The point of view in poetry depends on the relationship between the speaker and the events described. In LYRIC poetry, such as in the poems by Tuqan, Boland, and Baraka, the speaker represents one aspect, or a PERSONA, of the poet expressing a personal and intense reaction to a particular problem or situation. For example, when the speaker in Tuqan's "I Found It" says "I found it on a radiant day/After a long drifting," we share her joy in a direct way. We understand that the speaker in this work may represent Tuqan's mood at an earlier time.

In NARRATIVE poems, such as that of Kenny, the emphasis is less on the speaker's feeling than on the story the poem tells. In "Sometimes . . . Injustice" the speaker tells how events outside his control have shaped his life.

DESCRIPTIVE poetry is less personal than either lyric or narrative poetry. For example the description of a beautiful red azalea thriving in a harsh mountainous terrain in Xu Gang's "Red Azalea on the Cliff" suggests aspects of the speaker's sensibility indirectly through the quality of his perceptions.

Poems written from a DRAMATIC point of view are presented as speeches similar to those heard on the stage. Ted Hughes's "Examination at the Womb-Door" creates its effects through balanced contrasts, antitheses, and parallel assertions that create the illusion of a conversation between living figures that move, converse, and influence each other.

The playwright's way of telling a story is restricted to a single objective point of view. Drama offers an unrivaled sense of intensity and immediacy. We do not have a narrator commenting on events or characters, explaining motivation, or interpreting the significance of the actions characters perform on the stage. The reader or audience must draw conclusions solely through what the characters do and say. In watching a drama we have the sensation that we are witnessing events as they unfold and that we are listening to the conversation between the characters at that very moment.

Leonard Schrader's screenplay of Manuel Puig's novel, *Kiss of the Spider Woman*, differs from a conventional dramatic script in a number of important ways that illustrate the basic difference between film and theater. When you watch a play in the theater you are free to look at anything happening on the stage in any order you choose. A filmmaker, by contrast, manipulates the angle from which you see events by moving the camera to present the action from many different points of view. In one shot we may see the events as they appear from one actor's perspective. A succeeding shot may shift the angle so that the camera has moved above the scene and we are looking downward from an aerial view. In the space of a few moments we can be transported from an intimate close-up to a panoramic long shot from which the scene is viewed from a considerable distance. The camera angle not only dictates the point of view from which the scene is shot, but establishes our sense of closeness or distance to the figures in the scene. A screenplay stipulates how much of the action we can see, from what angle we can see it, how many characters will be included in the shot, and how long the image will remain on the screen.

An essay that investigates how screenplays achieve their unique effects might analyze how the separate scenes work together to tell a story in ways that are controlled by the manipulation of point of view through the placement and movement of the camera. Every choice determining what you see, and how much of it, whether from close up or far away, whether the frame includes one character, two or three characters, or a crowd, and how long you get to see it, is absolutely controlled by the camera angle the director has chosen. Not only does the camera angle dictate the point of view from which the scene is shot, but it establishes our sense of closeness to, or distance from, both figures and action.

In film, two images are juxtaposed to achieve an effect that is more significant for an audience than either of the individual shots. This principle is called MONTAGE and is the basis of storytelling in film. The analysis of any screenplay may reveal how scenes are shot and arranged for the express purpose of communicating an idea or emotion in the mind of the audience or reader. We can understand this method of composition by looking at the four short scenes after Molina has returned home from prison and has tried to resume his former life. In one scene we see him sitting with his "arm around his frail mother" watching television. In the next, he is alone, wearing the robe he wore in prison, staring at the red candy box he and Valentin had shared. He lifts his head and gazes across the skyline of the city toward the prison and finally leaves the apartment. In the next scene, he makes a phone call from an empty subway station. In the fourth scene in the sequence, Molina closes his account at the bank. The emotion or idea implanted in the audience's mind by the juxtaposition of images communicates elegantly and economically Molina's psychological turmoil, his inability to forget Valentin, and decision to risk everything in making contact with Valentin's group. The emotional and aesthetic effect is far more forceful than any of the individual shots would be. Through the combination of the four shots the audience is manipulated to intimately understand Molina's feelings and intentions.

Connections

1. How do the works by Reichel and al-Shaykh show how a girl's discovery of a suppressed truth changes her relationships with her parents and other adults?

2. How do both Buzzati's and Lispector's stories offer portraits of the psychological pressures that often characterize adolescence when young people reach beyond their families to find an identity through acceptance and friendship?

3. How do both Kosinski and Hughes dramatize how the impact of having to survive in harsh, violent environments shapes the protagonists?

4. How does the transformation of an ordinary person into someone with extraordinary gifts change both the lives of the protagonists and those around them in "Flowers for Algernon" and "China"?

5. How do Reichel's and Kosinski's works depict children coming to terms with the existence of violence and evil in the world during World War II?

6. How do Song, Boland, and Tuqan provide insight into the struggles facing the speakers in their efforts to cope with the need to have an independent identity?

7. In what ways are "Lisa's Ritual, Age 10," "An Agony. As Now," and "The Street" based on the concept of fragmented identity? What can you infer about the nature of the forces that led each of the speakers in the three poems to become dissociated?

8. How do the poems by Xu Gang and Tuqan show that only by great effort can one achieve what is most valuable?

9. What similarities and differences can you discover between how Maurice Kenny and Imamu Amiri Baraka portray the nature of forces that prevent individuals from becoming all that they can be?

10. Discuss the importance of friendship in finding one's own identity as shown in the works by Lispector, Johnson, and Puig.

3

Gender

"*Women have served all these centuries as looking-glasses possessing the magic and delicious power of reflecting the figure of man at twice its natural size.*"

— *Virginia Woolf*

"*The face of a lover is unknown, precisely because it is invested with so much of oneself. It is a mystery, containing, like all mysteries, the possibility of torment.*"

— *James Baldwin*

Culture plays an enormous role in shaping expectations attached to sex roles. This process, sometimes called socialization, determines how each of us assimilates our culture's ideas of what it means to act as a male or female. We tend to acquire a sense of our own sexual identity in conjunction with societal expectations. Yet, these expectations differ strikingly from culture to culture. For example, in male-dominated Islamic Mideastern societies, the sex roles and relationships between men and women are very different from those in modern industrial societies.

The writers in this chapter address questions of how some societies give authority and value to the roles of men while treating women as if they were invisible. This attitude is most apparent in how a particular society greets the birth of a female infant. Gender is not only a question of difference but of power, and concepts of masculinity and femininity vary widely in societies and in historical periods.

This chapter presents contemporary works by writers around the world that explore the complexities that arise in relationships between the sexes. The attitude toward female sexuality in Mideastern culture is powerfully explored by an Egyptian physician and feminist in her essay "The Mutilated Half." In "The Lion" we read a gentle tale of romantic love from a bygone era set in Russia. In "Amina," from Lebanon, we hear the story of a wife's anxiety lest she give birth to another girl. The trial of a woman in Mexico charged with five counts of bigamy calls into question basic attitudes toward gender in that culture, in "The Night Visitor." From Pakistan we learn of the dissolution of a marriage in "Facing the Light," and from the Republic of the Congo we read a satirical portrait of a male chauvinist in "The Esteemed Representative." A French-Canadian author unfolds a bizarre tale of erotic obsession in "The Red Boots." The poignant story of a late-blooming love affair set in Russia is told in "Nothing Special."

The poetry in Chapter 3 presents a wide range and rich selection of works illustrative of male and female relationships in many countries and cultures, including those of Mexico, Puerto Rico, Italy, Russia, Estonia, and, in the United States, the Mexican-American. These poems by Rosario Castellanos, Judith Ortiz Cofer, Jimmy Santiago Baca, Marta Fabiani, Anna Akhmatoba, Adrienne Rich, Doris Kareva, and Muriel Rukeyser present many aspects of gender relationships.

The Lion and the Jewel, a play by Africa's leading dramatist, Wole Soyinka, offers a delightful battle of the sexes in a ribald comedy about the courtship of a young, beautiful, and egotistical girl by the crafty old chief of the village intent on adding her to his retinue of wives.

Nawal el-Saadawi

The Mutilated Half

Nawal el-Saadawi is an Egyptian physician and internationally acclaimed writer whose work publicizing the injustices and brutalities to which Arab women are subject is well known throughout the world. Born in the village of Kafrtahla on the banks of the Nile in 1931, she completed her secondary and college education in Egypt and later studied at Columbia University in New York. She has worked as a physician and psychiatrist in both Cairo and rural areas of Egypt. She lost her position as Egypt's director of education in the Ministry of Health because of the outspoken views expressed in her first nonfiction book, Women and Sex *(1972). In it, she openly challenged the restrictions placed on women in Arab society. She was later imprisoned by Anwar Sadat, and her many books, including seven novels, four collections of short stories, and five works of nonfiction, are still banned in Egypt, Saudi Arabia, and Libya. Since her release from prison in 1982, she has continued to write and is an activist for women's rights in the Arab world. "The Mutilated Half" is drawn from* The Hidden Face of Eve: Women in the Arab World, *translated and edited by el-Saadawi's husband, Dr. Sherif Hetata, in 1980. In this work, el-Saadawi investigates the cultural origins of the widely practiced but rarely discussed procedure of female circumcision, an operation she herself endured at the age of eight.*

1   The practice of circumcising girls is still a common procedure in a number of Arab countries such as Egypt, the Sudan, Yemen and some of the Gulf states.

2   The importance given to virginity and an intact hymen in these societies is the reason why female circumcision still remains a very widespread practice despite a growing tendency, especially in urban Egypt, to do away with it as something outdated and harmful. Behind circumcision lies the belief that, by removing parts of girls external genital organs, sexual desire is minimized. This permits a female who has reached the "dangerous age" of puberty and adolescence to protect her virginity, and therefore her honour, with greater ease. Chastity was imposed on male attendants in the female harem by castration which turned them into inoffensive eunuchs. Similarly female circumcision is meant to preserve the chastity of young girls by reducing their desire for sexual intercourse.

3   Circumcision is most often performed on female children at the age of seven or eight (before the girl begins to get menstrual periods). On the scene appears the *daya* or local midwife. Two women members of the family grasp the child's thighs on either side and pull them apart to expose the external genital organs and to prevent her from struggling—

330

like trussing a chicken before it is slain. A sharp razor in the hand of the *daya* cuts off the clitoris.

During my period of service as a rural physician, I was called upon   4
many times to treat complications arising from this primitive operation, which very often jeopardized the life of young girls. The ignorant *daya* believed that effective circumcision necessitated a deep cut with the razor to ensure radical amputation of the clitoris, so that no part of the sexually sensitive organ would remain. Severe haemorrhage was therefore a common occurrence and sometimes led to loss of life. The *dayas* had not the slightest notion of asepsis, and inflammatory conditions as a result of the operation were common. Above all, the lifelong psychological shock of this cruel procedure left its imprint on the personality of the child and accompanied her into adolescence, youth and maturity. Sexual frigidity is one of the after-effects which is accentuated by other social and psychological factors that influence the personality and mental make-up of females in Arab societies. Girls are therefore exposed to a whole series of misfortunes as a result of outdated notions and values related to virginity, which still remains the fundamental criterion of a girl's honour. In recent years, however, educated families have begun to realize the harm that is done by the practice of female circumcision.

Nevertheless a majority of families still impose on young female   5
children the barbaric and cruel operation of circumcision. The research that I carried out on a sample of 160 Egyptian girls and women showed that 97.5% of uneducated families still insisted on maintaining the custom, but this percentage dropped to 66.2% among educated families.[1]

When I discussed the matter with these girls and women it tran-   6
spired that most of them had no idea of the harm done by circumcision, and some of them even thought that it was good for one's health and conducive to cleanliness and "purity." (The operation in the common language of the people is in fact called the cleansing or purifying operation.) Despite the fact that the percentage of educated women who have undergone circumcision is only 66.2%, as compared with 97.5% among uneducated women, even the former did not realize the effect that this amputation of the clitoris could have on their psychological and sexual health. The dialogue that occurred between these women and myself would run more or less as follows:

"Have you undergone circumcision?"   7
"Yes."   8
"How old were you at the time?"   9
"I was a child, about seven or eight years old."   10
"Do you remember the details of the operation?"   11
"Of course. How could I possibly forget?"   12

1. This research study was carried out in the years 1973 and 1974 in the School of Medicine, Ein Shams University, under the title: *Women and Neurosis*.

13   "Were you afraid?"

14   "Very afraid. I hid on top of the cupboard [in other cases she would say under the bed, or in the neighbour's house], but they caught hold of me, and I felt my body tremble in their hands."

15   "Did you feel any pain?"

16   "Very much so. It was like a burning flame and I screamed. My mother held my head so that I could not move it, my aunt caught hold of my right arm and my grandmother took charge of my left. Two strange women whom I had not seen before tried to keep me from moving my thighs by pushing them as far apart as possible. The *daya* sat between these two women, holding a sharp razor in her hand which she used to cut off the clitoris. I was scared and suffered such great pain that I lost consciousness at the flame that seemed to sear me through and through."

17   "What happened after the operation?"

18   "I had severe bodily pains, and remained in bed for several days, unable to move. The pain in my external genital organs led to retention of urine. Every time I wanted to urinate the burning sensation was so unbearable that I could not bring myself to pass water. The wound continued to bleed for some time, and my mother used to change the dressing for me twice a day."

19   "What did you feel on discovering that a small organ in your body had been removed?"

20   "I did not know anything about the operation at the time, except that it was very simple, and that it was done to all girls for purposes of cleanliness, purity and the preservation of a good reputation. It was said that a girl who did not undergo this operation was liable to be talked about by people, her behaviour would become bad, and she would start running after men, with the result that no one would agree to marry her when the time for marriage came. My grandmother told me that the operation had only consisted in the removal of a very small piece of flesh from between my thighs, and that the continued existence of this small piece of flesh in its place would have made me unclean and impure, and would have caused the man whom I would marry to be repelled by me."

21   "Did you believe what was said to you?"

22   "Of course I did. I was happy the day I recovered from the effects of the operation, and felt as though I was rid of something which had to be removed, and so had become clean and pure."

23   Those were more or less the answers that I obtained from all those interviewed, whether educated or uneducated. One of them was a medical student from Ein Shams School of Medicine. She was preparing for her final examinations and I expected her answers to be different, but in fact they were almost identical to the others. We had quite a long discussion which I reproduce here as I remember it.

24   "You are going to be a medical doctor after a few weeks, so how can

you believe that cutting off the clitoris from the body of a girl is a healthy procedure, or at least not harmful?"

"This is what I was told by everybody. All the girls in my family 25 have been circumcised. I have studied anatomy and medicine, yet I have never heard any of the professors who taught us explain that the clitoris had any function to fulfil in the body of a woman, neither have I read anything of the kind in the books which deal with the medical subjects I am studying."

"That is true. To this day medical books do not consider the science 26 of sex as a subject which they should deal with. The organs of a woman worthy of attention are considered to be only those directly related to reproduction, namely the vagina, the uterus and the ovaries. The clitoris, however, is an organ neglected by medicine, just as it is ignored and disdained by society."

"I remember a student asking the professor one day about the clitoris. The professor went red in the face and answered him curtly, saying that no one was going to ask him about this part of the female body during examinations, since it was of no importance."

My studies led me to try and find out the effect of circumcision on 28 the girls and women who had been made to undergo it, and to understand what results it had on the psychological and sexual life. The majority of the normal cases I interviewed answered that the operation had no effect on them. To me it was clear that in the face of such questions they were much more ashamed and intimidated than the neurotic cases were. But I did not allow myself to be satisfied with these answers, and would go on to question them closely about their sexual life both before and after the circumcision was done. Once again I will try to reproduce the dialogue that usually occurred.

"Did you experience any change of feeling or of sexual desire after 29 the operation?"

"I was a child and therefore did not feel anything." 30

"Did you not experience any sexual desire when you were a child?" 31

"No, never. Do children experience sexual desire?" 32

"Children feel pleasure when they touch their sexual organs, and 33 some form of sexual play occurs between them, for example, during the game of bride and bridegroom usually practised under the bed. Have you never played this game with your friends when still a child?"

At these words the young girl or woman would blush, and her eyes 34 would probably refuse to meet mine, in an attempt to hide her confusion. But after the conversation had gone on for some time, and an atmosphere of mutual confidence and understanding had been established, she would begin to recount her childhood memories. She would often refer to the pleasure she had felt when a man of the family permitted himself certain sexual caresses. Sometimes these caresses would be proffered by the domestic servant, the house porter, the private teacher or the neighbour's son. A college student told me that her brother had been wont to caress her sexual organs and that she used to experience acute enjoyment. However after undergoing circumcision she no longer had the same sensation of pleasure. A married woman admitted that during intercourse with her husband she had never experienced the slightest sexual enjoyment, and that her last memories of any form of pleasurable sensation went back twenty years, to the age of six, before she had undergone circumcision. A young girl told me that she had been accustomed to practise masturbation, but had given it up completely after removal of the clitoris at the age of ten.

35   The further our conversations went, and the more I delved into their lives, the more readily they opened themselves up to me and uncovered the secrets of childhood and adolescence, perhaps almost forgotten by them or only vaguely realized.

36   Being both a woman and a medical doctor I was able to obtain confessions from these women and girls which it would be almost impossible, except in very rare cases, for a man to obtain. For the Egyptian woman, accustomed as she is to a very rigid and severe upbringing built on a complete denial of any sexual life before marriage, adamantly refuses to admit that she has ever known, or experienced, anything related to sex before the first touches of her husband. She is therefore ashamed to speak about such things with any man, even the doctor who is treating her.

37   My discussions with some of the psychiatrists who had treated a number of the young girls and women in my sample, led me to conclude that there were many aspects of the life of these neurotic patients that remained unknown to them. This was due either to the fact that the psychiatrist himself had not made the necessary effort to penetrate deeply into the life of the woman he was treating, or to the tendency of the patient herself not to divulge those things which her upbringing made her consider matters not to be discussed freely, especially with a man.

38   In fact the long and varied interchanges I had over the years with the majority of practising psychiatrists in Egypt, my close association with a large number of my medical colleagues during the long periods I spent working in health centres and general or specialized hospitals and, finally, the four years I spent as a member of the National Board of the Syndicate of Medical Professions, have all led me to the firm conclusion that the medical profession in our society is still incapable of understanding the fundamental problems with which sick people are burdened, whether they be men or women, but especially if they are women. For the medical profession, like any other profession in society, is governed by the political, social and moral values which predominate, and like other professions is one of the institutions which is utilized more often than not to protect these values and perpetuate them.

39   Men represent the vast majority in the medical profession, as in

most professions. But apart from this, the mentality of women doctors differs little, if at all, from that of the men, and I have known quite a number of them who were even more rigid and backward in outlook than their male colleagues.

A rigid and backward attitude towards most problems, and in par- 40 ticular towards women and sex, predominates in the medical profession, and particularly within the precincts of the medical colleges in the Universities.

Before undertaking my research study on "Women and Neurosis" 41 at Ein Shams University, I had made a previous attempt to start it at the Kasr El Eini Medical College in the University of Cairo, but had been obliged to give up as a result of the numerous problems I was made to confront. The most important obstacle of all was the overpowering traditionalist mentality that characterized the professors responsible for my research work, and to whom the word "sex" could only be equated to the word "shame." "Respectable research" therefore could not possibly have sex as its subject, and should under no circumstances think of penetrating into areas even remotely related to it. One of my medical colleagues in the Research Committee advised me not to refer at all to the question of sex in the title of my research paper, when I found myself obliged to shift to Ein Shams University. He warned me that any such reference would most probably lead to fundamental objections which would jeopardize my chances of going ahead with it. I had initially chosen to define my subject as "Problems that confront the sexual life of modern Egyptian women," but after prolonged negotiations I was prevailed to delete the word "sexual" and replace it by "psychological." Only thus was it possible to circumvent the sensitivities of the professors at the Ein Shams Medical School and obtain their consent to go ahead with the research.

After I observed the very high percentages of women and girls who 42 had been obliged to undergo circumcision, or who had been exposed to different forms of sexual violation or assault in their childhood, I started to look for research undertaken in these two areas, either in the medical colleges or in research institutes, but in vain. Hardly a single medical doctor or researcher had ventured to do any work on these subjects, in view of the sensitive nature of the issues involved. This can also be explained by the fact that most of the research carried out in such institutions is of a formal and superficial nature, since its sole aim is to obtain a degree or promotion. The path of safety is therefore the one to choose, and safety means to avoid carefully all subjects of controversy. No one is therefore prepared to face difficulties with the responsible academic and scientific authorities, or to engage in any form of struggle against them, or their ideas. Nor is anyone prepared to face up to those who lay down the norms of virtue, morals and religious behaviour in society. All the established leaderships in the area related to such matters suffer from a pronounced allergy to the word "sex," and any of its implications, especially if it happens to be linked to the word "woman."

43   Nevertheless I was fortunate enough to discover a small number of medical doctors who had the courage to be different, and therefore to examine some of the problems related to the sexual life of women. I would like to cite, as one of the rare examples, the only research study carried out on the question of female circumcision in Egypt and its harmful effects. This was the joint effort of Dr. Mahmoud Koraim and Dr. Rushdi Ammar, both from Ein Shams Medical College, and which was published in 1965. It is composed of two parts, the first of which was printed under the title *Female Circumcision and Sexual Desire*,[2] and the second, under the title *Complications of Female Circumcision*.[3] The conclusions arrived at as a result of this research study, which covered 651 women circumcised during childhood, may be summarized as follows:

44   (1) Circumcision is an operation with harmful effects on the health of women, and is the cause of sexual shock to young girls. It reduces the capacity of a woman to reach the peak of her sexual pleasure (i.e., orgasm) and has a definite though lesser effect in reducing sexual desire.

45   (2) Education helps to limit the extent to which female circumcision is practised, since educated parents have an increasing tendency to refuse the operation for their daughters. On the other hand, uneducated families still go in for female circumcision in submission to prevailing traditions, or in the belief that removal of the clitoris reduces the sexual desire of the girl, and therefore helps to preserve her virginity and chastity after marriage.

46   (3) There is no truth whatsoever in the idea that female circumcision helps in reducing the incidence of cancerous disease of the external genital organs.

47   (4) Female circumcision in all its forms and degrees, and in particular the fourth degree known as Pharaonic or Sudanese excision, is accompanied by immediate or delayed complications such as inflammations, haemorrhage, disturbances in the urinary passages, cysts or swellings that can obstruct the urinary flow or the vaginal opening.

48   (5) Masturbation in circumcised girls is less frequent than was observed by Kinsey in girls who have not undergone this operation.

49   I was able to exchange views with Dr. Mahmoud Koraim during several meetings in Cairo. I learnt from him that he had faced numerous difficulties while undertaking his research, and was the target of bitter criticism from some of his colleagues and from religious leaders

---

2. *Female Circumcision and Sexual Desire*, Mahmoud Koraim and Rushdi Ammar (Ein Shams University Press, Cairo, 1965).

3. *Complications of Female Circumcision*, the same authors (Cairo, 1965).

who considered themselves the divinely appointed protectors of morality, and therefore required to shield society from such impious under-
takings, which constituted a threat to established values and moral codes.

The findings of my research study coincided with some of the con-   50
clusions arrived at by my two colleagues on a number of points. There
is no longer any doubt that circumcision is the source of sexual and
psychological shock in the life of the girl, and leads to a varying degree
of sexual frigidity according to the woman and her circumstances.
Education helps parents realize that this operation is not beneficial, and
should be avoided, but I have found that the traditional education
given in our schools and universities, whose aim is simply some certificate, or degree, rather than instilling useful knowledge and culture, is
not very effective in combating the long-standing, and established traditions that govern Egyptian society, and in particular those related to
sex, virginity in girls, and chastity in women. These areas are strongly
linked to moral and religious values that have dominated and operated
in our society for hundreds of years.

Since circumcision of females aims primarily at ensuring virginity   51
before marriage, and chastity throughout, it is not to be expected that
its practice will disappear easily from Egyptian society or within a short
period of time. A growing number of educated families are, however,
beginning to realize the harm that is done to females by this custom,
and are therefore seeking to protect their daughters from being among
its victims. Parallel to these changes, the operation itself is no longer
performed in the old primitive way, and the more radical degrees approaching, or involving, excision are dying out more rapidly.
Nowadays, even in Upper Egypt and the Sudan, the operation is limited to the total, or more commonly the partial, amputation of the clitoris. Nevertheless, while undertaking my research, I was surprised to
discover, contrary to what I had previously thought, that even in educated urban families over 50% still consider circumcision as essential to
ensure female virginity and chastity.

Many people think that female circumcision only started with the   52
advent of Islam. But as a matter of fact it was well known and
widespread in some areas of the world before the Islamic era, including
in the Arab peninsula. Mahomet the Prophet tried to oppose this custom since he considered it harmful to the sexual health of the woman.
In one of his sayings the advice reported as having been given by him
to Om Attiah, a woman who did tattooings and circumcision, runs as
follows: "If you circumcise, take only a small part and refrain from cutting most of the clitoris off . . . The woman will have a bright and
happy face, and is more welcome to her husband, if her pleasure is
complete."[4]

4. See *Dawlat El Nissa'a*, Abdel Rahman El Barkouky, first edition (Renaissance
Bookshop, Cairo, 1945).

53   This means that the circumcision of girls was not originally an Islamic custom, and was not related to monotheistic religions, but was practised in societies with widely varying religious backgrounds, in countries of the East and the West, and among peoples who believed in Christianity, or in Islam, or were atheistic . . . Circumcision was known in Europe as late as the 19th century, as well as in countries like Egypt, the Sudan, Somaliland, Ethiopia, Kenya, Tanzania, Ghana, Guinea and Nigeria. It was also practised in many Asian countries such as Sri Lanka and Indonesia, and in parts of Latin America. It is recorded as going back far into the past under the Pharaonic Kingdoms of Ancient Egypt, and Herodotus mentioned the existence of female circumcision seven hundred years before Christ was born. This is why the operation as practised in the Sudan is called "Pharaonic excision."

54   For many years I tried in vain to find relevant sociological or anthropological studies that would throw some light on the reasons why such a brutal operation is practised on females. However I did discover other practices related to girls and female children which were even more savage. One of them was burying female children alive almost immediately after they were born, or even at a later stage. Other examples are the chastity belt, or closing the aperture of the external genital organs with steel pins and a special iron lock.[5] This last procedure is extremely primitive and very much akin to Sudanese circumcision where the clitoris, external lips and internal lips are completely excised, and the orifice of the genital organs closed with a flap of sheep's intestines leaving only a very small opening barely sufficient to let the tip of the finger in, so that the menstrual and urinary flows are not held back. This opening is slit at the time of marriage and widened to allow penetration of the male sexual organ. It is widened again when a child is born and then narrowed down once more. Complete closure of the aperture is also done on a woman who is divorced, so that she literally becomes a virgin once more and can have no sexual intercourse except in the eventuality of marriage, in which case the opening is restored.

55   In the face of all these strange and complicated procedures aimed at preventing sexual intercourse in women except if controlled by the husband, it is natural that we should ask ourselves why women, in particular, were subjected to such torture and cruel suppression. There seems to be no doubt that society, as represented by its dominant classes and male structure, realized at a very early stage that sexual desire in the female is very powerful, and that women, unless controlled and subjugated by all sorts of measures, will not submit themselves to the moral, social, legal and religious constraints with which they have been surrounded, and in particular the constraints related to monogamy. The patriarchal system, which came into being when society had

5. Desmond Morris, *The Naked Ape* (Corgi, 1967). p. 76.

reached a certain stage of development and which necessitated the imposition of one husband on the woman whereas a man was left free to have several wives, would never have been possible, or have been maintained to this day, without the whole range of cruel and ingenious devices that were used to keep her sexuality in check and limit her sexual relations to only one man, who had to be her husband. This is the reason for the implacable enmity shown by society towards female sexuality, and the weapons used to resist and subjugate the turbulent force inherent in it. The slightest leniency manifested in facing this "potential danger" meant that woman would break out of the prison bars to which marriage had confined her, and step over the steely limits of a monogamous relationship to a forbidden intimacy with another man, which would inevitably lead to confusion in succession and inheritance, since there was no guarantee that a strange man's child would not step into the waiting line of descendants. Confusion between the children of the legitimate husband and the outsider lover would mean the unavoidable collapse of the patriarchal family built around the name of the father alone.

History shows us clearly that the father was keen on knowing who his real children were, solely for the purpose of handing down his landed property to them. The patriarchal family, therefore, came into existence mainly for economic reasons. It was necessary for society simultaneously to build up a system of moral and religious values, as well as a legal system capable of protecting and maintaining these economic interests. In the final analysis we can safely say that female circumcision, the chastity belt and other savage practices applied to women are basically the result of the economic interests that govern society. The continued existence of such practices in our society today signifies that these economic interests are still operative. The thousands of *dayas*, nurses, paramedical staff and doctors, who make money out of female circumcision, naturally resist any change in these values and practices which are a source of gain to them. In the Sudan there is a veritable army of *dayas* who earn a livelihood out of the series of operations performed on women, either to excise their external genital organs, or to alternately narrow and widen the outer aperture according to whether the woman is marrying, divorcing, remarrying, having a child or recovering from labour.[6]

Economic factors and, concomitantly, political factors are the basis upon which such customs as female circumcision have grown up. It is important to understand the facts as they really are, the reasons that lie behind them. Many are the people who are not able to distinguish between political and religious factors, or who conceal economic and po-

6. Rose Oldfield, "Female genital mutilation, fertility control, women's roles, and patrilineage in modern Sudan," *American Ethnologist*, Vol. II, No. 4, November 1975.

litical motives behind religious arguments in an attempt to hide the real forces that lie at the basis of what happens in society and in history. It has very often been proclaimed that Islam is at the root of female circumcision, and is also responsible for the under-privileged and backward situation of women in Egypt and the Arab countries. Such a contention is not true. If we study Christianity it is easy to see that this religion is much more rigid and orthodox where women are concerned than Islam. Nevertheless, many countries were able to progress rapidly despite the preponderance of Christianity as a religion. This progress was social, economic, scientific and also affected the life and position of women in society.

58   That is why I firmly believe that the reasons for the lower status of women in our societies, and the lack of opportunities for progress afforded to them, are not due to Islam, but rather to certain economic and political forces, namely those of foreign imperialism operating mainly from the outside, and of the reactionary classes operating from the inside. These two forces cooperate closely and are making a concerted attempt to misinterpret religion and to utilize it as an instrument of fear, oppression and exploitation.

59   Religion, if authentic in the principles it stands for, aims at truth, equality, justice, love and a healthy wholesome life for all people, whether men or women. There can be no true religion that aims at disease, mutilation of the bodies of female children, and amputation of an essential part of their reproductive organs.

60   If religion comes from God, how can it order man to cut off an organ created by Him as long as that organ is not diseased or deformed? God does not create the organs of the body haphazardly without a plan. It is not possible that He should have created the clitoris in woman's body only in order that it be cut off at an early stage in life. This is a contradiction into which neither true religion nor the Creator could possibly fall. If God has created the clitoris as a sexually sensitive organ, whose sole function seems to be the procurement of sexual pleasure for women, it follows that He also considers such pleasure for women as normal and legitimate, and therefore as an integral part of mental health. The psychic and mental health of women cannot be complete if they do not experience sexual pleasure.

61   There are still a large number of fathers and mothers who are afraid of leaving the clitoris intact in the bodies of their daughters. Many a time they have said to me that circumcision is a safeguard against the mistakes and deviations into which a girl may be led. This way of thinking is wrong and even dangerous because what protects a boy or a girl from making mistakes is not the removal of a small piece of flesh from the body, but consciousness and understanding of the problems we face, and a worthwhile aim in life, an aim which gives it meaning and for whose attainment we exert our mind and energies. The higher

the level of consciousness to which we attain, the closer our aims draw to human motives and values, and the greater our desire to improve life and its quality, rather than to indulge ourselves in the mere satisfaction of our senses and the experience of pleasure, even though these are an essential part of existence. The most liberated and free of girls, in the true sense of liberation, are the least preoccupied with sexual questions, since these no longer represent a problem. On the contrary, a free mind finds room for numerous interests and the many rich experiences of a cultured life. Girls that suffer sexual suppression, however, are greatly preoccupied with men and sex. And it is a common observation that an intelligent and cultured woman is much less engrossed in matters related to sex and to men than is the case with ordinary women, who have not got much with which to fill their lives. Yet at the same time such a woman takes much more initiative to ensure that she will enjoy sex and experience pleasure, and acts with a greater degree of boldness than others. Once sexual satisfaction is attained, she is able to turn herself fully to other important aspects of life.   62

In the life of liberated and intelligent women, sex does not occupy a disproportionate position, but rather tends to maintain itself within normal limits. In contrast, ignorance, suppression, fear and all sorts of limitations exaggerate the role of sex in the life of girls and women, and cause it to swell out of all proportion and to end up by occupying the whole, or almost the whole, of their lives.

Questions for Discussion and Writing

1. How does the event el-Saadawi describe permanently change her relationship with her parents, husband, colleagues, and her professional role as a physician with her female patients?
2. Why do you think el-Saadawi chooses to describe the procedure in such precise detail and objective language, given her own personal experiences and feelings about it? How does el-Saadawi's use of diction, and choice of denotative rather than connotative language, encourage the reader to share the writer's perception of this subject?
3. How does el-Saadawi use case histories documenting the emotional and physical consequences of female circumcision?
4. To what factors does she attribute the hostility she encountered as a physician in Egypt as she continued with her investigation?
5. In what places can we share her astonishment and anger as she tries to sort through various explanations and uncover the reasons why even other female physicians accept this practice as necessary?
6. In el-Saadawi's view, what cultural attitudes explain the use of circumcision as a form of social control intended to shape the attitude women have of themselves in Egyptian society?
7. Discuss the broad range of rhetorical means el-Saadawi uses to try to influence her readers to share her perspective of female circumcision. Consider

her use of her own experiences, incidents and stories that bear on the subject, case histories as examples, an analysis of the prevailing cultural attitudes, and the linguistic means (style, tone, diction, imagery) she uses to express her views and shape the reader's response.

8. Is there any outdated custom or practice you would wish to make a case against in contemporary society? Provide evidence and reasons to support your views and respond to objections those holding the opposite view might raise.

Evgeny Zamyatin

The Lion

Evgeny Ivanovich Zamyatin (1884–1937) was born in Lebedyan, Russia. His brilliant anti-utopian novel We *(1920) anticipated the speculative fiction of H. G. Wells and Aldous Huxley. The book describes a totalitarian future in a dehumanized society that reflects Zamyatin's disenchantment with the new Soviet state, although he was originally a Bolshevik. Zamyatin's later writings were openly critical of Soviet oppression. As a result, his work was banned and it was only through the intercession of the Russian writer, Maxim Gorky, that Zamyatin was permitted to emigrate to France, where he continued to write novels, plays, literary criticism, and short stories. Many of his works satirize bureaucratic conformity and are set in Russia during the period between the czarist regime and the new Soviet one. In "The Lion," translated by David Richards (1935), we see a good example of Zamyatin's art in which simplicity of language and gentle irony depict a young student out to impress the girl of his dreams.*

It all began with a most bizarre incident: the lion, great king of the beasts, was found hopelessly drunk. He kept tripping over all four paws and rolling onto his side. It was an utter catastrophe. 1

The lion was a student at Leningrad University and at the same time worked as an extra in the theatre. In that day's performance, dressed in a lionskin, he was to have stood on a rock, waiting to be struck down by a spear hurled at him by the heroine of the ballet; thereupon he was to fall onto a mattress in the wings. At rehearsals everything had gone off splendidly, but now suddenly, only half an hour before the curtain was due to go up for the première, the lion had taken it into his head to behave like a pig. No spare extras were available, but the performance couldn't be postponed since a cabinet minister from Moscow was expected to be there. An emergency conference was in session in the office of the theatre's Red director. 2

There was a knock on the door and the theatre fireman, Petya Zherebyakin, came in. The Red director (now he really was red—with anger) rounded on him. 3

"Well, what is it? What do you want? I've no time. Get out!" 4

"I . . . I . . . I've come about the lion, Comrade Director," said the fireman. 5

"Well, what about the lion?" 6

"Seeing, I mean, as our lion is drunk, that is, I'd like to play the lion, Comrade Director." 7

I don't know if bears ever have blue eyes and freckles but, if they do, then the enormous Zherebyakin in his iron-soled boots was much 8 more like a bear than a lion. But suppose by some miracle they could make a lion out of him? He swore that they could: he had watched all the rehearsals from backstage, and when he was in the army he had taken part in *Tsar Maximillian*. So, to spite the producer, who was grinning sarcastically, the director ordered Zherebyakin to put the costume on and have a try.

9   A few minutes later the orchestra was already playing, *con sordini*, the "March of the Lion" and Petya Zherebyakin was performing in his lion costume as if he had been born in the Libyan desert rather than in a village near Ryazan. But at the last moment, when he was supposed to fall off the rock, he glanced down and hesitated.

10   "Fall, damn you, fall!" whispered the producer fiercely.

11   The lion obediently plumped down, landed heavily on his back and lay there, unable to get up. Surely he was going to get up? Surely there was not to be another catastrophe at the last moment?

12   He was helped to his feet. He got out of the costume and stood there, pale, holding his back and giving an embarrassed smile. One of his upper front teeth was missing and this made the smile somewhat rueful and childlike (incidentally, there is always something rather childlike about bears, isn't there?).

13   Fortunately he appeared not to be seriously hurt. He asked for a glass of water, but the director insisted that a cup of tea be brought from his own office. Once Petya had drunk the tea the director began to chivvy him.

14   "Well, Comrade, you've appointed yourself lion, you'd better get into the costume. Come on, come on, lad, we'll soon be starting!"

15   Someone obligingly sprang forward with the costume, but the lion refused to put it on. He declared that he had to slip out of the theatre for a moment. What this unforeseen exigency was he wouldn't explain; he simply gave his embarrassed smile. The director flared up. He tried to order Zherebyakin to stay and reminded him that he was a candidate-member of the Party and a shockworker, but the shockworker-lion obstinately stood his ground. They had to give in, and with a radiant, gap-toothed smile Zherebyakin hurried off out of the theatre.

16   "Where the devil's he off to?" asked the director, red with anger again. "And what are all these secrets of his?"

17   Nobody could answer the Red director. The secret was known only to Petya Zherebyakin—and of course to the author of this story. And, as Zherebyakin runs through the autumnal St Petersburg rain, we can move for a while to that July night when his secret was born.

18   There was no night that night: it was the day lightly dozing off for a second, like a marching soldier who keeps in step but cannot distinguish dream from reality. In the rosy glass of the canals doze inverted trees, windows and columns—St Petersburg. Then suddenly, at the lightest of breezes, St Petersburg disappears and in its place is Leningrad. A red flag on the Winter Palace stirs in the wind, and by the

railings of the Alexandrovsky Park stands a policeman armed with a rifle.

The policeman is surrounded by a tight group of night tramworkers. Over their shoulders Petya Zherebyakin can see only the policeman's face, round as a Ryazan honeyapple. Then a very strange thing happens: somebody seizes the policeman's hands and shoulders, and one of the workers, thrusting his lips forward in the shape of a trumpet, plants an affectionate smacking kiss on his cheek. The policeman turns crimson and blows a loud blast on his whistle; the workers run away. Zherebyakin is left face to face with the policeman—and the policeman disappears, just as suddenly as the reflection of St Petersburg in the canal, puffed away by the breeze: in front of Zherebyakin stands a girl in a policeman's cap and tunic—the first policewoman to be stationed by the Revolution on Nevsky Prospekt. Her dark eyebrows met angrily over the bridge of her nose and her eyes flashed fire.

"You ought to be ashamed of yourself, Comrade," was all she said—but it was the way she said it! Zherebyakin became confused and muttered guiltily:

"But it wasn't me, honestly. I was just walking home."

"Come off it, and you a worker too!" The policewoman looked at him—but what a look!

If there had been a trapdoor in the roadway, as there is in the theatre, Zherebyakin would have fallen straight through it and been saved; but he had to walk away slowly, feeling her eyes burning into his back.

The next day brought another white night, and again Comrade Zherebyakin was walking home after his duty-turn in the theatre, and again the policewoman was standing by the railings of the Alexandrovsky Park. Zherebyakin wanted to slip past, but he noticed she was looking at him, so he gave a guilty, embarrassed nod. She nodded back. The twilight glinted on the glossy black steel of her rifle, turning it pink; and in the face of this pink rifle Zherebyakin felt more cowardly than before all the rifles which for five years had been fired at him on various fronts.

Not until a week later did he risk starting up a conversation with the policewoman. It turned out that she too was from Ryazan, just like Zherebyakin, and moreover she too remembered their Ryazan honeyapples—you know, the sweet ones with a slightly bitter taste; you can't get them here . . .

Every day on his way home Zherebyakin would stop by the Alexandrovsky Park. The white nights had gone quite mad: the green, pink and copper-coloured sky did not grow dark for a single second. The courting couples in the park had to look for shady spots to hide in just as if it were daytime.

One such night Zherebyakin, with bear-like awkwardness, suddenly asked the policewoman:

"Er, are you, that is, are policewomen allowed to get married like in the course of duty? I mean, not in the course of duty, but in general, seeing as your work is sort of military . . .?"

29   "Married?" said policewoman Katya, leaning on her rifle. "We're like men now: if we take a fancy to someone, we have him."

30   Her rifle shone pink. The policewoman lifted her face towards the feverishly blazing sky and then looked past Zherebyakin into the distance and completed her thought:

31   "If there was a man who wrote poetry like . . . or perhaps an actor who came out onto the stage and the whole audience started clapping . . ."

32   It was like the honey-apple—sweet and yet bitter at the same time. Petya Zherebyakin saw that he'd better be off and not come back there again, his cause was done for . . .

33   But no! Wonders haven't ceased! When there occurred that bizarre incident of the lion, thank the Lord, drinking himself silly, an idea flashed into Petya Zherebyakin's head and he flew into the director's room . . .

34   However, that is all in the past. Now he was hurrying through the autumn rain to Glinka Street. Luckily it wasn't far from the theatre and luckily he found policewoman Katya at home. She wasn't a policewoman now, but simply Katya. With her sleeves rolled up, she was washing a white blouse in a basin. Dewdrops hung on her nose and forehead. She had never looked sweeter than like this, in her domestic setting.

35   When Zherebyakin placed a free ticket in front of her and told her he had a part in the ballet that evening she didn't believe him at first; then she grew interested; then for some reason she became embarrassed and rolled her sleeves down; finally she looked at him (but what a look!) and said she would definitely come.

36   The bells were already ringing in the theatre smoking-room, in the corridors and in the foyer. The bald cabinet minister was in his box, squinting through a pince-nez. On the stage behind the curtain, which was still down, the ballerinas were smoothing their skirts with the movement swans use to clean their wings under the water. Behind the rock the producer and the director were both fussing round Zherebyakin.

37   "Don't forget, you're a shockworker. Mind you don't ruin everything!" whispered the director into the lion's ear.

38   The curtain rose, and behind the bright line of the footlights the lion suddenly saw the dark auditorium, packed to the roof with white faces. Long ago, when he was simply Zherebyakin, and had to climb out of trenches with grenades exploding in front of him, he used to shudder and automatically cross himself, but still run forward. Now, however, he felt unable to take a single step, but the producer gave him a shove and, somehow moving arms and legs which seemed not to belong to him, he slowly climbed up onto the rock.

On top of the rock, the lion raised his head and saw, right next to   39
him, policewoman Katya, leaning over the front barrier of one of the
second-row boxes. She was looking straight at him. The leonine heart
thumped once, twice, and then stopped. He was trembling all over. His
fate was about to be decided. Already the spear was flying towards him
. . . Ouch!—it struck him in the side. Now he had to fall. But suppose
he again fell the wrong way and ruined everything? He had never felt
so terrified in all his life—it was far worse than when he used to climb
out of the trenches . . .

The audience had already noticed that something wasn't right: the   40
mortally wounded lion was standing stock-still on top of the rock and
gazing down. The front rows heard the producer's terrible whisper:
"Fall, damn you, fall!"   41

Then they all saw a most bizarre thing: the lion raised its right paw,   42
quickly crossed itself, and plumped down off the rock like a stone . . .

There was a moment of numbed silence, then a roar of laughter ex-   43
ploded in the auditorium like a grenade. Policewoman Katya was
laughing so hard that she was in tears. The slain lion buried its muzzle
in its paws and sobbed.

Questions for Discussion and Writing

1. What circumstances bring Petya Zherebyakin into the theater to audition for
   the part of the lion?
2. What stylistic features of the story add to the reader's enjoyment? How
   would you characterize the OMNISCIENT NARRATOR from the way in which he
   uses language? How would you describe the TONE of the story?
3. What is ironic about the initial encounter between Petya and Katya?
4. What early details foreshadow the outcome?
5. Start at the point where the story ends and describe what you think happens
   next between Petya and Katya.
6. Have you ever acted a part on the stage? How did you cope with stage
   fright, if any? Did you have an ulterior motive similar to that of the protagonist in this story? Describe your experiences.
7. Have you ever observed a situation in which what the people were saying
   contrasted ironically with their actions at that moment? Relate the details of
   this incident.
8. Describe a recent or memorable occasion of flirting. Recreate the circumstances, what was said, gestures made, and what happened.
9. The young man's actions and reactions indicate that he is in love. What actions and reactions of your own or someone you know serve as sure-fire
   signs of being in love?

Shirley Saad

Amina

Shirley Saad was born in Cairo in 1947 to a Lebanese father and a Polish-Rumanian mother. Saad was educated at St. Clare's College by Irish nuns and spoke English, French, and Italian until the 1952 revolution in which Gamal Abdel Nasser gained power, after which the study of Arabic became mandatory in the schools. In 1961 her family moved to Lebanon. Largely self-taught, Saad was influenced by reading the novels of Hanan al-Shaykh and, while she lived in Abu Dhabi, started writing stories about restrictions imposed on women in the Arabic world. "Amina" sympathizes with the plight of a woman who has just given birth to a child and is apprehensive that her husband will take another wife if the child is not a son.

1   Amina opened her eyes and for a moment wondered where she was. Then she remembered and a moan escaped her lips. The English nurse hurried over and bent down, "Don't you worry now," she said. "You'll be fine and the baby is all right."

2   Amina asked, not daring to hope, "Is it a boy or a girl?"

3   "A girl," replied the nurse cheerfully. "A beautiful, bouncing, four kilograms girl. *Mabruk*, congratulations."

4   "*Allah yi barek fi omrek*," murmured Amina as she sank back on her pillows. Another girl!

5   What a catastrophe. What would happen to her now? She had brought four girls into the world, four girls in six years of marriage. She felt tears running down her cheeks, and remembered how happy and proud she had been when her mother told her that she was engaged to be married.

6   She had seen Hamid twice, once at her cousin's house when he arrived unexpectedly. The girls all scattered to their quarters to put on their masks and veils. The next time, he came with his father to ask for her hand in marriage. The houseboy serving the coffee told the Indian housegirl who in turn, ran and told her mistress. So, she had gone to peek through the partition between the men's and women's *majlis*. She saw Hamid and his father sipping coffee and being congratulated by all the men in the family. They embraced and rubbed noses, big smiles on everyone's faces.

7   Amina remembered her wedding, the noise and the bustle, her hennaed hands and feet, the whispers among the older women which frightened her and the anticipation. Finally, she found herself alone with this stranger, who had turned out to be very kind and gentle and considerate.

348

Well, there would be no henna and celebration for this girl. God, 8
why couldn't she have a boy? Just one, that's all she wanted, just one
little baby boy.

She wished the midwife hadn't told her when she had that miscar- 9
riage that it had been a boy. The only one in six years, and she had to
go and lose it. It was her fault too. She had no business climbing a ladder at five months. She slipped and fell and the doctors kept her in the
hospital for a week, then told her she was all right and could go home.
But there was no movement, no life, so she went back to the hospital
and after two weeks of tests and X-rays and hope and despair, they finally decided the baby was dead.

After that, she had two more girls, and now the fourth. 10

Would Hamid divorce her? Would he take a second wife? His older 11
brother had been pressing for two years now, urging him to take a second wife. Hamid loved Amina and his daughters, but he was human.
He did have all that money and the social and political position and no
boy to leave it to.

Her mother came in, then her sisters-in-law. Each one kissed her 12
and said "Mabruk," but she could tell they were not really happy. Her
mother was especially fearful for her daughter's future and felt that
some of the disgrace fell on her and the family too. The sisters-in-law
were secretly jubilant, because they had boys. Hamid's social status and
half his fortune would revert to their own sons if he never had any boys
of his own. Of course, he was still young and he and Amina might try
again. But for the moment the in-laws left reassured and falsely com-
miserated with Amina on her bad luck.

"It is God's will," they murmured, smiling under their masks. Their 13
mouths were sad, but Amina could see the twinkle in their eyes. "God's
will be done."

Friends started coming into the room. They kissed Amina and said 14
"Mabruk," then sat on the floor, cross-legged. Arranging their robes
around them, they sipped coffee from little thimble cups, eating fruits
and sweets.

Her cousin Huda came too. She wore a long, velvet dress, embroi- 15
dered on the sides and bodice, loose and flowing, to conceal her belly.
She was in her sixth month and looked radiantly serene. She sat on the
carpet and sipped her coffee.

Amina thought bitterly, "She already has two daughters and three 16
sons. What does she need another baby for? She's not so young any
more."

As if she had read her thoughts, Huda said, "This is my last baby. It 17
will be the baby for my old age. The others are married or away at
school all day. An empty house is a sad house. You need many sons
and daughters to keep your husband happy. You are still young,
Amina. God has given you four daughters, maybe the next four will be
boys. God's will be done."

18   "As God wills it, so be it," murmured the other ladies smugly.

19   Hamid came in and the ladies all stood up, saluted him deferen-
tially, and hastily went into the next room. The maid served them more
coffee. Hamid looked at his wife, tried to smile and searched for something nice to say. He thought she must be tired, disappointed, ashamed
of having failed him one more time and afraid of being repudiated.

20   He sat down near the bed and said, "Well, mother of my children,
we will just have to try again, won't we?"

21   Amina burst into tears of sorrow, shame and relief.

22   "Don't cry," he said, distressed. "The important thing is that you
and the girls are in good health," smiling. "As long as we are young,
we will try again, eh?"

23   Amina blushed under her mask and pulled her veil around her face.
He patted her hand, got up, and left the room.

24   The ladies came rushing back in, like a flock of crows, eager for the
news, good or bad.

25   Amina's mother said solicitously, "What did he say, my daughter?"

26   "He said better luck next time, Mother!"

27   The mother let out a sigh of relief. They had another year's reprieve.
The women congratulated Amina and left to spread the news.

28   Amina sank back on to her pillows and drifted off to sleep.

Questions for Discussion and Writing

1. What insight do you gain into the kind of societal and personal pressures
   Amina is under from the reactions of her mother and in-laws?
2. How is the story shaped to build up suspense first as to the sex of the child
   and second as to how Amina's husband will react to this news?
3. What does Amina's husband's reaction reveal about him and his feelings for
   her?
4. How would you characterize the author's attitude toward the events she describes—that is, the TONE of the story.
5. How would you evaluate the role DIALOGUE plays in the story in defining individual characters? For example, why are the condolences offered by
   Amina's sisters-in-law IRONIC?
6. How does the conflict between private affection and public obligation reveal
   the values that govern women's lives in Mideastern society?
7. What recent developments (for example, ultrasound clinics in India and ge-
   netic screening in the United States) illustrate the pressure on women to produce sons? You might discuss how the one-child policy in China and accompanying female infanticide have now resulted in an imbalance of 70 million
   more males.
8. Describe a conversation you have overheard between people you did not
   know that allowed you to infer the relationship between the speakers.
9. What physical obstacles (such as separation) or psychological tests (such as
   jealousy) have you overcome in a long-term romantic relationship?

Elena Poniatowska
The Night Visitor

Elena Poniatowska was born in Paris in 1933, daughter of a Mexican mother and a Polish father, and moved to Mexico at the age of ten. She began her career as a journalist in 1954, becoming the first woman to receive Mexico's National Journalism Award in 1977. Among her books that incorporate interviews are Massacre in Mexico, *an account of the 1968 Mexican student movement, as well as her major work of testimonial literature,* Hasta no verte Jesús mío (See you never sweet Jesus) *(1969). This novel tells the life story of Jesusa, a Mexican peasant woman, starting with her involvement in the Mexican Revolution and moving on to her life in modern times. Poniatowska's epistolary novel, written in the form of letters,* Dear Diego *(1978), is the story of the romance between a young Russian woman and the painter Diego Rivera. Poniatowska is internationally known for the major role she played in organizing relief efforts following the 1985 Mexico City earthquake; her writing brought the consequences of the devastation to the attention of the world, and she became actively involved in seeking to alleviate Mexico City's abysmal housing conditions for the poor. She is the widow of Guillermo Haro, a Mexican astronomer, and lives in Mexico with her three children. "The Night Visitor," translated by Catherine White-House (1979), displays Poniatowska's flair for authentic dialogue in this lighthearted tale of an affectionate, albeit naive woman, accused of bigamy by one of her five husbands.*

"But, you . . . don't you suffer?" 1

"Me?" 2

"Yes, you." 3

"A little, sometimes, like when my shoes are tight. . . ." 4

"I'm referring to your situation, Mrs. Loyden." He stressed the Mrs., 5
letting it fall to the bottom of Hell, Miss-sus, and all it implied. "Don't
you suffer because of it?"

"No." 6

"Wasn't it a lot of trouble to get where you are? Your family went to 7
a good deal of expense?"

The woman shifted in her seat. Her green eyes no longer questioned 8
the Public Ministry agent. She looked at the tips of her shoes. These
didn't hurt her. She used them every day.

"Don't you work in an institution that grew out of the Mexican 9
Revolution? Haven't you benefitted from it? Don't you enjoy the privileges of a class that yesterday had scarcely arrived from the fields and
today receives schooling, medical attention, and social welfare? You've
been able to rise, thanks to your work. Oh, I forgot. You have a curious
concept of work."

351

10 The woman protested in a clear voice, even though its intonations were childish.

11 "I'm a registered nurse. I can show you my license. Right now, if we go to my house."

12 "Your house?" said the Public Ministry agent ironically, "Your house? Which of your houses?"

13 The judge was old, pure worm-eaten wood, painted and repainted, but, strangely, the face of this Public Ministry agent didn't look so old, in spite of his curved shoulders and the shudders that shook them. His voice was old, his intentions old. His gestures were clumsy as was his way of fixing his eyes on her through his glasses and getting irritated like a teacher with a student who hasn't learned his lesson. "Objects contaminate people," she thought. "This man looks like a piece of paper, a drawer, an inkwell. Poor fellow." Behind her in the other armchairs there was no one, just a policeman scratching his crotch near the exit door, which opened to admit a short woman who reached up to the Public Ministry agent's desk and handed him a document. After looking at it, he admonished her in a loud voice, "The crimes must be classified correctly. . . . And at the end, you always forget the 'Effective Suffrage, No Re-Election.' Don't let it happen again, please!"

14 When they were alone, the accused inquired in her high voice, "Could I call home?"

15 The judge was about to repeat sharply, "Which one?" But he preferred a negative. He rounded his mouth in such a way that the wrinkles converged like they do on a chicken's ass.

16 "No."

17 "Why?"

18 "Because we-are-in-the-mid-dle-of-an-in-ter-ro-ga-tion. We are making a deposition."

19 "Oh, and if I have to go to the bathroom, do I have to wait?"

20 "My God, is this woman mentally retarded, or what? But if she were, how could she have received her diploma?"

21 He inquired with renewed curiosity, "To whom do you wish to speak?"

22 "My father."

23 "Her father . . . her-fa-ther," he mocked. "To top it off, you have a father!"

24 "Yes," she said, swinging her legs, "Yes, my daddy is still alive."

25 "Really? And does your father know what kind of a daughter he has?"

26 "I'm very much like him," said the child-woman with a smile. "We've always looked alike. Always."

27 "Really? And when do you see him, if you please?"

28 "Saturdays and Sundays. I try to spend the weekends with him."

29 The sweetness of her tone made the policeman stop scratching himself.

"Every Saturday and Sunday?"   30

"Well, not always. Sometimes an emergency comes up, and I don't   31
go. But I always let him know by phone."

"And the others? Do you let them know?"   32

"Yes."   33

"Don't waver, madam. You're in a court of law."   34

The woman looked with candid eyes at the ten empty chairs behind   35
her, the wooden counter painted gray, and the high file cabinets, government issue. On passing through the rooms on the way to the Public
Ministry agent's office, the metal desks almost overwhelmed her. They
too were covered with files piled every which way, some with a white
card between the pages as a marker. She almost knocked down one of
the tall stacks perched dangerously on a corner in front of a fat woman
eating her lunch, elbows on her desk. It was obvious that she had previously bitten into a sandwich, and now she was gleefully adding greasy
pieces of avocado to the opened bread cut with the paper knife. The
floor of the grayish, worn out granite was filthy even though it was
mopped daily. Windows that looked out on the street were very small
and had thick, closely spaced bars. The dirty panes let through a sad,
grime-choked light. It was clear that no one cared about the building,
that everyone fled from it as soon as work was finished. No air entered
the offices except through the door to the street that closed immediately. The fat lady put the remains of her sandwich that she meant to
finish later in a brown paper bag where there also was a banana. The
drawer shut with a coiled-spring sound. Then, with greasy hands, she
faced her typewriter. All the machines were tall, very old, and the rib-
bons never returned by themselves. The fat lady put her finger into the
carriage—the nail of her little finger—and began to return it. Then she
got tired. With an inky finger, she pulled open the middle desk drawer
and took out a ballpoint pen that she put in the center of the ribbon.
When she finished—now with her glasses on—she started work without bothering about the defendant in the antechamber reading the accusation: "The witness affirms that he wasn't at home at the time of the
events. . . ." The typist stopped to adjust the copies, wetting her
thumb and index finger. All the documents were made with ten copies
when five would do. That's why there was a great deal of used carbons
with government initials in the square gray wastebaskets. "Oh, boy,
what a lot of carbon paper! What do they want with so many copies?"
Everyone in the tribunal seemed immune to criticism. Some scratched
their sides, others their armpits, women fixed a bra strap, grimacing.
They grimaced on sitting down, but once seated they got up again to go
to another desk to consult whatever it was that made them scratch their
noses or pass their tongues several times over their teeth looking for
some prodigious milligram. Once they found it, they took it out with
their little finger. All in all, if they weren't aware of what they were doing, they weren't aware of the others either.

36   "Have them send Garcia to take a deposition."

37   "How many copies will they make?" asked the accused.

38   Nothing altered the clearness of her gaze, no shadow, no hidden motive on the shining surface.

39   The Public Ministry agent had to respond, "Ten."

40   "I knew it!"

41   "So, how many times have you been arrested?"

42   "None. This is the first time. I knew it because I noticed when we came in. I'm very observant," she said with a satisfied smile.

43   "You must be in order to have done what you've done for seven years."

44   She smiled, a fresh innocent smile, and the judge thought, "It's easy to see. . . ." He almost smiled. "I must keep this impersonal. But how can it be done when this woman seems to be playing, crossing and uncrossing her legs, showing her golden, round, perfectly shaped knees?"

45   "Let's see . . . your name is . . ."

46   "Esmeralda Loyden."

47   "Age?"

48   "Twenty-seven."

49   "Place of birth?"

50   "Mexico City."

51   "Native?"

52   "Yes." Esmeralda smiled again.

53   "Address?"

54   "27 Mirto, Apartment 3."

55   "District?"

56   "Santa Maria la Rivera."

57   "Postal zone?"

58   "Four."

59   "Occupation?"

60   "Nurse. Listen, Your Honor, the address I gave you is my father's." She shook her curly head. "You have the other ones."

61   "All right. Now we're going to look at your declaration. Are you getting this down, Garcia?"

62   "Yes, Your Honor."

63   "Catholic?"

64   "Yes."

65   "Practicing?"

66   "Yes."

67   "When?"

68   "I always go to mass on Sunday, Your Honor."

69   "Oh, really? And how is your conscience?"

70   "Fine, your honor. I especially like singing masses."

71   "And midnight masses? You must like those best," the old man said hoarsely.

72   "That's only once a year, but I like them, too."

"Oh, really? And who do you go with?"   73

"My father. I try to spend Christmas with him."   74

Esmeralda's green eyes, like tender, untrodden grass, got bigger.   75

"She almost looks like a virgin," thought the agent.   76

"Let's see, Garcia. We're ready to pronounce sentence in Case   77
132/6763, Thirtieth Tribunal, Second Penal Court on five counts of
bigamy."

"Five, your honor?"   78

"It's five, isn't it?"   79

"Yes, your honor, but only one accuses her."   80

"But she's married to five of them, isn't she?"   81

"Yes, sir."   82

"Put it down. Then, let's look at the first statement from Queretaro,   83
State of Queretaro. It says, 'United States of Mexico. In the name of the
Mexican Republic and as Civil State Judge of this place I make known
to those witnesses now present and certify to be true that in the Book
titled Marriages of the Civil Registry in my jurisdiction, on page 18,
of the year 1948, permission of government number 8577, File
351.2/49/82756 of the date June 12, 1948, F.M. at 8:00 P.M., before me
appeared the citizens, Pedro Lugo and Miss Esmeralda Loyden with
the object of matrimony under the rule of conjugal society.' Are you
getting this, Garcia? Like this one, there are four more certificates, all
properly certified and sealed. Only the names of the male correspon-
dents change because the female correspondent—horrors—is always
the same: Esmeralda Loyden. Here is a document signed in
Cuernavaca, Morelos; another in Chilpancingo, Guerrero; another in
Los Mochis, Sinaloa; and the fifth in Guadalajara, Jalisco. It appears
that, as well as bigamy, you like traveling, madam."

"Not so much, Your Honor. They're the ones that . . . well, you   84
know, for the honeymoon."

"Ah, yes."   85

"Yes, Your Honor. If it had been up to me, I would have stayed in   86
Mexico City." Her voice was melodious.

The short woman entered again with the folder. The exasperated   87
agent opened it and read aloud, "'. . . with visual inspections and
ministerial faith, so much of the injury caused during the course of the
above mentioned events in the clause immediately before . . .' Now
you can go on from there yourself. It's only a copy . . . Ah, and look!
You forgot the 'Effective Suffrage, No Re-election' again. Didn't I tell
you? Well, watch what you're doing. Don't let it happen again . . .
please."

When the dwarf shut the door, the judge hurried to say, "The names   88
of the male parties, Garcia, must appear in the Juridical Edict in strict
alphabetical order. Carlos Gonzales, Pedro Lugo, Gabriel Mercado,
Livio Martinez, Julio Vallarta . . . one . . . two . . . three . . . four
. . . five." The judge counted to himself. . . . "So you're Mrs.

Esmeralda Loyden Gonzalez, Mrs. Esmeralda Loyden Lugo, Mrs. Esmeralda Loyden Martinez, Mrs. Esmeralda Loyden Mercado, Mrs. Esmeralda Loyden Vallarta. . . . Hmmm. How does that sound to you, Garcia?"

89   "Fine."

90   "What do you mean, fine?"

91   "The names are all correct, Your Honor, but the only one who's accusing her is Pedro Lugo."

92   "I'm not asking you that, Garcia. I am pointing out the moral, legal, social and political implications of the case. They seem to escape you."

93   "Oh, that, Your Honor!"

94   "Have you ever encountered, Garcia, in your experience, a case like this?"

95   "No, Your Honor. Well, not with a woman because with men . . ." Garcia whistled in the air, a long whistle, like a passing train.

96   "Let's see what the accused has to say. But before that, let me ask you a personal question, Mrs. Esmeralda. Didn't you get Julio confused with Livio?"

97   Esmeralda appeared like a child in front of a marvelous kaleidoscope. She looked through the transparent waters of her eyes. It was a kaleidoscope only she could see. The judge, indignant, repeated his question, and Esmeralda jumped as if the question startled her.

98   "Get them confused? No, Your Honor. They're all very different!"

99   "You never had a doubt, a slip up?"

100   "How could I?" she responded energetically. "I respect them too much."

101   "Not even in the dark?"

102   "I don't understand."

103   She rested a clear, tranquil gaze on the old man, and the agent was taken aback.

104   "It's incredible," he thought. "Incredible. Now I'm the one who'll have to beg her pardon!"

105   Then he attacked. "Did she undergo a gynecological exam with the court doctor?"

106   "Why, no," protested Garcia. "It's not a question of rape."

107   "Ah, yes, that's true. They're the ones who have to have it," laughed the agent, rubbing his hands together.

108   The woman also laughed as if it had nothing to do with her. She laughed to be kind, to keep the old man company. This disconcerted him even more.

109   "So there are five?" He tapped on the grimy wooden table.

110   "Five of them needed me."

111   "And you were able to accommodate them?"

112   "They had a considerable urgency."

113   "And children? Do you have children?" he asked almost respectfully.

"How could I? They are my children. I take care of them and help them with everything. I wouldn't have time for others." 114

The judge couldn't go on. Jokes with double meaning, vulgarities, witty comments all went over her head. . . . And Garcia was a hairy beast, an ox. He even appeared to have gone over to her side. That was the limit! He couldn't be thinking of becoming. . . . The agent would have to wait until he was at the saloon with his cronies to tell them about this woman who smiled simply because smiling was part of her nature. 115

"I suppose you met the first one in the park." 116

"How did you know? Yes, I met Carlos in the Sunken Park. I was there reading Jose Emilio Pacheco's novel, *You Will Die Far Away*." 117

"So, you like to read?" 118

"No. He's the only one I've read and that's because I've met him." Esmeralda perked up. "I thought he was a priest. Imagine. We shared the same taxi, and when he got out I said, 'Father, give me your blessing.' He got very nervous and was even sweating. He handed me something black, 'Look. So you'll see I'm not what you think, I'm giving you my book.'" 119

"Well, what happened with Carlos?" 120

"Pedro . . . I mean, Carlos sat down on the bench where I was reading and asked me if the book was good. That's how everything started. Oh, no! Then something got in his eye—you know February is the month for dust storms. I offered to get it out for him. His eye was full of tears. I told him I was a nurse and then . . . I got it out. Listen, by the way, I've noticed that your left eye has been watering. Why don't you tell your wife to put some chamomile in it, not the kind from a package, but the fresh kind, with a good flower. Tell your wife . . . if I could I would do it for you. You have to make sure the cup is quite clean before boiling a tiny bit of chamomile of the good kind. Then you hold yourself like this with your head thrown back. About ten minutes, so it penetrates well. . . . You'll see how it soothes. Pure chamomile flower." 121

"So, you're the kind who offers herself . . . to help." 122

"Yes, Your Honor. It's my natural reaction. The same thing happened with Gabriel. He'd burned his arm. You should have seen how awful, one pustule after another. I treated it. It was my job to bandage him as ordered by Dr. Carrillo. Then when he was well, he told me—I don't know how many times—that what he loved best in the world—besides me—was his right arm because it was the reason. . . ." 123

Esmeralda Loyden's five tales were similar. One case followed another with little variation. She related her marriages with shining, confident eyes. Sometimes, she was innocently conceited. "Pedro can't live without me. He doesn't even know where his shirts are." On the Public Ministry agent's lips trembled the words "perversion," "perfidy," "depravity," "absolute shame." But an opportunity never arose to voice 124 them even though they were burning his tongue. With Esmeralda they lost all meaning. Her story was simple, without artifice. Mondays were Pedro's. Tuesdays Carlos's, and so on . . . until the week was complete. Saturdays and Sundays were set aside for washing and ironing clothes and preparing some special dish for Pedro, the most capricious of the five. When an emergency came up, a birthday, a saint's day, an outing, she gave up a Saturday or Sunday. No, no. They accepted everything, as long as they saw her. The only condition she always put was not giving up her nursing career.

125   "And they were agreeable to only having one day?"

126   "Sometimes they get an extra day. Besides, they work, too. Carlos is a traveling salesman, but manages to be in the City on Wednesdays. He doesn't miss those. Gabriel sells insurance. He also travels and is so intelligent they've offered him a job with IBM."

127   "None of them has ever wanted a child?"

128   "They never said so in so many words. When they talk about it, I tell them we've only been together a few years, that love matures."

129   "They accept this?"

130   "Yes, apparently."

131   "Well, apparently not. Now your game's up because they've denounced you."

132   "That was Pedro, the most temperamental, the most excitable. But at heart, Your Honor, he's a good fellow. He's generous. You know, like milk that boils over, then settles down. . . . You'll see."

133   "I'm not going to see anything because you are confined to jail. You've been separated for eight days. Or haven't you noticed, Mrs. Loyden? Don't you regret being locked up?"

134   "Not much. Everyone's very nice. Besides you lose track of time. I've slept at least eight hours a night. I was really tired."

135   "I imagine so. . . . Then things haven't gone badly for you?"

136   "No. I've never lost sleep from worrying."

137   And really, the girl looked good, her skin healthy and clean, her eyes shining with health, all of her a calm smoothness. Ah! Her hair also shone, hair like that of a newborn animal, fine hair that invited caressing, just as her turned up nose invited tweaking. The judge started furiously. He was fed up with so much nonsense.

138   "Don't you realize you lived in absolute promiscuity? You deceived. You de-ceive. Not only are you immoral, but amoral. You don't have principles. You're pornographic. Yours is a case of mental illness. Your näiveté is a sign of imbecility. Your . . . your . . ."—he began to stutter—"People like you undermine the base of our society. You destroy the family nucleus. You're a social menace! Don't you realize all the wrong you've done with your irresponsible conduct?"

139   "Wrong to who?" cried Esmeralda.

140   "The men you've deceived, yourself, society, the principles of the Mexican Revolution!"

"Why? Shared days are happy days! Harmonious. They don't hurt 141
anyone!"

"And the deceit?" 142

"What deceit? It's one thing not to say anything. It's another to de- 143
ceive."

"You're crazy. Moreover, the psychiatrist is going to prove it. For 144
sure."

"Really? Then what will happen to me?" 145

"Ah, hah! Now you're worried! It's the first time you've thought 146
about your fate."

"Yes, Your Honor. I've never been a worrier." 147

"What kind of a woman are you? I don't understand you. Either 148
you're mentally deficient . . . or . . . I don't know . . . a loose woman."

"Loose woman?"—Esmeralda got serious—"Tell Pedro that." 149

"Pedro, Juan, and the others. When they find out, they're going to 150
think the same thing."

"They won't think the same thing. They're all different. I don't think 151
the same as you, and I couldn't if I wanted to."

"Don't you realize your lack of remorse?" 152

The agent hit his fist on the table making the age-old dust fly. 153
"You're a wh . . . You act like a pros . . . (Curiously, he couldn't say
the words in front of her. Her smile inhibited him. Looking at her
closely . . . he'd never seen such a pretty girl. She wasn't so pretty at
first sight, but she grew in healthiness, cleanliness, freshness. She
seemed to have just bathed. That was it. What would she smell like?
Perhaps like vanilla? A woman with all her teeth. You could see them
when she threw her head back to laugh, because the shameless woman
laughed.)

"Well, and don't you sometimes see yourself as trash?" 154

"Me?" she asked, surprised. "Why?" 155

The agent felt disarmed. 156

"Garcia, call Lucita to take a statement." 157

Lucita was the one with the avocado and the banana. She carried 158
her shorthand tablet under her arm, her finger still covered with ink.
She sat down grimacing and muttered, "The defendant. . . ."

"No, look. Do it directly on the machine. It comes out better. What 159
have you to say in your defense, Mrs. Loyden?"

"I don't know legal terms. I wouldn't know how to say it. Why 160
don't you advise me, Your Honor, since you're so knowledgable?"

"It . . . it . . . it's too much," stuttered the agent, "Now I have to 161
advise her. Read the file, Lucita."

Lucita opened a folder with a white card in the middle and said, 162
"It's not signed."

"If you like," proposed Esmeralda, "I'll sign it." 163

"You haven't made a statement yet. How are you going to sign it?" 164

165 "It doesn't matter. I'll sign beforehand. After all, Gabriel told me that in the courts they write in whatever they want."

166 "Well, Gabriel's a liar, and I'm going to have the pleasure of sending him a subpoena accusing him of defamation."

167 "Will I be able to see him?" Esmeralda asked excitedly.

168 "Gabriel? I doubt very much he'll want to see you."

169 "But the day he comes, will you send for me?"

170 (Crazy, ignorant, animal-like, all women are crazy. They are vicious, degenerate, demented, bestial. To think she would get involved with five at a time and awaken fresh as the morning. Because the many nights on duty have not affected this woman at all. She doesn't even hear anything I say, for all I try to make her understand.)

171 "By that time you'll be behind bars in the Santa Marta Acatitla prison. For desecration of morality, for bigamy, for not being wise"—he thought of various other possible crimes—"for injuries to particular individuals, criminal association, incitement to rebellion, attacks on public property. Yes, yes. Didn't you meet Carlos in the park?"

172 "But, will I be able to see Gabriel?"

173 "Is he the one you love most?" asked the Public Minister, suddenly intrigued.

174 "No. I love them all, equally."

175 "Even Pedro who denounced you?"

176 "Oh, my sweet Pedro," she said rocking him between her breasts . . . which looked very firm because they stayed erect while she made the rocking gesture.

177 "That's the last straw!"

178 Lucita, with a pencil behind her ear, stuck in her greasy hair, crackled something in her hands, a brown paper bag. Perhaps so the agent would notice her or so he would stop shouting. For the past few moments, Lucita had been staring at the accused. In fact, four or five employees weren't missing a word of the confrontation. Carmelita left her *Tears and Laughs*, and Tere put away her photo novel. Carvajal was standing next to Garcia, and Perez and Mantecon were listening intently. In the courtroom, men wore ties, but everyone looked dirty and sweaty. Clothes stuck to them like poultices, their suits shiny and full of lint, and that horrible brown color that dark people like to wear. It makes them look like rancid chocolate. Lucita, though, fitted her short stature with screaming colors. A green skirt with a yellow nylon blouse, or was it the opposite? Pure circus combinations, but her face was so rapt now that she looked attractive. Interest ennobled them. They had quit scuffing their feet, scratching their bodies, and leaning against the walls. No indolence remained. They had come alive. They remembered they were once men, once young, once totally unattached to the paperwork and marking of cards. Drops of crystalline water shone on their foreheads. Esmeralda bathed them.

"The press is waiting outside," Lucita advised the Public Ministry 179
agent.

He stood up. He wasn't in the habit of making the press wait. It was 180
the fifth power.

Meanwhile, Lucita approached Esmeralda and patted her thigh. 181
"Don't worry, honey. I'm with you. I'm enjoying this because the bastard I married had another woman after a while. He even put her up in a house, and he's got me here working. How terrific that someone like you can get revenge. I'll help on that last interrogation. I swear I'll help. And not only me, but Carmelita, too. That's her desk over there. And Carvajal and Mantecon and Perez and Mr. Michael, who's a little old-fashioned, but nice. What can I say? You're better than divine Yesenia for us. Let's see. I'll start the statement, 'the defendant. . . .' (By now, Esmeralda, convicted or not, felt a drowsiness that made her curl up in the chair like a cat whom everyone likes, especially Lucita.)

Lucita's keys flew joyously through the legal terms—written, 182
they're obscure; spoken in a loud voice, they're incomprehensible. Lucita insisted on saying them out loud to Esmeralda to give proof of her loyalty. After typing, "Coordinated Services of Prevention and Social Adaptation," and realizing she got no response, Lucita spoke in Esmeralda's ear. "You're sleepy, honey. We're about done. I'll only need to add something about damages, a notification, and reprehension of the accused. It doesn't all fit. Oh, well, that's in accord with the law. Let'er know her rights and the time allowed for appeal. 'Dispatch,' I think it has a 't.' Oh, well. Now the warrants and extra copies. The word 'court' should be capitalized, but I didn't do it the other five times. It's not important. Okay, sweetie, sign it here and . . . listen. D'ya want a cold drink to perk you up? Here are the identifying markers. A formal decree presumes you're guilty and off to prison, but don't pay any attention. We won't let it happen. We need a medical certificate and a corresponding certificate of court appraisal . . . the law's conclusions. They'll all be favorable. You'll see, honey. I'll take care of it. For you, nothing can go wrong."

In her cell, after a good soup with chicken wing and thigh, 183
Esmeralda slept surrounded by sympathetic jailers. The next day, groups came to demonstrate, including feminine sectors of several political parties. Rene Cardona Junior wanted to make a film on the spot. The press had reported events in scandalous form. "Five, Like The Fingers On Her Hand," read the headline across eight columns in the police section. *Ovaciones*, in big black headlines, wrote "Five Winners And The Jockey Is A Woman." Three exclamation marks. An editorial writer somberly began his column ". . . Once more our primitive nature is confronted and put to the test." He went into detail about low instincts. Another writer, obviously a technician with a state agency, spoke of the multistratification of women; they were treated like ob-

jects; domestic work didn't allow them access to the higher realms of culture. There were other dangerous distortions which the readers promised to read later. All in all, it was a tiring day. Among the many visitors appeared two nuns, very excited. That didn't count nuns not wearing habits, progressive ones, usually French. There were many. "Oh, boy," thought Lucita, "What a day for us women! Even though Esmeralda might turn out a scapegoat, she's our rallying flag. Her struggle is ours as well."

184   The Public Ministry agent took it upon himself, seeing heated spirits, to throw cold water on them.

185   "The courtroom will be closed to the public."

186   Lucita disappeared behind the old typewriter with the ribbon she had to rewind by hand.

187   "In Iztapalapa, Federal District at 10:30 o'clock on the 22nd day, within the period of time specified by Article 19 of the Constitution, proceedings were initiated to resolve the juridical situation of Mrs. Esmeralda Loyden Gonzalez Lugo Martinez Mercado Vallarta whom the Public Minister accuses of committing five counts of adultery, considered bigamy, as described by Article 37, Paragraph 1 of the Penal Code of Penal Processes with the writ of damages presented by the accuser who in his civilian state is called Pedro Lugo, who, having sworn and having been warned in terms of the law to conduct himself truthfully, subject to sanctions applied to those who submit false testimony, declared the above to be his name, to be thirty-two years of age, married, Catholic, educated, employed, originally from Coatzacoalcos, state of Veracruz, who in the essential part of his accusation said that on Monday, May 28, when his wife did not arrive as she usually did at 8:00 P.M. on the dot on Mondays at their conjugal dwelling, located at 246 Patriotismo, Apartment 16, Colonia San Pedro of the Pines, Postal Zone 13, he went to look for her at the hospital where she said she worked and not finding her, he asked if she would be there the following night and was informed by the receptionist to go see the administration since her name did not appear on the night duty list, that she thought she probably worked during the day, but since she came on with the second shift she was not sure and could not tell him, since she got there la-"—here Lucita just put "la" because "later" didn't fit on the line and she let it go—"and therefore (on the next line) she saw the necessity of sending the plaintiff to the administration to get more information and that in the already mentioned administration the accuser was informed that the one he called his wife never worked the night shift, so the man had to be restrained, putting his hands behind his back, something two attendants had to do after being called by the director, who feared the man wasn't sane. They then saw the accuser leave staggering, beside himself, supporting himself on the walls since he did sustain with the witness sexual relations being her legitimate husband as testified by certificate number 13797, page 18, being the said

a pubescent, fecund woman, when he married her seven years ago. Afterward the accuser proceeded to subsequent inquiries adding what remains explained in file number 347597, without the knowledge of the defendant and managed to find out that the other four husbands were in the same situation and whom he proceeded to inform of the 'quintuplicity' of the accused. The presumed penal responsibility of the accused in the commission of the crimes committed with an original and five copies (the original for Pedro Lugo, being he, the first and principle accuser) as charged by the Social Representation, is found accredited to this moment, with the same elements of proof mentioned, in the consideration that precedes, with an emphasis on the direct imputation that the offended party makes and above all, the affidavit concerning the clothes and personal objects of the defendant at the five addresses mentioned as well as the numerous personal details, photographic proofs, inscriptions on photographs, letters and love missives lavishly written by the accused, brought together by the aggrieved and above all, the indisputableness and authenticity of the marriage certificates and the resulting acts derived from the aforesaid. And it can be said according to the five and to the accused herself, the marriages were dutifully and entirely consummated, to the full satisfaction of all, in the physical person of Esmeralda Loyden, so-called nurse by profession. That the defendant emitted declarations that are not supported by any proof that makes them credible, but on the contrary, proven worthless because of the elements which were alluded to [alluded with two "l"'s], that the defendant didn't manifest remorse at any moment, neither did she seem to realize that she was charged with five crimes, that she didn't voice any objection except that she was sleepy, that the defendant submits with notable docility to the administering of all tests, allowing all the procedures to be carried out that are necessary for the clarification of the facts, as well as those advanced by the parties, in accordance with the parts III, IV, and V of Article 20 of the Federal Constitution, be it notified and put into effect, the nature and cause of the accusation. On the same date, the Secretary of the Factions Clerk swears that the term for the parties to offer more proof in the present cause begins on this June 20 and concludes on next July 12. I swear this document to be true and valid."

When the Public Ministry Agent was about to put his signature at the bottom of the document, he yelled angrily, "Lucita, what's wrong with you? You forgot the 'Effective Suffrage, No Re-Election' again!" 188

Afterward, everything was rumor. Some say Esmeralda left with her jailkeepers for the jail wagon, followed by the faithful Lucita, who had prepared her a sandwich for the trip; by Garcia, the scribe, who kissed her hand; and by the affectionate gaze of the Public Ministry agent. 189

On saying good-bye, the agent again urged as he took her two hands between his own, moving each and everyone with his words: 190

"Esmeralda, look what happens when you get involved in such things. Listen to me. You're young. Get away from all this, Esmeralda. Be respectable. From now on, be proper."

191   Many spectators made the convicted woman smile when they applauded her gracious manner. Others, on the other hand, saw, in the middle of the crowd behind the gray wooden bannister, painted and repainted with an always thinner coat, Pedro Lugo, the accuser, pierce Esmeralda with his intense gaze. On the other side, some saw myopic Julio give her a friendly sign with his hand. Getting into the police wagon, Esmeralda didn't see Carlos, but did notice Livio with his shaved head and eyes filled with tears. She yelled to him, "Why did you cut it? You know I don't like short hair."

192   The journalists took notes. None of the husbands was missing, not even the travelling salesman. Authoritative voices said the five husbands had tried to stop the trial because they all wanted Esmeralda back. But the sentence was already dictated, and they couldn't appeal to the Supreme Court of Justice. The case had received too much publicity. Each one agreed, in turn, to conjugal visits at Santa Maria Acatitla. Things were nearly the same, *"de facto et in situ."* Before, they had seen her only one night a week. Now they all got together occasionally for Sunday visits. Each one brought a treat. They took a variety of things to please not only Esmeralda, but also Lucita, Carmelita, Tere, Garcia, Carvaal, Perez, Mantecon, and the Public Ministry agent, who from time to time quietly presented himself—he'd grown fond of Esmeralda's responses.

193   But from these facts a new case couldn't be made. Accusors and accused, judge and litigants, had repented of their haste in bringing the first action, number 479/32/875746, page 68. Everything, though, remained in the so-called book of life which is full of trivia and which preceded the book now used to note the facts. It has an ugly name: computer certification. I swear this document to be true and valid.

Effective Suffrage, No Re-Election

Questions for Discussion and Writing

1. How do the descriptions of Esmeralda's appearance, voice quality, and body language define what is unique about her? What role does CONNOTATIVE LANGUAGE play in creating this impression?
2. How does Esmeralda's apt use of language deflate the prosecutor in his attempt to browbeat her?
3. How would you characterize Poniatowska's attitude toward the characters and events in the story? What in the TONE of the story encourages the reader to share her attitude?
4. Why is Esmeralda's behavior perceived as being so threatening and outrageous? How does her behavior challenge the norms in Mexican culture? How does it explain why the female employees of the court rally around her?

6. How does the title refer to circumstances that led Pedro to discover the true facts about his marriage to Esmeralda? What is unusual about the other four husbands' reactions when they discover the others' existence?

7. Have you had any personal experiences involving double standards regarding sexual behavior in our society? Describe your experiences. You might choose to describe the event as if you were a court reporter or a journalist. Be sure to cover the five Ws (when, what, who, where, and why) and describe the people, places, actions, and dialogue as objectively as possible.

Talat Abbasi

Facing the Light

Talat Abbasi was born in Karachi, a seaport on the southwest coast of Pakistan, and was educated at the London School of Economics. Her stories have appeared in Feminist Studies, Asian Women's Anthology, *and* Short Story International. *A recent story, "Going to Baltistan," was published in* Massachusetts Review *(Winter 1988/89). Of her short stories, Abbasi observes, "I am on the whole a person of few words. I studied in a convent in Karachi where the nuns said, 'Economy in everything, including words.'" Abbasi's characteristic sensitivity to gender roles and class in Pakistani culture are revealed in "Facing the Light," which originally appeared in* Sudden Fiction International *(1989), a story that explores the moment in a relationship when illusions give way to truth.*

1   "I wish to be fair to you," he says and the head goes up as it always does when he wishes to be fair to her. And in sympathy, in solidarity, the eyebrows and nose rise to the occasion, positioning themselves upwards. And the mouth tightens into a straight line to underline it all. And together they all say the same thing: And now you may thank us, and now you may thank us. And she, bent over her sewing machine, pricks her finger with its needle which she is pretending to thread and snatches up a tissue, wipes off the drop of blood and tosses it in the direction of the maidservant. The woman springs out of the sea of silk and muslin on the Persian carpet, giggles as she catches it, darts across to the wastepaper basket and still giggling, leaps back into the pile of saris. The room is looking like a smuggler's den with trunks and suitcases spilling out hoards of dazzling material. And there is scarcely room to stand let alone sit for rolls of georgette are billowing on the sofa, brocades are draped over chairs and everything is flowing onto the carpet where a clean bedsheet has been spread.

2   The seasons are changing. Another few days and summer will be upon Karachi, stretching endlessly like the desert itself from which hot winds are already rising. The brush with cool weather a memory.

3   So they are right in the midst of sorting out her wardrobe, packing away the heavier silks and satins and unpacking the cool cottons and frothy chiffons and she is instructing the little maidservant—these for washing, these for dry cleaning, that black one throw over to me, I have just the magenta and purple border to liven it up. That petticoat for mending. And this whole lot kicked towards her, all that for throwing out. Yes yes of course that is what she meant—that she could have

366

them all. But no, again no, not this midnight blue chiffon sari, most certainly not. Is she in her senses that she can even ask again? A thousand, twelve hundred rupees for the embroidery alone, for these hundreds of silver sequins—real silver, each one of them, sprinkled all over like stars. And she, whenever she'd worn it, so like a goddess who on a summer night stepping out of heaven had hastily snatched a piece of the star-spangled sky to cover herself with. For after all, that had been the whole idea, she'd designed it herself with herself in mind. And now give it away to a servant? Just like that? Throw it down the drain? Preposterous. How did she dare ask again? How did she dare even think? Yes even if the silver was tarnished, even if every single star had blackened and the sari no more than a shabby rag. Which shouldn't have happened because she herself had packed it away at the end of last season, with these hands, trusting no one, wrapped it up in layer upon layer of muslin, buried it like a mummy, deep inside a steel trunk. Safe, airtight. She'd been so certain the Karachi air couldn't possibly get to it and tarnish the silver. But it had and had snuffed out the stars like candles. And now, on her lap, this veil of darkness, dullness.

As he chooses that precise moment to rap so loudly with his cane on   4
her bedroom door that the midnight blue sari slithers to her feet, an inky shadow. She quickly bends over her sewing machine, pretending to thread the needle. What's he doing here at this time, jamming the doorway of her bedroom? Never home for dinner why here even before tea? "Malik Sahib," announces the woman as though she needs assistance in recognizing her own husband of twenty-two—three—years. And rushes to evict a stack of summer cotton saris which have usurped the sofa. But he makes an impatient gesture with his hands and remains standing and immediately begins to be fair to her. So anxious is he to be fair to her.

"Go to your quarter," she says to the woman, for she cannot allow   5
him to be fair to her in front of the servants. Not when he's going out of his way to be fair to her and she can tell that he's going to outdo himself in fairness today. She can tell by that red flower which has blossomed overnight upon his chest and is now blazing out of his button hole. She can tell by that moustache, till yesterday steel grey, stiff as a rod, today henna red, oiled, curled softly, coaxed gently to a fine point at both edges. Like a pair of wings dipped in a rosy sunset! And as surely as a pair of wings ever did fly she can tell that that moustache will fly tonight.

"But the saris . . ." Such a thrill of excitement has shot through her,   6
lighting up the saucer eyes in the dark face as though car headlights have suddenly flashed in a tunnel. She must stay, she must listen. She mustn't miss a word of this.

"Later."   7

The woman dares not say another word and hurriedly picks up her   8
slippers at the door.

9   "Tea in half an hour," she says to the woman so he doesn't spend all evening being fair to her.

10   The door is closing after her and he is already stretching himself up to his full height—and beyond—in preparation for ultimate fairness to her. Striding over, he will come straight to the point. He will not waste his time blaming her for anything because he realizes that she cannot help herself. And because she will in any case pay for it, regret it all, regrets made more bitter by the remembrance of his own decency throughout, for after all how many men, how many men—but no, straight to the point. Looming over her, smiling, positively beaming down at her in anticipation of her shock at his news, he must tell her that it is too late for regrets. He is leaving. Yes. Leaving and this time it is final. She heard right. She did not imagine it. But in case she thinks she did, he will thump the ground with his cane. Three times he will thump the ground with his cane. And three times the ground reverberates. Final. Final. Final. Yet he will be fair to her. Indeed more than. He will be generous. Large hearted.

11   And so, his chest is swelling, expanding, the petals on it trembling as it grows larger and larger. In any case, he has a position to maintain and so she will be maintained in the style which she has always been used to and which—stretching himself further up, risking a launch into space in his determination to be fair to her—a man in his position can well afford. Therefore car, house, servants, nothing will change. And looking down at her as at a pebble he has just flung at the bottom of a well he reassures her: car, house, servants . . .

12   Car, house, servants! Tea in five minutes, she should've said. For—car, house, servants—what more was there? Her fault, her mistake, her stupidity thinking a half hour would be needed, thinking there was so much to say now when not a word had ever been spoken before.

13   Is she listening? Is she listening?

14   Noises. Just noises. Two prisoners in neighbouring cells and no one on the other side. Hence the tapping noises. One tap for food, two for money. Short taps, sharp taps, clear taps. And please, not too many. Just enough to pull along, I in my cell, you in yours.

15   Has she heard? Car, house, serv . . .

16   The lid crashes down on the sewing machine, the spool of cotton, the thimble, flying to the floor. The other side then! To the far end of the room, to the window, to her big brass bed, there to spread out the sari, all six yards of it, give it another look, every inch of it, one last chance, for surely, surely in the bright light of day, the sun shining directly on it, it would look different. Yes it would, of course it would, everything looks different in the light. So there by the open window, she would see it again, the sparkle of a thousand stars, lost here, in the shadows of the room. It would still be salvaged. Still be saved.

17   He cannot believe this. Getting up, walking away, right in the mid-

dle of his being fair to her. Leaving him talking as though to himself, turning her back to him . . .

Facing the light. The sari laid out on the bed. The curtains drawn aside. The sun streaming through the window, pouring down the skylight onto the bed, warming the brass, setting afire the ruby carpet. Yet here too, that veil of darkness, dullness, will not yield but instead spreads its claim everywhere. For now she sees that same layer of darkness, dullness, on everything. Nothing is safe then, for it is in the air, the very air. Nothing escapes. Nothing remains the same. The toughest metals suffer. Brass blackens. Silver loses its luster. Gold dulls. This bed. These bangles. Constantly being polished and repolished. Even these grilles on this window. Painted how long ago? A month? Two? And already here, there, in patches, the rust is cutting through. Everything is being attacked. As though an unseen force is snaking its way through the city, choosing its victims, the strongest, the most precious, stalking them, ferreting them out as they lie hidden under paint and polish, shrouded in trunks. Strikes them, robs them of their sparkle, their luster, their very light. 18

. . . as if he isn't there, as if he doesn't exist. Very well then. Out through that door. This instant. 19

And some things you simply cannot keep polishing and repolishing no matter how precious they are. Too fragile, the fabric. It will have to be discarded, thrown away on that heap of old clothes. She will have it after all. She will. There is no help for it, for it is in the air, the very air. And so, still facing the light, she begins to fold the sari. 20

Questions for Discussion and Writing

1. How do the METAPHORS with which the narrator describes her husband's mustache encourage the reader to share her sense of betrayal? Where else do STYLISTIC features of DICTION, phrasing, or IMAGERY contribute to the effect of the story?

2. What is IRONIC about the narrator's reaction once she becomes aware that her style of life will be maintained?

3. How does the contrast between the LITERAL meaning of the word *fair* and the way it is used create an unsympathetic impression of the husband?

4. How does the detail of pricking her finger underscore the puncturing of the illusion she has created of herself as a "goddess"?

5. How would you characterize the relationship of the wife with her maidservant? At what point does Abbasi shift so that events appear from the maidservant's POINT OF VIEW? How does this brief shift let the reader see events from another perspective?

6. How does Abbasi shed light on the relationship between the husband and wife by using the ANALOGY of the prisoner in a cell, tapping for food and money?

7. How do the LITERAL and FIGURATIVE images of hot winds and blazing light suggest the forces undermining the traditional role of women in Pakistani society?
8. How might the title "Facing the Light" be considered a metaphor describing the challenge facing the protagonist? How is this image related to the description of the tarnished silver beads on the blue sari?
9. Describe the breakup of a relationship in which you have been involved. Were there any similarities to the situation described in "Facing the Light"?
10. Rewrite any portion of the story you wish from the maid's perspective. How might the same events and conversations take on an entirely new meaning?
11. Describe a couple's first date and last date. How do they differ in terms of how they treat each other, what they say, and how they feel?

Henri Lopes
The Esteemed Representative

The eminent Congolese writer Henri Lopes was born in 1937 in Kinshasa. After receiving a university education in France, he returned to the Republic of the Congo to teach history. Lopes subsequently served in a succession of ministerial positions including minister of education, foreign affairs, finance, and, between 1973 and 1974, as prime minister. He now lives in Paris and serves as assistant director general of UNESCO. Lopes's experiences in government are reflected in his enlightened and satiric portrayals of characters in his collections of short stories. In addition to Tribaliks: Contemporary Congolese Stories *(1971), which won the Grand Prix Litteraire de L'Afrique Noir, he has written novels, including* The Laughing Cry *(1986), and poetry. Lopes's writings taken together offer a startlingly perceptive view of a postcolonial African nation and of the problems that confront educated black women in their attempt to transform the Republic of the Congo into a modern egalitarian state. "The Esteemed Representative," translated by Andrea Leskes, taken from* Tribaliks, *relates with compelling realism the predicament of the wife, daughters, and mistress of a government official whose private chauvinism contrasts with his public stance.*

". . . Colonization has imposed an economic system on us that has reduced our sisters to slaves. At the present stage, it's up to the men to liberate the underprivileged of our society in general, and our women in particular, from this economic servitude." (Applause.) "Our women have a right to certain jobs and they must be allowed to hold them. It is unacceptable in an independent country like ours, where thousands of girls are educated, that only the foreigners in our country get jobs as secretaries and saleswomen." (Applause.) "Sisters, let us take advantage of the occasion of your conference to publicly ask our National Assembly and our government, 'Why the delay?' What is holding up the passage of a law explicitly spelling out that all positions as waitresses in bars and night clubs are to be exclusively reserved for Africans, and prohibited to Europeans." (Everyone in the hall rose, and thundering applause drowned out the speaker.) "The salaries earned by our women in these jobs must be equal to those earned by European women." (Thunderous applause.) "Because as was said by—um—um—as was said by—uh—La Fontaine, I believe it was La Fontaine . . . (Applause.) . . . As I said, La Fontaine stated, 'Equal pay for equal work.' (Thundering applause.) It is also time that those fathers, who in the name of tradition still refuse to allow their daughters to continue their schooling, be disillusioned of their prejudices. Women have the same rights as men. Yet some men still refuse to accept this truth.

371

That is why I am turning to you, my sisters, and proclaiming that you women alone must liberate yourselves from masculine tyranny." (Applause.) "At the present time, when tribal divisions are strong and men throughout the world are mercilessly killing each other like lunatics, let me say in front of you, up here on this platform, that only women can help us to overcome tribal prejudices and win peace on earth." (Applause.)

2   Representative Ngouakou-Ngouakou continued to speak in this manner for twenty minutes, watch in hand. When he had finished, he wiped his brow. The crowd in the lecture room at the party headquarters broke out in a frenzied joy. Men and women congratulated each other with slaps on the back, laughed and shouted out, "Papa Ngouakou-Ngouakou! Is it Papa Ngouakou-Ngouakou?" "Yes, yes," responded another part of the room. Some of the women danced in place while the babies they carried on their backs grimaced at being so rudely awakened from their naps.

3   The bodyguard ceremoniously removed the official shoulder sash from the speaker and carried off the folder in which was sandwiched the text of the speech Ngouakou-Ngouakou had just delivered. The excited crowd, given over to rejoicing, could not calm down.

* * *

4   At 8 P.M. Ngouakou-Ngouakou returned home. His houseboy hurried to relieve him of his briefcase. He threw himself into an arm chair.

5   "Bouka, Bouka, come say hello to Papa."

6   The child climbed into his father's lap. Ngouakou-Ngouakou surveyed him proudly, his only son, his seventh child.

7   "Papa, you didn't buy me an Apollo XII."

8   "What in the world is that?"

9   "Akpa has one. His father bought it for him."

10   "Emilienne," shouted Ngouakou-Ngouakou. "Emilienne!"

11   "She is writing a paper for school," called her mother from the kitchen.

12   "Writing? A paper? Writing won't teach her how to please her husband. Tell her to bring me my slippers."

13   "Listen, Ngouakou-Ngouakou. Be a little more understanding of that poor child," said her mother.

14   "Tell me, woman, since when do wives talk back to their husbands? Are you going to teach me how to bring up my daughter?"

15   "Here, Papa, here are your slippers," said Bouka-Bouka.

16   "Thank you, son. At least you think of me. But this is really too much. Are we men going to have to do the work around here now?"

17   "Emilienne!"

18   Emilienne arrived, all distraught.

19   "Well now, how many times must I call you?"

20   "I'm sorry, Papa. I didn't hear you."

21   "Where were you?"

"In my room."   22

"In your room? You must have been dreaming."   23

"No, Papa, I was doing my maths homework."   24

"Dreaming and mathematics don't go together. If you were study-   25
ing maths, you should have been paying attention. And when one pays
attention, one hears people call. Bring me some whiskey."

Emilienne mechanically headed towards the cupboard. She was   26
dreaming of boarding school, and envying her friends who were far
from familial discipline. It must be nice to depend only on oneself.
Parents! They think they're acting for our benefit with all their rules.
They don't even see that we're judging them. Oh! The bottle is almost
empty. Emilienne searched in vain on all the shelves of the cupboard.

"How about my whiskey?"   27

"There isn't any more."   28

"What? There isn't any more? I forbid you to play with your friends   29
for two days."

"But Papa, it's not my fault."   30

"You have to learn that when the bottle is only half full, it's time to   31
go and buy another one. Bring me a beer, then."

He turned on the TV. Myriam Makeba was singing. Usually he en-   32
joyed listening to her, but that evening she got on his nerves. They were
showing the tape of her most recent concert in the city. Ngouakou-
Ngouakou knew it by heart, since it was broadcast at least twice a
week. When the TV producers run out of ideas for shows, they fall back
on something they have on hand, even if the public has already seen it
a hundred times. Ngouakou-Ngouakou was bored. He checked his
watch.

"When can we eat?"   33

"In five minutes," answered his wife from the kitchen.   34

"I'm hungry."   35

"The rice isn't quite ready yet."   36

"It's always the same story. Nothing is ever ready at the right time."   37

Myriam Makeba was singing "Malaïka." Ngouakou-Ngouakou let   38
himself be carried away by the music this time. He liked beautiful
songs. Then the South African singer chose one in which she clicked her
tongue and danced, swaying her backside about like a boat on the
waves.

"Dinner is ready," called his wife.   39

Ngouakou-Ngouakou did not answer.   40

"Dinner! It's getting cold."   41

Ngouakou-Ngouakou curbed his anger. He disliked being inter-   42
rupted when he was listening to music. He sat down at his place, facing
the TV. Myriam continued to sing.

"Rice and meat with sauce again?"   43

"At this time of year there isn't much choice at the market."   44

"Not much choice? Isn't there any fish?"   45

"That must be the first time I ever heard you offer any suggestions   46 about meals. It's a fine idea to vary the menu, but there are limits. In the morning when I ask you what you want for dinner, you grab your briefcase and dash off to the office."

47   "That's the last straw! Don't you think I have enough to handle without having to think about meals on top of it all? You don't go off to work in an office. I'm the one who brings in the money."

48   "I would gladly change places."

49   "What I do isn't woman's work. I know many women who dream of being in your place, of having a husband who provides the latest model gas stove, a refrigerator, money . . ."

50   "Money? With the money you give me every week I have to rack my brain to feed a large family like ours."

51   "Obviously you're not the one earning the money!" The newscaster began presenting the national news.

52   "Shut up all of you so I can hear!"

"Today marked the opening of the conference sponsored by the National Federation of Radical Women. Several speakers were on the day's roster. This is the second conference of the Federation since its inception. Those present included delegations invited from neighbouring African countries and from friendly countries in Europe, America and Asia."

53   Ngouakou-Ngouakou was furious. Tomorrow I'll speak with the Minister of Information about punishing the newscaster. He didn't even mention my speech. Ngouakou-Ngouakou pushed away his plate.

54   "I'm not hungry anymore."

55   The newscaster spoke about the war in Nigeria. Ngouakou-Ngouakou lit a cigarette, thinking how they always seemed to repeat the same things about the war.

56   "How about the girls? Can't they help you with the cooking and housework? Marcelline, how about you?"

57   "But Papa, I have a lot of work."

58   "Don't forget you're a woman. A woman's most important work is to keep house."

59   "Be a little more understanding," cautioned her mother. "You know perfectly well that Marcelline is in her last year at school and is preparing for her exams so she can receive her diploma."

60   "Do you think a diploma will help her keep her husband at home? Good food will help, yes, and something else too."

61   "You could at least be more discrete in what you say."

62   "Oh Papa," cried Bouka-Bouka, "Look!"

63   Featured on the television were young Biafran children. They looked like fat-bellied skeletons. The whole family fell silent.

64   "Why are those children so ugly?"

65   "It's not their fault," corrected his mother.

66   Ngouakou-Ngouakou stood up and went to his room. Whistling, he

threw his clothes on to the bed. His wife would tidy up after him. He pulled on a pair of light grey trousers, and a short, loose-fitting, bright-coloured shirt decorated with gold braiding on the sleeves, pockets and collar. He looked at himself in the mirror. He looked younger. He lit a cigarette and went out into the night, whistling.

* * *

The Peek-a-Boo bar is located on the outskirts of the city, on an unlit 67 street. The bar itself, though, has electricity. This came about because the owner, Marguerita, is a remarkably beautiful young widow with regular features, well-formed breasts peeping out from behind her camisole, and long fawn-like legs that are difficult to ignore when she wears her tight-fitting dresses and high-heeled shoes. Some mistake her for a mulatto, but those who have known her since birth say that her skin tint has lightened considerably since certain American products have been for sale in the Congo. Marguerita is very popular. And since she is unable to satisfy everyone at once, she has cousins living with her, cousins almost as beautiful as she is. Whenever a high-level official brings a group of visiting dignitaries to the Peek-a-Boo Bar, he flaunts his prowess by arranging for them to dance cheek to cheek with Marguerita. At about one in the morning he whispers in her ear and goes off to "make it" with her while her cousins "make it" with the foreign dignitaries. In exchange for these favours, Marguerita obtains what she wants. Two months of constant attention to the Minister of Energy resulted in the installation of electricity in her bar.

Marie-Therese had taken a taxi to reach that part of the city. She hes- 68 itated a moment before entering the bar. The electricity, used mostly to power the record player, hardly lit the room. The light bulbs were all painted red so that only red shadows were distinguishable moving about or seated at the bar. The room was divided into small compart-ments, separated by bamboo partitions. People seated in these compart-ments were protected from unwelcome glances. Marie-Therese chose one and sat down on a small, low, willow bench. Marguerita had seen her and signalled to one of her cousins who went over to the new cus-tomer, shuffling her feet.

"No thank you, nothing for the moment. I'm waiting for someone."   69

When the cousin returned to the bar, a man who had been seated on 70 a high stool grabbed her around the waist and led her off to dance the rumba. The cousin immediately lost her indifference. The two, pelvis to pelvis, moved with large, circular rubbing movements. They have noth-ing left to hide from each other, thought Marie-Therese. If the lights weren't so dim we would surely see that their eyes are closed. Marie-Therese felt embarrassed by the display.

When the dance ended, the man returned to the bar and flirted 71 laughingly with all the cousins. As the next dance began, he approached Marie-Therese. His self-assurance and beautiful eyes seemed to paralyse her.

72   "No thank you."

73   "Do you find me so unattractive?"

74   ". . ."

75   She turned her head away and just at that moment Ngouakou-Ngouakou entered.

76   "Oh, excuse me, Representative, Sir. Excuse me . . . I didn't know . . ."

77   Ngouakou-Ngouakou said nothing. He turned away, sat down and mumbled to himself: "It's that little idiot Bwala. He'll find out who he's talking to."

78   The cousin returned. She joked informally with the esteemed representative for a few minutes. They knew each other well. The Honourable Representative Ngouakou-Ngouakou is one of the humblest men in the world. He is a child of the proletariat and has no fear of renewing his relations with the masses. He ordered drinks. When the waitress returned with the order and the politician started to pay, she told him that it had already been taken care of by the man at the bar.

79   A *pachanga* was playing and Marie-Therese wanted to dance. Since no one else was on the floor, everyone at the bar watched as she danced with Ngouakou-Ngouakou, and they smiled. They smiled to see a young girl show off her youth through every movement of her hips, legs and shoulders as she moved to the music, smiling wholesomely. Were they also smiling tenderly at the fifty-year old man whose baldness and paunch did not inhibit his nimble movement? The man at the bar could not resist remarking:

80   "Yes, sister, that's Africa for you! Our negritude, our blackness. Ours is the civilization of the dance."

81   But the dancing couple took no notice of their audience at the bar. They were too engrossed in each other.

82   After three dances, Ngouakou-Ngouakou wanted to leave.

83   "Already!" she asked. "But it's so nice here."

84   "It'll be nicer somewhere else." He took her by the arm, helped her up, and disappeared with her into the dark night.

* * *

85   In front of the Hotel Relais, Ngouakou-Ngouakou repeated to Marie-Therese:

86   "I had my secretary reserve a room in the name of Miss Baker. Go to the reception desk, and ask for the key. Wait for me in the room. I'll join you there in fifteen minutes."

87   As she turned out the light, Marie-Therese felt herself engulfed by strong, well-muscled arms. The hair on her arms intermingled with her

partner's. He was panting already. It was always like that with him. He didn't caress her, but preferred to enter her immediately. She could not help crying out, from the depths of her throat, as if in pain.

"Am I hurting you?" 88

"No, just the opposite." 89

Her nails dug into his flesh. She felt his large muzzle move across 90 her face. She could no longer speak, but only pant, "yes, yes," and other things she could not make out herself. It always took him a long time, longer than the young men. She liked that. She knew she was damned. But so what. She vibrated, she lived, she was free.

Four times that night she whimpered and cried out, before finally 91 falling asleep. Each time she repeated:

"Oh, it feels so good! You're pitiless to satisfy me like that." 92

She dreamed that Ngouakou-Ngouakou came to pick her up in a 93 large, fancy American car. Dressed in black, she was elated. He told her that his wife was dead. He had come directly from the funeral to fetch her and take her abroad. She hardly dared believe it. She wanted to pack some *pagnes** and dresses to take along but Ngouakou-Ngouakou warned her not to waste time.

After helping her into the car, Ngouakou-Ngouakou sped to the air- 94 port. Along the way she saw many familiar faces in the street. Despite the speed of the car, she distinctly heard them condemning her for tak- ing an old man away from his children and accusing her of having killed Mrs Ngouakou-Ngouakou. Marie-Therese was dripping with sweat by the time they reached the airport. There was no room on the plane so they were put in the cockpit. Ngouakou-Ngouakou took com- mand of the controls and started the engines. The plane moved along the runway but did not manage to get more than ten feet off the ground. It seemed as if the black dog which had been following Marie- Therese would manage to jump into the plane.

Marie-Therese woke up and saw Ngouakou-Ngouakou already 95 dressed.

"I must leave now." 96

She reached out to him and smiled. He sat on the edge of the bed, 97 kissed her on the forehead and said: "I have to go."

"But I have something to tell you." 98

"You're just looking for a way to keep me here with you." 99

"No, it's important." 100

She took the man's hand and placed it on her belly under the sheet. 101

"I think I'm carrying your child." 102

"What? You're joking!" 103

"No, it's true." 104

"What proof do you have that it's mine?" 105

Marie-Therese turned on her stomach, buried her head in the pil- 106

---

*Cloth worn wrapped about the body. The traditional dress of African women.

low, bit and bit it, and started to cry. She beat the bed with her fists and
kicked her feet.

107   "What's wrong, honey?"

108   "Bastard, you bastard! Get out of here. Bastard, bastard, bastard . . ."

* * *

109   The sun poked its head over the horizon, and climbed slowly in the
sky, promising a hot day. Shining through the windows, the daylight
awakened Miss Ngouakou-Ngouakou. As was her custom every morning, she turned on the radio to keep herself from falling back to sleep.
She listened to the national news.

> "Yesterday Representative Ngouakou-Ngouakou presented a keynote
> address at the opening session of the Radical Women's Federation
> Conference. In his speech he stressed the need to liberate our women,
> who are not inferior beings but are men's equals."

Questions for Discussion and Writing

1. How does the NARRATOR's characterization of Ngouakou-Ngouakou use sarcasm to encourage the reader to see the hypocrisy in his behavior?
2. How does the speech Representative Ngouakou-Ngouakou delivers at the
   opening set up a discrepancy between appearance and reality that defines
   his relationship with women?
3. How does Lopes construct the unfolding action of the story using the principle of IRONIC juxtaposition? For instance, how are Ngouakou-Ngouakou's activities in the first scene contrasted with the different side of his personality
   that he reveals to his wife and daughters?
4. How does Ngouakou-Ngouakou's relationship with his mistress at the Peek-
   a-Boo Bar and his reaction to her pregnancy illustrate his hypocrisy?
5. Describe the most blatant example of hypocrisy you have ever encountered.
   Give details that illuminate the difference between what was thought to be
   the case and what was really the case.
6. Create a character sketch of a male or female chauvinist. Do you know anyone who might serve as an example? If so, describe him or her.
7. Describe the most blatant illustration of sexism and hypocrisy you ever encountered.

Jean-Yves Soucy

The Red Boots

Jean-Yves Soucy was born in 1945 in Causapscal, Quebec. In his twenties, he spent much time traveling in Quebec and in the southern United States, where he worked at a variety of jobs, including that of an accountant in a financial institution. He then moved to Montreal where he became a social worker for The Little Brothers of the Poor (Les petits frères des pauvres) from 1972 to 1976. Since then he has been a journalist with Radio-Canada International and Radio-Quebec. For the past few years he has been president of the Salon du Livre, an annual book fair in Montreal. Soucy's works include the novels Creatures of the Chase *(1976), a powerful naturalistic fable set in northern Quebec that was awarded the Prix de la Presse, and* Les Chevaliers de la Nuit *(1980), as well as a collection of fables, didactic tales, and realistic narratives titled* L'Étranger au ballon rouge *(1981), from which "The Red Boots," translated by Matt Cohen into English in 1986, is taken. This bizarre tale of erotic obsession tells how a sought-after pair of red boots turn the tables on the soft-spoken accountant who lusts after them.*

From the day that he saw them, Thouin was unable to forget them, and what he most feared, happened. During all his twenty-six years as a civil servant, he had taken special care to avoid disruption. Now he was thrown into turmoil. After a lifetime of mild desires, easily satisfied or suppressed, Thouin was now tortured by passion. He *had* to possess them, to have them all to himself, to be able to love them whenever he wanted. He struggled briefly, then turned around to inspect them. From that moment on, their image was with him all the time, even at work. Because of them he was unable to sleep. And during the day, the same upheaval. . . . 1

Exhausted and worn down, he made his decision. It was evening. He wanted them right away, but, of course, he had to wait until the next day. The hours stretched out endlessly. He tried to read a book. Then he switched on the television. Finally he went to bed hoping to fall asleep. It was no use. He saw them in all their beauty, imagined the softness of their skin and their odour. What would his life be like when they were his? Entirely different, that much was clear. 2

The next morning he called in sick: his first absence since that devastating flu nine years ago! Then he went to the bank so he could pay in cash. Suddenly he was seized by fear. Surely they were the only ones; what if they were gone? Now he regretted his stupid indecision and delays. He flagged a taxi and had to restrain himself from telling the driver to go more quickly. What a relief to see them. They were slender, aristocratic, absolutely elegant. He went inside. 3

379

4   "I want those red boots in the window."

5   "They're the only ones I have. I don't know if the size . . ."

6   "It doesn't matter," Thouin interrupted.

7   Buying new boots for his collection usually made him fearful and timid. Not this time. In fact he hardly recognized his own voice. The salesman seemed unsurprised and said nothing more. Thouin laid out the equivalent of a week's salary without blinking an eye and then left the shop, clutching the box to his chest. Crazy ideas filled his mind. He might be hit by a car and die without having a chance to touch the boots he had so lusted after; a thief might knock him over and run away with his parcel. Thouin walked faster, gripping his treasure more tightly.

8   Finally he was home. He delayed the moment of opening the package; when he decided to break the string his fingers trembled with emotion. Delicately he positioned the boots on the table, then hastily he pulled back his hands. Now he was intimidated! His reaction surprised him and he laughed aloud. But he didn't touch them again.

9   Afraid of disturbing the boots he perched at the corner of the table, hardly able to eat his dinner. Instead of contemplating them the way he wanted to, he could only glance at them surreptitiously. But they *were* superb! The light played on the contours of the glossy leather; the high heels and the arched insteps gave them an aristocratic bearing; the dozens of eyelets through which the laces disappeared were like so many pairs of eyes staring at Thouin.

10   He went into the next room and stretched out on the bed. He felt uncomfortable.

11   "That . . . *presence* in the kitchen."

12   Presence? For a moment he considered the idea. The whole thing was becoming ridiculous. These boots were beautiful, even extraordinarily beautiful, but they were only objects, just like the others piled up in the closet. He was going to get up, take them to bed, possess them. Then they would be his, just like the others. He sat up, decided.

13   "You're going to be put in your place."

14   As he picked them up his hands were uncertain, and he carried them at arm's length. He didn't want to hold them too close. That would show a lack of respect.

15   The he placed them on the bureau. The whole afternoon he watched them; and in an almost offensive way they stared back from on high.

16   The atmosphere in his apartment became so uncomfortable that he decided to go out for supper. A waitress came up to him and suddenly her flat, low-heeled, white shoes became the red boots. The illusion lasted only a second but was so strong that Thouin thought he could hear the tapping of high heels. He paid his bill and left.

17   Outside a woman approached. She was wearing red boots. Thouin watched closely and the mirage disappeared. But again he heard the same footsteps as in the restaurant. Agitated, Thouin went into a movie

theatre. As he expected, while he was still walking down the aisle, the red boots appeared on the screen; he left without even sitting down. On the way home he became furious. How many days had he lived as a mere extension of these boots? Because of them he had even missed work! Until now he had made sure that his shadow life was confined to its proper time and place. This obsession had lasted too long.

"Possession conquers desire." 18

That decided the matter. When he returned, the innumerable watching eyes were filled with terror. Terror mixed with contempt. He bore the accusation without flinching. 19

"I'm going to teach you a lesson." 20

To add to the humiliation he positioned other pairs of shoes on the furniture. They would be the audience. 21

When he awoke his sheets were all tangled up. One of the boots had fallen to the floor, the other was half hidden by a pillow. It was while shaving that he saw the marks on his body: here a scrape, there a scratch, somewhere else a bruise. He must have hurt himself on the sharp edges of the high heels as he turned in his sleep. He was late. Thouin picked up all the shoes and threw them in a heap in a corner of the room. Later they could be straightened out, but now he had barely enough time to make it to the office. That morning, finally freed from the stupid obsession, Thouin was in great spirits. He was able to work in peace. 22

Thouin loathed disorder. In the evening, even before eating, he tidied his apartment. The red boots were placed conspicuously on a table. They would not join the others in the cupboard immediately. 23

"They're not looking at me the way they used to." 24

No longer as haughty and stubborn, they had been tamed. Thouin embraced them tenderly. 25

The next morning, when he woke up, he had a shock. The boots were in his bed. But when he had gone to sleep they had been on the dresser; he distinctly remembered looking at them as he turned off the light. 26

"Don't tell me I'm a sleepwalker." 27

He had spoken aloud. It was reassuring to hear a voice, even his own. He pushed away the boot which was pressed close to him. 28

"It has the eyes of a lover." 29

He got up to put them in the cupboard, then threw them towards the back. He felt morose. It was depressing to think that he could be getting out of bed during the night and wandering around in a trance. He told himself he should never have brought the boots home. He decided to shove them into a corner and try to forget that they existed. 30

The following night he was wakened by a knocking at the door. He grumbled and got up. But was silenced when, to his amazement, he realized that the blows were coming from the cupboard. He switched on the light and the sounds stopped. Might he have been dreaming? Or 31 perhaps the noise came from the neighbour's. Then a thought occurred to him which he pushed away: the boots. It was too ridiculous. But he went closer to the cupboard door.

32   Fearfully, he pressed his ear to the wood. Nothing, of course. He had been dreaming. A nightmare. He went back to bed but he didn't turn off the lights. He tried to fall asleep but he was afraid that the noise would start again. That would eliminate the nightmare explanation. It was nearly dawn before he finally drifted off, but Thouin woke up at his usual time. Even before the alarm stopped ringing he screamed. The boots were with him in bed!

33   He rushed into the kitchen, gulped down a glass of water and tried to calm himself. A sentence ran ceaselessly through his mind: "They opened the cupboard door. They opened the cupboard door. . . ."

34   He could hardly convince himself that he had been sleepwalking again. Finally, he got up the courage to go back to his bedroom. The boots were lying on the bed, inert like any other ordinary object. There was just enough time for him to grab his clothes and rush off to the restaurant for breakfast.

35   Though no one said anything, everyone at the office saw that he was falling apart. All day he thought about the terrible night, relived again and again the moment of waking, and searched for some rational explanation. He was so distracted that for the first time ever he was reprimanded by the office manager—much to the delight of his fellow workers. Then, in the afternoon, he was called to the telephone for a personal call. But to his repeated, "Hello, hello . . ." there was no response. No voice, only the hammering of high heels.

36   Thouin hung up. Everything was going to pieces. He tried to tell himself that someone had discovered his secret and was playing a nasty joke on him. But the sound he had heard over the telephone was that of the high heels on the red boots, a sound which—until then—he had only imagined. No one else could know their peculiar rhythm and tone. Without offering any excuse he got up and rushed out of the office. He even forgot his briefcase.

37   For a while he wandered around, and then he had a preposterous idea. Finding a pay telephone, he dialed his own number. The telephone rang four times and he was about to hang up when someone picked up the receiver.

38   "Who is there?" Thouin demanded, in a broken voice.

39   No answer, just the hammering of the high heels. Thouin was livid and his heart pounded wildly, but he persisted.

40   "Is that you?"

41   A single tap of the heel.

42   "What do you want with me?"

43   A mewing, perhaps the gentle hiss of two pieces of leather rubbing against each other. Thouin shook so violently that he could hardly hang up. Tottering, he sank onto a bench. Gradually his body grew calm. But not his mind, which kept turning over questions to which he had no

answer. These moans of a cat in heat—they made him shiver. The boots were calling him, crying for him, reproaching him for his absence. Closing his eyes he saw them again: beautiful, proud, determined and stubborn.

"No. These are only objects, things without life. The truth is that I'm going insane."   44

This idea made him feel better but still he could not go home. Instead he found a hotel. Safely enclosed in his room he went over the events of the past few days and analyzed the situation.   45

"Hallucinations! My eccentricity has become an illness. I should see a psychiatrist. But that's unnecessary. I'm only exhausted. Overworked. On the edge of a nervous breakdown. Or right in the midst of one. I'm going to take a holiday and go somewhere for a while. To a country where people go barefoot or in sandals."   46

He dozed. Just after midnight came the knock at his door.   47
Immediately his fear returned, even worse than before. He reasoned with himself. The chain was in place. It was an employee, another guest, someone at the wrong door, even a fire. Anything rather than . . . More knocks, this time impatient.

"Yes, yes, I'm coming."   48

He touched the doorknob.   49

"Who is it?"   50

The mewing. He burst into tears.   51

"I'm crazy. I'm crazy. It's nothing but madness."   52

Again the cat's appeal. Panic-stricken, Thouin pushed a dresser   53
against the door and then threw himself sobbing onto the bed, his head buried under the pillow. In spite of the fact that he held his hands over his ears, he could still hear the boots pacing up and down the hallway, stopping from time to time in front of the door to growl in a low voice. This went on the whole night. Finally at dawn it was quiet. Thouin sank into a sleep filled with nightmares. He was wakened at noon and asked if he was going to keep his room another day. He paid his bill and left.

For hours he wandered through the city. He was exhausted, but he   54
had nowhere to go. Take a trip? The boots would search him out at the end of the world. Since it was useless to run, Thouin resolved to face the situation. He kept moving until evening, and gradually a plan took shape. He went back to his apartment. The boots were on the small table beside the telephone.

"As if they were waiting for a call."   55

Thouin saw both reproach and joy in their eyes. He took the boots in   56
his arms and pressed them close. At first reticent, the boots gradually warmed themselves in his heat. Finally they were limp in his arms. Thouin reached the bed. This was the moment he had chosen to act. He seized their throats and squeezed with all his strength. Instantly they understood his intention. Their eyes filled with hate. They struggled, they swung from side to side, they tried to hit him and he had to hold them at arm's length. As they fought Thouin felt muscular waves

rippling through the leather. But despite his disgust for these beasts, Thouin remained in control of himself and of the situation. The box was on the floor, open. He shut the boots inside and tied on the lid. The boots were still wriggling but they were cramped and couldn't get up enough momentum to break the cardboard.

57   Thouin realized he was sane after all and this observation only added to his terror. He was dealing with living beings, beings which had loved him and now hated him. Absurd, but nevertheless true. He didn't try to explain or understand. Now was the time to act. He had admitted the impossible and this brought with it the inevitable solution.

58   "To get rid of a living being, you kill it."

59   He went out with the box under his arms. The things kept struggling inside. He walked to the bridge and, battling his vertigo, began to cross it. Below, far below, flowed the river. In the middle of the bridge, in spite of the pleading woman's voice that he so distinctly heard, he let the box drop into the emptiness. As it fell it twisted. The string broke and the cover flew off. The box turned upside down, the air slowed its descent, the wind carried it off. Side by side the boots plunged into a swirl of water. They did not resurface.

60   Freed from his nightmare Thouin felt ten years younger. He would invent an explanation for his absence from work and everything would return to normal. In a little while he would no longer think about the red boots. In a month he would laugh at the whole affair, sure he had been dreaming. Already he was beginning to doubt his own memory. He had almost reached the end of the bridge when he heard a step behind him. He swung round: the sidewalk was empty.

61   "It's in your head. Take a deep breath. Calm down."

62   He continued on as though nothing had happened, but the step continued to echo his own. The characteristic tapping of the red boots! Gradually his assurance crumbled. While walking along a dark street he became so afraid that he began to run. The sound of the high heels tapping on pavement followed him like a shadow. And inside his skull, the same woman's voice was accusing him. . . .

63   "You killed us! You killed us!"

64   He had to escape. He plunged into an alleyway and though his lungs burned he ran at full speed. Success! No more sounds of pursuit. He was only a few steps from a well-lit street. After a few more cautious detours he would be back at his house. Suddenly he saw them, ghostly shapes in the semi-darkness, a reddish haze in the dull light. They were blocking the exit. He stopped, frozen to the spot, terrified. The boots were at least ten feet tall. He stood there with his mouth open, panting. He couldn't move. One of the boots, at least its ghost, tapped its toe impatiently on the pavement.

65   "Murderer. Murderer. You are condemned. We are going to crush you."

Run back down the alley? They would catch up to him in no time. Thouin was afraid, afraid, afraid. He was going to die in the shadows like a rat. Without thinking, he leapt over a gate and found himself in a courtyard which, luckily, led into the next street. His own agility surprised him. The light! He must stay close to it. As he walked—he couldn't run anymore—he zigzagged from one streetlight to the next. The sound of the red boots met him as he reached a main street all lit up with neon lights. 66

The eternal solitary now sought out the company of others; he lingered near a group on a streetcorner, mixed in with people leaving the movies, followed them discreetly. So long as he was in the company of other humans, in the light, the boots could do nothing to him. There was only the sound that followed him, a sound that he alone seemed to hear. 67

Gradually the sidewalks emptied. Thouin made the rounds of the bars and, when they closed, went from restaurant to restaurant. Eventually morning would come and with it, peace. The footsteps continued to pursue him but Thouin became so used to them that he no longer paid them any attention. Sometimes the silhouettes of the boots would appear in a driveway, sometimes in a darkened portico. Thouin turned his head away and kept on. 68

Daylight came. No more apparitions, and the hammering of the high heels faded. Already there were more people: labourers coming back from the factories or on their way to work. He could go home. 69

The bus stop was crowded. Thouin wished he was at home, asleep. Then, once again, he heard the sound. In the full light of day! It was clearer than ever. Would he never have peace and quiet? The sound came closer: a woman wearing boots emerged from the subway station. Red boots the same in every detail as the ones Thouin had thrown into the river. He leaned against the wall and closed his eyes. In spite of the cold he was sweating. 70

"Just a coincidence. An unbelievable, horrible coincidence." 71

But that unmistakable sound? 72

The woman took her place in the line and began to read a magazine. Thouin could only stare at the boots. They were so undeniably real that he could think of nothing else. Or, at least, his thoughts tumbled by so quickly that he didn't notice any particular one. Suddenly one of the boots began to tap on the pavement—just as the apparition had tapped in the alleyway. The two boots ogled him, their proud eyes full of hatred. 73

"We've caught up with you. Murderer." 74

The same voice. The same boots. Everything began to spin and Thouin, who had resisted terror the whole night through, now submitted. Howling, he leapt on the woman, threw her to the ground and began choking her. Her widened eyes turned up; her death rattle was over at the same moment that the boots ceased to struggle. Thouin 75 laughed derisively. The witnesses had been unable to separate them in time. The woman was dead. The man, suddenly calm, almost dazed, waited without moving for the police to come and get him.

76   This murder was impossible to figure out. No motive; the murderer didn't know the victim and the inquest established that he had led an exemplary life. His co-workers, nonetheless, pointed out that Thouin had seemed different the past few days. Insanity was considered, especially as the murderer offered no explanation. The judge referred the accused to the psychiatrists. Thouin, hoping for understanding and trusting that these professionals would be able to enlighten him with the help of a complicated Latin word, recounted his terrible story. The psychiatrists were unanimous. They declared Thouin unfit to stand trial and put him in a mental hospital.

77   The patient soon stopped claiming to be sane. He took life as it came. He was sheltered, fed and looked after. Finally his life unfolded smoothly and without surprises. He was a model patient, respectful of the rules, quiet and willing to help. He was . . . happy. As he had to take treatment and since he had to talk during these long appointments, Thouin amused himself by tracing the origin of his fetish. The psychiatrist viewed him with respect, almost friendship.

78   But the remission was short-lived. First there were footsteps in the night. Thouin was unable to sleep. Finally he talked about them with his doctor, who prescribed sedatives. Stunned by the drugs, Thouin now passed every night in a semi-coma. But instead he heard the boots during the day. They followed him on his walks, pursued him down the corridors of the hospital.

79   The model patient became irascible and unpredictable. He had crises. He complained about hearing voices. Then came the hallucinations. In spite of the drugs, he began to howl at night. Then his violence turned on himself. In the morning he was found covered with bruises and cuts. A real psycho. Every evening the sick man was tied to his bed.

80   The psychiatrist wasn't sure what to think: this man's fantasies seemed so real, he was so persuasive when he asked for help. Nor could the psychiatrist explain the footsteps that the orderlies said they heard at night, nor the footprints in the courtyard under the window of Thouin's room. Worst of all was the poor man's death. He was found one morning, still tied to his bed. The iron springs were all twisted and his bones were broken in dozens of places. Thouin was crushed like a tiny creature that you grind under your heel.

Questions for Discussion and Writing

1. How much of the dramatic effect of the story is due to the use of CONNOTA-TIVE, highly expressive and emotional, rather than LITERAL language to describe M. Thouin's reactions?

2. How would you characterize the kind of life M. Thouin has lived up to the point when he purchases the red boots?

3. Why is it significant that M. Thouin pays for them in cash and doesn't care what size they are?

4. How is the story shaped to follow M. Thouin's changing relationship with the red boots? How does he behave toward them initially? What changes do his co-workers notice in him? To what extent does M. Thouin's relationship with the boots have a "fatal attraction" quality?

5. What are the first indications that M. Thouin's obsession with the boots has crossed over from a fetish into madness?

6. In your view, what is the significance of the final scene? How does the ending of the story throw all the preceding events into an entirely new light?

7. In a short essay, define the characteristics of Soucy's unique STYLE and analyze the contribution that his DICTION, SYNTAX, RHYTHM, and IMAGERY make in bringing us into the mind of the protagonist.

8. Describe a situation that initially seems plausible, but in which the parameters of the real world soon are suspended.

9. What inanimate object would you choose to imbue with mystical and anthropomorphic qualities? Describe it and the qualities it has taken on.

10. Write a description of a place exaggerating every feature to the utmost, including noise, motion, sights, actions, and the characteristics of people and animals in the scene.

11. What would a double date be like between you and your date and M. Thouin and his "date"?

Viktoria Tokareva

Nothing Special

Viktoria Samoilovna Tokareva was born in 1937 in Leningrad (now Saint Petersburg). Although she graduated as a pianist from the Leningrad Music School, her ambition to work in films led her to enroll in 1963 in the Moscow State Institute of Cinematography; she published her first story a year later. After graduating from the scriptwriting department in 1967, Tokareva continued to write fiction and began writing scripts for television and film, including Ship of Widows, *based on I. Grekova's novel of the same name. She has received several film awards, including the Golden Prize at the Tenth Moscow International Film Festival in 1977 for* Mimino. *Tokareva's fiction offers sensitive and original insights into contemporary Russian society. She has the ability to create a highly individualized narrative voice dispensing generalizations about life in a breezy, ironic, and self-deprecatory tone. The effect is to distance her ingenuous protagonists, as well as the reader, from experiences that otherwise would seem unbearably painful. This sensitivity to human fallibility, so evident in "Nothing Special," translated by Helena Goscilo, brought her wide popularity not only in Russia, but internationally in the past decade.*

1   Margarita Poludeneva was a fortunate person.

2   For example, once, in the fourth grade, Vovka Korsakov, the boy sitting next to her, fell in love with her. Wishing to draw attention to himself, he threw a heavy metal flatiron at her from the sixth floor. The iron landed eleven centimeters from her foot. Fate stepped aside eleven centimeters. At that moment Margarita was fixing a stocking that had slipped down. She raised her head, saw Vovka at the window, and said, "Ah—it's you . . .," and went on her way in her two-peaked dark-blue velvet hood. She didn't take offense at Vovka. That was the kind of character she had. If he had killed or maimed her, then there would have been a reason to take offense. But, why take offense at something that hadn't happened?

3   Margarita had emerged unhurt, beside a stack of firewood. At that time firewood was used for heating. She grew up, finished school, and enrolled in a shipbuilding institute, Shiply for short. And at seventeen she became enamored of an Arab with the sumptuous name of Bedr el-Din Maria Muhammad. Two months after their acquaintance, Maria Muhammad returned to his harem. The complicated international situation wouldn't allow him to remain any longer in Leningrad. He had to return to the United Arab Republic. Bedr left her the name Margo—instead of Rita. And also a little son, Sashechka, with black eyes and light-brown hair, which, practically speaking, was a joy. She could have been left with nothing.

Officially Margo was considered a single mother, though it was 4 more correct grammatically to say unwed mother. If a woman has a child, and especially such a beautiful and precious one as Sashechka, she's definitely not single.

In addition, Bedr el-Din taught Margo to eat potatoes with vegetable 5 oil and lemon; it was tasty and cheap. So on closer examination, Bedr proved to be quite a lot of use. More than harm. Especially since he was useful consciously. And harmful unconsciously. After all, he couldn't influence complicated international relations. Love is helpless in the face of politics. Probably because love involves only two people, whereas politics involves many.

Time passed. Sashechka grew and was already enrolled in a board- 6 ing school, and on Saturdays and Sundays Margo would bring him home. Margo worked in a design office and awaited her happiness. She didn't simply wait, vaguely hoping; she abided in a state of permanent readiness to meet her happiness and to accept it joyfully without re-criminations for its tardiness. For such a long absence.

Once happiness appeared in the form of a Russianized Armenian 7 named Gena. Friends said, "Here we go again." They said that Margo specialized in the Middle East. They thought that Gena and Bedr were one and the same. Though the only thing they had in common was their hair color.

To Gena's credit, one must say that he had no intentions of pulling 8 the wool over Margo's eyes, and immediately, from the first day, he said that he didn't love her and didn't intend to. His heart belonged to another woman, but their relations were temporarily complicated. Gena studied at the conservatory in the woodwind department, and, to express it in musicians' language, complicated love was the dominant theme of his life. Whereas Margo played a subordinate part. His whole life was a symphonic "poem of ecstasy."

Gena was somewhat languid, not like an Armenian at all. He con- 9 stantly caught colds and coughed like a trumpet. Apparently the damp Leningrad climate didn't agree with him. He said that Leningrad was built on a swamp and he could never get warm there. Margo knitted warm things for him, cooked hot soups, and took him out for walks. As they walked down the street, she led him by the hand—not he her, but she him, holding his soft, limp fingers in her hand. Sometimes they would stop and kiss. That was wonderful.

The dominant theme interwove harmoniously with the subordinate 10 part. In music this is called polyphony.

Margo knew how to live for the moment and didn't look ahead. But 11 Gena was prone to self-analysis. He said that only the simplest infuso-rial microorganisms reproduce by simple division without looking ahead. A human is a human precisely so as to plan life and direct fate himself.

And so they planned. They got together with the Starostins from the 12 design office for their holiday. They set off for Gagra, but ended up in totally different places: Gena in the grave, and Margo in the hospital.

13   Margo recalled how they had driven onto a nearby road. Zinka Starostin had switched on "Maiak,"[1] and Pekhi's voice had launched into the old waltz, "Dunai, Dunai, oh, try to find whose gift is where. . . ." Starostin had glanced back and said, "The door's rattling," referring to the right rear door beside which Margo was sitting.

14   Gena said, "Go faster."

15   The speedometer leaped to a hundred and twenty kilometers; the car seemed to take off, leaving the ground, and you couldn't feel the friction of wheels at all. Margo looked at Gena, found his cool hand on the seat, squeezed his fingers, and said through tears:

16   "I'm happy."

17   That was the last thing she felt—happiness.

18   Then there was a gap in her memory. And then the surgeon's voice said:

19   "She's fortunate. She was born under a lucky star."

20   Margo's good fortune this time consisted of everyone else's having been smashed to death, whereas she'd been thrown out of the improperly closed door and suffered a ruptured spleen.

21   When a person's spleen is removed, the marrow assumes the blood-producing function, so that one can live as before without a spleen, without noticing whether it's there or not. After all, she could have had a ruptured liver, for example. Or heart. Or the door could have been closed properly.

22   Margo regained consciousness in the hospital when they were wheeling her into the operating room, and she didn't experience a single emotion: neither fear nor distress. Not even surprise. Apparently that's how the psyche's defense mechanism works. Had Margo been able to fully realize and experience what had happened to her, she'd have died of nerves alone. But she didn't care. Only one thing worried her—where to put her hands: to stretch them out along the seams or to let them hang down from the gurney. Margo folded her hands on her chest like a corpse who'd gone to meet her maker, and the surgeon on duty, Ivan Petrovich, covered her crossed hands with his large palm. His palm was warm, whereas her hands were cold because, on account of her internal bleeding, her blood pressure was disturbed and her end was literally near, for she was growing cold precisely from her "ends," her extremities—the hands and feet.

23   Ivan Petrovich walked beside Margo without taking his gaze off her, either keeping a professional eye on her or sympathizing with her as a human being—after all, she was young and pretty. No matter when death comes, it's always premature.

---

1. "Maiak"—since 1964, a twenty-four-hour nonstop radio program which broadcasts information and music. Also a brand of radio.

In the operating room Ivan Petrovich bent over Margo. From close   24
up she saw his blue eyes and light-brown beard. His beard had been
rinsed in some wonderful shampoo, and each hair shone and emitted a
gentle fragrance. Through her profound indifference, Margo suddenly
sensed that she wouldn't die because life was beckoning to her. She further understood that even right before death she was thinking of love.

Several hours later Margo awoke in intensive care. There were tubes   25
sticking out of her nose and stomach. She realized that she was alive;
this neither cheered nor depressed her. She didn't care one way or the
other.

From time to time nurses approached and gave her injections, drugs   26
with soporifics. That's why Margo either slept or remained in a rather
dazed state. Sometimes she would open her eyes and see Ivan
Petrovich above her, but even that fact left her indifferent.

Once Margo awoke during the night and heard one of the nurses   27
telling another that the operation hadn't been successful because Ivan
Petrovich had accidentally cut across some very important duct, that
during the operation they'd had to summon a special unit, and for five
hours they'd intricately sutured this important duct. Now no one knew
how things would work out, and her relatives could sue him and he'd
be put in prison if Margo died.

Margo thought about the fact that she had no relatives except Bedr   28
el-Din. She'd been an orphan from the age of thirteen. Her friends the
Starostins also weren't around. That meant that no one would complain
anywhere, and she should tell him so.

Ivan Petrovich came the next morning and started checking the   29
tubes that stuck out of Margo's stomach like flowers out of a modern
vase, with every stem pinned in place. Then he placed a can of cran-
berry juice on the night table beside her and told her to drink two
spoonfuls. He raised the spoon to her mouth and stretched his own
lips, as if duplicating her movements. The way mothers feed little children.

Then Ivan Petrovich took some manganic solution and cotton wads   30
from the nurse and started carefully washing the traces of dried blood
from Margo's stomach, scrupulously avoiding the tubes. Ivan Petrovich
was a surgeon, not an orderly, and this procedure wasn't part of his duties at all. But he couldn't entrust Margo into someone else's indifferent
hands.

Margo smiled gently, as if to say, "It's all right, we'll make it!" He   31
also smiled, but his smile came out as a grimace. And tears gathered in
his eyes. Margo was startled: it had been such a long time since anyone
had cried on her account. To be really honest, no one had ever cried on
her account, except perhaps Sashechka whenever she forbade him
something. Margo gazed at his face, inspired with sorrow, and suddenly she didn't regret her stomach at all. She was ready to surrender
both an arm and a leg. Let him cut. If only he would sit like that beside
her and cry on account of her.

32   Next day Margo asked the nurse for a mirror. No mirror could be found, and the nurse brought her a powder compact on the lid of which was written "Elena." Margo peered into the round mirror and saw her face in it. It wasn't pale, but bluish-white, like a blue-bleached pillowcase. And not thin, but simply shrunken to the bone. It looked good on her. A new expression had appeared—of sanctity. She also noticed that her chin and the tip of her nose were peeling. She wondered what that could mean, and recalled that the evening before the trip she and Gena had kissed. Gena had been unshaven, and his cheeks had scraped like a grater. And suddenly, for the first time in this whole period, she realized that he didn't exist. His kisses had not yet left her face, but he himself was no more. Nor were the Starostins.

33   For the first time, Margo burst out crying and couldn't bury her face in the pillow to hide it. She could lie only on her back. A nurse came over and said that under no circumstances was Margo allowed to cry, because getting upset was bad for her. Margo replied that she couldn't stop right away. Then the nurse dashed to the telephone and called Ivan Petrovich. He appeared literally in two minutes and ordered the nurse not to disturb Margo's crying; Margo should do whatever she wanted. And if she wanted to cry, then the nurse shouldn't forbid it, but should create all the right conditions for it.

34   The nurse went off in a huff because she'd been humiliated in front of a patient. And patients ranked lower in the hospital than did nurses and even orderlies. Ivan Petrovich brought a low stool from somewhere. He sat down beside Margo, his shoulders stooped. Their faces were on about the same level with each other. He took her hand in his and started breathing on her fingers as if her hand were a frozen bird and he was warming it with his breath. He seemed glad that Margo was crying. It was the first emotion she'd exhibited in all this time. It was a return to life.

35   He breathed on her hand, raising it close to his lips. He gazed at her with a look as though he were withdrawing a part of her suffering and absorbing it into himself. She really started feeling warmer from his breathing and better from his gaze. And she wanted to sit like that forever.

36   Two weeks later they pulled the tubes out of her and set up an x-ray. All the gurneys were in use for some reason. Not for some reason, but precisely because they were needed. The hospital observed its own procedures, according to which what was needed could never be found, and what wasn't, could. Ink for a fountain pen, for example. Ivan Petrovich spent half a day on operations, and half on writing up these operations. Who needed this writing? Not the doctor or the patient, in any event. Perhaps it was for the archives. Sometime, many generations later, descendants would have an idea of the state of affairs in medicine at the end of the twentieth century. So Ivan Petrovich spent half the day

for the sake of descendants. Although his contemporaries needed his time much more.

There were no gurneys handy, so Ivan Petrovich carried Margo in his arms. The x-ray room was located two floors down, and Ivan Petrovich carried Margo first along the entire corridor, then down two sets of stairs below. She was afraid that he'd drop her and all her seams, both outside and in, would burst, and she held him firmly around the neck, and smelled the delicate aroma of his mustache and beard. Once she'd experienced the same feeling, or one similar to it, at a downhill skiing resort, when she was riding on the ski lift to the top of the hill. A ravine yawned below—and she dangled between heaven and earth, breathless with fear and joy.

"Don't breathe in my ear," he requested. "It tickles. I'll drop you."

"That's okay," she responded, "If you drop me, you'll patch me up."

He continued to carry her, on and on, and it was the way not to the x-ray room but to eternity. In the Lord's arms.

No one had ever carried her in his arms. Only her parents when she was a child.

From that day, Margo started waiting for him. She lived from one hospital round to the next. She fell asleep with the thought that the next day she'd see him again. And she'd awaken with a sense of joy: soon the door would open, and she'd see his face and hear his voice.

Margo caught herself imitating his intonation and assuming his facial expression. She didn't see herself in the mirror, but she thought that she looked like him when she wore that expression. That was the beginning of love, when one "I" started becoming identical with another "I." When Margo's "I" didn't wish to exist independently, becoming a part of Ivan Petrovich's "I."

Each morning he would enter the ward at a half-run. Her life would enter the ward at a half-run, and fluids of joy would gush from her eyes and the crown of her head, like little fountains of water from a whale. He'd sit down on the edge of her bed, and he too would become happy because he'd entered the climatic zone of young love and because Margo was getting better and was in some sense like a creation of his.

She was happy. Her soul soared, like a bird that he'd warmed. And from the heights of her flight, difficulties and even physical pain seemed diminished.

Patients and nurses were surprised at the discrepancy between her mood and the seriousness of her condition. Her neighbor Alevtina, with the gall bladder problem, believed that prolonged anesthesia had affected her brain and now Margo "was not all there." Others thought that Margo possessed an exceptionally strong will. But Margo had neither strength nor will. She was simply happy because she loved her doctor, her Ivan Petrovich Korolkov[2] [Kingly], as she'd never loved anyone. This was, of course, betrayal as regards Gena. But she was tired of not being loved by him. Gena had acted as though his very presence were a favor. Margo had continuously entertained him and reminded herself of a nanny who dances and claps her hands in front of a capricious child to get him to eat a spoonful of gruel. But the child looks sullen and distrustfully pushes the spoon away, and the gruel trickles in a thin blob down the nanny's face.

47   She was fed up with self-abnegating love. Victimizing love. She needed compassionate love. Ivan Petrovich felt compassion for her. He spoon-fed her, carried her in his arms, and cried. Even if to some extent he was saving himself, he also saved her. That meant that their interests coincided. And love is just that—the coincidence of interests.

48   Ivan Petrovich didn't prevent Margo from loving him. She could love him as much as she wanted. And how she wanted. And he didn't prevent her—because he didn't know.

49   Her neighbor Alevtina fed Margo vitamins. Alevtina had visitors every day, several times a day, and the whole department could have lived off her parcels.

50   As a conversationalist Alevtina was a bore, because she was wholly engrossed in her illness and talked only about her gall bladder. Alevtina was absorbed with her breathing, digestion, and swallowing down the next piece of gourmet food; she would dive together with the piece into her esophagus, then would swim down to her stomach and hear how her gastric juices started their activity, and the piece would be processed and digested, tumbling like a jacket in a dry-cleaning machine. Her face would assume a fetal grimace. She loved no one in the world more than herself, and she had nothing left but to sustain and ensure her life processes.

51   Life in the hospital ran its habitual course. Laughter could be heard from the adjacent ward. Patients laughed, making fun of their illnesses, their helplessness, and each other. The healthy visited and cried. And the sick laughed. Because laughter was a means of surviving.

52   One fine overcast day, Ivan Petrovich arrived at the ward dressed up and jubilant, like a groom. From under his surgical coat peered a starched shirt and tie. He extended his arm to Margo and said:

53   "Please."

54   He was asking her to get up. But Margo was afraid of getting on her feet. In the course of her illness and her acquaintance with Alevtina, she'd had time to grow enamored of life, and more than anything she valued and trembled for her fragile existence.

55   "I'm scared," confessed Margo.

56   After the accident her feeling of insecurity and instability had in-

---

2. Korolkov—derived from *Korol'*, meaning "King." The name in its English equivalent would best be rendered as Kingly or Kingsley.

creased, as if her life were an empty shell. Someone was bound to step on it and—crack!—not even a trace would remain.

"I'm scared," repeated Margo. 57

"But my arm?" 58

Margo glanced at his crooked arm, which was strong and seemed 59 filled with extra strength. She placed her hand on it, withered like a cypress branch. And she got up.

"Are you standing?" he asked. 60

"I am," said Margo. 61

"Now walk." 62

She took a step. Then another. And he also took a step at her side. 63 Then another. They walked down the ward. They went out into the corridor.

Along the corridor a little blonde nurse was wheeling a tray with 64 medications. Beside her, helping to wheel the tray, was a black Cuban on whose dark face stood out white Band-Aid strips. The black was a patient on the floor above, in the male section, but every day he'd come down because he found the little blonde nurse's company more interesting.

The floor in the corridor was slippery and wet. Margo walked as if 65 on ice. She tired immediately, and large beads of sweat appeared on her forehead. She thought that that was the way it would be now, and it would never be any different. She'd never be able to walk just like that, as before, without expending any effort on a movement, without thinking about every step.

Margo's robe was wound almost four times around her. She was 66 pale, emaciated, marked by profound suffering. But Ivan Petrovich gazed on her and couldn't hide the joy spreading over his face. He gazed on her as no one had ever gazed on her, except perhaps her mother or father when she was little and they were teaching her to walk. But that was long ago, if it had ever been. She didn't remember it.

Thereafter Margo started wandering around the ward: at first bent 67 over double, holding onto her stomach. Then just slightly bent. Then almost upright. And—an amazing phenomenon—with what avidity her young organism was restored. Margo stood at the window, looking at the street, and felt the strength surging within her like juices from the ground along a stem.

Outside it was already November, dirt mixed with snow. People 68 were wearing dark clothes, their heads lowered gloomily. And she was utterly happy because she was alive and in love as she'd never been before, with anyone.

As soon as Margo started to improve, Ivan Petrovich lost interest in 69 her—at first sixty percent, then ninety percent. He hurriedly examined her stitches, said that she had reached the first stage of healing and that she was a real trooper. He would press his finger against her nose as if it were an alarm button and immediately would dash off. Other post-operative patients were waiting for him.

70   Ivan Petrovich was considered the best surgeon in the department, and all the most difficult cases were given to him.

71   Margo patrolled the corridor watching for him to appear. He'd appear and, with hand raised, sketch a greeting to her, his fingers scratching the air as if to say "so long," and would walk on. Behind him, like a retinue behind a military leader, trooped the interns.

72   Two other surgeons worked in the department—Anastasyev and Protsenko. Anastasyev was a good specialist but a bad person. If, for instance, a patient asked him before an operation: "Is it possible not to operate?" he'd answer, "It's possible. But you'll die." When a patient's relatives started asking questions, he would ask: "Are you a doctor?" The other person would reply: "No." "So what's the point of my giving you a lecture? You won't understand anything anyway." Anastasyev had several such witty responses ready, and whenever he had the chance to put them to use, he was pleased with himself. What the relatives or the patient felt—that didn't concern him.

73   He was good at operating. But when patients were discharged, they almost never said "thank you" to him. And each time he was surprised: why were people so ungrateful?

74   Anastasyev and Korolkov didn't like each other, like two prima donnas in one theater. Anastasyev—so Margo thought—was somewhat disappointed by the fact that she'd recovered and wandered about the corridor like a shadow of her forgotten ancestors. Naturally he didn't express this in any way, but she divined his thoughts on the basis of his fleeting glance, which barely brushed her.

75   There was also a third surgeon in the department—Raisa Fiodorovna Protsenko. She was a very sweet woman, though it was beyond comprehension why she worked in surgery and not in the registry or the kitchen. Her patients survived purely by chance, not owing to, but in spite of, Raisa's intervention. It was said that Raisa had got her job through some high connection, and to remove her was impossible. First it was necessary to remove her high-placed benefactor. Margo dreamed of having this benefactor brought in by ambulance someday and having him fall into Raisa's hands. Then the crime and the punishment would meet at the same point, and for a while moral balance would reign in nature. But the benefactor had other doctors. He couldn't come to Raisa. The crime flapped freely, like a sail in the wind.

76   Soon Margo was transferred to a convalescent ward. Raisa ran this ward. She came on her rounds and examined Margo, painfully pressing down on her stomach with hard fingers, and the expression on her face was one of disgust. Then she went to the sink and washed her hands at length with some slaked lime and carbolic acid so as to wash the traces of someone else's illness from her hands. Margo stared at her back, and

it struck her that a human being was an erect animal. He'd been straightened out and left to stand on his hind paws.

After Raisa left the ward, Margo suddenly saw herself through her eyes—a pallid, underpaid single mother, a semi-invalid, without parents and without even a lover. She buried her face in the pillow and started to cry. Now she had the opportunity to do so unnoticed. She pulled the blanket over herself, and no one could see that she was crying. And anyway, that was her private business. Margo no longer enjoyed the privileges of the seriously ill; she was a run-of-the-mill hospital in-patient. As a person who had lost her glory, Margo cried until nightfall. Until she realized that things wouldn't be any different. And tears would change nothing. Instead of enduring it, as the yogis teach, she had to find a way out. Margo realized that her way out was through the door. She should get discharged from the hospital and go back home. And rely only on herself. She shouldn't even rely on Sashechka, for children, as we know, are ingrates. 77

It was night. Raisa was on duty. 78

Margo approached her table and sat down on a little white stool. Raisa was writing up someone's case history. Her handwriting was remarkable, simply calligraphic. She should have worked in the passport office filling out passports. Or written out honor certificates. At least future generations won't have to agonize over bad handwriting, but will easily follow the course of operations performed by Raisa. 79

"Discharge me so I can go home," requested Margo. 80

"Got to be a bore for you, has it?" asked Raisa and glanced at the blue page of an analysis. 81

"Not at all. It's nice here," replied Margo evasively. 82

"It's very nice here," confirmed Raisa darkly. "Simply splendid. Monte Carlo. Roulette." 83

Apparently Raisa felt offended by someone. Even insulted. But discussing such matters with patients wasn't done. 84

"Don't do the laundry right away. And don't lift anything heavy. Nothing over two kilograms. Whom do you live with?" 85

"With my family," replied Margo. 86

In the corridor lay a patient, a middle-aged woman with a stomach like a dirigible. Margo glanced at her and thought that tomorrow she'd be transferred to the ward. To the spot just vacated. 87

The next day, Margo called her place of work to ask them to bring her some winter things. But the person who came to meet her wasn't from work; it was Zina Starostin's mother—Natalia Trofimovna, or, as Zina had called her, Natalie. Natalie was an incredibly fat old woman weighing around 150 kilos, with poignant pretensions to sophistication. She stood downstairs with a string shopping bag swollen with items and waited for Margo. 88

Margo descended the stairs dressed in a hospital gown, holding 89 onto the bannister. Once she stumbled a little, but she kept her balance, and for a few seconds she couldn't bring herself to go farther.

90   When she saw Margo, Natalie burst into such loud sobs that everyone froze. From the floors above, the curious started leaning over the staircase.

91   Margo didn't know what to do or how to comfort her. It seemed as if she were guilty of having survived, though she could have died twice, on the road and during the operation. And here she was alive and standing there. Whereas there was no Zina. And yet it could have been vice versa if Zina hadn't sat beside her husband, but in Margo's place.

92   Silently, with a sense of guilt, Margo changed into her worn leather jacket, which she'd bought before leather jackets became fashionable. She changed into her clothes and shoes and, supporting Natalie, led her out of the hospital.

93   They walked through the hospital yard. The air was damp and piercingly crisp. Natalie was utterly drained by her sobbing and simply clung to Margo. Margo walked along and expected all her stitches to burst. She was allowed to handle two kilos of weight, whereas Natalie weighed 150. Over seventy times the weight allowed. But Margo didn't feel sorry for herself. Her spirit had plummeted from a great height and lay insensible. And her spirit was indifferent to what was happening with her body.

94   Margo was so constituted that she could think of herself only in connection with someone else. What's one person? A pitiful half, incapable of reproducing someone like herself.

95 On official forms, Ivan Petrovich Korolkov wrote that he was Russian, was professionally employed, and had been born in 1937. He enrolled in school early, when not quite seven; he was the youngest in his class, then the youngest in his class at the institute, and also as an intern in the hospital. So he considered himself young until he noticed that two young generations had grown up after him.

96   Ivan Petrovich Korolkov had a salary of 180 rubles a month. A stomach ulcer without any symptoms. A fifteen-year-old daughter, Ksenia. A fifty-five-year-old wife, Nadezhda.[3] Nadezhda was ten years his senior. Formerly, in their youth, this had been noticeable. It was also noticeable now. Korolkov was thin, frail. Nadezhda was bulky, broad, like a sofa bed placed on its side.

97   Nadezhda worked as the director of studies in a school for young workers. They had met in the town of Toropets[4] in the Velikie Luki province, where Ivan Korolkov had been sent on assignment. He was in

3. Nadezhda—literally, "hope."
4. Toropets—town in the Kalinin oblast.

charge of the hospital, she of the school. And in the evenings, when there was nowhere to go, he'd visit her. They'd drink home-brew and sing, accompanied by a guitar, and they sang so well that people would stop outside the window to listen. As a result of these singalongs Nadezhda got pregnant. They were both young, but in different ways: Nadezhda's youth was ending, Ivan's was beginning.

Nadezhda calculated the character of the new doctor, Ivan Korolkov, precisely. His character consisted of two components: conscientiousness plus inertness. 98

The inertness was virtually guaranteed. He would continue to come and go, drinking and singing, until his assigned term ended. Then he would leave and send New Year's cards. Or he wouldn't send them. 99

His term was drawing to an end. Awaiting him were Leningrad, a guaranteed profession, twenty-six years, and all of life. It never occurred to him to marry Nadezhda. However, to drop her when she was pregnant would have been awkward: the town was small, it was impossible to keep anything secret. Had Nadezhda made demands and reproached him, had she said that it was his duty, he simply would have dressed in silence and left. But she exposed her throat, like a dog in an unequal fight. And he couldn't go for the jugular. 100

With a vague sense of shame, he recalled how he'd tried to persuade her not to have the baby. One evening they were walking along the street. Ahead of them towered the wall of a club that the builders hadn't finished constructing. 101

"If you have the baby, I'll smash my head against the wall," warned Korolkov. 102

"Go ahead," Nadezhda gave her permission. 103

Korolkov gathered momentum, threw himself against the wall, and lost consciousness. When he came to, Nadezhda was sitting above him, her face long and doleful and sheeplike. 104

Korolkov held no grudges against her, except one: she wasn't *the* one. Yet she wanted to take *her* place. She wanted to take away from him twenty-six years and his future life. 105

Half a year later a little girl was born with a partial dislocation of the hip joint; they put a simple gadget called a brace on her legs. At first she couldn't get used to the brace and yelled from morning till night and from night till morning. In turns they carried her in their arms, wandering the length and breadth of their small apartment. Once the little girl fell asleep at the break of dawn. Through the dawning light he saw the emerging contours of her little face with its look of childish helplessness, her short nose, like a little sparrow's, and then at daybreak he felt a sense of conscience germinating in him, growing like flowers and water plants, and releasing its roots not only into his soul but also into his brain and his capillaries. He realized then that he wouldn't be going anywhere. That this was, indeed, his life. 106

Fifteen years had passed since then. During that time almost half his 107 friends and acquaintances had got divorced and remarried. But he and Nadezhda continued to live on and on. Those who got divorced wanted to find happiness *à deux*. But a union accompanied by loneliness proved the most durable. With time Ivan Petrovich became used to, and even grew to like, his loneliness, and now he wouldn't want to exchange it for happiness. Happiness—that's an obligation, too. One has to work for it, it has to be maintained. And he had enough obligations toward his daughter and his patients. A surgeon is like an athlete. Always a routine. Always in good shape. Nadezhda created that routine and demanded nothing for herself. Life was comfortable and inert. And even her age was convenient, insofar as it didn't presuppose any surprises, any betrayal.

108   But Nadezhda understood more and more that, despite having figured out everything about him, she hadn't figured out the main thing: when there is no love in the foundation of a relationship, a person turns nasty. She started feeling sorry for herself, for her life, devoid of affection. She realized that she could have gotten married in the normal way and would have led a normal life. Whereas now—who needed her? A natural selection process by age. And how she wanted to be loved. How chilling it is to live and know that you're not loved.

109   Awaking in the morning, she felt the heaviness of her face. In the mirror she would see a new wrinkle forming a second layer beneath her eye, resembling an arrow shot into old age. Old age is fatigue. And one wants to age with dignity. Yet she had to pretend all the time.

110   Not feeling up to dealing on her own with things falling apart, Nadezhda would sit at the telephone and call her acquaintances.

111   "Rai," she would say to Raisa if the latter was home, "it's me here. I'm calling you. I'm so depressed I can't stand it."

112   And Raisa would reply: "And who's happy?"

113   It turned out that nobody was happy. And that meant that she was like everybody and could go on living.

114   Raisa, in her turn, complained about problems at work. Nadezhda gave Raisa support, saying that free medical treatment was the source of all evil. They sought evil not within themselves but around them, and easily found it. Neither one wanted to admit to herself or to the other that she was not in her proper niche. It was too late to set anything right. A ruined, twisted life.

115   But people don't write that on official forms.

116   Ivan Petrovich walked to work. He believed that half of life's illnesses were due to hypodynamics—lack of movement, slackness of the heart muscle.

117   Five years ago he'd had a car, but he sold it. After a certain incident.

118   Oksana[5] was nine years old then. They sent her off to camp for the summer. She became homesick and pined, ate little, and cried a lot. But

5. Oksana—a formal version of the name Kseniya.

there was nowhere to put her. They had to visit her often. Once Korolkov came during a weekday. The girl on duty at the gates asked: "Are you Oksana's dad?"

He was startled: "How'd you know?"   119

"You look alike," said the girl and rushed off to get Oksana, yelling   120
as she ran: "Korolkov! You've got a visitor!"

Oksana appeared. She approached quite restrainedly, although she   121
was all aglow inside. Korolkov watched her approach and saw that his
daughter resembled his wife, but that didn't stop him from loving her.

"So how are you finding it here?" he asked.   122

"It's okay. Only not enough affection and stroking."'   123

He took her into the wood, got some early tomatoes out of his brief-   124
case and some first-crop apricots. He started stroking his daughter—for
a week in advance so that she'd have enough stroking for the week. He
kissed each of her small fingers in turn, stroked the little grey wisps
of her hair. And she calmly waited until he finished, neither over- nor
undervaluing it all. Her father's love was a habitual condition for her,
like the earth under her feet and the sky above.

Then she told him the camp news: yesterday they'd had elections to   125
the advisers' squad.

"And were you elected to anything?" asked Korolkov.   126

"I was. But I refused," replied Oksana with dignity.   127

"What were you elected as?"   128

"Sanitary inspector. To check feet before we go to sleep."   129

Korolkov privately noted that in a collective his daughter was not a   130
leader. A common ant by heredity.

"And do you have dances?"   131

"Of course, I attend them,"bragged Oksana.   132

"And do boys invite you?"   133

"One does. Valerik."   134

Some boys were running down the soccer field. They were chasing a   135
ball.

"Is he here?" asked Korolkov, indicating the field.   136

"No. He's excused from phys ed."   137

"Some sort of invalid," noted Korolkov privately. "Also not a   138
leader."

They went over everyting. Two hours later Korolkov headed home.   139
Evening was just setting in. The sun was no longer hot. The road was
improbably beautiful. Korolkov drove, enjoying the beauty, peace,
movement, and the state of equilibrium that replaced joy for him.

The road opened onto a little village. The grey log huts emitted the   140
coziness of a healthy, simple existence. It would have been nice to get
out of the car and stay there forever. Or, in any event, for the summer.
On condition that a local hospital be nearby. He couldn't do without a
hospital. Suddenly he noticed, moving swiftly somewhere from the
depths of a vegetable garden, something resembling a small dog, yet

not a dog, for dogs don't have such bluish-grey coats. Korolkov realized that in a second they'd meet at some point and that the weight of
the Moskvich,[6] increased by the speed, would hit that "something" in
the side. He braked sharply. The something also braked sharply and
came to a halt on the side of the road. It looked at Korolkov. Korolkov
discerned that it was, nevertheless, a dog, which had slept the previous
night, and perhaps all past nights, on a pile of coal. That was why its
coat had acquired that unnatural hue. And if it were washed, what
would emerge was a white little mongrel with a clever, charming face
and eyes the color of golden syrup. Korolkov registered the color of its
eyes because the dog looked at him attentively and questioningly, as if
trying to determine what he intended to do next. To Korolkov it
seemed that the dog was making way for him, the superior force: go
ahead. Whereas the dog apparently thought that Korolkov was delaying, making it possible for it to run across, since it was in such a hurry.
Otherwise why would he have stopped? The dog came to that conclusion and abruptly darted onto the road. Korolkov stepped on the gas
and abruptly flung the car forward. They met. Korolkov heard a dull
thud. Then he felt his shuddering soul. He didn't turn around.
He couldn't turn around. He drove on. But he drove differently. The
world had become different. The beauty of the road had disappeared,
or rather, it was as before, but it didn't penetrate Korolkov's eyes.
His soul wailed like a siren, pounded inside him with its hands and
feet, like a child locked in a dark room. Like a mechanical robot
Korolkov continued to drive the car, changing gears and stepping on
the clutch.

141   Suddenly in the rearview mirror he saw a policeman on a motorcycle riding behind him. With his small head, short neck, and broad
frame, the policeman resembled a bag of flour. Korolkov didn't know
whether the policeman was coming to get him or was simply riding
along. He speeded up. The policeman also speeded up. He slowed
down. The policeman also slowed down. The fact unnerved him, and
his nerves refused to accept the additional burden. Korolkov stopped
the car. He got out. The policeman rode up to him. He got off the motorcycle. He asked:

142   "Was it you who killed the dog?"

143   "It was," said Korolkov.

144   "Why?"

145   "What do you mean, 'Why?'" Korolkov didn't understand.

146   "Why'd you kill it?"

147   "It was an accident," said Korolkov. "Surely you can understand
that?"

148   The policeman looked at him in silence, and it was obvious from his
face that he didn't believe Korolkov.

6. Moskvich—small Soviet car produced since 1946.

"We didn't understand each other," explained Korolkov, feeling it 149
necessary to justify himself. "It thought I was letting it pass, and I
thought it was letting me pass."

"You thought, it thought. . . . How do you know what it thought? 150
What did it do—tell you?"

"No." Korolkov was embarrassed. "It didn't tell me anything." They 151
were silent.

"Well?" asked the policeman. 152

"What do you mean, 'Well?'" 153

"Why'd you kill it?" 154

For a second everything appeared unreal to Korolkov: the road, the 155
dog, the policeman, the talk with its high degree of idiocy. The only
thing real was the rage starting up in him.

"What do you want? I don't understand," asked Korolkov quietly, 156
feeling the rage within himself and fearing it.

"You'd go back and clear it off the road," ordered the policeman. 157
"You're around when it comes to killing. But when it comes to clearing
it off, you're gone. And traffic will be coming. . . ."

"Okay," interrupted Korolkov. 158

He swung the car round and drove back. 159

The blue dog lay right where he'd left it. There was no evidence of 160
external injury. Evidently it had died of internal injuries. Korolkov
squatted above it and glanced into its eyes, the color of golden syrup.
Its eyes didn't reflect fear or pain. It hadn't had the time to grasp what
had happened to it and probably had continued to chase someone or
escape from someone, only in another temporal dimension.

He lifted it—scruffy, trusting, and foolish—in his arms, pressed it 161
to his shirt, and carried it across the road. Across the ditch. Into the dry
birch forest. There he found a square hollow overgrown with thick
grass and placed the dog on the bright-green, young June grass. He
covered it over with twigs and branches. He stood a while over the
grave. Then he went to the car, forcing himself not to turn around.

Before getting into the car he stood a while, leaning against the 162
door. He felt sick. He wanted to vomit up the whole day. And all of his
life.

He forced himself to get in and drive off. 163

Beside the police booth stood the "bag of flour." Seeing Korolkov, 164
he whistled.

Korolkov stopped the car. He got out. 165

"Did you clear it off?" 166

"I did." 167

"So tell me now: why did you kill the dog?" 168

Carefully, almost stealthily, Korolkov took hold of the policeman's 169
top button and tore it off with a piece of his tunic.

As if he'd just been waiting for that, the policeman actually cheered 170
up and readily blew his whistle.

171   Korolkov was taken away to a pretrial cell, and the door was closed behind him.

172   He looked around: there was a small barred window and a bed fastened to the wall like the upper berth in a train compartment. There was nothing to sit on. Korolkov sat on the floor. He leaned his head on his knees. And he suddenly felt that right then he wouldn't want to be anywhere else. He couldn't have gone home, sat down to drink tea with his wife, and then watched TV. He wanted at least some form of punishment for himself. To place a cool palm against the burning forehead of his sick conscience.

173   Who was to blame for what had happened? Or was no one to blame? It was simply an accident. Chance. A defect of fate. Or was it a preordained chance, inscribed at birth?

174   Korolkov sold the car; for the first time he was afraid of the steering wheel. Soon he became free of the memories. He was almost free. He was, after all, a surgeon. Death was part of his profession. People die. And how they die! What is one homeless mongrel more than a hundred kilometers from the city?

175   Time restored the balance between him and his conscience, between his "I" and his ideal of the "I." Life continued according to his beloved and indispensable inertness. But one day when he was on duty, a young woman was brought in, with big eyes the color of golden syrup. She looked at Korolkov, and the expression in her eyes, tranquil and even dreamy, didn't correspond in any way to the seriousness of her condition.

176   On the basis of her extreme pallor and thready pulse, Korolkov immediately diagnosed internal bleeding and ordered that she be wheeled into the operating room.

177   "I should call in Anastasyev," he thought for some reason. But there was no time for that. Her diastolic blood pressure was down to twenty. It turned out to be a ruptured spleen. Just as he'd surmised. One doesn't sew up the spleen. One removes it. And technically it's one of the most straightforward operations, even entrusted to interns.

178   Korolkov performed the operation with concentration, almost artistically, but he didn't experience that special feeling that usually possessed him during an operation. His anxiety and his near-certainty that something would happen prevented that. And when he cut through the pancreas, he wasn't surprised. He thought: and here it is.

179   It meant that the road had been his preordained destiny. The dog had merely chanced to be under the feet of his fate. And now fate was winding a new coil, and that new coil was called Margarita Poludneva.

180   During the entire postoperative period, he didn't stir a step from her side. He was afraid of peritonitis. He ate and slept in the hospital department. No one visited her. Korolkov would go to the market himself; he'd steam minced veal and press and squeeze out juices. And

when he felt that it was all behind them, that they were out of danger, he felt devastated. He'd got used to looking after her, and he didn't stop suffering on her account. His conscience plus inertness switched on. And it was a dangerous union.

Korolkov suddenly started noticing that something fascinating was taking place in the world. For example, the sky outside was cosmic, as in Baikonur,[7] where sputniks were launched. He'd never been in Baikonur, but was certain the sky there was just like that—gates to the cosmos. He could stand for long stretches and look at the sky, shaken at the insignificance and the greatness of man. Or, for example, the park in front of the hospital with the tame squirrels, shedding their coats after spring. People fed them and cats chased them at top speed—so that the squirrels flew all over the park on their chic tails with their shabby greyish-beige flanks. The cats probably thought that the squirrels were flying rats. But perhaps they didn't think anything—what difference did it make to them what they gorged themselves on? 181

The park had always been there. The tame squirrels had browsed in it for about ten years. And the sky, too, had existed long ago—much before Korolkov paid attention to it. Only now, however, did he notice all this. 182

"What's the matter with you?" Raisa asked him as she came off duty. "I think you've fallen in love." 183

"What makes you think that?" Korolkov became nervous. 184

"I understand the language," said Raisa vaguely and went off to engage in battle with the world. She felt more self-confident outside the walls of the hospital. 185

Love—if one were to define it chemically—is a thermonuclear reaction that necessarily ends in an explosion. An explosion into happiness. Or into unhappiness. Or into nowhere. 186

Korolkov had no faith in himself. What could he give her? His almost fifty years? More accurately, those that would remain after fifty? His salary of 180 rubles, or rather, what would remain from his salary? His intractable daughter, or rather, his pining after his daughter? His symptomless ulcer, which was a danger precisely because of its lack of symptoms and threatened to become perforated? What else did he have to offer the woman he loved? 187

But, my God, how he wanted love. He'd been waiting for it for so long. He'd been walking toward it for a long time. And he'd encountered it. And he'd recognized it. And he'd got cold feet. Perhaps he'd waited too long and had overstrained himself? Everything in life should come in its right time. Even death. 188

Korolkov transferred Poludneva to the recovery ward, and each day as he passed the ward he'd give himself the short command: "Move on! Move on!" And he'd move on. 189

7. Baikonur—launching base in Kazakhstan from which the cosmonaut Iurii Gagarin (1934–68) took off for his historic space flight in 1961.

190   Today he also said: "Move on." And he peeked in. Her bed was empty.

191   "Where's Poludneva?" asked Korolkov.

192   "She was discharged," said the patient from the next bed calmly. For her the fact that a patient had been discharged was a common and even happy event.

193   "When?"

194   "Yesterday."

195   Korolkov just stood there, as if waiting for something. The woman looked at him in surprise.

196   "Did she leave a message for me?" asked Korolkov.

197   "For you? No. Nothing."

198   Korolkov went into the interns' room, attempting to arrange all the chaos within him on the shelves. He had the sensation of having been betrayed. After all, he'd carried her in his arms out of the fire, even if he'd been the one who'd shot at her. And she'd left without even saying goodbye.

199   Raisa was standing in the interns' room. She hadn't yet had time to put on her cap, and her elaborate hairdo resembled a flowerbed.

200   "Did you discharge Poludneva?" asked Korolkov.

201   "Yes. She requested it," said Raisa.

202   Korolkov took the medical chart. He leafed through it.

203   "She requested it. . . . Her hemoglobin count is forty-five." He looked at Raisa with disgust.

204   "She'll increase it with natural vitamins."

205   Raisa had thick brows and restless eyes that sought advantage, like the eyes of a predator. A marten. Or a polecat. Although Korolkov had never seen a marten or a polecat.

206   "Her type wouldn't fall under a car," he thought. "And she wouldn't roll along with the car." Anastasyev came in. He looked at Korolkov and asked: "Are you dying your hair, Ivan?"

207   "What color?" asked Korolkov.

208   "I've no idea. Only it's got darker."

209   "I've got paler. My face has changed color, not my hair."

210   "Do you want me to remove your ulcer? Out of friendship."

211   "Thanks. No," replied Korolkov tonelessly.

212   Margarita Poludneva was lodged like a bone in his throat. He couldn't swallow her or spit her out. Suddenly he realized that he would choke if he didn't see her. He read her address on the cover page of her chart. He asked: "Who's Vavilov?"[8]

8. Nikolai Vavilov (1887–1943)—botanist and geneticist of enormous prestige until he opposed Lysenko's misguided theories about heredity. As a consequence, he was deposed as the head of the Academy of Agricultural Sciences (which he had founded) and arrested (1940); he perished in the Siberian concentration camps at Kolyma. His reputation was rehabilitated after Stalin's death. His brother Sergei Vavilov (1891–1951) was a physicist specializing in luminescence in condensed systems.

"What Vavilov?" Anastasyev didn't understand, thinking he was 213
talking about a patient.

"Vavilov Street," explained Korolkov. 214

"A revolutionary, most likely," prompted Raisa. 215

"Or perhaps a scholar," suggested Anastasyev. "Why?" 216

"No reason," replied Korolkov. 217

Anastasyev was surprised at the discrepancy between his expres- 218
sion and the gist of their conversation.

Korolkov left the hospital, caught a cab, and arrived at Vavilov 219
Street. Margo opened the door, saw him, heard a ringing in her ears, as
if bells had started chiming, and fell on his chest as if on a knife.

Their souls met, and ascended, and alighted on a little cloud, hand 220
in hand.

Margo gazed, scrutinizing his lowered face. In her whole life she'd 221
never seen anything more beautiful than the face bent over her. A work
of divine art. An original.

"All people are the same. But if gradually you pluck out everything 222
that's the same, what finally remains is what a person is in essence. A
mystery. You understand?"

She watched his lips moving. 223

"It's like restoration. You remove layer after layer, and finally you 224
find that which you . . . Does it hurt?"

"Let it!" 225

It hurt from the knife that pierced her solar plexus. Tears came to 226
her eyes.

He kissed her eyes. Then her lips. And she caught the taste of her 227
own tears.

"Where did you get this?" 228

"What?" 229

"This here . . ." She kept touching his face like a blind woman, her 230
fingers checking his eyebrows, cheeks, and lips. "Where did you get
this?"

"This is only for you. In general I don't have this. I'm totally differ- 231
ent with you. It's you."

They spoke in whispers about something for which there are no 232
words. And what happened can't be defined.

"When did you start loving me?" 233

"I? Right away. And you?" 234

"Also right away." 235

"And what did you imagine?" 236

"I was afraid." 237

"Of what?" 238

"I'm old, penniless, and sick." 239

"So what!" 240

"Now it's 'So what!' But later?" 241

242   "You shouldn't look ahead. There's no need to plan anything. It's enough that he made plans. . . ."

243   "Who?"

244   "It doesn't matter who it was. . . . History has a lot of examples. Hitler. Napoleon."

245   "Did you love until I came along?"

246   "Now it seems to me that I didn't."

247   "I ask you . . . while we're together, don't have anyone else. . . . "

248   "We'll always be together. Don't be afraid of anything. A real man shouldn't run away from love. He shouldn't be afraid of being weak, sick, and penniless."

249   "I'm not a real one. You're mistaking me for someone else. You don't know me."

250   "It's you who don't know yourself. You're strong and talented. You're the best person there is. You're simply very tired because you've been living a life that's not yours. You've been unhappy."

251   "How did you conclude that?"

252   "Look at yourself in the mirror. A happy person doesn't have a face like that."

253   "Really?"

254   "It gives the impression that you've lived your whole life and are still living it through inertia. Living by habit."

255   "You're still young. You don't have habits. You're not drawn to them."

256   "I have the habit of solitude."

257   "Do you like it?"

258   "What?"

259   "Solitude."

260   "Is it really possible to like solitude?"

261   "I did until I met you. Now I realize that I was really a beggar."

262   "And I know what you were like when you were small."

263   "What was I like?"

264   "Like you are now. You're still small, a child who's turned grey from horror. And you talk, you mutter like a reader in a church choir. You were probably scolded at school."

265   An old-fashioned clock chimed. Ivan closed his eyes and recalled how he'd been small. How long ago his life had begun. And how much it would still stretch out.

266   Margo flowed around him like a river, filling in all the bends, not letting either pain or a draft get through to him.

267   "What are you thinking about?"

268   "I'm happy. My soul is so at peace. In its very depths it's so quiet. That's all a person needs. Peace in his soul and a devoted woman with a light touch."

269   "And wrinkles," added Margo.

"And wrinkles that you yourself have put on her face. Wrinkles 270
from tears and laughter. When you made her happy, she laughed.
When you made her unhappy, she cried. That's the way a man takes a
young face that's beginning its life and draws according to his discre-
tion."

"And what if it's been drawn on before you?" 271

"I'll erase everything that came before me." 272

"You won't throw me over?" 273

"No. Will you me?" 274

"I'm your dog. I'll follow at your heels as long as you want. And if 275
you don't want, I'll keep my distance."

"Don't talk like that. . . ." 276

They intertwined their arms, bodies, and breath. And it was no 277
longer possible to disentangle them because you couldn't tell who was
where.

"Where are you off to?" 278

"To get cigarettes." 279

"I'm coming with you." 280

"Wait for me." 281

"I can't wait. I can't stand it without you." 282

"Do wait!" 283

"I can't. Honestly." 284

"Then count to ten. I'll be back." 285

He got up and left. 286

Margo started counting: "One . . . two . . . three . . . four . . . 287
five. . . ."

When he returned, Margo was standing in the middle of the room 288
looking at the door. Her nakedness emitted a soft glow because she was
the brightest object in the room. He went up to her and said, "You're
shining. Like a saint."

"Don't ever go away anywhere again," she requested seriously. 289

He gazed into her face. She seemed to him like his frozen scared 290
daughter.

His kisses on her face woke Margo. 291

She opened her eyes and said in profound fear, "No!" 292

"What do you mean, 'no'?" 293

"I know what you were about to say." 294

"What?" 295

"That you have to go to work." 296

"That's right. How did you know? Are you telepathic?" 297

"Where you're concerned, yes. I'll go with you." 298

"Where? To the operating room?" 299

"I'll sit on a bench and look at the windows behind which you'll be 300
standing."

"I'll cut somebody up. I ought to belong only to the patient. And 301
you'll be pulling me away. Do you understand?"

302   Head bent, Margo quietly burst into tears.

303   "I can't leave you when you're crying."

304   "I'm crying on your account."

305   "On mine?" Korolkov was startled.

306   "I feel so sorry to leave you without me. I'm afraid something will happen to you."

307   "I'd like to know . . . who's the doctor and who's the patient here?"

308   Margo raised her palms to her ears.

309   "There's a ringing in my ears. . . ."

310   "That's anemia."

311   "No. Those are bells. Tolling for you and me."

312   "What kind of nonsense is that?"

313   "You won't come again. . . ."

314   "I will. I'll come to you for good."

315   "When?"

316   "Tomorrow."

317   "And today?"

318   "Today is Oksana's birthday. She's sixteen. She's been growing and growing and has grown up."

319   "She's a big girl. . . ."

320   "Yes, she is. But also little."

321   "I'm scared. . . ."

322   "But why? All right, come with me if you want to. . . ."

323   "No. You'll cut somebody up. I'll be to blame. I'll wait for you here. I'll count to a million."

324   "Don't count. Work on something. Find something to do."

325   "But I have something to do."

326   "What?"

327   "Love."

328   Smells and shouts drifted through the house.

329   Nadezhda was setting the table, exchanging abuse with Oksana, who was in the bathroom and answered from the other side of the wall. The actual words weren't audible, but Korolkov grasped the gist of the conflict. Nadezhda wanted to sit at the table with the young people, whereas that was precisely what Oksana didn't want, and she cited as examples other mothers who not only didn't sit at the table, but even left the house on such occasions. Nadezhda shouted that she'd spent a week preparing the birthday celebration and her whole life bringing up Oksana, and she wasn't about to sit in the kitchen like a servant.

330   Korolkov lay on the couch in his room. His heart gave him pain, or rather, he felt it like heavy cobblestones laid in his chest. He lay and thought about how he'd leave and they'd continue to trade abuse from morning till night, because Oksana didn't know how to speak with her

mother, or Nadezhda with her daughter. She brought her up by belittling her. They ignited each other like a match on a box.

Korolkov knew by his own example: from him, too, it was possible to get something only by flattery. No truths. Still less belittlement. Flattery seemed to elevate his abilities, and he strove to raise himself to that new and pleasing limit. 331

The door opened, and Oksana entered in a new jacket in retro style, what she called a "retree." It's a great thing to advocate "retrees" at sixteen. 332

"Come on, Dad, tell her," Oksana complained loudly. "Why is she tearing my nerves to shreds?" 333

"Is that any way to speak with your mother?" Korolkov rebuffed her. 334

"But, Dad . . . why should she sit with us? I'll be tense the whole time. She's always blurting something out that makes everyone uncomfortable. . . ." 335

"What do you mean—blurting out?" 336

"So she won't blurt something out. She'll raise a toast to peace in the whole world. Or she'll start turning people's attention to me . . . or she'll start piling everyone's plates as though they're starving. . . ." 337

"You've never starved, whereas we did. . . ." 338

"But look when that was. Forty years ago she went hungry, and she still can't get enough now. The bread starts getting moldy and she doesn't throw it out." 339

"All right, that's enough, it's disgusting to listen to you," announced Korolkov. "You're talking like a complete egoist." 340

"Well, I'm sorry . . . but it is my birthday. I'm sixteen. Why can't things be done the way I want them on this day?" 341

Korolkov glanced at her clean-cut face, with its fresh, sparklingly white teeth, and thought that they'd loved her to excess as a child, and now they'd have to reap what they'd sown. He realized that his daughter needed him not when he had carried her in his arms and visited her in the Pioneer camp. Any decent fellow could have carried her and visited her. It was precisely now, at sixteen, when the foundation of her entire future life was being laid, that she needed her own father. And not in an ambulatory way, as doctors say—coming and going. But as an in-patient. Every day. Under constant observation. So as not to overlook possible complications. And complications, as he knew, were on the horizon. 342

The doorbell rang. Oksana disappeared in a flash together with her dissatisfaction, and in a second her voice could be heard—taut and tinkling like a stream released under pressure. Everything was fine for her. She had a celebration to look forward to, and life is like a celebration. 343

Korolkov imagined Margo sitting and counting. She wasn't living but was marking time. And he realized that he first had crippled her 344 body and now her soul. He had knocked her down on the road. Even if accidentally. For it to have been on purpose would have been the last straw.

345   His heart gave a jerk and started aching. The pain spilled into his shoulder and beneath his shoulder blade.

346   Korolkov rose and went into the kitchen.

347   He could hear the noise coming from Oksana's room.

348   "Mom!" yelled Oksana. "Make us some jam water."

349   Nadezhda took a can of sugared plum jam out of the refrigerator. They also had strawberry jam, but Nadezhda didn't waste it on guests, keeping it for family use.

350   Korolkov knew from Raisa that Nadezhda had called the hospital during the night and had learned that he wasn't there. If he wasn't at the hospital and wasn't at home, that meant that he was at some third place. And it would have been natural for Nadezhda as his wife to show an interest in what that third place was. But she kept silent, as though nothing had happened.

351   "You're a sly one," said Korolkov.

352   "Give me the sugar," ordered Nadezhda and glanced at him.

353   He saw her eyes—grey, pluvial, without lashes. Actually, there were some lashes—sparse and short, like a worn toothbrush. It had been a long time—ten years now—since Korolkov had looked at his wife. He'd got used to her the way people get used to their own arm or leg, and he no longer looked at her with an outsider's eye. But now he really saw her. And he shuddered with hatred. And precisely because of this hatred, he realized that he wouldn't leave for any place. Had he decided to leave, he would have felt sorry for Nadezhda and would have seen her differently.

354   "You're a sly one," he repeated, clutching at his heart.

355   "I'm old," replied Nadezhda.

356   "You weren't always old."

357   "With you, I've been an old woman since I was thirty-five."

358   "But you always knew what you were doing. You churned me about like meat in a meat grinder and got the product you wanted."

359   "Quiet," requested Nadezhda, "we've got guests. What will they think of us?"

360   "Why are you like that to me? What did I do to you?"

361   "Don't project onto me. I always did everything the way you wanted it. And I go on doing things the way you want them."

362   "I don't want it this way."

363   "Of course. You want everything at once. To permit yourself everything and not to answer for anything. Centaur!"

364   "Who?" Korolkov was astonished.

365   "Centaur—half-horse, half-man. And you're half-old man, half-child."

366   "Very well!" Korolkov was pleased. "I'm leaving."

"Go on!" answered Nadezhda calmly, and he was struck by how simply problems that had seemed insoluble could be resolved. 367

Korolkov went into the entrance hall. He dressed and left the apartment. 368

On the third floor he remembered that he'd forgotten his razor and stethoscope. He went back upstairs. 369

"I forgot my stethoscope," he explained. 370

"Take it," said Nadezhda. 371

Korolkov took his old briefcase, which had seen better days; he'd acquired it in Czechoslovakia during a tourist trip. Into it he threw his razor in its case, along with the stethoscope. 372

"Goodbye," he said. 373

Nadezhda didn't respond. 374

Korolkov pressed the elevator button. He went down, then remembered that he hadn't explained anything to Oksana. 375

He went back. 376

"I didn't tell Oksana anything" he explained, standing in the kitchen doorway. 377

"Tell her," Nadezhda gave her permission. 378

Korolkov glanced into Oksana's room. 379

The girls and boys were sitting around the table. He knew some of them—Fedotova and Max. 380

"You're like a Georgian, with your toasts," said Fedotova. 381

"I'm not 'like a Georgian,' I am a Georgian," Max corrected her. 382

"Georgians cherish traditions because they're a small nation," announced Oksana. 383

"Georgians cherish traditions because they cherish the past," replied Max. "Without a past there's no present. Even comets must have a tail." 384

"But tadpoles manage without a tail," Fedotova reminded him. 385

"And that's how we live, like tadpoles," replied Max. " As if everything began with us and will end after we're gone." 386

"Go on talking, go on," requested Oksana and propped her high cheekbones on her little fist. 387

"Talking? Saying what?" Max didn't understand. 388

"Anything you want. You talk very well." 389

Oksana noticed her father in coat and cap, standing in the doorway. 390

"Where are you off to?" she asked in surprise. 391

"Nowhere," replied Korolkov and left, heading for the kitchen. 392

"Sit down," said Nadezhda calmly, standing with her back to him. "Stop running back and forth." 393

"I don't feel well," said Korolkov, and his face became detached. 394

"You need to calm down. Have a drink!" 395

Nadezhda took a bottle of cognac out of the refrigerator. From time to time his patients would slip him these bottles. To take them was awkward. And not to take them was also awkward. It was a form of gratitude, within their powers, for a life saved. 396

397   Korolkov poured himself a glass and drank it down as if he were thirsty. He poured a second and drank the second.

398   He was pouring not cognac into himself, but anesthetic, so as not to feel anything, to wash away all his feelings, down to the last one. Otherwise there'd be a catastrophe, as if a patient were suddenly to awaken during an operation and to start blinking consciously. Music blared from Oksana's room. For a while through the door Korolkov saw them dancing, or rather, slowly swaying, like weeds in water. He just had time to think, for some reason, that youth is an essential condition for modern dancing. Then everything vanished.

399   . . . He was running along the highway—grey, smooth, and endless. It was difficult to breathe; his heart thumped in his throat, in his temples, and in the tips of his fingers. He felt he wouldn't make it.

400   But there was the familiar booth. In the booth was the familiar policeman, the "bag of flour." The top button of his tunic was torn off. So he hadn't sewn it on since then. He was sitting and drinking tea with a large bagel that was soft even in appearance. Korolkov knocked on the door as if he were being pursued. "The Bag" rose slowly, approached him, and slid open the bolt.

401   "Take me to a pretrial cell," requested Korolkov, gasping for breath.

402   "Why?" asked "The Bag" in surprise.

403   "I've committed a crime."

404   "What crime?" "The Bag" wiped his lips, brushing the crumbs from his face.

405   "I betrayed love."

406   "That's not a crime," "The Bag" soothed him. "There's no punishment for that nowadays."

407   "And formerly?"

408   "Depends when, formerly. Comrades' court, for example. Or a reprimand, with an entry made in your personal file."

409   "And earlier still?"

410   "Earlier still?" "The Bag" grew thoughtful. "A duel."

411   "But whom should I shoot it out with? I alone am to blame."

412   "So shoot it out with yourself."

413   "Give me a pistol."

414   "I don't have the right to. I'd have to answer for it."

415   Korolkov tugged at the holster and pulled it off the belt, expecting "The Bag" to blow his whistle, and to be taken away to a pretrial cell.

416   But "The Bag" didn't blow his whistle.

417   "Only not in the road," he cautioned. "Some vehicle might come along. . . ."

418   Korolkov went back along the highway, peering into the forest that bordered the road. He thought: "But where should I shoot—in the temple or the heart?"

419   He placed the pistol against his heart. He pressed the trigger. The

trigger was heavy as if it were rusty and moved sluggishly. Korolkov pressed harder, squeezing the muzzle against his chest so that it wouldn't make too much noise. But there was no sound at all. He only felt a strong blow in the chest, and a spot of pain started to burn. Then the fire from this spot traveled to his throat, to his stomach, and in an instant his whole chest was filled with an unbearable burning. He wanted to break open his chest so that the air could cool his heart.

"How painful it is to die," thought Korolkov, "Poor people. . . ." 420

Three years passed. 421

Korolkov recovered after his heart attack and as before walked to 422
work and back.

While he lay in the hospital, they discovered that he had never had 423
an ulcer at all. The pain from his heart had been radiating into his stomach.

Korolkov got the job of department head. His administrative duties 424
increased, taking him away from operations. On the other hand, he started getting twenty-five rubles more.

Life flowed on as before. His essential and beloved inertness re- 425
turned. He didn't think consciously about Margo. He was afraid that if he started thinking, his heart would split along the former seam.

Korolkov had known from his experience with his patients, and 426
now knew on the basis of his own case, that a man wants happiness when his heart is healthy. But when it's like a slow-acting mine with a timer and can explode any second, when his life is in danger, then he wants to live, and nothing more. Just to live and perform operations, both scheduled and emergency ones.

As formerly, squirrels raced among the trees, and as before, cats 427
chased them. But to Korolkov it seemed that in three years everything had changed. The squirrels had shed and aged, as if gnawed by time. The cats had grown more melancholy, and he had the impression that the cats and squirrels had also had a heart attack.

Oksana married, divorced, and was planning to marry again. When 428
Korolkov asked, "Is it serious?" she replied, "At the moment it's forever."

No changes occurred in Margo's life. 429

Korolkov had said, "Wait." And she waited. At first, each minute. 430
Then, each hour. Now, each day.

When the phone rang at work, she would turn her head and look at 431
the instrument seriously, intently. Her friends laughed at her, and she laughed at herself along with them. But in her heart of hearts she waited. After all, a person can't leave—just like that. And forever. If one believes in such a thing, then to live is impossible.

So that the wait would not be so monotonous, Margo took 432
Sashechka out of the boarding school and arranged for him to take

swimming and figure-skating lessons. She loaded his childhood to its limits because childhood is a very important time of life, and one shouldn't rush by it, like an express train past a small station.

433   In the winter it gets dark early. When Margo returned from work with bags and carryalls, it was already dark.

434   She and Sasheckha would sit down in the kitchen; and Margo would feed him, and she'd experience pride every time he swallowed, pride that the essential vitamins were going into the precious growing organism.

435   But Sashechka knew nothing of pride; he simply chewed, and his ears moved and his Adam's apple moved up when he swallowed. Sometimes a totally unfamiliar person would show through in him, and Margo with happy bewilderment would examine the Russian boy with light-brown hair and a Pharoh's manners. But at other times he was the spitting image of her in her childhood photographs, and then Margo felt as if she were sitting at the table with her own childhood.

436   Once at a subway crossing, she met Vovka Korsakov, the one who had thrown the iron at her.

437   "Ah . . . is it you?" Margo felt joy well up in her, and her face lit up with joy at meeting him.

438   Vovka said nothing and stood there, his face expressionless.

439   "Don't you recognize me?" asked Margo.

440   "Why? I recognize you," answered Vovka calmly. "You haven't changed at all."

441   In fact, there was something in her that did not succumb to time: trust in the world and its individual representatives. Although the representatives left her for various reasons, the trust remained. And it made her resemble her earlier self—the one beside the stack of firewood in a velvet two-peaked hood of the kind worn by jesters in Shakespeare's time.

442   "Well," Margo didn't believe him, "twenty years have passed. In twenty years even the climate changes."

443   "Perhaps the climate changes," agreed Vovka. "But you haven't changed a bit. You've only aged. . . ."

Questions for Discussion and Writing

1. What circumstances have led Margo to meet Ivan Petrovich? What recent events in Ivan's life might explain why he reacts as he does to Margo?
2. Who would you say was changed the most by the relationship? Margo or Ivan?
3. What advantage is there for Tokareva in retracing events from Ivan's perspective? For example, what is the significance of the incident involving Ivan's running over the dog?
4. Why does Ivan, during his daughter's sixteenth birthday party, decide to remain with his family even though he does not love his wife? In your opinion, is it love for his daughter, his own passivity, or some other reason that makes Ivan decide not to go back to Margo?

5. How would you characterize the narrator's attitude toward the characters and events depicted in the story? How does the TONE of the story invite the reader to share this response?
6. To what extent do the conversations that are reported express the characters' thoughts and feelings in ways that define them for the reader? Discuss at least two examples.
7. How does the story's title raise the question of whether special things can happen to people who view themselves as ordinary? To what extent does the closing episode show how this relationship has changed both Margo and Ivan?
8. Have you ever been in a situation where a conflict between you and another person was never fully resolved?
9. Describe an accident where the consequences were strange or unusual or where both parties were unexpectedly delighted.
10. Describe an accident that changed the lives of the parties involved (either negatively or positively).
11. Do you believe in love at first sight? Has this ever happened to you or anyone you know? Describe the experience.

Rosario Castellanos

Chess

_____

Rosario Castellanos (1925–1974), the distinguished poet, novelist, short story writer, and essayist, was born in Mexico City but grew up in the Chiapas region where her family was part of the property-owing aristocracy that was stripped of most of its holdings in the land reform program of 1941. As a consequence, Castellanos was forced to discover her own values, a process she undertook when she decided to study philosophy instead of literature at the National University. Her 1950 thesis, Feminine Culture, *written for her master's degree, began her lifelong search into the question of women's place in culture. After postgraduate work in Spain, she directed a theater troupe performing in remote towns and villages in Chiapas. She is best known for the tremendously important role she played in bringing to public awareness the plight of Mexican women in* The Nine Guardians *(1957). Castellanos taught at the universities of Wisconsin, Indiana, and Colorado and returned to Mexico to accept a chair in comparative literature at the National University. In 1971 she became Mexico's ambassador to Israel and was emerging as one of Mexico's major literary figures before her accidental death in 1974. In addition to four volumes of essays, drawn from articles she wrote for newspapers and magazines, three volumes of short stories, and two novels about the Tzotzil Indians, she wrote twelve books of poetry in which she brings extraordinary insight to everyday experiences. The poem "Chess," translated by Maureen Ahern (1988), describes how the relationship between two lovers changes when each plays to win a harmless game of chess.*

Because we were friends and sometimes loved each other,
perhaps to add one more tie
to the many that already bound us,
we decided to play games of the mind.

5   We set up a board between us:
equally divided into pieces, values,
and possible moves.
We learned the rules, we swore to respect them,
and the match began.

10   We've been sitting here for centuries, meditating
ferociously
how to deal the one last blow that will finally
annihilate the other one forever.

Questions for Discussion and Writing

1. How was the idea of playing a game of chess intended to strengthen an already strong relationship?

2. Why do you think Castellanos chose the game of chess to serve as a CONTROLLING IMAGE for the poem (rather than backgammon, checkers, poker, or any other game)? How do the qualities associated with chess in particular enhance your understanding of the tensions that arise between the couple?

3. How does the IMAGERY used to describe the changing nature of the relationship connect to the LITERAL and FIGURATIVE qualities of the game of chess? In your opinion, what destroys what had been a good relationship?

4. How would you characterize the TONE of the poem—that is, the attitude of the speaker toward the events being described?

5. From what POINT OF VIEW are the events in the poem related? How would the meaning of the poem change according to whether the two players were a man and a woman, two men, or two women?

6. Did you ever participate in an activity intended to strengthen a friendship only to discover the competitive nature of the game ended up undermining the relationship? Discuss your experience.

7. Write a dialogue between two people, one of whom has a secret while the other is trying to find out what it is.

Judith Ortiz Cofer
The Woman Who Was Left at the Altar

Judith Ortiz Cofer, a poet and novelist, was born in 1952 in Hormigueros, Puerto Rico. After her father, a career Navy officer, retired, the family settled in Georgia where Cofer attended Augusta College. During college she married, and with her husband and daughter moved to Florida where she finished a master's in English at Florida Atlantic University. A fellowship allowed her to pursue graduate work at Oxford University, after which she returned to Florida and began teaching English and writing poetry. Her first volume of poetry, Peregrina *(1985), won the Riverstone International Poetry Competition and was followed by two poetry collections,* Reaching for the Mainland *(1987), from which "The Woman Who was Left at the Altar" is taken, and* Terms of Survival *(1988). Her first novel,* The Line of the Sun *(1989), was listed as one of the "25 books to remember" of 1989 by the New York City Public Library system. In 1981 and 1982 she received scholarships to the Bread Loaf Writers' Conference, and she is currently on the faculty there. The underlying theme of Cofer's poetry is the viability of the relationships between men and women, as in the following poem that presents a haunting portrait of a woman whose life has been shaped by being left at the altar.*

She calls her shadow Juan,
looking back often as she walks.
She has grown fat, her breasts huge
as reservoirs. She once opened her blouse
5   in church to show the silent town
what a plentiful mother she could be.
Since her old mother died, buried in black,
she lives alone.
Out of the lace she made curtains for her room,
10   doilies out of the veil. They are now
yellow as malaria.
She hangs live chickens from her waist to sell,
walks to the town swinging her skirts of flesh.
She doesn't speak to anyone. Dogs follow
15   the scent of blood to be shed. In their hungry,
yellow eyes she sees his face. She takes him
to the knife time after time.

Questions for Discussion and Writing

1. How has the woman described in this poem been changed as a result of being left at the altar?
2. What is the significance of the uses to which she puts her bridal gown and veil?
3. What CONNOTATIONS does the color "yellow" acquire in the context in which it appears? What do the IMAGES involving this color suggest about the nature of the changes in the woman's personality?
4. How does the word SHADOW function both LITERALLY and FIGURATIVELY?
5. How is the poem constructed to touch on only those details that present significant consequences of the initial event?
6. Speculate about why a member of your family or relative acts the way he or she does. What clues from the past do you think account for this person's present behavior?

Jimmy Santiago Baca

Spliced Wire

Jimmy Santiago Baca was born in New Mexico in 1952. He currently lives on a small farm outside Albuquerque. Baca wrote the poems in the collection Immigrants in Our Own Land *(1979) while he was in prison. His most re-*

cent volume is Martin and Meditations on the South Valley *(1987), which consists of two long narrative poems. Baca has written the screenplay for the 1993 film,* Bound by Honor. *Baca's poetry often tells the story of mestizo outcasts who confront hurdles thrown up by American society that isolate those who do not fit in. Through this, Baca has established himself as an important force in Chicano literature. His poetry is a passionate exploration of life in the urban barrios and landscapes of New Mexico. The following poem, "Spliced Wire," from* What's Happening *(1982), confronts the realities of love and betrayal.*

I filled your house with light.
There was warmth in all corners
of the house. My words I gave you
like soft warm toast in early morning.
I brewed your tongue   5
to a rich dark coffee, and drank
my fill. I turned on the music for you,
playing notes along the crest
of your heart, like birds,
eagles, ravens, owls on rim of red canyon.   10

I brought reception clear to you,
and made the phone ring at your request,
from Paris or South America,
you could talk to any of the people,
as my words gave them life,   15
from a child in a boat with his father,
to a prisoner in a concentration camp,
all at your bedside.

And then you turned away, wanted
a larger mansion. I said no. I left you.   20
The plug pulled out, the house blinked out,
Into a quiet darkness, swallowing wind,
collecting autumn leaves like stamps
between its old boards where they stick.

You say, or carry the thought with you   25
to comfort you, that faraway somewhere,
lightning knocked down all the power lines.
But no my love, it was I,
pulling the plug. Others will come, plug in,
but often the lights will dim weakly   30
in storms, the music stop to a drawl,
the warmth shredded by cold drafts.

Questions for Discussion and Writing

1. From the speaker's POINT OF VIEW, what went wrong with the relationship? Keep in mind you are getting only one side of the story. To what extent does the TONE of the poem suggest the speaker is rationalizing to save his wounded ego?
2. How do the effects of the SIMILE in line 4 ("like soft warm toast") differ from those produced by the METAPHOR in lines 5 and 6 ("I brewed your tongue/to a rich dark coffee") in giving a sense of what the speaker feels he contributed to the relationship?
3. How does the phrase "spliced wire" serve as a CONTROLLING IMAGE in the poem?
4. What role does the IMAGE of a "spliced wire" play in advancing the speaker's claim as to what he brought to the relationship?
5. How do the everyday objects mentioned (such as telephone, light bulbs, radio) serve as METAPHORS for connections the speaker claims to have brought into the life of the person to whom the poem is addressed?
6. To what extent does the issue over which the couple break up involve jealousy and possessiveness? Have you ever broken up with someone because of these reasons? How might the events in the poem appear from the perspective of the other person?
7. Write about something that seems at first glance to be unrelated to your subject, but that serves as a metaphor for it, as Baca does in this poem.

Marta Fabiani

The Poetess

Marta Fabiani was born in Pavia, Italy, and now lives in Milan. She is a freelance writer. A collection of her poems, Maratona, has been published by a writers' cooperative called Cooperativa scrittori. She has edited Sylvia Plath's letters to her mother and has directed a series of radio plays in Switzerland. In this 1986 poem, "The Poetess," translated by Muriel Kittel, Fabiani offers a glimpse of the difficult balancing act a woman poet must perform in pursuing her vocation while also meeting the cultural expectations of contemporary Italian society.

The poetess has paragraphs of words
threads she unravels as phrases
unusual comparisons
among the gleams
5   of a kitchen stove.

She reaches the eternal
by little
unveilings,
the infinite is the leaking
faucet, the row   10
of empties to return.
The poetess weaves tapestries
in a seditious lodging:
at night she keeps a warm cup
for the monsters, there, on the landing.   15
We must be nice, she says.
We must be discreet so that she never hurls in your face
her foot fetish
never offers you
her great sore to lick.   20
Blood is red so that you may see it.
But she knows
that she cannot pass through Duchamp's door.
Her slippers, at most,
will be the four feathers of a starlet: 25
winking
from the shopping bag of milk cartons, a Gulliver's revolt.
It is still her job
to count the chambers in the pistol
to be sure everything is in order,   30
accountant even in this hateful occupation.

Questions for Discussion and Writing

1. How does the DICTION of the poem reveal the speaker's sense of bitterness in being forced to subordinate her rich inner life as a poet to menial housekeeping duties? What METAPHORS or SIMILES reveal the extent to which her imagination transforms even the most commonplace features of her domestic environment?
2. What considerations keep the speaker from revealing her true self?
3. What is the contrast between how the speaker sees herself and how her family sees her?
4. To what extent does the image in the last line suggest the self-destructive consequences of concealing her inner life?
5. Describe a person who seems to be one way on the surface but reveals clues of being a completely different person underneath.
6. What advice do you think the speaker in this poem would give her daughter on the day of her wedding?

Anna Akhmatova

Cinque

---

*Anna Akhmatova (1889–1966), one of the best-loved Russian poets of this cen-
tury, was born in Odessa and grew up in Saint Petersburg and Kiev. When she
traveled to Paris in 1911, Modigliani painted sixteen portraits of her. Her husband was executed in 1921 for his political activism and Akhmatova herself
was silenced as a poet for eighteen years during the Stalin regime. After
Stalin's death, she was restored to the writers' union, but then was expelled in
1946 and her son was arrested. Her legacy can be seen in the influence she had
over younger poets, such as Joseph Brodsky. She is as well known for her love
poetry as she is for her political poems, such as "Requiem 1935–1940" (1961),
an epic that transcends personal significance to describe a common fate of millions who had suffered losses similar to her own during the purges of the 1930s,
and "To the Defenders of Stalin" (1962). "Cinque," translated by Richard
McKane, is a series of five poems that describe the indelible impact of a love affair Akhmatova had with the Oxford philosopher Isaiah Berlin when he visited
Leningrad (now, again, Saint Petersburg) in 1945, a relationship Berlin describes in his book Personal Impressions (1947). These poems capture the
voice of the heart and reveal how even a brief encounter can change one's life
forever.*

> Autant que toi sans doute, il te sera fidèle,
> Et constant jusques à la mort.
> Baudelaire

1

The memory of your words
is like being on the edge of a cloud,

and my words made your
nights brighter than your days.

And so, wrenched from the earth,
we moved through space like stars.

Neither despair, nor shame,
not now, not after, not then.

In the reality of everyday
you hear me calling you.

I have no strength to slam
the door you opened just a little.

26th November 1945

2

Sounds smoulder to ashes in the air,
and the dawn pretended to be darkness.
Just two voices: yours and mine
in the eternally numbed world,
And under the wind from the invisible Ladoga lakes,   5
through a sound like the ringing of bells,
the night's conversation was turned
into the light sparkle of crossed rainbows.

    20th December 1945

3

I have never liked people to pity me,
even from days long ago,
but I go on with a drop of your pity
as though I carry the sun within me.
That's why the dawn is all around.   5
That's why I go on working miracles.

    20th December 1945

4

You know yourself that I will not begin to celebrate
that most bitter day of our meeting.
What can I leave you as a memory,
my shadow? What do you want with my shadow?
The dedication of a burnt drama,   5
from which there is no ash?
Or a terrifying New Year's portrait
suddenly coming out of the frame?
Or the whisper of birch embers
barely, barely heard?   10
Or that they failed
to convince me of a stranger's love?

    6th January 1946

5

We didn't breathe in soporific poppies,
and we do not know of what we are guilty.
Under just what star signs
were we born to bring each other grief?

What Hell's brew did   5
this January darkness bring?
And what unseen luminous delight
drove us out of our minds before dawn?

    11th January 1946

Questions for Discussion and Writing

1. What situation is described in this sequence of five poems? What does the speaker reveal about herself in terms of the initial impact the relationship had upon her and the ultimate way it changed her life after it was over?
2. What examples of FIGURATIVE LANGUAGE did you find especially effective in enabling you to share the speaker's feelings?
3. Briefly characterize the MOOD and TONE of each of the five poems. What specific features of language and IMAGERY help create the mood for each poem?
4. What role do the last four lines in the fifth poem play in throwing new light over all that has gone before?
5. Were you ever involved in a love relationship that was doomed from the start? Did you react in the same way as did the speaker? Describe your experiences.
6. How would the effect of this series of poems be changed if you imagined the voice of the speaker as being male rather than female? How does this reshape the emotional meaning of the text without changing the words?
7. Get together with four other students in your class and collaborate in writing a poem about love where each person in succession writes one stanza that elaborates on the preceding stanza.
8. Try your hand at writing a short letter in the form of a poem (known as an *epistle*) to someone you care about.

Adrienne Rich

Your Small Hands

Adrienne Rich, a prominent feminist poet, was born in 1929 in Baltimore, Maryland. Shortly after her graduation from Radcliffe College, she won distinction when her first book of poems and essays, A Change of World *(1951), received the Yale Younger Poets Award and was published with a laudatory preface by W. H. Auden. As the wife of a Harvard economics professor and mother of three sons, Rich was expected to conform to a life of domestic femininity, a constricting role she describes in her volume of poems* Snapshots of a Daughter-in-Law *(1963). After Rich's husband committed suicide in 1970, she wrote* Diving Into the Wreck *(1973), a collection of poetry that explores the depths of her anguish as she confronts the inherited myths of power and sexuality that have been handed down from generation to generation. Her work chronicles the evolution of feminist consciousness and illuminates the phases of her own personal development, through self-awareness, to her present role as lesbian/feminist.* On Lies, Secrets, and Silence: Selected Prose 1966–1978 *(1979) most clearly explores this transformation. In 1974 Rich received a National Book Award that she accepted with the poet Audre Lord on behalf of all women. Her best-known recent books include* The Fact of a Door Frame: Poems Selected and New, 1950–1984 *(1984) and* Your Native Land, Your Life *(1986). Her poetic voice is distinctive and powerful, blending lyricism with quotations and slogans representing feminist goals. Rich's poetry reflects her continuous search for a new language to define her new vision. Her poetry has always sought to provide a voice for the dispossessed by reconceptualizing a sense of what is essential and what is possible for women. In "Your Small Hands," Section 6 of a sequence of love poems to a female partner, Rich compiles a catalogue of images of hands performing constructive actions of nurture and repair that she juxtaposes to images of prevalent male violence directed against women.*

Your small hands, precisely equal to my own—
only the thumb is larger, longer—in these hands
I could trust the world, or in many hands like these,
handling power-tools or steering-wheel
or touching a human face. . . . Such hands could turn   5
the unborn child rightways in the birth canal
or pilot the exploratory rescue-ship
through icebergs, or piece together
the fine, needle-like sherds of a great krater-cup
bearing on its sides   10
figures of ecstatic women striding
to the sibyl's den or the Eleusinian cave—
such hands might carry out an unavoidable violence
with such restraint, with such a grasp
of the range and limits of violence   15
that violence ever after would be obsolete.

Questions for Discussion and Writing

1. How does the picture of the "small hands" serve as a CONTROLLING IMAGE or important unifying principle in connecting associations touched off in the speaker's memory?

2. How does the speaker's attitude or tone reveal that she trusts women more than she does men?

3. Do you agree with the speaker that women are intrinsically less capable of violence than men? Explain your answer.

4. How do images of women performing important roles in previous cultures, and taking on roles traditionally associated with men in contemporary society, underscore the impression the speaker wishes to communicate?

5. You have brought home your date, not necessarily of the opposite sex, to meet your family. If they did not approve, what would they say to you about him or her? What influence would their opinions have on your views of the person?

Doris Kareva

To Make One Life Visible

Doris Kareva was born in 1958 and lives in Tallinn, Estonia, a newly independent Baltic republic. Her six books of poetry include Secret Consciousness and a volume of selected poems, Days of Grace (1991). Kareva's poetry is spare, often despairing, and displays an uncompromising ethical stance. She believes that "a poem is like a dream—at once a memory and a fantasy; a genuineness that opens up not along the lines of life but the lines of fate; no, not the lot that befalls us, but an eternally present part of our world." "To make one life visible," translated by T. H. Ilves (1990), projects the hope of a spiritual union between two people.

To make one life visible,
and give it to many
to keep
is impossible.

5   There remains a distance,
there remains a tinge of estrangement.

Only deep wisdom,
spacious love,
drawn closer and unites
10   our differences.

This spirit of
light and freedom
which appears at once
in two bodies

15   and recognizes itself
in both.

Questions for Discussion and Writing

1. How would you paraphrase the ideas expressed in each of the five stanzas? What underlying assumptions explain the conclusions the speaker draws?
2. What images or phrases suggest that the speaker has thought about the issue for a long time and has finally reached a conclusion?
3. Why is the ability to see yourself as you appear from the other's perspective a condition that is only possible with two people, rather than many?
4. In what way does illumination or "light" serve as a CONTROLLING IMAGE in the

development of the poem? How does the change in this image reflect the differences in the way one person relates to another or to a group?

5. Would you rather have one best friend or lover or be popular with an entire group without being intimate with any one person? Explain why.
6. Write the thoughts and feelings of both a boy and a girl who have seen each other and like each other, but have never spoken.

Muriel Rukeyser

Myth

Muriel Rukeyser (1913–1980) lived most of her life in New York and was educated at Vassar College and Columbia University. Although from an affluent background, most of Rukeyser's friends were socialists, labor organizers, or artists, and her poetry from the outset was directed against racial, political, and economic injustice of the kind that led to the execution of the immigrants Sacco and Vanzetti. She began publishing her work in the early 1930s and along with Elizabeth Bishop and Mary McCarthy founded a literary magazine. Her first book of poetry, Theory of Flight *(1935), renounced the artificially poetic in favor of lyrical articulation of personal experience. Her poetry gave voice to the victimized in such volumes as* The Soul and Body of John Brown *(1940) and* The Green Wave *(1948); books that deal directly with social injustice in America and with the atrocities of World War II. Her later volumes,* Body of Waking *(1958),* The Speed of Darkness *(1968),* Breaking Open *(1973), and* The Gates *(1976) oppose the imagery of giving birth to the violence she witnessed and protested against in Korea and in Vietnam. In "Myth" (1973), Rukeyser presents a witty update of the encounter between Oedipus and the Sphinx to point out the limitations of a male-centered perspective.*

Long afterward, Oedipus, old and blinded, walked the
roads.   He smelled a familiar smell.   It was
the Sphinx.   Oedipus said, "I want to ask one question.
Why didn't I recognize my mother?"   "You gave the
wrong answer," said the Sphinx.   "But that was what   5
made everything possible," said Oedipus.   "No," she said.
"When I asked, What walks on four legs in the morning,
two at noon, and three in the evening, you answered,
Man.   You didn't say anything about woman."
"When you say Man," said Oedipus, "you include women   10
too. Everyone knows that."   She said, "That's what
you think."

Questions for Discussion and Writing

1. How does the DICTION of the poem imbue it with its qualities of wit, sarcasm, urbanity, and sophistication? How does this style make the poem seem modern despite the antiquity of the characters involved?
2. What perennial male attitudes does the poem satirize?
3. How is Oedipus's insensitivity made the subject of mockery rather than outright condemnation?
4. How does the visual appearance of the poem reinforce the sense of an ongoing debate between Oedipus and the Sphinx?
5. How is the wrong answer Oedipus gave to the Sphinx connected to his inability to recognize his own mother? To what extent is Oedipus's obtuse male chauvinism still evident in contemporary male attitudes toward females?
6. Write a dialogue in which two very different people emerge through their very different ways of speaking. For example, make one a glib, rapid talker conversing with a taciturn person.

Wole Soyinka

The Lion and the Jewel

Born Akinwande Oluwole Soyinka in 1934 in Abeokuta, Nigeria, Soyinka was educated at University College, Ibadan, Nigeria, and at Leeds University in England where he began his active career as a playwright, political reformer, and social critic. He worked for the Royal Court Theatre in London, where his plays were first produced. Returning to Nigeria, he founded the Orisun Players, a theater group, served as the coeditor of the literary journal Black Orpheus, *and taught drama and comparative literature at the universities of Ibadan, Lagos, and Ife. During the Nigerian civil war, he was imprisoned for two years, an experience he describes in his autobiography,* The Man Died *(1973). Soyinka's amazingly diverse works show him to be a playwright, novelist, poet, and critic of the highest caliber whose writing explores the relationship between African tribal culture and tradition and the pressures of modern society. In 1986 he was awarded the Nobel Prize for literature. Plays of his that have appeared in theaters around the world include* The Swamp Dweller *(1958),* A Dance of Forests *(1960),* Madmen and Specialists *(1970),* Death and the King's Horseman *(1976), and* Requiem for a Futurologist *(1985). Much of Soyinka's dramatic work explores the conflict between deeply rooted Yoruba traditions expressed in myths, religion, and customs, and the consequences of colonial exploitation. His plays often incorporate elements of tragedy, comedy, and farce in a unique combination that is exemplified by* The Lion and the Jewel *(1963). Popular with audiences in Europe and in Nigeria, this ribald comedy invites the audience to enjoy a battle of wits between the crafty and powerful chief of the village (known as Baroka, the "lion") and the beautiful young Sidi (the "jewel").*

CHARACTERS

SIDI   the Village Belle
LAKUNLE   School teacher
BAROKA   The "Bale" of Ilujinle
SADIKU   His head wife
THE FAVOURITE
VILLAGE GIRLS
A WRESTLER
A SURVEYOR
SCHOOLBOYS
ATTENDANTS ON THE "BALE"
Musicians, Dancers, Mummers,
Prisoners, Traders, the VILLAGE.

MORNING

A clearing on the edge of the market, dominated by an immense "odan" tree. It is the village centre. The wall of the bush school flanks the stage on the right, and a rude window opens on to the stage from the wall. There is a chant of the "Arithmetic Times" issuing from this window. It begins a short while before the action begins. Sidi enters from left, carrying a small pail of water on her head. She is a slim girl with plaited hair. A true village belle. She balances the pail on her head with accustomed ease. Around her is wrapped the familiar broad cloth which is folded just above her breasts, leaving the shoulders bare.

Almost as soon as she appears on the stage, the schoolmaster's face also appears at the window. (The chanting continues—"Three times two are six," "Three times three are nine," etc.) The teacher Lakunle, disappears. He is replaced by two of his pupils, aged roughly eleven, who make a buzzing noise at Sidi, repeatedly clapping their hands across the mouth. Lakunle now reappears below the window and makes for Sidi, stopping only to give the boys admonitory whacks on the head before they can duck. They vanish with a howl and he shuts the window on them. The chanting dies away. The schoolmaster is nearly twenty-three. He is dressed in an old-style English suit, threadbare but not ragged, clean but not ironed, obviously a size or two too small. His tie is done in a very small knot, disappearing beneath a shiny black waistcoat. He wears twenty-three-inch-bottom trousers, and blanco-white tennis shoes.

LAKUNLE: Let me take it.

SIDI: No.

LAKUNLE: Let me. (*Seizes the pail. Some water spills on him.*)

SIDI (*delighted.*):
    There. Wet for your pains.
    Have you no shame?

LAKUNLE: That is what the stewpot said to the fire.
    Have you no shame—at your age
    Licking my bottom? But she was tickled
    Just the same.

SIDI: The school teacher is full of stories
    This morning. And now, if the lesson
    Is over, may I have the pail?

LAKUNLE: No. I have told you not to carry loads
    On your head. But you are as stubborn
    As an illiterate goat. It is bad for the spine.
    And it shortens your neck, so that very soon
    You will have no neck at all. Do you wish to look
    Squashed like my pupils' drawings?

SIDI: Why should that worry me? Haven't you sworn
    That my looks do not affect your love?
    Yesterday, dragging your knees in the dust

You said, Sidi, if you were crooked or fat,
And your skin was scaly like a . . .
LAKUNLE: Stop!
SIDI: I only repeat what you said.
LAKUNLE: Yes, and I will stand by every word I spoke.
　　　　But must you throw away your neck on that account?
　　　　Sidi, it is so unwomanly. Only spiders
　　　　Carry loads the way you do.
SIDI (*huffily, exposing the neck to advantage.*):
　　　　Well, it is my neck not your spider.
LAKUNLE (*looks, and gets suddenly agitated.*):
　　　　And look at that! Look, look at that!
　　　　(*Makes a general sweep in the direction of her breasts.*)
　　　　Who was it talked of shame just now?
　　　　How often must I tell you, Sidi, that
　　　　A grown-up girl must cover up her . . .
　　　　Her . . . shoulders? I can see quite . . . quite
　　　　A good portion of—that! And so I imagine
　　　　Can every man in the village. Idlers
　　　　All of them, good-for-nothing shameless men
　　　　Casting their lustful eyes where
　　　　They have no business . . .
SIDI: Are you at that again? Why, I've done the fold
　　　　So high and so tight, I can hardly breathe.
　　　　And all because you keep at me so much.
　　　　I have to leave my arms so I can use them . . .
　　　　Or don't you know that?
LAKUNLE: You could wear something.
　　　　Most modest women do. But you, no.
　　　　You must run about naked in the streets.
　　　　Does it not worry you . . . the bad names,
　　　　The lewd jokes, the tongue-licking noises
　　　　Which girls, uncovered like you,
　　　　Draw after them?
SIDI: This is too much. Is it you, Lakunle,
　　　　Telling me that I make myself common talk?
　　　　When the whole world knows of the madman
　　　　Of Ilujinle, who calls himself a teacher!
　　　　Is it Sidi who makes the men choke
　　　　In their cups, or you, with your big loud words
　　　　And no meaning? You and your ragged books
　　　　Dragging your feet to every threshold
　　　　And rushing them out again as curses
　　　　Greet you instead of welcome. Is it Sidi
　　　　They call a fool—even the children—
　　　　Or you with your fine airs and little sense!

LAKUNLE (*first indignant, then recovers composure.*):
>For that, what is a jewel to pigs?
>If now I am misunderstood by you
>And your race of savages, I rise above taunts
>And remain unruffled.

SIDI (*furious, shakes both fists at him.*):
>O . . . oh, you make me want to pulp your brain.

LAKUNLE (*retreats a little, but puts her aside with a very lofty gesture.*):
>A natural feeling, arising out of envy;
>For, as a woman, you have a smaller brain
>Than mine.

SIDI (*madder still.*):
>Again! I'd like to know
>Just what gives you these thoughts
>Of manly conceit.

LAKUNLE (*very, very patronizing.*):
>No, no. I have fallen for that trick before.
>You can no longer draw me into arguments
>Which go above your head.

SIDI (*can't find the right words, chokes back.*):
>Give me the pail now. And if you ever dare
>To stop me in the streets again . . .

LAKUNLE: Now, now, Sidi . . .

SIDI: Give it or I'll . . .

LAKUNLE (*holds on to her.*):
>Please, don't be angry with me.
>I didn't mean you in particular.
>And anyway, it isn't what I say.
>The scientists have proved it. It's in my books.
>Women have a smaller brain than men
>That's why they are called the weaker sex.

SIDI (*throws him off.*):
>The weaker sex, is it?
>Is it a weaker breed who pounds the yam
>Or bends all day to plant the millet
>With a child strapped to her back?

LAKUNLE: That is all part of what I say.
>But don't you worry. In a year or two
>You will have machines which will do
>Your pounding, which will grind your pepper
>Without it getting in your eyes.

SIDI: O-oh. You really mean to turn
>The whole world upside down.

LAKUNLE: The world? Oh, that. Well, maybe later.
>Charity, they say, begins at home.
>For now, it is this village I shall turn

Inside out. Beginning with that crafty rogue,
Your past master of self-indulgence—Baroka.
SIDI: Are you still on about the Bale?
What has he done to you?
LAKUNLE: He'll find out. Soon enough, I'll let him know.
SIDI: These thoughts of future wonders—do you buy them
Or merely go mad and dream of them?
LAKUNLE: A prophet has honour except
In his own home. Wise men have been called mad
Before me and after, many more shall be
So abused. But to answer you, the measure
Is not entirely of my own coinage.
What I boast is known in Lagos, that city
Of magic, in Badagry where Saro women bathe
In gold, even in smaller towns less than
Twelve miles from here . . . .
SIDI: Well go there. Go to these places where
Women would understand you
If you told them of your plans with which
You oppress me daily. Do you not know
What name they give you here?
Have you lost shame completely that jeers
Pass you over?
LAKUNLE: No. I have told you no. Shame belongs
Only to the ignorant.
SIDI: Well, I am going.
Shall I take the pail or not?
LAKUNLE: Not till you swear to marry me.
(Takes her hand, instantly soulful.)
Sidi, a man must prepare to fight alone.
But it helps if he has a woman
To stand by him, a woman who . . .
Can understand . . . like you.
SIDI: I do?
LAKUNLE: Sidi, my love will open your mind
Like the chaste leaf in the morning, when
The sun first touches it.
SIDI: If you start that I will run away.
I had enough of that nonsense yesterday.
LAKUNLE: Nonsense? Nonsense? Do you hear?
Does anybody listen? Can the stones
Bear to listen to this? Do you call it
Nonsense that I poured the waters of my soul
To wash your feet?
SIDI: You did what!
LAKUNLE: Wasted! Wasted! Sidi, my heart

Bursts into flowers with my love.
But you, you and the dead of this village
Trample it with feet of ignorance.

SIDI (*shakes her head in bafflement.*):
If the snail finds splinters in his shell
He changes house. Why do you stay?

LAKUNLE: Faith. Because I have faith.
Oh Sidi, vow to me your own undying love
And I will scorn the jibes of these bush minds
Who know no better. Swear, Sidi,
Swear you will be my wife and I will
Stand against earth, heaven, and the nine
Hells . . .

SIDI: Now there you go again.
One little thing
And you must chirrup like a cockatoo.
You talk and talk and deafen me
With words which always sound the same
And make no meaning.
I've told you, and I say it again
I shall marry you today, next week
Or any day you name.
But my bride-price must first be paid.
Aha, now you turn away.
But I tell you, Lakunle, I must have
The full bride-price. Will you make me
A laughing-stock? Well, do as you please.
But Sidi will not make herself
A cheap bowl for the village spit.

LAKUNLE: On my head let fall their scorn.

SIDI: They will say I was no virgin
That I was forced to sell my shame
And marry you without a price.

LAKUNLE: A savage custom, barbaric, out-dated,
Rejected, denounced, accursed,
Excommunicated, archaic, degrading,
Humiliating, unspeakable, redundant.
Retrogressive, remarkable, unpalatable.

SIDI: Is the bag empty? Why did you stop?

LAKUNLE: I own only the Shorter Companion
Dictionary, but I have ordered
The Longer One—you wait!

SIDI: Just pay the price.

LAKUNLE (*with a sudden shout.*):
An ignoble custom, infamous, ignominious
Shaming our heritage before the world.

Sidi, I do not seek a wife
To fetch and carry,
To cook and scrub,
To bring forth children by the gross . . .

SIDI: Heaven forgive you! Do you now scorn
Child-bearing in a wife?

LAKUNLE: Of course I do not. I only mean . . .
Oh Sidi, I want to wed
Because I love,
I seek a life-companion . . .
(*pulpit-declamatory.*)
"And the man shall take the woman
And the two shall be together
As one flesh."
Sidi, I seek a friend in need.
An equal partner in my race of life.

SIDI (*attentive no more. Deeply engrossed in counting the beads on her neck.*):
Then pay the price.

LAKUNLE: Ignorant girl, can you not understand?
To pay the price would be
To buy a heifer off the market stall.
You'd be my chattel, my mere property.
No, Sidi! (*very tenderly.*)
When we are wed, you shall not walk or sit
Tethered, as it were, to my dirtied heels.
Together we shall sit at table
—Not on the floor—and eat,
Not with fingers, but with knives
And forks, and breakable plates
Like civilized beings.
I will not have you wait on me
Till I have dined my fill.
No wife of mine, no lawful wedded wife
Shall eat the leavings off my plate—
That is for the children.
I want to walk beside you in the street,
Side by side and arm in arm
Just like the Lagos couples I have seen
High-heeled shoes for the lady, red paint
On her lips. And her hair is stretched
Like a magazine photo. I will teach you
The waltz and we'll both learn the foxtrot
And we'll spend the week-end in night-clubs at Ibadan.
Oh I must show you the grandeur of towns
We'll live there if you like or merely pay visits.
So choose. Be a modern wife, look me in the eye

And give me a little kiss—like this.
(*Kisses her.*)

SIDI (*backs away.*):
No, don't! I tell you I dislike
This strange unhealthy mouthing you perform.
Every time, your action deceives me
Making me think that you merely wish
To whisper something in my ear.
Then comes this licking of my lips with yours.
It's so unclean. And then,
The sound you make—"Pyout!"
Are you being rude to me?

LAKUNLE (*wearily.*):   It's never any use.
Bush-girl you are, bush-girl you'll always be;
Uncivilized and primitive—bush-girl!
I kissed you as all educated men—
And Christians—kiss their wives.
It is the way of civilized romance.

SIDI (*lightly.*):   A way you mean, to avoid
Payment of lawful bride-price.
A cheating way, mean and miserly.

LAKUNLE (*violently.*):   It is not.
(*Sidi bursts out laughing. Lakunle changes his tone to a soulful one,
both eyes dreamily shut.*)
Romance is the sweetening of the soul
With fragrance offered by the stricken heart.

SIDI (*looks at him in wonder for a while.*):
Away with you. The village says you're mad,
And I begin to understand.
I wonder that they let you run the school.
You and your talk. You'll ruin your pupils too
And then they'll utter madness just like you.
(*Noise off-stage.*)
There are people coming
Give me the bucket or they'll jeer.
(*Enter a crowd of youths and drummers, the girls being in various
stages of excitement.*)

FIRST GIRL: Sidi, he has returned. He came back just as
he said he would.

SIDI: Who has?

FIRST GIRL: The stranger. The man from the outside world.
The clown who fell in the river for you.
(*They all burst out laughing.*)

SIDI: The one who rode on the devil's own horse?

SECOND GIRL: Yes, the same. The stranger with the one-eyed box.
(*She demonstrates the action of a camera amidst admiring titters.*)

THIRD GIRL: And he brought his new horse right into the village
   square this time. This one has only two feet. You should
   have seen him. B-r-r-r-r.
   (*Runs around the platform driving an imaginary motor-bike.*)
SIDI: And has he brought . . . ?
FIRST GIRL: The images? He brought them all. There was hardly
   any part of the village which does not show in the book.
   (*Clicks the imaginary shutter.*)
SIDI: The book? Did you see the book?
   Had he the precious book
   That would bestow upon me
   Beauty beyond the dreams of a goddess?
   For so he said.
   The book which would announce
   This beauty to the world—
   Have you seen it?
THIRD GIRL: Yes, yes, he did. But the Bale is still feasting his eyes
   on the images. Oh, Sidi, he was right. You *are* beautiful.
   On the cover of the book is an image of you from here
   (*touches the top of her head*) to here (*her stomach*). And in the
   middle leaves, from the beginning of one leaf right across
   to the end of another, is one of you from head to toe. Do
   you remember it? It was the one for which he made you
   stretch your arms towards the sun. (*Rapturously.*) Oh, Sidi,
   you looked as if, at that moment, the sun himself had
   been your lover. (*They all gasp with pretended shock at this
   blasphemy and one slaps her playfully on the buttocks.*)
FIRST GIRL: The Bale is jealous, but he pretends to be proud of
   you. And when this man tells him how famous you are in
   the capital, he pretends to be pleased, saying how much
   honour and fame you have brought to the village.
SIDI (*with amazement.*):   Is not Baroka's image in the book at all?
SECOND GIRL (*contemptuous.*):   Oh yes, it is. But it would have
   been much better for the Bale if the stranger had omitted
   him altogether. His image is in a little corner somewhere
   in the book, and even that corner he shares with one of
   the village latrines.
SIDI: Is that the truth? Swear! Ask Ogun to
   Strike you dead.
GIRL: Ogun strike me dead if I lie.
SIDI: If that is true, then I am more esteemed
   Than Bale Baroka,
   The Lion of Ilujinle.
   This means that I am greater than
   The Fox of the Undergrowth,
   The living god among men . . .

LAKUNLE (*peevishly.*): And devil among women.

SIDI: Be silent, you.
			You are merely filled with spite.

LAKUNLE: I know him what he is. This is
			Divine justice that a mere woman
			Should outstrip him in the end.

SIDI: Be quiet;
			Or I swear I'll never speak to you again.
			(*Affects sudden coyness.*)
			In fact, I am not so sure I'll want to wed you now.

LAKUNLE: Sidi!

SIDI: Well, why should I?
			Known as I am to the whole wide world,
			I would demean my worth to wed
			A mere village school teacher.

LAKUNLE (*in agony.*): Sidi!

SIDI: And one who is too mean
			To pay the bride-price like a man.

LAKUNLE: Oh, Sidi, don't!

SIDI (*plunging into an enjoyment of Lakunle's misery.*):
			Well, don't you know?
			Sidi is more important even than the Bale.
			More famous than that panther of the trees.
			He is beneath me now—
			Your fearless rake, the scourge of womanhood!
			But now,
			He shares the corner of the leaf
			With the lowest of the low—
			With the dug-out village latrine!
			While I—How many leaves did my own image take?

FIRST GIRL: Two in the middle and . . .

SIDI: No, no. Let the school teacher count!
			How many were there, teacher-man?

LAKUNLE: Three leaves.

SIDI (*threateningly.*): One leaf for every heart that I shall break.
			Beware!
			(*Leaps suddenly into the air.*)
			Hurray! I'm beautiful!
			Hurray for the wandering stranger!

CROWD: Hurray for the Lagos man!

SIDI (*wildly excited.*): I know. Let us dance the dance of the lost
			Traveller.

SHOUTS: Yes, let's.

SIDI: Who will dance the devil-horse?
			You, you, you and you.
			(*The four girls fall out.*)

A python. Who will dance the snake?
Ha ha! Your eyes are shifty and your ways are sly.
(*The selected youth is pushed out amidst jeers.*)
The stranger. We've got to have the being
From the mad outer world . . . You there,
No, you have never felt the surge
Of burning liquor in your milky veins.
Who can we pick that knows the walk of drunks?
You? . . . No, the thought itself
Would knock you out as sure as wine . . . Ah!
(*Turns round slowly to where Lakunle is standing with a kindly,
    fatherly smile for the children at play.*)
Come on book-worm, you'll play his part.

LAKUNLE: No, no. I've never been drunk in all my life.

SIDI: We know. But your father drank so much,
He must have drunk your share, and that
Of his great grandsons.

LAKUNLE (*tries to escape.*):   I won't take part.

SIDI: You must.

LAKUNLE: I cannot stay. It's nearly time to take
Primary four in Geography.

SIDI (*goes over to the window and throws it open.*):
Did you think your pupils would remain in school
Now that the stranger has returned?
The village is on holiday, you fool.

LAKUNLE (*as they drag him towards the platform.*):
No, no. I won't. This foolery bores me.
It is a game of idiots. I have work of more importance.

SIDI (*bending down over Lakunle who has been seated forcibly on the plat-
    form.*):
You are dressed like him
You look like him
You speak his tongue
You think like him
You're just as clumsy
In your Lagos ways—
You'll do for him!

(*This chant is taken up by all and they begin to dance round Lakunle, speaking
the words in a fast rhythm. The drummers join in after the first time, keeping
up a steady beat as the others whirl round their victim. They go faster and
faster and chant faster and faster with each round. By the sixth or seventh,
Lakunle has obviously had enough.*)

LAKUNLE (*raising his voice above the din.*):   All right! I'll do it.
Come now, let's get it over with.

(*A terrific shout and a clap of drums. Lakunle enters into the spirit of the dance with enthusiasm. He takes over from Sidi, stations his cast all over the stage as the jungle, leaves the right top-stage clear for the four girls who are to dance the motor-car. A mime follows of the visitor's entry into Ilujinle, and his short stay among the villagers. The four girls crouch on the floor, as four wheels of a car. Lakunle directs their spacing, then takes his place in the middle, and sits on air. He alone does not dance. He does realistic miming. Soft throbbing drums, gradually swelling in volume, and the four "wheels" begin to rotate the upper halves of their bodies in perpendicular circles. Lakunle clowning the driving motions, obviously enjoying this fully. The drums gain tempo, faster, faster, faster. A sudden crash of drums and the girls quiver and dance the stall. Another effort at rhythm fails, and the "stalling wheels" give a corresponding shudder, finally, and let their faces fall on to their laps. Lakunle tampers with a number of controls, climbs out of the car and looks underneath it. His lips indicate that he is swearing violently. Examines the wheels, pressing them to test the pressure, betrays the devil in him by seizing his chance to pinch the girls' bottoms. One yells and bites him on the ankle. He climbs hurriedly back into the car, makes a final attempt to re-start it, gives it up and decides to abandon it. Picks up his camera and his helmet, pockets a flask of whisky from which he takes a swig, before beginning the trek. The drums resume beating, a different, darker tone and rhythm, varying with the journey. Full use of "gangan" and "iya ilu." The "trees" perform a subdued and unobtrusive dance on the same spot. Details as a snake slithering out of the branches and poising over Lakunle's head when he leans against a tree for a rest. He flees, restoring his nerves shortly after by a swig. A monkey drops suddenly in his path and gibbers at him before scampering off. A roar comes from somewhere, etc. His nerves go rapidly and he recuperates himself by copious draughts. He is soon tipsy, battles violently with the undergrowth and curses silently as he swats the flies off his tortured body.*

Suddenly, from somewhere in the bush comes the sound of a girl singing. The Traveller shakes his head but the sound persists. Convinced he is suffering from sun-stroke, he drinks again. His last drop, so he tosses the bottle in the direction of the sound, only to be rewarded by a splash, a scream and a torrent of abuse, and finally, silence again. He tip-toes, clears away the obstructing growth, blinks hard and rubs his eyes. Whatever he has seen still remains. He whistles softly, unhitches his camera and begins to jockey himself into a good position for a take. Backwards and forwards, and his eyes are so closely glued to the lens that he puts forward a careless foot and disappears completely. There is a loud splash and the invisible singer alters her next tone to a sustained scream. Quickened rhythm and shortly afterwards, amidst sounds of splashes, Sidi appears on the stage, with a piece of cloth only partially covering her. Lakunle follows a little later, more slowly, trying to wring out the water from his clothes. He has lost all his appendages except the camera. Sidi has run right across the stage, and returns a short while later, accompanied by the Villagers. The same cast has disappeared and re-forms behind Sidi as the Villagers. They are in an ugly mood, and in spite of his protests, haul him off to the town centre, in front of the "Odan" tree.

Everything comes to a sudden stop as Baroka the Bale, wiry, goateed, tougher than his sixty-two years, himself emerges at this point from behind the tree. All go down, prostrate or kneeling with the greetings of "Kabiyesi" "Baba" etc. All except Lakunle who begins to sneak off.)

BAROKA:　Akowe. Teacher wa. Misita Lakunle.
　　　　(As the others take up the cry "Misita Lakunle" he is forced to stop. He returns and bows deeply from the waist.)
LAKUNLE:　A good morning to you sir.
BAROKA:　Guru morin guru morin, ngh-hn! That is
　　　　All we get from "alakowe." You call at his house
　　　　Hoping he sends for beer, but all you get is
　　　　Guru morin. Will guru morin wet my throat?
　　　　Well, well our man of knowledge, I hope you have no
　　　　Query for an old man today.
LAKUNLE:　No complaints.
BAROKA:　And we are not feuding in something
　　　　I have forgotten.
LAKUNLE:　Feuding sir? I see no cause at all.
BAROKA:　Well, the play was much alive until I came.
　　　　And now everything stops, and you were leaving
　　　　Us. After all, I knew the story and I came in
　　　　Right on cue. It makes me feel as if I was
　　　　Chief Baseje.
LAKUNLE:　One hardly thinks the Bale would have the time
　　　　For such childish nonsense.
BAROKA:　A-ah Mister Lakunle. Without these things you call
　　　　Nonsense, a Bale's life would be pretty dull.
　　　　Well, now that you say I am welcome, shall we
　　　　Resume your play?
　　　　(Turns suddenly to his attendants.)
　　　　Seize him!
LAKUNLE *(momentarily baffled.):*　What for? What have I done?
BAROKA:　You tried to steal our village maidenhead
　　　　Have you forgotten? If he has, serve him a slap
　　　　To wake his brain.

(An uplifted arm being proffered, Lakunle quickly recollects and nods his head vigorously. So the play is back in performance. The Villagers gather round threatening, clamouring for his blood. Lakunle tries bluff, indignation, appeasement in turn. At a sudden signal from the Bale, they throw him down prostrate on his face. Only then does the Chief begin to show him sympathy, appear to understand the Stranger's plight, and pacify the villagers on his behalf. He orders dry clothes for him, seats him on his right and orders a feast in his honour. The Stranger springs up every second to take photographs of the party, but most of the time his attention is fixed on Sidi dancing with abandon.

Eventually he whispers to the Chief, who nods in consent, and Sidi is sent for. The Stranger arranges Sidi in all sorts of magazine postures and takes innumerable photographs of her. Drinks are pressed upon him; he refuses at first, eventually tries the local brew with scepticism, appears to relish it, and drinks profusely. Before long, however, he leaves the party to be sick. They clap him on the back as he goes out, and two drummers who insist on dancing round him nearly cause the calamity to happen on the spot. However, he rushes out with his hand held to the mouth. Lakunle's exit seems to signify the end of the mime. He returns almost at once and the others discard their roles.)

SIDI (*delightedly.*):   What did I say? You played him to the bone,
       A court jester would have been the life for you,
       Instead of school.
       (*Points contemptuously to the school.*)
BAROKA: And where would the village be, robbed of
       Such wisdom as Mister Lakunle dispenses
       Daily? Who would tell us where we go wrong?
       Eh, Mister Lakunle?
SIDI (*hardly listening, still in the full grip of her excitement.*):
       Who comes with me to find the man?
       But Lakunle, you'll have to come and find sense
       In his clipping tongue. You see book-man
       We cannot really do
       Without your head.
       (*Lakunle begins to protest, but they crowd him and try to bear him down. Suddenly he breaks free and takes to his heels with all the women in full pursuit. Baroka is left sitting by himself—his wrestler, who accompanied him on his entry, stands a respectful distance away—staring at the flock of women in flight. From the folds of his agbada he brings out his copy of the magazine and admires the heroine of the publication. Nods slowly to himself.*)
BAROKA: Yes, yes . . . it is five full months since last
       I took a wife . . . five full months . . .

NOON

A road by the market. Enter Sidi, happily engrossed in the pictures of herself in the magazine. Lakunle follows one or two paces behind carrying a bundle of firewood which Sidi has set out to obtain. They are met in the centre by Sadiku, who has entered from the opposite side. Sadiku is an old woman, with a shawl over her head.

SADIKU: Fortune is with me. I was going to your house to see you.
SIDI (*startled out of her occupation.*):   What! Oh, it is you, Sadiku.
SADIKU: The Lion sent me. He wishes you well.

SIDI: Thank him for me.
  (*Then excitedly.*)
  Have you seen these?
  Have you seen these images of me
  Wrought by the man from the capital city?
  Have you felt the gloss? (*Caresses the page.*)
  Smoother by far than the parrot's breast.

SADIKU: I have. I have. I saw them as soon as the city man
  came . . . Sidi, I bring a message from my lord. (*Jerks
  her head at Lakunle.*) Shall we draw aside a little?

SIDI: Him? Pay no more heed to that
  Than you would a eunuch.

SADIKU: Then, in as few words as it takes to tell, Baroka wants
  you for a wife.

LAKUNLE (*bounds forward, dropping the wood.*):
  What! The greedy dog!
  Insatiate camel of a foolish, doting race;
  Is he at his tricks again?

SIDI: Be quiet, 'Kunle. You get so tiresome.
  The message is for me, not you.

LAKUNLE (*down on his knees at once. Covers Sidi's hands with kisses.*):
  My Ruth, my Rachel, Esther, Bathsheba
  Thou sum of fabled perfections
  From Genesis to the Revelations
  Listen not to the voice of this infidel . . .

SIDI (*snatches her hand away.*):
  Now that's your other game;
  Giving me funny names you pick up
  In your wretched books.
  My name is Sidi. And now, let me be.
  My name is Sidi, and I am beautiful.
  The stranger took my beauty
  And placed it in my hands.
  Here, here it is. I need no funny names
  To tell me of my fame.
  Loveliness beyond the jewels of a throne—
  That is what he said.

SADIKU (*gleefully.*):   Well, will you be Baroka's own jewel?
  Will you be his sweetest princess, soothing him on weary
  nights? What answer shall I give my lord?

SIDI (*wags her finger playfully at the woman.*):
  Ha ha. Sadiku of the honey tongue.
  Sadiku, head of the Lion's wives.
  You'll make no prey of Sidi with your wooing tongue
  Not this Sidi whose fame has spread to Lagos
  And beyond the seas.

(*Lakunle beams with satisfaction and rises.*)

SADIKU: Sidi, have you considered what a life of bliss awaits
you? Baroka swears to take no other wife after you.
Do you know what it is to be the Bale's last wife?
I'll tell you. When he dies—and that should not be long;
even the Lion has to die sometime—well, when he does,
it means that you will have the honour of being the senior
wife of the new Bale. And just think, until Baroka dies,
you shall be his favourite. No living in the outhouses for
you, my girl. Your place will always be in the palace;
first as the latest bride, and afterwards, as the head of the
new harem . . . It is a rich life, Sidi. I know, I have been
in that position for forty-one years.

SIDI: You waste your breath.
Why did Baroka not request my hand
Before the stranger
Brought his book of images?
Why did the Lion not bestow his gift
Before my face was lauded to the world?
Can you not see? Because he sees my worth
Increased and multiplied above his own;
Because he can already hear
The ballad-makers and their songs
In praise of Sidi, the incomparable,
While the Lion is forgotten.
He seeks to have me as his property
Where I must fade beneath his jealous hold.
Ah, Sadiku,
The school-man here has taught me certain things
And my images have taught me all the rest.
Baroka merely seeks to raise his manhood
Above my beauty
He seeks new fame
As the one man who has possessed
The jewel of Ilujinle!

SADIKU (*shocked, bewildered, incapable of making any sense of Sidi's words.*):
But Sidi, are you well? Such nonsense never passed
your lips before. Did you not sound strange, even in your
own hearing? (*Rushes suddenly at Lakunle.*) Is this your
doing, you popinjay? Have you driven the poor girl mad
at last? Such rubbish . . . I will beat your head for this!

LAKUNLE (*retreating in panic.*): Keep away from me, old hag.

SIDI: Sadiku, let him be.
Tell your lord that I can read his mind,
That I will none of him.
Look—judge for yourself.
(*Opens the magazine and points out the pictures.*)

He's old. I never knew till now,
He was that old . . .
(*During the rest of her speech, Sidi runs her hand over the surface of
the relevant part of the photographs, tracing the contours with her
fingers.*)
   . . . To think I took
No notice of my velvet skin.
How smooth it is!
And no man ever thought
To praise the fulness of my breasts . . .
LAKUNLE (*laden with guilt and full of apology.*):
Well, Sidi, I did think . . .
But somehow it was not the proper thing.
SIDI (*ignores the interruption.*):
See I hold them to the warm caress
(*unconsciously pushes out her chest.*)
Of a desire-filled sun.
(*Smiles mischievously.*)
There's a deceitful message in my eyes
Beckoning insatiate men to certain doom.
And teeth that flash the sign of happiness,
Strong and evenly, beaming full of life.
Be just, Sadiku,
Compare my image and your lord's—
An age of difference!
See how the water glistens on my face
Like the dew-moistened leaves on a Harmattan morning
But he—his face is like a leather piece
Torn rudely from the saddle of his horse,
(*Sadiku gasps.*)
Sprinkled with the musty ashes
From a pipe that is long over-smoked.
And this goat-like tuft
Which I once thought was manly;
It is like scattered twists of grass—
Not even green—
But charred and lifeless, as after a forest fire!
Sadiku, I am young and brimming; he is spent.
I am the twinkle of a jewel
But he is the hind-quarters of a lion!
SADIKU (*recovering at last from helpless amazement.*):   May Sango
restore your wits. For most surely some angry god has
taken possession of you. (*Turns around and walks away.
Stops again as she remembers something else.*) Your ranting
put this clean out of my head. My lord says that if you
would not be his wife, would you at least come to supper
at his house tonight. There is a small feast in your honour.

He wishes to tell you how happy he is that the great capital
city has done so much honour to a daughter of Ilujinle.
You have brought great fame to your people.

SIDI: Ho ho! Do you think that I was only born
Yesterday?
The tales of Baroka's little suppers,
I know all.
Tell your lord that Sidi does not sup with
Married men.

SADIKU: They are lies, lies. You must not believe everything
you hear. Sidi, would I deceive you? I swear to you . . .

SIDI: Can you deny that
Every woman who has supped with him one night,
Becomes his wife or concubine the next?

LAKUNLE: Is it for nothing he is called the Fox?

SADIKU (advancing on him.): You keep out of this, or so Sango
be my witness . . .

LAKUNLE (retreats just a little, but continues to talk.):
His wiliness is known even in the larger towns.
Did you never hear
Of how he foiled the Public Works attempt
To build the railway through Ilujinle?

SADIKU: Nobody knows the truth of that. It is all hearsay.

SIDI: I love hearsays. Lakunle, tell me all.

LAKUNLE: Did you not know it? Well sit down and listen.
My father told me, before he died. And few men
Know of this trick—oh he's a die-hard rogue
Sworn against our progress . . . yes . . . it was . . . some-
where here
The track should have been laid just along
The outskirts. Well, the workers came, in fact
It was prisoners who were brought to do
The harder part . . . to break the jungle's back . . .
(Enter the prisoners, guarded by two warders. A white surveyor examines his map (khaki helmet, spats, etc.) The foreman runs up with
his camp stool, table etc., erects the umbrella over him and unpacks
the usual box of bush comforts—soda siphon, whisky bottle and
geometric sandwiches. His map consulted, he directs the sweat team
where to work. They begin felling, matchet swinging, log dragging,
all to the rhythm of the work gang's metal percussion (rod on gong
or rude triangle, etc.) The two performers are also the song leaders
and the others fill the chorus. "N'ijo itoro," "Amuda el'ebe l'aiya"
"Gbe je on'ipa" etc.)

LAKUNLE: They marked the route with stakes, ate
Through the jungle and began the tracks. Trade,
Progress, adventure, success, civilization,
Fame, international conspicuousity . . . it was

All within the grasp of Ilujinle . . .

(*The wrestler enters, stands horrified at the sight and flees. Returns later with the Bale himself who soon assesses the situation.*

They disappear. The work continues, the surveyor occupies himself with the fly-whisk and whisky. Shortly after, a bull-roarer is heard. The prisoners falter a little, pick up again. The bull-roarer continues on its way, nearer and farther, moving in circles, so that it appears to come from all round them. The foreman is the first to break and then the rest is chaos. Sole survivor of the rout is the surveyor who is too surprised to move.

Baroka enters a few minutes later accompanied by some attendants and preceded by a young girl bearing a calabash bowl. The surveyor, angry and threatening, is prevailed upon to open his gift. From it he reveals a wad of pound notes and kola nuts. Mutual understanding is established. The surveyor frowns heavily, rubs his chin and consults his map. Re-examines the contents of the bowl, shakes his head. Baroka adds more money, and a coop of hens. A goat follows, and more money. This time "truth" dawns on him at last, he has made a mistake. The track really should go the other way. What an unfortunate error, discovered just in time! No, no, no possibility of a mistake this time, the track should be much further away. In fact (scooping up the soil) the earth is most unsuitable, couldn't possibly support the weight of a railway engine. A gourd of palm wine is brought to seal the agreement and a kola nut is broken. Baroka's men help the surveyor pack and they leave with their arms round each other followed by the surveyor's booty.)

LAKUNLE (*as the last of the procession disappears, shakes his fist at them, stamping on the ground.*):
Voluptuous beast! He loves this life too well
To bear to part from it. And motor roads
And railways would do just that, forcing
Civilization at his door. He foresaw it
And he barred the gates, securing fast
His dogs and horses, his wives and all his
Concubines . . . ah, yes . . . all those concubines
Baroka has such a selective eye, none suits him
But the best . . .
(*His eyes truly light up. Sidi and Sadiku snigger, tip-toe off stage.*)
    . . . Yes, one must grant him that.
Ah, I sometimes wish I led his kind of life.
Such luscious bosoms make his nightly pillow.
I am sure he keeps a time-table just as
I do at school. Only way to ensure fair play.
He must be healthy to keep going as he does.
I don't know what the women see in him. His eyes
Are small and always red with wine. He must
Possess some secret . . . No! I do not envy him!

Just the one woman for me. Alone I stand
For progress, with Sidi my chosen soul-mate, the one
Woman of my life . . . Sidi! Sidi where are you?
(*Rushes out after them, returns to fetch the discarded firewood and
runs out again.*)

*

(*Baroka in bed, naked except for baggy trousers, calf-length. It is a rich
bedroom covered in animal skins and rugs. Weapons round the
wall. Also a strange machine, a most peculiar contraption with a
long lever. Kneeling beside the bed is Baroka's current Favourite,
engaged in plucking the hairs from his armpit. She does this by first
massaging the spot around the selected hair very gently with her
forefinger. Then, with hardly a break, she pulls out the hair between
her finger and the thumb with a sudden sharp movement. Baroka
twitches slightly with each pull. Then an aspirated "A-ah," and a
look of complete beatitude spreads all over his face.*)

FAVOURITE: Do I improve my lord?

BAROKA: You are still somewhat over-gentle with the pull
As if you feared to hurt the panther of the trees.
Be sharp and sweet
Like the swift sting of a vicious wasp
For there the pleasure lies—the cooling aftermath.

FAVOURITE: I'll learn, my lord.

BAROKA: You have not time, my dear.
Tonight I hope to take another wife.
And the honour of this task, you know,
Belongs by right to my latest choice.
But—A-ah—Now that was sharp.
It had in it the scorpion's sudden sting
Without its poison.
It was an angry pull; you tried to hurt
For I had made you wrathful with my boast.
But now your anger flows in my blood-stream.
How sweet it is! A-ah! That was sweeter still.
I think perhaps that I shall let you stay,
The sole out-puller of my sweat-bathed hairs.
Ach!
(*Sits up suddenly and rubs the sore point angrily.*)
Now that had far more pain than pleasure
Venegeful creature, you did not caress
The area of extraction long enough!
(*Enter Sadiku. She goes down on her knees at once and bows her head
into her lap.*)
Aha! Here comes Sadiku.
Do you bring some balm,

To soothe the smart of my misused armpit?
Away, you enemy!
(*Exit the Favourite.*)
SADIKU: My lord . . .
BAROKA: You have my leave to speak.
What did she say?
SADIKU: She will not, my lord. I did my best, but she will have
none of you.
BAROKA: It follows the pattern—a firm refusal
At the start. Why will she not?
SADIKU: That is the strange part of it. She says you're much
too old. If you ask me, I think that she is really off her head.
All this excitement of the books has been too much for her.
BAROKA (*springs to his feet.*):
She says . . . That I am old
That I am much too old? Did a slight
Unripened girl say this of me?
SADIKU: My Lord, I heard the incredible words with my ears,
and I thought the world was mad.
BAROKA: But is it possible, Sadiku? Is this right?
Did I not, at the festival of Rain,
Defeat the men in the log-tossing match?
Do I not still with the most fearless ones,
Hunt the leopard and the boa at night
And save the farmers' goats from further harm?
And does she say I'm old?
Did I not, to announce the Harmattan,
Climb to the top of the silk-cotton tree,
Break the first pod, and scatter tasselled seeds
To the four winds—and this but yesterday?
Do any of my wives report
A failing in my manliness?
The strongest of them all
Still wearies long before the Lion does!
And so would she, had I the briefest chance
To teach this unfledged birdling
That lacks the wisdom to embrace
The rich mustiness of age . . . if I could once . . .
Come hither, soothe me, Sadiku
For I am wroth at heart.
(*Lies back on the bed, staring up as before. Sadiku takes her place at the
foot of the bed and begins to tickle the soles of his feet. Baroka turns
to the left suddenly, reaches down the side, and comes up with a
copy of the magazine. Opens it and begins to study the pictures. He
heaves a long sigh.*)
That is good, Sadiku, very good.
(*He begins to compare some pictures in the book, obviously his own and*

Sidi's. Flings the book away suddenly and stares at the ceiling for a
second or two. Then, unsmiling.)
　　Perhaps it is as well, Sadiku.
SADIKU:　My lord, what did you say?
BAROKA:　Yes, faithful one, I say it is as well.
　　The scorn, the laughter and the jeers
　　Would have been bitter.
　　Had she consented and my purpose failed,
　　I would have sunk with shame.
SADIKU:　My Lord, I do not understand.
BAROKA:　The time has come when I can fool myself
　　No more. I am no man, Sadiku. My manhood
　　Ended near a week ago.
SADIKU:　The gods forbid.
BAROKA:　I wanted Sidi because I still hoped—
　　A foolish thought I know, but still—I hoped
　　That, with a virgin young and hot within,
　　My failing strength would rise and save my pride.
　　(Sadiku begins to moan.)
　　A waste of hope. I knew it even then.
　　But it's a human failing never to accept
　　The worst; and so I pandered to my vanity.
　　When manhood must, it ends.
　　The well of living, tapped beyond its depth,
　　Dries up, and mocks the wastrel in the end.
　　I am withered and unsapped, the joy
　　Of ballad-mongers, the aged butt
　　Of youth's ribaldry.
SADIKU *(tearfully.)*:　The Gods must have mercy yet.
BAROKA *(as if suddenly aware of her presence, starts up.)*:
　　I have told this to no one but you,
　　Who are my eldest, my most faithful wife.
　　But if you dare parade my shame before the world . . .
　　(Sadiku shakes her head in protest and begins to stroke the soles of his
　　　feet with renewed tenderness. Baroka sighs and falls back slowly.)
　　How irritable I have grown of late
　　Such doubts to harbour of your loyalty . . .
　　But this disaster is too much for one
　　Checked thus as I upon the prime of youth.
　　That rains that blessed me from my birth
　　Number a meagre sixty-two;
　　While my grandfather, that man of teak,
　　Fathered two sons, late on sixty-five.
　　But Okiki, my father beat them all
　　Producing female twins at sixty-seven.
　　Why then must I, descendant of these lions

Forswear my wives at a youthful sixty-two
My veins of life run dry, my manhood gone!
(*His voice goes drowsy; Sadiku sighs and moans and caresses his feet.*
His face lights up suddenly with rapture.)
Sango bear witness! These weary feet
Have felt the loving hands of much design
In women.
My soles have felt the scratch of harsh,
Gravelled hands.
They have borne the heaviness of clumsy,
Gorilla paws.
And I have known the tease of tiny,
Dainty hands,
Toy-like hands that tantalized
My eager senses,
Promised of thrills to come
Remaining
Unfulfilled because the fingers
Were too frail
The touch too light and faint to pierce
The incredible thickness of my soles.
But thou Sadiku, thy plain unadorned hands
Encase a sweet sensuality which age
Will not destroy. A-ah,
Oyayi! Beyond a doubt Sadiku,
Thou art the queen of them all.
(*Falls asleep.*)

NIGHT

The village centre. Sidi stands by the Schoolroom window, admiring her photos as before. Enter Sadiku with a longish bundle. She is very furtive. Unveils the object which turns out to be a carved figure of the Bale, naked and in full detail. She takes a good look at it, bursts suddenly into derisive laughter, sets the figure standing in front of the tree. Sidi stares in utter amazement.

SADIKU: So we did for you too did we? We did for you in the
      end. Oh high and mightly lion, have we really scotched you?
      A—ya-ya-ya . . . we women undid you in the end. I was
      there when it happened to your father, the great Okiki.
      I did for him, I, the youngest and freshest of the wives. I
      killed him with my strength. I called him and he came at
      me, but no, for him, this was not like other times. I, Sadiku,
      was I not flame itself and he the flax on old women's
      spindles? I ate him up! Race of mighty lions, we always

consume you, at our pleasure we spin you, at our whim
we made you dance; like the foolish top you think the
world revolves around you . . . fools! fools! . . . it is you
who run giddy while we stand still and watch, and draw
your frail thread from you, slowly, till nothing is left but
a runty old stick. I scotched Okiki, Sadiku's unopened
treasure-house demanded sacrifice, and Okiki came with
his rusted key. Like a snake he came at me, like a rag
he went back, a limp rag, smeared in shame. . . . (*Her
ghoulish laugh re-possesses her.*) Ah, take warning my
masters, we'll scotch you in the end . . .   (*With a yell she
leaps up, begins to dance round the tree, chanting.*)
Take warning, my masters
We'll scotch you in the end.
(*Sidi shuts the window gently, comes out. Sadiku, as she comes round
again, gasps and is checked in mid-song.*)

SADIKU: Oh it is you my daughter. You should have chosen
a better time to scare me to death. The hour of victory is
no time for any woman to die.

SIDI: Why? What battle have you won?

SADIKU: Not me alone girl. You too. Every woman. Oh my
daughter, that I have lived to see this day . . . To see him
fizzle with the drabbest puff of a mis-primed "sakabula."
(*Resumes her dance.*)
Take warning, my masters
We'll scotch you in the end.

SIDI: Wait Sadiku. I cannot understand.

SADIKU: You will my girl. You will.
Take warning my masters . . .

SIDI: Sadiku, are you well?

SADIKU: Ask no questions my girl. Just join my victory dance.
Oh Sango my lord, who of us possessed your lightning
and ran like fire through that lion's tail . . .

SIDI (*holds her firmly as she is about to go off again.*):
Stop your loose ranting. You will not
Move from here until you make some sense.

SADIKU: Oh you are troublesome. Do you promise to tell no one?

SIDI: I swear it. Now tell me quickly.
(*As Sadiku whispers, her eyes widen.*)
O-ho-o-o-o-!
But Sadiku, if he knew the truth, why
Did he ask me to . . .
(*Again Sadiku whispers.*)
Ha ha! Some hope indeed. Oh Sadiku
I suddenly am glad to be a woman.
(*Leaps in the air.*)

We won! We won! Hurray for womankind!
(*Falls in behind Sadiku.*)
Take warning, my masters
We'll scotch you in the end. (*Lakunle enters unobserved.*)

LAKUNLE: The full moon is not yet, but
The women cannot wait.
They must go mad without it.
(*The dancing stops. Sadiku frowns.*)

SADIKU: The scarecrow is here. Begone fop! This is the world of
women. At this moment our star sits in the centre of the
sky. We are supreme. What is more, we are about to
perform a ritual. If you remain, we will chop you up, we
will make you the sacrifice.

LAKUNLE: What is the hag gibbering?

SADIKU (*advances menacingly.*):   You less than man, you less than
the littlest woman, I say begone!

LAKUNLE (*nettled.*):   I will have you know that I am a man
As you will find out if you dare
To lay a hand on me.

SADIKU (*throws back her head in laughter.*):   You a man? Is Baroka
not more of a man than you? And if he is no longer a man,
then what are you? (*Lakunle, understanding the meaning,
stands rooted, shocked.*) Come on, dear girl, let him look
on if he will. After all, only *men* are barred from watching
this ceremony.
Take warning, my masters
We'll . . .

SIDI: Stop. Sadiku stop. Oh such an idea
Is running in my head. Let me to the palace for
This supper he promised me. Sadiku, what a way
To mock the devil. I shall ask forgiveness
For my hasty words . . . No need to change
My answer and consent to be his bride—he might
Suspect you've told me. But I shall ask a month
To think on it.

SADIKU (*somewhat doubtful.*):   Baroka is no child you know, he
will know I have betrayed him.

SIDI: No, he will not. Oh Sadiku let me go.
I long to see him thwarted, to watch his longing
His twitching hands which this time cannot
Rush to loosen his trouser cords.

SADIKU: You will have to match the Fox's cunning. Use your
bashful looks and be truly repentant. Goad him my child,
torment him until he weeps for shame.

SIDI: Leave it to me. He will never suspect you
of deceit.

SADIKU (*with another of her energetic leaps.*):   Yo-rooo o! Yo-rororo o!
     Shall I come with you?
SIDI: Will that be wise? You forget
     We have not seen each other.
SADIKU: Away then. Away woman. I shall bide here.
     Haste back and tell Sadiku how the no-man is.
     Away, my lovely child.
LAKUNLE (*he has listened with increasing horror.*):
     No, Sidi, don't. If you care
     One little bit for what I feel,
     Do not go to torment the man.
     Suppose he knows that you have come to jeer—
     And he will know, if he is not a fool—
     He is a savage thing, degenerate
     He would beat a helpless woman if he could . . .
SIDI (*running off gleefully.*):   Ta-raa school teacher. Wait here for me.
LAKUNLE (*stamps his foot helplessly.*):
     Foolish girl! . . . And this is all your work.
     Could you not keep a secret?
     Must every word leak out of you
     As surely as the final drops
     Of mother's milk
     Oozed from your flattened breast
     Generations ago?
SADIKU: Watch your wagging tongue, unformed creature!
LAKUNLE: If any harm befalls her . . .
SADIKU: Woman though she is, she can take better care of herself
     than you can of her. Fancy a thing like you actually wanting
     a girl like that, all to your little self. (*Walks round him and
     looks him up and down.*) Ah! Oba Ala is an accommodating
     god. What a poor figure you cut!
LAKUNLE: I wouldn't demean myself to bandy words
     With a woman of the bush.
SADIKU: At this moment, your betrothed is supping
     with the Lion.
LAKUNLE (*pleased at the use of the word "Betrothed."*):
     Well, we are not really betrothed as yet,
     I mean, she is not promised yet.
     But it will come in time, I'm sure.
SADIKU (*bursts into her cackling laughter.*):   The bride-price, is that paid?
LAKUNLE: Mind your own business.
SADIKU: Why don't you do what other men have done? Take a
     farm for a season. One harvest will be enough to pay the
     price, even for a girl like Sidi. Or will the smell of the wet
     soil be too much for your delicate nostrils?
LAKUNLE: I said mind your own business.

SADIKU: A—a—ah. It is true what they say then. You are going to
    convert the whole village so that no one will ever pay the
    bride-price again. Ah, you're a clever man. I must admit
    that it is a good way for getting out of it, but don't you
    think you'd use more time and energy that way than you
    would if . . .

LAKUNLE (*with conviction.*):   Within a year or two, I swear,
    This town shall see a transformation
    Bride-price will be a thing forgotten
    And wives shall take their place by men.
    A motor road will pass this spot.
    And bring the city ways to us.
    We'll buy saucepans for all the women
    Clay pots are crude and unhygienic
    No man shall take more wives than one
    That's why they're impotent too soon.
    The ruler shall ride cars, not horses
    Or a bicycle at the very least.
    We'll burn the forest, cut the trees
    Then plant a modern park for lovers
    We'll print newspapers every day
    With pictures of seductive girls.
    The world will judge our progress by
    The girls that win beauty contests.
    While Lagos builds new factories daily
    We only play "ayo" and gossip.
    Where is our school of Ballroom dancing?
    Who here can throw a cocktail party?
    We must be modern with the rest
    Or live forgotten by the world
    We must reject the palm wine habit.
    And take to tea, with milk and sugar.
    (*Turns on Sadiku who has been staring at him in terror. She retreats,
        and he continues to talk down at her as they go round, then down
        and off-stage, Lakunle's hectoring voice trailing away in the
        distance.*)
    This is my plan, you withered face
    And I shall start by teaching you.
    From now you shall attend my school
    And take your place with twelve-year-olds.
    For though you're nearly seventy,
    Your mind is simple and unformed.
    Have you no shame that at your age,
    You neither read nor write nor think?
    You spend your days as senior wife,
    Collecting brides for Baroka.

And now because you've sucked him dry,
You send my Sidi to his shame. . . .
(*The scene changes to Baroka's bedroom. On the left in a one-knee-on-floor posture, two men are engaged in a kind of wrestling, their arms clasped round each other's waist, testing the right moment to leave. One is Baroka, the other a short squat figure of apparent muscular power. The contest is still in the balanced stage. In some distant part of the house, Sidi's voice is heard lifted in the familiar general greeting, addressed to no one in particular.*)

SIDI: A good day to the head and people
Of this house.
(*Baroka lifts his head, frowns as if he is trying to place the voice.*)
A good day to the head and people
Of this house.
(*Baroka now decides to ignore it and to concentrate on the contest. Sidi's voice draws progressively nearer. She enters nearly backwards, as she is still busy admiring the room through which she has just passed. Gasps on turning round to see the two men.*)

BAROKA (*without looking up.*):   Is Sadiku not at home then?

SIDI (*absent-mindedly.*):   Hm?

BAROKA: I asked, is Sadiku not at home?

SIDI (*recollecting herself, she curtsys quickly.*):   I saw no one, Baroka.

BAROKA: No one? Do you mean there was no one
To bar unwanted strangers from my privacy?

SIDI (*retreating.*):   The house . . . seemed . . . empty.

BAROKA: Ah, I forget. This is the price I pay
Once every week, for being progressive.
Prompted by the school teacher, my servants
Were prevailed upon to form something they call
The Palace Workers' Union. And in keeping
With the habits—I am told—of modern towns,
This is their day off.

SIDI (*seeing that Baroka seems to be in a better mood, she becomes somewhat bolder. Moves forward—saucily.*):
Is this also a day off
For Baroka's wives?

BAROKA (*looks up sharply, relaxes and speaks with a casual voice.*):
No, the madness has not gripped them—yet.
Did you not meet with one of them?

SIDI: No, Baroka. There was no one about.

BAROKA: Not even Ailatu, my favourite?
Was she not at her usual place,
Beside my door?

SIDI (*absently. She is deeply engrossed in watching the contest.*):
Her stool is there. And I saw
The slippers she was embroidering.

BAROKA: Hm. Hm. I think I know
    Where she'll be found. In a dark corner
    Sulking like a slighted cockroach.
    By the way, look and tell me
    If she left her shawl behind.
    (*So as not to miss any part of the tussle, she moves backwards, darts a
        quick look round the door and back again.*)

SIDI: There is a black shawl on the stool

BAROKA (*a regretful sigh.*):
    Then she'll be back tonight. I had hoped
    My words were harsh enough
    To free me from her spite for a week or more.

SIDI: Did Ailatu offend her husband?

BAROKA: Offend? My armpit still weeps blood
    For the gross abuse I suffered from one
    I called my favourite.

SIDI (*in a disappointed voice.*):
    Oh. Is that all?

BAROKA: Is that not enough? Why child?
    What more could the woman do?

SIDI: Nothing. Nothing, Baroka. I thought perhaps—
    Well—young wives are known to be—
    Forward—sometimes—to their husbands.

BAROKA: In an ill-kept household perhaps. But not
    Under Baroka's roof. And yet,
    Such are the sudden spites of women
    That even I cannot foresee them all.
    And child—if I lose this little match
    Remember that my armpit
    Burns and itches turn by turn.
    (*Sidi continues watching for some time, then clasps her hand over her
        mouth as she remembers what she should have done to begin with.
        Doubtful how to proceed, she hesitates for some moments, then
        comes to a decision and kneels.*)

SIDI: I have come, Bale, as a repentant child.

BAROKA: What?

SIDI (*very hesitantly, eyes to the floor, but she darts a quick look up
        when she thinks the Bale isn't looking.*):
    The answer which I sent to the Bale
    Was given in a thoughtless moment . . .

BAROKA: Answer, child? To what?

SIDI: A message brought by . . .

BAROKA (*groans and strains in a muscular effort.*):
    Will you say that again? It is true that for supper
    I did require your company. But up till now
    Sadiku has brought no reply.

SIDI (*amazed.*):   But the other matter! Did not the Bale
        Send . . . did Baroka not send . . . ?

BAROKA (*with sinister encouragement.*):
        What did Baroka not, my child?

SIDI (*cowed, but angry, rises.*):
        It is nothing, Bale. I only hope
        That I am here at the Bale's invitation.

BAROKA (*as if trying to understand, he frowns as he looks at her.*):
        A-ah, at last I understand. You think
        I took offence because you entered
        Unannounced?

SIDI: I remember that the Bale called me
        An unwanted stranger.

BAROKA: That could be expected. Is a man's bedroom
        To be made naked to any flea
        That chances to wander through?
        (*Sidi turns away, very hurt.*)
        Come, come, my child. You are too quick
        To feel aggrieved. Of course you are
        More than welcome. But I expected Ailatu
        To tell me you were here.
        (*Sidi curtsys briefly with her back to Baroka. After a while, she turns
            round. The mischief returns to her face. Baroka's attitude of denial
            has been a set-back but she is now ready to pursue her mission.*)

SIDI: I hope the Bale will not think me
        Forward. But, like everyone, I had thought
        The Favourite was a gentle woman.

BAROKA: And so had I.

SIDI (*slyly.*):   One would hardly think that *she*
        Would give offence without a cause.
        Was the Favourite . . . in some way . . .
        Dissatisfied . . . with her lord and husband?
        (*With a mock curtsy, quickly executed as Baroka begins to look up.*)

BAROKA (*slowly turns towards her.*):
                                Now that
        Is a question which I never thought to hear
        Except from a school teacher. Do you think
        The Lion has such leisure that he asks
        The whys and wherefores of a woman's
        Squint?
        (*Sidi steps back and curtsys. As before, and throughout this scene, she
            is easily cowed by Baroka's change of mood, all the more easily as
            she is, in any case, frightened by her own boldness.*)

SIDI: I meant no disrespect . . .

BAROKA (*gently.*):   I know. (*Breaks off.*) Christians on my
        Father's shrines, child!
        Do you think I took offence? A—aw

Come in and seat yourself. Since you broke in
Unawares, and appear resolved to stay,
Try, if you can, not to make me feel
A humourless old ram. I allow no one
To watch my daily exercise, but as we say,
The woman gets lost in the woods one day
And every wood deity dies the next.
(*Sidi curtsys, watches and moves forward warily, as if expecting the
two men to spring apart too suddenly.*)

SIDI: I think he will win.

BAROKA: Is that a wish, my daughter?

SIDI: No, but—(*Hesitates, but boldness wins.*)
                     If the tortoise cannot tumble
It does not mean that he can stand.
(*Baroka looks at her, seemingly puzzled. Sidi turns away, humming.*)

BAROKA: When the child is full of riddles, the mother
                Has one water-pot the less.
(*Sidi tiptoes to Baroka's back and pulls asses' ears at him.*)

SIDI: I think he will win.

BAROKA: He knows he must. Would it profit me
                To pit my strength against a weakling?
                Only yesterday, this son of—I suspect—
                A python for a mother, and fathered beyond doubt
                By a blubber-bottomed baboon,
                (*The complimented man grins.*)
                Only yesterday, he nearly
                Ploughed my tongue with my front teeth
                In a friendly wrestling bout.

WRESTLER (*encouraged, makes an effort.*): Ugh. Ugh.

SIDI (*bent almost over them. Genuinely worried.*):
                Oh! Does it hurt?

BAROKA: Not yet . . . but, as I was saying
                I change my wrestlers when I have learnt
                To throw them. I also change my wives
                When I have learnt to tire them.

SIDI: And is this another . . . changing time
          For the Bale?

BAROKA: Who knows? Until the finger nails
                Have scraped the dust, no one can tell
                Which insect released his bowels.
                (*Sidi grimaces in disgust and walks away. Returns as she thinks up a
                new idea.*)

SIDI: A woman spoke to me this afternoon.

BAROKA: Indeed. And does Sidi find this unusual—
                That a woman speak with her in the afternoon?

SIDI (*stamping.*): No. She had the message of a go-between.

BAROKA: Did she? Then I rejoice with you.

(*Sidi stands biting her lips. Baroka looks at her, this time with deliberate appreciation.*)
And now I think of it, why not?
There must be many men who
Build their loft to fit your height.

SIDI (*unmoving, pointedly.*): Her message came from one
With many lofts.

BAROKA: Ah! Such is the greed of men.

SIDI: If Baroka were my father
(*aside*)—which many would take him to be—
(*Makes a rude sign.*)
Would he pay my dowry to this man
And give his blessings?

BAROKA: Well, I must know his character.
For instance, is the man rich?

SIDI: Rumour has it so.

BAROKA: Is he repulsive?

SIDI: He is old. (*Baroka winces.*)

BAROKA: Is he mean and miserly?

SIDI: To strangers—no. There are tales
Of his open-handedness, which are never
Quite without a motive. But his wives report
—To take one little story—
How he grew the taste for ground corn
And pepper—because he would not pay
The price of snuff!
(*With a sudden burst of angry energy, Baroka lifts his opponent and throws him over his shoulder.*)

BAROKA: A lie! The price of snuff
Had nothing to do with it.

SIDI (*too excited to listen.*): You won!

BAROKA: By the years on my beard, I swear
They slander me!

SIDI (*excitedly.*): You won. You won!
(*She breaks into a kind of shoulder dance and sings.*)
Yokolu Yokolu. Ko ha tan bi
Iyawo gb'oko san'le
Oko yo'ke . . .
(*She repeats this throughout Baroka's protests. Baroka is pacing angrily up and down. The defeated man, nursing a hip, goes to the corner of the room and lifts out a low "ako" bench. He sits on the floor, and soon, Baroka joins him; using only their arms now, they place their elbows on the bench and grip hands. Baroka takes his off again, replaces it, takes it off again and so on during the rest of his outburst.*)

BAROKA: This means nothing to me of course. Nothing!
But I know the ways of women, and I know

Their ruinous tongues.
Suppose that, as a child—only suppose—
Suppose then, that as a child, I—
And remember, I only use myself
To illustrate the plight of many men . . .
So, once again, suppose that as a child
I grew to love "tanfiri"—with a good dose of pepper
And growing old, I found that—
Sooner than die away, my passion only
Bred itself upon each mouthful of
Ground corn and pepper I consumed.
Now, think child, would it be seemly
At my age, and the father of children,
To be discovered, in public
Thrusting fistfuls of corn and pepper
In my mouth? Is it not wise to indulge
In the little masquerade of a dignified
Snuff-box?—But remember, I only make
A pleading for this prey of women's
Malice. I feel his own injustice,
Being myself, a daily fellow-sufferer!
(*Baroka seems to realize for the first time that Sidi has paid no attention
to his explanation. She is, in fact, still humming and shaking her
shoulders. He stares questioningly at her. Sidi stops, somewhat
confused and embarrassed, points sheepishly to the wrestler.*)

SIDI: I think this time he will win.
(*Baroka's grumbling subsides slowly. He is now attentive to the present bout.*)

BAROKA: Now let us once again take up
The questioning. (*Almost timidly.*) Is this man
Good and kindly?

SIDI: They say he uses well
His dogs and horses.

BAROKA (*desperately.*):
Well is he fierce then? Reckless!
Does the bush cow run to hole
When he hears his beaters' Hei-ei-wo-rah!

SIDI: There are heads and skins of leopards
Hung around his council room.
But the market is also
Full of them.

BAROKA: Is he not wise? Is he not sagely?
Do the young and old not seek
His counsel?

SIDI: The Fox is said to be wise
So cunning that he stalks and dines on
New-hatched chickens.

BAROKA (*more and more desperate.*):
>Does he not beget strength on wombs?
>Are his children not tall and stout-limbed?

SIDI: Once upon a time.

BAROKA: Once upon a time?
>What do you mean, girl?

SIDI: Just once upon a time.
>Perhaps his children have of late
>Been plagued with shyness and refuse
>To come into the world. Or else
>He is so tired with the day's affairs
>That at night, he turns his buttocks
>To his wives. But there have been
>No new reeds cut by his servants,
>No new cots woven.
>And his household gods are starved
>For want of child-naming festivities
>Since the last two rains went by.

BAROKA: Perhaps he is a frugal man.
>Mindful of years to come,
>Planning for a final burst of life, he
>Husbands his strength.

SIDI (*giggling. She is actually stopped, half-way, by giggling at the cleverness of her remark.*):
>To husband his wives surely ought to be
>A man's first duties—at all times.

BAROKA: My beard tells me you've been a pupil,
>A most diligent pupil of Sadiku.
>Among all shameless women,
>The sharpest tongues grow from that one
>Peeling bark—Sadiku, my faithful lizard!
>(*Growing steadily warmer during this speech, he again slaps down his opponent's arm as he shouts "Sadiku."*)

SIDI (*backing away, aware that she has perhaps gone too far and betrayed knowledge of the "secret."*):
>I have learnt nothing of anyone.

BAROKA: No more. No more.
>Already I have lost a wrestler
>On your account. This town-bred daring
>Of little girls, awakes in me
>A seven-horned devil of strength.
>Let one woman speak a careless word
>And I can pin a wriggling—Bah!
>(*Lets go the man's arm. He has risen during the last speech but held on to the man's arm, who is forced to rise with him.*)
>The tappers should have called by now.
>See if we have a fresh gourd by the door.

(*The wrestler goes out. Baroka goes to sit on the bed, Sidi eyeing him,*
   doubtfully.)
What an ill-tempered man I daily grow
Towards. Soon my voice will be
The sand between two grinding stones.
But I have my scattered kindliness
Though few occasions serve to herald it.
And Sidi, my daughter, you do not know
The thoughts which prompted me
To ask the pleasure that I be your host
This evening. I would not tell Sadiku,
Meaning to give delight
With the surprise of it. Now, tell me, child
Can you guess a little at this thing?

SIDI: Sadiku told me nothing.

BAROKA: You are hasty with denial. For how indeed
    Could Sadiku, since I told her
    Nothing of my mind. But, my daughter,
    Did she not, perhaps . . . invent some tale?
    For I know Sadiku loves to be
    All-knowing.

SIDI: She said no more, except the Bale
    Begged my presence.

BAROKA (*rises quickly to the bait.*):
    Begged? Bale Baroka begged?
    (*Wrestler enters with gourd and calabash-cups. Baroka relapses.*)
    Ah! I see you love to bait your elders.
    One way the world remains the same,
    The child still thinks she is wiser than
    The cotton head of age.
    Do you think Baroka deaf or blind
    To little signs? But let that pass.
    Only, lest you fall victim to the schemes
    Of busy women, I will tell you this—
    I know Sadiku plays the match-maker
    Without the prompting. If I look
    On any maid, or call her name
    Even in the course of harmless, neighbourly
    Well-wishing—How fares your daughter?
    —Is your sister now recovered from her
    Whooping cough?—How fast your ward
    Approaches womanhood! Have the village lads
    Begun to gather at your door?—
    Or any word at all which shows I am
    The thoughtful guardian of the village health,
    If it concerns a woman, Sadiku straightway
    Flings herself into the role of go-between

And before I even don a cap, I find
Yet another stranger in my bed!

SIDI: It seems a Bale's life
Is full of great unhappiness.

BAROKA: I do not complain. No, my child
I accept the sweet and sour with
A ruler's grace. I lose my patience
Only when I meet with
The new immodesty with women.
Now, my Sidi, you have not caught
This new and strange disease, I hope.

SIDI (*curtsying.*): The threading of my smock—
Does Baroka not know the marking
Of the village loom?

BAROKA: But will Sidi, the pride of mothers,
Will she always wear it?

SIDI: Will Sidi, the proud daughter of Baroka,
Will she step out naked?
(*A pause. Baroka surveys Sidi in an almost fatherly manner and she
bashfully drops her eyes.*)

BAROKA: To think that once I thought,
Sidi is the eye's delight, but
She is vain, and her head
Is feather-light, and always giddy
With a trivial thought. And now
I find her deep and wise beyond her years.
(*Reaches under his pillow, brings out the now familiar magazine, and
also an addressed envelope. Retains the former and gives her the
envelope.*)
Do you know what this means?
The trim red piece of paper
In the corner?

SIDI: I know it. A stamp. Lakunle receives
Letters from Lagos marked with it.

BAROKA (*obviously disappointed.*):
Hm. Lakunle. But more about him
Later. Do you know what it means—
This little frippery?

SIDI (*very proudly.*):
Yes. I know that too. Is it not a tax on
The habit of talking with paper?

BAROKA: Oh. Oh. I see you dip your hand
Into the pockets of the school teacher
And retrieve it bulging with knowledge.
(*Goes to the strange machine, and pulls the lever up and down.*)
Now this, not even the school teacher can tell

What magic this performs. Come nearer,
It will not bite.

SIDI: I have never seen the like.

BAROKA: The work dear child, of the palace blacksmiths
Built in full secrecy. All is not well with it—
But I will find the cause and then Ilujinle
Will boast its own tax on paper, made with
Stamps like this. For long I dreamt it
And here it stands, child of my thoughts.

SIDI (*wonder-struck.*): You mean . . . this will work some day?

BAROKA: Ogun has said the word. And now my girl
What think you of that image on the stamp
This spiderwork of iron, wood and mortar?

SIDI: Is it not a bridge?

BAROKA: It is a bridge. The longest—so they say
In the whole country. When not a bridge,
You'll find a print of groundnuts
Stacked like pyramids,
Or palm trees, or cocoa-trees, and farmers
Hacking pods, and workmen
Felling trees and tying skinned logs
Into rafts. A thousand thousand letters
By road, by rail, by air,
From one end of the world to another,
And not one human head among them;
Not one head of beauty on the stamp?

SIDI: But I once saw Lakunle's letter
With a head of bronze.

BAROKA: A figurehead, my child, a lifeless work
Of craft, with holes for eyes, and coldness
For the warmth of life and love
In youthful cheeks like yours,
My daughter . . .
(*Pauses to watch the effect on Sidi.*)
. . . Can you see it, Sidi?
Tens of thousands of these dainty prints
And each one with this legend of Sidi.
(*Flourishes the magazine, open in the middle.*)
The village goddess, reaching out
Towards the sun, her lover.
Can you see it, my daughter!
(*Sidi drowns herself totally in the contemplation, takes the magazine
but does not even look at it. Sits on the bed.*)

BAROKA (*very gently.*):
I hope you will not think it too great
A burden, to carry the country's mail

All on your comeliness.
(*Walks away, an almost business-like tone.*)
                    Our beginnings will
Of course be modest. We shall begin
By cutting stamps for our own village alone.
As the schoolmaster himself would say—
Charity begins at home.
(*Pause. Faces Sidi from nearly the distance of the room.*)
                    For a long time now,
The town-dwellers have made up tales
Of the backwardness of Ilujinle
Until it hurts Baroka, who holds
The welfare of his people deep at heart.
Now, if we do this thing, it will prove more
Than any single town has done!

(*The wrestler, who has been listening open-mouthed, drops his cup in admiration. Baroka, annoyed, realizing only now in fact that he is still in the room, waves him impatiently out.*)

I do not hate progress, only its nature
Which makes all roofs and faces look the same.
And the wish of one old man is
That here and there,
(*Goes progressively towards Sidi, until he bends over her, then sits beside her on the bed.*)
Among the bridges and the murderous roads,
Below the humming birds which
Smoke the face of Sango, dispenser of
The snake-tongue lightning; between this moment
And the reckless broom that will be wielded
In these years to come, we must leave
Virgin plots of lives, rich decay
And the tang of vapour rising from
Forgotten heaps of compost, lying
Undisturbed . . . But the skin of progress
Masks, unknown, the spotted wolf of sameness . . .
Does sameness not revolt your being,
My daughter?
(*Sidi is capable only of a bewildered nod, slowly.*)
BAROKA (*sighs, hands folded piously on his lap.*):
I find my soul is sensitive, like yours,
Indeed, although there is one—no more think I—
One generation between yours and mine,
Our thoughts fly crisply through the air
And meet, purified, as one.

And our first union
Is the making of this stamp.
The one redeeming grace on any paper-tax
Shall be your face. And mine,
The soul behind it all, worshipful
Of Nature for her gift of youth
And beauty to our earth. Does this
Please you, my daughter?

SIDI: I can no longer see the meaning, Baroka.
Now that you speak
Almost like the school teacher, except
Your words fly on a different path,
I find . . .

BAROKA: It is a bad thing, then, to sound
Like your school teacher?

SIDI: No Bale, but words are like beetles
Boring at my ears, and my head
Becomes a jumping bean. Perhaps after all,
As the school teacher tells me often,
(*Very miserably.*)
I have a simple mind.

BAROKA (*pats her kindly on the head.*):
No, Sidi, not simple, only straight and truthful
Like a fresh-water reed. But I do find
Your school teacher and I are much alike.
The proof of wisdom is the wish to learn
Even from children. And the haste of youth
Must learn its temper from the gloss
Of ancient leather, from a strength
Knit close along the grain. The school teacher
And I, must learn one from the other.
Is this not right?
(*A tearful nod.*)

BAROKA: The old must flow into the new, Sidi,
Not blind itself or stand foolishly
Apart. A girl like you must inherit
Miracles which age alone reveals.
Is this not so?

SIDI: Everything you say, Bale,
Seems wise to me.

BAROKA: Yesterday's wine alone is strong and blooded, child,
And though the Christians' holy book denies
The truth of this, old wine thrives best
Within a new bottle. The coarseness
Is mellowed down, and the rugged wine
Acquires a full and rounded body . . .

Is this not so—my child?

(*Quite overcome, Sidi nods.*)

BAROKA: Those who know little of Baroka think

His life one pleasure-living course.

But the monkey sweats, my child,

The monkey sweats,

It is only the hair upon his back

Which still deceives the world . . .

(*Sidi's head falls slowly on the Bale's shoulder. The Bale remains in his final body-weighed-down-by-burdens-of-State attitude.*

Even before the scene is completely shut off a crowd of dancers burst in at the front and dance off at the opposite side without slackening pace. In their brief appearance it should be apparent that they comprise a group of female dancers pursuing a masked male. Drumming and shouts continue quite audibly and shortly afterwards. They enter and re-cross the stage in the same manner.

The shouts fade away and they next appear at the market clearing. It is now full evening. Lakunle and Sadiku are still waiting for Sidi's return. The traders are beginning to assemble one by one, ready for the evening market. Hawkers pass through with oil-lamps beside their ware. Food sellers enter with cooking-pots and foodstuffs, set up their "adogan" or stone hearth, and build a fire.

All this while, Lakunle is pacing wretchedly, Sadiku looks on placidly.)

LAKUNLE (*he is pacing furiously.*):

He's killed her.

I warned you. You know him,

And I warned you.

(*Goes up all the approaches to look.*)

She's been gone half the day. It will soon

Be daylight. And still no news.

Women have disappeared before.

No trace. Vanished. Now we know how.

(*Checks, turns round.*)

And why!

Mock an old man, will you? So?

You can laugh? Ha ha! You wait.

I'll come and see you

Whipped like a dog. Baroka's head wife

Driven out of the house for plotting

With a girl.

(*Each approaching footstep brings Lakunle to attention, but it is only a hawker or a passer-by. The wrestler passes. Sadiku greets him familiarly. Then, after he has passed, some significance of this breaks on Sadiku and she begins to look a little puzzled.*)

LAKUNLE: I know he has dungeons. Secret holes

Where a helpless girl will lie

And rot for ever. But not for nothing

Was I born a man. I'll find my way
To rescue her. She little deserves it, but
I shall risk my life for her.

(*The mummers can now be heard again, distantly. Sadiku and Lakunle
become attentive as the noise approaches, Lakunle increasingly
uneasy. A little, but not too much notice is paid by the market
people.*)

What is that?

SADIKU: If my guess is right, it will be mummers.

(*Adds slyly.*)

Somebody must have told them the news.

LAKUNLE: What news?

(*Sadiku chuckles darkly and comprehension breaks on the School
teacher.*)

Baroka! You dared . . . ?
Woman, is there no mercy in your veins?
He gave you children, and he stood
Faithfully by you and them.
He risked his life that you may boast
A warrior-hunter for your lord . . . But you—
You sell him to the rhyming rabble
Gloating in your disloyalty . . .

SADIKU (*calmly dips her hand in his pocket.*):
Have you any money?

LAKUNLE (*snatching out her hand.*):
Why? What? . . . Keep away, witch! Have you
Turned pickpocket in your dotage?

SADIKU: Don't be a miser. Will you let them go without
giving you a special performance?

LAKUNLE: If you think I care for their obscenity . . .

SADIKU (*wheedling.*):   Come on, school teacher. They'll expect
it of you . . . The man of learning . . . the young sprig of
foreign wisdom . . . You must not demean yourself in
their eyes . . . you must give them money to perform for
your lordship . . .

(*Re-enter the mummers, dancing straight though [more centrally this time] as
before. Male dancer enters first, pursued by a number of young women and
other choral idlers. The man dances in tortured movements. He and about half
of his pursuers have already danced off-stage on the opposite side when Sadiku
dips her hand briskly in Lakunle's pocket, this time with greater success. Before
Lakunle can stop her, she has darted to the drummers and pressed a coin apiece
on their foreheads, waving them to possession of the floor. Tilting their heads
backwards, they drum her praises. Sadiku denies the credit, points to Lakunle
as the generous benefactor. They transfer their attention to him where he
stands biting his lips at the trick. The other dancers have now been brought
back and the drummers resume the beat of the interrupted dance. The treasurer*

removes the coins from their foreheads and places them in a pouch. Now begins the dance of virility which is of course none other than the Baroka story. Very athletic movements. Even in his prime, "Baroka" is made a comic figure, held in a kind of tolerant respect by his women. At his decline and final downfall, they are most unsparing in their taunts and tantalizing motions. Sadiku has never stopped bouncing on her toes through the dance, now she is done the honour of being invited to join at the kill. A dumb show of bashful refusals, then she joins them, reveals surprising agility for her age, to the wild enthusiasm of the rest who surround and spur her on.

With "Baroka" finally scotched, the crowd dances away to their incoming movement, leaving Sadiku to dance on oblivious of their departure. The drumming becomes more distant and she unwraps her eyelids. Sighs, looks around her and walks contentedly towards Lakunle. As usual he has enjoyed the spectacle in spite of himself, showing especial relish where "Baroka" gets the worst of it from his women. Sadiku looks at him for a moment while he tries to replace his obvious enjoyment with disdain. She shouts "Boo" at him, and breaks into a dance movement, shakes a sudden leg at Lakunle.)

SADIKU: Sadiku of the duiker's feet . . . that's what the men
                used to call me. I could twist and untwist my waist with
                the smoothness of a water snake. . . .
LAKUNLE: No doubt. And you are still just as slippery.
                I hope Baroka kills you for this.
                When he finds out what your wagging tongue
                Has done to him, I hope he beats you
                Till you choke on your own breath . . .
                (*Sidi bursts in, she has been running all the way. She throws herself on
                    the ground against the tree and sobs violently, beating herself on
                    the ground.*)
SADIKU (*on her knees beside her.*):   Why, child. What is the matter?
SIDI (*pushes her off.*):
                Get away from me. Do not touch me.
LAKUNLE (*with a triumphant smile, he pulls Sadiku away and takes her
                place.*):
                Oh, Sidi, let me kiss your tears . . .
SIDI (*pushes him so hard that he sits down abruptly.*):
                Don't touch me.
LAKUNLE (*dusting himself.*):
                He must have beaten her.
                Did I not warn you both?
                Baroka is a creature of the wilds,
                Untutored, mannerless, devoid of grace.
                (*Sidi only cries all the more, beats on the ground with clenched fists
                    and stubs her toes in the ground.*)
                Chief though he is,
                I shall kill him for this . . .
                No. Better still, I shall demand

Redress from the central courts.
I shall make him spend
The remainder of his wretched life
In prison—with hard labour.
I'll teach him
To beat defenceless women . . .

SIDI (*lifting her head.*):
Fool! You little fools! It was a lie.
The frog. The cunning frog!
He lied to you, Sadiku.

SADIKU: Sango forbid!

SIDI: He told me . . . afterwards, crowing.
It was a trick.
He knew Sadiku would not keep it to herself,
That I, or maybe other maids would hear of it
And go to mock his plight.
And how he laughed!
How his frog-face croaked and croaked
And called me little fool!
Oh how I hate him! How I loathe
And long to kill the man!

LAKUNLE (*retreating.*): But Sidi, did he . . . ? I mean . . .
Did you escape?
(*Louder sobs from Sidi.*)
Speak, Sidi, this is agony.
Tell me the worst; I'll take it like a man.
Is it the fright which effects you so,
Or did he . . . ? Sidi, I cannot bear the thought.
The words refuse to form.
Do not unman me, Sidi. Speak
Before I burst in tears.

SADIKU (*raises Sidi's chin in her hand.*):
Sidi, are you a maid or not?
(*Sidi shakes her head violently and bursts afresh in tears.*)

LAKUNLE: The Lord forbid!

SADIKU: Too late for prayers. Cheer up. It happens to the best
of us.

LAKUNLE: Oh heavens, strike me dead!
Earth, open up and swallow Lakunle.
For he no longer has the wish to live.
Let the lightning fall and shrivel me
To dust and ashes . . .
(*Recoils.*)
No, that wish is cowardly. This trial is my own.
Let Sango and his lightning keep out of this. It
Is my cross, and let it not be spoken that
In the hour of need, Lakunle stood

Upon the scales and was proved wanting.
My love is selfless—the love of spirit
Not of flesh.
(*Stands over Sidi.*)
Dear Sidi, we shall forget the past.
This great misfortune touches not
The treasury of my love.
But you will agree, it is only fair
That we forget the bride-price totally
Since you no longer can be called a maid.
Here is my hand; if on these terms,
You'll be my cherished wife.
We'll take an oath, between us three
That this shall stay
A secret to our dying days . . .
(*Takes a look at Sadiku and adds quickly.*)
Oh no, a secret even after we're dead and gone.
And if Baroka dares to boast of it,
I'll swear he is a liar—and swear by Sango too!
(*Sidi raises herself slowly, staring at Lakunle with unbelieving
      eyes. She is unsmiling, her face a puzzle.*)

SIDI: You would? You would marry me?

LAKUNLE (*puffs out his chest.*):   Yes.
(*Without a change of expression, Sidi dashes suddenly off the stage.*)

SADIKU: What on earth has got into her?

LAKUNLE: I wish I knew
She took off suddenly
Like a hunted buck.
(*Looks off-stage.*)
I think—yes, she is,
She is going home.
Sadiku, will you go?
Find out if you can
What she plans to do.
(*Sadiku nods and goes. Lakunle walks up and down.*)
And now I know I am the biggest fool
That ever walked this earth.
There are women to be found
In every town or village in these parts,
And every one a virgin.
But I obey my books.
(*Distant music. Light drums, flutes, box-guitars, "sekere."*)
"Man takes the fallen woman by the hand"
And ever after they live happily.
Moreover, I will admit,
It solves the problem of her bride-price too.

> A man must live or fall by his true
> Principles. That, I had sworn,
> Never to pay.
> (*Enter Sadiku.*)

SADIKU: She is packing her things. She is gathering her clothes
and trinkets together, and oiling herself as a bride does
before her wedding.

LAKUNLE: Heaven help us! I am not impatient.
Surely she can wait a day or two at least.
There is the asking to be done,
And then I have to hire a praise-singer,
And such a number of ceremonies
Must firstly be performed.

SADIKU: Just what I said but she only laughed at me and called
me a . . . a . . . what was it now . . . a bra . . . braba . . .
brabararian. It serves you right. It all comes of your
teaching. I said what about the asking and the other
ceremonies. And she looked at me and said, leave all that
nonsense to savages and brabararians.

LAKUNLE: But I must prepare myself.
I cannot be
A single man one day and a married one the next.
It must come gradually.
I will not wed in haste.
A man must have time to prepare,
To learn to like the thought.
I must think of my pupils too:
Would they be pleased if I were married
Not asking their consent . . . ?
(*The singing group is now audible even to him.*)
What is that? The musicians?
Could they have learnt so soon?

SADIKU: The news of a festivity travels fast. You ought to
know that.

LAKUNLE: The goddess of malicious gossip
Herself must have a hand in my undoing.
The very spirits of the partial air
Have all conspired to blow me, willy-nilly
Down the slippery slope of grim matrimony.
What evil have I done . . . ? Ah, here they come!
(*Enter crowd and musicians.*)
Go back. You are not needed yet. Nor ever.
Hence parasites, you've made a big mistake.
There is no one getting wedded; get you home.
(*Sidi now enters. In one hand she holds a bundle, done up in a rich-
ly embroidered cloth: in the other the magazine. She is radiant,*

jewelled, lightly clothed, and wears light leather-thong sandals.
They all go suddenly silent except for the long-drawn O-Ohs
of admiration. She goes up to Lakunle and hands him the book.)

SIDI: A present from Sidi.
        I tried to tear it up
        But my fingers were too frail.
        (*To the crowd.*)
        Let us go.
        (*To Lakunle.*)
        You may come too if you wish,
        You are invited.

LAKUNLE (*lost in the miracle of transformation.*):
        Well I should hope so indeed
        Since I am to marry you.

SIDI (*turns round in surprise.*):
        Marry who . . . ? You thought . . .
        Did you really think that you, and I . . .
        Why, did you think that after him,
        I could endure the touch of another man?
        I who have felt the strength,
        The perpetual youthful zest
        Of the panther of the trees?
        And would I choose a watered-down,
        A beardless version of unripened man?

LAKUNLE (*bars her way.*):
        I shall not let you.
        I shall protect you from yourself.

SIDI (*gives him a shove that sits him down again, hard against the tree base.*):
        Out of my way, book-nourished shrimp.
        Do you see what strength he has given me?
        That was not bad. For a man of sixty,
        It was the secret of God's own draught
        A deed for drums and ballads.
        But you, at sixty, you'll be ten years dead!
        In fact, you'll not survive your honeymoon . . .
        Come to my wedding if you will. If not . . .
        (*She shrugs her shoulders. Kneels down at Sadiku's feet.*)
        Mother of brides, your blessing . . .

SADIKU (*lays her hand on Sidi's head.*):   I invoke the fertile gods.
        They will stay with you. May the time come soon when
        you shall be as round-bellied as a full moon in a low sky.

SIDI (*hands her the bundle.*):
        Now bless my wordly goods.
        (*Turns to the musicians.*)
        Come, sing to me of seeds
        Of children, sired of the lion stock.
        (*The Musicians resume their tune. Sidi sings and dances.*)

Mo te'ni. Mo te'ni.
Mo te'ni. Mo te'ni.
Sun mo mi, we mo mi
Sun mo mi, fa mo mi
Yarabi lo m'eyi t'o le d'omo . . .

(Festive air, fully pervasive. Oil lamps from the market multiply as traders desert their stalls to join them. A young girl flaunts her dancing buttocks at Lakunle and he rises to the bait. Sadiku gets in his way as he gives chase. Tries to make him dance with her. Lakunle last seen, having freed himself of Sadiku, clearing a space in the crowd for the young girl.
The crowd repeat the song after Sidi.)

Tolani Tolani
T'emi ni T'emi ni
Sun mo mi, we mo mi
Sun mo mi, fa mo mi
Yarabi lo m'eyi t'o le d'omo.

Questions for Discussion and Writing

1. In the opening scene, how does the argument over tribal customs versus urbanized western values serve to characterize Sidi and Lakunle? Why haven't they married?
2. How does the DIALOGUE between Sidi and Lakunle suggest Sidi's narcissism and Lakunle's pedantry?
3. What impact did the picture the white photographer took of Sidi have on Baroka and on Sidi herself?
4. Why does Sidi turn down Baroka's offer of marriage (as presented by Sadiku) and even refuse to have supper with him?
5. How does Lakunle's report of how Baroka outsmarted colonial surveyors depict Baroka as a defender of tribal values?
6. Why does Baroka tell his gossipy eldest wife, Sadiku, about his "impotence"?
7. What role does Baroka's distinctive use of METAPHORS and FIGURES OF SPEECH play in his seduction of Sidi?
8. How does Sidi's dismissal of Lakunle represent the victory of tribal values over western ones?
9. Where in the play does IRONY contribute to the humor of any particular scene?
10. Using an interesting photograph of yourself and/or a relative or friend, recreate the events at the time the picture, either posed or candid, was taken. Describe the circumstances under which the picture was taken and the memories triggered by this photograph.
11. Having never seen a bicycle, the people in the community describe it as an "iron horse." Describe some commonplace object (for example, piano, word processor, toilet, refrigerator, roller-blades, comb) as if you were the proverbial visitor from Mars. Speculate on its possible function.

WRITING ABOUT LANGUAGE

STYLE embodies the author's unique vision of his or her material and is established by the writer's choice of words, or DICTION; SYNTAX, or how the author arranges phrases, sentences, and paragraphs; and FIGURATIVE LANGUAGE, or how he or she uses IMAGERY and METAPHORS. The expressive and emotional qualities of language result from the use of figurative rather than literal images, sensitivity to the sounds of words and rhythm of phrases, and an emphasis on the CONNOTATIVE rather than the DENOTATIVE meaning of words.

Although style encompasses a complete range of linguistic resources of diction, syntax, rhythm, and imagery, TONE refers to the narrator's or speaker's attitude toward the characters and events depicted in the story. Whether sympathetic, indifferent, amused, disapproving, or outraged, the tone encourages the reader to feel a certain way about the work and even a slight shift in tone may alter the reader's perception. For example, when the narrator in Viktoria Tokareva's "Nothing Special" says that "officially Margo was considered a single mother, though it was more correct grammatically to say unwed mother. If a woman has a child, and especially such a beautiful and precious one as Sashechka, she's definitely not single," we are encouraged to be sympathetic toward Margo and her child, and scorn pedantic moralists. Tone invites the reader to share the writer's response to the subject. It can be developed through word choice, as in Tokareva, through imagery, or through irony. When the narrator in Talat Abbasi's "Facing the Light" says of her husband's oiled and curled mustache, "like a pair of wings dipped in a rosy sunset! and as surely as a pair of wings ever did fly she can tell that mustache will fly tonight," the reader is encouraged to feel the narrator's scorn. The metaphor instills a sense of sympathy for the wife and a shared feeling with the narrator's perception of her philandering husband.

IRONY is one of the most easily recognizable expressions of tone. Irony results from a clash between appearance and reality, expectation and outcome, or when there is a discrepancy between the literal meaning of words and the intent. VERBAL IRONY conveys the opposite of what is said, either through UNDERSTATEMENT or OVERSTATEMENT (HYPERBOLE). For example, when the narrator in Henri Lopes's "The Esteemed Representative" describes the protagonist's visit to a bar to pick up a girl, we read "the honorable representative Ngouakou-Ngouakou is one of the humblest men in the world. He is a child of the proletariat and has no fear of renewing his relations with the masses. He ordered drinks." The understated sarcasm strips away the pompous facade of the protagonist and encourages a hostile attitude toward Ngouakou-

478

Ngouakou. The story develops SITUATIONAL or DRAMATIC IRONY in scenes that contrast the protagonist's oppressive treatment of his wife and children with the grand speech he has delivered in public that day.

One useful approach in planning an essay on language, style, and tone is to define first the characteristics of the writer's style and then to analyze the extent to which the writer's diction, syntax, rhythm, and imagery contribute to our impression of the characters and incidents.

Effective poetry has the capacity to reveal new insights into common human emotions and to open new vistas of perception in ways that are both compelling and artistically satisfying. Poems rely on the carefully selected, concentrated use of words that appeal to the senses and are capable of evoking a range of emotional associations. That is, poets rely on CONNOTATIVE rather than simply the DENOTATIVE meaning of words. For example, the connotations of "the house blinked out" in Baca's poem suggests an impression of futility and hopelessness that gives the reader more insight than would the factually correct denotative phrase "the lights in the house went out."

Another way poets use language to communicate the emotional overtones of experiences is through IMAGERY. Images can be either LITERAL or FIGURATIVE. Literal images convey sensory impressions through straightforward, concrete representations through which the reader shares the sight, taste, touch, and sound described (for example, when Baca writes "but often the lights will dim weakly/in storms"). By contrast, when the poet compares a literal image to something else, the writer is using language figuratively to express an abstract idea through concrete means. If the comparison is explicit and involves the words "like" or "as" it is called a SIMILE. If the comparison equates things that are essentially unlike each other but eliminates comparative words, it is called a METAPHOR. We can see both operating in Baca's "Spliced Wire" ("my words I gave you/like soft warm toast in the early morning./I brewed your tongue to a rich dark coffee, and drank my fill"). Imagery acts as a kind of bridge to make the abstract tangible, the unfamiliar accessible, and opens the subjective realm of feeling to empathetic imagination. Imagery enables the reader to participate in the emotions of the speaker.

A single image that dominates an entire poem is called a CONTROLLING IMAGE as, for example, Adrienne Rich's "Your Small Hands" is ruled by the image of a woman's hands, and in Rosario Castellanos's "Chess," the image of a chess game encompasses the subordinate image.

In creating the overall effect of the poem, the sound the words create is as important as the imagery and the emotional associations these images call to mind. The stylistic analysis of sound and rhythm in poetry is known as PROSODY. Poets use patterns of sound and rhythm to create emotional involvement.

They do this in four ways: (1) by varying the pitch, tempo, and intensity of sounds; (2) by introducing patterns of repetition of consonants and vowels known respectively as ALLITERATION (as in the phrase "buried in black" in Cofer's poem) and ASSONANCE (as in the phrase "house blinked out" in Baca's poem); (3) by using RHYME and METER in various forms (such as ballad, sonnet, couplet); and (4) by introducing pauses known as CAESAURAE and by strategically placed moments of emphasis, as Rich does in "Your Small Hands," in the lines "your small hands, precisely equal to my own—/ only the thumb is larger, longer—in these hands . . ."

In writing about language in poetry try to understand why you like the poem. You might describe how it affects you. Explain the feelings or ideas the poem communicates, and discuss why the poet's use of language is striking or memorable. Is the poem one you feel you will remember for a long time? Explain why you feel as you do, quoting from the poem to support your statements. What connotations heighten the emotional impact of the poem? You might consider the connection between the subject of the poem and the imagery through which the subject is depicted and analyze which images are literal and which are figurative. Does the poem contain a controlling image to which other images are subordinated? When you read the poem aloud does it have a definite rhythm? You might wish to mark stressed syllables in the poem and underline repetitive sound patterns. How do they create a sense of progression and movement and make the poem more effective?

In drama, the language the audience hears as the conversation between characters is known as dramatic DIALOGUE. To be effective, dialogue must give full and coherent expression to each character's thoughts and feelings, thereby delineating that character to the audience. It is through the dialogue that the playwright presents the conflict that advances the plot. As one character converses and argues with another, the dialogue sets up a pattern of assertion and counterassertion that reveals the conflict at the heart of the play. For example, the argument between Lakunle, the schoolmaster, and Sidi, the village beauty, in the opening scene of Wole Soyinka's *The Lion and the Jewel*, turns on Lakunle's unwillingness to pay "the full bride-price" and Sidi's refusal to marry him until he does.

In writing an essay that analyzes the playwright's use of language you might wish to concentrate on how the dialogue acts to define the characters, and how each character's speech is particularly suited to him or her. For example, what qualities in Soyinka's play communicate Sidi's narcissism, Lakunle's pedantry, and Baroka's shrewdness? You might choose to analyze one scene in depth to show how the pattern of assertion and denial reveals the conflict between opposing motivations, views, and desires in ways that advance the plot.

As in analyzing fiction or poetry, you might explain how the characters' use of certain figures of speech, metaphors, or images define them as individuals (as when Baroka says, "What an ill-tempered man I daily grow / Towards. Soon my voice will be / The sand between two grinding stones"). In what terms can the author's language be characterized—highly figurative or symbolic? abstract? colloquial? What are the sources, if any, of verbal humor? Is it used for contrast, diversion, satire? If it is satiric, what is being mocked?

Connections

1. How do the works by Saad and Tokareva illuminate how unequal distribution of social status and power between the sexes leads to differences in speech between men and women? You might wish to compare how women's speech in these works takes the form of avoiding confrontation, phrasing observations in passive form, exaggerated politeness, and talking around the issues as ways of negotiating with the authority of the male characters in the stories. You might wish to compare this kind of speech to the interaction between Oedipus and the Sphinx in Rukeyser's poem, and to that between the female characters and the chief in Soyinka's play.

2. How does the male perspective of the speaker in Baca's poem present a quite different viewpoint of the breakup of a relationship from the female perspective of the speaker in Castellanos's poem? How does Akhmatova's account of her brief, passionate affair in "Cinque" provide a different perspective on the end of a relationship?

3. What cultural differences can you observe between separation and divorce as represented in Talat Abbasi's story set in Pakistan and in Shirley Saad's "Amina" set in Lebanon?

4. What similarities can you discover in the husbands' attitudes toward their wives in "Facing the Light" and in "The Esteemed Representative"? What different cultural attitudes about the status of women in Pakistan and in the Republic of the Congo can you infer from these stories?

5. How do the works "Facing the Light," "The Esteemed Representative," "The Poetess," and "The Woman Who Was Left at the Altar" explore the issue of living arrangements forced upon women by men?

6. To what extent do the three stories written by men in this chapter ("The Lion," "The Esteemed Representative," and "The Red Boots") differ from those written by women in terms of the extent to which they support or criticize underlying patriarchal values in their respective societies?

7. How do both el-Saadawi's essay and Rich's poem explore in different contexts and cultures the issue of violence against women?

8. How do both Soucy's story and Fabiani's poem explore the tension between an outer-controlled and staid existence and the protagonists' rebellion against this atmosphere of predictability?

9. How is the color red in "The Red Boots" and in "The Esteemed Representative" a depiction of danger, excitement, sexuality, and unpredictability that exemplifies an aspect of women that is threatening to men?

10. How does the archetype of the "lion" change in the different contexts in which it appears in "Myth," "The Lion," and The Lion and the Jewel and how does the depiction of the "lion" express each of the three authors' attitudes toward the opposite sex?

11. What characterizes the speech of women who have power? How does the speech of women in "The Esteemed Representative," "The Red Boots," "Nothing Special," "Cinque," "Your Small Hands," "Myth," "Chess," "The Woman Who Was Left at the Altar," and *The Lion and the Jewel* display features of mockery, irony, directness, control, and confidence?

12. To what extent is the expression of anger conditioned by gender role? Analyze circumstances where anger would be warranted, whether or not it is expressed, and if so by whom in "Facing the Light," "The Esteemed Representative," "Nothing Special," "The Poetess," "The Woman Who Was Left at the Altar" and "The Mutilated Half."

13. How do both poems, "Your Small Hands" by Adrienne Rich and "Myth" by Muriel Rukeyser, appropriate and subvert the dominant masculine perspective?

14. How do the authors of the works in this chapter—set in Egypt, Lebanon, Pakistan, Republic of the Congo, Mexico, Italy, and Nigeria—dramatize the extent to which these cultures give authority and value to the roles and activities of men, exclude women from social and political power, and limit them to exercising power from behind the scenes in a separate domestic realm?

15. "The Red Boots" and *The Lion and the Jewel* draw an equivalence between women having beauty and being powerful. To what extent do these works also show that men's attitudes toward beautiful women is of the trophy mentality, as ornaments that reflect their own power?

16. Discuss how Lopes and Poniatowska each satirize the sexual double standard and male chauvinism in their respective cultures of the Republic of the Congo and Mexico.

17. What opposing views are dramatized by Soyinka in his play and Poniatowska in her story as regards polygamy and polyandry?

4

Class

> *"I used to think I was poor. Then they told me I wasn't poor, I was needy.
> Then they told me it was self-defeating to think of myself as needy, I was
> deprived. Then they told me deprived was a bad image, I was underprivileged.
> Then they told me underprivileged was overused, I was disadvantaged. I still
> don't have a dime. But I sure have a great vocabulary."*
>
> — Jules Feiffer

> *"A hungry man is an angry man."*
>
> — James Howell

Every society is capable of being characterized in terms of social class. Although principles by which class is identified vary widely from culture to culture, from the amount of money you earn in the United States to what kind of accent you speak with in England to what religious caste you are born into in India, class serves to set boundaries around individuals in terms of opportunities and possibilities. Conflicts based on inequalities of social class are often intertwined with those of race because minorities usually receive the least amount of education, have less political clout, earn the least income, and find work in occupations considered menial without the possibility of advancement. Class conditions our entire lives by setting limitations that determine, more than we might like to admit, who we can be friends with, what our goals are, and even who we can marry.

Selections in this chapter take up the crucial and often unrecognized relationships among race, sense of identity, and class, through works of fiction and nonfiction that explore positions of power and powerlessness. The Croatian writer, Slavenka Drakulić, in her essay "Pizza in Warsaw, Torte in Prague," reveals how obtaining common foods reflects widely different economic circumstances between Eastern Europe and the United States. An essay by the Native American writer, Linda Hogan, "Hearing Voices," explains how Hogan, a Chickasaw, sees poetry as a means to reaffirm the human value of Native Americans marginalized in American society.

A timeless story, "Désirée's Baby" by Kate Chopin, explores conflicts of class and racism in turn-of-the-century Louisiana. An offbeat story by Australian writer Murray Bail, "The Drover's Wife," tells of a

483

successful dentist whose wife runs off with a cattle drover. Catherine Lim in "Paper" tells how the lure of easy money destroys a couple's life in Singapore. Krishnan Varma in "The Grass-Eaters," creates a shocking depiction of homelessness in modern-day Calcutta, and Sheila Roberts in "The Weekenders" reveals how class loyalty prevents a rape victim from identifying her attackers in a story set in South Africa. Rosanna Yamagiwa Alfaro in "Professor Nakashima and Tomiko the Cat" describes how a Japanese-American professor, denied tenure, reevaluates his relationship with friends for whom he is house-sitting. The spoiled children of an upper-middle-class black family make life a living hell for their new housekeeper in Ntozake Shange's "Betsey Brown." Fernando Sorrentino in "The Life of the Party" shows how a couple on the cocktail party circuit in Buenos Aires discourage social climbing would-be friends.

The poems continue this chapter's exploration of class, sense of identity, and self-esteem in various countries. The voices heard in these poems are those of men and women of different races and several nations.

From Germany, Mascha Kaléko, in "Mannequins," contrasts the meager backstage life of fashion models with their glamorous public image. Léon Damas from French Guiana in "Hiccup" recreates his mother's litany of complaints regarding his failings to mimic white social etiquette. Ana Castillo, a poet whose work reflects the experiences of Mexican-Americans, in "Napa, California," creates a moving appeal for migrant workers to achieve dignity through their labor. Yannis Ritsos, a popular Greek poet, in "Greek Carters" defines the timeless character of Greek workers. Linda Hogan, of the Chickasaw Indian tribe, explores, in "Workday," the profound social gulf between the world of Native Americans and the dominant white values of the university community where she teaches. John Agard, in "Listen Mr Oxford Don," creates a mocking tribute to the upper-class language patterns the British sought to impose on Guyana.

Playwright Dario Fo's dark comedy, *We Won't Pay! We Won't Pay!*, depicts what happens when a typical law-abiding worker in modern-day Italy has to face the fact that his wife has been stealing food to make ends meet and that those with power do not have his best interests at heart.

Slavenka Drakulić

Pizza in Warsaw, Torte in Prague

Slavenka Drakulić is a leading Croatian journalist and novelist. Her insightful commentary on East European affairs first appeared in her columns in the magazine Danas *published in Zagreb. She is a regular contributor to* The Nation, The New Republic, *and* The New York Times Magazine. *Drakulić is the author of a novel,* Holograms of Fear *(1992), and several works of nonfiction, including* How We Survived Communism and Even Laughed *(1991), from which "Pizza in Warsaw, Torte in Prague" is taken. Her recent book of essays,* The Balkan Express *(1993), presents a heartfelt account of the war involving Serbia, Croatia, and Bosnia-Herzegovina from which she escaped to live in New York. "Pizza in Warsaw, Torte in Prague" offers an incisive analysis of what day-to-day life was like in eastern Europe under communism.*

We were hungry, so I said "Let's have a pizza!" in the way you would think of it in, say, New York, or any West European city—meaning "Let's go to a fast-food place and grab something to eat." Jolanta, a small, blond, Polish translator of English, looked at me thoughtfully, as if I were confronting her with quite a serious task. "There are only two such places," she said in an apologetic tone of voice. Instantly, I was overwhelmed by the guilt of taking pizza in Poland for granted. "Drop it," I said. But she insisted on this pizza place. "You must see it," she said. "It's so different from the other restaurants in Warsaw."

We were lucky because we were admitted without reservations. This is a privately owned restaurant, one of the very few. We were also lucky because we could afford a pizza and beer here, which cost as much as dinner in a fancy hotel. The restaurant was a small, cozy place, with just two wooden tables and a few high stools at the bar—you couldn't squeeze more than twenty people in, even if you wanted to.

It was raining outside, a cold winter afternoon in Warsaw. Once inside, everything was different: two waiters dressed in impeccable white shirts, with bow ties and red aprons, a bowl of fresh tropical fruit on the bar, linen napkins and the smell of pizza baked in a real charcoal-fired oven. Jolanta and I were listening to disco music, eating pizza, and drinking Tuborg beer from long, elegant glasses. Perhaps this is what you pay for, the feeling that you are somewhere else, in a different Warsaw, in a dreamland where there is everything—pizza, fruit juice, thick grilled steaks, salads—and the everyday life of shortages and poverty can't seep in, at least, for the moment.

Yet to understand just how different this place is, one has to see a "normal" coffee shop, such as the one in the modernistic building of

485

concrete and glass that we visited the same day. Inside neon lights flicker, casting a ghostly light on the aluminum tables and chairs covered with plastic. This place looks more like a bus terminal than like a *kawiarnia*. It's almost empty and the air is thick with cigarette smoke. A bleached blond waitress slowly approaches us with a very limited menu: tea, some alcoholic beverages, Coke, coffee. "With milk?" I ask.

5   "No milk," she shakes her head.

6   "Then, can I get a fruit juice perhaps?" I say, in the hopes of drinking just one in a Polish state-owned restaurant.

7   "No juice." She shakes her head impatiently (at this point, of course, there is no "sophisticated" question about the kind of juice one would perhaps prefer). I give up and get a cup of coffee. It's too sweet. Jolanta is drinking Coke, because there is Coke everywhere—in the middle of Warsaw as, I believe, in the middle of the desert. There may be neither milk nor water, but there is sure to be a bottle of Coke around. Nobody seems to mind the paradox that even though fruit grows throughout Poland, there is no fruit juice yet Coke is everywhere. But here Coke, like everything coming from America, is more of a symbol than a beverage.

8   To be reduced to having Coke and pizza offered not only as fancy food, but, what's more, as the idea of choice, strikes me as a form of imperialism, possibly only where there is really very little choice. Just across the street from the private restaurant, where Jolanta parked her tiny Polski Fiat, is a grocery store. It is closed in the afternoon, so says a handwritten note on the door. Through the dusty shop window we can see the half-empty shelves, with a few cans of beans, pasta, rice, cabbage, vinegar. A friend, a Yugoslav living in Warsaw, told me that some years ago vinegar and mustard were almost all you could find in the stores. At another point, my friend noticed that shelves were stocked with prune compote. One might easily conclude that this is what Poles probably like the best or why else would it be in stores in such quantities? But the reason was just the opposite: Prune compote was what they had, not what they liked. However, the word "like" is not the best way to explain the food situation (or any situation) in Poland. Looking at a shop window where onions and garlic are two of the very few items on display, what meaning could the word "like" possibly have?

9   Slowly, one realizes that not only is this a different reality, but that words have a different meaning here, too. It makes you understand that the word "like" implies not only choice but refinement, even indulgence, *savoir-vivre*—in fact, a whole different attitude toward food. It certainly doesn't imply that you stuff yourself with whatever you find at the farmer's market or in a grocery that day. Instead, it suggests a certain experience, a knowledge, a possibility of comparing quality and taste. Right after the overthrow of the Ceausescu government in Romania in December 1989, I read a report in the newspaper about life

in Bucharest. There was a story about a man who ate the first banana in his life. He was an older man, a worker, and he said to a reporter shyly that he ate a whole banana, together with the skin, because he didn't know that he had to peel it. At first, I was moved by the isolation this man was forced to live in, by the fact that he never read or even heard what to do with a banana. But then something else caught my attention: "It *tasted good*," he said. I can imagine this man, holding a sweet-smelling, ripe banana in his hand, curious and excited by it, as by a forbidden fruit. He holds it for a moment, then bites. It tastes strange but "good." It must have been good, even together with a bitter, tough skin, because it was something unachievable, an object of desire. It was not a banana that he was eating, but the promise, the hope of the future. So, he liked it no matter what its taste.

One of the things one is constantly reminded of in these parts is not to be thoughtless with food. I remember my mother telling me that I had to eat everything in front of me, because to throw away food would be a sin. Perhaps she had God on her mind, perhaps not. She experienced World War II and ever since, like most of the people in Eastern Europe, she behaves as if it never ended. Maybe this is why they are never really surprised that even forty years afterwards there is a lack of sugar, oil, coffee, or flour. To be heedless—to behave as if you are somewhere else, where everything is easy to get—is a sin not against God, but against people. Here you have to think of food, because it has entirely diverse social meanings. To bring a cake for dessert when you are invited for a dinner—a common gesture in another, more affluent country—means you invested a great deal of energy to find it if you didn't make it yourself. And even if you did, finding eggs, milk, sugar, and butter took time and energy. That makes it precious in a very different way from if you had bought it in the pastry shop next door.

When Jaroslav picked me up at Prague airport, I wanted to buy a torte before we went to his house for dinner. It was seven o'clock in the evening and shops were already closed. Czechs work until five or six, which doesn't leave much time to shop. "The old government didn't like people walking in the streets. It might cause them trouble," said Jaroslav, half joking. "Besides, there isn't much to buy anyway." My desire to buy a torte after six o'clock appeared to be quite an extravagance, and it was clear that one couldn't make a habit of bringing a cake for dessert. In the Slavia Café there were no pastries at all, not to mention a torte. The best confectioner in Prague was closed, and in the Hotel Zlatá Husa restaurant a waitress repeated "Torte?" after us as if we were in the wrong place. Then she shook her head. With every new place, my desire to buy a torte diminished. Perhaps it is not that there are no tortes—it's just hard to find them at that hour. At the end, we went to the only shop open until eight-thirty and bought ice cream. There were three kinds and Jaroslav picked vanilla, which is what his boys like the best.

12   On another occasion, in the Bulgarian capital Sofia, Evelina is preparing a party. I am helping her in the small kitchen of the decaying apartment that she shares with a student friend, because as an assistant professor at the university, she cannot afford to rent an apartment alone. I peel potatoes, perhaps six pounds of them. She will make a potato salad with onions. Then she will bake the rest of them in the oven and serve them with . . . actually nothing. She calls it "a hundred-ways potato party"—sometimes humor is the only way to overcome depression. There are also four eggs for an omelet and two cans of sardines (imported from Yugoslavia), plus vodka and wine, and that's it, for the eight people she has invited.

13   We sit around her table: a Bulgarian theater director who lives in exile in Germany, three of Evelina's colleagues from the university, a historian friend and her husband, and the two of us. We eat potatoes with potatoes, drink vodka, discuss the first issue of the opposition paper *Demokratia*, the round-table talks between the Union of Democratic Forces and the communist government, and calculate how many votes the opposition will get in the forthcoming free elections—the first. Nobody seems to mind that there is no more food on the table—at least not as long as a passionate political discussion is going on. "*This* is our food," says Evelina. "We are used to swallowing politics with our meals. For breakfast you eat elections, a parliament discussion comes for lunch, and at dinner you laugh at the evening news or get mad at the lies that the Communist Party is trying to sell, in spite of everything." Perhaps these people can live almost without food—either because it's too expensive or because there is nothing to buy, or both—without books and information, but not without politics.

14   One might think that this is happening only now, when they have the first real chance to change something. Not so. This intimacy with political issues was a part of everyday life whether on the level of hatred, or mistrust, or gossip, or just plain resignation during Todor Živkov's communist government. In a totalitarian society, one *has* to relate to the power directly; there is no escape. Therefore, politics never becomes abstract. It remains a palpable, brutal force directing every aspect of our lives, from what we eat to how we live and where we work. Like a disease, a plague, an epidemic, it doesn't spare anybody. Paradoxically, this is precisely how a totalitarian state produces its enemies: politicized citizens. The "velvet revolution" is the product not only of high politics, but of the consciousness of ordinary citizens, infected by politics.

15   Before you get here, you tend to forget newspaper pictures of people standing in line in front of shops. You think they serve as proof in the ideological battle, the proof that communism is failing. Or you take them as mere pictures, not reality. But once here, you cannot escape the *feeling* of shortages, even if you are not standing in line, even if you don't see them. In Prague, where people line up only for fruit, there

was enough of all necessities, except for oranges or lemons, which were considered a "luxury." It is hard to predict what will be considered a luxury item because this depends on planning, production, and shortages. One time it might be fruit, as in Prague, or milk, as in Sofia. People get used to less and less of everything. In Albania, the monthly ration for a whole family is two pounds of meat, two pounds of cheese, ten pounds of flour, less than half a pound each of coffee and butter. Everywhere, the bottom line is bread. It means safety—because the lack of bread is where real fear begins. Whenever I read a headline "No Bread" in the newspaper, I see a small, dark, almost empty bakery on Vladimir Zaimov Boulevard in Sofia, and I myself, even without reason, experience a genuine fear. It makes my bread unreal, too, and I feel as if I should grab it and eat it while it lasts.

Every mother in Bulgaria can point to where communism failed, from the failures of the planned economy (and the consequent lack of food, milk), to the lack of apartments, child-care facilities, clothes, disposable diapers, or toilet paper. The banality of everyday life is where it has really failed, rather than on the level of ideology. In another kitchen in Sofia, Ana, Katarine and I sit. Her one-year-old daughter is trying to grab our cups from the table. She looks healthy. "She is fine now," says Ana, "but you should have seen her six months ago. There was no formula to buy and normal milk you can hardly get as it is. At one point our shops started to sell Humana, imported powdered milk from the dollar shops, because its shelf life was over. I didn't have a choice. I had to feed my baby with that milk, and she got very, very sick. By allowing this milk to be sold, our own government poisoned babies. It was even on TV; they had to put it on because so many babies in Sofia got sick. We are the Third World here." 16

If communism didn't fail on bread or milk, it certainly failed on strawberries. When I flew to Warsaw from West Berlin, I bought cosmetics, oranges, chocolates, Nescafé, as a present for my friend Zofia— as if I were going home. I also bought a small basket of strawberries. I knew that by now she could buy oranges or even Nescafé from street vendors at a good price—but not strawberries. I bought them also because I remembered when we were together in New York for the first time, back in the eighties, and we went shopping. In a downtown Manhattan supermarket, we stood in front of a fruit counter and just stared. It was full of fruits we didn't know the names of—or if we did, like the man with the banana in Bucharest, we didn't know how they would taste. But this sight was not a miracle; we somehow expected it. What came as a real surprise was fresh strawberries, even though it was December and decorated Christmas trees were in the windows already. In Poland or Yugoslavia, you could see strawberries only in spring. We would buy them for children or when we were visiting a sick relative, so expensive were they. And here, all of a sudden—strawberries. At that moment, they represented all the difference between the world we 17 lived in and this one, so strange and uncomfortably rich. It was not so much that you could see them in the middle of the winter, but because you could afford them. When I handed her the strawberries in Warsaw, Zofia said: "How wonderful! I'll save them for my son." The fact that she used the word "save" told me everything: that almost ten years after we saw each other in New York, after the victory of Solidarity, and private initiatives in the economy, there are still no strawberries and perhaps there won't be for another ten years. She was closer to me then, that evening, in the apartment where she lives with her sick, elderly, mother (because there is nobody else to take care of her and to put your parent in a state-run institution would be more than cruelty, it would be a crime). Both of them took just one strawberry each, then put the rest in the refrigerator "for Grzegorz." This is how we tell our kids we love them, because food is love, if you don't have it, or if you have to wait in lines, get what you can, and then prepare a decent meal. Maybe this is why the chicken soup, cabbage stew, and mashed potatoes that evening tasted so good.

18   All this stays with me forever. When I come to New York and go shopping at Grace Balducci's Marketplace on Third Avenue and 71st Street, I think of Zofia, my mother, my friend Jasmina who loves Swiss chocolates, my daughter's desire for Brooklyn chewing gum, and my own hungry self, still confused by the thirty kinds of cheese displayed in front of me. In an article in *Literaturnaya Gazeta* May 1989 the Soviet poet Yevgenii Yevtushenko tells of a *kolkhoz* woman who fainted in an East Berlin shop, just because she saw twenty kinds of sausages. When she came back to her senses, she repeated in despair: "Why, but why?" How well I understand her question—but knowing the answer doesn't really help.

Questions for Discussion and Writing

1. How does Drakulić's request in Warsaw, "Let's have a pizza," lead her to understand how what to her is a simple matter could be an extraordinary event?
2. How does the availability of any kind of food, for example, prune compote, in Warsaw, change what the word "like" means?
3. How does the episode of the banana illustrate the value attached to a normally unobtainable food?
4. How does bringing a cake for dessert mean very different things in Eastern European countries from what it would in the West?
5. Why is it ironic that Drakulić runs into as much difficulty in trying to obtain a torte, an Eastern European dessert, in Prague as she did in getting a pizza in Warsaw?
6. How does the episode in Bulgaria with the "hundred-ways potato party" or the availability of powdered milk or strawberries reveal how food itself becomes politicized in Eastern European countries?
7. At what points in reading this essay did you anticipate very different out

comes to events from those that actually occurred? For example, in the conversation with the waitress in the coffee shop, what did you imagine Drakulić would eventually be served?

8. In your opinion, what is the significance of the story of the woman who "fainted in an East Berlin shop, just because she saw twenty kinds of sausages. When she came back to her senses, she repeated in despair 'Why, but why?'" You might choose to use this quote as a jumping-off point to explore differences in class expectations in a consumer society. In what way is being poor in the United States similar to being the average citizen in terms of food choices in Eastern Europe?

9. Describe the process and psychology underlying reciprocal gift-giving in your family and among your friends.

10. If money was no object, what would you serve at a party for your friends or a special occasion such as a wedding?

Linda Hogan

Hearing Voices

Linda Hogan, Chickasaw poet, novelist, and essayist, was born in 1947 in Denver, Colorado, grew up in Oklahoma, and earned an M.A. in English and creative writing from the University of Colorado at Boulder in 1978. She worked as a poet in the public schools for Colorado and Oklahoma from 1980 to 1984 and was also a teacher of creative writing. She served on the faculty of Colorado College in The Tribes program from 1982 to 1984, and from 1984 through 1991 taught American Indian Studies at the University of Minnesota. At present, she is a professor of American Studies and American Indian Studies at the University of Colorado. Hogan's writing has evolved from her deep commitment to the community at all levels. She has had a lifelong interest in wildlife rehabilitation and continues to work in the conservation and rehabilitation programs for birds of prey. Her poetry has been collected in Daughters, I Love You *(1981),* Eclipse *(1983), and* Seeing Through the Sun *(1985), which received an American Book Award from The Before Columbus Foundation.* Savings *(1988) is her most recent book of poetry. As a writer of fiction, she has published two collections of short stories,* That Horse *(1985) and* The Big Woman *(1987). A first novel,* Mean Spirit, *was published in 1990. She has received a National Endowment for the Arts grant, a Minnesota Arts Board Grant, a Colorado Writer's Fellowship, and the Five Civilized Tribes Museum playwriting award for her three-act play,* A Piece of Moon *(1981). In "Hearing Voices" (1991), which first appeared in* The Writer on Her Work, *edited by Janet Sternburg, Hogan describes how her writing evolves as an effort to retrieve the deepest sources of psychic and spiritual strength for an endangered community.*

1   When Barbara McClintock was awarded a Nobel Prize for her work on gene transposition in corn plants, the most striking thing about her was that she made her discoveries by listening to what the corn spoke to her, by respecting the life of the corn and "letting it come."

2   McClintock says she learned "the stories" of the plants. She "heard" them. She watched the daily green journeys of growth from earth toward sky and sun. She knew her plants in the way a healer or mystic would have known them, from the inside, the inner voices of corn and woman speaking to one another.

3   As an Indian woman, I come from a long history of people who have listened to the language of this continent, people who have known that corn grows with the songs and prayers of the people, that it has a story to tell, that the world is alive. Both in oral traditions and in mythology—the true language of inner life—account after account tells of the stones giving guidance, the trees singing, the corn telling of inner

earth, the dragonfly offering up a tongue. This is true in the European traditions as well: Psyche received direction from the reeds and the ants, Orpheus knew the languages of earth, animals, and birds.

This intuitive and common language is what I seek for my writing, work in touch with the mystery and force of life, work that speaks a few of the many voices around us, and it is important to me that McClintock listened to the voices of corn. It is important to the continuance of life that she told the truth of her method and that it reminded us all of where our strength, our knowing, and our sustenance come from.

It is also poetry, this science, and I note how often scientific theories lead to the world of poetry and vision, theories telling us how atoms that were stars have been transformed into our living, breathing bodies. And in these theories, or maybe they should be called stories, we begin to understand how we are each many people, including the stars we once were, and how we are in essence the earth and the universe, how what we do travels clear around the earth and returns. In a single moment of our living, there is our ancestral and personal history, our future, even our deaths planted in us and already growing toward their fulfillment. The corn plants are there, and like all the rest we are forever merging our borders with theirs in the world collective.

Our very lives might depend on this listening. In the Chernobyl nuclear accident, the wind told the story that was being suppressed by the people. It gave away the truth. It carried the story of danger to other countries. It was a poet, a prophet, a scientist.

Sometimes, like the wind, poetry has its own laws speaking for the life of the planet. It is a language that wants to bring back together what the other words have torn apart. It is the language of life speaking through us about the sacredness of life.

This life speaking life is what I find so compelling about the work of poets such as Ernesto Cardenal, who is also a priest and was the Nicaraguan Minister of Culture. He writes: "The armadilloes are very happy with this government. . . . Not only humans desired liberation/the whole ecology wanted it." Cardenal has also written "The Parrots," a poem about caged birds who were being sent to the United States as pets for the wealthy, how the cages were opened, the parrots allowed back into the mountains and jungles, freed like the people, "and sent back to the land we were pulled from."

How we have been pulled from the land! And how poetry has worked hard to set us free, uncage us, keep us from split tongues that mimic the voices of our captors. It returns us to our land. Poetry is a string of words that parades without a permit. It is a lockbox of words to put an ear to as we try to crack the safe of language, listening for the right combination, the treasure inside. It is life resonating. It is sometimes called Prayer, Soothsaying, Complaint, Invocation, Proclamation, Testimony, Witness. Writing is and does all these things. And like that parade, it is illegitimately insistent on going its own way, on being part of the miracle of life, telling the story about what happened when we were cosmic dust, what it means to be stars listening to our human atoms.

10   But don't misunderstand me. I am not just a dreamer. I am also the practical type. A friend's father, watching the United States stage another revolution in another Third World country, said, "Why doesn't the government just feed people and then let the political chips fall where they may?" He was right. It was easy, obvious, even financially more reasonable to do that, to let democracy be chosen because it feeds hunger. I want my writing to be that simple, that clear and direct. Likewise, I feel it is not enough for me just to write, but I need to live it, to be informed by it. I have found over the years that my work has more courage than I do. It has more wisdom. It teaches me, leads me places I never knew I was heading. And it is about a new way of living, of being in the world.

11   I was on a panel recently where the question was raised whether we thought literature could save lives. The audience, book people, smiled expectantly with the thought. I wanted to say, Yes, it saves lives. But I couldn't speak those words. It saves spirits maybe, hearts. It changes minds, but for me writing is an incredible privilege. When I sit down at the desk, there are other women who are hungry, homeless. I don't want to forget that, that the world of matter is still there to be reckoned with. This writing is a form of freedom most other people do not have. So, when I write, I feel a responsibility, a commitment to other humans and to the animal and plant communities as well.

12   Still, writing has changed me. And there is the powerful need we all have to tell a story, each of us with a piece of the whole pattern to complete. As Alice Walker says, We are all telling part of the same story, and as Sharon Olds has said, Every writer is a cell on the body politic of America.

13   Another Nobel Prize laureate is Betty William, a Northern Ireland co-winner of the 1977 Peace Prize. I heard her speak about how, after witnessing the death of children, she stepped outside in the middle of the night and began knocking on doors and yelling, behaviors that would have earned her a diagnosis of hysteria in our own medical circles. She knocked on doors that might have opened with weapons pointing in her face, and she cried out, "What kind of people have we become that we would allow children to be killed on our streets?" Within four hours the city was awake, and there were sixteen thousand names on petitions for peace. Now, that woman's work is a lesson to those of us who deal with language, and to those of us who are dealt into silence. She used language to begin the process of peace. This is the living, breathing power of the word. It is poetry. So are the names of those who signed the petitions. Maybe it is this kind of language that saves lives.

14   Writing begins for me with survival, with life and with freeing life,

saving life, speaking life. It is work that speaks what can't be easily said. It originates from a compelling desire to live and be alive. For me, it is sometimes the need to speak for other forms of life, to take the side of human life, even our sometimes frivolous living, and our grief-filled living, our joyous living, our violent living, busy living, our peaceful living. It is about possibility. It is based in the world of matter. I am interested in how something small turns into an image that is large and strong with resonance, where the ordinary becomes beautiful. I believe the divine, the magic, is here in the weeds at our feet, unacknowledged. What a world this is. Where else could water rise up to the sky, turn into snow crystals, magnificently brought together, fall from the sky all around us, pile up billions deep, and catch the small sparks of sunlight as they return again to water?

These acts of magic happen all the time; in Chaco Canyon, my sister has seen a kiva, a ceremonial room in the earth, that is in the center of the canyon. This place has been uninhabited for what seems like forever. It has been without water. In fact, there are theories that the ancient people disappeared when they journeyed after water. In the center of it a corn plant was growing. It was all alone and it had been there since the ancient ones, the old ones who came before us all, those people who wove dog hair into belts, who witnessed the painting of flute players on the seeping canyon walls, who knew the stories of corn. And there was one corn plant growing out of the holy place. It planted itself yearly. With no water, no person to care for it, no overturning of the soil, this corn plant rises up to tell its story, and that's what this poetry is.

Questions for Discussion and Writing

1. How does Hogan use the example of Barbara McClintock's research in developing her essay? What is the connection between McClintock's work and the importance of listening to nature?
2. In your own words, explain what you think Hogan means when she says the function of poetry is to be a "language that wants to bring back together what the other words have torn apart."
3. How is the practice of poetry for Hogan a kind of witnessing of the plight of the disadvantaged, those excluded from power, and others whose lives are authentic, but unrecognized?
4. How does the story of Betty William illustrate the theme of responsibility that Hogan believes poetry should accomplish?
5. Evaluate Hogan's unusual blend of images—drawn from nature, the cutting edge of scientific research, Greek mythology, politics, and items in the news—in developing her thesis.
6. To what extent did reading this essay change your perception as to what poetry is and what it might accomplish? Do you agree or disagree with Hogan's thesis? Explain your reasons.

Kate Chopin
Désirée's Baby

Kate Chopin (1851–1904) was born Katherine O'Flaherty, the daughter of a successful St. Louis businessman and his French Creole wife. After her father died in 1855, Kate was raised by her mother and great-grandmother. When she was nineteen, she married Oscar Chopin and accompanied him to New Orleans where he established himself as a cotton broker. After his business failed, they moved to his family plantation in Louisiana where he opened a general store. After his sudden death in 1883, Chopin managed the plantation for a year, but then decided to return to St. Louis with her six children. She began to submit stories patterned on the realistic fiction of Guy de Maupassant to local papers and national magazines, including the Saturday Evening Post *and* Atlantic Monthly. *Her stories of Creole life were widely praised for their realistic delineation of Creole manners and customs and were later collected in* Bayou Folk *(1894) and* A Night in Acadie *(1897). Her novel* The Awakening *(1899), although widely praised as a masterpiece for its frank depiction of its heroine's sexual awakening and need for self-fulfillment, created a public controversy. Chopin's uncompromising delineation of the pressures of class and race in Louisiana at the time are clearly seen in the poignant story "Désirée's Baby" (1899).*

1   As the day was pleasant, Madame Valmondé drove over to L'Abri to see Désirée and the baby.

2   It made her laugh to think of Désirée with a baby. Why, it seems but yesterday that Désirée was little more than a baby herself; when Monsieur in riding through the gateway of Valmondé had found her lying asleep in the shadow of the big stone pillar.

3   The little one awoke in his arms and began to cry for "Dada." That was as much as she could do or say. Some people thought she might have strayed there of her own accord, for she was of the toddling age. The prevailing belief was that she had been purposely left by a party of Texans, whose canvas-covered wagon, late in the day, had crossed the ferry that Coton Maïs kept, just below the plantation. In time Madame Valmondé abandoned every speculation but the one that Désirée had been sent to her by a beneficent Providence to be the child of her affection, seeing that she was without child of the flesh. For the girl grew to be beautiful and gentle, affectionate and sincere—the idol of Valmondé.

4   It was no wonder, when she stood one day against the stone pillar in whose shadow she had lain asleep, eighteen years before, that Armand Aubigny riding by and seeing her there, had fallen in love

496

with her. That was the way all the Aubignys fell in love, as if struck by a pistol shot. The wonder was that he had not loved her before; for he had known her since his father brought him home from Paris, a boy of eight, after his mother died there. The passion that awoke in him that day, when he saw her at the gate, swept along like an avalanche, or like a prairie fire, or like anything that drives headlong over all obstacles.

Madame Valmondé bent her portly figure over Désirée and kissed her, holding her an instant tenderly in her arms. Then she turned to the child.

"This is not the baby!" she exclaimed, in startled tones. French was the language spoken at Valmondé in those days.

"I knew you would be astonished," laughed Désirée, "at the way he has grown. The little *cochon de lait!*[1] Look at his legs, mamma, and his hands and fingernails,—real fingernails. Zandrine had to cut them this morning. Isn't it true, Zandrine?"

The woman bowed her turbaned head majestically, "Mais si, Madame."

"And the way he cries," went on Désirée, "is deafening. Armand heard him the other day as far away as La Blanche's cabin."

Madame Valmondé had never removed her eyes from the child. She lifted it and walked with it over to the window that was lightest. She scanned the baby narrowly, then looked as searchingly at Zandrine, whose face was turned to gaze across the fields.

"Yes, the child has grown, has changed," said Madame Valmondé, slowly, as she replaced it beside its mother. "What does Armand say?"

Désirée's face became suffused with a glow that was happiness itself.

"Oh, Armand is the proudest father in the parish, I believe, chiefly because it is a boy, to bear his name; though he says not—that he would have loved a girl as well. But I know it isn't true. I know he says that to please me. And mamma," she added, drawing Madame Valmondé's head down to her, and speaking in a whisper, "he hasn't punished one of them—not one of them—since baby is born. Even Négrillon, who pretended to have burnt his leg that he might rest from work—he only laughed, and said Négrillon was a great scamp. Oh, mamma, I'm so happy; it frightens me."

What Désirée said was true. Marriage, and later the birth of his son, had softened Armand Aubigny's imperious and exacting nature greatly. This was what made the gentle Désirée so happy, for she loved him desperately. When he frowned she trembled, but loved him. When he smiled, she asked no greater blessing of God. But Armand's dark, handsome face had not often been disfigured by frowns since the day he fell in love with her.

When the baby was about three months old, Désirée awoke one day

[1]Literally "pig of milk"—a big feeder.

to the conviction that there was something in the air menacing her peace. It was at first too subtle to grasp. It had only been a disquieting suggestion; an air of mystery among the blacks; unexpected visits from far-off neighbors who could hardly account for their coming. Then a strange, an awful change in her husband's manner, which she dared not ask him to explain. When he spoke to her, it was with averted eyes, from which the old love light seemed to have gone out. He absented himself from home; and when there, avoided her presence and that of her child, without excuse. And the very spirit of Satan seemed suddenly to take hold of him in his dealings with the slaves. Désirée was miserable enough to die.

16   She sat in her room, one hot afternoon, in her *peignoir*, listlessly drawing through her fingers the strands of her long, silky brown hair that hung about her shoulders. The baby, half naked, lay asleep upon her own great mahogany bed, that was like a sumptuous throne, with its satin-lined half canopy. One of La Blanche's little quadroon boys— half naked too—stood fanning the child slowly with a fan of peacock feathers. Désirée's eyes had been fixed absently and sadly upon the baby, while she was striving to penetrate the threatening mist that she felt closing about her. She looked from her child to the boy who stood beside him; and back again, over and over. "Ah!" It was a cry that she could not help, which she was not conscious of having uttered. The blood turned like ice in her veins, and a clammy moisture gathered upon her face.

17   She tried to speak to the little quadroon boy; but no sound would come, at first. When he heard his name uttered, he looked up, and his mistress was pointing to the door. He laid aside the great, soft fan, and obediently stole away, over the polished floor, on his bare tiptoes.

18   She stayed motionless, with gaze riveted upon her child, and her face the picture of fright.

19   Presently her husband entered the room, and without noticing her, went to a table and began to search among some papers which covered it.

20   "Armand," she called to him, in a voice which must have stabbed him, if he was human. But he did not notice. "Armand," she said again. Then she rose and tottered towards him. "Armand," she panted once more, clutching his arm, "look at our child. What does it mean? Tell me."

21   He coldly but gently loosened her fingers from about his arm and thrust the hand away from him. "Tell me what it means!" she cried despairingly.

22   "It means," he answered lightly, "that the child is not white; it means that you are not white."

23   A quick conception of all that this accusation meant for her nerved her with unwonted courage to deny it. "It is a lie; it is not true, I am white! Look at my hair, it is brown; and my eyes are gray, Armand, you

know they are gray. And my skin is fair," seizing his wrist. "Look at my
hand, whiter than yours, Armand," she laughed hysterically.

"As white as La Blanche's," he returned cruelly, and went away   24
leaving her alone with their child.

When she could hold a pen in her hand, she sent a despairing letter   25
to Madame Valmondé.

"My mother, they tell me I am not white. Armand has told me I am   26
not white. For God's sake tell them it is not true. You must know it is
not true. I shall die. I must die. I cannot be so unhappy, and live."

The answer that came was as brief: 27

"My own Désirée: Come home to Valmondé; back to your mother   28
who loves you. Come with your child."

When the letter reached Désirée she went with it to her husband's   29
study, and laid it open upon the desk before which he sat. She was like
a stone image: silent, white, motionless after she placed it there.

In silence he ran his cold eyes over the written words. He said noth-   30
ing. "Shall I go, Armand?" she asked in tones sharp with agonized suspense.

"Yes, go."   31

"Do you want me to go?"   32

"Yes, I want you to go."   33

He thought Almighty God had dealt cruelly and unjustly with him;   34
and felt, somehow, that he was paying Him back in kind when he
stabbed thus into his wife's soul. Moreover he no longer loved her, because of the unconscious injury she had brought upon his home and his
name.

She turned away like one stunned by a blow, and walked slowly to-   35
wards the door, hoping he would call her back.

"Good-by, Armand," she moaned.   36

He did not answer her. That was his last blow at fate.   37

Désirée went in search of her child. Zandrine was pacing the sombre   38
gallery with it. She took the little one from the nurse's arms with no
word of explanation, and descending the steps, walked away, under
the live-oak branches.

It was an October afternoon; the sun was just sinking. Out in the still   39
fields the Negroes were picking cotton.

Désirée had not changed the thin white garment nor the slippers   40
which she wore. Her hair was uncovered and the sun's rays brought a
golden gleam from its brown meshes. She did not take the broad,
beaten road which led to the far-off plantation of Valmondé. She
walked across a deserted field, where the stubble bruised her tender
feet, so delicately shod, and tore her thin gown to shreds.

She disappeared among the reeds and willows that grew thick along   41
the banks of the deep, sluggish bayou; and she did not come back
again.

·   ·   ·   ·   ·   ·   ·   ·   ·

42   Some weeks later there was a curious scene enacted at L'Abri. In the centre of the smoothly swept back yard was a great bonfire. Armand Aubigny sat in the wide hallway that commanded a view of the spectacle; and it was he who dealt out to a half dozen negroes the material which kept this fire ablaze.

43   A graceful cradle of willow, with all its dainty furbishings, was laid upon the pyre, which had already been fed with the richness of a priceless *layette*. Then there were silk gowns, and velvet and satin ones added to these; laces, too, and embroideries; bonnets and gloves; for the *corbeille*[2] had been of rare quality.

44   The last thing to go was a tiny bundle of letters; innocent little scribblings that Désirée had sent to him during the days of their espousal. There was the remnant of one back in the drawer from which he took them. But it was not Désirée's; it was part of an old letter from his mother to his father. He read it. She was thanking God for the blessing of her husband's love:

45   "But, above all," she wrote, "night and day, I thank the good God for having so arranged our lives that our dear Armand will never know that his mother, who adores him, belongs to the race that is cursed with the brand of slavery."

[2]Basket; linens, clothing, and accessories collected in anticipation of a baby's birth.

Questions for Discussion and Writing

1. Based on the information about Désirée's background and Madame Valmondé's response on first seeing Désirée's baby, what ASSUMPTIONS did you make regarding the outcome?
2. What can you INFER about Armand's character, and his past behavior, from the fact that he had not punished one slave since his baby was born? How does Armand's behavior toward Désirée change after the baby is three months old?
3. What did you assume Désirée would do when she realizes that Armand values his social standing more than he does her? What did you think she would do? Were you surprised by her reaction?
4. In retrospect, what clues might have allowed you to fill in the gaps in ways that would have pointed to the truth disclosed at the end of the story?
5. In a short essay, discuss the picture you formed of the society in which this story took place and the extent to which considerations of race and class determined people's behavior.
6. Have you ever been in a situation where someone who was unaware of your racial or ethnic background referred to your group in a disparaging way? How did you feel and what did you do?

Murray Bail

The Drover's Wife

Murray Bail was born in 1941 in Adelaide, South Australia. An internationally respected art critic, he served as trustee of the Australian National Gallery from 1976 to 1981. Bail is equally talented as a novelist and writer of short stories and is considered a major force in contemporary Australian literature. His first novel, Homesickness (1980), *about a group of Australians undergoing a world tour, won both the Book of the Year Award and the National Book Council Award in Australia. A second novel,* Holden's Performance (1987), *focusing on an Australian civil servant who befriends eccentric characters, won the 1988 Victorian Premier's Award. "The Drover's Wife" is taken from his 1984 collection of short stories,* The Drover's Wife and Other Stories, *that offer new perspectives on seemingly ordinary situations. Both his talents as a writer and as an art critic come together in this offbeat and inventive tale that was inspired by Australian artist Russell Drysdale's painting of the same name: in it, a dentist comes across a portrait of his wife, painted many years after she had abandoned him and their daughter to run away with a cattle drover.*

There has perhaps been a mistake—but of no great importance—made in the denomination of this picture. The woman depicted is not "The Drover's Wife." She is my wife. We have not seen each other now . . . it must be getting on thirty years. This portrait was painted shortly after she left—and had joined him. Notice she has very conveniently hidden her wedding hand. It is a canvas 20×24 inches, signed l/r "Russell Drysdale." 1

I say "shortly after" because she has our small suitcase—Drysdale has made it look like a shopping bag—and she is wearing the sandshoes she normally wore to the beach. Besides, it is dated 1945. 2

It is Hazel all right. 3

How much can you tell by a face? That a woman has left a husband and two children? Here, I think the artist has fallen down (though how was he to know?). He has Hazel with a resigned helpless expression—as if it was all my fault. Or, as if she had been a country woman all her ruddy life. 4

Otherwise the likeness is fair enough. 5

Hazel was large-boned. Our last argument I remember concerned her weight. She weighed—I have the figures—12 st 4 ozs. And she wasn't exactly tall. I see that she put it back on almost immediately. It doesn't take long. See her legs. 6

She had a small, pretty face, I'll give her that. I was always surprised by her eyes. How solemn they were. The painting shows that. Overall, a 7

501

gentle face, one that other women liked. How long it must have lasted up in the drought conditions is anybody's guess.

8   A drover! Why a drover? It has come as a shock to me.

9   "I am just going round the corner," she wrote, characteristically. It was a piece of butcher's paper left on the table.

10   Then, and this sounded odd at the time: "Your tea's in the oven. Don't give Trev any carrots."

11   Now that sounded as if she wouldn't be back, but after puzzling over it, I dismissed it.

12   And I think that is what hurt me most. No "Dear" at the top, not even "Gordon." No "love" at the bottom. Hazel left without so much as a goodbye. We could have talked it over.

13   Adelaide is a small town. People soon got to know. They . . . shied away. I was left alone to bring up Trevor and Kay. It took a long time—years—before, if asked, I could say: "She vamoosed. I haven't got a clue to where."

14   Fancy coming across her in a painting, one reproduced in colour at that. I suppose in a way that makes Hazel famous.

15   The picture gives little away though. It is the outback—but where exactly? South Australia? It could easily be Queensland, West Australia, the Northern Territory. We don't know. You could never find that spot.

16   He is bending over (feeding?) the horse, so it is around dusk. This is borne out by the length of Hazel's shadow. It is probably in the region of 5 P.M. Probably still over the hundred mark. What a place to spend the night. The silence would have already begun.

17   Hazel looks unhappy. I can see she is having second thoughts. All right, it was soon after she had left me; but she is standing away, in the foreground, as though they're not speaking. See that? Distance = doubts. They've had an argument.

18   Of course, I want to know all about him. I don't even know his name. In Drysdale's picture he is a silhouette. A completely black figure. He could have been an Aborigine; by the late forties I understand some were employed as drovers.

19   But I rejected that.

20   I took a magnifying glass. I wanted to see the expression on his face. What colour is his hair? Magnified, he is nothing but brush strokes. A real mystery man.

21   It is my opinion, however, that he is a small character. See his size in relation to the horse, to the wheels of the cart. Either that, or it is a ruddy big horse.

22   It begins to fall into place.

23   I had an argument with your youngest, Kay, the other day. Both she and Trevor sometimes visit me. I might add, she hasn't married and has her mother's general build. She was blaming me, said people said mum was a good sort.

Right. I nodded.   24
"Then why did she scoot?"   25
"Your mother," I said thinking quickly, "had a silly streak."   26
If looks could kill!   27
I searched around—"She liked to paddle in water!"   28
Kay gave a nasty laugh, "What? You're the limit. You really are."   29

Of course, I hadn't explained properly. And I didn't even know then   30
she had gone off with a drover.

Hazel was basically shy, even with me: quiet, generally non-com-   31
mittal. At the same time, I can imagine her allowing herself to be
painted so soon after running off without leaving even a phone number
or forwarding address. It fits. It sounds funny, but it does.

This silly streak. Heavy snow covered Mt Barker for the first time   32
and we took the Austin up on the Sunday. From a visual point of view
it was certainly remarkable. Our gum trees and stringy barks somehow
do not go with the white stuff, not even the old Ghost Gum. I mentioned this to Hazel but she just ran into it and began chucking snow-
balls at me. People were laughing. Then she fell in up to her knees,
squawking like a schoolgirl. I didn't mean to speak harshly, but I went
up to her, "Come on, don't be stupid. Get up." She went very quiet. She
didn't speak for hours.

Kay of course wouldn't remember that.   33

With the benefit of hindsight, and looking at this portrait by   34
Drysdale, I can see Hazel had a soft side. I think I let her clumsiness get
me down. The sight of sweat patches under her arms, for example,
somehow put me in a bad mood. It irritated me the way she chopped
wood. I think she enjoyed chopping wood. There was the time I caught
her lugging into the house the ice for the ice chest—this is just after the
war. The ice man didn't seem to notice; he was following, working out
his change. It somehow made her less attractive in my eyes, I don't
know why. And then of course she killed that snake down at the beach
shack we took one Christmas. I happened to lift the lid of the
incinerator—a black brute, its head bashed in. "It was under the
house," she explained.

It was a two-roomed shack, bare floorboards. It had a primus stove,   35
and an asbestos toilet down the back. Hazel didn't mind. Quite the contrary; when it came time to leave she was downcast. I had to be at town
for work.

The picture reminds me. It was around then Hazel took to wearing   36
just a slip around the house. And bare feet. The dress in the picture
looks like a slip. She even used to burn rubbish in it down the back.

I don't know.   37

"Hello, missus!" I used to say, entering the kitchen. Not perfect per-   38
haps, especially by today's standards, but that is my way of showing affection. I think Hazel understood. Sometimes I could see she was
touched.

39   I mention that to illustrate our marriage was not all nitpicking and argument. When I realized she had gone I sat for nights in the lounge with the lights out. I am a dentist. You can't have shaking hands and be a dentist. The word passed around. Only now, touch wood, has the practice picked up to any extent.

40   Does this explain at all why she left?

41   Not really.

42   To return to the picture. Drysdale has left out the flies. No doubt he didn't want Hazel waving her hand, or them crawling over her face. Nevertheless, this is a serious omission. It is altering the truth for the sake of a pretty picture, or "composition." I've been up around there—and there are hundreds of flies. Not necessarily germ carriers, "bush flies" I think these are called; and they drive you mad. Hazel of course accepted everything without a song and dance. She didn't mind the heat, or the flies.

43   It was a camping holiday. We had one of those striped beach tents shaped like a bell. I thought at the time it would prove handy—visible from the air—if we got lost. Now that is a point. Although I will never forget the colours and the assortment of rocks I saw up there I have no desire to return, none. I realized one night. Standing a few yards from the tent, the cavernous sky and the silence all round suddenly made me shudder. I felt lost. It defied logic. And during the day the bush, which is small and prickly, offered no help (I was going to say "sympathy"). It was stinking hot.

44   Yet Hazel was in her element, so much so she seemed to take no interest in the surroundings. She acted as if she were part of it. I felt ourselves moving apart, as if I didn't belong there, especially with her. I felt left out. My mistake was to believe it was a passing phase, almost a form of indolence on her part.

45   An unfortunate incident didn't help. We were looking for a camp site. "Not yet. No, not there," I kept saying—mainly to myself, for Hazel let me go on, barely saying a word. At last I found a spot. A tree showed in the dark. We bedded down. Past midnight we were woken by a terrifying noise and lights. The children all began to cry. I had pitched camp alongside the Adelaide–Port Augusta railway line.

46   Twenty or thirty miles north of Port Augusta I turned back. I had to. We seemed to be losing our senses. We actually met a drover somewhere around there. He was off on the side making tea. When I asked where were his sheep, or the cattle, he gave a wave of his hand. For some reason this amused Hazel. She squatted down. I can still see her expression, silly girl.

47   The man didn't say much. He did offer tea though. "Come on," said Hazel, smiling up at me.

48   Hazel and her silly streak—she knew I wanted to get back. The drover, a diplomat, poked at the fire with a stick.

49   I said: "You can if you want. I'll be in the car."

That is all.   50

I recall the drover as a thin head in a khaki hat, not talkative, with   51
dusty boots. He is indistinct. Is it him? I don't know. Hazel—it is Hazel
and the rotten landscape that dominate everything.

Questions for Discussion and Writing

1. How do the circumstances connected with the picture which the dentist encounters create a GAP or mystery that encourages the reader to speculate
   why the dentist's wife would have left him to run off with a cattle drover?
2. How does the narrator's account of his wife's actions during the camping
   trip provide you with important CLUES as to why she would not have been
   put off by the rugged nature of a drover's life? What other clues suggest
   that she was not free to be herself in the middle-class world of the dentist?
3. What does the dentist reveal about himself in the course of commenting on
   his wife that would allow you to INFER why she left him?
4. What aspects of a drover's life might have appealed to Hazel, given the
   clues we get from the dentist's commentary?
5. How do class expectations explain the dentist's shock at his wife's actions?
6. Would you have EXPECTED that to this day the daughter does not blame her
   mother for leaving? Why or why not?
7. What insights does the story offer into how different the outback in
   Australia is from its urban civilized areas?
8. Do you know anyone who voluntarily dropped out of a middle-class life-
   style to rough it? Describe their experiences.
9. Using an interesting photograph of yourself and/or a relative or friend, either posed or candid, re-create the events at the time the picture was taken.
   Describe the circumstances under which the picture was taken and the
   memories triggered by it.
10. For any painting or photograph, imagine that you are inside the picture,
    writing from the point of view of a person or object in the picture, or write a
    dialogue between the person in the picture and the person looking at it.

Catherine Lim

Paper

Catherine Lim is one of Singapore's foremost writers. She currently works for the Curriculum Development Institute of Singapore, writing English language instructional materials for use in the primary schools. Her widely praised collections of short stories include Little Ironies—Stories of Singapore *(1978), from which "Paper" is taken,* Or Else, The Lightning God and Other Stories *(1980), and* The Shadow of a Shadow of a Dream—Love Stories of Singapore *(1981). She is also the author of two novels,* They Do Return *(1982) and* The Serpent's Tooth *(1983). Her short stories have been compared to those of Guy de Maupassant for their accuracy of observation, clarity in presentation of character, and precise detail. Lim's stories reveal a wealth of information about the forces, customs, and pressures that shape the lives of the Chinese community in Singapore, a densely populated metropolis in which Chinese, Malay, and Indian cultures coexist and thrive. "Paper" is set against the turbulent background of the Singapore Stock Exchange, a volatile financial market reflecting the seemingly limitless possibilities of one of the world's most productive financial, industrial, and commercial centers. This story dramatically explores how the lure of easy money leads a man and his wife to tragic consequences.*

1   He wanted it, he dreamed of it, he hankered after it, as an addict after his opiate. Once the notion of a big beautiful house had lodged itself in his imagination, Tay Soon nurtured it until it became the consuming passion of his life. A house. A dream house such as he had seen on his drives with his wife and children along the roads bordering the prestigious housing estates on the island, and in the glossy pages of *Homes* and *Modern Living*. Or rather, it was a house which was an amalgam of the best, the most beautiful aspects of the houses he had seen. He knew every detail of his dream house already, from the aluminum sliding doors to the actual shade of the dining room carpet to the shape of the swimming pool. Kidney. He rather liked the shape. He was not ashamed of the enthusiasm with which he spoke of the dream house, an enthusiasm that belonged to women only, he was told. Indeed, his enthusiasm was so great that it had infected his wife and even his children, small though they were. Soon his wife Yee Lian was describing to her sister Yee Yeng, the dream house in all its perfection of shape and decor, and the children were telling their cousins and friends, "My daddy says that when our house is ready . . ."

2   They talked of the dream house endlessly. It had become a reality stronger than the reality of the small terrace house which they were sharing with Tay Soon's mother, to whom it belonged. Tay Soon's

mother, whose little business of selling bottled curries and vegetable preserves which she made herself, left her little time for dreams, clucked her tongue and shook her head and made sarcastic remarks about the ambitiousness of young people nowadays.

"What's wrong with this house we're staying in?" she asked petu- 3 lantly. "Aren't we all comfortable in it?"

Not as long as you have your horrid ancestral altars all over the 4 place, and your grotesque sense of colour—imagine painting the kitchen wall bright pink. But Yee Lian was tactful enough to keep the remarks to herself, or to make them only to her sister Yee Yeng, otherwise they were sure to reach the old lady, and there would be no end to her sharp tongue.

The house—the dream house—it would be a far cry from the little 5 terrace house in which they were all staying now, and Tay Soon and Yee Lian talked endlessly about it, and it grew magnificently in their imaginations, this dream house of theirs with its timbered ceiling and panelled walls and sunken circular sitting room which was to be car- peted in rich amber. It was no empty dream, for there was much money in the bank already. Forty thousand dollars had been saved. The house would cost many times that, but Tay Soon and Yee Lian with their good salaries would be able to manage very well. Once they took care of the down payment, they would be able to pay back monthly over a period of ten years—fifteen, twenty—what did it matter how long it took as long as the dream house was theirs? It had become the symbol of the peak of earthly achievement, and all of Tay Soon's energies and devo- tion were directed towards its realisation. His mother said, "You're a show-off; what's so grand about marble flooring and a swimming pool? Why don't you put your money to better use?" But the forty thousand grew steadily, and after Tay Soon and Yee Lian had put in every cent of their annual bonuses, it grew to forty eight thousand, and husband and wife smiled at the smooth way their plans were going.

It was a time of growing interest in the stock market. The quotations 6 for stocks and shares were climbing the charts, and the crowds in the rooms of the broking houses were growing perceptibly. Might we not do something about this? Yee Lian said to her husband. Do you know that Dr. Soo bought Rustan Banking for four dollars and today the shares are worth seven dollars each? The temptation was great. The re- wards were almost immediate. Thirty thousand dollars' worth of NBE became fifty-five thousand almost overnight. Tay Soon and Yee Lian whooped. They put their remaining eighteen thousand in Far East Mart. Three days later the shares were worth twice that much. It was not to be imagined that things could stop here. Tay Soon secured a loan from his bank and put twenty thousand in OHTE. This was a particu- larly lucky share; it shot up to four times its value in three days.

"Oh, this is too much, too much," cried Yee Lian in her ecstasy, and 7 she sat down with pencil and paper, and found after a few minutes' calculation that they had made a cool one hundred thousand in a matter of days.

8   And now there was to be no stopping. The newspapers were full of it, everybody was talking about it, it was in the very air. There was plenty of money to be made in the stock exchange by those who had guts—money to be made by the hour, by the minute, for the prices of stocks and shares were rising faster than anyone could keep track of them! Dr. Soo was said—he laughingly dismissed it as a silly rumour— Dr. Soo was said to have made two million dollars already. If he sold all his shares now, he would be a millionaire twice over. And Yee Yeng, Yee Lian's sister, who had been urged with sisterly goodwill to come join the others make money, laughed happily to find that the shares she had bought for four twenty on Tuesday had risen to seven ninety-five on Friday—she laughed and thanked Yee Lian who advised her not to sell yet, it was going further, it would hit the ten dollar mark by next week. And Tay Soon both laughed and cursed—cursed that he had failed to buy a share at nine dollars which a few days later had hit seventeen dollars! Yee Lian said reproachfully, "I thought I told you to buy it, darling," and Tay Soon had beaten his forehead in despair and said, "I know, I know, why didn't I! Big fool that I am!" And he had another reason to curse himself—he sold five thousand West Parkes at sixteen twenty-three per share, and saw, to his horror, West Parkes climb to eighteen ninety the very next day!

9   "I'll never sell now," he vowed. "I'll hold on. I won't be so foolish." And the frenzy continued. Husband and wife couldn't talk or think of anything else. They thought fondly of their shares—going to be worth a million altogether soon. A million! In the peak of good humour, Yee Lian went to her mother-in-law, forgetting the past insults, and advised her to join the others by buying some shares; she would get her broker to buy them immediately for her, there was sure money in it. The old lady refused curtly, and to her son later, she showed great annoyance, scolding him for being so foolish as to put all his money in those worthless shares. "Worthless!" exploded Tay Soon. "Do you know, Mother, if I sold all my shares today, I would have the money to buy fifty terrace houses like the one you have?"

10   His wife said, "Oh, we'll just leave her alone. I was kind enough to offer to help her make money. But since she's so nasty and ungrateful, we'll leave her alone." The comforting, triumphant thought was that soon, very soon, they would be able to purchase their dream house; it would be even more magnificent than the one they had dreamt of, since they had made almost a—Yee Lian preferred not to say the sum. There was the old superstitious fear of losing something when it is too often or too directly referred to, and Yee Lian had cautioned her husband not to make mention of their gains.

11   "Not to worry, not to worry," he said jovially, not superstitious like his wife. "After all, it's just paper gains so far."

The downward slide, or the bursting of the bubble as the newspa- 12 pers dramatically called it, did not initially cause much alarm. For the speculators all expected the shares to bounce back to their original strength and thence continue the phenomenal growth. But that did not happen. The slide continued.

Tay Soon said nervously, "Shall we sell? Do you think we should 13 sell?" but Yee Lian said stoutly, "There is talk that this decline is a technical thing only—it will be over soon, and then the rise will continue. After all, see what is happening in Hong Kong and London and New York. Things are as good as ever."

"We're still making, so not to worry," said Yee Lian after a few 14 days. Their gains were pared by half. A few days later, their gains were pared to marginal.

There is talk of a recovery, insisted Yee Lian. Do you know, Tay 15 Soon, Dr. Soo's wife is buying up some OHTE and West Parkes now? She says these two are sure to rise. She has some inside information that these two are going to climb past the forty-dollar mark—

Tay Soon sold all his shares and put the money in OHTE and West 16 Parkes. OHTE and West Parkes crashed shortly afterwards. Some began to say the shares were not worth the paper of the certificates.

"Oh, I can't believe, I can't believe it," gasped Yee Lian, pale and 17 sick. Tay Soon looked in mute horror at her.

"All our money was in OHTE and West Parkes," he said, his lips 18 dry.

"That stupid Soo woman!" shrieked Yee Lian. "I think she deliber- 19 ately led me astray with her advice! She's always been jealous of me— ever since she knew we were going to build a house grander than hers!"

"How are we going to get our house now?" asked Tay Soon in deep 20 distress, and for the first time he wept. He wept like a child, for the loss of all his money, for the loss of the dream house that he had never stopped loving and worshipping.

The pain bit into his very mind and soul, so that he was like a mad- 21 man, unable to go to his office to work, unable to do anything but haunt the broking houses, watching with frenzied anxiety for OHTE and West Parkes to show him hope. But there was no hope. The decline continued with gleeful rapidity. His broker advised him to sell, before it was too late, but he shrieked angrily, "What! Sell at a fraction at which I bought them! How can this be tolerated!"

And he went on hoping against hope. 22

He began to have wild dreams in which he sometimes laughed and 23 sometimes screamed. His wife Yee Lian was afraid and she ran sobbing to her sister who never failed to remind her curtly that all her savings were gone, simply because when she had wanted to sell, Yee Lian had advised her not to.

"But what is your sorrow compared to mine," wept Yee Lian, "see 24 what's happening to my husband. He's cracking up! He talks to himself, he doesn't eat, he has nightmares, he beats the children. Oh, he's finished!"

25   Her mother-in-law took charge of the situation, while Yee Lian, wide-eyed in mute horror at the terrible change that had come over her husband, shrank away and looked to her two small children for comfort. Tight-lipped and grim, the elderly woman made herbal medicines for Tay Soon, brewing and straining for hours, and got a Chinese medicine man to come to have a look at him.

26   "There is a devil in him," said the medicine man, and he proceeded to make him a drink which he mixed with the ashes of a piece of prayer paper. But Tay Soon grew worse. He lay in bed, white, haggard and delirious, seeming to be beyond the touch of healing. In the end, Yee Lian, on the advice of her sister and friends, put him in hospital.

27   "I have money left for the funeral," whimpered the frightened Yee Lian only a week later, but her mother-in-law sharply retorted, "You leave everything to me! I have the money for his funeral, and I shall give him the best! He wanted a beautiful house all his life; I shall give him a beautiful house now!"

28   She went to the man who was well-known on the island for his beautiful houses, and she ordered the best. It would come to nearly a thousand dollars, said the man, a thin, wizened fellow whose funereal gauntness and pallor seemed to be a concession to his calling.

29   That doesn't matter, she said, I want the best. The house is to be made of superior paper, she instructed, and he was to make it to her specifications. She recollected that he, Tay Soon, had often spoken of marble flooring, a timbered ceiling and a kidney-shaped swimming pool. Could he simulate all these in paper?

30   The thin, wizened man said, "I've never done anything like that before. All my paper houses for the dead have been the usual kind—I can put in paper furniture and paper cars, paper utensils for the kitchen and paper servants, all that the dead will need in the other world. But I shall try to put in what you've asked for. Only it will cost more."

31   The house when it was ready, was most beautiful to see. It stood seven feet tall, a delicate framework of wire and thin bamboo strips covered with finely worked paper of a myriad colours. Little silver flowers, scattered liberally throughout the entire structure, gave a carnival atmosphere. There was a paper swimming pool (round, as the man had not understood "kidney") which had to be fitted inside the house itself, as there was no provision for a garden or surrounding grounds. Inside the house were paper figures; there were at least four servants to attend to the needs of the master who was posed beside two cars, one distinctly a Chevrolet and the other a Mercedes.

32   At the appointed time, the paper house was brought to Tay Soon's grave and set on fire there. It burned brilliantly, and in three minutes was a heap of ashes on the grave.

Questions for Discussion and Writing

1. How do the events in each of the four scenes into which the story is divided encourage you to anticipate what would happen next? Did you have to revise your EXPECTATIONS as you read the story? Describe your reactions.

2. What details suggest the extent to which Tay Soon has identified himself with the magnificent dream house he wishes to buy? What does it represent for him? Why is he unwilling to settle for a lesser house that he could afford?

3. What role does Tay's mother play in the story? How do her values differ from those of Tay and his wife?

4. What role does Tay's wife, Yee Lian, play in the entire venture?

5. Why is the final image of the burning miniature paper house ironic?

6. How did the recurrent mention of the word "paper" (paper profits, certificates of paper, prayer paper, a paper house, and shares not worth the paper they are printed on) focus your attention on one of the story's central *themes*?

7. What is your attitude toward deferring material gratification? Did you find yourself valuing the fantasies you had about a vacation, car, clothes, jewelry, or whatever in ways that were comparable to the feelings of Tay Soon?

8. To discover what you really value, consider the following hypothetical situation: a raging fire has started where you live. You can save only one item other than another person or a pet. What item would you save? How does the value of this item (material, sentimental, or both) imply what is really important to you? Discuss your reactions.

Krishnan Varma

The Grass-Eaters

Krishnan Varma was born in Kerala, a southwestern state of India. Varma's stories, in both English and Malayalam (an Indian language), have been published in India, the United States, and Canada. "The Grass-Eaters" was first published in Wascana Review, *1985. In this tale of the fate of a teacher and his wife in modern-day Calcutta, a city of fourteen million beset by extreme poverty, overcrowding, and high unemployment, Varma challenges Western assumptions by showing how it is possible to accept conditions that initially appear unthinkable.*

1   For some time several years ago I was tutor to a spherical boy (now a spherical youth). One day his ovoid father, Ramaniklal Misrilal, asked me where I lived. I told him.

2   Misrilal looked exceedingly distressed. "A pipe, Ajit Babu? Did you say—a *pipe*, Ajit Babu?"

3   His cuboid wife was near to tears. "A *pipe*, Ajit Babu? How can you live in a pipe?"

4   It was true: at that time I was living in a pipe with my wife, Swapna. It was long and three or four feet across. With a piece of sack cloth hung at either end, we had found it far more comfortable than any of our previous homes.

5   The first was a footpath of Chittaranjan Avenue. We had just arrived in Calcutta from East Bengal where Hindus and Muslims were killing one another. The footpath was so crowded with residents, refugees like us and locals, that if you got up at night to relieve yourself you could not be sure of finding your place again. One cold morning I woke to find that the woman beside me was not Swapna at all but a bag of bones instead. And about fifty or sixty or seventy years old. I had one leg over her too. I paid bitterly for my mistake. The woman very nearly scratched out my eyes. Then came Swapna, fangs bared, claws out . . . I survived, but minus one ear. Next came the woman's husband, a hill of a man, whirling a tree over his head, roaring. That was my impression, anyway. I fled.

6   Later in the day Swapna and I moved into an abandoned-looking freight wagon at the railway terminus. A whole wagon to ourselves—a place with doors which could be opened and shut—we did nothing but open and shut them for a full hour—all the privacy a man and wife could want—no fear of waking up with a complete stranger in your arms . . . it was heaven. I felt I was God.

7   Then one night we woke to find that the world was running away

512

from us: we had been coupled to a freight train. There was nothing for it but to wait for the train to stop. When it did, miles from Calcutta, we got off, took a passenger train back, and occupied another unwanted-looking wagon. That was not the only time we went to bed in Calcutta and woke up in another place. I found it an intensely thrilling experience, but not Swapna.

She wanted a stationary home; she insisted on it. But she would not 8 say why. If I persisted in questioning her she snivelled. If I tried to persuade her to change her mind, pointing out all the advantages of living in a wagon—four walls, a roof and door absolutely free of charge, and complete freedom to make love day or night—she still snivelled. If I ignored her nagging, meals got delayed, the rice undercooked, the curry over-salted. In the end I gave in. We would move, I said, even if we had to occupy a house by force, but couldn't she tell me the reason, however irrelevant, why she did not like the wagon?

For the first time in weeks Swapna smiled, a very vague smile. 9 Then, slowly, she drew the edge of her sari over her head, cast her eyes down, turned her face from me, and said in a tremulous, barely audible whisper that she (short pause) did (long pause) not want (very long pause) her (at jet speed) baby-to-be-born-in-a-running-train. And she buried her face in her hands. Our fourth child. One died of diphtheria back home (no longer our home) in Dacca; two, from fatigue, on our long trek on foot to Calcutta. Would the baby be a boy? I felt no doubt about it; it would be. Someone to look after us in our old age, to do our funeral rites when we died. I suddenly kissed Swapna, since her face was hidden in her hands, on her elbow, and was roundly chided. Kissing, she holds, is a western practice, unclean also, since it amounts to licking, and should be eschewed by all good Hindus.

I lost no time in looking for a suitable place for her confinement. She 10 firmly rejected all my suggestions: the railway station platform (too many residents); a little-used overbridge (she was not a kite to live so high above the ground); a water tank that had fallen down and was empty (Did I think that she was a frog?). I thought of suggesting the municipal primary school where I was teaching at the time, but felt very reluctant. Not that the headmaster would have objected if we had occupied one end of the back veranda: a kindly man, father of eleven, all girls, he never disturbed the cat that regularly kittened in his in-tray. My fear was: suppose Swapna came running into my class, saying, "Hold the baby for a moment, will you? I'm going to the l-a-t-r-i-n-e." Anyway, we set out to the school. On the way, near the Sealdah railway station, we came upon a cement concrete pipe left over from long-ago repairs to underground mains. Unbelievably, it was not occupied and, with no prompting from me, she crept into it. That was how we came to live in a pipe.

"It is not proper," said Misrilal, "not at all, for a school master to 11 live in a pipe." He sighed deeply. "Why don't you move into one of my buildings, Ajit Babu?"

12 The house I might occupy, if I cared to, he explained, was in Entally, not far from where the pipe lay; I should have no difficulty in locating it; it was an old building and there were a number of old empty coal tar drums on the roof; I could live on the roof if I stacked the drums in two rows and put a tarpaulin over them.

13 We have lived on that roof ever since. It is not as bad as it sounds. The roof is flat, not gabled, and it is made of cement concrete, not corrugated iron sheets. The rent is far less than that of other tenants below us—Bijoy Babu, Akhanda Chatterjee and Sagar Sen. We have far more light and ventilation than they. We don't get nibbled by rats and mice and rodents as often as they do. And our son, Prodeep, has far more room to play than the children below.

14 Prodeep is not with us now; he is in the Naxalite underground. We miss him, terribly. But there is some compensation, small though it is. Had he been with us, we would have had to wear clothes. Now, we don't. Not much, that is. I make do with a loin cloth and Swapna with a piece slightly wider to save our few threadbare clothes from further wear and tear. I can spare little from my pension for new clothes. Swapna finds it very embarrassing to be in my presence in broad daylight so meagerly clad and so contrives to keep her back turned to me. Like a chimp in the sulks. I am fed up with seeing her backside and tell her that she has nothing that I have not seen. But she is adamant; she will not turn around. After nightfall, however, she relents: we are both nightblind.

15 When we go out—to the communal lavatory, to pick up pieces of coal from the railway track, to gather grass—we do wear clothes. Grass is our staple food now: a mound of green grass boiled with green peppers and salt, and a few ladles of very thin rice gruel. We took to eating it when the price of rice started soaring. I had a good mind to do as Bijoy Babu below us is believed to be doing. He has a theory that if you reduce your consumption of food by five grams each day, you will not only not notice that you are eating less but after some time you can do without any food at all. One day I happened to notice that he was not very steady on his feet. That gave me pause. He can get around, however badly he totters, because he has two legs; but I have only one. I lost the other after a fall from the roof of a tram. In Calcutta the trams are always crowded and if you can't get into a carriage you may get up on its roof. The conductor will not stop you. If he tries to, the passengers beat him up, set fire to the tram and any other vehicles parked in the vicinity, loot nearby shops, break street lamps, take out a procession, hold a protest meeting, denounce British imperialism, American neo-colonialism, the central government, capitalism and socialism, and set off crackers. I don't mind my handicap at all; I need wear only one sandal and thereby save on footwear.

So, on the whole, our life together has been very eventful. The events, of course, were not always pleasant. But, does it matter? We have survived them. And now, we have no fears or anxieties. We have a home made of coal tar drums. We eat two square meals of grass every day. We don't need to wear clothes. We have a son to do our funeral rites when we die. We live very quietly, content to look at the passing scene: a tram burning, a man stabbing another man, a woman dropping her baby in a garbage bin.

16

Questions for Discussion and Writing

1. How is the story structured as a series of flashbacks composed of all the places Ajit and Swapna have lived before their present home? How do the circumstances in which Swapna's two previous children died make it so important to her to have a home in which her forthcoming child can be born?
2. At what points in the story did the surrealistic descriptions create GAPS or AMBIGUITIES that you were forced to interpret?
3. What evidence can you cite that being a teacher is important to Ajit in maintaining his self-esteem? How is this need related to his initial rejection of the offer his headmaster makes to let him live on the veranda of the school?
4. What details underscore the vast differences in social class and life circumstances between the headmaster, Misrilal and his family, and Ajit and Swapna and their son?
5. What is the significance of Ajit's reference to the fact that Misrilal's eleven children are all girls? What ASSUMPTIONS can you make about underlying cultural values in India from this reference?
6. How is the story structured to force the reader to accept the reality of events that would be unthinkable at the outset? In effect, how does the process of the story put the reader in Ajit and Swapna's situation? How did you revise your EXPECTATIONS as to what would happen as the story went along?
7. In your opinion, what is Varma's attitude toward the characters and events depicted in the story? Does he find Ajit's acceptance of the most horrible circumstances admirable or is he critical of the tradition of passive acceptance of one's karma?
8. Are you aware of homeless people in your town or city whose conditions might not be comparable to that of Ajit and Swapna, but whose lives are just as desperate? Discuss your response to the issue of homelessness from any angle you wish.

Sheila Roberts

The Weekenders

Sheila Roberts was born in 1942 in Johannesburg, South Africa. She received a doctorate from the University of Pretoria in 1970 and has taught African and Commonwealth literature at Michigan State University. She currently is on the faculty of the University of Wisconsin, Milwaukee, in the English Department. A highly acclaimed writer, she received the Olive Schreiner Award for Prose from the English Academy of South Africa in 1975 for her first collection of short stories, Outside Life's Feast. *Her other works include a volume of poetry,* Lou's Life and Other Poems *(1976), and the novels* He's My Brother *(1977),* Johannesburg Requiem *(1980),* The Weekenders *(1981), which is based on the story reprinted here,* Don Jacobson *(1981), and* This Time of Year *(1983). Roberts's strongest work explores the conditions of the disenfranchised—blacks, women, children, failures—in South Africa. In "The Weekenders," the reason the wife of a wealthy businessman refuses to identify her attackers lies at the center of this thought-provoking story.*

1   I used to be a nurse but I didn't finish my training. It's not nice work, you know. Man, you're on your feet the whole day and the pay's not good. And after a while people get you down, always wanting attention for the slightest thing. You don't get used to pain and blood and all the mess, people wetting themselves, old people who can't wait for the bedpan, the enemas, the bedsores, the catheters, and having to wash the dead. A lot of girls think they'll end up marrying doctors, but I can tell you, the students'll screw and drink with you but they mostly end up marrying their senior partners' daughters once they've finished with their internship. Some of the younger doctors are already caught: they married so that their wives could work and help put them through med school. And the older doctors usually have a lot of bloody kids. They're not even worth having affairs with. The Afrikaners are building up the South African nation, the Catholics won't use birth control, and the Jews don't believe in abortion. Another thing, if a doctor can stick up a family photo with a ton of kids on it, his female patients think he's a nice guy and they don't mind stripping.

2   Nursing's no life, man. They say you get hardened to all the cruelty and misery in life, but I don't know. Maybe I didn't stay long enough to test the truth of that. I just gave it up after two years. I think my talent is for getting on with people. I like people, especially men.

3   So when I saw that job advertised by Champagne Inns, I said to myself, now honestly, Annette, what training do you need to be a hostess and chauffeur? None at all, just a pleasant personality, the ability to

516

keep smiling, and a driver's licence. I applied, and they seemed to be impressed with my nursing experience. Also, I'm not bad-looking and I look nice in tailored skirts and blazers, especially in shades of blue. They first put me to work at the small inn at Umhlanga Rocks and then offered me the job in the new inn out here. I was tired of the heat and humidity of Natal, so I said yes. I was one of the first women they sent out and I really enjoyed myself. There was the construction team and all the contractors all over the bloody place. I was the driver they used to send out to the airport to fetch Venner and Robinson and the others whenever they flew in. We all used to have a lot of fun at night, especially when they started installing the roulette tables. We gambled for small amounts just for fun and, God, we used to drink!

Once they tried to start training Black staff things weren't so good. I 4
was telling the others this when we were going to drive those people to that stupid picnic. I can't associate with a Black on equal terms. I don't know why, I'm just uneasy. As soon as they talk right and smarten up they seem to be thinking themselves great, and it gets my back up. I hate it when Tshithaban men make passes at me in the street, I could kill them. I'll soon be transferring to Milner Park, I hope.

At first I fancied that Arthur Robinson, I can tell you. He's a damn 5
good-looker, with those big shoulders and straight back, and, man, I like the way he walks. But he kept to himself, didn't seem to want to know me. And then I noticed him with that snob-face, Gretchen. She was among the first of the croupiers to be sent out. I'm bloody glad now I didn't let that Arthur put his shoes under *my* bed. My conscience would worry me something awful now. His poor wife so badly hurt by those terrorists. Not that I liked her much when I did meet her. One of those people who look as if they've got the whole bloody world on their shoulders. Concerned about the Blacks all the time, and talking about this being right and that being right and the next thing being wrong. It gets you down. And the men she was with, the skinny *ou*[1] and the American, on that picnic, just went to show what her taste was like. No wonder her husband was screwing around. Though, actually, I always feel sympathetic to the woman. Men mess around whether they've got reason to or not.

I hope the police round those crooks up. Then they can turn them 6
over to me, one by one. I could think of some tortures for them. First I'd cut off their pricks with a blunt scissors.

On the one hand my nursing experience was a good thing: it got me 7
this job. But, on the other, it's been a damn nuisance. Every time somebody cuts himself, the cry goes up, Annette, Annette, where are you? Once one of the Blacks got his finger cut off in a saw. What did he do? He put the damn thing in a match-box and brought it to me! What must I do? Stitch it on again? And every time one of the girls gets a period

---

[1]guy

pain, she'll come and tell me all about it. If people only knew how boring they are. But I have been of help occasionally, like that time when Yvette fainted and when Marcia decided to take an overdose of sleeping pills, stupid thing.

8   So naturally when that bearded American found the sack in front of the hotel and realized there was a body in it, everybody started screaming for Annette. Thank goodness there was a doctor in the hotel, poor devil, trying to have a bit of a holiday. They got him up right away, feeling it was only right that he should cut open the sack. And people were pushing me forward to help. God's truth! I'd never seen anything like it!

9   The smell was terrible! Down her mouth and all over her chin and breasts was this drying mixture of vomit and semen, you could just smell it! Those bladdy Black bastards. Honestly, if a Black came in my mouth I'd just die. Her crotch and backside and thighs and everything were sticky with blood and shit. It was to be expected. Her body was stiff, her knees clenched to her chest, but she was conscious. Every now and then her body would tremble and then be still.

10   "God, who *did* this to you?" I asked her as we lifted her on to a stretcher.

11   Doctor Steinberg told me to shut up.

12   She didn't answer but her eyes looked. Twice in my life I've seen that look. It frightens you. At school back in Daspoort there was this kid with very dark skin and krissy[2] hair. We all knew he had the tarbrush, and some of the boys used to beat him up bad. I remember once when Hansi Schoen beat him so badly that his collar bone was broken, he got this look in his eyes. Kind of hard, but faraway, and very steady. I've seen it in a woman before too. There was this woman in the General with cancer, they told her she had about two years to live. Her kids were tiny and apparently she'd had great trouble conceiving them. I came to straighten her bed and she looked at me and said, out of the blue like that, I am certainly not going to die yet. And Arthur Robinson's wife too. It's hard to explain. It's as if the person's soul has changed shape. I don't know whether people have souls. I read in a book once that somebody was weighing souls. Weigh the body before death and weigh it immediately after death. The human soul weighs twenty-one grams. What do you know? Anyway, Robinson's wife had this look in her eyes. A devilish look, as if nothing could ever really move her again, you know, to pity or tears. Something that says, forget it man, I am going to survive even if it means hating God.

13   But, man, she wouldn't talk. Not at all, for nobody. Doctor Steinberg wanted to put her out altogether, but there was no anaesthetist to be had or anything. He got supplies of local anaesthetic from the nearby

2kinky

clinic and he gave her a couple of shots so that he could do some stitching. Myself and Gretchen (it serves her right), we had to put on overalls and help wash her down, very carefully of course, while Doctor Steinberg treated the burns and cuts and bruises. He himself washed her head and put antiseptic on it and bandaged it, telling us he didn't need us. Man, he had tears in his eyes, which is a very rare thing for a doctor. Meanwhile, Gretchen was throwing up in the bucket, things had finally got to her. Then the South African police arrived from the border post. The Tshithaba police had already put in an appearance, looked around, and taken themselves off.

But she wouldn't talk, not at all. The officer tried very gently to ask her questions. But her mouth was closed. Just her eyes stared at nobody.   14

"I honestly don't think Mrs Robinson is in any condition to answer questions," said Doctor Steinberg.   15

"We understand, Doctor," said the lieutenant. "But we'd like to apprehend the people who did this to her . . . as soon as possible."   16

"I know," said the doctor. "But I am seriously worried about her . . . her mental condition . . . as well as her physical . . . I think you will simply have to make do with questioning the other people . . . involved."   17

"Yes, we will have to do that."   18

So the police left.   19

She turned her head away when her husband came tiptoeing in. She would not look at him even when he whispered her name. He stood there, stiff as a post, white in the face. He really didn't persist. Had I been her and if I had a husband, I would have expected him to fling himself across my bed and howl like a lost soul. But men these days . . . Anyway, he just stood there, looking down at her as if it all was her own fault. And she just looked at the wall.   20

Let me tell you my own theory about why those bastards did this: they were surprised, you see, when the White people came riding up— they thought the game was up. So they nabbed them and threw them into that hut. But something, there must have been something about Joanne Robinson that caught their attention. Something unusual. So they took her and raped her. But to their surprise, she didn't scream or cry or anything. So they lit cigarettes and burnt her. But she still didn't cry. Maybe she didn't want to frighten the others by letting them hear her screams. Stupid woman! Anyway, then they raped her up her arse and her flesh tore. I've seen it happen in childbirth. But by that stage the tissue can be numb, I hope it was in her case. But she still keeps quiet, and they can't understand it. It makes them mad, crazy, so they take out knives and make little cuts on her, but she remains dumb. They are infuriated, but they're also a little bit scared. But what really grips them is her unnatural silence. Why won't she scream? At last they get a fine idea. A white woman's hair. Madam at the hairdressers. Cut   21 it off. But they don't have a scissors, so they use their knives and they hack the stuff off her head.

22   I think if Blacks admire *anything*, it's strength. Why do you think Idi Amin stayed in power that long hey? They see her silence as enormous strength, and probably it is. So they decide not to kill her. But she is a terrible sight, so they get a mealie sack and pull it over her and tie it closed. They want to show the White people a thing or three. And they want the money and the political prisoners or whoever to be released. So they dump it in front of the hotel.

23   Man, the truth is, Joanne Robinson should have screamed and screamed like hell to begin with and she would have got off with just being raped.

24   Things have at least cleared up, or should I say settled themselves. Joanne has left me and is living with her sister. I knew the break was coming even before she left the hospital and so had taken the time to discuss with Advocate du Toit my chances of gaining custody of the children. He thought they were good, particularly in view of Joanne's obviously disturbed mental state. But, believe it or not, she didn't even ask to take the children with her. She told me she wanted to leave and when I said it would be very sensible if I instituted divorce proceedings, she agreed without a fuss. I then said very reasonably, I thought, touching her on the shoulder, that I felt it would be best if the children stayed with me, and again she agreed, just nodding her head silently. You know, the more I see of female behaviour, the more I am convinced that men are more deeply parental than they are. Anyway, Laurie and Ronald seem to be doing perfectly all right, what with my mother's constant visits, Gretchen's kindness in coming over each night to cook for them and me, and the Black servants' truly indulgent attention. I feel an immense relief being able to come home at night to smiling faces and not having to anticipate solemn discussion about poverty and misery and the political cock-up when all I want to do is relax with my family. Gretchen is also a fine woman to have in bed. She rouses easily, expresses her enjoyment, and comes without any difficulty. I've never understood why so many women turn sex into a complicated business when it's essentially a very simple human activity.

25   The trial is over too, thank goodness. I was bloody glad that Black swine got life, and glad that the judge agreed to Joanne's testimony being brief. It was hard for me to believe that the person standing in the witness box was my wife. She didn't look like the woman I'd married. The loss of her hair has certainly changed her appearance, not only in that it somehow alters the shape of her head, I mean the very short curly hair-style she wears, but also in that it distorts her facial expression. Of course, some of the facial scars are still there and have an effect, but all the same there is now an intangible unfamiliarity about her and I am certainly glad she decided to leave. I mean, after *that* experience I

could not have asked her to leave and have retained my image with the Company. People, not understanding, would have been disgusted with me. And I don't think I would have liked my face in the mirror when I shaved in the morning. It's all so very complex.

She doesn't wear the same pretty clothes either any more. The outfit she wore in court was not old but it looked dowdy and mannish, and the other day when she came to get the children for an afternoon she wore old jeans, tennis shoes and a loose tee-shirt. Nor had she tried to disguise the remaining scars with make-up. She looked like a released convict. Actually, she looks now, frankly, more like the class to which she belongs. Let's face the fact, Joanne married *up*. Certainly, she put herself through university and easily learned to copy the manners and ways of the upper middle class, but there remained something ineradicably working class about her. She never learnt to avoid unpleasant subjects of conversation (I always felt uneasy when I took her to Company functions), her sense of humour was at times bawdy and dull, and she never even tried to hide her origins. I persisted in referring in public to her parents' little plot of ground near Vanderbijl as "the farm," but she would not play along with me, telling several people the truth, that her father was a retired NCO from the Permanent Force! Why could she not have transformed him into a farmer for my sake? [26]

Things are going well with me at Champagne Inns. Venner has taken me off the Kwa' Metse job and sent me to start the ball rolling with the Lichtenburg Inn. He thinks I don't know why, but I do. Ever since all the newspapers splashed the story of Joanne's kidnapping and rape and the way the other three hotel guests were kept locked up in a hut, the Inn has been doing brisk business. The horse-riding guide now takes all riders along the very path Joanne and Stella and McLaren and Bob took and shows them where the incident occurred. Venner also had the Board of Directors vote to pay me a most acceptable compensation for my embarrassment and, since Joanne and I separated, my relationships with other women have become easy and flattering. I was discussing this with Freddie Mostert the other day and he said that in his opinion Joanne was the kind of woman that made other women uneasy about getting off with me, something to do with her sincerity, he said. But then Freddie always did like Joanne a lot. I always thought he was in love with her hair. To tell the truth that's what I fell in love with myself. [27]

At first I wasn't very happy about the magistrate's ruling that I pay Joanne a monthly sum for two years to enable her to improve her qualifications, but I must say when I see how she lives I don't feel so bad. She doesn't waste a penny on herself. She is continuing her studies with an obvious compulsion, never goes out, buys very few clothes, and seems to see no one but her sister and, twice a week, the children. I thought it would be worth my while to have her watched: I mean R260 [28] a month for two years adds up to R6,240: a down-payment on a new car. But the detective confirmed what her sister had told me—Joanne is becoming a studious recluse. Fine. I also have outstanding bills to submit to my medical insurance fund for her and more will be coming because she has to have another stint of plastic surgery to her face and more patching up to the lower bowel. But after that the accounts should stop coming in.

29 Gretchen has marvellous taste and is full of great ideas of how we could renovate the house. I really admire a woman who can transform a home into a work of art. I love beautiful furniture and hangings and don't mind at this time spending some money on a few objets d'art and a statuette or two. It always used to annoy me that Joanne was indifferent to whatever shade of carpet or curtain we put in the rooms of that house. I remember how, when it was first built, she left the choice of colours and designs to me. She wasn't very good at entertaining more than about six guests either. Bronwen Mostert could set out a delicious spread to feed twenty, while poor Joanne would make the sea-food sauce too thin, the French fries too dry, the steak too rare, and the salad dressing too sour. She just could not cook well. She did nothing well, really. She didn't have first-class dress-sense; she didn't run the house meticulously; she didn't organize the servants efficiently (Gretchen has remarked how very easy both Nimrod and Nomhla take things. "If you don't watch it, this house'll turn into the Robinson Hotel," she said half-jokingly the other day); she was never quite sexy enough for me; she was obsessed by but badly informed on politics—an annoying combination. She had no awareness of how her behaviour could affect my position—she never tried to influence the right people, and Goddammit, she *would* buy me things I didn't like. It took her so long to learn that I don't like others buying me clothes. I never wore the clothes my mother bought me as surprises, and I couldn't stand the pullovers and shirts and ties that Joanne would bring home for me. I like things to be perfect, exact, and totally appropriate. I'm not one of those easy mix-and-matchers when it comes to clothing. Things must fit properly and the colours must blend superbly or I'm just not interested!

30 The latest in-thing for men is coarse-lace shirts. The guys are wearing them unbuttoned to below the sternum with no undershirts but with chains or pendants round their necks. Last Saturday I wore mine with the fine gold chain Lillian bought me and my black Calvin Kleins. Gretchen told me on the way home that she had overheard one woman say to the other, "Who is that gorgeous creature in the black pants?" I had a good laugh.

31 In a couple of years Joanne should qualify herself to get a decent job, say, with a law firm or even with the legislature. I foresee her taking to tweedy skirts and flat shoes, but also becoming a pillar of strength when it comes to the matter of organizing Laurie and Ronald's

education. I am very thankful that freedom from marital duties hasn't turned her into a gad-about: that would have been so bad for my position. If there is one thing that does bother me, though, it's the curious detachment in her manner. I am friendly, even jovial with her when she comes to see the children, and I have even recently offered her more money if she needs it for necessities. I tell her of things that have happened in the office, and show her the improvements I've made to the house and the things I've bought, but she just listens politely while giving the impression that she hasn't heard a word I'm saying.

I must admit this too. Sometimes I am sad. She used to be a beautiful woman and she did love me. Honestly, sometimes it just seems to me that this country screws up everything. Luckily I have Gretchen and my job is doing well. But, this country . . . really you know, sometimes I wonder. 32

Look at the urban terrorist situation. Not good, man, not good. We've had trains derailed, bombs in shopping centres, shootings out in banks. The government and the police should be doing their job better. We all should be better informed, I say. 33

Those Blacks easily take over the police station at Mazelspoort. They kill a Black constable and they hold three Whites, including a lieutenant, hostage. They want money and the release of Mtlatla and Sigwili. They know, man, they *know*, the S.A.P. don't negotiate. Again, there's a shoot-out. Three of the Blacks are killed, the White sergeant wounded and the White lieutenant dies in hospital. It turns out that the poor bloody lieutenant has five kids, one of whom has had polio, and the man has been supporting a sickly mother. The result? A big fright for us all in the papers, and there's Joanne lying in hospital refusing to speak while they're stitching her up all over. What a wholesale bloody disaster! 34

At least the fourth criminal stood trial and got life. I'm sure he would have got the death sentence had it not been for Joanne's vague and sometimes incomprehensible testimony. 35

"Is this one of the men who raped you, Mrs Robinson?" 36
"I think so." 37
"But you are not sure?" 38
"No." 39
"Do you not recognize him?" 40
"I'm not sure." 41
"Is he one of those who inflicted other injuries on you?" 42
"No." 43
"Did he help to cut at your hair?" 44
"No." 45
"Were you able to identify among the corpses which man it was who inflicted those multiple injuries on you?" 46
"No." 47
"Thank you, Mrs Robinson." 48

49   Oh well. I know the best thing for me is not to look back, but to look forward to a better, more comfortable life with Gretchen and the children.

Questions for Discussion and Writing

1. How is each narrator CHARACTERIZED? From what Annette tells you about herself, and her reasons for leaving the hospital to work at the hotel, would you have ASSUMED that she would be more sympathetic to Joanne or to Arthur?
2. In what respects are Annette's and Arthur's versions of events similar to or different from each other? To what extent are their differences in interpretation due to differences in social class?
3. Would the class differences between Arthur and Joanne have led you to infer that he would react to her being raped in the way that he did?
4. How is the story shaped to create suspense as to why Joanne would not cooperate with the police and identify her attackers? What clues in the text could you rely on in forming your hypothesis that might explain her unusual reaction?
5. Describe a person whom you admire or even envy, revealing how you feel in your description without stating it directly.

Rosanna Yamagiwa Alfaro

Professor Nakashima and Tomiko the Cat

Rosanna Yamagiwa Alfaro grew up in an area in the Midwest where she was the only Asian-American. She has written many short stories, poems, and plays about the predicament of Asian-Americans. Her work has appeared in magazines such as The Harvard Advocate, Descant, *and* The Capilano Review. Behind Enemy Lines, *her play about Japanese-American internment camps, was produced by the People's Theatre in Cambridge, Massachusetts, in 1981 and by the Pan Asian Repertory Theater in New York in 1982. A drama,* Mishima, *based on the life of the great Japanese writer, Yukio Mishima, was produced by the East West Players in Los Angeles in 1988. Another drama based on the life of Martha Mitchell, was produced by Theater Center in Philadelphia, also in 1988. In "Professor Nakashima and Tomiko the Cat" the protagonist is led to rethink his entire life while house-sitting for friends.*

Professor Nakashima held Tomiko under his arm and waved goodbye to the Sobels. Tomiko was a large Persian cat who had been with the Sobels all of her eighty-seven cat years. Whenever the Sobels went away on their summer and winter vacations she worked herself into such a state that she would moult until she was nearly bald. "Don't call us when it happens," said Amy. "Just keep her away from drafts and remember, it all grows back as soon as we return." 1

Amy was Japanese-American and obstinately cheery. She had been brought up in postwar Southern California like himself. They had, in fact, been childhood sweethearts, lost touch when they went their separate ways to college, then, inevitably it seemed, gotten back together when he and Amy's husband Tom discovered they were colleagues at Brandeis. 2

The snow was beginning to fall again when Professor Nakashima, Tomiko held tightly under his arm, retreated into the Sobels' house. The new flurries would freshly dust the piles of snow that had slowly accumulated over the past month. The only challenge to all that whiteness were the nests of dog shit, often still steaming on the edges of the shoveled paths, and the urine stains in the snow banks at every driveway. It was extraordinary, thought Professor Nakashima, the quantities of urine that must seep unnoticed into the ground during the summertime. 3

Once inside the Sobels' large house Professor Nakashima sat back on the great flowered sofa that Amy had spent an entire summer reupholstering. Tomiko drew blood as she sprang out of his arms. In one motion she displaced herself from armchair to bookcase to mantlepiece 4 and began washing herself vigorously, anxious, no doubt, to rid herself of any trace of his human scent.

5   Professor Nakashima, out of work for 398 days, detested cats, which hadn't prevented him from leaving his small bachelor quarters to catsit in his ex-colleague's house for the Christmas vacation. Tom and Amy had stashed their two small children with the grandparents and were off to Puerto Rico for a month. Never mind that the university vacation was only three weeks long. Tom, to whom tenure and all other things came easily, had arranged it so he'd be away the entire month.

6   Even the heavens went out of their way to contribute to Tom's happiness, thought Professor Nakashima as he untied his shoes and sank back into the great sofa. The snow flurries had come down at just the right moment to heighten Tom's anticipation of escaping to warmer climes. Lying back, Professor Nakashima, who had put on a fair amount of weight since his enforced retirement, felt like a beached whale.

7   Later it seemed to him that he had spent most of his first three weeks there on the down-filled cushions of Amy's sofa. He simply found it very difficult to move. Even when he executed a slow turn from one side to the other he heard a thin whistle that seemed to be coming from his heart, as if it were letting out a little air. Spiritually, however, he moved more rapidly, going pleasantly from book to book, not from Tom's esoteric library, which reminded him too much of his own, but from Amy's Book-of-the-Month Club selections.

8   Since he had been denied tenure, Professor Nakashima had not opened a single book of Far-Eastern history. Of course, neither had many of his ex-colleagues, including Tom, a committee rat, who had taught the same courses for five years in a row and devoted his considerable talents entirely to administrative matters. There were even rumors afloat that Tom was the one who might most naturally take over the department once the present chairman retired.

9   For Professor Nakashima life made simpler demands—telephone messages to jot down, the cat to feed. Tomiko, perversely enough, had developed an attachment to him. She jumped on his lap and sat all over any book he happened to be reading. She wove back and forth ahead of him as he made his way to the kitchen, rubbing her cheeks on his stockinged feet. Since Amy, with her compulsive Japanese tidiness, had left the cans of catfood neatly stacked, all he had to do was alternate the tuna with the chicken liver. But Professor Nakashima soon discovered he hated the smell of cat food and couldn't bring himself to wash out Tomiko's bowl for over a week. At that point he gingerly threw the bowl into the garbage and thereafter Tomiko ate directly from the can.

10   Once in the kitchen there was also the matter of his own meals. The Sobels kept a well-stocked larder. Tom gave him the keys to the liquor cabinet and Amy said he was to help himself to anything he could find in the pantry. Though Professor Nakashima couldn't bring himself to

touch a drop of Tom's liquor, he felt no compunctions about raiding the pantry. In the morning he poured milk into the miniature cereal boxes Amy bought for the children, thereby saving himself the bother of doing the breakfast dishes. He found pickled herring and sesame crackers for lunch, bottled chicken and truffles for dinner, and though he snacked continually he hardly made a dent in the pantry stores. How fortunate for Tom that Amy was so provident.

Whenever he felt a pang of guilt for poaching on the Sobel preserves he reminded himself that they, after all, owed him several meals of his own choosing. In the beginning Amy had invited him with other members of the history department for special Japanese meals she knew he would particularly enjoy. But lately, especially after the tenure decision, she tended to invite him alone on what he immediately recognized as the leftovers of some banquet they had had without him the night before. Not that they didn't enjoy his company. He still retained a special place in their household, much like a pet of long standing to whom one fed the best scraps under the table.

Within two weeks Professor Nakashima had poked through all the shelves, even finding the cookie jar where Amy stashed her jewels. Professor Nakashima ran the necklaces through his fingers, his long mandarin fingers that stayed thin and elegant in spite of his great weight. He could not remember Amy even wearing the simplest pin, but here was a wealth of gold and silver, emeralds and diamonds squirreled prudently away for a rainy day. He warmed a fat ruby brooch in his palm before letting it drop back into the cookie jar. Poor but honest, he thought, grimly calculating its worth in porterhouse steaks and smoked salmon.

Tom and his other Anglo-American friends cherished the illusion that Professor Nakashima had achieved his impressive girth on sake and sushi, when living on welfare as he did, he usually had to settle for beer and chips. Even when he was still receiving his assistant professor's wages he generally preferred Chinese to Japanese cuisine, finding it more varied and opulent, catering more to the palate than to the eye.

His appetites being what they were, Professor Nakashima took pains to weigh himself at the thinnest moment of every day—in the morning between urinating and having breakfast—and found he had lately been gaining weight at the rate of a pound a week. Having no full-length mirror in his bachelor's quarters, he had not fully appreciated the extent of his enormity. He knew he spilled over his belt, that he was a snug fit in Tom's leather Corbusier armchair, but turning sideways in front of the hall mirror was a revelation of such proportions that he instantly despaired of any diet or exercise.

And in the Sobel house, although he had yet to go out for groceries, he was growing, not shrinking. His shirts were all tight at the armpits. The few that used to hang straight now took the shape of his stomach. One day he tried on one of Tom's jackets and heard something rip at the shoulder. Then he discovered a wide denim smock of Amy's in the laundry bin and found it so much to his liking that he wore it an entire week both waking and sleeping.

16   In the bathroom the Sobels had a small magnifying mirror surrounded with lights and in it he discovered his first white hairs, not one but five all at once. As a child he had carefully pulled out a black hair and a white hair from his mother's head so he could examine them under a microscope. The black hair was thin, the white hair thick with a center that resembled the core of a carrot. His own white hairs, which he also pulled out, were stiff and curly. Professor Nakashima's sleek black hair had always been his sole point of vanity.

17   The time passed quickly or rather did not pass at all. He barely gave a thought to the snowy streets outside. At the end of the fourth week a postcard arrived from Amy complaining that Tom had decided to leave Puerto Rico a week early to attend a medieval history symposium in Ohio before flying home. The idea of leaving a tropical paradise early to return to wintry climes seemed absurd to Amy. Tom could travel without her. She would remain by herself in the sun.

18   Professor Nakashima derived a certain amount of satisfaction from the peevishness of Amy's note. Why she had married Tom in the first place had always been a source of mystery to him. He had naturally assumed that she would marry a Japanese-American like himself. He still averted his eyes whenever she addressed the tall bearded Tom with an endearment or when she stood, as she often did, with her arm around his waist. On the other hand, particularly lately, he found himself wondering what Tom could possibly see in Amy, built short and squat like a soup can. Poor Amy had never been thin but, like himself, had recently gained six hundred pounds. Unlike himself, she had Japanese-American stamped on her forehead, determined, tidy, sensible to a fault. She had probably sniffed out Tom's administrative potential from the beginning.

19   Amy's postcard also served as a reminder that he was not on his own turf, that the Sobels would be back in a week. That was all well and good, thought Professor Nakashima, since Tomiko was beginning to get on his nerves. It seemed he couldn't leave the room without her following at his heels. She was always with him, asleep on his lap, playing with his shoelaces, or even squatting on the toilet seat to watch him as he took his bath. The smell of cat was in the air and on his clothes. Also, as Amy had forewarned him, she was beginning to moult. Balls of cat hair would blow across the floor like tumbleweed. There was also the matter of the kitty litter. He had noticed after the second week that it had gotten permanently wet and lumpy, but overcome by an immense lethargy, he couldn't quite bring himself to change it.

20   Professor Nakashima suddenly decided that just as Amy felt the need for a vacation away from Tom, he owed it to himself to spend a few days away from Tom's namesake. Letting Tomiko out was

impossible. She was one of those housecats that had never once set foot on the grass, accustomed all her life to the feel of wall-to-wall carpets. No wonder she was so neurotic and spent many of her waking hours on the window sill looking out longingly at the snow.

Fortunately the house was big enough for both of them. Professor Nakashima in one master stroke picked up his belongings from the guest bedroom and moved into the master bedroom with its own bathroom attached, complete with the only Japanese bath in Waltham. For his five day retreat he provided himself with a basket of supplies from Amy's pantry along with a large parcel of interesting tinned and bottled delicacies from Japan which had just arrived in a Christmas package from Amy's aunt and which he had absentmindedly opened. 21

For Tomiko he poured a large saucepan of milk and opened up five cans of cat food which he placed side by side on the floor. He even watered the plants, which Amy had thoughtfully gathered together on the kitchen table lest they fall victim to his benign neglect. Professor Nakashima watered them thoroughly, waiting until the water came out of the holes at the bottom of the flower pots. Then, having discharged all his responsibilities, he said goodbye to Tomiko and settled back on the crisp gingham spread of the Sobels' emperor size bed. 22

These were perhaps the most perfect days that Professor Nakashima ever spent in his adult life. Even Tomiko couldn't spoil his five day idyll though at first she sat outside his door for hours at a time, meowing pitifully, sticking her paw under the door and trying to pull it open. At night she would gallop up and down the hall like a horse, chasing some small object—a child's marble, perhaps, or a mouse. 23

But, generally speaking, Professor Nakashima settled back to enjoy his cans of eel and cuttlefish, his bottles of pickled tofu, mushrooms, ferns and leeks. New Year's Eve, he poured water into the large sunken tub just before midnight and splashed happily about, relishing the fact that his bath spanned two years. He was a great lover of the bath—in that one respect his Japanese genes seemed to assert themselves over his American environment. Or maybe it was because the bath was as close as he ever got these days to the sea. Even as a child he had been as graceful in the water as he was clumsy on land. Swimming, he displaced himself as effortlessly as the seals and walruses. Walking, he was out of his element. 24

The sunken bath, which was obviously also enjoyed by the Sobel children, had on its edge several small colorful bath toys which he examined at his leisure. A small wind-up turtle that flapped its way across the tub and a toy pump were his favorites. They reminded him pleasantly of his own childhood when his mother, a large woman, took him into the bath with her and allowed him to dock his boats on her island tummy. His own stomach was now so large he had difficulty in viewing his private parts. 25

It was on his fifth night in the Sobels' room that Professor 26

Nakashima received a midnight telephone call that effectively put an end to his holiday. It was Amy. She was sorry, she said, for waking him, but naturally she wanted to take advantage of the cheapest phone rates. "Of course, of course, how sensible," he said, adding pleasantly, "how Japanese."

27   The connection was bad. It seemed to him that her voice was coming from another planet. He slowly pieced together what it was she was saying, and trying to shake himself awake from the nightmare said, "You what?" and then, "For Christ's sake, Amy," because the woman he had known and in his own way adored ever since childhood, the woman with whom he had grown comfortably middle-aged and fat was now telling him she would be a week late because she was having as she put it, "a last ditch stab at happiness, freedom, love, whatever you want to call it" with, from all he could gather, a dermatologist attending a cosmetics colloquium in San Juan.

28   "Listen," she was saying, "You're the only person I can count on to square things with Tom. I'm not asking you to understand. I know we're the same age, but it's different for a woman. All these years I've been the typical housewife with nothing in my future except teenaged children, an empty nest, and menopause."

29   Professor Nakashima was stunned. He cut Amy short saying, "This must be costing you a small fortune." Never in his life had he come face to face with an act of such vulgarity, such wanton abandonment. How could Amy have gotten herself into such a mess? He had, for God's sake, been her devoted admirer for twenty years and never once thought of asking more.

30   And now that he had hung up on her, how was he to face Tom who like everyone else had taken Amy so much for granted as the fine dependable Japanese wife she used to be? Professor Nakashima was a sensitive man. He thought of the house, once tidy, now a pig's pen. He pictured himself in Amy's denim smock, welcoming the lord and master home, and Tom's sharp eyes instantly assessing the external damages. Well, even he was now in position to tell poor Tom a thing or two about putting the house in order.

31   Professor Nakashima slept fitfully. Each time he woke he had a tingling sensation in the scalp as if his hair were in the process of turning white or falling out. Early the next morning he opened the door and surveyed the disaster of the last five days.

32   The air was thick and sweet. In the kitchen all the cat food was gone but the milk was untouched and had curdled. Most likely Tomiko had eaten all the cat food in the first day and gone hungry for four. Also she had probably not had a drop to drink. The scatter rugs were askew in the hall. Cat hair was matted on all of the diningroom chairs. Still, he reflected, there was nothing he couldn't put back in order—he had a couple of days left before Tom returned. But then he saw the dark stains on Amy's flowered sofa. Looking more carefully, he discovered

that Tomiko in her anger had defecated in the center of each down-filled cushion.

Sometime later he found the culprit under the radiator by the front   33
door. She pretended not to recognize him but finally pulled herself out from her hiding place and sniffed at the crack under the door. She had shed a great deal in the last three days, giving her a thin patchy appearance.

"You've never been out in your life. What would an old cat like you   34
do in all the snow?" he asked aloud, looking out through the leaded panes of the door. Outside there were flurries. Usually in Waltham the snow alternated with the slush, but this winter it never rained and never got above freezing. Nothing was washed away, all was accumulated.

Tomiko meowed pitifully. He felt sorry for her, the poor old cat who   35
had never had a taste of freedom in all her eighty-seven years. Professor Nakashima realized he was perspiring. Perhaps one of the reasons Tomiko was moulting in winter was simply because the house was kept too hot. He felt his ankles tingle and knew that he would never be able to set things right before Tom came home. Summoning all his strength, he pushed open the door against the wind and watched as Tomiko, her long thin hair trailing behind her like a mandarin's beard, streaked out into the bright snow.

Questions for Discussion and Writing

1. Did anything in Professor Nakashima's behavior alert you to the possibility that he might react as he did to Amy's midnight telephone call? Why was this such a big disappointment to him?
2. How do issues of social class help explain why Amy and Tom are treating Nakashima differently than they did in the past?
3. How does the failure to be granted tenure change Professor Nakashima's self-image and behavior?
4. In what ways are Tomiko's and Nakashima's circumstances similar? In what way might Nakashima's actions toward the cat in the final scene reflect his view of Tom and Amy?
5. Where in the story would you have been unable to anticipate what would happen next? To what extent did your inability to imagine what would happen next depend on your ASSUMPTIONS as to how a college professor would behave?
6. Have you ever taken care of someone's house and/or pets? Discuss your experiences.
7. Describe someone whose self-image was shattered. What view of themselves did they initially have and what changed it?
8. What does the name you gave your pet reveal about the character traits that are important to you and your family in bestowing an identity?

Ntozake Shange

Betsey Brown

Ntozake Shange, playwright, poet, and novelist, was educated at Barnard College and the University of Southern California. She has captivated audiences with her fiery speech since the 1976 Broadway debut of for colored girls who have considered suicide/when the rainbow is enuf. *Both an OBIE Award winner and a critically acclaimed PBS production,* for colored girls *was soon followed by three extraordinary plays—*Spell No. 7 *(1981), A* Photograph: Lovers in Motion *(1981), and* Boogie Woogie Landscapes *(1981)—that also integrate poetry, dance, and music. Shange is the author of several volumes of poetry and criticism, including* A Daughter's Geography *(1983),* From Okra to Greens *(1978), and* See No Evil *(1984). Her first novel was* Sassafras, Cypress, and Indigo *(1982), followed by* Betsey Brown *(1985), and most recently* Riding the Moon in Texas *(1992). Drawn from her novel of the same name, "Betsey Brown" is an autobiographical work that was also adapted as a musical and first presented at the McCarter Theater in Princeton, New Jersey, in 1991. This story relates how the spoiled children of an upper-middle-class black family sabotage the efforts of their new black housekeeper to bring order into their chaotic household.*

1   "Goddammit, Greer! Do you understand anything I ever say to you?"

2   Jane looked at her wedding picture, satiny, a patina of thirteen years veiling her young foolish face. She wanted to push the gilded edges of the damn thing through Greer's head the way he used scalpels to take bullets outta the hoodlums he loved so much.

3   "Did you hear me? Where were you when I needed you? Me? Jane, your wife! Not some lowly sick acting-the-fool stinking niggahs so dumb they can't find the goddamn clinic! Do you hear me? I am talking to you!"

4   Greer looked up from *Digest for Surgical Procedures* and nodded. Jane froze. She held her breath and started again. She was going to be decent about this one more time.

5   "Where were you when the police brought our children home? Don't you realize what could have happened to them? Where were you, dammit! Answer me!"

6   Jane picked up his stethoscope and threw it at him. Greer caught it in his left hand and went right on reading.

7   "I was at the Johnsons'. He's been bleeding again since he left the hospital, and I wanted to check on him. He's an old man, Jane, he can't get up and run to the clinic on one leg."

8   "But I suppose your children could be in jail or dead on accounta

poor Mr. Johnson, who's got so many benefits he's forgotten what money looks like."

Jane walked around the bed to Greer and pulled the *Digest* from his hands. "Did Mr. Johnson pay you something today? Or you so holy you can give your services away? Who do you think you are, Saint Francis? I have a house full of children who need clothes, shoes, dental work, eyeglasses, dance classes, food, and a father. And where is their father? Why, seeing Mr. Johnson! Mr. Johnson doesn't live here, Greer. We live here with five children and my beloved mother, who was right that the race definitely needs some improving!" 9

Jane began to beat the dresser with the *Digest*. Then she started tearing it to pieces, when Greer slowly wrapped her in his arms, saying: "Aren't the boys all right?" Jane didn't respond. "Aren't the police going to leave them alone if they act right?" Jane said nothing. "Look, honey, they're not in jail. Charlie was just having a little fun." 10

"Charlie was having fun, was he? Well, this is St. Louis, Missouri, my dear. You ask Chuck Berry how much fun the police let blacks have when it comes to white girls." Jane snatched Greer's loosened tie from around his neck. 11

"I am going to tell you one more time. I cannot run this house as if I were the father and the mother. Now I know you are a doctor, and you have a public responsibility, but if you don't put this household first in your life, I swear 'fore Jesus you're going to be in for a big surprise." 12

Greer knew Jane in these moods. He didn't understand why she couldn't see he was working himself half to death to keep the family exactly the way she wanted. She didn't understand that poor colored people didn't get decent treatment at the clinic, and by going by to see them he was building a clientele for his real practice. Damn, Greer thought, for such an intelligent woman, Jane didn't have much foresight. 13

"I got home as soon as I could." With that, Greer took his tie out of Jane's hands and picked up the latest issue of *MD* magazine. 14

Jane sat at her vanity table staring at Greer, who had the audacity to read when her boys had been touched by Southern police. What gall! What an ass she'd married! What ever was she going to do? She took the emery boards from the top left drawer and started doing her nails. She was going to play bridge, but before she did that she was going to have a scotch and soda and play a game of solitaire with the prettiest hands a woman with this many problems could have. Not another word passed between them, not one that was spoken, at any rate, not a word anyone else would understand. 15

Betsey thought she understood it. She thought she knew that the problem was there were too many of them. Too many children. Too wild. Too much noise. Too trying for her delicate mother's nature. Why, Mama wasn't raised to tend to a bunch of ruffians like Sharon and them, especially not Charlie, who'd awready been put out of 16 schools in the North. No, Betsey knew when her parents were arguing it was most likely on accounta the children. Then there was the problem of the white people and money. White folks and money seemed to go hand in hand. Whenever a black mentioned one, he mentioned the other, like the white folks had took up all the money and were hiding it from the blacks, like they kept the nice houses for themselves, and the good schools, and the restaurants and motels. Just for themselves.

17   "You did not win," Charlie screeched down the back stairs. The basketball ricocheted from one wall to the other all the way down the stairway.

18   "Betsey! Would you see what's the matter?" Jane called tiredly from her manicure and highball.

19   "He did, too!"

20   "He didn't." Margot and Sharon began tussling with each other over the issue of whether or not Allard had won, when it was clear it was none of their business.

21   "He didn't what?" Betsey screamed into the house from her terrace, where she'd gone to escape the chaos of the house.

22   "Betsey! Didn't I ask you to see about these children?" Jane leaped up, exasperated. "Betsey, where are you?"

23   "That's not yours," Margot tried to pull the ball and jacks from Sharon.

24   "Who threw this ball down the stairs?" Vida hollered up.

25   "I don't know, Grandma," Betsey hollered down.

26   "Well, come along here and get it. It certainly doesn't belong in the kitchen."

27   "Grandma, I didn't have anything to do with that ball!"

28   "I'ma tell on you. You pull my hair one more time, ya hear?"

29   "Give it back then."

30   "I will not either."

31   "Allard, put those matches down! I see you. Where'd you start the fire?" Betsey ran after Allard, who'd only set a small fire on the third floor to get back at Charlie, who was a big bully anyway. By the time Betsey'd put the fire out, the second floor was going crazy.

32   "I'ma tell Mama. You tore my dress."

33   "If you do, I'ma knock one of those buck teeth of yours out!"

34   "Where's my basketball?"

35   "I'ma tell Mama."

36   "Mama, Mama, please make her stop."

37   "Mama, please make her stop."

38   "Mama, Allard got holdt to some matches again, but everything's awright."

39   "Sharon, stop it, I say."

40   "You're hurtin' my arm!"

41   "Mama, please, come help me," Margot cried.

42   "Mama, she's lying on me," Sharon moaned.

"Mama, I didn't start a big fire," Allard explained.   43

"Aunt Jane, tell Grandma to give me back my basketball."   44

"Mama, please! Come help."   45

Jane shut the door to her room and played solitaire, betting against   46
herself. Greer'd fallen asleep. He'd been on call two nights in a row.
Betsey went to her terrace for some cloud peace and air. The children
just went on as children will do. Jane's thoughts veered to her wedding
vows, "in sickness and in health." Wasn't anything about in madness or
white folks.

Betsey took a deep breath 'cause the South may be full of ugly   47
things but it's not in the air. The air is flowers, leaves, and spaces divine, when you're up high enough to climb onto a sturdy branch of
your very own oak tree. If she climbed out to the middle of the tree,
Betsey thought, she'd be a bird and sing a colored child's bird song, a
colored child's blues song, or a hot jump and rag song. From the middle of her tree, where she was sure she was not supposed to be, Betsey
listened real close for her city to sing to her so she could respond.
Everybody knows any colored child could sing, specially one from a
river city. A hankering blues-ridden, soft-swaying grace of a place like
her home would surely answer her first melody.

From her vantage point through the myriad leaves, Betsey saw what   48
looked to her mind like a woman in need of some new clothes and a
suitcase. Who ever heard of carrying one's belongings in two shopping
bags, while wearing a hat with five different-colored flowers on it? And
she was singing a Mississippi muddy song:

humm hum, hum hum, hum uh

well, my name is bernice & i come a long way
up from arkansas & i'm here to stay
i got no friends & i ain't got no ma
but i'ma make st. louis give me a fair draw

hum hum, hum hum, hum hum, uh

there's some pretty young men
in these mighty fine jobs
got pomade in their hair
& they move like the light
i'ma set my sights
on a st. louis guy
with some luck by my side
i'ma dress up my best
& bring me a st. louis mess of a man

humm hum, hum hum, hum hum, hum uh

i'ma show them white folks in arkansas
that a good woman can get what she want
how she want and when/humm humm, humm humm

my name is bernice & i come a long way
i'ma makin' my business in st. louis to stay

The song moved as if it weren't usedta having shoes on its feet. The lips blurred like the slurs of her lines, losing definition into flat pimply cheeks and a head of hair in need of pressing underneath that hat. Bernice hadda way about her. A country honor that came from knowing hard work too soon, and being rid of it too late. The children's noises coming from this big ol' house gladdened her heart.

49   "I told you to give me my jacks!"

50   "No ball playing beneath the chandelier, do you hear me, you piece of Northern trash! Even if you are my grandchild, you ain't right."

51   "Mama, Mama, please come see to Sharon."

52   "Jane, you best come out your room and see to these chirren 'fore they tear your house down."

53   Bernice waddled up the stairs from the curb, glanced at Betsey in the tree, took a breath and hummed her song. She had been walking around this rich colored neighborhood all day looking for work, and she was determined to stay in St. Louis. She was going to help this family out. She was what was missing, an eye on these hinckety misbehaving brats. Bernice kept on up the stairs to the front door in time to the yelps and hollers careening through the screens of every floor. Seemed like not a child in there could talk decent. All of them screaming and hollering like they were out on the farm. Bernice rang the front doorbell.

54   "Mama, there's somebody at the door."

55   "Mama, there's a colored woman at the door."

56   "Mama, there's a fat lady at the door."

57   "Jane, you've got a visitor."

58   "Aunt Jane, there's something at the door."

59   Jane tied her robe around her waist while looking at Greer asleep in his clothes. That damned green surgical outfit sprawled all over her fresh linen. But that was the man she'd married. She bent over and gave him a peck of a kiss, a long caress where the evening shadow was beginning to appear on his chin.

60   "Jane, I say, you've got a caller!"

61   By the time Jane reached the front door, all the children were crowded around her like the woman who lived in a shoe. It was claustrophobic. She had a hard time opening the front door for all the feet pressed up against it. What she saw was a heavyset, no-funny-business country woman with the most peculiar hat.

"Good evening, ma'am." 62

"Yes, may I help you? I'm Mrs. Brown." 63

"Yes, ma'am, Mrs. Brown. I see you've got some chirrens and I 64
thought you might be in need of some he'p. I'ma hardworkin' gal. I
come up from Arkansas to raise myse'f up. I'm ready to tend after 'em,
and see to they meals and hair and such."

Jane smiled, thinking the Lord moves in mysterious ways. 65

"Well, come in, miss—uh . . ." 66

"My name is Bernice Calhoun, ma'am." 67

"Well, Miss Calhoun, please come in. This is Allard. Here is Sharon. 68
This is Margot. And my nephew Charles. Oh, I wonder where Betsey is.
Mama, have you seen Betsey?" Jane called.

"No, I haven't," Vida answered from the kitchen. 69

"Miss Calhoun, have you worked with children before?" 70

"Why, yes, ma'am, in Arkansas." 71

"Do you have any references you could show me?" 72

"Well, I could tell you the names of the families I worked for, and 73
you could call them. But down South they's mighty informal, so I don't
have anything writ down that I could show you."

"Oh, my." Jane sighed. "I think the best thing to do, Miss Calhoun, 74
is for you to give me the names and addresses of your former employers. I shall write them. In the meantime you may work here on a proba-
tionary basis till I've heard from them."

"Oh, that's fine, ma'am." 75

Vida was approaching Jane to say she had no idea where Betsey 76
was. Instead she interrupted, "Who's this?"

"Oh, Mama, this is Bernice Calhoun, who's going to stay on to help 77
with the children. Isn't that wonderful? Miss Calhoun, this is my
mother, Mrs. Murray."

Vida took one look at Bernice and went back to the kitchen, shaking 78
her head about what the race had to offer.

"I can't figure out where Betsey is right now, Bernice, but she's my 79
oldest girl and she'll be a big help to you."

Bernice pursed her lips, thinking now would be the time to get in 80
good with Mrs. Brown. Show her what a sharp eye she had for chirrens.

"Might she be that one out there, up in that tree, ma'am?" 81

Jane forgot the time of day. She stiffened and ran out on the front 82
porch to the far end. Right above her head, in the middle of a huge tree,
sat her daughter Betsey.

"Betsey, you come down from there right this instant! How do you 83
expect to set an example behaving like a jackass? Come down from
there, right this minute! Do you hear me, Elizabeth!"

When Jane called Betsey "Elizabeth," it was serious. Betsey cut her 84
eyes at Bernice Calhoun, who didn't realize what a mistake she'd made.
Honeying up to Jane wasn't going to do her any good. Jane wasn't

home half the day; Betsey Brown was. Now, Betsey Brown was more than mad 'cause some fool Mississippi song had given away her sacred hiding place. Made her mama call her Elizabeth.

85   "I'll be right out, Mother. I'm so sorry. I can't imagine what got into me." Betsey oozed, not fooling Jane at all. "I want to meet the company. I'm coming right now."

86   Jane watched in amazement as her daughter maneuvered herself along the limbs of the tree to the edge of the terrace and through the window. In a flash Betsey presented herself.

87   "Hello, my name is Elizabeth Brown. How are you?"

88   Jane was proud of her daughter again. Bernice thought she'd made a friend.

89   "Betsey, I told you, Miss Calhoun."

90   "Oh, ma'am, the chirrens can call me Bernice."

91   "I told Bernice that you would help her with the children and the running of the house. Show her to her room on the third floor and tell her about the neighborhood and the children's chores."

92   Betsey took Bernice by the hand. Charlie reluctantly picked up her paper bags filled with God only knew what, and up they traipsed through the back stairway to the top of the house. It was against Jane's principles to put a black in the basement. It was against the children's principles to accept somebody who was going to tell on them all the time. Betsey had some very special plans for Miss Calhoun.

93   "I hope you'll be very happy with us, Bernice. The girls are very smart, and Allard never causes any trouble, and Charlie is practically a grown-up awready."

94   "Why, thank-ya, 'Liz'beth."

95   "Uh, Betsey is just fine, Bernice, if you don't mind."

96   "Well, I say to ya again, thank ya, Miss Betsey."

97   Betsey gave the secret sign of a fist behind her back with two fingers outstretched to indicate it was time for a children's meeting in the basement. Who did this Bernice think she was, giving away secrets like that? Why, Jane hadn't even known about the tree reaching over the porch until Bernice came. Betsey was going to see to it that Bernice paid. Boy, would she pay. The line, led by Charlie dribbling the basketball down the stairs, headed straight for the bowels of the house.

98   Bernice didn't know it, as she examined the tilted curved ceilings of her new quarters. Jane didn't know it, as she curled up next to Greer behind the locked door of their room above the lilacs. Only the children in the darkest, smallest corner of the basement knew what Bernice had coming her way. Vida in the kitchen over chicken fricassee could only think of her Frank and how much he liked the meat to fall off the bone over the rice and onions. And there was nothing any one of the grown-ups could have done had they known what was up in the basement.

99   The basement was a secret of its own. There were rooms that led to

other rooms and back around to the first room. There were closets that went way back against the walls of the house until it smelled like the earth was coming right on in. There were rooms to have seances and see cats have kittens. Corners to whisper make-believe apologies and dreams. There was the smell of many folks having lived in the dark for many years, and there was the children's favorite meeting place that no one bigger than them had ever seen. In the far left-hand corner of the longest closet with the lowest ceilings and plywood walls painted green long before Christ was born, the Brown children had their powwow.

"How's she gonna do something with us?" Betsey was riled, and 100 her little temper was cavorting in the shadows with her small horde of followers. "She can't even talk. Imagine callin' me 'Lizabeth. Why, that ain't even a name, 'Lizabeth!"

"And she tol' on you, too, Betsey," Sharon chimed in. 101

"Mama didn't know nothing 'bout that tree," Margot added. 102

"Not now, Allard. Now we've got to figure out a way to get this 103 woman out of our house."

"Not only can't she talk, she can't hardly walk," Charlie quipped 104 with the basketball twirling on his finger, then behind his back.

"So how's she gonna do something with us?" Allard decried. 105

"She's not. Just wait till morning." And Betsey dismissed the crowd. 106

Betsey was not a vindictive child. She was a child of special places 107 and times of her own. She tried not to hurt anybody or anything, but Bernice'd given the whole family access to her privacy. Now when they went looking for her, they'd all know to go to her beloved tree. Search its branches for the dreamer and make noises that would disrupt Betsey's current reveries. No, Betsey wasn't being evil; to her mind she was protecting herself. God only knew what else that Bernice would uncover and deliver over to Jane and Greer. Heaven forbid she ever found that long closet in the basement! That's where everybody practiced writing nasty words like "pussy" and "dick," though only Charlie admitted to knowing where all these things were. Margot just liked to write them in big red letters with nail polish she'd borrowed from her mother's collection of toiletries. Allard just liked making the letters and then asking what the word was.

Meanwhile, in the upper reaches of the house, Bernice was hanging 108 her limited wardrobe in the armoire next to a single bed just 'bout big enough to accommodate her rotund brown body. Yes, she thought, looking at the red dress with the lace on one sleeve, St. Louis was gointa be just fine. She'd have every Friday and Saturday night off, to meet some nice hardworking fella, maybe one of them from down her way, not too citified. Bernice looked out her window down on the garden, thinking how lucky she'd been to run into the Brown family. That poor Mrs. Brown, so frail, with all these chirren, and Mrs. Murray with her nose all up in the air on accounta a body didn't have good hair. She'd win them over. That's what she'd do.

109   In the morning the children tumbled down the stairs into a fine chaos. First, Betsey told Allard it was all right to rub the goldfish together. Then Sharon and Margot decided to swing on the curtain rod separating the living room from the parlor. Charlie decided he'd practice throwing his basketball around the chandelier. Of course, Jane and Greer were relaxing for a change, relieved to have Bernice handling everything. Even Vida had gone out to see to her dahlias in the back. So it was just Bernice and the Brown children.

110   "Look, Bernice, somebody peed in the bed." Margot came running through the kitchen with a dank sheet wrapped around her head.

111   "Bernice, you wanta see me make fires? We could use these matches right under here." Allard crawled through Bernice's legs to the cupboard where the fireplace matches were kept. He really liked those. They were so long and the fire was very tiny at first, till you threw it somewhere. Then whamo. Big flame.

112   Yet Bernice was undaunted. She was gointa stay in St. Louis, no matter what.

113   "Bring that nappy head on 'round heah. No, don't carry no comb, bring me a brush. A comb ain't gointa go through all that mess."

114   Bernice'd made breakfast of grits and eggs that no one ate, claimin' the grits were stiff and the eggs too hard.

115   "Allard, didn't you say you wanted to climb out the window? The one in my room is open. Sharon, there's some money in Bernice's sweater pocket if you want to buy some Snickers today."

116   All this was going on while Bernice was trying to make some sense of the mass of braids on the girls' heads. Bernice shouted, "Put them goldfish down. I want my money in my pocket right now." It didn't sit right with her. This Betsey was supposed to be her friend, and here she was undermining everything.

117   "Bernice, the fish are dying."

118   "Well, put 'em back in the water, fool."

119   "I'ma tell Mama you callt me a fool."

120   "That's right, Allard, you tell Mama."

121   "Betsey, bring that head over heah, I tol' you."

122   "Bernice, I'm hungry."

123   "Well. Eat your breakfast."

124   "I don't want breakfast, I want some chicken."

125   "That's for dinner."

126   "I want some chicken now!"

127   "Well, awright, then. Charlie, get that basketball out this house."

128   "Oh, Bernice, I spilled all the chicken grease."

129   Bernice stood up with an Arkansas fire in her eyes, screaming, "You better eat them grits 'cause that's all you gonna get! Put them goldfish down! I tell ya whoever took my money bettah pray for they soul! I ain't going nowhere, and y'all best mind, 'cause I'm in St. Louis to stay."

"How you gonna do something with us?" 130

"You can't even talk." 131

"I say bring that nappy head on over heah!" 132

The ruckus sent Jane flying down the stairs to find the blinds at a 45- 133
degree angle in the front room. The curtains in the parlor all over.
Six crystals from her chandelier on the floor. Chicken grease on the
kitchen floor. A table full of grits and eggs. Not one combed head.
Allard with matches in both pockets. Betsey quietly gazing out the window at Vida working with her dahlias. Plus, no one had brought up
the morning's coffee. Now this was just too much. No coffee and the
house in a shambles. It was better with her mother tending to the children, even though it was hard on her heart. The likes of this never happened.

"And, Miss Calhoun, just what do you call yourself doing this 134
morning?"

"Well, ma'am, I fixed the chirren they breakfast. Then I put the 135
chicken on for dinner. Then I was 'bout to start doing heads, but
Betsey told them they could climb through windows and steal my
money, take them fish out the water. Oh, Mrs. Brown, they been a mess
today."

"Bernice, don't you wanta see me make fires?" Allard grinned. Jane 136
grabbed the matches from his hands and all his pockets, slapped his
backside good. She turned to Miss Calhoun with Sharon between her
legs wrapped up in the wet sheet smelling of urine.

"Miss Calhoun, I just don't think this is going to work out." 137

At that moment Vida was about to come into the kitchen through 138
the back door. Betsey ran to her aid. "Oh, Grandma, be careful. Bernice
left chicken grease all on the floor. You hold onto me or you might slip
and fall."

Vida cut her eyes first at Jane, then at Bernice. "Well, I should have 139
known that a body with no upbringing couldn't very well bring up
these chirren of mine. Thank you, Betsey, you are always so helpful."

The children ran gleefully to school, shouting: "How's she gonna do 140
something with us. She can't even talk. She can't even walk. How's she
gonna do something with us."

Bernice sat glumly on her small bed. She felt such a big fool. Mrs. 141
Brown had let her go in one day, she hadn't even had one Friday night
off to wear her red dress. She couldn't hardly begin to pack her things.
She heard the folks in Arkansas laughing at her. Big ol' flat-faced
Bernice goin'ta to St. Louis. Hahahaha.

Jane made her own coffee, sat at the kitchen table with the chil- 142
dren's breakfasts surrounding her, and played a game of solitaire.
There was no way in the world she could go to work today. Thank God
for Betsey. There was one child with a head on her shoulders. Jane tried
to think of what might have happened if Betsey hadn't been there to
mind the children.

Questions for Discussion and Writing

1. What can you INFER about the role social class plays in the lives of Jane and Greer from their disagreement over whether Greer should continue to treat patients at the clinic and from comments the grandmother makes?

2. What details suggest how much Jane and Greer have lost control over their household and need someone to take charge of the children?

3. How are class issues involved in the way in which Bernice is perceived by the family? Why is Betsey particularly out to get rid of her?

4. Does the story tend to make you more sympathetic toward Betsey or Bernice? Explain your reactions.

5. Describe a disagreement where the people argued about trivialities as a way of avoiding dealing with deeper issues.

6. Describe a nonviolent prank that you played on someone or someone played on you.

7. What places do you go to be alone? How do you act in ways that are different there than when you are around other people?

Fernando Sorrentino

The Life of the Party

Fernando Sorrentino, short story writer, novelist, editor, teacher, and literary critic, was born in Buenos Aires in 1942 into a lower-middle-class family of Italian and Argentine ancestry. In 1968, Sorrentino graduated from the Mariano Acosta, a school attended earlier by Julio Cortázar. Sorrentino began writing short stories; their publication in 1969 brought him international renown. Collections of his short stories include The Best of All Possible Worlds *(1976),* In Self-Defense *(1982), and* The Remedy for the Blind King *(1984). He is also the author of a book-length series of interviews with Jorge Luis Borges (1982). He founded the journal* Lucanor *in 1986. His writing is characterized by a sparkling humor, Kafkaesque narratives, witty dialogue, and satires of the excessive materialism and senseless bureaucracy that characterize much of the modern age. Sorrentino is considered by many to be the brightest new talent in contemporary Argentine literature. His detestation of greed, vanity, and stupidity is immediately apparent in the satire of social conventions and social climbers in "The Life of the Party," translated by Thomas Meehan, from* Sanitary Centennial and Selected Short Stories *(1988).*

1

My wife's name is Graciela; mine is Arthur. "They're such a charming couple," our friends are always saying. They're right, we are a bright, young, elegant, cosmopolitan married couple, good conversationalists and financially secure. As a result, a large part of our life is spent at social gatherings. People vie to invite us, and we must frequently choose between one party and another. 1

The essential feature of our conduct is that we never have to be begged. We hate giving the impression that we're aware of our qualities and, hence, when accepting their invitations, that we are bestowing a great honor upon our hosts. But they do consider it an honor, and this fact also weighs in favor of our reputation as generous, magnanimous people, free of pettiness and suspiciousness. 2

I swear we make no effort whatsoever to stand out. Nevertheless— and I'm speaking impartially—Graciela and I are always the best looking, the nicest, and the most intelligent. We are the life of the party. 3

Graciela is surrounded by the gentlemen; I, by the ladies. Naturally, we're strangers to jealousy and distrust; we know that no man, except Arthur, is worthy of Graciela; that no woman, except Graciela, is worthy of Arthur. 4

How many people must doubtlessly envy our social success! And 5

543

yet, Graciela and I detest social life, we abhor gatherings, we hate parties. Moreover, we are actually shy, contemplative individuals given to silence and solitude, to reading and intimate conversation; persons who despise crowds, dances, loud music, frivolity, small talk, and forced smiles.

6   Well then, why the devil are we so urbane? Why can't we turn down even a single invitation to a social gathering?

7   The truth of the matter is that deep down Graciela and I have no willpower and we don't dare say no. On our way to a party, we're submerged in gloomy thoughts, bitter tribulations, and painful guilt feelings. But once we enter into the noisy whirlwind of the throng, the voices, faces, smiles, and jokes all make us forget the annoyance of being there against our will.

8   But then, home once again, how it hurts us to consider how fragile our personality is! How painful our feeling of helplessness! How horrible to see ourselves always obliged to be the life of the party!

9   Burdened by a problem similar to ours, two ordinary people might have fallen into despair. But, far from that, Graciela and I are in the midst of a campaign to avoid further invitations, to cease being the life of the party. We have devised a plan, the purpose of which is to make ourselves unpleasant, obnoxious, abhorrent.

10   Now, then, when we're at parties, we don't have the courage to appear unpleasant, much less obnoxious or abhorrent; to such a degree are we imbued with our role as the life of the party. But in our own home, where serenity invites contemplation and where the pernicious influence of parties doesn't reach, we are transforming ourselves into pariahs of refined society, turning into the antithesis of the glorious life of the party.

11   When we put our plan into practice—some two months ago—it still suffered from many shortcomings. Our inexperience, our excitement, our lack of cold-bloodedness at first caused us to make some serious mistakes. But people learn throughout their lives; little by little, Graciela and I were improving. I'd be exaggerating if I said we've achieved perfection; I can state, however, that we feel pleased, satisfied, even proud of our latest performance. We are now awaiting the fruits of our labors.

2

12   There's always some couple that's especially friendly toward us and wants to be invited to our home. We have no objection to doing so, but we take the liberty of delaying to the maximum the moment of extending the invitation. When it does come, the couple, whether it's a pair of young nonconformists living together or a ripe old married couple, is waiting for nothing else and rushes to accept it.

13   We made the Vitavers wait a long time, a very long time, before

inviting them. The point is that, given their dangerous qualities, with that kind of people one had to be careful. I preferred not to improvise, and I wanted us to be very well prepared.

Beneath his false air of the respectable gentleman, Mr. Vitaver is 14 semi-illiterate. His lack of culture, an unlimited bad faith, a total disregard for his fellow man, and an implacable dishonesty have, of course, led him to make a fortune. After all kinds of marginally legal businesses, he has established himself as a pornographic book publisher. Hence, one of his favorite expressions is, "We, the disseminators of culture . . ." Needless to say, I despise Vitaver: his spiritual emptiness, his greed, his coarse humor, his eagerness to please, his impeccably shaved face, his unscrupulous beady little tradesman's eyes, his exquisite clothes, his manicured fingernails, his suspiciousness, his desperate need to be respected, to make a proper place for himself. For my taste and character, all these wretched features combined to paint an atrocious portrait. And Vitaver sought out my friendship; my supposed connections with what he called "the world of letters" were important to him. He doubtlessly cherished the idea that my frequent contact with novelists, critics, or poets would act by way of osmosis on him, taking the rough edges off his mercantile crudeness. He never suspected that the majority of those writers—as brutish and uncultured as he himself—were concealing what was only stupidity beneath extravagant attitudes that sought to be shocking.

Vitaver's wife is not his wife, but his concubine. This fact, which 15 should be immaterial, irrelevant to approval or reproof, fills the Vitavers with pride. They imagine that such daring covers them with a glorious halo of modernity and open-mindedness; they never miss an opportunity to talk about it. I don't know what her name is; Vitaver calls her *Adidine*, a nickname that, although it evokes shades of prostitution, also sounds like a pharmaceutical product. The latter is an attribute that fits her very badly, however, for there is nothing aseptic about Mrs. Vitaver. On the contrary, her taut, shiny, moist oily skin evokes all the possible humors of the human body. In general, when both dimensions are compatible, she tends more to width than to length: her fingers are short and fat; her hands are short and fat; her face is wide and fat. All of her is broad and fat. And she is obtuse, and she is ignorant, and she is pompous, and she is dyed, and she is daubed, and she is bejeweled, and she is repugnant.

And so, Vitaver and Adidine, based on grossly commercial reasons, 16 sought our friendship, the friendship of the life of the party. And we were sick of being the life of the party, and we were sick of these Vitavers in particular and of the hundreds of Vitavers who tormented us weekly with their stupidity, their frivolity, their mercantilism.

At that point, we invited the Vitavers to dinner at our home. 17

3

18   Graciela and I are neither princes nor paupers. But we live comfortably, we can renew our wardrobes often, and we have a small car and
lots of books. We own our apartment. It takes up the entire second floor
of a house on Emilio Ravignani Street, a house built in 1941, a solid
house with very thick walls, fine wood, and very high ceilings, a house
that has not yet succumbed to demolition and the subsequent construction of a fragile apartment building with apartments heaped up on top
of one another.

19   On the ground floor there's a hardware store; then there's the entrance to the flat below us and, right next to it, the door to ours. The
door opens directly on a steep stairway made of black marble that leads
up to the second floor, where our home actually begins.

20   We like the flat. It's larger than we need, so in case of emergency we
can change the furniture from one room to another and carry out other
strategic maneuvers.

21   The heavy rain that fell the night of the Vitavers' visit was a challenge to my creative spontaneity. Although it wasn't foreseen in my
plans, I knew how to take advantage of it to the maximum.

22   From behind the closed shutters on the second floor, we peeked out
at the ostentatious arrival of Vitaver's enormous car, we saw how he
parked at the curb across the street (there's no parking on our side);
with delight, we observed the Vitavers get out, encumbered by rain-
coats and umbrellas, and we watched them cross the street on the run
and rush headlong against our door like two fighting bulls. Unfortunately, we have a balcony, and it sheltered them a bit from the
rain.

23   Beside our door there are two doorbells, each with a little cardboard
nameplate. The first announces my last name; on the other it says MR.
JABBERWOCKY, a name I took from a poem in *Through the Looking Glass*.
Besieged by the whirlwinds of freezing rain, which the wind pelted at
him every little while, Vitaver rang the doorbell corresponding to my
name once, twice, and once again. That noise, monotonous, of course,
sounded to us like celestial music. Vitaver rang, and rang, and rang;
Graciela and I did not answer.

24   At last, Vitaver inevitably rang the Jabberwocky's doorbell, from
which he received the little electric discharge I had foreseen. Naturally,
it's Vitaver's fault; who told him to ring the doorbell of an unknown
person?

25   Our ears pressed to the shutters, Graciela and I listened with glee to
the Vitavers' conjectures: "I tell you, the doorbell gave me a shock!"

26   "It just seemed that way to you."

27   "You ring, you'll see."

28   "Ow! Me too!"

29   "Didjuh see? Can the bell be ringing upstairs?"

"Is the number of the house right?" 30

"Of course. Besides, there's his last name." 31

Then I barely stuck my head out through the shutters and, pru- 32
dently covered with a waterproof hat and an umbrella, I shouted from
the second floor: "Vitaver! Vitaver!"

Happy to hear my voice, he ran out to the edge of the sidewalk to 33
try to see me, because of which he got much wetter. He tilted his head
back and completely neglected to hold his umbrella up. "How are you,
Arthur?" he shouted, squinting his eyes against the rain lashing his
face.

"Fine, just fine, thank you." I replied cordially. "And your wife? 34
You can't have come alone, have you?"

"Here I am," said Adidine, obligingly rushing out next to Vitaver. It 35
was wonderful to behold the way the water was running down over
her tightly set hairdo and her fur coat.

"Hello, there, Adidine. How are you? Always so pretty, eh . . .," I 36
said. "What a downpour! And just this morning the weather was beautiful. Who could have imagined that? But . . . Well! Don't just stand
there getting soaked! Get up against the wall, and I'll let you in right
away."

I closed the window and let ten minutes go by. Finally, I called out 37
again: "Vitaver! Vitaver!"

He was obliged to go back out to the curb. 38

"Please excuse the delay," I said. "I couldn't find the key to save my 39
life."

With great difficulty, Vitaver etched a woeful smile of understand- 40
ing on his face.

"Here comes the key," I added. "Catch it and go right ahead and 41
open the door yourself, if you will. Just take it for granted you're in
your own home."

I threw it to him with such bad aim that the key ended up falling 42
into the water in the gutter. Vitaver had to squat down and stir around
in the dark water for a while with his hand. When he stood up, having
now salvaged the key, he was wetter than a mackerel.

He finally opened the door and came in. I already pointed out that 43
the stairway marble is black; so it barely gets dark and you can't see a
thing. Vitaver groped around on the wall in the darkness until he found
the light switch. From upstairs I heard *click, click, click*, but the light
didn't go on. Then I shouted: "Vitaver, it looks like the light bulb burnt
out just this minute. Come up very slowly, so you don't fall."

Clutching the two railings with an iron grip and in the uncertain 44
light of short-lived matches, the Vitavers came hesitantly up the stairs.
Graciela and I awaited them above, wearing our warmest smiles. "How
are the charming Vitavers?"

Vitaver was getting ready to shake hands with us when a shriek of 45
horror from Graciela turned him to stone.

46   "What have you got on your hands?! Oh, my God, look how you're all stained! How awful, your clothes! And Adidine's beautiful coat!"

47   Huge red stains covered Vitaver's right side and Adidine's left side.

48   "Damn!" I became indignant, clenching my fists in a rage. "What'll you bet Cecilia took it into her head this very day to paint the stairway railings? What a stupid girl!"

49   "Cecilia is the maid," sighed Graciela, considering the matter at an end. "She's driving us crazy with her dumb tricks."

50   "Domestic help is getting worse every day," Adidine said heroically, as she looked out of the corner of her eye at the hairs of her mink coat all stuck together. "I just don't know how we well-to-do families are going to get along!"

51   She had no idea to what extent this last statement worsened her situation.

52   "Tomorrow without fail," I insisted with a dire look on my face and an admonishing index finger, "I'm putting Cecilia right out in the street."

53   "Oh, the poor girl," said Graciela. "Just now, when she was beginning to learn? And she's already like a member of the family."

54   "Right out in the street!" I repeated with greater emphasis.

55   "But consider the fact that poor Cecilia is an unwed mother, that she has two babies. Don't be inhuman!"

56   "I'm not inhuman," I specified. "I'm being just, which is quite different."

57   "Justice cannot be upheld without a humanitarian foundation," Graciela adduced. "Epictetus said that . . ."

58   And leaving the Vitavers disdainfully forgotten, Graciela and I engaged in a learned debate, abounding in apocryphal quotations and authors, concerning justice, equity, morals, goodness, and other values remotely applicable to the case of the nonexistent Cecilia.

59   The Vitavers listened to our conversation, anxious to intervene but—inept as they were—without knowing what to say. Evidently, they were suffering, they were suffering a great deal. But how artfully they concealed it! They too aspired to be as worldly wise and as congenial as we are; they assumed that, in a similar predicament, Graciela and I would not have lost our smiles.

60   We finally remembered the existence of the Vitavers and helped them rid themselves of their rainwear, umbrellas, and coats. Vitaver was wearing a magnificent, black dinner jacket, a shirt with narrow lace edging, and a bow tie; he was elegant to the extent that such an outfit could refine his rough, underworld nature. Adidine was wearing a long white sparkling evening gown; she was profusely jewelled, finely perfumed.

61   "Oh, Adidine!" Graciela exclaimed with admiration when the intense dining room light fell fully on those wonders. "How elegant, how

lovely you look! What a beautiful gown! And those shoes! What I wouldn't give to have clothes like that! But we're so poor. Look what I had to put on. These are my best clothes."

The Vitavers had already seen our apparel and had already pretended not to notice anything unusual about it. But Graciela and I, implacable, were not about to exempt them from the unpleasant experience of looking over our garb while they, in turn, were attentively observed by us. 62

"Look, Adidine, just look," Graciela repeated, twirling around like an advertising model. "Look, look." She was all disheveled and had no make-up on. She was wearing a very old mended blouse and a plain skirt covered with big grease spots and with the hem unstitched. She had on silk stockings perforated with big holes and long runs and, over the stockings, a pair of brown anklets that partially disappeared inside some dilapidated slippers. "Look, Adidine, look." Adidine didn't know what to say. 63

"And I, what am I to say?" I intervened. "I don't even have a shirt!" 64

In effect, I had put on a grayish municipal street sweeper's smock right over a heavy woolen undershirt full of holes. Around my bare neck I had tied a frayed old necktie. A pair of baggy, dirty-white bricklayer's pants and black hemp sandals rounded out my attire. 65

"That's life," I said philosophically, as I scratched my five-day beard and chewed on a toothpick. "That's life, friend Vitaver, that's life." 66

Completely disoriented, Vitaver vaguely nodded his head. "That's life," he repeated like a parrot. 67

"That's life," I insisted yet once again. " 'So goes the world, Don Laguna, / Old pardner, nothin' lasts, / Fortune smiles on us today, / Tomorrow it'll give us a lash.' *Faust*, by Estanislao del Campo. What do you think?"[1] 68

"Huh? Oh, yeah," he said hurriedly. "I read it. I remember that old Vizcacha . . ."[2] 69

"You know what Manrique said about the gifts of fortune, don't you?" I interrupted him. "He said: 'For they are gifts of Lady Fortune, / who swiftly spins her wheel . . .' "[3] 70

Then, with an affected voice and grandiose gestures, I recited five or six stanzas for him, something I love to do. "Do you get it, Vitaver?" 71

"Yes, yes, how fabulous!" He hadn't understood a word, and that wretched adjective of his was tantamount to making his crimes worse. 72

"Today you're loaded with money," I added, poking his chest with my index finger. "You have social status. You have intelligence. You're cultured. You have *savoir faire*. You have a beautiful wife. You have everything, right?" I stopped and stared at him, obliging him to answer. 73

"Well, maybe not everything," he smiled conceitedly; he actually thought he possessed all those endowments! 74

"Tomorrow you could lose it all," I then said in a gloomy tone, to show him another facet of the drama of life. "You could lose your for- 75 tune. You could end up in jail. You could become seriously ill. Your intelligence could atrophy, your culture become watered down. Your *savoir faire* might be scorned. Your wife could be unfaithful to you."

76   I went on haranguing him for a long time with the vision of an atrocious future made up of imprisonment, illnesses, and misfortune. We were acting out an odd scene: a ragged beggar was solemnly pontificating before a gentleman dressed in strict formal attire. Together, we constituted a kind of allegory on the disillusionments of the world.

77   While I soliloquized, the Vitavers' fretful little eyes were leaping here and there. How humiliating! To have worn their best clothes and be received by two grimy, woebegone, melancholy tramps! "How can this be?" they seemed to be thinking. "And what about the clothes, the jewelry, and the elegance they always displayed at parties?"

78   "We've been left with nothing, friend Vitaver," I said, as if responding to their thoughts. "Yesterday we even had to sell the dining room furniture at a loss."

79   Then—as if it were necessary—the Vitavers cast a stupid glance over the obviously empty dining room.

80   "*Ubi sunt? Ubi sunt?*" I emphasized. "Tell me, Vitaver: *Ubi sunt? Ubi sunt? Ubi sunt mensa et sellae sex?*"[4]

81   "And so," said Graciela, "we have no choice but to have dinner in the kitchen."

82   "Oh please! That's quite all right," said Adidine.

83   "And we don't have a table in the kitchen, either, so we'll have to eat on the marble counter top. If you'd like to come this way."

84   I knew the condition the kitchen was in, and I watched the Vitavers' faces as stupefaction, disbelief, and repressed anger swiftly passed over them.

85   The kitchen was a kind of monument paying homage to disorder, laziness, filth, and abandonment. In the sink, semisubmerged in water so greasy it was thick and on which floated the remains of meals, were heaped dishes, pots, platters, silverware, and sticky saucepans. Thrown here and there on the floor were about ten days of damp old newspapers. There stood against one wall an enormous trash can overflowing with garbage, with swarms of flies, cockroaches, and worms running and wriggling over it. In the air there floated the smell of grease, fried things, wet paper, and stagnant water.

86   The Vitavers looked very solemn.

87   "In just a jiffy," said Graciela, trying in vain to give her words an optimistic tone, "in just a jiffy I'll spread the tablecloth"—and she pointed at the marble sink counter, also covered with remains of meals and empty cans of mackerel—"and we'll eat . . . although . . . although . . . ."

88   Graciela burst into loud weeping. Playing the role of humanitarian, Adidine tried to console her. "Oh, poor Graciela! What's the matter? For heaven's sake!"

"It's, it's just that . . .," Graciela stammered between sobs and hiccups, "it's just that we don't have a tablecloth either."

Indignant over this breach of confidence, I let fly a furious punch against the wall. But Graciela was unrestrainable: "Everything , we've lost everything!" she howled. "We have nothing! Everything, everything sold at a loss! Even my first-communion dress! Everything, everything lost . . . and all through his fault!" And she pointed a tragic, accusing finger at me.

"Graciela!!" I roared melodramatically, giving her to understand that a single word more from her could drive me into committing an irreparable act.

"Yes, yes, yes!" she insisted, wailing louder and louder and looking to the Vitavers, as if calling upon them as witnesses to her misfortunes. "All because of him! I was happy in my parents' home! We were rich, we lived in San Isidro,[5] in a cheerful home with a rose garden. One ominous day, that happiness was cut short. One ominous day, a monster appeared, a monster that was stalking my youth and beauty, a monster that took advantage of my innocence."

"Graciela!!!" I insisted with concentrated rage.

Ignoring me, she continued on, always addressing the Vitavers: "The monster had a human shape and it had a name; its name was . . . Arthur!" And she emphasized this name by pressing her clenched fist against her forehead. "And this monster took me from my home, wrenched me away from the affection of my parents, and carried me off with him. And he put me through a life of privation, and he squandered my entire fortune at the race track and the gambling casino. And when he gets drunk on absinthe and vodka, he scourges my back with barbed wire."

Blind with rage, I hurled myself at Graciela and dealt her a resounding slap across the face: "Silence, thou vile insane woman!" I shouted, addressing her with the archaic form, *thou*, so everything would seem more theatrically tragic. "How dare you reproach me? *Me*, the pitiful victim of your whims, your insolence, and your adulteries? How can you offend in such a way the proud, worthy man who, by pulling you up out of the slime, redeemed you from sin and guilt by marrying you?"

And I, too, began to cry and compete with Graciela over who could scream the loudest. Such weeping! We cried with so much conviction that there came a moment when we really couldn't hold back our tears.

The Vitavers, pale and glum, were completely baffled. They had come to our home—the home of the life of the party—in the hope of enjoying a pleasant evening, and now, dressed in their luxurious outfits, they were like spectators at an incomprehensible fight between a poverty-stricken married couple.

They were saying something to us, but, intent on the pleasure of our weeping, we paid no attention to them. Patting me affectionately on the back, Vitaver dragged me over to the wall, near the garbage can. "Better times lie ahead, man," he said. "The Lord'll test you, but He won't break you."

99   That *man*, together with his habitual use of *you know* and *I seen*, gave me renewed courage for the struggle.

100   "You mustn't despair," he insisted, but he was the desperate one; it was quite obvious he wanted to disappear as quickly as possible.

101   Now Adidine came to my side, holding up the fainting Graciela; now they were urging us to make peace; now we were making up.

102   Drying her tears and blowing her nose, Graciela cleared the counter top by indifferently shoving aside the cans and dishes with her arm until they fell into the dirty water in the sink. But the counter was still covered anyway with crumbs and the somewhat moist, greasy remains of meals. By way of a tablecloth, she spread over those bulging things one of the newspapers she picked up off the floor. On the newspaper she set out four plates laced with cracks, four yellowish spoons, three everyday glasses of different styles and colors, and a large cup for café au lait.

103   "We only have three glasses," she explained. "I'll drink out of the cup."

104   How dirty, how greasy, how sticky everything was! How the flies flitted about over our heads! How the cockroaches ran up and down the walls! How the worms wriggled about on the floor!

105   The four of us sat up against the sink counter and our knees kept bumping the doors of the cupboards built in below it. We were extremely uncomfortable. Vitaver cut a strange figure, seated in the midst of that sort of garbage dump, with his dinner jacket, his shirt with narrow lace edging, and black bow tie, next to his wife, with her low-cut white evening gown and luxurious jewels. On the other hand, Graciela and I were in complete harmony with that filthy, sordid atmosphere.

106   "There's just one course," said Graciela, apologizing. "Noodle soup."

107   "How delicious!" exclaimed Adidine. (As if anyone in the world could consider that fare for sick people as delicious!)

108   "Yes, it is delicious," Graciela agreed. "It's a pity that, because of the fight, it got a little burned."

109   And from a pot all oozing over and stained, she began to take out some shapeless tangles of dried out, burnt, and now cold noodles and distributed them onto the plates.

110   "Adidine," said Graciela, "since you're by the sink, could you please fill the glasses with water? We have no wine."

111   Adidine stood up submissively and turned on the tap. Just as we had foreseen, the water shot out with extraordinary pressure, bounced off the gelatinous utensils in the sink, and spattered Adidine's white gown with the remains of food.

112   With what disgusted faces the Vitavers ate! And how they tried to conceal it so as not to offend us! And how bewildered they were! Were

we really the life of the party? Might we not be a pair of imposters? Constantly surrounded by the grease, the stench, the cockroaches, and the flies, they finished their dried-up burnt soup as well as they could and drank a little water from the cracked glasses. With their clothing stained, their stomachs upset, and spirits chagrined, they said they had to leave, that they had some commitment or other. Despite our urging them repeatedly to have some more soup, they insisted they had to leave, a discourtesy that grieved us, of course. They put on their coats, covered up with their rainwear, and went down the stairs.

"Don't touch the railing," I warned them. "It's just freshly painted, 113 you know."

Before they got in their car, we bade them an affectionate farewell 114 through the window: "So long, dear friends! It's been a real pleasure! Wish we could have these delightful get-togethers more often! Come back anytime!"

They waved at us quickly and rushed headlong into their car, which 115 pulled away with uncommon speed.

4

Two weeks have now passed. During that interval, we have relied 116 on the Vitavers to slander us enough to dissuade anyone from inviting us to another party. I know Vitaver well and I can foresee his wicked-ness; I know he will have said awful things about us. However, our reputation is too strong; it won't be easy to bring it down through slan-der.

So now we find ourselves at another party. We're sporting our best 117 clothes, and we're perfumed with the finest fragrances. We display our most expensive jewelry, wear our most sophisticated smiles, and show the warmest cordiality.

We see the Vitavers, each with a drink and smiling, smiling forced 118 smiles. The Vitavers see us and the smile freezes on their faces. Without letting them react, we shake hands with them very naturally and quickly begin to converse with the Carracedos.

We don't like the Carracedos either, for reasons similar to those 119 which make us reject the Vitavers. On the other hand, the Carracedos are desirous of becoming friendly with us; they admire us and hope to gain material advantage from a relationship with us. He is a prosperous businessman, an expert swindler, adept at defrauding. To strengthen the bonds between us, he believes it the opportune moment to appeal to confidences: he tells me about his financial plans, describes the future expansion of his businesses, and tips me off to some tricks about how to make some illegal money and go unpunished.

Carracedo smiles, he smiles a forced smile, proud of his commercial 120 shrewdness, smug about being so able to multiply his wealth, happy with his possessions, his weekend home, and his foreign car.

121   The Carracedos are so courteous, so cordial, and so friendly toward us that, well, not to invite them to dinner at our home would be inconceivably rude, an act of blatant discourtesy unworthy of the life of the party. So, we invited them; they're coming on Saturday.

122   And then we, Graciela and Arthur, now thoroughly caught up in the whirlwind of the party, go flitting from room to room, lavishing smiles, kisses, and handshakes. We dance, we tell and laugh at jokes, we are brilliant and admired, and everyone feels appreciation, but also envy, toward us. "They're such a charming couple," our friends always say. Because Graciela and I are always the best looking, the nicest, the most intelligent. Because Graciela and I are still the life of the party.

    1. In del Campo's famous Argentine gaucho poem (*Fausto*, 1866), a gaucho (Anastasio el Pollo) describes to his crony, Laguna, a performance of Gounod's opera *Faust*, which he had witnessed by chance when he wandered into the old Colón Theatre during a visit to Buenos Aires. Part of the poem's artistry and humor resides in the gaucho's interpreting the opera's incidents as real and in the recounting of them in the rustic, picturesque (but stylized) gaucho dialect of the pampas. (My translation of verses from *Fausto*.) [trans. notes]

    2. With ironic humor, Sorrentino unmasks Vitaver's ignorance by having him recall here an almost unforgettable character who appears, however, not in *Fausto* but in *Martín Fierro* (1872; 1879) by José Hernández. The latter work is undoubtedly the most famous and finest gaucho poem and is read by most Argentine schoolchildren. Had Vitaver read the poems, he could not possibly make such a blunder. [trans. notes]

    3. Arthur now quotes from what may well be the most famous poem in the Spanish language, Jorge Manrique's *Coplas a la muerte del Maestro don Rodrigo, su padre* [Verses on the death of Commander Rodrigo, his father]. Rodrigo Manrique was an eminent, fifteenth-century Spanish nobleman and knight-commander (*Maestro*) of the military chivalric Order of Santiago [St. James]. When Rodrigo Manrique died, his son, Jorge, was so deeply grieved that he composed this immortal elegy in his father's memory. Among other medieval themes included in the poem are a solemn meditation on the transitory nature of wealth and other worldly, material things and a consideration of the brevity of power, beauty, nobility, and human life. (My translation of verses.) In mythology, Fortune is often depicted as a goddess with a wheel; her constant turning of this "wheel of fortune" raises the unfortunate to lofty heights of wealth and power, only to cast them down again, and vice versa. Arthur's subsequent recitation of "five or six stanzas" more of Manrique's poem then prompts him to expand on the medieval work's meaning for the crass, phony Vitaver. The explanation reaches a humorous crescendo with Arthur's reference to Adidine's possible future infidelity to her husband. [trans. notes]

    4. Latin: "Where are they? Where are they? etc. Where are the table and six chairs?" The words *ubi sunt* ("Where are . . . ?"), in Latin and other European languages, were frequent opening lines as well as the principal motif and theme of many European medieval poems emphasizing the transitory nature of all things. Perhaps the best-known example is François Villon's ballade with its famous line "*Mais ou sont les neiges d'antan?*" [But where are the snows of yesteryear?]. *Ubi sunt* is now a term used to identify the theme of such works, which have continued to be written on down to modern and contemporary times. Arthur's insistent repetition of the phrase is particularly appropriate in light of his previous quotation from Jorge Manrique's *Coplas a la muerte del . . . su padre*, the principal theme of which is, of course, *ubi sunt*. [trans. notes]

    5. A Buenos Aires suburb. [trans. notes]

Questions for Discussion and Writing

1. From the way the NARRATOR describes himself and his wife Graciela, would you have ever expected them to treat the Vitavers the way they do? If not, why not?

2. How does the humor of the story depend on the contrast between what the Vitavers expect and what they encounter?

3. How does Arthur's characterization of the Vitavers encourage the reader to side with Arthur and Graciela rather than with the Vitavers?

4. Aside from the physical discomforts the Vitavers undergo (being kept waiting in the rain, dark stairway, wet paint, burnt noodles for dinner, and so on), what other psychological tortures do Arthur and Graciela inflict on them? In each case, how does social class enter into each torture?

5. In a short essay discuss the difference between having "class" and having money, although they are often seen as identical. What qualities do you associate with having "class"?

6. Have you ever known anyone like the Vitavers? Describe them in detail. Invent your own torturous evening for them and describe what you would do.

7. Imagine you have arrived at a party where the host or hostess asks you to introduce yourself. You decide on impulse to invent a wild story about who you are and what you have accomplished in order to impress the other guests. What would you say?

8. Did you ever "put someone on" in ways that confirmed their worst fears? Did you later reveal your purpose in doing so?

Mascha Kaléko

Mannequins

Mascha Kaléko (1912–1975) began contributing poems to local Berlin newspapers while studying there. She soon became famous throughout Germany for her ironic depiction of urban life and her satiric wit, tempered by an essentially romantic and melodic style. Kaléko's work provides witty, ironic descriptions of petit-bourgeois life in Berlin during the Weimar Republic. In her Das lyrische Stenogrammheft (The Lyrical Stenographer's Notebook) *(1933), love can be expressed only in shorthand on one's afternoon off. In 1938, she was forced to emigrate and lived in New York City and Jerusalem until her death thirty-seven years later. Other works include* Kleines Lesebuch für Grosse *(1934; reprinted in 1956), and* Verse für Zeitgenossen *(1945; reprinted in 1980). The appeal of her poetry to contemporary audiences continues to grow, something we can easily appreciate from reading "Mannequins," a sardonic backstage glimpse of the less than glamorous private life of fashion models, translated by Susan L. Cocalis (1986).*

> *Wanted: Model, with a size 6 figure.*
> *Easy, pleasant work . . .*

Just smiling and flattering the whole day through . . .
It gets you down.
—Whatever they promise to do:
We remain sound.
5 We show off in silks the *dernier cri*,
Knowing: they will never belong to me.
That door is closed to us.
We wear the rags from the stockroom,
And say to the damsels with figures "in bloom":
10 "Madam, . . . it's marvelous!"

We live from day to day on bread, butter, and tea.
We have to make do.
And sometimes a gentleman takes us to eat . . .
 . . . If we want to.
15 What good is this wrapping of crèpe satin—
You are what you are: just a mannequin.
That's nothing to laugh at.
We worry about every cent at night,
Yet we must, like toy dolls, appear bright
20 Lest the customers complain about that.

Our legs are our working capital,
And our references.
Salary: as high as our hips are small.
Logical consequences . . .
Condition: well-proportioned, discreet, and—lovely,   25
(For that's the store's policy.)
And if men have something off-color to say,
Don't cry "No!" and don't show your shame.
It's all part of the company's name
And part of your pay.   30

Questions for Discussion and Writing

1. How does the situation depicted in the poem contrast IRONICALLY with the expectations conveyed in the lines of the want ad?
2. What details suggest the extent to which mannequins must reshape their bodies to reflect society's fantasies about what women should look like and also suppress their real feelings toward their customers?
3. How does the poem undercut illusions or ASSUMPTIONS you may have had about the glamorous lives of models?
4. What are some other professions that require women to appear to be what they are not to suit masculine fantasies and societal expectations?
5. Create a word portrait of someone by describing only his or her clothes, whether they are stylish, colorful, or dull, as well as hair style and makeup. Based on your observations or memory, describe someone at work according to the actions he or she performs. Use vivid, concrete, and descriptive details.
6. Which parts of your body are you happy with and which are you dissatisfied with? To what extent do you feel your views are influenced by societal expectations promoted through advertising?

Léon Gontran Damas

Hiccup

Léon Damas was born in 1912 in the capital city of Cayenne, French Guiana—in the shadow of Devil's Island—the son of a middle-class mulatto family conscious of its intellectual and social position. His childhood was dominated by a mother imbued with ultra-white values. Chronic asthma kept Damas virtually bedridden until the age of six. Eventually, he was well enough to be sent to Fort-de-France, Martinique, to attend Lycée Schoelcher where he first met the poet Aime Cesarie. From there, he went to Paris to continue his education, devoting himself at first to law and Oriental languages. He gained considerable prestige with his collection of poetry, Pigments *(1936), which appeared as the first substantial artistic work in the movement known as* negritude, *an international literary movement promoting the awareness of black culture. This volume of poetry was seized and banned by the government that, on the eve of World War I, found the inflammatory verse dangerous to French security in the colonies. Ironically, Damas served with the French Armed Forces in World War II, earning several decorations for meritorious conduct. After the war he was elected a deputy to the National Assembly from French Guiana and has since served in a variety of positions with the Ministry of Foreign Affairs. Volumes of his work include poetry in* Graffiti *(1952) and* Black-Label *(1956), a collection of essays,* Return to Guiana *(1938), and a volume of short stories,* Veillées noires *(1943). "Hiccup," translated by Norman R. Shapiro (1970), is an amusing portrait of the extent to which Damas as a boy was never able to fulfill his mother's expectations.*

And it doesn't help to swallow seven gulps of water
three or four times every twenty-four hours
back comes my childhood
in a hiccup that jolts
5   my instinct
like the cop shaking the tramp

Disaster
tell me about the disaster
tell me about it

10   My mother hoping for a very table-manners son
                Hands on the table
                bread is not cut
                bread is broken
                bread is not wasted
15   bread the gift of God
                bread of the sweat of your Father's brow
                bread of the bread

                A bone is eaten with restraint and discretion
                a stomach should be polite
20   and every polite stomach
                learns not to belch
                a fork is not a tooth-pick
                you must not blow your nose
                so everyone can see
25   and hear
                and besides sit up straight
                a well-bred nose
                does not mop up the plate

                And besides this besides that
30   and besides in the name of the Father

the Son
the Holy Ghost
at the end of every meal

And besides this besides that
and then disaster   35
tell me about the disaster
tell me about it

My mother hoping for a syllabus son

Unless you learn your history lesson
you shall not go to mass   40
on Sunday
in all your Sunday best

This child will bring disgrace upon our name
this child will be for Heaven's sake
                                                                    45
Be still
How often have I told you that you must speak French
the French of France
the Frenchman's French
French French
                                                                    50
Disaster
tell me about the disaster
tell me about it

My Mother hoping for a son
just like his mother
                                                                    55
You didn't say hello to Madame next door
and your shoes all dirty again
just let me catch you playing in the street
or on the grass or the Savane
under the War Memorial   60
playing games
running around with little So-and-so
with So-and-so who wasn't even baptised

Disaster
tell me about the disaster
tell me about it   65

My Mother hoping for a son who was very do
    very re
    very mi

very fa
70   very sol
very la
very si
very do
re-mi-fa
75   sol-la-si
do

I understand that once again you missed
your vi-o-lin lesson
A banjo
80   you said a banjo
is that what you said
a banjo
you really said
a banjo
85   Oh no young man
you must learn that our kind of people frown
on ban
and jo
and gui
90   and tar
that's not for us *mulattos*
that kind of thing is only for the *blacks*

Questions for Discussion and Writing

1. How do the mother's values and social expectations result in her constantly finding fault with the speaker's table manners, language, choice of play-mates, and musical preferences?
2. Why is the hiccup a good symbol for the speaker's inability to control when he will remember his mother's complaints about his manners and etiquette?
3. How is the humor of the poem enhanced by the PARADOX that the mother finds all of the speaker's transgressions to be equally reprehensible?
4. How is the poem structured to intensify the conflicts between the speaker and his mother to allow us to hear the two voices arguing?
5. How do considerations of race and class explain why the mother becomes so upset over the speaker's preference for a banjo over a violin?
6. Were you ever subject to any attempts to improve your table manners or speech, or to make you learn how to play a musical instrument in order to allow you to pass as a member of a higher social class? How did you react?
7. Describe a person, using words and sentences that suggest the person's appearance and character (active verbs for an aggressive person, passive sentences for a shy person, short sentences for someone who is edgy, and so forth).
8. Try to get into the spirit of Damas's poem by composing an insult poem in which you tell the truth about someone, using humor and exaggeration. For example, a lead-off line might be "You think that's bad, well, he or she just . . ."

Ana Castillo

Napa, California

Ana Castillo was born in 1953 in Chicago and earned a bachelor's degree from Northeastern Illinois University in 1975. She served as an associate editor and reviewer for Third Woman Magazine. Castillo, in addition to being a widely published poet, is a novelist, essayist, translator, editor, and teacher. She is the author of several volumes of poetry—Otro Canto (1977), The Invitation (1979), Women Are Not Roses (1984), and My Father Was a Toltec: Poems (1988). An innovative novelist as well, Castillo has written The Mixquiahuala Letters (1986), an epistolary novel that explores the changing role of Hispanic women in the United States and Mexico. Comprised of thirty-eight letters written over a ten-year period from Teresa, a California poet, to a college friend, Alicia, a New York artist, the novel chronicles their relationship and their travels together to Mexico as well as their separate personal lives. Castillo created three possible versions—for the "Conformist," the "Cynic," and the "Quixotic"—by numbering the letters and supplying varying orders in which to read them, each with a different tone and resolution. Her recent novels include Sapognia (1989) and So Far from God (1993). She is recognized as one of the most important voices in Chicano literature and has received many awards, including a grant from the National Endowment for the Arts. "Napa, California" (1984) lets us hear the voices of migrant workers struggling to achieve a fair wage and human dignity.

Dedicado al Sr. Chávez, Sept. '75

We pick
   the bittersweet grapes
   at harvest
   one
      by   5
         one
   with leather worn hands
         as they pick
            at our dignity
            and wipe our pride   10
            away
            like the sweat we wipe
            from our sun-beaten brows
            at midday
In fields   15
   so vast
   that our youth seems
   to pass before us

```
              and we have grown
20            very
                 very
                    old
                       by dusk . . .
                       (bueno pues, ¿qué vamos a hacer, Ambrosio?
25                     ¡bueno pues, seguirle, comparde, seguirle!
                       ¡Ay, Mama!
                       Sí pues, ¿qué vamos a hacer, compadre?
                       ¡Seguirle, Ambrosio, seguirle!)¹
          We pick
30           with a desire
             that only survival
             inspires
          While the end
             of each day only brings
35           a tired night
             that waits for the sun
             and the land
             that in turn waits
             for us . . .
```

[1]Well then, what are we going to do, Ambrosio?
Well then, follow him, my good friend, follow him!
Mama!
Yes, well, what are we going to do, friend?
Follow him, Ambrosio, follow him!

Questions for Discussion and Writing

1. How is the poem constructed to take the reader inside the lives of migrant workers in ways that create an illusion of real people speaking? Do you find this kind of approach more effective than a narrative account of the same situation?

2. How does the METAPHOR of harvesting also apply to the workers themselves? In what way are they picked and thrown away?

3. How do the lines in Spanish in the second stanza heighten the sense of desperation the workers are experiencing? If you didn't understand Spanish, how would this section of the poem function as a GAP into which you would project your own ASSUMPTION about what is going on?

4. Given the title and the dedication of the poem, which details underscore the need for a leader to work on the migrants' behalf to bring about reforms?

5. At which points in the poem must the reader supply HYPOTHESES to fill in BLANKS? What were your hypotheses?

6. How is the meaning of the poem expressed in its form as well as its ideas, images, and actual words?

Yannis Ritsos

Greek Carters

Yannis Ritsos (1909–1992), one of the most distinguished poets of modern Greece, is also one of the most celebrated. His poetry has been translated into forty-four languages. He was born in Monemvasia, Greece, and worked as a law clerk, editor, and proofreader before becoming a full-time writer. His poems have achieved wide popularity through being set to music by such composers as Mikis Theodorakis. Two themes run throughout Ritsos's work: his political commitment and a mood of introspection, a dual focus evident as early as "Epitaphios" (1936), a lyrical lament of a mother for her son who was shot down by police during a political demonstration. Collections of his poetry include Romiosini *(1954), a long poem celebrating the essence of Greek identity as a struggle against oppression. This poem was composed as a tribute to the Greek forces who fought against the Germans during World War II. Other major poems include* Farewell, Stone Age, *and* The Neighborhoods of the World, *all written in 1957. When a right-wing military junta seized control of Greece in 1967, Ritsos was arrested and sent to a prison island from which he was released in 1971 because of worldwide protest. From the suffering Ritsos endured for his beliefs, he wrought remarkable poetry, not so much for its espousal of a particular ideology as in its celebration of human freedom and the independence of the Greek people. As a poet, his gift for original and striking metaphors can be seen in "Greek Carters," from* The Fourth Dimension, *translated by Rae Dalven (1977). The poem extols the collective consciousness of the Greek people against the backdrop of a sharply defined, typically Greek landscape.*

Slowly, at noon, after they sell their products
in the market—vegetables, grapes, pears—
dripping with sweat, they and their horses
return with their carts along the seashore road
to their little farms far off—   5
with their paper money tied in their handkerchiefs
and the coins jingling in their pockets,
foolish, exhausted, almost fierce,
with the fury of an unknown delay or an injustice,
with the tufts of their coarse hair full of dust and sweat   10
constructed under their caps.

But, as they turn off the highway, as they meet
the first deserted sandy beach, they unyoke their horses,
undress hastily, throw their clothes on the pebbles,
and go into the sea to wash their horses.   15

And then, soaking wet, stark naked and golden, men and horses
sparkle in the sun with a lofty nobility
industrious and omnipotent, as if they had stepped out
of the ancient legends. The youngest carter,
20   barely eighteen, all glittering in midday,
riding nude on his horse, galloped along the sea,
while a white cloud marked his shadow in the blue.

And the carts at the seashore, they too all golden,
shone in the circular reflections of their wheels
25   like glorious chariots of ancient Greek games
that had stopped here and would start again from here.

Questions for Discussion and Writing

1. How does the sequence in which the events in the poem are described compel the reader to put aside initial ASSUMPTIONS and EXPECTATIONS about the Greek workers?
2. How are the carters transformed when they leave the marketplace after a day of selling their products and go down to the beach to wash themselves and their horses?
3. How does Ritsos use the IMAGERY of light to suggest that the splendor of ancient Greece is still recoverable despite the obscuring of its essence by the commercialism of centuries?
4. Do you know people who change dramatically when they leave work and seem to be very different people when they are away from their jobs? If so, describe them.
5. Describe an experience where you become aware that a person you knew only through his or her role at work had a "real" life aside from that. For example, have you ever seen one of your teachers at a shopping mall, movie, or supermarket?

Linda Hogan

Workday

See the biographical sketch on page 492, as well as Linda Hogan's essay "Hearing Voices." In "Workday" (1988) Hogan uses the occasion of a bus ride as she returns home from work at the university to explore the gap between Native Americans and her middle-class white co-workers.

I go to work
though there are those who were missing today
from their homes.
I ride the bus
and I do not think of children without food   5
or how my sisters are chained to prison beds.

I go to the university
and out for lunch
and listen to the higher-ups
tell me all they have read   10
about Indians
and how to analyze this poem.
They know us
better than we know ourselves.

I ride the bus home   15
and sit behind the driver.
We talk about the weather
and not enough exercise.
I don't mention Victor Jara's mutilated hands
or men next door   20
in exile
or my own family's grief over the lost child.

When I get off the bus
I look back at the light in the windows
and the heads bent   25
and how the women are all alone
in each seat
framed in the windows
and the men are coming home,
then I see them walking on the Avenue,   30
the beautiful feet,
the perfect legs
even with their spider veins,
the broken knees
with pins in them,   35
the thighs with their cravings,
the pelvis
and small back
with its soft down,
the shoulders which bend forward   40
and forward and forward
to protect the heart from pain.

Questions for Discussion and Writing

1. What is the situation in which the SPEAKER finds herself?
2. How would you characterize the VOICE you hear? How is the mood, tone, or spirit of the situation communicated through the choice of individual words, DICTION, phrasing, and structure?
3. What IMAGES in the poem express the speaker's sense of grief at the psychological and physical costs for Native Americans trying to survive in mainstream American society?
4. How does the sequence in which the thoughts are presented require the reader to question whether the speaker has irrevocably lost touch with her own people by working at a university in which she is little more than a token Native American? Seen in this way, how does the poem function as a gesture to connect her with the Indian laborers on the bus?
5. Did you ever work at a place where you felt alienated from the other workers because of differences in race or class? Describe your experience.
6. In high school, was there an individual or group of people who were regarded as being different (in terms of race, ethnicity, physical disabilities, or social class) and who were ostracized because of it? How did you feel about this person or group at the time and how do you feel now? What accounts for your change in attitude, if any?
7. Describe a place where you or someone you know works. Reveal how you feel about the place, using sensory details to create a sense of atmosphere.

John Agard

Listen mr oxford don

Born in 1930 in Guyana, John Agard is a poet, short story writer, journalist, and actor. He has been a frequent contributor to the magazines Expression *and* Plexis *as well as to Guyana's newspaper, the* Sunday Chronicle. *Agard's poetry has been collected in* Shoot Me with Flowers *(1985). The most important link between Agard's poetry and the wealth of West Indian oral tradition of song, speech, and performance in the forms of reggae, calypso, work songs, dub (an early form of "rap") poetry, and political satire is that of voice. In "Listen Mr Oxford Don" we hear a voice that reflects the speech patterns and rhythm of steel-pan music as the speaker launches a witty assault on British colonialism.*

Me not no Oxford don
me a simple immigrant
from Clapham Common
I didn't graduate
5   I immigrate

But listen Mr Oxford don
I'm a man on de run
and a man on de run
is a dangerous one

I ent have no gun   10
I ent have no knife
but mugging de Queen's English
is the story of my life

I dont need no axe
to split/ up yu syntax   15
I dont need no hammer
to mash up yu grammar

I warning you Mr Oxford don
I'm a wanted man
and a wanted man   20
is a dangerous one

Dem accuse me of assault
on de Oxford dictionary/
imagin a concise peaceful man like me/
dem want me serve time   25
for inciting rhyme to riot
but I tekking it quiet
down here in Clapham Common

I'm not a violent man Mr Oxford don
I only armed wit muh human breath   30
but human breath
is a dangerous weapon

So mek dem send one big word after me
I ent serving no jail sentence
I slashing suffix in self-defence   35
I bashing future wit present tense
and if necessary

I making de Queen's English accessory/to my offence

Questions for Discussion and Writing

1. What INFERENCES did you draw about the nature of the crime of which the
   speaker is supposedly guilty? How does his defense depend on "making de
   Queen's English accessory" by citing the effect of British colonial domination
   of Guyana?

2. What elements in the poem contribute to its TONE, humor, and satiric wit?

3. How does the speaker's sophisticated mastery of the language, albeit non-standard English, refute the ASSUMPTIONS you might have had about the crime of which he stands accused?

4. How does the poem arrange to carry forward the argument through skillfully varied parallel assertions, contrasts, and antitheses?

5. Does this poem trigger any memories where you were judged by the way you used colloquial or nonstandard English?

6. To discover the extent to which you associate "voice" with social class, imagine this poem substituting the "voice" of someone from Maine, Texas, Italy, or any other place associated with a distinctive style of expression. How does this change in tone affect your interpretation of the poem?

7. What is the best example of current rap you have heard? What similarities can you discover between rap and Agard's poem in terms of the rhythmic beat, the story told, and the speaker's tone or attitude? You might wish to make up your own rap by telling a story you know well to a beat.

hands like this (over ears). If you don't like what you see, you put your hands like this (over eyes). And if you don't like what you see and what you hear, you don't want to get involved, you raise your hands like this (Fuck-you gesture). Please feel free to practice that at any time during the show. Perhaps you would all like to practice a little before we start. You don't like what you hear . . . (ad lib practice).

We know that you will enjoy the show, and, remember, if you are planning a trip to Italy, be sure to see me at intermission or after the show and I will be happy to help you with anything but airline reservations. In sympathy with your air traffic controllers' strike, the controllers in my country have decided to show up for work and it is a very dangerous situation. For those of you undecided about visiting my country, I brought a brochure. This one is for . . . (improvisation off brochure).

There are many tours available. One of the more popular in this part of the country is "The Mediterranean Sea: Cradle of Civilization and Home of the Fruit Fly." For those of you of the Catholic faith, there is the "Cardinal Cody Tour," with all expenses paid for single women over seventy.

I only brought one of these, so I will give it to you, and you can pass it around, always remembering the words of that great French Marxist, Alexander Dumas: "All for one and one for all."

Have a good evening, and ciao.

ACT ONE

A modest working class apartment. To the right, a table; a cupboard, a refrigerator, a gas range, and, close by, two gas tanks hooked up for welding. Along one wall, a daybed and a wardrobe.

A woman, ANTONIA, *enters, followed by a younger woman,* MARGHERITA. *They are loaded with shopping bags, filled to overflowing, and with different plastic bags stuffed with goods, which they place on the table and daybed.*

ANTONIA: It's really lucky that I ran into you today . . . If not, I really don't know how I'd have managed to drag all this stuff here.

MARGHERITA: But where did you find the money to buy all this stuff?

ANTONIA: I told you, I didn't buy it, I won it with green stamps . . . and then, in a box of laundry powder, I found a prize. I happened to find a gold coin . . .

MARGHERITA: Sure, go tell that to someone else . . . a gold coin, c'mon!

ANTONIA: You don't believe my story?

MARGHERITA: Of course not!

ANTONIA: Okay, then, I'll tell you another one.

MARGHERITA: Ciao.

ANTONIA: Where are you going?

MARGHERITA: See ya!

ANTONIA: No, no, hold on, I'll tell you the truth.

MARGHERITA (*rushes to sit*):   Okay, tell me.

ANTONIA: Well, I went to the supermarket, and there was a bunch of women and a few men, too, raising hell over the prices going up so much that it's enough to make you sick.

MARGHERITA: You said it, enough to make you sick!!

ANTONIA: Pasta and sugar, it's awful not to mention meat and canned goods . . . And there was the manager, trying to calm us down: "It's not my fault," he kept saying, "it's management that sets the prices . . . and they've decided to raise them." Decided? With whose permission? "With nobody's permission, it's legal; that's free enterprise, free competition!" Free competition, against who? Against us? And we're supposed to take it? Your money or your life! You're a bunch of thieves—I yelled that myself, and then hid.

MARGHERITA: Good for you!

ANTONIA: Then one woman said, "We've had it! Basta! This time *we're* setting the prices. We'll only pay the same as last year. And if you object, we'll take the stuff away without paying at all. Got it? Take it or leave it!" You should have seen him: the manager went white as a sheet. "But you're all crazy! I'm calling the police!" So he shoots like a rocket over to the checkout counter to telephone . . . but the telephone isn't working; somebody has cut the wire. "Excuse me, let me get to my office, excuse me!" But he couldn't get through . . . all those women around him . . . he starts pushing and one woman pretends that she's hit . . . she makes like she'd just passed out.

MARGHERITA: Oh, beautiful! Che bello!

ANTONIA: Then a great big fat woman started hollering, "You coward! You picked on a poor woman . . . who's probably pregnant, too! If she loses the baby, you'll see what'll happen to you! We'll send you to jail! Murderer!" Then everybody yelled: "Baby killer!" "Baby killer!" "Baby killer!"

MARGHERITA: Oh, I wish I'd been there.

ANTONIA: Yeah, it was quite a sight.

MARGHERITA: And then what happened?

ANTONIA: Well, it happened that that fool of a manager . . . completely terrified . . . gave in . . . and we paid what we'd wanted to. I must say that one woman overdid it; she wanted to take the stuff on credit, and wouldn't give her name. "I can't tell you where I live," she said, "because you're liable to turn me in to the police . . . I know you guys! You'll just have to put your faith in trust. Trust is the soul of business . . . don't you always say that? Well, Arriverderci! Trust me!"

MARGHERITA: Oh, boy!

ANTONIA: Then someone started yelling: "The police!" It was a false alarm, but everybody took off . . . some dropped their packages, others burst out crying they were so scared. Then these workers from the factory near there . . . started saying, "Calma, calma! What's all this chickenshit, why be afraid of the police? For god's sake! You're right to pay what's fair! Hey, this is a strike, in fact, better, because in a strike the workers always lose money . . . and now this is a strike where the boss loses out!" "We women can even go one better: We won't pay! We won't pay! And that goes for all the money you've been stealing from us in the years we've been coming here to shop!" So I made up my mind and did my shopping all over again. I was yelling: "We won't pay! We won't pay!" And all the other women too: "We won't pay! We won't pay!" It was like the storming of the Bastille!

MARGHERITA: Beautiful!

ANTONIA: Yeah, it was really like a party, but not so much because we didn't pay for the stuff, but because we suddenly found ourselves all together, men and women, doing something really right and brave against those crooks. We really caught 'em off balance! Now they're beginning to get scared, and in some supermarkets they've already brought down the prices.

MARGHERITA: Sure, you all did great, but now what are you going to tell your husband? You're not gonna feed him that story about the green stamps, are you?

ANTONIA: You don't think he'll swallow it?

MARGHERITA: Of course not.

ANTONIA: Well, maybe it is a bit far-fetched. Trouble is, he's such a law-abiding citizen he'll shit a brick. I ran out of money today so tomorrow I won't have a cent for the gas and electricity. At least I don't worry about the rent. I haven't paid it for four months!

MARGHERITA: Well, for that matter, I don't have any money left either! And *I* haven't paid the rent for *five* months! And I didn't even manage to go shopping like you did today . . .

ANTONIA: Now, to start with, we have to hide everything. Do me a favor and take some of this stuff yourself. (*gives her a sack*)

MARGHERITA: No, no, really, thanks, but I don't want it . . . I already told you I haven't got a cent to pay you.

ANTONIA: Look, don't be silly. It's gift merchandise! Today we're giving credit!

MARGHERITA: Sure, and then what am I gonna tell my husband? "Look, this stuff is only half-stolen!" He'll half kill me!

ANTONIA: Mine won't; he won't kill me, but he'll drive me nuts with his ranting and raving . . . he'll bring up the honor of his sullied name . . . "Better to drop dead from hunger than to break the law! I've always paid for everything to the last penny . . . Poor, but honest . . . Hold my head high among the people," and on and on

. . . a pain in the ass. But what did I get? (*examines the sack on the table*) What's in this jar? (*reading*) "Reconstituted meat for dogs and cats?" Look! (*She hands the jar to her friend.*)

MARGHERITA: What's this, "Homogenized with different flavors." Why did you get it?

ANTONIA: I really don't know . . . I guess in the confusion . . . I just grabbed what I found . . . And look at this! (*shows a packet*) "Select millet bird seed!"

MARGHERITA: Bird seed?

ANTONIA: Thank goodness it's all stuff I didn't pay for; otherwise I'd be mad. (*shows a box*) Frozen rabbit heads!

MARGHERITA: Come on! Rabbit heads?!

ANTONIA: Well, that's what it says: "To enrich your chicken feed . . . ten heads, two hundred lira!"

MARGHERITA: But that's crazy. And you want me to take this crap home?

ANTONIA: No, not the rabbit heads; I want them. You can take the ordinary stuff: oil, pasta . . . Quick, get going! Your husband is working the night shift, you've plenty of time to hide it.

MARGHERITA: Sure, hide it, and then the police come to search the building house by house!

ANTONIA: Don't talk garbage; the police! The whole neighborhood was at the supermarket today . . . And there are at least ten thousand families here. (*She goes over and glances out the window.*) Can you imagine the police coming to check us out one by one . . . When would they finish up, by Easter? Madonna, my husband! He's coming up; he's already downstairs. Quick, take this stuff. (*She gives her a bag;* MARGHERITA *moves to leave.*) No, put it under your coat! Help put mine under the bed . . . No, don't help me, I'll do it myself. (MARGHERITA *quickly arranges the various bags under her coat and exits.* ANTONIA *hides all the bags under the bed. Only the one containing the pet food is left out.*) Get going! Get going!

(GIOVANNI *comes in, and runs into* MARGHERITA *in the doorway.*)

MARGHERITA: Hello, Giovanni!

GIOVANNI: Oh, hi, Margherita . . . How's it going?

MARGHERITA: Pretty good, thanks. Ciao, Antonia, see ya' later.

ANTONIA: Yeah, see 'ya later; say hi to your Luigi for me. (GIOVANNI *stands there in confusion, having seem* MARGHERITA *leaving, with her body all puffed up.* ANTONIA *takes the plastic bag with the millet, etc., and puts it in the cupboard.*) Well, Giovanni, what are you gaping it? It was about time you got home. Where have you been all this time? (*She starts sweeping, tidying up.*)

GIOVANNI: Hey, what's wrong with Margherita?

ANTONIA: Why, is something wrong with her?

GIOVANNI: She's all big in front, a huge belly!

ANTONIA: Why, is this the first time you've seen a married woman with a big belly before?

GIOVANNI: You mean she's pregnant?

ANTONIA: Well, that's the least that can happen to a woman who has sex.

GIOVANNI: But how far along is she? I saw her just last Sunday, and she didn't seem . . .

ANTONIA: Since when have you ever understood anything about women? Last Sunday is a week ago . . . a lot can happen in one week. (*She becomes very busy tidying up the house, but it's clear she's doing all this just to seem nonchalant.*)

GIOVANNI: Listen, I'm not as stupid as that. And anyway her husband, Luigi, didn't tell me about it. We work on the same assembly line, and he always tells me everything about himself and his wife.

ANTONIA: Well, there are—certain things it might bother someone to talk about—

GIOVANNI: What do you mean, bother him? Are you crazy? Why should it bother him to say his wife's pregnant? Are people supposed to be ashamed of having a baby nowadays?

ANTONIA: Well, then, in this case he doesn't know about it yet. And if he doesn't know, how could he go and tell you about it?

GIOVANNI: What do you mean, he doesn't know?

ANTONIA: Well, in this case, she didn't want to tell him.

GIOVANNI: What do you mean she didn't want to tell him?

ANTONIA: Well, Luigi is always going on with Margherita about how it's too soon, it isn't the right moment, we're in the middle of a depression, first they have to get settled . . . and if she gets pregnant, the company she works for will fire her. In fact, he always made her take the pill.

GIOVANNI: And if he made her take the pill, how could she get pregnant?

ANTONIA: Well, in this case the pill didn't work. It happens, you know!

GIOVANNI: But if it happens, why did she keep it a secret from her husband; why should she feel guilty about it?

ANTONIA: Well, in this case, maybe the pill didn't work because she wasn't taking it. And if you don't take the pill then it happens that the pill doesn't work in this case!

GIOVANNI: What are you talking about?

ANTONIA: Oh, you know she's a real religious Catholic; and since the Pope said, "It's a sin to take the pill" . . .

GIOVANNI: What's the matter, you got rocks in your head? You're talking like a nut; the pill not working because she isn't taking it, the Pope, her looking like she's nine months pregnant and her husband not even noticing?

ANTONIA: But how could he notice it, if she bound herself up?

GIOVANNI: Bound herself up?

ANTONIA: Yeah, wound herself around real tight with bandages so as not to attract attention. In fact, just today I told her: "You're crazy, do you want to lose the baby? You're suffocating him. Take off those bandages this minute and who gives a damn if they fire you! The baby is more important!" Did I do the right thing?

GIOVANNI: Sure you did the right thing. Sure!

ANTONIA: Was I good?

GIOVANNI: Sure, sure you were good.

ANTONIA: Well, so then Margherita made up her mind to unwind the bandages and, ploff! her belly popped right out. And then I told her, "If your Luigi starts giving you trouble, tell him to come over here, because my Giovanni is home and he'll straighten him out." Did I do the right thing?

GIOVANNI: Sure you did the right thing.

ANTONIA: Was I good?

GIOVANNI: Yes, yes, sure!

ANTONIA: You hear that, yes, yes, sure . . . what sort of answer is that? Listen, are you mad at me? Come on: what have I done?

GIOVANNI: No, no, I'm not mad at you . . . I'm *mad* because of what happened today in the factory.

ANTONIA: Why, what happened?

GIOVANNI: Well, at lunch time we went down to the cafeteria, and four or five troublemakers began making a stink about the food—saying it was lousy, it was garbage, and all that . . .

ANTONIA: And it really was good stuff—"Excellent food, generous portions" . . . ?

GIOVANNI: No, no . . . it was really slop . . . but there was no need to form a mob and raise hell like that!

ANTONIA: What d'ya mean, a mob? You said there were four or five guys!

GIOVANNI: Yeah, at the beginning! But then everybody joined in. They all ate and then walked out without paying.

ANTONIA: Them too?

GIOVANNI: What do you mean, them too?

ANTONIA: Yeah, I mean not only those four or five guys, but everybody else too.

GIOVANNI: Yeah, even the union reps—they should set a good example . . . not join the extremists.

ANTONIA: I'll say!

GIOVANNI: But that's not all; I go out, and on my way to the streetcar I see a whole bunch of women by the supermarket—there must have been a hundred of them shouting, and coming out of the market loaded with stuff. I asked what was going on, and they told me they'd fixed their own prices for the goods! Imagine!

ANTONIA: Ooh, can you beat that!

GIOVANNI: But in fact—they really just took the stuff themselves because most of them walked out without paying!

ANTONIA: Them too?

GIOVANNI: What do you mean, them too?

ANTONIA: Yes, I mean like those troublemakers in your factory who wouldn't pay for the cafeteria meal.

GIOVANNI: That's right, them too. And they even roughed up the manager.

ANTONIA: Which manager, the one in the supermarket or the one in the cafeteria?

GIOVANNI: Both!

ANTONIA: Ooh, can you beat that! I'm just standing here with my mouth hanging open!

GIOVANNI: That's right! Those goddamn ignorant rabble, goddamn provocateurs, goddamned judas pigs who play into the goddamn bosses' hands . . . so they can go around saying the workers rip stuff off, calling us a bunch of goddamn crooks . . .

ANTONIA: But what do the workers have to do with it? At the supermarket it was the women taking the stuff at cut prices, wasn't it?

GIOVANNI: Yeah, but when they get home, their husbands pretend not to notice anything . . . or they even say, "Brava, you did the right thing, stealing stuff." Instead of smashing them over the head with every can and package, one by one. Because "*if*" my wife pulled something like that, I'd make her eat the tin can along with the little key. So you better not get any bright ideas about stealing, because "*if*" I ever hear you grabbed stuff at the supermarket without paying, or took a discount on even one can of anchovies, I'll . . . I'll . . .

ANTONIA: . . . you'll make me eat it along with the little key!

GIOVANNI: No, more than that, I'll leave this house. I'll pack my bags and disappear for good! In fact, first I'll kill you and then I'll file for divorce!

ANTONIA: Listen, if you're going to talk like that, you can leave right now, without waiting for a divorce. How dare you insinuate that I—listen, rather than bring home stuff I haven't paid the legal price for, I'd let you die of starvation!

GIOVANNI: Right, I'd rather you did! And speaking of starvation, what's for supper? With that circus in the cafeteria today, I even missed my lunch. So, what do we eat?

ANTONIA: This! (*She places the two cans of pet food on the table.*)

GIOVANNI: What's this stuff?

ANTONIA: Can't you read? It's special meat by-products for dogs and cats.

GIOVANNI: What?

ANTONIA: It's very good!

GIOVANNI: It may be very good for dogs!

ANTONIA: That's all there was. Besides, it's cheap, "nutritious . . . rich in proteins . . . delicious!" Look, it says so right here!

GIOVANNI: Are you trying to make a fool out of me?

ANTONIA: Who's trying to make a fool out of you? Hey, do you ever go and do the grocery shopping? You know how much they're charging for oil, meat, ham—everything costs twice as much as it used to, and besides, you can't find anything: they're hoarding it all, so they can set up a black market. It's worse than in wartime!

GIOVANNI: Don't exaggerate—wartime! Anyway, I'm not a dog yet . . . and I won't do it! I refuse.

ANTONIA: Refuse all you want. Because maybe you're not a dog yet— in fact, you're definitely not—but the boss doesn't see it that way. He thinks we're lower than dogs!

GIOVANNI: OK, OK! Take this crap away. You eat it if it really appeals to you. Look, I'll just have a glass of milk, that'll do.

ANTONIA: I'm sorry, there isn't any milk.

GIOVANNI: What do you mean, there isn't any?

ANTONIA: Oh, don't you know? This morning the milk truck came, and a rumor started that they'd raised the price again . . . and then a bunch of troublemakers, irresponsible jerks, including some Communist Party members, jumped on the truck and began giving the milk out to all the women at half price. And did you expect me to run downstairs and take it at that price? Half stolen milk! Would you have done it? And then drunk it?

GIOVANNI: Oh, no, not on your life.

ANTONIA: Good: then don't drink it!

GIOVANNI: But isn't there anything else?

ANTONIA: Yes, I could make you some soup . . .

GIOVANNI: Out of what?

ANTONIA: Birdseed for canaries.

GIOVANNI: Birdseed for canaries?

ANTONIA: Yes, it's delicious. It's good for diabetes!

GIOVANNI: But I don't have diabetes!

ANTONIA: Well, I can't help that. Besides, it's half the price of rice. And anyway, there wasn't any long grain rice left.

GIOVANNI: Oh, no, that's too much: first you make out I'm a dog, then a cat, now a canary—

ANTONIA: Oh, quit your bellyaching. Michela, who lives across the hall here, says she makes it every day for her husband, and she swears it's great.

GIOVANNI: For her husband. Yeah, I noticed that he's growing feathers.

ANTONIA: The entire secret is in the stock. Look, I got some rabbit heads too.

GIOVANNI: Rabbit heads?

ANTONIA: Sure. You certainly are ignorant! Birdseed soup is made with rabbit heads—only the heads: frozen! You're not going to tell me you're against frozen food, now?

GIOVANNI: All right, all right . . . I get it . . . So long!

ANTONIA: Where are you going?

GIOVANNI: Where do you think? Out, to some cafe.

ANTONIA: And what about money?

GIOVANNI: Give me some cash.

ANTONIA: What cash?

GIOVANNI: What do you mean, what cash? You're not going to tell me you're broke already!

ANTONIA: No, but did you forget that tomorrow we have to pay the gas and electricity bill, and the rent? Or do you want them to send us an eviction notice and cut off the light and gas!?

GIOVANNI: Of course not.

ANTONIA: Well then, you can forget about the cafe. But don't worry, I'll get you something. (*She puts on her coat.*)

GIOVANNI: Where are you going?

ANTONIA: Over to Margherita's. She went shopping today; she'll lend me some stuff. Don't worry, I'll be back in a minute. In the meantime, read your paper . . . or else go over there and watch TV, I'm sure that the prime minister will be on the screen talking about the economic recession, which is serious but not desperate, saying how we all have to stick together, rich and poor . . . Tighten our belts, have patience, understanding, faith in the government and in "Let's Make a Deal." So, while you're having faith in the government and in "Let's Make a Deal," I'll be right back.

GIOVANNI: OK, but without rabbit heads, please.

ANTONIA: Don't worry, this time I'll bring you the paws! (*exits*)

GIOVANNI: Okay, be a smart ass, go ahead . . . when I'm so hungry I could even eat . . . (*He looks, and reads:*) a tidbit for your little doggie and kitty friends! (*He has picked up a jar and is turning it around in his hands.*) How do you open it? Oh, great; as usual she forgot to get a key. Wait a minute, it's got a screw top. For dogs and cats they make screw top jars!? (*opens the jar*) Here goes! (*sniffs it*) Well, it doesn't smell bad . . . it's like pickled marmalade with a base of chopped kidneys, seasoned with cod liver oil. Boy, dogs and cats must really be retarded to eat this crap. Well, I'm going to taste it. But with a few drops of lemon juice to guard against cholera . . . (*From outside comes the whine of a police siren, screams of men and women, and military commands.*) What's this racket? (*He glances out the imaginary window and gestures to someone on the other side, in the facing apartment block.*) Aldo, hey, Aldo! What's going on? Yeah, I can see it's the police, but what do they want? Wow, look at all those police vans! What? Something about the supermarket? . . . What supermarket? What, here too: The one in this neighborhood? But when

. . . Today? . . . But who . . . Everybody? What do you mean, everybody? A thousand women. No, my wife wasn't there, you can be sure about that. She's so much against these ripoffs that she bought me rabbit heads instead . . . yeah, frozen! Besides, today she didn't even leave the house. She had to unwind a girlfriend's belly. No, unravel the bandages, bust it open . . . because her husband, Luigi, doesn't want her to get pregnant, and she obeyed the Pope and so the pill didn't work and she puffed up so much in one week . . . you wouldn't believe it . . . !! What d'you mean, you don't understand? (*He looks down into the street; orders and cries are heard.*) Wow, they're searching everywhere! Are they really trying to go house by house? Well, if they come here to my place, I'll show them! Because this is a clear provocation! A spit in the face. A frame-up. Sure, so they can blame things on us, "those lazy, good-for-nothing thieves, the workers!"

(*a knock at the door*)

VOICE FROM OUTSIDE: Permesso!

GIOVANNI: Who is it?

VOICE: Polizia! Open up!

GIOVANNI: Police! (*opens the door*) What do you want with me?

POLICE SERGEANT: Search. Here's the warrant. Search in the whole block.

GIOVANNI: Why, what are you looking for?

POLICE SERGEANT (*relaxed, and tired*): Look, you didn't just fall out of the clouds. You know yourself, everybody knows that the supermarket here was looted today. We're looking for the stolen goods, or if you prefer, the merchandise obtained at a five-finger discount.

GIOVANNI: And you're coming to look here, in my house? Meaning I'm a crook, a thug, a bum!

POLICE SERGEANT: Look, take it anyway you like. It's got nothing to do with me. I've got my orders and I have to carry them out.

GIOVANNI: Go right ahead and carry them out . . . but I warn you, this is a provocation. In fact, it's worse: it's a kick in the ass! You come here to fuck around with us, besides starving us to death. Look what I have to eat here: mixed dog and cat rations. (*holds the can out to the officer*)

POLICE SERGEANT: What?

GIOVANNI: Look, look. Smell this crap! And you know why! Because everything costs an arm and a leg! And I don't mean a chicken leg: look here, frozen rabbit heads! (*sticks the package of frozen rabbit heads under the officer's nose*) We can't afford decent stuff—we can't even find it, because it disappears: they hoard it!

SERGEANT: You mean you really eat this stuff?

GIOVANNI: I have no choice . . . anyway, it's not bad, you know! Would you like to try some? Come on, don't stand on ceremony . . . a squeeze of lemon and it goes down like cat shit. Taste it! It's good for sciatica.

SERGEANT: No thanks. I never throw up before meals.

GIOVANNI: Maybe you'd like me to fix you a nice birdseed soup?

SERGEANT: Birdseed soup? Are you fucking around with me now?

GIOVANNI: I wouldn't dream of it, here it is. It's half the cost of rice . . . eat this and you'll start singing like a canary—you know, tweet, tweet, tweet!

SERGEANT: Boy, you sure are in bad shape! But for that matter it's the same for us, on our wages, it's no joke, my wife has to scrimp and scrape too—even with me getting my meals at the station. Look, I really do understand. And . . . I shouldn't say this, but I also understand all these women in the neighborhood who forced the stores to sell out today. They are right. Personally, I sympathize with them entirely: expropriation is the only defense against robbery!

GIOVANNI: Huh? What? You think they're right?

SERGEANT: Well, sure, things can't go on like this. You may not believe it, but it makes me sick to come around here playing the cop . . . going through this lousy search. And who am I doing it for, anyway?—a bunch of dirty speculators who grab stuff, rip it off—they're the ones that are doing the stealing!

GIOVANNI: Excuse me, sergeant . . . that's right, isn't it, you are a sergeant?

SERGEANT: Yes, I'm a sergeant.

GIOVANNI: Good . . . is that a proper way to talk? A policeman, for crying out loud! You know you're talking like an extremist?

SERGEANT: Extremist, nothing, I'm a person who uses his head. And gets pissed off, too—you have to stop considering ordinary policemen a bunch of morons who just jump whenever they hear a whistle: Attention! At your orders! Quick, bark, bite—like guard dogs! And God help you if you try to talk, discuss things . . . never express your own opinions . . . Shut up! Lie down and be good!

VOICE FROM OUTSIDE: Sergeant! Now where did he go? Sergeant!

SERGEANT (goes to door, yells): Here I am, on the second floor . . . I'm doing a house search. You go on upstairs, to the other floors. (returns to discussion)

GIOVANNI: All right, OK . . . I guess I'll go along with what the Party Secretary Belinguer says, that you're workers too, "sons of the people," . . . but—

SERGEANT: Sons of the people, my ass—we're guard dogs. They turn us into lackeys of the people in power, the boss's thugs . . . We're supposed to enforce respect for their laws, and dirty tricks.

GIOVANNI: Wait a moment: if that's how you think, why did you
  choose this job?
SERGEANT: Who chose what? Just like you chose to eat this crap for
  dogs and cats, rabbit heads, and that other garbage for canaries?
GIOVANNI: No, that's all there was!
SERGEANT: There you are! That's all there was for me too . . . take it
  or drop dead. I happen to be a college graduate.
A MALE VOICE FROM OUTSIDE: Sergeant, we've finished here . . .
  What should we do now, go on ahead?
SERGEANT (*goes to door, yells:*): Of course, don't just stand there giving
  me a pain in the ass! (*returns to discussion*) As I was saying, I'm a
  college graduate. My father went without for years so that I could
  go to school . . . And in the end what did I find? A city job sweeping streets, waiting on tables in Switzerland, or the police force! I
  had to take this job! "Join the police force and learn the ways of the
  world." Boy, some ways! Some world! A world of bastards,
  swindlers, and suckers!
GIOVANNI: Yeah, but not everybody thinks that way. Some guys get
  along fine in the police force.
SERGEANT: Oh, sure, the ones snowed by propaganda: "A sense of
  honor and sacrifice." To feel they're somebody these guys have to
  repress other people, give orders, and bust a few heads; they're the
  retarded sons of this nation of sheep!
GIOVANNI (*to audience*): It's unbelievable . . . if I hadn't heard it with
  my own two ears, I'd never believe it. (*to* SERGEANT) But in the end
  we need the police . . . don't we? Maybe a little more democratic,
  but we need them. If not, we'd have chaos! Just because it comes
  into your head that something's right doesn't mean you can act on it
  . . . (*Without noticing it, he's shaking the rabbit heads.*) . . . like going
  shopping and paying whatever you think is right. You've got to
  obey the law!
SERGEANT: And what if the law's rotten, just a cover for grand larceny?
GIOVANNI: Well, then there's a parliament, there are the parties . . .
  democratic methods of struggle . . . and laws can be reformed—
SERGEANT: What d'you mean, reforms? What reforms, where? A con,
  that's what they are. For twenty years, they've been promising us
  reforms . . . and the only ones that have passed are those that pull
  the grafters up by *our* bootstraps: reforms that raise the price of
  gasoline, telephone, electricity . . . what about the one that handed
  out forty billion lire to the political parties for their election
  campaigns. First they steal in business, and then as punishment we
  let these fucking thieves in the government, where they decide to
  finance themselves . . . another ripoff, this time legalized! And the
  Communist Party's in it too!
GIOVANNI: Well, you're right about that—I didn't like that pig shit
  either.

SERGEANT: Believe me, the only serious reforms will be made by the people, in their own name, when they really start thinking. Because as long as the people "delegate . . .," "put their trust . . .," "have patience, a sense of responsibility, understanding, self-control, self-discipline" and on and on like this . . . *nothing changes!* And now, please excuse me, I have to go and do my job.

GIOVANNI: There, you see! First you act the Maoist subversive, and then, when it comes down to it, you put on your cap, and go back to being a cop.

SERGEANT: You're right, I'm just one of those guys who's all talk. I let off steam and that's that. Obviously, I don't have enough courage and consciousness. For now, I'm just a shit-slinger.

GIOVANNI: Right! All talk . . . The poor college graduate who has to be a cop because he's got no other choice! D'you expect me to cry over your problems? "But I can't really emigrate, you know, I'"m a college graduate." In fact, you should have emigrated too, or else swept streets, like other guys in your home town . . . *They've* made a man's choice—because they've got dignity. Got it! It's a matter of dignity! But guys like you are always ready with an excuse so they never risk anything. Yeah, and tomorrow you'll be there in front of the factory as usual ready to beat me up when there's a strike.

SERGEANT: Correct; you're right again. But you never know . . . maybe one of these days you'll hear that some cops have refused to go do the dirty work for the bosses . . . that they've even gone over to the other side!

GIOVANNI: Oh, I'll wait for the day. But first I expect to see the Pope dressed as an Indian!

SERGEANT: Look, the world's changing. It's changing a lot. So long and have a nice meal!

GIOVANNI: So now you're taking off like that, without even doing a little search? Now I'm offended! Take a little peek, just for fun . . . under the bed, in the closet . . . for instance.

SERGEANT: What for? Just to find a package of pig food and a can of meal for home-grown trout? Thanks, but there's no need. So long, and buon appetite! (*exits*)

GIOVANNI: Altre tanto! Boy, the number of weirdos you run into! A cop who's a wild red subversive! I've met fascists, thugs, and bullies, and now. So here's where the political extremists wind up . . . in the police force . . . and he stands there criticizing the Communist Party as not revolutionary enough! If only they knew it. Some "sons of the people." Ah, now I get it . . . he's a provocateur. The wise guy comes here to try and put words into my mouth: "We have to loot the supermarkets . . . the police should revolt" . . . and if I'd fallen for it like an asshole and agreed with him, he'd have pounced on me: "hands up . . . Red Brigades . . . you're under

arrest . . . where've you hidden Moro." . . . Oh, yeah! You found
the fish who'd bite all right. (*Absent-mindedly he grabs the package of
birdseed.*) . . . the fish who'd swallow the bait and the hook too?
. . . No. Here the fish only eats canary food!

(ANTONIA *enters with* MARGHERITA, *the latter's belly still swollen up and
covered with her overcoat.* MARGHERITA *peeks in the doorway, then quickly
backs off.*)

ANTONIA: Have they been here too?
GIOVANNI: Who?
ANTONIA: Don't you know what's going on? . . . That they're search-
   ing house by house?
GIOVANNI: Sure I know it.
ANTONIA: They even arrested the Mambettis and the Fosanis . . .
   They found stuff in lots of apartments and confiscated everything.
GIOVANNI: It serves them right, that'll teach 'em to act so smart.
ANTONIA: But they even took stuff that was fully paid for.
GIOVANNI: Sure, it's always the same; when a few creeps rip stuff off,
   people who don't have anything to do with it get into trouble
   —For instance, they came here and . . .
ANTONIA: They came? Here?
GIOVANNI: Sure.
ANTONIA: What did they find?
GIOVANNI: Why? What should they have found?
ANTONIA: No, I mean . . . you never know . . . sometimes you
   think you don't have anything in the house, and then . . .
GIOVANNI: And then?
ANTONIA: And then?
GIOVANNI: And then?
ANTONIA: And then they plant the stuff there themselves, to frame
   you . . . It wouldn't be the first time. For instance, they searched at
   Rosa's son's place, and just like that, pop! they snuck in a pistol
   under the pillow and a pack of leaflets under the bed.
GIOVANNI: Ma che brava! You think they'd come here to put packages
   of pasta and sugar under the bed?
ANTONIA: Well, maybe not under the bed, no . . . You know what I
   mean . . .
GIOVANNI: Yeah, I know . . . but maybe you're right . . . You never
   know . . . I'll have a look.
ANTONIA: No!
GIOVANNI: What d'you mean, no?
ANTONIA: Well, I mean . . . you'll put your dirty hands all over the
   pillow . . . I'll take a look myself . . . You let in Margherita.
GIOVANNI: Margherita? Where is she?
MARGHERITA (*loud cry*):   Ahhh!

GIOVANNI: Where?

MARGHERITA: Here!

ANTONIA: There, outside the door. (*She pretends to look under the bed.*) No, nothing here.

GIOVANNI: But why'd you leave her standing out there? Oh, good god, MARGHERITA, what are you doing there? Come in, come in. (MARGHERITA *enters, sobbing.*) What happened to her?

ANTONIA: Ah, she was all alone in her apartment, poor kid . . . and when she saw all those cops charging in, she got scared. Imagine, there was a lieutenant who wanted to feel her belly.

MARGHERITA: (*loud cry*)

GIOVANNI: Bastard! Why?

ANTONIA: Because he got the idea that instead of a baby up there, she had packages of pasta and other stuff.

GIOVANNI: What a dirty sonofabitch!

ANTONIA: You said it . . . C'mere, Margherita, sit down on the bed. So I told her to come to our place. Did I do the right thing?

GIOVANNI: Sure you did the right thing. But take off your coat, Margherita.

MARGHERITA: No thanks.

GIOVANNI: Come on, don't be so formal. Take it off.

ANTONIA: Ah, let her be. She said she'd rather keep it on. Maybe she's cold.

GIOVANNI: But it's hot in here.

ANTONIA: You find it hot, but she finds it cold. Maybe she even has a fever!

GIOVANNI: A fever? Is she sick?

ANTONIA: Sure; she's having labor pains!

MARGHERITA: (*two loud cries*)

GIOVANNI: Already?

ANTONIA: Whaddya mean, already? What do you know about it? Half an hour ago you didn't even know she was pregnant, and now you're amazed that she's having labor pains!

GIOVANNI: Well, it seems to me . . . I dunno . . . It seems to me a little premature!

ANTONIA: There he goes again! What do you know about it, if it's premature or not? You think you know more about it than she does? She's having the pains! Come on, get undressed . . . undress and get under the covers. And you: do me a favor: turn around.

GIOVANNI: Sure, sure, I'll turn around. (*does it*)

ANTONIA: Come on! Don't tremble like that . . . don't cry . . . it's all over now.

GIOVANNI: But if she's having labor pains, we'd better call a doctor. Or maybe even an ambulance.

ANTONIA: Aren't you bright: an ambulance! And then we'll go on a nice wild goose chase to every hospital in town . . . back and forth

. . . because we'll never find an empty bed! Oh boy, what a great way for the baby to be born! Don't you know that with the chaos they've got in the hospitals, people like us on the health plan, have to reserve a bed at least a month in advance?

GIOVANNI: So how come she didn't preregister?

ANTONIA: Oh, yeah, sure, why didn't she preregister: Us women always have to take care of everything: we have to do the running around, we have the kids, we make the reservations; And why didn't her husband do it?

GIOVANNI: But how could he, if he didn't know about it?

ANTONIA: That's a great excuse: he didn't know . . . You men are always like that—take the easy way out. You hand us the paycheck and then you say, "You take care of it; you work it out!" You make love—because you've got a sacred right—you get us pregnant, and then it's, "you work it out. Take the pill." And who gives a damn if the poor wife, who's a devout Catholic, every night dreams of the Pope saying to her: "you're committing a sin; you must procreate!"

GIOVANNI: So the Pope comes to mess you up even in your dreams, and even on television saying, "love one anotherski, we're all God's childrenski, rich and poor—especially the rich!" But what I mean, or rather what I want to know, is: when did Margherita get pregnant?

ANTONIA: What's it to you? And what's all this putting down the Popeski?

GIOVANNI: No, I mean—if they haven't even been married five months?

ANTONIA: So, they couldn't have started having sex earlier? Or are you a goddamn moralist, too, worse than the Pope?

GIOVANNI: No, but her husband, Luigi, told me that they made love for the first time only after they were married!

MARGHERITA: Did my Luigi tell you all that?

ANTONIA: But that's incredible—going around telling intimate things like that to anyone who comes along!

GIOVANNI: I'm not anyone who comes along! I'm his friend! His best friend! And he always tells me everything, asks me for advice . . . because I'm older and more experienced.

ANTONIA: Oh, get that: more experienced! (*another knock at the door*) Who is it?

VOICE FROM OUTSIDE: Police, open up!

GIOVANNI: Again?

MARGHERITA: Omigod!

GIOVANNI (*opening the door*): Buono serra . . . is it you again? (*In fact, we see the same actor who played the role of the* POLICE SERGEANT, *but now he is wearing the insignia of a lieutenant in the Carabinieri, and has a mustache.*)

LIEUTENANT: What do you mean, you again?

GIOVANNI: Oh, sorry, I thought you were the one who was here before.

LIEUTENANT: Which one was here before?

GIOVANNI: A police sergeant.

LIEUTENANT: Well, I happen to be a lieutenant in the Carabinieri.

GIOVANNI: I can see that, besides, you have a mustache. Okay, what is it you want?

LIEUTENANT: We have to make a search.

GIOVANNI: But your fellow-officers in the police department already just made one.

LIEUTENANT: That doesn't matter! We'll do it over again.

GIOVANNI: Ah, you don't trust them, so you came back to make sure we haven't pulled any fast ones! Then maybe the Treasury Department will come to check up on you; then they'll send in the secret police and finally, the Marines.

LIEUTENANT: Stop wisecracking—get over there and let us do our job.

ANTONIA: Of course, everybody has to get on with his job! We break our backs in the factory for eight hours a day at the looms . . . you put in eight hours on the assembly line, like a bunch of animals . . . and they work to make sure we toe the line—that we pay the price the bosses ask for their merchandise! (*The Carabiniere opens the cupboard and closet.*) Do you ever happen by any chance to check on whether the bosses are following their contracts and not killing us with piece-work or dumping us on unemployment? Check to make sure they're following the health and safety regulations?

(*The* LIEUTENANT *continues his search undisturbed.*)

GIOVANNI: No, you shouldn't talk like that, because it disgusts them too! Isn't that right, Lieutenant, that it makes you sick to carry out these searches and arrests for the bosses? You tell my wife how you policemen are fed up to here with taking orders every time a whistle blows—Attention! Jump up! Bark! Bite! like guard dogs—and god help you if you argue. Lie down, heel.

LIEUTENANT: Say that again. What's this about guard dogs?

GIOVANNI: Yes, I said you aren't sons of the people, like the communists say . . . you're servants of the ruling class—the boss's thugs!

LIEUTENANT: Handcuffs! (*removes cuffs from self*)

GIOVANNI: Handcuffs? Why, what for?

LIEUTENANT: For offense and insult to a public officer.

GIOVANNI: What d'you mean, insulting? I'm not the one who said those things—it was your fellow officer, a little while ago, he was the one who said you feel like lackeys of the ruling class!

LIEUTENANT: You, who? Us carabinieri?

GIOVANNI: No, he said you, meaning them—the ones in the Police Department.

LIEUTENANT: Oh, well, if those guys in the police force feel like lackeys, that's their problem. But watch what you say!

GIOVANNI: Sure, sure, I'll watch it. Boy, are these separate institutions ever separate!

(The Carabinieri goes on with his search, now approaching the bed.)

ANTONIA (*to* MARGHERITA):   Start moaning! Come on, cry.

MARGHERITA: Aiaooaoo!

ANTONIA: Louder!

MARGHERITA (*moaning as if in extreme pain*):   Ahiouua! Aiaaooioo!

LIEUTENANT: What's going on? What's the matter with her?

ANTONIA: She's having labor pains, poor kid!

GIOVANNI: Premature delivery, five months at the most.

ANTONIA: She got into a state a little while ago . . . because some cops tried to feel her stomach, poor kid!

LIEUTENANT: Feel her stomach?

GIOVANNI: Sure, to see if, instead of a baby, she maybe had a couple of packages of rice or pasta stuffed up there. Go on, why don't you help yourself. Sure, she's just a poor factory worker, you won't get into any trouble . . . you're allowed. Now if you took liberties with Princess Grace or poked your finger up Pirelli's wife you'd get thrown straight out of the force. But there's no risk here—one poke to a customer.

LIEUTENANT: Listen, stop that! You're provoking us!

ANTONIA: Yeah, you're overdoing it—cut it out!

MARGHERITA (*very loud*):   Aiuaaiiiaaiiiii! Auhiaaa!

ANTONIA: Don't you overdo it too.

LIEUTENANT: But did you call an ambulance?

ANTONIA: An ambulance?

LIEUTENANT: Well, you can't leave this poor woman here to maybe die. And if it's premature like you say, she could lose the baby.

GIOVANNI: He's right. You see, you see how understanding the Lieutenant is? I told you before you should call an ambulance.

ANTONIA: And I told you before that without a reservation they won't accept her. They'll send her chasing from one hospital to another all over town. That way she'll croak in the ambulance! (*The howling of a siren is heard outside.*)

LIEUTENANT (*going over and looking out the window*): There, an ambulance is coming to pick up that other woman who got sick on the next floor down. Come on, give me a hand. Let's load her on too.

ANTONIA (*resisting*): No, for heaven's sake . . . don't go to any trouble.

MARGHERITA: No, I don't want to go to the hospital!

ANTONIA: You see, she doesn't want to.

MARGHERITA: I want my husband, my husband . . . Ahio! Ahiuuaoo!

ANTONIA: You hear, she wants her husband . . . But he can't be here because he's on the night shift. I'm sorry, but without her husband's consent, we can't take this responsibility.

GIOVANNI: Oh, no, we can't take it.

LIEUTENANT: You won't take it, eh? But you'd take the responsibility for letting her drop dead here?

ANTONIA: Instead of the hospital?

LIEUTENANT: At the hospital they could save her, and maybe the baby, too!

GIOVANNI: But it's premature, I told you!

MARGHERITA: Yes, yes, I'm premature . . .

ANTONIA: And with the ambulance jolting she'll give birth! And how can a five-months' old baby survive?

LIEUTENANT: Obviously you have no idea of modern medical progress. Didn't you ever read about test-tube babies?

ANTONIA: Yes, I did, but what do test-tubes have to do with it? And you can't put a five-month baby in an oxygen tent!

GIOVANNI: That's right, such a teeny thing, under a tent—doing what, anyway? Camping out?

LIEUTENANT: It's clear that you're starved for information.

ANTONIA AND GIOVANNI: Oh yes, we're starved, all right!

LIEUTENANT: Where have you been hiding out? Haven't you ever seen the equipment they've got now, right here in Milan, at the gynecology clinic? I was on duty in there five months ago, and I saw they're even doing transplants.

MARGHERITA, ANTONIA, AND GIOVANNI: A transplant of what?

LIEUTENANT: A premature baby transplant. (*He demonstrates.*) They took a four-and-a-half month baby out of the womb of a woman who couldn't carry him, and they fixed him in another woman's womb.

GIOVANNI: Right inside her?

LIEUTENANT: Just like that. Caesarian: they transplanted it with the placenta and everything . . . sewed her up, and four months later—just last month, in fact, out came the baby again, as fine and healthy as a fish.

GIOVANNI: A fish?

LIEUTENANT: Yep!

GIOVANNI: Must be a trick.

ANTONIA: Trick, nothing, I read about it too. Sure it's incredible—a baby born twice . . . a kid with two mothers!

MARGHERITA: No, no, I don't want to! Ahiouu!

ANTONIA: She's right, poor kid . . . hell, I'd never let another woman give birth to my child either!

MARGHERITA: I don't want to, I don't want to! I won't give my consent!

ANTONIA: There, you hear. She won't give her consent . . . so we can't take her away from here.

LIEUTENANT: Well then, I'll give my consent; I'll take the responsibility! I don't want trouble for neglecting to provide necessary aid!

ANTONIA: But that's just plain force and violence: first they poke all over the house, then they handcuff us . . . now they want to shove us into an ambulance. You won't let us live, OK, but at least let us die where we choose!

LIEUTENANT: No, you can't die where you choose.

GIOVANNI: Sure, we have to die where the law decides!

LIEUTENANT: And you watch it with the snide remarks. I already warned you—

GIOVANNI: So who's making snide remarks?

ANTONIA: Take it from me, Giovanni, this isn't the right moment. Come on, let's carry her down.

LIEUTENANT: Should I call for the stretcher?

ANTONIA: No, no, she can come by herself. You can walk, can't you? Now we'll just help her up . . .

MARGHERITA: Yes, yes—oh, no, no—it's slipping out!

ANTONIA: Omigod! Do you mind going out for a minute? My friend is kind of undressed, and I have to help her get her clothes back on.

LIEUTENANT: Right, let's go. (*All the men exit.*)

ANTONIA: C'mon, hurry, lift up these bags. Dammit, that lousy ambulance was all we needed!

MARGHERITA: I knew it would end badly! And what'll happen at the hospital when they find out I'm pregnant with pasta, rice and canned goods?

ANTONIA: Nothing will happen, because we won't get to the hospital.

MARGHERITA: Sure, because we'll get arrested first!

ANTONIA: Just cut out the whining: once we're inside the ambulance, we'll tell the medical assistants what's going on . . . They're good people, those guys, they're on our side . . . they'll help us out for sure.

MARGHERITA: What if they're not on our side? And they report us?

ANTONIA: Cut it out, they won't report us!

MARGHERITA: It's slipping down; I'm losing another bag!

ANTONIA: Hold onto it! Good grief, what a pain in the ass!

MARGHERITA: No, don't push . . . Dammit, something just broke open . . . a packet of olives in juice! Yech!

(*At this moment* GIOVANNI *appears, followed by the* LIEUTENANT.)

GIOVANNI: What's going on now?

MARGHERITA: It's coming out; it's all coming out!

GIOVANNI: The baby's coming out! The baby's coming out! Quick, Lieutenant, help me carry her!

LIEUTENANT: Let me do that!

ANTONIA: There we are . . . good . . . keep her horizontal.

LIEUTENANT: What's this wet spot?

ANTONIA: Oh, she must be losing water.

GIOVANNI: Quick; if we don't hurry, she'll be having the baby in here!

ANTONIA: Cool down, cool down, take it easy!

MARGHERITA: It's coming, it's coming out!

ANTONIA (*sotto voce to* MARGHERITA): I know it's coming out! (*to others*) Hold on, let's wrap her up in this blanket. Take it easy, Lieutenant!

GIOVANNI: Wait a minute, I'll get my jacket and come too.

ANTONIA: No, stay at home! You take a cloth and wipe up the floor where it's all wet. This is women's business. (*exit, all except* GIOVANNI)

GIOVANNI (*grabs the rag and goes to wipe up the floor*): Yeah, sure . . . I'll take a rag and wipe . . . that's men's business. What a mess! Luigi'll have a surprise when he comes off the shift tomorrow . . . and finds himself a father all at one stroke . . . He'll *have* a stroke! And when he finds out his baby has been transplanted into another woman, he'll have another stroke . . . and that'll finish him off! I'd better speak to him first, prepare him gradually, kind of come in through the back door! I know! I'll begin by talking about the Pope . . . "My brothers in Christ!" (*He's down on all fours, wiping the floor with the rag.*) Wow, look at all that water! What a weird odor, it smells like vinegar . . . yes, like olive juice, sure! I never knew that . . . that before we're born, we spend nine months in olive juice! Oh look . . . what's this? An olive? We sit in juice with olives? I can't believe it! That's crazy! The olive's got nothing to do with it. (*Once again the howl of a siren is heard;* GIOVANNI *gets up and returns to the window.*) Well, they're driving off. Let's hope everything comes out alright . . . But where'd this olive come from? And look, another one: two olives? If they weren't of such uncertain origin . . . I'd eat them, I'm so hungry! I'm almost tempted to make a soup with birdseed for real. Maybe it's even good. The water's on the stove already . . . I'll just put in a couple of bouillon cubes . . . and a head of garlic . . . (*opens the refrigerator*) I knew it! No bouillon cubes, and not a single head of garlic . . . I guess I have put in a rabbit head instead! I feel like the witch in Snow White fixing up the poison potion. Then you'll see, I eat the soup and bam! I turn into a frog! (*Without thinking he grabs the starter.*) Hey, what's my portable starter doing here? How many times do I have to tell that idiot Antonia that she shouldn't use it to light the stove, it's dangerous! And besides, it runs down the batteries.

(LUIGI *looks in from the door.*)

LUIGI: Can I come in? Anybody home?

GIOVANNI: Ciao, Luigi! Aren't you on the night shift? What are you doing here at this hour?

LUIGI: Something happened on the way to the factory . . . I'll explain later. Right now, do you know where my wife is? I might as well throw my keys away. (*He throws them onto the cupboard.*) I was just home, and everything's wide open, but nobody's there.

GIOVANNI: Right; your wife was here ten minutes ago, and left with Antonia.

LUIGI: Where'd they go? And what for?

GIOVANNI: Well, you know; "women's business."

LUIGI: What do you mean, "women's business"?

GIOVANNI: Hey, cool down! What's got into you? When I say, "women's business," I mean things that aren't men's business.

LUIGI: But why shouldn't it be any of my business? It *is* my business!

GIOVANNI: Oh, sure, it's your business. Well then, how come you didn't make it your business to reserve a bed a month ago, like everybody else does?

LUIGI: A bed? A bed for what?

GIOVANNI: Oh, yeah, that's women's business, isn't it! The usual song and dance! We shove our paycheck at 'em and then tell 'em: "You work it out!" We have sex, and we tell 'em: "Take the pill!" We get 'em pregnant and, "It's your problem!" They have the baby, and they're the ones that have to take it to nursery school, pick it up . . .

LUIGI: What the hell are you talking about?

GIOVANNI: I'm talking about that they're right; we really are irresponsible jerks! We're exploiters, the same as the bosses!

LUIGI: But what's all this got to do with the fact that Margherita leaves the apartment door wide open and disappears just like that, without even leaving me a note?

GIOVANNI: Why should she leave you a note? Aren't you supposed to be at the plant on the night shift? So how come you're already back?

LUIGI: Well, the train was held up.

GIOVANNI: Who held it up?

LUIGI: All of us workers, because those sons-a-bitches raised the price of our commuter pass thirty percent!

GIOVANNI: And for that you held up the train?

LUIGI: Sure, we pulled the emergency cord, and everybody jumped down on the tracks! We blocked the whole line. Even the Rome express and the International for Paris! You should have seen how pissed off the first-class passengers were!

GIOVANNI: Ah, a great party? Very impressive! Sorry, but in my book only brainless troublemakers would pull a stunt like that. Dumb, shithead tricks, playing into the hands of the reactionaries!

LUIGI: Yeah, you're right, they're dumb shithead tricks! I even told them, "There is no point in making this stink over raising the price; we shouldn't be paying for the pass in the first place!"

GIOVANNI: Oh, bravo . . . you're really crazy! Not pay for the pass!

LUIGI: Sure, the company ought to pay for our transportation! And they ought to pay us for the time we spend in the train too! Portal to portal pay. Because all that traveling isn't for sightseeing; we get up two hours early and come home two hours later . . . all for the company.

GIOVANNI: Are you serious? Who've you been talking to? Those wild men on the far left, I bet . . . they're all police agents and provacateurs!

LUIGI: Don't talk horseshit, provocateurs! Is Tonino a provocateur?

GIOVANNI: Tonino that works the presses?

LUIGI: Yeah, him. And Marco, and the three Calabrians from my home town?

GIOVANNI: So, you've been listening to those southern Italians? Those Arab hijackers!

LUIGI: No, I thought it all on my own. It's obvious that things can't go on like this; we gotta move without waiting for the good wishes of the government, or the intervention of the unions or a good word from the party. We gotta stop waiting for permission to do every thing even taking a piss. "Wait," "have faith," "sense of responsibility," "be understanding." No, we've got to get things moving ourselves.

GIOVANNI: Tell me: have you been talking to that police sergeant with out a mustache who's the spitting image of the Carabinieri lieutenant with a mustache?

LUIGI: Who?

GIOVANNI: Yeah, that cop, the maoist provocateur who says we gotta go shoplifting in the supermarkets; that guy makes the same brainless hothead speeches you do!

LUIGI: Never heard of him. (*He tastes the contents of the open jar.*) Hm, not bad, this stuff. What is it?

GIOVANNI: Huh? You ate the stuff in that jar?

LUIGI: Sure, it's not bad. Sorry, but I was hungry.

GIOVANNI: Without lemon?

LUIGI: Yes, why, do you eat it with lemon?

GIOVANNI: Bah, I don't know. Sure it's good?

LUIGI: Wonderful.

GIOVANNI: Let me taste . . . Well, I thought it'd be worse; it's almost better than that concentrate they use for carp fishing. Would you mind opening this other jar too?

LUIGI: Sure, but what is it?

GIOVANNI: It's a kind of paté for rich dogs and cats.

LUIGI: Paté for dogs and cats? Are you nuts?

GIOVANNI: No, I'm an eccentric . . . a gourmet. Try this. (*He brings* LUIGI *a bowl of soup*.) Taste it, taste it!

LUIGI: Huh, not bad. What is it?

GIOVANNI: Oh, a speciality of mine: canary seed in a broth of frozen rabbit heads.

LUIGI: Canary seed and rabbit heads?

GIOVANNI: Sure, it's a Chinese dish; they call it Mush a la Deng Xiaoping . . . Revisionist cooking.

LUIGI: But the birdseed's a bit raw . . .

GIOVANNI: What d'you mean? It's birdseed pilaf, it's always served a bit crisp . . . Yes, crispy birdseed and crappy rabbit heads. That's the way they started the cultural counterrevolution in China! By the way, who ate the olive that was sitting here?

LUIGI: I did. Why, wasn't I supposed to?

GIOVANNI: No, you were not supposed to! It was your wife's olive! Man, you'll even steal your newborn baby's food!

LUIGI: What? My wife's olive . . . my newborn baby?

GIOVANNI: Ah, yes, because when you're born, you see, the juice comes out . . . Well, forget it, I'd better go slowly . . . start with the Pope . . . Now, His Eminence John Paul . . .

LUIGI: Look, Giovanni, are you feeling OK? What kind of talk is this?

GIOVANNI: Talk? Oh yeah; you're the one who knows the right way to talk. The boss should pay for our ticket because we travel for him . . . and for the time we spend on the train too . . . Next you'll be saying he should pay us for the time we sleep, because we're resting up for his sake, so we can be nice and fresh for work the next day; and he should even pay for our movies and our TV set because that junk helps us unwind our nerves after working on the line. And he ought to pay our wives, too, every time they have sex with us because it makes us feel better so we produce more!

LUIGI: Ecco Bravo! And isn't it true that our wives really slave for the boss without pay? And when the boss makes us mad, we take it out on them? All that—what do you call it—alienation we get from the factory. We come back home and quarrel like dogs in a compound. (*imitating two puppet voices:*)

        M: Where's the milk?
        F: There is no milk.
        M: Why no milk?
        F: There is no money.
        M: What you mean, no money!
        M & F (*Both fight.*)

Husband and wife!

GIOVANNI: Don't exaggerate now. Life isn't all that shitty, come on. Things are better than they used to be! Almost everybody has a house now, even if it's lousy. Some of us even have a car, and everybody has a refrigerator, and a TV set . . .

LUIGI: What do I care about a refrigerator, a car, or a TV set, when the work I do makes me want to puke? Jesus Christ! Our job is like a trained monkey act: a weld, a rap with the hammer, a shot with the drill, a weld, a rap, one part gone, another in place . . . a weld and (GIOVANNI *begins to pick up the motion of the assembly-line work; gradually he speaks with* LUIGI, *then he adds sounds, building:*) . . . a rap . . . the line speeds up . . . a weld . . .

GIOVANNI with LUIGI: . . . rap . . . a shot with the drill . . . one part gone, another in place . . . A weld . . .

GIOVANNI (*breaking the rhythm*): Hey, for Chrissake, what are you making me do? You're scrambling my brain, too!

LUIGI: No, it's not me who's scrambling your brain, it's the boss! The same boss that messes you up inside everywhere: at the movies with stories about impossible fucks with little asses all over the place . . . women acting like panthers in heat . . . talking and moving their mouth and tongue like they're licking an ice cream cone, and I don't know what else. And that's what they call adult movies.

GIOVANNI: Yeah! And what about when you leave the movies? You're taking a nice little relaxing stroll with your wife and you pass those billboards with more tits and ass, advertising ball point pens, toothpaste, cheese spread. There's your wife, walking next to you. You look at her . . . she doesn't have her hair washed in Dreck, "soft, manageable, and lustrous," she doesn't wear nail polish with "glowing color," she doesn't wear perfume, "Love me tender!" Her tits are just plain round things . . . they don't even bounce. Her behind is only a behind; it's not a "little ass" like the ones in the movies. She has swollen feet and chapped hands; I take one look at her and get the urge to knock her into the first ditch I see!

LUIGI: Right! There you are, good! You know what happens to me? When I have sex with my wife? I don't make love with her, I make love with Signal toothpaste, the one with the red stripes . . . with Black Velvet Scotch, "smooth and blonde," and with Aqua Velva!

GIOVANNI: Man, it really makes you sick!

LUIGI: It makes you sick because the bosses have made it that way. You've been infected all over. They've poisoned the air we breathe, they've poisoned our rivers, they've turned the sea into a sewer. They've made human relations into a cesspool, love into sewage and people into shit . . . even the food you eat!

GIOVANNI: Well, not everything. For instance, this birdseed soup isn't bad!

LUIGI: Everything's going to pot . . . look: factories closing; layoffs, unemployment . . . and the collapse of that bank where even the Pope had his billions stashed.

GIOVANNI: It serves him right, that old scarecrow going around in a white dress, giving women a pain in the ass about getting pregnant!

LUIGI: What d'you mean, the Pope's getting pregnant?

GIOVANNI: No, not him . . . though he'd probably like it . . . I'm talking about your wife.

LUIGI: What's my wife got to do with the Pope?

GIOVANNI: Oh, you're pretending you don't know?

LUIGI: No, I *don't* know! What's this thing about the Pope?

GIOVANNI: There you are! Instead of making love with striped tooth-paste and Aqua Velva, if you paid attention to what your wife dreams at night, when his Eminence John Paul comes in his white robe and starts saying "Brothers in Christ, I come to tell you that the pill is God's curse . . . For Christ's sake, don't take the pill!"

LUIGI: Well, in fact Margherita doesn't take the pill.

GIOVANNI: Ah, so you knew it. Who told you?

LUIGI: Who was supposed to tell me? She doesn't need to take it since she can't have babies anyway, something's wrong inside, can't re-member exactly.

GIOVANNI: You're the one who's got something wrong in your head! Your wife is fit as a fiddle, and can have babies! In fact she's got one now!

LUIGI: She has a baby? Since when?

GIOVANNI: Since right now! It's probably already born, five months premature!

LUIGI: Don't give me that crap; five months! She didn't even have a belly!

GIOVANNI: No, she didn't have one because she'd bandaged herself up; then Antonia untied her, and ploof! a belly that looked like nine months . . . or maybe even eleven!

LUIGI: Listen, are you fuckin' around with my head!

GIOVANNI: Not me! Fact is, if you really want to know, my wife's gone with her to the hospital in an ambulance, because she was almost about ready to have the baby here.

LUIGI: Have the baby here!

GIOVANNI: She was already losing water . . . look, I wiped it up myself.

LUIGI: You wiped up my wife's water?

GIOVANNI: Well, water . . . Maybe it would be more accurate to call it "juice" with an olive or two, which actually you've just eaten.

LUIGI: Quit kidding around! Where's my wife?

GIOVANNI: I told you, at the hospital.

LUIGI: Which hospital?

GIOVANNI: Who knows? If you'd preregistered, now we'd know. But this way she may be going from one place to the other, with the baby coming out in the ambulance, poor little bambino, among all the olives!

LUIGI: Stop acting like an asshole! Always making wisecracks, and kidding even about serious things! Tell me what hospital they took her to or I'll smack you in the teeth!

GIOVANNI: Hey, cool it! I told you, I don't know . . . Wait a minute, maybe they went to that place, whaddyacallit, the geanological clinic.

LUIGI: The gynecological clinic?

GIOVANNI: Yeah, where they also transplant premature babies.

LUIGI: Transplant babies?

GIOVANNI: Yeah, really. Where have you been? It's obvious you're starved for information about premature birth so I'll just explain. They do it like this: there's this big oxygen tent . . . They take the woman with the premature baby, four and a half, maybe five months . . . Then they take this woman who's the second mother . . . do a Caesarian on her . . . put the baby in her belly, sew up the placenta and everything . . . and then after four months (*pauses*) . . . a fish.

LUIGI: Cut it out about transplants and Caesarians . . . just tell me where this goddam gynecological clinic is. You got a phone book?

GIOVANNI: No, I don't. What would I do with it, without a phone? I guess I could read it for fun, just to find out who's in town!

LUIGI: Then let's go downstairs to the bar. They've got a phone there.

GIOVANNI: It just came back to me, the gynecological clinic is in Niguarda!

LUIGI: Niguarda?

GIOVANNI: Yeah, it's at least twenty kilometers from here.

LUIGI: But why'd they go there?

GIOVANNI: I told you; God, what a shithead. It's because that's where they do the transplants; they take another woman, the first volunteer . . . Another woman? My wife! Antonia would do it for sure . . . She'd be the first volunteer! She's so dumb! Get going! She'll let them do the transplant for sure, and she'll come back home pregnant!

CURTAIN

ACT TWO

LUIGI *and* GIOVANNI *cross apron, on their way to the hospital, singing "Avanti Popolo." Curtain.* ANTONIA *and* MARGHERITA *are coming back into the apartment.* MARGHERITA *is whining, she still has her big belly.*

ANTONIA: Hurry up, Margherita, come in. (*calling out*) Giovanni, Giovanni! Not here, he must have gone to work already. What time is it? (*looks at the alarm clock on the cupboard*) Five-thirty. Madonna, what with one thing and another, we've been gone more than four hours. (*goes to glance into the other room*) Yeah, he really has gone. And he didn't even get to bed, poor guy.

MARGHERITA: It's all your fault; why did I listen to you! Now look, we're in shit up to our ears.

ANTONIA: Stop moaning, dammit, you really are a crybaby! So what happened finally? Everything went as smooth as silk, didn't it? Didn't you see how nice those guys in the ambulance were? We just told them: "Look, the kid here isn't pregnant, just big with loot," and they jumped at the chance to help us. They even congratulated us! "Che brave! You women are terrific! It's great what you did! Those thieving profiteers at the supermarket deserve a good beating!" And you were so worried: you should learn to trust people! (*She looks in the refrigerator.*) Hey, who stole my butter? No, no, here it is. Now I'll make you some soup. Oh, the rice, give me a package of rice. (MARGHERITA *pulls a package of rice out of a bag hidden under her coat.* ANTONIA *goes to the stove and sees the pan there.*) But what's this stuff? Birdseed? That big deficient Giovanni really made himself some soup with the birdseed and rabbit heads! Do you believe it! You can't even tell him a lie without him swallowing it.

MARGHERITA: Look, if you're making the soup just for me, don't bother, I'm not hungry. My stomach has all closed up . . .

ANTONIA: Well, I'll open it for you again. You shouldn't get so panicked. You know your problem is that you really don't trust people. You've got to realize that people are OK . . . Well, not everybody . . . I mean people like us . . . the ones who break their asses trying to make ends meet. People like that are on our side, if you show them you're not asleep, that you're ready to fight the bosses, to defend your rights and not wait for the Angel of the Lord to come floating down on his wings together with Holy Providence! I remember when I was working in that factory, making breadsticks. It was murder working in damp heat, but it was just enough money to make ends meet. Suddenly the owners decided to shut down. They *said* the factory wasn't making enough money. They just wanted to kick us out. So we went and occupied the factory: three hundred of us. But the unions wouldn't support us. "You're crazy!" they told us. "You'll never make it! It's a losing battle! Who's going to give you capital to buy the flour? And who'll buy your products? If you don't have a market, you're screwed!"

MARGHERITA: And they were right, weren't they?

ANTONIA: But we tried it just the same. We all put in money. One woman even sold the tiny flat she'd just managed to pay for after years of scrimping. Lots of us took stuff to the pawnshop, even sheets and mattresses. That's how we bought the first sacks of flour. Then we took the breadsticks and we went out to sell them to the shops. We even sold them in front of the factories; and the workers saw our courage and supported us. They made a big deal everytime we showed up and even bought stuff they didn't need. And do you know what they did in the end?

MARGHERITA: What?

ANTONIA: They set up a subscription fund among the workers in all the factories in and around Milan. And they raised more than eighty million lire. Eighty million! If I hadn't been there myself, right in the middle of things, I'd never have believed it. When the workers came to bring all that money to use in the factory . . . I'll never forget it as long as I live . . . We were all there kneading the dough and we began to cry, tears falling into the flour . . . we mixed tears and flour for breadsticks and saved on salt! (*On hearing this story,* MARGHERITA *is deeply moved.*) But what are you bawling about, now?

MARGHERITA: It's a very moving story, that's all!

ANTONIA: Instead of just being moved, you should think about what I've told you; it isn't just a pretty story about human kindness. Hey, what are you up to now?

MARGHERITA: I am removing these packages and bags . . . You don't expect me to keep them on me the rest of my natural life, do you?

ANTONIA: No, but don't take them out here; we've got to take them to the shed in the garden allotment . . .

MARGHERITA: What shed?

ANTONIA: . . . behind the railroad tracks. We'll take it all over there, with the stuff under the bed. I'll make myself a nice belly too. Come here, help me. In two or three trips we can move everything. (*She takes some pillow cases from a drawer, and with pins and ribbon, makes two sacks to hang from the shoulders.*)

MARGHERITA: What's all this about a shed?

ANTONIA: I told you, by the railroad tracks, just across the street. My father-in-law has a garden there . . . ten square meters of land . . . just enough to keep us in salad greens. It's a safe hiding place.

MARGHERITA: No, thanks, I've had it. I'm fed up with your crazy ideas. Sorry, but I'm leaving everything here. I don't even want one package of spaghetti.

ANTONIA: Do as you like . . . but you're an idiot!

MARGHERITA: Oh, *I'm* an idiot! If you're so clever and bright, think of something for me to tell your husband when he sees me again minus the belly and without even a baby?

ANTONIA: I've already got it figured out; we'll tell him you had a hysterical pregnancy.

MARGHERITA: Hysterical?

ANTONIA: Yeah, it's common for a woman to think she's pregnant . . . her belly gets big and then when she goes to have the baby, all that comes out is air.

MARGHERITA: Go on, only air! And how did I get this hysterical pregnancy?

ANTONIA: From the Pope. He's the one who always comes in your dreams and tells you: "Have a baby, have a baby." And you obeyed him; you've had a baby . . . an air baby. Just the soul of the baby!

MARGHERITA: Oh great, drag the Pope into our business as well!

ANTONIA: Well, one good turn deserves another, doesn't it? (*Meanwhile*, MARGHERITA *has unloaded herself;* ANTONIA *on the other hand has built a swollen belly under her coat.*) OK, that's it. Now look: keep your eye on the pan there on the stove, and I'll be back in ten minutes.

MARGHERITA: Buy why don't you just grab a couple more shopping bags and take over everything in one trip, instead of doing this song and dance routine about the pregnant mommy?

ANTONIA: Because I'm not an idiot like you who'd get herself busted right away. Look down there out front, in the street. Come here; see that! It's a police wagon. And what do you think they're doing there, so early? They're waiting specially for suckers like you who go walking around with shopping bags to hide stuff early in the morning . . . and pop! they catch you on the fly! (*She turns to the gas range for a moment.*) Listen, if the gas goes out, there's this portable gizmo of Giovanni's. It works like this . . . it lights up.

MARGHERITA: But doesn't it get red hot?

ANTONIA: No, because it's not made of iron . . . it's special stuff they call antimony which goes up to 2000 degrees without ever getting red. It's made specially for lighting the gas.

MARGHERITA (*glancing out the window*):   Look down there, it's Maria from the fourth floor; she's got herself pregnant too . . . there she goes crossing . . .

ANTONIA: They're all stealing our idea; next you'll see pregnant dogs in their little coats, and men with big humps.

MARGHERITA: Listen, I've changed my mind, I'm going with you. (*She takes the bags again and arranges them on he stomach.*)

ANTONIA: Good, but hurry up . . . Even those like you who get so scared they pee in their pants . . . sooner or later they get brave. (*affectionately*) Get going, you big dummy! (*She caresses her own belly.*) I'll go and get the key to the shed. You know something? This big belly makes me feel sentimental; it reminds me of my baby.

MARGHERITA: Your baby?

ANTONIA: Well, actually, he's already over nineteen but for me he's still my baby . . . Fulvio. Even if he is living on his own, with a girl. She left home and everything too.

MARGHERITA: Well, I left home early too!

ANTONIA: I know . . . as soon as they manage to earn two cents of their own, they're off.

MARGHERITA: They're right; personally I couldn't take it at home anymore. What sort of home was it? We never saw each other . . . we never managed to talk . . . and even when you do get to talk, all we did was quarrel, like dogs in a compound. Any excuse to say nasty things to each other, to vent our rage.

ANTONIA: So, my boy, Fulvio, took off too. But pretty soon now he'll have a child of his own and the old story will start again from the beginning; the kids always take off thinking that they're escaping from the compound, but really they're still here inside the fence! It's no good, until we break down the fence and get rid of the keeper!

MARGHERITA: And male chauvinism too!

ANTONIA: Well, let's go. Today really is mother's day!

CURTAIN

(*In front of curtain.* LUIGI *and* GIOVANNI *enter from stage left, as if walking along the street.* LUIGI *takes out a cap and puts it on his head.* GIOVANNI *does the same.*)

LUIGI: Now it's even beginning to rain.

GIOVANNI: Shit.

LUIGI: Lousy government.

GIOVANNI: They told you on the phone that your wife's not a patient, so why did we have to go traipsing around like this?

LUIGI: With that circus of an administration, who can you trust?

GIOVANNI: Well, I've had it. Now I'm going to the station and take the train and go to work. They'll probably dock me an hour already. (*He goes; then, at center, he stops, looking toward the audience.*) Look! Over there! Oh shit, what a disaster!

LUIGI (*moves to* GIOVANNI): It's a truck . . . no, two! Those eight-axle rigs! They've turned over!

GIOVANNI: No wonder, with this rain . . . you brake on a wet spot . . . and pata pum!

(*Enter the* POLICE SERGEANT *we have already met.*)

SERGEANT: Get back, get back! Keep away, it's dangerous! They could be carrying inflammable material! It might blow up any minute!

GIOVANNI: Hi there, Sergeant: We always run into each other on happy occasions, don't we?

SERGEANT: Oh, it's you. You see what an easy life we have? (*speaking to the back of the house*) Hey, down there, you, on the embankment! What are these idiots doing? Get back, you too! . . . (*turns to the left*) Hey, over there! Keep moving, get going . . . go to work! Don't you have enough accidents at work? You gotta come looking for them here too!

LUIGI: Eh, you really know this guy?

GIOVANNI: Sure, we're bosom buddies. A red hot Maoist. I think he's an infiltrator.

LUIGI: An infiltrator, in the police?

GIOVANNI: Sure. Hey, Sergeant . . . look on the side of the truck, it says "caustic soda," and that stuff doesn't blow up.

SERGEANT: I know, "caustic soda" is written on the outside; but you don't know what's on the inside.

GIOVANNI: Oh, you're always so suspicious, Sergeant. Those are two "International Transport" trucks, stuff that goes out of the country. With all the inspections they have, there's no way they could put on a fake label. You'll see, it won't blow up!

SERGEANT: I know, I know, the truck won't blow up, but my balls might. You know, what with one thing and another, I've been on my feet since yesterday morning.

GIOVANNI: Ah, and you think we've had it any better; "Move it, move it, keep the torch hot. On the job!"

SERGEANT: Ecco bravo! You're all ready to join the police force . . . why don't you take my place?

GIOVANNI: Well, in your place, to begin with, *I'd* clear away all these sacks that fell out on the embankment. 'Cause if it *is* caustic soda, with the rain that's coming down it'll soon begin boiling. You'll get a smoking mush that'll be really dangerous! "Caustic" means that it burns, right?!

SERGEANT: Right, OK, so now you can give me a hand . . . I always like people who show initiative and a cooperative spirit. Let's go, get a move on!

GIOVANNI: Goddam me and all my bright ideas!

LUIGI: You said it! You really do have this fault; you get these jerkie ideas!

SERGEANT (*turns to the rear of the house*):   Come on, you too! Give us a hand! Let's save these sacks. Do it for the truck drivers . . . You've got to support those in trouble.

(*The action of passing the sacks from hand to hand begins. The sacks plop on to stage left.*)

GIOVANNI: Look! Everybody's coming over to give us a hand. You're always such a pessimist. And they'll probably be late for work, and get their pay docked.

SERGEANT: *I* never said that the people aren't generous.

GIOVANNI: Oh no: you just say that we've got to look sharp since the world is full of crooks and you can't trust anybody. You know, you really remind me of my first boss: a suspicious old bastard who had a dog older than he was—half deaf, but a ferocious watchdog. And since the old guy didn't trust anybody else, he went out and had a hearing aid made specially for the dog.

SERGEANT: A hearing aid for a dog?

GIOVANNI: Yeh. A really strong, battery-operated one. He tied it to the inside of the dog's leg. But as soon as the dog lifted his leg to piss, he pissed on the battery—short circuit—and zapp! he got electrocuted.

SERGEANT: Well, I'll try not to raise my leg. By the way . . . do you know what happened to the truck drivers?

LUIGI: Where did they go? O Jesus! Were they crushed inside the cab?

SERGEANT: They weren't crushed; they got out.

GIOVANNI: Thank goodness!

SERGEANT: They got out right away and took off like a couple of rockets!

GIOVANNI: Why?

SERGEANT: Because just as I thought these sacks we're rescuing with such love and generosity don't have caustic soda in them, but refined sugar!

GIOVANNI: Sugar? There's sugar in there?

LUIGI (opening a sack to check): Yep, it's really sugar.

SERGEANT: These are sugar, those others first grade flour.

GIOVANNI: The bastards! But where were they taking it?

SERGEANT: The first load was going to Switzerland and the other one to Germany. You were the one who said that these guys never put on a fake label. Real honest folks: "You know, with all the inspections they have!"

GIOVANNI: How *do* they get around the inspection? Don't they have one?

SERGEANT: Oh yeah, they have one at the beginning of the trip and that's that. Then seal it up and away they go; nobody stops them again!

LUIGI: Unless they happen to roll over on the highway.

GIOVANNI: Well, there's always a God in heaven who trips up the smart guys . . . you get what they do, these industrialist sons-of-bitches? First they make the stuff disappear from the shops: "We've run out," they tell you. And then, here it is . . . where it's really going. They're not satisfied with sending the money they earned from the sweat of our backs over the border, now they're even ripping off the food we eat! Goddam bandits!

SERGEANT: Well, good for you! Work it off, get indignant! Indignation is the real weapon of the asshole!

GIOVANNI: Oh, thanks a lot! I'm an asshole! (*turns to* LUIGI) You see what good friends we've become! (*to* SERGEANT) And what do you do, then, besides fucking around with people?

SERGEANT: I sequester! Sequester and confiscate! Thanks to your help, we're saving the merchandise from destruction. Then we'll write a nice report and bring charges. And then, the TV news will report today's brilliant police operation. So the guilty industrialists, warned in advance, will have all the time they need to beat it out of the country. The judge will sentence them to four months "in absentia."

The President of the Republic will grant them a swift pardon. And that's that.

GIOVANNI: That's that, huh! And what about the merchandise?

SERGEANT: That will be restored to its proper owners, upon payment of a large fine against which the same industrialists will keep appealing until they're allowed to pay only for the storage!

GIOVANNI: No, I don't believe it . . . that would be too much!

SERGEANT: Sure! I don't even believe it myself! I'm not allowed to believe it; my uniform and my rank prohibit it! But it's different for you . . . let's put it this way . . . you can't believe it because . . .

GIOVANNI: Because I'm an asshole . . . I get the point!

SERGEANT: If you insist! (*moving a few steps toward stage right*) Hey, where are those guys going? Jesus Christ, they're ripping off the sacks! They found out that there was sugar and flour inside!

GIOVANNI: Well, aren't you going to stop them? If you stand there with your finger up your ass, the others'll take off too . . . with the whole truck!

LUIGI: But what's it to you? Now you want to be an informer? You really are an asshole!

GIOVANNI: Oh no, not you too!

SERGEANT: There you are, ideas spread. And why are you getting so hot and bothered about a couple of miserable sacks of soda?

GIOVANNI: What do you mean, soda, you know perfectly well . . .

SERGEANT: No, I don't know anything . . . I stick to what's written on the truck: "caustic soda." It's not up to me to check . . . The inspection has to be made by my direct superior, and he'll get here in a couple of hours. That's the regulation! And I'm sticking to it! In fact, since the regulation also says that "in case of a traffic accident the primary duty of the squad-leader is to place himself in the roadway where he is to concern himself with directing traffic, and with no other incidental duty." So, I'll leave the incidental to you and attend to the primary duty of directing traffic! Arrivederci! (*He exits, singing "Arrivederci Roma."*)

GIOVANNI: Where's he going? That guy is really off his rocker!

LUIGI: No, we're the ones who are off our rocker! We stay here hauling sacks to save the stuff for those thieving bastards! You know what I say? I'm just about ready to pick up a couple of these sacks and take them home with me!

GIOVANNI: Are you nuts? You don't want to put yourself on the same level as those stupid bums. I tell you, those guys aren't workers, they're a mob, a bunch of lazy, do-nothings who refuse to work!

LUIGI: Refuse to work? The "Knight of Labor" has spoken. But "refuse to work" means "strike." Don't you ever go on strike?

GIOVANNI: Sure I go on strike, but I don't rip off stuff that's not mine.

LUIGI: Oh, it's not yours? And who makes this stuff? Who grows it? Who makes the machines to process it? Processes it? Isn't it us?

Always us, and nobody else? And the so-called entrepreneurs, aren't they the ones who always rip it off us?

GIOVANNI: So then since we're in a land of crooks, let's start stealing too. Hooray! The slickest is the guy who grabs the most! And anybody who doesn't rip stuff off is an asshole! Well, you know what I say? I'm proud to be an asshole in a world of swindlers and crooks!

LUIGI: I know; that's what they call the pride of the asshole!

GIOVANNI: You said it! Because you talk just like those lumpen, those desperadoes, who don't see any solution but to hustle. Everybody for himself, each for numero uno! And then, my two-bit revolutionary, all you get is chaos, which is just what the bosses want so that they will arrive at the "inescapable necessity" of having to call in the military to restore order!

LUIGI: You're wrong. They only show up when us workers don't understand what's going on. Not when we move to take what belongs to us.

GIOVANNI: Well, that's what the union struggles are for. And don't tell me that the unions are sleeping because I'd like to know who organized the campaign to pay half price for the gas and electricity in Turin? The Union! And who organized the campaign to reduce the fare for commuters? The Unions!

LUIGI: Sure they organized it, but only after the rank and file started first.

GIOVANNI (ironic): Oh sure, the unions always show up afterwards, when the job's already done . . . Don't you even believe in the unions now?

LUIGI: Sure I believe in them . . . but only when *we* run *them*.

(*The* CARABINIERI LIEUTENANT *enters.*)

LIEUTENANT: Hey, what's going on here?

LUIGI: What's going on is that we're heaving sacks; we're saving the country!

LIEUTENANT: Saving the country nothing—you're having a raiding party here!

GIOVANNI: Oh, look who's here! The lieutenant with a mustache! Doesn't he look like the sergeant who was here before?

LUIGI: Oh yeah, the guy that talked according to regulations.

(*The remaining sacks are removed, as the two workers who were helping to pass the sacks take off, with some sacks.*)

LIEUTENANT: Hey, halt! Put down that stuff! Put down those sacks or I'll shoot! (*runs across stage*) Yellow bastards, they ran away. (*turns to* GIOVANNI *and* LUIGI) And you guys, who gave you permission to touch these sacks?

LUIGI: There, you see, on top of everything else we're going to get shot!

GIOVANNI: Listen, Lieutenant, keep cool! And be careful not to trip with that pistol in your hand; because whenever you carabinieri trip you kill somebody. You have easy-trip-pistols.

LIEUTENANT: Don't be a wise guy, you! I already told you!

GIOVANNI: Okay, but we're doing you a favor; if we don't the stuff will all rot.

LIEUTENANT: We don't need any favors . . . go on, clear out!

GIOVANNI: Gladly, but listen, the sergeant over there told us to do this!

LIEUTENANT: What sergeant, over where?

GIOVANNI: The one who's doing the incidental duty of directing traffic.

LIEUTENANT: Well, then keep on. No, halt . . . wait till I go check it out. Hey, sergeant! (*exits*)

LUIGI: Orders! Counter orders! You see, we're already in the ranks!

GIOVANNI: Yeah, he does come off like a pig . . . but look, deep down he's a good guy; he's the one who loaded your wife on the ambulance with the baby and the olives and everything!

LUIGI: Oh yeah? Wait a minute, I was going to tell you something . . .

GIOVANNI: What?

LUIGI: It's about those well-planned and organized struggles we've been talking about. Starting tomorrow, we're all on a three day week.

GIOVANNI: Who told you?

LUIGI: I found out yesterday on the train; they're cutting all six thousand of us back to 24 hours; then, in a couple of months, they're shutting down.

GIOVANNI: Shutting down the plant? But why should they shut it down? They're not in a crisis; in fact, they've got enough orders for the rest of the year!

LUIGI: What do they care about orders? If they move everything to Spain, they make more money . . . and in Brazil even more . . .

GIOVANNI: Because of labor costs, huh?

LUIGI: Not just that; frozen wages, no unions, no strikes, a fascist government that guarantees social peace . . . What do you bet?

GIOVANNI: Pass me that sack . . . and that other one, too . . . and those two over there! You too; load on all you can, and move it.

LUIGI: Hey, where's the pride of being a law-abiding democratic asshole?

GIOVANNI: You're right, but there comes a day when even the assholes wake up! *We* worked, didn't we . . . so now we're getting paid! (*They exit, loaded down. The* LIEUTENANT *yells from farstage.*)

LIEUTENANT: Hey, you two, where are you going? Halt! Stop or I'll shoot! I'll shoot! (*tries to get his gun out*)

GIOVANNI: Sure, shoot; shoot your balls off!

LIEUTENANT: Those bastards! And they were pretending to work . . . "we're saving the goods . . . we're doing a favor!" And everybody says Naples is bad. (*leaves, after them; lights down*)

(*Curtain slides open, revealing* GIOVANNI *and* ANTONIA's *apartment. The two women, with big bellies, are returning.*)

ANTONIA: Quick, Margherita, hurry up . . . come in and shut the door.

MARGHERITA: Give me some water. I'm thirsty.

ANTONIA: Let's empty this bundle and take another load . . . this really will be the last one.

MARGHERITA: Yeah, yeah, load, unload, I feel like a truck!

ANTONIA: Oh, always complaining! (MARGHERITA *has begun to unbutton her coat, and pulls out from underneath it some salad greens and cabbages.*)

MARGHERITA: Look at this, we have enough salad to eat for a month.

ANTONIA: Yeah, maybe it's a little too much . . . but then we had to load ourselves up this way; if the cops in the wagon first see us crossing with a big belly and then see us come back without . . . and going again with a belly . . . as lame as they are, even they'd get the point sooner or later!

MARGHERITA: Well, you're right there.

ANTONIA (*Concerned, she runs over to the stove.*): My God, we forgot the soup . . . it must have turned into glue. (*She raises the cover of the pan.*) No, it didn't even cook! There's no gas. Those bastards really cut it off! I bet they'll cut off the electricity pretty soon too! (*A knock is heard at the door.*) Who is it?

VOICE FROM OUTSIDE: Friends.

ANTONIA: What friends?

VOICE: I work with your husband. He told me to come and tell you something.

ANTONIA: O, my God! Something's happened to him. (*goes to open the door*)

MARGHERITA: Wait a second until I put the greens back inside.

ANTONIA: Hang on, one minute . . . I'm undressed. (*She opens the door and the* LIEUTENANT *appears.*) Oh, it's you. What kind of joke is this?

LIEUTENANT: Stop right where you are! This time I've caught you! There they are, both of them pregnant now! How those bellies grow! I knew right away that it was a trick!

ANTONIA: But you're nuts! What trick are you talking about?

MARGHERITA (*collapsing on the bed, exhausted*): There, now we've had it! I knew it! I knew it!

LIEUTENANT (*to* MARGHERITA): I'm pleased to see that you didn't lose your little one. But you, madam, did even better. Congratulations!

In five hours you've had sex, become a mommy, and already arrived at the ninth month . . . What speed!

ANTONIA: Look, Lieutenant, you're making a big mistake.

LIEUTENANT: No, I made a mistake before . . . when I fell for that little drama about the labor pains and the premature birth! But now I'm not falling for anything anymore; out with the stolen goods!

ANTONIA: But you're nuts! What stolen goods?

LIEUTENANT: Don't try to be tricky, because this time it won't work! It's too obvious now; the husbands go out on a raiding party, then they pass the sacks to their wives who fix up a big belly and off they go! All day long I've been seeing pregnant women walking back and forth! How come all the women in this neighborhood conceived at the same time? I know the proverbial fecundity of lower-class women—but this is going too far! Grown women, teenagers, little girls—I even saw a little eighty year old lady going by today, with a belly that could be carrying twins!

ANTONIA: I know, but it's not for the reason you think . . . really . . . it's for the feast of our patron saint . . .

LIEUTENANT: What's this new story about the patron saint?

ANTONIA: But, of course, for Saint . . .

MARGHERITA: Eulalie . . .

ANTONIA: . . . you know, that saint who couldn't have children, and then, when she reached the ripe old age of sixty, by the grace of the Eternal Father, she got pregnant.

LIEUTENANT: At sixty?

ANTONIA: Sure; and imagine, her husband was over eighty!

LIEUTENANT: Wow!

ANTONIA: Well, you know the power of faith! But they say that the husband died almost right away. And to commemorate this miracle all the women in the neighborhood go around for three days with a fake belly.

LIEUTENANT: What a beautiful tradition! Good for you! So that's why you empty the supermarket shelves—just so you can get stuff to make your false bellies?! Now, isn't it amazing what the religious spirit of the people can do . . . Let's go! Cut the circus act and show me what you've got under there, or I'll lose my patience!

ANTONIA: You'll lose your patience, and then what? Are you going to tear off our clothes? I'm warning you that if you even lay one finger on us, if you insist on looking, something terrible will happen to you!

LIEUTENANT: Don't make me laugh, what kind of terrible thing?

ANTONIA: The same one that happened to Saint Eulalie's husband, that unbeliever! The old guy had no faith, and he didn't believe her: "What d'you mean, pregnant; quit telling me tales! Show me what you have underneath . . . and I'm warning you, if you really are pregnant, I'll kill you, because that'll mean I'm not the father!" So then Saint Eulalie suddenly opened up her dress and the second miracle: from her belly came roses, a shower of roses!

LIEUTENANT: Oh, listen to that, what a lovely miracle!

ANTONIA: Yes, but the story isn't over. Suddenly darkness came over the husband's eyes: "I can't see anymore, I can't see anymore," he cried, "I'm blind! God has punished me!" "And now you believe, faithless one," said Saint Eulalie. "Yes, I believe!" and then, third miracle: from the roses a baby sprouted, already ten months old and talking, and he said: "Daddy, daddy, the Lord pardons you, now you can die in peace!" He laid his little hand on the old man's head, and he died on the spot!

LIEUTENANT: Very interesting! Now stop telling stories and show me the roses . . . No, I mean . . . well, hurry up because I've already wasted a lot of time and I'm a bit nervous!

ANTONIA: Okay; so you don't believe in the miracle?

LIEUTENANT: No, I don't.

ANTONIA: You're not afraid of bad luck?

LIEUTENANT: No, I told you!

ANTONIA: Okay, you asked for it. But don't say I didn't warn you. (to MARGHERITA) Come on, get on your feet and we'll both open up our clothes:

> St. Eulalie of the swollen womb-a
> Bring forth on the unbelieving
> The curse that seals his doom-ba
>
> Black and darken his eyesightness
> Your Holiness
> Saint Eulalie
> Give him a crack on the head

(ANTONIA *and* MARGHERITA *open their coats*). Amen.

LIEUTENANT: What is this stuff?

ANTONIA: What stuff . . . Well, I never, it looks like salad greens!

LIEUTENANT: Salad greens?

ANTONIA: Yes, it really is salad: chicory, endive, red lettuce, even a cabbage!

MARGHERITA: Me too, me too, a cabbage!

LIEUTENANT: What's all this? Why did you hide all these greens in your belly?

ANTONIA: But we didn't hide them! It must be a miracle!

LIEUTENANT: Sure, a miracle of the cabbages.

ANTONIA: Well, you make miracles with whatever greens you happen to have around! Anyhow, whether you believe in it or not, what's wrong with it? Is there some law that says the Italian citizen, especially if of the feminine sex, can't carry chicory, endive and cabbage on her belly?

LIEUTENANT: No, no, of course, there's no law . . . but I don't understand why you put all this stuff inside your clothes?

ANTONIA: I told you, to swell up our bellies according to the belief in the miracle of Saint Eulalie! We're supposed to carry it around for three days. And whoever doesn't believe in it will have bad luck! (*Very slowly, the light dims.*)

ANTONIA AND MARGHERITA: Saint Eulalie of the swollen womb, bring forth on the unbelieving . . .

LIEUTENANT: What's going on now? Is the light going out?

ANTONIA: What light?

LIEUTENANT: But don't you see that the light's getting dimmer . . . it's getting dark!

ANTONIA: What do you mean, dark, I can see. Can you see?

MARGHERITA: Yes, I can see . . .

ANTONIA: We can see just as usual . . . maybe your eyesight's going bad. (MARGHERITA *gropes toward* ANTONIA.)

MARGHERITA (*whispers*): The light's gone out, everywhere, except outside.

LIEUTENANT: Stop kidding around! The switch, where's the switch?

MARGHERITA (*moving through the darkness*): Here it is, can't you see it? Wait, I'll do it . . . (*She makes the click of the switch.*) There now it's off, now it's on . . . can't you see?

LIEUTENANT: No, I can't see.

ANTONIA: Oh, dio mio, he's gone blind! Bad luck fell on him!

LIEUTENANT: Stop it! Open the window; I want to look outside!

ANTONIA: But the window is open!

MARGHERITA: Yes, the window's open, can't you see?

ANTONIA: Come here, come here and look. (*She grabs him by a sleeve.*) There you are. (*places him in front of a chair*) Watch out for the chair! (*He bumps against it.*)

LIEUTENANT: Ow! That hurt!

ANTONIA: Watch where you put your feet!

LIEUTENANT: But how can I if I can't see anything?

ANTONIA: You're right, poor man, you can't see. Here's the window. (*She leads him to the cupboard.*)

MARGHERITA: Watch out . . . there you are, lean on the window sill and we'll open the shutters . . . touch them . . . see, the shutters are open! (*The* LIEUTENANT *does this gropingly.*)

ANTONIA: Look at all those lights in the street! What day is it today? Oh, of course, it's all lit up for Saint Eulalie . . . Can't you see?

LIEUTENANT (*head in cupboard*): No, I can't see! Dammit, what's happened to me? A match, light a match!

ANTONIA: Right away . . . stay there while I get one. Here! I've got something better than a match . . . here I've got a gas burner . . . (*She lights it.*) Look, look at the beautiful flame!

LIEUTENANT: No, I don't see it and I don't believe that there is a flame . . . let me touch it . . .

ANTONIA: No, no, look out, it's getting hot! It's all red!

LIEUTENANT: Let me touch it, I said. An . . . ah . . . owww! I've burned my hand!

ANTONIA: That's what you get for never wanting to believe!

LIEUTENANT: La miseria. So I really am blind!

ANTONIA: That's right, you're blind . . . ! It was the curse!

LIEUTENANT: I've got to get out . . . where's the door? Let me out!

ANTONIA: Wait a second, I'll go with you . . . here it is . . . here's the door. (*She opens the door of the wardrobe; the* LIEUTENANT *hurls himself forward and bangs his head against the inside; staggering backwards, he falls to the floor on his back.*)

LIEUTENANT: Oh, Christ, what a bump!

MARGHERITA: He's busted his head!

LIEUTENANT: Owwwwwwww! I'm dying . . . my head . . . what happened?

ANTONIA: The baby . . . "it's the baby who put his little hand on your forehead!"

LIEUTENANT: Musta been wearin' brass knuckles.

ANTONIA: Lieutenant? Lieutenant! Oh shit, he passed out!

MARGHERITA: Now you've done it! Maybe he's dead!

ANTONIA: Always the optimist, huh? He's not dead . . . get the flashlight . . . (MARGHERITA *does.*) . . . Hurry up . . .

MARGHERITA: He's dead, he's dead, he's stopped breathing!

ANTONIA: No, he's just gotten sick . . . He's breathing, he's not breathing!

MARGHERITA: Oh God! We've killed a carabiniere!

ANTONIA: Yeah, maybe we carried things a bit too far. What are we going to do now?

MARGHERITA: You're asking me? What've I got to do with it? You did everything . . . Sorry, but I'm going back to my apartment . . . The keys . . . where did I put the keys to the apartment?

ANTONIA: A fine friend you are; leaving me here, just like that: Great solidarity!

MARGHERITA (*finds a bunch of keys on the cupboard*): Oh, there they are! But I had another pair in my pocket, two bunches of keys! These are my husband's. So he's been here . . . he came looking for me, and forgot them!

ANTONIA: So if he forgot them, he'll come back soon to pick them up.

MARGHERITA: He must have run into your husband, who told him the whole story about my being pregnant! And what am I going to tell him, now? Sorry, but I'm not moving from here. Now you get me out of this mess . . . You tell him everything yourself!

ANTONIA: Sure I'll tell him . . . My shoulders are nice and broad. (*She observes the* LIEUTENANT.) But this guy really did have a stroke.

MARGHERITA: You see what happens when you joke around with miracles?

ANTONIA: No, he's the one who was joking around . . . I told him: watch out for the curse; 'cause Saint Eulalie's a powerful saint! (*She raises his arms, then lowers them.*)

MARGHERITA: Now what are you up to?

ANTONIA: Artificial respiration.

MARGHERITA: But what good will that do? They don't do that anymore . . . You've got to give him mouth-to-mouth resuscitation like for drowning . . .

ANTONIA: Oh yeah, now I'm going to kiss a carabiniere? If my husband ever finds out about it . . . Margherita, you kiss him!

MARGHERITA: Not me. What we really need is an oxygen tank.

ANTONIA (*thinks for a second*): I've got it! There's the one from the welder, it is oxygen! One is hydrogen and the other is oxygen. Come here, help me . . . Now I close the valve on the hydrogen tank . . . like that . . . and open the oxygen.

MARGHERITA: Are you sure it works?

ANTONIA: Oh, of course . . . I saw it done in the movies!

MARGHERITA: Oh, well, if you saw it done in the movies . . .

ANTONIA: Look . . . you see? He's beginning to breathe . . . Look how his stomach's moving . . . see! It's going up . . . there . . . you'll see, now it'll go down.

MARGHERITA: Seems to me like it's just going up . . . his belly as well, look . . . stop! You're inflating him!

ANTONIA: Damn! I made a mistake and now I can't get the tube out of his mouth, he's biting it! Turn it off . . . go shut the valve! Hurry up! No, no, the other way . . . turn it the other way.

MARGHERITA: There, it's done.

ANTONIA: Mamma mia, what a belly! Now we've gotten a carabiniere pregnant!

(*The curtain closes. The lights come up slowly.* GIOVANNI *and* LUIGI *on apron.*)

LUIGI: It was a good idea coming to my place instead of yours. At least we shook off the lieutenant.

GIOVANNI: We can't stand on the landing for hours like a couple of doormats. Listen, I'm going to see if I can bust down the door with my shoulder.

LUIGI: It's no good, the door's bolted and there are two locks.

GIOVANNI: Why all the paraphernalia?

LUIGI: It's my wife who had it installed. She's terrified of thieves.

GIOVANNI: So, now when us thieves are trying to get back in the house, we're screwed, stuck here outside the door like a couple of dumbbells. You too, dammit—a crook, who loses the keys to his own house!

LUIGI: Cut out that stuff about crooks! Jesus! Now I remember; I didn't lose the keys, I left them at your apartment . . . that's it . . . on the cupboard.

GIOVANNI: Are you sure?

LUIGI: Absolutely. Give me the keys to your place and I'll go and pick mine up.

GIOVANNI: Sure, smartass, with the lieutenant there, waiting to swoop down on us like a hawk: zap!

LUIGI: No, no, by now he must have left.

GIOVANNI: That's what you think; that guy's worse than a bulldog . . . I tell you, that guy has planted himself there for the rest of his natural life . . . I can't ever think about going home. I'll have to emigrate!

LUIGI: Come off it.

GIOVANNI: Why the hell did I ever go along with this asshole idea of yours!? (*sound of approaching footsteps*) Goddam, somebody's coming.

LUIGI: Calm down, it's probably some neighbor.

GIOVANNI: Cover up the sacks! Hide them! (*takes off his jacket and throws it on top of the stolen goods*)

LUIGI: What's the matter with you? Are you afraid they're going to tell on you? These people are on our side; they wouldn't blab.

GIOVANNI: You never know.

VOICE FROM FARSTAGE: Excuse me, could you give me some information?

GIOVANNI: Now we're really screwed.

LUIGI: Screwed? Why?

GIOVANNI: It's the lieutenant . . . don't you recognize him? You see, somebody did tell on us!

LUIGI: No, no it's not him. It looks like him, but it's not him.

GIOVANNI: No, you're right, it's not him.

UNDERTAKER'S ATTENDANT (*coming onstage always moving in a rhythmic halting trot*): Pardon me, did you say something? Were you talking to me?

GIOVANNI: No, nothing, I just thought I recognized you.

LUIGI: Holy shit, he does look like him, though.

UNDERTAKER'S ATTENDANT: Look like who?

GIOVANNI: A lieutenant in the carabinieri with a mustache who's the spitting image of a police sergeant without a mustache. I feel like I'm in a cheap production I saw once where they couldn't afford enough actors to play all the roles, so they hired one actor to play all the cops.

UNDERTAKER: Actually, I'm not a cop!

GIOVANNI: Oh, no? What role are you playing, then?

UNDERTAKER: I'm from the public funeral parlor.* Could you tell me if Sergio Prampolini lives here?

LUIGI: Yeah, upstairs, on the third floor. But I know for a fact he's not home. He's in the hospital. Poor guy, he's always sick—a terrible life!

UNDERTAKER: Yes, in fact he died. I'm supposed to deliver the casket I left downstairs.

LUIGI: Well, I'm sure his son will come home tonight, maybe you ought to take the casket to the hospital, since that's where he died.

UNDERTAKER: I've just come from there. But unfortunately, the corpse isn't there anymore. I was hoping to find it here, but it looks like they've taken it to another relative's house—God knows where.

GIOVANNI: Oh well, just leave it down in the entrance hall.

UNDERTAKER: No, no, I can't . . . After all, a funeral casket . . . just left there, with all those people going by . . . kids climbing in and playing Indians in a canoe . . . Besides, I need to have the delivery order signed by a reliable person.

LUIGI: In that case, we really wouldn't know what to advise you.

UNDERTAKER: You seem like reliable folks to me. You live here, don't you?

LUIGI: Yes, I live right here.

UNDERTAKER: OK, then it's all taken care of—I'll give you the casket, we'll put it into your house . . . and when the son of the deceased gets back this evening . . .

GIOVANNI: A funeral casket in the house?

UNDERTAKER: Just a matter of learning to live with it.

LUIGI: I know, I know. But the fact is that we can't get it in because I don't have the key. We're locked out ourselves.

UNDERTAKER: Oh, too bad! Well then, I have no choice but to carry it all the way back to the warehouse.

GIOVANNI: No, listen . . . maybe there's another solution: we'll take it over to my place, just across the street. If you'll trust me, I can keep it for you.

UNDERTAKER: Why, of course I trust you. In fact, I can't thank you enough.

GIOVANNI: Don't mention it. But now you have to do *me* a favor.

UNDERTAKER: Certainly, what is it?

GIOVANNI: Could you let us put these bags inside the casket? You know, since it's raining . . . This is delicate stuff, and if it gets wet it will be a real mess.

UNDERTAKER: Oh, of course.

GIOVANNI: Well—let's go, then.

---

*The two cover their balls.

UNDERTAKER: Yes, yes; let's go. I'll run down and take the casket out of the wagon. (*Exits.* GIOVANNI *and* LUIGI *gather up the sacks.*)

GIOVANNI: The cops will never dare stick their noses in a funeral casket!

LUIGI: Hot damn, I must say you really got a great idea—where did it come from?

GIOVANNI: The Vietcong. I got the idea from the Vietcong. Remember how they transported all their weapons in the city funeral wagons—and then they raised all that hell.

LUIGI: Oh, yeah, you mean in the Tet Offensive.

GIOVANNI: That's it. No doubt about it, you can always learn from the Vietcong.

LUIGI: Then learn from the Vietcong how you're going to get around that sonofabitch lieutenant, if he's still there waiting for us?!

UNDERTAKER (*offstage*):   Hey, we're ready—are you coming down?

GIOVANNI: God damn, I've just thought of something. The Vietcong didn't leave their caskets empty. I mean inside they carried weapons, but there was always a dead body on top to hide them!

LUIGI: And where are we going to find a dead body?

GIOVANNI: Right here! I'll be the dead man and you can be the guy from the funeral parlor who carries the casket. Hope I don't die laughing!

(*They exit. Darkness. Curtain opens, revealing* MARGHERITA *with flashlight on* ANTONIA *who is filling her bag with stuff from under the bed.*)

MARGHERITA: Well, besides being careless I'd say you're nuts. Madonna, here we are with a dead man . . .

ANTONIA: Come over here and give me a hand putting him away, 'cause if somebody comes . . .

MARGHERITA: Where are you gong to put him?

ANTONIA: In the wardrobe.

MARGHERITA: In the wardrobe?

ANTONIA: Where else? Haven't you ever seen any suspense movies? They always put dead bodies in the wardrobe—it's the rule! (*They lift the carabiniere to his feet.*)

MARGHERITA: Well, if it's the rule . . . God almighty, he weighs a ton—this is what they call dead weight, huh? (*They move the carabiniere's body around, finally managing to place it in the wardrobe.*)

ANTONIA: There we are. Wait, let's put this coat hanger under his jacket . . . like that . . . OK, now pick him up so we can hang him from the pole . . . perfect! God damn it, his belly is so puffed up the door won't even close. Push—help me! There! (*They shut the wardrobe door.*)

MARGHERITA: Look, it's getting light!! Let's open the shutters. (*opens them*) It's raining cats and dogs.

ANTONIA: I can see that. Wait, I'll go put on my galoshes and get my umbrella. (*goes offstage to other room*)

(*The door opens and* LUIGI *comes in wearing the Undertaker Attendant's cap.*)

LUIGI (*glancing around, almost in a whispe*r):   Hey, anybody home? Is the lieutenant here?

MARGHERITA: Who is it? Luigi, is that you? What are you doing in that getup?

LUIGI: Margherita, honey, at last! How are you—let me see? But don't you have a big belly? And the baby—where's the baby? How is it? Did you lose him?

MARGHERITA: No, no . . . Don't worry, everything went fine . . .

LUIGI: Everything fine, really? And you're OK? Tell me—

MARGHERITA: Later, later . . . Antonia can tell you about it . . . she'll explain the whole thing.

LUIGI: Why Antonia?

UNDERTAKER (*from offstage*):   Hey, this casket is heavy! Should we come in or not?

LUIGI: Sure, sure, come on in. The lieutenant's not here; nobody's here.

(*At that moment, the wardrobe door opens briefly, revealing the Carabiniere hanging there.* MARGHERITA *closes it with lightning speed.*)

LUIGI: Come on, Giovanni, you can get out of the casket now. We have to turn it on its side to get it through the doorway. (MARGHERITA *runs into the other room.*)

GIOVANNI (*from offstage*):   Too bad, I was so comfortable in there—I even fell asleep . . . (*He enters, carrying a large funeral casket.*) And I dreamed the lieutenant died and Antonia pumped him up with the hydrogen tank so his belly got bigger and rounder until he floated up into the sky like a balloon. (*The wardrobe door opens up again. Without noticing,* GIOVANNI, *who is backing in carrying the funeral casket with the* UNDERTAKER, *closes it once more.*) Incredible dreams!

MARGHERITA (*from the other room*):   Antonia, Antonia, come on out. Hurry up!

ANTONIA (*from the other room also*):   What is it? For crying out loud, can't I even piss in peace?

GIOVANNI: Are both the girls back?

LUIGI: Yes, everything went fine . . . they're just fine.

GIOVANNI: Thank God for that. (*to* UNDERTAKER) Thanks for every thing.

LUIGI: So long. Oh, thanks for your hat. (*give sit to him*)

UNDERTAKER: Don't mention it. (*offstage*)

GIOVANNI: Now how are we going to explain this dead man's box to

Antonia? This time it'll take more than the Vietcong to save us . . .

LUIGI: Listen, I've got an idea. We'll lock the bedroom door and shut the girls in there for a moment while we unload everything. We can hide the stuff under that bed and set the casket upright inside the wardrobe.

GIOVANNI: Right. Go turn the key, and get rid of this lid. (*They carry out the plan, busily removing the bags from the casket and putting them under the bed.*)

MARGHERITA (*from the other room*): Antonia, are you coming? I have to tell you something.

ANTONIA (*from other room also*): OK, coming, I'm getting dressed again . . . everything's falling out here!

GIOVANNI: There, that's it . . . the bags are all hidden. Push, we have to push them right under the bed.

LUIGI: Hidden, my ass. With all this pushing, we've shoved them under one side—and they've come out the other. (*bending over to look under the bed*) Look at all this stuff! It didn't seem such a lot inside the casket. Looks like twice as much now!

GIOVANNI: Of course, if you look at it with your head down, every thing seems bigger. That's called the Yoga effect. Come on, help me set this casket upright . . . (*They take the casket and put it in the wardrobe. Without realizing it, they have exactly fitted the casket over the lieutenant's body.*)

LUIGI: OK. Now what's this about the Yoga effect?

GIOVANNI: Yeah, the people in India use it . . . poor folks, when they don't have anything to eat . . . and those people have gone hungry for plenty long. They stand on their heads, and with their heads down they can imagine anything they want. Food, drinks . . . more, more, more; . . . Kissinger taught them to do it.

LUIGI: And do they stop feeling hungry?

GIOVANNI: No, that goes on. That's it, push!

LUIGI: Ah, so they just enjoy the illusion. Is that it?

GIOVANNI: Yeah, I guess . . . (*tries to close the wardrobe door*)

LUIGI: You know, after I put my head down, I got an illusion too?

GIOVANNI: I know, you told me.

LUIGI: No, no, another one. I thought I saw the lieutenant inside the wardrobe.

GIOVANNI: The lieutenant? (*rapidly flings open the wardrobe door*) Good thing it was just an illusion. Better not let me catch you with your head down again, eh . . . Leave that game to the Indians. Dammit it won't close! (*fruitlessly pushes the door, which remains half-open*)

MARGHERITA (*from off*): Listen, Antonia, I'm fed up. I'll wait for you in the other room.

GIOVANNI: Go and unlock the door; I can't move. (LUIGI *runs to open up;* MARGHERITA *enters.*)

MARGHERITA: Thanks, nice of you. (*sees* GIOVANNI) Oh, hi, Giovanni!

GIOVANNI: Hey, hey, your husband told me everything went fine. So was the baby born or not?

ANTONIA (*bursting in*): What was it you wanted to tell me? (*stands rooted to the spot*) Ahh . . . you're back? About time!

GIOVANNI: Antonia! Your belly—did you get . . .

GIOVANNI AND LUIGI: the transplant?!

ANTONIA: Well, yes, sort of.

GIOVANNI: What do you mean, sort of! You got it, didn't you?

ANTONIA: Yes, but I mean, it was something sort of, almost, that is . . .

GIOVANNI: I knew it, I knew it. What did I tell you . . . that woman's an idiot—she's at the top of the idiot list! (*moves from the wardrobe door, but immediately has to move back to stop it opening*) Did they do a Caesarian section on you?

ANTONIA: Yes, but just a small one.

GIOVANNI: What do you mean, a small one?

ANTONIA: Well, the right size, I mean.

LUIGI: And did they do a Caesarian section on you too?

MARGHERITA: Mm, yes . . . I don't know—did they do one on me, Antonia?

LUIGI: How come you're asking her don't you know?

ANTONIA: Oh, no, poor kid, they put her to sleep. So how could she know it when she was asleep?

GIOVANNI: But you mean they operated on *you* while you were *awake*?

ANTONIA: Oh, come on, that's enough! What is this, the third degree? (*Stamps her foot; wardrobe door opens; all rush to close it. Cupboard doors, then bedroom door, all open, then wardrobe. Each time one or more of the characters rushes to close them.*) The coward didn't even ask how I am, if we're alive, or about to drop dead. Considering that to keep you from worrying we got out of bed like a couple of cretins. When the hospital staff was against it. And what was I supposed to do? This woman was about to lose her baby, I could save it. Didn't I have to show solidarity? Aren't you always saying we have to help each other out—and that a communist ought to be a person who—

GIOVANNI: Yes, yes, you're right . . . sorry . . . maybe you did the right thing—in fact, of course you did . . .

LUIGI: Thanks for what you've done, Antonia, you are a fine woman.

GIOVANNI: Yes, yes, you're a fine woman!

LUIGI: You tell her too. Come on . . .

MARGHERITA: It's true, Antonia, you really are a good woman!

ANTONIA: OK, that's enough . . . you're making me cry.

GIOVANNI: Here . . . come over here. You shouldn't be on your feet. (*makes her sit down on the bed*) With a Caesarian, you know . . . Maybe you should have stayed in the hospital a while longer.

ANTONIA: Oh, go on. Besides, I'm fine. I didn't feel a thing!

GIOVANNI: Yes . . . you look fine. And look at that nice big tummy! (*nearly caresses her stomach*) Hey, am I mistaken or is it already moving!?

LUIGI: Moving? 'Scuse me, Antonia, could I feel it too?

MARGHERITA: No, you're not feeling a damn thing.

LUIGI: Hey, it's my child too, you know!

GIOVANNI: Yeah, right . . . now we're close relatives! I'm the expectant father of an Arab terrorist!

MARGHERITA: And what about me? Antonia steals the show, and I don't even count any more?

ANTONIA: She's right; make a fuss over her, too. Quit crowding my space. I have to go out, anyway. (*She gets up and quickly goes toward the exit.*)

GIOVANNI (*blocking her path*): Go out? What for? You're crazy! You're not moving from here. You get right into bed, nice and warm . . . We'll move the bed over there, near the radiator. (*prepares to move bed*)

LUIGI (*everybody rushes over to bed*): Stop! What the hell are you doing? Dumb jerk!

GIOVANNI: You're right. It's dangerous, too dangerous to move it . . . the hydrogen tanks are over there . . .

ANTONIA: What is that lid thing?

GIOVANNI: Where?

ANTONIA: Over there. (*points to the lid of the casket*)

GIOVANNI: Oh, yeah; that's not a lid, it's a cradle! Luigi bought it the minute he found out about the baby: rock-a-bye baby . . . It's the latest design; you see, it hangs from the ceiling by ropes and swings—

ANTONIA: Isn't it a bit long?

GIOVANNI: Well, if he grows, you know. We're all tall in my family. Besides, it was on sale.

(*An elderly man appears at the doorway. It is the same all-purpose actor wearing different clothes.*)

OLD MAN: Can I come in? Am I interrupting anything?

GIOVANNI: Oh papa, this is a nice surprise. Come on in.

ANTONIA: Ciao, papa!

GIOVANNI: Have you met my friends? This is my father.

OLD MAN: Pleased to meet you.

LUIGI: Shit, another look-alike. Giovanni, have you noticed that—

GIOVANNI: Sure, sure, but don't pay any attention to it. My father's a little slow in the head.

OLD MAN: Don't you start that—I'm not one bit slow in the head! (*turns to* MARGHERITA) How's my Antonia! Gee, you're looking fine . . . much younger.

GIOVANNI: No, papa, that's not Antonia . . . Antonia's over here.

OLD MAN: Oh, really?

ANTONIA: Yes, papa, it's me.

OLD MAN: What are you doing there in bed? Don't you feel well?

GIOVANNI: No, she's expecting a kid.

OLD MAN: She is? And where did the child go? Don't worry, he'll come back, you'll see. (*looks at* LUIGI *as if seeing him for the first time*) Oh, there he is, back already. Wow, hasn't he gotten to be a big boy! But you know, you shouldn't keep your mom waiting like that . . .

GIOVANNI: Papa, this is a friend.

OLD MAN: Bravo! You should always be friends with your children. Now, I really came to inform you that you're about to be evicted.

GIOVANNI: By who?

OLD MAN: The landlord of this building. They sent the eviction notice to my place by mistake. Here it is. It says you haven't paid the rent in four months.

GIOVANNI: No, you've got it wrong, let me see. Antonia always paid the rent every month, right, Antonia?

ANTONIA: Yes, of course.

OLD MAN: At any rate, they're going to clear out the whole building, because almost nobody has paid up for months—and the few people who have been paying have sent in only half the rent.

GIOVANNI: Who told you that?

OLD MAN: The police chief. He's going around all the apartments forcing the tenants out. Great Guy! (*There is an almost imperceptible sound of voices, mingled with some shouted orders.*)

LUIGI (*looking out of the imaginary window*):   Take a look down in the street! What a lot of police!

GIOVANNI: Yes. Just look at that . . . like in a war. And all those trucks!

OLD MAN: Sure, to haul away the furniture. All for free! (*The sound of voices becomes louder. Crying women and children are heard, along with more commands.*)

GIOVANNI: Hey, this eviction notice really is addressed to us. My God, Antonia, what's going on here?

ANTONIA: Don't shout, you'll scare the baby.

GIOVANNI: OK, I'll lower my voice. It says here we haven't paid the rent in four months. Come on, Antonia, I want an answer.

ANTONIA: Oh, all right: it's true, I haven't paid for four months, and I haven't paid the gas and electric bills either. As a matter of fact, they've cut off our service.

GIOVANNI: They've cut off our gas and electric? But how come you didn't pay?

ANTONIA: Because with all the money both of us earn together, I just barely manage to feed you—not very well, either—

MARGHERITA: Luigi, I have to tell you something: I haven't been able to pay the rent either.

LUIGI: Oh, isn't that just great!

ANTONIA: You see, I told you—us women always get it in the neck. Along with all the other women in this apartment building, and the one across the way, and that one over there . . . all of us.

GIOVANNI: For chrissakes, why didn't you tell me you didn't have the money?

ANTONIA: Why, what would you have done then—gone out stealing maybe?

GIOVANNI: No, of course not. But I mean . . .

ANTONIA: But you mean you would have started cursing me out, calling me a disgrace—cursing the day you married me. (sobs)

LUIGI: But did you at least pay the gas and electric bills?

MARGHERITA: Yes, yes, I did pay the gas and electric!

LUIGI: That's something.

GIOVANNI: Come on, don't cry, besides, it's bad for the baby!

OLD MAN: Sure, sure. Everything will turn out OK. That reminds me, I came here to deliver some stuff. Hang on, I left it right outside. (leaves and returns at once) I'm getting absent-minded. Here it is. (returns carrying a large bag, which he empties on the table) I found this inside my shed. Must be your stuff.

LUIGI: What is it? Butter, flour, canned tomatoes?

ANTONIA: Nothing to do with me.

GIOVANNI: No, no, papa—it can't be our stuff.

OLD MAN: Sure it is! It's your stuff; I saw Antonia coming out of the shed this morning!

ANTONIA: OK, OK, it's stuff I bought yesterday at half price.

GIOVANNI: At the supermarket?

ANTONIA: Yes, I paid for half of it and I swiped the rest.

GIOVANNI: Swiped? You've started stealing?

ANTONIA: Yes.

LUIGI: You too?

MARGHERITA: Yes, me too.

ANTONIA: No, it's not true—she's a liar; she didn't do anything! She just gave me a hand afterwards.

POLICEMAN'S VOICE (played by the OLD MAN): Attenzione! Attenzione! Is this the Bardi residence? (All nod.) Is that you? (All nod.) Here's the order to vacate. You've got half an hour. Start moving!

GIOVANNI: This is crazy—I'm losing my mind.

LUIGI: Cool it, Giovanni. We'd better shut up about stolen goods.

GIOVANNI: Shut up? That's not the point . . . We're out in the street, don't you realize? This goddamned woman—this dumb, dishonest—

ANTONIA: Sure, you're right. Now call me a whore who's dishonored you, who's dragging your poor but honest name through the mud—who's played on your finest paternal sentiments, because, I'd better tell you, the story of the baby isn't true either. All bullshit. Here's what I was hiding in my belly: pasta, rice, sugar . . . stuff to eat . . . all ripped off! (*She angrily pulls it out from under her coat.*)

LUIGI: What . . . the baby, (*sobs*) the transplant, (*sobs*) . . . Margherita?

GIOVANNI: Oh, no, nossir—this is too much! No, I'm going to murder her! I'll kill her!

OLD MAN: Well, now I've given you all the news . . . so long, kids. And don't forget, always keep your sunny side up. (*He exits, singing "When You're Smiling" in Italian: "Quando Sorridi."*)

(*From outside, the babble of voices grows increasingly louder; men and women yelling, shouted commands, wailing sirens.*)

GIOVANNI: Lying cheat! Fooling me with a story about a baby! (LUIGI *restrains him by force.*) Let me go!

ANTONIA: He's right, let him go . . . just let him kill me, I mean it. Because I'm sick and tired of this wretched life too! Even more than you are! And I'm especially sick and tired of your windbag speeches—responsibility, sacrifice . . . the dignity of tightening our belts, the pride of the working class. So what is this working class; who are these workers? They're us, you know that? And goddam mad, just like us. Dirt poor, and desperate like all those people they're throwing out of their homes right now . . . Look at them, look down there—worse than deportees! (*The clamor grows even louder.*) But you don't want to see how things really are, you want to keep a blindfold over your eyes! You're not even a communist anymore—you've turned into a left-wing church-warden. An asshole!

GIOVANNI: There we are, now the circle's complete! Why don't you take your turn too, Margherita—Nossir, I am not an asshole! I can figure out how things are really going myself, I can see my party's push-and-pull games with the Christian Democrats in order to get into the government. And the workers are right to be so pissed off! I'm pissed off myself. And the reason I'm mad isn't because of you . . . it's because of myself, not being able to do anything, feeling screwed. The party's not here now; it's not with us, it's not down there in the street with those desperate people! And tomorrow the papers will write that we're a bunch of irresponsible troublemakers!

ANTONIA: What's happening to you, Giovanni? Is that you really talking, Giovanni? Have you got a screw loose? Have you changed sides?

LUIGI: Yeah, have those extremists gotten to you, too?

GIOVANNI: No, I've always thought this way . . . except that maybe you're right, Antonia, I have a church-warden complex . . . And I'll tell you another thing, while we're about it: I've been stealing too, with Luigi. Move over—look here, under the bed: bags of sugar and flour!

ANTONIA: You stole?

LUIGI: Yes, but only when he found out they're putting us on half-time.

GIOVANNI: No, that was only the last straw. Look at all this stuff. Now I'm feeling the Yoga effect standing up! But that's not all. You might as well know this isn't a cradle, but the lid of a funeral casket! Here it is, right here—give me a hand, Luigi . . . it was my idea, for carrying the stuff! (*He goes toward the closet.*)

ANTONIA: Stop, what are you doing?

GIOVANNI: I'm doing what I have to do. You've got to know the whole story. (*They take out the casket, revealing the* LIEUTENANT, *who is regaining consciousness.*)

GIOVANNI AND LUIGI: The Lieutenant!

LIEUTENANT: I can see! I can see! (*getting out of the closet*) Saint Eulalie has pardoned me! She showed me mercy! My belly! I'm pregnant! Oh, blessed Saint Eulalie . . . I thank you for this too! I'm going to be a mother! A mother! Thank you, Saint Eulalie! Thank you! (*exits*)

(*Gunshots and cries are heard outside.*)

GIOVANNI (*all at the window*): Look, the women are pulling their stuff down off the trucks. The police are shooting!

LUIGI: Yeah, but look at those kids on the roofs—they're throwing stuff down: roof tiles, bricks . . . !

ANTONIA: And over there—look at that woman with the hunting rifle—there, she's shooting from that window!

GIOVANNI: The police are shooting at the crowd . . . They hit a kid—

MARGHERITA: Oh god, these cops are out to kill for real.

CHORUS: Murderers, bastards!

ANTONIA: They're running away! The cops are running away!

MARGHERITA: They left the truck and everything just standing there!

ANTONIA: And the women are pulling their stuff down off the trucks!

GIOVANNI: Good for them! Hey, good for you! Bravo! That's the way.

ANTONIA: That poor kid . . . they're carrying him away.

GIOVANNI: Bastards. There you see them, the sons of the people— those murderers!

LUIGI: You finally caught on!

GIOVANNI: Today I've found out it's time to change the tune.

ANTONIA: Yes . . . like those workers were saying yesterday at the supermarket: it's a new sort of strike, in which the bosses have to pay!

LUIGI: Sure, 'cause the bosses aren't going to respond to loving persuasion!

GIOVANNI: Damn right they aren't—you can't tell them: "Excuse me, would you mind moving over a bit—to let us breathe a little more air?" No, the only way to persuade these guys is to throw them in the toilet . . . and then pull the chain! Then we really would have a decent world, maybe with fewer shiny store windows and freeways, but with fewer corrupt bureaucrats in the government, too—fewer capitalist crooks. And a world where there would be real justice! Where people like us, who've always carried the load to support them all, would finally start supporting ourselves—organizing our own lives! Like human men and women.

ANTONIA: A world where you can notice that there's a sky . . .

LUIGI: That plants and trees flower . . .

MARGHERITA: That there's even springtime . . .

GIOVANNI: With children laughing and singing!

ALL: And at the end, when you die, it wasn't just an old worn-out mule that dropped dead; it was a human being that died; a person who lived happy and free, along with free other people! (*music; singing*) "Avanti Popolo . . ."

Questions for Discussion and Writing

1. How does the prologue set up the audience's EXPECTATIONS that the play will explore political, cultural, and religious aspects of Italian life in terms of class conflicts?

2. Why can't Antonia tell her husband, Giovanni, the truth about how she obtained the groceries she has brought home from the supermarket? What does Giovanni's response to Antonia's various stories tell you about him?

3. How are each of the following issues a source of humor in the play: the masculine self-image in Italian society; the role of the pope and the Catholic Church; the corruption in government, unions, and big business; the fantasy values promoted by the media and films; the mystique and authority of science?

4. How does Fo CHARACTERIZE and mock authority figures in the play (for example, the Lieutenant or Giovanni's elderly father)?

5. How do props (for example, the gas starter, cupboard, bed, casket, and packet of olives) play a particularly important role at crucial points in the play?

6. How do Giovanni's experiences change him from the law-abiding citizen he was at the beginning of the play?

7. In a short essay, discuss how the effect of any given scene depends on having the reader or audience anticipate how a character will respond to a surprising turn of events or unbelievable situation (baby transplants or the "miracle" of Saint Eulalie).

8. Describe a situation (other than mealtime) where food played a central role in the interaction between two or more people.

9. Describe the most preposterous story you ever heard that, at the time, you accepted as true.

WRITING ABOUT READER EXPECTATION

Although it is something we have done most of our lives, when we look at it closely, reading is a rather mysterious activity. The individual interpretations readers bring to characters and events in the text make every story mean something slightly different to every reader. There are, however, some strategies all readers use: we instinctively draw on our own knowledge of human relationships in interpreting characters and incidents, we simultaneously draw on clues in the text to anticipate what will happen next, and we continuously revise our past impressions as we encounter new information.

For example, consider the mental gymnastics a reader would go through while reading Murray Bail's "The Drover's Wife." Like most authors, Bail cannot imagine the entire story for the reader. The details he includes are selective and the reader must fill in the missing pieces of information by working with the clues Bail supplies. Bail tells the story of a middle-class, middle-aged dentist in Australia who has seen a portrait titled "The Drover's Wife" that he believes is a portrait of his wife, who left him and their young son and daughter thirty years before. As readers, we must piece together the entire story from the dentist's comments about the picture. The reader's first reaction would be to wonder whether in fact the woman in the picture really is his wife and, if so, what prompted her to leave him and their children to run off with a cattle drover. When the narrator describes the camping trip they took together and how she enjoyed chopping wood and lugging ice, or the time she killed the snake down at the beach shack while the narrator was terrified, we can participate in the text by imagining how the narrator reacted to these vents and begin to create a hypothesis as to why she left him to run off with a cattle drover. The most important clues are provided by all those things that concern the dentist, such as imprecision in labeling the picture, bush flies, the hardships of camping, the value he puts on propriety and decorum, and his standing in the community. Cumulatively they provide the reader with the information necessary to draw inferences that create a meaning for the story.

It is precisely this process of active involvement that makes reading such an enjoyable activity. The reader plays an important role in creating the meaning for any short story, poem, or play. Anyone who has ever returned to a favorite story, poem, or play only to discover something new in it can see how much the reader contributes to creating a meaning for any work; the text remains the same, and any new insights must be attributable to changes in the reader. Reading at its most satisfying is a cooperative venture between the reader and the text. Every text embodies particular ideas, experiences, and assumptions that reflect the personal attitudes of the author as well as the societal norms and literary conventions of the time and place in which the text was written. These assumptions, beliefs, and perspectives may be quite different from your own. For example, the view of what would serve as acceptable living conditions for a husband and wife in Calcutta in Krishnan Varma's story "The Grass-Eaters" ("and now we have no fears or anxieties. We have a home made of coal tar drums. We eat two square meals of grass a day") would probably differ greatly from your own expectations.

In addition to differences in personal backgrounds and cultural perspectives, readers differ in terms of their assumptions as to what literature is. Some readers view fiction as an escape from reality and enjoy the twists and turns of a suspenseful plot. Other readers associate poetry with what is high-minded and beautiful and believe a poem has to rhyme in order to be a poem. Those readers might have trouble with a poem like Damas's "Hiccup," whose form and content challenge conventional assumptions about poetry. However, most readers cannot resist speculating on the next disaster the speaker would be accused of by his berating mother. In effect, we project ourselves into the poem by imagining what lies ahead, and we draw from our own memories of childhood in interpreting the characters and incidents the poem describes.

An essay in which you explore the personal, literary, and cultural assumptions you bring to reading a particular text is called a RESPONSE STATEMENT. If you wish, such an essay may be written as a first-person statement, describing your interaction with the text in terms of how it made you feel, and what particular thoughts, memories, and associations it triggered. Why did you like or dislike the work? How would you account for your reaction in terms of any of the literary elements—CHARACTERIZATION, SETTING, POINT OF VIEW, LANGUAGE, TONE, STYLE, and EFFECTIVE USE OF IMAGERY? Was the narrative logic of the story (chronological, associative, surreal, and so on) sustained? For example, if ghosts can't pass through walls in the beginning of the story, has the author forgotten this by the end of story?

At what points in the work were you required to imagine or anticipate what would happen next? How did you make use of the information the author gave you to generate a hypothesis about what lay ahead? To what extent do your own past experiences—gender, age, race, class, and culture—differ from those of the characters in the story, poem, or play? How might your reading of the text differ from that of other readers? Has the writer explored all the possibilities raised within the work? Has she or he missed any opportunities that you as the writer would have explored?

Connections

1. What similarities in sources of humor, methods of satire, and farce can you discover in Sorrentino's story and Fo's play?
2. How do Shange and Bail develop the theme that one's feeling of value as a person is conditioned by social class, as displayed in the attitude of the upper-middle class toward the working poor?
3. To what extent does acting "white" play a part in establishing class values in "Hiccup" and "Betsey Brown"? What is the attitude of Damas and Shange respectively toward such actions?
4. How do both Kate Chopin and Sheila Roberts explore the relationship between class and race in terms of the behavior of the husbands in both stories?
5. How do the stories by Alfaro and Bail provide complementary views from different angles on how a shift in status and social class results in changed attitudes?
6. How do both Lim and Sorrentino illustrate the differences between having money and having class?
7. To what extent do the works by Bail, Roberts, Alfaro, and Shange present criticisms of the upper-middle-class bourgeoise as shallow, self-righteous, provincial, and fearful of slipping back into a lower class?
8. How do Kaléko's poem and Varma's story show the differences in cultural values attached to getting enough food in western Europe and in Calcutta?
9. How do the works by Kaléko, Shange, and Alfaro reflect connections between social class and weight?
10. How do the poems by Ritsos and Hogan reveal the author's assumptions that a rise in social class means losing touch with humanity?
11. To what extent are the poems by Hogan and Castillo offered as expressions of those who cannot speak for themselves?
12. How do Agard and Shange reveal very different attitudes toward both the use of proper "white" middle-class speech patterns and how social class is connected to the language you speak?
13. To what extent do the works by Fo and Castillo address the issue of exploitation of workers?
14. How do Drakulić and Sorrentino offer insight into how the kinds of food served to guests imply class values in Warsaw, Prague, and Buenos Aires?
15. How is Hogan's discussion in her essay, "Hearing Voices," of what she is trying to achieve by writing poetry illustrated in her poem "Workday"?

5

The Individual and the State

"*You only have power over people so long as you don't take everything away from them. But when you've robbed a man of everything he's no longer in your power—he's free again.*"

— *Alexander Solzhenitsyn*

In no area are the conflicts between different points of view more dramatic than between individual citizens and the nation-states to which they relinquish a degree of freedom in order to gain benefits that can be achieved only through the nation-state's collective political and social institutions (such as the military, the legal system, or health care). The allegiance individuals owe their governments, and the protection of individual rights that citizens expect in return, has been the subject of intense analysis down through the ages.

A politicized environment within a state has an intensely corrosive and debilitating effect on personal relationships when individual loyalties, codes of values, and sense of honor come into conflict with officially decreed allegiances. Authors in many countries and cultures describe the seductive and persuasive powers the state can mobilize through threat of force and propaganda to manipulate the perceptions of the citizens under its control. Regimes also remain in power by channeling existing resentments of one group against another. In individuals, this takes the form of encouraging people to hate themselves and see themselves as helpless as a way of keeping control. This psychological dimension has been the basis of a wide range of stories, poems, and plays that explore the predicaments of ordinary citizens trying to survive in repressive military and political regimes.

In "Roller Ball Murder" William Harrison foresees a day when international corporations that have replaced nations compete against each other in a deadly blood sport. In "We Have Arrived in Amritsar," Bhisham Sahni evokes the spectre of factional and religious violence among Hindus, Muslims, and Sikhs, and the communal riots that have torn India apart. In "The Censors," Luisa Valenzuela dramatizes the corrupting effect of power on an idealistic young man in Argentina. In an accompanying essay, "Writing with the Body," Valenzuela speaks with candor of the difficulties of trying to be a writer under the fascist regime in her country. "Gregory," by Panos Ioannides, explores the conflict between personal loyalty and military duty during the Cypriot rebellion. From Nicaragua, Ernesto Cardenal in "The Swede" relates how a Swede imprisoned in Central America acts as an unwilling intermediary and translator between the president and his Swedish lady. In "Cervicide," Gloria Anzaldúa tells the poignant story of a Mexican-American girl who has to kill her pet deer to save her father from going to jail. A delightful fable, "The Elephant," by the Polish satirist Slawomir Mrożek, spoofs the absurdities of life under a centralized bureaucracy. The devastating consequences of apartheid for both blacks and whites in South Africa is the subject of Jan Rabie's modern-day parable, "Drought." In the heartfelt tale "A Pair of Socks with Love," the Taiwanese author P'an Jen-mu portrays the strength of personal loyalty against ideological fervor during the Cultural Revolution. In "The Torture and Death of Her Little Brother," Rigoberta Menchú, winner of the 1992 Nobel Peace Prize, recounts the horrifying murder of her younger brother by the military regime in Guatemala.

Poetry by writers of conscience who in many cases have survived oppressive regimes, imprisonment, physical and psychological torture in Poland, Vietnam, Armenia, the United States, Greece, South Africa, and Israel provides a unique insight into the human consequences of political turmoil and oppression. Students will hear the voices of Wisława Szymborska, a popular Polish poet satirizing censorship; Nguyen Chi Thien, who survived twenty years in a North Vietnam prison; Diana Der Hovanessian, writing of coming to terms with what had been denied by the world; Etheridge Knight, who began writing poetry while serving time in Indiana State Prison; Eleni Fourtouni, a Greek resistance fighter against the Nazis; and Yehuda Amichai, with a thoughtful reflection on relationships between Jews and Arabs.

In the play *How I Got That Story*, Amlin Gray presents a nightmarishly funny vision of American involvement in a fictionalized Southeast Asian country called Am-bo Land. A naive reporter from Iowa comes to cover the war and becomes addicted to covering the story long after common sense would suggest cutting his losses. *Protest*, a one-act play by Václav Havel, the president of the Czech Republic, offers a theatrical realization of the meeting between a dissident writer (based on Havel's own experiences before being sentenced to four and a half years in prison for his political activities) and a successful hack who has compromised his political ideals and has put his talent at the service of those in power.

William Harrison

Roller Ball Murder

William Harrison is a native of Dallas, Texas, where he was born in 1933. He was educated at Texas Christian University and Vanderbilt. His works include The Theologian (1965), several other novels, and a collection of short fiction, Roller Ball Murder and Other Stories (1974). He also coauthored the script for the film Rollerball (1975), which was based upon his story and starred James Caan and John Houseman. Harrison teaches creative writing at the University of Arkansas. In this story, which takes place in the twenty-first century, international corporations, known as the Six Majors, have replaced nations as we know them and entertain and control the masses through a blood sport (roller ball) that combines motorcycling, football, jai alai, the roller derby, and hand-to-hand combat. The protagonist, Jonathan E, embodies the last vestiges of individualism in this quasi-totalitarian world of the future.

1   The game, the game: here we go again. All glory to it, all things I am and own because of Roller Ball Murder.

2   Our team stands in a row, twenty of us in salute as the corporation hymn is played by the band. We view the hardwood oval track which offers us the bumps and rewards of mayhem: fifty yards long, thirty yards across the ends, high banked, and at the top of the walls the cannons which fire those frenzied twenty-pound balls—similar to bowling balls, made of ebonite—at velocities over three hundred miles an hour. The balls career around the track, eventually slowing and falling with diminishing centrifugal force, and as they go to ground or strike a player another volley fires. Here we are, our team: ten roller skaters, five motorbike riders, five runners (or clubbers). As the hymn plays, we stand erect and tough; eighty thousand sit watching in the stands and another two billion viewers around the world inspect the set of our jaws on multivision.

3   The runners, those bastards, slip into their heavy leather gloves and shoulder their lacrosselike paddles—with which they either catch the whizzing balls or bash the rest of us. The bikers ride high on the walls (beware, mates, that's where the cannon shots are too hot to handle) and swoop down to help the runners at opportune times. The skaters, those of us with the juice for it, protest: we clog the way, try to keep the runners from passing us and scoring points, and become the fodder in the brawl. So two teams of us, forty in all, go skating and running and biking around the track while the big balls are fired in the same direction as we move—always coming up behind us to scatter and maim

630

us—and the object of the game, fans, as if you didn't know, is for the runners to pass all skaters on the opposing team, field a ball, and pass it to a biker for one point. Those bikers, by the way, may give the runners a lift—in which case those of us on skates have our hands full overturning 175cc motorbikes.

No rest periods, no substitute players. If you lose a man, your team plays short. 4

Today I turn my best side to the cameras. I'm Jonathan E, none other, and nobody passes me on the track. I'm the core of the Houston team and for the two hours of play—no rules, no penalties once the first cannon fires—I'll level any bastard runner who raises a paddle at me. 5

We move: immediately there are pileups of bikes, skaters, referees, and runners, all tangled and punching and scrambling when one of the balls zooms around the corner and belts us. I pick up momentum and heave an opposing skater into the infield at center ring; I'm brute speed today, driving, pushing up on the track, dodging a ball, hurtling downward beyond those bastard runners. Two runners do hand-to-hand combat and one gets his helmet knocked off in a blow which tears away half his face; the victor stands there too long admiring his work and gets wiped out by a biker who swoops down and flattens him. The crowd screams and I know the cameramen have it on an isolated shot and that viewers in Melbourne, Berlin, Rio, and L.A. are heaving with excitement in their easy chairs. 6

When an hour is gone I'm still wheeling along, naturally, though we have four team members out with broken parts, one rookie maybe dead, two bikes demolished. The other team, good old London, is worse off. 7

One of their motorbikes roars out of control, takes a hit from one of the balls, and bursts into flame. Wild cheering. 8

Cruising up next to their famous Jackie Magee, I time my punch. He turns in my direction, exposes the ugly snarl inside his helmet, and I take him out of action. In that tiniest instant, I feel his teeth and bone give way and the crowd screams approval. We have them now, we really have them, we do, and the score ends 7–2. 9

The years pass and the rules alter—always in favor of the greater crowd-pleasing carnage. I've been at this more than fifteen years, amazing, with only broken arms and collarbones to slow me down, and I'm not as spry as ever, but meaner—and no rookie, no matter how much in shape, can learn this slaughter unless he comes out and takes me on in the real thing. 10

But the rules. I hear of games in Manila, now, or in Barcelona with no time limits, men bashing each other until there are no more runners left, no way of scoring points. That's the coming thing. I hear of Roller Ball Murder played with mixed teams, men and women, wearing tear- 11 away jerseys which add a little tit and vulnerable exposure to the action. Everything will happen. They'll change the rules until we skate on a slick of blood, we all know that.

12 Before this century began, before the Great Asian war of the 1990s, before the corporations replaced nationalism and the corporate police forces supplanted the world's armies, in the last days of American football and the World Cup in Europe, I was a tough young rookie who knew all the rewards of this game. Women: I had them all—even, pity, a good marriage once. I had so much money after my first trophies that I could buy houses and land and lakes beyond the huge cities where only the executive class was allowed. My photo, then, as now, was on the covers of magazines, so that my name and the name of the sport were one, and I was Jonathan E, no other, a survivor and much more in the bloodiest sport.

13 At the beginning I played for Oil Conglomerates, then those corporations became known as ENERGY; I've always played for the team here in Houston, they've given me everything.

14 "How're you feeling?" Mr. Bartholemew asks me. He's taking the head of ENERGY, one of the most powerful men in the world, and he talks to me like I'm his son.

15 "Feeling mean," I answer, so that he smiles.

16 He tells me they want to do a special on multivision about my career, lots of shots on the side screens showing my greatest plays, and the story of my life, how ENERGY takes in such orphans, gives them work and protection, and makes careers possible.

17 "Really feel mean, eh?" Mr. Bartholemew asks again, and I answer the same, not telling him all that's inside me because he would possibly misunderstand; not telling him that I'm tired of the long season, that I'm lonely and miss my wife, that I yearn for high, lost, important thoughts, and that maybe, just maybe, I've got a deep rupture in the soul.

18 An old buddy, Jim Cletus, comes by the ranch for the weekend. Mackie, my present girl, takes our dinners out of the freezer and turns the rays on them; not so domestic, that Mackie, but she has enormous breasts and a waist smaller than my thigh.

19 Cletus works as a judge now. At every game there are two referees—clowns, whose job it is to see nothing amiss—and the judge who records the points scored. Cletus is also on the International Rules Committee and tells me they are still considering several changes.

20 "A penalty for being lapped by your own team, for one thing," he tells us. "A damned simple penalty, too: they'll take off your helmet."

21 Mackie, bless her bosom, makes an O with her lips.

22 Cletus, once a runner for Toronto, fills up my oversized furniture and rests his hands on his bad knees.

"What else?" I ask him. "Or can you tell me?" 23

"Oh, just financial things. More bonuses for superior attacks. Bigger 24
bonuses for being named World All-Star—which ought to be good
news for you again. And, yeah, talk of reducing the two-month off-
season. The viewers want more."

After dinner Cletus walks around the ranch with me. We trudge up 25
the path of a hillside and the Texas countryside stretches before us.
Pavilions of clouds.

"Did you ever think about death in your playing days?" I ask, 26
knowing I'm a bit too pensive for old Clete.

"Never in the game itself," he answers proudly. "Off the track— 27
yeah, sometimes I never thought about anything else."

We pause and take a good long look at the horizon. 28

"There's another thing going in the Rules Committee," he finally ad- 29
mits. "They're considering dropping the time limit—at least, god help
us, Johnny, the suggestion has come up officially."

I like a place with rolling hills. Another of my houses is near Lyons 30
in France, the hills similar to these although more lush, and I take my
evening strolls there over an ancient battleground. The cities are too
much, so large and uninhabitable that one has to have a business passport to enter such immensities as New York.

"Naturally I'm holding out for the time limit," Cletus goes on. "I've 31
played, so I know a man's limits. Sometimes in that committee, Johnny,
I feel like I'm the last moral man on earth sitting there and insisting that
there should be a few rules."

The statistical nuances of Roller Ball Murder entertain the multitudes as 32
much as any other aspect of the game. The greatest number of points
scored in a single game: 81. The highest velocity of a ball when actually
caught by a runner: 176 mph. Highest number of players put out of action in a single game by a single skater: 13—world's record by yours
truly. Most deaths in a single contest: 9—Rome vs. Chicago, December
4, 2012.

The giant lighted boards circling above the track monitor our pace, 33
record each separate fact of the slaughter, and we have millions of
fans—strange, it always seemed to me—who never look directly at the
action, but just study those statistics.

A multivision survey established this. 34

Before going to the stadium in Paris for our evening game, I stroll un- 35
der the archways and along the Seine.

Some of the French fans call to me, waving and talking to my body- 36
guards as well, so I become oddly conscious of myself, conscious of my
size and clothes and the way I walk. A curious moment.

I'm six foot three inches and weigh 255 pounds. My neck is 18½ 37
inches. Fingers like a pianist. I wear my conservative pinstriped jump

suit and the famous flat Spanish hat. I am 34 years old now, and when I grow old, I think, I'll look a lot like the poet Robert Graves.

38 The most powerful men in the world are the executives. They run the major corporations which fix prices, wages, and the general economy, and we all know they're crooked, that they have almost unlimited power and money, but I have considerable power and money myself and I'm still anxious. What can I possibly want, I ask myself, except, possibly, more knowledge?

39 I consider recent history—which is virtually all anyone remembers—and how the corporate wars ended, so that we settled into the Six Majors: ENERGY, TRANSPORT, FOOD, HOUSING, SERVICES, and LUXURY. Sometimes I forget who runs what—for instance, now that the universities are operated by the Majors (and provide the farm system for Roller Ball Murder), which Major runs them? SERVICES or LUXURY? Music is one of our biggest industries, but I can't remember who administers it. Narcotic research is now under FOOD, I know, though it used to be under LUXURY.

40 Anyway, I think I'll ask Mr. Bartholemew about knowledge. He's a man with a big view of the world, with values, with memory. My team flings itself into the void while his team harnesses the sun, taps the sea, finds new alloys, and is clearly just a hell of a lot more serious.

41 The Mexico City game has a new wrinkle: they've changed the shape of the ball on us.

42 Cletus didn't even warn me—perhaps he couldn't—but here we are playing with a ball not quite round, its center of gravity altered, so that it rumbles around the track in irregular patterns.

43 This particular game is bad enough because the bikers down here are getting wise to me; for years, since my reputation was established, bikers have always tried to take me out of a game early. But early in the game I'm wary and strong and I'll always gladly take on a biker—even since they put shields on the motorbikes so that we can't grab the handlebars. Now, though, these bastards know I'm getting older—still mean but slowing down, as the sports pages say about me—so they let me bash it out with the skaters and runners for as long as possible before sending the bikers after me. Knock out Jonathan E, they say, and you've beaten Houston; and that's right enough, but they haven't done it yet.

44 The fans down here, all low-class FOOD workers mostly, boil over as I manage to keep my cool—and the oblong ball, zigzagging around at lurching speeds, hopping two feet off the track at times, knocks out virtually their whole team. Finally, some of us catch their last runner/clubber and beat him to a pulp, so that's it: no runners, no points. Those dumb FOOD workers file out of the stadium while we show off and score a few fancy and uncontested points. The score 37–4. I feel wonderful, like pure brute speed.

Mackie is gone—her mouth no longer makes an O around my villa or ranch—and in her place is the new one, Daphne. My Daphne is tall and English and likes photos—always wants to pose for me. Sometimes we get out our boxes of old pictures (mine as a player, mostly, and hers as a model) and look at ourselves, and it occurs to me that the photos spread out on the rug are the real us, our public and performing true selves, and the two of us here in the sitting room, Gaelic gray winter outside our window, aren't too real at all.

"Look at the muscles in your back!" Daphne says in amazement as she studies a shot of me at the California beach—and it's as though she never before noticed.

After the photos, I stroll out beyond the garden. The brown waving grass of the fields reminds me of Ella, my only wife, and of her soft long hair which made a tent over my face when we kissed.

I lecture to the ENERGY-sponsored rookie camp and tell them they can't possibly comprehend anything until they're out on the track getting belted.

My talk tonight concerns how to stop a biker who wants to run you down. "You can throw a shoulder right into the shield," I begin. "And that way it's you or him."

The rookies look at me as though I'm crazy.

"Or you can hit the deck, cover yourself, tense up, and let the bastard flip over your body," I go on, counting on my fingers for them and doing my best not to laugh. "Or you can feint, sidestep up hill, and kick him off the track—which takes some practice and timing."

None of them knows what to say. We're sitting in the infield grass, the track lighted, the stands empty, and their faces are filled with stupid awe. "Or if a biker comes at you with good speed and balance," I continue, "then naturally let the bastard by—even if he carries a runner. That runner, remember, has to dismount and field one of the new odd-shaped balls which isn't easy—and you can usually catch up."

The rookies begin to get a smug look on their faces when a biker bears down on me in the demonstration period.

Brute speed. I jump to one side, dodge the shield, grab the bastard's arm, and separate him from his machine in one movement. The bike skids away. The poor biker's shoulder is out of socket.

"Oh yeah," I say, getting back to my feet. "I forgot about that move."

Toward midseason when I see Mr. Bartholemew again he has been deposed as the chief executive at ENERGY. He is still very important, but lacks some of the old certainty; his mood is reflective, so that I decide to take this opportunity to talk about what's bothering me.

We lunch in Houston Tower, viewing an expanse of city. A nice Beef Wellington and Burgundy. Daphne sits there like a stone, probably imagining that she's in a movie.

58   "Knowledge, ah, I see," Mr. Bartholemew replies in response to my topic. "What're you interested in, Jonathan? History? The arts?"

59   "Can I be personal with you?"

60   This makes him slightly uncomfortable. "Sure, naturally," he answers easily, and although Mr. Bartholemew isn't especially one to inspire confession I decide to blunder along.

61   "I began in the university," I remind him. "That was—let's see—more than seventeen years ago. In those days we still had books and I read some, quite a few, because I thought I might make an executive."

62   "Jonathan, believe me, I can guess what you're going to say," Mr. Bartholemew sighs, sipping the Burgundy and glancing at Daphne. "I'm one of the few with real regrets about what happened to the books. Everything is still on tapes, but it just isn't the same, is it? Nowadays only the computer specialists read the tapes and we're right back in the Middle Ages when only the monks could read the Latin script."

63   "Exactly," I answer, letting my beef go cold.

64   "Would you like me to assign you a specialist?"

65   "No, that's not exactly it."

66   "We have the great film libraries: you could get a permit to see anything you want. The Renaissance. Greek philosophers. I saw a nice summary film on the life and thought of Plato once."

67   "All I know," I say with hesitation, "is Roller Ball Murder."

68   "You don't want out of the game?" he asks warily.

69   "No, not at all. It's just that I want—god, Mr. Bartholemew, I don't know how to say it: I want *more*."

70   He offers a blank look.

71   "But not things in the world," I add. "More for *me*."

72   He heaves a great sigh, leans back, and allows the steward to refill his glass. Curiously, I know that he understands; he is a man of sixty, enormously wealthy, powerful in our most powerful executive class, and behind his eyes is the deep, weary, undeniable comprehension of the life he has lived.

73   "Knowledge," he tells me, "either converts to power or it converts to melancholy. Which could you possibly want, Jonathan? You *have* power. You have status and skill and the whole masculine dream many of us would like to have. And in Roller Ball Murder there's no room for melancholy, is there? In the game the mind exists for the body, to make a harmony of havoc, right? Do you want to change that? Do you want the mind to exist for itself alone? I don't think you actually want that, do you?"

74   "I really don't know," I admit.

75   "I'll get you some permits, Jonathan. You can see video films, learn something about reading tapes, if you want."

76   "I don't think I really *have* any power," I say, still groping.

"Oh, come on. What do *you* say about that?" he asks, turning to   77
Daphne.

"He definitely has power," she answers with a wan smile.   78

Somehow the conversation drifts away from me; Daphne, on cue,   79
like the good spy for the corporation she probably is, begins feeding
Mr. Bartholemew lines and soon, oddly enough, we're discussing my
upcoming game with Stockholm.

A hollow space begins to grow inside me, as though fire is eating   80
out a hole. The conversation concerns the end of the season, the All-Star
Game, records being set this year, but my disappointment—in what,
exactly, I don't even know—begins to sicken me.

Mr. Bartholemew eventually asks what's wrong.   81

"The food," I answer. "Usually I have great digestion, but maybe   82
not today."

In the locker room the dreary late-season pall takes us. We hardly   83
speak among ourselves, now, and, like soldiers or gladiators sensing
what lies ahead, we move around in these sickening surgical odors of
the locker room.

Our last training and instruction this year concerns the delivery of   84
deathblows to opposing players; no time now for the tolerant shoving
and bumping of yesteryear. I consider that I possess two good
weapons: because of my unusually good balance on skates, I can often
shatter my opponent's knee with a kick; also, I have a good backhand
blow to the ribs and heart, if, wheeling along side by side with some
bastard, he raises an arm against me. If the new rules change removes a
player's helmet, of course, that's death; as it is right now (there are rumors, rumors every day about what new version of RBM we'll have
next) you go for the windpipe, the ribs or heart, the diaphragm, or anyplace you don't break your hand.

Our instructors are a pair of giddy Oriental gentlemen who have all   85
sorts of anatomical solutions for us and show drawings of the human
figure with nerve centers painted in pink.

"What you do is this," says Moonpie, in parody of these two.   86
Moonpie is a fine skater in his fourth season and fancies himself an old-
fashioned drawling Texan. "What you do is hit 'em on the jawbone and
drive it up into their ganglia."

"Their *what*?" I ask, giving Moonpie a grin.   87

"Their goddamned *ganglia*. Bunch of nerves right here underneath   88
the ear. Drive their jawbones into that mess of nerves and it'll ring their
bells sure."

Daphne is gone now, too, and in this interim before another companion   89
arrives, courtesy of all my friends and employers at ENERGY, Ella
floats back into my dreams and daylight fantasies.

I was a corporation child, some executive's bastard boy, I always   90 preferred to think, brought up in the Galveston section of the city. A big kid, naturally, athletic and strong—and this, according to my theory, gave me healthy mental genes, too, because I take it now that strong in body is strong in mind: a man with brute speed surely also has the capacity to mull over his life. Anyway, I married at age fifteen while I worked on the docks for Oil Conglomerates. Ella was a secretary, slim with long brown hair, and we managed to get permits to both marry and enter the university together. Her fellowship was in General Electronics—she was clever, give her that—and mine was in Roller Ball Murder. She fed me well that first year, so I put on thirty hard pounds and at night she soothed my bruises (was she a spy, too, I've sometimes wondered, whose job it was to prime the bull for the charge?) and perhaps it was because she was my first woman ever, eighteen years old, lovely, that I've never properly forgotten.

91   She left me for an executive, just packed up and went to Europe with him. Six years ago I saw them at a sports banquet where I was presented an award: there they were, smiling and being nice, and I asked them only one question, just one, "You two ever had children?" It gave me odd satisfaction that they had applied for a permit, but had been denied.

92   Ella, love; one does consider: did you beef me up and break my heart in some great design of corporate society?

93   There I was, whatever, angry and hurt. Beyond repair, I thought at the time. And the hand which stroked Ella soon dropped all the foes of Houston.

94   I take sad stock of myself in this quiet period before another woman arrives; I'm smart enough, I know that: I had to be to survive. Yet, I seem to know nothing—and can feel the hollow spaces in my own heart. Like one of those computer specialists, I have my own brutal technical know-how; I know what today means, what tomorrow likely holds, but maybe it's because the books are gone—Mr. Bartholemew was right, it's a shame they're transformed—that I feel so vacant. If I didn't remember my Ella—this I realize—I wouldn't even *want* to remember because it's love I'm recollecting as well as those old university days.

95   Recollect, sure: I read quite a few books that year with Ella and afterward, too, before turning professional in the game. Apart from all the volumes about how to get along in business, I read the history of the kings of England, that pillars of wisdom book by T. E. Lawrence, all the forlorn novels, some Rousseau, a bio of Thomas Jefferson, and other odd bits. On tapes now, all that, whirring away in a cool basement someplace.

96   The rules crumble once more.

97   At the Tokyo game, we discover that there will be three oblong balls in play at all times.

Some of our most experienced players are afraid to go out on the track. Then, after they're coaxed and threatened and finally consent to join the flow, they fake injury whenever they can and sprawl in the infield like rabbits. As for me, I play with greater abandon than ever and give the crowd its money's worth. The Tokyo skaters are either peering over their shoulders looking for approaching balls when I smash them, or, poor devils, they're looking for me when a ball takes them out of action. [98]

One little bastard with a broken back flaps around for a moment like a fish, then shudders and dies. [99]

Balls jump at us as though they have brains. [100]

But fate carries me, as I somehow know it will: I'm a force field, a destroyer. I kick a biker into the path of a ball going at least two hundred miles an hour. I swerve around a pileup of bikes and skaters, ride high on the track, zoom down, and find a runner/clubber who panics and misses with a roundhouse swing of his paddle; without much ado, I belt him out of play with the almost certain knowledge—I've felt it before—that he's dead before he hits the infield. [101]

One ball flips out of play soon after being fired from the cannon, jumps the railing, sails high, and plows into the spectators. Beautiful. [102]

I take a hit from a ball, one of the three or four times I've ever been belted. The ball is riding low on the track when it catches me and I sprawl like a baby. One bastard runner comes after me, but one of our bikers chases him off. Then one of their skaters glides by and takes a shot at me, but I dig him in the groin and discourage him, too. [103]

Down and hurting, I see Moonpie killed. They take off his helmet, working slowly—it's like slow motion and I'm writhing and cursing and unable to help—and open his mouth on the toe of some bastard skater's boot. Then they kick the back of his head and knock out all his teeth—which rattle downhill on the track. Then kick again and stomp: his brains this time. He drawls a last groaning good-bye while the cameras record it. [104]

And later I'm up, pushing along once more, feeling bad, but knowing everyone else feels the same; I have that last surge of energy, the one I always get when I'm going good, and near the closing gun I manage a nice move: grabbing one of their runners with a headlock, I skate him off to limbo, bashing his face with my free fist, picking up speed until he drags behind like a dropped flag, and disposing of him in front of a ball which carries him off in a comic flop. Oh, god, god. [105]

Before the All-Star Game, Cletus comes to me with the news I expect: this one will be a no-time-limit extravaganza in New York, every multivision set in the world tuned in. The bikes will be more high-powered, four oblong balls will be in play simultaneously, and the referees will blow the whistle on any sluggish player and remove his helmet as a penalty. [106]

107   Cletus is apologetic.

108   "With those rules, no worry," I tell him. "It'll go no more than an hour and we'll all be dead."

109   We're at the Houston ranch on a Saturday afternoon, riding around in my electrocart viewing the Santa Gertrudis stock. This is probably the ultimate spectacle of my wealth: my own beef cattle in a day when only a few special members of the executive class have any meat to eat with the exception of mass-produced fish. Cletus is so impressed with my cattle that he keeps going on this afternoon and seems so pathetic to me, a judge who doesn't judge, the pawn of a committee, another feeble hulk of an old RBM player.

110   "You owe me a favor, Clete," I tell him.

111   "Anything," he answers, not looking me in the eyes.

112   I turn the cart up a lane beside my rustic rail fence, an archway of oak trees overhead and the early spring bluebonnets and daffodils sending up fragrances from the nearby fields. Far back in my thoughts is the awareness that I can't possibly last and that I'd like to be buried out here—burial is seldom allowed anymore, everyone just incinerated and scattered—to become the mulch of flowers.

113   "I want you to bring Ella to me," I tell him. "After all these years, yeah: that's what I want. You arrange it and don't give me any excuses, okay?"

114   We meet at the villa near Lyons in early June, only a week before the All-Star Game in New York, and I think she immediately reads something in my eyes which helps her to love me again. Of course I love her: I realize, seeing her, that I have only a vague recollection of being alive at all, and that was a long time ago, in another century of the heart when I had no identity except my name, when I was a simple dock worker, before I ever saw all the world's places or moved in the rumbling nightmares of Roller Ball Murder.

115   She kisses my fingers. "Oh," she says softly, and her face is filled with true wonder, "what's happened to you, Johnny?"

116   A few soft days. When our bodies aren't entwined in lovemaking, we try to remember and tell each other everything: the way we used to hold hands, how we fretted about receiving a marriage permit, how the books looked on our shelves in the old apartment in River Oaks. We strain, at times, trying to recollect the impossible; it's true that history is really gone, that we have no families or touchstones, that our short personal lives alone judge us, and I want to hear about her husband, the places they've lived, the furniture in her house, anything. I tell her, in turn, about all the women, about Mr. Bartholemew and Jim Cletus, about the ranch in the hills outside Houston.

117   Come to me, Ella. If I can remember us, I can recollect meaning and time.

118   It would be nice, I think, once, to imagine that she was taken away

from me by some malevolent force in this awful age, but I know the truth of that: she went away, simply, because I wasn't enough back then, because those were the days before I yearned for anything, when I was beginning to live to play the game. But no matter. For a few days she sits on my bed and I touch her skin like a blind man groping back over the years.

On our last morning together she comes out in her traveling suit with her hair pulled up underneath a fur cap. The softness has faded from her voice and she smiles with efficiency, as if she has just come back to the practical world; I recall, briefly, this scene played out a thousand years ago when she explained that she was going away with her executive. 119

She plays like a biker, I decide; she rides up there high above the turmoil, decides when to swoop down, and makes a clean kill. 120

"Good-bye, Ella," I say, and she turns her head slightly away from my kiss so that I touch her fur cap with my lips. 121

"I'm glad I came," she says politely. "Good luck, Johnny." 122

New York is frenzied with what is about to happen. 123

The crowds throng into Energy Plaza, swarm the ticket offices at the stadium, and wherever I go people are reaching for my hands, pushing my bodyguards away, trying to touch my sleeve as though I'm some ancient religious figure, a seer or prophet. 124

Before the game begins I stand with my team as the corporation hymns are played. I'm brute speed today, I tell myself, trying to rev myself up; yet, adream in my thoughts, I'm a bit unconvinced. 125

A chorus of voices joins the band now as the music swells. 126

The game, the game, all glory to it, the music rings, and I can feel my lips move with the words, singing. 127

Questions for Discussion and Writing

1. How does information about Jonathan E's background and life experiences encourage the reader to view him as the last individualist in a totalitarian society? How will proposed rule changes make it impossible for even Jonathan E to survive?

2. What overall picture of society do you get from this story? What role does the game play in this futuristic society?

3. What evidence can you cite that the power of the state in alliance with corporations has become all-encompassing and a form of totalitarianism? Under what circumstances do you need passports? Why is it significant that the universities are run by the Majors? For what kinds of things do citizens need to get permits from the government? Putting all these references together, what picture of a future society does this story present? Which of the elements depicted in this story have already become apparent in today's world?

4. In what way is Jonathan E's encounter with Ella a TURNING POINT that decides the issue of whether he should continue playing?
5. Describe your favorite sports hero. How is this person similar to and different from Jonathan E? To what extent are corporations and sports more closely related nowadays than they were when "Roller Ball Murder" was written some twenty years ago? What sports have already started to resemble "roller ball"?
6. To what extent do national sports reveal important features of their respective cultures? For example, what aspects of American culture are embodied in football or baseball?

Bhisham Sahni

We Have Arrived in Amritsar

The Hindi writer Bhisham Sahni was born in 1915. He has published five novels, eight collections of short stories, three full-length plays, and a biography of his brother, the actor and writer Balraj Sahni. Bhisham Sahni received the Distinguished Writer Award from the Punjab government in 1974, the Sahitya Akademi Prize for his novel Tamas *in 1975, the Lotus Award of the Afro-Asian Writer's Association in 1981, the Sovietland Nehru Award in 1983, and two awards from the Uttar Pradesh Hindi Samsthan Association. In "We Have Arrived in Amritsar," translated into English by the author, deteriorating relationships among the Hindus, Muslims, and Sikh passengers sharing a compartment on a train traveling between New Delhi and Amritsar mirror the upsurge in sectarian violence that occurred throughout India following the partition in 1947 that created the country of Pakistan.*

There were not many passengers in the compartment. The Sardarji, sitting opposite me, had been telling me about his experiences in the war. He had fought on the Burmese front, and every time he spoke about the British soldiers, he had a hearty laugh at their expense. There were three Pathan[1] traders too, and one of them, wearing a green *salwar kameez*,[2] lay stretched on one of the upper berths. He was a talkative kind of a person and had kept up a stream of jokes with a frail-looking *babu*[3] who was sitting next to me. The *babu*, it seemed, came from Peshawar[4] because off and on they would begin to converse with each other in Pushto.[5] In a corner, under the Pathan's berth, sat an old woman telling beads on her rosary, with her head and shoulders covered by a shawl. These were the only passengers that I can recollect being in the compartment. There might have been others too, but I can't remember them now.

The train moved slowly and the passengers chatted away. Outside the breeze made gentle ripples across the ripening wheat. I was happy because I was on my way to Delhi to see the Independence Day celebrations.

Thinking about those days it seems to me that we had lived in a kind of mist. It may be that as time goes by all the activities of the past

[1]Muslim community near Afghanistan.
[2]A long knee-length cotton shirt.
[3]Generic term for any male.
[4]City located in Pakistan.
[5]A type of dialect.

643

begin to float in a mist, which seems to grow thicker and thicker as we move away further into the future.

4   The decision about the creation of Pakistan had just been announced and people were indulging in all kinds of surmises about the pattern of life that would emerge. But no one's imagination could go very far. The Sardarji sitting in front of me repeatedly asked me whether I thought Mr Jinnah would continue to live in Bombay after the creation of Pakistan or whether he would resettle in Pakistan. Each time my answer would be the same, "Why should he leave Bombay? I think he'll continue to live in Bombay and keep visiting Pakistan." Similar guesses were being made about the towns of Lahore[6] and Gurdaspur[7] too, and no one knew which town would fall to the share of India and which to Pakistan. People gossiped and laughed in much the same way as before. Some were abandoning their homes for good, while others made fun of them. No one knew which step would prove to be the right one. Some people deplored the creation of Pakistan, others rejoiced over the achievement of independence. Some places were being torn apart by riots, others were busy preparing to celebrate Independence. Somehow we all thought that the troubles would cease automatically with the achievement of freedom. In that hazy mist there came the sweet taste of freedom and yet the darkness of uncertainty seemed continuously to be with us. Only occasionally through this darkness did one catch glimpses of what the future meant for us.

5   We had left behind the city of Jhelum when the Pathan sitting on the upper berth untied a small bundle, took out chunks of boiled meat and some bread, and began distributing it among his companions. In his usual jovial manner he offered some of it to the *babu* next to me.

6   "Eat it, *babu*, eat it. It will give you strength. You will become like us. Your wife too will be happy with you. You are weak because you eat *dal*[8] all the time. Eat it, *dalkhor*."[9]

7   There was laughter in the compartment. The *babu* said something in Pushto but kept smiling and shaking his head.

8   The other Pathan taunted him further.

9   "O *zalim*,[10] if you don't want to take it from our hands, pick it up yourself with your own hand.[11] I swear to God that it is only goat's meat and not of any other animal."

10   The third Pathan joined in: "O son of a swine, who is looking at you here? We won't tell your wife about it. You share our meat and we shall share your *dal* with you."

---

6 & 7 Border towns.

[8] Type of thick soup made of cereal grain.

[9] Insulting term, meaning one who eats "dal", that is, a vegetarian.

[10] "Cruel" person.

[11] Brahmin, the highest caste, will not eat food touched by another caste.

There was a burst of laughter. But the emaciated clerk continued to 11
smile and shake his head.

"Does it look nice that we should eat and you should merely look 12
on?" The Pathans were in good humour.

The fat Sardarji joined in and said, "He doesn't accept it because 13
you haven't washed your hands," and burst out laughing at his own
joke. He was reclining on the seat with half his belly hanging over it.
"You just woke up and immediately started to eat. That's the reason
babuji won't accept food from your hands. There isn't any other reason." As he said this he gave me a wink and guffawed again.

"If you don't want to eat meat, you should go and sit in a ladies' 14
compartment. What business have you to be here?"

Again the whole compartment had a good laugh. All the passengers 15
had been together since the beginning of the journey, a kind of infor-
mality had developed amongst them.

"Come and sit with me. Come, rascal, we shall sit and chat about 16
kissakhani."[12]

*

The train stopped at a wayside station and new passengers barged into 17
the compartment. Many of them forced their way in.

"What is this place?" someone asked. 18

"Looks like Wazirabad to me," I replied, peering out of the window. 19

The train only stopped for a short time, but during the stop a minor 20
incident occurred. A man got down from a neighbouring compartment
and went to the tap on the platform for water. He had hardly filled his
glass with water when suddenly he turned round and started running
back towards his compartment. As he ran the water spilt out of the
glass. The whole manner of his dash was revealing to me. I had seen
people running like this before and knew immediately what it meant.
Two or three other passengers, who were queuing at the tap also began
running towards their compartments. Within a matter of seconds the
whole platform was deserted. Inside our compartment, however, people were still chatting and laughing as before.

Beside me the babu muttered: "Something bad is happening." 21

Something really had happened but none of us could figure it out. I 22
had seen quite a number of communal riots and had learnt to detect the
slightest change in the atmosphere; people running, doors shutting,
men and women standing on housetops, an uncanny silence all
round—these were signs of riots.

Suddenly the sound of a scuffle was heard from the back-entrance 23
to the compartment. Some passenger was trying to get into the compartment.

[12]Literally, "news and stories," that is, chit-chat.

24   "No, you can't come in here," someone shouted. "There is no place here. Can't you see? No, no. Go away."

25   "Shut the door," someone else remarked. "People just walk in as though it was their uncle's residence."

26   Several voices were heard, speaking simultaneously.

27   As long as a passenger is outside a compartment and is trying desperately to get in, he faces strong opposition from those inside. But once he succeeds in entering, the opposition subsides and he is soon accepted as a fellow traveller, so much so that at the next stop, he too begins to shout at the new passengers trying to get in.

28   The commotion increased. A man in soiled, dirty clothes and with drooping moustache forced his way into the compartment. From his dirty clothes he appeared to be a sweet-vendor. He paid no attention to the shouts of protest of the passengers. He squeezed himself inside and turned around to try and haul in his enormous black trunk.

29   "Come in, come in, you too climb," he shouted, addressing someone behind him. A frail, thin woman entered the door followed by a young dark girl of sixteen or seventeen. People were still shouting at them. The Sardarji had got up on his haunches.

30   Everyone seemed to be shouting at the same time: "Shut the door. Why don't you?" "People just come barging in." "Don't let anyone in." "What are you doing?" "Just push him out, somebody. . . ."

31   The man continued hauling in his trunk, while his wife and daughter shrank back and stood against the door of the toilet, looking anxious and frightened.

32   "Can't you go to some other compartment? You have brought womenfolk with you too. Can't you see this is a men's compartment?"

33   The man was breathless and his clothes were drenched with perspiration. Having pulled in the trunk, he was now busy collecting the other sundry items of his baggage.

34   "I am a ticketholder. I am not travelling without tickets. There was no choice. A riot has broken out in the city. It was an awful job, reaching the railway station. . . ."

35   All the passengers fell silent except the Pathan who was sitting on the upper berth. He leaned forward and shouted, "Get out of here! Can't you see there is no room here?"

36   Suddenly he swung out his leg and kicked the man. Instead of hitting the man, his foot landed squarely on the wife's chest. She screamed with pain, and collapsed on the floor.

37   There was no time for argument. The sweet-vendor continued to assemble his baggage into the compartment. Everybody was struck silent. After pulling in the heavy bundle he was struggling with the bars of a dismantled *charpoy*.[13] The Pathan lost all patience.

38   "Turn him out, who is he anyway?" he shouted.

---

[13]A cot.

One of the other Pathans sitting on the lower berth got up and pushed the man's trunk out of the compartment.   39

In that silence only the old woman could be heard. Sitting in the corner, she muttered abstractedly, "Good folk, let them come in. Come, child, come and sit with me. We shall manage to pass the time somehow. Listen to me. Don't be so cruel. . . ."   40

The train began to move.   41

"Oh, the luggage! What shall I do about my luggage!" the man shouted, bewildered and nervous.   42

"*Pitaji*,[14] half our luggage is still outside! What shall we do?" the girl cried out, trembling.   43

"Get down. Let's get down. There is no time," the man shouted nervously, and throwing the big bundle out of the door, he caught hold of the door-handle, and hurried down. He was followed by his trembling daughter and his wife who still clutched at her chest and moaned with pain.   44

"You are bad people!" the old woman shouted. "You have done a very bad thing. All human feeling has died in your hearts. He had his young daughter with him. There is no pity in your hearts. . . ."   45

The train left the deserted platform and steamed ahead. There was an uneasy silence in the compartment. Even the old woman had stopped muttering. No one had the courage to defy the Pathans.   46

Just then the *babu* sitting next to me touched my arm and whispered agitatedly, "Fire! Look! There is a fire out there!"   47

By now the platform had been left far behind and all we could see was clouds of smoke rising from the leaping flames.   48

"A riot has started! That's why the people were running about on the platform. Somewhere a riot has broken out!"   49

The whole city was aflame. When the passengers realized what was happening, they all rushed to the windows to get a better view of the inferno.   50

*

There was an oppressive silence in the compartment. I withdrew my head from the window and looked about. The feeble-looking *babu* had turned deathly pale, the sweat on his forehead was making it glisten in the light. The passengers were looking at each other nervously. A new tension could now be felt between them. Perhaps a similar tension had arisen in each compartment of the train. The Sardarji got up from his seat and came over and sat down next to me. The two Pathans sitting on the lower berth climbed up to the upper berth where their compatriot was sitting. Perhaps the same process was on in other compartments also. All dialogue ceased. The three Pathans, perched side by   51

[14]"Father."

side on the upper berth, looked quietly down. The eyes of each passenger were wide with apprehension.

52   "Which railway station was that?" asked someone.

53   "That was Wazirabad."

54   The answer was followed by another reaction. The Pathans looked perceptibly relieved. But the Hindu and Sikh passengers grew more tense. One of the Pathans took a small snuffbox out of his waistcoat and sniffed it. The other Pathans followed suit. The old woman went on with her beads but now and then a hoarse whisper could be heard coming from her direction.

55   A deserted railway platform faced us when the train stopped at the next station. Not even a bird anywhere. A watercarrier, his water-bag on his back, came over to the train. He crossed the platform and began serving the passengers with water.

56   "Many people killed. Massacre, massacre," he said. It seemed as though in the midst of all that carnage he alone had come out to perform a good deed.

57   As the train moved out again people suddenly began pulling down the shutters over the windows of the carriage. Mingled with the rattle of wheels, the clatter of closing shutters must have been heard over a long distance.

58   The babu suddenly got up from his seat and lay down on the floor. His face was still deathly pale. One of the Pathans perched above the others said mockingly: "What a thing to do! Are you a man or a woman? You are a disgrace to the very name of man!" The others laughed and said something in Pushto. The babu kept silent. All the other passengers too were silent. The air was heavy with fear.

59   "We won't let such an effeminate fellow sit in our compartment," the Pathan said. "Hey babu, why don't you get down at the next station and squeeze into a ladies' compartment?"

60   The babu stammered something in reply, and fell silent. But after a little while he quietly got up from the floor, and dusting his clothes went and sat down on his seat. His whole action was completely puzzling. Perhaps he was afraid that there might soon be stones pelting the train or firing. Perhaps that was the reason why the shutters had been pulled down in all the compartments.

61   Nothing could be said with any sense of certainty. It may be that some passengers, for some reason or the other had pulled down a shutter and that others had followed suit without thinking.

*

62   The journey continued in an atmosphere of uncertainty. Night fell. The passengers sat silent and nervous. Now and then the speed of the train would suddenly slacken, and the passengers would look at one another with wide-open eyes. Sometimes it would come to a halt, and the

silence in the compartment would deepen. Only the Pathans sat as before, unruffled and relaxed. They too, however, had stopped chatting because there was no one to take part in their conversation.

Gradually the Pathans began to doze off while the other passengers 63 sat staring into space. The old woman, her head and face covered in the folds of her shawl, her legs pulled up on the seat, dozed off too. On the upper berth, one of the Pathans awoke, took a rosary out of his pocket and started counting the beads.

Outside, the light of the moon gave the countryside an eerie look of 64 mystery. Sometimes one could see the glow of fire on the horizon. A city burning. Then the train would increase its speed and clatter through expanses of silent country, or slow down to an exhausted pace.

Suddenly the feeble-looking *babu* peeped out of the window and 65 shouted, "We have passed Harbanspura!" There was intense agitation in his voice. The passengers were all taken aback by this outburst and turned round to stare at him.

"Eh, *babu*, why are you shouting?" the Pathan with the rosary said, 66 surprised. "Do you want to get down here? Shall I pull the chain?" He laughed jeeringly. It was obvious that he knew nothing about the significance of Harbanspura. The location and the name of the town conveyed nothing to the Pathan.

The *babu* made no attempt to explain anything. He just continued to 67 shake his head as he looked out of the window.

Silence descended on the passengers of the compartment once 68 again. The engine sounded its whistle and slowed its pace immediately. A little later, a loud clicking sound was heard; perhaps the train had changed tracks. The *babu* peeping out of the window looked towards the direction in which the train was advancing.

"We are nearing some town," he shouted. "It is Amritsar." He 69 yelled at the top of his voice and suddenly stood up and, addressing the Pathan sitting on the upper berth, shouted, "You son of a bitch, come down!"

The *babu* started yelling and swearing at the Pathan, using the 70 foulest language. The Pathan turned round and asked, "What is it, *babu*? Did you say something to me?"

Seeing the *babu* in such an agitated state of mind, the other passen- 71 gers too pricked up their ears.

"Come down, *haramzade*.[15] You dared kick a Hindu woman, you son 72 of a. . . ."

"Hey, control your tongue, *babu*! You swine, don't swear or I'll pull 73 out your tongue!"

"You dare call me a swine!" the *babu* shouted and jumped on to his 74 seat. He was trembling from head to foot.

"No, no, no quarrelling here," the Sardarji intervened, trying to 75

[15]Bastard.

pacify them. "This is not the place to fight. There isn't much of the journey left. Let it pass quietly."

76   "I'll break your head," the *babu* shouted, shaking his fist at the Pathan. "Does the train belong to your father?"

77   "I didn't say anything. Everyone was pushing them out. I also did the same. This fellow here is abusing me. I shall pull out his tongue."

78   The old woman again spoke beseechingly, "Sit quietly, good folk. Have some sense. Think of what you are doing."

79   Her lips were fluttering like those of a spectre, and only indistinct, hoarse whispers could be heard from her mouth.

80   The *babu* was still shouting, "You son of a bitch, did you think you would get away with it?"

*

81   The train steamed into Amritsar railway station. The platform was crowded with people. As soon as the train stopped they rushed towards the compartments.

82   "How are things there? Where did the riot take place?" they asked anxiously.

83   This was the only topic they talked about. Everyone wanted to know where the riot had taken place. There were two or three hawkers, selling *puries*[16] on the platform. The passengers crowded round them. Everyone had suddenly realized that they were very hungry and thirsty. Meanwhile two Pathans appeared outside our compartment and called out for their companions. A conversation in Pushto followed. I turned round to look at the *babu*, but he was nowhere to be seen. Where had he gone? What was he up to? The Pathans rolled up their beddings and left the compartment. Presumably they were going to sit in some other compartment. The division among the passengers that had earlier taken place inside the compartments was now taking place at the level of the entire train.

84   The passengers who had crowded round the hawkers began to disperse to return to their respective compartments. Just then my eyes fell on the *babu*. He was threading his way through the crowd towards the compartment. His face was still very pale and on his forehead a tuft of hair was hanging loose. As he came near I noticed that he was carrying an iron rod in one of his hands. Where had he got that from? As he entered the compartment he furtively hid the rod behind his back, and as he sat down, he quickly pushed it under the seat. He then looked up towards the upper berth and not finding the Pathans there grew agitated and began looking around.

85   "They have run away, the bastards! Sons of bitches!"

86   He got up angrily and began shouting at the passengers: "Why did

16A type of fluffy fried wheat bread.

you let them go? You are all cowards! Impotent people!" But the compartment was crowded with passengers and no one paid any attention to him.

The train lurched forward. The old passengers of the compartment had stuffed themselves with *puries* and had drunk enormous quantities of water; they looked contented because the train was now passing through an area where there was no danger to their life and property. The new entrants into the compartment were chatting noisily. Gradually the train settled down to an even pace and people began to doze. The *babu*, wide awake, kept staring into space. Once or twice he asked me about the direction in which the Pathans had gone. He was still beside himself with anger.

In the rhythmical jolting of the train I too was overpowered by sleep. There wasn't enough room in the compartment to lie down. In the reclining posture in which I sat my head would fall, now to one side, now to the other. Sometimes I would wake up with a start and hear the loud snoring of the Sardarji who had gone back to his old seat and had stretched himself full length on it. All the passengers were lying or reclining in such grotesque postures that one had the impression that the compartment was full of corpses. The *babu* however sat erect, and now and then I found him peeping out of the window.

Every time the train stopped at a wayside station, the noise from the wheels would suddenly cease and a sort of desolate silence descend over everything. Sometimes a sound would be heard as of something falling on the platform or of a passenger getting down from a compartment, and I would sit up with a start.

*

Once when my sleep was broken, I vaguely noticed that the train was moving at a very slow pace. I peeped out of the window. Far away, to the rear of the train, the red lights of a railway signal were visible. Apparently the train had left some railway station but had not yet picked up speed.

Some stray, indistinct sounds fell on my ears. At some distance I noticed a dark shape. My sleep-laden eyes rested on it for some time but I made no effort to make out what it was. Inside the compartment it was dark, the light had been put out some time during the night. Outside the day seemed to be breaking.

I heard another sound, as of someone scraping the door of the compartment. I turned round. The door was closed. The sound was repeated. This time it was more distinct. Someone was knocking at the door with a stick. I looked out of the window. There was a man there; he had climbed up the two steps and was standing on the footboard and knocking away at the door with a stick. He wore drab, colourless clothes, and had a bundle hanging from his shoulder. I also noticed his thick, black beard and the turban on his head. At some distance, a woman was running alongside the train. She was barefooted and had two bundles hanging from her shoulders. Due to the heavy load she was carrying, she was not able to run fast. The man on the footboard was again and again turning towards her and saying in a breathless voice: "Come on, come up, you too come up here!"

93   Once again there was the sound of knocking on the door.

94   "Open the door, please. For the sake of Allah, open the door."

95   The man was breathless.

96   "There is a woman with me. Open the door or we shall miss the train. . . ."

97   Suddenly I saw the *babu* get up from his seat and rush to the door.

98   "Who is it? What do you want? There is no room here. Go away."

99   The man outside again spoke imploringly: "For the sake of Allah, open the door, or we shall miss the train."

100   And putting his hand through the open window, he began fumbling for the latch.

101   "There's no room here. Can't you hear? Get down, I am telling you," the *babu* shouted, and the next instant flung open the door.

102   "Ya Allah!" the man exclaimed, heaving a deep sigh of relief.

103   At that very instant I saw the iron rod flash in the *babu's* hand. He gave a stunning blow to the man's head. I was aghast at seeing this; my legs trembled. It appeared to me as though the blow with the iron rod had no effect on the man, for both his hands were still clutching the door-handle. The bundle hanging from his shoulder had, however, slipped down to his elbow.

104   Then suddenly two or three tiny streams of blood burst forth and flowed down his face from under his turban. In the faint light of the dawn I noticed his open mouth and his glistening teeth. His eyes looked at the *babu*, half-open eyes which were slowly closing, as though they were trying to make out who his assailant was and for what offence had he taken such a revenge. Meanwhile the darkness had lifted further. The man's lips fluttered once again and between them his teeth glistened. He seemed to have smiled. But in reality his lips had only curled in terror.

105   The woman running along the railway track was grumbling and cursing. She did not know what had happened. She was still under the impression that the weight of the bundle was preventing her husband from getting into the compartment, from standing firmly on the footboard. Running alongside the train, despite her own two bundles, she tried to help her husband by stretching her hand to press his foot to the board.

106   Then, abruptly, the man's grip loosened on the door-handle and he fell headlong to the ground, like a slashed tree. No sooner had he fallen than the woman stopped running, as though their journey had come to an end.

The *babu* stood like a statue, near the open door of the compartment. 107
He still held the iron rod in his hand. It looked as though he wanted to
throw it away but did not have the strength to do so. He was not able to
lift his hand, as it were. I was breathing hard; I was afraid and I continued staring at him from the dark corner near the window where I sat.

Then he stirred. Under some inexplicable impulse he took a short 108
step forward and looked towards the rear of the train. The train had
gathered speed. Far away, by the side of the railway track, a dark heap
lay huddled on the ground.

The *babu's* body came into motion. With one jerk of the hand he 109
flung out the rod, turned round and surveyed the compartment. All the
passengers were sleeping. His eyes did not fall on me.

For a little while he stood in the doorway undecided. Then he shut 110
the door. He looked intently at his clothes, examined his hands carefully to see if there was any blood on them, then smelled them. Walking
on tiptoe he came and sat down on his seat next to me.

The day broke. Clear, bright light shone on all sides. No one had 111
pulled the chain to stop the train. The man's body lay miles behind.
Outside, the morning breeze made gentle ripples across the ripening
wheat.

The Sardarji sat up scratching his belly. The *babu*, his hands behind 112
his head, was gazing in front of him. Seeing the *babu* facing him, the
Sardarji giggled and said, "You are a man with guts, I must say. You
don't look strong, but you have real courage. The Pathans got scared
and ran away from here. Had they continued sitting here you would
certainly have smashed the head of one of them. . . ."

The *babu* smiled—a horrifying smile—and stared at the Sardarji's 113
face for a long time.

Questions for Discussion and Writing

1. How does the opening of this story provide important background information through the narrator? In what way is the dramatic situation depicted
   in the story a microcosm of the CONFLICTS among the millions of Hindus,
   Muslims, and Sikhs in India and Pakistan?
2. How does the clash between the Pathan traders and the Hindu *babu* illustrate the larger societal CONFLICT taking place between India and Pakistan?
3. Why is it significant that Sahni tells the story from the perspective of an on-
   looker who himself did nothing to intervene in the events he witnessed?
4. How do the events in the story disprove the ASSUMPTION expressed by those
   in the train compartment that after partition a Muslim could continue to live
   in India?
5. How is the story STRUCTURED to focus on changes in the behavior of the *babu*
   over the course of the journey? How would you characterize these changes?
   By choosing to focus on the transformation of this mild-mannered individual, what is Sahni saying about the human consequences of the highly politicized environment that gripped people at the time?

6. In what way is the episode of the Sikh and his wife trying to get on the train foreshadowed by the earlier episode of the Hindu sweet-vendor and his wife?
7. Discuss present-day developments in India or Pakistan that reflect the conflicts described in this story.
8. Have you ever taken a bus, train, or plane trip where you discovered surprising things about your traveling companions?

Luisa Valenzuela
Writing with the Body

Luisa Valenzuela was born in Buenos Aires, Argentina, in 1938 and grew up in a literary atmosphere. Jorge Luis Borges often visited her home and coauthored stories with her mother, the well-known novelist Luisa Mercedes Levinson. After attending the University of Buenos Aires, Valenzuela began her career writing for magazines and working on the editorial staff of La Nación. *She traveled widely in the United States, Europe, and Latin America and lived for three years in France. Her first book,* Clara: Thirteen Stories and a Novel *(1966), explores themes relating to the subjugation of women in Argentina. Her next publication was a collection of stories,* Strange Things Happen Here *(1976), reflecting the horrors perpetrated by the Argentine military regime in the late 1970s. As civil liberties disappeared with the imposition of censorship, the bombing of publishers' offices, and individuals—known as the "disappeared"—being removed without a trace by the military police, Valenzuela fled Argentina to live in New York City. During her years in the United States, she taught creative writing at Columbia University and has written a novel,* The Lizard's Tale *(1983), and a short story collection,* The Open Door *(1988). She recently returned to Argentina where she is at work on a novel and a play. In her essay, "Writing with the Body," translated by Janet Sternburg and Cynthia Ventura (1991), Valenzuela candidly discloses the challenges she faced in continuing to write under the fascist regime in her country.*

As I leave the ambassador's residence in Buenos Aires early one morning in 1977, at the height of my country's military dictatorship, and walk through the dark, tree-lined streets, I think I am being followed. I have been hearing political testimony from people who sought asylum in the Mexican embassy. Enemies of the de facto government. I think that I can be abducted at any moment. Yet I feel immensely vital, filled with an inexplicable strength that may come from my having reached some kind of understanding. I walk back home through those streets that appear to be empty, and take all the precautions I can to make sure that I'm not being followed, that I'm not being aimed at from some doorway, and I feel alive. I would say happy.

Now I know why.

The answer is simple, now, so many years later. I felt—at this moment, I feel—happy because I was—am—writing with the body. Writing that lingers in the memory of my pores. Writing with the body? Yes. I am aware of having done this throughout my life, at intervals, although it may be almost impossible for me to describe. I'm afraid that it's a matter of a secret action or a mode of being that may be ineffable.

655

4   But I don't believe in the ineffable. The struggle of every person who writes, of every true writer, is primarily against the demon of that which resists being put into words. It is a struggle that spreads like an oil stain. Often, to surrender to the difficulty is to triumph, because the best text can sometimes be the one that allows words to have their own liberty.

5   While writing with the body one also works with words, sometimes completely formed in one's mind, sometimes barely suggested. Writing with the body has nothing to do with "body language." It implies being fully committed to an act which is, in essence, a literary act.

6   At the Mexican embassy that night in 1977, I had just spoken at length with an ex-president who was a political refugee, as well as with a terrorist who had also sought asylum. Both men were sitting at the same table; we were all somewhat drunk and, because of that, more sincere. Then I walked down the streets and as I was walking, I was writing with the body. And not just because of a letter that I was mentally addressing to my friend, Julio Cortázar. I was telling him in the letter—because I knew that I was risking my life and was afraid—that I don't want to play "duck": when I get into the water, I choose to get wet.

7   I was writing with the body, and fear had much to do with this.

8   Fear.

9   I was the kind of child who always poked around wherever there was fear: to see what kind of a creature fear was. I played at being a snake, a snail, or a hippopotamus in a warm African river. Among the animals I avoided was the ostrich. I wanted nothing to do with hiding my head in the sand. I don't know what crazy, morbid impulse made me run through the dark long hallways to the foyer at the entrance of my house, in the middle of the night, when the clock—controlled by witches—struck the hour. Nor do I know what made me go to the terrace where there was supposed to be a two-headed eagle, or behind the house where all kinds of dangers were lurking. I would have preferred hiding my head under the covers. But then who would reassure me? How could my eyes face daylight if they couldn't face shadows in the night? This is why I would go to look, and maybe because I looked came the need, sometime much later, to tell what I had seen.

10   Why?

11   Because of surprise

12   Because of adventure

13   Because of a question, and a gut rejection of any answers.

14   You tend to ask yourself why write with your entire body when you have that simple upper extremity which, thanks to the evolution of the species, has an opposable thumb especially made for holding a pen.

15   You also ask yourself—and this is really overwhelming—why write at all? In my case, I belong, body and soul and mind, to the

so-called Third World where certain needs exist that are not at all literary.

Then other responses (or perhaps they are excuses) come to mind. 16
The need to preserve collective memory is undoubtedly one of them.

There is yet another good excuse: writing as one's destined voca- 17
tion. But I don't know if literature was my destiny. I wanted to be a
physicist, or a mathematician, and, before that, an archaeologist or anthropologist, and for a long time I wanted to be a painter. Because I was
raised in a house full of writers and that wasn't for me. No, ma'am. No
thanks.

Fernando Alegría now describes that moment and place as the 18
Buenos Aires Bloomsbury and this description isn't as crazy as it may
appear. In our old house in the Belgrano section of town, the habitués
were named Borges, Sábato, Mallea. My mother, the writer Luisa
Mercedes Levinson, was the most sociable person in the world when
she wasn't in bed, writing.

When I was a child, I would look from the door of her room and she 19
would be in her bed surrounded by papers, all day until sunset when
the others arrived. I would watch her with admiration and with the
conviction that that life wasn't for me. I wanted a different future.

Disguises I chose for Carnivals: 20

Aviatrix 21

Woman Explorer 22

Robin Hood 23

Those were the masks that belonged to the official Carnival. But 24
other masks at other times also took the shape of exploration and adventure. I would climb onto the roofs of the neighboring houses to try
and reach the end of the block, something which was impossible to do
because of the gardens in between. On those days when I felt really
daring, I would climb up to a stone angel that clung to a column and
that needed my presence, because otherwise no one would ever see it. I
would also sneak into empty lots, or explore an abandoned house
around the block. I was always looking for treasures that changed according to my ambitions: colorful figurines, stamps, coins. There was
an old guard at the abandoned house who would let us in and was our
friend. Until one afternoon, after exploring the basement looking for secret passages—at that time we pretended that the house belonged to
German spies or was it a smuggler's hideout?—the old guard greeted
us with his fly open and all those strange things hanging out. I ran
away with my best friend in tow. I never went back, but years, thousands of years later, I wondered if that was the treasure for which we
searched.

Now I know: with that small adventure around the block and with 25
those big stories I made up, I began the slow learning process of writing
with the body

26   Because

27   pores or ink, it is the same thing

28   the same stakes.

29   Clarice Lispector knew it and in her books focused on that love-hate, that happiness-misfortune we call literature. Her novels appear to be about love and the search for knowledge but they are also different ways of speaking about writing.

30   One's happiness is greatest when the story flows like a stream of clear water, even if the worst abominations are being narrated. It is only during the reading of those passages that the fear of what has flowed from one's own pen takes over.

31   There is another misfortune in writing and it is perhaps the most painful. It is inscribed during times of silence, when nothing is written with the body or mind or hand. Periods of drought which seem to be of nonexistence.

32   This is why I say sometimes that writing is a full-time curse.

33   I also say that, in its best moments, writing a novel is a euphoric feeling, like being in love.

34   And to think that my mother, the writer, is to blame for all of this. Not because of the example she set, nor because of my emulation of her, which I acknowledge. She is to blame because when I was in the sixth grade in elementary school, my teacher asked her to help me with my compositions. "Your daughter is so bright in science," my teacher told her, "it's a shame that her grade should go down because she can't write." So my mother, overzealous in trying to help me, wrote a composition as she thought a tender eleven-year-old would.

35   I didn't think it was a very dignified text. From that moment on, I decided to assume the responsibility of my own writings. And that's how things are.

36   Because writing is the path that leads to the unknown. The way back is made of reflection, trying to come to terms with yourself and with that which has been produced. I strongly believe in the fluctuation from intuition to understanding. Placing ourselves right there

37   at the border

38   between two currents

39   at the center of the whirlpool,

40   the eye of the tornado?

41   "You are too intelligent to be beautiful" is what many of us have been told at some time by a man we've loved. Or, supposing literature is your profession: "You are too intelligent to be a good writer." Contrasting, of course, that ugly, masculine thing which is intelligence with female intuition. You wouldn't tell that to Susan Sontag is what someone with clearer ideas would reply. But those marks were made on young and tender skin, and from that moment on, one will always have a feeling of inadequacy.

Incapable, inactive, unproductive. I think all of us, from the time 42 we're very young, feel at some time what could be called a nostalgia for imprisonment: the crazy, romantic fantasy that a prisoner has all the time to herself, to write. Only later do we realize that writing is an exercise of liberty.

From exigencies and from temptations, the stuff of literature is 43 made. And from reflection, also. From everything. There is no unworthy material, although a great deal must be discarded.

When I was seventeen years old, I started working in journalism. 44 For many years it was the perfect combination, one that allowed me to be part of all the disciplines, to go everywhere, and, at the same time, to write. A gift of ubiquity wrapped in words. I had the tremendous luck, almost a miracle, of having a boss who was a true teacher. Ambrosio Vencino was not a journalist; he was a displaced man of letters. To him I owe my obsessive precision with language.

I owe my travels to myself, to my need to touch the world with my 45 own hands. I never paid attention to the premise that you don't have to leave your own bedroom to know the world. I traveled, I continue traveling, and I sometimes think that in all those displacements, parts of my self are being left behind.

Rodolfo Walsh, the Argentine writer and activist, once told me 46 when I was complaining about how much I went from one place to the next and how little I wrote: "Your writing is also made from your travels."

Many years later, my writing was also made from another of 47 Rodolfo Walsh's lessons to which I didn't pay much attention at the time. One day he showed me the difficult physical exercises that Cuban guerrillas practiced then in the Sierra Maestra. That physical guerrilla wisdom seemed to stand me in good stead in 1975 and 1976, when I sat in the cafes of Buenos Aires, devastated by state terrorism, and wrote stories that were, in a way, guerrilla exercises.

I put my body where my words are. 48

The physical loss hasn't been as great for me as it has been for oth- 49 ers. I haven't been tortured, beaten, or persecuted. Knock on wood. I've been spared, perhaps because my statements aren't frontal; they are visions from the corner of my eye, oblique. I think we must continue writing about the horrors so that memory isn't lost and history won't repeat itself.

As a teenager, I was a voracious reader and I bragged about it but 50 there were two books that I read in secret: *Freud* by Emil Ludwig and *The Devil in the Flesh* (*Le Diable au Corps*) by Raymond Radiguet. With these two books I may not have gone very far in terms of pornographic material but it's clear that my libido was already acting up.

That writing with the body known as the act of love happened later, 51 as it should have, and turned out quite well, with great style, but with more of an inclination toward the short story than the novel.

52   I love the short story for being round, suggestive, insinuating, microcosmic. The story has both the inconvenience and the fascination of new beginnings.

53   The novel, on the other hand, requires more concentration, more time, a state of grace. I love it because of the joy in opening new paths as words progress.

54   Paths to the unknown, the only interesting ones.

55   What I already know bores me, makes me repetitive. This is why whenever I have had a good plot that was clearly thought out, I was forced to give it up or at least to compress it, trying to squeeze out the juice that wasn't visible at first sight.

56   If I had to write my creed, I would first mention humor:

57   I believe in having a sense of humor at all costs

58   I believe in sharp, black humor

59   I believe in the absurd

60   in the grotesque

61   in everything which allows us to move beyond our limited thinking, beyond self-censorship and the censorship by others, which tends to be much more lethal. Taking a step to one side to observe the action as it is happening. A necessary step so that the vision of political reality is not contaminated by dogmas or messages.

62   I have nothing to say.

63   With luck, something will be said through me, despite myself, and I might not even realize it.

64   It is said that women's literature is made of questions.

65   I say that women's literature consequently is much more realistic.

66   Questions, uncertainties, searches, contradictions.

67   Everything is fused, and sometimes confused, and implicates us. The true act of writing with the body implies being fully involved. I am my own bet; I play myself, as though lying on the roulette table, calling out "All or nothing!"

68   What is interesting about the literary wager is that we do wager everything, but we don't know against what.

69   They say that women's literature is made of fragments.

70   I repeat that it is a matter of realism.

71   It is made of rips, shreds of your own skin which adhere to the paper but are not always read or even legible. Shreds that can be of laughter, of sheer delight.

72   Sometimes while writing, I have to get up to dance, to celebrate the flow of energy transforming itself into words. Sometimes the energy becomes words that are not printed, not even with the delicate line of a fountain pen, which is the most voluptuous in the act of writing. You must always celebrate when—whether in a cafe or subway—a happy combination of words, a fortuitous allusion, elicits associations that unwind the mental thread of writing without a mark. The mark comes

next. And I will do my best to retain the freshness of that first moment of awe and transformation.

Questions for Discussion and Writing

1. For Valenzuela, how does the way of writing she refers to as "writing with the body" allow her to recover an authenticity and self-awareness she first experienced as a child? How do the conditions in which she now finds herself strengthen the need to "write with the body"? In your view, what does she mean by this phrase?

2. Of all the people and experiences she mentions in explaining the forces that shaped her choice of vocation as a writer, which do you see as the most influential?

3. Where in this essay is it apparent that Valenzuela is less interested in providing an account of objective truth than in trying to evolve a personal viewpoint that takes into account political realities and her own values? What means does she use to try to influence readers to value "writing with the body" as highly as she does?

4. To what extent does Valenzuela's description of the pleasures and terrors of writing duplicate your own experiences?

5. Imagine you are a successful author who has written books of all kinds, including nonfiction—memoirs, travel, sports, cooking—as well as poetry and fiction, both short stories and novels—romance, horror, science fiction, mysteries, and westerns. What are the titles of the books that you have written?

6. Try to put yourself into a state of intense awareness of yourself and the surroundings, sensations, and sounds in your immediate environment that Valenzuela describes as "writing with the body" and describe this moment. Organize your description by the way your sensations move from one sense to another.

7. Describe a place that always produces a unique, identifiable feeling. It might be your church, your grandparent's house, or your favorite store.

Luisa Valenzuela

The Censors

*Luisa Valenzuela's short story, "The Censors," translated by David Unger,
first appeared in* The Open Door *(1988), a collection of stories whose title she
chose because "The Open Door is the name of the most traditional, least threatening lunatic asylum in Argentina." In this ironic fable, Valenzuela explores
how a treacherous political atmosphere and the corrupting lure of power can se-
duce even the most idealistic individual into collusion with the state. (For further information on Luisa Valenzuela, see the biographical sketch for "Writing
with the Body" on page 655.)*

1   Poor Juan! One day they caught him with his guard down before he
could even realize that what he had taken as a stroke of luck was really
one of fate's dirty tricks. These things happen the minute you're careless, as one often is. Juancito let happiness—a feeling you can't trust
—get the better of him when he received from a confidential source
Mariana's new address in Paris and knew that she hadn't forgotten
him. Without thinking twice, he sat down at his table and wrote her a
letter. *The* letter that now keeps his mind off his job during the day and
won't let him sleep at night (what had he scrawled, what had he put on
that sheet of paper he sent to Mariana?).

2   Juan knows there won't be a problem with the letter's contents, that
it's irreproachable, harmless. But what about the rest? He knows that
they examine, sniff, feel, and read between the lines of each and every
letter, and check its tiniest comma and most accidental stain. He knows
that all letters pass from hand to hand and go through all sorts of tests
in the huge censorship offices and that, in the end, very few continue
on their way. Usually it takes months, even years, if there aren't any
snags; all this time the freedom, maybe even the life, of both sender and
receiver is in jeopardy. And that's why Juan's so troubled: thinking that
something might happen to Mariana because of his letters. Of all people, Mariana, who must finally feel safe there where she always dreamt
she'd live. But he knows that the *Censor's Secret Command* operates all
over the world and cashes in on the discount in air fares; there's nothing to stop them from going as far as that hidden Paris neighborhood,
kidnapping Mariana, and returning to their cozy homes, certain of having fulfilled their noble mission.

3   Well, you've got to beat them to the punch, do what everyone tries
to do: sabotage the machinery, throw sand in its gears, get to the bottom of the problem so as to stop it.

4   This was Juan's sound plan when he, like many others, applied for a

662

censor's job—not because he had a calling or needed a job: no, he applied simply to intercept his own letter, a consoling albeit unoriginal idea. He was hired immediately, for each day more and more censors are needed and no one would bother to check on his references.

Ulterior motives couldn't be overlooked by the *Censorship Division*, but they needn't be too strict with those who applied. They knew how hard it would be for the poor guys to find the letter they wanted and even if they did, what's a letter or two when the new censor would snap up so many others? That's how Juan managed to join the *Post Office's Censorship Division*, with a certain goal in mind.

The building had a festive air on the outside that contrasted with its inner staidness. Little by little, Juan was absorbed by his job, and he felt at peace since he was doing everything he could to get his letter for Mariana. He didn't even worry when, in his first month, he was sent to *Section K* where envelopes are very carefully screened for explosives.

It's true that on the third day, a fellow worker had his right hand blown off by a letter, but the division chief claimed it was sheer negligence on the victim's part. Juan and the other employees were allowed to go back to their work, though feeling less secure. After work, one of them tried to organize a strike to demand higher wages for unhealthy work, but Juan didn't join in; after thinking it over, he reported the man to his superiors and thus got promoted.

You don't form a habit by doing something once, he told himself as he left his boss's office. And when he was transferred to *Section J*, where letters are carefully checked for poison dust, he felt he had climbed a rung in the ladder.

By working hard, he quickly reached *Section E* where the job became more interesting, for he could now read and analyze the letters' contents. Here he could even hope to get hold of his letter, which, judging by the time that had elapsed, had gone through the other sections and was probably floating around in this one.

Soon his work became so absorbing that his noble mission blurred in his mind. Day after day he crossed out whole paragraphs in red ink, pitilessly chucking many letters into the censored basket. These were horrible days when he was shocked by the subtle and conniving ways employed by people to pass on subversive messages; his instincts were so sharp that he found behind a simple "the weather's unsettled" or "prices continue to soar" the wavering hand of someone secretly scheming to overthrow the Government.

His zeal brought him swift promotion. We don't know if this made him happy. Very few letters reached him in *Section B*—only a handful passed the other hurdles—so he read them over and over again, passed them under a magnifying glass, searched for microprint with an electronic microscope, and tuned his sense of smell so that he was beat by the time he made it home. He'd barely manage to warm up his soup, eat some fruit, and fall into bed, satisfied with having done his duty.

Only his darling mother worried, but she couldn't get him back on the right track. She'd say, though it wasn't always true: Lola called, she's at the bar with the girls, they miss you, they're waiting for you. Or else she'd leave a bottle of red wine on the table. But Juan wouldn't overdo it: any distraction could make him lose his edge and the perfect censor had to be alert, keen, attentive, and sharp to nab cheats. He had a truly patriotic task, both self-denying and uplifting.

12   His basket for censored letters became the best fed as well as the most cunning basket in the whole *Censorship Division*. He was about to congratulate himself for having finally discovered his true mission, when his letter to Mariana reached his hands. Naturally, he censored it without regret. And just as naturally, he couldn't stop them from executing him the following morning, another victim of his devotion to his work.

Questions for Discussion and Writing

1. What is Juan's initial motivation for applying for the job of censor?
2. How does Juan's growing skill and increasing commitment at his new task introduce an element of potential CONFLICT in the story?
3. What details suggest that Juan becomes adept at discerning the censorable contents in the letters of others and has grown zealously committed to his new vocation?
4. In what way does Juan's mother represent the values of the normal life that he has cast aside?
5. How does the choice of what to do with his own letter (the very reason that he became a censor) bring the CONFLICT to a CRISIS?
6. Discuss the issue Valenzuela dramatizes in this story. What can you infer about the political environment in Argentina when she wrote this story?
7. Have you or anyone you know "bought into" a system without admitting that this was in fact the case? Describe what happened.
8. Draft a set of rules and regulations that would have been posted in the official government office telling censors what to look for. Your description of these rules might satirize the mindset of the bureaucracy.

Panos Ioannides

Gregory

Panos Ioannides was born in Cyprus in 1935 and was educated in Cyprus, the United States, and Canada. He has been the head of television programs at Cyprus Broadcasting Corporation and is the author of many plays that have been staged or telecast internationally; he has also written novels, short stories, and radio scripts. Ioannides has won many awards for his prose works, such as his novel Census *(1968) and his short story collections* Epics of Cyprus *(1971) and* The Unseen View *(1973). "Gregory" was written in 1963 and first appeared in* The Charioteer, *a Review of Modern Greek Literature (1965). The English translation is by Marion Byron Raizis and Catherine Raizis. This compelling story is based on a true incident that took place during the Cypriot liberation struggle against the British in the late 1950s. Ioannides takes the unusual approach of letting the reader experience the torments of a soldier ordered to shoot a prisoner, Gregory, who had saved his life and was his friend.*

My hand was sweating as I held the pistol. The curve of the trigger was biting against my finger. 1

Facing me, Gregory trembled. 2

His whole being was beseeching me, "Don't!" 3

Only his mouth did not make a sound. His lips were squeezed tight. If it had been me, I would have screamed, shouted, cursed. 4

The soldiers were watching . . . 5

The day before, during a brief meeting, they had each given their opinions: "It's tough luck, but it has to be done. We've got no choice." 6

The order from Headquarters was clear: "As soon as Lieutenant Rafel's execution is announced, the hostage Gregory is to be shot and his body must be hanged from a telegraph pole in the main street as an exemplary punishment." 7

It was not the first time that I had to execute a hostage in this war. I had acquired experience, thanks to Headquarters which had kept entrusting me with these delicate assignments. Gregory's case was precisely the sixth. 8

The first time, I remember, I vomited. The second time I got sick and had a headache for days. The third time I drank a bottle of rum. The fourth, just two glasses of beer. The fifth time I joked about it, "This little guy, with the big pop-eyes, won't be much of a ghost!" 9

But why, dammit, when the day came did I have to start thinking that I'm not so tough, after all? The thought had come at exactly the wrong time and spoiled all my disposition to do my duty. 10

You see, this Gregory was such a miserable little creature, such a puny thing, such a nobody, damn him. 11

12   That very morning, although he had heard over the loudspeakers that Rafel had been executed, he believed that we would spare his life because we had been eating together so long.

13   "Those who eat from the same mess tins and drink from the same water canteen," he said, "remain good friends no matter what."

14   And a lot more of the same sort of nonsense.

15   He was a silly fool—we had smelled that out the very first day Headquarters gave him to us. The sentry guarding him had got dead drunk and had dozed off. The rest of us with exit permits had gone from the barracks. When we came back, there was Gregory sitting by the sleeping sentry and thumbing through a magazine.

16   "Why didn't you run away, Gregory?" we asked, laughing at him, several days later.

17   And he answered, "Where would I go in this freezing weather? I'm O.K. here."

18   So we started teasing him.

19   "You're dead right. The accommodations here are splendid . . ."

20   "It's not bad here," he replied. "The barracks where I used to be are like a sieve. The wind blows in from every side . . ."

21   We asked him about his girl. He smiled.

22   "Maria is a wonderful person," he told us. "Before I met her she was engaged to a no-good fellow, a pig. He gave her up for another girl. Then nobody in the village wanted to marry Maria. I didn't miss my chance. So what if she is second-hand. Nonsense. Peasant ideas, my friend. She's beautiful and good-hearted. What more could I want? And didn't she load me with watermelons and cucumbers every time I passed by her vegetable garden? Well, one day I stole some cucumbers and melons and watermelons and I took them to her. 'Maria,' I said, 'from now on I'm going to take care of you.' She started crying and then me, too. But ever since that day she has given me lots of trouble—jealousy. She wouldn't let me go even to my mother's. Until the day I was recruited, she wouldn't let me go far from her apron strings. But that was just what I wanted . . ."

23   He used to tell this story over and over, always with the same words, the same commonplace gestures. At the end he would have a good laugh and start gulping from his water jug.

24   His tongue was always wagging! When he started talking, nothing could stop him. We used to listen and nod our heads, not saying a word. But sometimes, as he was telling us about his mother and family problems, we couldn't help wondering, "Eh, well, these people have the same headaches in their country as we've got."

25   Strange, isn't it!

26   Except for his talking too much, Gregory wasn't a bad fellow. He was a marvelous cook. Once he made us some apple tarts, so delicious we licked the platter clean. And he could sew, too. He used to sew on

all our buttons, patch our clothes, darn our socks, iron our ties, wash our clothes . . .

How the devil could you kill such a friend? 27

Even though his name was Gregory and some people on his side 28 had killed one of ours, even though we had left wives and children to go to war against him and his kind—but how can I explain? He was our friend. He actually liked us! A few days before, hadn't he killed with his own bare hands a scorpion that was climbing up my leg? He could have let it send me to hell!

"Thanks, Gregory!" I said then, "Thank God who made you . . ." 29

When the order came, it was like a thunderbolt. Gregory was to be 30 shot, it said, and hanged from a telegraph pole as an exemplary punishment.

We got together inside the barracks. We sent Gregory to wash some 31 underwear for us.

"It ain't right." 32

"What is right?" 33

"Our duty!" 34

"Shit!" 35

"If you dare, don't do it! They'll drag you to court-martial and then 36 bang-bang . . ."

Well, of course. The right thing is to save your skin. That's only logi- 37 cal. It's either your skin or his. His, of course, even if it was Gregory, the fellow you've been sharing the same plate with, eating with your fingers, and who was washing your clothes that very minute.

What could I do? That's war. We had seen worse things. 38

So we set the hour. 39

We didn't tell him anything when he came back from the washing. 40 He slept peacefully. He snored for the last time. In the morning, he heard the news over the loudspeaker and he saw that we looked gloomy and he began to suspect that something was up. He tried talking to us, but he got no answers and then he stopped talking.

He just stood there and looked at us, stunned and lost . . . 41

Now, I'll squeeze the trigger. A tiny bullet will rip through his chest. Maybe 42 *I'll lose my sleep tonight but in the morning I'll wake up alive.*

Gregory seems to guess my thoughts. He puts out his hand and asks, 43 *"You're kidding, friend! Aren't you kidding?"*

What a jackass! Doesn't he deserve to be cut to pieces? What a thing to ask 44 *at such a time. Your heart is about to burst and he's asking if you're kidding. How can a body be kidding about such a thing? Idiot! This is no time for jokes. And you, if you're such a fine friend, why don't you make things easier for us? Help us kill you with fewer qualms? If you would get angry—curse our Virgin, our God—if you'd try to escape it would be much easier for us and for you.*

45   *So it is now.*

46   *Now, Mr. Gregory, you are going to pay for your stupidities wholesale. Because you didn't escape the day the sentry fell asleep; because you didn't escape yesterday when we sent you all alone to the laundry—we did it on purpose, you idiot! Why didn't you let me die from the sting of the scorpion?*

47   *So now don't complain. It's all your fault, nitwit.*

48   *Eh? What's happening to him now?*

49   *Gregory is crying. Tears flood his eyes and trickle down over his clean-shaven cheeks. He is turning his face and pressing his forehead against the wall. His back is shaking as he sobs. His hands cling, rigid and helpless, to the wall.*

50   *Now is my best chance, now that he knows there is no other solution and turns his face from us.*

51   *I squeeze the trigger.*

52   *Gregory jerks. His back stops shaking up and down.*

53   *I think I've finished him! How easy it is . . . But suddenly he starts crying out loud, his hands claw at the wall and try to pull it down. He screams, "No, no . . ."*

54   *I turn to the others. I expect them to nod, "That's enough."*

55   *They nod, "What are you waiting for?"*

56   *I squeeze the trigger again.*

57   *The bullet smashes into his neck. A thick spray of blood spurts out.*

58   *Gregory turns. His eyes are all red. He lunges at me and starts punching me with his fists.*

59   *"I hate you, hate you . . ." he screams.*

60   I emptied the barrel. He fell and grabbed my leg as if he wanted to hold on.

61   He died with a terrible spasm. His mouth was full of blood and so were my boots and socks.

62   We stood quietly, looking at him.

63   When we came to, we stooped and picked him up. His hands were frozen and wouldn't let my legs go.

64   I still have their imprints, red and deep, as if made by a hot knife.

65   "We will hang him tonight," the men said.

66   "Tonight or now?" they said.

67   I turned and looked at them one by one.

68   "Is that what you all want?" I asked.

69   They gave me no answer.

70   "Dig a grave," I said.

71   Headquarters did not ask for a report the next day or the day after. The top brass were sure that we had obeyed them and had left him swinging from a pole.

They didn't care to know what happened to that Gregory, alive or 72
dead.

Questions for Discussion and Writing

1. Much of the story's ACTION takes place during the few seconds when the narrator must decide whether to pull the trigger. What function do FLASHBACKS serve in generating and sustaining SUSPENSE? Why do you think Ioannides chooses to tell the story from the executioner's POINT OF VIEW rather than from Gregory's?

2. How is the STRUCTURE of the story designed to bring the psychological CONFLICT experienced by the narrator to the point of crisis? Why does the narrator's past intensify his CONFLICT?

3. What details illustrate that Gregory has become a friend to the narrator and other soldiers rather than just a prisoner? In what way does Gregory embody the qualities of humanity, decency, and domestic life that the soldiers were forced to leave behind? Why is his innocence a source of both admiration and irritation?

4. How does Gregory's decision to marry Maria suggest the kind of person he is and answer the question of why he doesn't try to escape when he is told he is going to be killed?

5. How does the question "Why didn't you let me die from the sting of the scorpion?" reveal the anguish the narrator feels as he is faced with the order to kill his friend Gregory?

6. At the end, how does the narrator's order not to hang Gregory's body reveal his distress after shooting Gregory? Why is it IRONIC that the higher-ups never inquire whether their orders have been carried out? What does this imply and why does it make the narrator feel even worse?

7. If you were in the narrator's shoes, what would you have done? Do you think you would have had to make yourself hate Gregory, as the narrator did, in order to be able to kill him?

Ernesto Cardenal

The Swede

Ernesto Cardenal was born in 1925 in Granada, Nicaragua. He attended the University of Mexico and Columbia University. After his conversion to Christianity in 1956, he studied to become a priest in Gethsemani, Kentucky, with Thomas Merton, the scholar, poet, and Trappist monk. The poetry Cardenal wrote during this period expresses feelings of love, social criticism, political passion, and the quest for a transcendent spiritual life, themes that continue throughout his life, as in The Gospel in Solentinamo *(1976). Cardenal is well known in the United States as a spokesman for justice and self-determination for Latin America. His poetry frequently touches on events in the history of Nicaragua, as in the volume* With Walker in Nicaragua and Other Early Poems, 1949–1954 *(1985). He was ordained a Roman Catholic priest in 1965 and became a prominent voice of "liberation theology" in Central America, a stance that brought him into conflict in the 1980s with Pope John Paul II. He served as the Minister of Culture in Nicaragua in the government of Daniel Ortega, following the overthrow of Somoza in 1979. In addition to many collections of poetry, including, most recently,* From Nicaragua With Love: Poems 1979–1986 *(1986), Cardenal's writing includes short stories and religious meditations. "The Swede," translated by John Lyons (1992), depicts an unusual triangle involving a Swede inexplicably imprisoned while traveling in Central America, the dictatorial president of the country, and a beautiful girl in Sweden with whom both men are in love.*

1   I'm Swedish. And I begin by declaring that I am Swedish because this simple fact is the cause of all the strange things that have happened to me (which some will judge to be beyond belief) which I now propose to relate. So, as I was saying, I'm Swedish, and many years ago, I came, for a short visit, to this small and wretched Central American republic—where I still find myself—in search of an example of a curious species of the *Iguanidae* family not catalogued by my fellow countryman, Linnaeus, and which I consider to be a descendant of the dinosaur (although in the scientific community its existence is still the subject of controversy).

2   I had the ill-fortune that hardly had I crossed the border when I was arrested. Why I was arrested don't expect me to explain; for I've never managed to explain it to myself satisfactorily, however much I've tried to explain it to myself over the years, and there's no one in the world who can explain it. It's true that the country was in the throes of a revolution at the time and my Nordic appearance may have aroused suspicions, in addition to which I had committed the imprudence of coming to this country without knowing the language. You will say to me that

670

none of these reasons sufficiently justifies being arrested; but I've already said that there was no satisfactory reason. Quite simply: I was arrested.

Trying to make them understand, in an unintelligible language, that I was Swedish did not help me in the least. My firm conviction that my country's representative would arrive to rescue me later vanished, when I discovered that this representative not only could not communicate with me, since he knew no Swedish and had never had the slightest relationship with my country, but also that he was a deaf old man and in poor health, and also he himself, frequently, was arrested. 3

In prison I met a great number of important people in the republic, who were also accustomed to being frequently arrested: ex-presidents, senators, army officers, respectable ladies and bishops, and even including on one occasion the chief of police himself. The arrival of these people, which occurred generally in large groups, upset the prison routine with all sorts of visitors, messages, food parcels, bribes to jailers, riots, and even on occasions escapes. These great floods of prisoners around the time of conspiracies always modified the situation of those of us who enjoyed, so to speak, a more permanent character in the prison, and from a single—relatively comfortable—cell you could be transferred to an immense cell crammed with people and where scarcely another would fit, or to an individual hole in which a person could scarcely fit, or even to the torture chamber—if the rest of the prison being full—this place was not in use. 4

But I'm not being accurate when I say the prison, since it wasn't one prison but many, and many times we were moved from one to another for no apparent reason: I believe I've been through almost all of them. Although a prominent member of the opposition who was in prison— and previously he'd been a prominent figure in the Government—once told me that there was one single prison; that the entire country was a prison, and that some were in "the prison" within that prison, others were under house arrest, but everyone was imprisoned in the country. 5

In these prisons one frequently comes across old trusted prisoners, who are serving a very long sentence for some crime, turned jailers, as also former jailers turned prisoners; and just as important men in the Government are sometimes arrested, equally there have been important Opposition prisoners who afterwards have gone on to occupy high Government positions (I can testify to one, who was held in this prison and who, so other prison companions have told me, even participated in an assassination attempt, yet is presently Minister of State), but the confusion grows even further with the secret agents and the prison spies, about whom one cannot be certain whether they are false Government spies in prison for having dealings with the Opposition or false prisoners put in prison by the Government to spy on the Opposition. 6

With regard to the Opposition, I should relate here what one of the 7 most influential members of the Opposition once told me in confidence: "The Opposition—he told me—in reality does not exist; it's a fiction maintained by the Government, just as the Government Party likewise is another fiction. It ceased to exist long ago, but it suits us too to maintain this fiction of Opposition, although we are sometimes arrested on account of it." And whether this is true or not, I can't be sure. But a much more extraordinary—and more incredible—revelation was that made to me, in the greatest of secrecy, by one of the President's closest friends who—converted now into one of his most bitter enemies—found himself in prison. "The President—he told me—doesn't exist! He's a double! He ceased to exist a long time ago!" According to him, the President had had a double whom he used to foil attempts on his life, which frequently were false and hatched by the President himself, in order to see which of his friends fell into the trap with a view to getting rid of them (although this game also proved dangerous to him, as well as complicated, because it lent itself to the possibility that real conspirators might devise a false plot with his assistance with the intention of really getting rid of him) and it seems to be the case that one day either some plan of the President's failed or some plot of his enemies had succeeded (perhaps with the complicity of the double himself—whether out of personal ambition to replace the President or self-defence seeing his life threatened in the cruel role of double—although my informant didn't know the details or didn't wish to tell me them) but the fact had been that the double assumed the President's place; and whether all this is pure invention, or lies, or the truth, or a joke, or the ravings of a mind unbalanced by confinement, I cannot say, neither did I discover whether my informant's friendship, or his betrayal, related to the first President or to his supposed double, or both.

8   As you will appreciate, I had by now come to grips with the language, and acquired, in prison, a perfect knowledge of the entire country, and had had close dealings with the most influential figures of the Opposition (and even the Government as I've mentioned) who in prison confided in me matters which outside are not confided to a wife, nor even to fellow conspirators. It may be said then that the only important person in the country with whom I was not acquainted was the President. And here's where the most extraordinary part of my story begins: not only did I get to know the President, but furthermore I got to know him in a much more intimate way than any other individual from the Opposition or from the Government with whom to date I had had dealings. But let's not run ahead of the events.

9   At the beginning, when I was arrested, I repeated tirelessly that I was Swedish, but finally I stopped doing so, convinced that just as to me it was absurd that they should imprison me for being Swedish, to them it was equally absurd to release me for the simple reason of being Swedish. I'd been in this situation which I have related for many years, and lost hope that at the end of the President's term of office I'd see

myself released (because he had re-elected himself), when some Government agents called at the prison to ask me—much to my astonishment—whether I was Swedish. Not without stammering for a moment, owing to the unexpectedness of the question and the interest which they displayed in asking it, I told them I was, and immediately they made me bathe, they shaved me and cut my hair (things they'd never done) and gave me a dress suit to wear. At first I thought that relations with my country had improved remarkably, although on the other hand so many preparations and ceremony—especially the dress suit—induced a deep fear in me, thinking that perhaps they were taking me to be killed. To some extent this fear faded when I discovered that they were taking me to the President.

Immediately I arrived all the doors were thrown open until I entered the office of the President, who appeared to be waiting for me. The moment he saw me he greeted me politely: "Hello. How's it going?" Although I believe his question was rather insincere. Before I could respond he asked me whether I was Swedish. With a crisp "yes" I answered him, and again he asked: "Then you can speak Swedish?" I told him that this was so too, and I could see my reply pleased him. He then handed me a letter written in delicate female script in the language of my country, ordering me to translate it. (I later learned that when this letter arrived they had scoured the country high and low, to no avail, for someone who could read it, until somebody, fortunately, recalled having heard a prisoner cry out that he was Swedish.) The letter was from a girl who requested the President to send her a few of those beautiful gold coins which, so she'd heard, were in circulation here, expressing at the same time her admiration for the President of this exotic country, to whom she was also sending her picture: the photograph of the most beautiful girl that I have ever seen in my life!

After listening to my translation, the President, delighted by the letter and above all the girl's picture, dictated a reply to me not without romantic insinuations, in which he gladly acceded to the sending of the gold coins, a generous amount, while explaining nevertheless that this was expressly forbidden by the Law. I faithfully translated his thoughts into the Swedish language, firmly convinced that my unexpected usefulness might earn me not only my freedom, but perhaps even a modest position, or at least official backing for the tracking down of the desired *Iguanidae*. But as a measure of prudence for whatever might happen, I took the precaution of adding a few lines to the letter the President dictated to me, explaining my situation and imploring my beautiful compatriot to take steps to secure my freedom.

I was soon congratulating myself for this initiative, because the moment my work was over, to my great disappointment I was taken back to the prison, where the dress suit was removed, restoring me to my previous miserable state. Nonetheless the days from then on were now full of hope: the image of my beautiful saviour never left my mind, and not long after, a fresh bath and shave and the reappearance of the dress suit announced to me that the desired reply had arrived.

13 And so it proved to be. Just as I had foreseen, this letter referred almost exclusively to myself, imploring the President to release me, but (and this too I had already foreseen) I couldn't read that letter to the President, because, either he'd think that I was making it all up, or he would discover that I had previously inserted words of my own into his letter, punishing my boldness perhaps to the point of death.

14 So I found myself obliged to skip all references to my freedom, replacing them sadly with words of adulation for the President. But on the other hand in the chivalrous reply which he dictated to me, I had the opportunity to give a more detailed account of my story, dismissing at the same time the romantic idea she had of the President and revealing to her what in truth he was like.

15 From then on the beautiful girl began to write frequently, showing an ever-increasing interest in my affair, so that shaves and baths and wearing of the dress suit increased, as at the same time did my hopes of freedom.

16 I gradually acquired ever more intimacy with her through the replies which the President dictated to me, which I took advantage of in order to unburden my own feelings. I must confess that during the long and monotonous intervals that occurred between one letter and another, the thought of my freedom (linked to the thought of the wonderful girl who might obtain it for me) never left my mind, and both thoughts frequently coalesced into a single thought, to the point that I no longer knew whether it was on account of my desire for freedom that I thought of her, or whether on account of desire for her that I thought of my freedom (she and my freedom were the same thing for me, as I told her so many times while the President was dictating). To put it more clearly: I'd fallen in love. It will appear improbable to those who read this narrative (being on the outside) that someone can fall in love, within the confines of a prison, with a woman far away, known to him only by her photograph. But I can assure you that I fell in love in this prison and with an intensity that those who are free cannot even imagine. Yet, to my misfortune, the President, that most cruel, misanthropic, solitary, extravagant man, had also fallen in love, or pretended to have done so, and, what was worse, I had been the instigator and promoter of that love, making him believe, with the aim of sustaining the correspondence, that the letters were for him.

17 In my long and anxious periods of confinement, I passed the time thoroughly preparing the next letter that I would read to the President, which was indispensable to me, since he never permitted me to read it through first to myself before proceeding to translate it, insisting rather that I should translate at the same time as I was reading, and furthermore (whether out of distrust of me or for the pleasure that it afforded him) he made me read the same letter three and even four times on the

trot. And equally I prepared the fresh reply that I would write, polishing each sentence and striving to put into them all the poetry and traditional beauty of the Swedish language and even including from time to time my own brief compositions in verse.

In order to prolong my letters even further I made up for the President all sorts of questions about the history, customs and the political situation in the country, to which he always responded with great gusto. Thus, he then dictated to me long epistles, speaking of his Government and the Opposition and the affairs of State and consulting and asking his girlfriend's advice. So it transpired that, from a prison, I was giving advice to the Government and held in my hands the destiny of the country, without anyone, not even the President himself, being aware of this, and I secured the return of those in exile. I commuted sentences and set many of my prison companions free, although none of them was able to thank me for it. Yet the only person on whose behalf I could not intercede was myself. 18

One of the greatest pleasures of those days of dictation was to be able to look again at her picture, which the President brought out of hiding, so he said "to inspire himself." I asked her to send us more pictures and she did so, although as you will appreciate, they all ended up in the President's hands. My revenge consisted in the presents he sent her, which were numerous and of considerable value, which she received more as though they came from me. 19

Yet at the same time as my love had been growing so too had a dread within me, and it was that huge collection of letters which were piling up on the President's desk, and in which finally, we did not even mention him except from time to time, and then so as to insult him. In a manner of speaking, each of those letters bore my death warrant. 20

The theme of freedom as you'd expect is the one that dominated our correspondence. We were forever dreaming up all sorts of plans or imagining possible stratagems. My first plan had been to go on strike, to refuse to translate further letters, unless I was granted my freedom; but then I was condemned to bread and water, and this, together with the even greater agony of not reading any more of her letters (which by now had become indispensable to me) broke my will. I then proposed as a condition that at least the shave and the bath and the decent clothes could be accorded to me on a regular basis and not merely on letter days (which was not only impracticable but also humiliating) but not even this was conceded, and then I had to submit unconditionally. 21

Later she proposed to travel out here so as to call on the President and make arrangements for my release (a plan which had the advantage of counting on the resolute support of the President, who for some time had been urging her to do so with some impatience) but I was utterly opposed to it, because without doubt it would mean losing her (and losing myself as well possibly). My proposal, on the other hand, that some other woman should come in her place, she rejected as some- 22 thing dangerous, besides being impossible. Another of her plans which really was on the point of being put into practice, was to obtain a forceful protest on the part of my Government and even a breaking off of relations, but I made her see in time that such a measure not only would not improve my situation, but rather would considerably worsen it and I'd never be heard of again. I was much more in favour of trying to improve relations between the two countries, then in such a lamentable state, but as she pointed out quite rightly: how to convince the Swedish Government to improve its relations on the basis that one of its citizens should have been unjustly imprisoned? But the most preposterous idea, suggested by a lawyer friend of hers, was that of demanding my extradition as a wanted criminal (to which I objected) failing to realise that if I was already being held for no reason, there being a charge against me, the President would have me put to death there and then.

23   But do not think that we were the only ones who were making plans, for all the prisoners (and even the whole country) lived all the time elaborating the most diverse and contradictory plans: the general strike or attempts on his life, civic action, revolution, alliance with the Government, rebellion, palace plot, violence and terrorism, passive resistance, poisoning, bombs, guerilla warfare, whispering campaigns, prayer, psychic powers. There was even a prisoner (a professor of mathematics) who was working on a very abstruse plan to overthrow the Government by means of mathematical laws (he conceived of an almost cosmic clandestine organisation which would continue to grow in geometric proportion and within a few weeks would be as large as the number of inhabitants in the whole country, and a few days later, having continued to grow, the inhabitants of the entire globe would not be sufficient, yet he failed to take into account that those who did not join the organisation would also increase in geometric proportion).

24   As for me, a fresh worry had come to join the others, and it was that of seeing how day by day I was becoming more dangerous in the President's eyes on account of the tremendous secret (together with the innumerable lesser confidences) of which I was the depository; although it is true that his love, real or feigned, constituted my greatest security, because he would not kill me while he required my services (but this security brought me anguish on another count, because needing my services it was more improbable that he would let me go). And the same hope I had at the beginning that one of my fellow countrymen might happen to pass through, had been transformed into the main fear, because the President might proudly show him a letter, and my deception would be uncovered.

25   There we were she and I, busy in the elaboration of a new plan which might prove to be more effective, when suddenly, that which most anxiously terrified me and with all the strength of my mind I had tried to avoid, came about: the President stopped being in love. His was not, to my misfortune, a gradual falling out of love, but sudden,

without giving me time to prepare myself. Quite simply, the letters which arrived were no longer answered but thrown into the basket, and I was not called upon, except on the odd afternoon so as to read something or other, more out of curiosity and boredom, dictating to me afterwards cold, laconic replies with the aim of putting a stop to the affair. All the desperation and mortal anguish of my soul were poured into those lines and in the few letters that I still had the good fortune to read to the President. I in turn put the tenderest, the most affectionate and passionate entreaties of love that any woman has ever expressed, but with so little success he cut short the reading in the middle of a letter. To cap it all, the letters she wrote were above all reproachful of me, for not replying to her, raising doubts that I was still a prisoner and even coming to insinuate that I had never been a prisoner. The last occasion, when I was not even brought in dress suit to the Presidential Residence but rather in the prison itself, an utterly definitive break was dictated to me by a guard, I understood that she, my freedom and everything, had come to an end, and my final, heart-rending words of farewell had been written.

The remaining sheets of paper and the pen were left for me in the cell, in case some other letter from me was again required, I presume. And whether the President did not have me killed because he remained grateful to me, or in case some other person writes from Sweden, or simply because he forgot about me, I don't know (and I still think of the possibility that they might have killed him—although this is unlikely—and that he who exists is another double). Neither do I know whether she has continued to write to me or if she now no longer remembers me, and the terrible absurd idea has even occurred to me that perhaps she never existed, but rather it was all hatched by someone from the Opposition in exile, in order to make fun of the President or to make fun of me (or by the President himself who is a cruel maniac) owing to a custom of thinking absurd ideas which lately I have developed in prison. Did you love me too, Selma Borjesson, as I loved you madly in this prison? 26

Much time has passed since then, and now once again I have lost hope of seeing myself released at the end of the President's term of office, because once again he has re-elected himself. The paper which was left over, and now serves no purpose, I have used to tell my story. I write in Swedish so the President will not understand it, should this fall into his hands. I end here because the paper is running out and perhaps it may be years before I have paper again (and perhaps I have only a few days left to live). In the remote case that some fellow countryman of mine should happen to read these pages, I implore him to remember Erik Hjalmar Ossiannilsson, if I am still not yet dead. 27

NOTE: *A friend of mine who was arrested found this manuscript in the prison, almost destroyed by damp, under a brick. It would appear to have been* 28 *written many years ago. And years later an employee of the Ericksonn Telephone Company translated it for us. We have been unable to trace any data referring to the person who wrote it. I have published the text as it was given to me, making obvious corrections to the style and grammar.*

Questions for Discussion and Writing

1. What circumstances have led the NARRATOR to correspond with Selma on behalf of the president? How does being in this position create a CONFLICT that sets the story in motion?
2. Through what phases does the relationship between the president and Selma (via the narrator) fluctuate? What consequence does each of these have for the narrator?
3. Why is the president's suddenly falling out of love with Selma a crucial turning point in the narrator's life?
4. What equivalences does the story suggest between being imprisoned by a dictator in a Central American country and being subject to the whims of one with whom you are in love?
5. How does the note added to the end of the story change your perception of Erik or any of the events?
6. Write a letter in which you say something you wish you had said earlier but lacked the courage to say at the time.

Gloria Anzaldúa

Cervicide

Gloria Anzaldúa is a Chicana poet and fiction writer who grew up in south Texas. She has edited several highly praised anthologies. This Bridge Called My Back: Writings by Radical Women of Color *won the 1986 Before Columbus Foundation American Book Award.* Borderlands—La Frontera, the New Mestiza *was selected as one of the best books of 1987 by* Library Journal. *Her most recent work is* Making Face, Making Soul *(1990). She has been a contributing editor for* Sinister Wisdom *since 1984 and has taught Chicano studies, feminist studies, and creative writing at the University of Texas at Austin, San Francisco State University, and the University of California, Santa Cruz. "Cervicide" first appeared in* Labyris *(vol. 4, no. 11, Winter 1983). In it, Anzaldúa tells the poignant story of a Mexican-American family living on the Texas border who are forced to kill a pet deer whose detection by the game warden would result in an unaffordable fine or the father's imprisonment.*

La venadita. The small fawn. They had to kill their pet, the fawn. The game warden was on the way with his hounds. The penalty for being caught in possession of a deer was $250 or jail. The game warden would put *su papi en la cárcel.*

How could they get rid of the fawn? Hide it? No, *la guardia's* hounds would sniff Venadita out. Let Venadita loose in the *monte?* They had tried that before. The fawn would leap away and seconds later return. Should they kill Venadita? The mother and Prieta looked toward *las carabinas* propped against the wall behind the kitchen door—the shiny barrel of the .22, the heavy metal steel of the 40-40. No, if *they* could hear his pickup a mile and a half down the road, he would hear the shot.

Quick, they had to do something. Cut Venadita's throat? Club her to death? The mother couldn't do it. She, Prieta, would have to be the one. The game warden and his *perros* were a mile down the road. Prieta loved her *papí.*

In the shed behind the corral, where they'd hidden the fawn, Prieta found the hammer. She had to grasp it with both hands. She swung it up. The weight folded her body backwards. A thud reverberated on

Cervicide—the killing of a deer. In archetypal symbology the Self appears as a deer for women.

    su papí en la cárcel—her father in jail
    monte—the woods
    Prieta—literally one who is dark-skinned, a nickname

Venadita's skull, a wave undulated down her back. Again, a blow behind the ear. Though Venadita's long lashes quivered, her eyes never left Prieta's face. Another thud, another tremor. *La guardia* and his hounds were driving up the front yard. The *venadita* looked up at her, the hammer rose and fell. Neither made a sound. The tawny, spotted fur was the most beautiful thing Prieta had ever seen. She remembered when they had found the fawn. She had been a few hours old. A hunter had shot her mother. The fawn had been shaking so hard, her long thin legs were on the edge of buckling. Prieta and her sister and brothers had bottle-fed Venadita, with a damp cloth had wiped her skin, had watched her tiny, perfectly formed hooves harden and grow.

5   Prieta dug a hole in the shed, a makeshift hole. She could hear the warden talking to her mother. Her mother's English had suddenly gotten bad—she was trying to stall *la guardia*. Prieta rolled the fawn into the hole, threw in the empty bottle. With her fingers raked in the dirt. Dust caked on her arms and face where tears had fallen. She patted the ground flat with her hands and swept it with a dead branch. The game warden was strutting toward her. His hounds sniffing, sniffing, sniffing the ground in the shed. The hounds pawing pawing the ground. The game warden, straining on the leashes *les dio un tirón, sacó los perros*. He inspected the corrals, the edge of the woods, then drove away in his pickup.

les dio un tirón, sacó los perros—jerked the dogs out

Questions for Discussion and Writing

1. How does the beginning of the story provide necessary background information that frames the dramatic situation in which the CONFLICT occurs?
2. To what pressures is the family subject because they are illegal immigrants?
3. How does Anzaldúa's characterization of the PROTAGONIST and the ANTAGONISTS sharpen the dilemma leading to the moment of crisis?
4. How does being forced to choose between a deer that she loves and her father whom she loves illustrate the kind of predicament in which those without power find themselves?
5. Discuss the consequences for the narrator of having to make such a choice and perform such an action. In your opinion, how will she be different from now on? In what sense might the deer symbolize the self that can no longer exist?
6. Would you ever consider killing your pet for food if you were in a circumstance where you and your children were starving?

Slawomir Mrożek

The Elephant

Slawomir Mrożek was born in 1930 in Borzecin, Poland, and studied architecture and Oriental culture in Krakow. He has gained international acclaim as Poland's preeminent contemporary satirist and playwright. He worked as a caricaturist and journalist for the weekly publication Szpilki *and other newspapers and magazines. He also directed, edited, and produced several films. Mrożek's gift for caricature of the absurdity of life under communist rule, in plays such as* The Police *(1958) and* Tango *(1964), produced such an uproar that the authorities banned his work and he was forced to emigrate in 1968 to Paris. Despite political liberalization in Poland since this period, Mrożek has chosen to live in Paris permanently. His satirical short stories have been widely translated and are collected in two volumes,* The Elephant *(1962) and* The Ugupu Bird *(1968). "The Elephant," translated by Konrad Syrop (1962), displays Mrożek's typical blend of deliberate ambiguity, sharp irony, and irreverent spoofing of bureaucratic inanity to elevate an absurd situation to sublime satire.*

The director of the Zoological Gardens had shown himself to be an upstart. He regarded his animals simply as stepping stones on the road of his own career. He was indifferent to the educational importance of his establishment. In his zoo the giraffe had a short neck, the badger had no burrow and the whistlers, having lost all interest, whistled rarely and with some reluctance. These shortcomings should not have been allowed, especially as the zoo was often visited by parties of schoolchildren.

The zoo was in a provincial town, and it was short of some of the most important animals, among them the elephant. Three thousand rabbits were a poor substitute for the noble giant. However, as our country developed, the gaps were being filled in a well-planned manner. On the occasion of the anniversary of the liberation, on 22nd July, the zoo was notified that it had at long last been allocated an elephant. All the staff, who were devoted to their work, rejoiced at this news. All the greater was their surprise when they learned that the director had sent a letter to Warsaw, renouncing the allocation and putting forward a plan for obtaining an elephant by more economic means.

"I, and all the staff," he had written, "are fully aware how heavy a burden falls upon the shoulders of Polish miners and foundry men because of the elephant. Desirous of reducing our costs, I suggest that the elephant mentioned in your communication should be replaced by one of our own procurement. We can make an elephant out of rubber, of the correct size, fill it with air and place it behind railings. It will be

681

carefully painted the correct color and even on close inspection will be indistinguishable from the real animal. It is well known that the elephant is a sluggish animal and it does not run and jump about. In the notice on the railings we can state that this particular elephant is particularly sluggish. The money saved in this way can be turned to the purchase of a jet plane or the conservation of some church monument.

4   "Kindly note that both the idea and its execution are my modest contribution to the common task and struggle.

5   "I am, etc."

6   This communication must have reached a soulless official, who regarded his duties in a purely bureaucratic manner and did not examine the heart of the matter but, following only the directive about reduction of expenditure, accepted the director's plan. On hearing the Ministry's approval, the director issued instructions for the making of the rubber elephant.

7   The carcass was to have been filled with air by two keepers blowing into it from opposite ends. To keep the operation secret the work was to be completed during the night because the people of the town, having heard that an elephant was joining the zoo, were anxious to see it. The director insisted on haste also because he expected a bonus, should his idea turn out to be a success.

8   The two keepers locked themselves in a shed normally housing a workshop, and began to blow. After two hours of hard blowing they discovered that the rubber skin had risen only a few inches above the floor and its bulge in no way resembled an elephant. The night progressed. Outside, human voices were stilled and only the cry of the jackass interrupted the silence. Exhausted, the keepers stopped blowing and made sure that the air already inside the elephant should not escape. They were not young and were unaccustomed to this kind of work.

9   "If we go on at this rate," said one of them, "we shan't finish by morning. And what am I to tell my missus? She'll never believe me if I say that I spent the night blowing up an elephant."

10   "Quite right," agreed the second keeper. "Blowing up an elephant is not an everyday job. And it's all because our director is a leftist."

11   They resumed their blowing, but after another half-hour they felt too tired to continue. The bulge on the floor was larger but still nothing like the shape of an elephant.

12   "It's getting harder all the time," said the first keeper.

13   "It's an uphill job, all right," agreed the second. "Let's have a little rest."

14   While they were resting, one of them noticed a gas pipe ending in a valve. Could they not fill the elephant with gas? He suggested it to his mate.

15   They decided to try. They connected the elephant to the gas pipe, turned the valve, and to their joy in a few minutes there was a full-sized beast standing in the shed. It looked real: the enormous body, legs like

columns, huge ears and the inevitable trunk. Driven by ambition the director had made sure of having in his zoo a very large elephant indeed.

"First class," declared the keeper who had the idea of using gas. "Now we can go home." 16

In the morning the elephant was moved to a special run in a central position, next to the monkey cage. Placed in front of a large real rock it looked fierce and magnificent. A big notice proclaimed: "Particularly sluggish. Hardly moves." 17

Among the first visitors that morning was a party of children from the local school. The teacher in charge of them was planning to give them an object-lesson about the elephant. He halted the group in front of the animal and began: 18

"The elephant is a herbivorous mammal. By means of its trunk it pulls out young trees and eats their leaves." 19

The children were looking at the elephant with enraptured admiration. They were waiting for it to pull out a young tree, but the beast stood still behind its railings. 20

". . . The elephant is a direct descendant of the now-extinct mammoth. It's not surprising, therefore, that it's the largest living land animal." 21

The more conscientious pupils were making notes. 22

". . . Only the whale is heavier than the elephant, but then the whale lives in the sea. We can safely say that on land the elephant reigns supreme." 23

A slight breeze moved the branches of the trees in the zoo. 24

". . . The weight of a fully grown elephant is between nine and thirteen thousand pounds." 25

At that moment the elephant shuddered and rose in the air. For a few seconds it swayed just above the ground, but a gust of wind blew it upward until its mighty silhouette was against the sky. For a short while people on the ground could see the four circles of its feet, its bulging belly and the trunk, but soon, propelled by the wind, the elephant sailed above the fence and disappeared above the treetops. Astonished monkeys in the cage continued staring into the sky. 26

They found the elephant in the neighboring botanical gardens. It had landed on a cactus and punctured its rubber hide. 27

The schoolchildren who had witnessed the scene in the zoo soon started neglecting their studies and turned into hooligans. It is reported that they drink liquor and break windows. And they no longer believe in elephants. 28

Questions for Discussion and Writing

1. What can you infer about the motives behind the zoo director's suggestions? How does the way the elephant is constructed, what it is filled with, and how it is labeled present an ironic contrast between appearance and reality?

2. What details lead you to believe that Mrożek might be drawing equivalences between the way the zoo is run and what life was like in Poland under the communist regime? Looked at in this way, what features of the centralized bureaucracy is he mocking?
3. How do the schoolchildren's reactions suggest the disillusionment citizens experience when they see through the propaganda dispensed by their leaders?
4. Discuss any recent incident that seems to you to express the CONFLICT between appearance and reality (as does Mrożek's political allegory)—such as, perhaps, the instant renovations that precede the visit of a high-ranking personage where roads are suddenly paved and streets are devoid of embarrassing litter.
5. Discuss any recent incident that made you aware of the extent to which any political event might be staged or how political rhetoric is used to disguise reality. In each case, what really happened and how was it made to appear?
6. How does your favorite zoo compare with the one described in the story? Try to include all five senses in your detailed description.

Jan Rabie

Drought

Jan Rabie was born in the Cape region in South Africa in 1920. A critic, short story writer, and novelist, Rabie returned to the Cape after spending several years in Paris and on the island of Crete. He gained prominence among the group of Afrikaans prose writers (Afrikaans is the language of South Africa developed from seventeenth-century Dutch) who brought about a renewal of South African fiction in the 1960s and include among their number Etiénne Leroux and André P. Brink. In 1969, his novel, A Man Apart, a historical work dealing with racial issues, appeared and was widely praised. Throughout his career, Rabie has been interested in internationalizing the interests of Afrikaans literature and has worked actively to bring about the recognition of the value and usefulness of tribal literature and culture. "Drought" (1962), translated by the author, is a compelling parable which addresses the relationship of the races under the apartheid system of South Africa. It has been included in the South African public school syllabus as required reading.

Whirling pillars of dust walk the brown floor of the earth. Trembling, the roots of the withered grass await the rain; thirsty for green love the vast and arid plain treks endlessly out to its horizon. One straight ruler-laid railway track shoots from under the midday sun's glare towards where a night will be velvet-cool with stars. The landscape is that of drought. Tiny as two grains of sand, a white man and a black man build a wall. Four walls. Then a roof. A house. 1

The black man carries blocks of stone and the white man lays them in place. The white man stands inside the walls where there is some shade. He says: "You must work outside. You have a black skin, you can stand the sun better than I can." 2

The black man laughs at his muscles glistening in the sun. A hundred years ago his ancestors reaped dark harvests with their assegais, and threshed out the fever of the black sun in their limbs with the Ngoma-dance. Now the black man laughs while he begins to frown. 3

"Why do you always talk of my black skin?" he asks. 4

"You are cursed," the white man says. "Long ago my God cursed you with darkness." 5

"Your God is white," the black man angrily replies. "Your God lies! I love the sun and I fear the dark." 6

The white man speaks dreamily on: "Long ago my forefathers came across the sea. Far they came, in white ships tall as trees, and on the land they built them wagons and covered them with the sails of their ships. Far they travelled and spread their campfire ashes over this vast barbaric land. But now their children are tired, we want to build houses 7

685

and teach you blacks how to live in peace with us. It is time, even if your skins will always be black . . ."

8   Proudly the black man counters: "And my ancestors dipped their assegais in the blood of your forefathers and saw that it was red as blood. Red as the blood of the impala that our young men run to catch between the two red suns of the hills!"

9   "It's time you forgot the damned past," the white man sadly says. "Come, you must learn to work with me. We must build this house."

10   "You come to teach me that God is white. That I should build a house for the white man." The black man stands with folded arms.

11   "Kaffir!" the white man shouts, "will you never understand anything at all! Do what I tell you!"

12   "Yes, Baas," the black man mutters.

13   The black man carries blocks of stone and the white man lays them in place. He makes the walls strong. The sun glares down with its terrible eye. Far, as the only tree in the parched land, a pillar of dust walks the trembling horizon.

14   "This damned heat!" the white man mutters, "if only it would rain."

15   Irritably he wipes the sweat from his forehead before he says: "Your ancestors are dead. It's time you forgot them."

16   Silently the black man looks at him with eyes that answer: Your ancestors, too, are dead. We are alone here.

17   Alone in the dry and empty plain the white man and the black man build a house. They do not speak to each other. They build the four walls and then the roof. The black man works outside in the sun and the white man inside in the shade. Now the black man can only see the white man's head. They lay the roof.

18   "Baas," the black man asks at last, "why has your house no windows and no doors?"

19   The white man has become very sad. "That, too, you cannot understand," he says. "Long ago in another country my forefathers built walls to keep out the sea. Thick, watertight walls. That's why my house, too, has no windows and no doors."

20   "But there's no big water here!" the black man exclaims, "the sand is dry as a skull!"

21   You're the sea, the white man thinks, but is too sad to explain.

22   They lay the roof. They nail the last plank, the last corrugated iron sheet, the black man outside and the white man inside. Then the black man can see the white man no more.

23   "Baas!" he calls, but hears no answer.

24   The Inkoos cannot get out, he thinks with fright, he cannot see the sky or know when it is day or night. The Inkoos will die inside his house!

25   The black man hammers with his fists on the house and calls: "But Baas, no big water will ever come here! Here it will never rain for forty days and forty nights as the Book of your white God says!"

He hears no answer and he shouts: "Come out, Baas!" 26

He hears no answer. 27

With his fists still raised as if to knock again, the black man raises 28 his eyes bewilderedly to the sky empty of a single cloud, and stares around him at the horizon where red-hot pillars of dust dance the fearful Ngoma of the drought.

Alone and afraid, the black man stammers: "Come out, Baas . . . 29 Come out to me . . ."

Questions for Discussion and Writing

1. What words and phrases most effectively create the scene? How might the landscape parched for rain reflect the title? What might the comparison of the two men to grains of sand suggest? Why is it significant that they are building "a wall"? What might the wall represent?
2. Why is it significant that, in building the wall, the black man is the laborer, carrying "blocks of stone," while the white man takes on the role of supervisor?
3. How does the STRUCTURE of the parable take the form of a debate that explores the CONFLICT between the black man and the white man? How does the black man's response refute the white man's claim that before the white man's arrival Africa was a "vast barbaric land"?
4. Why does the black man resent the white man's attempt to justify all his actions on the assumptions that God is white and has supposedly cursed the black man? What lines in the parable most forcefully express the black man's rejection of this rationale and its conclusion that he should always accept a subservient role? In your opinion, why does the black man, at this point, continue to build the house for the white man?
5. At what point in the story does the construction of the windowless, doorless house from which there is no escape become irreversible? How is this the moment of CRISIS beyond which the CONFLICT cannot continue?
6. How does the equation of the black man to the sea ("You're the sea") give you an insight into the white man's attitude toward the black man—which might explain why, from the white man's point of view, it was necessary to build such a house?
7. What insight did "Drought" give you into the network of psychological interdependency between the races in South Africa? In what sense did the parable formulate both a history and a criticism of the system of apartheid? What kind of scarcity might the title symbolize?

P'an Jen-mu

A Pair of Socks with Love

P'an Jen-mu was born in 1920 in Liaoning Province, Manchuria, grew up in Beijing, and graduated from the National Central University in Nanking with a B.A. in English. She spent three years teaching in Sinkiang, in western China, between Mongolia and Tibet, an experience that provided her with material for a number of her short stories. After moving to Taiwan, she served as editor in chief of the Children's Reading Program, sponsored by the Ministry of Education. Her publications include two prize-winning novels, My Cousin Lien-yi (1951) and Nightmare (1953), as well as a collection of short stories, Sorrow and Happiness in a Small World (1981). Translated by Chen I-djen, "A Pair of Socks with Love" was first published in 1985 in the Central Daily News in Taiwan. The story presents an image of the prerevolutionary Chinese family and society, told from the perspective of a little girl in an upper-class family. The relationships between her parents, and between them and their servant, are presented in positive human terms. At the same time, the story exposes the oppression of the poor through a sensitive portrayal of the family's servant and the impoverished living conditions of beggars outside the village. "A Pair of Socks with Love" relates how the child's request that her servant be given real store-bought socks comes full circle, many years later, during the Cultural Revolution.

1   I left home many decades ago and feel as if I have just been drifting along all these years. I often dream of home, but the one happy dream that I cherished the most was about my mother coming into my room, a smile on her face, to prepare and warm my bedding for me. It was a wintery night, and I was only seven or eight years old. The oil lamp cast a weak shadow as she folded my mauve-colored comforter into a Chinese style envelope, our version of a sleeping bag, and watched me take off my felt shoes and get into bed, which we called a *k'ang*.[1] I slid my legs into the folded comforter slowly; I took off my cotton wool padded maroon-colored raw silk gown, my fur vest, my blue cotton wool padded pants that were bound at the ankles. I would then be wearing only a white undergarment, an old pair of underpants, a red band around my stomach and was ready to ease myself into my comforter. The garments I shed would be placed on top of my bedding in the order they were taken off, one on top of the other, to make it easier to put them back on the next morning without having to search for them.

---

[1]A brick bed which can be kept warm by a fire fed from an adjoining room, usually the kitchen.

The last item to be taken off would be my cotton socks, which I handed to my mother. The next morning there would be a pair of clean socks in my felt shoes, one in each shoe.

I loved this moment when my mother prepared my bedding for me; still more, I loved the way she looked at me. She would gaze at me all the while I was undressing. I felt that she loved me, really loved me. After I left home, whenever I remembered that look in her eyes, I would begin to cry. Even when I dreamt about it, I would wake up crying.

After I slid all the way into my folded quilt she would then put a blanket on top of my feet, a threadbare Russian blanket. And she always added, "Don't kick it off." Always.

In our home we had the kind of bed known as a "fire k'ang," which was always built against a window. One slept with one's feet facing the window and head towards the room. The window was papered on the outside and smeared with tung oil to prevent the rain and snow from dampening the window. It also protected it from gale winds. Cracks along the window were sealed with some coarse paper but still the cold wind would find its way in. The glass pane in the middle of the window would be frosted by the cold air outside, so it was always colder where one's feet were. I remembered very clearly one night when it was time to take off my socks, I said hesitantly, folding my hands, "Ma, may I sleep with my socks on tonight?"

"Sleep with your socks on? That won't do. What're you up to now? Figuring on getting into our k'ang, isn't that it?"

"No!"

"What is it then? If you sleep with your socks on your feet will feel like those of the hairy legged chicks. Try it if you don't believe me. It'll really make you feel awkward."

"How do you know, Ma?"

"I wore them to sleep on my wedding night. Just that once and it was awkward beyond words."

"I would also do it only once."

"Not even once. If you sleep with them on you may tend to kick your bedding off. If that happened you would find yourself frozen stiff in the wee hours of the morning. Have you forgotten that last year on the eighth day of the twelfth lunar month you caught a bad cold because you kicked off your bedding? You were feverish and sneezing like mad. Chung Jen had to get Chang the Lama to treat you. All that because you kicked off your bedding. Have you forgotten already? Now take them off right away."

"I won't do it this time, won't kick them off. If I do, may the skin around my eyes rot."

"So, you have learned to swear! Whom did you learn it from? Rotting of the skin around the eyes is harder to cure than colds and fever. The old monk from the temple would have to be fetched, and he would stick you with a needle."

15   "But, Ma, the old monk from the temple only knows how to grow cucumbers. He won't know what to do with a needle. That much I know."

16   "Nonetheless he knows how to look for a spike of sorghum to prop open the eyelids of little children with rotting skin around the eyes. Would you like that?"

17   "I won't kick, Ma! Then nothing would happen."

18   "I merely urge you to take off your socks. I really cannot figure out why it should cause so much difficulty. I heard you mention to Erh-niu in the south court only the day before yesterday, 'Don't you ever sleep in your socks! If you do your toes will stack up one against the other like your mother's. Notice how ugly they look in shoes?' Weren't those your very words?"

19   "The day before yesterday? The day before yesterday I had on a pair of cotton socks. Of course I had to say it was better to sleep without them. And what do I have on today? Don't you remember? A pair of imported knitted Dark Chrysanthemum brand socks! Look!"

20   As I argued with her I felt that reason was on my side and I began to sob.

21   Ma could only let me have my way; she probably agreed with me.

22   To this day I cherish a special feeling for this Dark Chrysanthemum brand of imported socks. It was the first article which served in my "modernization." Some fifty or sixty years ago everything I wore was homemade, everything except the string for my hair, the binding strips for my leggings, and the felt shoes I wore in the winter. Of all these homemade items the socks were the most uncomfortable things to wear. As one tried to pull them up beyond the heels one had to pull really hard. Children couldn't do it, and they often ended up on their backs with all four limbs kicking in the air.

23   At first, only Papa wore imported socks. Everyone in the household from Mama down treated them as something special. They were laundered in a separate basin, and the brand name was etched in everyone's memory. The paper that bore the trademark of this Dark Chrysanthemum brand of imported socks had only two colors: black and white, a black chrysanthemum on white, very striking. I was not entitled to wear imported socks, but the privilege of peeling off the trademark label was solely mine. If he should overlook having it pass through my hands before putting on a new pair of socks, I would stand outside in the snow if it were winter, and in the summer I would walk out and stand under the sun. I would not even come in to eat. Let them suffer!

24   I called the label I collected calico paper, and I saved it as I did cards from packages of cigarettes. I left my mark on all of them, a tiny little black fish. I issued them to those schoolmates of mine who were my friends. It was very useful in organizing a gang or a following.

25   Once when Papa took a trip to the provincial seat, for some

unknown reason he went all out and bought Dark Chrysanthemum brand imported socks for every member of the family. He bought several dozens of them, some were made of cotton thread, some woolen or lisle. The ones for Mama were natural color lisle socks and over the knee. Since the word for knee sounded the same in our language as the word for a feast, I thought it stood to reason that the longer socks were meant for such occasions.

After I was settled in bed, Mama would turn down the wick and tiptoe out. But I wasn't sleeping; how could I? The cozy feeling I experienced this morning when I put on my socks was still circulating all through my body. They fit so well and felt so soft that it was like stepping on a cloud. In school I stuck my feet out to show my schoolmates. They all wanted to feel them and asked if they were expensive. 26

The peddler hawking peanuts, watermelon seeds and candied crab apples went by, and shortly after, I heard Papa returning. I knew he would come in to see me soon, so I pretended to be asleep. 27

At first Papa and Ma talked in whispers, then they talked louder, and Ma said, "Don't! The child may see us." 28

"Isn't she asleep?" 29

"Oh, you're cold." 30

"It's very cold outside, dry and cold, the way it is toward the end of the year." 31

"What's keeping you so busy? You're very late!" 32

"The detention room was rebuilt. It was made into living quarters. I went to inspect it." 33

"So that was what kept you busy! Where did you eat supper?" 34

"At the training factory; I ate with them. I got workers from the training factory to install glass panes on the windows for us. All the windows are Western style. This is the best room in the whole office compound. Yet no one dares to move in. Have to ask Chung Jen to move in." 35

"Did anybody ever die in that room?" 36

"Very likely, it was already there during the Ch'ing Dynasty." 37

"They say there used to be huge sticks, torture bars, and water torture benches there. Where are they now?" 38

"They have been moved to the hall." 39

"How come? They used to do it secretively, and now you want to punish openly?" 40

"Can't let the criminals think that I am not going to punish them at all." 41

"A little beating, and a little threat should be enough. Even criminals have parents and are the darlings of their fathers and mothers. I have often thought that if ever our own family or our children commit any offence, I wish they would be treated with mercy . . ." 42

"My goodness, how you let your thoughts wander! We won't com- 43 mit any crime, and the first thing we teach our children would be not to commit any crime. The law of the land is improving day by day, and law-abiding citizens will not be wrongfully accused."

44 "Our ancestors were kind and merciful, thereby earning merit points with the gods and laying the foundation to build your future on. We should do the same for future generations; earn some merit points for them. Law is law, mercy is mercy, temper law with mercy."

45 I loved it when they talked about such official business. I knew where the torture chamber was. Whenever I had to pass that way, I always walked around it. I was afraid that the hand of a ghost would grab me and pull me into it. Now it would be all right; the torture chamber had been eliminated, and our houseboy Chung Jen was to move in.

46 Mama and Papa talked some more, still very softly. Then I sensed that they had walked around the screen, lifted the curtain and come into my room. I could smell the cold air brought in by Papa's blue silk fur robe. I opened my eyes ever so slightly and stole a look at him by dint of the light that came in with them. Today Papa was wearing a pair of copper-colored woolen Dark Chrysanthemum brand socks and black woolen shoes. I had taken off the trademark label before he put them on and it made me feel exceedingly filial to him.

47 Both of them bent down to look at me. Ma's breath was sweet and soft, and she tucked me in. I liked the feeling of her gold bracelet brushing against my cheeks. I also liked the smell of Papa, the smell of a mixture of paper and ink from the tip of his sleeves, the smell of the cold air and the smell of his black brocade vest. It was the smell of Papa and there was nothing that could take its place.

48 "Don't touch her; your hands are cold," Mama said very softly.

49 "I just touched her hair; no harm done."

50 "Still, it could have wakened her."

51 "Those tiny feet are sticking out from the bedding. How come this child is sleeping with her socks on?"

52 "Today is the first time she is wearing imported socks; no amount of arguing could make her take them off. She promised, and even swore that she would not kick off her bedding. Now as soon as she falls asleep, she has kicked them off." Ma stuck my feet back in and patted them.

53 "Take them off while she is sleeping."

54 "You know what would happen then. She would raise a ruckus tomorrow early in the morning."

55 "Where did she get that temper? Tell me."

56 "Don't! The child may see us. Don't."

57 They walked out quietly. Don't! Don't what? I stole a look. They walked out hand in hand. I had long suspected that they did something behind my back and now I had caught them at it. So that's what they do, hold hands!

I slept soundly, totally relaxed.   58

Sure enough, I woke up early, frozen. Mama was right; sleeping   59
with socks on really made me feel like a hairy-legged chick. Not only
had I kicked off my bedding, what was thrown over my feet now became cushions for them. My tummy was icy cold. Frost had formed on
the window pane like feathers, very thick feathers. I quietly took my
comb and went to look for Chun-hsi in the kitchen. She always got up
early to cook sorghum gruel, the watery part of which was to be used
to cook eggs for Papa.

"Chun-hsi, braid my hair for me. Hurry! And don't make it too   60
tight."

Whenever Chun-hsi did my hair she always hurt me as if she were   61
taking it out on me. She said it was because I had too much hair and it
tended to knot. After a bout with typhoid I almost lost all my hair. My
new head of hair was thicker than ever, but very short. My braid was
very thick at the root and tapered off to a thin end. It looked very
strange. When she finished braiding me she laughed and said, "I have
never seen such a funny-looking broomlike braid as yours."

I, however, felt that it was more like a slippery black fish, very shiny   62
and fresh out of water. "Chun-hsi, look at my imported socks!"

"Didn't you show them to me eight times already yesterday? Do   63
I have to look at them again? Find Chung Jen and show them to
him."

Of course I wanted to look for Chung Jen; I did not need her to ar-   64
range my itinerary for me. I had to find him to take me to school for the
morning review session before breakfast, not to show off. He too had
seen them eight times. I needed him to take me because on the way to
school I had to pass a few homes that had dogs, also the grotto of the
local god on a big stone tablet, which was put there to ward off evil
spirits, the residence of a divorcee, also several huts out in the field
where the beggars congregated. All these places looked especially scary
early in the morning before the sun was up and there were few pedestrians around.

That torture chamber looked really different now with all new   65
Western style windows. Nonetheless I felt intimidated as I approached
it. I could only bring myself to call out for him in a small voice, "Chung
Jen! Chung Jen!" I had to knock on the window pane a few times before
waking him up. He yawned and muttered, "Here!"

Ma told me that little girls may not enter a man's bedroom, even if   66
the man is a work hand or a servant from your own household. This
room, however, had glass windows all over, unlike the one he had before, which had papered windows. I tried not to look, but even from the
outside, with a slight turn of my head I saw clearly the procedure he
followed rising from his bed.

He, too, had piled layer after layer of clothing on top of his bedding.   67
He too put them on in the order they were laid out. Except, when it

came to the last item, the socks, he did it very differently. In addition to his socks he put an extra layer of something on his feet.

68   First he laid out a piece of cloth measuring about two feet square. It was homespun and a dirty gray color. Then he stuck out his big foot on top of the cloth, and using both hands he started wrapping, his thick lips tightly pursed as three deep furrows appeared on his forehead as if they were assisting him in his task. After his foot was thus wrapped up he brought out a cotton sock from under the bedding, which was already adjusted to the shape of his foot from previous wear. Very carefully and with his lips still tightly pursed he stuffed his foot into it. He then proceeded to wrap the other foot.

69   How many years did I have to wait? No wonder it took him so long every day! I was both cold and anxious. If it dragged on like this the sun would be up and I would be late getting to school.

70   "Hurry up! Hurry up! This is really unbelievable, taking so long to put on socks!"

71   At long last his feet wrapped, socks on, he stuffed them into his old cotton padded shoes and got off the bed. Now, with me walking in front and him following behind we were on our way to the county primary school for girls. It was Mama's ruling that he should follow behind within a distance of five to ten paces.

72   This, however, was easier said than done. Chung Jen was like a grasshopper, tall and skinny. He had legs long and wide apart like the crane's and could overtake me in two or three steps. Ma said he wasn't like this when he first came to work for us at fifteen. He was a mere child, shortish and withered looking. He didn't even have a name; when asked he said it was Second Pillar. His pa was a criminal; he was sued for not paying his debts and was also otherwise involved and had to be sent to the provincial capital. He and his ma were left behind. They were very poor and had no way of making a living. Papa felt sorry for him and told him to come to work for us. Even then Ma had said, "This Second Pillar may look like a caterpillar, but how he can eat nonstop. He is no help at all, but he is honest and can be trusted." Later, when he was seventeen Papa found a wife for him and sent the wife to the countryside to wait on her mother-in-law while waiting for the return of her father-in-law. As for himself, he was promoted to office boy and was given the name Chung Jen. Ever since Papa had given him his name he liked to test people to see if they were literate. "Do you know how to read? Can you write my name?" Now he had surely come up in this world. He sent money home every month, and he learned to say, "I serve in the Pan's residence." (Even I did not know the meaning of the word "serve," but I pretended I did.) The only thing was that he would turn red all the way down to his neck at the mention of his wife. Mama let him go home once a month. And he was always given a basket full of food such as cakes and cookies to take back.

The county primary school was not far from home. It could be reached in less time than it took to finish a pipe. But he always had a lot to say on the way, to help slow him down and to show off what he knew, I guessed. He told me the names of all the dogs along the way, that Lao Wang's woman lent money out at high interest rates, the age of Lao Li's calf, and how many soybean cakes Lao Liu had made that year, and so forth. Incidentally, the first step toward making bean paste was to cook the soybeans and make them into cakes for fermentation. 73

I was in no mood to listen to that. There were no other children on the road; most likely I was late. It was all his fault. 74

"Chung Jen, you walk in front of me." 75

"That will never do. Mistress's order, I have to walk behind you." 76

"You walk fast. If I follow you, I would be walking faster too. Otherwise I'll be late and the teacher will make me stand in the corner." 77

"We are here at this time every day; why should we be late today? What are you up to? Don't try to take advantage of me. I won't listen to you, only to Mistress." 78

"If you walk in front of me then I can see if you walk funny with your feet wrapped in cloth, and if you look like a hairy-legged chick when you walk." 79

"Have you ever seen a hairy-legged chick my size?" 80

"Don't you feel uncomfortable wearing a piece of cloth inside your sock?" 81

"No more than having sand or pebbles in them." 82

"Does the cloth remain flat, or does it narrow into strips or become knotted?" 83

"They are wrapped around my feet." 84

"Don't they come loose? You did not tie them or fasten them in any manner." 85

"Should they become loose, there're always my socks to keep them in place." 86

"Do your socks fit that tightly? You must be very uncomfortable. Do your second and third toes double up one on top of another?" 87

He did not answer but followed quietly behind. 88

"You have to tell me why you wrap your feet in cloth." He pretended not to have heard. 89

I unexpectedly dashed up an earthen mound and ran around at the top against the wind, the black fish flying behind me and knocking against my neck. It scared Chung Jen and he screamed at me, "Come down quickly, please. You may find people urinating on the other side of the mound." 90

Sure enough there were people doing that on the other side, so I came down. 91

"You have to tell me why you must wrap them up; otherwise I'm going up there again." 92

"To save wear and tear of the socks." 93

94 "What's the sense of saving the wear and tear of such ragged old cotton socks? Don't you always bring back new ones every time you return from your home visit? Why are you so stingy? Why are you so careful? Your wife can make you more." I had turned around, stopped short, and asked with my arms akimbo.

95 "She . . . she doesn't know how."

96 "She doesn't know how to make socks? How can she be your wife when she doesn't even know how to make socks? What good is she anyway?"

97 Chung Jen found no answer, but he blushed all the way down his neck.

98 "Who made your socks for you?" We were on our way again.

99 "My ma made them."

100 I saw a beggar push open the door of the beggars' house, and I was scared into total silence. Funny that I should be so afraid of a beggar. What was so scary about a beggar?

101 I was really late that day. It was my fault. Teacher had told us at the end of school the day before that the morning review session was to be held half an hour earlier, because he had to prepare for the arrival of an inspector. I was so happy with my imported Dark Chrysanthemum socks that I had forgotten about it. I was not punished for being late, but it was unsettling to be the last one to walk into the room and to have all eyes trained on me.

102 After the review session was over, all the other children went home for breakfast, but Chung Jen was not there yet to fetch me. I figured the others might be having a second helping of their sorghum gruel already when a tall figure with two long cranelike legs hopped in through the front door.

103 "You're late. If I should be late returning to school you have to make it up to me. Today the Inspector is coming. Whoever is late bringing his charge back to school will be beaten. Just watch out."

104 "I did not do it on purpose. The mistress wanted me to deliver bean rolls to the beggars."

105 On my way home I took an extra look at the beggars' house. It was by then completely under the morning sun. If it were a huge piece of candy, it would have been halfway melted already. The reason I thought of it as such was because our teacher once told us a story about a witch who built a candy house to tempt little children.

106 It seemed to me that since Ma gave them all those bean rolls, all the beggars should be squatting on their heels along the wall and wolfing them down now, yet there was not a single one in sight.

107 "Why give them bean rolls? They're not hungry."

108 "The bean rolls were frozen hard as rock."

109 "I was asking why should they be given the rolls."

110 "It's close to the New Year. Mistress sends them these things on all

three festivals of the year. This is to earn merit points with the gods. You mustn't talk about it."

"What's she trying to earn? Merit points with the gods? What kind 111 of a card is that? What can you exchange them for? Dark Chrysanthemum imported socks?"

"Child, sometimes you're very smart, and sometimes really dumb. 112 How do I know what one can get in exchange for merit points? Maybe longevity or something of the sort."

"Is giving bean rolls to the beggars the only way to earn merit 113 points?"

"All good deeds count. Your papa's abolishing torture and sending 114 minor criminal offenders to the training factory to learn a trade is also a way of earning points."

"But to find you a wife who cannot make socks is not. For you now 115 have to be very careful about wearing them out and have to wrap your feet in cloth."

"How you do ramble on." 116

"In the spring when hot air comes up from the earth do you still 117 have to wrap them?" I remembered seeing hot air bubbling up from the waste land where the beggars' low and dilapidated house was. It always happened in the spring, and it was like the earth was making steamed rolls. This hot air could only be seen from a distance; it rippled like the waves bending the dried weeds and small trees in its way.

"Have to. Socks wear out faster when hot air rises from the earth. If 118 I don't wrap my feet my ma would die of exhaustion."

"Ma! Chung Jen's ma is going to die from exhaustion." I couldn't 119 wait to get home to make the pronouncement.

"What?" 120

"This morning he caused me to be late all because he had to wrap 121 those smelly feet of his; took him an awful long time to do that."

"What about his mother?" 122

"He said if he did not wrap his feet in cloth he would be wearing 123 out his socks too soon and his mother would die of exhaustion from making more socks."

"Ah." 124

"Ma, I have a solution." 125

"What is it?" 126

"Didn't Papa buy a whole lot of those Dark Chrysanthemum socks? 127 I beg you to give him a few pairs; won't that take care of it?"

"Why? They're expensive." 128

"If he had imported socks to wear, he wouldn't need cotton socks; if 129 he need not wear cotton socks, he would not have to wrap his feet in cloth. This way his mother would not die of exhaustion and I would not be late for school. Right?"

The following day Ma brought out two pairs of Papa's old imported 130 socks and a brand new pair, which was white, a color Papa did not much care for.

131   "Give them to Chung Jen. You must not tear off the calico paper since it is a present. No itchy fingers!" Ma was talking about the trademark label. I was not going to let it go at that. What right had Chung Jen to be special? I could do that even with Papa's socks. I drew a black fish on the paper as always; my way of saying, "This too belongs to me."

132   Although Chung Jen now had three pairs of imported socks, some old, some new, he could not bring himself to wear them. He continued to wrap his feet in cloth and wear the cotton socks his ma made for him. When he reached twenty-five, he had saved enough money to buy a piece of land and went home to work his own land.

133   After I grew up, I left home and traveled to a distant land, but whenever I thought of home I always remembered Chung Jen. I remembered reading a story book for children. In it there was a picture of long-legged John, the idiot carrying his donkey home on his back. He reminded me of Chung Jen.

134   It has been more than thirty years since I left home and I never received any word from my family. In 1980 after the iron curtain of mainland China was opened slightly, I received this letter from my nephew:

. . . In the Spring of 1967 Grandma had a stroke, and she became quite confused. The Red Guards came and they confiscated everything. Grandpa was accused of being a rightist; they accused him for serving as the provincial governor of an illegal regime. He was badly beaten and was dragged along and paraded on the streets, and was sent back to his native province. Eventually he was beaten to death at a mass rally. Grandpa never said a single word in defence of himself. It would have been useless any way. All he said was: I did nothing against the law! My conscience is clear. He died with his clothes totally shredded. After he died they dragged him off the stage. He was completely covered with blood, his two bare feet twitching as if they wanted to linger a little longer. My sister and I were forced to witness this violent act, but none of us dared to come forward. We had to draw a clear line of demarcation. Just then a white-haired old fellow with very long legs staggered up and blocked their way. He produced a brand new pair of white socks, tore the brand name paper off in haste and put the socks on Grandpa's feet. He muttered something unintelligible. The socks were instantly covered with blood, but Grandpa would not be going to the other world barefoot.

I picked up the badly trodden paper with the trade name and kept it as a souvenir. It was a piece of white paper with the picture of a black chrysanthemum. The words "Dark Chrysanthemum brand" were printed on it, and there was also the picture of a small black fish. The paper had yellowed with age. It must have been an old relic. I wonder who was that old fellow and how was he connected with our family? I wanted to catch him and find out, but he disappeared in the crowd. Aunt, can you figure out who it could have been . . .

I could not finish the letter. Tears were running down my cheeks. I tried to wipe them away with my hands, but they kept coming. I had a blurred vision, through my tears, of a seven- or eight-year-old little girl walking in the front and followed by a long-legged servant of the family. A young and beautiful mother, her eyes full of love and tenderness holding the hand of the father as they watch a daughter walk toward the county primary school for girls. Suddenly the girl turned around and held on to the long legs of the servant and began to sob, as the shadows of Father and Mother shattered into pieces and faded away.

Questions for Discussion and Writing

1. How does the STRUCTURE of the story make it possible for the reader to discern the pattern of emerging CONFLICTS more clearly? What role do the FLASHBACKS play in providing necessary background information about the childhood of the NARRATOR in China before Mao Tse Tung came to power?
2. How do the perceptions of the little girl as a NAIVE NARRATOR create possibilities for the reader to understand the significance of events that the child cannot? How is the child's inference that her parents hold hands at night an example of a naive narrator's perception? What does this tell you about their relationship?
3. How would you characterize the narrator's relationship with Chung-Jen?
4. To what extent is the child strikingly ignorant of the improverished conditions in which most people live, outside of her own privileged family and high social class? How does the visit of the girl to the beggar's house reveal this?
5. What religious and ethical assumptions seem to guide the parents' behavior in terms of the father's activities, the mother's charity work, and their treatment of their servant, Chung-Jen?
6. What chain of circumstances leads to the unusual event of a servant, Chung-Jen, being given a pair of real store-bought socks?
7. How does the letter received from the nephew in 1980, after the narrator has been out of China for thirty years, provide information on the excesses of the Cultural Revolution?
8. What significance can you discover in the gesture of Chung-Jen putting the store-bought socks on his former master's feet after the master has been executed during Mao's Cultural Revolution? To what extent does this last gesture affirm the importance of human ties over and above political considerations?
9. Is there any idea or belief so important to you that you would be prepared to undergo imprisonment and torture to defend it?

Rigoberta Menchú

The Torture and Death of Her Little Brother

Rigoberta Menchú, a Quiché Indian, was born in the hamlet of Chimel in northwestern Guatemala in 1959. Her life reflects experiences common to ethnic Indians in communities throughout Central America. When she was eight years old she started picking coffee and cotton for pennies a pound. She later left the Guatemalan highlands, home of her native Quiché people, for Guatemala City to work as a maid for a family that expected her to submit to sex with their sons. She survived a genocide that destroyed her family and community: her brother, father, and mother were all killed in acts of savagery after the coming to power of the Garcia Lucas regime in 1978. She fled to Mexico in 1981 after receiving death threats for her human rights work. There she met the anthropologist Elisabeth Burgos-Debray, herself from Latin America, who undertook an ambitious program of interviews with Menchú. The result is a book unique in contemporary literature, I . . . Rigoberta Menchú: An Indian Woman in Guatemala (1983), translated by Ann Wright, a powerful work that speaks of the struggle to maintain Indian culture and tradition. In recognition of her work as an international activist for the rights of Guatemalan Indians, Menchú was awarded the Nobel Prize for peace in 1992. The Guatemalan government denounced the award. This chapter, from I . . . Rigoberta Menchú, "The Torture and Death of Her Little Brother," graphically describes the horrifying incidents of savagery on the part of the army that destroyed Menchú's family and drove her into exile.

> *My mother said that when a woman sees her son tortured, burnt alive, she is incapable of forgiving, incapable of getting rid of her hate.*
>
> — *Rigoberta Menchú*

> *. . . but next winter the requital will come [they thought], and they fed the blaze with branches of the great thorn trees, because in the fire of warriors, which is the fire of war, even the thorns weep.*
>
> — *Miguel Angel Asturias,* Men of Maize

1   It was in 1979, I remember, that my younger brother died, the first person in my family to be tortured. He was sixteen years old. After the family's farewell, each of us went their own way: he stayed in the community since, as I said, he was secretary of the community. He was the youngest of my brothers, though I have two little sisters who are younger. One of them went with my mother and the other stayed in the community, learning and training in self-defence. My mother, unable to find any other solution had gone off somewhere else. My brothers too,

700

because they were being hunted, and so as not to expose the community to danger. . . . The thing is that the government put about this image of us, of our family, as if we were monsters, as if we were some kind of foreigners, aliens. But my father was Quiché, he was no Cuban. The government called us communists and accused us of being a bad influence. So, in order not to expose the community to danger and to weed out this "bad influence," we had to go away to different places. But my young brother had stayed there in the community.

On 9 September 1979 my brother was kidnapped. It was a Sunday, and he'd gone down to another village—he worked in other villages as well as his own. His name was Petrocinio Menchú Tum—Tum is my mother's name. Well, my brother had a job to do. He was very fond of organising work. So he went round organising in various places, and the army discovered him and kidnapped him. After 9 September my mother and the rest of us began to worry. At that time—and I still thank God they didn't kill all of us—my mother nonetheless went to the authorities to enquire after him. If they kill me because of my son, she said, let them kill me. I wasn't there at the time; I was in Huehuetenango when my brother was captured. They say that the day he fell, my mother was at home and my other brothers were not far away. Mother went into the village to find out where her son was, but nobody could give her any news of his whereabouts. However, he had been betrayed by someone in the community. As I said before, there are people who'll turn their hand to anything when you least expect it. Out of pure necessity, often they'll sell their own brothers. This man from the community had been a *compañero*, a person who'd always collaborated and who had been in agreement with us. But, they offered him fifteen *quetzals*—that's to say fifteen dollars—to turn my brother in, and so he did. The army didn't know who he was. That day my brother was going to another village with a girl when they caught him. The girl and her mother followed along after him. From the first moment they tied his hands behind his back, they started to drive him along with kicks. My brother fell, he couldn't protect his face. The first part of him to begin to bleed was his face. They took him over rough ground where there were stones, fallen treetrunks. He walked about two kilometres being kicked and hit all the time. Then they started to threaten the girl and her mother. They were risking their lives by following my brother and finding out where he was being taken. Apparently they said to them: "Do you want us to do the same to you, do you want us to rape you right here?" That's what this thug of a soldier said. And he told the *señora* that if they didn't go away they'd be tortured just like he was going to be because he was a communist and a subversive, and subversives deserved to be punished and to die.

It's an unbelievable story. We managed to find out how he died, what tortures they inflicted on him from start to finish. They took my brother away, bleeding from different places. When they'd done with him, he didn't look like a person any more. His whole face was disfigured with beating, from striking against the stones, the tree-trunks; my brother was completely destroyed. His clothes were torn from his falling down. After that they let the women go. When he got to the camp, he was scarcely on his feet, he couldn't walk any more. And his face, he couldn't see any more, they'd even forced stones into his eyes, my brother's eyes. Once he arrived in the camp they inflicted terrible tortures on him to make him tell where the guerrilla fighters were and where his family was. What was he doing with the Bible, they wanted to know, why were the priests guerrillas? Straight away they talked of the Bible as if it were a subversive tract, they accused priests and nuns of being guerrillas. They asked him what relationship the priests had with the guerrillas, what relationship the whole community had with the guerrillas. So they inflicted those dreadful tortures on him. Day and night they subjected him to terrible, terrible pain. They tied him up, they tied his testicles, my brother's sexual organs, they tied them behind with string and forced him to run. Well, he couldn't stand that, my little brother, he couldn't bear that awful pain and he cried out, he asked for mercy. And they left him in a well, I don't know what it's called, a hole with water and a bit of mud in it, they left him naked there all night. There were a lot of corpses there in the hole with him and he couldn't stand the smell of all those corpses. There were other people there who'd been tortured. He recognized several catechists there who'd been kidnapped from other villages and were suffering as badly as he was. My brother was tortured for more than sixteen days. They cut off his fingernails, they cut off his fingers, they cut off his skin, they burned parts of his skin. Many of the wounds, the first ones, swelled and were infected. He stayed alive. They shaved his head, left just the skin, and also they cut the skin off his head and pulled it down on either side and cut off the fleshy part of his face. My brother suffered tortures on every part of his body, but they took care not to damage the arteries or veins so that he would survive the tortures and not die. They gave him food so that he'd hold out and not die from his wounds. There were twenty men with him who had been tortured or were still undergoing torture. There was also a woman. They had raped her and then tortured her.

4　　　As soon as she heard, my mother got in touch with me and I came home. My brother had been missing for three days when I got home. Most of all it was a matter of comforting my mother, because we knew that our enemies were criminals and, well, we wouldn't be able to do anything. If we went to claim him, they'd kidnap us at once. Mother did go, the first days, but they threatened her and said that if she came again she'd get the same treatment as her son was getting. And they told her straight out that her son was being tortured, so not to worry.

5　　　Then, on 23 September, we heard that the military were putting out bulletins around the villages. They didn't come to my village because they knew the people were prepared, ready for them at a moment's notice. In other villages, where we also had *compañeros*, they handed out bulletins and propaganda announcing punishment for the guerrillas. Saying they had such and such a number of guerrillas in their power and that they were going to carry out punishment in such and such a place. Well, when we got this news, it must have been about 11 in the morning, I remember, on the 23rd, my mother said: "My son will be among those who are punished." It was going to be done in public, that is, they were calling the people out to witness the punishment. Not only that, a bulletin said (we'd managed to get hold of a copy) that any who didn't go to witness the punishment were themselves accomplices of the guerrillas. That was how they threatened the people. So my mother said: "Come along then, if they're calling out everyone, we'll have to go." My father also came home at once, saying it was an opportunity we couldn't miss, we must go and see. We were in a frenzy. My brothers arrived. We were all together at home, my brothers, my little sisters, Mother, Father and me. We were preparing the midday meal when we heard the news and we didn't even finish preparing it or remember to take a bit of food to eat on the way. We just went.

We had to cross a long mountain ridge to get to another village— Chajul, where the punishment took place. Mother said: "We've got to be there tomorrow!" We knew it was a long way off. So we set out at 11 in the morning on the 23rd for Chajul. We crossed long stretches of mountain country on foot. We walked through some of the night, with pine torches, in the mountains. About 8 o'clock the next morning we were entering the village of Chajul. The soldiers had the little village surrounded. There were about five hundred of them. They'd made all the people come out of their houses, with threats that if they didn't go to watch the punishments they'd suffer the same punishment, the same tortures. They stopped us on the road, but they didn't know we were relatives of one of the tortured. They asked us where we were going. My father said: "To visit the saint at Chajul." There's a saint there that many people visit. The soldier said: "No chance of that, get going, go over there. And if you get there, you'll see that no-one leaves this village." We said, "All right." About twenty soldiers, it must have been, stopped us at different points before we reached the village. They all threatened us the same way. They were waiting for the men whom they hadn't found when they emptied the houses, in case they'd gone to work, to make them come back to the village to see the punishments.

When we reached the village there were many people who'd been there since early morning: children, women, men. Minutes later, the army was surrounding the people who were there to watch. There were machines, armoured cars, jeeps, all kinds of weapons. Helicopters started to fly over the village so that the guerilla fighters wouldn't come. That's what they were afraid of. The officer opened the meeting. I remember he started by saying that a group of guerrillas they'd caught were about to arrive and that they were going to suffer a little punishment. A little punishment, because there were greater punishments, he said, but you'll see the punishment they get. And that's for being communists! For being Cubans, for being subversives! And if you get mixed up with communists and subversives, you'll get the same treatment as these subversives you'll be seeing in a little while. My mother was just about 100 per cent certain her son would be amongst those being brought in. I was still not sure, though, because I knew my brother wasn't a criminal and didn't deserve such punishments.

8   Well, a few minutes later three army lorries came into the village. One went a little ahead, the middle one carried the tortured people and the third one brought up the rear. They guarded them very closely, even with armoured cars. The lorry with the tortured came in. They started to take them out one by one. They were all wearing army uniforms. But their faces were monstrously disfigured, unrecognisable. My mother went closer to the lorry to see if she could recognise her son. Each of the tortured had different wounds on the face. I mean, their faces all looked different. But my mother recognized her son, my little brother, among them. They put them in a line. Some of them were very nearly, half dead, or they were nearly in their last agony, and others, you could see that they were; you could see that very well indeed. My brother was very badly tortured, he could hardly stand up. All the tortured had no nails and they had cut off part of the soles of their feet. They were barefoot. They forced them to walk and put them in a line. They fell down at once. They picked them up again. There was a squadron of soldiers there ready to do exactly what the officer ordered. And the officer carried on with his rigmarole, saying that we had to be satisfied with our lands, we had to be satisfied with eating bread and chile, but we mustn't let ourselves be led astray by communist ideas. Saying that all the people had access to everything, that they were content. If I remember aright, he must have repeated the word "communist" a hundred times. He started off with the Soviet Union, Cuba, Nicaragua; he said that the same communists from the Soviet Union had moved on to Cuba and then Nicaragua and that now they were in Guatemala. And that those Cubans would die a death like that of these tortured people. Every time he paused in his speech, they forced the tortured up with kicks and blows from their weapons.

9   No-one could leave the meeting. Everyone was weeping. I, I don't know, every time I tell this story, I can't hold back my tears, for me it's a reality I can't forget, even though it's not easy to tell of it. My mother was weeping; she was looking at her son. My brother scarcely recognized us. Or perhaps . . . My mother said he did, that he could still smile at her, but I, well, I didn't see that. They were monstrous. They were all fat, fat, fat. They were all swollen up, all wounded. When I drew closer to them, I saw that their clothes were damp. Damp from the moisture oozing out of their bodies. Somewhere around half-way

through the speech, it would be about an hour and a half, two hours on, the captain made the squad of soldiers take the clothes off the tortured people, saying that it was so that everyone could see for themselves what their punishment had been and realize that if we got mixed up in communism, in terrorism, we'd be punished the same way. Threatening the people like that, they wanted to force us to do just as they said. They couldn't simply take the clothes off the tortured men, so the soldiers brought scissors and cut the clothes apart from the feet up and took the clothes off the tortured bodies. They all had the marks of different tortures. The captain devoted himself to explaining each of the different tortures. This is perforation with needles, he'd say, this is a wire burn. He went on like that explaining each torture and describing each tortured man. There were three people who looked like bladders. I mean, they were inflated, although they had no wounds on their bodies. But they were inflated, inflated. And the officer said, that's from something we put in them that hurts them. The important thing is that they should know that it hurts and that the people should know it's no easy thing to have that done to your body.

In my brother's case, he was cut in various places. His head was shaved and slashed. He had no nails. He had no soles to his feet. The earlier wounds were suppurating from infection. And the woman *compañera*, of course I recognized her; she was from a village near ours. They had shaved her private parts. The nipple of one of her breasts was missing and her other breast was cut off. She had the marks of bites on different parts of her body. She was bitten all over, that *compañera*. She had no ears. All of them were missing part of the tongue or had had their tongues split apart. I found it impossible to concentrate, seeing that this could be. You could only think that these were human beings and what pain those bodies had felt to arrive at that unrecognizable state. All the people were crying, even the children. I was watching the children. They were crying and terrified, clinging to their mothers. We didn't know what to do. During his speech, the captain kept saying his government was democratic and gave us everything. What more could we want? He said that the subversives brought foreign ideas, exotic ideas that would only lead us to torture, and he'd point to the bodies of the men. If we listened to these exotic slogans, he said, we'd die like them. He said they had all kinds of weapons that we could choose to be killed with. The captain gave a panoramic description of all the power they had, the capacity they had. We, the people, didn't have the capacity to confront them. This was really all being said to strike terror into the people and stop anyone from speaking. My mother wept. She almost risked her own life by going to embrace my brother. My other brothers and my father held her back so she wouldn't endanger herself. My father was incredible; I watched him and he didn't shed a tear, but he was full of rage. And that was a rage we all felt. But all the rest of us began to weep, like everyone else. We couldn't believe it, I couldn't be-

10

lieve that had happened to my little brother. What had he done to deserve that? He was just an innocent child and that had happened to him.

11   After he'd finished talking the officer ordered the squad to take away those who'd be "punished," naked and swollen as they were. They dragged them along, they could no longer walk. Dragged them along to this place, where they lined them up all together within sight of everyone. The officer called to the worst of his criminals—the *Kaibiles*, who wear different clothes from other soldiers. They're the ones with the most training, the most power. Well, he called the *Kaibiles* and they poured petrol over each of the tortured. The captain said, "This isn't the last of their punishments, there's another one yet. This is what we've done with all the subversives we catch, because they have to die by violence. And if this doesn't teach you a lesson, this is what'll happen to you too. The problem is that the Indians let themselves be led by the communists. Since no-one's told the Indians anything, they go along with the communists." He was trying to convince the people but at the same time he was insulting them by what he said. Anyway, they lined up the tortured and poured petrol on them; and then the soldiers set fire to each one of them. Many of them begged for mercy. They looked half dead when they were lined up there, but when the bodies began to burn they began to plead for mercy. Some of them screamed, many of them leapt but uttered no sound—of course, that was because their breathing was cut off. But—and to me this was incredible—many of the people had weapons with them, the ones who'd been on their way to work had machetes, others had nothing in their hands, but when they saw the army setting fire to the victims, everyone wanted to strike back, to risk their lives doing it, despite all the soldiers' arms. . . . Faced with its own cowardice, the army itself realized that the whole people were prepared to fight. You could see that even the children were enraged, but they didn't know how to express their rage.

12   Well, the officer quickly gave the order for the squad to withdraw. They all fell back holding their weapons up and shouting slogans as if it were a celebration. They were happy! They roared with laughter and cried, "Long live the Fatherland! Long live Guatemala! Long live our President! Long live the army, long live Lucas!" The people raised their weapons and rushed at the army, but they drew back at once, because there was the risk of a massacre. The army had all kinds of arms, even planes flying overhead. Anyway, if there'd been a confrontation with the army, the people would have been massacred. But nobody thought about death. I didn't think that I might die, I just wanted to do something, even kill a soldier. At that moment I wanted to show my aggression. Many people hurried off for water to put out the fires, but no-one fetched it in time. It needed lots of people to carry the water—the water supply is in one particular place and everyone goes there for it—but it was a long way off and nothing could be done. The bodies were

twitching about. Although the fire had gone out, the bodies kept twitching. It was a frightful thing for me to accept that. You know, it wasn't just my brother's life. It was many lives, and you don't think that the grief is just for yourself but for all the relatives of the others: God knows if they found relatives of theirs there or not! Anyway, they were Indians, our brothers. And what you think is that Indians are already being killed off by malnutrition, and when our parents can hardly give us enough to live on, and make such sacrifices so that we can grow up, then they burn us alive like that. Savagely. I said, this is impossible, and that was precisely the moment for me, personally, when I finally felt firmly convinced that if it's a sin to kill a human being, how can what the regime does to us not be a sin?

Everyone set to work, so that in two hours there were coffins for all the bodies. Everyone busied themselves with finding a blanket to put over them. I remember they picked bunches of flowers and put them beside them. The people of Guatemala are mostly Christian. They express their faith one way or another; they went to fetch the priest (I suppose that priest's since been murdered as well) to ask him, since he was a long way from the village, to bless the blanket to put over the corpses. When the fires died out, for a while nobody knew what to do: it was both terrifying to see the burned, tortured bodies and at the same time it gave you courage, strength to keep on going. My mother was half dead with grief. She embraced her son, she spoke to him, dead and tortured as he was. She kissed him and everything, though he was burnt. I said to her: "Come, let's go home." We couldn't bear to watch, we couldn't bear to keep looking at the dead. It wasn't through cowardice, rather that it filled us with rage. It was intolerable. So, all the people promised to give all the dead and tortured a Christian burial. Then my mother said, "I can't stay here." So we had to go, to leave it all behind and leave off looking. My father and my brothers were there, grieving. We just saw that the people . . . there were flowers, there was everything. The people decided to bury them there, not to take them home. There would have been a wake in one of the houses, but the people said, they didn't die in a house, it's fitting that this place should be sacred to them. We left them there. And it started to rain; it rained heavily. There they were getting wet, the people watching over the corpses. None of them left that spot. They all stayed. 13

But we went home. It was as though we were drunk or struck dumb; none of us uttered a word. When we got home Father said: "I'm going back to work." Then he started to talk to us. He said, rightly, that if so many people were brave enough to give their lives, their last moments, their last drop of blood, then wouldn't we be brave enough to do the same? And my mother, too, said: "It's not possible that other mothers should suffer as I have suffered. The people cannot endure that, their children being killed. I've decided too to abandon everything. I shall go away." And we all said the same: there was nothing 14 else you could say. Though, for myself, I didn't know what would be the most effective: to take up arms, to go to fight—which was what I most wanted to do—or to go to some other village and continue consciousness-raising among the people. My father said: "I may be old, but I'm joining the guerrillas. I'll avenge my son with arms." But I also considered that the community was important, since I had experience in organising people. We concluded that the most important thing was to organise the people so that they wouldn't have to suffer the way we had, see that horror film that was my brother's death.

15　　The next day my father sorted out his things and left the house without delay. "Whether I return or not," he said, "I know the house will remain. I'll try to attend to everything in the community; that's always been my dream. Well, I'm going now." And my father left. Mother stayed in the house, not knowing what to do. She couldn't bear it, she remembered the whole thing. She cried from moment to moment, remembering. But most of the time she didn't cry; she tried to be cheerful. She said that her son was the one who had been a lot of trouble to bring up, because he'd nearly died as a little child. She had to go into a lot of debt to cure him. And then for this to happen to him. It made her very sad. But there were times when she cheered up. I remember that during this time Mother was very close to the *compañeros* in the mountains. Since we still had my brother's clothes—his trousers and shirts—my mother gave them away to one of the *compañeros* in the mountains, saying it was only just that they should be used by the *compañeros* because they were her son's clothes and her son had always been against the whole situation we were facing. And since the *compañeros* were against it too, they should use the clothes. Sometimes my mother was mad. All the neighbours would come and look. And mother thought: "If I start crying in front of the neighbours, what sort of example will that be?" "No crying; fighting's what we want," she'd say, and she'd act tough, and in spite of the fact that she was always a little ill and felt very tired, she'd battle on.

16　　I stayed in the house a week longer. Then I made up my mind and said: "I must go." So I left, keener than ever to work. I knew that my mother also had to leave home. There was hardly any communication between us, either about where we were going or what we were going to do. I had the chance to say goodbye to my brothers, but I didn't know what they were going to do either. Each of us took our own decision. And so I left.

Questions for Discussion and Writing

1. Why would it be so important for Menchú to find out how her younger brother died and to describe his murder in such exact detail? In your view, what purpose is her account designed to achieve?
2. What picture do you get of the political environment in Guatemala? Why did the government stage this event in the way that they did?

3. How is the captain's narration of the manifold varieties of torture intended to make the villagers feel helpless in the face of the powerful government?

4. How would you characterize the effect this terrible spectacle has on the villagers, on Menchú's father and mother, and on Menchú herself? To what extent was the reaction very different from what the government's soldiers intended?

5. What can you infer about Menchú from the sheer fact that she is able to relate these atrocities that happened to her brother?

6. Describe any action involving two or more people engaged in a wordless conflict (such as wrestling, looking at each other, moving into each other's path). Use as many action words as you can.

Wisława Szymborska

An Opinion on the Question of Pornography

Born in 1923, Wisława Szymborska has lived in Cracow since the age of eight.
Since 1952, she has published eight volumes of poetry, including most recently
The People on the Bridge (1986) as well as translations of French poetry and
collections of essays. Important collections of her poetry, including There But
for the Grace (1972), A Great Number (1976) (as yet untranslated), and
Sounds, Feelings, Thoughts: Seventy Poems by Wisława Szymborska,
translated by Magnus J. Krynski and Robert A. Maguire (1981), have made
her the most popular woman poet living in Poland today. A consistent defender
of the individual, Szymborska's poetry often takes a paradoxical and ironic
stance toward dogmatic authority. "An Opinion on the Question of
Pornography," translated by Stanisław Barańczak and Clare Cavanaugh, presents the voice of a bureaucrat who is as scandalized by free thought as if it
were a form of pornography.

There's nothing more debauched than thinking.
This sort of wantonness runs wild like a wind-borne weed
on a plot laid out for daisies.

Nothing's sacred for those who think.
5   Calling things brazenly by name,
risqué analyses, salacious syntheses,
frenzied, rakish chases after the bare facts,
the filthy fingering of touchy subjects,
discussion in heat—it's music to their ears.

10   In broad daylight or under cover of the night
they form circles, triangles, or pairs.
The partners' age and sex are unimportant.
Their eyes glitter, their cheeks are flushed.
Friend leads friend astray.
15   Degenerate daughters corrupt their fathers.
A brother pimps for his little sister.

They prefer the fruits
from the forbidden tree of knowledge
to the pink buttocks found in glossy magazines—
20   all that ultimately simplehearted smut.
The books they relish have no pictures.

What variety they have lies in certain phrases
marked with a thumbnail or a crayon.

It's shocking, the positions,
the unchecked simplicity with which   25
one mind contrives to fertilize another!
Such positions the Kamasutra itself doesn't know.

During these trysts of theirs the only thing that's steamy is the tea.
People sit on their chairs and move their lips.
Everyone crosses only his own legs   30
so that one foot is resting on the floor,
while the other dangles freely in midair.
only now and then does somebody get up,
go to the window
and through a crack in the curtains   35
take a peep out at the street.

Questions for Discussion and Writing

1. How does the apparent solemnity with which the speaker condemns free-thinking suggest the poem is meant as a tongue-in-cheek satire on censorship?
2. Which IMAGES or phrases depend on double entendres (phrases that can be understood in two ways) to express the CONFLICT at the heart of the poem—expressed through the speaker's horror at the freedom to discuss any subject from any position?
3. How does the STRUCTURE of the poem make it possible for the reader to clearly see the development of the CONFLICT the poem explores? In what way do the last lines represent a decisive TURNING POINT in the speaker's attitude?
4. Create your own dramatic monologue written in poetry or prose in which you assail something as a menace to the public that really is rather trivial.
5. Describe one of your character traits (for example, penny-pinching) or habits (for example, always being late) and write two paragraphs on it. In the first adopt a scolding or haranguing tone, and in the second switch to a congratulatory tone and praise yourself for having this same habit or trait.

Nguyen Chi Thien

I Kept Silent

Nguyen Chi Thien is a poet who was first detained in 1959 for speaking against the authorities. He is reported to have spent the past twenty years of his life in prison camps. In 1979, a collection of his poems was smuggled out of North Vietnam with a covering letter imploring the world outside to publicize the conditions in the prison camps. "I Kept Silent," translated by Nguyen Huu Hieu, first appeared in the Index on Censorship *(vol. 11, no. 3, 1982), a journal comprised of the works of writers whose manuscripts have been confiscated and banned in their original countries. Through the efforts of Amnesty International and P.E.N. International, Thien was finally released from prison in 1992.*

I kept silent when I was tortured by my enemy:
With iron and with steel, soul faint in agony—
The heroic stories are for children to believe.
I kept silent because I kept telling myself:
5   Has anyone, who entered the jungle and who was
      run over by the wild beast
Been stupid enough to open his mouth and ask for mercy?

Questions for Discussion and Writing

1. How is the poem shaped as an exploration of possible reasons why the speaker kept silent under torture?
2. What elements in the poem serve as FLASHBACKS that help explain how the speaker came to find himself in the situation he describes?
3. Explain why you think the speaker kept silent. Do his reasons make sense to you? Why or why not?
4. Interview a male member of your family who lived through a war as either a soldier or a civilian. Points to explore might include how he felt about going, if he volunteered or was drafted, what happened to him in the service and when he returned home, and how he felt about his experiences then and now.
5. Describe a room that contains the physical devices and/or psychological tortures that would be hardest for you to endure.
6. Would you rather be the torturer or the tortured in a situation such as Thien found himself in? Explain why.

Diana Der Hovanessian

Looking at Cambodian News Photos

Diana Der Hovanessian, born in New England, is an accomplished Armenian-American poet and translator. She is the author of ten books of poetry and translations and has won international and national awards and fellowships, including prizes from the Poetry Society of America, the Columbia/P.E.N. Translation Center, and the Massachusetts Arts Council. She is president of the New England Poetry Club and serves on the governing board of the Poetry Society of America. She has been writer in residence and guest lecturer at various universities. Her first book, How to Choose Your Past, *was published in 1978 and a recent volume of poetry is called* About Time (1987). *She won the Barcelona Peace Prize in 1985 for the poem "Songs of Bread," the title poem of a group entitled* Songs of Bread, Songs of Salt (1990), *in which she takes on the persona of the martyred Armenian poet Daniel Varoujan who was executed in 1915. In "Looking at Cambodian News Photos," from* Songs of Bread, Songs of Salt, *seeing the photos of massacred Cambodians evokes the speaker's pent-up grief and forces her to confront the psychological effects of the Armenian massacre by the Turks that took place over half a century before.*

My sack of tiny
bones, bird
bones, my baby
with head so large
your thin neck bends,   5
my flimsy bag of breath,
all my lost cousins
unfed
wearing your pink flesh
like cloth   10
my pink rag doll
with head that grows
no hair,
eyes that cannot close,
my unborn past,   15
heaving your dry tears.

Questions for Discussion and Writing

1. How have the photographs of Cambodian victims of the Khmer Rouge massacre triggered the speaker's suppressed awareness of the Turkish massacre of Armenians generations before?
2. What words or phrases suggest that the poet is experiencing a great psycho-

logical CONFLICT in finally confronting the issue that has burdened her for many years?

3. How does the repetition of "my" and "your" and other key words suggest the speaker is projecting herself and her lost relatives into the photographs of the Cambodians?

4. Do you think writing this poem served as a kind of catharsis in accepting what had happened to her relatives? If not, why not?

5. How do the short, clipped, halting images and phrases in the very form of the poem suggest the difficulty the speaker is having confronting her emotions?

6. Imagine you are an eyewitness to some recent historic event and describe it from the POINT OF VIEW of someone who was directly affected by it.

7. Select a news photo and describe the action the photo contains, adding words that bring out any latent conflict implicit in the picture.

Etheridge Knight

Hard Rock Returns to Prison from the Hospital for the Criminal Insane

---

Etheridge Knight was born in 1931 in Corinth, Mississippi, into a poor family with seven children, and was able to complete only the ninth grade. At age sixteen he enlisted in the army and later fought in the Korean war. He became addicted to drugs as a result of being treated with narcotics for a shrapnel wound. After his discharge from the service, he learned the art of telling toasts (long narrative poems from the black oral tradition that are acted out in a theatrical manner) and performed them in bars and pool halls. From these experiences, Knight developed his gift for writing poetry as a transcribed form of oral poetry. He was arrested for purse snatching and in 1960 was sentenced to serve a 10- to 25-year term in Indiana State Prison. Embittered by his lengthy sentence, Knight turned to the Autobiography of Malcolm X *and other prison works as an outlet for his rage. As he has said, "I died in 1960 from a prison sentence and poetry brought me back to life." His poetry, much of it written in prison, is powerful, as is evident in "Hard Rock Returns to Prison from the Hospital for the Criminal Insane." Knight's works include* Poems From Prison *(1968),* Belly Song and Other Poems *(1973), and* The Essential Etheridge Knight *(1986), which won an American Book Award.*

Hard Rock was "known not to take no shit
From nobody," and he had the scars to prove it:
Split purple lips, lumped ears, welts above
His yellow eyes, and one long scar that cut

Across his temple and plowed through a thick   5
Canopy of kinky hair.

The WORD was that Hard Rock wasn't a mean nigger
Anymore, that the doctors had bored a hole in his head,
Cut out part of his brain, and shot electricity
Through the rest. When they brought Hard Rock back,   10
Handcuffed and chained, he was turned loose,
Like a freshly gelded stallion, to try his new status.
And we all waited and watched, like indians at a corral,
To see if the WORD was true.

As we waited we wrapped ourselves in the cloak   15
Of his exploits: "Man, the last time, it took eight
Screws to put him in the Hole."[1] "Yeah, remember when he
Smacked the captain with his dinner tray?" "He set
The record for time in the Hole—67 straight days!"
"Ol Hard Rock! man, that's one crazy nigger."   20
And then the jewel of a myth that Hard Rock had once bit
A screw on the thumb and poisoned him with syphilitic spit.

The testing came, to see if Hard Rock was really tame.
A hillbilly called him a black son of a bitch
And didn't lose his teeth, a screw who knew Hard Rock   25
From before shook him down and barked in his face.
And Hard Rock did *nothing*. Just grinned and looked silly,
His eyes empty like knot holes in a fence.

And even after we discovered that it took Hard Rock
Exactly 3 minutes to tell you his first name,   30
We told ourselves that he had just wised up,
Was being cool; but we could not fool ourselves for long,
And we turned away, our eyes on the ground. Crushed.
He had been our Destroyer, the doer of things
We dreamed of doing but could not bring ourselves to do,   35
The fears of years, like a biting whip,
Had cut grooves too deeply across our backs.

[1]Solitary confinement. *Screws*: guards.

Questions for Discussion and Writing

1. How does each STANZA of the poem describe one stage in the ACTION and create SUSPENSE as to how Hard Rock has reacted to his "treatment" in the prison hospital?
2. What details make it clear that the story the poem tells is described from the point of view of the inmates who have a lot riding on the outcome? Why

should Hard Rock's transformation into a model prisoner be so devastating to them?

3. How is the fact that we never know the prisoner's real name—only that he is known as "Hard Rock," lend the poem an epic quality?

4. How does the condition in which Hard Rock returns bring all the preceding events to a dramatic CLIMAX?

5. As a research project, you might compare the events described in this poem with issues developed in Ken Kesey's 1965 novel, *One Flew Over the Cuckoo's Nest*.

6. Etheridge Knight became a writer while in prison. The form most prison writing takes is of the dream that begins in the world outside and ends with the dreamer waking up inside prison. Try your hand at composing one of these dream stories or poems.

7. What would a day be like in an institution for the criminally insane? Describe the interactions between the doctors, staff, and patients in a serious or satiricial way.

Eleni Fourtouni

Child's Memory

Eleni Fourtouni was born in Sparta, Greece, in 1933. In 1953 she came to the United States as an exchange student where she studied social studies at Nasson College in Maine. Fourtouni's poetry springs from her translations of nine journals kept by Greek women political prisoners during World War II in Greece. These journals, published as Greek Women of the Resistance, *were compiled by the poet Victoria Theodorou, an inmate of the prison camp and a writer of one of the journals. In 1974, Fourtouni spent several months in Greece, which was still controlled by a military junta, and conceived the idea of translating the work of young Greek poets whose voices had been silenced. Fourtouni's work includes a collection of poetry,* Monovassia (1976), *and an anthology she edited and translated,* Contemporary Greek Women Poets (1978), *in which "Child's Memory" first appeared. A mother's memories of the horrors she witnessed under the Nazi occupation of Greece are triggered when her young son brings her a fish he has just caught.*

Every time I think of it
there's a peculiar tickle
on my throat
especially when I clean fish—
5 the fish my blond son brings me
proud of his catch—
and I must cut off the heads

my hand
holding the blade
hesitates
that peculiar tickle again 10
I set aside the knife
fleetingly I scratch my throat
I bring the knife
down
on the thick scaly neck— 15
not much of a neck really
just below the gills—
I hack at the slippery hulk of bass
my throat itches
my hands stink fish 20
they drip blood
my knife cuts through

the great head is off
I breathe 25

once again the old image comes
into focus
the proud, blond soldier
his shining black boots
his spotless green uniform 30
smiling
he lugs a sack
into the schoolyard

the children, curious, gather
he dips his ruddy hand inside the sack 35
the children hold their breath

what is it, what?
he must have been in our gardens again
looting the cabbage
the children think 40
their brown hands
fly to their eyes
No
we mustn't look
at it 45
it's too horrible

but we're full of curiosity
between our spread fingers
we see . . .

50   the soldier's laughter is gleefully loud
as he pulls out
the heads of two Greek partisans

quickly I rinse the blood off my knife

Questions for Discussion and Writing

1. How does the way in which the poem begins suggest that the traumatic events of the past are never far from the speaker's consciousness?
2. How does the way the poem is constructed build up SUSPENSE as to exactly what the event was that was so horrible as to cast a shadow over the poet's life in the present?
3. In your opinion, how has the poet's relationship with her young son been affected by FLASHBACKS to her own childhood during wartime?
4. What insight does the poem offer into the relationship between the local Greek population and the German army that occupied the town during World War II?
5. Were there any events in the lives of your parents from which they tried to shield you? What were they and how did you react when you heard about them?
6. Interview a female member of your family whose life was deeply changed because of a wartime situation. Report on what you discovered.

Yehuda Amichai

An Arab Shepherd Is Searching for His Goat on Mount Zion

Yehuda Amichai, one of the finest poets writing in modern Hebrew, was born in 1924 in Wurzburg, Germany, of German-Jewish parents who emigrated to Jerusalem in 1936. During World War II, he fought in the British army's Jewish Brigade and served with distinction in the 1948 Israeli War of Independence and in subsequent conflicts in 1956 and 1973. Amichai has published six volumes of poetry, including Songs of Jerusalem and Myself *(1973),* Time *(1979), and* Great Tranquility: Questions and Answers *(1983); a collection of short stories,* The World Is a Room *(1984); and two novels, only one of which,* Not of This Time, Not of This Place *(1968), has been translated into English. Amichai has an unusual gift for transforming personal situations into universal ones, often by setting the present moment against the background of biblical places and religious legends. Many of his poems are set in Jerusalem and draw on its history and landscape to affirm the importance of human connections in a divided country and a troubled world. The tragic overtones of the Palestinian-Israeli conflict are apparent in "An Arab Shepherd Is Searching for His Goat on Mount Zion," translated by Chana Bloch.*

An Arab shepherd is searching for his goat on Mount Zion
and on the opposite mountain I am searching
for my little boy.
An Arab shepherd and a Jewish father
both in their temporary failure.   5
Our voices meet
above the Sultan's Pool in the valley between us.
neither of us wants
the child or the goat to get caught in the wheels
of the terrible *Had Gadya* machine.   10

Afterward we found them among the bushes
and our voices came back inside us, laughing and crying.

Searching for a goat or a son
has always been the beginning
of a new religion in these mountains.   15

Questions for Discussion and Writing

1. How does the action of the poem allude to an age-old historical antagonism going back to biblical times?
2. How does the poem create a story to explore whether individuals can give up automatic responses and timeworn animosities to avoid losing something they value?
3. How does the STRUCTURE of the poem more sharply define the CONFLICT between Arab and Jew and increase the SUSPENSE as to whether they can transcend their differences in order to help each other?
4. Did you ever find yourself in a situation where you and another person had to give up mutual mistrust to achieve a common goal? Describe your experiences.
5. Discuss a belief you once held that you no longer hold. What experiences raised doubts in your mind and led to the change? What actions have you taken that reflect your new attitude?

Amlin Gray

How I Got That Story

American dramatist Amlin Gray was born in 1946. He is currently a play-wright in residence at the Milwaukee Repertory Theater. A prolific playwright, Gray has written numerous works, including Kingdom Come *(1984),* Mickey's Teeth *(1992), and* Bindle Stiff *(1992). He achieved national recog-nition for his play,* How I Got That Story, *which won an OBIE Award in 1981. The play presents a nightmarishly funny vision of American involve-ment in a fictionalized southeast Asian country, Am-bo Land, and is based in part on Gray's experience as a medic during the Vietnam War. To represent the complexity of Vietnam, Gray created a tour de force, multicharacter role called* The Historical Event. *This character is the foil to a naive American reporter fresh from East Dubuque, Iowa. Armed with his pad, tape recorder, and pencil, The Reporter doggedly pursues his goal of finding out what's happening and reporting the events honestly, but is constantly thwarted by The Historical Event (a role that requires one actor to play more than twenty characters of both sexes, different nationalities, and all social strata, including a Buddist monk, an American army lieutenant, and an Ambonese prostitute). The Reporter's pained bewilderment and gradual disintegration become a parable of the tragic experience of the United States in Vietnam. Gray's gifts are many, including an uncommonly sharp ear for idiosyncratic speech and an ability to involve the audience as cocreators of the play through imagination.*

This play is dedicated to Sharon Ott

CHARACTERS

THE REPORTER. An eager young man in his late twenties

THE HISTORICAL EVENT. The actor playing this part appears at times as the entire EVENT, at other times as people who make up parts of the EVENT, as follows:

THE DEPUTY COORDINATOR
MR. KINGSLEY
AN AMBONESE PEDESTRIAN
A BONZE
MADAME ING
A STREET URCHIN
A G.I. IN MIMI'S FLAMBOYANT
LIEUTENANT THIBODEAUX (Pronounced "TIH-buh-doe")
PFC PROCHASKA
A GUERRILLA
SERGEANT PEERS
LI (Pronounced "Lee")
A CIVILIAN FLIGHT ANNOUNCER
AN AMERICAN PHOTOGRAPHER
AN AIR FORCE PILOT
AN AMBONESE PSYCHOLOGICAL WARFARE OFFICER
AN AMBONESE SOLDIER
A GUERRILLA INFORMATION OFFICER
OFFICER X
AN AMBONESE NUN

Every sound effect in the play is made, live or on tape, by the EVENT actor. Where possible, the audience should be able to recognize his voice.

SCENES

One	1	ACCREDITATION
	2	TIP
	3	AUDIENCE
	4	STRIP
	5	FIELD
	6	IMPRINTMENT
	7	PLANES
	8	RUN
Two	1	VILLAGE
	2	SELF-CRITICISM
	3	RESCUE
	4	PROPOSAL
	5	WORK
	6	ORPHANAGE
	7	HOME

SETTING

A wide, shallow space, as bare of props and set pieces as possible. This will help to characterize the EVENT as the REPORTER sees it: broadly, shallowly, and in sharply isolated fragments.

The back wall should be textured in a range of shades from green to greenish brown, perhaps with collage materials (bamboo, scraps of Asian writing, etc.) blended in. The backdrop must serve alike for city scenes and scenes set in the countryside. To facilitate the EVENT's transformations, masked breaks should be provided in the back wall. Slides announcing the titles of the scenes, etc., appear on the back wall, as do photographs of the EVENT, as described.

As the audience is just about getting settled, the EVENT *walks into the playing area, stands utterly impassive, and, his mouth moving minimally, begins to articulate a strange and Asian-sounding musical piece. If any stage light is on him, it goes out with the house lights. He continues his instrumental-sounding version of the foreign melody in the darkness.*

SLIDE: HOW I GOT THAT STORY
SLIDE: starring

SLIDE: (ACTOR'S NAME) as THE REPORTER

(*A light comes up as the slide goes off, showing the* REPORTER *with pencil poised over his notepad, trying to locate the source of the elusive music. The light goes out.*)

SLIDE: and

SLIDE: (ACTOR'S NAME) as THE HISTORICAL EVENT

(*A light comes up on the* EVENT, *from whose passive presence music continues to issue. He is now standing on his head.*)

ACT ONE

SLIDE: ACCREDITATION

(*Lights come up on the* REPORTER. *He is wearing a rumpled lightweight jacket with ink stains around the pockets. He holds a somewhat crushed felt hat in one hand and speaks to the audience.*)

REPORTER: Hello there. This is Am-bo Land. My new job with the TransPanGlobal Wire Service brought me here. It's not the safest place right now, but this is how I figure it. The last two years I've been reporting on the western part of East Dubuque. A lot goes on there. If you add it all up right, then you've got western East Dubuque. That's fine. But if you add up Am-bo Land, it's everyplace. It's *it*. It's what the world is like. If I just keep my eyes wide open I can understand the whole world. That's how I figure it. These are the Am-bo Land offices of TransPanGlobal. Good-sized outfit, hey? I'm here to pick up my accreditation card so I can work incountry. Spell that word without a hyphen.

VOICE: Next. (*The* REPORTER *walks over to a desk. The* DEPUTY COORDINATOR *is sitting behind it.*)

COORDINATOR: May I help you?

REPORTER: I'm here to see Mr. Kingsley.

COORDINATOR: May I ask your business?

REPORTER: I'm just picking up my card so I can work incountry.

COORDINATOR: You'll see Mr. Kingsley.

REPORTER: Thank you.

COORDINATOR: Straight back, third door to the right, first left, and down the hall.

REPORTER: Thanks.

COORDINATOR: He's expecting you.

REPORTER: He is?

COORDINATOR: Yes.

REPORTER: How?

COORDINATOR: You said you work for TransPanGlobal?

REPORTER: Yes.

COORDINATOR: I'm sure you know, then, that our business is communication.

REPORTER: Thank you very much. (*He moves off and into the maze of the* COORDINATOR'S *directions. When he gets to* KINGSLEY'S *office,* KINGSLEY *is waiting for him. He stands up from his desk and shakes the* REPORTER'S *hand.*)

KINGSLEY: I'm so happy to meet you. Please sit down. (*He indicates a chair in front of his desk. The* REPORTER *sits.*) Don't mind if I stare. It's one of the little pleasures of my job when a byline changes to a face. You look quite like your byline, I might say. I couldn't be more pleased.

REPORTER: Well, thank you.

KINGSLEY: I admire your work. Before I'd read two pages of the samples that you sent us, I said, "Bob"—please call me Bob, that's what I call myself—

REPORTER: Okay, Bob.

KINGSLEY: I said, "Bob, this is a man for TransPanGlobal. An impartial man. He views all sides and then he writes the truth as he believes it."

REPORTER: If I may, sir—

KINGSLEY: Bob.

REPORTER: Bob, I'm not sure I'd put it quite that way. I don't think belief is too much help to a reporter. What I try to do is *see*, then write the truth—Bob—as I *see* it.

KINGSLEY: My mistake. Poor choice of words. My meaning was, you don't allow some pietistic preconception to subvert your objectivity. You write what you see.

REPORTER: That's very nicely said, Bob. I'll subscribe to that.

KINGSLEY: On the other hand, you don't write *everything* you see.

REPORTER: I'm not quite sure I—

KINGSLEY: If your wife farts in church you don't run it on the human interest page.

REPORTER: I'm not married.

KINGSLEY: No, I know you're not. That was a figure of speech.

REPORTER: (*"Go on."*) Okay.

KINGSLEY: To bring this down to cases. The Government of Madame Ing is fighting for its life. You probably know that the guerrillas don't confine themselves to Robert's Rules of Order. Madame Ing is forced, in kind, to bite and scratch a little. You may see a few examples. Some abridgement of the freedom of internal opposition. Some abridgement of the outer limbs of those involved. These things may rock you. Nothing wrong with that—as long as you keep one thing very firmly in mind. When we send out reports, the nearest terminal for them is the Imperial Palace. Madame Ing eats ticker tape like eel in fish sauce. That's the A-1 delicacy here, you'll have to try it. Can you handle chopsticks?

REPORTER: Yes, I—

KINGSLEY: Madame Ing is very sensitive to how she's viewed from overseas. Let's face it. When we applied for permission to set up an agency here, we didn't apply to the guerrillas. It's Ing who allowed us to come here, and it's Ing who has the power to send us back. (*Sliding a card across the desk to the* REPORTER.) Let's have a signature.

REPORTER: What's this?

KINGSLEY: Your press card.

REPORTER (*Pleased.*):   Oh. (*He signs.*)

KINGSLEY (*Deftly seals the card in plastic.*):   You'll find this plastic proof against the rainy season, jungle rot—. I took a card like this intact right off the body of a newsman who had all but decomposed.

REPORTER: What happened to him?

KINGSLEY: Madame Ing expelled him but he didn't leave. The will of a developing government will find a way. (*He hands the* REPORTER *his sealed card.*) We're very glad you're with us.

(*Grey-out.* KINGSLEY *disappears as the* REPORTER, *somewhat overloaded, retraces his steps through the maze of "corridors" and out onto the streets. His journey is accompanied by the sounds—made on tape, like all the sounds that follow, by the voice of the* EVENT—*of a ticker-tape machine, crossfading with the putt-beep-swish of Hondas.*)

SLIDE: TIP

(*Lights full up on the* REPORTER, *still a bit nonplussed as he makes his way along the street. He puts the press card in his hatband and the hat back on his head. The tape ends with a whooshing sound as a sudden wind blows the* REPORTER *to a standstill, makes him grab his hat. He stands quite puzzled.*)

REPORTER: That was odd. A sudden breeze, now nothing. (*He wets his finger and holds it up; shrugs.*) Oriental weather. (*Starts walking again.*) I've heard that the guerrillas move so fast you feel a wind and don't see anything, but sitting in your pocket is a bomb. (*A moment's delay, then frantically he pats his pockets from the chest down. Gives a sigh of relief. Then, registering something, returns to the first pocket that he checked. Slowly he draws out a neatly folded sheet of rice paper. Carefully he opens it. It contains a single wooden match. He reads the message on the paper.*) "Han Sho Street and Perfume Boulevard in twenty minutes. A man will ask you for a light." (*Checking his watch.*) Twenty minutes. That would be at two o'clock. What time is it now? (*Checking.*) Twenty minutes of two! Excuse me, sir? (*A* MAN *in a conical reed hat has walked on.*) Sir. Han Sho Street and Perfume Boulevard. Which way? (*The* MAN *snatches the* REPORTER'S *hat off his head and runs. Chasing him.*) Hey! Hey! (*A chase ensues, with the* MAN *appearing from unexpected places, then vanishing, the* REPORTER *farther and farther behind him. A continuation of the street sounds tape accompanies the chase.*) Hey, come back here! Stop! I need that! (*Finally the* MAN *strolls on with his reed hat in his hand and the* REPORTER'S *on his head. Puffing, the* REPORTER *comes in sight.*) Sir, it's not the hat I want. I won't begrudge you that. I know you probably live in very straitened circumstances. I just want the press card. (*The* MAN *points at an offstage sign.*) Oh. Han Sho Street and Perfume Boulevard. (*The* MAN *holds out his own hat, bottom up. The* REPORTER *puts money in it. The* MAN *takes the* REPORTER'S *hat from his head and flips it to its owner. Then he ambles off, counting his money.*) I made it. No one here though. (*He takes the match out of his pocket and holds it awkwardly in front of him. After a moment.*) I'll take the opportunity to absorb a little atmosphere. (*Writing in a little spiral notebook.*) Busy intersection. People. Hondas. Over there a big pagoda. Lots of Buddhists in the windows, dressed in saffron robes. (*As he goes on, the* BONZE—*in saffron robes*—*comes on, unseen by him. The* BONZE *is carrying a large red gasoline can.*) All ages. Every window filled with faces. They're all looking over here in my direction. Not at me, though. I don't *think* at me. (*The* BONZE *has "poured" a pool of gasoline on the pavement.*) I can smell their incense. (*The* BONZE *has set the can down and come up behind the* REPORTER. *The* REPORTER *spins around.*) Oh! You startled me. (*Pause. The* BONZE *just stands there.*) Are you my contact? (*Pause.*) You're supposed to ask me something. (*The* BONZE *stands. The* REPORTER *starts to hold the match up again, to give the man a hint. The* BONZE *takes it.*) That's not incense! That's gas! (*In one resolute movement, the* BONZE *walks back to the puddle of gas and sits down cross-legged in the middle of it. He "empties" the rest of the can over his head.*)

BONZE: Down with Madame Ing! Down with the repressive government of Am-bo Land! (*He scrapes the match on the pavement and at once is "burning" [a red special and a piece of paper crackled in each hand can give the effect]. The* REPORTER *stands rooted with horror.*)

REPORTER: Oh my god. He's burning. People up and down the street are watching. I am too. I'm watching. (*Quickly.*) *I'm* not watching. I'm not here! I'm a reporter! I'm recording this! (*He writes.*) "The monk was sitting in the center of a column of fire. From time to time a light wind blew the flames away from his face. His face was twisted with the pain." The pain, my god—! (*To himself.*) No! You're not here. You're just recording this. You look at it, you take the pencil, and you write it down. (*The* BONZE *topples sideways.*) My god. (*He forces his pencil to his pad and writes. Tape fades up: a low repeating chant in an Asian-sounding language.*) ". . . Charred black . . . black circle on the pavement . . . wisps of orange fabric drifted down the street . . ." (*The lights fade out. The chant continues in the darkness.*)

SLIDE: AUDIENCE

(*Lights come up on the* REPORTER, *still shaken from his experience at the street corner.*)

REPORTER: I went and talked this morning to the Reverend Father of the Han Sho Street Pagoda. Here. (*He takes out his notebook.*) I think I've got it clear now. He explained to me that the—what's that? (*He can't read his writing.*)—the immolation was a political act and a spiritual act at the same time. There are six thousand monks in Ambo Land. Of these six thousand, one hundred and fifty have applied for permission to kill themselves. They wish to demonstrate their faith. But the Reverend Father withholds permission till the worldly motive—political protest—is sufficient by itself to justify the act. (*Quoting.*) "The spiritual act must be politically pure; the political act must be spiritually pure." It's both at once. And so it's sort of—neither . . . If I'd had some sand or water—or I might have tried to damp the fire with my jacket—but that would have been unethical . . . I've got it all down here, though. (*A gong sounds. The* REPORTER *starts.*) The most amazing thing has happened! I'm about to talk to Madame Ing! She summoned me! Reporters have waited years without getting an audience. I can't believe this is happening. (*The gong sounds again, a little louder. The* REPORTER *walks awestruck into the Presence.* MADAME ING *is seated, regally.*)

ING: Here I sit and stand.

REPORTER: Um . . . yes. (*At a loss what to say.*) I've seen you on the cover of *Time* magazine.

ING: Do not mention that loathsome publication in my presence.

REPORTER: But they named you "Woman of the Year."

ING: What year?

REPORTER: Why, last year.

ING: Why not this year?

REPORTER: They never give it to anyone twice in a row.

ING: In my country one must grow in honor as one grows in years.

Time should have named me "Woman of the Decade," next year "Woman of the Century," and so on. I have summoned you.

REPORTER: I'm flabbergasted.

ING: I wish not to know what that word means.

REPORTER: To what do I owe the extraordinary honor of your summons?

ING: To your crime.

REPORTER: My crime?

ING: You bribed the monks of Han Sho Street Pagoda to set one of their fellows on fire.

REPORTER: What?

ING: They filled his veins with morphine till his blood was thin. They led him to the street and they set fire to him.

REPORTER: That's not true.

ING: Not true?

REPORTER: No. The man was alone. Nobody led him to the street.

ING: Then he was hypnotized.

REPORTER: He wasn't.

ING: How do you know?

REPORTER: Because I heard him speak.

ING: A man can speak under hypnosis.

REPORTER: Well, I'm sure he wasn't hypnotized.

ING: Men of the press are expected to have documentation for what they say. Do you have proof?

REPORTER: I saw him.

ING: Look at me. You see my face?

REPORTER: Yes . . .

ING: Am I smiling?

REPORTER (*Peering as through darkness at her unreadable expression.*):   I don't know.

ING: The monk was hypnotized.

REPORTER: *You* have no proof.

ING: I know. You have admitted you do not know. Madame Ing has won that argument.

REPORTER: All right, then, let's just say that he was hypnotized. What makes you think I was behind it?

ING: I have proof.

REPORTER: What proof?

ING: Sheer logic. Highly valued in the West. Tell me what reason might this monk have had to light himself on fire?

REPORTER: Well, I've done a little work on that. His motives were political, exclusively—and therefore they were purely of the spirit. Only by being entirely the one and not at all the other could they be entirely the other and I really thought I had that.

ING: On his first day in my country, a reporter puts this barbecue on ticker tapes that go to every land. Is this not good for his career?

REPORTER: No—!

ING: No?

REPORTER: Well, yes—

ING: You are the one man with a motive for this foolishness.

REPORTER: I didn't do it.

ING: You have proof?

REPORTER: No—.

ING: I have shown you *my* proof. Madame Ing has won *that* argument. It is time to do my dance for you. (*She breaks toward a standing screen.*)

REPORTER: Madame Ing, I hope you won't expel me.

ING: No. You may be wrong.

REPORTER: Wrong?

ING: You may *not* have bribed the monks to burn their friend. (*The gong sounds.* MADAME ING *passes behind the screen; emerges draped in a flowing costume.*) I have an army and I have a private army. (*Dancing a prelude.*) My private army is made up entirely of women.

REPORTER: Yes, I know.

ING (*Silencing him.*): I speak to speak. I do not speak to give you information. Objections have been raised because I pay my women more than my regular army. But my women are all officers, down to the lowest private. Now I present the guerrilla chief. (*She assumes the posture of a bent-haunched, quavering man.*) And this is the lowest of my Paramilitary Girls. (*She strikes the stance of a tall, fierce woman. In the dance that follows—a solo version of the entire Peking Opera—the Paramilitary Girl fights with the guerrilla and defeats him.* ING *withdraws behind her screen. Unseen, she uses a device to alter her voice—say, a #10 can. Reverberant.*) You find us inscrutable here in the East.

REPORTER: It's not just you. It's the Americans here too. I can't—

ING: Be patient. Soon you will understand even less. Your ignorance will be whipped with wind until it is pure as mist above the mountains. But you must await this time with patience—patient as the rocks. We will never be perfectly inscrutable to you till we have killed you and you do not know why. (*The gong sounds.*)

REPORTER: Does that mean I go now? (*Silence. The* REPORTER *starts off as the lights fade out. Slides: on the back wall appear glimpses of parts of the face of the actor playing the* EVENT. *Each slide shows just a single feature. The slides are in exaggerated half-tone—broken into dots as if for reproduction—and thus suggestive of pictures in a newspaper. If the slides come from more than one projector, they should alternate arrhythmically.*)

SLIDE: STRIP

(*The* REPORTER *is standing on the sidewalk of the Strip.*)

REPORTER: These people in power are a little hard to fathom. So I've come here, to the street they call the Strip. This is where the real people come, the normal, regular people. And what better place to look for the reality of this moment in history? Who better to talk to than the G.I.'s and the Government troops, the bar girls and the peddlers, people trying just to get along, to live their lives, to snatch a moment of pleasure or excitement in the midst of the horror and confusion of this war? (*He starts to walk.*) The bars have names like China Doll, Las Vegas, there's the Dragon Bar, that one's the Playboy. Up and down the street are skinny men in short sleeves selling local soda dyed bright red and blue. Little barefoot boys are selling dirty pictures. That is, I'm sure they're dirty. I assume they're dirty. Filthy, probably. (*A* BOY *has pattered on. He thrusts three or four pictures at the* REPORTER, *arrayed like playing cards.*) No thank you, I don't want to see them. No, but wait a minute. I should look. They're part of local color. (*He pays the* BOY *and takes the pictures. Quickly joking to the audience.*) Nope, they're black-and-white. (*Back to the pictures.*) That's awful. Would you look at that? That's terrible. (*Putting the pictures in his pocket.*) These are documents. These say it all. (*A* G.I. *passes the* REPORTER. *He is looking very wired.*) There's a G.I. going into that bar. I'm going to interview him. (*Reading the sign above the "door" the* G.I. *has gone through.*) "Mimi's Flamboyant." Here I go—(*He chokes off, coughing, fans the smoke away from his face. There is a blast of instrumental music—a tinny imitation of Western rock-and-roll, say, "Satisfaction."*) The music's so loud I can hardly see the people's faces. Where did my G.I. go? It's dark in here but all the girls are wearing sunglasses. The girls look very young. They're pretty. No, that's not objective. Stick to what's objective. But they are. (*The* G.I. *comes in from the back, carrying a drink. He looks spent. He sits down at a table.*) Look, there's my G.I. now. Excuse me, soldier, can I talk to you?

G.I. (*Looks at him stonily.*):   About what?

REPORTER: All this.

G.I.:   All what?

REPORTER: The whole thing.

G.I.:   You in the army?

REPORTER: No.

G.I.:   Then what in the fuck are you doin over here?

REPORTER: It's my beat. I'm a reporter.

G.I.:   A reporter? All right. Ask your questions.

REPORTER: What's it like?

G.I.:   What's what like?

REPORTER: Combat.

G.I.:   Scary.

REPORTER: Scary?

G.I.:   What the fuck you think?

REPORTER: I figured it was scary.

G.I.:   You're a fuckin genius. Ask some more.

REPORTER: I don't think we've exhausted that subject yet.

G.I.: Naw, you got it figured, man. It's scary. You got that one fuckin *down*.

REPORTER: Tell me some stories.

G.I.: Stories?

REPORTER: Anecdotes. Some things that happened.

G.I.: Only one thing happens, baby. You're out there in the jungle, right? The fuckin boonies. Everything is green. And then the bullet comes. Your name is on it. That's the story.

REPORTER: Your name is on it?

G.I.: That's a rodge.

REPORTER: What if your name's not on it?

G.I.: Then it misses you and hits your buddy.

REPORTER: Do you have to duck?

G.I.: What?

REPORTER: Do you duck?

G.I.: Your mama drop you on your head when you was little?

REPORTER: So you duck then?

G.I.: Man, you hug that ground like it was Raquel fuckin Welch.

REPORTER: But if the bullet hasn't got your name, it isn't going to hit you.

G.I.: Right.

REPORTER: And if it's got your name—

G.I.: Man, if it's got your name, you can dig a hole and roll an APC on top of you, don't make no never mind.

REPORTER: Then why do you duck?

G.I.: Someone's shooting at your ass, you duck!

REPORTER: It still seems like a contradiction. Guess you've got to go out there and see it for yourself.

G.I.: Out where?

REPORTER: The boonies.

G.I.: Are you batshit?

REPORTER: Huh?

G.I.: You're going out there?

REPORTER: Yeah.

GI: What for?

REPORTER: I want to see. (*Showing his notebook.*) I've got a job to do.

G.I.: You want to see. Tomorrow morning you wake up in your hotel room, you say, fine day, think I'll grab a chopper, go on out and hump the boonies. That ain't it, man. You can't want to go. Somebody got to make you go. Some mean old sergeant, damnfool captain got to tell you, soldier, grab your gear and get your ass out there and hump. You can't want to go.

REPORTER: I won't get out there if it's not by choice. I have to want to.

G.I.: I'm gonna tell you something, hombre. I'm gonna tell you once, so listen. You go out there if you're gonna, but you don't come near my unit. Do you read me? We get hit for sure. You're *bad luck*. You come close to my platoon, I'm gonna waste your ass. You'll never know what hit you. (*Exiting into the back.*) Mama! Mamasan! Hey mama!

(*Blackout. Tape: the sound of helicopters in flight, then setting down—without, however, turning off their rotors.*)

SLIDE: FIELD

(*The* REPORTER *in the field. He has put a mottled green flak jacket over his shirt, and is wearing a tiger-fatigue hat with his accreditation card tucked in the camouflage band. He speaks into the microphone of a cassette recorder that hangs off his hip.*)

REPORTER: This is your correspondent in Am-bo Land, reporting from the field. I've gone out with an American reconnaissance platoon. The choppers dropped us in a clearing. We've regrouped behind the treeline. (*Lights up on* LIEUTENANT THIBODEAUX, *speaking to the troops.*)

LIEUTENANT: Sweet Jesus fuckin string my balls and hang me from a fuckin tree, Christ fuckin motherfuck god damn! Because this war has taught me two things, men. It's taught me how to kill and it's taught me how to swear. God fuckin crap-eye son of a bee, and cunt my fuckin jungle rot and hang me fuckin upside-down and jangle my cojones. Joy roll! Fuckin-A! You hear me, men?

REPORTER: That's Lieutenant Thibodeaux. He's trying to help his troops achieve the right aggressive attitude.

LIEUTENANT: You hear me, men?

SOLDIERS (*On tape; with no trace of enthusiasm.*): Yeah

LIEUTENANT: Sound off like you got a pair! We're Airborne! Say it!

SOLDIERS: Airborne.

LIEUTENANT: Well, that's not outstanding, but it's better. Slip my disc and tie my tubes, god damn and fuckin motherfuck!

REPORTER: He has to win the absolute confidence of the men in his command. If he's not able to, in combat, when he's giving them an order that requires them to risk their lives, it's possible that one of them may shoot him in the back. The soldiers call this "fragging."

LIEUTENANT: I won't lie to you. This is a dangerous mission. But I want you to know, men, I've been out there and I've come back. I've come back every god damn time. That's every motherloving asslick shit-brick pick your nose and fuck me time. I don't wear decorations in the field, but if any man here doesn't believe me he can come to my hootch when this thing is over and I'll show him my Sharpshooter's Badge with four bars and my two Good Conduct Medals. Suck my dick and kick my ass six ways from Sunday. Sing it with me.
I wanna be an Airborne Ranger
I wanna be an Airborne Ranger
I wanna lead a life of danger.

SOLDIERS (*Barely audible.*):   I wanna lead a life of danger.

LIEUTENANT: 'Cause I fight out there beside by men. And here's one thing I promise you. If I give any of you men an order that requires you to lay down your life, it's because I'm wearing army green. I love this uniform. I love the army. Good luck, men. Let's move out! (*He turns and takes a step away. A shot rings out.* THIBODEAUX'S *limbs sprawl outwards as the lights black out. Almost immediately, the lights pick up the* REPORTER *in the same spot where he stood at the beginning of the scene. Once more, he speaks into his tape recorder.*)

REPORTER: This is your correspondent in Am-bo Land, reporting from the field. Our mission was almost aborted by a circumstance the facts aren't quite all in on yet. We'll proceed with Sergeant Peers in charge. He's forming the platoon into a line. I'm supposed to walk at the end. The men say that'll give me the best view of everything that happens. (*He walks in a circle, falling in behind the last soldier—* PFC PROCHASKA. PROCHASKA *carries an M-16 rifle. They hump the boonies during the following, the* REPORTER *carefully copying everything* PROCHASKA *does.*) Excuse me? Soldier?

PFC (*Turning.*):   Yeah? Hey, stagger!

REPORTER: Stagger?

PFC: Don't walk in a line with me! Some sniper hits you gets me too.

REPORTER (*Sidestepping.*):   Check. Soldier?

PFC: Don't call me soldier. I got drafted. Call me Prochaska.

REPORTER: Check.

PFC: And keep it down.

REPORTER (*More quietly.*):   Is this your first patrol?

PFC: Do pigs shit ice cream?

REPORTER (*Not understanding.*):   No . . . (*Speaking furtively into his cassette recorder.*) "Do pigs shit ice cream?" Look that up. (*To* PROCHASKA.) What's the purpose—the objective—of this patrol?

PFC: Find the enemy.

REPORTER: Do you expect it to succeed?

PFC: I hope not.

REPORTER: Are you afraid?

PFC: Do cows have titties?

REPORTER: Yes . . . (*Into his recorder.*) Check "Do cows have titties?" (*To* PROCHASKA.) You don't think I'm bad luck, do you?

PFC: No, you good luck, brother.

REPORTER: Good luck? Super. Although it would defeat my entire purpose to affect the outcome of the mission in any way. But why am I good luck?

PFC: You're walking behind me.

REPORTER: Huh?

PFC: Go-rillas spring an ambush, the man in the back gets shot first.

REPORTER: Sure. That stands to reason.

PFC: You're not carrying a rifle either. They gonna take you for a medic.

REPORTER: What does that mean?

PFC: First they shoot the officer. Then they shoot the medic.

REPORTER: I thought they shot the man in back first.

PFC: Brother, either way . . .

REPORTER: I want to get this straight. Let's say for now that I'm not here, so you're the man in back. Good. Now the officer is Sergeant Peers, and there's the medic. Okay. So, the man in back and the officer get shot before the medic. But which of you gets shot first?

PFC: Man, we all get shot if you keep talking.

REPORTER: The sergeant is raising his hand. What does that mean?

PFC: Break time. You smoke?

REPORTER: No.

PFC: Save me your ciggies from your C's, okay?

REPORTER: Sure.

PFC: Don't sit near the radio. You do, they shoot you first. (*He walks off. The* REPORTER *sits in place.*)

REPORTER: When PFC Prochaska said "C's," his reference was to C-rations, the G.I.'s meal-in-a-box. I'm about to open my first box of C's. (*He takes a small box out of his pack. Reading.*) "Meal, Combat, Individual." (*He opens the box and finds a paper napkin on top; tucks it into his shirt like a bib. Then he goes through the assorted tins and packets, reading their printed contents.*) Cigarettes. (*He puts the little four-pack of cigarettes aside for* PROCHASKA.) Beans with Frankfurter Chunks in Tomato Sauce. Towel, Paper, Cleansing, Wet, Antiseptic. Interdental Stimulator. Cream substitute, Dry, Non-dairy. Chiclets. (*He takes out a book of matches with an olive-drab cover.*) "These matches are designed especially for damp climates. They will not light when wet." (*While the* REPORTER *has been busy with his C's, a* GUERRILLA *has appeared behind him, wearing foliage for camouflage. He has watched the* REPORTER *for a moment, inhumanly still; then, with very small gestures to right and left, has closed in his fellow guerrillas—who are unseen—around the Americans for an ambush, and has vanished. Now the* REPORTER *fingers a small white wad.*) Toilet paper. (*The ambush is sprung. The* REPORTER *holds up his accreditation card. The firing is deafening, intolerably loud. It continues longer than its intensity would seem to allow, then quite suddenly it stops completely; all at once explodes again. The* REPORTER *low-crawls frantically away, nearly running into* SERGEANT PEERS, *who, having reached low ground, starts tuning in the field phone he is carrying. It has a receiver like a regular telephone, leaving one of the* SERGEANT's *ears free.*)

SERGEANT (*To the* REPORTER.): Cover my back.

REPORTER: What? Sergeant Peers, it's—(*He was going to say* "*me.*")

SERGEANT: All behind my back's your field of fire.

REPORTER: I haven't got a weapon.

SERGEANT (*Looking at him for the first time.*):   Christ, it's that one. (*He goes back to the radio.*)

REPORTER: What happens now?

SERGEANT: I try and get my god damn channel.

REPORTER: Where's the radio man?

SERGEANT: Which piece of him?

REPORTER (*Taking out his notebook.*):   What was his name?

SERGEANT (*Into the radio.*):   HQ!

REPORTER: Was he a draftee or did he enlist?

SERGEANT: At ease, god damn it!

REPORTER: Sarge, I've got to get some facts. If I'm not getting facts there isn't any purpose to my being here.

SERGEANT: HQ!

REPORTER: I mean, consider for a moment what my situation is. I don't know anything I didn't know before I got here. What if I get killed? I don't know why that monk was burning, what my boss wants—. What's the word for this? Condition Red?

SERGEANT (*Into the phone.*):   HQ! We're pinned down. Our coordinates are 5730 by 9324.

REPORTER: What's your serial number?

SERGEANT: Will you shut the fuck up?

REPORTER: I'm not getting any news! If I'm not getting any news then what in Christ's name am I doing here? (*A grenade bursts. The* REPORTER *is hit in the rump.*) I'm hit.

SERGEANT: Don't move. (*He quickly checks the wound.*) You're all right.

REPORTER: No I'm not all right. I'm hit.

SERGEANT: You're okay.

REPORTER: Is there blood?

SERGEANT: No sweat. You're gonna see that girl. (*Handing him a pressure dressing.*) Here. Hold this on the wound.

REPORTER: It hurts! I'm going to die! They're going to kill me! Get me out of here! Christ Jesus, get me out of here! (*A whistling.*)

SERGEANT: Here comes the artillery! Flatten!

(*With the* SERGEANT'S *last word there comes a blackout, then a monstrous crashing, ten times louder than before. The barrage continues in the darkness.*)

SLIDE: IMPRINTMENT

(*Lights come up on the* REPORTER *in a hospital bed. He is sleeping. There is a little cabinet next to the bed, with a phone on it. The* REPORTER'S *field clothes are folded on a shelf underneath. His cassette recorder is on top. A knock comes at the door—a very soft one. The* REPORTER *doesn't register it, but he stirs, rearranges himself for more sleep—sees the audience.*)

REPORTER: Where am I? (*He sits partway up and feels a rush of pain.*) Ow! Excuse me. (*Discreetly, he lifts the sheet and turns his hip; remembers.*) Oh yeah. What day is this? The last thing I remember is the medic and the morphine. I should find out where I am. (*He makes a move to get up; stops mid-motion.*) I feel dizzy. (*The soft knock is repeated.*) Come in? (Lɪ *enters: a small, pretty Ambonese bar girl. She walks with little steps into the room.*) Hello.

Lɪ: You sleep?

REPORTER: No, I'm awake. Are you the nurse?

Lɪ: My name Li. Bar girl. I work Coral Bar. You know?

REPORTER: Um—no, I've never been there.

Lɪ: I come here too. Man downstairs who sometime let me in. Are you G.I.?

REPORTER: No.

Lɪ: See? I know you not G.I. I like you better than G.I. (*Coming further into the room.*) You very nice.

REPORTER (*Holding her off.*): No, I'm not nice. I'm a reporter.

Lɪ: Li not understand.

REPORTER: I'm someone who's not here—who's here but can't—do anything, except report.

Lɪ: (*Puzzled.*): You like I go away?

REPORTER: No, you don't have to go away . . .

Lɪ: You lonely.

REPORTER: No I'm not. Not *lonely* . . .

Lɪ: Yes, you lonely. I see.

REPORTER: I'm *alone*. It's a condition of the job.

Lɪ: You tired.

REPORTER: Well, they've given me some medication . . .

Lɪ: You lie down.

REPORTER: I'm lying down.

Lɪ: You lie down all the way—

REPORTER (*Escapes by jumping out of bed—he is wearing blue institutional pyjamas.*): I've got a wonderful idea.

Lɪ: No, where you go?

REPORTER: You sit down. Sit down on the bed. (*Going into the pockets of his field clothes.*) Look, here's some money for your time. There's fifty hoi. Is that enough? I'm going to interview you.

Lɪ (*Not knowing the word.*): In-ter-view?

(*The* REPORTER *has laid two small colored bills on the bed.* Lɪ *picks them up and, somewhat uncertainly, sits down on the bed. The* REPORTER *sets up his tape recorder.*)

REPORTER: I've been feeling, lately, quite confused. I think that maybe, if I just can try and understand one person who's involved in all this, then I might be onto something. Will you tell me your story?

LI: Oh, you like me tell you *story*. Now I see. I have G.I. friend teach
      me tell him your Jack and the Beanstalk. When I get to part where
      beanstalk grow I stop and he say "Fee Fi Fo Fum"—

REPORTER: Not that kind of story. Just your life. Where do you come
      from?

LI: Where you like I come from?

REPORTER: From wherever you were born.

LI: Okay. I try. (*Thinks a second, sizing the* REPORTER *up.*) I was born in
      little village. I hate the guerrillas. Was so glad when many heli-
      copters come all full of big Americans. Americans with big guns.
      You have gun?

REPORTER: No.

LI: Yes you do. I know you have gun.

REPORTER: No, I don't.

LI: Yes, great big huge big gun and shoot so straight—

REPORTER (*Turns off the tape.*):   No, no. That isn't what I want, Li. I
      just want your story. Nothing else.

LI: You shy.

REPORTER: It's just a question of professional procedure.

LI: You like woman to be like a man. I see now. Now I tell my story.

REPORTER: Wait. (*He switches on his tape.*) Go.

LI: I am spy. My name not Li at all.

REPORTER: What is it?

LI: My name *Gad Da Lai I Rang Toi Doung*. That mean Woman Who
      Love to Watch Foreigners Die. I hate Americans.

REPORTER: Now we're getting down to cases. I'll bet all you girls hate
      Americans.

LI (*Encouraged.*):   Yes. I love to kill them.

REPORTER: Have you killed very many?

LI: Every day I kill one or I no can sleep. I like to pull their veins out
      with my little white sharp teeth. This is only thing can make Li
      happy with a man.

REPORTER (*Getting drawn in.*):   Wow. That's *political*.

LI: I like to climb on top of you and bite you, chew your neck until
      your bones are in my teeth and then I crack them—

REPORTER: Stop! You're making this up too. Li, don't you under-
      stand? I want your real story. (LI *has found the light switch on the wall
      above the bed and turned it off.*) Li, turn the lights back on.

LI: You tired.

REPORTER: I'm not tired, I just *feel* tired.

LI: You come here.

REPORTER: I'll bring the tape recorder and we'll talk some more.

LI: You like it in my country?

REPORTER (*Sitting on the bed.*):   No. I hate it. I don't understand what
      anybody's doing. I don't like it here at all.

LI: You like I turn lights on?

REPORTER: Yes.

LI: There. (*The lights are still off.*)

REPORTER: There what?

LI: You no see lights? Then you have eyes closed.

REPORTER: No—

LI: I turn lights off again. (*She leaves them off.*) You like that?

REPORTER: Are they on or off?

LI: You lie down.

REPORTER (*Does.*): Do you wear sunglasses indoors? At Mimi's all the girls wear very dark dark glasses. Are you touching me? You're not supposed to touch me.

LI: I no touch you. (*She is touching him.*)

REPORTER: I saw a man burn with a lot of people watching. I saw Ing dance. I was in the jungle and a piece of flying metal flew so fast you couldn't see it but it stopped inside my body. I'm in Am-bo Land. (*The phone rings.*) The phone? (*He picks it up.*) Hello? (*Pause.*) Mr. Kingsley, yes, hello! (*Pause.*) You're here? Wait just a little second, Mr. Kingsley. (*Turning the lights on.*) Li? (*She is gone. The* REPORTER *looks puzzled but relieved. He takes the phone back up—interrupts his movement to make a quick check under the bed, but* LI *is truly gone. Into the phone.*) I'm sorry, sir—Hello? (*KINGSLEY bursts in, bearing flowers.*)

KINGSLEY: Hey there, how's the Purple Heart?

REPORTER: Hello, sir—

KINGSLEY (*Points a mock-stern finger at him.*): Sir?

REPORTER: Bob! Hello, Bob. You're so thoughtful to come visit me.

KINGSLEY (*Seeing the cassette recorder, which is still in the* REPORTER'S *lap.*): I see you made a tape. You gonna pay the girl residuals? (*The* REPORTER *looks at the machine, then turns it off.*) I got here half an hour ago and saw her coming in here. Figured this'd give you time enough. Hell, just in from the field most guys don't need but twenty seconds. (*He plunks down the flowers on the cabinet.*)

REPORTER: I was interviewing her.

KINGSLEY: Here's something else you'll need. (*He takes a red-white-and-blue card out of his vest pocket and hands it to the* REPORTER.)

REPORTER: What's this?

KINGSLEY: A business card.

REPORTER (*Looks at it.*): It's just a number.

KINGSLEY: You hold onto that.

REPORTER (*Slips it in his shirt pocket.*): Who is it?

KINGSLEY: Officer X.

REPORTER: Who's that?

KINGSLEY: He's probably lots of people. First-rate resource. He's got access to army supply lines. Got a couple of straws in the Ambonese milkshake too. You'll want a stereo system for starters. And an ice machine.

REPORTER: I don't need—

KINGSLEY: It's all on TransPanGlobal. X already has your name. Hey, you're our boy! We wouldn't want you cooped up here without a few amenities.

REPORTER: I've only got a flesh wound. I'll be out of here tomorrow, or today.

KINGSLEY: Today. Tomorrow.

REPORTER: Next day at the latest.

KINGSLEY: I guess you know you got off pretty easy.

REPORTER: Yes, I guess I did.

KINGSLEY: Good luck, huh?

REPORTER: Guess it was.

KINGSLEY: Good luck for you. Bad luck for TransPanGlobal.

REPORTER: How?

KINGSLEY: This thing has hit us right smack in the middle of a gore gap.

REPORTER: Gore gap?

KINGSLEY: Little guy from *Aujourd'hui* lost his esophagus last week. Two weeks ago some wop from *Benvenuto* got his ear blown off. We haven't had an injury for five months. God damn outlets don't believe you're really covering a war unless some blood flows with the ink. So let's say we announce your little contretemps the way it really happened. "On such-and-such a day our correspondent sallied forth to get the news. In the performance of his duty, he was wounded." (*As a questioner.*) "Where?" "He took a little shrapnel." "Where?" "He took a little shrapnel in the ass." (*To the* REPORTER.) Not too impressive. Let me ask you something. Why should we accept that you were wounded where you were and let the whole of TransPanGlobal look like shitheads—are you with me?—when a half a foot—six inches—from your perforated fanny is your spine?

REPORTER: My spine?

KINGSLEY: We're going to say the shrapnel lodged aginst your lower vertebrae. That's nothing that a brilliant surgeon, luck, and a short convalescence can't cure.

REPORTER: How short?

KINGSLEY: Three months.

REPORTER: Three months?

KINGSLEY: The spine's a very tricky area.

REPORTER: Why do you assume I'll go along with this?

KINGSLEY: We brought you here.

REPORTER: You brought me where?

KINGSLEY: To Am-bo Land.

REPORTER: That's supposed to make me grateful?

KINGSLEY: Don't you like it here?

REPORTER: What makes you even possibly imagine that I like it here?

KINGSLEY: By this point in their tour, we've found that most reporters have experienced imprintment.

REPORTER: What's—

KINGSLEY: Imprintment. A reporter goes to cover a country and the country covers him.

REPORTER: You think that Am-bo Land is covering me?

KINGSLEY: It's just a guess.

REPORTER: A guess.

KINGSLEY: That's all.

REPORTER: All right. I'm going to show you just how good a guess it is. (*He gets out of bed.*)

KINGSLEY: What are you doing?

REPORTER (*Getting his clothes out of the cabinet.*):   You see these socks? They're decomposing with the climate. Not the rain and mud. The *air.* The air is putrid in this country. When I go to put on clean socks in the morning they all smell as if some stranger took and *wore* them in the night. (*He flings the socks away and starts to pull on his field clothes over his pyjamas.*) I can't *believe* you thought that Am-bo Land was covering me. It's true that I can't do my job, if that's the same thing. I can never tell what's going on. Nobody ever gives me any answers. If they do I'm asking stupid questions. That's not how my life is supposed to go! I won't accept that! I refuse! It doesn't rain here when it rains. It sweats. The palm leaves drip sweat even in the sunshine. Have you tried the beer? It's great. Tastes like the inside of a monkey's armpits.

KINGSLEY: Where are you going?

REPORTER: First I'm going to the airbase. That's four miles. From there, eleven thousand miles to East Dubuque.

KINGSLEY: You're leaving?

REPORTER: That's eleven thousand-four miles. I'll be counting every centimeter.

KINGSLEY: What about the gore gap?

REPORTER: Blow your brains out. That'll fill it.

Kingsley: This is highly unprofessional. You know that.

REPORTER: No I don't. I don't know anything. I only know I'm going.

KINGSLEY: If you're going, I won't try to stop you.

REPORTER: Great. Goodbye. (*Limping slightly, he starts out.*)

KINGSLEY: You're sure you want to go?

REPORTER: I'm sure!

KINGSLEY: Enjoy your flight.

REPORTER: You bet I will! I'll savor every second! (*He slams out. Blackout. Tape:* A CIVILIAN FLIGHT ANNOUNCER *speaks over an outdoor loudspeaker.*)

FLIGHT ANNOUNCER (*In a voice that reeks routine.*):   Attention on the runway please . . . Attention on the runway please . . . Lone Star

Airlines Flight 717 has completed its boarding procedure . . . Clear the runway please . . . Please clear the runway . . . No more passengers may board at this time . . . (*With a little more urgency.*) Will the gentleman please clear the runway . . . Flight 717 is taking off . . . The gentleman is standing in the backblast . . . Will the gentleman please limp a little faster, he is about to be cremated . . .

SLIDE: PLANES

(*Simultaneously with the slide, the* REPORTER *shouts from offstage.*)

REPORTER (*Live.*):   Okay! Okay! (*Lights up on a black-and-yellow barrier with the legend,* "DO NOT PASS BEYOND THIS POINT.")

FLIGHT ANNOUNCER (*Still on tape.*):   Will the gimp in the pyjama top accelerate his pace please . . .

REPORTER (*Still offstage, but closer.*):   Yes, o-kay!

FLIGHT ANNOUNCER: Now will the moron kindly haul his ass behind the yellow barrier and await the next plane out at that location.

REPORTER (*Rushing on in total disarray.*):   Yes, all *right*! I'm here! I'm *here*!

(*He crawls under the barrier, ending up on the downstage side. The* PHOTOGRAPHER *hobbles on from the opposite direction. He is missing an arm. One foot is in a huge cast. His clothes are multi-layered and multi-colored, and include a Clint Eastwood-style serape. Sundry cameras, lens cases, filter cases hang from straps around his neck and shoulders. A sign on his floppy field hat reads,* "SAY CHEESE.")

PHOTOGRAPHER: Hey man, I need a little help with something, can you help me out?

REPORTER (*Just sits on the asphalt, panting.*):   Damn it! *Damn* it!

PHOTOGRAPHER: Missed your plane, huh? That's a drag.

REPORTER: There's not another plane for seven hours.

PHOTOGRAPHER: There's one in fifteen minutes. That's the help I need.

REPORTER (*Pulls himself up by the barrier.*):   In fifteen minutes? Where?

PHOTOGRAPHER (*Pointing offstage.*):   Right over there. The Weasel. See? She's sleeping. But in fifteen minutes she'll be up there in the sky. It fucks your mind up.

REPORTER: That's a bomber.

PHOTOGRAPHER: Dig it.

REPORTER: I need a passenger plane.

PHOTOGRAPHER (*Enlightened.*):   You mean a plane to *go* somewhere. Okay, man. Not too zen, but—. Wanna help me out?

REPORTER: If I can.

PHOTOGRAPHER (*Extends his foot cast to be pulled off like a boot.*):   Here. Help me ditch this plaster, willya?

REPORTER: What's it on for?

PHOTOGRAPHER: German paper that I sometimes sell my snaps to wanted pictures of a minefield. Who knows why, right? Only, dig it man, the thing about a minefield is it looks like any other field. I mean like that's the whole idea, right? So I tramped a lot of paddies before I found one. Got an action shot, though. KRUUMP!

REPORTER: What happened to your arm?

PHOTOGRAPHER: Ooh that was righteous. It was night time. I was standing getting pictures of the tracer patterns. BAMMO! from behind! I got an incredible shot of that arm flying off. WHOOSH! Little bit underexposed, but something else, man. WHOOSH!

REPORTER: I think you ought to take my flight with me.

PHOTOGRAPHER: You wouldn't wanna leave if you could make these bomb runs.

REPORTER: I could make the bomb runs.

PHOTOGRAPHER: Nix. They just give seats to newsmen.

REPORTER: I'm a reporter.

PHOTOGRAPHER: Yeah? Well shit man, what you waiting for? Come help me get my foot up in the cockpit and then climb on in yourself.

REPORTER: No way. I've got a plane to catch.

PHOTOGRAPHER: These babies drop their goodies and they come right back. Takes half an hour.

REPORTER: They come back in half an hour?

PHOTOGRAPHER: Like a boomerang. Come on.

REPORTER: Not me.

PHOTOGRAPHER: I'm telling you, these flights are ab-*stract*.

REPORTER: Even if I wanted to, I couldn't.

PHOTOGRAPHER: Why not?

REPORTER: 'Cause they wouldn't let me on.

PHOTOGRAPHER: You're a reporter.

REPORTER: No I'm not. I was. I quit.

PHOTOGRAPHER: You quit?

REPORTER: That's right.

PHOTOGRAPHER: You give your card back?

REPORTER (*Lies.*): —Yes.

PHOTOGRAPHER: You didn't, man. It's right there on your hat.

REPORTER (*Taking it out of the hatband.*): I still have the *card*.

PHOTOGRAPHER: Come on! We're gonna miss the takeoff! It's outrageous, man, it pulls your smile till it's all the way back of your head! (*He disappears.*)

REPORTER (*Calling after him.*): I'm not going to go. I'll help you load your cast in, but I'm not going to go.

PHOTOGRAPHER (*Off.*): Come *on*, man!

REPORTER: Okay, but I'm only going to help you with your cast . . .

(*He follows the* PHOTOGRAPHER *off. Blackout. Tape: an orientation by the* AIR FORCE PILOT, *crackling as if over earphones in a helmet.*)

PILOT: I'm gonna tell you right off I don't want you here. I don't know why they let reporters on bomb runs and I'm damned if I'm gonna worry about you. This is a vertical mission. If they hit us while we're diving, I'll try to get the plane in a horizontal position, then I'll jump.

SLIDE: RUN

PILOT: That means there won't be any pilot, so you'll probably want to jump too. (*Lights come up on the* REPORTER *and the* PHOTOGRAPHER *seated in the plane. They are both wearing helmets. As the* PILOT *continues, the* REPORTER *tries to locate the devices he mentions.*) There are two handles beside your seat. Move the one on the right first down then up. Your seat will eject you and your chute will open automatically. If the chute doesn't open you've got a spare, pull the cord on the front of your flight jacket. If that chute doesn't open you can lodge a complaint. Have a good flight and don't bother me. (*The* REPORTER *and the* PHOTOGRAPHER *lurch backwards in their seats as the plane takes off.*)

PHOTOGRAPHER: Okay, man. When the pilot dives, you push a button on the left side of your helmet.

REPORTER: What does that do?

PHOTOGRAPHER: Try it, man. You see the nozzle there? Pure oxygen! (*He takes a hit. The* REPORTER *follows suit.*) You dive. The jungle gets closer and closer like it's flying up to slam you. You can see the tree that's going to hit you, then the leaves on the tree, then the veins on the leaves—and then the pilot pulls out and he starts to climb. The sky comes crushing down on you, your eyes go black, it's like you're being crushed by darkness. Then you level off and everything goes back to normal. Then you dive again. It's outa sight.

REPORTER: Can you see the victims on the ground?

PHOTOGRAPHER: Man, you can see their *faces*! You can see the little lights coming out of the end of their machine guns. Bullets flying up at just below the speed of sound, you screaming straight down toward 'em. Hit one and you cashed your checks!

REPORTER: One bullet couldn't bring a plane down.

PHOTOGRAPHER: Man, at that speed a stiff stream of piss could bring a plane down. Hey! We're diving!

REPORTER: Wait! I haven't got my background done! What's the pilot's home town? I don't even know what the pilot's home town is!

PHOTOGRAPHER: Wooo!

REPORTER: Stop the plane! I have to do an interview!

PHOTOGRAPHER: I thought you quit.

REPORTER: I did, but—(*The plane pitches sharply as it steepens its dive.*) Oh-h-h—

PHOTOGRAPHER: Fifty meters in two seconds! Woo! This guy is good!

REPORTER: My stomach just went out with the exhaust fumes.

PHOTOGRAPHER: See that little man? Guerrilla. Look, he's waiting. Now he's lifting up his rifle.

REPORTER: Pull out!

PHOTOGRAPHER: The pilot let the bombs go. See? They're traveling down right next to us.

REPORTER: Those?

PHOTOGRAPHER: Uh-huh.

REPORTER: Those are bombs?

PHOTOGRAPHER: Yep.

REPORTER: If they slipped a half a foot they'd blow us up. They're getting closer!

PHOTOGRAPHER: Little man down there is firing!

REPORTER (*To the bomb outside his window.*): Down there! Get him! We're your friends!

PHOTOGRAPHER: Yah! Little fucker hit the pilot! Good shot! Woo! (*He starts snapping pictures.*)

REPORTER: We're going to crash!

PHOTOGRAPHER: You bet your ass! We're going down!

REPORTER: Bail out!

PHOTOGRAPHER: You go. I'm staying. You don't think I'm gonna miss this!

REPORTER: Miss what?

PHOTOGRAPHER: When's the last time you saw shots of a plane crash taken *from the plane*?

REPORTER: I'm going! (*He "bails out."*)

PHOTOGRAPHER: Great shot of your ass, Jim! Wooo! (*He whoops and snaps pictures as the scream of the descent increases. The stage goes black as the crash is heard—a colossal explosion. House lights up for:*)

SLIDE: INTERMISSION

ACT TWO

SLIDE: VILLAGE

(*Tape: the voice of the* EVENT *renders the Ambonese national anthem, which is jerry-built and grandiose. As the lights come up, an* AMBONESE PSYCHOLOGICAL WARFARE OFFICER *is taking his place in front of a group of unseen villagers. He carries a small table arrayed with assorted apparatus for the demonstration he is about to perform. A small cassette player on the table is the source of the anthem.*

The REPORTER *is seated on the ground between us and the* OFFICER, *slightly off to one side. He is dressed like a villager, in black-pyjama pants, a conical hat, and sandals. By his feet is a small bundle. He is sitting on his haunches Asian-style, quite relaxed and placid, waiting for the* OFFICER *to start. The* OFFICER *clicks off the cassette.)*

OFFICER: Citizens of So Bin Village, you have done a hard day's work. The Government wishes to submit to you a presentation. (*He arranges his apparatus, which includes a bowl of rice, a basin, chopsticks, a towel, and a quart jug of thick, fetid, poisonous-looking green liquid. While he is thus employed, the* REPORTER *turns to the audience.*)

REPORTER: I drifted in my parachute what seemed like miles and miles and I landed over there. I love this village. I've been here—I don't know how long. I think this is my third week. If I had to write a dateline, I'd be out of luck. I don't, though.

OFFICER (*Holding up the jug of green gunk.*):   This is defoliant. Our friends the Americans use it to improve the jungle so our enemy cannot use it for a hiding place. The enemy has told you that this harmless liquid poisons you and makes your babies come out of your stomachs with no arms and legs. This is not so. You will see for yourself when I have poured some defoliant in this bowl. (*He does. Then "acting" stiffly.*) My but it was hot today. My face is very dirty. I have need to wash my hands and face. (*He does so, dipping and turning his hands in the green liquid, then splashing it on his face. He looks as happy as the people in TV soap commercials.*) Ah! That is refreshing! (*He wipes himself dry.*)

REPORTER (*To the audience.*):   A company of Government soldiers has been using this village an an outpost. They were here when I arrived. Today at dusk some transport choppers will be coming in to pick them up. I mean to pick *us* up. I'll catch a lift to the airbase, then a plane home. Home *America.* (*Bemusedly.*) I don't know why I said that. Home where else?

OFFICER: Mm, my hard day's work has given me an appetite. I think that I will eat some rice. No fish sauce? Very well then, I will pour on some of this. (*He pours defoliant over the bowl of rice and eats it with the chopsticks.*)

REPORTER (*To the audience, referring to his squatting posture.*):   The villagers all sit this way. I started it because my wound reopened when I hit the ground. But after you get used to it, it's really very comfortable.

OFFICER (*Wiping his mouth.*):   My! That was good! But now my hearty meal has made me very thirsty. Ah! (*He "discovers" the defoliant again and drinks the rest of it, straight from the jug; sets the empty on the table with a bang.*) The guerrillas are liars. The Government speaks the truth. Goodbye. (*He clicks the anthem back on and, to its accompaniment, walks off with his gear.*)

REPORTER: It's very peaceful in this village. I've picked up bits and snatches of the language and I'm learning how to harvest rice. I spent the morning threshing. When you get the rhythm you can thresh all day. You slap the stalks against a board. The grains go sliding down and drop into a basket. That's all. Slap, slap, slap, slap . . . Nothing to write about there. No hook. No angle. Slap, slap, slap . . . (*A* GOVERNMENT SOLDIER *comes on. He is tying the legs of a chicken with a cord that hangs from his belt.*) There goes the last of the soldiers. I should go with him. Before I do, I want to show you what I've learned. (*To the* SOLDIER.) *Tay dap moung.* (*Translating for the audience.*) That means, "Stop please." (*To the* SOLDIER, *in a complimentary tone and with a gesture toward the chicken.*) *Kin wau ran faun to bak im brong.* (*The* SOLDIER *stares at him in complete incomprehension. To the audience.*) I understand the language better than I speak it. (*To the* SOLDIER *again, more slowly.*) *Kin wau ran faun to bak im brong.*

SOLDIER: *Fop nah in gao breet? Rew ksawn ep lam?*

REPORTER (*To the* SOLDIER, *waving away his own words.*): *Manh.* (*To the audience.*) The trouble is that Ambonese has all these tones. You say the right sounds but the wrong tones and you've got a different meaning. Apparently I told him that his nose was like a bite of tree farm.

SOLDIER (*Challengingly.*): *Op feo ting ko bi dang?*

REPORTER: Why? Because I *want* to speak your language. I want to *duc fi rop* what you are saying and to *fan bo doung* to you.

SOLDIER: *Ken hip yan geh wim parn ti brong, ip yuh rat.*

REPORTER (*To the audience.*): He says his chicken speaks his language better, and it's dead. That's an Ambonese joke.

SOLDIER (*Indicating the* REPORTER'S *clothes.*): *Fawn tip si bah?*

REPORTER: Am I a villager? Yes. Sure. Why not? *Meo.* I'm a villager. I'm happy here.

SOLDIER: *Prig paw yan tsi mah strak.*

REPORTER: You're not protecting me. I landed in a village you were occupying. *Nik kwan tap.* I wish you hadn't been here.

SOLDIER: *Wep ksi—*

REPORTER (*Cutting him off.*): I'm not afraid of the guerrillas. *Manh kip.*

SOLDIER: *Manh kip?*

REPORTER: *Manh.* I'm not their enemy. In fact, I'd like to meet them. If you think I'm scared, you go ahead without me.

SOLDIER: *Sep?*

REPORTER: You go and catch your helicopter. I'm not leaving yet. *Ping dop.*

SOLDIER: *Ping dop?*

REPORTER: There'll be more troops through here. I can get a ride out any time. America won't disappear. *Ping dop.* Go catch your helicopter. (*The* SOLDIER *shrugs and starts out.*) Goodbye.

SOLDIER (*Turns*): *Dik ram vi clao brong.*

REPORTER (*Translating for himself.*): "Now you'll enjoy your chicken." Good.

SOLDIER: *Wep ksi ren—*

REPORTER: Yes, the guerrillas—?

SOLDIER: *—vi clao—*

REPORTER: "—will enjoy—"

SOLDIER (*Points emphatically at the* REPORTER.):   *—seng.* (*He goes off.*)

REPORTER (*To the audience.*):   There'll be troops coming back to the village. I won't be here long. And the guerrillas—well, all right, if I
surprise them, then it's dangerous. I won't though. Probably they almost know already that I've stayed behind. They'll know before
they come. And so I'll have a chance to talk to them. They'll see I'm
not their enemy. (*He looks up at the sky.*) It's getting dark now. (*He
crosses to his bundle and unwraps it.*) I've been sleeping over here.
Sometimes it's rained, and then I've made a lean-to with my
parachute. Tonight it looks like I can use it for a pillow. (*He "fluffs
up" his parachute—which is mottled shades of green—and stretches out.*)
I love the sky at night here. It's not a pretty sky, but it's alive. You
can see the storms far off in all directions. The clouds are grey, and
when the sheet lightning flashes behind them they look like flaps of
dead skin, twitching. I know that that sounds ugly, but it's beautiful. (*A* GUERRILLA *comes in silently behind him.*) The guerrillas can pretend they're animals. They talk to each other in the dark that way.
They also can pretend they're trees and bushes, rocks and branches,
vines. Sometimes they pretend they're nothing at all. That's when
you know they're near. The world is never quite that still. You don't
have to tell me. This time I know he's there. (*Carefully but decisively,
the* REPORTER *stands up and turns to face the* GUERRILLA. *Blackout. Tape:
jungle sounds—strange clicking, dripping, hissing of snakes, animal cries,
etc.*)

SLIDE: SELF-CRITICISM

(*A small, bare hut. The* REPORTER *is sleeping on the floor. His head is covered
by a black hood and his hands are tied behind his back. A* GUERRILLA
INFORMATION OFFICER *comes in carrying a bowl of rice.*)

GUERRILLA: Stand up, please.

REPORTER (*Coming awake.*):   What?

GUERRILLA: Please stand up.

REPORTER: It's hard with hands behind the back.

GUERRILLA: I will untie them.

REPORTER: That's all right. I'll make it. (*With some clumsiness, he gets to
his feet.*) There I am.

GUERRILLA: I offered to untie your hands.

REPORTER: I'd just as soon you didn't. When you know that you can
trust me, then untie my hands. I'd let you take the hood off.

GUERRILLA (*Takes the hood off.*):   Tell me why you think that we should
trust you.

REPORTER: I'm no threat to you. I've never done you any harm.

GUERRILLA: No harm?

REPORTER: I guess I've wasted your munitions. Part of one of your grenades wound up imbedded in my derriere—my backside.

GUERRILLA: I speak French as well as English. You forget—the French were here before you.

REPORTER: Yes.

GUERRILLA: You told us that you came here as a newsman.

REPORTER: Right.

GUERRILLA: You worked within the system of our enemies and subject to their interests.

REPORTER: Partly subject.

GUERRILLA: Yet you say that you have never done us any harm.

REPORTER: All I found out as a reporter was I'd never find out anything.

GUERRILLA: Do we pardon an enemy sniper if his marksmanship is poor?

REPORTER: Yes, if he's quit the army.

GUERRILLA: Ah, yes. You are not a newsman now.

REPORTER: That's right.

GUERRILLA: What are you?

REPORTER: What am I? (*The* GUERRILLA *is silent.*) I'm what you see.

GUERRILLA: What do you do?

REPORTER: I live.

GUERRILLA: You live?

REPORTER: That's all.

GUERRILLA: You live in Am-bo Land.

REPORTER: I'm here right now.

GUERRILLA: Why?

REPORTER: Why? You've got me prisoner.

GUERRILLA: If you were not a prisoner, you would not be here?

REPORTER: No.

GUERRILLA: Where would you be?

REPORTER: By this time, I'd be back in East Dubuque.

GUERRILLA: You were not leaving when we captured you.

REPORTER: I was, though. I was leaving soon.

GUERRILLA: Soon?

REPORTER: Yes.

GUERRILLA: When?

REPORTER: I don't know exactly. Sometime.

GUERRILLA: Sometime.

REPORTER: Yes.

GUERRILLA: You have no right to be here even for a minute. Not to draw one breath.

REPORTER: You have no right to tell me that. I'm here. It's where I am.

GUERRILLA: We are a spectacle to you. A land in turmoil.

REPORTER: I don't have to lie to you. Yes, that attracts me.

GUERRILLA: Yes, You love to see us kill each other.

REPORTER: No. I don't.

GUERRILLA: You said you didn't have to lie.

REPORTER: I'm not. It does—excite me that the stakes are life and death here. It makes everything—intense.

GUERRILLA: The stakes cannot be life and death unless some people die.

REPORTER: That's true. But I don't make them die. They're dying anyway.

GUERRILLA: You just watch.

REPORTER: That's right.

GUERRILLA: Your standpoint is aesthetic.

REPORTER: Yes, all right, yes.

GUERRILLA: You enjoy our situation here.

REPORTER: I'm filled with pain by things I see.

GUERRILLA: And yet you stay.

REPORTER: I'm here.

GUERRILLA: You are addicted.

REPORTER: Say I am, then! I'm addicted! Yes! I've said it! I'm addicted!

GUERRILLA: Your position in my country is morbid and decadent. It is corrupt, reactionary, and bourgeois. You have no right to live here.

REPORTER: This is where I live. You can't pass judgment.

GUERRILLA: I have not passed judgment. You are useless here. A man must give something in return for the food he eats and the living space he occupies. This is not a moral obligation but a practical necessity in a society where no one is to be exploited.

REPORTER: Am-bo Land isn't such a society, is it?

GUERRILLA: Not yet.

REPORTER: Well, I'm here right now. If you don't like that then I guess you'll have to kill me.

GUERRILLA: We would kill you as we pick the insects from the skin of a valuable animal.

REPORTER: Go ahead, then. If you're going to kill me, kill me.

GUERRILLA: We are not going to kill you.

REPORTER: Why not?

GUERRILLA: For a reason.

REPORTER: What's the reason?

GUERRILLA: We have told the leadership of TransPanGlobal Wire Service when and where to leave one hundred thousand dollars for your ransom.

REPORTER: Ransom? TransPanGlobal?

GUERRILLA: Yes.

REPORTER: But that's no good. I told you, I don't work there anymore.

GUERRILLA: Your former employers have not made the separation public. We have made our offer public. You will not be abandoned in the public view. It would not be good business.

REPORTER (*Truly frightened for the first time in the scene.*):   Wait. You have to think this out. A hundred thousand dollars is too much. It's much too much. You might get ten.

GUERRILLA: We have demanded one hundred.

REPORTER: They won't pay that. Take ten thousand. That's a lot to you.

GUERRILLA: It is. But we have made our offer.

REPORTER: Change it. You're just throwing away money. Tell them ten. They'll never pay a hundred thousand.

GUERRILLA: We never change a bargaining position we have once set down. This is worth much more than ten thousand dollars or a hundred thousand dollars.

REPORTER: Please—

GUERRILLA: Sit down.

REPORTER (*Obeys; then, quietly.*):   Please don't kill me.

GUERRILLA: Do not beg your life from me. The circumstances grant your life. Your employers will pay. You will live.

REPORTER: You sound so sure.

GUERRILLA: If we were not sure we would not waste this food on you. (*He pushes the bowl of rice towards the* REPORTER.)

REPORTER: How soon will I know?

GUERRILLA: Soon. Ten days.

REPORTER: That's not soon.

GUERRILLA: This war has lasted all my life. Ten days is soon. (*Untying the* REPORTER'S *hands.*) You will be fed on what our soldiers eat. You will think that we are starving you, but these are the rations on which we march toward our inevitable victory. Eat your rice. In three minutes I will tie you again. (*He goes out. The* REPORTER *eats as best he can. Blackout. Slides: the face of the* EVENT, *each frame now showing two of his features, in somewhat finer half-tone.*)

SLIDE: RESCUE

(*Lights up on* MR. KINGSLEY, *seated at his desk. He is talking on the telephone.*)

KINGSLEY: Sure they're going to bring him here, but hell, Dave, you don't really want to talk to him. Why put a crimp in your imagination? Make sure you don't contradict our bulletins. Beyond that, go to town. The sky's the limit. (*The* REPORTER *appears at the door.*) Dave, I've got to sign off. Get to work on this right now, check? I'll be firing some more ideas your way as they occur to me. Over and out. (*The* REPORTER *wanders into the office. He looks blown out. He is still in his villager clothes.*) So here you are. How far they bring you?

REPORTER: Three guerrillas brought me to the border of the City. Then they gambled with some sticks. One brought me here. He's gone.

KINGSLEY: You look all shot to shit. Sit down.

REPORTER (*Unthinkingly sits down on his haunches; then continues.*):   He had the longest knife I ever saw. Strapped here, across his back. It would have gone right through me. He took off his thongs and hid them in the underbrush and put on shoes. We started through the streets. He wasn't used to shoes. They came untied. He didn't know how to tie them. So he stood still and I tied them for him. All the time he had this knife. The longest knife I ever saw. (*Pause.*) I'd have gone back out with him if he'd have let me.

KINGSLEY: How you fixed for cash?

REPORTER: I have some. (*He takes some rumpled, pale bills of different colors out of his shirt.*) Here.

KINGSLEY: I wasn't asking you to give it to me.

REPORTER: I owe it to you.

KINGSLEY: No you don't.

REPORTER: A hundred thousand dollars.

KINGSLEY: Just forget about it.

REPORTER: Am I supposed to work for you now? I can probably do some kind of work. I can't report the news.

KINGSLEY: We're square. We'll get our value for the hundred grand. You're a four-part feature. Maybe six if we can stretch it. We might try some kind of angle with a girl guerrilla. That's a thought. (*He picks up the phone.*) Get me Dave Feltzer again. (*To the* REPORTER.) No, all we ask of you is don't give information to the rival press. We want a clean exclusive. We'll be signing your name to the story, by the way. Don't be surprised.

REPORTER: Why should I be surprised?

KINGSLEY: Well, when you read it.

REPORTER: I won't read it.

KINGSLEY: Okay. Want to catch the movie if you can. We're trying to interest Redford. (*Into the phone.*) Yeah, hold on, Dave. (*To the* REPORTER.) I think that's all then.

REPORTER: That's all? (*Pause.* KINGSLEY *just sits with the phone in his hand.*) Okay. Goodbye, Bob. (*He turns and leaves.*)

KINGSLEY (*Into the phone.*):   Yeah Dave. Got a little brainstorm for the sequence in the punji pit. He's down there, right, he's got this bamboo sticking through his feet, and he looks up and sees an AK-47 clutched in little tapered fingers and the fingernails are painted red . . . (*Blackout. Tape: tinny Asian-Western rock-and-roll as in Act I, Scene 4 [Strip]; this time a ballad—say, "Ruby Tuesday."*)

SLIDE: PROPOSAL

(*Lights up on* LI's *room at the Coral Bar. A bed, a doorway made of hanging beads, a screen.* LI *is behind the screen, dressing. The* REPORTER *is lying on the bed. They have just had sex. The* REPORTER *lies quietly a while before he speaks.)*

REPORTER: Li?

LI: Yes?

REPORTER: It's good here. It's so good with you.

LI (*Professionally.*): It's good with you too.

REPORTER: When I look in your eyes, your eyes look back. I love that. That's so important to me.

LI: I love that too.

REPORTER: I love to be with you.

LI: I love to be with you too.

REPORTER: Do you love me, Li? You don't, I know.

LI: I love you. Love you best of all my men.

REPORTER: Do you know what? When I come here I pretend we short-time just because we both just want to. I pretend you wouldn't take my money only Mai Wah makes you take it.

LI: Mai Wah makes me or I no take money.

REPORTER: Would you short-time me for love?

LI: Yes.

REPORTER: Are you sure you would?

LI: Yes.

REPORTER: Are you absolutely sure?

LI: Yes.

REPORTER: Li, I don't have any money.

LI (*Emerging from behind the screen.*): What you say?

REPORTER: I'm broke. No money.

LI: No. You joke with Li.

REPORTER: I had to see you and I didn't want to spoil it by telling you till after.

LI: I have to pay myself now. Mai Wah writes it down, who comes here, how much time. Now you no pay I have to pay myself.

REPORTER: I didn't know that.

LI: Now you know.

REPORTER: I paid a lot of times, Li. Maybe it's fair that you pay once.

LI: Get out of here.

REPORTER: Li—

LI: Next time I see money first, like you G.I. I thought you nice. You trick me. You get out of here.

REPORTER: Li, marry me.

LI: What you say?

REPORTER: I say I want us to get married.

LI: Now you really joke. You bad man.

REPORTER: I'm not joking, Li. I mean it.

LI: Yes? You marry me?

REPORTER: That's right.

LI: You take me to America?

REPORTER: America? No.

LI: Marry me, not take me to America? You leave me here?

REPORTER: I stay with you, Li. I'm not going to America.

LI: You lie. Sometime you go.

REPORTER: I'm never going to go. I'm going to stay here.

LI: No. America is good. Here no good. You marry me and take me to America.

REPORTER: If I wanted to go to America, I wouldn't want to marry you.

LI: Li just good enough for Am-bo Land. You have round-eye wife, go back to her. I know.

REPORTER: You're wrong. Li. I am never going back.

LI: You say then why you want to marry me.

REPORTER: You make me feel at home here and this country *is* my home. I want to sleep with you, wake up with you. I want to look at you and see you looking back.

LI: Where you live now?

REPORTER: Well, really nowhere just this minute. See, I haven't got a job right now—

LI: You go now.

REPORTER: Wait, Li—

LI: You come back, you show me money first. You owe me for three short-times because you stay so long.

REPORTER: Li, listen—

LI: No. You go away. Not be here when I come back. (*She goes out through the beaded curtain. Blackout. Tape: a distant foghorn.*)

SLIDE: WORK

(*Dim lights up on the* REPORTER. *It is dusk. He is waiting for someone.* OFFICER X *appears. He wears a stateside class-A army overcoat with the bronze oak leaves of a major on the lapels.*)

REPORTER: Officer X? Then you *are* an officer. I didn't know if that might be a code name.

X: What's with the gook suit?

REPORTER: It's just my clothes.

X: They've gotta go. Hawaiian shirts and shiny Harlem slacks is best for couriers. You have to blend in. Give me the card that Kingsley gave you. (*The* REPORTER *hands him the red-white-and-blue card from Act I, Scene 6* [Imprintment].) You know the number?

REPORTER: No.

X (*Hands back the card.*): Learn it. (*The* REPORTER *starts to put the card back in his pocket.*) Learn it now. (*The* REPORTER *reads the card, trying to memorize the number. The effort of concentration is hard for him.* OFFICER X *takes the card back.*) What's the number?

REPORTER (*With difficulty.*): 7 . . . 38 . . . 472 . . . 4.

X: Again.

REPORTER: 738 . . . 47 . . . 24.

X (*Pockets the card.*):   Remember it. Don't write it down. Here. (*He hands the* REPORTER *a packet wrapped in paper, tied with string.*)

REPORTER: What is it?

X: Don't ask what, ask where.

REPORTER: Where?

X: Lin Cho District. Tan Hoi Street. Number 72.

REPORTER: Number 72 Tan Hoi Street.

X: Better put it under your shirt. But get an overcoat with inside pockets.

REPORTER (*Hiding the package as directed.*):   I can speak some Ambonese.

X: When we need that, we have interpreters. Be back here with the money in two hours. (*The* REPORTER *starts out.*) Hold on. Do you have a weapon?

REPORTER: —Yes.

X: Let's see it. (*The* REPORTER *doesn't move.* X *takes out a handgun.*) Here.

REPORTER: That's okay.

X: You'll pay me back in trade. Here, take it.

REPORTER: I don't need it.

X: Hell you don't.

REPORTER: I don't.

X: You've got to have it.

REPORTER: I don't want it.

X: I'll just ask you one more time. You gonna take the pistol? (*The* REPORTER *looks at it but doesn't answer.*) Give me back the package.

REPORTER: I can get it where it's going.

X: Give it.

REPORTER: Number 72 Tan Hoi—

X: Nobody carries goods for me unless they're able to protect them.

REPORTER: I'll protect them.

X: If you won't use the gun, don't think I won't. (*He points the pistol at the* REPORTER. *The* REPORTER *gives him the packet.*)

REPORTER: I can speak some Ambonese.

X: You told me. What's my number?

REPORTER: 7 . . . 7 . . . 38 . . . 738 . . . (*His face goes blank.*)

X: Good. Don't remember it again. (*He leaves the way he came. Blackout. Tape: babies crying.*)

SLIDE: ORPHANAGE

(*The crying of the babies continues into the scene. Lights come up on an* AMBONESE NUN *tending children who are imagined to be in a long row of cribs between her and the audience. The* REPORTER *comes in left.*)

REPORTER: Excuse me, Sister.

NUN: Yes?

REPORTER: The Mother Superior told me to come up here.

NUN: Yes?

REPORTER: I'm going to adopt a child.

NUN (*Scanning his garments; gently.*):   Adopt a child?

REPORTER: Yes.

NUN: Have you been interviewed?

REPORTER: Not yet. I have to get a bit more settled first. But the Mother Superior said I could come upstairs and if I chose a child she would keep it for me.

NUN: Ah. How old a child would you want?

REPORTER: He should probably not be very young. And tough. He should be tough. I don't have lots of money.

NUN: You said "he."

REPORTER: A girl would be all right. A girl would be nice.

NUN: It must be a girl. The Government has a law that only girls may be adopted. The boys are wards of the State. When they are older, they will go into the army.

REPORTER: Well, a girl is fine.

NUN (*Starting down the line with him, moving left.*):   This girl is healthy.

REPORTER: Hello. You're very pretty. You have cheekbones like a grownup, like your mommy must have had. Look. If I pull back my skin as tight as I can, I still don't have skin as tight as you. (*He pulls his skin back toward his temples. One effect is that this gives him slanted eyes.*) Why won't you look at me?

NUN: She is looking at you.

REPORTER: She doesn't trust me. (*To the child.*) I won't hurt you. I just want to have a child of your country. Will you be my child? (*To the* NUN.) She doesn't like me. Do you see that child down the line there? (*Pointing right.*) That one's looking at me. Let's go talk to that child.

NUN: That section is boys. This way. (*She leads him to the next crib to the left.*)

REPORTER: She's asleep but, look, her little fists are clenched. She wouldn't like me. I don't want to wake her up.

NUN: Here is another.

REPORTER (*To the third child.*):   Do you like me? I'll take care of you. I understand that you need food, and I'll try and be a friend to you. (*To the* NUN.) She doesn't even hear my voice.

NUN: Here.

REPORTER: These aren't children! These are ancient people, shrunken down! Look at their eyes! They've looked at everything! They'll never look at me!

NUN: You're upsetting the children.

REPORTER (*Pointing toward the boys' section.*):   That child sees me. He's been looking at me since I came in the room. I want that child.

NUN: I've told you that you cannot have a boy—. Wait. Which child?

REPORTER: The one who's standing up and looking at me.

NUN: The child in green?

REPORTER: Yes.

NUN: You can have the child in green. The Government will not object to that. The boy is blind.

REPORTER: Blind?

NUN: Yes.

REPORTER: He isn't blind. He's looking at me.

NUN: He can't see you.

REPORTER: Yes he can.

NUN: He can't.

REPORTER: That child's the only one who sees me. How can he be blind?

NUN: He can't see.

REPORTER: He's looking at me! Can't you see? He's looking at me!

NUN: You'd better go now. Come back when you have made an application and have been approved. The boy will be here.

REPORTER: He's blind.

NUN: Yes.

REPORTER: I'm going to go now. (*He doesn't move.*)

NUN: Yes, please go now.

REPORTER: He's blind. (*He starts out the way he came.*)

NUN: God be with you. (*Blackout.*)

SLIDE: HOME

(*A street in the City. It is dead of night. The* REPORTER *is walking along the street. He is nearly stumbling from exhaustion. When the lights come up, it is as if—from the* REPORTER'S *point of view—they came up on the audience. He looks at the audience quizzically.*)

REPORTER: Hello. You look familiar. I believe I used to talk to you. Are you my readers? I'm doing very well. Last night I found a refrigerator carton that would shelter a whole family with their pigs and chickens. Next to it a trash pile I can live off for a week. If I can find my way back. I kind of get lost on these streets sometimes. (*Pause.*) Sometimes I can stand like this and drift in all directions through the City, soaking up the sounds . . . (*Sitting down on the pavement.*) There's a firefight out there beyond the border of the City. Tracers from a helicopter gunship, see, they're streaming down like water from a hose. Green tracers coming up to meet them now, they climb up towards the ship and then they drop and their green fire goes out. They fall and hit some tree somewhere. The lumber industry is almost dead in Am-bo Land. A fact I read. The trees are all so full of metal that the lumber mills just break their sawblades. (*The lights take on bodiless whiteness.*) Magnesium flares. They're floating down on little parachutes. I floated down like that once. Everything is turning silver and the shadows are growing and growing. The street looks like the surface of the moon. And listen. (*The* EVENT'S *voice, on tape, has come softly on: elusive Asian music from the opening titles of the play. The* REPORTER *shuts his eyes. As the sounds continue, he falls into a position almost too awkward to be sleep; a position that suggests a drunken stupor or a state of shock. The* EVENT *makes more sounds, blending them together almost soothingly: a helicopter passing overhead; distant mortar and automatic weapons fire; more Asian music, very lulling. From far along the street is heard the creaking sound of dolly wheels. The* PHOTOGRAPHER *comes on, now legless, propelling himself on a platform.*)

PHOTOGRAPHER: Hey, is that a body, man? God damn, a Yankee dressed up like a gook. Yeah, that's a picture. Hold it. Smile, Charlie. (*He takes a flash photo. Simultaneously with the flash, the stage goes black and the picture appears on the screen. It is the head and shoulders of a body in the same position as the* REPORTER'S, *and dressed identically. The face is that of the* EVENT. *The picture holds for several seconds, then clicks off.*)

SLIDE: HOW I GOT THAT STORY

Questions for Discussion and Writing

1. How is the reporter characterized? What do we know about him, his skills, his cultural background, and his former experience that might help explain the difficulties he experiences in trying to "get the story"?
2. What is at stake for the reporter in his encounter with the Buddhist monk?
3. How does the reporter's naiveté become a source of humor in his encounter with PFC Prochaska?
4. How does having one actor play a multitude of parts known collectively as the "historical event" connect isolated events in a way that the reporter cannot grasp? How does the audience's objective POINT OF VIEW contrast with the reporter's subjective first-person perspective?
5. How does Kingsley try to convert the reporter's injury into a news story? Why does the reporter go along?
6. How would you define the phenomenon of "imprintment" in your own words? Why is this concept important to understanding why the reporter cannot bring himself to leave Am-bo Land? How could this be understood as his TRAGIC FLAW? In what ways is imprintment a form of addiction?
7. How does the photographer FORESHADOW what the reporter will become if he persists in trying to "get the story"?
8. How does the reporter's addiction to staying in Amboland reveal itself in his relationships with Kingsley, Li, the Bar Girl, and in the orphanage scene? Why does being recognized become all-important to him given the preceding events in the play?
9. How does the CONFLICT in any individual scene reveal the reporter's inability to look at events from the perspective or POINT OF VIEW of any other character?
10. In a short essay, discuss the extent to which this play reflects your under-

standing of the involvement of the United States in Southeast Asia during the war in Vietnam. What features of America's participation might Gray be emphasizing in his characterization of the reporter?

11. Have you ever known anyone who was drawn into an addictive and/or abusive situation and remained in it long after common sense would have suggested it was time to get out? Did the psychological phenomenon of imprintment or addiction operate in the same way as in the play?

12. In what way did the war in Vietnam differ from previous or subsequent military actions in terms of any of the following: congressional approval, public support, international backing, draft versus volunteer army, objectives, media coverage, weaponry, treatment of POWs, cultural differences, duration, casualties, attitude toward returning soldiers, unresolved issues stemming from the conflict (for example, Agent Orange), MIAs, drug addiction, war orphans?

Václav Havel

Protest

Václav Havel was born in Prague, Czechoslovakia, in 1936. Prevented from attending high school, he earned a diploma by attending night class and working as a laboratory assistant during the day. By age twenty, Havel was publishing his first articles in literary and theatrical magazines. He worked as a stagehand at several theaters in Prague and rose to the position of resident playwright at the Ballustrade Theater. His first play, Autostop *(1961), cowritten with Ivan Vyskocil, is a satire on society's preoccupation with automobiles. Havel's first full-length play,* The Garden Party *(1963), is widely regarded as the play that began the theater of the absurd in Czechoslovakia. A second full-length play,* The Memorandum *(1965), continued to articulate Havel's exploration of conflict between citizens and the political system. The play earned an OBIE Award when it was produced at the 1968 New York Shakespeare Festival. Months after Havel's third play,* The Increased Difficulty of Concentration *(1968), appeared, Havel discovered he was under government surveillance and was being watched twenty-four hours a day. Government censorship prevented him from finding a publisher or having his plays produced, and he resorted to circulating his works privately—even as foreign productions of his plays won him an international reputation. His best-known works of the 1970s are his three one-act plays, often called The Vaněk Trilogy after the main character. All three plays—*Audience, Private View, *and* Protest—*focus on how the system intrudes into the lives of common citizens who are not dissidents. Throughout this period, Havel was repeatedly interrogated, held for detention, and imprisoned. He managed to write* Protest, *translated by Vera Blackwell, in 1979 while under surveillance and house arrest before being sentenced to prison for four and a half years. The accounts of his imprisonment, from which he was released in 1983 when he became violently ill, are in his nonfiction works,* Living in Truth *(1989),* Disturbing the Peace *(1990), and* Letters to Olga *(1990), a volume of letters written to his wife. The "Velvet Revolution" that brought down the communist government in 1989 led to Havel's becoming the first freely elected president of Czechoslovakia. In 1993 he was reelected as the president of the newly credited Czech Republic. In* Protest, *the dissident writer Vaněk, a semiautobiographical figure, is confronted by Staněk, a successful writer who has made his peace with the system. Staněk's attempt to justify his own behavior is perhaps the most brilliant theatrical realization of pseudoreasoning and rationalization of political cowardice ever presented on a stage.*

CHARACTERS

VANĚK
STANĚK

PLACE

Staněk's study, Prague.

Staněk's study. On the left, a massive writing desk, on it a typewriter, a telephone, reading glasses, and many books and papers; behind it, a large window with a view into the garden. On the right, two comfortable arm chairs and between them a small table. The whole back wall is covered by bookcases, filled with books and with a built-in bar. In one of the niches there is a tape recorder. In the right back corner, a door; on the right wall, a large surrealist painting. When the curtain rises, Staněk and Vaněk are on stage: Staněk, standing behind his desk, is emotionally looking at Vaněk, who is standing at the door holding a briefcase and looking at Staněk with signs of embarrassment. A short, tense pause. Then Staněk suddenly walks excitedly over to Vaněk, takes him by the shoulders with both arms, shakes him in a friendly way, calling out.)

STANĚK: Vaněk!—Hello!
(*Vaněk smiles timidly. Staněk lets go, trying to conceal his agitation.*) Did you have trouble finding it?
VANĚK: Not really—
STANĚK: Forgot to mention the flowering magnolias. That's how you know it's my house. Superb, aren't they?
VANĚK: Yes—
STANĚK: I managed to double their blossoms in less than three years, compared to the previous owner. Have you magnolias at your cottage?
VANĚK: No—
STANĚK: You must have them! I'm going to find you two quality saplings and I'll come and plant them for you personally. (*Crosses to the bar and opens it.*) How about some brandy?
VANĚK: I'd rather not—
STANĚK: Just a token one. Eh?
(*He pours brandy into two glasses, hands one glass to Vaněk, and raises the other for a toast.*) Well—here's to our reunion!
VANĚK: Cheers—
(*Both drink; Vaněk shudders slightly.*)
STANĚK: I was afraid you weren't going to come.
VANĚK: Why?
STANĚK: Well, I mean, things got mixed up in an odd sort of way— What?—Won't you sit down?
VANĚK (*Sits down in an armchair, placing his briefcase on the floor beside him.*): Thanks—
STANĚK (*Sinks into an armchair opposite Vaněk with a sigh.*): That's more like it! Peanuts?
VANĚK: No, thanks—

STANĚK (*Helps himself. Munching.*): You haven't changed much in all these years, you know?

VANĚK: Neither have you—

STANĚK: Me? Come on! Getting on for fifty, going gray, aches and pains setting in—Not as we used to be, eh? And the present times don't make one feel any better either, what? When did we see each other last, actually?

VANĚK: I don't know—

STANĚK: Wasn't it at your last opening night?

VANĚK: Could be—

STANĚK: Seems like another age! We had a bit of an argument—

VANĚK: Did we?

STANĚK: You took me to task for my illusions and my over-optimism. Good Lord! How often since then I've had to admit to myself you were right! Of course, in those days I still believed that in spite of everything some of the ideals of my youth could be salvaged and I took you for an incorrigible pessimist.

VANĚK: But I'm not a pessimist—

STANĚK: You see, everything's turned around! (*Short pause.*) Are you—alone?

VANĚK: How do you mean, alone?

STANĚK: Well, isn't there somebody—you know—

VANĚK: Following me?

STANĚK: Not that I care! After all, it was me who called you up, right?

VANĚK: I haven't noticed anybody—

STANĚK: By the way, suppose you want to shake them off one of these days, you know the best place to do it?

VANĚK: No—

STANĚK: A department store. You mingle with the crowd, then at a moment when they aren't looking you sneak into the washroom and wait there for about two hours. They become convinced you managed to slip out through a side entrance and they give up. You must try it out sometime! (*Pause.*)

VANĚK: Seems very peaceful here—

STANĚK: That's why we moved here. It was simply impossible to go on writing near that railway station! We've been here three years, you know. Of course, my greatest joy is the garden. I'll show you around later—I'm afraid I'm going to boast a little—

VANĚK: You do the gardening yourself?

STANĚK: It's become my greatest private passion these days. Keep puttering about out there almost every day. Just now I've been rejuvenating the apricots. Developed my own method, you see, based on a mixture of natural and artificial fertilizers plus a special way of waxless grafting. You won't believe the results I get! I'll find some cuttings for you later on—

(*Staněk walks over to the desk, takes a package of foreign cigarettes out of a drawer, brings matches and an ashtray, and puts it all on the table in front of Vaněk.)* Ferdinand, do have a cigarette.

VANĚK: Thanks—

(Vaněk takes a cigarette and lights it; Staněk sits in the other chair; both drink.)

STANĚK: Well now, Ferdinand, tell me—How are you?

VANĚK: All right, thanks—

STANĚK: Do they leave you alone—at least now and then?

VANĚK: It depends—

(Short pause.)

STANĚK: And how was it in there?

VANĚK: Where?

STANĚK: Can our sort bear it at all?

VANĚK: You mean prison? What else can one do?

STANĚK: As far as I recall, you used to be bothered by hemorrhoids. Must have been terrible, considering the hygiene in there.

VANĚK: They gave me suppositories—

STANĚK: You ought to have them operated on, you know. It so happens a friend of mine is our greatest hemorrhoid specialist. Works real miracles. I'll arrange it for you.

VANĚK: Thanks—

(Short pause.)

STANĚK: You know, sometimes it all seems like a beautiful dream—all the exciting opening nights, private views, lectures, meetings—the endless discussions about literature and art! All the energy, the hopes, plans, activities, ideas—the wine-bars crowded with friends, the wild booze-ups, the madcap affrays in the small hours, the jolly girls dancing attendance on us! And the mountains of work we managed to get done, regardless!—That's all over now. It'll never come back!

VANĚK: Mmn—

(Pause. Both drink.)

STANĚK: Did they beat you?

VANĚK: No—

STANĚK: Do they beat people up in there?

VANĚK: Sometimes. But not the politicals—

STANĚK: I thought about you a great deal!

VANĚK: Thank you—

(Short pause.)

STANĚK: I bet in those days it never even occurred to you—

VANĚK: What?

STANĚK: How it'll all end up! I bet not even you had guessed that!

VANĚK: Mmn—

STANĚK: It's disgusting, Ferdinand, disgusting! The nation is governed by scum! And the people? Can this really be the same nation which not very long ago behaved so magnificently? All that horrible cringing, bowing and scraping! The selfishness, corruption and fear wherever you turn! What have they made of us, old pal? Can this really be us?

VANĚK: I don't believe things are as black as all that—

STANĚK: Forgive me, Ferdinand, but you don't happen to live in a normal environment. All you know are people who manage to resist this rot. You just keep on supporting and encouraging each other. You've no idea the sort of environment I've got to put up with! You're lucky you no longer have anything to do with it. Makes you sick at your stomach!

(*Pause. Both drink.*)

VANĚK: You mean television?

STANĚK: In television, in film studios—you name it.

VANĚK: There was a piece by you on the T.V. the other day—

STANĚK: You can't imagine what an ordeal that was! First they kept blocking it for over a year, then they started changing it around— changed my whole opening and the entire closing sequence! You wouldn't believe the trifles they find objectionable these days! Nothing but sterility and intrigues, intrigues and sterility! How often I tell myself—wrap it up, chum, forget it, go hide somewhere— grow apricots—

VANĚK: I know what you mean—

STANĚK: The thing is though, one can't help wondering whether one's got the right to this sort of escape. Supposing even the little one might be able to accomplish today can, in spite of everything, help someone in some way, at least give him a bit of encouragement, uplift him a little.—Let me bring you a pair of slippers.

VANĚK: Slippers? Why?

STANĚK: You can't be comfortable in those boots.

VANĚK: I'm all right—

STANĚK: Are you sure?

VANĚK: Yes. Really—

(*Both drink.*)

STANĚK (*Pause.*): How about drugs? Did they give you any?

VANĚK: No—

STANĚK: No dubious injections?

VANĚK: Only some vitamin ones—

STANĚK: I bet there's some funny stuff in the food!

VANĚK: Just bromine against sex—

STANĚK: But surely they tried to break you down somehow!

VANĚK: Well—

STANĚK: If you'd rather not talk about it, it's all right with me.

VANĚK: Well, in a way, that's the whole point of pre-trial interrogations, isn't it? To take one down a peg or two—

STANĚK: And to make one talk!

VANĚK: Mmn—

STANĚK: If they should haul me in for questioning—which sooner or later is bound to happen—you know what I'm going to do?

VANĚK: What?

STANĚK: Simply not answer any of their questions! Refuse to talk to them at all! That's by far the best way. Least one can be quite sure one didn't say anything one ought not to have said!

VANĚK: Mmn—

STANĚK: Anyway, you must have steel nerves to be able to bear it all and in addition to keep doing the things you do.

VANĚK: Like what?

STANĚK: Well, I mean all the protests, petitions, letters—the whole fight for human rights! I mean the things you and your friends keep on doing—

VANĚK: I'm not doing so much—

STANĚK: Now don't be too modest, Ferdinand! I follow everything that's going on! I know! If everybody did what you do, the situation would be quite different! And that's a fact. It's extremely important there should be at least a few people here who aren't afraid to speak the truth aloud, to defend others, to call a spade a spade! What I'm going to say might sound a bit solemn perhaps, but frankly, the way I see it, you and your friends have taken on an almost superhuman task: to preserve and to carry the remains, the remnant of moral conscience through the present quagmire! The thread you're spinning may be thin, but—who knows—perhaps the hope of a moral rebirth of the nation hangs on it.

VANĚK: You exaggerate—

STANĚK: Well, that's how I see it, anyway.

VANĚK: Surely our hope lies in all the decent people—

STANĚK: But how many are there still around? How many?

VANĚK: Enough—

STANĚK: Are there? Even so, it's you and your friends who are the most exposed to view.

VANĚK: And isn't that precisely what makes it easier for us?

STANĚK: I wouldn't say so. The more you're exposed, the more responsibility you have towards all those who know about you, trust you, rely on you and look up to you, because to some extent you keep upholding their honour, too! (*Gets up.*) I'll get you those slippers!

VANĚK: Please don't bother—

STANĚK: I insist. I feel uncomfortable just looking at your boots. (*Pause. Staněk returns with slippers.*)

VANĚK: (*Sighs.*)

STANĚK: Here you are. Do take those ugly things off, I beg you. Let me—

(*Tries to take off Vaněk's boots.*) Won't you let me—Hold still—

VANĚK (*Embarrassed.*):　No—please don't—no—I'll do it—(*Struggles out of his boots, slips on slippers.*) There—Nice, aren't they? Thank you very much.

STANĚK:　Good gracious, Ferdinand, what for?—(*Hovering over Vaněk.*) Some more brandy?

VANĚK:　No more for me, thanks—

STANĚK:　Oh, come on. Give me your glass!

VANĚK:　I'm sorry, I'm not feeling too well—

STANĚK:　Lost the habit inside, is that it?

VANĚK:　Could be—But the point is—last night, you see—

STANĚK:　Ah, that's what it is. Had a drop too many, eh?

VANĚK:　Mmn—

STANĚK:　I understand. (*Returns to his chair.*) By the way, you know the new wine-bar, "The Shaggy Dog"?

VANĚK:　No—

STANĚK:　You don't? Listen, the wine there comes straight from the cask, it's not expensive and usually it isn't crowded. Really charming spot, you know, thanks to a handful of fairly good artists who were permitted—believe it or not—to do the interior decoration. I can warmly recommend it to you. Lovely place. Where did you go, then?

VANĚK:　Well, we did a little pub-crawling, my friend Landovský and I—

STANĚK:　Oh, I see! You were with Landovský, were you? Well! In that case, I'm not at all surprised you came to a sticky end! He's a first class actor, but once he starts drinking—that's it! Surely you can take one more brandy! Right?

VANĚK:　(*Sighs.*)

(*Drinks are poured. They both drink. Vaněk shudders.*)

STANĚK (*Back in his armchair. Short pause.*):　Well, how are things otherwise? You do any writing?

VANĚK:　Trying to—

STANĚK:　A play?

VANĚK:　A one-act play—

STANĚK:　Another autobiographical one?

VANĚKK:　More or less—

STANĚK:　My wife and I read the one about the brewery[1] the other day. We thought it was very amusing.

VANĚK:　I'm glad—

STANĚK:　Unfortunately we were given a rather bad copy.[2] Very hard to read.

---

[1]Staněk is referring to *Audience.*

[2]Literary works circulating as *samizdat* texts in typescript are understandably often of poor quality. If one gets to read the, say, sixth carbon copy on onion skin, the readability of the script leaves much to be desired.

VANĚK: I'm sorry—

STANĚK: It's a really brilliant little piece! I mean it! Only the ending seemed to me a bit muddy. The whole thing wants to be brought to a more straightforward conclusion, that's all. No problem. You can do it.

(*Pause. Both drink. Vaněk shudders.*)

STANĚK: Well, how are things? How about Pavel?[3] Do you see him?

VANĚK: Yes—

STANĚK: Does he do any writing?

VANĚK: Just now he's finishing a one-act, as well. It's supposed to be performed together with mine—

STANĚK: Wait a minute. You don't mean to tell me you two have teamed up also as authors!

VANĚK: More or less—

STANĚK: Well, well!—Frankly, Ferdinand, try as I may, I don't get it. I don't. I simply can't understand this alliance of yours. Is it quite genuine on your part? Is it?—Good heavens! Pavel! I don't know! Just remember the way he started! We both belong to the same generation, Pavel and I, we've both—so to speak—spanned a similar arc of development, but I don't mind telling you that what he did in those days—Well! It was a bit too strong even for me!—Still, I suppose it's your business. You know best what you're doing.

VANĚK: That's right—

(*Pause. Both drink.*)

STANĚK: Is your wife fond of gladioli?

VANĚK: I don't know. I think so—

STANĚK: You won't find many places with such a large selection as mine. I've got thirty-two shades, whereas at a common or garden nursery you'll be lucky to find six. Do you think your wife would like me to send her some bulbs?

VANĚK: I'm sure she would—

STANĚK: There's still time to plant them you know. (*Pause.*) Ferdinand—

VANĚK: Yes?

STANĚKK: Weren't you surprised when I suddenly called you up?

VANĚK: A bit—

STANĚK: I thought so. After all, I happen to be among those who've still managed to keep their heads above water and I quite understand that—because of this—you might want to keep a certain distance from me.

VANĚK: No, not I—

STANĚK: Perhaps not you yourself, but I realize that some of your friends believe that anyone who's still got some chance today has either abdicated morally, or is unforgivably fooling himself.

---

[3]Staněk means Pavel Kohout.

VANĚK: I don't think so—

STANĚK: I wouldn't blame you if you did, because I know only too well the grounds from which such prejudice could grow. (*An embarrassed pause.*) Ferdinand—

VANĚK: Yes?

STANĚK: I realize what a high price you have to pay for what you're doing. But please don't think it's all that easy for a man who's either so lucky, or so unfortunate as to be still tolerated by the official apparatus, and who—at the same time—wishes to live at peace with his conscience.

VANĚK: I know what you mean—

STANĚK: In some respects it may be even harder for him.

VANĚK: I understand.

STANĚK: Naturally, I didn't call you in order to justify myself! I don't really think there's any need. I called you because I like you and I'd be sorry to see you sharing the prejudice which I assume exists among your friends.

VANĚK: As far as I know nobody has ever said a bad word about you—

STANĚK: Not even Pavel?

VANĚK: No—

STANĚK (*Embarrassed pause.*):   Ferdinand—

VANĚK: Yes?

STANĚK: Excuse me—(*Gets up. Crosses to the tape recorder. Switches it on: Soft, nondescript background music. Staněk returns to his chair.*) Ferdinand, does the name Javurek mean anything to you?

VANĚK: The pop singer? I know him very well—

STANĚK: So I expect you know what happened to him.

VANĚK: Of course. They locked him up for telling a story during one of his performances. The story about the cop who meets a penguin in the street—

STANĚK: Of course. It was just an excuse. The fact is, they hate his guts because he sings the way he does. The whole thing is so cruel, so ludicrous, so base!

VANĚK: And cowardly—

STANĚK: Right! And cowardly! Look, I've been trying to do something for the boy. I mean, I know a few guys at the town council and at the prosecutor's office, but you know how it is. Promises, promises! They all say they're going to look into it, but the moment your back is turned they drop it like a hot potato, so they don't get their fingers burnt! Sickening, the way everybody looks out for number one!

VANĚK: Still, I think it's nice of you to have tried to do something—

STANĚK: My dear Ferdinand, I'm really not the sort of man your friends obviously take me for! Peanuts?

VANĚK: No, thanks—

STANĚK (*Short pause.*):   About Javurek—

VANĚK: Yes?

STANĚK: Since I didn't manage to accomplish anything through private intervention, it occurred to me perhaps it ought to be handled
in a somewhat different way. You know what I mean. Simply write
something—a protest or a petition? In fact, this is the main thing I
wanted to discuss with you. Naturally, you're far more experienced
in these matters than I. If this document contains a few fairly well-
known signatures—like yours, for example—it's bound to be published somewhere abroad which might create some political pressure. Right? I mean, these things don't seem to impress them all that
much, actually—but honestly, I don't see any other way to help the
boy. Not to mention Annie—

VANĚK: Annie?

STANĚK: My daughter.

VANĚK: Oh? Is that your daughter?

STANĚK: That's right.

VANĚK: Well, what about her?

STANĚK: I thought you knew.

VANĚK: Knew what?

STANĚK: She's expecting. By Javurek—

VANĚK: Oh, I see. That's why—

STANĚK: Wait a minute! If you mean the case interests me merely because of family matters—

VANĚK: I didn't mean that—

STANĚK: But you just said—

VANĚK: I only wanted to say, that's how you know about the case
at all; you were explaining to me how you got to know about
it. Frankly, I wouldn't have expected you to be familiar with
the present pop scene. I'm sorry if it sounded as though I
meant—

STANĚK: I'd get involved in this case even if it was someone else expecting his child! No matter who—

VANĚK: I know—

(*Embarrassed pause.*)

STANĚK: Well, what do you think about my idea of writing
some sort of protest?

(*Vaněk begins to look for something in his briefcase, finally finds a paper,
and hands it to Staněk.*)

VANĚK: I guess this is the sort of thing you had in mind—

STANĚK: What?

VANĚK: Here—

STANĚK (*Grabs the document.*):   What is it?

VANĚK: Have a look—

(*Staněk takes the paper from Vaněk, goes quickly to the writing desk,
picks up his glasses, puts them on, and begins to read attentively. Lengthy*

pause. Staněk shows signs of surprise. When he finishes reading, he puts aside his glasses and begins to pace around in agitation.)

STANĚK: Now isn't it fantastic! That's a laugh, isn't it? Eh? Here I was cudgeling my brains how to go about it, finally I take the plunge and consult you—and all this time you've had the whole thing wrapped up and ready! Isn't it marvellous? I knew I was doing the right thing when I turned to you! (*Staněk returns to the table, sits down, puts on his glasses again, and rereads the text.*) There! Precisely what I had in mind! Brief, to the point, fair, and yet emphatic. Manifestly the work of a professional! I'd be sweating over it for a whole day and I'd never come up with anything remotely like this!

VANĚK: (*Embarrassed.*)

STANĚK: Listen, just a small point—here at the end—do you think "willfulness" is the right word to use? Couldn't one find a milder synonym, perhaps? Somehow seems a bit misplaced, you know. I mean, the whole text is composed in very measured, factual terms—and this word here suddenly sticks out, sounds much too emotional, wouldn't you agree? Otherwise it's absolutely perfect. Maybe the second paragraph is somewhat superfluous; in fact, it's just a rehash of the first one. Except for the reference here to Javurek's impact on nonconformist youth. This is excellent and must stay in! How about putting it at the end instead of your "willfulness"? Wouldn't that do the trick?—But these are just my personal impressions. Good heavens! Why should you listen to what I have to say! On the whole the text is excellent, and no doubt it's going to hit the mark. Let me say again, Ferdinand, how much I admire you. Your knack for expressing the fundamental points of an issue, while avoiding all needless abuse, is indeed rare among our kind!

VANĚK: Come on—you don't really mean that—
           (*Staněk takes off his glasses, goes over to Vaněk, puts the paper in front of him, sits again in the easy chair, and sips his drink. Short pause.*)

STANĚK: Anyway, it's good to know there's somebody around whom one can always turn to and rely on in a case like this.

VANĚK: But it's only natural, isn't it?

STANĚK: It may seem so to you. But in the circles where I've to move such things aren't in the least natural! The natural response is much more likely to be the exact opposite. When a man gets into trouble everybody drops him as soon as possible, the lot of them. And out of fear for their own positions they try to convince all and sundry they've never had anything to do with him; on the contrary, they sized him up right away, they had his number! But why am I telling you all this, you know best the sort of thing that happens! Right? When you were in prison your long-time theatre pals held forth against you on television. It was revolting—

VANĚK: I'm not angry with them—

STANĚK: But I am! And what's more I told them so. In no uncertain terms! You know, a man in my position learns to put up with a lot of things, but—if you'll forgive me—there are limits! I appreciate it might be awkward for you to blame them, as you happen to be the injured party. But listen to me, you've got to distance yourself from the affair! Just think: Once we, too, begin to tolerate this sort of muck—we're *de facto* assuming co-responsibility for the entire moral morass and indirectly contributing to its deeper penetration. Am I right?

VANĚK: Mmn—

STANĚK (*Short pause.*): Have you sent it off yet?

VANĚK: We're still collecting signatures—

STANĚK: How many have you got so far?

VANĚK: About fifty—

STANĚK: Fifty? Not bad! (*Short pause.*) Well, never mind, I've just missed the boat, that's all.

VANĚK: You haven't—

STANĚK: But the thing's already in hand, isn't it?

VANĚK: Yes, but it's still open—I mean—

STANĚK: All right, but now it's sure to be sent off and published, right? By the way, I wouldn't give it to any of the agencies, if I were you. They'll only print a measly little news item which is bound to be overlooked. Better hand it over directly to one of the big European papers, so the whole text gets published, including all the signatures!

VANĚK: I know—

STANĚK (*Short pause.*): Do they already know about it?

VANĚK: You mean the police?

STANĚK: Yes.

VANĚK: I don't think so. I suppose not—

STANĚK: Look here, I don't want to give you any advice, but it seems to me you ought to wrap it up as soon as possible, else they'll get wind of what's going on and they'll find a way to stop it. Fifty signatures should be enough! Besides, what counts is not the number of signatures, but their significance.

VANĚK: Each signature has its own significance!

STANĚK: Absolutely, but as far as publicity abroad is concerned, it is essential that some well-known names are represented, right? Has Pavel signed?

VANĚK: Yes—

STANĚK: Good. His name—no matter what one may think of him personally—does mean something in the world today!

VANĚK: No question—

STANĚK (*Short pause.*): Listen, Ferdinand—

VANĚK: Yes?

STANĚK: There's one more thing I wanted to discuss with you. It's a bit delicate, though—

VANĚK: Oh?

STANĚK: Look here, I'm no millionaire, you know, but so far I've been able to manage—

VANĚK: Good for you—

STANĚK: Well, I was thinking—I mean—I'd like to—Look, a lot of your friends have lost their jobs. I was thinking—would you be prepared to accept from me a certain sum of money?

VANĚK: That's very nice of you! Some of my friends indeed find themselves in a bit of a spot. But there are problems, you know. I mean, one is never quite sure how to go about it. Those who most need help are often the most reluctant to accept—

STANĚK: You won't be able to work miracles with what I can afford, but I expect there are situations when every penny counts. (*Takes out his wallet, removes two banknotes, hesitates, adds a third, hands them to Vaněk.*) Here—please—a small offering.

VANĚK: Thank you very much. Let me thank you for all my friends—

STANĚK: Gracious, we've got to help each other out, don't we? (*Pause.*) Incidentally, there's no need for you to mention this little contribution comes from me. I don't wish to erect a monument to myself. I'm sure you've gathered that much by now, eh?

VANĚK: Yes, Again many thanks—

STANĚK: Well now, how about having a look at the garden?

VANĚK: Mr. Staněk—

STANĚK: Yes?

VANĚK: We'd like to send it off tomorrow—

STANĚK: What?

VANĚKK: The protest—

STANĚK: Excellent! The sooner the better!

VANĚK: So that today there's still—

STANĚK: Today you should think about getting some sleep! That's the main thing! Don't forget you've a bit of a hangover after last night and tomorrow is going to be a hard day for you!

VANĚK: I know. All I was going to say—

STANĚK: Better go straight home and unplug the phone. Else Ladovský rings you up again and heaven knows how you'll end up!

VANĚK: Yes, I know. There're only a few signatures I've still got to collect—it won't take long. All I was going to say—I mean, don't you think it would be helpful—as a matter of fact, it would, of course, be sensational! After all, practically everybody's read your *Crash*!

STANĚK: Oh, come on, Ferdinand! That was fifteen years ago!

VANĚK: But it's never been forgotten!

STANĚK: What do you mean—sensational?

VANĚK: I'm sorry, I had the impression you'd actually like to—

STANĚK: What?

VANĚK: Participate—

STANĚK: Participate? Wait a minute. Are you talking about (*points to the paper*) this? Is that what you're talking about?

VANĚK: Yes—

STANĚK: You mean I—

VANĚK: I'm sorry, but I had the impression—

(*Staněk finishes his drink, crosses to the bar, pours himself a drink, walks over to the window, looks out for a while, whereupon he suddenly turns to Vaněk with a smile.*)

STANĚK: Now that's a laugh, isn't it?

VANĚK: What's a laugh?

STANĚK: Come on, can't you see how absurd it is? Eh? I ask you over hoping you might write something about Javurek's case—you produce a finished text and what's more, one furnished with fifty signatures! I'm bowled over like a little child, can't believe my eyes and ears, I worry about ways to stop them from ruining your project— and all this time it hasn't occurred to me to do the one simple, natural thing which I should have done in the first place! I mean, at once sign the document myself! Well, you must admit it's absurd, isn't it?

VANĚK: Mmn—

STANĚK: Now, listen Ferdinand, isn't this a really terrifying testimony to the situation into which we've been brought? Isn't it? Just think: even I, though I know it's rubbish, even I've got used to the idea that the signing of protests is the business of local specialists, professionals in solidarity, dissidents! While the rest of us—when we want to do something for the sake of ordinary human decency—automatically turn to you, as though you were a sort of service establishment for moral matters. In other words, we're here simply to keep our mouths shut and to be rewarded by relative peace and quiet, whereas you're here to speak up for us and to be rewarded by blows on earth and glory in the heavens! Perverse, isn't it?

VANĚK: Mmn—

STANĚK: Of course it is! And they've managed to bring things to such a point that even a fairly intelligent and decent fellow—which, with your permission, I still think I am—is more or less ready to take this situation for granted! As though it was quite normal, perfectly natural! Sickening, isn't it? Sickening the depths we've reached! What do you say? Makes one puke, eh?

VANĚK: Well—

STANĚK: You think the nation can ever recover from all this?

VANĚK: Hard to say—

STANĚK: What can one do? What can one do? Well, seems clear, doesn't it? In theory, that is. Everybody should start with himself. What? However! Is this country inhabited only by Vaněks? It really doesn't seem that everybody can become a fighter for human rights.

VANĚK: Not everybody, no—

STANĚK: Where is it?

VANĚK: What?

STANĚK: The list of signatures, of course.

VANĚK (*Embarrassed pause.*):   Mr. Staněk—

STANĚK: Yes?

VANĚK: Forgive me, but—I'm sorry, I've suddenly a funny feeling
that perhaps—

STANĚK: What funny feeling?

VANĚK: I don't know—I feel very embarrassed—Well, it seems to me
perhaps I wasn't being quite fair—

STANĚK: In what way?

VANĚK: Well, what I did—was a bit of a con trick—in a way—

STANĚK: What are you talking about?

VANĚK: I mean, first I let you talk, and only then I ask for your signature—I mean, after you're already sort of committed by what
you've said before, you see—

STANĚK: Are you suggesting that if I'd known you were collecting signatures for Javurek, I would never have started talking about him?

VANĚK: No, that's not what I mean—

STANĚK: Well, what do you mean?

VANĚK: How shall I put it—

STANĚK: Oh, come on! You mind I didn't organize the whole thing
myself, is that it?

VANĚK: No, that's not it—

STANĚK: What is it then?

VANĚK: Well, it seems to me it would've been a quite different matter
if I'd come to you right away and asked for your signature. That
way you would've had an option—

STANĚK: And why didn't you come to me right away, actually? Was it
because you'd simply written me off in advance?

VANĚK: Well, I was thinking that in your position—

STANĚK: Ah! There you are! You see? Now it's becoming clear what
you really think of me, isn't it? You think that because now and then
one of my pieces happens to be shown on television, I'm no longer
capable of the simplest act of solidarity!

VANĚK: You misunderstand me.—What I meant was—

STANĚK: Let me tell you something, Ferdinand. (*Drinks. Short pause.*)
Look here, if I've—willy-nilly—got used to the perverse idea that
common decency and morality are the exclusive domain of the dissidents—then you've—willy-nilly—got used to the idea as well!
That's why it never crossed your mind that certain values might be
more important to me than my present position. But suppose even I
wanted to be finally a free man, suppose even I wished to renew my
inner integrity and shake off the yoke of humiliation and shame? It
never entered your head that I might've been actually waiting for
this very moment for years, what? You simply placed me once and
for all among those hopeless cases, among those whom it would be

pointless to count on in any way. Right? And now that you found I'm not entirely indifferent to the fate of others—you made that slip about my signature! But you saw at once what happened, and so you began to apologize to me. Good God! Don't you realize how you humiliate me? What if all this time I'd been hoping for an opportunity to act, to do something that would again make a man of me, help me to be once more at peace with myself, help me to find again the free play of my imagination and my lost sense of humour, rid me of the need to escape my traumas by minding the apricots and the blooming magnolias! Suppose even I prefer to live in truth! What if I want to return from the world of custom-made literature and the proto-culture of television to the world of art which isn't geared to serve anyone at all?

VANĚK: I'm sorry—forgive me! I didn't mean to hurt your feelings—. Wait a minute, I'll—just a moment—

(*Vaněk opens his briefcase, rummages in it for a while, finally extracts the sheets with the signatures and hands them to Staněk. Staněk gets up slowly and crosses with the papers to the desk, where he sits down, puts on his glasses, and carefully studies the sheets nodding his head here and there. After a lengthy while, he takes off his glasses, slowly rises, thoughtfully paces around, finally turning to Vaněk.*)

STANĚK: Let me think aloud. May I?

VANĚK: By all means—

STANĚK (*Halts, drinks, begins to pace again as he talks.*): I believe I've already covered the main points concerning the subjective side of the matter. If I sign the document, I'm going to regain—after years of being continually sick to my stomach—my self-esteem, my lost freedom, my honour, and perhaps even some regard among those close to me. I'll leave behind the insoluble dilemmas, forced on me by the conflict between my concern for my position and my conscience. I'll be able to face with equanimity Annie, myself, and even that young man when he comes back. It'll cost me my job, though my job brings me no satisfaction—on the contrary, it brings me shame—nevertheless, it does support me and my family a great deal better than if I were to become a night watchman. It's more than likely that my son won't be permitted to continue his studies. On the other hand, I'm sure he's going to have more respect for me that way, than if his permission to study was bought by my refusal to sign the protest for Javurek, whom he happens to worship.—Well then. This is the subjective side of the matter. Now how about the objective side? What happens when—among the signatures of a few well-known dissidents and a handful of Javurek's teenage friends—there suddenly crops up—to everybody's surprise and against all expectation—my signature? The signature of a man who hasn't been heard from regarding civic affairs for years! Well? My co-signatories—as well as many of those who don't sign documents of this sort, but who nonetheless deep down side with those who do—are naturally go-

ing to welcome my signature with pleasure. The closed circle of habitual signers—whose signatures, by the way, are already beginning to lose their clout, because they cost practically nothing. I
mean, the people in question have long since lost all ways and
means by which they could actually pay for their signatures. Right?
Well, this circle will be broken. A new name will appear, a name the
value of which depends precisely on its previous absence. And of
course, I may add, on the high price paid for its appearance! So
much for the objective "plus" of my prospective signature. Now
what about the authorities? My signature is going to surprise, annoy, and upset them for the very reasons which will bring joy to the
other signatories. I mean, because It'll make a breach in the barrier
the authorities have been building around your lot for so long and
with such effort. All right. Let's see about Javurek. Concerning his
case, I very much doubt my participation would significantly influence its outcome. And if so, I'm afraid it's more than likely going to
have a negative effect. The authorities will be anxious to prove they
haven't been panicked. They'll want to show that a surprise of this
sort can't make them lose their cool. Which brings us to the consideration of what they're going to do to me. Surely, my signature is
bound to have a much more significant influence on what happens
in my case. No doubt, they're going to punish me far more cruelly
than you'd expect. The point being that my punishment will serve
them as a warning signal to all those who might be tempted to follow my example in the future, choose freedom, and thus swell the
ranks of the dissidents. You may be sure they'll want to show them
what the score is! Right? The thing is—well, let's face it—they're no
longer worried all that much about dissident activities within the
confines of the established ghetto. In some respects they even seem
to prod them on here and there. But! What they're really afraid of is
any semblance of a crack in the fence around the ghetto! So they'll
want to exorcize the bogey of a prospective epidemic of dissent by
an exemplary punishment of myself. They'll want to nip it in the
bud, that's all. (*Drinks. Pause.*) The last question I've got to ask myself is this: what sort of reaction to my signature can one expect
among those who, in one way or another, have followed what you
might call "the path of accommodation." I mean people who are, or
ought to be, our main concern, because—I'm sure you'll agree—our
hope for the future depends above all on whether or not it will be
possible to awake them from their slumbers and to enlist them to
take an active part in civic affairs. Well, I'm afraid that my signature
is going to be received with absolute resentment by this crucial section of the populace. You know why? Because, as a matter of fact,
these people secretly hate the dissidents. They've become their bad
conscience, their living reproach! That's how they see the dissidents.
And at the same time, they envy them their honour and their inner
freedom, values which they themselves were denied by fate. This is

why they never miss an opportunity to smear the dissidents. And precisely this opportunity is going to be offered to them by my signature. They're going to spread nasty rumours about you and your friends. They're going to say that you who have nothing more to lose—you who have long since landed at the bottom of the heap and, what's more, managed to make yourselves quite at home in there—are now trying to drag down to your own level an unfortunate man, a man who's so far been able to stay above the salt line. You're dragging him down—irresponsible as you are—without the slightest compunction, just for your own whim, just because you wish to irritate the authorities by creating a false impression that your ranks are being swelled! What do you care about losing him his job! Doesn't matter, does it? Or do you mean to suggest you'll find him a job down in the dump in which you yourselves exist? What? No—Ferdinand! I'm sorry. I'm afraid I'm much too familiar with the way these people think! After all, I've got to live among them, day in day out. I know precisely what they're going to say. They'll say I'm your victim, shamelessly abused, misguided, led astray by your cynical appeal to my humanity! They'll say that in your ruthlessness you didn't shrink even from making use of my personal relationship to Javurek! And you know what? They're going to say that all the humane ideals you're constantly proclaiming have been tarnished by your treatment of me. That's the sort of reasoning one can expect from them! And I'm sure I don't have to tell you that the authorities are bound to support this interpretation, and to fan the coals as hard as they can! There are others, of course, somewhat more intelligent perhaps. These people might say that the extraordinary appearance of my signature among yours is actually counterproductive, in that it concentrates everybody's attention on my signature and away from the main issue concerning Javurek. They'll say it puts the whole protest in jeopardy, because one can't help asking oneself what was the purpose of the exercise: was it to help Javurek, or to parade a newborn dissident? I wouldn't be at all surprised if someone were to say that, as a matter of fact, Javurek was victimized by you and your friends. It might be suggested his personal tragedy only served you to further your ends—which are far removed from the fate of the unfortunate man. Furthermore, it'll be pointed out that by getting my signature you managed to dislodge me from the one area of operation—namely, backstage diplomacy, private intervention—where I've been so far able to manoeuvre and where I might have proved infinitely more helpful to Javurek in the end! I do hope you understand me, Ferdinand. I don't wish to exaggerate the importance of these opinions, nor am I prepared to become their slave. On the other hand, it seems to be in the interests of our case for me to take them into account. After all, it's a matter of a political decision and a good politician must consider all the issues which are likely to influence the end result of his action. Right? In these circumstances the question one must resolve is as follows: what do I prefer? Do I prefer the inner liberation which my signature is going to bring me, a liberation paid for—as it now turns out—by a basically negative objective impact—or do I choose the other alternative. I mean, the more beneficial effect which the protest would have without my signature, yet paid for by my bitter awareness that I've again—who knows, perhaps for the last time—missed a chance to shake off the bonds of shameful compromises in which I've been choking for years? In other words, if I'm to act indeed ethically—and I hope by now you've no doubt I want to do just that—which course should I take? Should I be guided by ruthless objective considerations, or by subjective inner feelings?

VANĚK: Seems perfectly clear to me—

STANĚK: And to me—

VANĚK: So that you're going to—

STANĚK: Unfortunately—

VANĚK: Unfortunately?

STANĚK: You thought I was—

VANNĚK: Forgive me, perhaps I didn't quite understand—

STANĚK: I'm sorry if I've—

VANĚK: Never mind—

STANĚK: But I really believe—

VANĚK: I know—

(Both drink. Vaněk shudders. Lengthy embarrassed pause. Staněk takes the sheets and hands them with a smile to Vaněk who puts them, together with the text of the letter of protest, into his briefcase. He shows signs of embarrassment. Staněk crosses to the tape recorder, unplugs it, comes back and sits down.)

STANĚK: Are you angry?

VANĚK: No—

STANĚK: You don't agree, though—

VANĚK: I respect your reasoning—

STANĚK: But what do you think?

VANĚK: What should I think?

STANĚK: That's obvious, isn't it?

VANĚK: Is it?

STANĚK: You think that when I saw all the signatures, I did, after all, get the wind up!

VANĚK: I don't—

STANĚK: I can see you do!

VANĚK: I assure you—

STANĚK: Why don't you level with me?! Don't you realize that your benevolent hypocrisy is actually far more insulting than if you gave it to me straight?! Or do you mean I'm not even worthy of your comment?!

VANĚK: But I told you, didn't I, I respect your reasoning—

STANĚK: I'm not an idiot, Vaněk!

VANĚK: Of course not—

STANĚK: I know precisely what's behind your "respect"!

VANĚK: What is?

STANĚK: A feeling of moral superiority!

VANĚK: You're wrong—

STANĚK: Only, I'm not quite sure if you—you of all people—have any right to feel so superior!

VANĚK: What do you mean?

STANĚK: You know very well what I mean!

VANĚK: I don't—

STANĚK: Shall I tell you?

VANĚK: Please do—

STANĚK: Well! As far as I know, in prison you talked more than you should have!

(*Vaněk jumps up, wildly staring at Staněk, who smiles triumphantly. Short tense pause. The phone rings. Vaněk, broken, sinks back into his chair. Staněk crosses to the telephone and lifts the receiver.*)

STANĚK: Hello—yes—what? You mean—Wait a minute—I see—I see—Where are you? Yes, yes, of course—absolutely!—good—You bet!—Sure—I'll be here waiting for you! Bye bye. (*Staněk puts the receiver down and absent-mindedly stares into space. Lengthy pause. Vaněk gets up in embarrassment. Only now Staněk seems to realize that Vaněk is still there. He turns to him abruptly.*) You can go and burn it downstairs in the furnace!

VANĚK: What?

STANĚK: He's just walked into the canteen! To see Annie.

VANĚK: Who did?

STANĚK: Javurek! Who else?

VANĚK (*Jumps up.*): Javurek? You mean he was released? But that's wonderful! So your private intervention did work, after all! Just as well we didn't send off the protest a few days earlier! I'm sure they would've got their backs up and kept him inside!

(*Staněk searchingly stares at Vaněk, then suddenly smiles, decisively steps up to him, and with both hands takes him by the shoulders.*)

STANĚK: My dear fellow, you mustn't fret! There's always the risk that you can do more harm than good by your activities! Right? Heavens, if you should worry about this sort of thing, you'd never be able to do anything at all! Come, let me get you those saplings—

Questions for Discussion and Writing

1. What is the nature of the relationship between Vaněk and Staněk? What can you infer about their past relationship from what they reveal about themselves at the beginning of the play?

2. What is the occasion that has prompted this meeting between Vaněk and Staněk after many years?

3. What implications can you draw from the fact that Staněk lives in a house with land while Vaněk lives in a small cottage? How does Staněk's offer of magnolia cuttings, names of medical specialists, brandy, and slippers alert you to the fact that he wants something from Vaněk? What is it that he wants?

4. How does Havel use the incident of drawing up and signing the petition to reveal the kind of person Staněk has become?

5. To what extent does Havel reveal the human dimensions of the STEREOTYPES of the political dissident and of the writer who has sold out to the establishment?

6. How have Staněk's reactions to events in the play changed your perception of him from what it was at the beginning?

7. Have you had an experience where differences in political ideology created conflicts in a personal relationship? Describe what happened.

WRITING ABOUT CONFLICT AND STRUCTURE

The storyline, or sequence of interrelated incidents that happen to characters in fiction, is known as the PLOT. Rather than being randomly selected, these incidents are causally connected. Moreover, the particular sequence of incidents of which the story is composed is meaningful because of the changes it produces in a character's situation, self-awareness, or relationships with others. To be effective, plot must lead readers to speculate on both the causes and consequences of the character's motivations and actions. By seeing plot as a set of events capable of changing the lives of the characters caught in those events, we can better understand the intrinsic dramatic structure of most stories.

The most effective arrangement of events is the one that allows the author to generate and sustain the element of CONFLICT. In most stories, the INTRODUCTION or EXPOSITION provides necessary background information, establishes the setting, introduces the reader to the major characters, and frames the dramatic situation in which the conflict of the story will occur. Then a COMPLICATION instigates a clash between one character and another or between a character and the forces of nature or society that sets the plot in motion. The character with whom we are encouraged to identity is known as the PROTAGONIST, and the opposing character or force is called the ANTAGONIST. Succeeding complications escalate what is at stake for the protagonist by creating more obstacles for him or her to overcome in pursuing the desired goal. An important means writers use in preparing readers for a significant future event in the story is through FORESHADOWING. Foreshadowing not only heightens suspense in a story but lends it a sense of artistic unity.

In the CLIMAX of the story, the opposing forces reach a TURNING POINT, or CRISIS, that is the moment of truth for the protagonist. Before this point, it is possible for either side to win. After this point, the situation can never return to what it was at the beginning of the story. Events have led to an irreversible change in a character's situation, knowledge, or understanding. The RESOLUTION of a story settles the crisis, and the CONCLUSION then ties up loose ends or clarifies the implications of the events that have been resolved.

Looking at Luisa Valenzuela's story "The Censors" in this way, we see that it presents a conflict, or crisis, in the life of Juan, the protagonist. Valenzuela first establishes the setting of the story in Argentina during a time of political repression, introduces the major character, Juan, and provides essential background information that allows the reader to understand how concerned Juan is over the letter he has written to his friend Mariana in Paris. The complication that sets the plot in motion occurs when Juan decides to become a government censor in hopes of retrieving his letter. Complications escalate as Juan is promoted from one department to another because he proves so adept at discerning censorable contents in the letters of others. Finally, the moment of greatest tension occurs when he confronts his own letter and is faced with the choice of betraying his newfound vocation as censor, to which he has become zealously committed, or concealing the letter's existence. Both the resolution of the crisis and the inexorable conclusion quickly follows: "Naturally, he censored it without regret. And just as naturally, he couldn't stop them from executing him the following morning, another victim of his devotion to his work." Notice how Valenzuela focuses on a single conflict in one character's life rather than a series of dilemmas.

The STRUCTURE, or form, of a literary work reflects the author's decision about what organization of events and scenes will best reveal the interplay between character and action. A plot develops CHRONOLOGICALLY if incidents unfold or are related in the order in which they occurred, as in Mrożek's "The Elephant," Valenzuela's "The Censors," or William Harrison's "Roller Ball Murder." Stories that are told retrospectively, though flashbacks, shift the action to events that happened earlier, such as in Cardenal's "The Swede," Sahni's "We Have Arrived in Amritsar," and Ioannides's "Gregory."

Structure is not important for its own sake but exists within a work only to make it possible for the reader or audience to discern the pattern of emerging conflicts more clearly. In discovering how all the parts of a work are mutually interrelated, try to discover what the main conflict is, who the hero, or PROTAGONIST, is and who the ANTAGONIST, which conflicts are external and which internal and psychological. Does the work focus on a conflict between individuals (as in "We Have Arrived in Amritsar"), between an individual and the community (as in "Roller Ball Murder"), or on a conflict within the speaker's mind (as in "Gregory")? What elements of foreshadowing permit the reader to foresee the eventual outcome of the action? Where does the main climax of the work occur? How is it resolved?

In poetry, writing about conflict and structure involves understanding how the form of the poem sharpens the dilemma the poem explores. For example, consider how Etheridge Knight divides the action of his poem into separate stanzas that create the framework in which the action of the poem is to occur. Knight generates suspense by revealing how much is at stake for the inmates in Hard Rock's continued resistance. Each stanza then escalates the tension by withholding, and then revealing the permanent change Hard Rock has undergone. The form of the poem organizes the confrontation into easily discernible stages. Thien, Hovanessian, Fortouni, and Amichai do this in less formal ways, but each of these poets sets up a basic situation, introduces a complication that escalates to a crisis that leads to a change, however subtle, in the speaker's situation or self-awareness. For example, the speaker in Diana Der Hovanessian's poem will never again repress her awareness of the Armenian holocaust to save herself anguish. The Jewish father and the Arab shepherd in Yehuda Amichai's poem have permanently altered their views of one another in order to cooperate for their mutual self-interest.

As you analyze a poem, try to identify how the poet uses stanzas, line lengths, and rhyme schemes to emphasize the issue the poem explores. Look for the pattern of a developing conflict that is resolved by the end of the poem.

As in fiction, the sequence of interrelated incidents and actions that comprise the plot in drama lead audiences through a typical progression of exposition, complication, climax, and resolution. We can discern these elements in the construction of any modern play, whether of one, two, or three acts. In addition, each scene within a play not only advances the plot but has its own pattern of developing and concluding conflict.

For example, Amlin Gray's drama *How I Got That Story* takes the form of a two-act play, further divided into eight scenes in Act One and seven scenes in Act Two. Act One presents the exposition, introduces the characters, initiates the main conflict, and advances the action through any number of complications that make the protagonist's problem (how to "get that story") more difficult to solve. The second act escalates the conflict by raising the stakes for the protagonist to a point of great emotional intensity as unexpected challenges and obstacles from the antagonist (symbolized by the Historical Event that is the story the reporter has come to cover) oppose him at every turn. At the climax of the play, in Scene Six ("Orphanage"), the series of related events that make up the plot finally lead the reporter to a moment of self-awareness in which he recognizes the futility of his endeavor. At this point the events of the play have been decided. The reporter has lost.

The last scene presents the consequences of this moment of recognition. If we were to examine each of the scenes, we would find that each one functions in much the same manner as the play as a whole. That is, each scene contains a conflict that leads to a crisis in which the reporter is confronted by a choice. For example, in Act One, Scene One ("Accreditation"), the issue is whether the reporter will avoid incidents that embarrass the government. In Scene Two, the issue is whether the reporter can accept that he is causing the news to happen—for example, that a Buddhist monk immolated himself *because* the reporter was there to cover the event. Each scene in effect is a miniature play that contributes to the overall structure—that is, scenes within the play are structured so that each develops a miniconflict by confronting the reporter with different problems, difficulties, and obstacles that impede his progress toward his goal (getting that story).

Thus, in writing about conflict and structure your essay should clarify how each distinct part, whether act or scene, contributes to the central conflict that lies at the core of the play. How does the playwright set the stage for the action to follow and then initiate the conflict? What sort of conflict does the play explore? Who is the protagonist? What is his or her objective? What opposing forces—whether other characters, nature, society, or some aspect of the protagonist's self—create obstacles, problems, or difficulties that impede the protagonist's desire to pursue a goal? How does the dialogue in individual scenes dramatize this collision of opposing forces as well as advance the overall plot? What means does the playwright use to keep the balance between protagonist and antagonist nearly equal to produce suspense (as Amlin Gray does in leaving open the possibility to the very last moment that the reporter will simply leave Am-bo Land)? Where does the climactic moment of truth and recognition occur? For example, in Havel's *Protest*, how does Staněk's long final monologue serve as the turning point, or climax, of the entire play? In what way have events led to a change in the protagonist's situation, knowledge, or self-awareness? What consequences result from this insight?

Connections

1. How do "Roller Ball Murder," "The Censors," *Protest*, and *How I Got That Story* explore the issue of what makes some individuals buy into the system whereas others remain uncorruptible?

2. How does "Writing with the Body" provide insight into the political climate that existed in Argentina when Valenzuela wrote "The Censors"?

3. Compare Jonathan E in Harrison's story with the speaker in Thien's poem "I Kept Silent." To what extent are both individualists who are realistic about the situations in which they find themselves?

4. How do both "We Have Arrived in Amritsar" and "Gregory" illustrate that the ultimate price of abstract political hatreds is becoming dehumanized?

5. How does Amichai's poem and "We Have Arrived in Amritsar" allow the reader to understand the psychological causes of religious intolerance?

6. How might both "The Elephant" and Knight's poem be viewed as parables exploring the relationship between the individual and the system? What differences in the authors' attitudes toward authority explain the difference in tone between the two works?

7. What might you infer about the predicament of blacks in South Africa and in the United States from "Drought" and the poem "Hard Rock"?

8. What do both "Gregory" and the poem "Child's Memory" reveal about how atrocities are used for propaganda and shock value during wartime?

9. Compare the use of letters as a narrative device in "The Swede" and "The Censor." How do both stories revolve around the issue of what is or is not in a particular letter?

10. How do the narrative effects of "A Pair of Socks with Love," and "Child's Memory" depend on events seen from the perspective of a child?

11. What differences and similarities can you discover in the predicaments confronting the narrators in "Cervicide" and "Gregory"?

12. How do both "A Pair of Socks with Love" and "Gregory" illustrate a conflict between political allegiance and personal loyalty?

13. How are psychological conflicts in the present triggered by memories from the past in "Looking at Cambodian News Photos" and "Child's Memory"?
14. How do the authors of "The Censors" and "An Opinion on the Question of Pornography" satirize ideological zeal associated with censorship?
15. How does the concept of the scapegoat in different guises enter "Hard Rock," "Drought," "Amritsar," "Cervicide," and *How I Got That Story*?

6

Exile

In some ways, our age—the age of the refugee, the displaced person, and mass immigration—is defined by the condition of exile. As communications, immigration, and travel make the world grow smaller, the potential for cross-cultural misunderstandings accelerates. Customs and rituals that may seem bizarre or strange to an outsider appear entirely normal and natural to those within the culture. Unfortunately, the potential for conflict exists as soon as cultures whose "natural" ways do not coincide make contact. Correspondingly, the need to become aware of the extent to which our and other people's conclusions about the world are guided by different cultural presuppositions grows.

For some exiles, ironically, the condition of *not* belonging, of being caught between two cultures provides the chance to see things from outside the controlling frame of reference of their particular culture. For most, however, the jarring, intense, and often painful emotional experience produced by having to redefine oneself in a strange land, and trying to reconcile conflicting cultural values, forces a surrender of all ideas of safety, and the comfort of familiar surroundings and a common language.

The short stories, essay, poems, and plays in this chapter explore the condition of exiles, whether refugees, immigrants, or travelers who are caught between two cultures, at home in neither. The need of those who have left home to make sense of their lives in a new place is the theme explored by Mark Mathabane (South Africa) in his essay "I Leave South Africa." The difficulties faced by Korean women who immigrate to the United States is the subject of Kim Chi-Wŏn's "A Certain Beginning." The fate of two naturalists stranded on the out-islands of New Zealand is the basis of Keri Hulme's enigmatic story, "Unnamed Island in the Unknown Sea." The poignant story by Mahdokht Kashkuli, "The Button," tells of a boy's reaction to being placed in an orphanage (Iran). Neil Bissoondath (Trinidad) tells the amusing story of a patriarch's misguided preparations for his future immigration to Toronto. In "Visiting Places," Arun Mukherjee describes how an immigrant to Canada unwisely chooses to return to India as a guide for her new Canadian friends. A bizarre malady, as upsetting to the narrator as it is comical to the reader, prevents a writer from adjusting to a new environment in "Letter to a Young Lady in Paris" by Julio Cortázar (Argentina). The classic tale "The Guest," by Albert Camus, explores the existential implications of exile in the story of a Frenchman torn by divided loyalties in Algeria. In Mahasweta Devi's "Giribala" (Bengal/India), a mother chooses to leave her husband and community in order to save her youngest daughter from being sold into prostitution as were her sisters.

Like the short stories, the poems in this chapter offer many perspectives—by writers from Poland, Sweden, Hawaii, Israel, China, Chile, the United States, and Japan—on what it is to be exiled. We share the experience of learning a new language (Czeslaw Milosz, "My Faithful Mother Tongue"), of the void created by a failure to communicate (Lennart Sjögren, "The Roses") of the intolerance of the dominant Anglo culture toward minorities (Wing Tek Lum, "Minority Poem"), of experiencing mixed feelings of vulnerability and bravado (Rahel Chalfi, "Porcupine Fish"), and of having always to be ready to emigrate (Pablo Neruda, "Goodbyes"). In other poems, the state of exile is seen as an opportunity to dismantle barriers and celebrate new landscapes and visions (Diane Wakoski, "The Orange") and to create new possibilities and opportunities for oneself (Mitsuye Yamada, "I Learned to Sew").

In *The Dance and the Railroad*, the Chinese-American playwright David Henry Hwang dramatizes the predicament of the Chinese immigrants who came to America to pursue the dream of the "gold mountain." Hwang uses the 1867 railroad workers' strike as a framework to explore the extent to which both artists and immigrants as exiles can help each other face their common challenge. The Latina playwright Milcha Sanchez-Scott in *The Cuban Swimmer* offers an empathetic and imaginative account of a Cuban family who must pull together to help their daughter survive a marathon swim between San Pedro and Catalina Island.

Mark Mathabane

I Leave South Africa

Mark Mathabane was born in 1960 in South Africa, where his family suffered under apartheid (forced segregation of the races). His childhood and youth were spent in Alexandra, a notorious ghetto in which poverty and oppression, midnight raids by police, and other atrocities were routine. Miraculously under these circumstances, Mathabane learned to play tennis well enough to receive an athletic scholarship to attend a small college in the United States. Mathabane's account of his experiences growing up in South Africa and emigrating to America with the help of the tennis star Stan Smith is contained in Kaffir Boy *(1986) and* Kaffir Boy in America *(1989), from which the following essay is taken. Mathabane relates his initial encounters in the United States after having just left the repressive regime of his homeland. He currently lives in Kernersville, North Carolina, with his wife and daughter.*

1   The plane landed at Atlanta's International Airport the afternoon of September 17, 1978. I double-checked the name and description of Dr. Killion's friend who was to meet me. Shortly after the plane came to a standstill at the gate, and I was stashing Dr. Killion's letter into my tote-bag, I felt a tap on my shoulder, and turning met the steady and unsettling gaze of the Black Muslim.

2   "Are you from Africa?" he asked as he offered to help me with my luggage.

3   "Yes." I wondered how he could tell.

4   "A student?"

5   "Yes." We were aboard a jumbo jet, almost at the back of it. From the throng in front it was clear that it would be some time before we disembarked, so we fell into conversation. He asked if it was my first time in the United States and I replied that it was. He spoke in a thick American accent.

6   "Glad to meet you, brother," he said. We shook hands. "My name is Nkwame."

7   "I'm Mark," I said, somewhat intimidated by his aspect.

8   "Mark is not African," he said coolly. "What's your African name, brother?"

9   "Johannes."

10 "That isn't an African name either."

11 I was startled by this. How did he know I had an African name? I hardly used it myself because it was an unwritten rule among black youths raised in the ghettos to deny their tribal identity and affiliation,

786

and that denial applied especially to names. But I didn't want to offend this persistent stranger, so I gave it to him. "Thanyani."

"What does it stand for?" 12

How did he know that my name stood for something? I wondered 13
in amazement. My worst fears were confirmed. Black Americans did indeed possess the sophistication to see through any ruse an African puts up. Then and there I decided to tell nothing but the truth.

"The wise one," I said, and quickly added, "but the interpretation is 14
not meant to be taken literally, sir."

We were now headed out of the plane. He carried my tennis rackets. 15

"The wise one, heh," he mused. "You Africans sure have a way with 16
names. You know," he went on with great warmth, "one of my nephews is named after a famous African chief. Of the Mandingo tribe, I believe. Ever since I saw 'Roots' I have always wanted to know where my homeland is."

I found this statement baffling for I thought that as an American his 17
homeland was America. I did not know about "Roots."

"Which black college in Atlanta will you be attending, Thanyani?" 18
he asked. "You will be attending a black college, I hope?"

Black colleges? I stared at him. My mind conjured up images of the 19
dismal tribal schools I hated and had left behind in the ghetto. My God, did such schools exist in America?

"No, sir," I stammered. "I won't be attending school in Atlanta. I'm 20
headed for Limestone College in South Carolina."

"Is Limestone a black college?" 21

"No, sir," I said hastily. 22

"What a pity," he sighed. "You would be better off at a black col- 23
lege."

I continued staring at him. 24

He went on. "At a black college," he said with emphasis, "you can 25
meet with your true brothers and sisters. There's so much you can teach them about the true Africa and the struggles of our people over there. And they have a lot to teach you about being black in America. And, you know, there are lots of black colleges in the South."

I nearly fainted at this revelation. Black schools in America? Was I 26
hearing things or what? I almost blurted out that I had attended black schools all my life and wanted to have nothing to do with them. But instead I said, "Limestone College is supposed to be a good college, too, sir. It's integrated."

"That don't mean nothing," he snapped. "Integrated schools are the 27
worst places for black folks. I thought you Africans would have enough brains to know that this integration business in America is a fraud. It ain't good for the black mind and culture. Integration, integration," he railed. "What good has integration done the black man? We've simply become more dependent on the white devil and forgotten how to do things for ourselves. Also, no matter how integrated we become, white

folks won't accept us as equals. So why should we break our backs trying to mix with them, heh? To them we will always be niggers."

28   I was shaken by his outburst. I longed to be gone from him, especially since he had drawn me aside in the corridor leading toward customs. The Black Muslim must have realized that I was a complete
stranger to him, that his bitter tone terrified and confused me, for he
quickly recollected himself and smiled.

29   "Well, good luck in your studies, brother," he said, handing me my
rackets. "By the way, where in Africa did you say you were from?
Nigeria?"

30   "No. South Africa."

31   "South what!" he said.

32   "South Africa," I repeated. "That place with all those terrible race
problems. Where black people have no rights and are being murdered
every day."

33   I expected my statement to shock him; instead he calmly said, "You
will find a lot of South Africa in this country, brother. Keep your eyes
wide open all the time. Never let down your guard or you're dead. And
while you're up there in South Carolina, watch out for the Ku Klux
Klan. That's their home. And don't you ever believe that integration
nonsense."

34   He left. I wondered what he meant by his warning. I stumbled my
way to customs. There was a long queue and when my turn came the
white, somber-faced immigration official, with cropped reddish-brown
hair, seemed transformed into an Afrikaner bureaucrat. I almost
screamed. He demanded my passport. After inspecting it, he asked to
see my plane ticket. I handed it to him.

35   "It's a one-way ticket," he said.

36   "Yes, sir. I couldn't afford a return ticket," I answered, wondering
what could be wrong.

37   "Under the student visa regulations you're required to have a return
ticket," he said icily. "Otherwise how will you get back home? You intend returning home after your studies, don't you?"

38   "Yes, sir."

39   "Then you ought to have a return ticket."

40   I remained silent.

41   "Do you have relatives or a guardian in America?"

42   I speedily handed him a letter from Stan Smith, along with several
completed immigration forms indicating that he had pledged to be my
legal guardian for the duration of my stay in the States. The immigration official inspected the documents, then left his cubicle and went to
consult his superior. I trembled at the thought that I might be denied
entry into the United States. But the one-way ticket, which created the
impression that I was coming to America for good, was hardly my
fault. Having had no money to purchase a ticket of my own, I had de-
pended on the charity of white friends, and I was in no position to in-

sist that they buy me a return ticket. The immigration official came back. He stamped my passport and welcomed me to the United States. I almost fell on my knees and kissed the hallowed ground.

"Welcome to America, Mark," a tall, lean-faced white man greeted me as I came out of customs. It was Dr. Waller. 43

His kind voice and smiling face, as he introduced himself and asked me if I had a good flight, raised my spirits. As we walked toward the baggage claim area I stared at everything about me with childlike wonder. I scarcely believed I had finally set foot in *the* America. I felt the difference between South Africa and America instantly. The air seemed pervaded with freedom and hope and opportunity. Every object seemed brighter, newer, more modern, fresher, the people appeared better dressed, more intelligent, richer, warmer, happier, and full of energy—despite the profound impersonality of the place. 44

"I would like to use the lavatory," I told Dr. Waller. 45

"There should be one over there." He pointed to a sign ahead which read RESTROOMS. "I'll wait for you at the newsstand over there." 46

When I reached the restroom I found it had the sign MEN in black and white on it. Just before I entered I instinctively scoured the walls to see if I had missed the other more important sign: BLACKS ONLY or WHITES ONLY, but there was none. I hesitated before entering: this freedom was too new, too strange, too unreal, and called for the utmost caution. Despite what I believed about America, there still lingered in the recesses of my mind the terror I had suffered in South Africa when I had inadvertently disobeyed the racial etiquette, like that time in Pretoria when I mistakenly boarded a white bus, and Granny had to grovel before the irate redneck driver, emphatically declare that it was an insanity "not of the normal kind" which had made me commit such a crime, and to appease him proceeded to wipe, with her lovely tribal dress, the steps where I had trod. In such moments of doubt such traumas made me mistrust my instincts. I saw a lanky black American with a mammoth Afro enter and I followed. I relieved myself next to a white man and he didn't die. 47

The black American washed his hands and began combing his Afro. I gazed at his hair with wonder. In South Africa blacks adored Afros and often incurred great expense cultivating that curious hairdo, in imitation of black Americans. Those who succeeded in giving their naturally crinkly, nappy, and matted hair, which they loathed, that buoyant "American" look were showered with praise and considered handsome and "glamorous," as were those who successfully gave it the permanent wave or jerry-curl, and bleached their faces white with special creams which affected the pigmentation. 48

I remember how Uncle Pietrus, on my father's side, a tall, athletic, handsome man who earned slave wages, was never without creams such as Ambi to bleach his face, and regularly wore a meticulously combed Afro greased with Brylcreem. Many in the neighborhood con- 49 sidered him the paragon of manly beauty, and women were swept away by his "American" looks.

50   From time to time he proudly told me stories of how, in the center of Johannesburg, whites who encountered black men and women with bleached faces, Afros, or straightened hair, and clad in the latest fashion from America, often mistook them for black Americans and treated them as honorary whites. A reasonable American accent made the masquerade almost foolproof. So for many blacks there were these incentives to resemble black Americans, to adopt their mannerisms and lifestyles. And the so-called Coloureds (mixed race), with their naturally lighter skin and straightened hair, not only frequently took advantage of this deception but often passed for whites. But they were rarely secure in their false identity. And in their desperation to elude discovery and humiliation at being subjected to fraudulent race-determining tests like the pencil test (where the authorities run a pencil through one's hair: if the pencil slides smoothly through, one gets classified white; if it gets tangled, that's "positive" proof of being black), they often adopted racist attitudes toward blacks more virulent than those of the most racist whites.

51   I had sense enough to disdain the practice of whitening one's skin. I considered it pathetic and demeaning to blacks. As for the companies which manufactured these popular creams, they are insidiously catering to a demand created by over three hundred years of white oppression and domination. During that traumatic time the black man's culture and values were decimated in the name of civilization, and the white man's culture and values, trumpeted as superior, became the standards of intelligence, excellence, and beauty.

52   I left the bathroom and rejoined Dr. Waller at the newsstand. I found him reading a magazine.

53   "There's so much to read here," I said, running my eyes over the newspapers, magazines, and books. Interestingly, almost all had white faces on the cover, just as in South Africa.

54   "Yes," replied Dr. Waller.

55   I was shocked to see pornography magazines, which are banned in South Africa, prominently displayed. The puritan and Calvinistic religion of the Afrikaners sought to purge South African society of "influences of the devil" and "materials subversive to the state and public morals" by routinely banning and censoring not only books by writers who challenged the status quo, but also publications like *Playboy*.

56   "So many black people fly in America," I said.

57   "A plane is like a car to many Americans," said Dr. Waller.

58   "To many of my people cars are what planes are to Americans."

59   At the baggage-claim area I saw black and white people constantly rubbing shoulders, animatedly talking to one another, and no one seemed to mind. There were no ubiquitous armed policemen.

"There truly is no apartheid here," I said to myself. "This is indeed 60
the Promised Land."

I felt so happy and relieved that for the first time the tension that 61
went with being black in South Africa left me. I became a new person.

Questions for Discussion and Writing

1. Where in the essay can you see Mathabane trying to reconcile opposing feelings on what it means to be black from a South African as opposed to an American perspective? To what extent does the essay not only chart his arrival in the United States but represent his struggle to understand his new identity in this new culture?
2. What different attitudes, values, and assumptions separate Mark from Nkwame? What do you infer Nkwame expected Mark to be like, having just arrived from Africa?
3. What differences in cultural assumptions explain why Nkwame and Mark view the prospect of attending a black college so differently?
4. How do Mark's first experiences in the United States (searching for the restroom, seeing a black American combing his Afro, seeing the kinds of magazines displayed on newsstands, and so forth) challenge his preconceptions about what life would be like in the United States?
5. What features in your current environment do you take for granted that you would miss most if you had to live somewhere else?

Kim Chi-Wŏn

A Certain Beginning

Kim Chi-Wŏn was born in 1943 in Kyonggi Province, Korea, into a preeminent literary family. She is the daughter of Ch'oe Chong-Hui, one of the most popular woman writers in twentieth-century Korea. She graduated in English literature from Ewha University in 1965 and made her literary debut in 1974 with "A Certain Beginning," translated by Bruce and Ju-Chan Fulton. Since the 1970s she has been living in the New York City area and has written many stories that explore the difficulties faced by Korean immigrant women in American cities. Like the work of other current women writers in Korea, Kim Chi-Wŏn's fiction displays a less sentimental, less deterministic outlook than did that of previous generations. Her unique mastery of style, technique, plotting, and characterization can be seen in this poignant story of late-blooming love.

1   Yun-ja floated on the blue swells, her face toward the dazzling sun. At first the water had chilled her, but now it felt agreeable, almost responding to her touch. Ripples slapped about her ears, and a breeze brushed the wet tip of her nose. Sailboats eased out of the corner of her eye and into the distance. She heard the drone of powerboats, the laughter of children, and the babble of English, Spanish, and other tongues blending indistinguishably like faraway sounds in a dream. Her only reaction to all this was an occasional blink. She felt drugged by the sun.

2   Yun-ja straightened herself in the water and looked for Chŏng-il. There he was, sitting under the beach umbrella with his head tilted back, drinking something. From her distant vantage point, twenty-seven-year-old Chŏng-il looked as small as a Boy Scout. He reminded her of a houseboy she had seen in a photo of some American soldiers during the Korean War.

3   "Life begins all over after today," Yun-ja thought. She had read in a women's magazine that it was natural for a woman who was alone after a divorce, even a long-awaited one, to be lonely, to feel she had failed, because in any society a happy marriage is considered a sign of a successful life. And so a divorced woman ought to make radical changes in her life-style. The magazine article had suggested getting out of the daily routine—sleeping as late as you want, eating what you want, throwing a party in the middle of the week, getting involved in new activities. "My case is a bit different, but like the writer says, I've got to start over again. But how? How is my life going to be different?" Yun-ja hadn't the slightest idea how to start a completely new life. Even

792

if she were to begin sleeping all day and staying up all night, what difference would it make if she hadn't changed inwardly? Without a real change the days ahead would be boring and just blend together, she thought. Day would drift into night; she would find herself hardly able to sleep and another empty day would dawn. And how tasteless the food eaten alone; how unbearable to hear only the sound of her own chewing. These thoughts hadn't occurred to her before. "He won't be coming anymore starting tomorrow," she thought. The approaching days began to look meaningless.

Several days earlier, Chŏng-il had brought some soybean sprouts and tofu to Yun-ja's apartment and had begun making soybean-paste soup. Yun-ja was sitting on the old sofa, knitting. 4

"Mrs. Lee, how about a trip to the beach to celebrate our 'marriage'? A honeymoon, you know?" 5

Yun-ja laughed. She and Chŏng-il found nothing as funny as the word *marriage*. Chŏng-il also laughed, to show that his joke was innocent. 6

"Marriage" to Chŏng-il meant the permanent resident card he was obtaining. He and Yun-ja were already formally married, but it was the day he was to receive the green card he had been waiting for that Chŏng-il called his "wedding day." 7

Chŏng-il had paid Yun-ja fifteen hundred dollars to marry him so that he could apply for permanent residency in the U.S. Until his marriage he had been pursued by the American immigration authorities for working without the proper visa. 8

"Americans talk about things like inflation, but they're still a superpower. Don't they have anything better to do than track down foreign students?" Chŏng-il had said the day he met Yun-ja. His eyes had been moist with tears. 9

Now, almost two months later, Chŏng-il had his permanent resident card and Yun-ja the fifteen hundred dollars. And today their relationship would come to an end. 10

Chŏng-il ambled down the beach toward the water, his smooth bronze skin gleaming in the sun. He shouted to Yun-ja and smiled, but she couldn't make out the words. Perhaps he was challenging her to a race, or asking how the water was. 11

Yun-ja had been delighted when Ki-yŏng's mother, who had been working with her at a clothing factory in Chinatown, sounded her out about a contract marriage with Chŏng-il. "He came here on a student visa," the woman had explained. "My husband tells me his older brother makes a decent living in Seoul. . . . The boy's been told to leave the country, so his bags are packed and he's about to move to a different state. . . . It's been only seven months since he came to America. . . . Just his luck—other Korean students work here without getting caught. . . ." 12

"Why not?" Yun-ja had thought. If only she could get out of that 13 sunless, roach-infested Manhattan basement apartment that she had been sharing with a young Chinese woman. And her lower back had become stiff as a board from too many hours of piecework at the sewing machine. All day long she was engulfed by Chinese speaking in strange tones and sewing machines whirring at full tilt. Yun-ja had trod the pedals of her sewing machine in the dusty air of the factory, the pieces of cloth she handled feeling unbearably heavy. Yes, life in America had not been easy for Yun-ja, and so she decided to give herself a vacation. With the fifteen hundred dollars from a contract marriage she could get a sunny room where she could open the window and look out on the street.

14   And now her wish had come true. She had gotten a studio apartment on the West Side, twenty minutes by foot from the end of a subway line, and received Chŏng-il as a "customer," as Ki-yŏng's mother had put it.

15   After quitting her job Yun-ja stayed in bed in the morning, listening to the traffic on the street below. In the evening, Chŏng-il would return from his temporary accounting job. Yun-ja would greet him like a boardinghouse mistress, and they would share the meal she had prepared. Her day was divided between the time before he arrived and the time after.

16   Thankful for his meals, Chŏng-il would sometimes go grocery shopping and occasionally he would do the cooking, not wishing to feel obligated to Yun-ja.

17   Chŏng-il swam near. "Going to stay in forever?" he joked. His lips had turned blue.

18   "Anything left to drink?" she asked.

19   "There's some Coke, and I got some water just now."

20   Chŏng-il had bought everything for this outing—Korean-style grilled beef, some Korean delicacies, even paper napkins.

21   "Mrs. Lee, this is a good place for clams—big ones too. A couple of them will fill you up—or so they say. Let's go dig a few. Then we can go home, steam them up, and have them with rice. A simple meal, just right for a couple of tired bodies. What do you think?"

22   Instead of answering, Yun-ja watched Chŏng-il's head bobbing like a watermelon. "So he's thinking about dropping by my place. . . . Will he leave at eleven-thirty again, on our last day? Well, he has to go there anyway to pick up his things." While eating lunch, she had mentally rehearsed some possible farewells at her apartment: "I guess you'll be busy with school again pretty soon," or "Are you moving into a dorm?"

23   Yun-ja was worried about giving Chŏng-il the impression that she was making a play for him. At times she had wanted to hand Chŏng-il a fresh towel or some lotion when he returned sopping wet from the shower down the hall, but she would end up simply ignoring him.

24   Yun-ja thought about the past two months. Each night after dinner at her apartment Chŏng-il would remain at the table and read a book or

newspaper. At eleven-thirty he would leave to spend the night with a friend who lived two blocks away. Chŏng-il had been told by his lawyer that a person ordered out of the country who then got married and applied for a permanent resident card could expect to be investigated by the Immigration and Naturalization Service. And so he and Yun-ja had tried to look like a married couple. This meant that Chŏng-il had to be seen with Yun-ja. He would stay as late as he could at her apartment, and he kept a pair of pajamas, some old shoes, and other belongings there.

Tick, tick, tick. . . . Yun-ja would sit knitting or listening to a 25 record, while Chŏng-il read a book or wrote a letter. Pretending to be absorbed in whatever they were doing, both would keep stealing glances at their watches. . . . Tick, tick, tick. . . .

At eleven-thirty Chŏng-il would strap on his watch and get up. 26 Jingling his keys, he would mumble "Good night" or "I'm going." Yun-ja would remain where she was and pretend to be preoccupied until his lanky, boyish figure had disappeared out the door.

It hadn't always been that way. During the first few days after their 27 marriage they would exchange news of Korea or talk about life in America—U.S. immigration policy, the high prices, the unemployment, or whatever. And when Chŏng-il left, Yun-ja would see him to the door. The silent evenings had begun the night she had suggested they live together. That night Chŏng-il had brought some beer and they had sung some children's ditties, popular tunes, and other songs they both knew. The people in the next apartment had pounded on the wall in protest. Chŏng-il and Yun-ja had lowered their voices, but only temporarily. It was while Chŏng-il was bringing tears of laughter to Yun-ja, as he sang and clowned around, that she had broached the subject: Why did Chŏng-il want to leave right at eleven-thirty every night only to sleep at a friend's apartment where he wasn't really welcome? He could just as easily curl up in a corner of her apartment at night and the two of them could live together like a big sister and her little brother— now wouldn't that be great? Immediately Chŏng-il's face had hardened and Yun-ja had realized her blunder. That was the last time Chŏng-il had brought beer to the apartment. The lengthy conversations had stopped and Chŏng-il no longer entertained Yun-ja with songs.

Yun-ja had begun to feel resentful as Chŏng-il rose and left like 28 clockwork each night. "Afraid I'm going to bite, you little stinker!" she would think, pouting at the sound of the key turning in the door. "It's a tug-of-war. You want to keep on my good side, so you sneak looks at me to see how I'm feeling. You're scared I might call off the marriage. It's true, isn't it—if I said I didn't want to go through with it, what would you do? Where would you find another unmarried woman with a green card? Would you run off to another state? Fat chance!"

The evening following her ill-advised proposal to live together, 29

Yun-ja had left her apartment around the time Chŏng-il was to arrive. She didn't want him to think she was sitting around the apartment waiting for him. She walked to a nearby playground that she had never visited before and watched a couple of Asian children playing with some other children. She wondered if being gone when Chŏng-il arrived would make things even more awkward between them. She wanted to return and tell him that her suggestion the previous evening had had no hidden meaning. Yun-ja had no desire to become emotionally involved with Chŏng-il. This was not so much because of their thirteen-year age difference (though Yun-ja still wasn't used to the idea that she was forty), but because Yun-ja had no illusions about marriage.

30   The man Yun-ja had married upon graduating from college had done well in business, and around the time of their divorce seven years later he had become a wealthy man, with a car and the finest house in Seoul's Hwagok neighborhood.

31   "Let's get a divorce; you can have the house," he had said one day.

32   Yun-ja was terribly shocked.

33   "But why? . . . Is there another woman?"

34   "No, it's not that. I just don't think I'm cut out for marriage."

35   In desperation Yun-ja had suggested a trial separation. But her husband had insisted on the divorce, and one day he left, taking only a toiletry kit and some clothes. Yun-ja had wept for days afterward. She was convinced that another woman had come on the scene, and sometimes she secretly kept an eye on her husband's office on T'oegye Avenue to try to confirm this.

36   "Was there really no other woman?" she asked herself at the playground. "Did he want the divorce because he was tired of living with me?" Their only baby had been placed in an incubator at birth, but the sickly child had died. Being a first-time mother had overwhelmed Yun-ja. "Maybe he just got sick and tired of everything. Or maybe he just wanted to stop living with me and go somewhere far away—that's how I felt toward him when he stayed out late." She had heard recently that he had remarried.

37   "Are you Korean?"

38   Yun-ja looked up to see a withered old Korean woman whose hair was drawn into a bun the size of a walnut. Yun-ja was delighted to see another Korean, though she couldn't help feeling conspicuous because of the older woman's traditional Korean clothing, which was made of fine nylon gauze.

39   Before Yun-ja could answer, the woman plopped herself down and drew a crimson pack of cigarettes from the pocket of her bloomers.

40   "Care for one, miss?"

41   "No, thank you."

42   The old woman lit a cigarette and began talking as if she were ripe for a quarrel: "Ah me, this city isn't fit for people to live in. It's a place for animals, that's what. In Korea I had a nice warm room with a

laminated floor, but here no one takes their shoes off and the floors are all messy."

"Can't you go back to Korea?" 43

"Are you kidding? Those darn sons of mine won't let me. I have to 44 babysit their kids all day long. Whenever I see a plane I start crying—I tell you! To think that I flew over here on one of those damned things!"

The old woman's eyes were inflamed, as if she cried every day, and 45 now fresh tears gathered. Yun-ja looked up and watched the plane they had spotted. It had taken off from the nearby airport and seemed to float just above them as it climbed into the sky. Its crimson and emerald green landing lights winked.

"I don't miss my hometown the way this grandmother does. And I 46 don't feel like crying at the sight of that plane," thought Yun-ja. Her homeland was the source of her shame. She had had to get away from it—there was no other way.

It was around seven when Yun-ja returned from the playground. 47

Chŏng-il opened the door. "Did you go somewhere?" he asked po- 48 litely, like a schoolboy addressing his teacher.

Yun-ja was relieved to have been spoken to first. 49

"I was talking with an elderly Korean woman." 50

"The one who goes around in Korean clothes? Was she telling you 51 how bad it is here in America?"

"You know her?" 52

"Oh, she's notorious—latches on to every Korean she sees." 53

This ordinary beginning to the evening would eventually yield to a 54 silent standoff, taut like the rope in a tug-of-war.

Chŏng-il's joking reference to "marriage" the evening he had offered to 55 take Yun-ja to the beach had come easily because his immigration pa- pers had finally been processed. All he had to do was see his lawyer and sign them, and he would get his permanent resident card.

Though it was six o'clock, it was still bright as midday. It was a 56 muggy August evening, and the small fan in the wall next to the win- dow stuttered, as if it were panting in the heat of Yun-ja's top-floor apartment.

Realizing that Chŏng-il was only joking, Yun-ja stopped knitting. 57 She got up and put a record on. The reedy sound of a man's mellow voice unwound from the cheap stereo:

Now that we're about to part
Take my hand once again. . . .

Yun-ja abruptly turned off the stereo. "Listening to songs makes me feel even hotter," she said.

Several days later, after Chŏng-il had obtained his permanent resi- 58 dent card, he borrowed a car and took Yun-ja to the beach, as promised. Yun-ja had thought it a kind of token of his gratitude, like the flowers or wine you give to the doctor who delivered your baby, or a memento you give to your teacher at graduation.

59   They stayed late at the beach to avoid the Friday afternoon rush hour. As the day turned to evening, the breeze became chilly and the two of them stayed out of the water, sitting together on the cool sand. Whether it was because they were outside or because this was their last day together, Yun-ja somehow felt that the tug-of-war between them had eased. But the parting words a couple might have said to each other were missing: "Give me a call or drop me a line and let me know how things are going." Chŏng-il did most of the talking, and Yun-ja found his small talk refreshing. He told her about getting measles at age nine, practicing martial arts in college, and going around Seoul in the dog days of summer just to get a driver's license so he could work while going to school in America. And he talked about a book he'd read, entitled *Papillon*.

60   "If you have Papillon's will, the sky's the limit on what you can do in America. You've heard Koreans when they get together here. They're always talking about the Chinese. The first-generation Chinese saved a few pennies doing unskilled labor when the subways were built. The second generation opened up small laundries or noodle stands. Buying houses and educating the kids didn't happen until the third generation. Whenever I hear that, I realize that Koreans want to do everything in a hurry—I'm the same way. They sound like they want to accomplish in a couple of years what it took the Chinese three generations to do. . . . When I left Korea I told my friends and my big brother not to feel bad if I didn't write, because I might not be able to afford the postage. My brother bought me an expensive fountain pen and told me that if I went hungry in the States I should sell it and buy myself a meal. And then my older sister had a gold ring made for me. I put the damned thing on my finger, got myself decked out in a suit for the plane ride, and then on the way over I was so excited I couldn't eat a thing—not a thing. The stewardess was probably saying to herself, 'Here's a guy who's never been on a plane before.' That damned ring—I must have looked like a jerk!"

61   Yun-ja related a few details about the elderly Korean woman she had met in the park. (Why did her thoughts return so often to this grandmother?) Then she told Chŏng-il a little about herself, realizing he had probably already learned through Ki-yŏng's mother that she was just another divorcée with no one to turn to.

62   The cool wind picked up as the sunlight faded, and they put their clothes on over their swimsuits. Chŏng-il's shirt was inside out, and Yun-ja could read the brand name on the neck tag.

63   "Your shirt's inside out."

64   Chŏng-il roughly pulled the shirt off and put it on right side out. Her steady gaze seemed to annoy him.

The beach was deserted except for a few small groups and some 65 young couples lying on the sand nearby, exchanging affections. Hundreds of sea gulls began to gather. The birds frightened Yun-ja. Their wings looked ragged; their sharp, ceaselessly moving eyes seemed treacherous. Yun-ja felt as if their pointed beaks were about to bore into her eyes, maybe even her heart. She folded the towel she had been sitting on and stood up.

"Let's get going." 66

More gulls had alighted on the nearly empty parking lot, which 67 stretched out as big as a football field.

"Want to get a closer look?" Chŏng-il asked as he started the car. 68

"They'll fly away." 69

"Not if we go slow. God, there must be thousands of them." 70

The car glided in a slow circle around the sea gulls. Just as Chŏng-il 71 had said, the birds stayed where they were. Yun-ja watched them through the window, her fear now gone.

They pulled out onto the highway and the beach grew distant. A 72 grand sunset flared up in the dark blue sky. The outline of distant hills and trees swung behind the car and gradually disappeared. Yun-ja noticed that Chŏng-il had turned on the headlights.

"You must be beat," Chŏng-il said. "Why don't you lean back and 73 make yourself comfortable."

Perhaps because he was silent for a time, Yun-ja somehow felt his 74 firm, quiet manner in the smooth, steady motion of the car. She wondered what to do when they arrived at her apartment. Invite him in? Arrange to meet him somewhere the following day to give him his things? But the second idea would involve seeing him again. . . . The tide hadn't been low, so they hadn't been able to dig clams. . . . "I'll bet I've looked like a nobody to him, a woman who's hungry for love and money." Yun-ja recalled something Chŏng-il had once told her: "After I get my degree here, write a couple of books, and make a name for myself, I'd like to go back to Korea. Right now there are too many Ph.D.'s over there. I know I wouldn't find a job if I went back with just a degree."

"And for the rest of your life," Yun-ja now thought, "I'll be a cheap 75 object for you to gossip about. You'll say, 'I was helpless when they told me to leave the country—so I bought myself a wife who was practically old enough to be my mother. What a pain in the neck—especially when she came up with the idea of living together.' And at some point in the future when you propose to your sweetheart, maybe you'll blabber something like 'I have a confession to make—I've been married before. . . .'"

Chŏng-il drove on silently. His hand on the steering wheel was fine 76 and delicate—a student's hand. Yun-ja felt like yanking that hand, biting it, anything to make him see things her way, to make him always speak respectfully of her in the future.

77   Chŏng-il felt Yun-ja's gaze and stole a glance at her. The small face that had been angled toward his was now looking straight ahead. "She's no beauty—maybe it's that thin body of hers that makes her look kind of shriveled up—but sometimes she's really pretty. Especially when it's hot. Then that honey-colored skin of hers gets a nice shine to it and her eyelashes look even darker." But Chŏng-il had rarely felt comfortable enough to examine Yun-ja's face.

78   "Mrs. Lee, did you ever have any children?"

79   "One—it died."

80   Chŏng-il lit a cigarette. Her toneless voice rang in his ears. "She doesn't seem to have any feelings. No expression, no interest in others, it even sounds as if her baby's death means nothing to her. True—time has a way of easing the pain. I don't show any emotion either when I tell people that my father died when I was young and my mother passed away when I was in college. Probably it's the same with her. But her own baby? How can she say 'It died' just like that?"

81   He had known from the beginning, through Ki-yŏng's mother, that Yun-ja was a single woman with no money. It had never occurred to him when he paid Ki-yŏng's mother the first installment of the fifteen hundred dollars that a woman with such a common name as Yun-ja might have special qualities. What had he expected her to be like, this woman who was to become his wife in name only? Well, a woman who had led a hard life, but who would vaguely resemble Ki-yŏng's mother—short permed hair, a calf-length sack dress, white sandals—a woman in her forties who didn't look completely at ease in Western-style clothing. But the woman Ki-yŏng's father had taken him to meet at the bus stop was thin and petite with short, straight hair and a sleeveless dress. Her eyelids had a deep double fold, and her skin had a dusky sheen that reminded Chŏng-il of Southeast Asian women. She was holding a pair of sunglasses, and a large handbag hung from her long, slender arm.

82   As they walked the short distance to Ki-yŏng's mother's for dinner that first night, Chŏng-il had felt pity for this woman who didn't even come up to his shoulders. He had also felt guilty and ill at ease. But Yun-ja had spoken nonchalantly: "So you're a student? Well, I just found an apartment yesterday. I'll be moving in three days from now. We can go over a little later and I'll show you around. It's really small—kitchen, bathroom, living room, and bedroom all in one." To Chŏng-il this breezy woman of forty or so acted like an eighteen-year-old girl. "This woman's marrying me for money." He felt regretful, as if he were buying an aging prostitute.

83   "Why don't you two forget about the business part of it and get married for real?" Ki-yŏng's mother had said at dinner. And when she sang a playful rendition of the wedding march, Chŏng-il had felt like crawling under the table. Yun-ja had merely laughed.

84   The traffic between the beach and the city was heavy, occasionally

coming to a standstill. Among the procession of vehicles Yun-ja and Chŏng-il noticed cars towing boats, cars carrying bicycles, cars with tents and shovels strapped to their roof racks.

As Chŏng-il drove by shops that had closed for the day, he thought of all the time he had spent on the phone with his older brother in Korea, of all the hard-earned money he had managed to scrounge from him (did his sister-in-law know about that?)—all because of this permanent resident card. And now he couldn't even afford tuition for next semester. These thoughts depressed him. But then he bucked up: Now that he had his green card (his chest swelled at the idea), there was no reason he couldn't work. "I'll take next semester off, put my nose to the grindstone, and by the following semester I'll have my tuition." And now that he was a permanent resident, his tuition would be cut in half. He made some mental calculations: How much could he save by cutting his rent and food to the bone? "But you can't cut down on the food too much," Chŏng-il reminded himself. There were students who had ended up sick and run-down, who couldn't study or do other things as a result. "This woman Yun-ja really has it easy—doesn't have to study. All she has to do is eat and sleep, day after day." Chŏng-il felt it was disgraceful that a young, intelligent Korean such as himself was living unproductively in America, as if he had no responsibilities to his family or country. "Why am I busting my butt to be here? Is the education really that wonderful?" In English class back in Korea he had vaguely dreamed of studying in America. Or rather he had liked the idea of hearing people say he had studied there. More shameful than this was the impulse he had to stay on in America. "What about the other people from abroad who live in the States—do they feel guilty about their feelings for their country, too?" He had read diatribes about America's corrupt material civilization. But he couldn't figure out what was so corrupt about it, and that bothered him. He wanted to see just what a young Korean man could accomplish in the world, and he wanted to experience the anger of frustration rather than the calm of complacency. He wanted knowledge, and recognition from others. But this woman Yun-ja didn't even seem to realize she was Korean.

The car pulled up on a street of six-story apartment buildings whose bricks were fading. Children were running and bicycling on the cement sidewalk; elderly couples strolled hand in hand, taking in the evening. Chŏng-il got out, unpacked the cooler and the towels, and loaded them on his shoulder. He and Yun-ja had the elevator to themselves. Yun-ja felt anxious and lonely, as if she had entered an unfamiliar neighborhood at dusk. She braced herself against the side of the elevator as it accelerated and slowed. When she was young it seemed the world belonged to her, but as time went on these "belongings" had disappeared; now she felt as if she had nothing. When it came time to part from someone, her heart ached as if she were separating from a lover. "Am I so dependent on people that I drove my husband away? Nobody wants to be burdened with me, so they all leave—even my baby. . . . I wonder if that old woman at the playground went back to Korea. Maybe she's still smoking American cigarettes and bending the ear of every Korean she sees here. Maybe I'll end up like her when I'm old. Already my body feels like a dead weight because of my neuralgia—God forbid that I latch on to just anybody and start telling a sob story."

87   Yun-ja unlocked the door to the apartment and turned on the light.

88   Today the small, perfectly square room looked cozy and intimate to them. They smelled the familiar odors, which had been intensified by the summer heat.

89   But Chŏng-il felt awkward when he saw that Yun-ja had packed his trunk and set it on the sofa. If only he could unpack it and return the belongings to their places.

90   "You must feel pretty sticky—why don't you take a shower?" Yun-ja said.

91   Chŏng-il returned from washing his salt-encrusted body to find Yun-ja cleaning the sand from the doorway. She had changed to a familiar, well-worn yellow dress. The cooler had been emptied and cleaned, the towels put away. Yun-ja had shampooed, and comb marks were still visible in her wet hair. Chŏng-il tried to think of something to say, gave up, and tiptoed to the sofa to sit down. "She's already washed her hair, changed, and started sweeping up," he thought. As Yun-ja bustled about, she looked to Chŏng-il as if she had just blossomed.

92   "Shouldn't I offer him some dinner?" Yun-ja thought as she swept up the sand. "He went to the trouble of borrowing a car and taking me out—the least I can do is give him a nice meal. And where would he eat if he left now? He'd probably fill up on junk food. . . . But if I offer to feed him, he might think I had something in mind. And when I've paid people for something, they never offered me dinner, did they?"

93   "How about some music?" Chŏng-il mumbled. He got up, walked stiffly to the stereo, and placed the needle on the record that happened to be on the turntable. The rhythm of a Flamenco guitar filled the room. Although Chŏng-il didn't pay much attention to the music Yun-ja played, it seemed that this was a new record. "Why have I been afraid of this woman? You'd think she was a witch or something."

94   "If that woman sinks her hooks into you, you've had it." Chŏng-il had heard this from his roommate, Ki-yŏng's father, and goodness knows how many others. "Nothing happened again today?" the roommate would joke when Chŏng-il returned in the evening from Yun-ja's apartment. "When it comes to you-know-what, nothing beats a middle-aged woman. I hope you're offering good service in return for those tasty meals you're getting."

95   The shrill voices of the children and the noise of airplanes and traffic were drowned out by the guitar music. The odor of something rotten outside wafted in with the heat of the summer night.

Chŏng-il began to feel ashamed. Here he was about to run out on this woman he'd used in return for a measly sum of money—a woman whose life he had touched. He had visited this room for almost two months, and now he wished he could spend that time over again. "Why didn't I try to make it more enjoyable?" he asked himself. He and Yun-ja had rarely listened to music, and when they had gone strolling in the nearby park after dinner he had felt uneasy, knowing that they did this only so that others would see the two of them together. 96

Yun-ja finished sweeping the sand up and sat down at the round dinner table. "If you're hungry, why don't you help yourself to some leftovers from yesterday's dinner? There's some lettuce and soybean paste and a little rice too." 97

Yun-ja's hair had dried, and a couple of strands of it drooped over her forehead. She looked pretty to Chŏng-il. 98

"And some marinated peppers," she continued. 99

Chŏng-il's body stiffened. This offer of dinner was a signal that it was time for him to leave. He rose and fumbled for something appropriate to say about the past two months. The blood rushed to his head and his face burned. Finally he blurted out, "What would you say if I . . . proposed to you?" Then he flung open the door as if he were being chased out. In his haste to leave he sent one of Yun-ja's sandals flying from the doorway toward the gas range. The door slammed shut behind him. 100

Yun-ja sprang up from the table. "What did he say?" Her body prickled, as if she were yielding to a long-suppressed urge to urinate. "I don't believe in marriage," she told herself. "Not after what I went through." She rushed to the door and looked through the peephole into the hall. She saw Chŏng-il jab futilely at the elevator button and then run toward the stairway. 101

"The boy proposed to me—I should be thankful," Yun-ja thought. Like water reviving a dying tree, hot blood began to buzz through her sleepy veins. This long-forgotten sensation of warmth made her think that maybe their relationship had been pointing in this direction all along. "It was fun prettying myself up the day I met him. And before that, didn't I expect some good times with him even though we weren't really married?" 102

Yun-ja turned and looked around the room. There was Chŏng-il's trunk on the sofa. "But he'd end up leaving me too." Suddenly she felt very vulnerable. Everything about her, starting with her age and the divorce, and then all the little imperfections—the wrinkles around the eyes, the occasional drooling in her sleep—reared up in her mind. "But I'm not going to let my shortcomings get me down," she reassured herself. "It's time to make a stand." 103

Questions for Discussion and Writing

1. What impression did you get of the relationship between Yun-ja and Chŏng-il from the description of their outing to the beach? Were you surprised to discover that she was so much older than he was and the reasons for their marriage? In a sentence or two, describe why each of them has entered into this arrangement.
2. What picture do we get of Yun-ja's life as a divorced woman in Korea? What striking differences in the two CULTURES explain why she immigrated to the United States?
3. What is the significance of Yun-ja's encounter with the old Korean woman at the playground?
4. How does the author underscore different stages in the relationship between Yun-ja and Chŏng-il with different kinds of songs and music played on the stereo?
5. What additional insight do you gain as a result of the author's shift in POINT OF VIEW so that the events previously described from Yun-ja's viewpoint are now seen as they appeared to Chŏng-il? What had prevented Chŏng-il from acting on his true feelings?
6. How does the ALLUSION to *Papillon* (1970) by H. Charrière relate to Chŏng-il's predicament?
7. In a short essay, discuss any of the issues raised in the story regarding the plight of divorced women in Korea, the way in which Yun-ja had to support herself in the United States, the relationship between Koreans and the Chinese community, and the pressures on Korean students to obtain green cards. In what way does the story suggest that people of different generations and in different CULTURAL CONTEXTS interpret the world in very different ways?
8. In the story, music is important in the developing relationship between the two people. Describe the mental images or pictures that form in your mind while listening to your favorite piece of music. Does the music go beyond separate images to suggest a narrative or story line?
9. Write your own ending to this story, extending the events over the next few years.
10. Describe or imagine what it was like at the time your forebears immigrated to the United States.

Keri Hulme

Unnamed Island in the Unknown Sea

Keri Hulme was born in 1947 in Christchurch, New Zealand. She attended the University of Canterbury and has worked as a fisher, television director, and cook. She was writer in residence at Otago University, Dunedin, New Zealand, in 1978 and at the University of Canterbury in Christchurch in 1985. Her mother's people, the Kai Tahu, were the first south island people to encounter Europeans. Hulme currently lives in Okarito, New Zealand, in a remote area in a village whose population is fourteen. She is best known for her highly acclaimed first novel, The Bone People *(1984), about the stormy relationships among three social outcasts, praised for its dazzling word play and psychological insight into native Maori culture and sensibility. This work won the New Zealand Book Award in 1984 and England's Booker McConnell Prize in 1985. Much of Hulme's writing draws on her own Maori heritage. Hulme has also written a volume of poetry,* The Silences Between *(1982), and a collection of short stories,* Te Kaihau: The Wind Eater *(1986), from which "Unnamed Island in the Unknown Sea" is taken. Her writing is distinguished by a style that incorporates both the vernacular and archaic, the poetic and the prosaic, to express tensions between different psychological and social perspectives. This story relates the events in the last days of a journalist and naturalist stranded on one of the New Zealand out-islands as seen through the eyes of a bureaucratic government investigator.*

[*The Contents:*

damned dear. In the last crazy hours before you died, I saw sights   1
through your eyes, sealions tombstoning, albatrosses with weary
hearts, eggs with pink yolks. Now I am myself alone again, I must balance what I saw with what I know surrounds me. This reality before
the next.

1: the overhang. It juts like the prow of any ship but is massive. It   2
   broods over me. One day it will fall but I do not fear that. It has
   anciently hung here—remember the bones? Moa you said, and I
   believe that. They were old old bones, so old the rats hadn't bothered them.
2: the pile of seaweed at the left end. I have rewoven it, more   3
   tightly. It makes a ragged screen.
3: your sleeping bag. I washed it, beat it against the rock until all   4
   your sweated pain & foulness fled. It is nearly dry. I have rolled
   it, so it serves me as a backrest. I am undecided whether to sleep
   in it tonight. I think I might.

805

5   4: the rocky floor. It slopes towards the sea. Did it never strike you
     as odd? The roof rears heavenward and all our floor tries to slip
     away from us, downwards, outwards, away.

6   5: the fire—o yes. I haven't let it go out. Even if I go swimming, I
     want it there to look back to. I feed it dried kelp butts, and twigs
     from the mikkimik and detritus from the moon, feathers and sun-
     dried bladders and a piece of polystyrene float.

7   6: twelve mussels in their shells. They are placed in an arc by my
     feet. They make small popping and hissing sounds, as though
     they had minute mouths that cared to suck air. Kissing sounds.
     They are tea.

8   Then there is me clad in my despair & wet clothes; my raw feet; your
     weatherbeaten seabattered notebook. My notebook. My pen. I hope to
     God it doesn't run out.

9   (As you were ultimately your last clear analytic words, so I shall be
     these pages. And maybe they will be found by someone who doesn't
     understand, who doesn't read English even, or just can't be bothered
     reading such stained and faded script, and so burns them. As I burned
     those poor brown remnants of moa, which had maybe stored all the
     song of its living in those bones. Did moas sing?)

10   I have eaten the mussels. Thin meat, mussels. Even the peacrabs
     don't add much more than crunch. And I used to love them, mussels
     succulent on a scrubbed shining navy shell, topped with garlic butter or
     richly robed in melted cheese—

11   Better to remember Day 2, my feet already butchered by those
     bloody rocks, and me despairing because you couldn't keep the mus-
     sels or limpets down and that was all I could gather. And suddenly the
     waves flung a fish on the beach. It flopped weakly, one flank deeply
     gashed—a couta you said. I managed to hit it on the head—indeed hit
     with a savagery I didn't know inhabited me.

12   Cooking mussels and limpets had been easy—arrange them care-
     fully in the embers and let them toast. But that red cod? Easy, you said.
     You sounded very tired, and you were huddled over. That seaweed,
     that bullkelp? Get some thickish fronds off it and split them and stick
     the cod inside. Never mind the guts.

13   You kept down the soft flesh. But it wasn't enough. Maybe it wors-
     ened matters.

14   I can't remember the order of days after Day 2. It could be as long as
     nine days I've been here.

15   Sometimes during the nights—ten? Eight?—sometimes during
     the nights we saw lights far out at sea. Distant ships perhaps, though
     some grew at a strangely fast rate and others stayed abnormally
     steady, beacons through the night, winking out at dawn. We saw lights?
     The only time you showed awareness of any of them was that night
     the waves danced, alive with phosphorescence. Porotitiwai, you

whispered, porotitiwai, and I never thought to ask you what that means.

Do you know I have always been scared of the sea? Don't laugh. It 16 is remorseless. There is no humanity in it.

You would have laughed at that. 17

I am cold and smoked and damp and so alone that I feel all the rest 18 of the world has deliberately gone home, leaving me in the dark. I miss your laughter. O God I miss the way your arms felt either side of me as you paddled. A jaunt you said. Only thirty *k* to that island, and look at the sea. Flat as a pancake. I can get us there and back between dawn and dusk, hell I've paddled Cook Strait! And to my demur you said Think! No one's set foot on that island for bloody years! Now that's a story! And then added, your eyes full of a wicked glinting glee, That's if you came to get a story and not just see me.

I said very primly that I Am A Journalist Albeit Freelance, and a 19 story was what I came for, and writing about scruffy field assistants cutting transects won't sell *anywhere*, so lead on MacDuff. McLeay actually, you said. From the whisky actually.

This is pointless. The rats'll eat it. 20

Who's going to come looking for a freelance peripatetic journo? 21

I don't want to say what bottle I have sent out on the waves— 22

I used to love reading about islands as a child. Being shipwrecked 23 on one would be heaven. You'd use the materials from your wrecked ship, and feast on the island's provender and finally when it was getting a little boring, you'd light an enormous bonfire which would hail a passing cruise ship and you'd sail happily home a better and a richer man.

God knows when I heard the plane I tried. I grabbed anything I 24 thought would burn and a piece of smouldering kelp and rushed out on the halfmoon of gravel that is the only beach. And the drizzle made everything sodden. The fire was only smoke and a few sullen flickers of flame. Desperate—o how *weak* that reads! *desperate*! I would have burnt my hair had it been longer, I would have fed my clothes to those flames if they hadn't been wetter than the driftwood! I raced back under the overhang and grabbed my sleeping bag and folded it round the smoulder. I prayed. My feet ached so much from the running I cried. The plane droned away and as it got further and further towards the horizon the sleeping bag suddenly flared into a glorious bonfire. Nobody saw it. Just me.

It has been silent since then, if anywhere near the sea is silent. There 25 were silences before. You would say something, mainly a coherent few sentences—

"Do you know they shake penguins out of their skins before they 26 eat them? Catch them underwater and surface with them and shake 'em so viciously quick that the bird flies out of its skin. Then the leopard seal dines."

27   Up until these few days ago I had never *heard* of a leopard seal.

28   I wanted to ask more but you had closed your eyes and there was another silence that lasted all night.

29   The days are silent too, mainly. At least, the first few—three? Four?—days. Your belly blackens. The haematoma spreads up to your collar-bones. You bleed to death inside but it all takes silent time. At least, mainly silent.

30   You start to curl up, going from sitting-up huddle, to lying-down hunch. And as you curl slowly into your beginning shape, you want me to see some other island. You talk against the unremitting pain.

31   It was a harsh place, this island you loved. A bleak volcanic terrain, sere and disordered. Some subantarctic place where the waters teemed with whitepointers and the winds never ceased.

32   There was mist around our island, closing the world down to just our size.

33   It was either cliff or swamp, you said, but we had hardwood-plant tracks and so could walk through the headhigh tussock. We could walk past the peat bogs. But if you went off the planks you got quickly lost in the draco . . . and you'd come to a cairn where there was may-be a body underneath, as though the cairn called you. Or arrive at a still inland tarn and there, deep in the water, was an unrusting try-pot. We'd been there, people had been there, lots of people, but the land felt *unlived on* and somehow, it wanted people living on it, people as well as the elephant seals and the sealions and the skuas and the alba-tross.

34   This Godforsaken rock, *this* island is lived on. It doesn't want us. It already has rats and shags and the mikkimik. The rats live on the shags and each other I think. Presumably the shags live off the sea. They aren't nesting at the moment. The adult birds shuffle but they shuffle faster than I can limp. And the guano burns my feet horribly.

35   You said weakly, "The wind is in my ears."

36   It is so still outside. The mist hides even the sea.

37   There is always the wind you say, and nearly always the rain or the snow. Ninety-knot winds . . . I used to worry about the birds. And how did the cattle stand it? That small shotabout fearful herd—did they crouch into the gullies, die finally in the peaty bogs?

38   It was then your breathing changed.

39   Between gasps you say, "Sometimes there is an unnatural quiet, a threatening calm, as the wind holds still for an hour, deciding its next quarter."

40   O God he can't have spoken like that. It got hard. The blood on his lungs. I can do nothing, could do nothing. Collect limpets and mussels and stew the juice out of them and have it ready in the thermos flask so when he is ready he can sup soup. The mist pools on the rocks. We have water. The mist makes it hard to breathe. My own lungs are husking.

41   But your lungs are heaving in and out harnh harnh every hard intake, the sound pitching higher and higher until you are screaming—

I stay outside for the screaming—   42

remember thinking, But I screamed too. I screamed, What was it?   43
What *was* it? We lay in a tangle a crush in the froth on shore. You had
just laughed and pulled the right side of the paddle down hard.
"Landing!" you yelled. And then the sea lurched. Something sleek and
bulky and sinuous, a grey fast violent hulk punched into the kayak
punched past me into you fled past us into the onshore surf. I screamed
What *was* it? until you had caught your breath. You grunted, "Leopard
seal. Wanted to get out to sea. We were in the way." You grinned. Your
last grin. "We probably scared it to hell."

None of the kayak has washed ashore.   44

I can do nothing now. I fold myself beside you and hold your hand.   45
You say, the screaming finished, the breathing nearly finished, you say
in that tired hoarse whisper,

"At new moons there are bigger currents than normal. Huge shoals   46
of fish are swept close inshore. The sharks feed hard. Sometimes they
will get in amongst a group of Hooker sealions that are also feeding
hard. And then you will see the sealions tombstone—bodies rigid in
the water, heads sticking straight out, while the white pointers circle
and threaten and crazily decide whether to take one or to take all. They
can't take all. Islands don't work like that."

And somehow I am behind your eyes and I see the cliffs that arrow   47
out of the grey seas to terminate in mean blade edges. I see the sheep,
feral Drysdales gone surefooted like goats, gaze fearlessly down on
climbing humans. I see the albatross effortfully trudge over a ridge
down to the hollow where its chick roosts safely out of the wind. I see it
feed the chick. I see a skua pluck a pink-yolked penguin's egg and then
hungrily cruise on. I see it take the albatross's chick, a limp-necked vulnerable downy sac. I see the albatross halfway down the ridge, watch;
then turn and stagger back up to the top of the ridge and launch into
the wind.

And then suddenly the shags outside wave their snaky necks and   48
shoot stinking excrement onto the rocks.

And there is no one behind your eyes.   49

But you did say, watching the sad lumbering albatross, you did say,   50
because I heard you there behind your eyes.

"Don't be afraid. We are all islands but the sea connects us, every-   51
one. Swim."

And I had enough heart and mind left to laugh at a swimming is-   52
land as you died.

I gave you to the sea. I rolled you down the sloping floor onto   53
a quartermoon of gravel and let the sea take you. The waves toyed
with your beautiful black hair, the waves toyed with your scarred
strong hands. Then they too rolled you over and swam you out of
sight.

I have given my message to the sea, my bottle, my message.   54

It is unbearable.]   55

[*The Notebook from the Unnamed Island off Breaksea Sound:*

56   It is a standard field notebook, issue item 1065, 18 cm × 13 cm. black elastic closure band, forty-six double pages lined each side, and divided by a midpage column, with red, waterstained, covers. The standard issue pen is missing from the side holder. The last ten pages, and the first two pages, have been torn out.

57   The notebook was found inside a plastic sandwich container (Tupperware, item CT 106), which had been wrapped in a light down sleeping bag ("Camper," manufactured by Arthur Ellis, Dunedin). The sleeping bag, which had been extensively damaged by rats, was found tucked in the far corner on the overhang described in "Contents."

58   There was no other sign of human intervention or habitation on the island.]

[*Conclusion:*

59   Many people have speculated on the identity of the writer of this notebook since its recovery by two crew members from the fishing boat "Motu" (Dunedin registration 147 DN). The unnamed "you" may be Jacob Morehu, a field assistant employed by the DSIR on Resolution Island during the recent blue penguin (*Eudyptula minor*) counts. Two possible indicators for this identification are:
Morehu was employed during the '84 season on Campbell Island (by the DSIR), and
Morehu disappeared shortly before the now-infamous Skinned Body corpse was discovered at Goose Cove. (Morehu is not implicated. He was an ardent kayak enthusiast, and his kayak vanished at the same time. The area round Breaksea Island is marked "reputed dangerous" on all charts, and this pertains to the unnamed small island beyond.)

60   However, it is much more probable the notebook is an obscure joke perpetrated by a person or persons unknown. The indicators for this Conclusion, which is that of the Department, are:

   a] *nobody else* was reported missing from the *entire South Island* at the time Morehu went missing;
   b] the "Skinned Body" was almost certainly murder, and is thought to have been committed by the eccentric gunship shooter, Mike Corely, who fell into the notorious giant eel tarn in Fiordland National Park two days before the body was discovered;
   c] nobody has explained satisfactorily to me why two sleeping bags should be taken on what is described as a *day-trip* in a kayak. A plastic container of sandwiches, yes, but two light sleeping bags suitable only for indoor use?]

Questions for Discussion and Writing

1. Under what circumstances did the journalist record her observations in the naturalist's log? Reconstruct the sequence of events that preceded the writing of this log.

2. What is the significance of the ALLUSION to *Robinson Crusoe* by Daniel DeFoe (1719) as it relates to the journey undertaken by the couple? How does the reference place Hulme's story in a particular LITERARY CONTEXT?

3. How does the detail about the way leopard seals kill penguins tie into the physical condition of the body mentioned by the investigator?

4. In what sense is the investigator's unsympathetic and objective response to the contents of the diary linked thematically with the harsh and inhospitable environment of the island?

5. To what extent does the story suggest that the naturalist, journalist, and bureaucrat in charge of the investigation understand the world only in terms of the CONTEXT of their respective disciplines? How do these differences help define them as individuals?

6. How does this story use a physical environment to dramatize the psychological effects of alienation? How might the title of the story be taken to refer METAPHORICALLY to the radical differences that separate people from each other? How does the physical landscape reflect this estrangement?

7. Describe how a natural landscape or an unusually harsh climate affect the people who live in that area. Is there anything dangerous about living there?

8. Describe a place (real or imaginary) to which you have always wanted to go.

9. Describe a time you were caught in a snowstorm, hailstorm, landslide, flood, volcanic eruption, hurricane, or tornado, when your survival skills and resourcefulness were tested.

10. If you were stranded in a desert and could have only two things with you, what would those be and why?

Mahdokht Kashkuli

The Button

Mahdokht Kashkuli was born in 1950 in Teheran, Iran. She was married at age fourteen and, unlike similar marriages, hers did not prevent her from pursuing her education. She succeeded in obtaining her bachelor of arts in performing literature from Teheran University. By 1982 she had completed two masters' degrees, one in library science and one in linguistics, and a doctorate in the language, culture, and religion of Ancient Iran from the same university. She started her career first as a researcher for Iranian Educational Television from 1975 to 1985 and then as a professor of performing literature at Teheran University. Her short stories, including "The Fable of Rain in Iran," "The Fable of Creation in Iran," "Our Customs, Our Share," "The Pearl and the Moon," and "Tears and Water" have won her national recognition. She is presently working on a novel. "The Button," translated by Soraya Sullivan, was first published in the summer of 1978 in the periodical Arash. *This short story explores the heartbreaking consequences of a family's poverty in contemporary Iran.*

1   My sister was perched in the doorway, sobbing bitterly; her curly, russet hair was stuck to her sweaty forehead. My mother was doing her wash by the pond, paying no attention to my sister's sobs or my father's shouts, "Hurry up Reza! Move it!" I was holding on to the edge of the mantle shelf tightly, wishing that my hand would remain glued there permanently. It was only a few nights ago that I had heard, with my own ears, my father's voice whispering to my mother, "Woman, stop grumbling! God knows that my heart is aching too, but we don't have a choice. I can't even provide them with bread. What else can I do? This way, we'll have one less mouth to feed." I had cocked my ears to hear who that "one less mouth to feed" was. I remained frozen, holding my breath for a few minutes; then I heard my father say, "Reza is the naughtiest of all; the most restless. Akbar and Asghar are more tame, and we can't send the girls away. It's not wise." Suddenly a dry cough erupted from my mouth. My father called out, "Reza! Reza! Are you awake?" I did not answer him. He fell silent, and then my mother's snorts followed the awkward silence. My father went on, "Woman, who said the orphanage is a bad place? They teach the kids, they feed them, they clothe them. At least this one will have a chance to live a good life." My mother's snorts stopped. She groaned, "I don't know. I don't know anything. Just do what you think is best." And then there was silence.

2   Why are they going to make me the "one less mouth to feed"? What

is an orphanage? I wish I hadn't nibbled the bread on my way home from the bakery; I wish I hadn't quarreled with Asghar; I wish I hadn't messed around with my mother's yarn, as if it were a ball; I wish I hadn't pulled the bottle out of Kobra's mouth, and drunk her milk; I wish I could stay still, like the mannequin in the clothing store at the corner. Then they wouldn't make me the "one less mouth to feed." My pillow was soaked with tears.

I ran outside with puffy eyes the next morning. Ahmad was stand- 3 ing at the other end of the alley, keeping watch for Husain so he could pick a fight with him. I yelled, "Ahmad, Ahmad! What's an orphan- age?" Keeping his eyes still on the door to Husain's house, Ahmad said, "It's a place where they put up poor people's children." "Have you been there?" I asked. He shouted indignantly, "Listen to this goddamn wretch! You can't be nice to anyone these days!" I ran back to the house, scared. If Ahmad hadn't been waiting for Husain, he surely would have beaten me up.

My father's screams shot up again, "Are you deaf? Hurry up, it's 4 late!" I released my grip on the shelf and went down the stairs. The saltiness of my tears burned my face. My father said, "What's wrong? Why are you crying? Come, my boy! Come wash your face!" Then he took my hand and led me to the pond and splashed a handful of the murky water on my face. He wiped my face with his coat lining. I be- came uneasy. My father seldom showed signs of affection; I suspected that he was being affectionate because he had decided to make me the "one less mouth to feed." We walked towards the door. He pulled aside the old cotton rug hanging before the door with his bony hands. Then he said, in a tone as if he were talking to himself, "One thousand . . . God knows, I had to pull a thousand strings before they agreed to ad- mit you."

I asked, while I kept my head down, "Why?" My father screamed 5 angrily, "He asks why again! Because!" I lowered my head. My eyes met his shoes. They were strangely crooked and worn out; maybe he had them on wrong. . . . The lower part of his long underwear showed from beneath his pants. He was wearing a belt to hold his loose pants up, and they creased like my mother's skirt. "I'm telling you, Reza, a thousand strings," he repeated. "You must behave when you get there." I didn't look at him but said grudgingly, "I don't want to be- have!"

He threw a darting glance at me and raved, his hand rising to cuff 6 me on the back of the neck but he changed his mind and said instead, "They'll teach you how to behave yourself." Indignantly I said, "I don't want to go to an orphanage, and if you take me there, I'll run away." I pulled my hand out of his quickly and ran ahead, knowing that he'd hit me this time. But he didn't. He only said, "You think they admit every- one? I've been running around for a year, resorting to everyone I know." I said, "Dad, I don't want to go to the orphanage. They keep poor children there." "What, do you think you are, rich?" my father said. "Listen to him use words bigger than his mouth!" And he broke out laughing. When he laughed I saw his gold teeth. There were two of them. I thought to myself, "What does it take to be rich? My father has gold teeth, my mother has gold teeth, and my brother has a fountain pen." I looked at his face. He wasn't laughing anymore; his face had turned gray. I said spontaneously, "Dad, is the landlord rich?" He didn't hear me, or it seemed he didn't, and said absentmindedly, "What?" I said, "Nothing."

7   I thought about the landlord. He sends his oldest son or his young daughter to collect the rent two weeks before the rent is due. His oldest son enters my father's shop and stands in the front of the mirror, scrutinizing himself, resting one hand on his waist. My father rushes to him and says, "Do you want a haircut?" The landlord's son responds, "No. You just gave me one on Thursday." My father says politely, "What can I do for you, then?" The landlord's son says, "Is the rent ready?" My father answers, "Give me a few more days. Tell Haji Agha I'll pay before the due date." And the next day his young daughter shows up in the shop. She is so small that she can hardly see herself in the mirror. She holds her veil tightly under her chin with those tiny, delicate hands, and says, "Hello!" My father smiles and says, "Hello, cutie pie! What can I do for you?" The girl laughs cheerfully and says, "My father sent me after the rent. If it's ready, give it to me." My father picks a sugar cube out of the sugar bowl, puts it gently in her palm, and says, "Tell Haji Agha, fine!"

8   We reached the intersection. My father held my hand in his tightly and stopped to look around. We then crossed the street. He was mumbling to himself, "The damn thing is so far away. . . ."

9   I felt sick. I said, "Wait a minute!" He eyed me curiously and said, "Why, what's wrong?" I said, "I'm tired; I don't want to go to the orphanage." He mimicked me, pursing his lips, and said, "You don't understand! You were always dumb, dense!"

10   I remembered that my father was always unhappy with me, although I swept the shop everyday and watered the China roses he had planted in front of the shop. I would take my shirt off on hot summer afternoons and jump in the brook with my underpants. The elastic of my pants was always loose and I always tried to tie it into a knot, never succeeding to make it tight enough to stay. In the brook, I held my pants with one hand while I watered the China roses with a small bowl. It felt nice and cool there. Flies would gather around my shoulders and arms. Grandmother used to say, "God made flies out of wax." But I didn't understand why they didn't melt in the hot sun; they flew off my body and landed on the China rose flowers and I shook the branches with my bowl to disperse them. The flowers were my father's and no fly was allowed to sit on them. In spite of all my efforts, my father was always unhappy with me; he was unhappy with my mother, with my

sisters and brothers, with the landlord, and with the neighbors. But he was happy with one person: God. He would sigh, tap himself hard on the forehead, and say, "Thank God!"

I said to him one day, "Why are you thanking God, Dad?" 11 Suddenly, he hit me in the mouth with the back of his hand. My upper lip swelled and my mouth tasted bloody. I was used to the taste of blood because whenever I bled in the nose, I tasted blood in my mouth. I covered my mouth, walked to the garden and spat in the dirt. I looked at the bubbles on my spittle, tapped myself on the forehead and said, "Thank God!" Then I picked up a piece of watermelon skin lying on the brook and smacked it on the head of a yellow dog that always used to nap by the electric post. The yellow dog only opened its eyes, looked at me indifferently, and shut its eyes again, thanking God, perhaps.

We passed another street before we got to the bus station. A few 12 people were waiting in line; one of them was sitting at the edge of the brook. My father took my hand and led me to the front of the bus line. Someone said, "This is not the end of the line, old man!" I only looked at my father.

He said to me, "Ignore him. Just stay right here!" The bus came and 13 my father pushed me towards it. I tore my feet off the ground and jumped on the coach-stop, feeling as if I were floating in the air. Someone said, "Old man, the end of the line is on the other side! Look how people give you a headache on a Monday morning!" My father didn't hear him; he pushed me forward. I was stuck between a seat and the handle bar. . . . So, today is Monday. . . . Every week on Monday my mother does her wash. The clothesline spread around the entire yard. I liked the smell of damp clothes. In spite of my mother's curses, I liked cupping my hands underneath the dripping clothes so that the water that dripped could tickle my palms. Every Monday we had yogurt soup for lunch. My brother and I would take a bowl to the neighborhood dairy store to buy yogurt. On the way back, we took turns licking the surface of the yogurt. When we handed the bowl to my mother, she would scream at us and beat the first one of us she could get her hands on. . . . I felt depressed. I wished I could jump out the window.

The bus stopped at a station and we got off. My father walked 14 ahead of me while I dragged my feet along behind him.

He waited for me to catch up, then he said, "Move it! He walks like 15 a corpse. Hurry up, it's late!" I stopped momentarily and said, "Dad, I don't want to go. I don't want to go to the orphanage." My father froze in his spot. He said incredulously, "What did you say? You think you know what's good for you? Don't you want to become a decent human being some day? They have rooms, there. They have food, and they'll teach you everything you need to learn to get a decent job." I sobbed, "To hell with anyone who has a decent job. To hell with decent jobs. I don't want one! I like staying home. I like playing with Asghar and

Akbar. I want to sell roasted corn with the kids from the neighborhood in the summer. I want to help you out in the shop. I don't want to go."

16   My father sprang towards me, but suddenly retreated and became affectionate. He said, "Let's go, good boy! We're almost there." I felt sorry for him because every time he was kind he looked miserable. My father was walking ahead of me and I was following him, dragging my feet on the street like that yellow dog. On the next street, we stopped in front of a big metal door. A chair was placed inside the door to keep it ajar. A man was sitting on the chair, playing with a ring of prayer beads. He had on a navy blue coat with metal buttons. His eyes were half-closed and his mouth was open. His cheeks were puffy, as if he had a toothache. My father greeted him and said, "Mr. Guard!" The man opened his eyes. Strands of blood ran through the white of his eyes. He said with a gloomy voice, "What is it, what do you want?" My father thrust his hand in both his pockets, took out an envelope and extended it toward the guard with both hands. The man looked at my father, then threw a threatening glance at me. He yawned, stared at the envelope for a while (I didn't believe he could read), shook his head, coughed, and said, "They won't leave you alone; one leaves, another comes!" Then he pushed the door with the tip of his shoes. The door opened just enough to let me in.

17   After my father walked through the doorway behind me, the guard gave him the envelope and said, "The first door!" My father was walking fast, and when he opened the hallway door, my heart started beating violently and I started to cry. He said, "My boy, my sweet Reza, this is a nice place. The people here are nice, the kids are all your own age. . . ."

18   He didn't finish his sentence. He pushed on the door. The door opened and I saw a woman inside the room. I wished she were my mother, but she was heavier than my mother, with a deep vertical wrinkle between her eyebrows. She wore a blue uniform and her hair was a bleached blonde.

19   My father pushed me further in and said, "Greet her, Reza! Greet her!" I didn't feel like greeting anyone.

20   My father handed the woman the envelope. She opened it, pulled the letter out halfway, and started reading it. Then she turned to my father and said, "Go to the office so they can complete his file."

21   My father leaped and ran out the door. Then, as though he had remembered something, he returned and stood in front of the door, rubbing his hand on the wood frame of the door. He raised one hand to tap on his forehead and say, "Thank God," but stopped, rubbed his forehead gently and sighed. His eyes were as moist and shiny as the eyes of the yellow dog hanging around his shop. Her head still lowered on the letter, the woman said, "Go, old man! What are you waiting for? Go to the office!" Father took a few steps backwards, then tore himself from the door and disappeared into the corridor.

The woman looked at me, then turned her gaze toward the window 22
and fixed it there. While she had her back to me, she said, "Don't cry,
boy! Please don't, I'm not in the mood!" Then she turned around and
put her hands on my shoulders. Her hands were as heavy as my
mother's but not as warm. She took my hand and walked me toward
the door. We passed one corridor, and entered another. Then we entered a room, then another corridor and another room. There were a
few people in the room. One was sitting in the doorway, whistling; one
was leaning against the desk; one was sitting in a chair writing something. Although the room was furnished with chairs and desks, it was
not warm. The woman said, "Say hello to these people!" I looked at her
but didn't say anything. I didn't feel like talking to them. I didn't hear
what they said to each other, either. I only wanted to sit still and look at
them. We left that room and went into another. There was another
woman there. I wished she were my mother. She was wearing a blue
uniform and had a red scarf around her neck. I think she had a cold because she sniffled constantly. As soon as she saw me, she checked me
out thoroughly and spoke with a nasal voice, "Is he new here? I don't
know where we're going to put him." She then opened a closet, took
out a uniform and said to me, "Take your jacket off and wear this!"
Then she continued, "Take your shirt off, too. How long has it been
since your last shower?" I didn't answer. Her words hit my ears and
bounced right off. She went toward the closet again and asked, "Are
you done?" I looked around and then looked at myself, my eyes becoming fixed on my jacket. It had only one button. The button had belonged to my mother's jacket before she used it to replace my missing
button. The woman's voice went on, "Quit stalling, boy! Hurry up, I
have tons of work to do!"

I put my hand on the button and pulled it out, then hid it in my 23
palm. The woman said, "Are you done?" I said, "Yes!"

I thrust the button in my uniform pocket and wiped my tears with 24
the back of my hand.

Questions for Discussion and Writing

1. Of what imagined crimes does the narrator accuse himself that might explain why he is the one to be sent to an orphanage instead of one of his sib-
   lings?
2. How would you characterize the boy's relationship with his father? In your
   view, what has caused the father to choose him to be the one to be sent to an
   orphanage?
3. What insight does this story provide into the prevailing economic and social
   conditions in modern Iranian society? Why would you have to understand
   the SOCIAL CONTEXT to appreciate more fully why the father is forced to take
   such an action?
4. How does Reza's attitude toward the button reveal his feelings and emotions?

5. Have you ever known anyone who was raised in an orphanage, foster home, or away from his or her family? What circumstances led to the separation and how did this experience affect the person?
6. Do you have a memento such as the button that symbolizes a past relationship? Describe the object and the memories you have associated with it.
7. Write about one of your grandparents or parents as seen through an object you connect with him or her. Under what circumstances did you first come across this object? What associations connect this object with your parent or grandparent?

Neil Bissoondath

Insecurity

Neil Bissoondath was born in 1955 in Sangre Grande, a small market town in Trinidad, into a family who originally came to the West Indies from India. Bissoondath moved to Canada in 1973 to study French at York University. He presently lives in Toronto. He is the nephew of V. S. and Shiva Naipaul, both well-known writers. For eight years Bissoondath taught English to immigrants and French-speaking Canadians while writing at night. With the success of his collection of stories, Digging Up the Mountains *(1986), from which "Insecurity" is taken, he became a full-time writer. His much praised novel,* A Casual Brutality, *was published in 1988. "Insecurity" is set in Trinidad, an island nation off the coast of Venezuela that was a Spanish and then an English colony before achieving independence in 1964. In this story, a well-to-do resident of Trinidad makes plans to emigrate to Canada as the threat of revolution becomes greater, and secretly sends money for safekeeping to his son in Toronto.*

"We're very insecure in this place, you know." Alistair Ramgoolam 1
crossed his fat legs and smiled beatifically, his plump cheeks, gouged by bad childhood acne, quivering at the effect his words had had. "You fly down here, you look around, you see a beautiful island, sun, co-conut trees, beaches. But I live here and I see a different reality. I see the university students parading Marx and Castro on the campus, I see more policemen with guns, I see people rioting downtown, I see my friends running away to Vancouver and Miami. So you can see, we are very insecure down here. That is why I want you to put the money your company owes me into my Toronto bank account. It is my own private insurance. The bank will notify me the money has been deposited and the government here won't notice a thing."

Their business concluded, the visitor pocketed Mr Ramgoolam's ac- 2
count number and stood ready to leave. He asked to use the phone. "I'd like to call a taxi. My flight leaves early in the morning."

"No, no." Mr Ramgoolam gestured impatiently with his plump arm. 3
"Vijay will drive you into town. You're staying at the Hilton, not so?"

The visitor nodded. 4

"Vijay! Vijay!" Mr Ramgoolam's silver hair—stirred, the visitor no- 5
ticed, by the slightest movement—jumped as if alive.

Vijay's voice rattled like a falling can as it came in irritated response 6
from the bowels of the house. "Coming, Pa, coming."

The tick-tock of Vijay's table-tennis game continued and Mr 7
Ramgoolam, chest heaving, bellowed, "Vijay!"

8   Still smiling beatifically, Mr Ramgoolam turned to his visitor and said, "So when you'll be coming back to the islands again?"

9   The visitor shrugged and smiled. "That depends on the company. Not for a long time probably."

10   "You like Yonge Street too much to leave it again soon, eh?" Mr Ramgoolam chuckled. The visitor smiled politely.

11   Vijay, rake thin and wild-eyed, shuffled into the living room.

12   Mr Ramgoolam saw the visitor to Vijay's sports car, the latest model on the road. "You won't forget to get the letter to my son, eh? Remember, it's Markham Street, the house number and phone number on the envelope. You won't forget, eh?"

13   "I won't forget," the visitor said. They shook hands.

14   Mr Ramgoolam was back in his house before the gravel spat up by the tyres of the car had settled. He followed the tail-lights through a heavily burglar-proofed window—Vijay was speeding again, probably showing off; he'd need another talking to. Nodding ponderously, he muttered, "We're very insecure in this place, yes, very insecure."

15   Alistair Ramgoolam was a self-made man who thought back with pride to his poor childhood. He credited this poverty with preventing in him the aloofness he often detected in his friends: a detachment from the island, a sneering view of its history. He had, he felt, a fine grasp on the island, on its history and its politics, its people and its culture. He had developed a set of "views" and anecdotes which he used to liven up parties. It distressed him that his views and anecdotes rarely had the desired effect, arousing instead only a deadpan sarcasm. He had written them down and had them privately published in a thin volume. Except for those he'd given away as gifts, all five hundred copies were collecting dust in cardboard boxes under the table-tennis board.

16   Mr Ramgoolam had seen the British when they were the colonial masters and he had attended the farewell ball for the last British governor. He had seen the Americans arrive with the Second World War, setting up their bases on large tracts of the best agricultural land; and he had seen the last of them leave, the Stars and Stripes tucked securely under the commander's arm, more than twenty years after the end of the war. He had seen the British, no longer masters and barely respected, leave the island in a state of independence. And he had seen that euphoric state quickly degenerate into a carnival of radicals and madmen.

17   His life at the fringe of events, he felt, had given him a certain authority over and comprehension of the past. But the present, with its confusion and corruption, eluded him. The sense of drift nurtured unease in Mr Ramgoolam.

18   He would always remember one particular day in late August, 1969. He had popped out of his air-conditioned downtown office to visit the chief customs officer at the docks. As an importer of foreign foods and

wines, Mr Ramgoolam made it his business to keep the various officials who controlled the various entry stamps happy and content. On that day, he was walking hurriedly past the downtown square when a black youth, hair twisted into worm-like pigtails, thrust a pink leaflet into his unwilling hands. It was a socialist tract, full of new words and bombast. Mr Ramgoolam had glanced irritatedly at it, noticed several spelling mistakes, crumpled it up, and thrown it on the sidewalk. Then he remembered he was a member of the Chamber of Commerce Keep-Our-City-Clean Committee and he picked it up. Later that evening he found it in his pants pocket. He smoothed it out, read it, and decided it was nothing less than subversion and treason. At the next party he attended, he expounded his views on socialism. He was told to stop boring everyone.

Not long after the party, riots and demonstrations—dubbed "Black   19
Power" by the television and the newspaper—occurred in the streets. Mr Ramgoolam's store lost a window pane and the walls were scribbled with "Socialism" and "Black Communism." The words bedevilled the last of Mr Ramgoolam's black hairs into the mass of silver.

As he watched the last black stripe blend in, Mr Ramgoolam re-   20
alised that, with an ineffectual government and a growing military, one night could bring the country a change so cataclysmic that the only issue would be rapid flight. And failing that, poverty, at best.

He had no desire to return to the moneyless nobility of his child-   21
hood: pride was one thing, stupidity quite another, and Alistair Ramgoolam was acutely aware of the difference.

He began looking for ways of smuggling money out of the island to   22
an illegal foreign bank account. A resourceful man, he soon found several undetectable methods: buying travellers' cheques and bank drafts off friends, having money owed him by foreign companies paid into the illegal account, buying foreign currency from travellers at generous rates of exchange. His eldest son was attending university in Toronto, so it was through him that Mr Ramgoolam established his account.

The sum grew quickly. Mr Ramgoolam became an exporter of is-   23
land foods and crafts, deflating the prices he reported to the island's government and inflating those he charged the foreign companies. The difference was put into the Toronto account. Every cent not spent on his somewhat lavish lifestyle was poured into his purchases of bank drafts and travellers' cheques.

The official mail service, untrustworthy and growing more expen-   24
sive by the day, was not entrusted with Mr Ramgoolam's correspondence with his son. Visitors to or from Toronto, friend or stranger, were asked to perform favours.

Over the years, with a steadily developing business and ever-   25
increasing foreign dealings, Mr Ramgoolam's account grew larger and larger, to more than forty thousand dollars.

He contemplated his bankbooks with great satisfaction. Should   26 flight be necessary—and the more time passed, the more Mr Ramgoolam became convinced it would—there would be something to run to beyond bare refuge.

27   The more insecure he saw his island becoming, the more secure he himself felt. From this secure insecurity a new attitude, one of which he had never before been aware, arose in him. The island of his birth, on which he had grown up and where he had made his fortune, was transformed by a process of mind into a kind of temporary home. Its history ceased to be important, its present turned into a fluid holding pattern which would eventually give way. The confusion had been prepared for, and all that was left was the enjoyment that could be squeezed out of the island between now and then. He could hope for death here but his grandchildren, maybe even his children, would continue the emigration which his grandfather had started in India, and during which the island had proved, in the end, to be nothing more than a stopover.

28   When the Toronto account reached fifty thousand dollars, Mr Ramgoolam received a letter from his eldest son. He reminded his father that Vijay would be coming to Toronto to study and that the fifty thousand dollars was lying fallow in the account, collecting interest, yes, but slowly. Wouldn't it be better to invest in a house? This would mean that Vijay—Mr Ramgoolam noticed his eldest son had discreetly left himself out—would not have to pay rent and, with the rapidly escalating property prices in Toronto, a modest fifty-thousand-dollar house could be resold later at a great profit.

29   His first reading of the letter brought a chuckle to Mr Ramgoolam's throat. His independent-minded son, it seemed, was looking for a way of not paying rent. But then he felt a ripple of quiet rage run through him: his son had always made an issue of being independent, of making it on his own. Paying for the privilege, Mr Ramgoolam thought, was the first requisite of independence. He put the suggestion out of his mind.

30   Later that night, just before bed, he read the letter aloud to his wife. This had long been their custom. She complained continually of "weakness" in the eyes. As he lay in bed afterwards, the words "great profit" stayed with him.

31   His wife said, "You going to buy it?"

32   He said, "Is not such a bad idea. I have to think."

33   When he awoke at four the next morning for his usual Hindu devotions, Mr Ramgoolam's mind was made up. He walked around the garden picking the dew-smothered flowers with which he would garland the deities in his private prayer room and, breathing in the cool, fresh air of the young dawn's semi-light, he became convinced that the decision was already blessed by the beauty of the morning.

34   After a cold shower, Mr Ramgoolam draped his fine cotton *dhoti* around his waist and prayed before his gods, calling their blessings on to himself, his wife, his sons, and the new house soon to be bought,

cash, in Toronto. It was his contention that blessed business dealings were safer than unblessed ones.

He spent the rest of the morning writing a letter to his son, giving 35 instructions that before any deals were made he was to be consulted. He didn't want any crooked real estate agent fooling his son, Toronto sophisticate or not. He also warned that the place should be close enough to Vijay's school that he wouldn't have to travel too far: a short ride on public transportation was acceptable but his son should always remember that it was below the station of a Ramgoolam to depend on buses and trains.

That was an important point, Mr Ramgoolam thought. It might 36 force his independent son to raise his sights a little. He probably used public transportation quite regularly in Toronto, whereas here on the island he would not have heard of sitting in a bus next to some sweaty farmer. The letter, Mr Ramgoolam hoped, would remind his eldest son of the standards expected of a member of his family.

The letter was dispatched that evening with the friend of a friend of 37 a friend who just happened to be leaving for Toronto.

A week passed and Mr Ramgoolam heard nothing from his son. He 38 began to worry: if *he* were buying a house, you could be sure *he'd* have found a place and signed the deal by now. That son of his just had no business sense: didn't he know that time was money? A week could mean the difference of a thousand dollars! Mr Ramgoolam said to his wife, "I just wish he'd learn to be independent on somebody else's money."

He was walking in the garden worrying about his money and kick- 39 ing at the grass when Vijay shouted from the house, "Pa, Pa! Toronto calling."

Mr Ramgoolam hurried in, his cheeks jiggling. "Hello." It was the 40 real estate agent calling.

The operator said, "Will you accept the charges?" 41

Accept the charges? Mr Ramgoolam was momentarily unsettled. 42 "No." He slammed the phone down. He glared at Vijay sitting at the dining table. "What kind of businessman he is anyway? Calling collect. He's getting my money and he expects me to pay for his business call? He crazy or what, eh?" Incensed, he ran out into the garden. Every few minutes, Vijay could hear him muttering about "cheapness."

The telephone rang again half an hour later. 43

This call was from his son and, luckily, not collect. The first thing Mr 44 Ramgoolam said was, "Get rid of that cheap agent. I don't trust him. Get somebody else."

The son agreed. Then he asked whether his father would be willing 45 to go above fifty thousand, to, say, sixty or sixty-five. Only such a sum would assure a good house in a proper location. Less would mean a good house, yes, but a long way on public transportation for Vijay.

Mr Ramgoolam pictured Vijay riding on some rickety bus with a 46 smelly fish vendor for company. He broke out in a cold sweat. "Now wait up a minute . . . awright, awright, sixty or sixty-five. But not a cent more. And close the deal quickly. Time is money, you know."

47 Time dragged by. Nothing was heard from Toronto for a week. Mr Ramgoolam began to worry. What was that no-good son of his up to now? Wasting time as usual, probably running off somewhere being independent.

48 Another week went by and Mr Ramgoolam began brooding over the house in Toronto. He couldn't get his mind off it. He stopped going to the office. Not even prayer seemed to ease his growing doubts. Wasn't it better to have the cash safely in the bank, slowly but surely collecting its interest? And what about Vijay? The money for his schooling was to have come from that account: now he'd have to take money with him, and Mr Ramgoolam hadn't counted on that. Above all, the house was going to cost ten to fifteen thousand more than the Toronto account contained; that was a lot of money to smuggle out. Would it mean a mortgage? He hated mortgages and credit. He hated owing. Buy only when you could pay: it was another of his convictions.

49 After three more days and a sleepless night, Mr Ramgoolam eased himself out of bed at 3.30 am. He might as well pray. It always helped, eased the mind however little.

50 There was very little light that morning and the flowers he collected were wilted and soggy. He stubbed his toe on a stone and cursed, softly, in Hindi. The cold shower felt not so much refreshing as merely cold.

51 He prayed, his *dhoti* falling in careless folds, his gods sad with their colourless flowers.

52 When he finished he wrote a quick letter to his son, ordering him to leave all the money in the bank and to forget about buying a house. He couldn't afford it at the present time, he said.

53 He signed it and sealed it. He wondered briefly whether he should telephone or telegram but decided they were both too expensive. The next problem was to find someone who was going to Toronto. That was easy: the representative of his biggest Toronto client, the one staying at the Hilton, would be coming to the house this evening to finalise a deal and to get the Toronto account number. He could take the letter.

54 Five days passed and Mr Ramgoolam heard nothing from his eldest son. Once more he began to worry. Couldn't the fool call to say he'd got the letter and the money was safe? He spent the morning in bed nursing his burning ulcer.

55 On the morning of the sixth day the call came.

56 "Hello, Pa?" His son's voice was sharp and clear, as if he were calling from across the street. "You're now the proud owner of a house in Toronto. The deal went through yesterday. It's all finalised."

Mr Ramgoolam's jaw fell open. His cheeks quivered. "What? You 57
didn't get my letter?"

"You mean the one the company rep brought up? Not yet. He just 58
called me last night. I'm going to collect the letter this evening, before
the ballet."

"Be-be-be-fore the ballet?" Mr Ramgoolam ran his pudgy fingers 59
down the length of his perspiring face. He could feel his heart thump-
ing heavily against the fat in his chest.

"Yes, I'm going to the ballet tonight. Good news about the house, 60
eh? I did exactly as you told me, Pa. I did it as quickly as possible. Time
is money, as you always say."

"Yes-yes," said Mr Ramgoolam. "Time is money, son, time is 61
money. We're very insecure in this place, you know."

His son said, "What?" 62

"Nothing." Mr Ramgoolam ran his hand, trembling, through his 63
hair. "Goodbye." He replaced the receiver. The wooden floor seemed to
dance beneath him and, for a moment, he had a sense of slippage, of
life turned to running liquid. He saw his son sitting in the living room
of the Toronto house—sitting, smiling, in a room Mr Ramgoolam knew
to be there, but the hardened outlines of which he could not distinguish—and he suddenly understood how far his son had gone. Just as
his father had grown distant from India; just as he himself had grown
even further from the life that, in memory, his father had represented
and then, later in life, from that which he himself had known on the island, so too had his eldest son gone beyond. Mr Ramgoolam had been
able to picture the money sitting in the bank, piles of bills; but this
house, and his son sitting there with ballet tickets in his hand: this was
something softer, hazier, less graspable. He now saw himself as being
left behind, caught between the shades of his father and, unexpectedly,
of his son. And he knew that his insecurity, until then always in the
land around him, in the details of life daily lived, was now within him.
It was as if his legs had suddenly gone hollow, two shells of utter
fragility.

There was only one thing left, one thing to hold on to. He hurried to 64
his room and, brushing his wife aside, dressed quickly. Then he swallowed two hefty gulps of his stomach medicine and called out to Vijay
to drive him to the office.

Questions for Discussion and Writing

1. What information about the political environment and SOCIAL CONTEXT does
   the story provide that would explain why Alistair Ramgoolam is sending
   money out of the country to his son in Toronto?
2. Why doesn't Alistair think of Trinidad as being his real home anymore?

3. How would you characterize the relationship between Alistair and his son in Toronto? In what respects does his relationship with this son mirror the kind of relationship he had with his own father?

4. How does the difference between Alistair's expectations and what his son is really doing in Toronto create an ironic contrast?

5. With whom are you more sympathetic, the father or the son, and why? Have there been experiences in your own life that would enable you to better understand Alistair's son?

6. Do a lot of young people who grew up in your town or area choose to leave, and if so where do they want to go?

7. How does someone born in a place experience that place differently from someone who has just arrived there as a result of forced immigration?

Arun Mukherjee

Visiting Places

Arun Mukherjee was born in Lahore in 1946, eleven months before the parti-tion of India. When she was eleven months old her family journeyed to Tikamgarh, a small town in Madyha Pradesh, India. She came to Canada in 1971 to do graduate work at the University of Toronto. She has taught at sev-eral Canadian universities, including York University. She has published nu-merous articles and is the author of two books of cultural criticism, The Gospel of Wealth in the American Novel *(1983) and* Toward An Aesthetic of Opposition: Essays on Culture, Literature and Cultural Imperialism *(1987). She is currently working on a book on feminist literary theory and the question of race. Mukherjee speaks four languages, including her native Punjabi and her husband's Bengali. Mukherjee's fiction depicts North American life from the perspective of a multilingual, multicultural, non-white immigrant woman. "Visiting Places" (1990) explores the unforeseen consequences of a Hindu woman's decision to take on the role of guide in India for her new Canadian friends.*

1 "Well, that's it folks! Our great trip to India," Jim said, as the last slide went off the screen. The small group of friends chipped in with words like wonderful, spectacular, romantic. "And, of course," Jim said, "as you saw for yourself, we could never have learned and enjoyed so much if it hadn't been for *Vineeta* here." Jim mispronounced my name in the typical Canadian fashion, putting the stress on the wrong place and retroflexing the "ta" ending.

2 Jenny and Roy and Janet all turned toward me now. Someone said, "Yes, it is just so-o different. Being with the families, eating what they eat, living the way they live."

3 Susan and Fred are always travelling somewhere. At least whenever I phone them, I find out about their latest bicycle trip to Scotland or their safari in Kenya or their backpacking in the canyons. They have a cottage somewhere and I have often fished for an invitation, unsuccess-fully.

4 I keep telling my Canadian friends about my great curiosity to expe-rience cottage-living, hoping some day someone will invite me. I heard Susan say to me, "We have never travelled in Asia but we hope to get to all those lovely places some day. Kathmandu, Sri Nagar, Agra, Jaipur. It would be marvellous if our plans coincided. Then we could have as much fun as Jim and Sara here."

5 "Wouldn't that be wonderful," I said in the spirit of the occasion. But I could feel my teeth gritting and my jaws beginning to hurt, some-thing that happens to me when I am under stress. For I must admit, Jim

and Sara had all the fun while I had all the dregs: the double anger of the whites and the natives had descended on me and made a wreck of me. So much so that I was hardly civil when I bid good bye to Jim and Sara at Palam airport in New Delhi. You see, I was awfully tired and depressed and one can hardly be civil under those circumstances. Even an Indian woman.

6   Fortunately, Jim and Sara seemed not to have noticed. And they had either forgotten those dreadful experiences in India or they hadn't really noticed what I had gone through. Anyway, their India was now a beautiful slide show: historical buildings, colourful clothes, wayside barbers, performing monkeys, even a snake charmer.

7   But the slide show inside my head at times begins to run automatically and brings back memories I so badly want to suppress.

8   There are so many things in my life I want to suppress. The contradictions of being a non-white Indian woman living in Canada, loving it and hating it, loving my white friends but hating them too. Just like my relationship with my parents, my in-laws, and with mother India herself.

9   I could start way way back, with my now shame-inducing desire of becoming a "foreign returned" Indian, like everybody else who mattered in Delhi U. But let me start with Jim and Sara. For starting the former way is much too painful and would require the narrating of a whole history of colonialism, something which George Woodcock would have no patience for and it would make him write a merciless review in *Canadian Literature*. So, let me just tell you about me with Jim and Sara.

10   Jim and Sara and I spent a couple of weeks together in India one winter. I was in Delhi researching Indian feminism for my thesis when I got their telegram. Yes, they were really coming, and that's when I began to get nervous. I was living with my brother, in his two rooms, one of which contained a portable gas burner and a cylinder.

11   "Are they coming *here*?" he asked. "Where will they *live*? They can't be expected to live like our Indian guests who crash in whether we want them or not."

12   Surely not. The rooms were awfully messy and small. Running water lasted hardly two hours in the morning. And there was, of course, no toilet paper.

13   "Maybe, I will go to the airport and bring them here, offer them some tea, and tell them they can live here if they can take it. Otherwise, they should go to a hotel." That was my way of opening a delicate negotiation with my brother to let them stay with us if they would.

14   I cleaned up as much as I could in the next couple of days, went to Connaught Place to buy some toilet paper and we were set.

15   When they arrived, they decided to stay with us even after seeing the rooms. "We won't be here much anyway," Jim said, "So why waste money on hotels."

I should have seen them off two days later but foolishly accepted 16 their invitation to travel with them. I pretended lack of funds at first, but when they offered to pay my expenses, how could I refuse!

They wanted to travel like Indians do, by train. So we went to 17 Baroda House the next day to get our tickets. However, by the time Jim and Sara and I got there, it was already 11:30 and the booking clerks were busy. At one, they promptly closed their windows and told us to come back at two. That is when I began to see how different we, the Indians, were from them, the whites. For they were whites there, not Canadians. Such fine distinctions do not matter in India.

"We have lost a whole day just for buying train tickets," Sara cried. 18 "We could be doing something exciting, but here we sit, waiting for him to open when he pleases and listening to him talk of his sons in America!"

True, the clerk had been garrulously chatting away. The atmosphere 19 had been more of gossip than of work.

"Why can't they learn to be more efficient? That's why these coun- 20 tries don't make any progress."

I made a feeble protest about the inhumanity of too much efficiency. 21 I malevolently suggested that Sara enjoy the beautiful gardens of Baroda House which were full of bird noises and extremely colourful bougainvellia at this time of the year. The sky was dark blue and there were a few white clouds merrily floating along. At such aesthetic mo- ments, I become proudly patriotic.

But Sara was really upset and not the least bit interested in com- 22 muning with nature. The last straw came when the clerk told us at two that Baroda House did not do second class reservations: the class Jim and Sara wanted to "experience."

I will spare you a detailed description of the explosion which fol- 23 lowed: Sara, beside herself with anger, Jim trying to appear calm and in control but hardly succeeding, and I stubbornly refusing to criticize anything Indian. When our tempers cooled, we finally went to the right place, stood in a long line-up as second class travellers do in India and got our tickets.

But what happened on the train remains indelibly in my memory. 24 The ticket collector had as usual sold an excess number of tickets in or- der to supplement his salary and, as a result, there was barely room enough for us to sit. The hard wooden bench, the mixed smells of sweat, smoke and food—typical of Indian railways by the way—were more than Jim could take. He screamed, fought, even got off the train to complain but to no avail. He wanted to stretch his limbs and didn't care what happened to the illegals. Sara and I got sent to the empty berths in the ladies' section and Sara even managed to fall asleep, but I kept thinking of Jim doing his *Tandava* dance in the aisles. Finally, the con- ductor made two of the rustic-looking illegals sit on the floor, and Jim could lie down, but only in the fetal position, as two other illegals re- fused to vacate their portion of the bench.

25   I could hear their entire conversation. "These *gora log*, you know, they have no strength. No Indian would have made such a fuss just for one night." "Absolutely. We say one should have space in one's heart. Then one can share even the little that one has."

26   "What do these white bastards think? *Han ji*? Are they still ruling us that we should be polite to them?"

27   And so it went, on and on, thankfully in Hindi. I was embarrassed but not entirely in disagreement.

28   The ambiguity of my position became clear to me when we checked in at a hotel in Amritsar the next day. While Jim and Sara went to their room to catch up on their sleep, I decided to stand in the corridor and look at the view. I was soon accosted by a type of Indian male I hate and fear from the bottom of my heart: the well-fed, government officer who exudes power from every pore and who drives hundreds of kilometers in a government jeep to see the latest movie in the big city; the type Shyam Benegal portrays so well in his movies, dining and wining with the contractors and womanizing at *their* expense. He hadn't even bothered to put on his *kurta*. "Haven't I seen you somewhere before?" he said, almost touching me.

29   This is a typical come-on Indian men learn from Hindi movies and I immediately said "no" while moving several steps back to keep my distance. "Are you sure? Weren't you at Agra Tourist Lodge last month with a party?"

30   Oh, my God. He thinks I am a call girl or something, I thought. Going around with foreigners.

31   I hurriedly made my retreat to my room and bolted it from the inside. Fortunately, our trip occurred long before Operation Blue Star. After Jim and Sara rested, we leisurely toured the Golden Temple, the narrow bazaars, and finally went to the house of the brother of a friend of theirs. He insisted we stay with them in their huge British bungalow, which we gladly did.

32   The man and his wife happened to be running a Christian missionary centre of some sort. Their children were home from Woodstock for the winter break and they talked of how Woodstock students had the whole city of Mussoorie under their thumbs.

33   Our hosts talked to Jim and Sara about the stupidity of Hindus for building a shelter for old cows while human beings went starving on the street. However, an Indian woman is trained to be polite, obedient, accommodating, and I continued to smile.

34   Our next stop was Mussoorie. By now, Jim and Sara had decided to skip the experience of travelling second class. The first class was much more roomy and had thick "dunlopillo" cushions and the journey went uneventfully, except for the stench of sugar mills en route.

35   We took a deluxe bus from Dehra Dun to Mussoorie. While they had the address of a teacher in Woodstock, supplied by the friend's brother, I remembered that a classmate of mine was teaching in the Government College and decided to impose on his hospitality.

But to get to our destination we had to hire coolies to take our suit- 36
cases up the hill. It was a stiff climb and I was panting hard within five
minutes. That's when Jim started: "You know, it is really cruel of us to
burden this human being with our stuff. Their hearts get enlarged carrying so much weight and they have a very short life span." I protested,
"But they are used to it, Jim," and immediately wished I could have bit
my tongue, for we Indians use "used to" for practically everything.
There was definitely a point to what Jim was saying. But my nationalis-
tic pride wouldn't give up. "They've got to make a living, haven't
they?" I said.

We parted company, only to meet in the market the next day. Jim 37
and Sara had obviously been bored by the Woodstock teacher and they
followed me and my friend's family home.

"These whites," Lal was saying to me. "They have exploited us for 38
centuries and now they come touring here, looking for the exotic
India."

I tried to explain to Lal that Jim and Sara were not imperialists, just 39
ordinary Canadians. But he wouldn't listen. "I don't care. They are all
alike. They go back home with photographs of sunsets and minarets
and publish a collection of poetry. I had a bunch of them teaching me a
course on Canadian Literature this summer."

I didn't tell Lal that one of his teachers had indeed published a 40
much-acclaimed volume of poems after his return from India, embellished with haunting photographs of minarets in sunset. I tried to keep
on smiling and began to talk in English so that Jim and Sara could join
in.

Jim and Sara needed travellers' cheques cashed and Lal obliged us 41
by taking us to his bank. It was a beautiful walk. One could see way
down in the valley. The air smelt of firs and deodars. I like the mountains in India.

But apparently Sara was not enjoying herself. She, of course, is not 42
used to walking and was very tired. And by now I had come to realize
that when she is tired she can be awfully difficult. I couldn't believe my
ears when she said, "Why aren't we doing something exciting? Why
can't we go mountain climbing?" "Because you don't have the right
shoes," Jim said. But Sara was in a rotten mood. "I can't believe how
awful it has all been. Why can't we do anything else except buy tickets
and cash cheques? When are we really going to *see* the country?"

I could have killed her then, I was so angry. She was simply provid- 43
ing more ammunition to Lal's hatred. He winked at me triumphantly. I
felt like crying, so I had to walk ahead of everybody to hide my tears.
The beauty of the snow-capped Himalayas had been entirely ruined for
me by Sara's whining.

At the bank, an unexpected disaster happened. Lal's friend insisted 44
that we be served tea while the paperwork was being done, a typical
Indian thing. Sara loves tea and she immediately agreed. However,
when the tea came, it was Indian style. Leaves, milk, sugar, water, ev-

erything boiled together. Very strong and very sweet. I don't like it much either, but I often drink it out of politeness. Sara, however, had one sip and said, "It's awful." I wished I could disappear in the ground like Sita in the *Ramayana*. Lal's friend said, "I am sorry." He wanted to order a fresh supply but I told him not to because I knew his peon would only repeat the first attempt.

45   We decided to leave Mussoorie that night since Jim and Sara didn't want to spend any more time with the Woodstock teacher. We took the midnight bus leaving for Delhi. Lal was worried because a bus had been stopped en route a couple of weeks before and cash and jewelry seized from the passengers. I decided not to worry Jim and Sara about it. So they slept, or snoozed in their seats while I kept squirming all the way.

46   All three of us, by now, had our fill of "sightseeing" and decided to take it easy for the next day or two. Unluckily, it meant that Jim and Sara were home when little Kuttan came to sweep the rooms and do the dishes. "Don't tell me you have child labour in India," Jim said in a shocked voice. I was in a terribly embarrassing spot now, as a con-doner, if not a direct employer, of child labour. As usual, Kuttan's blasted mother had sent her ten-year-old daughter, as though on pur-pose to embarrass me in front of my Canadian friends.

47   When we Indians, I mean comfortably off Indians, are in such spots, we say, "What about you!" and go on to talk about our having not yet recovered from the colonial legacy. But that sort of argument works only in the general sense, not when one is directly involved. Here I was, seeing our ten-year-old Kuttan wash our dishes in Delhi's awful December cold and going on as though everything was fine and dandy about the world. I mumbled something about Kuttan's mother forcing her to do it and left it at that. Talking about salad pickers in California and coffee pickers in Colombia would not have helped my floundering conscience. The fact that bothered me was how I had become so "used to" taking Kuttan's labour for granted.

48   Another embarrassing memory emerged at this moment. It was that of the wife of a visiting professor of American Literature in Delhi University. Our Chairman had asked me and the other girls in the class to go visit her at the university guest house. She had pointed to the con-struction workers outside her window, busily working at their tasks in the midday heat of the fierce April sun and said how pained she was by their misery. I had just hung my head in shame for not having felt it be-fore.

49   And so it went on. The next few days were spent together touring the sights of Delhi. The only jarring elements were the beggars who missed no opportunity to harrass us. They would come and push their hands into our taxi while it waited at the traffic lights. I was dead set against giving alms and it only prolonged the embarrassing encounters. One shabby beggar with a child even tugged at my sleeve, which com-

pletely upset me so that I moved my arm with a big jerk which resulted in her child falling down. I felt so contrite that I handed her a *chavanni* which the beggar immediately used to buy ice cream for the screaming child.

One final embarrassment still awaited me. One day, my police-inspector uncle visited my brother's rooms and insisted, again in the typical Indian fashion, that I bring Jim and Sara to dinner at their place. Meanwhile, he left his chauffeur-driven car—purchased and maintained through corrupt money, I was sure—for my guests' pleasure. We were driven around in great style, but I burned all day because I had never been shown this preferential treatment by my uncle. 50

So what was embarrassing about that, you might ask. Nothing, I suppose. It is what happened at dinner that still rankles me. My brazen cousin who runs around chasing girls on a scooter, and is also rumoured to be involved in smuggling, asked Jim at the dinner table if he would consider selling his camera! "Jeans etc. I don't care about," he smirked. "They are really easy to get, but I really like your camera." 51

I wished for the umpteenth time, then, for mother earth to break open and welcome me in her lap as it had done for Sita. But no such luck. I heard Jim mumble that it was an old camera and that he was really attached to it. My cousin didn't seem to mind a bit. "Oh well. Suit yourself," is what he said, to my infinite surprise, and proceeded to tell us how easy it was to buy imported goods in Delhi if you had the right kind of "dough." 52

It is torment enough to have such relatives but to expose them to the wide world! I shuddered at what Jim and Sara were going to think of me and my family and India from now on. 53

It was sheer luck that they were leaving the next day for the next leg of their Asia tour and my uncle regretted that he couldn't show them around, as his naughty niece hadn't told him about their visit. He regretted his inability to demonstrate to them the world-famous Indian hospitality and seemed to go on in that vein for a great length of time. 54

The next day, I bid Jim and Sara farewell at Palam, where we were driven in my uncle's car in the company of my cousin, dressed in his imported regalia. 55

I was a total wreck for about a week with exhaustion, depression, anger, frustration, shame and I don't know what else. I lost my temper fairly easily and screamed indiscriminately at my brother, at Kuttan, at the milkman, at the *subziewallah*, almost anybody who would allow me. 56

I even did something one day that put me through a terribly traumatic experience. Normally, you see, Indian women don't retaliate against people who feel their breasts and fall all over them in the crowded Delhi buses. But in this raw mood of mine, I just couldn't help knuckling a policeman who had been falling all over me as the crowd jostled in the bus. The bastard was sitting beside me on the ladies' seat while several women stood, too polite to ask him to get up. I, of course, 57 pretended that the sharp turn had made me do it. But the policeman was much too smart. "You think you are very beautiful, woman, but I wouldn't waste a rupee to fuck you," he said. Lots of people heard him but nobody dared say anything.

58   I got off at the next stop and cried my fill. For the next several days I couldn't face the world, or myself. Then I sobered up and went back to my interrupted research on Indian feminism.

59   I didn't hear from Jim and Sara for a long time. When I came back to Canada and saw Sara at the Roberts Library, we picked up again. She was as bubbly as ever and immediately began to talk of what a wonderful time we'd had together.

60   Well, I am glad she and Jim remember nothing of what I do. Is it that they are good actors? Or is it that they must, for their own sakes, believe that they did have a wonderful time? Now they are off to Jamaica for Christmas. One of Jim's friends has a beautiful house near the beach in Kingston . . .

Questions for Discussion and Writing

1. To what extent does Vineeta's decision to act as Jim and Sara's guide in India allow her to participate in their lives in a way that she has wanted to but was never permitted to do in Canada?
2. How do the episodes regarding cashing checks versus responding to the perfume of the trees, being served tea in authentic Indian style, and traveling as second-class passengers on the train make the reader realize that despite Jim and Sara's expressed wish to experience authentic Indian life, their real desire is to impress their friends at home?
3. What assumptions do Sara and Tom bring with them to their new environment that Vineeta sees as false, and why are these assumptions inappropriate in the CONTEXT of Indian CULTURE? How does Vineeta's relationship with Jim and Sara change after she goes to India with them?
4. Have you ever served as a "guide" in some capacity and to what extent did your experiences differ from Vineeta's?
5. Have you ever ignored warning signs and found yourself in a situation that made you extremely uncomfortable, such as the narrator found herself in? Describe the circumstances, how you felt—and reacted, if it applies—and the extent to which other people made you feel so uncomfortable. What did you ignore or not notice that would have alerted you to avoid the situation?
6. Discuss any situation, such as interactions between parents and children, displaying affection in public, conceptions of privacy, and so on, where you became aware that people from different cultures relied on very different assumptions in interpreting the situation.

Julio Cortázar

Letter to a Young Lady in Paris

Julio Cortázar (1914–1984), one of the most widely recognized Spanish-American writers outside the Spanish-speaking world, was born in Brussels of Argentine parents, who returned to Buenos Aires when he was four. He grew up in Buenos Aires, attended the university there, and started publishing his first stories in Argentina's leading literary journals with the help of Jorge Luis Borges, who became his mentor and friend. In 1952, Cortázar moved to France to escape the censorship imposed by the regime of Juan Perón. In Paris, Cortázar worked as a free-lance translator for UNESCO and began his lifelong series of experiments with fiction that blurred the boundary between reality and fantasy in narratives that broke away from traditional forms. Cortázar received international recognition with the publication of his novel Hopscotch *(1963), which makes use of the collage technique and is written in seemingly dissociative sequences that force the reader to recompose the narrative in order to understand the aspirations of the protagonist, Oliveira. Typically, Cortázar's characters pursue something undefinable that they need to bring them an inner harmony. This elusive authenticity is made more poignant by the surrealistic undercurrents and unforeseen imaginative possibilities that undercut and compromise the everyday world of his protagonists.*

Cortázar's freewheeling, improvisational style playfully challenges conventional language and syntax through irony, myth, and elements of the absurd. Two of his stories have been the basis for movies, Antonioni's Blow-Up *(1966) and Godard's* Weekend *(1968). His stories have been collected in* All Fires the Fire *(1973),* A Change of Light and Other Stories *(1980), and* We Love Glenda So Much and Other Tales *(1983). Besides* Hopscotch, *his innovative novels include* 62: A Model Kit *(1968) and* A Manual for Manuel *(1973), in which Cortázar assails political repression in Latin America by incorporating the horrors of torture into a nightmarish tale that breaks away from conventional categories of narrative. His translations, poetry, essays, and literary criticism are collected into* Miscellanies: Around the Day in Eighty Worlds *(1967) and* Ultimo Round *(1969). "Letter to a Young Lady in Paris," translated by P. Blackburn, first appeared in* The End of the Game and Other Stories *(1967). In this bizarre tale, the normal world is displaced by unsettling surrealistic events that might appear comic to the reader but that have tragic implications for the protagonist.*

Andrea, I didn't want to come live in your apartment in the calle 1
Suipacha. Not so much because of the bunnies, but rather that it offends me to intrude on a compact order, built even to the finest nets of air, networks that in your environment conserve the music in the lavender, the heavy fluff of the powder puff in the talcum, the play between

the violin and the viola in Ravel's quartet. It hurts me to come into an ambience where someone who lives beautifully has arranged everything like a visible affirmation of her soul, here the books (Spanish on one side, French and English on the other), the large green cushions there, the crystal ashtray that looks like a soap-bubble that's been cut open on this exact spot on the little table, and always a perfume, a sound, a sprouting of plants, a photograph of the dead friend, the ritual of tea trays and sugar tongs . . . Ah, dear Andrea, how difficult it is to stand counter to, yet to accept with perfect submission of one's whole being, the elaborate order that a woman establishes in her own gracious flat. How much at fault one feels taking a small metal tray and putting it at the far end of the table, setting it there simply because one has brought one's English dictionaries and it's at this end, within easy reach of the hand, that they ought to be. To move that tray is the equivalent of an unexpected horrible crimson in the middle of one of Ozenfant's painterly cadences, as if suddenly the strings of all the double basses snapped at the same time with the same dreadful whiplash at the most hushed instant in a Mozart symphony. Moving that tray alters the play of relationships in the whole house, of each object with another, of each moment of their soul with the soul of the house and its absent inhabitant. And I cannot bring my fingers close to a book, hardly change a lamp's cone of light, open the piano bench, without a feeling of rivalry and offense swinging before my eyes like a flock of sparrows.

2   You know why I came to your house, to your peaceful living room scooped out of the noonday light. Everything looks so natural, as always when one does not know the truth. You've gone off to Paris, I am left with the apartment in the calle Suipacha, we draw up a simple and satisfactory plan convenient to us both until September brings you back again to Buenos Aires and I amble off to some other house where perhaps . . . But I'm not writing you for that reason, I was sending this letter to you because of the rabbits, it seems only fair to let you know; and because I like to write letters, and maybe too because it's raining.

3   I moved last Thursday in a haze overlaid by weariness, at five in the afternoon. I've closed so many suitcases in my life, I've passed so many hours preparing luggage that never manages to get moved anyplace, that Thursday was a day full of shadows and straps, because when I look at valise straps it's as though I were seeing shadows, as though they were parts of a whip that flogs me in some indirect way, very subtly and horribly. But I packed the bags, let your maid know I was coming to move in. I was going up in the elevator and just between the first and second floors I felt that I was going to vomit up a little rabbit. I have never described this to you before, not so much, I don't think, from lack of truthfulness as that, just naturally, one is not going to explain to people at large that from time to time one vomits up a small rabbit. Always I have managed to be alone when it happens, guarding the fact much as we guard so many of our privy acts, evidences of our

physical selves which happen to us in total privacy. Don't reproach me for it, Andrea, don't blame me. Once in a while it happens that I vomit up a bunny. It's no reason not to live in whatever house, it's no reason for one to blush and isolate oneself and to walk around keeping one's mouth shut.

When I feel that I'm going to bring up a rabbit, I put two fingers in my mouth like an open pincer, and I wait to feel the lukewarm fluff rise in my throat like the effervescence in a sal hepatica. It's all swift and clean, passes in the briefest instant. I remove the fingers from my mouth and in them, held fast by the ears, a small white rabbit. The bunny appears to be content, a perfectly normal bunny only very tiny, small as a chocolate rabbit, only it's white and very thoroughly a rabbit. I set it in the palm of my hand, I smooth the fluff, caressing it with two fingers; the bunny seems satisfied with having been born and waggles and pushes its muzzle against my skin, moving it with that quiet and tickling nibble of a rabbit's mouth against the skin of the hand. He's looking for something to eat, and then (I'm talking about when this happened at my house on the outskirts) I take him with me out to the balcony and set him down in the big flowerpot among the clover that I've grown there with this in mind. The bunny raises his ears as high as they can go, surrounds a tender clover leaf with a quick little wheeling motion of his snout, and I know that I can leave him there now and go on my way for a time, lead a life not very different from people who buy their rabbits at farmhouses.

Between the first and the second floors, then, Andrea, like an omen of what my life in your house was going to be, I realized that I was going to vomit a rabbit. At that point I was afraid (or was it surprise? No, perhaps fear of the same surprise) because, before leaving my house, only two days before, I'd vomited a bunny and so was safe for a month, five weeks, maybe six with a little luck. Now, look, I'd resolved the problem perfectly. I grew clover on the balcony of my other house, vomited a bunny, put it in with the clover and at the end of a month, when I suspected that any moment . . . then I made a present of the rabbit, already grown enough, to señora de Molina, who believed I had a hobby and was quiet about it. In another flowerpot tender and propitious clover was already growing, I awaited without concern the morning when the tickling sensation of fluff rising obstructed my throat, and the new little rabbit reiterated from that hour the life and habits of its predecessor. Habits, Andrea, are concrete forms of rhythm, are that portion of rhythm which helps to keep us alive. Vomiting bunnies wasn't so terrible once one had gotten into the unvarying cycle, into the method. You will want to know why all this work, why all that clover and señora de Molina. It would have been easier to kill the little thing right away and . . . Ah, you should vomit one up all by yourself, take it in two fingers, and set it in your opened hand, still attached to yourself by the act itself, by the indefinable aura of its proximity, barely now broken away. A month puts a lot of things at a distance; a month is size, long fur, long leaps, ferocious eyes, an absolute difference. Andrea, a month is a rabbit, it really makes a real rabbit; but in the maiden moment, the warm bustling fleece covering an inalienable presence . . . like a poem in its first minutes, "fruit of an Idumean night" as much one as oneself . . . and afterwards not so much one, so distant and isolated in its flat white world the size of a letter.

6   With all that, I decided to kill the rabbit almost as soon as it was born. I was going to live at your place for four months: four, perhaps with luck three—tablespoonsful of alcohol down its throat. (Do you know pity permits you to kill a small rabbit instantly by giving it a tablespoon of alcohol to drink? Its flesh tastes better afterward, they say, however, I . . . Three or four tablespoonsful of alcohol, then the bathroom or a package to put in the rubbish.)

7   Rising up past the third floor, the rabbit was moving in the palm of my hand. Sara was waiting upstairs to help me get the valises in . . . Could I explain that it was a whim? Something about passing a pet store? I wrapped the tiny creature in my handkerchief, put him into my overcoat pocket, leaving the overcoat unbuttoned so as not to squeeze him. He barely budged. His miniscule consciousness would be revealing important facts: that life is a movement upward with a final click, and is also a low ceiling, white and smelling of lavender, enveloping you in the bottom of a warm pit.

8   Sara saw nothing, she was too fascinated with the arduous problem of adjusting her sense of order to my valise-and-footlocker, my papers and my peevishness at her elaborate explanations in which the words "for example" occurred with distressing frequency. I could hardly get the bathroom door closed; to kill it now. A delicate area of heat surrounded the handkerchief, the little rabbit was extremely white and, I think, prettier than the others. He wasn't looking at me, he just hopped about and was being content, which was even worse than looking at me. I shut him in the empty medicine chest and went on unpacking, disoriented but not unhappy, not feeling guilty, not soaping up my hands to get off the feel of a final convulsion.

9   I realized that I could not kill him. But that same night I vomited a little black bunny. And two days later another white one. And on the fourth night a tiny grey one.

10   You must love the handsome wardrobe in your bedroom, with its great door that opens so generously, its empty shelves awaiting my clothes. Now I have them in there. Inside there. True, it seems impossible; not even Sara would believe it. That Sara did not suspect anything, was the result of my continuous preoccupation with a task that takes over my days and nights with the singleminded crash of the portcullis falling, and I go about hardened inside, calcined like that starfish you've

put above the bathtub, and at every bath I take it seems all at once to swell with salt and whiplashes of sun and great rumbles of profundity.

They sleep during the day. There are ten of them. During the day they sleep. With the door closed, the wardrobe is a diurnal night for them alone, there they sleep out their night in a sedate obedience. When I leave for work I take the bedroom keys with me. Sara must think that I mistrust her honesty and looks at me doubtfully, every morning she looks as though she's about to say something to me, but in the end she remains silent and I am that much happier. (When she straightens up the bedroom between nine and ten, I make noise in the living room, put on a Benny Carter record which fills the whole apartment, and as Sara is a *saetas* and *pasodobles* fan, the wardrobe seems to be silent, and for the most part it is, because for the rabbits it's night still and repose is the order of the day.) 11

Their day begins an hour after supper when Sara brings in the tray with the delicate tinkling of the sugar tongs, wishes me good night— yes, she wishes me, Andrea, the most ironic thing is that she wishes me good night—shuts herself in her room, and promptly I'm by myself, alone with the closed-up wardrobe, alone with my obligation and my melancholy. 12

I let them out, they hop agilely to the party in the living room, sniffing briskly at the clover hidden in my pockets which makes ephemeral lacy patterns on the carpet which they alter, remove, finish up in a minute. They eat well, quietly and correctly; until that moment I have nothing to say, I just watch them from the sofa, a useless book in my hand—I who wanted to read all of Giraudoux, Andrea, and López's Argentine history that you keep on the lower shelf—and they eat up the clover. 13

There are ten. Almost all of them white. They lift their warm heads toward the lamps in the living room, the three motionless suns of their day; they love the light because their night has neither moon nor sun nor stars nor streetlamps. They gaze at their triple sun and are content. That's when they hop about on the carpet, into the chairs, ten tiny blotches shift like a moving constellation from one part to another, while I'd like to see them quiet, see them at my feet and being quiet— somewhat the dream of any god, Andrea, a dream the gods never see fulfilled—something quite different from wriggling in behind the portrait of Miguel de Unamuno, then off to the pale green urn, over into the dark hollow of the writing desk, always fewer than ten, always six or eight and I asking myself where the two are that are missing, and what if Sara should get up for some reason, and the presidency of Rivadavia which is what I want to read in López's history. 14

Andrea, I don't know how I stand up under it. You remember that I came to your place for some rest. It's not my fault if I vomit a bunny from time to time, if this moving changed me inside as well—not 15 nominalism, it's not magic either, it's just that things cannot alter like that all at once, sometimes things reverse themselves brutally and when you expect the slap on the right cheek—. Like that, Andrea, or some other way, but always like that.

16   It's night while I'm writing you. It's three in the afternoon, but I'm writing you during their night. They sleep during the day. What a relief this office is! Filled with shouts, commands, Royal typewriters, vice presidents and mimeograph machines! What relief, what peace, what horror, Andrea! They're calling me to the telephone now. It was some friends upset about my monasterial nights, Luis inviting me out for a stroll or Jorge insisting—he's bought a ticket for me for this concert. I hardly dare to say no to them, I invent long and ineffectual stories about my poor health, I'm behind in the translations, any evasion possible. And when I get back home and am in the elevator—that stretch between the first and second floors—night after night, hopelessly, I formulate the vain hope that really it isn't true.

17   I'm doing the best I can to see that they don't break your things. They've nibbled away a little at the books on the lowest shelf, you'll find the backs repasted, which I did so that Sara wouldn't notice it. That lamp with the porcelain belly full of butterflies and old cowboys, do you like that very much? The crack where the piece was broken out barely shows, I spent a whole night doing it with a special cement that they sold me in an English shop—you know the English stores have the best cements—and now I sit beside it so that one of them can't reach it again with its paws (it's almost lovely to see how they like to stand on their hind legs, nostalgia for that so-distant humanity, perhaps an imitation of their god walking about and looking at them darkly; besides which, you will have observed—when you were a baby, perhaps—that you can put a bunny in the corner against the wall like a punishment, and he'll stand there, paws against the wall and very quiet, for hours and hours).

18   At 5 A.M. (I slept a little stretched out on the green sofa, waking up at every velvety-soft dash, every slightest click) I put them in the wardrobe and do the cleaning up. That way Sara always finds everything in order, although at times I've noticed a restrained astonishment, a stopping to look at some object, a slight discoloration in the carpet, and again the desire to ask me something, but then I'm whistling Franck's *Symphonic Variations* in a way that always prevents her. How can I tell you about it, Andrea, the minute mishaps of this soundless and vegetal dawn, half-asleep on what staggered path picking up butt-ends of clover, individual leaves, white hunks of fur, falling against the furniture, crazy from lack of sleep, and I'm behind in my Gide, Troyat I haven't gotten to translating, and my reply to a distant young lady who will be asking herself already if . . . why go on with all this, why go on with this letter I keep trying to write between telephone calls and interviews.

Andrea, dear Andrea, my consolation is that there are ten of them   19
and no more. It's been fifteen days since I held the last bunny in the
palm of my hand, since then nothing, only the ten of them with me,
their diurnal night and growing, ugly already and getting long hair,
adolescents now and full of urgent needs and crazy whims, leaping on
top of the bust of Antinoös (it is Antinoös, isn't it, that boy who looks
blindly?) or losing themselves in the living room where their movements make resounding thumps, so much so that I ought to chase them
out of there for fear that Sara will hear them and appear before me in a
fright and probably in her nightgown—it would have to be like that
with Sara, she'd be in her nightgown—and then . . . Only ten, think
of that little happiness I have in the middle of it all, the growing calm
with which, on my return home, I cut past the rigid ceilings of the first
and second floors.

I was interrupted because I had to attend a committee meeting. I'm con-   20
tinuing the letter here at your house, Andrea, under the soundless grey
light of another dawn. Is it really the next day, Andrea? A bit of white
on the page will be all you'll have to represent the bridge, hardly a period on a page between yesterday's letter and today's. How tell you
that in that interval everything has gone smash? Where you see that
simple period I hear the circling belt of water break the dam in its fury,
this side of the paper for me, this side of my letter to you I can't write
with the same calm which I was sitting in when I had to put it aside to
go to the committee meeting. Wrapped in their cube of night, sleeping
without a worry in the world, eleven bunnies; perhaps even now, but
no, not now— In the elevator then, or coming into the building; it's not
important now where, if the when is now, if it can happen in any now
of those that are left to me.

Enough now, I've written this because it's important to me to let you   21
know that I was not all that responsible for the unavoidable and helpless destruction of your home. I'll leave this letter here for you, it would
be indecent if the mailman should deliver it some fine clear morning in
Paris. Last night I turned the books on the second shelf in the other direction; they were already reaching that high, standing up on their hind
legs or jumping, they gnawed off the backs to sharpen their teeth—not
that they were hungry, they had all the clover I had bought for them, I
store it in the drawers of the writing desk. They tore the curtains, the
coverings on the easy chairs, the edge of Augusto Torres' self-portrait,
they got fluff all over the rug and besides they yipped, there's no word
for it, they stood in a circle under the light of the lamp, in a circle as
though they were adoring me, and suddenly they were yipping, they
were crying like I never believed rabbits could cry.
    I tried in vain to pick up all the hair that was ruining the rug, to   22
smooth out the edges of the fabric they'd chewed on, to shut them up

again in the wardrobe. Day is coming, maybe Sara's getting up early. It's almost queer, I'm not disturbed so much about Sara. It's almost queer, I'm not disturbed to see them gamboling about looking for something to play with. I'm not so much to blame, you'll see when you get here that I've repaired a lot of the things that were broken with the cement I bought in the English shop, I did what I could to keep from being a nuisance . . . As far as I'm concerned, going from ten to eleven is like an unbridgeable chasm. You understand: ten was fine, with a wardrobe, clover and hope, so many things could happen for the better. But not with eleven, because to say eleven is already to say twelve for sure, and Andrea, twelve would be thirteen. So now it's dawn and a cold solitude in which happiness ends, reminiscences, you and perhaps a good deal more. This balcony over the street is filled with dawn, the first sounds of the city waking. I don't think it will be difficult to pick up eleven small rabbits splattered over the pavement, perhaps they won't even be noticed, people will be too occupied with the other body, it would be more proper to remove it quickly before the early students pass through on their way to school.

Questions for Discussion and Writing

1. Under what circumstances do the bunnies appear in the narrator's life? How had he set up his life to accommodate this phenomenon?
2. How do the narrator's comments about his unwillingness to move even a "small metal tray" imply that keeping control over his environment is the single most important value in his life?
3. What details emphasize the extent to which the bunnies have taken over the narrator's life? For example, what had he planned to do in the apartment and what is he actually able to do?
4. In light of the narrator's original comments about how careful he would want to be with Andrea's possessions, why would the destruction of her books and other items by the bunnies make him feel guilty? How, in this matter, is he his own severest judge?
5. How did the circumstances that precipitate the narrator's suicide suggest that he finds the inability to control himself or his environment intolerable?
6. What advantage is there for Cortázar in telling this story in the form of a letter that the narrator stops and continues at different times? How could this letter be understood as a suicide note?
7. What features of the story might be characterized as belonging to the type of writing known as MAGICAL REALISM? How does the displacement of normalcy by increasingly bizarre events suggest the psychological deterioration of the narrator?
8. How might the events in this story be interpreted in the context of what is known about the OCD (Obsessive Compulsive Disorder) syndrome?
9. Describe a situation that initially seems plausible, but in which the parameters of the real world soon are suspended.

10. Describe a dream or fantasy that involves a strange and incongruous combination of images, situations, or characters that cross the line into the bizarre in ways that give you insight into the way the unconscious works.

11. Writing in the first person, perhaps as a diary entry as the narrator in this story does, describe activities, events, feelings, and thoughts of someone during a day that ends with the person being committed to a mental institution. Try to imitate Cortázar's style and tone; that is, write about someone who treats bizarre occurrences as if they were ordinary.

Albert Camus

The Guest

Albert Camus (1913–1960) was born in Mondavi, Algeria (then a colony of France), in 1913 to Breton and Spanish parents. Despite the hardships of poverty and his bouts with tuberculosis, Camus excelled as both an athlete and scholarship student at the University of Algiers. Camus lived and worked as a journalist in Algeria until 1940 when he traveled to France and became active in the Resistance, serving as editor of the clandestine paper Combat. *Internationally recognized for his essays and novels, Camus received the Nobel Prize for Literature in 1957, a few years before he was killed in an automobile accident. Camus was closely associated with Jean-Paul Sartre and the French existentialist movement, but broke with Sartre and developed his own concept of the absurd that asserts the importance of human solidarity as the only value capable of redeeming a world without meaning. Although Camus began as a journalist, his work soon extended far beyond journalism to encompass novels, such as* The Stranger *(1942), the play* Caligula *(1944), and a lengthy essay defining his concept of the "absurd" hero, in* The Myth of Sisyphus *(1942). Camus's second novel,* The Plague *(1947), uses the description of a plague in a quarantined city to depict the human struggle against physical and spiritual evil in all its forms, a position Camus outlined in great detail in his nonfiction work* The Rebel *(1951). "The Guest," translated by Justin O'Brien, is drawn from his last collection of short stories,* Exile and the Kingdom *(1957). In this story, Camus returns to the landscape of his native Algeria to depict the poignant dilemma of his protagonist, Daru, a rural schoolteacher who resists being forced into complicity with the French during the war between France and Algeria, which lasted from 1954 to 1962. Set against the background of the Algerian struggle for independence, the story masterfully explores all the important themes of the burdens of freedom, brotherhood, responsibility, moral ambiguity, and the inevitability of choice that Camus grappled with throughout his life.*

1   The schoolmaster was watching the two men climb toward him. One was on horseback, the other on foot. They had not yet tackled the abrupt rise leading to the schoolhouse built on the hillside. They were toiling onward, making slow progress in the snow, among the stones, on the vast expanse of the high, deserted plateau. From time to time the horse stumbled. Without hearing anything yet, he could see the breath issuing from the horse's nostrils. One of the men, at least, knew the region. They were following the trail although it had disappeared days ago under a layer of dirty white snow. The schoolmaster calculated that it would take them half an hour to get onto the hill. It was cold; he went back into the school to get a sweater.

He crossed the empty frigid classroom. On the blackboard the four   2
rivers of France, drawn with four different colored chalks, had been
flowing toward their estuaries for the past three days. Snow had suddenly fallen in mid-October after eight months of drought without the
transition of rain, and the twenty pupils, more or less, who lived in the
villages scattered over the plateau had stopped coming. With fair
weather they would return. Daru now heated only the single room that
was his lodging, adjoining the classroom and giving also onto the
plateau to the east. Like the class windows, his window looked to the
south too. On that side the school was a few kilometers from the point
where the plateau began to slope toward the south. In clear weather
could be seen the purple mass of the mountain range where the gap
opened onto the desert.

Somewhat warmed, Daru returned to the window from which he   3
had first seen the two men. They were no longer visible. Hence they
must have tackled the rise. The sky was not so dark, for the snow had
stopped falling during the night. The morning had opened with a dirty
light which had scarcely become brighter as the ceiling of clouds lifted.
At two in the afternoon it seemed as if the day were merely beginning.
But still this was better than those three days when the thick snow was
falling amidst unbroken darkness with little gusts of wind that rattled
the double door of the classroom. Then Daru had spent long hours in
his room, leaving it only to go to the shed and feed the chickens or get
some coal. Fortunately the delivery truck from Tadjid, the nearest village to the north, had brought his supplies two days before the bliz-
zard. It would return in forty-eight hours.

Besides, he had enough to resist a siege, for the little room was clut-   4
tered with bags of wheat that the administration left as a stock to distribute to those of his pupils whose families had suffered from the
drought. Actually they had all been victims because they were all poor.
Every day Daru would distribute a ration to the children. They had
missed it, he knew, during these bad days. Possibly one of the fathers
or big brothers would come this afternoon and he could supply them
with grain. It was just a matter of carrying them over to the next harvest. Now shiploads of wheat were arriving from France and the worst
was over. But it would be hard to forget that poverty, that army of
ragged ghosts wandering in the sunlight, the plateaus burned to a cin-
der month after month, the earth shriveled up little by little, literally
scorched, every stone bursting into dust under one's foot. The sheep
had died then by thousands and even a few men, here and there, sometimes without anyone's knowing.

In contrast with such poverty, he who lived almost like a monk in   5
his remote schoolhouse, nonetheless satisfied with the little he had and
with the rough life, had felt like a lord with his whitewashed walls, his
narrow couch, his unpainted shelves, his well, and his weekly provision of water and food. And suddenly this snow, without warning,

without the foretaste of rain. This is the way the region was, cruel to live in, even without men—who didn't help matters either. But Daru had been born here. Everywhere else, he felt exiled.

6   He stepped out onto the terrace in front of the schoolhouse. The two men were now halfway up the slope. He recognized the horseman as Balducci, the old gendarme he had known for a long time. Balducci was holding on the end of a rope an Arab who was walking behind him with hands bound and head lowered. The gendarme waved a greeting to which Daru did not reply, lost as he was in contemplation of the Arab dressed in a faded blue jellaba, his feet in sandals but covered with socks of heavy raw wool, his head surmounted by a narrow, short *chèche*. They were approaching. Balducci was holding back his horse in order not to hurt the Arab, and the group was advancing slowly.

7   Within earshot, Balducci shouted: "One hour to do the three kilometers from El Ameur!" Daru did not answer. Short and square in his thick sweater, he watched them climb. Not once had the Arab raised his head. "Hello" said Daru when they got up onto the terrace. "Come in and warm up." Balducci painfully got down from his horse without letting go the rope. From under his bristling mustache he smiled at the schoolmaster. His little dark eyes, deep-set under a tanned forehead, and his mouth surrounded with wrinkles made him look attentive and studious. Daru took the bridle, led the horse to the shed, and came back to the two men, who were now waiting for him in the school. He led them into his room. "I am going to heat up the classroom," he said. "We'll be more comfortable there." When he entered the room again, Balducci was on the couch. He had undone the rope tying him to the Arab, who had squatted near the stove. His hands still bound, the *chèche* pushed back on his head, he was looking toward the window. At first Daru noticed only his huge lips, fat, smooth, almost Negroid; yet his nose was straight, his eyes were dark and full of fever. The *chèche* revealed an obstinate forehead and, under the weathered skin now rather discolored by the cold, the whole face had a restless and rebellious look that struck Daru when the Arab, turning his face toward him, looked him straight in the eyes. "Go into the other room," said the schoolmaster, "and I'll make you some mint tea." "Thanks," Balducci said. "What a chore! How I long for retirement." And addressing his prisoner in Arabic: "Come on, you." The Arab got up and, slowly, holding his bound wrists in front of him, went into the classroom.

8   With the tea, Daru brought a chair. But Balducci was already enthroned on the nearest pupil's desk and the Arab had squatted against the teacher's platform facing the stove, which stood between the desk and the window. When he held out the glass of tea to the prisoner, Daru hesitated at the sight of his bound hands. "He might perhaps be untied." "Sure," said Balducci, "that was for the trip." He started to get to his feet. But Daru, setting the glass on the floor, had knelt beside the Arab. Without saying anything, the Arab watched him with his feverish

eyes. Once his hands were free, he rubbed his swollen wrists against each other, took the glass of tea, and sucked up the burning liquid in swift little sips.

"Good," said Daru. "And where are you headed?" 9

Balducci withdrew his mustache from the tea. "Here, son." 10

"Odd pupils! And you're spending the night?" 11

"No. I'm going back to El Ameur. And you will deliver this fellow to Tinguit. He is expected at police headquarters." 12

Balducci was looking at Daru with a friendly little smile. 13

"What's this story?" asked the schoolmaster. "Are you pulling my leg?" 14

"No, son. Those are the orders." 15

"The orders? I'm not . . ." Daru hesitated, not wanting to hurt the old Corsican. "I mean, that's not my job." 16

"What! What's the meaning of that? In wartime people do all kinds of jobs." 17

"Then I'll wait for the declaration of war!" 18

Balducci nodded. 19

"O.K. But the orders exist and they concern you too. Things are brewing, it appears. There is talk of a forthcoming revolt. We are mobilized, in a way." 20

Daru still had his obstinate look. 21

"Listen, son," Balducci said. "I like you and you must understand. There's only a dozen of us at El Ameur to patrol throughout the whole territory of a small department and I must get back in a hurry. I was told to hand this guy over to you and return without delay. He couldn't be kept there. His village was beginning to stir; they wanted to take him back. You must take him to Tinguit tomorrow before the day is over. Twenty kilometers shouldn't faze a husky fellow like you. After that, all will be over. You'll come back to your pupils and your comfortable life." 22

Behind the wall the horse could be heard snorting and pawing the earth. Daru was looking out the window. Decidedly, the weather was clearing and the light was increasing over the snowy plateau. When all the snow was melted, the sun would take over again and once more would burn the fields of stone. For days, still, the unchanging sky would shed its dry light on the solitary expanse where nothing had any connection with man. 23

"After all," he said, turning around toward Balducci, "what did he do?" And, before the gendarme had opened his mouth, he asked: "Does he speak French?" 24

"No, not a word. We had been looking for him for a month, but they were hiding him. He killed his cousin." 25

"Is he against us?" 26

"I don't think so. But you can never be sure." 27

"Why did he kill?" 28

29   "A family squabble, I think. One owed the other grain, it seems. It's not at all clear. In short, he killed his cousin with a billhook. You know, like a sheep, *kreezk!*"

30   Balducci made the gesture of drawing a blade across his throat and the Arab, his attention attracted, watched him with a sort of anxiety. Daru felt a sudden wrath against the man, against all men with their rotten spite, their tireless hates, their blood lust.

31   But the kettle was singing on the stove. He served Balducci more tea, hesitated, then served the Arab again, who, a second time, drank avidly. His raised arms made the jellaba fall open and the schoolmaster saw his thin, muscular chest.

32   "Thanks, kid," Balducci said. "And now, I'm off."

33   He got up and went toward the Arab, taking a small rope from his pocket.

34   "What are you doing?" Daru asked dryly.

35   Balducci, disconcerted, showed him the rope.

36   "Don't bother."

37   The old gendarme hesitated. "It's up to you. Of course, you are armed?"

38   "I have my shotgun."

39   "Where?"

40   "In the trunk."

41   "You ought to have it near your bed."

42   "Why? I have nothing to fear."

43   "You're crazy, son. If there's an uprising, no one is safe, we're all in the same boat."

44   "I'll defend myself. I'll have time to see them coming."

45   Balducci began to laugh, then suddenly the mustache covered the white teeth.

46   "You'll have time? O.K. That's just what I was saying. You have always been a little cracked. That's why I like you, my son was like that."

47   At the same time he took out his revolver and put it on the desk.

48   "Keep it; I don't need two weapons from here to El Ameur."

49   The revolver shone against the black paint of the table. When the gendarme turned toward him, the schoolmaster caught the smell of leather and horseflesh.

50   "Listen, Balducci," Daru said suddenly, "every bit of this disgusts me, and first of all your fellow here. But I won't hand him over. Fight, yes, if I have to. But not that."

51   The old gendarme stood in front of him and looked at him severely.

52   "You're being a fool," he said slowly. "I don't like it either. You don't get used to putting a rope on a man even after years of it, and you're even ashamed—yes, ashamed. But you can't let them have their way."

53   "I won't hand him over," Daru said again.

54   "It's an order, son, and I repeat it."

"That's right. Repeat to them what I've said to you: I won't hand 55
him over."

Balducci made a visible effort to reflect. He looked at the Arab and 56
at Daru. At last he decided.

"No, I won't tell them anything. If you want to drop us, go ahead; 57
I'll not denounce you. I have an order to deliver the prisoner and I'm
doing so. And now you'll just sign this paper for me."

"There's no need. I'll not deny that you left him with me." 58

"Don't be mean with me. I know you'll tell the truth. You're from 59
hereabouts and you are a man. But you must sign, that's the rule."

Daru opened his drawer, took out a little square bottle of purple ink, 60
the red wooden penholder with the "sergeant-major" pen he used for
making models of penmanship, and signed. The gendarme carefully
folded the paper and put it into his wallet. Then he moved toward the
door.

"I'll see you off," Daru said. 61

"No," said Balducci. "There's no use being polite. You insulted me." 62

He looked at the Arab, motionless in the same spot, sniffed pee- 63
vishly, and turned away toward the door. "Good-by, son," he said. The
door shut behind him. Balducci appeared suddenly outside the window and then disappeared. His footsteps were muffled by the snow.
The horse stirred on the other side of the wall and several chickens fluttered in fright. A moment later Balducci reappeared outside the window leading the horse by the bridle. He walked toward the little rise
without turning around and disappeared from sight with the horse following him. A big stone could be heard bouncing down. Daru walked
back toward the prisoner, who, without stirring, never took his eyes off
him. "Wait," the schoolmaster said in Arabic and went toward the bedroom. As he was going through the door, he had a second thought,
went to the desk, took the revolver, and stuck it in his pocket. Then,
without looking back, he went into his room.

For some time he lay on his couch watching the sky gradually close 64
over, listening to the silence. It was this silence that had seemed painful
to him during the first days here, after the war. He had requested a post
in the little town at the base of the foothills separating the upper
plateaus from the desert. There, rocky walls, green and black to the
north, pink and lavender to the south, marked the frontier of eternal
summer. He had been named to a post farther north, on the plateau itself. In the beginning, the solitude and the silence had been hard for
him on these wastelands peopled only by stones. Occasionally, furrows
suggested cultivation, but they had been dug to uncover a certain kind
of stone good for building. The only plowing here was to harvest rocks.
Elsewhere a thin layer of soil accumulated in the hollows would be
scraped out to enrich paltry village gardens. This is the way it was: bare
rock covered three quarters of the region. Towns sprang up, flourished,
then disappeared; men came by, loved one another or fought bitterly,

then died. No one in this desert, neither he nor his guest, mattered. And yet, outside this desert neither of them, Daru knew, could have really lived.

65   When he got up, no noise came from the classroom. He was amazed at the unmixed joy he derived from the mere thought that the Arab might have fled and that he would be alone with no decision to make. But the prisoner was there. He had merely stretched out between the stove and the desk. With eyes open, he was staring at the ceiling. In that position, his thick lips were particularly noticeable, giving him a pouting look. "Come," said Daru. The Arab got up and followed him. In the bedroom, the schoolmaster pointed to a chair near the table under the window. The Arab sat down without taking his eyes off Daru.

66   "Are you hungry?"

67   "Yes," the prisoner said.

68   Daru set the table for two. He took flour and oil, shaped a cake in a frying-pan and lighted the little stove that functioned on bottled gas. While the cake was cooking, he went out to the shed to get cheese, eggs, dates, and condensed milk. When the cake was done he set it on the window sill to cool, heated some condensed milk diluted with water, and beat up the eggs into an omelette. In one of his motions he knocked against the revolver stuck in his right pocket. He set the bowl down, went into the classroom, and put the revolver in his desk drawer. When he came back to the room, night was falling. He put on the light and served the Arab. "Eat," he said. The Arab took a piece of the cake, lifted it eagerly to his mouth, and stopped short.

69   "And you?" he asked.

70   "After you. I'll eat too."

71   The thick lips opened slightly. The Arab hesitated, then bit into the cake determinedly.

72   The meal over, the Arab looked at the schoolmaster. "Are you the judge?"

73   "No, I'm simply keeping you until tomorrow."

74   "Why do you eat with me?"

75   "I'm hungry."

76   The Arab fell silent. Daru got up and went out. He brought back a folding bed from the shed, set it up between the table and the stove, perpendicular to his own bed. From a large suitcase which, upright in a corner, served as a shelf for papers, he took two blankets and arranged them on the camp bed. Then he stopped, felt useless, and sat down on his bed. There was nothing more to do or to get ready. He had to look at this man. He looked at him, therefore, trying to imagine his face bursting with rage. He couldn't do so. He could see nothing but the dark yet shining eyes and the animal mouth.

77   "Why did you kill him?" he asked in a voice whose hostile tone surprised him.

78   The Arab looked away.

"He ran away. I ran after him."

He raised his eyes to Daru again and they were full of a sort of woeful interrogation. "Now what will they do to me?"

"Are you afraid?"

He stiffened, turning his eyes away.

"Are you sorry?"

The Arab stared at him openmouthed. Obviously he did not understand. Daru's annoyance was growing. At the same time he felt awkward and self-conscious with his big body wedged between the two beds.

"Lie down there," he said impatiently. "That's your bed."

The Arab didn't move. He called to Daru:

"Tell me!"

The schoolmaster looked at him.

"Is the gendarme coming back tomorrow?"

"I don't know."

"Are you coming with us?"

"I don't know. Why?"

The prisoner got up and stretched out on top of the blankets, his feet toward the window. The light from the electric bulb shone straight into his eyes and he closed them at once.

"Why?" Daru repeated, standing beside the bed.

The Arab opened his eyes under the blinding light and looked at him, trying not to blink.

"Come with us," he said.

In the middle of the night, Daru was still not asleep. He had gone to bed after undressing completely; he generally slept naked. But when he suddenly realized that he had nothing on, he hesitated. He felt vulnerable and the temptation came to him to put his clothes back on. Then he shrugged his shoulders; after all, he wasn't a child and, if need be, he could break his adversary in two. From his bed he could observe him, lying on his back, still motionless with his eyes closed under the harsh light. When Daru turned out the light, the darkness seemed to coagulate all of a sudden. Little by little, the night came back to life in the window where the starless sky was stirring gently. The schoolmaster soon made out the body laying at his feet. The Arab still did not move, but his eyes seemed open. A faint wind was prowling around the schoolhouse. Perhaps it would drive away the clouds and the sun would reappear.

During the night the wind increased. The hens fluttered a little and then were silent. The Arab turned over on his side with his back to Daru, who thought he heard him moan. Then he listened for his guest's breathing, become heavier and more regular. He listened to that breath so close to him and mused without being able to go to sleep. In this room where he had been sleeping alone for a year, this presence bothered him. But it bothered him also by imposing on him a sort of brother-hood he knew well but refused to accept in the present circumstances. Men who share the same rooms, soldiers or prisoners, develop a strange alliance as if, having cast off their armor with their clothing, they fraternized every evening, over and above their differences, in the ancient community of dream and fatigue. But Daru shook himself; he didn't like such musings, and it was essential to sleep.

99   A little later, however, when the Arab stirred slightly, the school-master was still not asleep. When the prisoner made a second move, he stiffened, on the alert. The Arab was lifting himself slowly on his arms with almost the motion of a sleepwalker. Seated upright in bed, he waited motionless without turning his head toward Daru, as if he were listening attentively. Daru did not stir, it had just occurred to him that the revolver was still in the drawer of his desk. It was better to act at once. Yet he continued to observe the prisoner, who, with the same slithery motion, put his feet on the ground, waited again, then began to stand up slowly. Daru was about to call out to him when the Arab be-gan to walk, in a quite natural but extraordinarily silent way. He was heading toward the door at the end of the room that opened into the shed. He lifted the latch with precaution and went out, pushing the door behind him but without shutting it. Daru had not stirred. "He is running away," he merely thought. "Good riddance!" Yet he listened attentively. The hens were not fluttering; the guest must be on the plateau. A faint sound of water reached him, and he didn't know what it was until the Arab again stood framed in the doorway, closed the door carefully, and came back to bed without a sound. Then Daru turned his back on him and fell asleep. Still later he seemed, from the depths of his sleep, to hear furtive steps around the schoolhouse. "I'm dreaming! I'm dreaming!" he repeated to himself. And he went on sleeping.

100   When he awoke, the sky was clear; the loose window let in a cold, pure air. The Arab was asleep, hunched up under the blankets now, his mouth open, utterly relaxed. But when Daru shook him, he started dreadfully, staring at Daru with wild eyes as if he had never seen him and such a frightened expression that the schoolmaster stepped back. "Don't be afraid. It's me. You must eat." The Arab nodded his head and said yes. Calm had returned to his face, but his expression was vacant and listless.

101   The coffee was ready. They drank it seated together on the folding bed as they munched their pieces of the cake. Then Daru led the Arab under the shed and showed him the faucet where he washed. He went back into the room, folded the blankets and the bed, made his own bed and put the room in order. Then he went through the classroom and out onto the terrace. The sun was already rising in the blue sky; a soft, bright light was bathing the deserted plateau. On the ridge the snow was melting in spots. The stones were about to reappear. Crouched on

the edge of the plateau, the schoolmaster looked at the deserted expanse. He thought of Balducci. He had hurt him, for he had sent him off in a way as if he didn't want to be associated with him. He could still hear the gendarme's farewell and, without knowing why, he felt strangely empty and vulnerable. At that moment, from the other side of the schoolhouse, the prisoner coughed. Daru listened to him almost despite himself and then, furious, threw a pebble that whistled through the air before sinking into the snow. That man's stupid crime revolted him, but to hand him over was contrary to honor. Merely thinking of it made him smart with humiliation. And he cursed at one and the same time his own people who had sent him this Arab and the Arab too who had dared to kill and not managed to get away. Daru got up, walked in a circle on the terrace, waited motionless, and then went back into the schoolhouse.

The Arab, leaning over the cement floor of the shed, was washing   102
his teeth with two fingers. Daru looked at him and said: "Come." He went back into the room ahead of the prisoner. He slipped a hunting-jacket on over his sweater and put on walking-shoes. Standing, he waited until the Arab had put on his *chèche* and sandals. They went into the classroom and the schoolmaster pointed to the exit, saying: "Go ahead." The fellow didn't budge. "I'm coming," said Daru. The Arab went out. Daru went back into the room and made a package of pieces of rusk, dates, and sugar. In the classroom, before going out, he hesitated a second in front of his desk, then crossed the threshold and locked the door. "That's the way," he said. He started toward the east, followed by the prisoner. But, a short distance from the schoolhouse, he thought he heard a slight sound behind them. He retraced his steps and examined the surroundings of the house; there was no one there. The Arab watched him without seeming to understand. "Come on," said Daru.

They walked for an hour and rested beside a sharp peak of lime-   103
stone. The snow was melting faster and faster and the sun was drinking up the puddles at once, rapidly cleaning the plateau, which gradually dried and vibrated like the air itself. When they resumed walking, the ground rang under their feet. From time to time a bird rent the space in front of them with a joyful cry. Daru breathed in deeply the fresh morning light. He felt a sort of rapture before the vast familiar expanse, now almost entirely yellow under its dome of blue sky. They walked an hour more, descending toward the south. They reached a level height made up of crumbly rocks. From there on, the plateau sloped down, eastward, toward a low plain where there were a few spindly trees and, to the south, toward outcroppings of rock that gave the landscape a chaotic look.

Daru surveyed the two directions. There was nothing but the sky on   104
the horizon. Not a man could be seen. He turned toward the Arab, who was looking at him blankly. Daru held out the package to him. "Take

it," he said. "There are dates, bread, and sugar. You can hold out for two days. Here are a thousand francs too." The Arab took the package and the money but kept his full hands at chest level as if he didn't know what to do with what was being given him. "Now look," the schoolmaster said as he pointed in the direction of the east, "there's the way to Tinguit. You have a two-hour walk. At Tinguit you'll find the administration and the police. They are expecting you." The Arab looked toward the east, still holding the package and the money against his chest. Daru took his elbow and turned him rather roughly toward the south. At the foot of the height on which they stood could be seen a faint path. "That's the trail across the plateau. In a day's walk from here you'll find pasturelands and the first nomads. They'll take you in and shelter you according to their law." The Arab had now turned toward Daru and a sort of panic was visible in his expression. "Listen," he said. Daru shook his head: "No, be quiet. Now I'm leaving you." He turned his back on him, took two long steps in the direction of the school, looked hesitantly at the motionless Arab, and started off again. For a few minutes he heard nothing but his own step resounding on the cold ground and did not turn his head. A moment later, however, he turned around. The Arab was still there on the edge of the hill, his arms hanging now, and he was looking at the schoolmaster. Daru felt something rise in his throat. But he swore with impatience, waved vaguely, and started off again. He had already gone some distance when he again stopped and looked. There was no longer anyone on the hill.

105   Daru hesitated. The sun was now rather high in the sky and was beginning to beat down on his head. The schoolmaster retraced his steps, at first somewhat uncertainly, then with decision. When he reached the little hill, he was bathed in sweat. He climbed it as fast as he could and stopped, out of breath, at the top. The rock-fields to the south stood out sharply against the blue sky, but on the plain to the west a steamy heat was already rising. And in that slight haze, Daru, with heavy heart, made out the Arab walking slowly on the road to prison.

106   A little later, standing before the window of the classroom, the schoolmaster was watching the clear light bathing the whole surface of the plateau, but he hardly saw it. Behind him on the blackboard, among the winding French rivers, sprawled the clumsily chalked-up words he had just read: "You handed over our brother. You will pay for this." Daru looked at the sky, the plateau, and, beyond, the invisible lands stretching all the way to the sea. In his vast landscape he had loved so much, he was alone.

Questions for Discussion and Writing

1. What do you know about Daru's background that would explain why in his present circumstances he does not wish to step outside of his role as

teacher to enforce the rulings of the authorities? Between what conflicting loyalties is Daru torn?

2. What can you infer about Daru's past relationship with Balducci from his reaction to Balducci's request?

3. What is the crime of which the Arab has been accused? How is it related to the food shortage afflicting the community?

4. How do the descriptions of the physical environment (the stones, the sudden snow and melting that follows) underscore the human drama?

5. How does Daru's feeling of common humanity make it increasingly difficult for him to turn the Arab over to the authorities? How does Daru try to avoid the responsibility for turning in the Arab?

6. How are Daru's actions toward the Arab misunderstood by the local populace who are spying on him? What is the significance of the message written on the blackboard?

7. What outside sources of knowledge about HISTORICAL and LITERARY CONTEXTS would be useful in interpreting this story? Why would it be helpful to know something about existentialism, the history of the Algerian revolt, or Camus's own childhood growing up as a non-Arab French citizen in Algeria?

8. Why, in your opinion, does the Arab choose to go to the place where he will be imprisoned or even executed although he now has money, food, and the freedom to go wherever he wants?

9. Describe the last time a guest stayed with you or your family, or a time when you were a guest in someone else's home. What insight did these experiences give you into Camus's story?

10. Just as the protagonist in the story finds he cannot live a private life outside of public events, do you remember where you were and what you thought immediately before and after you heard the news of a historical event that made the problems of everyday life insignificant (for example, the 1986 *Challenger* disaster)?

Mahasweta Devi

Giribala

Mahasweta Devi was born in East Bengal in 1926, moved to West Bengal as an adolescent, and studied at Visva-Bharati and Calcutta universities where she received a master's degree in English. From a family with widespread literary and political influence, Devi joined the Gananatya, a group of highly accomplished, keenly political actors and writers who took the revolutionary step of bringing theater, on themes of burning interest in rural Bengal, to villages. Subsequently, she became a writer and journalist while holding a job as a college teacher in Calcutta. Over a period of years she has studied and lived among the tribal and outcast communities in southwest Bengal and southeast Bihar. Her stories, collected in Agnigarbha (Womb of fire) (1978), focus on the semi-landless tribals and untouchables who are effectively denied rights guaranteed by the constitution, including a legal minimum wage. Her unique style of narrative realism reflects this emphasis on observations drawn from actual situations, persons, dialects, and idioms. "Giribala," translated into English from Bengali by Bardhan Kalpana, was first published in the magazine Prasad (Autumn 1982), a journal Devi created as a kind of people's magazine, which she still edits. Like her other stories, "Giribala" reflects carefully researched information Devi gathered directly from the lives of the rural underclass. This story tells the shocking tale of a woman whose husband sells their young daughters into prostitution.

1   Giribala[1] was born in a village called Talsana, in the Kandi subdivision of Murshidabad district.[2] Nobody ever imagined that she could think on her own, let alone act on her own thought. This Giribala, like so many others, was neither beautiful nor ugly, just an average-looking girl. But she had lovely eyes, eyes that somehow made her appearance striking.

2   In their caste, it was still customary to pay a bride-price. Aulchand gave Giri's father eighty rupees[3] and a heifer before he married her. Giri's father, in turn, gave his daughter four tolas[4] of silver, pots and pans, sleeping mats, and a cartload of mature bamboo that came from the bamboo clumps that formed the main wealth of Giri's father. Aulchand had told him that only because his hut had burned down did he need the bamboo to rebuild it. This was also the reason he gave for having to leave her with them for a few days—so that he could go to build a home for them.

[1]Literally, "mountain girl."
[2]In the United Province, near New Delhi.
[3]Approximately $20.
[4]One tola = .40 ounce.

Aulchand thus married Giri, and left. He did not come back soon.   3

Shortly after the marriage, Bangshi Dhamali,[5] who worked at the   4
sub-post office in Nishinda, happened to visit the village. Bangshi enjoyed much prestige in the seven villages in the Nishinda area, largely
due to his side business of procuring patients for the private practice of
the doctor who was posted at the only hospital in the area. That way,
the doctor supplemented his hospital salary by getting paid by the patients thus diverted from the hospital, and Bangshi supplemented his
salary of 145 rupees from the sub-post office with the commission he
got for procuring those patients. Bangshi's prestige went up further after he started using the medical terms he had picked up from being
around the doctor.

For some reason that nobody quite recalled, Bangshi addressed   5
Giri's father as uncle. When Bangshi showed up on one of his patient-
procuring trips, he looked up Giri's father and remarked disapprovingly about what he had just learned from his trip to another village,
that he had given his only daughter in marriage to Aulchand, of all
people.

"Yes. The proposal came along, and I thought he was all right."   6

"Obviously, you thought so. How much did he pay?"   7

"Four times twenty and one."   8

"I hope you're ready to face the consequences of what you've   9
done."

"What consequences?"   10

"What can I say? You know that I'm a government servant myself   11
and the right-hand man of the government doctor. Don't you think you
should have consulted me first? I'm not saying that he's a bad sort, and
I will not deny there was a time when I smoked ganja[6] with him. But I
know what you don't know—the money he gave you as bride-price
was not his. It's Channan's. You see, Channan's marriage had been arranged in Kalhat village. And Aulchand, as Channan's uncle, was
trusted with the money to deliver as bride-price on behalf of Channan.
He didn't deliver it there."

"What?"   12

"Channan's mother sat crying when she learned that Aulchand,   13
who had been living under their roof for so long, could cheat them like
that. Finally, Channan managed to get married by borrowing from several acquaintances who were moved by his plight."

"He has no place of his own? No land for a home to stand on?"   14

"Nothing of the sort."   15

"But he took a cartload of my bamboo to rebuild the hut on his   16
land!"

"I was going to tell you about that too. He sold that bamboo to   17

---

[5]Literally, mischievious.
[6]Marijuana cigarettes, also known as "pip."

Channan's aunt for a hundred rupees and hurried off to the Banpur fair."

18   Giri's father was stunned. He sat with his head buried in his hands. Bangshi went on telling him about other similar tricks Aulchand had been pulling. Before taking leave, he finally said, perhaps out of mercy for the overwhelmed man, "He's not a bad one really. Just doesn't have any land, any place to live. Keeps traveling from one fair to another, with some singing party or other. That's all. Otherwise, he's not a bad sort."

19   Giri's father wondered aloud, "But Mohan never told me any of these things! He's the one who brought the proposal to me!"

20   "How could he, when he's Aulchand's right hand in these matters?"

21   When Giri's mother heard all this from Giri's father, she was livid. She vowed to have her daughter married again and never to send her to live with the cheat, the thief.

22   But when after almost a year Aulchand came back, he came prepared to stop their mouths from saying what they wanted to say. He brought a large taro root, a new sari for his bride, a squat stool of jackfruit wood for his mother-in-law, and four new jute sacks for his father-in-law. Giri's mother still managed to tell him the things they had found out from Bangshi. Aulchand calmly smiled a generous, forgiving smile, saying, "One couldn't get through life if one believed everything that Bangshi-*dada* said.[7] Your daughter is now going to live in a brick house, not a mere mud hut. That's true, not false."

23   So, Giri's mother started to dress her only daughter to go to live with her husband. She took time to comb her hair into a nice bun, while weeping and lamenting, partly to herself and partly to her daughter, "This man is like a hundred-rooted weed in the yard. Bound to come back every time it's been pulled out. What he just told us are all lies, I know that. But with what smooth confidence he said those lies!"

24   Giri listened silently. She knew that although the groom had to pay a bride-price in their community, still a girl was only a girl. She had heard so many times the old saying: "A daughter born, To husband or death, She's already gone." She realized that her life in her own home and village was over, and her life of suffering was going to begin. Silently she wept for a while, as her mother tended to grooming her. Then she blew her nose, wiped her eyes, and asked her mother to remember to bring her home at the time of Durga puja[8] and to feed the red-brown cow that was her charge, adding that she had chopped some hay for the cow, and to water her young *jaba* tree that was going to flower someday.

---

[7]*Dada*, meaning elder brother, is also used to refer politely to or to address a friend or acquaintance older than oneself, but not old enough to be referred to or addressed as uncle. [Author's note.]

[8]Rituals designed to worship a household goddess of good fortune.

Giribala, at the age of fourteen, then started off to make her home 25
with her husband. Her mother put into a bundle the pots and pans that
she would be needing. Watching her doing that, Aulchand remarked,
"Put in some rice and lentils too. I've got a job at the house of the *babu*.
Must report to work the moment I get back. There'll be no time to buy
provisions until after a few days."

Giribala picked up the bundle of rice, lentils, and cooking oil and 26
left her village, walking a few steps behind him. He walked ahead, and
from time to time asked her to walk faster, as the afternoon was starting
to fade. He took her to another village in Nishinda, to a large brick
house with a large garden of fruit trees of all kinds. In the far corner of
the garden was a crumbling hovel meant for the watchman. He took
her to it. There was no door in the door opening. As if answering her
thought, Aulchand said, "I'll fix the door soon. But you must admit the
room is nice. And the pond is quite near. Now go on, pick up some
twigs and start the rice."

"It's dark out there! Do you have a kerosene lamp?" 27

"Don't ask me for a kerosene lamp, or this and that. Just do what 28
you can."

A maid from the babu's household turned up and saved Giri. She 29
brought a kerosene lamp from the house and showed Giri to the pond,
complaining about Aulchand and cautioning her about him. "What
kind of heartless parents would give a tender young girl to a no-good
ganja addict? How can he feed you? He has nothing. Gets a pittance
taking care of the babu's cattle and doing odd jobs. Who knows how he
manages to feed himself, doing whatever else he does! If you've been
brought up on rice, my dear, you'd be wise enough to go back home tomorrow to leave behind the bits of silver that you have got on you."

But Giri did not go back home the next day for safekeeping her sil- 30
ver ornaments. Instead, in the morning she was found busy plastering
with mud paste the exposed, uneven bricks of the wall of the crumbling
room. Aulchand managed to get an old sheet of tin from the babu and
nailed it to a few pieces of wood to make it stand; then he propped it up
as a door for the room. Giri promptly got herself employed in the babu
household for meals as her wage. After a few months, Aulchand remarked about how she had managed to domesticate a vagabond like
him, who grew up without parents, never stayed home, and always
floated around.

Giri replied, "Go, beg the babus for a bit of the land. Build your own 31
home."

"Why will they give me land?" 32

"They will if you plead for the new life that's on its way. Ask them 33
if a baby doesn't deserve to be born under a roof of its own. Even beggars and roving street singers have some kind of home."

"You're right. I too feel sad about not having a home of my own. 34
Never felt that way before, though."

35   The only dream they shared was a home of their own.

36   However, their firstborn, a daughter they named Belarani,[9] was born in the crumbling hovel with the tin door. Before the baby was even a month old, Giri returned to her work in the babu household, and, as if to make up for her short absence from work, she took the heavy sheets, the flatweave rugs, and the mosquito nets to the pond to wash them clean. The lady of the house remarked on how she put her heart into the work and how clean her work was!

37   Feeling very magnanimous, the lady then gave Giri some of her children's old clothes, and once in a while she asked Giri to take a few minutes' break from work to feed the baby.

38   Belarani was followed by another daughter, Poribala, and a son, Rajib, all born in the watchman's hovel at the interval of a year and a half to two years. After the birth of her fourth child, a daughter she named Maruni,[10] she asked the doctor at the hospital, where she went for this birth, to sterilize her.

39   By then Aulchand had finally managed to get the babu's permission to use a little area of his estate to build a home for his family. He had even raised a makeshift shack on it. Now he was periodically going away for other kinds of work assigned to him.

40   He was furious to learn that Giri had herself sterilized, so furious that he beat her up for the first time. "Why did you do it? Tell me, why?"

41   Giri kept silent and took the beating. Aulchand grabbed her by the hair and punched her a good many times. Silently she took it all. After he had stopped beating because he was tired and his anger temporarily spent, she calmly informed him that the Panchayat[11] was going to hire people for the road building and pay the wages in wheat.

42   "Why don't you see your father and get some bamboo instead?"

43   "What for?"

44   "Because you're the one who has been wanting a home. I could build a good one with some bamboo from your father."

45   "We'll both work on the Panchayat road and have our home. We'll save some money by working harder."

46   "If only we could mortgage or sell your silver trinkets, . . ."

47   Giribala did not say anything to his sly remark; she just stared at him. Aulchand had to lower his eyes before her silent stare. Giri had put her silver jewelry inside the hollow of a piece of bamboo, stuffed it up and kept it in the custody of the lady of the house she worked for. Belarani too started working there, when she was seven years old, doing a thousand odd errands to earn her meals. Bela was now ten, and

---

[9]Literally, "pretty queen."

[10]Literally meaning a girl likely to die; the name is perhaps intended to repel death, following the belief that death takes first the lives people want to cling to most. [Author's note.]

[11]Governing body of the local village, usually made up of five officials ("pancha" means "five").

growing like a weed in the rainy season. Giri would need the silver to get her married someday soon. All she had for that purpose was the bit of silver from her parents and the twenty-two rupees she managed to save from her years of hard work, secretly deposited with the mistress of the house, away from Aulchand's reach.

"I'm not going to sell my silver for a home. My father gave all he could for that, a whole cartload of bamboo, one hundred and sixty-two full stems, worth a thousand rupees at that time even in the markets of Nishinda." 48

"The same old story comes up again!" Aulchand was exasperated. 49

"Don't you want to see your own daughter married someday?" 50

"Having a daughter only means having to raise a slave for others. Mohan had read my palm and predicted a son in the fifth pregnancy. But, no, you had to make yourself sterile, so you could turn into a whore." 51

Giri grabbed the curved kitchen knife and hissed at him, "If ever I hear you say those evil things about me, I'll cut off the heads of the children and then my own head with this." 52

Aulchand quickly stopped himself, "Forget I said it. I won't, ever again." 53

For a few days after that he seemed to behave himself. He was sort of timid, chastised. But soon, probably in some way connected with the grudge of being chastised by her, the vile worm inside his brain started to stir again; once again Mohan, his trick master, was his prompter. 54

Mohan had turned up in the midst of the busy days they were spending in the construction of a bus road that was going to connect Nishinda with Krishnachawk.[12] Giri and Aulchand were both working there and getting as wages the wheat for their daily meals. Mohan too joined them to work there, and he sold his wheat to buy some rice, a pumpkin, and occasionally some fish to go with the wheat bread. He had remained the same vagabond that he always was, only his talking had become more sophisticated with a bohemian style picked up from his wanderings to cities and distant villages. He slept in the little porch facing the room occupied by Giri and her family. 55

Sitting there in the evenings, he expressed pity for Aulchand, "Tch! Tch! You seem to have got your boat stuck in the mud, my friend. Have you forgotten all about the life we used to have?" 56

Giri snapped at him, "You can't sit here doing your smart talking, which can only bring us ruin." 57

"My friend had such a good singing voice!" 58

"Perhaps he had that. Maybe there was money in it too. But that money would never have reached his home and fed his children." 59

Mohan started another topic one evening. He said that there was a great shortage of marriage-age girls in Bihar,[13] so that the Biharis with 60

[12]A major junction.
[13]A state near Bengal.

money were coming down for Bengali brides and paying a bundle for that! He mentioned that Sahadeb Bauri, a fellow he knew, a low-caste fellow like themselves, received five hundred rupees for having his daughter married to one of those bride-searching Biharis.

61   "Where is that place?" Aulchand's curiosity was roused.

62   "You wouldn't know, my friend, even if I explained where it is. Let me just say that it's very far and the people there don't speak Bengali."

63   "They paid him five hundred rupees?" Aulchand was hooked in.

64   "Yes, they did."

65   The topic was interrupted at that point by the noise that rose when people suddenly noticed that the cowshed of Kali-babu,[14] the Panchayat big shot, was on fire. Everybody ran in that direction to throw bucketfuls of water at it.

66   Giri forgot about the topic thus interrupted. But Aulchand did not.

67   Something must have blocked Giri's usual astuteness because she suspected nothing from the subsequent changes in her husband's tone.

68   For example, one day he said, "Who wants your silver? I'll get my daughter married and also my shack replaced with bricks and tin. My daughter looks lovelier every day from the meals in the babu home!"

69   Giri's mind sensed nothing at all to be alerted to. She only asked, "Are you looking for a groom for her?"

70   "I don't have to look. My daughter's marriage will just happen."

71   Giri did not give much thought to this strange answer either. She merely remarked that the sagging roof needed to be propped up soon.

72   Perhaps too preoccupied with the thought of how to get the roof propped up, Giri decided to seek her father's help and also to see her parents for just a couple of days. Holding Maruni to her chest and Rajib and Pori by the hand, she took leave of Belarani, who cried and cried because she was not being taken along to visit her grandparents. Giri, also crying, gave her eight annas to buy sweets to eat, telling her that she could go another time because both of them could not take off at the same time from their work at the babu's place, even if for only four days, including the two days in walking to and from there.

73   She had no idea that she was never to see Bela again. If she had, she would not only have taken her along, but she would also have held her tied to her bosom, she would not have let her out of her sight for a minute. She was Giri's beloved firstborn, even though Giri had to put her to work at the babu household ever since she was only seven; that was the only way she could have her fed and clothed. Giri had no idea when she started for her parents' village, leaving Bela with a kiss on her forehead.

74   "A daughter born, To husband or death, She's already gone." That must be why seeing the daughter makes the mother's heart sing! Her

---

[14]Kali means dark complexion; literally, "black."

father had been very busy trying to sell his bamboo and acquiring two *bighas*[15] of land meanwhile. He was apologetic about not being able in all this time to bring her over for a visit, and he asked her to stay on a few more days once she had made the effort to come on her own. Her mother started making puffed rice and digging up the taro root she had been saving for just such a special occasion. While her hands worked making things for them to eat, she lamented about what the marriage had done to her daughter, how it had tarnished her bright complexion, ruined her abundant hair, and made her collarbones stick out. She kept asking her to stay a few more days, resting and eating to repair the years of damage. Giri's little brother begged her to stay for a month.

For a few days, after many years, Giri found rest and care and heaping servings of food. Her father readily agreed to give her the bamboo, saying how much he wanted his daughter to live well, in a manner he could be proud of. Giri could easily have used a few tears and got some other things from her father. Her mother asked her to weep and get a maund[16] of rice too while he was in the giving mood. But Giri did not do that. Giri was not going to ask for anything from her loved ones unless she absolutely had to. She walked over to the corner of the yard, to look at the hibiscus she had planted when she was a child. She watched with admiration its crimson flowers and the clean mud-plastered yard and the new tiles on the roof. She also wondered if her son Rajib could stay there and go to the school her brother went to. But she mentioned nothing to her parents about this sudden idea that felt like a dream. 75

She just took her children to the pond, and, with the bar of soap she had bought on the way, she scrubbed them and herself clean. She washed her hair too. Then she went to visit the neighbors. She was feeling lighthearted, as if she were in heaven, without the worries of her life. Her mother sent her brother to catch a fish from the canal, the new irrigation canal that had changed the face of the area since she last saw it. It helped to raise crops and catch fish throughout the year. Giri felt an unfamiliar wind of fulfillment and pleasure blowing in her mind. There was not the slightest hint of foreboding. 76

Bangshi Dhamali happened to be in the village that day, and he too remarked on how Giri's health and appearance had deteriorated since she went to live with that no-good husband of hers. He said that if only Aulchand were a responsible father and could look after the older kids, she could have gone to work in the house of the doctor who was now living in Bahrampur town, and after some time she could take all the children over there and have them all working for food and clothing. 77

Giri regarded his suggestion with a smile, and asked him instead, 78

---

[15]One *bigha* is roughly one-third of an acre. [Author's note.]
[16]Equal to approximately 85 pounds.

"Tell me, dad, how is it that when so many destitute people are getting little plots of land from the government, Rajib's father can't?"

79   "Has he ever come to see me about it? Ever sought my advice on anything? I'm in government service myself, and the right-hand man of the hospital doctor as well. I could easily have gotten him a plot of land."

80   "I'm going to send him to you as soon as I get back."

81   It felt like a pleasant dream to Giri, that they could have a piece of land of their own for a home of their own. She knew that her husband was a pathetic vagabond. Still, she felt a rush of compassion for him. A man without his own home, his own land. How could such a man help being diffident and demoralized?

82   "Are you sure, Bangshi-dada? Shall I send him to you then?"

83   "Look at your own father. See how well he's managed things. He's now almost a part of the Panchayat. I don't know what's the matter with uncle, though. He could have seen to it that Aulchand got a bit of the land being distributed. I once told him as much, and he insulted me in the marketplace, snapped at me that Aulchand should be learning to use his own initiative."

84   Giri decided to ignore the tendentious remark and keep on pressing Bangshi instead, "Please, Bangshi-dada, you tell me what to do. You know how impractical that man is. The room he's put up in all these years doesn't even have a good thatch roof. The moon shines into it all night and the sun all day. I'm hoping to get Bela married someday soon. Where am I going to seat the groom's party? And, dada, would you look for a good boy for my daughter?"

85   "There is a good boy available. Obviously, you don't know that. He's the son of my own cousin. Just started a grocery store of his own."

86   Giri was excited to learn that, and even Rajib's face lit up as he said that he could then go to work as a helper in his brother-in-law's shop and could bring home salt and oil on credit. Giri scolded him for taking after his father, wanting to live on credit rather than by work.

87   Giri ended up staying six days with her parents instead of two. She was about to take leave, wearing a sari without holes that her mother gave her, a bundle of rice on her head, and cheap new shirts and pants on her children. Just then, like the straw suddenly blown in, indicating the still unseen storm, Bangshi Dhamali came in a rush to see her father.

88   "I don't want to say if it is bad news or good news, uncle, but what I just heard is incredible. Aulchand had told Bela that he was going to take her to see her grandparents. Then with the help of Mohan, he took her to Kandi town, and there he got the scared twelve-year-old, the timid girl who had known only her mother, married to some strange man from Bihar. There were five girls like Bela taken there to be married to five unknown blokes. The addresses they left are all false. This kind of business is on the rise. Aulchand got four hundred rupees in

cash. The last thing he was seen doing was, back from drinking with Mohan, crying and slobbering, 'Bela! Bela!' while Kali-babu of the village Panchayat was shouting at him."

The sky seemed to come crashing down on Giribala's head. She 89 howled with pain and terror. Her father got some people together and went along with her, vowing to get the girl back, to break the hands of the girl's father, making him a cripple, and to finish Mohan for good.

They could not find Mohan. Just Aulchand. On seeing them, he kept 90 doing several things in quick succession. He vigorously twisted his own ears and nose to show repentance, he wept, perhaps with real grief, and from time to time he sat up straight, asserting that because Bela was his daughter it was nobody else's business how he got her married off.

They searched the surrounding villages as far as they could. Giri 91 took out the silver she had deposited with the mistress of the house and went to the master, crying and begging him to inform the police and get a paid announcement made over the radio about the lost girl. She also accused them, as mildly as she could in her state of mind, for letting the girl go with her father, knowing as they did the lout that he was.

The master of the house persuaded Giri's father not to seek police 92 help because that would only mean a lot of trouble and expense. The terrible thing had happened after all; Bela had become one more victim of this new business of procuring girls on the pretext of marriage. The police were not going to do much for this single case; they would most probably say that the father did it after all. Poor Bela had this written on her forehead!

Finally, that was the line everybody used to console Giri. The master 93 of the house in which she and Bela worked day and night, the neighbors gathered there, even Giri's father ended up saying that—about the writing on the forehead that nobody could change. If the daughter was to remain hers, that would have been nice, they said in consolation, but she was only a daughter, not a son. And they repeated the age-old saying: "A daughter born, To husband or death, She's already gone."

Her father sighed and said with philosophical resignation, "It's as if 94 the girl sacrificed her life to provide her father with money for a house."

Giri, crazed with grief, still brought herself to respond in the im- 95 plied context of trivial bickering, "Don't send him any bamboo, father. Let the demon do whatever he can on his own."

"It's useless going to the police in such matters," everybody said. 96

Giri sat silently with her eyes closed, leaning against the wall. Even 97 in her bitter grief, the realization flashed through her mind that nobody was willing to worry about a girl child for very long. Perhaps she should not either. She too was a small girl once, and her father too gave her away to a subhuman husband without making sufficient inquiries.

98   Aulchand sensed that the temperature in the environment was
dropping. He started talking defiantly and defending himself to her father by blaming Giri and answering her remark about him. "Don't
overlook your daughter's fault. How promptly she brought out her silver chain to get her daughter back! If she had brought it out earlier,
then there would have been a home for us and no need to sell my
daughter. Besides, embarrassed as I am to tell you this, she had the operation to get cleaned out, saying, 'What good was it having more children when we can't feed the ones we've got?' Well, I've shown what
good it can be, even if we got more daughters. So much money for a
daughter!"

99   At this, Giri started hitting her own head against the wall so violently that she seemed to have suddenly gone insane with grief and
anger. They had to grapple with her to restrain her from breaking her
head.

100   Slowly the agitation died down. The babu's aunt gave Giri a choice
nugget of her wisdom to comfort her. "A daughter, until she is married,
is her father's property. It's useless for a mother to think she has any
say."

101   Giri did not cry any more after that night.

102   Grimly, she took Pori to the babu's house, to stay there and work in
place of Bela, and told her that she would kill her if she ever went anywhere with her father. In grim silence, she went through her days of
work and even more work. When Aulchand tried to say anything to
her, she did not answer; she just stared at him. It scared Aulchand. The
only time she spoke to him was to ask, "Did you really do it only because you wanted to build your home?"

103   "Yes. Believe me."

104   "Ask Mohan to find out where they give the children they buy full
meals to eat. Then go and sell the other three there. You can have a
brick and concrete house. Mohan must know it."

105   "How can you say such a dreadful thing, you merciless woman?
Asking me to sell the children. Is that why you got sterilized? And why
didn't you take the bamboo that your father offered?"

106   Giri left the room and lay down in the porch to spend the night
there. Aulchand whined and complained for a while. Soon he fell
asleep.

107   Time did the ultimate, imperceptible talking! Slowly Giri seemed to
accept it. Aulchand bought some panels of woven split-bamboo for the
walls. The roof still remained covered with leaves. Rajib took the work
of tending the babu's cattle. Maruni, the baby, grew into a child, playing by herself in the yard. The hardest thing for Giri now was to look at
Pori because she looked so much like Bela, with Bela's smile, Bela's way
of watching things with her head tilted to one side. The mistress of the
house was full of similar praise for her work and her gentle manners.

108   Little Pori poured her heart into the work at the babu household, as

if it were far more than a means to the meals her parents couldn't provide, as if it were her vocation, her escape. Perhaps the work was the disguise for her silent engagement in constant, troubling thoughts. Why else would she sweep all the rooms and corridors ten times a day, when nobody had asked her to? Why did she carry those jute sacks for paddy storage to the pond to wash them diligently? Why else would she spend endless hours coating the huge unpaved yard with a rag dipped in mud-dung paste until it looked absolutely smooth from end to end?

When Pori came home in the evening, worn out from the day's constant work, Giri, herself drained from daylong work, would feed her some puffed rice or chickpea flour that she might happen to have at home. Then she would go and spend most of the evening roaming alone through the huge garden of the babus, absently picking up dry twigs and leaves for the stove and listening to the rustle of leaves, the scurrying of squirrels in the dark. The night wind soothed her raging despair, as it blew her matted hair, uncombed for how long she did not remember. 109

The gentle face of her firstborn would then appear before her eyes, and she would hear the sound of her small voice, making some little plea on some little occasion. "Ma, let me stay home today and watch you make the puffed rice. If they send for me, you can tell them that Bela would do all the work tomorrow, but she can't go today. Would you, Ma, please?" 110

Even when grown up, with three younger ones after her, she loved to sleep nestled next to her mother. Once her foot was badly cut and bruised. The squat stool that the babu's aunt sat on for her oil massage had slipped and hit her foot. She bore the pain for days, until applying the warm oil from a lamp healed it. Whenever Giri had a fever, Bela somehow found some time in between her endless chores at the babu household to come to cook the rice and run back to work. 111

> Bela, Belarani, Beli—
> Her I won't abandon.
> Yet my daughter named Beli,
> To husband or death she's gone!

Where could she be now? How far from here? In which strange land? Giri roamed the nights through the trees, and she muttered absently, "Wherever you are, my daughter, stay alive! Don't be dead! If only I knew where you were, I'd go there somehow, even if I had to learn to fly like birds or insects. But I don't know where you were taken. I wrote you a letter, with the babu's help, to the address they left. You couldn't have got it, daughter, because it's a false address." 112

Absently Giri would come back with the twigs, cook the rice, feed Maruni, eat herself, and lie down with her children, leaving Aulchand's rice in the pot. 113

The days without work she stayed home, just sitting in the porch. 114

The days she found work, she went far—by the bus that now plied along the road they had worked on a few years ago, the bus that now took only an hour and a half to reach Kandi town. There, daily-wage work was going on, digging feeder channels from the main canal. The babu's son was a labor contractor there. He also had the permit for running a bus. Giri took that bus to work.

115   There, one day she came across Bangshi Dhamali. He was sincere when he said that he had difficulty recognizing her. "You've ruined your health and appearance. Must be the grief for that daughter. But what good is grieving going to do after all?"

116   "Not just that. I'm now worried about Pori. She's almost ten."

117   "Really! She was born only the other day, the year the doctor built his house, and electricity came to Nishinda. Pori was born in that year."

118   "Yes! If only I had listened to what you said to me about going to work at the doctor's house and taken the children to town! My son now tends the babu's cattle. If I had gone then, they could all be in school now!"

119   "Don't know about your children being able to go to school. But I do know that the town is now flooded with jobs. You could put all your children to work at least for daily meals."

120   Giri was aware that her thinking of sending her children to school annoyed Bangshi. She yielded, "Anyway, Bangshi-dada. What good is it being able to read a few pages if they've to live on manual labor anyway? What I was really going to ask you is to look for a boy for my Pori."

121   "I'll tell Aulchand when I come to know of one."

122   "No. No. Make sure that you tell me."

123   "Why are you still so angry with him? He certainly made a mistake. Can't it be forgiven? Negotiating a daughter's wedding can't be done with the mother. It makes the groom's side think there's something wrong in the family. When it comes to your son's wedding, the bride's side would talk to you. It's different with the daughter."

124   "At least let me know about it all, before making a commitment."

125   "I'll see what I can do. I happen to know a rickshaw plier in Krishnachawk. Not very young, though. About twenty-five, I think."

126   "That's all right. After what happened to Bela, the groom's age is not my main concern."

127   "Your girl will be able to live in Krishnachawk. But the boy has no land, he lives by plying a rented rickshaw, which leaves him with barely five rupees a day. Makes a little extra by rolling bidis[17] at night. Doesn't have a home yet. He wants to get married because there's nobody to cook for him and look after him at the end of the day."

128   "You try for him. If it works out, I'd have her wedding this winter."

129   The total despondency in her mind since losing Bela suddenly

---

[17]Tobacco cigarettes rolled with leaves.

moved a little to let in a glimmer of hope for Pori. She went on hope-
fully, saying, "I'll give her everything I've got. After that, I'll have just
Maruni to worry about. But she's still a baby. I'll have time to think. Let
me tell you Bangshidada, and I'm saying this not because she's my
daughter, my Pori looks so lovely at ten. Perhaps the meals at the babu
house did it. Come dada, have some tea inside the shop."

Bangshi sipped the tea Giri bought him and informed her that her
father was doing very well for himself, adding to his land and his stores
of paddy, and remarked what a pity it was that he didn't help her
much!

"It may not sound nice, sister. But the truth is that blood relation is
no longer the main thing these days. Uncle now mixes with his equals,
those who are getting ahead like himself, not with those gone to the
dogs, like your man, even if you happen to be his daughter."

Giri just sighed, and quietly paid for the tea with most of the few
coins tied in one end of the sari and tucked in her waist. Before taking
leave, she earnestly reminded Bangshi about her request for finding a
good husband for Pori.

Bangshi did remember. When he happened to see Aulchand shortly
after that, he mentioned the rickshaw plier. Aulchand perked up, saying that he too was after a boy who plied a rickshaw, though his did it
in Bahrampur, a bit further away but a much bigger place than
Krishnachawk. The boy had a fancy beard, mustache, and hair, and he
talked so smart and looked so impressive in some dead Englishman's
pants and jacket he had bought for himself at the second-hand market.
Aulchand asked Bangshi not to bother himself anymore about the rickshaw plier he had in mind.

Next time Giri saw Bangshi, she asked him if he had made contact
with the rickshaw plier in Krishnachawk. He said that he had talked
with Aulchand about it meanwhile and that she need not worry about
it.

Aulchand then went looking for Mohan, his guide in worldly matters. And why not? There was not a place Mohan hadn't been to, all the
nearby small towns in West Bengal that Aulchand had only heard of:
Lalbagh, Dhulian, Jangipur, Jiaganj, Farakka. In fact, Aulchand didn't
even know that Mohan was now in a business flung much further,
procuring girls for whorehouses in the big cities, where the newly rich
businessmen and contractors went to satisfy their newfound appetite
for the childlike, underdeveloped bodies of Bengali pubescent girls. Fed
well for a few months, they bloomed so deliciously that they yielded
back within a couple of years the price paid to procure them.

But it was very important to put up a show of marriage to procure
them. It was no longer possible to get away with just paying some
money for the girl. Any such straight procurer was now sure to get a
mass beating from the Bengali villagers. Hence, the need for stories
about a shortage of marriage-age girls in Bihar and now the need for

something even more clever. The weddings now had to look real, with a priest and all that. Then there would have to be some talk about the rituals that must be performed at the groom's place according to their local customs to complete the marriage, and so with the family's permission they must get back right away.

137   The "grooms from Bihar looking for brides in Bengal" story had circulated long enough. Newer tactics became necessary. The local matchmakers, who got a cut in each deal, were no longer informed enough about what was going on, but they sensed that it held some kind of trouble for their occupation. They decided not to worry too much about exactly how the cheating was done. They just took the position that they were doing what the girl's parents asked them to do—to make contact with potential grooms. They played down their traditional role as the source of information about the groom's family and background.

138   The girls' families too decided to go ahead despite the nonperformance of their usual source of information. Their reason for not talking and investigating enough was that the high bride-price they were offered and the little dowry they were asked to pay might then be revealed, and, because there was no dearth of envious people, someone might undo the arrangement. In some cases, they thought that they had no choice but an out-of-state groom because even in their low-caste communities, in which bride-price was customary, the Bengali grooms wanted several thousands of rupees in watches, radios, bicycles, and so on.

139   Since the incident of Bela, Kali-babu of the Panchayat refused to hire Aulchand on the road project or any other construction under the Panchayat. Aulchand found himself a bit out of touch, but, with plenty of free time, he went away for a few days trying to locate Mohan.

140   Mohan, meanwhile, was doing exceedingly well considering that he never got past the fourth grade in school. He had set up another business like a net around the block development office of Nishinda, to catch the peasants who came there for subsidized fertilizers and loans, part of which they somehow managed to lose to Mohan before they could get back to their village. Mohan was an extremely busy man these days.

141   He firmly shook his head at Aulchand's request, saying, "Count me out. Mohan Mandal has done enough of helping others. To help a father get his daughter married is supposed to be a virtue. You got the money. What did I get? The other side at least paid me forty rupees in broker's fee. And you? You used your money all on bamboo wall-panels. Besides, I'm afraid of your wife."

142   "She's the one who wants a rickshaw plier in a nearby town."

143   "Really?"

144   "Yes. But listen. You stay out of the thing and just put me in touch with a rickshaw plier boy in a big town like Bahrampur. My daughter

will be able to live there; we'll go there to visit them. I'd like nothing better. Bela's mother too might be pleased with me."

"You want to make up with your wife this way, right?" 145

"I'd like to. The woman doesn't think of me as a human being. I 146 want to show her that I can get my daughter married well without anyone's help. Only you can supply me that invisible help."

Mohan laughed and said, "All right. But I'll not get involved. I'll 147 just make the contact, that's all. What if the big-town son-in-law has a long list of demands?"

"I'll have to borrow." 148

"I see. Go home now. I'll see what I can do." 149

Mohan gave it some thought. He must be more careful this time. He 150 must keep the "groom from Bihar" setup hidden one step away and have a rickshaw plier boy in front, the one who will do the marrying and then pass her on. Aulchand's plea thus gave birth to a new idea in Mohan's head, but first he had to find a rickshaw plier boy. Who could play the part? He must go to town and check with some of his contacts.

Talking about Pori's marriage did reduce the distance between 151 Giribala and Aulchand. Finally, one day Mohan informed Aulchand that he had the right match. "How much does he want?" Aulchand asked.

"He's already got a watch and a radio. He plies a cycle-rickshaw, so 152 he wants no bicycle. Just the clothes for bride and groom, bed, shoes, umbrella, stuff like that. Quite a bargain, really."

"How much will he pay in bride-price?" 153

"One hundred rupees." 154

"Does he have a home for my daughter to live in?" 155

"He has a rented room. But he owns the cycle-rickshaw." 156

Aulchand and Giri were happy. When the future groom came to see 157 the bride, Giri peeked from behind the door, studying him intently. Big, well-built body, well-developed beard and mustache. He said that his name was Manohar Dhamali. In Bahrampur, there was indeed a rickshaw plier named Manohar Dhamali. But this man's real name was Panu. He had just been acquitted from a robbery charge, due to insufficient evidence. Aulchand didn't know about this part. After getting out of jail, Panu had just married a girl like Poribala in Jalangi, another in Farakka, and delivered them to the "groom from Bihar" gang. He was commissioned to do five for five hundred rupees. Not much for his efforts, he thought, but not bad with his options at the moment. Panu had plans to move further away, to Shiliguri, to try new pastures as soon as this batch was over and he had some money in hand.

At the time of Bela's marriage, no relative was there, not even 158 Giribala. This time, Giri's parents came. Women blew conch shells and ululated happily to solemnize each ritual. Giri, her face shining with sweat and excited oil glands, cooked rice and meat curry for the guests. She brought her silver ornaments from the housemistress and put them on Pori, who was dressed in a new sari that Giri's mother had brought. Her father had brought a sackful of rice for the feast. The babu family contributed fifty rupees. The groom came by bus in the company of five others. Pori looked even more like Bela. She was so lovely in the glow on her skin left from the turmeric rub and in the red *alta*[18] edging her small feet.

159   Next day, with the groom she took the bus and left for the town.

160   That was the last time Giri saw Pori's face. The day after, Aulchand went to the town with Rajib and Giri's young brother to visit the newly married couple, as the custom required. The night advanced, but they did not return. Very, very late in the night, Giri heard the sound of footsteps of people coming in, but silently. Giri knew at once. She opened the door, and saw Bangshi Dhamali holding Rajib's hand. Rajib cried out, "Ma!" Giri knew the terrible thing had happened again. Silently she looked on them. Giri's brother told her. There wasn't much to tell. They did find a Manohar Dhamali in the town, but he was a middle-aged man. They asked the people around and were told that it must be another of Panu's acts. He was going around doing a lot of marrying. He seemed to be linked with some kind of gang.

161   Giri interrupted to ask Bangshi, "And Mohan is not behind this?"

162   "He's the mastermind behind this new play."

163   "And where's Rajib's father? Why isn't he with you?"

164   "He ran to catch Mohan when he heard that Mohan got five to seven hundred rupees from it. He left shouting incoherently, 'I want my daughter. I want my money.'"

165   Giri's little porch was again crowded with sympathetic, agitated people, some of them suggesting that they find Mohan and beat him up, others wanting to go to the police station, but all of them doing just a lot of talking. "Are we living in a lawless land?" Lots of words, lots of noise.

166   Close to dawn, Aulchand came home. Overwhelmed by the events, he had finally gone to get drunk and he was talking and bragging, "I found out where he got the money from. Mohan can't escape Aulchand-sardar.[19] I twisted his neck until he coughed up my share of the money. Why shouldn't I get the money? The daughter is mine, and he'll be the one to take the money from putting her in a phony marriage? Where's Pori's mother? Foolish woman, you shouldn't have done that operation. The more daughters we have, the more money we can have. Now I'm going to have that home of ours done. Oh-ho-ho, my little Pori!"

167   Aulchand cried and wept and very soon he fell asleep on the porch. Giribala called up all her strength to quietly ask the crowd to go home. After they left, Giri sat by herself for a long time, trying to think what she should do now. She wanted to be dead. Should she jump into the

---

[18]Colored design traditionally worn before a marriage.
[19]Literally, "chief"; in the context, a form of self-praise.

canal? Last night, she heard some people talking, correctly perhaps, that the same fate may be waiting for Maruni too.

"Making business out of people's need to see their daughters married. Giri, this time you must take it to the police with the help of the babu. Don't let them get away with it. Go to the police, go to court." 168

Giri had looked on, placing her strikingly large eyes on their faces, then shaking her head. She would try nothing! Aulchand got his money at his daughter's expense. Let him try. Giri firmly shook her head. 169

Bangshi had remarked before leaving, "God must have willed that the walls come from one daughter and the roof from the other." 170

Giri had silently gazed at his face too with her striking eyes. 171

After some time, Aulchand was crying and doing the straw roof at the same time. The more tears he shed, the more dry-eyed Giri became. 172

The babu's elderly aunt tried to console her with her philosophy of cliches, "Not easy to be a daughter's mother. They say that a daughter born is already gone, either to husband or to death. That's what happened to you. Don't I know why you aren't crying? They say that one cries from a little loss, but turns into stone with too much loss. Start working again. One gets used to everything except hunger." 173

Giri silently gazed at her too, as she heard the familiar words coming out of her mouth. Then she requested her to go and tell the babu's wife that Giri wanted to withdraw her deposited money immediately. She went to collect the money. She put it in a knot in her sari and tucked the knot in her waist. 174

She came back and stood by the porch, looking at the home Aulchand was building. Nice room. The split-bamboo woven panels of the wall were neatly plastered with mud and were now being topped with a new straw roof. She had always dreamed of a room like this. Perhaps that was wanting too much. That was why Beli and Pori had to become prostitutes—yes, prostitutes. No matter what euphemism is used, nobody ever sets up home for a girl bought with money. 175

Nice room. Giri thought she caught a flitting glimpse of Aulchand eyeing little Maruni while tying up the ends of the straw he had laid on the roof. Giri silently held those striking eyes of hers steadily on Aulchand's face for some time, longer than she had ever done before. And Aulchand thought that no matter how great her grief was, she must be impressed with the way their home was turning out after all. 176

The next morning brought the biggest surprise to all. Before sunrise, Giribala had left home, with Maruni on her hip and Rajib's hand held in hers. She had walked down to the big road and caught the early morning bus to the town. Later on, it also became known that at the Nishinda stop she had left a message for Pori's father with Bangshi Dhamali. The message was that Giri wanted Aulchand to live in his new room happily forever. But Giri was going away from his home to work in other people's homes in order to feed and raise her remaining 177 children. And if he ever came to the town looking for her, she would put her neck on the rail line before a speeding train.

178   People were so amazed, even stunned by this that they were left speechless. What happened to Bela and Pori was happening to many others these days. But leaving one's husband was quite another matter. What kind of woman would leave her husband of many years just like that? Now, they all felt certain that the really bad one was not Aulchand, but Giribala. And arriving at this conclusion seemed to produce some kind of relief for their troubled minds.

179   And Giribala? Walking down the unfamiliar roads and holding Maruni on her hip and Rajib by the hand, Giribala only regretted that she had not done this before. If she had left earlier, then Beli would not have been lost, then Pori would not have been lost. If only she had had this courage earlier, her two daughters might have been saved.

180   As this thought grew insistent and hammered inside her brain, hot tears flooded her face and blurred her vision. But she did not stop even to wipe her tears. She just kept walking.

Questions for Discussion and Writing

1. Under what circumstances had Aulchand married Giribala? How does the reality of Giribala's married life contrast with the promises Aulchand had made to her and her parents? In what respects had he deceived them?
2. What insights does the story provide into how the caste system and cultural traditions such as the bride price function in the SOCIAL CONTEXT of Bengali culture?
3. How would you characterize the relationship between Aulchand and his right-hand man, Mohan? Who in your opinion is more to blame for what happens?
4. To what extent is the effectiveness of Devi's story a result of the matter-of-fact, objective tone she uses in describing such shocking events? Devi is active in promoting social reform for women in Bengal and throughout India and her works are written in part to bring about these reforms. How might "Giribala" have this effect?
5. What circumstances lead Aulchand to sell their young daughter, Bela? How does Bela's fate echo that of her mother, Giribala?
6. What measures does Giribala take to prevent Pori, another young daughter, from suffering the same fate as Bela? Why do her efforts come to nought?
7. To what extent does Giribala accept responsibility for what has happened?
8. Why is it ironic that the villagers blame Giribala for leaving her husband? What does this reveal about prevailing social views in Bengal?

Czeslaw Milosz

My Faithful Mother Tongue

One of the greatest twentieth-century Polish poets and essayists, and arguably one of the most important figures in world literature, Czeslaw Milosz was born in 1911 in Seteiniai, Lithuania (then part of the Russian empire). Milosz spent a good part of his youth in the city of Vilnius where he attended high school, and in 1929 he entered King Stefan Batory University. In 1930, he made his writing debut in a student journal and together with several other poets and critics founded a literary group, Zagary. In 1931, on a trip to Paris, Milosz met his distant relative, the French symbolist poet Oscar V. de L. Milosz, who influenced the evolution of his work. His first books of poetry, published when he was twenty-one, were greeted with critical acclaim. During World War II he worked with the underground Resistance movement against the Nazis and after the war he held posts in the Polish diplomatic service. While in Paris, in 1951, he sought political asylum and later moved to the United States where he still lives. In addition to numerous volumes of poetry, Milosz, during this period, wrote The Captive Mind (1953), a study of the capitulation of Eastern European intellectuals to Stalinism; a political novel, The Seizure of Power (1953); and Native Realm, a long treatise in verse on poetry's relation to nature and history (1957). In 1961, he took a position as professor of Slavic languages at the University of California, Berkeley, where he currently resides. Most of the poetry he has written since the 1960s is available in English translation in Selected Poems (1973), Bells in Winter (1978), The Witness of Poetry (1983), The Separate Notebooks (1984), and Unattainable Earth (1986). He also began the extraordinarily ambitious project of translating the Bible into modern Polish, and to date has translated a number of books from both the Old and New Testaments. Recognition of his incomparable influence in areas as diverse as politics, poetics, history, and metaphysics came in the form of the Neustadt International Literary Prize in 1978 and the Nobel Prize for literature in 1980. Milosz's poetry is characterized by a strong historical sense and a constant awareness of personal transience; the speaker seems to oscillate between his private concerns and contemplations of social and global problems. This predicament is eloquently presented in "My Faithful Mother Tongue" (1968), from The Collected Poems, 1931–1987 (1988).

Faithful mother tongue
I have been serving you.
Every night, I used to set before you little bowls of colors
so you could have your birch, your cricket, your finch
as preserved in my memory.   5

This lasted many years.
You were my native land; I lacked any other.

I believed that you would also be a messenger
between me and some good people
10   even if they were few, twenty, ten
or not born, as yet.

Now, I confess my doubt.
There are moments when it seems to me I have squandered my life.
For you are a tongue of the debased,
15   of the unreasonable, hating themselves
even more than they hate other nations,
a tongue of informers,
a tongue of the confused,
ill with their own innocence.

20   But without you, who am I?
Only a scholar in a distant country,
a success, without fears and humiliations.
Yes, who am I without you?
Just a philosopher, like everyone else.

25   I understand, this is meant as my education:
the glory of individuality is taken away,
Fortune spreads a red carpet
before the sinner in a morality play
while on the linen backdrop a magic lantern throws
30   images of human and divine torture.

Faithful mother tongue,
perhaps after all it's I who must try to save you.
So I will continue to set before you little bowls of colors
bright and pure if possible,
35   for what is needed in misfortune is a little order and beauty.

Questions for Discussion and Writing

1. What images, words, and phrases demonstrate how being Polish is the ultimate CONTEXT (historical, psychological, and literary) in which the speaker
   defines his identity?
2. What would the speaker lose were he to write his poetry in English and
   what would he gain? Ultimately, what factors prove most important to him?
3. If your situation is similar to that of the speaker in the poem, describe the
   feelings you experienced in deciding whether or not to continue to speak
   and write in your original language.
4. If English is not your first language, what experiences did you have upon entering schools where English is the required language?

Lennart Sjögren

The Roses

Lennart Sjögren (born 1930) lives in Oland, Sweden, in an agricultural community where he was born and grew up. He studied art in Gothenberg in the 1950s, and although he still paints, he is best known for his poetry. He has produced nearly twenty books, chiefly of poems, but also short stories, lyrical prose, and essays. His most recent collection of poems is Selected Poems *(1980). Sjögren's writing has the qualities of classic still-life paintings that present a self-contained world that conveys a paradoxical sense of life standing still. His work creates a sense of mystery, partly because the reader has to infer so much from a minimum of details. "The Roses," translated by Robin Fulton (1990), is a short prose piece (a genre practiced by many Swedish poets) in which a fragment of a total situation is subtly suggested through carefully chosen details.*

The phones ring in the empty house, both upstairs and down. The carpets hear them ringing, so do the windows, and the faces inside the picture-frames. But these are all fixed in their places. They trust in Silence to hurry to the phone. The wallpaper roses are imprisoned in the walls and the cutlery is lying, in spite of its sheen, piled together in their compartments like life-time prisoners.

Silence leaps up from his chair, reaches the phone at the third ring, lifts the receiver and replies. But whoever is ringing hears nothing and calls hello in vain.

"It's about someone who's bleeding to death. Answer, for God's sake! Answer, and prevent a tragedy!"

"It's about the sharing out of an inheritance, it's a family matter. You must answer, your silence could have unforeseeable legal consequences."

"It's about someone who's just been born. About the umbilical cord, you must realize!"

"It's about an impending accident which only your voice can prevent. A fateful mistake. Aren't you listening, you must listen!"

Again and again Silence calls out his reply into the receiver. But his voice cannot be transmitted through such wires.

"It's about some flowers that were ordered. Can the roses be delivered?"

But no matter how often the phone rings, nothing helps. The pictures persist with their wailing, and the window-panes still dream of being able to burst free. Silence sits in his chair paralyzed.

The unstopped bleeding proves fatal. The misunderstandings multiply. The umbilical cord is not cut. The inheritance goes to the wrong person. And the roses are left without a recipient.

Questions for Discussion and Writing

1. How does the poem suggest a state of psychological estrangement by evoking a variety of different situations where a required response fails to take place?
2. Although we normally expect a writer to achieve a sense of dramatic conflict with human characters, how does Sjögren use household objects and furnishings to suggest an inability to communicate?
3. How do the different images in which the color red occurs suggest the very qualities that would enable the unseen occupants to break out of their isolation? How do the undelivered real roses symbolize what has been lost?
4. In what way does the medium of the poem act as a LITERARY CONTEXT? How does the fact that this poem is written in prose ALLUDE to qualities that underscore the prosaic rather than poetic?
5. Speculate on the behind-the-scenes story that might explain the alienation described in this poem.
6. Write about something that seems at first glance unrelated to something else but that serves as a metaphor for it in the way Sjögren does in this poem.
7. Write a short piece that can be a story, a fable, a joke, or meditation using figurative language that looks like a prose passage, but has the qualities of poetry.
8. Describe all the features and contents (furniture, paintings, rugs, colors, textures, knickknacks) of a room in such a way as to allow the reader to infer the identity of its inhabitants.

Wing Tek Lum

Minority Poem

_____

Wing Tek Lum was born in 1946 in Honolulu, Hawaii. Lum was educated at Brown University and the Union Theological Seminary in New York City, and worked in New York's Chinatown for four years. During his stay in New York, he received the Poetry Center's Discovery Award in 1970. He lived in Hong Kong for three years employed as a social worker before returning to Honolulu, where he helps operate the family real estate business. His first collection of poems, Expounding the Doubtful Points *(1987), won the Creative Literature Award from the Association for Asian American Studies in 1988 and The Before Columbus Foundation American Book Award in 1989. Most of Lum's*

*poems deal with familial and domestic experiences in the context of Chinese-
American-Hawaiian associations and cultural constructs. "Minority Poem"
counters the myth of a pluralistic United States with an acerbic look at the
deep, underlying intolerance of the dominant Anglo culture that pays lip service to the ideals of multiculturalism.*

Why
we're just as American
as apple pie—
that is, if you count
the leftover peelings   5
lying on the kitchen counter
which the cook has forgotten about
or doesn't know
quite what to do with
except hope that the maid   10
when she cleans off the chopping block
will chuck them away
into a garbage can she'll take out
on leaving for the night.

Questions for Discussion and Writing

1. How does the poem use dramatic irony to satirize the traditional concept of
   American mainstream culture by revealing how much of it is supported by
   the unacknowledged labor of various ethnic groups?
2. How is the choice of what goes into making an apple pie and what gets left
   over an effective way of ALLUDING to cultural STEREOTYPES?
3. In what way does the poem assail conventional assumptions as to who is in
   the mainstream and who is marginal within a culture?
4. How does the way the speaker uses language and characterizes the situation
   express a particular kind of personality and his attitude toward the events in
   the poem? How would you describe this person through the VOICE you
   hear—for example, bitter, or witty?
5. In your own words, present the case the speaker is making. How does the
   poem argue for broadening the concept of what being an American means?
6. Describe the contributions of a particular ethnic group to the spirit and culture of your town or community.

Rahel Chalfi

Porcupine Fish

Born in Israel, but reared in Mexico, Rahel Chalfi has been acclaimed as one of
the most talented writers of Hebrew poetry. She is also a well-known playwright who has received a number of awards in both Israel and abroad, including best original play award in 1967 from Israel's Committee for Culture and
Literature. Her play Felicidad was published in English in 1974. She has also
received the 1971 Shubert Playwriting Award from the University of California, Berkeley, the 1983 Film Award by the Israeli Film Institute, and the
1989 Prime Minister's Award for Literature by Israel's Committee for Culture
and Literature. She has published five volumes of poetry, including Submarine
and Other Poems (1976), Free Fall (1979), Chameleon, or the Principle of
Uncertainty (1987), Underwater and Other Poems (1989), and Matter
(1990). Chalfi's gifts as a poet reflect her remarkable sensitivity to a whole spectrum of minute feelings, sensations, and states of consciousness that have no
corresponding words. The experience that is of special interest to her is the ineffable multifaceted quality of the single moment. "Porcupine Fish," translated
by Robert Friend (1977), explores the tension between the need to show bravado
and feelings of vulnerability.

Apparently a fish like you and me.
But there is something nail-like about him.

Slowly he glides,
examining himself in that great mirror called water
and asking why,
why these nails planted in his flesh,
why this need for endless wariness
that sharpens him, keeps him from being one
with the blue enfolding softness.

And then
the waters breathe,
something moves,
something alien perhaps,
certainly malign.
His spines bristle.
He turns into something else—
a swollen ball,
a small mountain of fear—
all roar, if one could hear.

His mouth—small, tight, rectangular—   20
distorts into a smile.
And his eyes, tiny pools in a suddenly vast forehead,
whirl violent images in his brain.

This time, however,
it was nothing really.   25

And he subsides
into the rigid destiny
of his nail-like self.

Questions for Discussion and Writing

1. What details effectively suggest a sense of a menacing environment? How does Chalfi's use of DICTION and FIGURATIVE LANGUAGE enhance your awareness of the unusual features the porcupine fish possesses to scare off would-be predators?

2. How does PERSONIFICATION of the porcupine fish enhance a sense of psychological realism and create a distinctive TONE?

3. To what extent might this poem refer to the geographical location and HISTORICAL CONTEXT in which Israelis find themselves in relation to their Arab neighbors?

4. To what extent is the poem built around the contrast between the normal state of the porcupine fish and the warlike appearance it adopts to ward off would-be predators?

5. Describe an object, animal, or natural force, using metaphor or similes, but in the form of a riddle, without telling the reader what the answer is. Your description should use active verbs that help your readers imagine the answer to the riddle.

6. Create a word portrait of an animal that is most like you, telling how it moves, sounds, and looks. Then provide an inside portrait of its thoughts and feelings in a first-person monologue.

Pablo Neruda

Goodbyes

Pablo Neruda was born in Parral, a central Chilean town, in 1904, the son of a railroad worker and a schoolteacher who died a month after his birth. His father's second wife assumed the role of mother. The family soon moved to Temuco, in the forest south of Chile, a setting that would give the future poet a wealth of symbolic natural imagery. While studying to be a French teacher, he began to show literary talent and his first published books date from the early 1920s. He began his long career as a diplomat and was stationed in Burma, Ceylon, and Singapore. After returning to Chile, he continued as consul in Buenos Aires and in Spain until the eruption of the Spanish Civil War. He occupied other consulate posts in Mexico from 1940 to 1943 and then returned to Chile when, in 1945, he was elected a senator. In 1948, the anticommunist government ordered Neruda's arrest and he began a period of exile that lasted until 1952. Neruda was a candidate for president of Chile but withdrew in support of the socialist Salvador Allende. He served as ambassador to France in 1971 and 1972 but had to resign because of failing health. He died in 1973, two years after receiving the Nobel Prize for literature.

Throughout his life, Neruda insisted on the connection between poetry and politics. He is considered to have been one of the greatest modern poets writing in Spanish who gave voice to the hitherto unexpressed aspirations of people in the Third World. He was influenced by such diverse poets as Blake, Rimbaud, Whitman, Tagore, and especially Dario, who imbued him with the concept of the poet as a socially conscious being. In 1932 he published the first part of his collection of poetry, Residence on Earth, which transformed poetry written in the Spanish language with its dynamic fusion of symbolism and surrealism. His poetry in the 1930s reflects his increasingly committed leftist stance. After a trip to Peru, where he visited the ancient ruins of Macchu Picchu, he wrote the inspired Heights of Macchu Picchu (1966). In 1968 he published one of his most popular collections of poems, The General Song, that celebrated the greatness of Latin America's land and history while providing a clarion call for the downtrodden and politically dispossessed, who Neruda saw as carrying the promise of the future. A posthumous collection of his poetry is titled Five Decades, a Selection: Poems 1925–1970 (1974). His poetry, ranging from works on specific political issues to heartfelt love poems and thoughtful meditations, is characterized by emotional associations that build up a composite portrait by a spontaneous synthesis of different moods that reflect the flow of sensation and thought. In this he is reminiscent of Whitman in his capacity for moving, within one poem, over enormous distances by incremental enumeration. "Goodbyes," translated by Alastair Reid, first appeared in Fully Empowered (1975). The poem gives us access to the thoughts of a constant traveler who discovers the need to live within himself wherever he happens to be.

Goodbye, goodbye, to one place or another,
to every mouth, to every sorrow,
to the insolent moon, to weeks
which wound in the days and disappeared,
goodbye to this voice and that one stained   5
with amaranth, and goodbye
to the usual bed and plate,
to the twilit setting of all goodbyes,
to the chair that is part of the same twilight,
to the way made by my shoes.   10

I spread myself, no question;
I turned over whole lives,
changed skin, lamps, and hates,
it was something I had to do,
not by law or whim,   15
more of a chain reaction;
each new journey enchained me;
I took pleasure in place, in all places.

And, newly arrived, I promptly said goodbye
with still newborn tenderness   20
as if the bread were to open and suddenly
flee from the world of the table.
So I left behind all languages,
repeated goodbyes like an old door,
changed cinemas, reasons, and tombs,   25
left everywhere for somewhere else;
I went on being, and being always
half undone with joy,
a bridegroom among sadnesses,
never knowing how or when,   30
ready to return, never returning.

It's well known that he who returns never left,
so I traced and retraced my life,
changing clothes and planets,
growing used to the company,   35
to the great whirl of exile,
to the great solitude of bells tolling.

Questions for Discussion and Writing

1. How does the SPEAKER's readiness to leave each place as he arrives change the way he looks at these places?
2. How does the speaker use the IMAGE of an indelible purple dye made from a

perishable flower to develop the theme of what can be preserved in the experience of being uprooted?

3. In what way does the speaker use the METAPHOR of being a bridegroom to express his mood as he arrives in each new place?

4. Do you agree or disagree with the speaker's assertion that the best attitude to have is never to become identified with any particular place? Have you had the experience of moving from one place to another? How did it affect you psychologically?

5. Write a poem the subject of which is saying goodbye or hello to a friend, love, parent, relative, pet, place, or object.

6. How might the attitude the speaker advocates be characterized as a belief in nonattachment espoused in Hindu and Buddhist philosophy? Do you think it would be possible to develop this attitude and not identify with property and material goods?

Diane Wakoski

The Orange

Diane Wakoski was born in Whittier, California, in 1927. She was educated at the University of California, Berkeley, and settled in New York City in the early 1960s where she worked in a bookstore and taught English in a junior high school until 1969. During this period she wrote and published such volumes as Coins and Coffins *(1962),* The George Washington Poems *(1967), and* Inside the Blood Factory *(1968). Since then she has taught at various universities, given poetry readings, and conducted verse-writing workshops. Volumes of her poetry at this time include* Waiting for the King of Spain *(1976) and* The Man Who Shook Hands *(1978). Her most recent collections include* Emerald Ice: Selected Poems 1962–1987 *(1988), which won the Poetry Society of America's William Carlos Williams Award and* Medea the Sorceress *(1990), in which "The Orange" appears. She is currently writer in residence at Michigan State University. Taken as a whole, Wakoski's poetry projects an imaginary autobiography in which fantastic leaps of the imagination and surrealistic images allow her to reinvent her identity in ways that are typically American. As is typical of poetry of self-transformation, "The Orange" relies on digressions and tangential wanderings through imagery and fantasy to explore the speaker's sensation of freedom from emotional entanglements while driving from Los Angeles to Las Vegas.*

Driving through the desert at night in summer
can be
like peeling an orange,

the windows rolled down, the prickly scent
of mesquite and sage
blowing through the car, the   5
perfume
of the twilight shadowed earth lingering,
as if the sticky juice
of the orange   10
were shading and matting your hands,
the acrid spray of the peel;
with its meaty white pillow
nestles into your fingers.

You are driving from Los Angeles to Las Vegas,   15
running from your loneliness, an empty house,
an ocean which brings neither father nor lover.

For one hour, the wind streams through
your car, a
three-year-old Pontiac you have named Green Greed;   20
for one hour, the scent of all the desert
plants makes you feel
loved, makes you
forget you have no one
to talk to. You do not care about the   25
myth of the West, about
the City of Angels and its beaches.

You are not yet even slightly
interested in
gambling.   30
You are 32
and feel you have a destiny. Somehow
in that car,
on that night, alone on the wind-cooled highway between California
and Nevada, for one hour,   35
the fragrance of sage, especially,
made you complete,
moving swiftly over your face, through
nostrils, the car, you warm,
from desert day fire.   40

You were not even looking
yet, for Beethoven in Las Vegas,
Snake Mother in the desert.
Your life was over, or
had not yet begun. Did you see   45

a map of Michigan filling your hand
as you peeled the big navel orange,
the one which glowed like fireflies
that wink
50   in Michigan summer nights?
The white membrane, the orange raindrop
textured meat of the fruit
saturating your hands with sugar
as you drive, as you drove,
55   as you remembered one
beginning?

Questions for Discussion and Writing

1. From what POINT OF VIEW is the poem written? What details and ALLUSIONS suggest that the poem is written by an older person describing how she was when she was young?
2. What details suggest that the speaker has gained a new perspective because she has found herself between involvements, obligations, and responsibilities?
3. How do tactile and sensory IMAGES associated with a desert environment and the peeling of an orange allow the reader to experience what the speaker feels at this moment?
4. How do references to important figures in history, literature, and music suggest that the speaker's development as a person has been enhanced through these wider CONTEXTS?
5. How does the speaker's emerging sense of a plan to guide her life contrast with the momentary freedom from responsibilities and entanglements she experiences while driving through the desert?
6. Have you ever experienced this momentary sense of freedom when you were between involvements, obligations, and attachments? If so, describe your experience.
7. If you can locate a photograph of yourself taken some time ago, describe the clues that tell you when it might have been taken and how anything in the picture has changed since it was taken, including transportation, landscape, buildings, clothes, advertisements, and so on. Discuss how you are different now from the person you were in the picture.

Mitsuye Yamada

I Learned to Sew

Mitsuye Yamada was born in 1923 in Fukuoka, Japan. Yamada's parents were U.S. residents at the time of her birth but were on a prolonged visit when she was born. She came to the United States in 1926 and became a naturalized citizen in 1955. She was raised in Seattle until the outbreak of World War II, when she and her family were interned at Minidoka Relocation Center in Idaho. She and the Chinese-American poet Nelly Wong were the subjects of a National PBS documentary on Asian-American women. She taught English at Fullerton College, California, from 1966 to 1969 and was a professor of English at Cypress College in southern California from 1969 until she retired in 1991. She is the founder of the Multi-cultural Woman Writers of Orange County and chairperson of the Pacific Asian American Center. She received the Vesta Award in 1982 and was awarded a writer's residency at Yaddo in New York state in 1984. Her first book of poetry, Camp Notes and Other Poems, *was published in 1976. Her most recent volume of poetry is* Desert Run: Poems and Stories *(1988), from which "I Learned to Sew" was taken. Yamada's lifelong search for her cultural heritage makes her writing at once both intensely personal and universal, qualities that can be seen in "I Learned to Sew," a poignant saga of determination in the face of rejection.*

How can I say this?
My child
My life is nothing
There is nothing to tell

My family in Japan was too poor   5
to send me to school
I learned to sew
always I worked to help my family
when I was seventeen years old
and no one made marriage offer   10
a friend in our village who was going
to Hawaii a picture bride
said to me
Come with me.

I did not want to   15
my parents did not want me to
my picture was sent to a stranger anyway
a young man's photograph and letter came
I was already seventeen years old

887

20 I went to the island of Hawaii to marry
this photograph.

This man came to the boat
he was too shy to talk to me
the Immigration man said to him
25 Here
sign here for her
He walked away
The Immigration man came to me
Don't you have relatives in Hawaii?

30 I said
Yes I have that man who will marry me
He said
Go back to Japan on the next boat
I said
35 I will wait here for my man
The Immigration man said
No
your man is not coming back
he told me he does not want you
40 he said you are too ugly for him
why don't you go back to Japan
on the next boat?
I said
No
45 I am not going back
I am staying here

  Just
  A minute
  My child
50 Put that pen down
  Do not write this
  I never told this to anybody
  Not even to my oldest son, your father
  I now tell this story
55 To you first time in sixty years

I sat at Immigration for a long time
people came and people went
I stayed
I could not see the sky
60 I could not see the sun

outside the window
I saw a seaweed forest
the crickets made scraping sounds
the geckos went tuk tuk tuk
sometimes a gecko would come into my room   65
but I was not afraid to talk to it
it came and it went as it pleased.

I was thinking about Urashima Taro
you know the story?
Urashima disappeared into the sea   70
lived in the undersea world
married a beautiful princess
returned to his village
a very old man
I was thinking   75
I will leave this place
only when I am an old lady.

Pretty soon the Immigration man came to me
We found your cousin
In two weeks a cousin I met once   80
in Japan came for me
I stayed with him and his wife until
my cousin found a job for me
I worked doing housework
I did this for one year.   85

My cousin found a husband for me
he was a merchant
we had a small store
and sold dry goods
my husband died after three sons   90
your father, my oldest son, was six years old
I could not keep the store
I could not read
I could not write
the only thing I knew how to do was sew.   95

I took the cloth from our store
sewed pants and undergarments
put the garments on a wooden cart
ombu the baby on my back
we went from plantation to plantation   100
sold my garments to the workers

I was their only store
sewed more garments at night
I did this for five years.

105   Your father grew up to love study and books
my friends called him the professor
he was then eleven years old
I said to him you need a father
He said I want to go to college
110   I said to him I will marry any man you say
I will marry any man
who will send you to college.

One day he came home and said
I went to a matchmaker and
115   found a husband for you
he will marry a widow with three sons
will send them to college
he is a plantation foreman.

I married this man.

120   By and by my oldest son went away
to college in Honolulu
but my husband's boss told him
I need workers
your three sons must work
125   on my plantation like the others.
My husband said
No
He kept his word to my oldest son
and lost his job.

130   After that we had many hard times
I am nothing
know nothing
I only know how to sew
I now sew for my children and grandchildren
135   I turn to the sun every day of my life
pray to Amaterasu Omikami
for the health and
education of my children
for me that is enough

140   My child
Write this

There   take your pen
There   write it
Say that I am not going back
I am staying here

145

Questions for Discussion and Writing

1. How does the choice the speaker confronts as described in the last few lines explain why, after all these years, she is telling her grandaughter the story of her life?

2. How has the speaker's life been determined at crucial points by whom she was supposed to marry and whom she did marry? How would you characterize her relationship with each of her husbands?

3. What information does the poem provide about the SOCIAL CONTEXTS in which the speaker has lived? What kinds of expectations existed for women in Japan at the time she came to the United States?

4. How does learning to sew come to stand for the speaker's ability to survive in a new place, to withstand personal tragedies, and to take care of herself?

5. What is the significance of the speaker's ALLUSION to the mythic figure Amaterasu Omikami? This figure is a female deity in the Shinto religion who, although abandoned, becomes a mighty warrior. In Japanese myths and legends she is connected with the silk worm and the art of spinning silk and sewing.

6. Interview a male and a female relative who overcame obstacles to immigrate to the United States and compare the two accounts.

7. What stories would you tell to your grandchildren about your adolescence or childhood?

David Henry Hwang

The Dance and the Railroad

<hr/>

*David Henry Hwang was born in 1957 in Los Angeles, educated at Stanford
(B.A. 1979), and attended Yale University School of Drama from 1980 to 1981.
Hwang gained widespread praise for his first play, F.O.B. (fresh off the boat)
(1980), which developed out of a playwriting seminar led by Sam Shepard. In
the process of exploring his identity as a Chinese-American, Hwang became in-
terested in Chinese folklore, history, and myth. Joseph Papp produced F.O.B. in
New York, where it won an OBIE Award as the best new play of the season.
Hwang's next two plays,* The Dance and the Railroad *(1981) and* Family
Devotions *(1981), continue this exploration of Chinese-American history. The*
Dance and the Railroad *evolved out of his collaboration with the actor John
Lone (who starred in* F.O.B. *and who was trained in the traditions of Chinese
opera in Hong Kong). The play attempts to create a cultural fusion of Asian
and Western theater. Hwang gave the characters the names of John Lone and
Tzi Ma, the actors who played the parts. In the play, Hwang portrays two nineteenth-century Chinese men working on the transcontinental railroad. By contrast,* Family Devotions *looks at a well-established Chinese-American family
in the twentieth century. Hwang's 1988 play* M. Butterfly *was based on the
true story of a French diplomat and his Chinese lover, who turned out to be not
only a spy but a man; the play earned a Pulitzer Prize nomination and the
Tony Award. It was heralded for its exploration of East-West relations and the
wider concerns of race, gender, and culture.*

The Dance and the Railroad *is set in California in 1867 at the time of a
strike by Chinese railroad workers and explores the confrontation between a
new arrival, Ma, and Lone, who has been in America for two years. Their conflict sets the image of traditional Chinese culture (the dance) against the counter-
image of working to make one's way in the new world (represented by the railroad).*

CHARACTERS

LONE, twenty years old, ChinaMan railroad worker.
MA, eighteen years old, ChinaMan railroad worker.

PLACE

A mountaintop near the transcontinental railroad.

TIME

June, 1867.

SYNOPSIS OF SCENES

Scene One. Afternoon.
Scene Two. Afternoon, a day later.
Scene Three. Late afternoon, four days later.
Scene Four. Late that night.
Scene Five. Just before the following dawn.

SCENE ONE

A mountaintop. LONE *is practicing opera steps. He swings his pigtail around like a fan.* MA *enters, cautiously, watches from a hidden spot.* MA *approaches* LONE.

LONE: So, there are insects hiding in the bushes.
MA: Hey, listen, we haven't met, but—
LONE: I don't spend time with insects.

(LONE *whips his hair into* MA's *face;* MA *backs off;* LONE *pursues him, swiping at* MA *with his hair*)

MA: What the—? Cut it out!

(MA *pushes* LONE *away*)

LONE: Don't push me.
MA: What was that for?
LONE: Don't ever push me again.
MA: You mess like that, you're gonna get pushed.
LONE: Don't push me.
MA: You started it. I just wanted to watch.
LONE: You "just wanted to watch." Did you ask my permission?
MA: What?
LONE: Did you?
MA: C'mon.

LONE: You can't expect to get in for free.

MA: Listen. I got some stuff you'll wanna hear.

LONE: You think so?

MA: Yeah. Some advice.

LONE: Advice? How old are you, anyway?

MA: Eighteen.

LONE: A child.

MA: Yeah. Right. A child. But listen—

LONE: A child who tries to advise a grown man—

MA: Listen, you got this kind of attitude.

LONE: —is a child who will never grow up.

MA: You know, the ChinaMen down at camp, they can't stand it.

LONE: Oh?

MA: Yeah. You gotta watch yourself. You know what they say? They call you "Prince of the Mountain." Like you're too good to spend time with them.

LONE: Perceptive of them.

MA: After all, you never sing songs, never tell stories. They say you act like your spit is too clean for them, and they got ways to fix that.

LONE: Is that so?

MA: Like they're gonna bury you in the shit buckets, so you'll have more to clean than your nails.

LONE: But I don't shit.

MA: Or they're gonna cut out your tongue, since you never speak to them.

LONE: There's no one here worth talking to.

MA: Cut it out, Lone. Look, I'm trying to help you, all right? I got a solution.

LONE: So young yet so clever.

MA: That stuff you're doing—it's beautiful. Why don't you do it for the guys at camp? Help us celebrate?

LONE: What will "this stuff" help celebrate?

MA: C'mon. The strike, of course. Guys on a railroad gang, we gotta stick together, you know.

LONE: This is something to celebrate?

MA: Yeah. Yesterday, the weak-kneed ChinaMen, they were running around like chickens without a head: "The white devils are sending their soldiers! Shoot us all!" But now, look—day four, see? Still in one piece. Those soldiers—we've never seen a gun or a bullet.

LONE: So you're all warrior-spirits, huh?

MA: They're scared of us, Lone—that's what it means.

LONE: I appreciate your advice. Tell you what—you go down—

MA: Yeah?

LONE: Down to the camp—

MA: Okay.

LONE: To where the men are—

MA: Yeah?

LONE: Sit there—

MA: Yeah?

LONE: And wait for me.

MA: Okay. (*Pause*) That's it? What do you think I am?

LONE: I think you're an insect interrupting my practice. So fly away. Go home.

MA: Look, I didn't come here to get laughed at.

LONE: No, I suppose you didn't.

MA: So just stay up here. By yourself. You deserve it.

LONE: I do.

MA: And don't expect any more help from me.

LONE: I haven't gotten any yet.

MA: If one day, you wake up and your head is buried in the shit can—

LONE: Yes?

MA: You can't find your body, your tongue is cut out—

LONE: Yes.

MA: Don't worry, 'cuz I'll be there.

LONE: Oh.

MA: To make sure your mother's head is sitting right next to yours.

(MA *exits*)

LONE: His head is too big for this mountain.

(*Returns to practicing*)

SCENE TWO

Mountaintop. Next day. LONE *is practicing.* MA *enters.*

MA: Hey.

LONE: You? Again?

MA: I forgive you.

LONE: You . . . what?

MA: For making fun of me yesterday. I forgive you.

LONE: You can't—

MA: No. Don't thank me.

LONE: You can't forgive me.

MA: No. Don't mention it.

LONE: You—! I never asked for your forgiveness.

MA: I know. That's just the kinda guy I am.

LONE: This is ridiculous. Why don't you leave? Go down to your friends and play soldiers, sing songs, tell stories.

MA: Ah! See? That's just it. I got other ways I wanna spend my time. Will you teach me the opera?

LONE: What?

MA: I wanna learn it. I dreamt about it all last night.

LONE: No.

MA: The dance, the opera—I can do it.

LONE: You think so?

MA: Yeah. When I get outa here, I wanna go back to China and perform.

LONE: You want to become an actor?

MA: Well, I wanna perform.

LONE: Don't you remember the story about the three sons whose parents send them away to learn a trade? After three years, they return.
The first one says, "I have become a coppersmith." The parents say,
"Good. Second son, what have you become?" "I've become a silver-
smith." "Good—and youngest son, what about you?" "I have become an actor." When the parents hear that their son has become
only an actor, they are very sad. The mother beats her head against
the ground until the ground, out of pity, opens up and swallows
her. The father is so angry he can't even speak, and the anger builds
up inside him until it blows his body to pieces—little bits of his skin
are found hanging from trees days later. You don't know how you
endanger your relatives by becoming an actor.

MA: Well, I don't wanna become an "actor." That sounds terrible. I
just wanna perform. Look, I'll be rich by the time I get out of here,
right?

LONE: Oh?

MA: Sure. By the time I go back to China, I'll ride in gold sedan chairs,
with twenty wives fanning me all around.

LONE: Twenty wives? This boy is ambitious.

MA: I'll give out pigs on New Year's and keep a stable of small birds
to give to any woman who pleases me. And in my spare time, I'll
perform.

LONE: Between your twenty wives and your birds, where will you
find a free moment?

MA: I'll play Gwan Gung and tell stories of what life was like on the
Gold Mountain.

LONE: Ma, just how long have you been in "America"?

MA: Huh? About four weeks.

LONE: You are a big dreamer.

MA: Well, all us ChinaMen here are—right? Men with little dreams—
have little brains to match. They walk with their eyes down, trying
to find extra grains of rice on the ground.

LONE: So, you know all about "America"? Tell me, what kind of stories will you tell?

MA: I'll say, "We laid tracks like soldiers. Mountains? We hung from
cliffs in baskets and the winds blew us like birds. Snow? We lived
underground like moles for days at a time. Deserts? We—"

LONE: Wait. Wait. How do you know these things after only four weeks?

MA: They told me—the other ChinaMen on the gang. We've been telling stories ever since the strike began.

LONE: They make it sound like it's very enjoyable.

MA: They said it is.

LONE: Oh? And you believe them?

MA: They're my friends. Living underground in winter—sounds exciting, huh?

LONE: Did they say anything about the cold?

MA: Oh, I already know about that. They told me about the mild winters and the warm snow.

LONE: Warm snow?

MA: When I go home, I'll bring some back to show my brothers.

LONE: Bring some—? On the boat?

MA: They'll be shocked—they never seen American snow before.

LONE: You can't. By the time you get snow to the boat, it'll have melted, evaporated, and returned as rain already.

MA: No.

LONE: No?

MA: Stupid.

LONE: Me?

MA: You been here awhile, haven't you?

LONE: Yes. Two years.

MA: Then how come you're so stupid? This is the Gold Mountain. The snow here doesn't melt. It's not wet.

LONE: That's what they told you?

MA: Yeah. It's true.

LONE: Did anyone show you any of this snow?

MA: No. It's not winter.

LONE: So where does it go?

MA: Huh?

LONE: Where does it go, if it doesn't melt? What happens to it?

MA: The snow? I dunno. I guess it just stays around.

LONE: So where is it? Do you see any?

MA: Here? Well, no, but . . . (*Pause*) This is probably one of those places where it doesn't snow—even in winter.

LONE: Oh.

MA: Anyway, what's the use of me telling you what you already know? Hey, c'mon—teach me some of that stuff. Look—I've been practicing the walk—how's this? (*Demonstrates*)

LONE: You look like a duck in heat.

MA: Hey—it's a start, isn't it?

LONE: Tell you what—you want to play some *die siu*?

MA: *Die siu*? Sure.

LONE: You know, I'm pretty good.

MA: Hey, I play with the guys at camp. You can't be any better than Lee—he's really got it down.

(LONE *pulls out a case with two dice*)

LONE: I used to play till morning.

MA: Hey, us too. We see the sun start to rise, and say, "Hey, if we got to sleep now, we'll never get up for work." So we just keep playing.

LONE (*Holding out dice*): Die or siu?

MA: Siu.

LONE: You sure?

MA: Yeah!

LONE: All right. (*He rolls*) Die!

MA: Siu!

(*They see the result*)

MA: Not bad.

(*They continue taking turns rolling through the following section;* MA *always loses*)

LONE: I haven't touched these in two years.

MA: I gotta practice more.

LONE: Have you lost much money?

MA: Huh? So what?

LONE: Oh, you have gold hidden in all your shirt linings, huh?

MA: Here in "America"—losing is no problem. You know—End of the Year Bonus?

LONE: Oh, right.

MA: After I get that, I'll laugh at what I lost.

LONE: Lee told you there was a bonus, right?

MA: How'd you know?

LONE: When I arrived here, Lee told me there was a bonus, too.

MA: Lee teach you how to play?

LONE: Him? He talked to me a lot.

MA: Look, why don't you come down and start playing with the guys again?

LONE: "The guys."

MA: Before we start playing, Lee uses a stick to write "Kill!" in the dirt.

LONE: You seem to live for your nights with "the guys."

MA: What's life without friends, huh?

LONE: Well, why do *you* think I stopped playing?

MA: Hey, maybe you were the one getting killed, huh?

LONE: What?

MA: Hey, just kidding.

LONE: Who's getting killed here?

MA: Just a joke.

LONE: That's not a joke, it's blasphemy.

MA: Look, obviously you stopped playing 'cause you wanted to practice the opera.

LONE: Do you understand that discipline?

MA: But, I mean, you don't have to overdo it either. You don't have to
treat 'em like dirt. I mean, who are you trying to impress?

(*Pause.* LONE *throws dice into the bushes*)

LONE: Oooops. Better go see who won.

MA: Hey! C'mon! Help me look!

LONE: If you find them, they are yours.

MA: You serious?

LONE: Yes.

MA: Here.

(*Finds the dice*)

LONE: Who won?

MA: I didn't check.

LONE: Well, no matter. Keep the dice. Take them and go play with
your friends.

MA: Here. (*He offers them to* LONE) A present.

LONE: A present? This isn't a present!

MA: They're mine, aren't they? You gave them to me, right?

LONE: Well, yes, but—

MA: So now I'm giving them to you.

LONE: You can't give me a present. I don't want them.

MA: You wanted them enough to keep them two years.

LONE: I'd forgotten I had them.

MA: See, I know, Lone. You wanna get rid of me. But you can't. I'm
paying for lessons.

LONE: With my dice.

MA: Mine now. (*He offers them again*) Here.

(*Pause.* LONE *runs* MA's *hand across his forehead*)

LONE: Feel this.

MA: Hey!

LONE: Pretty wet, huh?

MA: Big deal.

LONE: Well, it's not from playing *die siu*.

MA: I know how to sweat. I wouldn't be here if I didn't.

LONE: Yes, but are you willing to sweat after you've finished sweating? Are you willing to come up after you've spent the whole day chipping half an inch off a rock, and punish your body some more?

MA: Yeah. Even after work, I still—

LONE: No, you don't. You want to gamble, and tell dirty stories, and dress up like women to do shows.

MA: Hey, I never did that.

LONE: You've only been here a month. (*Pause*) And what about "the guys"? They're not going to treat you so well once you stop playing with them. Are you willing to work all day listening to them whisper, "That one—let's put spiders in his soup"?

MA: They won't do that to me. With you, it's different.

LONE: Is it?

MA: You don't have to act that way.

LONE: What way?

MA: Like you're so much better than them.

LONE: No. You haven't even begun to understand. To practice every day, you must have a fear to force you up here.

MA: A fear? No—it's 'cause what you're doing is beautiful.

LONE: No.

MA: I've seen it.

LONE: It's ugly to practice when the mountain has turned your muscles to ice. When my body hurts too much to come here, I look at the other ChinaMen and think, "They are dead. Their muscles work only because the white man forces them. I live because I can still force my muscles to work for me." Say it. "They are dead."

MA: No. They're my friends.

LONE: Well, then, take your dice down to your friends.

MA: But I want to learn—

LONE: This is your first lesson.

MA: Look, it shouldn't matter—

LONE: It does.

MA: It shouldn't matter what I think.

LONE: Attitude is everything.

MA: But as long as I come up, do the exercises—

LONE: I'm not going to waste time on a quitter.

MA: I'm not!

LONE: Then say it.—"They are dead men."

MA: I can't.

LONE: Then you will never have the dedication.

MA: That doesn't prove anything.

LONE: I will not teach a dead man.

MA: What?

LONE: If you can't see it, then you're dead too.

MA: Don't start pinning—

LONE: Say it!

MA: All right.
LONE: What?
MA: All right. I'm one of them. I'm a dead man too.

(*Pause*)

LONE: I thought as much. So, go. You have your friends.
MA: But I don't have a teacher.
LONE: I don't think you need both.
MA: Are you sure?
LONE: I'm being questioned by a child.

(LONE *returns to practicing. Silence*)

MA: Look, Lone, I'll come up here every night—after work—I'll spend my time practicing, okay? (*Pause*) But I'm not gonna say that they're dead. Look at them. They're on strike; dead men don't go on strike, Lone. The white devils—they try and stick us with a ten-hour day. We want a return to eight hours and also a fourteen-dollar-a-month raise. I learned the demon English—listen: "Eight hour a day good for white man, all same good for ChinaMan." These are the demands of live ChinaMen, Lone. Dead men don't complain.
LONE: All right, this is something new. No one can judge the ChinaMen till after the strike.
MA: They say we'll hold out for months if we have to. The smart men will live on what we've hoarded.
LONE: A ChinaMan's mouth can swallow the earth. (*He takes the dice*) While the strike is on, I'll teach you.
MA: And afterwards?
LONE: Afterwards—we'll decide then whether these are dead or live men.
MA: When can we start?
LONE: We've already begun. Give me your hand.

SCENE THREE

LONE *and* MA *are doing physical exercises.*

MA: How long will it be before I can play Gwan Gung?
LONE: How long before a dog can play the violin?
MA: Old Ah Hong—have you heard him play the violin?
LONE: Yes. Now, he should take his violin and give it to a dog.
MA: I think he sounds okay.
LONE: I think he caused that avalanche last winter.
MA: He used to play for weddings back home.
LONE: Ah Hong?
MA: That's what he said.

LONE: You probably heard wrong.

MA: No.

LONE: He probably said he played for funerals.

MA: He's been playing for the guys down at camp.

LONE: He should play for the white devils—that will end this stupid strike.

MA: Yang told me for sure—it'll be over by tomorrow.

LONE: Eight days already. And Yang doesn't know anything.

MA: He said they're already down to an eight-hour day and five-dollar raise at the bargaining sessions.

LONE: Yang eats too much opium.

MA: That doesn't mean he's wrong about this.

LONE: You can't trust him. One time—last year—he went around camp looking in everybody's eyes and saying, "Your nails are too long. They're hurting my eyes." This went on for a week. Finally, all the men clipped their nails, made a big pile, which they wrapped in leaves and gave to him. Yang used the nails to season his food—he put it in his soup, sprinkled it on his rice, and never said a word about it again. Now tell me—are you going to trust a man who eats other men's fingernails?

MA: Well, all I know is we won't go back to work until they meet all our demands. Listen, teach me some Gwan Gung steps.

LONE: I should have expected this. A boy who wants to have twenty wives is the type who demands more than he can handle.

MA: Just a few.

LONE: It takes years before an actor can play Gwan Gung.

MA: I can do it. I spend a lot of time watching the opera when it comes around. Every time I see Gwan Gung, I say, "Yeah. that's me. The god of fighters. The god of adventurers. We have the same kind of spirit."

LONE: I tell you, if you work very hard, when you return to China, you can perhaps be the Second Clown.

MA: Second Clown?

LONE: If you work hard.

MA: What's the Second Clown?

LONE: You can play the *p'i p'a*, and dance and jump all over.

MA: I'll buy them.

LONE: Excuse me?

MA: I'm going to be rich, remember? I'll buy a troupe and force them to let me play Gwan Gung.

LONE: I hope you have enough money, then, to pay audiences to sit through your show.

MA: You mean, I'm going to have to practice here every night—and in return, all I can play is the Second Clown?

LONE: If you work hard.

MA: Am I that bad? Maybe I shouldn't even try to do this. Maybe I
should just go down.

LONE: It's not you. Everyone must earn the right to play Gwan Gung.
I entered opera school when I was ten years old. My parents decided to sell me for ten years to this opera company. I lived with
eighty other boys and we slept in bunks four beds high and hid our
candy and rice cakes from each other. After eight years, I was studying to play Gwan Gung.

MA: Eight years?

LONE: I was one of the best in my class. One day, I was summoned by
my master, who told me I was to go home for two days because my
mother had fallen very ill and was dying. When I arrived home,
Mother was standing at the door waiting, not sick at all. Her first
words to me, the son away for eight years, were, "You've been playing while your village has starved. You must go to the Gold
Mountain and work."

MA: And you never returned to school?

LONE: I went from a room with eighty boys to a ship with three hundred men. So, you see, it does not come easily to play Gwan Gung.

MA: Did you want to play Gwan Gung?

LONE: What a foolish question!

MA: Well, you're better off this way.

LONE: What?

MA: Actors—they don't make much money. Here, you make a bundle, then go back and be an actor again. Best of both worlds.

LONE: "Best of both worlds."

MA: Yeah!

(LONE *drops to the ground, begins imitating a duck, waddling and quacking*)

MA: Lone? What are you doing? (LONE *quacks*) You're a duck? (LONE
quacks) I can see that. (LONE *quacks*) Is this an exercise? Am I supposed to do this? (LONE *quacks*) This is dumb. I never seen Gwan
Gung waddle. (LONE *quacks*) Okay. All right. I'll do it. (MA *and* LONE
quack and waddle) You know, I never realized before how uncomfortable a duck's life is. And you have to listen to yourself quacking all
day. Go crazy! (LONE *stands up straight*) Now, what was that all
about?

LONE: No, no. Stay down there, duck.

MA: What's the—

LONE (*Prompting*):   Quack, quack, quack.

MA: I don't—

LONE: Act your species!

MA: I'm not a duck!

LONE: Nothing worse than a duck that doesn't know his place.
MA: All right. (*Mechanically*) Quack, quack.
LONE: More.
MA: Quack.
LONE: More!
MA: Quack, quack, quack!

(MA *now continues quacking, as* LONE *gives commands*)

LONE: Louder! It's your mating call! Think of your twenty duck wives!
   Good! Louder! Project! More! Don't slow down! Put your tail feathers into it! They can't hear you!

(MA *is now quacking up a storm.* LONE *exits, unnoticed by* MA)

MA: Quack! Quack! Quack! Quack. Quack . . . quack. (*He looks
   around*) Quack . . . quack . . . Lone? . . . Lone? (*He waddles
   around the stage looking*) Lone, where are you? Where'd you go? (*He
   stops, scratches his left leg with his right foot*) C'mon—stop playing
   around. What is this? (LONE *enters as a tiger, unseen by* MA) Look,
   let's call it a day, okay? I'm getting hungry. (MA *turns around, notices*
   LONE *right before* LONE *is to bite him*) Aaaaah! Quack, quack, quack!

(*They face off, in character as animals. Duck-*MA *is terrified*)

LONE: Grrrr!
MA (*As a cry for help*):   Quack, quack, quack!

(LONE *pounces on* MA. *They struggle, in character.* MA *is quacking
madly, eyes tightly closed.* LONE *stands up straight.* MA *continues to quack*)

LONE: Stand up.
MA (*Eyes still closed*):   Quack, quack, quack!
LONE (*Louder*):   Stand up!
MA (*Opening his eyes*):   Oh.
LONE: What are you?
MA: Huh?
LONE: A ChinaMan or a duck?
MA: Huh? Gimme a second to remember.
LONE: You like being a duck?
MA: My feet fell asleep.
LONE: You change forms so easily.
MA: You said to.
LONE: What else could you turn into?
MA: Well, you scared me—sneaking up like that.

LONE: Perhaps a rock. That would be useful. When the men need to rest, they can sit on you.

MA: I got carried away.

LONE: Let's try . . . a locust. Can you become a locust?

MA: No. Let's cut this, okay?

LONE: Here. It's easy. You just have to know how to hop.

MA: You're not gonna get me—

LONE: Like this.

(*He demonstrates*)

MA: Forget it, Lone.

LONE: I'm a locust.

(*He begins jumping toward* MA)

MA: Hey! Get away!

LONE: I devour whole fields.

MA: Stop it.

LONE: I starve babies before they are born.

MA: Hey, look, stop it!

LONE: I cause famines and destroy villages.

MA: I'm warning you! Get away!

LONE: What are you going to do? You can't kill a locust.

MA: You're not a locust.

LONE: You kill one, and another sits on your hand.

MA: Stop following me.

LONE: Locusts always trouble people. If not, we'd feel useless. Now, if you became a locust, too . . .

MA: I'm not going to become a locust.

LONE: Just stick your teeth out!

MA: I'm not gonna be a bug! It's stupid!

LONE: No man who's just been a duck has the right to call anything stupid.

MA: I thought you were trying to teach me something.

LONE: I am. Go ahead.

MA: All right. There. That look right?

LONE: Your legs should be a little lower. Lower! There. That's adequate. So how does it feel to be a locust?

(LONE *gets up*)

MA: I dunno. How long do I have to do this?

LONE: Could you do it for three years?

MA: Three years? Don't be—

LONE: You couldn't, could you? Could you be a duck for that long?

MA: Look, I wasn't born to be either of those.

LONE: Exactly. Well, I wasn't born to work on a railroad, either. "Best of both worlds." How can you be such an insect!

(Pause)

MA: Lone . . .

LONE: Stay down there! Don't move! I've never told anyone my story—the story of my parents' kidnapping me from school. All the time we were crossing the ocean, the last two years here—I've kept my mouth shut. To you, I finally tell it. And all you can say is, "Best of both worlds." You're a bug to me, a locust. You think you understand the dedication one must have to be in the opera? You think it's the same as working on a railroad.

MA: Lone, all I was saying is that you'll go back too, and—

LONE: You're no longer a student of mine.

MA: What?

LONE: You have no dedication.

MA: Lone, I'm sorry.

LONE: Get up.

MA: I'm honored that you told me that.

LONE: Get up.

MA: No.

LONE: No?

MA: I don't want to. I want to talk.

LONE: Well, I've learned from the past. You're stubborn. You don't go. All right. Stay there. If you want to prove to me that you're dedicated, be a locust till morning. I'll go.

MA: Lone, I'm really honored that you told me.

LONE: I'll return in the morning.

(Exits)

MA: Lone? Lone, that's ridiculous. You think I'm gonna stay like this? If you do, you're crazy. Lone? Come back here.

SCENE FOUR

Night. MA, *alone, as a locust.*

MA: Locusts travel in huge swarms, so large that when they cross the sky, they block out the sun, like a storm. Second Uncle—back home—when he was a young man, his whole crop got wiped out by locusts one year. In the famine that followed, Second Uncle lost his eldest son and his second wife—the one he married for love. Even to this day, we look around before saying the word "locust," to make sure Second Uncle is out of hearing range. About eight years ago, my brother and I discovered Second Uncle's cave in back of the stream near our house. We saw him come out of it one day around noon. Later, just before the sun went down, we sneaked in. We only looked once. Inside, there must have been hundreds—maybe five hundred or more—grasshoppers in huge bamboo cages—and around them—stacks of grasshopper legs, grasshopper heads, grasshopper antennae, grasshoppers with one leg, still trying to hop but toppling like trees coughing, grasshoppers wrapped around sharp branches rolling from side to side, grasshoppers legs cut off grasshopper bodies, then tied around grasshoppers and tightened till grasshoppers died. Every conceivable kind of grasshopper in every conceivable stage of life and death, subject to every conceivable grasshopper torture. We ran out quickly, my brother and I—we knew an evil place by the thickness of the air. Now, I think of Second Uncle. How sad that the locusts forced him to take out his agony on innocent grasshoppers. What if Second Uncle could see me now? Would he cut off my legs? He might as well. I can barely feel them. But then again, Second Uncle never tortured actual locusts, just weak grasshoppers.

SCENE FIVE

Night. MA *still as a locust.*

LONE (*Off, singing*):

Hit your hardest
Pound out your tears
The more you try
The more you'll cry
At how little I've moved
And how large I loom
By the time the sun goes down

MA: You look rested.
LONE: Me?
MA: Well, you sound rested.
LONE: No, not at all.
MA: Maybe I'm just comparing you to me.
LONE: I didn't even close my eyes all last night.
MA: Aw, Lone, you didn't have to stay up for me. You coulda just come up here and—
LONE: For you?
MA: —apologized and everything woulda been—
LONE: I didn't stay up for you.
MA: Huh? You didn't?
LONE: No.

MA: Oh. You sure?

LONE: Positive. I was thinking, that's all.

MA: About me?

LONE: Well . . .

MA: Even a little?

LONE: I was thinking about the ChinaMen—and you. Get up, Ma.

MA: Aw, do I have to? I've gotten to know these grasshoppers real
       well.

LONE: Get up. I have a lot to tell you.

MA: What'll they think? They take me in, even though I'm a little
       large, then they find out I'm a human being. I stepped on their kids.
       No trust. Gimme a hand, will you? (LONE *helps* MA *up, but* MA's *legs
       can't support him*) Aw, shit. My legs are coming off.

(*He lies down and tries to straighten them out*)

LONE: I have many surprises. First, you will play Gwan Gung.

MA: My legs will be sent home without me. What'll my family think?
       Come to port to meet me and all they get is two legs.

LONE: Did you hear me?

MA: Hold on. I can't be in agony and listen to Chinese at the same
       time.

LONE: Did you hear my first surprise?

MA: No. I'm too busy screaming.

LONE: I said, you'll play Gwan Gung.

MA: Gwan Gung?

LONE: Yes.

MA: Me?

LONE: Yes.

MA: Without legs?

LONE: What?

MA: That might be good.

LONE: Stop that!

MA: I'll become a legend. Like the blind man who defended Amoy.

LONE: Did you hear?

MA: "The legless man who played Gwan Gung."

LONE: Isn't this what you want? To play Gwan Gung?

MA: No, I just wanna sleep.

LONE: No, you don't. Look. Here. I brought you something.

MA: Food?

LONE: Here. Some rice.

MA: Thanks, Lone. And duck?

LONE: Just a little.

MA: Where'd you get the duck?

LONE: Just bones and skin.

MA: We don't have duck. And the white devils have been blockading
       the food.

LONE: Sing—he had some left over.

MA: Sing? That thief?

LONE: And something to go with it.

MA: What? Lone, where did you find whiskey?

LONE: You know, Sing—he has almost anything.

MA: Yeah. For a price.

LONE: Once, even some thousand-day-old eggs.

MA: He's a thief. That's what they told me.

LONE: Not if you're his friend.

MA: Sing don't have any real friends. Everyone talks about him bein' tied in to the head of the klan in San Francisco. Lone, you didn't have to do this. Here. Have some.

LONE: I had plenty.

MA: Don't gimme that. This cost you plenty, Lone.

LONE: Well, I thought if we were going to celebrate, we should do it as well as we would at home.

MA: Celebrate? What for? Wait.

LONE: Ma, the strike is over.

MA: Shit, I knew it. And we won, right?

LONE: Yes, the ChinaMen have won. They can do more than just talk.

MA: I told you. Didn't I tell you?

LONE: Yes. Yes, you did.

MA: Yang told me it was gonna be done. He said—

LONE: Yes, I remember.

MA: Didn't I tell you? Huh?

LONE: Ma, eat your duck.

MA: Nine days, we civilized the white devils. I knew it. I knew we'd hold out till their ears started twitching. So that's where you got the duck, right? At the celebration?

LONE: No, there wasn't a celebration.

MA: Huh? You sure? ChinaMen—they look for any excuse to party.

LONE: But I thought *we* should celebrate.

MA: Well, that's for sure.

LONE: So you will play Gwan Gung.

MA: God, nine days. Shit, it's finally done. Well, we'll show them how to party. Make noise. Jump off rocks. Make the mountain shake.

LONE: We'll wash your body, to prepare you for the role.

MA: What role?

LONE: Gwan Gung. I've been telling you.

MA: I don't wanna play Gwan Gung.

LONE: You've shown the dedication required to become my student, so—

MA: Lone, you think I stayed up last night 'cause I wanted to play Gwan Gung?

LONE: You said you were like him.

MA: I am. Gwan Gung stayed up all night once to prove his loyalty.

Well, now I have too. Lone, I'm honored that you told me your story.

LONE: Yes . . . That is like Gwan Gung.

MA: Good. So let's do an opera about *me*.

LONE: What?

MA: You wanna party or what?

LONE: About you?

MA: You said I was like Gwan Gung, didn't you?

LONE: Yes, but—

MA: Well, look at the operas he's got. I ain't even got one.

LONE: Still, you can't—

MA: You tell me, is that fair?

LONE: You can't do an opera about yourself.

MA: I just won a victory, didn't I? I deserve an opera in my honor.

LONE: But it's not traditional.

MA: Traditional? Lone, you gotta figure any way I could do Gwan Gung wasn't gonna be traditional anyway. I may be as good a guy as him, but he's a better dancer. (*Sings*)

Old Gwan Gung, just sits about
Till the dime-store fighters have had it out
Then he pitches his peach pit
Combs his beard
Draws his sword
And they scatter in fear

LONE: What are you talking about?

MA: I just won a great victory. I get—whatcha call it?—poetic license. C'mon. Hit the gongs. I'll immortalize my story.

LONE: I refuse. This goes against all my training. I try and give you your wish and—

MA: Do it. Gimme my wish. Hit the gongs.

LONE: I never—I can't.

MA: Can't what? Don't think I'm worth an opera? No, I guess not. I forgot—you think I'm just one of those dead men.

(*Silence.* LONE *pulls out a gong.* MA *gets into position.* LONE *hits the gong. They do the following in a mock-Chinese-opera style*)

MA: I am Ma. Yesterday, I was kicked out of my house by my three elder brothers, calling me the lazy dreamer of the family. I am sitting here in front of the temple trying to decide how I will avenge this indignity. Here comes the poorest beggar in this village. (*He cues* LONE) He is called Fleaman because his body is the most popular meeting place for fleas from around the province.

LONE (*Singing*):

> Fleas in love,
> Find your happiness
> In the gray scraps of my suit

MA: Hello, Flea—
LONE (*Continuing*):

> Fleas in need,
> Shield your families
> In the gray hairs of my beard

MA: Hello, Flea—

(LONE *cuts* MA *off, continues an extended improvised aria*)

MA: Hello, Fleaman.
LONE: Hello, Ma. Are you interested in providing a home for these fleas?
MA: No!
LONE: This couple here—seeking to start a new home. Housing today is so hard to find. How about your left arm?
MA: I may have plenty of my own fleas in time. I have been thrown out by my elder brothers.
LONE: Are you seeking revenge? A flea epidemic on your house? (*To a flea*) Get back there. You should be asleep. Your mother will worry.
MA: Nothing would make my brothers angrier than seeing me rich.
LONE: Rich? After the bad crops of the last three years, even the fleas are thinking of moving north.
MA: I heard a white devil talk yesterday.
LONE: Oh—with hair the color of a sick chicken and eyes round as eggs? The fleas and I call him Chicken-Laying-an-Egg.
MA: He said we can make our fortunes on the Gold Mountain, where work is play and the sun scares off snow.
LONE: Don't listen to chicken-brains.
MA: Why not? He said gold grows like weeds.
LONE: I have heard that it is slavery.
MA: Slavery? What do you know, Fleaman? Who told you? The fleas? Yes, I will go to Gold Mountain.

(*Gongs.* MA *strikes a submissive pose to* LONE)

LONE: "The one hundred twenty-five dollars passage money is to be paid to the said head of said Hong, who will make arrangements with the coolies, that their wages shall be deducted until the debt is absorbed."

(MA *bows to* LONE. *Gongs. They pick up fighting sticks and do a water-crossing dance. Dance ends. They stoop next to each other and rock*)

MA: I have been in the bottom of this boat for thirty-six days now. Tang, how many have died?
LONE: Not me. I'll live through this ride.
MA: I didn't ask how you are.
LONE: But why's the Gold Mountain so far?
MA: We left with three hundred and three.
LONE: My family's depending on me.
MA: So tell me, how many have died?
LONE: I'll be the last one alive.
MA: That's not what I wanted to know.
LONE: I'll find some fresh air in this hole.
MA: I asked, how many have died.
LONE: Is that a crack in the side?
MA: Are you listening to me?
LONE: If I had some air—
MA: I asked, don't you see—?
LONE: The crack—over there—
MA: Will you answer me, please?
LONE: I need to get out.
MA: The rest here agree—
LONE: I can't stand the smell.
MA: That a hundred eighty—
LONE: I can't see the air—
MA: Of us will not see—
LONE: And I can't die.
MA: Our Gold Mountain dream.

(LONE/TANG *dies;* MA *throws his body overboard. The boat docks.* MA *exits, walks through the streets. He picks up one of the fighting sticks, while* LONE *becomes the mountain*)

MA: I have been given my pickax. Now I will attack the mountain.

(MA *does a dance of labor.* LONE *sings*)

LONE:

Hit your hardest
Pound out your tears
The more you try
The more you'll cry
At how little I've moved
And how large I loom
By the time the sun goes down

(*Dance stops*)

MA: This mountain is clever. But why shouldn't it be? It's fighting for its life, like we fight for ours.

(*The* MOUNTAIN *picks up a stick.* MA *and the* MOUNTAIN *do a battle dance. Dance ends*)

MA: This mountain not only defends itself—it also attacks. It turns our strength against us.

(LONE *does* MA's *labor dance, while* MA *plants explosives in midair. Dance ends*)

MA: This mountain has survived for millions of years. Its wisdom is immense.

(LONE *and* MA *begin a second battle dance. This one ends with them working the battle sticks together.* LONE *breaks away, does a warrior strut*)

LONE: I am a white devil! Listen to my stupid language: "Wha che doo doo blah blah." Look at my wide eyes—like I have drunk seventy-two pots of tea. Look at my funny hair—twisting, turning, like a snake telling lies. (*To* MA) Bla bla doo doo tee tee.
MA: We don't understand English.
LONE (*Angry*): Bla bla doo doo tee tee!
MA (*With Chinese accent*): Please you-ah speak-ah Chinese?
LONE: Oh. Work—uh—one—two—more—work—two—
MA: Two hours more? Stupid demons. As confused as your hair. We will strike!

(*Gongs.* MA *is on strike*)

MA (*In broken English*): Eight hours day good for white man, all same good for ChinaMan.
LONE: The strike is over! We've won!
MA: I knew we would.
LONE: We forced the white devil to act civilized.
MA: Tamed the barbarians!
LONE: Did you think—
MA: Who woulda thought?
LONE: —it could be done?
MA: Who?
LONE: But who?
MA: Who could tame them?
MA *and* LONE: Only a ChinaMan!

(*They laugh*)

LONE: Well, c'mon.
MA: Let's celebrate!
LONE: We have.
MA: Oh.
LONE: Back to work.
MA: But we've won the strike.
LONE: I know. Congratulations! And now—
MA: —back to work?
LONE: Right.
MA: No.
LONE: But the strike is over.

(LONE *tosses* MA *a stick. They resume their stick battle as before, but* MA *is heard over* LONE's *singing*)

LONE:	MA:
Hit your hardest	Wait.
Pound out your	I'm tired of this!
tears	How do we end it?
The more you try	Let's stop now, all
The more you'll cry	right?
At how little I've	Look, I said enough!
moved	
And how large I	
loom	
By the time the	
sun goes down.	

(MA *tosses his stick away, but* LONE *is already aiming a blow toward it, so that* LONE *hits* MA *instead and knocks him down*)

MA: Oh! Shit . . .
LONE: I'm sorry! Are you all right?
MA: Yeah. I guess.
LONE: Why'd you let go? You can't just do that.
MA: I'm bleeding.
LONE: That was stupid—where?
MA: Here.
LONE: No.
MA: Ow!
LONE: There will probably be a bump.
MA: I dunno.
LONE: What?

MA: I dunno why I let go.

LONE: It was stupid.

MA: But how were we going to end the opera?

LONE: Here. (*He applies whiskey to* MA's *bruise*) I don't know.

MA: Why didn't we just end it with the celebration? Ow! Careful.

LONE: Sorry. But Ma, the celebration's not the end. We're returning to work. Today. At dawn.

MA: What?

LONE: We've already lost nine days of work. But we got eight hours.

MA: Today? That's terrible.

LONE: What do you think we're here for? But they listened to our demands. We're getting a raise.

MA: Right. Fourteen dollars.

LONE: No. Eight.

MA: What?

LONE: We had to compromise. We got an eight-dollar raise.

MA: But we wanted fourteen. Why didn't we get fourteen?

LONE: It was the best deal they could get. Congratulations.

MA: Congratulations? Look, Lone, I'm sick of you making fun of the ChinaMen.

LONE: Ma, I'm not. For the first time. I was wrong. We got eight dollars.

MA: We wanted fourteen.

LONE: But we got eight hours.

MA: We'll go back on strike.

LONE: Why?

MA: We could hold out for months.

LONE: And lose all that work?

MA: But we just gave in.

LONE: You're being ridiculous. We got eight hours. Besides, it's already been decided.

MA: I didn't decide. I wasn't there. You made me stay up here.

LONE: The heads of the gangs decide.

MA: And that's it?

LONE: It's done.

MA: Back to work? That's what they decided? Lone, I don't want to go back to work.

LONE: Who does?

MA: I forgot what it's like.

LONE: You'll pick up the technique again soon enough.

MA: I mean, what it's like to have them telling you what to do all the time. Using up your strength.

LONE: I thought you said even after work, you still feel good.

MA: Some days. But others . . . (*Pause*) I get so frustrated sometimes. At the rock. The rock doesn't give in. It's not human. I wanna claw it with my fingers, but that would just rip them up. I wanna throw myself head first onto it, but it'd just knock my skull open. The rock would knock my skull open, then just sit there, still, like nothing had happened, like a faceless Buddha. (*Pause*) Lone, when do I get out of here?

LONE: Well, the railroad may get finished—

MA: It'll never get finished.

LONE: —or you may get rich.

MA: Rich. Right. This is the Gold Mountain. (*Pause*) Lone, has anyone ever gone home rich from here?

LONE: Yes. Some.

MA: But most?

LONE: Most . . . do go home.

MA: Do you still have the fear?

LONE: The fear?

MA: That you'll become like them—dead men?

LONE: Maybe I was wrong about them.

MA: Well, I do. You wanted me to say it before. I can say it now: "They are dead men." Their greatest accomplishment was to win a strike that's gotten us nothing.

LONE: They're sending money home.

MA: No.

LONE: It's not much, I know, but it's something.

MA: Lone, I'm not even doing that. If I don't get rich here, I might as well die here. Let my brothers laugh in peace.

LONE: Ma, you're too soft to get rich here, naïve—you believed the snow was warm.

MA: I've got to change myself. Toughen up. Take no shit. Count my change. Learn to gamble. Learn to win. Learn to stare. Learn to deny. Learn to look at men with opaque eyes.

LONE: You want to do that?

MA: I will. 'Cause I've got the fear. You've given it to me.

(*Pause*)

LONE: Will I see you here tonight?

MA: Tonight?

LONE: I just thought I'd ask.

MA: I'm sorry, Lone. I haven't got time to be the Second Clown.

LONE: I thought you might not.

MA: Sorry.

LONE: You could have been a . . . fair actor.

MA: You coming down? I gotta get ready for work. This is gonna be a terrible day. My legs are sore and my arms are outa practice.

LONE: You go first. I'm going to practice some before work. There's still time.

MA: Practice? But you said you lost your fear. And you said that's what brings you up here.

LONE: I guess I was wrong about that, too. Today, I am dancing for no reason at all.

MA: Do whatever you want. See you down at camp.

LONE: Could you do me a favor?

MA: A favor?

LONE: Could you take this down so I don't have to take it all?

(LONE *points to a pile of props*)

MA: Well, okay. (*Pause*) But this is the last time.

LONE: Of course, Ma. (MA *exits*) See you soon. The last time. I suppose so.

(LONE *resumes practicing. He twirls his hair around as in the beginning of the play. The sun begins to rise. It continues rising until* LONE *is moving and seen only in shadow*)

Questions for Discussion and Writing

1. Under what circumstances has Ma come up the mountain to visit Lone?

2. How are Ma and Lone characterized in relationship to each other? What circumstances have led each to journey to the United States? What expectations does each have?

3. How does Ma's naïveté about working conditions in the United States define him as a newcomer and serve as a source of humor?

4. How do ALLUSIONS to the Chinese opera evoke traditional LITERARY and CULTURAL CONTEXTS? How does Lone's continuing desire to master this form of art in his new environment define him as someone quite different from Ma?

5. How does the railroad serve as a contrasting image representing making one's way in a new land even at the cost of losing touch with traditional Chinese culture?

6. How does the play develop as a personalized drama between these two conflicting value systems?

7. How does the dance Ma and Lone perform in which they take on the parts of the mountain, fleas, and other characters, provide insight into the HISTORICAL CONTEXT of the time? What insight does the play offer into the actual conditions Chinese immigrants endured in emigrating to the United States and into the dangerous working conditions they were forced to confront?

8. How do the various creatures and insects referred to in the course of the play comment on the human characters?

9. By the end of the play, how have Ma and Lone changed in relationship to each other? Why is it significant that Ma no longer aspires to play the lead role in the opera and why is it equally significant that Lone has decided to come down off the mountain?

10. In a short essay, discuss how the play offers insight into the problems an artist moving from one culture into another might face.
11. If you are familiar with the story of any group of immigrants, discuss how the play reflects the choices immigrants face between maintaining aspects of their traditional culture and assimilating into the new culture.
12. Describe or imagine what it was like at the time your forebears immigrated to the United States.
13. What Lone and Ma say to each other has a great effect on how each character feels about himself. What is the most effective (negative or positive) thing someone has said to you in the last few years? In what context were the words spoken? Why did the words have so much meaning for you? How did they make you feel?

Milcha Sanchez-Scott
The Cuban Swimmer

Milcha Sanchez-Scott was born in Bali in 1955 to a mother of Indonesian, Chinese, and Dutch heritage and a Colombian father. She emigrated with her family when she was a teenager to La Jolla, California, and currently lives in Los Angeles. Sanchez-Scott's first play, Latina, was premiered by L.A. Theatre Works in 1980 and received seven Drama-Logue Awards. Two one-act plays, Dog Lady and The Cuban Swimmer, were written during the next two years and were developed as a special project of L.A. Theatre Works in 1982. In 1983, Sanchez-Scott won the Vesta Award, given each year to a West Coast woman artist, and in 1983 and 1984 she was a member of INTAR's Hispanic Playwrights in Residence Laboratory, directed by Maria Irene Fornes. Her first full-length play, Roosters, was produced in Los Angeles in 1987. She is also the author of Evening Star (1988) and The Architect Piece (1991). The Cuban Swimmer presents an empathetic and imaginative account of how a family that has fled Cuba to live in the United States confronts a unique challenge. Sanchez-Scott is unusually skilled in paralleling the long-standing personal and cultural conflicts the Suárez family must resolve with the physical and psychological obstacles that Margarita must overcome as she attempts to swim the channel between San Pedro and Catalina Island off the California coast.

CHARACTERS

MARGARITA SUÁREZ, the swimmer
EDUARDO SUÁREZ, her father, the coach
SIMÓN SUÁREZ, her brother
AÍDA SUÁREZ, her mother
ABUELA, her grandmother
VOICE OF MEL MUNSON
VOICE OF MARY BETH WHITE
VOICE OF RADIO OPERATOR

Live conga drums can be used to punctuate the action of the play.

TIME

Summer.

PLACE

The Pacific Ocean between San Pedro and Catalina Island.

SCENE ONE

Pacific Ocean. Midday. On the horizon, in perspective, a small boat enters
U.L., crosses to U.R. and exits. Pause. Lower on the horizon, the same boat, in
larger perspective, enters U.R., crosses and exits U.L. Blackout.

SCENE TWO

Pacific Ocean. Midday. The swimmer, Margarita Suárez, is swimming. On
the boat following behind her are her father, Eduardo Suárez, holding a mega-
phone, and Simón, her brother, sitting on top of the cabin with his shirt off,
punk sunglasses on, binoculars hanging on his chest.

EDUARDO (*Leaning forward, shouting in time to Margarita's swimming.*):
    Uno, dos, uno, dos. Y uno, dos . . . keep your shoulders parallel to
    the water.
SIMÓN: I'm gonna take these glasses off and look straight into the sun.
EDUARDO (*Through megaphone.*):   *Muy bien, muy bien* . . . but punch
    those arms in, baby.
SIMÓN (*Looking directly at the sun through binoculars.*):   Come on, come
    on, zap me. Show me something. (*He looks behind at the shoreline and
    ahead at the sea.*) Stop! Stop, Papi! Stop! (*Aída Suárez and Abuela, the
    swimmer's mother and grandmother, enter running from the back of the
    boat.*)
AÍDA *and* ABUELA: *Qué? Qué es?*
AÍDA: *Es un* shark?
EDUARDO: Eh?
ABUELA: *Que es un* shark *dicen?* (*Eduardo blows whistle. Margarita looks
    up at the boat.*)
SIMÓN: No, Papi, no shark, no shark. We've reached the halfway
    mark.
ABUELA (*Looking into the water.*):   *A dónde está?*
AÍDA: It's not in the water.
ABUELA: Oh no? Oh no?
AÍDA: No! *A poco* do you think they're gonna have signs in the water
    to say you are halfway to Santa Catalina? No. It's done very scien-
    tific. *A ver, hijo,* explain it to your grandma.
SIMÓN: Well, you see Abuela—(*He points behind.*) There's San Pedro.
    (*He points ahead.*) And there's Santa Catalina. Looks halfway to me.
    (*Abuela shakes her head and is looking back and forth, trying to make the
    decision, when suddenly the sound of a helicopter is heard.*)
ABUELA (*Looking up.*):   *Virgencita de la Caridad del Cobre. Qué es eso?*
    (*Sound of helicopter gets closer. Margarita looks up.*)
MARGARITA: Papi, Papi! (*A small commotion on the boat, with everybody
    pointing at the helicopter above. Shadows of the helicopter fall on the boat.
    Simón looks up at it through binoculars.*) Papi—*qué es?* What is it?
EDUARDO (*Through megaphone.*):   Uh . . . uh . . . uh *un momentico* . . .
    mi hija. . . . Your papi's got everything under control, understand?

Uh . . . you just keep stroking. And stay . . . uh . . . close to the boat.

SIMÓN: Wow, Papi! We're on TV man! Holy Christ, we're all over the fucking U.S.A.! It's Mel Munson and Mary Beth White!

AÍDA: *Por Dios*! Simón, don't swear. And put on your shirt. (*Aída fluffs her hair, puts on her sunglasses and waves to the helicopter. Simón leans over the side of the boat and yells to Margarita.*)

SIMÓN: Yo, Margo! You're on TV, man.

EDUARDO: Leave your sister alone. Turn on the radio.

MARGARITA: Papi! *Qué está pasando?*

ABUELA: *Que es la televisión dicen?* (*She shakes her head.*) *Porque como yo no puedo ver nada sin mis espejuelos.* (*Abuela rummages through the boat, looking for her glasses. Voices of Mel Munson and Mary Beth White are heard over the boat's radio.*)

MEL'S VOICE: As we take a closer look at the gallant crew of La Havana . . . and there . . . yes, there she is . . . the little Cuban swimmer from Long Beach, California, nineteen-year-old Margarita Suárez. The unknown swimmer is our Cinderella entry . . . a bundle of tenacity, battling her way through the choppy, murky waters of the cold Pacific to reach the Island of Romance . . . Santa Catalina . . . where should she be the first to arrive, two thousand dollars and a gold cup will be waiting for her.

AÍDA: Doesn't even cover our expenses.

ABUELA: *Qué dice?*

EDUARDO: Shhhh!

MARY BETH'S VOICE: This is really a family effort, Mel, and—

MEL'S VOICE: Indeed it is. Her trainer, her coach, her mentor is her father, Eduardo Suárez. Not a swimmer himself, it says here, Mr. Suárez is head usher of the Holy Name Society and the owner-operator of Suárez Treasures of the Sea and Salvage Yard. I guess it's one of those places . . .

MARY BETH'S VOICE: If I might interject a fact here, Mel, assisting in this swim is Mrs. Suárez who is a former Miss Cuba.

MEL'S VOICE: And a beautiful woman in her own right. Let's try and get a closer look. (*Helicopter sound gets louder. Margarita, frightened, looks up again.*)

MARGARITA: Papi!

EDUARDO (*Through megaphone.*):   *Mi hija*, don't get nervous . . . it's the press. I'm handling it.

AÍDA: I see how you're handling it.

EDUARDO (*Through megaphone.*):   Do you hear? Everything is under control. Get back into your rhythm. Keep your elbows high and kick and kick and kick and kick . . .

ABUELA (*Finds her glasses and puts them on.*):   *Ay sí, es la televisión . . .* (*She points to helicopter.*) *Qué lindo mira . . .* (*She fluffs her hair, gives a big wave.*) *Alo América! Viva mi Margarita, viva todo los Cubanos en los Estados Unidos!*

AÍDA: *Ay por Dios*, Cecilia, the man didn't come all this way in his helicopter to look at you jumping up and down, making a fool of yourself.

ABUELA: I don't care. I'm proud.

AÍDA: He can't understand you anyway.

ABUELA: *Viva* . . . (*She stops.*) *Simón, comó se dice viva?*

SIMÓN: Hurray.

ABUELA: Hurray for *mi* Margarita *y* for all the Cubans living *en* the United States, *y un abrazo* . . . Simón, *abrazo* . . .

SIMÓN: A big hug.

ABUELA: *Sí*, a big hug to all my friends in Miami, Long Beach, Union City, except for my son Carlos who lives in New York in sin! He lives . . . (*She crosses herself.*) in Brooklyn with a Puerto Rican woman in sin! *No decente* . . .

SIMÓN: Decent.

ABUELA: Carlos, *no decente*. This family, *decente*.

AÍDA: Cecilia, *por Dios*.

MEL'S VOICE: Look at that enthusiasm. The whole family has turned out to cheer little Margarita on to victory! I hope they won't be too disappointed.

MARY BETH'S VOICE: She seems to be making good time, Mel.

MEL'S VOICE: Yes, it takes all kinds to make a race. And it's a testimonial to the all-encompassing fairness . . . the greatness of this, the Wrigley Invitational Women's Swim to Catalina, where among all the professionals there is still room for the amateurs . . . like these, the simple people we see below us on the ragtag La Havana, taking their long-shot chance to victory. *Vaya con Dios!* (*Helicopter sound fading as family, including Margarita, watch silently. Static as Simón turns radio off. Eduardo walks to bow of boat, looks out on the horizon.*)

EDUARDO (*To himself.*): Amateurs.

AÍDA: Eduardo, that person insulted us. Did you hear, Eduardo? That he called us a simple people in a ragtag boat? Did you hear . . . ?

ABUELA (*Clenching her fist at departing helicopter.*): *Mal-Rayo los parta!*

SIMÓN (*Same gesture.*): Asshole! (*Aída follows Eduardo as he goes to side of boat and stares at Margarita.*)

AÍDA: This person comes in his helicopter to insult your wife, your family, your daughter . . .

MARGARITA (*Pops her head out of the water.*): Papi?

AÍDA: Do you hear me, Eduardo? I am not simple.

ABUELA: *Sí*.

AÍDA: I am complicated.

ABUELA: *Sí, demasiada complicada.*

AÍDA: Me and my family are not so simple.

SIMÓN: Mom, the guy's an asshole.

ABUELA (*Shaking her fist at helicopter.*): Asshole!

AÍDA: If my daughter was simple she would not be in that water swimming.

MARGARITA: Simple? Papi . . . ?

AÍDA: *Ahora*, Eduardo, this is what I want you to do. When we get to Santa Catalina I want you to call the TV station and demand *un* apology.

EDUARDO: *Cállete mujer! Aquí mando yo.* I will decide what is to be done.

MARGARITA: Papi, tell me what's going on.

EDUARDO: Do you understand what I am saying to you, Aída?

SIMÓN (*Leaning over side of boat, to Margarita.*): Yo Margo! You know that Mel Munson guy on TV? He called you a simple amateur and said you didn't have a chance.

ABUELA (*Leaning directly behind Simón.*): *Mi hija, insultó a la familia. Desgraciado!!*

AÍDA (*Leaning in behind Abuela.*): He called us peasants! And your father is not doing anything about it. He just knows how to yell at me.

EDUARDO (*Through megaphone*): Shut up! All of you! Do you want to break her concentration? Is that what you are after? Eh? (*Abuela, Aída and Simón shrink back. Eduardo paces before them.*) Swimming is rhythm and concentration. You win a race *aquí*. (*Pointing to his head.*) Now . . . (*To Simón.*) you, take care of the boat, Aída y Mama . . . do something. Anything. Something practical. (*Abuela and Aída get on knees and pray in Spanish.*) Hija, give it everything, eh? . . . *por la familia. Uno . . . dos . . .* You must win. (*Simón goes into cabin. The prayers continue as lights change to indicate bright sunlight, later in the afternoon.*)

SCENE THREE

Tableau for a couple of beats. Eduardo on bow with timer in one hand as he counts strokes per minute. Simón is in the cabin steering, wearing his sunglasses, baseball cap on backwards. Abuela and Aída are at the side of the boat, heads down, hands folded, still muttering prayers in Spanish.

AÍDA *and* ABUELA (*Crossing themselves.*): *En el nombre del Padre, del Hijo y del Espíritu Santo amén.*

EDUARDO (*Through megaphone.*): You're stroking seventy-two!

SIMÓN (*Singing.*): Mama's stroking, Mama's stroking seventy-two . . .

EDUARDO (*Through megaphone.*): You comfortable with it?

SIMÓN (*Singing*): Seventy-two, seventy-two, seventy-two for you.

AÍDA (*Looking at the heavens.*): Ay, Eduardo, *ven acá,* we should be grateful that *Nuestro Señor* gave us such a beautiful day.

ABUELA (*Crosses herself.*): *Sí, gracias a Dios.*

EDUARDO: She's stroking seventy-two, with no problem. (*He throws a kiss to the sky.*) It's a beautiful day to win.

Aída: *Qué hermoso!* So clear and bright. Not a cloud in the sky. *Mira! Mira!* Even rainbows on the water . . . a sign from God.

Simón (*Singing.*):   Rainbows on the water . . . you in my arms . . .

Abuela and Eduardo (*Looking the wrong way.*):   *Dónde?*

Aída (*Pointing toward Margarita.*):   There, dancing in front of Margarita, leading her on . . .

Eduardo: Rainbows on . . . *Ay coño!* It's an oil slick! You . . . you . . . (*To Simón.*) Stop the boat. (*Runs to bow, yelling.*) Margarita! Margarita! (*On the next stroke, Margarita comes up all covered in black oil.*)

Margarita: Papi! Papi! (*Everybody goes to the side and stares at Margarita, who stares back. Eduardo freezes.*)

Aída: *Apúrate* Eduardo, move . . . what's wrong with you . . . *no me oíste,* get my daughter out of the water.

Eduardo (*Softly.*):   We can't touch her. If we touch her, she's disqualified.

Aída: But I'm her mother.

Eduardo: Not even by her own mother. Especially by her own mother. . . . You always want the rules to be different for you, you always want to be the exception. (*To Simón*) And you . . . you didn't see it, eh? You were playing again?

Simón: Papi, I was watching . . .

Aída (*Interrupting.*):   *Pues,* do something Eduardo. You are the big coach, the monitor.

Simón: Mentor! Mentor!

Eduardo: How can a person think around you? (*He walks off to bow, puts head in hands.*)

Abuela (*Looking over side.*):   *Mira como todos los* little birds are dead. (*She crosses herself.*)

Aída: Their little wings are glues to their sides.

Simón: Christ, this is like the La Brea tar pits.

Aída: They can't move their little wings.

Abuela: *Esa niña tiene que moverse.*

Simón: Yeah Margo, you gotta move, man. (*Abuela and Simón gesture for Margarita to move. Aída gestures for her to swim.*)

Abuela: *Anda niña, muévete.*

Aída: Swim, *hija,* swim or the *aceite* will stick to your wings.

Margarita: Papi?

Abuela (*Taking megaphone.*):   Your papi say "move it!" (*Margarita with difficulty starts moving.*)

Abuela, Aída and Simón (*Laboriously counting.*):   *Uno, dos . . . uno, dos . . . anda . . . uno, dos.*

Eduardo (*Running to take megaphone from Abuela.*):   *Uno, dos . . .* (*Simón races into cabin and starts the engine. Abuela, Aída and Eduardo count together.*)

Simón (*Looking ahead.*):   Papi, it's over there!

EDUARDO: Eh?

SIMÓN (*Pointing ahead and to* R.): It's getting clearer over there.

EDUARDO (*Through megaphone.*): Now pay attention to me. Go to the right. (*Simón, Abuela, Aída and Eduardo all lean over side. They point ahead and to* R., *except Abuela, who points to* R.)

FAMILY (*Shouting together.*): *Para yá! Para yá!* (*Lights go down on boat. A special light on Margarita, swimming through the oil, and on Abuela, watching her.*)

ABUELA: *Sangre de mi sangre,* you will be another to save us. *En Bolondron,* where your great-grandmother Luz Suárez was born, they say one day it rained blood. All the people, they run into their houses. They cry, they pray, *pero* your great-grandmother Luz she had *cojones* like a man. She run outside. She look straight at the sky. She shake her fist. And she say to the evil one, "*Mira* . . . (*Beating her chest.*) *coño, Diablo, aquí estoy si me quieres.*" And she open her mouth, and she drunk the blood.

(*Blackout.*)

SCENE FOUR

Lights up on boat. Aída and Eduardo are on deck watching Margarita swim.

We hear the gentle, rhythmic lap, lap, lap, of the water, then the sound of inhaling and exhaling as Margarita's breathing becomes louder. Then Margarita's heartbeat is heard, with the lapping of the water and the breathing under it. These sounds continue beneath the dialogue to the end of the scene.

AÍDA: *Dios mío.* Look how she moves through the water . . .

EDUARDO: You see, it's very simple. It is a matter of concentration.

AÍDA: The first time I put her in water she came to life, she grew before my eyes. She moved, she smiled, she loved it more than me. She didn't want my breast any longer. She wanted the water.

EDUARDO: And of course, the rhythm. The rhythm takes away the pain and helps the concentration. (*Pause. Aída and Eduardo watch Margarita.*)

AÍDA: Is that my child, or a seal . . .

EDUARDO: Ah a seal, the reason for that is that she's keeping her arms very close to her body. She cups her hands and then she reaches and digs, reaches and digs.

AÍDA: To think that a daughter of mine . . .

EDUARDO: It's the training, the hours in the water. I used to tie weights around her little wrists and ankles.

AÍDA: A spirit, an ocean spirit, must have entered my body when I was carrying her.

EDUARDO (*To Margarita.*): Your stroke is slowing down. (*Pause. We hear Margarita's heartbeat with the breathing under, faster now.*)

AÍDA: Eduardo, that night, the night on the boat . . .

EDUARDO: Ah, the night on the boat again . . . the moon was . . .

AÍDA: The moon was full. We were coming to America. . . . *Qué romantico.* (*Heartbeat and breathing continue.*)

EDUARDO: We were cold, afraid, with no money, and on top of everything, you were hysterical, yelling at me, tearing at me with your nails. (*Opens his shirt, points to the base of his neck.*) Look, I still bear the scars . . . telling me that I didn't know what I was doing . . . saying that we were going to die. . . .

AÍDA: You took me, you stole me from my home . . . you didn't give me a chance to prepare. You just said we have to go now, now! Now, you said. You didn't let me take anything. I left everything behind . . . I left everything behind.

EDUARDO: Saying that I wasn't good enough, that your father didn't raise you so that I could drown you in the sea.

AÍDA: You didn't let me say even a goodbye. You took me, you stole me, you tore me from my home.

EDUARDO: I took you so we could be married.

AÍDA: That was in Miami. But that night on the boat, Eduardo. . . . We were not married, that night on the boat.

EDUARDO: *No pasó nada!* Once and for all get it out of your head, it was cold, you hated me and we were afraid. . . .

AÍDA: *Mentiroso!*

EDUARDO: A man can't do it when he is afraid.

AÍDA: Liar! You did it very well.

EDUARDO: I did?

AÍDA: *Sí.* Gentle. You were so gentle and then strong . . . my passion for you so deep. Standing next to you . . . I would ache . . . looking at your hands I would forget to breathe, you were irresistible.

EDUARDO: I was?

AÍDA: You took me into your arms, you touched my face with your fingertips . . . you kissed my eyes . . . *la esquina de la boca y* . . .

EDUARDO: *Sí, sí,* and then . . .

AÍDA: I look at your face on top of mine, and I see the lights of Havana in your eyes. That's when you seduced me.

EDUARDO: Shhh, they're gonna hear you. (*Lights go down. Special on Aída.*)

AÍDA: That was the night. A woman doesn't forget those things . . . and later that night was the dream . . . the dream of a big country with fields of fertile land and big, giant things growing. And there by a green, slimy pond I found a giant pea pod and when I opened it, it was full of little, tiny baby frogs. (*Aída crosses herself as she watches Margarita. We hear louder breathing and heartbeat.*)

MARGARITA: Santa Teresa. Little Flower of God, pray for me. San Martín de Porres, pray for me. Santa Rosa de Lima, *Virgencita de la Caridad del Cobre*, pray for me. . . . Mother pray for me.

SCENE FIVE

Loud howling of wind is heard, as lights change to indicate unstable weather, fog and mist. Family on deck, braced and huddled against the wind. Simón is at the helm.

AÍDA: *Ay Dios mío, qué viento.*

EDUARDO (*Through megaphone.*): Don't drift out . . . that wind is pushing you out. (*To Simón*) You! Slow down. Can't you see your sister is drifting out?

SIMÓN: It's the wind, Papi.

AÍDA: Baby, don't go so far. . . .

ABUELA (*To heaven.*): *Ay Gran Poder de Dios, quita esta maldito viento.*

SIMÓN: Margo! Margo! Stay close to the boat.

EDUARDO: Dig in. Dig in hard. . . . Reach down from your guts and dig in.

ABUELA (*To heaven.*): *Ay Virgen de la Caridad del Cobre, por lo más tú quieres a pararla.*

AÍDA (*Putting her hand out, reaching for Margarita.*): Baby, don't go far. (*Abuela crosses herself. Action freezes. Lights get dimmer, special on Margarita. She keeps swimming, stops, starts again, stops, then, finally exhausted, stops altogether. The boat stops moving.*)

EDUARDO: What's going on here? Why are we stopping?

SIMÓN: Papi, she's not moving! Yo Margo! (*The family all run to the side.*)

EDUARDO: *Hija!* . . . *Hijita!* You're tired, eh?

AÍDA: *Por supuesto* she's tired. I like to see you get in the water, waving your arms and legs from San Pedro to Santa Catalina. A person isn't a machine, a person has to rest.

SIMÓN: Yo, Mama! Cool out, it ain't fucking brain surgery.

EDUARDO (*To Simón*): Shut up, you. (*Louder to Margarita.*) I guess your mother's right for once, huh? . . . I guess you had to stop, eh? . . . Give your brother, the idiot . . . a chance to catch up with you.

SIMÓN (*Clowning like Mortimer Snerd.*): Dum dee dum dee dum ooops, ah shucks. . . .

EDUARDO: I don't think he's Cuban.

SIMÓN (*Like Ricky Ricardo.*): Oye Lucy! I'm home! Ba ba lu!

EDUARDO (*Joins in clowning, grabbing Simón in a headlock.*): What am I gonna do with this idiot, eh? I don't understand this idiot. He's not like us Margarita. (*Laughing.*) You think if we put him into your bathing suit with a cap on his head . . . (*He laughs hysterically.*) You think anyone would know . . . huh? Do you think anyone would know? (*Laughs.*)

SIMÓN (*Vamping.*): *Ay, mi amor.* Anybody looking for tits would know. (*Eduardo slaps Simón across the face, knocking him down. Aída runs to Simón's aid. Abuela holds Eduardo back.*)

MARGARITA: *Mía culpa! Mía culpa!*

ABUELA: *Quí dices hija?*

MARGARITA: Papi, it's my fault, it's all my fault. . . . I'm so cold, I can't move. . . . I put my face in the water . . . and I hear them whispering . . . laughing at me. . . .

AÍDA: Who is laughing at you?

MARGARITA: The fish are all biting me . . . they hate me . . . they whisper about me. She can't swim, they say. She can't glide. She has no grace. . . . Yellowtails, bonita, tuna, man-o'-war, snub-nose sharks, los baracudas . . . they all hate me . . . only the dolphins care . . . and sometimes I hear the whales crying . . . she is lost, she is dead. I'm so numb, I can't feel. Papi! Papi! Am I dead?

EDUARDO: *Vamos,* baby, punch those arms in. Come on . . . do you hear me?

MARGARITA: Papi . . . Papi . . . forgive me. . . . (*All is silent on the boat. Eduardo drops his megaphone, his head bent down in dejection. Abuela, Aída, Simón all leaning over the side of the boat. Simón slowly walks away.*)

AÍDA: *Mi hija, qué tienes?*

SIMÓN: Oh Christ, don't make her say it. Please don't make her say it.

ABUELA: Say what? *Qué cosa?*

SIMÓN: She wants to quit, can't you see she's had enough?

ABUELA: *Mira, para eso. Esta niña* is turning blue.

AÍDA: *Oyeme, mi hija.* Do you want to come out of the water?

MARGARITA: Papi?

SIMÓN (*To Eduardo.*):   She won't come out until *you* tell her.

AÍDA: Eduardo . . . answer your daughter.

EDUARDO: *Le dije* to concentrate . . . concentrate on your rhythm. Then the rhythm would carry her . . . ay it's a beautiful thing, Aída. It's like yoga, like meditation, the mind over matter . . . the mind controlling the body . . . that's how the great things in the world have been done. I wish you . . . I wish my wife could understand.

MARGARITA: Papi?

SIMÓN (*To Margarita.*):   Forget him.

AÍDA (*Imploring.*):   Eduardo, *por favor.*

EDUARDO (*Walking in circles.*):   Why didn't you let her concentrate? Don't you understand, the concentration, the rhythm is everything. But no, you wouldn't listen. (*Screaming to the ocean.*) Goddam Cubans, why, God, why do you make us go everywhere with our families? (*He goes to back of boat.*)

AÍDA (*Opening her arms.*):   *Mi hija, ven,* come to Mami. (*Rocking.*) Your mami knows. (*Abuela has taken the training bottle, puts it in a net. She and Simón lower it to Margarita.*)

SIMÓN: Take this. Drink it. (*As Margarita drinks, Abuela crosses herself.*)

ABUELA: *Sangre de mi sangre.* (*Music comes up softly. Margarita drinks, gives the bottle back, stretches out her arms, as if on a cross. Floats on her back. She begins a graceful backstroke. Lights fade on boat as special lights come up on Margarita. She stops. Slowly turns over and starts to swim, gradually picking up speed. Suddenly as if in pain she stops, tries again, then stops in pain again. She becomes disoriented and falls to the bottom of the sea. Special on Margarita at the bottom of the sea.)*

MARGARITA: *Ya no puedo . . .* I can't . . . A person isn't a machine . . . *es mi culpa . . .* Father forgive me . . . Papi! Papi! One, two. *Uno, dos.* (*Pause.*) Papi! *A dónde estás?* (*Pause.*) One, two, one, two. Papi! Ay Papi! Where are you . . . ? Don't leave me. . . . Why don't you answer me? (*Pause. She starts to swim, slowly.*) *Uno, dos, uno, dos.* Dig in, dig in. (*Stops swimming.*) *Por favor,* Papi! (*Starts to swim again.*) One, two, one, two. Kick from your hip, kick from your hip. (*Stops swimming. Starts to cry.*) Oh God, please. . . . (*Pause.*) Hail Mary, full of grace . . . dig in, dig in . . . the Lord is with thee. . . . (*She swims to the rhythm of her Hail Mary.*) Hail Mary, full of grace . . . dig in, dig in, . . . the Lord is with thee . . . dig in, dig in. . . . Blessed art thou among women. . . . Mommie it hurts. You let go of my hand. I'm lost. . . . And blessed is the fruit of thy womb, now and at the hour of our death. Amen. I don't want to die, I don't want to die. (*Margarita is still swimming. Blackout. She is gone.*)

SCENE SIX

Lights up on boat, we hear radio static. There is a heavy mist. On deck we see only black outline of Abuela with shawl over her head. We hear the Voices of Eduardo, Aída and Radio Operator.

EDUARDO'S VOICE: La Havana! Coming from San Pedro. Over.

RADIO OPERATOR'S VOICE: Right. DT6-6, you say you've lost a swimmer.

AÍDA'S VOICE: Our child, our only daughter . . . listen to me. Her name is Margarita Inez Suárez, she is wearing a black one-piece bathing suit cut high in the legs with a white racing stripe down the sides, a white bathing cap with goggles and her whole body covered with a . . . with a . . .

EDUARDO'S VOICE: With lanolin and paraffin.

AÍDA'S VOICE: *Sí . . . con* lanolin and paraffin. (*More radio static. Special on Simón, on the edge of the boat.*)

SIMÓN: Margo! Yo Margo! (*Pause*) Man don't do this. (*Pause.*) Come on. . . . Come on. . . . (*Pause.*) God, why does everything have to be so hard? (*Pause.*) Stupid. You know you're not supposed to die for this. Stupid. It's his dream and he can't even swim. (*Pause.*) Punch those arms in. Come home. Come home. I'm your little brother. Don't forget what Mama said. You're not supposed to leave me behind. *Vamos,* Margarita, take your little brother, hold his hand tight when you cross the street. He's so little. (*Pause.*) Oh Christ, give us a sign. . . . I know! I know! Margo, I'll send you a message

. . . like mental telepathy. I'll hold my breath, close my eyes and I'll bring you home. (*He takes a deep breath; a few beats.*) This time I'll beep . . . I'll send out sonar signals like a dolphin. (*He imitates dolphin sounds. The sound of real dolphins takes over from Simón, then fades into sound of Abuela saying the Hail Mary in Spanish, as full lights come up slowly.*)

SCENE SEVEN

Eduardo coming out of cabin, sobbing, Aída holding him. Simón anxiously scanning the horizon. Abuela looking calmly ahead.

EDUARDO: *Es mi culpa, sí, es mi culpa.* (*He hits his chest.*)

AÍDA: *Ya, ya viejo* . . . it was my sin . . . I left my home.

EDUARDO: Forgive me, forgive me. I've lost our daughter, our sister, our granddaughter, *mi carne, mi sangre, mis ilusiones.* (*To heaven.*) *Dios mío* take me . . . take me, I say . . . Goddammit, take me!

SIMÓN: I'm going in.

AÍDA *and* EDUARDO: No!

EDUARDO (*Grabbing and holding Simón, speaking to heaven.*):   God, take me, not my children. They are my dreams, my illusions . . . and not this one, this one is my mystery . . . he has my secret dreams. In him are the parts of me I cannot see. (*Eduardo embraces Simón. Radio static becomes louder.*)

AÍDA: I . . . I think I see her.

SIMÓN: No it's just a seal.

ABUELA (*Looking out with binoculars.*):   *Mi nietacita, dónde estás?* (*She feels her heart.*) I don't feel the knife in my heart . . . my little fish is not lost. (*Radio crackles with static. As lights dim on boat, voices of Mel and Mary Beth are heard over the radio.*)

MEL'S VOICE: Tragedy has marred the face of the Wrigley Invitational Women's Race to Catalina. The Cuban swimmer, little Margarita Suárez, has reportedly been lost at sea. Coast Guard and divers are looking for her as we speak. Yet in spite of this tragedy the race must go on because . . .

MARY BETH'S VOICE (*Interrupting loudly.*):   Mel!

MEL'S VOICE (*Startled.*):   What!

MARY BETH'S VOICE: Ah . . . excuse me, Mel . . . we have a winner. We've just received word from Catalina that one of the swimmers is just fifty yards from the breakers . . . it's oh, it's Margarita Suárez! (*Special on family in cabin listening to radio.*)

MEL'S VOICE: What? I thought she died! (*Special on Margarita, taking off bathing cap, trophy in hand, walking on the water.*)

MARY BETH'S VOICE: Ahh . . . unless . . . unless this is a tragic. . . . No . . . there she is, Mel. Margarita Suárez! The only one in the race wearing a black bathing suit cut high in the legs with a racing stripe down the side. (*Family cheering, embracing.*)

SIMÓN (*Screaming.*): Way to go Margo!

MEL'S VOICE: This is indeed a miracle! It's a resurrection! Margarita Suárez with a flotilla of boats to meet her, is now walking on the waters, through the breakers . . . onto the beach, with crowds of people cheering her on. What a jubilation! This is a miracle! (*Sound of crowds cheering. Pinspot on Abuela.*)

ABUELA: *Sangre de mi sangre* you will be another to save us, . . . to say to the evil one, *Coño Diablo, aqui estoy si me quieres.* (*Lights and cheering fade. Blackout.*)

Questions for Discussion and Writing

1. In a phrase or two, how would you characterize each of the members of Margarita's family? What is at stake for the Suárez family in Margarita's participation in swimming the channel between San Pedro and Catalina?

2. How do the attitudes of Mel Munson and Mary Beth White toward Margarita and her family illustrate the attitudes prevalent in the mainstream SOCIAL CONTEXT with which they must contend?

3. What images serve to connect Margarita with women in her family who have always been regarded as rescuers?

4. How do the circumstances under which Eduardo and Aída left Cuba create a personal conflict that surfaces during Margarita's swim? What can you infer about the SOCIAL and POLITICAL CONTEXT in Cuba at the time they left?

5. How does Sanchez-Scott use physical obstacles that Margarita faces outside the boat (such as an oil slick, fog, mist) to reflect the psychological conflicts the family faces inside the boat? For example, how is Simón's jealousy over his sister's importance paralleled in the same scene when Margarita says "The fish are all biting me . . . they hate me"?

6. How does Simón's attitude toward Margarita change over the course of the play?

7. To what extent do children in immigrant families bear an extraordinary burden in having to succeed not only for themselves but for their entire family to justify the sacrifices made in coming to the United States? If appropriate, draw on your own experiences or those of people you know.

8. Describe the route taken by family members who traveled from one town to another, one state to another, or one country to another. Tell the reasons for the journey, how they traveled, and any unusual experiences they had along the way and upon their arrival.

9. Have you ever experienced the phenomenon known as "culture shock"? Describe the new circumstances that challenged your expectations and proved so unsettling.

WRITING ABOUT CONTEXT

Since no short story, poem, drama, or essay is written in a vacuum, another useful way of studying works of literature entails discovering the extent to which a work reflects or incorporates the historical, cultural, literary, and personal context in which it was written. Although works vary in what they require readers to know already, in most cases knowing more about the contexts in which the work was written will enhance a reader's pleasure and understanding.

Investigating the biographical or psychological contexts in which the work was written assumes that the facts of an author's life are particularly relevant to a full understanding of the work. For example, the predicament confronting the speaker in Milosz's poem "My Faithful Mother Tongue" articulates a problem that the poet confronted in his own life. Similarly, we can assume that the acerbic look at Anglo culture expressed by the speaker in Wing Tek Lum's "Minority Poem" grew out of experiences and feelings of the author. Like the heroine of her story, Kim Chi-Wŏn emigrated from Korea and has been living in New York City; she might well have known Korean women facing the dilemma depicted in "A Certain Beginning." So, too, Arun Mukherjee, who came to Canada from India, like her protagonist in "Visiting Places" has almost certainly had similar experiences. Notwithstanding the presumed relevance of an author's life, especially if the work seems highly autobiographical, we should remember that literature doesn't simply report events but imaginatively re-creates experience.

You can often better understand a single story, poem, or play by comparing how the same author treated similar subjects and concerns in other works. Speeches, interviews, lectures, and essays by authors often provide important insights into the contexts in which a particular literary work was created. For example, Albert Camus's classic nonfiction work *The Rebel* (1951) would provide the philosophical background on alienation that enters so significantly into "The Guest."

Placing individual works within the author's total repertoire is another way of studying works in their context. You can compare different works by the same author, or compare different stages in the composition of the same work by studying subsequent revisions or different published versions of a story, poem, or play. For example, many of David Henry Hwang's plays (such as *F.O.B.* and *Family Devotions*) deal with problems of adjustment to American life on the part of Chinese-American immigrants. By studying these works in relationship to *The Dance and the Railroad*, we can see the evolution of his handling of this theme.

Authors often address themselves to the important political and social developments of their time. For example, Mahasweta Devi has for many years lived and worked among the tribal and outcaste communities in southwest Bengal, India. Her stories reflect the information she has gleaned directly from the lives of the rural and urban underclass. We can see this in her unique style of narrative realism. Her story "Giribala" is based on observations drawn from actual situations and accurately reflects social values in Bengal. Her work can be understood as a reaction to the appalling social attitudes that keep women from being treated as human beings in Bengali culture.

In studying the social context of a work, ask yourself what dominant social values the work dramatizes and try to determine whether the author approves or disapproves of particular social values and trends by the way in which characters are portrayed. Or, you might choose to analyze how the author describes or draws upon the manners, mores, customs, rituals, or codes of conduct of that particular society at that particular time, as does Mitsuye Yamada in "I Learned to Sew," a poem that looks at the human consequences of the practice of arranged marriage.

Studying the historical context within which a work is written means identifying how features of the work reveal important historical, political, economic, social, intellectual, or religious currents and problems of the time. Think how useful it would be, for example, to know what the important issues were in the conflict between France and Algeria that are reflected in Albert Camus's "The Guest." When you approach these works to discover the circumstances in which they were written, you gain a broader understanding of individual works than you might otherwise obtain.

David Henry Hwang's play *The Dance and the Railroad* is set against the backdrop of the 1867 railroad workers' strike, and draws on historical events that Chinese immigrants experienced in the United States between 1849 and 1870. In studying the historical background of a work of literature such as this, it is important to first determine what elements, ideas, or characters can be clearly related to a specific historical period. Equally important to know is how the author's use of history reflects his or her own purposes. Has the writer chosen to interweave real historical incidents and figures with characters and events of his or her own creation, and if so, to what effect?

When we look at the actual historical circumstances during the time of Hwang's play, we discover that great numbers of émigrés left China's port cities on the south coast to make the harrowing, month-long voyage to work in California. Conditions aboard these ships for the seven-thousand-mile trip were so tortuous that fewer than half of those who sailed survived the voyage. Once in California, over ten thousand Chinese immigrants were employed in building the transcontinental railroad under difficult and dangerous circumstances, requiring workers to tunnel and blast through mountains and survive blinding snowstorms and avalanches. Dehumanizing working conditions precipitated the strike of 1867, which finally ended with concessions granted to the workers.

When we look at Hwang's play as a mirror of the events, we discover he has interwoven real events with imaginary incidents and characters of his own creation. It would be difficult for readers with no knowledge of the historical background to tell what was real and what was imagined. For example, Ma is not indulging in poetic hyperbole when he says "we hung from cliffs in baskets and the winds blew us like birds." In fact, Chinese workers were considered so expendable by their employers that they were often lowered down cliffs in baskets to plant explosives.

An essay that explores personal, social, or historical contexts would try to determine which elements in a work were preexisting and which represent the author's original contribution. In analyzing any work, the title, names of characters, references to places and events, or topical allusions may provide important clues to the work's original sources. Simply knowing more about the circumstances under which a work was written will add to your enjoyment and give you a broader understanding of the short story, poem, or play.

Connections

1. How do both Mathabane and Camus illustrate that individuals continue to be seen in stereotyped ways when they move into a new culture and are not accepted for who they are, but rather for what they represent?
2. How do the protagonists in "Visiting Places" and "A Certain Beginning" hope to transcend the roles they find themselves in and, through accommodation, gain acceptance?
3. In what way is bureacracy shown as a limiting force in Hulme's and Kim Chi-Wŏn's stories?
4. How are the protagonists in the works by Cortázar, Mukherjee, Kashkuli, and Bissoondath shown to be unable to reestablish themselves in new environments? To what extent does this put them at the mercy of others?
5. How do the works by Wing Tek Lum and Milcha Sanchez-Scott reveal the extent to which minorities face scorn and condescension in the process of seeking acceptance by the mainstream culture?
6. Contrast the metaphors Sjögren, Chalfi, and Cortázar use to symbolize alienation from one's environment.
7. Compare the circumstances under which marriages of convenience are arranged and the extent to which the protagonists are at the mercy of the situation in both Devi's and Chi-Wŏn's stories.
8. To what extent are the poems by Neruda and Wakoski based on the realization that no place is ever permanent?
9. How do the protagonists of "A Certain Beginning" and "I Learned to Sew" cope with their initial rejection by intended spouses?
10. What insight into arranged marriages in different cultures do you get from the works by Devi, Yamada, and Chi-Wŏn?

11. How do the works by Hwang and Milosz try to come to terms with the issue of what elements of their traditional cultures, China and Poland, they can hope to keep in their new environment? How are the problems artists face in a new culture different from and similar to those that others confront?

12. How do the works by Mathabane and Sanchez-Scott use sports as a metaphor to express the hurdles immigrants must surmount in order to gain acceptance in a new culture?

7

The Spiritual Dimension

"I think it pisses God off if you walk by the color purple in a field somewhere and don't notice it."

— *Alice Walker*

"It is beyond our power to explain either the prosperity of the wicked or the afflictions of the righteous."

— *The Talmud*

At one time or another in their lives, most people reflect on their relationship to a higher order of existence, whether one perceives it as an eternal force, the universe around us, a defined spiritual entity, or a concept that answers to a basic human need for a sense of order behind the turbulent appearance of everyday life. Some people are content to continue within the religious traditions in which they were raised, while others are drawn toward systems of belief that they find match their needs and perceptions of this spiritual dimension. If literature from around the world illustrates anything, it is this extraordinary multiplicity of different responses to the universal, or cosmic.

This chapter presents works that reflect how people in many different cultures and societies throughout the world look at themselves in relationship to the absolute, the eternal, the supernatural, or the concept of an ultimate truth. Octavio Paz (Mexico) describes in "Day of the Dead" how Mexican fiestas stop time and introduce a sense of transcendence into everyday life. Inés Arredondo (Mexico) in "The Shunammite" dramatizes the conflict between the flesh and the spirit in a modern retelling of an ancient biblical story. Naguib Mahfouz (Egypt) challenges the usual perceptions of time in his intriguing parable, "Half a Day." Tayeb Salih (Sudan) presents a mysterious encounter that raises basic questions of good and evil in "The Cypriot Man." François Barcelo (Canada), in "The Man Who Stopped Trains," presents the unusual tale of a jogger who discovers he has an extraordinary gift. Peter Carey (Australia) creates an eerie parable in "The Last Days of a Famous Mime," showing how an artistic quest may become a spiritual one. An encounter between an ornithologist and an egotistical talking canary raises basic questions about how we perceive the world in "A

Canary's Ideas," by Joaquim María Machado de Assis (Brazil). A classic story, "An Old Man" by Guy de Maupassant (France), dramatizes the absurdity of a life lived without spiritual values. A son's reappearance to his mother, after his death, repays her lifelong devotion in the bitter-sweet ghost story, "Life Is Sweet at Kumansenu," by Abioseh Nicol (Sierra Leone). A decree by the village gods sets off a chain of tragic consequences in Chinua Achebe's "Things Fall Apart" (Nigeria). Leslie Marmon Silko (Laguna Pueblo, United States), in "Language and Literature from a Pueblo Indian Perspective," reveals the unusual per-spective of Native Americans toward the interconnection between the natural and spiritual worlds.

The poems in this chapter present a vividly realized range of works exploring the relationships of individuals to their perception of a higher power, the universe, the eternal, or the cosmic. Jorge Luis Borges (Argentina), in "Afterglow," explores how the encroaching darkness after sunset and his own growing blindness makes his quest for a spiritual meaning to existence more urgent. Ma Lihua (Tibet) reveals the influence of Taoist and Buddhist thought in her sequence of four poems, "My Sun." In "The Wake," Rita Dove (African-American, United States) describes how her mother's death created a void. Anna Kamieńska (Poland) offers a wryly provoking view of the human con-dition in "Funny." Nelly Sachs (Sweden), in "Chorus of the Dead," affirms the unity of life despite the furnaces of the crematoria. In "Preliminary Investigation of an Angel," Zbigniew Herbert (Poland) creates a thought-provoking parable in which spiritual grace survives a tortuous inquisition. Bella Akhmadulina (Russia), in "The Garden," voices her belief that if imagination houses reality, then real time is time remembered. Vasko Popa in "The Lost Red Boot" (Yugoslavia) invokes the image of his irrepressible grandmother to inspire his poetry. A vi-sion of the return of Christ prophesied in the New Testament gives way to a terrifying embodiment of inhuman barbarism in "The Second Coming" by William Butler Yeats (Ireland).

In Sister Mary Ignatius Explains It All for You, Christopher Durang (United States), at his most iconoclastic, presents four students (an un-wed mother, a homosexual, a suicidal alcoholic wife-beater, and a rape victim) who return to confront their former teacher, a nun who victim-ized and terrified them, for her failure to prepare them for life.

Octavio Paz

The Day of the Dead

Octavio Paz, born on the outskirts of Mexico City in 1914, is a poet, essayist, and unequaled observer of Mexican society. He served as a Mexican diplomat in France and Japan and as ambassador to India before resigning from the diplomatic service to protest the Tlatelolco Massacre (the government massacre of three hundred students in Mexico City) in 1968. His many volumes of poetry include Sun Stone *(1958), a new reading of Aztec myths,* Marcel Duchamp *(1968),* The Children of the Mire *(1974), and* The Monkey Grammarian *(1981). In 1990, Paz was awarded the Nobel Prize for literature. A writer of exceptional talents, Paz's many volumes of essays cover subjects as diverse as poetic theory (*The Bow and the Lyre*), studies on structuralism and modern art (in books on Levi-Strauss and Marcel Duchamp), meditations on the erotic (*Conjunctions and Disjunctions*), and his monumental study of Sor Juana Inés de la Cruz. As an essayist whose works have helped redefine the concept of Latin American culture, Paz has written* The Labyrinth of Solitude, *translated by Lysander Kemp (1961), from which "The Day of the Dead" is taken, and* The Other Mexico *(1972). In the following essay, Paz offers insight, conveyed with his typical stylistic grace, and erudition, concerning how fiestas fulfill deep psychological needs in Mexican culture.*

1   The solitary Mexican loves fiestas and public gatherings. Any occasion for getting together will serve, any pretext to stop the flow of time and commemorate men and events with festivals and ceremonies. We are a ritual people, and this characteristic enriches both our imaginations and our sensibilities, which are equally sharp and alert. The art of the fiesta has been debased almost everywhere else, but not in Mexico. There are few places in he world where it is possible to take part in a spectacle like our great religious fiestas with their violent primary colors, their bizarre costumes and dances, their fireworks and ceremonies and their inexhaustible welter of surprises: the fruit, candy, toys and other objects sold on these days in the plazas and open-air markets.

2   Our calendar is crowded with fiestas. There are certain days when the whole country, from the most remote villages to the largest cities, prays, shouts, feasts, gets drunk and kills, in honor of the Virgin of Guadalupe or Benito Juárez. Each year on the fifteenth of September, at eleven o'clock at night, we celebrate the fiesta of the *Grito*[1] in all the plazas of the Republic, and the excited crowds actually shout for a whole hour . . . the better, perhaps, to remain silent for the rest of the

---

[1]Padre Hidalgo's call-to-arms against Spain, 1810.—*Tr.*

year. During the days before and after the twelfth of December,[2] time comes to a full stop, and instead of pushing us toward a deceptive tomorrow that is always beyond our reach, offers us a complete and perfect today of dancing and revelry, of communion with the most ancient and secret Mexico. Time is no longer succession, and becomes what it originally was and is: the present, in which past and future are reconciled.

But the fiestas which the Church and State provide for the country as a whole are not enough. The life of every city and village is ruled by a patron saint whose blessing is celebrated with devout regularity. Neighborhoods and trades also have their annual fiestas, their ceremonies and fairs. And each one of us—atheist, Catholic, or merely indifferent—has his own saint's day, which he observes every year. It is impossible to calculate how many fiestas we have and how much time and money we spend on them. I remember asking the mayor of a village near Mitla, several years ago, "What is the income of the village government?" "About 3,000 pesos a year. We are very poor. But the Governor and the Federal Government always help us to meet our expenses." "And how are the 3,000 pesos spent?" "Mostly on fiestas, señor. We are a small village, but we have two patron saints."

This reply is not surprising. Our poverty can be measured by the frequency and luxuriousness of our holidays. Wealthy countries have very few: there is neither the time nor the desire for them, and they are not necessary. The people have other things to do, and when they amuse themselves they do so in small groups. The modern masses are agglomerations of solitary individuals. On great occasions in Paris or New York, when the populace gathers in the squares or stadiums, the absence of people, in the sense of *a* people, is remarkable: there are couples and small groups, but they never form a living community in which the individual is at once dissolved and redeemed. But how could a poor Mexican live without the two or three annual fiestas that make up for his poverty and misery? Fiestas are our only luxury. They replace, and are perhaps better than, the theater and vacations, Anglo-Saxon weekends and cocktail parties, the bourgeois reception, the Mediterranean café.

In all of these ceremonies—national or local, trade or family—the Mexican opens out. They all give him a chance to reveal himself and to converse with God, country, friends or relations. During these days the silent Mexican whistles, shouts, sings, shoots off fireworks, discharges his pistol into the air. He discharges his soul. And his shout, like the rockets we love so much, ascends to the heavens, explodes into green, red, blue, and white lights, and falls dizzily to earth with a trail of golden sparks. This is the night when friends who have not exchanged

---

[2]Fiesta of the Virgin of Guadalupe.—*Tr.*

more than the prescribed courtesies for months get drunk together, trade confidences, weep over the same troubles, discover that they are brothers, and sometimes, to prove it, kill each other. The night is full of songs and loud cries. The lover wakes up his sweetheart with an orchestra. There are jokes and conversations from balcony to balcony, sidewalk to sidewalk. Nobody talks quietly. Hats fly in the air. Laughter and curses ring like silver pesos. Guitars are brought out. Now and then, it is true, the happiness ends badly, in quarrels, insults, pistol shots, stabbings. But these too are part of the fiesta, for the Mexican does not seek amusement: he seeks to escape from himself, to leap over the wall of solitude that confines him during the rest of the year. All are possessed by violence and frenzy. Their souls explode like the colors and voices and emotions. Do they forget themselves and show their true faces? Nobody knows. The important thing is to go out, open a way, get drunk on noise, people, colors. Mexico is celebrating a fiesta. And this fiesta, shot through with lightning and delirium, is the brilliant reverse to our silence and apathy, our reticence and gloom.

6   According to the interpretation of French sociologists, the fiesta is an excess, an expense. By means of this squandering the community protects itself against the envy of the gods or of men. Sacrifices and offerings placate or buy off the gods and the patron saints. Wasting money and expending energy affirms the community's wealth in both. This luxury is a proof of health, a show of abundance and power. Or a magic trap. For squandering is an effort to attract abundance by contagion. Money calls to money. When life is thrown away it increases; the orgy, which is sexual expenditure, is also a ceremony of regeneration; waste gives strength. New Year celebrations, in every culture, signify something beyond the mere observance of a date on the calendar. The day is a pause: time is stopped, is actually annihilated. The rites that celebrate its death are intended to provoke its rebirth, because they mark not only the end of an old year but also the beginning of a new. Everything attracts its opposite. The fiesta's function, then, is more utilitarian than we think: waste attracts or promotes wealth, and is an investment like any other, except that the returns on it cannot be measured or counted. What is sought is potency, life, health. In this sense the fiesta, like the gift and the offering, is one of the most ancient of economic forms.

7   This interpretation has always seemed to me to be incomplete. The fiesta is by nature sacred, literally or figuratively, and above all it is the advent of the unusual. It is governed by its own special rules, that set it apart from other days, and it has a logic, an ethic and even an economy that are often in conflict with everyday norms. It all occurs in an enchanted world: time is transformed to a mythical past or a total present; space, the scene of the fiesta, is turned into a gaily decorated world of its own; and the persons taking part cast off all human or social rank and become, for the moment, living images. And everything takes place

as if it were not so, as if it were a dream. But whatever happens, our actions have a greater lightness, a different gravity. They take on other meanings and with them we contract new obligations. We throw down our burdens of time and reason.

In certain fiestas the very notion of order disappears. Chaos comes back and license rules. Anything is permitted: the customary hierarchies vanish, along with all social, sex, caste, and trade distinctions. Men disguise themselves as women, gentlemen as slaves, the poor as the rich. The army, the clergy, and the law are ridiculed. Obligatory sacrilege, ritual profanation is committed. Love becomes promiscuity. Sometimes the fiesta becomes a Black Mass. Regulations, habits and customs are violated. Respectable people put away the dignified expressions and conservative clothes that isolate them, dress up in gaudy colors, hide behind a mask, and escape from themselves. 8

Therefore the fiesta is not only an excess, a ritual squandering of the goods painfully accumulated during the rest of the year; it is also a revolt, a sudden immersion in the formless, in pure being. By means of the fiesta society frees itself from the norms it has established. It ridicules its gods, its principles, and its laws: it denies its own self. 9

The fiesta is a revolution in the most literal sense of the word. In the confusion that it generates, society is dissolved, is drowned, insofar as it is an organism ruled according to certain laws and principles. But it drowns in itself, in its own original chaos or liberty. Everything is united: good and evil, day and night, the sacred and the profane. Everything merges, loses shape and individuality and returns to the primordial mass. The fiesta is a cosmic experiment, an experiment in disorder, reuniting contradictory elements and principles in order to bring about a renascence of life. Ritual death promotes a rebirth; vomiting increases the appetite; the orgy, sterile in itself, renews the fertility of the mother or of the earth. The fiesta is a return to a remote and undifferentiated state, prenatal or presocial. It is a return that is also a beginning, in accordance with the dialectic that is inherent in social processes. 10

The group emerges purified and strengthened from this plunge into chaos. It has immersed itself in its own origins, in the womb from which it came. To express it in another way, the fiesta denies society as an organic system of differentiated forms and principles, but affirms it as a source of creative energy. It is a true "re-creation," the opposite of the "recreation" characterizing modern vacations, which do not entail any rites or ceremonies whatever and are as individualistic and sterile as the world that invented them. 11

Society communes with itself during the fiesta. Its members return to original chaos and freedom. Social structures break down and new relationships, unexpected rules, capricious hierarchies are created. In the general disorder everybody forgets himself and enters into otherwise forbidden situations and places. The bounds between audience 12 and actors, officials and servants, are erased. Everybody takes part in the fiesta, everybody is caught up in its whirlwind. Whatever its mood, its character, its meaning, the fiesta is participation, and this trait distinguishes it from all other ceremonies and social phenomena. Lay or religious, orgy or saturnalia, the fiesta is a social act based on the full participation of all its celebrants.

13   Thanks to the fiesta the Mexican opens out, participates, communes with his fellows and with the values that give meaning to his religious or political existence. And it is significant that a country as sorrowful as ours should have so many and such joyous fiestas. Their frequency, their brilliance and excitement, the enthusiasm with which we take part, all suggest that without them we would explode. They free us, if only momentarily, from the thwarted impulses, the inflammable desires that we carry within us. But the Mexican fiesta is not merely a return to an original state of formless and normless liberty: the Mexican is not seeking to return, but to escape from himself, to exceed himself. Our fiestas are explosions. Life and death, joy and sorrow, music and mere noise are united, not to re-create or recognize themselves, but to swallow each other up. There is nothing so joyous as a Mexican fiesta, but there is also nothing so sorrowful. Fiesta night is also a night of mourning.

14   If we hide within ourselves in our daily lives, we discharge ourselves in the whirlwind of the fiesta. It is more than an opening out: we rend ourselves open. Everything—music, love, friendship—ends in tumult and violence. The frenzy of our festivals shows the extent to which our solitude closes us off from communication with the world. We are familiar with delirium, with songs and shouts, with the monologue . . . but not with the dialogue. Our fiestas, like our confidences, our loves, our attempts to reorder our society, are violent breaks with the old or the established. Each time we try to express ourselves we have to break with ourselves. And the fiesta is only one example, perhaps the most typical, of this violent break. It is not difficult to name others, equally revealing: our games, which are always a going to extremes, often mortal; our profligate spending, the reverse of our timid investments and business enterprises; our confessions. The somber Mexican, closed up in himself, suddenly explodes, tears open his breast and reveals himself, though not without a certain complacency, and not without a stopping place in the shameful or terrible mazes of his intimacy. We are not frank, but our sincerity can reach extremes that horrify a European. The explosive, dramatic, sometimes even suicidal manner in which we strip ourselves, surrender ourselves, is evidence that something inhibits and suffocates us. Something impedes us from being. And since we cannot or dare not confront our own selves, we resort to the fiesta. It fires us into the void; it is a drunken rapture that burns itself out, a pistol shot in the air, a skyrocket.

Questions for Discussion and Writing

1. What factors contribute to the popularity of fiestas in Mexico, especially in relation to the Mexican national character, as described by Paz?

2. What relationship does Paz see between "solitude" as a cultural phenomenon and the widespread love of fiestas in Mexico?

3. How does Paz use economic information about the cost and frequency of fiestas to underscore the importance of fiestas in Mexican society?

4. In what ways does the fiesta create its own world, set off from time, demarcated in space, and encourage forms of behavior normally not permitted in everyday life?

5. In your own words explain the psychology of sacrifice to attract abundance that is revealed in the lavish preparations for each fiesta.

6. How does the experience of time during the fiesta period (what might be termed "ritual time") qualitatively differ from "clock time" (normal time as it is experienced during the rest of the year)?

7. How does Paz use the fiesta to symbolize what, for him, is the distinctive quality of Mexican life when he uses such phrases as "our fiestas, like our confidences, our loves, our attempts to reorder our society, our violent breaks with the old or the established"?

8. Have you ever been at a party that came close in spirit to the Mexican fiesta where people used the occasion to renew friendships, get drunk together, and discover kinships? If so, describe your experiences and discuss the similarities and differences in terms of emotional transformation such celebrations encourage.

9. Create an entirely new ritual or tradition, either serious or whimsical, or revise a celebration for an existing holiday such as New Year's Eve, Halloween, or an occasion such as a wedding or graduation. Alternatively, you might choose to describe a real ritual with which other people are not familiar, such as Kwanzaa ("fruit of the harvest," in Swahili).

Inés Arredondo

The Shunammite

The Mexican writer Inés Arredondo was born in 1928, and has written exten-sively about the north coast of the San Lorenzo River, especially in her collec-tion of stories titled La Senal (The Sign), *1965. As a short story writer, her work has been strongly influenced by D. H. Lawrence. Although Arredondo ex-plores the extent to which women in Mexico become sacrificial victims in a male-dominated society, she often creates stories that bring to life archetypal fe-male figures such as Eve, Jocasta, and Medea. In "The Shunammite," trans-lated by Albert Manguel (1986), Arredondo recasts the biblical story in a mod-ern context.*

> So they sought for a fair damsel throughout all
> the coasts of Israel, and found Abishag, a
> Shunammite, and brought her to the king. . . .
>
> And the damsel was very fair, and
> cherished the king, and ministered to him;
> but the king knew her not.
> KINGS I: 1, 3–4

1 The summer had been a fiery furnace. The last summer of my youth.

2 Tense, concentrated in the arrogance that precedes combustion, the city shone in a dry and dazzling light. I stood in the very midst of the light, dressed in mourning, proud, feeding the flames with my blonde hair, alone. Men's sly glances slid over my body without soiling it, and my haughty modesty forced them to barely nod at me, full of respect. I was certain of having the power to dominate passions, to purify any-thing in the scorching air that surrounded but did not singe me.

3 Nothing changed when I received the telegram; the sadness it brought me did not affect in the least my feelings towards the world. My uncle Apolonio was dying at the age of seventy-odd years and wanted to see me. I had lived as a daughter in his house for many years and I sincerely felt pain at the thought of his inevitable death. All this was perfectly normal, and not a single omen, not a single shiver made me suspect anything. Quickly I made arrangements for the journey, in the very same untouchable midst of the motionless summer.

4 I arrived at the village during the hour of siesta.

5 Walking down the empty streets with my small suitcase, I fell to daydreaming, in that dusky zone between reality and time, born of the excessive heat. I was not remembering; I was almost reliving things as

944

they had been. "Look, Licha, the *amapas* are blooming again." The clear voice, almost childish. "I want you to get yourself a dress like that of Margarita Ibarra to wear on the sixteenth." I could hear her, feel her walking by my side, her shoulders bent a little forwards, light in spite of her plumpness, happy and old. I carried on walking in the company of my aunt Panchita, my mother's sister. "Well, my dear, if you *really* don't like Pepe . . . but he's such a *nice* boy. . . ." Yes, she had used those exact words, here, in front of Tichi Valenzuela's window, with her gay smile, innocent and impish. I walked a little further, where the paving stones seemed to fade away in the haze, and when the bells rang, heavy and real, ending the siesta and announcing the Rosary, I opened my eyes and gave the village a good, long look: it was not the same. The *amapas* had not bloomed and I was crying, in my mourning dress, at the door of my uncle's house.

The front gate was open, as always, and at the end of the courtyard   6 rose the bougainvillea. As always: but not the same. I dried my tears, and felt that I was not arriving: I was leaving. Everything looked motionless, pinioned in my memory, and the heat and the silence seemed to wither it all. My footsteps echoed with a new sound, and Maria came out to greet me.

"Why didn't you let us know? We'd have sent . . ."   7

We went straight into the sick man's room. As I entered, I felt cold.   8 Silence and gloom preceded death.

"Luisa, is that you?"   9

The dear voice was dying out and would soon be silent for ever.   10

"I'm here, uncle."   11

"God be praised! I won't die alone."   12

"Don't say that; you'll soon be much better."   13

He smiled sadly; he knew I was lying but he did not want to make   14 me cry.

"Yes, my daughter. Yes. Now have a rest, make yourself at home   15 and then come and keep me company. I'll try to sleep a little."

Shrivelled, wizened, toothless, lost in the immense bed and floating   16 senselessly in whatever was left of his life, he was painful to be with, like something superfluous, out of place, like so many others at the point of death. Stepping out of the overheated passageway, one would take a deep breath, instinctively, hungry for light and air.

I began to nurse him and I felt happy doing it. This house was *my*   17 house, and in the morning, while tidying up, I would sing long-forgotten songs. The peace that surrounded me came perhaps from the fact that my uncle no longer awaited death as something imminent and terrible, but instead let himself be carried by the passing days towards a more or less distant or nearby future, with the unconscious tenderness of a child. He would go over his past life with great pleasure and enjoy imagining that he was bequeathing me his images, as grandparents do with their children.

18   "Bring me that small chest, there, in the large wardrobe. Yes, that one. The key is underneath the mat, next to Saint Anthony. Bring the key as well."

19   And his sunken eyes would shine once again at the sight of all his treasures.

20   "Look: this necklace—I gave it to your aunt for our tenth wedding anniversary. I bought it in Mazatlan from a Polish jeweller who told me God-knows-what story about an Austrian princess, and asked an impossible price for it. I brought it back hidden in my pistol-holder and didn't sleep a wink in the stagecoach—I was so afraid someone would steal it!"

21   The light of dusk made the young, living stones glitter in his callused hands.

22   ". . . this ring, so old, belonged to my mother; look carefully at the miniature in the other room and you'll see her wearing it. Cousin Begona would mutter behind her back that a sweetheart of hers . . ."

23   The ladies in the portraits would move their lips and speak, once again, would breathe again—all these ladies he had seen, he had touched. I would picture them in my mind and understand the meaning of these jewels.

24   "Have I told you about the time we travelled to Europe, in 1908, before the Revolution? You had to take a ship to Colima. . . . And in Venice your aunt Panchita fell in love with a certain pair of ear-rings. They were much too expensive, and I told her so. 'They are fit for a queen.' . . . Next day I bought them for her. You just can't imagine what it was like because all this took place long, long before you were born, in 1908, in Venice, when your aunt was so young, so . . ."

25   "Uncle, you're getting tired, you should rest."

26   "You're right, I'm tired. Leave me a while and take the small chest to your room. It's yours."

27   "But, uncle . . ."

28   "It's all yours, that's all! I trust I can give away whatever I want!"

29   His voice broke into a sob: the illusion was vanishing and he found himself again on the point of dying, of saying good-bye to the things he had loved. He turned to the wall and I left with the box in my hands, not knowing what to do.

30   On other occasions he would tell me about "the year of the famine," or "the year of the yellow corn," or "the year of the plague," and very old tales of murderers and ghosts. Once he even tried to sing a *corrido* from his youth, but it shattered in his jagged voice. He was leaving me his life, and he was happy. The doctor said that yes, he could see some recovery, but that we were not to raise our hopes, there was no cure, it was merely a matter of a few days more or less.

31   One afternoon of menacing dark clouds, when I was bringing in the clothes hanging out to dry in the courtyard, I heard Maria cry out. I stood still, listening to her cry as if it were a peal of thunder, the first of

the storm to come. Then silence, and I was left alone in the courtyard, motionless. A bee buzzed by and the rain did not fall. No one knows as well as I do how awful a foreboding can be, a premonition hanging above a head turned towards the sky.

"Lichita, he's dying! He's gasping for air!" 32

"Go get the doctor. . . . No! I'll go. . . . But call Dona Clara to stay 33 with you till I'm back."

"And the priest . . . fetch the priest." 34

I ran, I ran away from that unbearable moment, blunt and asphyxi- 35 ating. I ran, hurried back, entered the house, made coffee; I greeted the relatives who began to arrive dressed in half-mourning; I ordered candles; I asked for a few holy relics; I kept on feverishly trying to fulfill my only obligation at the time, to be with my uncle. I asked the doctor: he had given him an injection, so as not to leave anything untried, but he knew it was useless. I saw the priest arrive with the Eucharist, even then I lacked the courage to enter. I knew I would regret it afterwards. *Thank God, now I won't die alone*—but I couldn't. I covered my face with my hands and prayed.

The priest came and touched my shoulder. I thought that all was 36 over and I shivered.

"He's calling you. Come in." 37

I don't know how I reached the door. Night had fallen and the 38 room, lit by a bedside lamp, seemed enormous. The furniture, larger than life, looked black, and a strange clogging atmosphere hung about the bed. Trembling, I felt I was inhaling death.

"Stand next to him," said the priest. 39

I obeyed, moving towards the foot of the bed, unable to look even at 40 the sheets.

"Your uncle's wish, unless you say otherwise, is to marry you *in ar-* 41 *ticulo mortis*, so that you may inherit his possessions. Do you accept?"

I stifled a cry of horror. I opened my eyes wide enough to let in the 42 whole terrible room. "Why does he want to drag me into his grave?" I felt death touching my skin.

"Luisa. . ." 43

It was uncle Apolonio. Now I had to look at him. He could barely 44 mouth the words, his jaw seemed slack and he spoke moving his face like that of a ventriloquist's doll.

". . . please." 45

And he fell silent with exhaustion. 46

I could take no more. I left the room. That was not my uncle, it did 47 not even look like him. Leave everything to me, yes, but not only his possessions, his stories, his life . . . I didn't want it, his life, his death. I didn't want it. When I opened my eyes I was standing again in the courtyard and the sky was still overcast. I breathed in deeply, painfully.

"Already? . . " The relatives drew near to ask, seeing me so dis- 48 traught.

49 I shook my head. Behind me, the priest explained.

50 "Don Apolonio wants to marry her with his last breath, so that she may inherit him."

51 "And you won't?" the old servant asked anxiously. "Don't be silly, you are the only one to deserve it. You were a daughter to them, and you have worked very hard looking after him. If you don't marry him, the cousins in Mexico City will leave you without a cent. Don't be silly!"

52 "It's a fine gesture on his part. . . ."

53 "And afterwards you'll be left a rich widow, as untouched as you are now." A young cousin laughed nervously.

54 "It's a considerable fortune, and I, as your uncle several times removed, would advise you to . . ."

55 "If you think about it, not accepting shows a lack of both charity and humility."

56 "That's true, that's absolutely true."

57 I did not want to give an old man his last pleasure, a pleasure I should, after all, be thankful for, because my youthful body, of which I felt so proud, had not dwelt in any of the regions of death. I was overcome by nausea. That was my last clear thought that night. I woke from a kind of hypnotic slumber as they forced me to hold his hand covered in cold sweat. I felt nauseous again, but said "yes."

58 I remember vaguely that they hovered over me all the time, talking all at once, taking me over there, bringing me over here, making me sign, making me answer. The taste of that night—a taste that has stayed with me for the rest of my life—was that of an evil ring-around-the-rosies turning vertiginously around me, while everyone laughed and sang grotesquely

> This is the way the widow is wed,
> The widow is wed, the widow is wed

while I stood, a slave, in the middle. Something inside me hurt, and I could not lift my eyes.

59 When I came to my senses, all was over, and on my hand shone the braided ring which I had seen so many times on my aunt Panchita's finger: there had been no time for anything else.

60 The guests began to leave.

61 "If you need me, don't hesitate to call. In the meantime give him these drops every six hours."

62 "May God bless you and give you strength."

63 "Happy honeymoon," whispered the young cousin in my ear, with a nasty laugh.

64 I returned to the sickbed. "Nothing has changed, nothing has changed." My fear certainly had not changed. I convinced Maria to stay and help me look after uncle Apolonio. I only calmed down once I saw dawn was breaking. It had started to rain, but without thunder or lightning, very still.

It kept on drizzling that day and the next, and the day after. Four 65 days of anguish. Nobody came to visit, nobody other than the doctor and the priest. On days like these no one goes out, everyone stays indoors and waits for life to start again. These are the days of the spirit, sacred days.

If at least the sick man had needed plenty of attention my hours 66 would have seemed shorter, but there was little that could be done for him.

On the fourth night Maria went to bed in a room close by, and I 67 stayed alone with the dying man. I was listening to the monotonous rain and praying unconsciously, half asleep and unafraid, waiting. My fingers stopped working, turning the rosary, and as I held the beads I could feel through my fingertips a peculiar warmth, a warmth both alien and intimate, the warmth we leave in things and which is returned to us transformed, a comrade, a brother foreshadowing the warmth of others, a warmth both unknown and recollected, never quite grasped and yet inhabiting the core of my bones. Softly, deliciously, my nerves relaxed, my fingers felt light, I fell asleep.

I must have slept many hours: it was dawn when I woke up. I knew 68 because the lights had been switched off and the electric plant stops working at two in the morning. The room, barely lit by an oil lamp at the feet of the Holy Virgin on the chest of drawers, made me think of the wedding night, my wedding night. . . . It was so long ago, an empty eternity.

From the depth of the gloomy darkness don Apolonio's broken and 69 tired breathing reached me. There he still was, not the man himself, simply the persistent and incomprehensible shred that hangs on, with no goal, with no apparent motive. Death is frightening, but life mingled with death, soaked in death, is horrible in a way that owes little to either life or death. Silence, corruption of the flesh, the stench, the monstrous transformation, the final vanishing act, all this is painful, but it reaches a climax and then gives way, dissolves into the earth, into memory, into history. But not this: this arrangement worked out between life and death—echoed in the useless exhaling and inhaling—could carry on forever. I would hear him trying to clear his anaesthetized throat and it occurred to me that air was not entering that body, or rather, that it was not a human body breathing the air: it was a machine, puffing and panting, stopping in a curious game, a game to kill time without end. That thing was no human being: it was somebody playing with huffs and snores. And the horror of it all won me over: I began to breathe to the rhythm of his panting; to inhale, stop suddenly, choke, breathe, choke again . . . unable to control myself, until I realized I had been deceived by what I thought was the sense of the game. What I really felt was the pain and shortness of breath of an animal in pain. But I kept on, on, until there was one single breathing, one single inhuman breath, one single agony. I felt calmer, terrified but calmer: I had lifted the barrier, I could let myself go and simply wait for the common end. It seemed to me that by abandoning myself, by giving myself up unconditionally, the end would happen quickly, would not be allowed to continue. It would have fulfilled its purpose and its persistent search in the world.

70 Not a hint of farewell, not a glimmer of pity towards me. I carried on the mortal game for a long, long while, from someplace where time had ceased to matter.

71 The shared breathing became less agitated, more peaceful, but also weaker. I seemed to be drifting back. I felt so tired I could barely move, exhaustion nestling in forever inside my body. I opened my eyes. Nothing had changed.

72 No: far away, in the shadows, is a rose. Alone, unique, alive. There it is, cut out against the darkness, clear as day, with its fleshy, luminous petals, shining. I look at it and my hand moves and I remember its touch and the simple act of putting it in a vase. I looked at it then, but I only understand it now. I stir, I blink, and the rose is still there, in full bloom, identical to itself.

73 I breathe freely, with my own breath. I pray, I remember, I doze off, and the untouched rose mounts guard over the dawning light and my secret. Death and hope suffer change.

74 And now day begins to break and in the clean sky I see that at last the days of rain are over. I stay at the window a long time, watching everything change in the sun. A strong ray enters me and the suffering seems a lie. Unjustified bliss fills my lungs and unwittingly I smile. I turn to the rose as if to an accomplice but I can't find it: the sun has withered it.

75 Clear days came again, and maddening heat. The people went to work, and sang, but don Apolonio would not die; in fact he seemed to get better. I kept on looking after him, but no longer in a cheerful mood—my eyes downcast, I turned the guilt I felt into hard work. My wish, now clearly, was that it all end, that he die. The fear, the horror I felt looking at him, at his touch, his voice, were unjustified because the link between us was not real, could never be real, and yet he felt like a dead weight upon me. Through politeness and shame I wanted to get rid of it.

76 Yes, don Apolonio was visibly improving. Even the doctor was surprised and offered no explanation.

77 On the very first morning I sat him up among the pillows, I noticed that certain look in my uncle's eyes. The heat was stifling and I had to lift him all by myself. Once I had propped him up I noticed: the old man was staring as dazed at my heaving chest, his face distorted and his trembling hands unconsciously moving towards me. I drew back instinctively and turned my head away.

78 "Please close the blinds, it's too hot."

79 His almost dead body was growing warm.

"Come here, Luisa, sit by my side. Come." 80

"Yes, uncle." I sat, my knees drawn up, at the foot of the bed, with- 81
out looking at him.

"Polo, you must call me Polo." His voice was again sweet and soft. 82
"You'll have a lot to forgive me. I'm old and sick, and a man in my condition is like a child."

"Yes." 83

"Let's see. Trying saying, 'Yes, Polo.'" 84

"Yes, Polo." 85

The name on my lips seemed to me an aberration, made me nause- 86
ated.

Polo got better, but became fussy and irritable. I realized he was 87
fighting to be the man he had once been, and yet the resurrected self
was not the same, but another.

"Luisa, bring me . . . Luisa, give me . . . Luisa, plump up my pil- 88
lows . . . pour me some water . . . prop up my leg. . . ."

He wanted me to be there all day long, always by his side, seeing to 89
his needs, touching him. And the fixed look and distorted face kept
coming back, more and more frequently, growing over his features like
a mask.

"Pick up my book. It fell underneath the bed, on this side." 90

I kneeled and stuck my head and almost half my body underneath 91
the bed, and had to stretch my arm as far as it would go, to reach it. At
first I thought it had been my own movements, or maybe the bed-
clothes, but once I had the book in my hand and was shuffling to get
out, I froze, stunned by what I had long foreseen, even expected: the
outburst, the scream, the thunder. A rage never before felt raced
through me when the realization of what was happening reached my
consciousness, when his shaking hand, taking advantage of my amazement, became surer and heavier, and enjoyed itself, adventuring with
no restraints, feeling and exploring my thighs—a fleshless hand glued
to my skin, fingering my body with delight, a dead hand searching impatiently between my legs, a bodyless hand.

I rose as quickly as I could, my face burning with shame and deter- 92
mination, but when I saw him I forgot myself: he had become a figure
in a nightmare. Polo was laughing softly, through his toothless mouth.
And then, suddenly serious, with a coolness that terrified me, he said:

"What? Aren't you my wife before God and men? Come here, I'm 93
cold, heat my bed. But first take off your dress, you don't want to get it
creased."

What followed, I know, is my story, my life, but I can barely remem- 94
ber it; like a disgusting dream I can't even tell whether it was long
or short. Only one thought kept me sane during the early days: "This
can't go on, it can't go on." I imagined that God would not allow it,
would prevent it in some way or another. He, personally, God, would

interfere. Death, once dreaded, seemed my only hope. Not Apolonio's
—he was a demon of death—but mine, the just and necessary death for
my corrupted flesh. But nothing happened. Everything stayed on, sus-
95 pended in time, without future. Then, one morning, taking nothing
with me, I left.

96 It was useless. Three days later they let me know that my husband
was dying, and they called me back. I went to see the father confessor
and told him my story.

97 "What keeps him alive is lust, the most horrible of all sins. This isn't
98 life, Father, it's death. Let him die!"
99 "He would die in despair. I can't allow it."
"And I?"
"I understand, but if you don't go to him, it would be like murder.
100 Try not to arouse him, pray to the Blessed Virgin, and keep your mind
on your duties. . . ."
I went back. And lust drew him out of the grave once more.
Fighting, endlessly fighting, I managed, after several years, to overcome
101 my hatred, and finally, at the very end, I even conquered the beast:
Apolonio died in peace, sweetly, his old self again.

But I was not able to go back to who I was. Now wickedness, malice, shine in the eyes of the men who look at me, and I feel I have become an occasion of sin for all, I, the vilest of harlots. Alone, a sinner,
totally engulfed by the never-ending flames of this cruel summer which
surrounds us all, like an army of ants.

Questions for Discussion and Writing

1. How does the quotation from the Bible evoke an archetypal situation re-
enacted by the characters in this story? In what respects does the
Shunammite's fate foreshadow Luisa's?
2. How would you characterize Luisa's past relationship with her Uncle
Apolonio and her Aunt Panchita?
3. Why does Luisa agree to marry her Uncle Apolonio despite her initial
qualms?
4. How do the jewelry and other material treasures Uncle Apolonio has acquired function as a SYMBOL for his greed and foreshadow his hunger for life?
5. What details suggest Luisa feels that she has betrayed herself in marrying
her uncle? How do changes in the rose SYMBOLIZE changes in Luisa?
6. How do the descriptions of Apolonio suggest that the person who comes
back to life has changed drastically from the uncle she knew? What details
suggest his renewal is unnatural?
7. How does the "disgusting dream" Luisa is living change her from the person
she was? Why doesn't she simply leave?
8. How can the story be understood as a universal FABLE of innocence and self-
betrayal, and the war between the flesh and the spirit?
9. Describe an abstract idea such as love, hate, depression, benevolence, and
anthropomorphize it by describing it as if it had a personality.

Naguib Mahfouz

Half a Day

Naguib Mahfouz was born in 1911 in Ganaliyya—an old quarter of Cairo that served as a setting for several of his novels—to a family that earned its living from trade. In 1930 he entered the Secular University in Cairo where he studied philosophy. Like his predecessor, Tewfik al-Hakim, Mahfouz developed a narrative technique through which he could criticize the government without running the risk of antagonizing the authorities. In this way, Mahfouz veiled his criticism of the ruling powers through the framework of historical novels set in ancient Egypt, most notably in The Mockery of Fate *(1939),* Radobais *(1943), and* The Struggle of Thebes *(1944). In the late 1940s and 1950s he turned to a more realistic style, setting his stories in modern Egypt. Between 1956 and 1957 he produced his famous Cairo Trilogy, a sequence of novels that chronicles the changes in three generations of a middle-class Cairo family.*

Widely regarded as Egypt's leading literary figure, Naguib Mahfouz is the first Arabic-language author awarded the Nobel Prize in literature (1988) and only the second from the African continent (Wole Soyinka, a Nigerian, had won two years earlier). Generations of Arabs have read his works and sixteen of his novels have been adapted for films in Egypt. He brought enormous changes to Arab prose by synthesizing traditional literary style and modern speech to create a language understood by Arabs everywhere.

Mahfouz's prose works have been compared in spirit and tone to the social realism of Balzac and Dickens because of both the extent to which they reflect Egypt's volatile political history, and their accurate depiction of the distressing conditions under which the poor live. He has held a variety of government posts and has served as director of the Foundation for Support of the Cinema. In 1989, when Mahfouz spoke out against the Ayatollah Khomeini's death sentence on Salman Rushdie (for his novel The Satanic Verses*), Mahfouz was himself subject to death threats by Muslim fundamentalists. In English, his most recently translated works include* Midag Alley *(1981),* Miramar *(1983), and* The Time and The Place and Other Stories *(1991), in which "Half a Day," translated by Davies Denys-Johnson, first appeared. This story is typical of Mahfouz's later works in its extensive use of allegory, symbolism, and experimental narrative techniques to explore spiritual themes.*

I proceeded alongside my father, clutching his right hand, running to keep up with the long strides he was taking. All my clothes were new: the black shoes, the green school uniform, and the red tarboosh. My delight in my new clothes, however, was not altogether unmarred, for this was no feast day but the day on which I was to be cast into school for the first time.

My mother stood at the window watching our progress, and I

1

2

would turn toward her from time to time, as though appealing for help. We walked along a street lined with gardens; on both sides were extensive fields planted with crops, prickly pears, henna trees, and a few date palms.

3   "Why school?" I challenged my father openly. "I shall never do anything to annoy you."

4   "I'm not punishing you," he said, laughing. "School's not a punishment. It's the factory that makes useful men out of boys. Don't you want to be like your father and brothers?"

5   I was not convinced. I did not believe there was really any good to be had in tearing me away from the intimacy of my home and throwing me into this building that stood at the end of the road like some huge, high-walled fortress, exceedingly stern and grim.

6   When we arrived at the gate we could see the courtyard, vast and crammed full of boys and girls. "Go in by yourself," said my father, "and join them. Put a smile on your face and be a good example to others."

7   I hesitated and clung to his hand, but he gently pushed me from him. "Be a man," he said. "Today you truly begin life. You will find me waiting for you when it's time to leave."

8   I took a few steps, then stopped and looked but saw nothing. Then the faces of boys and girls came into view. I did not know a single one of them, and none of them knew me. I felt I was a stranger who had lost his way. But glances of curiosity were directed toward me, and one boy approached and asked, "Who brought you?"

9   "My father," I whispered.

10   "My father's dead," he said quite simply.

11   I did not know what to say. The gate was closed, letting out a pitiable screech. Some of the children burst into tears. The bell rang. A lady came along, followed by a group of men. The men began sorting us into ranks. We were formed into an intricate pattern in the great courtyard surrounded on three sides by high buildings of several floors; from each floor we were overlooked by a long balcony roofed in wood.

12   "This is your new home," said the woman. "Here too there are mothers and fathers. Here there is everything that is enjoyable and beneficial to knowledge and religion. Dry your tears and face life joyfully."

13   We submitted to the facts, and this submission brought a sort of contentment. Living beings were drawn to other living beings, and from the first moments my heart made friends with such boys as were to be my friends and fell in love with such girls as I was to be in love with, so that it seemed my misgivings had had no basis. I had never imagined school would have this rich variety. We played all sorts of different games: swings, the vaulting horse, ball games. In the music room we chanted our first songs. We also had our first introduction to language. We saw a globe of the Earth, which revolved and showed the

various continents and countries. We started learning the numbers. The story of the Creator of the universe was read to us, we were told of His present world and of His Hereafter, and we heard examples of what He said. We ate delicious food, took a little nap, and woke up to go on with friendship and love, play and learning.

As our path revealed itself to us, however, we did not find it as totally sweet and unclouded as we had presumed. Dust-laden winds and unexpected accidents came about suddenly, so we had to be watchful, at the ready, and very patient. It was not all a matter of playing and fooling around. Rivalries could bring about pain and hatred or give rise to fighting. And while the lady would sometimes smile, she would often scowl and scold. Even more frequently she would resort to physical punishment. 14

In addition, the time for changing one's mind was over and gone and there was no question of ever returning to the paradise of home. Nothing lay ahead of us but exertion, struggle, and perseverance. Those who were able took advantage of the opportunities for success and happiness that presented themselves amid the worries. 15

The bell rang announcing the passing of the day and the end of work. The throngs of children rushed toward the gate, which was opened again. I bade farewell to friends and sweethearts and passed through the gate. I peered around but found no trace of my father, who had promised to be there. I stepped aside to wait. When I had waited for a long time without avail, I decided to return home on my own. After I had taken a few steps, a middle-aged man passed by, and I realized at once that I knew him. He came toward me, smiling, and shook me by the hand, saying, "It's a long time since we last met—how are you?" 16

With a nod of my head, I agreed with him and in turn asked, "And you, how are you?" 17

"As you can see, not all that good, the Almighty be praised!" 18

Again he shook me by the hand and went off. I proceeded a few steps, then came to a startled halt. Good Lord! Where was the street lined with gardens? Where had it disappeared to? When did all these vehicles invade it? And when did all these hordes of humanity come to rest upon its surface? How did these hills of refuse come to cover its sides? And where were the fields that bordered it? High buildings had taken over, the street surged with children, and disturbing noises shook the air. At various points stood conjurers showing off their tricks and making snakes appear from baskets. Then there was a band announcing the opening of a circus, with clowns and weight lifters walking in front. A line of trucks carrying central security troops crawled majestically by. The siren of a fire engine shrieked, and it was not clear how the vehicle would cleave its way to reach the blazing fire. A battle raged between a taxi driver and his passenger, while the passenger's wife called out for help and no one answered. Good God! I was in a daze. 19

My head spun. I almost went crazy. How could all this have happened in half a day, between early morning and sunset? I would find the answer at home with my father. But where was my home? I could see only tall buildings and hordes of people. I hastened on to the crossroads between the gardens and Abu Khoda. I had to cross Abu Khoda to reach my house, but the stream of cars would not let up. The fire engine's siren was shrieking at full pitch as it moved at a snail's pace, and I said to myself, "Let the fire take its pleasure in what it consumes." Extremely irritated, I wondered when I would be able to cross. I stood there a long time, until the young lad employed at the ironing shop on the corner came up to me. He stretched out his arm and said gallantly, "Grandpa, let me take you across."

Questions for Discussion and Writing

1. What can you infer about the boy's relationship with his father from their conversation on the way to school?
2. When did you suspect that the events in the story covered more than the narrator's first day at school?
3. How does the boy's encounter with the middle-aged man, and what the boy discovers when he returns to the street where he expects to find his home, suggest something out of the ordinary has happened?
4. How does the image of fire at the end of the story SYMBOLIZE the effect of time on people, places, and things?
5. In what way is the story an expression of the journey ARCHETYPE? How does the structure of the story personalize this universal theme?
6. Have you ever had experiences that made you aware that time is more subjective than simply counting minutes that pass on the clock?
7. What images or pictures come to mind in connection with the term *infinity*? What literal description can you offer that would represent infinity for you?

Tayeb Salih

The Cypriot Man

*Tayeb Salih was born in the northern province of the Sudan, the largest coun-
try on the African continent, in 1929. He was head of drama in the BBC's
Arabic Service and now works for UNESCO in Paris. His writing includes a
novel,* Season of Migration to the North *(1969), and the collection of stories
titled* The Wedding of Zein *(1978). Like many of Salih's other stories, "The
Cypriot Man," translated by Denys Johnson-Davies (1983), looks at the connection between ethical behavior and the ideas behind established religious systems, here examined through an encounter between an Everyman and a mysterious figure whose decisions are final in matters of life and death.*

Nicosia in July was as though Khartoum had been transplanted to   1
Damascus. The streets, as laid out by the British, were broad, the desert
was that of Khartoum, but there was that struggle between the east and
west winds that I remember in Damascus.

It was British from head to toe, despite all that blood that had been   2
spilt. I was surprised for I had expected a town of Greek character. The
man, though, did not give me time to pursue my thought to its conclusion but came and sat himself beside me at the edge of the swimming-
pool. He made a slight gesture with his head and they brought him a
cup of coffee.

"Tourist?" he said.   3

"Yes."   4

He made a noise the import of which I did not follow—it was as   5
though he were saying that the likes of me didn't deserve to be a tourist
in Nicosia, or that Nicosia didn't deserve to have the likes of me being a
tourist in it.

I turned my attention from him so as to examine a woman with a   6
face like that of one of Raphael's angels, and a body like that of
Gauguin's women. Was she the wife or the other woman? Again he cut
through the thread of my thoughts:

"Where are you from?"   7

"The Sudan."   8

"What do you do?"   9

"I'm in government service."   10

I laughed for in fact I didn't work for the government; anyway gov-   11
ernments have broad shoulders.

"I don't work," he said. "I own a factory."   12

"Really?"   13

"For making women's clothes."   14

"How lovely."   15

16   "I've made a lot of money. I worked like a black. I made a fortune. I don't work any longer—spend all my time in bed."

17   "Sleeping?"

18   "You must be joking. What does a man do in bed?"

19   "Don't you get tired?"

20   "You're joking. Look at me—what age do you think I am?"

21   Sometimes fifty, sometimes seventy, but I didn't want to encourage him.

22   "Seventy," I said to him.

23   This did not upset him as I had presumed. He gave a resounding laugh and said:

24   "Seventy-five in actual fact, but no one takes me for more than fifty. Go on, be truthful."

25   "All right, fifty."

26   "Why do you think it is?"

27   "Because you take exercise."

28   "Yes, in bed, I bash away—white and black, red and yellow: all colours. Europeans, negresses, Indians, Arabs, Jewesses; Muslims, Christians, Buddhists: all religions."

29   "You're a liberal-minded man."

30   "Yes, in bed."

31   "And outside."

32   "I hate Jews."

33   "Why do you hate Jews?"

34   "Just so. Also they play with skill."

35   "What?"

36   "The game of death. They've been at it for centuries."

37   "Why does that make you angry?"

38   "Because I . . . because I . . . it's of no consequence."

39   "Are they not defeated?"

40   "They all give up in the end."

41   "And their women?"

42   "There's no one better than them in bed. The greater your hatred for them, the greater your enjoyment with their women. They are my chosen people."

43   "And the negroes of America?"

44   "My relationship with them has not reached the stage of hatred. I must pay them more attention."

45   "And the Arabs?"

46   "They provoke laughter or pity. They give up easily, these days anyway. Playing with them is not enjoyable because it's one-sided."

47   I thought: if only they had accepted Cyprus, if only Balfour had promised them it.

48   The Cypriot man gave his resounding laugh and said:

49   "Women prolong one's life. A man must appear to be at least twenty years younger than he is. That's what being smart is."

"Do you fool death?"   50

"What is death? Someone you meet by chance, who sits with you as   51
we are sitting now, who talks freely with you, perhaps about the
weather or women or shares on the stock market. Then he politely sees
you to the door. He opens the door and signs for you to go out. After
that you don't know."

A grey cloud stayed overhead for a while, but at that moment I did not   52
know that the divining arrows had been cast and that the Cypriot man
was playing a hazardous game with me.

The wave of laughter broadened out and enfolded me. They were a   53
sweet family which I had come to like since sitting down: the father
with his good-natured face and the mother with her English voice
which was like an Elizabethan air played on the strings of an ancient
lyre, and four daughters, the eldest of whom was not more than twelve,
who would go in and out of the pool, laughing and teasing their parents. They would smile at me and broaden the compass of their happiness till it included me. There came a moment when I saw on the father's face that he was about to invite me to join them; it was at that
moment that the Cypriot man descended upon me. The eldest girl got
up and stepped gracefully towards the pool. With the girl having suddenly come to a stop as though some mysterious power had halted her,
the Cypriot man said:

"This one I'd pay a hundred pounds sterling for."   54

"What for?" I said to him in alarm.   55

The Cypriot man made an obscene gesture with his arm.   56

At that moment the girl fell face-down on to the stone and blood   57
poured from her forehead. The good-natured family started up, like
frightened birds, and surrounded the girl. I immediately got up from
beside the man, feeling for him an overwhelming hatred, and seated
myself at a table far away from him. I remembered my own daughters
and their mother in Beirut and was angry. I saw the members of the delightful family making their departures, sadly, the daughters clinging
to their mother, the mother reproaching the father, and I became more
angry. Then I quietened down and the things around me quietened
down. The clamour died away and there came to me my friend Taher
Wad Rawwasi and sat beside me: on the bench in front of Sa'eed's
shop. His face was beaming, full of health and energy.

"Really," I said to him, "why is it that you haven't grown old and   58
weak though you're older than all of them?"

"From when I first became aware of the world," he said, "I've been   59
on the move. I don't remember ever not moving. I work like a horse
and if there's no work to be done I create something to busy myself
with. I go to sleep at any old time, early or late, and wake up directly
the *muezzin* says 'God is great, God is great,' for the dawn prayer."

"But you don't pray?"   60

61   "I say the *shahada*[1] and ask God's forgiveness after the *muezzin* has finished giving the call to prayers, and my heart finds assurance that the world is going along as it always has. I take a nap for half an hour or so. The odd thing is that a nap after the call to prayers is for me equal to the whole night's sleep. After that I wake up as though I've been woken by an alarm clock. I make the tea and wake Fatima up. She performs the dawn prayer. We drink tea. I go down to meet the sun on the Nile's surface and say to God's morning Hello and Welcome. However long I'm away I come back to find the breakfast ready. We sit down to it, Fatima and I and any of God's servants that destiny brings to us. For more than fifty years it's been like this."

62   One day I'll ask Taher Wad Rawwasi about the story of his marriage to Fatima bint Jabr ad-Dar, one of Mahjoub's four sisters. His loyalty was not to himself but to Mahjoub, and he used to make fun both of himself and of the world. Would he become a hero? It was clear that if it really came to it he would sacrifice himself for Mahjoub. Should I ask him now? However, off his own bat, he uttered a short phrase compounded of the fabric of his whole life:

63   "Fatima bint Jabr ad-Dar—what a girl!"

64   "And Mahjoub?"

65   Taher Wad Rawwasi gave a laugh that had the flavour of those bygone days; it indicated the extent of his love for Mahjoub. Even mentioning his name would fill him with happiness, as though the presence of Mahjoub on the face of the earth made it less hostile, better, in Taher Wad Rawwasi's view. He laughed and said, laughing:

66   "Mahjoub's something else; Mahjoub's made of a different clay."

67   Then he fell silent and it was clear to me that he didn't, at that time, wish to say any more on that particular subject. After a time I asked him:

68   "Abdul Hafeez said you'd never in your whole life entered a mosque. Is that so?"

69   "Just once I entered a mosque."

70   "Why? What for?"

71   "Only the once. It was one winter, in *Touba* or *Amsheer*,[2] God knows best."

72   "It was in *Amsheer*," I said to him, "after you'd buried Maryam at night."

73   "That's right. How did you know?"

74   "I was there with you."

75   "Where? I didn't see you that morning, though the whole village had collected on that day in the mosque."

---

[1]The doctrinal formula of Islam: "There is no god but God and Mohammed is the Messenger of God."
[2]Winter months in the Coptic calendar.

"I was by the window, appearing and disappearing till you said 76
'And not those who are astray. Amen.' "[3]

"And then?" 77

"God be praised. Poor Meheimeed was calling out 'Where's the man 78
who was here gone to?' "

"And then?" 79

Suddenly the dream bird flew away. Wad Rawwasi disappeared, as 80
did Wad Hamid[4] with all its probabilities. Where he had been sitting I
saw the Cypriot man, I heard his voice and my heart contracted. I heard
his shouting and the hubbub, the slapping of the water against the
sides of the swimming-pool, with spectres shaped in the form of naked
women and naked men and children leaping about and shrieking. The
voice was saying:

"For this one I'd only pay fifty pounds sterling." 81

I pressed down on my eyes so as to be more awake. I looked at the 82
goods on offer in the market. It was that woman. She was drinking orange juice at the moment at which the Cypriot man had said what he
did. She spluttered and choked; a man leapt to his feet to help her, then
a woman; servants and waiters came along, people gathered, and they
carried her off unconscious. It was as if a magician had waved his wand
and, so it seemed to me, the people instantly vanished; and the darkness too, as though close at hand, awaiting a signal from someone,
came down all at once. The Cypriot man and I on our own with the
light playing around on the surface of the water. Between the light and
the darkness he said to me:

"Two American girls arrived this morning from New York. They're 83
very beautiful, very rich. One's eighteen and she's mine; the other's
twenty-five and she's for you. They're sisters; they own a villa in
Kyrenia. I've got a car. The adventure won't cost you a thing. Come
along. They'll be really taken by your colour."

The darkness and the light were wrestling around the swimming- 84
pool, while it was as if the voice of the Cypriot man were supplying the
armies of darkness with weapons. Thus I wanted to say to him All
right, but another sound issued from my throat involuntarily, and I
said to him, as I followed the war taking place on the water's surface:

"No, thank you. I didn't come to Nicosia in search of that. I came to 85
have a quiet talk with my friend Taher Wad Rawwasi because he refused to visit me in London and I failed to meet him in Beirut."

Then I turned to him—and what a ghastly sight met my eyes. Was I 86
imagining things, or dreaming, or mad? I ran, ran to take refuge with
the crowd in the hotel bar. I asked for something to drink; I drank it,
without recollecting the taste of it or what it was. I calmed down a little.

---

[3]The final words of the *Fatiha*, the equivalent in Islam of the Lord's Prayer.
[4]The village in which most of the writer's novels and short stories are placed.

But the Cypriot man came and sat down with me. He had bounded along on crutches. He asked for whisky, a double. He said that he had lost his right leg in the war. What war? One of the wars, what did it matter which one? His wooden leg had been smashed this morning. He had climbed up a mountain. He was waiting for a new leg from London. Sometimes his voice was English, sometimes it had a German accent; at others it seemed French to me; he used American words.

87   "Are you . . ."

88   "No, I'm not. Some people think I'm Italian, some that I'm Russian; others German . . . Spanish. Once an American tourist asked me whether I was from Basutoland. Just imagine. What's it matter where I'm from? And Your Excellency?"

89   "Why do you say to me Your Excellency?"

90   "Because you're a very fine person."

91   "And what's my importance?"

92   "You exist today and you won't exist tomorrow—and you won't recur."

93   "That happens to every person—what's important about that?"

94   "Not every person is aware of it. You, Excellency, are aware of your position in time and place."

95   "I don't believe so."

96   He put down his drink in one gulp and stood up, on two sound legs, unless I was imagining things, or was dreaming or mad, and it was as though he were the Cypriot man. He bowed with very affected politeness, and it was as though his face as I had seen it at the edge of the pool made you sense that life had no value.

97   "I won't say goodbye," he said, "but *au revoir*, Excellency."

98   It was ten o'clock when I went to bed. I did everything possible to bring sleep about, being tired and having swum all day. I tried talking to Taher Wad Rawwasi. I asked him about the story of his marriage to Fatima bint Jabr ad-Dar. I asked him about his attendance at dawn prayers on that memorable day. I asked him about that singing which was linking the two banks with silken threads, while poor Meheimeed was floundering about in the waves in pursuit of Maryam's phantom, but he did not reply. Music was of no help to me, neither was reading. I could have gone out, gone to a night club or for a walk, or I could have sat in the hotel bar. There was nothing I could do. Then the pain began: a slight numbness at the tips of the toes which gradually began to advance upwards until it was as though terrible claws were tearing at my stomach, chest, back and head: the fires of hell had all at once broken out.

99   I would lose consciousness then enter into a terrible vortex of pains and fires; the frightful face would show itself to me between unconsciousness and a state of semi-wakefulness, leaping from chair to chair, disappearing and reappearing all over the room. Voices I did not un-

derstand came to me from the unknown, faces I did not know, dark and scowling. There was nothing I could do. Though in some manner in a state of consciousness, I was incapable of lifting up the receiver and calling a doctor, or going down to reception in the hotel, or crying out for help. There was a savage and silent war taking place between me and unknown fates. I certainly gained some sort of a victory, for I came to to the sound of four o'clock in the morning striking, with the hotel and the town silent. The pains had gone except for a sensation of exhaustion and overwhelming despair, as though the world, the good and the evil of it, were not worth a gnat's wing. After that I slept. At nine o'clock in the morning the plane taking me to Beirut circled above Nicosia; it looked to me like an ancient cemetery.

On the evening of the following day in Beirut the doorbell rang. It 100 was a woman clad in black carrying a child. She was crying and the first sentence she said was:

"I'm Palestinian—my daughter has died."   101

I stood for a while looking at her, not knowing what to say; how- 102 ever, she entered, sat down and said:

"Will you let me rest and feed my child?"   103

While she was telling me her story the doorbell rang. I took a tele- 104 gram and opened it, with the Palestinian woman telling me her formidable misfortune, while I was engrossed in my own.

I crossed seas and deserts, wanting to know before all else when 105 and how he had died. They informed me that he had as usual worked in the garden in his field in the morning and had done those things he usually did during his day. He had not complained of anything. He had entered his relations' homes, sat with his friends here and there; he'd brought some half-ripe dates and drunk coffee with them. My name had cropped up in his conversation several times. He had been awaiting my arrival impatiently, for I had written to him that I was coming. He supped lightly as usual, performed the evening prayer, then about ten o'clock the harbingers of death had come to him; before the dawn prayer he had departed this world, and when the aeroplane was bearing me from Nicosia to Beirut they had just finished burying him.

At forenoon I stood by his grave, with the Cypriot man sitting at the 106 side of the grave, in his formal guise, listening to me as I gave prayers and supplications. He said to me in a voice that seemed to issue from the earth and sky, encompassing me from all sides:

"You won't see me again in this guise other than at the last moment 107 when I shall open the door to you, bow quietly and say to you 'After you, Your Excellency.' You will see me in other and various guises. You may encounter me in the form of a beautiful girl, who will come to you and tell you she admires your views and opinions and that she'd like to do an interview with you for some paper or magazine; or in the shape of a president or a ruler who offers you some post that makes your heart lose a beat; or in the form of one of life's pranks that gives you a lot of money without your expending any effort; perhaps in the form of a vast multitude that applauds you for some reason you don't know; or perhaps you'll see me in the form of a girl twenty years younger than you, whom you desire and who'll say to you: 'Let's go to an isolated hut way up in the mountains.' Beware. Your father will not be there on the next occasion to give his life for you. Beware. The term of life is designated, but we take into consideration the skill shown in playing the game. Beware for you are now ascending towards the mountain peak."

Questions for Discussion and Writing

1. What kind of person does the narrator seem to be? How do his comments about spiritual beauty, sexuality, and government service suggest he is well cast as the ARCHETYPAL Everyman? Under what circumstances does he encounter the Cypriot man?

2. In what way does the unusual coincidence of the girl's death following the Cypriot man's comments about paying one hundred pounds sterling for her suggest that the mysterious stranger may be a PERSONIFICATION of evil? How do the Cypriot man's allusions to his age, sexual proclivities, and his attitudes towards Jews, Negroes, Arabs, and death add to this feeling?

3. What details suggest that the narrator's friend, Taher Wad Rawwasi, SYMBOLIZES goodness? In what sense does the story develop as an ALLEGORY in which an Everyman has to choose between good and evil?

4. Why is it significant that the narrator turns down the Cypriot man's offer of one of the sisters after the Cypriot man has demonstrated his death-dealing powers a second time? How might the Cypriot man's next appearance, on crutches, SYMBOLIZE the setback of having his offer rejected?

5. How does the information that reaches the narrator about his father the next day move the "contest" a step forward?

6. Why does the Cypriot man let the narrator live? Under what circumstances does the Cypriot man say he will be entitled to claim the narrator's soul? What is the common element, or theme, that links together these seemingly diverse situations?

7. Begin by describing a person who seems quite ordinary, then describe how the person changes; gradually add details until the person turns into a monster, both physically and psychologically, such as a werewolf or Dr. Jekyll/Mr. Hyde.

8. Analyze this story in terms of the elements traditionally associated with the horror tale (the inhuman foe, righteous hero)—for example, Dracula versus Von Helsing, or the F.B.I. agent pitted against Hannibal Lector in the 1991 movie, Silence of the Lambs. To what extent is the horror of the story based on the fear that the hero or heroine will become contaminated by contact with the "monster"?

9. Imagine you have made a pact with the Devil. What do you want in return for your soul?

François Barcelo

The Man Who Stopped Trains

François Barcelo, one of Quebec's most imaginative contemporary authors, was born in Montreal in 1941. After receiving his master's degree in French litera-ture from L' Université de Montreal in 1963, he became an advertising copy-writer. In 1981, his first two novels, Agenor, Agenor, Agenor et Agenor *and* La Tribu, *were published. In 1982, a third,* Ville Dieu, *appeared. In addi-tion to his novels, Barcelo has written several short stories and the introduction to* Montreal, *a book of photographs with a bilingual text. He has also written a runner's guide to Montreal and, like the hero of "The Man Who Stopped Trains," translated by Matt Cohen (1983), runs about three thousand kilome-ters a year. This story, as are his other works, is witty and lucid, a satiric cau-tionary tale. In it, the protagonist lives to regret his wish that his life take an exciting turn.*

Like most amateur runners Gonzague Gagnon feared and detested the stretch between the first third and the halfway mark. 1

Along the small dirt road where he ran ten kilometres every day be-fore turning around and walking back, he had planted stakes to mark the main stages of his course: a tenth of the way, a fifth, a quarter, a third, halfway, two-thirds, etc. 2

The first third went by most easily because Gonzague Gagnon did not yet feel tired and because this third was divided into numerous fractions, which gave the impression of rapid progress. 3

But as soon as he had passed the stake signalling the one-third mark, Gonzague Gagnon moved into a no-man's-land: one and two-thirds kilometres without any stake, only the temptation to give up be-cause his legs were beginning to hurt. 4

As he was not very well educated Gonzague Gagnon didn't realize that due to a bizarre mathematical caprice, the gap between a third and a half is actually twice as large as that between a quarter and a third. He thought it was only an illusion. And so it amounted to the same thing. 5

Even worse, about a third of the way along, the winding road that was so pleasantly shaded where it followed a small stream turned into the open countryside and straightened out as it travelled between two flat and treeless fields. To the right was a little-used railway track. To the left, in the distance, flowed a river which at this point was very wide and not the least bit interesting or attractive. 6

The stake signalling the half-way mark was just on the other side of the narrow wooden bridge that crossed the St Nicol River. After that the road became shaded again, and full of those thousand and one dis- 7

965

tractions that transform the most monotonous course into a constantly changing experience. It made you think you were going a lot faster than in the open field.

8   So once the halfway mark was passed, everything went more easily and Gonzague Gagnon knew that the hard part was over. There was no point in giving up then. Soon he would reach the two-thirds stake, soon after that the three-quarters, the four-fifths, and finally the stake marking the end.

9   Had it not been for that diabolic stretch from the third to the half, he would have found the run very easy—too easy perhaps. And on the rare occasion when he had to give up and walk back, it happened somewhere between these two stakes.

10   Gonzague Gagnon manned a gas pump at the Gagnon garage, the only service station in St Nicol. There was a small apartment above the garage which he shared with Gaston Gagnon, garage mechanic and vague relation—everyone in St Nicol being more or less related and called Gagnon. But Gonzague and Gaston had nothing more in common than their employer and their apartment. They hardly ever talked to each other because they had nothing to say. Gaston found Gonzague's passion for running ridiculous. And Gonzague found it ridiculous not to have such a passion.

*

11   He'd never seen statistics on the subject but Gonzague Gagnon knew that most men die at about seventy years of age. He told himself that his running habit would help him live a little longer than the old men of St Nicol. Maybe until he was seventy-five.

12   When Gonzague Gagnon turned twenty-five, he calculated that he had arrived at the one-third mark of his life. He resigned himself to facing the most difficult part of his existence, between twenty-five and thirty-seven-and-a-half: that flat and lengthy stretch between the third and the half.

13   Not that the first third of his life had been particularly eventful. His birth, six years at school, the death of his mother, the hundreds of thousands of litres he had poured into the same cars and trucks week after week had been the only milestones in his life so far. But he had not found the time long, because this first third of his existence was only the first, and what he experienced during it was for the first time.

14   The beginning of the second third seemed excessively repetitive and monotonous—all the more so since he had twelve years and six months to go before reaching another important fraction of his life.

15   He began to seek out distractions.

16   Television put him to sleep as did drinking more than one bottle of beer. So the two principal amusements of the Nicolois didn't help him at all.

17   During his first twenty-five years Gonzague Gagnon had been con-

tent to daydream in his rocking chair which he didn't even rock—during the summer, on the balcony behind the Gagnon garage, looking out on the fields where the cows grazed nearly motionless; during the winter, in his room with the door shut to block out the sound of Gaston Gagnon's television.

But when he became aware that he was in the long, boring stretch between the third and halfway points of his life the time seemed even more boring and endless than before.   18

It was then that a public library opened in St Nicol. The mayor had decided to take advantage of a grant that had been set up for this purpose because the fire-truck needed repairs. He requested the necessary amount from the Department for the Propagation of Culture in Deprived Regions. Since about a hundred dollars remained after the repairs, the mayor, being a man of conscience, designated this money for the establishment of a public library. He had a shelf put up at the fire station. And he had the town of St Nicol subscribe to a series entitled *Great Mysteries of the Universe*.   19

According to an advertisement in the TV guide this series was made up of marvellous books, elegantly bound and embellished with numerous photographs and illustrations—many in colour. It seemed to the mayor of St Nicol that the series would please people who liked reading, people who liked leather-bound books and people who liked photographs and illustrations in black and white or colour. When the funds for the library were exhausted he had the subscription cancelled. And he looked with satisfaction at the first nine volumes of *Great Mysteries of the Universe* that were carefully lined up on their shelf in the fire station.   20

Gonzague Gagnon was a volunteer fireman. But this was only a very occasional distraction, since fires were infrequent in St Nicol. And anyway, whenever there was a fire, the firemen always came too late. Gonzague Gagnon had applied to be a volunteer out of a sense of duty, because he was the fastest runner in the village and was always the first to arrive at the scene.   21

One day Gonzague Gagnon discovered the dust-covered volumes. He had never read a book, had never even held one in his hands—except for some greasy, well-thumbed school books with many of their pages pulled out.   22

The first book in the series was called *And If You Could. . . .* Gonzague Gagnon read it in two nights, sitting in the driver's seat of the fire truck. Then he went to the other books, even though he read slowly and could not grasp the meaning of words without saying them out loud. But his favourite by far was *And If You Could. . . .* He re-read it a dozen times. The author claimed that each and every human being has special powers but that most people live in ignorance of their gift. But with a bit of systematic research, everyone could discover their own extraordinary powers.   23

The last chapter of *And If You Could . . .* was made up of a list of   24 nine hundred and one parapsychological powers. Each was preceded by two boxes, "yes" and "no," in which the reader could make a mark depending on whether or not he was gifted with this faculty. Here are some examples from the list.

Yes	No	
☐	☐	Bend forks at a distance
☐	☐	Levitate small animals (birds, cats, rabbits, etc.)
☐	☐	Levitate furniture (chairs, pianos, television sets)
☐	☐	Change the colour of objects without painting them
☐	☐	Make rain
☐	☐	Stop snowstorms

25   This list took up twenty pages and opened up some fascinating possibilities to Gonzague Gagnon.

26   He tried every experiment. Hunting with his eyes, for example, which would have allowed him to bring down partridges or rabbits with a simple wink. Heating water by plunging his hands into it. Instantly giving the answer to any complicated arithmetic calculation.

27   But nothing worked for him. The partridges continued their flight without even slowing down. The rabbits took off at full speed. The water stayed cold in the pot. And Gonzague Gagnon gave the most absurd replies to the simplest problems.

28   The author of *And If You Could . . .* specified that these powers weren't necessarily permanent, that one could acquire or lose them during the aging process, that for certain people certain powers only worked on Mondays, that the inexplicable powers had by definition the tendency to inexplicably appear or disappear.

29   That is why Gonzague Gagnon re-read the list several times a week, although he knew it almost by heart. And this activity helped him pass the time between the third and the halfway points of his life.

30   Although the author of *And If You Could . . .* asserted that he had undertaken in-depth research in order to draw up the most complete list possible, he encouraged his readers to carry out their own experiments.

31   So Gonzague Gagnon gave free reign to his imagination. His daily run gave him numerous opportunities. Transform the waters of the St Nicol River into milk . . . make buckwheat grow through snow . . . move houses closer together . . . shape clouds in his own image . . . make cows sing the "Kyrie" . . . turn fenceposts into Easter candles. . . . Why not? All he had to do was to keep trying. One day something would work.

32   Telepathy held his attention for a long time. It seemed more "normal" than making cows fly or snakes sing. Had it not often happened, without planning, that he and his employer would broach the same subject?

"It must be about time to change the oil in the Ford," they would both say at once. 33

When, at the age of thirteen, Gonzague Gagnon had entered into his vocation, he had invented a game: to guess if the driver of the car approaching the service station was going to ask for regular or super. But he had to give up the game when he knew which cars took regular and which took super. Anyway this game didn't really help pass the time since it could only be played when a car was approaching— the very moment when Gonzague Gagnon would have something to do. 34

So several years later Gonzague Gagnon returned to telepathy, telling himself that perhaps he had a gift for it. 35

He began by trying to transmit thoughts. For example, he would stare at his employer's neck when he turned his back and try to give him commands: ``Lean over. Take out your wallet. Scratch your left buttock." But his employer never responded. Except once, when he turned towards Gonzague Gagnon—who was ordering him to turn towards him—and said, "Why are you looking at me like that? What's wrong with you?" 36

The gas station attendant mumbled: "A dog does well to watch his master." To which his employer had shrugged his shoulders and gone back to dismantling the transmission of Nésime Gagnon's Chevrolet. 37

Forced to concede that he didn't have the power of mental projection, Gonzague Gagnon concluded that he must, on the contrary, excel at thought reception. 38

Fortunately he lived with an ideal subject: Gaston Gagnon, who spent hours in front of his television, watching programs that didn't seem to interest him—and therefore spent hours thinking. 39

For several evenings Gonzague sat in the armchair next to Gaston's. He closed his eyes, emptied his mind and concentrated, ready to seize the least reflection, the smallest image, the tiniest scrap of words or ideas emanating from his colleague. 40

But, perhaps because Gaston never thought about anything, Gonzague never perceived anything. 41

He had more success with Groaner, his boss's dog, a bastard albino who loved to pretend to be vicious but was actually afraid of field mice. During the summer, Gonzague Gagnon would sit on a chair in front of the service station, a few steps from Groaner's kennel. And Groaner would sit on his hind legs and watch him. Gonzague Gagnon would tell him what to do: "Bend your head, fold back your left ear, blink your eyes." And Groaner would obey. But Gonzague found little to be proud of in this because the dog did not respond to more complex instructions: "Bark five times, do a somersault, say hello." 42

There was no glory in making a stupid dog do stupid things. 43

*

44   By the time he had reached his thirty-fifth birthday, Gonzague Gagnon had given up trying to discover paranormal powers within himself.

45   Of the first half of his life, only two years and six months remained.
Surely then the months and the years would begin to whizz by as
quickly as the kilometres after he was halfway through his run.

46   The morning of his birthday, Gonzague Gagnon laced on his running shoes, determined to make an assault on a goal he had set long
ago: to run ten kilometres in thirty-five minutes on his thirty-fifth birthday. For many years he had made similar goals: thirty-two minutes
at thirty-two, thirty-three minutes at thirty-three years, and so on. He'd
never succeeded. But as the years went by, the goal became easier. And
last week he had managed to run the distance in thirty-six minutes.

47   It was six o'clock in the morning, which meant that he had two
hours in which to run his ten kilometres, walk back, take a shower and
go down to work.

48   It was a beautiful morning and Gonzague Gagnon congratulated
himself once more on being born in May, rather than having been conceived in the spring and then born in November or December, like most
of the villagers. He ran the first two kilometres at an easy pace, to make
sure his legs were warmed up. Then he lengthened his stride and began
to speed up. He reached the one-third stake three minutes later. As always, he began to feel a bit out of breath. But if he wanted to get in under thirty-five minutes, he couldn't slow down, even though every step
seemed to drag.

49   From a distance, Gonzague Gagnon saw the St Nicol River. Just on
the other side he would find the five-kilometre marker. But his legs
were growing heavy. Should he slow down and risk not doing his ten
kilometres in thirty-five minutes? Or maintain or even accelerate his
pace, and risk not finishing?

50   A far-away rumbling attracted his attention. It was the passenger
train. It gave a long whistle and Gonzague Gagnon couldn't resist the
temptation to turn his head, even though he knew he would lose a fraction of a second.

51   The train was quickly catching up to him, along the railway track
that ran parallel to the road.

52   It was always the same train, no doubt always with the same passengers and the same conductor.

53   Once more Gonzague Gagnon looked ahead. The wooden bridge
that straddled the St Nicol River was now at most a hundred feet away.

54   At that moment Gonzague Gagnon realized that he had not tried to
exercise his powers on anything mechanical. Why had he always tried
to move tables, chairs and other immobile objects? Was it not mobile
things like cars, trucks or trains that he—Gonzague Gagnon, apprentice
mechanic—would be the most likely to affect?

55   He glanced to the right. The train was about to draw up level with

him and would soon begin to cross the metal railway bridge upstream from the wooden one.

"Stop," said Gonzague Gagnon.   56

He had spoken in an undertone, for fear of appearing ridiculous.   57
But even if the train had had ears and hadn't been making so much noise, it could hardly have heard him from such a distance.

Nevertheless the train braked. Its wheels locked and screeched,   58
sending up great showers of sparks. Then the engine stopped, just a few turns of the wheel from the metal bridge.

Gonzague Gagnon also came to a halt, a few steps from the wooden   59
bridge.

Out came the engineer and the brakeman, gesturing wildly, the for-   60
mer shouting abuse apparently directed at the latter. They leaned over the track, inspected the wheels, then climbed back up. The train started up again, advancing slowly and with caution. Gonzague Gagnon watched as it gathered speed and pulled away.

He forgot his running. "I can stop trains," he said to himself over   61
and over again as he walked back home. But upon due reflection, he had to conclude that the experiment was not conclusive.

He waited impatiently for the train to appear again the following   62
week. Just as it was on the point of crossing the St Nicol River, he said, as he had the last time, "Stop." And the train stopped.

For several weeks that summer, Gonzague Gagnon took great plea-   63
sure in commanding the train to stop and watching the engineers leap frantically onto the track. Each time, the locomotive carried more in-spectors, more mechanics, more people whom Gonzague Gagnon guessed to be specialists of all kinds, from places farther and farther away, from positions which were more and more exalted.

The authorities had a length of the track replaced. Nothing changed.   64
In the village people began to talk about a curse, about a haunted rail-way track. When they brought the subject up with Gonzague Gagnon he smiled but said nothing.

Finally, when a team came to demolish the old metal bridge in order   65
to replace it with a new one, Gonzague Gagnon told himself that he had gone too far. The authorities were delighted that the new bridge had solved the problem of the inexplicable stoppages of the train, even if the stoppages themselves remained unexplained.

*

"Today my life is half over," Gonzague Gagnon realized one fine   66
December morning.

He brushed his teeth and put on his tights and his tracksuit, taking   67
special care to slide into place a little handkerchief folded in four. It kept the cold from a particularly sensitive part of his anatomy.

His usual road was well ploughed, but with a base of slippery ice   68 that encouraged caution. For this reason, Gonzague Gagnon was unable to achieve his goal of thirty-seven-and-one-half minutes at thirty-seven-and-one-half years of age. "That pleasure will be for my thirty-eighth birthday." He came to this conclusion philosophically, though his recent failures might have led him into bitterness. For a long time he had been convinced that eventually it would be easy to run the ten kilometres in the number of minutes equal to his age. But age was weakening him, and each year he needed more than an extra minute to run his distance.

69   On this particular morning he ran without any precise goal, without pushing himself, with no purpose other than enjoying the outdoors and feeling the harmonious working of his thirty-seven-and-a-half-year-old body.

70   He was even taking pleasure in musing that since he had now reached the middle of his life, the rest would be easy and full of excitement. Soon he would be two-thirds of the way through, then three-quarters. Never again would he be as bored as he had been between the third and the halfway mark.

71   Approaching the halfway point, the St Nicol River, he ran easily though without great speed. He was getting ready to cross the wooden bridge when he noticed a black silhouette against the frozen white bank of the river.

72   He slowed down. Sitting on a log, waving a short rod above a hole in the ice, someone was fishing in the river.

73   The fisherman suddenly raised his eyes towards him, as though he had sensed his presence.

74   Gonzague Gagnon stopped short. The fisherman was a woman. He had seen women fish before, but a woman fisherman alone, on the river—he had never seen that.

75   He decided to go closer and crossed the ditch at the edge of the road, aware of the snow working its way into his shoes. He advanced with difficulty, sinking to mid-thigh with each step.

76   Soon he was on the river. The wind had swept it clean of snow. The woman watched as he came near. He saw that she was beautiful. That frightened Gonzague Gagnon. He wanted to turn back. But what would she think after having seen him come towards her? That he was afraid?

77   Of course he was afraid. More and more afraid as the woman became more and more beautiful. What was he going to say to her?

78   He stopped a few steps away from her.

79   "Hello," he said.

80   "Hello."

81   "Are they biting?"

82   She didn't reply. Gonzague Gagnon only needed to look at the fish that surrounded her on the ice—ten perch and two pike. The most re-

cently caught still flopped about before freezing and dying—or dying and freezing.

For a few moments he stood still, watching her. Suddenly the 83 woman jerked her rod. Then she stood up and pulled out a beautiful perch, wriggling through the hole. Gonzague Gagnon moved forward to take the fish off the hook.

"I can do it," said the woman, removing her gloves. 84

Gonzague Gagnon stepped back. He would have liked to spend the 85 day there, not speaking, just watching her. But he felt he should speak. He searched for a subject of conversation that would be interesting or, better still, would make him interesting.

"I'm a runner," he finally said. 86

"So it seems." 87

He ought to have added that he was an apprentice mechanic. But 88 for the first time in his life, he was ashamed of his trade. Not that it suddenly seemed too humble. But too ordinary. Doubtless every village in the world had at least one apprentice mechanic, and maybe there were hundreds in the city that this woman came from—it seemed certain that she came from a city.

Again Gonzague Gagnon made his silent search for something to 89 say. Then there was a faint trembling in the air, hardly noticeable.

"It's the train," thought Gonzague Gagnon, pricking up his ears. 90

In fact the trembling had become a deep and far-away rumbling. 91

"It's the passenger train," said Gonzague Gagnon. 92

The woman nodded her head distractedly. All of her attention was 93 on the tip of her fishing rod, which she was shaking in brief staccato bursts.

Gonzague Gagnon turned to watch the train. It was now visible, 94 and rapidly growing larger.

"I can stop trains," he said. 95

Immediately he regretted having spoken. The woman had given 96 him a look that was both incredulous and indifferent, as if he were insane.

"I'm going to show her," he said to himself. And then, aloud: 97 "You'll see."

But suddenly he feared that his power might have weakened with 98 the passage of time. He ran towards the railway track, to be closer to the train.

A second doubt seized him: what if the young woman found his 99 ability to stop trains absolutely useless? Would he not be more sure of impressing her if at the same time he demonstrated his courage?

He climbed the embankment and positioned himself on a railway 100 tie, facing the train. The train was only about a hundred metres away. Gonzague Gagnon could feel the track vibrating beneath his feet. He waited a few seconds. Then he crossed his arms and closed his eyes.

101   "Stop," he said in a firm voice, loud enough for the young woman to hear.

102   The screeching of the wheels was enough to shatter his eardrums—but the noise reassured him of his power. The train came to a stop so close that he felt the heat of the engine on his cheeks.

103   He opened his eyes and looked towards the woman. She was still there, standing up, a black silhouette in the middle of her circle of fish. She was too far away for him to be able to see if she was watching him. But how could she not?

104   Voices drew his attention.

105   "This hasn't happened for years," Gonzague Gagnon heard one rough voice say.

106   A moment later he was facing two men in overalls.

107   "What are you doing?" the larger of the two asked him.

108   "I just wanted to stop the train," stammered Gonzague Gagnon.

109   "You think you're funny?" the big man asked.

110   The smaller of the two said nothing, but threw a punch at Gonzague Gagnon's nose.

111   This tiny fellow was a former boxing champion, which explains how Gonzague Gagnon was literally lifted from the earth. He flapped his arms in the air, expecting to land on the railway track or roll down the embankment.

112   But he was so close to the bridge that he fell into the river, in a place where the ice was thin.

113   He was immediately snatched up by the current. He tried to use his nails to grasp the rough surface of the ice above him: but the current was too strong. Then he said to himself that it would be better to let go and hold his breath: the open river wasn't far away and a fit man like himself had only to let himself be carried along under the ice until he was in the clear.

114   He stayed on his back in the water, pushing with his palms against the ice to make himself go more quickly.

115   He saw a long shadow across the ice and at the end of this shadow two darker patches. This must be the woman, he thought. Now he should tell her not to worry, that he would be back soon. But he reminded himself that he was under water. So he kept his mouth closed tight even though his lungs were beginning to burn. A few seconds later he decided to swallow just a little water, because that would be less painful than continuing to hold his breath.

116   Through the ice he saw the shadows of the great willow trees that flanked the river. He thought that he would soon be safe.

117   After that he saw nothing more.

118   "Impossible," he thought. "I am only half-way through my life."

*

When spring came Gaston Gagnon, who was religious, nailed a cross- 119
bar onto the stake which, on the other side of the river, had marked the
half-way point of Gonzague Gagnon.

Questions for Discussion and Writing

1. What details suggest that the divisions of the course that Gonzague runs
   each day can be seen as SYMBOLIC of the stages in his life?
2. What circumstances lead Gonzague to try to discover whether he possesses
   strange powers? Why would the prospect of having special powers be so important to Gonzague?
3. What circumstances lead Gonzague to discover that he can stop trains? Why
   does he cease doing so and then go back on his resolution?
4. How are the circumstances under which Gonzague dies an ironic commentary on his life?
5. Which would you prefer, a short eventful life in which you had unusual
   powers, or a long uneventful life? Explain your answer.
6. Describe a significant event that happened in your community in the past
   decade. It might be a natural disaster, crime, or an occasion for community
   action. You can use accounts from the newspapers, diaries, letters, or eyewit-
   nesses in compiling your report. Is there anything about the event like that
   described in Barcelo's story that still remains unexplained?
7. Jogging was a daily ritual for Gonzague Gagnon. What personal rituals do
   you or your family members carry out, such as at mealtimes or in preparation for going on a trip? Rituals can be patterns of conversation as well as actions that have developed over time with family or friends.

Peter Carey

The Last Days of a Famous Mime

Peter Carey was born in 1943 in Bacchus Marsh, Victoria, Australia, and was educated at Monash University. His most important short stories are collected in The Fat Man in History *(1974), in which "The Last Days of a Famous Mime" appeared, and in* War Crimes *(1979). His novels include* Bliss *(1981),* Illywhacker *(1985), and* Oscar and Lucinda *(1988), for which he won the Booker Prize. Carey's work suggests a wittily perverse intelligence behind his narratives, some of which are fantastically disturbing in their subversion of humanistic pieties. His stories constitute a fundamental challenge to the ethical and aesthetic values traditionally found in Australian short fiction. In "The Last Days of a Famous Mime," Carey describes an artist who sacrifices his life to accommodate his audience's needs.*

1.

1   The Mime arrived on Alitalia with very little luggage: a brown paper parcel and what looked like a woman's handbag.

2   Asked the contents of the brown paper parcel he said, "String."

3   Asked what the string was for he replied: "Tying up bigger parcels."

4   It had not been intended as a joke, but the Mime was pleased when the reporters laughed. Inducing laughter was not his forte. He was famous for terror.

5   Although his state of despair was famous throughout Europe, few guessed at his hope for the future. "The string," he explained, "is a prayer that I am always praying."

6   Reluctantly he untied his parcel and showed them the string. It was blue and when extended measured exactly fifty-three meters.

7   The Mime and the string appeared on the front pages of the evening papers.

2.

8   The first audiences panicked easily. They had not been prepared for his ability to mime terror. They fled their seats continually. Only to return again.

9   Like snorkel divers they appeared at the doors outside the concert hall with red faces and were puzzled to find the world as they had left it.

976

3.

Books had been written about him. He was the subject of an award- 10
winning film. But in his first morning in a provincial town he was distressed to find that his performance had not been liked by the one
newspaper's one critic.

"I cannot see," the critic wrote, "the use of invoking terror in an au- 11
dience."

The Mime sat on his bed, pondering ways to make his performance 12
more light-hearted.

4.

As usual he attracted women who wished to still the raging storms of 13
his heart.

They attended his bed like highly paid surgeons operating on a dif- 14
ficult case. They were both passionate and intelligent. They did not suffer defeat lightly.

5.

Wrongly accused of merely miming love in his private life he was 15
somewhat surprised to be confronted with hatred.

"Surely," he said, "if you now hate me, it was you who were imitat- 16
ing love, not I."

"You always were a slimy bastard," she said. "What's in that par- 17
cel?"

"I told you before," he said helplessly, "string." 18

"You're a liar," she said. 19

But later when he untied the parcel he found that she had opened it 20
to check on his story. Her understanding of the string had been perfect.
She had cut it into small pieces like spaghetti in a lousy restaurant.

6.

Against the advice of the tour organizers he devoted two concerts en- 21
tirely to love and laughter. They were disasters. It was felt that love and
laughter were not, in his case, as instructive as terror.

The next performance was quickly announced. 22

TWO HOURS OF REGRET

Tickets sold quickly. He began with a brief interpretation of love using 23
it merely as a prelude to regret which he elaborated on in a complex
and moving performance which left the audience pale and shaken. In a
final flourish he passed from regret to loneliness to terror. The audience

devoured the terror like brave tourists eating the hottest curry in an Indian restaurant.

7.

24 "What you are doing," she said, "is capitalizing on your neuroses. Personally I find it disgusting, like someone exhibiting their clubfoot, or Turkish beggars with strange deformities."

25   He said nothing. He was mildly annoyed at her presumption: that he had not thought this many, many times before.

26   With perfect misunderstanding she interpreted his passivity as disdain.

27   Wishing to hurt him, she slapped his face.

28   Wishing to hurt her, he smiled brilliantly.

8.

29 The story of the blue string touched the public imagination. Small brown paper packages were sold at the door of his concert.

30   Standing on stage he could hear the packages being noisily unwrapped. He thought of American matrons buying Muslim prayer rugs.

9.

31 Exhausted and weakened by the heavy schedule he fell prey to the doubts that had pricked at him insistently for years. He lost all sense of direction and spent many listless hours by himself, sitting in a motel room listening to the air conditioner.

32   He had lost confidence in the social uses of controlled terror. He no longer understood the audience's need to experience the very things he so desperately wished to escape from.

33   He emptied the ashtrays fastidiously.

34   He opened his brown paper parcel and threw the small pieces of string down the cistern. When the torrent of white water subsided they remained floating there like flotsam from a disaster at sea.

10.

35 The Mime called a press conference to announce that there would be no more concerts. He seemed small and foreign and smelt of garlic. The press regarded him without enthusiasm. He watched their hovering pens anxiously, unsuccessfully willing them to write down his words.

36   Briefly he announced that he wished to throw his talent open to broader influences. His skills would be at the disposal of the people, who would be free to request his services for any purpose at any time.

37   His skin seemed sallow but his eyes seemed as bright as those on a nodding fur mascot on the back window ledge of an American car.

11.

Asked to describe death he busied himself taking Polaroid photographs 38
of his questioners.

12.

Asked to describe marriage he handed out small cheap mirrors with 39
MADE IN TUNISIA written on the back.

13.

His popularity declined. It was felt that he had become obscure and be- 40
yond the understanding of ordinary people. In response he requested
easier questions. He held back nothing of himself in his effort to please
his audience.

14.

Asked to describe an airplane he flew three times around the city, only 41
injuring himself slightly on landing.

15.

Asked to describe a river, he drowned himself. 42

16.

It is unfortunate that this, his last and least typical performance, is the 43
only one which has been recorded on film.

There is a small crowd by the riverbank, no more than thirty people. 44
A small, neat man dressed in a gray suit picks his way through some
children who seem more interested in the large plastic toy dog they are
playing with.

He steps into the river, which, at the bank, is already quite deep. His 45
head is only visible above the water for a second or two. And then he is
gone.

A policeman looks expectantly over the edge, as if waiting for him 46
to reappear. Then the film stops.

Watching this last performance it is difficult to imagine how this 47
man stirred such emotions in the hearts of those who saw him.

Questions for Discussion and Writing

1. How does the form of the story reproduce the experience of a mime performing blackout skits in the theater?
2. How does the Mime's performance SYMBOLIZE reactions to basic forces and
   limits of human existence (the way traditional mimes react to presence of
   wind, walls, and so on, in ways that suggest their existence)?

3. How has the Mime transformed terror into his specialty to enable audiences to confront what they ordinarily would avoid? How does art generally make it possible to enjoy events on stage that would be terrifying if they happened to you personally?

4. How does the length of string symbolize the Mime's goal of encompassing more of human life within his act? What evidence does the story provide that the Mime is willing to change his act, to sacrifice his happiness, and even give up his life in the effort to more accurately reflect or "mime" reality for his audience?

5. How do the references to the bad spaghetti, tourism, the plastic dog, and prayer rugs raise the issue of the difference between popular, mass-produced art versus true art?

6. Why do the artist's personal relationships with women fail?

7. To what extent does the Mime's relationship to his audience, the miracle he performs by flying three times around the city, his rebuke of the questions asked him, and the way he dies, suggest events described in the New Testament? What are the similarities and what are the differences? For example, how is the description of the reporter's account of the Mime's last days similar to the accounts in the Gospels recorded after Christ's death?

8. How does Carey draw on both UNIVERSAL SYMBOLS and create highly personal CONTEXTUAL ones in formulating his FABLE of the artist? Discuss the extent to which the story suggests that a true artist's life has a sacrificial aspect to it.

9. Describe a funny or serious situation where meaning is communicated without words.

10. Describe an object that defies the laws of reality—for example, a one-sided coin.

Joaquim María Machado de Assis

A Canary's Ideas

Joaquim María Machado de Assis (1839–1908) was born in Rio de Janiero where he lived most of his life. His father, a house painter, was a mulatto Brazilian, the son of former slaves; his mother was a white Portuguese immigrant from the Azores. Machado attended only five years of elementary school. Beyond that, he educated himself and became fluent in several languages, including French, Spanish, and English. He began supporting himself at age fifteen, working at a variety of jobs, including typesetting, proofreading, and editing. In 1874 he entered the civil service in the Ministry of Agriculture and for the last thirty-four years of his life led the quiet, unturbulent life of a happily married, but childless, government bureaucrat. He used the financial security of his civil service position to carry on an astonishingly prolific career as a writer. Machado's early love was the theater, and by the time he was thirty he had written nineteen plays and opera librettos, most of them produced by theater companies in the city. He was also a skilled poet and regular newspaper columnist. After 1870, he turned his attention primarily to short stories and novels. His first great success was Epitaph of a Small Winner *(1881), written from a startlingly original point of view, namely the posthumous memoirs of the narrator, Braz Cubas—a tongue-in-cheek account of his life.*

Machado's second novel, Philosopher or Dog? *(1891), and his acknowledged masterpiece,* Dom Casmurro *(1900), both feature protagonists who are reflective skeptics tinged with madness. These unreliable narrators are a feature of his work. His close attention to the protagonist's stream of consciousness, his cool irony, unexpected juxtaposition of times, characters, and value systems conveyed in a forceful, unique style anticipate many features of the twentieth-century novel. He is now acknowledged by critics to be a master of the early modern novel, equal to Gustave Flaubert and Henry James. His complete works fill thirty-one volumes, and he is the author of over one hundred short stories, of which "A Canary's Ideas," translated by Jack Schmitt and Lorie Ishimatsu (1976), is typical. In this story, an egocentric, reasoning canary forms his impression of the universe by what surrounds him at the moment.*

A man by the name of Macedo, who had a fancy for ornithology, related to some friends an incident so extraordinary that no one took him seriously. Some came to believe he had lost his mind. Here is a summary of his narration. 1

At the beginning of last month, as I was walking down the street, a carriage darted past me and nearly knocked me to the ground. I escaped by quickly side-stepping into a secondhand shop. Neither the racket of the horse and carriage nor my entrance stirred the proprietor, dozing in a folding chair at the back of the shop. He was a man of 2 shabby appearance: his beard was the color of dirty straw, and his head was covered by a tattered cap which probably had not found a buyer. One could not guess that there was any story behind him, as there could have been behind some of the objects he sold, nor could one sense in him that austere, disillusioned sadness inherent in the objects which were remnants of past lives.

3   The shop was dark and crowded with the sort of old, bent, broken, tarnished, rusted articles ordinarily found in secondhand shops, and everything was in that state of semidisorder befitting such an establishment. This assortment of articles, though banal, was interesting. Pots without lids, lids without pots, buttons, shoes, locks, a black shirt, straw hats, fur hats, picture frames, binoculars, dress coats, a fencing foil, a stuffed dog, a pair of slippers, gloves, nondescript vases, epaulets, a velvet satchel, two hatracks, a slingshot, a thermometer, chairs, a lithographed portrait by the late Sisson, a backgammon board, two wire masks for some future Carnival—all this and more, which I either did not see or do not remember, filled the shop in the area around the door, propped up, hung, or displayed in glass cases as old as the objects inside them. Further inside the shop were many objects of similar appearance. Predominant were the large objects—chests of drawers, chairs, and beds—some of which were stacked on top of others which were lost in the darkness.

4   I was about to leave, when I saw a cage hanging in the doorway. It was as old as everything else in the shop, and I expected it to be empty so it would fit in with the general appearance of desolation. However, it wasn't empty. Inside, a canary was hopping about. The bird's color, liveliness, and charm added a note of life and youth to that heap of wreckage. It was the last passenger of some wrecked ship, who had arrived in the shop as complete and happy as it had originally been. As soon as I looked at the bird, it began to hop up and down, from perch to perch, as if it meant to tell me that a ray of sunshine was frolicking in the midst of that cemetery. I'm using this image to describe the canary only because I'm speaking to rhetorical people, but the truth is that the canary thought about neither cemetery nor sun, according to what it told me later. Along with the pleasure the sight of the bird brought me, I felt indignation regarding its destiny and softly murmured these bitter words:

5   "What detestable owner had the nerve to rid himself of this bird for a few cents? Or what indifferent soul, not wishing to keep his late master's pet, gave it away to some child, who sold it so he could make a bet on a soccer game?"

6   The canary, sitting on top of its perch, trilled this reply:

7   "Whoever you may be, you're certainly not in your right mind. I had no detestable owner, nor was I given to any child to sell. Those are the delusions of a sick person. Go and get yourself cured, my friend . . ."

"What?" I interrupted, not having had time to become astonished. 8
"So your master didn't sell you to this shop? It wasn't misery or laziness that brought you, like a ray of sunshine, to this cemetery?"

"I don't know what you mean by 'sunshine' or 'cemetery.' If the ca- 9
naries you've seen use the first of those names, so much the better, because it sounds pretty, but really, I'm sure you're confused."

"Excuse me, but you couldn't have come here by chance, all alone. 10
Has your master always been that man sitting over there?"

"What master? That man over there is my servant. He gives me food 11
and water every day, so regularly that if I were to pay him for his services, it would be no small sum, but canaries don't pay their servants.
In fact, since the world belongs to canaries, it would be extravagant for
them to pay for what is already in the world."

Astonished by these answers, I didn't know what to marvel at 12
more—the language or the ideas. The language, even though it entered
my ears as human speech, was uttered by the bird in the form of
charming trills. I looked all around me so I could determine if I were
awake and saw that the street was the same, and the shop was the
same dark, sad, musty place. The canary, moving from side, was waiting for me to speak. I then asked if it were lonely for the infinite blue
space . . .

"But, my dear man," trilled the canary, "what does 'infinite blue 13
space' mean?"

"But, pardon me, what do you think of this world? What is the 14
world to you?"

"The world," retorted the canary, with a certain professorial air, "is 15
a secondhand shop with a small rectangular bamboo cage hanging
from a nail. The canary is lord of the cage it lives in and the shop that
surrounds it. Beyond that, everything is illusion and deception."

With this, the old man woke up and approached me, dragging his 16
feet. He asked me if I wanted to buy the canary. I asked if he had acquired it in the same way he had acquired the rest of the objects he sold
and learned that he had bought it from a barber, along with a set of razors.

"The razors are in very good condition." he said. 17

"I only want the canary." 18

I paid for it, ordered a huge, circular cage of wood and wire, and 19
had it placed on the veranda of my house so the bird could see the garden, the fountain, and a bit of blue sky.

It was my intention to do a lengthy study of this phenomenon, with- 20
out saying anything to anyone until I could astound the world with my
extraordinary discovery. I began by alphabetizing the canary's language in order to study its structure, its relation to music, the bird's appreciation of aesthetics, its ideas and recollections. When this philologi-
cal and psychological analysis was done, I entered specifically into the
study of canaries: their origin, their early history, the geology and flora

of the Canary Islands, the bird's knowledge of navigation, and so forth. We conversed for hours while I took notes, and it waited, hopped about, and trilled.

21   As I have no family other than two servants, I ordered them not to interrupt me, even to deliver a letter or an urgent telegram or to inform me of an important visitor. Since they both knew about my scientific pursuits, they found my orders perfectly natural and did not suspect that the canary and I understood each other.

22   Needless to say, I slept little, woke up two or three times each night, wandered about aimlessly, and felt feverish. Finally, I returned to my work in order to reread, add, and emend. I corrected more than one observation, either because I had misunderstood something or because the bird had not expressed it clearly. The definition of the world was one of these. Three weeks after the canary's entrance into my home, I asked it to repeat to me its definition of the world.

23   "The world," it answered, "is a sufficiently broad garden with a fountain in the middle, flowers, shrubbery, some grass, clear air, and a bit of blue up above. The canary, lord of the world, lives in a spacious cage, white and circular, from which it looks out on the rest of the world. Everything else is illusion and deception."

24   The language of my treatise also suffered some modifications, and I saw that certain conclusions which had seemed simple were actually presumptuous. I still could not write the paper I was to send to the National Museum, the Historical Institute, and the German universities, not due to a lack of material but because I first had to put together all my observations and test their validity. During the last few days, I neither left the house, answered letters, nor wanted to hear from friends or relatives. The canary was everything to me. One of the servants had the job of cleaning the bird's cage and giving it food and water every morning. The bird said nothing to him, as if it knew the man was completely lacking in scientific background. Besides, the service was no more than cursory, as the servant was not a bird lover.

25   One Saturday I awoke ill, my head and back aching. The doctor ordered complete rest. I was suffering from an excess of studying and was not to read or even think, nor was I even to know what was going on in the city or the rest of the outside world. I remained in this condition for five days. On the sixth day I got up, and only then did I find out that the canary, while under the servant's care, had flown out of its cage. My first impulse was to strangle the servant—I was choking with indignation and collapsed into my chair, speechless and bewildered. The guilty man defended himself, swearing he had been careful, but the wily bird had nevertheless managed to escape.

26   "But didn't you search for it?"

27   "Yes, I did, sir. First it flew up to the roof, and I followed it. It flew to a tree, and then who knows where it hid itself? I've been asking around since yesterday. I asked the neighbors and the local farmers, but

no one has seen the bird."

I suffered immensely. Fortunately, the fatigue left me within a few   28
hours, and I was soon able to go out to the veranda and the garden.
There was no sign of the canary. I ran everywhere, making inquiries
and posting announcements, all to no avail. I had already gathered my
notes together to write my paper, even though it would be disjointed
and incomplete, when I happened to visit a friend who had one of the
largest and most beautiful estates on the outskirts of town. We were
taking a stroll before dinner when this question was trilled to me:

"Greetings, Senhor Macedo, where have you been since you disap-   29
peared?"

It was the canary, perched on the branch of a tree. You can imagine   30
how I reacted and what I said to the bird. My friend presumed I was
mad, but the opinions of friends are of no importance to me. I spoke
tenderly to the canary and asked it to come home and continue our conversations in that world of ours, composed of a garden, a fountain, a
veranda, and a white circular cage.

"What garden? What fountain?"   31

"The world, my dear bird."   32

"What world? I see you haven't lost any of your annoying professo-   33
rial habits. The world," it solemnly concluded, "is an infinite blue
space, with the sun up above."

Indignant, I replied that if I were to believe what it said, the world   34
could be anything—it had even been a secondhand shop . . .

"A secondhand shop?" it trilled to its heart's content. "But is there   35
really such a thing as a secondhand shop?"

Questions for Discussion and Writing

1. How is the narrator characterized? In what way is he defined by his zealous
   private pursuit of ornithology?
2. In what different circumstances does the narrator encounter the canary?
   How does the canary redefine its conception of the world to suit each new
   environment in which it finds itself?
3. How might the story be understood as a FABLE about egocentrism? Seen in
   this way, how might the canary be seen as SYMBOLIC of the narrator's intro-
   version and solipsism?
4. Marlon Brando once defined an actor as "a guy who, if you ain't talking
   about him, ain't listening." Describe the most egocentric person you have
   ever known.
5. How do pets often reflect submerged aspects of their owner's personalities?
6. Create a fable with supernatural elements, using animal characters, that
   makes a point about human nature.
7. What actions did a pet of yours ever take that led you to believe it possessed
   self-awareness and could communicate its intentions and feelings to you?

Guy de Maupassant

An Old Man

Guy de Maupassant (1850–1893), in his relatively brief life, wrote almost three hundred short stories, six novels, and more than two hundred sketches for newspapers and magazines, as well as essays on travel and dramatic adaptations. His best stories appear at first to be little more than brief anecdotes, but they reveal a wealth of psychological insight and an unusual balance of detachment and sympathy for the human condition. De Maupassant was born in Rouen, Normandy, near the seacoast town of Dieppe, in France. He received his early education from his literate and cultured mother before being enrolled at the age of thirteen in a seminary from which he was soon expelled for insubordination. He served as a soldier in the Franco-Prussian War of 1870–1871 and then settled in Paris as a clerk in the Naval Ministry. He became a protégé of Flaubert and was part of the famous literary circle in Paris that included Turgenev, Edmond Goncourt, Alphonse Daudet, and Émile Zola. His fame was assured with the publication of the short story "Boulle de Suif" (Ball of Fat) (1880) in an anthology edited by Zola. His novels include Une Vie *(1883),* Bel Ami *(1885), and* Pierre et Jean *(1888). Collections of his short stories include* La Maison Tellier *(1881),* Mademoiselle Fifi *(1882), and* Contes et Nouvelles *(1885), among others. A dissolute life led de Maupassant to contract syphilis, which led to an untimely death at the age of forty-two. "An Old Man," translated by Roger Colet, epitomizes de Maupassant's narrative technique. In its use of irony, precise detail, and the surprise ending, this story illustrates why de Maupaussant is widely recognized as a master of the short story form.*

1   All the newspapers had carried this advertisement:

> The new spa at Rondelis offers all the advantages desirable for a lengthy stay or even for permanent residence. Its ferruginous waters, recognized as the best in the world for countering all impurities of the blood, also seem to possess special qualities calculated to prolong human life. This remarkable circumstance may be due in part to the exceptional situation of the little town, which lies in a mountainous region, in the middle of a forest of firs. The fact remains that for several centuries it has been noted for cases of extraordinary longevity.

2   And the public came along in droves.

3   One morning the doctor in charge of the springs was asked to call on a newcomer, Monsieur Daron, who had arrived a few days before and had rented a charming villa on the edge of the forest. He was a little old man of eighty-six, still quite sprightly, wiry, healthy and active, who went to infinite pains to conceal his age.

He offered the doctor a seat and started questioning him straight 4
away.

"Doctor," he said, "if I am in good health, it is thanks to careful liv- 5
ing. Though not very old, I have already attained a respectable age, yet
I keep free of all illnesses and indispositions, even the slightest
malaises, by means of careful living. It is said that the climate here is
very good for the health. I am perfectly prepared to believe it, but before settling down here I want proof. I am therefore going to ask you to
come and see me once a week to give me the following information in
detail.

"First of all I wish to have a complete, absolutely complete, list of all 6
the inhabitants of the town and the surrounding area who are over
eighty years old. I also need a few physical and physiological details regarding each of them. I wish to know their professions, their way of
life, their habits. Every time one of those people dies you will be good
enough to inform me, giving me the precise cause of death and describing the circumstances."

Then he added graciously, "I hope, Doctor, that we shall become 7
good friends," and held out his wrinkled little hand. The doctor shook
it, promising him his devoted co-operation.

Monsieur Daron had always had an obsessive fear of death. He had de- 8
prived himself of nearly all the pleasures of this world because they
were dangerous, and whenever anyone expressed surprise that he
should not drink wine—wine, that purveyor of dreams and gaiety—he
would reply in a voice in which a note of fear could be detected: "I
value my life." And he stressed the word *my*, as if that life, *his* life, possessed some special distinction. He put into that *my* such a difference
between his life and other people's lives that any rejoinder was out of
the question.

For that matter he had a very special way of stressing the possessive 9
pronouns designating parts of his person and even things which belonged to him. When he said "my eyes, my legs, my arms, my hands,"
it was quite obvious that there must be no mistake about this: those organs were not at all like other people's. But where this distinction was
particularly noticeable was in his references to his doctor. When he said
"my doctor," one would have thought that that doctor belonged to him
and nobody else, destined for him alone, to attend to his illnesses and
to nothing else, and that he was superior to all the other doctors in the
world, without exception.

He had never regarded other men as anything but puppets of a sort, 10
created to fill up an empty world. He divided them into two classes:
those he greeted because some chance had put him in contact with
them, and those he did not greet. But both these categories of individuals were equally insignificant in his eyes.

However, beginning with the day when the Rondelis doctor 11

brought him the list of the seventeen inhabitants of the town who were over eighty, he felt a new interest awaken in his heart, an unfamiliar solicitude for these old people whom he was going to see fall by the wayside one by one. He had no desire to make their acquaintance, but he formed a very clear idea of their persons, and when the doctor dined with him, every Thursday, he spoke only of them. "Well, doctor," he would say, "and how is Joseph Poinçot today? We left him feeling a little ill last week." And when the doctor had given him the patient's bill of health, Monsieur Daron would suggest changes in his diet, experiments, methods of treatment which he might later apply to himself if they had succeeded with the others. Those seventeen old people provided him with an experimental field from which he learnt many a lesson.

12   One evening the doctor announced as he came in: "Rosalie Tournel has died."

13   Monsieur Daron gave a start and immediately asked, "What of?"

14   "Of a chill."

15   The little old man gave a sigh of relief. Then he said, "She was too fat, too heavy; she must have eaten too much. When I get to her age I'll be more careful about my weight." (He was two years older than Rosalie Tournel, but he claimed to be only seventy.)

16   A few months later it was the turn of Henri Brissot. Monsieur Daron was very upset. This time it was a man, and a thin man at that, within three months of his own age, and careful about his health. He did not dare to ask any questions, but waited anxiously for the doctor to give him some details.

17   "Oh, so he died just like that, all of a sudden," he said. "But he was perfectly all right last week. He must have done something silly, I suppose, Doctor?"

18   The doctor, who was enjoying himself, replied: "I don't think so. His children told me he had been very careful."

19   Then, unable to contain himself any longer, and filled with fear, Monsieur Daron asked: "But . . . but . . . what did he die of, then?"

20   "Of pleurisy."

21   The little old man clapped his dry hands in sheer joy.

22   "I told you so! I told you he had done something silly. You don't get pleurisy for nothing. He must have gone out for a breath of air after his dinner and the cold must have gone to his chest. Pleurisy! Why, that's an accident, not an illness. Only fools die of pleurisy."

23   And he ate his dinner in high spirits, talking about those who were left.

24   "There are only fifteen of them now, but they are all hale and hearty, aren't they? The whole of life is like that: the weakest go first; people who live beyond thirty have a good chance of reaching sixty; those who pass sixty often get to eighty; and those who pass eighty nearly always live to be a hundred, because they are the fittest, toughest and most sensible of all."

Another two disappeared during the year, one of dysentery and the 25
other of a choking fit. Monsieur Daron was highly amused by the death
of the former and concluded that he must have eaten something stimu-
lating the day before.

"Dysentery is the disease of careless people. Dammit all, Doctor, 26
you ought to have watched over his diet."

As for the man who had been carried off by a choking fit, his death 27
could only be due to a heart condition which had hitherto gone unnoticed.

But one evening the doctor announced the decease of Paul Timonet, 28
a sort of mummy of whom it had been hoped to make a centenarian
and an advertisement for the spa.

When Monsieur Daron asked, as usual: "What did he die of?" the 29
doctor replied, "Bless me, I really don't know."

"What do you mean, you don't know. A doctor always knows. 30
Hadn't he some organic lesion?"

The doctor shook his head. 31

"No, none." 32

"Possibly some infection of the liver or the kidneys?" 33

"No, they were quite sound." 34

"Did you check whether the stomach was functioning properly? A 35
stroke is often caused by poor digestion."

"There was no stroke." 36

Monsieur Daron, very perplexed, said excitedly: "Look, he must 37
have died of something! What do you think it was?"

The doctor threw up his hands. 38

"I've no idea, no idea at all. He died because he died, that's all." 39

Then Monsieur Daron, in a voice full of emotion, asked: "Exactly 40
how old was that one? I can't remember."

"Eighty-nine." 41

And the little old man, at once incredulous and reassured, ex- 42
claimed:

"Eighty-nine! So whatever it was, it wasn't old age . . ." 43

Questions for Discussion and Writing

1. With what objective in mind has Monsieur Daron come to the town? How
   does he come to know the doctor? How does Monsieur Daron's reaction to
   the death of each of the aged residents of Rondelis define him as a character?
2. Do you detect a change in the doctor's attitude toward Daron with each new
   case? Why does the doctor appear to derive pleasure from describing the
   death of the eighty-nine-year-old resident, Paul Timonet?
3. What universal aspects of human nature is de Maupassant portraying in his
   CHARACTERIZATION of Monsieur Daron? How does the story embody the
   ARCHETYPE of the QUEST for immortality? How does the TONE of the story
   express de Maupassant's attitude toward Daron's quest?

4. What interesting stories can you elicit from the oldest member of your family that would give you insight into what the world was like when he or she was young?

5. Write from the point of view of how you think you will be when you are the age of the protagonist in this story. You might choose to invent a dialogue between yourself now and yourself in sixty years.

Abioseh Nicol

Life Is Sweet at Kumansenu

Abioseh Nicol (whose given name was Davidson Sylvester Hector Willoughby Nicol) was born in 1924 in Sierra Leone. As a child he was educated in both his native Sierra Leone and in Nigeria. He received a medical degree from Cambridge University and has worked as a physician in both England and Africa and as a school administrator in Sierra Leone. He has also held a wide range of posts with the United Nations. Although he has published many articles on medical subjects, education, and politics, it was only through the efforts of the late African-American writer Langston Hughes that his poetry and short stories were published. Collections of his works include The Truly Married Woman and Other Stories *(1965) and* Two African Tales *(1972). "Life Is Sweet at Kumansenu" is typical of Nicol's work in its mixture of the old and the new in Africa, showing authentic and traditional animistic beliefs coexisting with urban culture.*

The sea and the wet sand to one side of it; green tropical forest on the other; above it the slow tumbling clouds. The clean round blinding disc of sun and the blue sky covered and surrounded the small African village, Kameni.

A few square mud houses with roofs like helmets, here thatched and there covered with corrugated zinc where the prosperity of cocoa and trading had touched the head of the family.

The widow Bola stirred her palm-oil stew and thought of nothing in particular. She chewed a kola nut[1] rhythmically with her strong toothless jaws and soon unconsciously she was chewing in rhythm with the skipping of Asi, her granddaughter. She looked idly at Asi as the seven-year-old brought the twisted palm-leaf rope smartly over her head and jumped over it, counting in English each time the rope struck the ground and churned up a little red dust. Bola herself did not understand English well, but she could count easily up to twenty in English for market purposes. Asi shouted six and then said nine, ten. Bola called out that after six came seven. And I should know, she sighed. Although now she was old, there was a time when she bore children regularly every two years. Six times she had borne a boy child and six times they had died. Some had swollen up and with weak plaintive cries had faded away. Others had shuddered in sudden convulsions, with burning skins, and had rolled up their eyes and died. They had all died. Or rather he had died, Bola thought, because she knew it was one child all the time whose spirit had crept up restlessly into her womb to

---

[1] *kola nut*, the bitter seed of an African evergreen tree, used in making medicines and soft drinks.

be born and to mock her.² The sixth time Musa, the village magician whom time had transformed into a respectable Muslim, had advised her and her husband to break the bones of the quiet little corpse and mangle it so that it couldn't come back to torment them alive again. But she held on to the child, and refused to let them handle it. Secretly she had marked it with a sharp pointed stick at the left buttock before it was wrapped in a mat and they had taken it away. When, the seventh time she had borne a son, and the purification ceremonies had taken place, she had turned it slyly to see whether the mark was there. It was. She showed it to the old woman who was the midwife and asked her what that was, and she had forced herself to believe the other who said it was an accidental scratch made whilst the child was being scrubbed. But this child had stayed. Meji, he had been called. And he was now thirty years of age and a second-class clerk in government offices in a town ninety miles away. Asi, his daughter, had been left with her to do the things an old woman wanted a small child for, to run and take messages to the neighbors, to fetch a cup of water from the earthenware pot in the kitchen, to sleep with her and be fondled.

4   She threw the washed and squeezed cassava³ leaves into the red boiling stew, putting in a finger's pinch of salt, and then went indoors, carefully stepping over the threshold to look for the dried red pepper. She found it, and then dropped it, leaning against the wall with a little cry. He turned round from the window and looked at her with a twisted half smile of love and sadness. In his short-sleeved, open-necked white shirt and gray gabardine trousers, a gold wristwatch and brown suede shoes, he looked like the pictures in African magazines of a handsome clerk who would get to the top because he ate the correct food, or regularly took the correct laxative, which was being advertised. His skin was grayish brown and he had a large handkerchief tied round his neck.

5   "Meji, God be praised," Bola cried. "You gave me quite a turn. My heart is weak and I can no longer take surprises. When did you come? How did you come? By lorry,⁴ by fishing boat? And how did you come into the house? The front door was locked. There are so many thieves nowadays. I'm so glad to see you, so glad," she mumbled and wept, leaning against his breast.

6   Meji's voice was hoarse, and he said: "I am glad to see you too, Mother," beating her back affectionately.

7   Asi ran in and cried, "Papa, Papa," and was rewarded with a lift and a hug.

8   "Never mind how I came, Mother," Meji said, laughing. "I'm here, and that's all that matters."

² One child . . . to mock her, a reference to a West African belief in a spirit-child who does not live to maturity but returns in a series of rebirths.
³ cassava (kä sä′vä), a tropical plant with starchy roots.
⁴ lorry, truck. [British]

"We must make a feast, we must have a big feast. I must tell the neighbors at once. Asi, run this very minute to Mr. Addai, the catechist, and tell him your papa is home. Then to Mami Gbera to ask her for extra provisions, and to Pa Babole for drummers and musicians . . ." 9

"Stop," said Meji raising his hand. "This is all quite unnecessary. I don't want to see *anyone*, no one at all; I wish to rest quietly and completely. No one is to know I'm here." 10

Bola looked very crestfallen. She was proud of Meji, and wanted to show him off. The village would never forgive her for concealing such an important visitor. Meji must have sensed this because he held her shoulder comfortingly and said: "They will know soon enough. Let us enjoy each other, all three of us, this time. Life is too short." 11

Bola turned to Asi, picked up the packet of pepper, and told her to go and drop a little into the boiling pot outside, taking care not to go too near the fire or play with it. After the child had gone, Bola said to her son, "Are you in trouble? Is it the police?" 12

He shook his head. "No," he said, "it's just that I like returning to you. There will always be this bond of love and affection between us, and I don't wish to share it. It is our private affair and that is why I've left my daughter with you," he ended up irrelevantly; "girls somehow seem to stay with relations longer." 13

"And don't I know it," said Bola. "But you look pale," she continued, "and you keep scraping your throat. Are you ill?" She laid her hand on his brow. "And you're cold, too." 14

"It's the cold wet wind," he said, a little harshly. "I'll go and rest now if you can open and dust my room for me. I'm feeling very tired. Very tired indeed. I've traveled very far today and it has not been an easy journey." 15

"Of course, my son, of course," Bola replied, bustling away hurriedly but happily. 16

Meji slept all afternoon till evening, and his mother brought his food to his room, later took the empty basins away. Then he slept again till morning. 17

The next day, Saturday, was a busy one, and after further promising Meji that she would tell no one he was about, Bola went off to market. Meji took Asi for a long walk through a deserted path and up into the hills. She was delighted. They climbed high until they could see the village below in front of them, and the sea in the distance, and the boats with their wide white sails. Soon the sun had passed its zenith and was halfway towards the west. Asi had eaten all the food, the dried fish and the flat tapioca pancakes and the oranges. Her father said he wasn't hungry, and this had made the day perfect for Asi, who had chattered, eaten, and then played with her father's fountain pen and other things from his pocket. They soon left for home because he had promised they would be back before dark; he had carried her down some steep boulders and she had held on to his shoulders because he had said his neck 18 hurt so and she must not touch it. She had said: "Papa, I can see behind you and you haven't got a shadow. Why?"

19   He had then turned her round to face the sun. Since she was getting drowsy, she had started asking questions, and her father had joked with her and humored her. "Papa, why has your watch stopped at twelve o'clock?" "Because the world ends at noon." Asi had chuckled at that. "Papa, why do you wear a scarf always round your neck?" "Because my head would fall off if I didn't." She had laughed out loud at that. But soon she had fallen asleep as he bore her homewards.

20   Just before nightfall, with his mother dressed in her best, they had all three, at her urgent request, gone to his father's grave, taking a secret route and avoiding the main village. It was a small cemetery, not more than twenty years or so old, started when the Rural Health Department had insisted that no more burials take place in the backyards of households. Bola took a bottle of wine and a glass and four split halves of kola, each a half sphere, two red and two white. They reached the graveside and she poured some wine into the glass. Then she spoke to the dead man softly and caressingly. She had brought his son to see him, she said. This son whom God had given success, to the confusion and discomfiture of their enemies. Here he was, a man with a pensionable clerk's job and not a farmer, fisherman, or a mechanic. All the years of their married life people had said she was a witch because her children had died young. But this boy of theirs had shown that she was a good woman. Let her husband answer her now, to show that he was listening. She threw the four kola nuts up into the air and they fell on the grave. Three fell with the flat face upwards and one with its flat face downwards. She picked them up again and conversed with him once more and threw the kola nuts up again. But still there was an odd one or sometimes two.

21   They did not fall with all four faces up, or with all four faces down, to show that he was listening and was pleased. She spoke endearingly, she cajoled, she spoke sternly. But all to no avail. Then she asked Meji to perform. He crouched by the graveside and whispered. Then he threw the kola nuts and they rolled a little, Bola following them eagerly with her sharp old eyes. They all ended up face downwards. Meji emptied the glass of wine on the grave and then said that he felt nearer his father at that moment than he had ever done before in his life.

22   It was sundown, and they all three went back silently home in the short twilight. That night, going outside the house near her son's room window, she found, to her sick disappointment, that he had been throwing away all the cooked food out there. She did not mention this when she went to say goodnight, but she did sniff and say that there was a smell of decay in the room. Meji said he thought there was a dead rat up in the rafters, and he would clear it away after she had gone to bed.

23   That night it rained heavily, and sheet lightning turned the darkness

into brief silver daylight for one or two seconds at a time. Then the darkness again and the rain. Bola woke soon after midnight and thought she could hear knocking. She went to Meji's room to ask him to open the door, but he wasn't there. She thought he might have gone out for a while and been locked out by mistake. She opened the door quickly, holding an oil lamp upwards. He stood on the veranda, curiously unwet, and refused to come in.

"I have to go away," he said hoarsely, coughing.   24

"Do come in," she said.   25

"No," he said, "I have to go, but I wanted to thank you for giving   26
me a chance."

"What nonsense is this?" she said. "Come in out of the rain."   27

"I did not think I should leave without thanking you."   28

The rain fell hard, the door creaked, and the wind whistled.   29

"Life is sweet, Mother dear, good-by, and thank you."   30

He turned round and started running.   31

There was a sudden diffuse flash of lightning and she saw that the   32
yard was empty. She went back heavily, and fell into a restless sleep. Before she slept she said to herself that she must see Mr. Addai next morning, Sunday, or, better still, Monday, and tell him about this in case Meji was in trouble. She hoped Meji would not be annoyed. He was such a good son.

But it was Mr. Addai who came instead, on Sunday afternoon, quiet   33
and grave, and saw Bola sitting on an old stool in the veranda, dressing Asi's hair in tight thin plaits.

Mr. Addai sat down and, looking away, he said: "The Lord giveth   34
and the Lord taketh away." And soon half the village were sitting round the veranda and in the yard.

"But I tell you, he was here on Friday and left Sunday morning,"   35
Bola said. "He couldn't have died on Friday."

Bola had just recovered from a fainting fit after being told of her   36
son's death in town. His wife, Asi's mother, had come with the news, bringing some of his property. She said Meji had died instantly at noon on Friday and had been buried on Saturday at sundown. They would have brought him to Kameni for the burial. He had always wished that. But they could not do so in time as bodies did not last much after a day.

"He was here, he was here," Bola said, rubbing her forehead and   37
weeping.

Asi sat by quietly. Mr. Addai said comfortingly, "Hush, hush, he   38
couldn't have been, because no one in the village saw him."

"He said we were to tell no one," Bola said.   39

The crowd smiled above Bola's head, and shook their heads. "Poor   40
woman," someone said, "she is beside herself with grief."

"He died on Friday," Mrs. Meji repeated, crying. "He was in the of- 41
fice and he pulled up the window to look out and call the messenger.

Then the sash broke. The window fell, broke his neck, and the sharp edge almost cut his head off; they say he died at once."

42   "My papa had a scarf around his neck," Asi shouted suddenly.

43   "Hush," said the crowd.

44   Mrs. Meji dipped her hand into her bosom and produced a small gold locket and put it round Asi's neck, to quieten her. "Your papa had this made last week for your Christmas present. You may as well have it now."

45   Asi played with it and pulled it this way and that.

46   "Be careful, child," Mr. Addai said, "it was your father's last gift."

47   "I was trying to remember how he showed me yesterday to open it." Asi said.

48   "You have never seen it before," Mrs. Meji said sharply, trembling with fear mingled with anger.

49   She took the locket and tried to open it.

50   "Let me have it," said the village goldsmith, and he tried whispering magic words of incantation. Then he said, defeated, "It must be poor-quality gold; it has rusted. I need tools to open it."

51   "I remember now," Asi said in the flat complacent voice of childhood.

52   The crowd gathered round quietly and the setting sun glinted on the soft red African gold of the dangling trinket. The goldsmith handed the locket over to Asi and asked in a loud whisper: "How did he open it?"

53   "Like so," Asi said and pressed a secret catch. It flew open and she spelled out gravely the word inside: "ASI."

54   The silence continued.

55   "His neck, poor boy," Bola said a little wildly, "that is why he could not eat the lovely meals I cooked for him."

56   Mr. Addai announced a service of intercession after vespers that evening. The crowd began to leave quietly.

57   Musa, the magician, was one of the last to leave. He was now very old and bent. In times of grave calamity, it was known that even Mr. Addai did not raise objection to Musa being consulted.

58   He bent over further and whispered in Bola's ear: "You should have had his bones broken and mangled thirty-one years ago when he went for the sixth time and then he would not have come back to mock you all these years by pretending to be alive. I told you so. But you women are naughty and stubborn."

59   Bola stood up, her black face held high, her eyes terrible with maternal rage and pride.

60   "I am glad I did not," she said, "and that is why he came back specially to thank me before he went for good."

61   She clutched Asi to her. "I am glad I gave him the opportunity to come back, for life is sweet. I do not expect you to understand why I did so. After all, you are only a man."

Questions for Discussion and Writing

1. Why did Bola refuse to perform the ritual Musa recommended after her first six sons had died in infancy?
2. Why is it significant that the mark Bola placed on the body of her sixth dead son reappeared on Meji?
3. How is Meji's visit an expression of gratitude to Bola for the chance to have lived?
4. How might each of the following details serve as a clue to Meji's true state: his hoarse voice, his pallor and temperature, the fact he casts no shadow, his joke to his daughter when she asks him about the handkerchief tied around his neck, the fact that he does not eat anything his mother offers him, the flash of lightning that marks his departure? What other clues can you cite?
5. What role does the locket play in convincing the skeptical villagers that Meji had really returned? How does the emphasis placed on this object signal its SYMBOLIC status?
6. Did you ever have a premonition of someone's death? Describe the setting and descriptive details that would allow the reader to experience your premonition the way you did.
7. What folktales were related to you when you were growing up? These might include ghost stories, tall tales, superstitions, beliefs about dreams, and so forth.
8. Did you ever have a lucky charm, talisman, or amulet? How did you acquire it and how has it brought you good luck?
9. Have you ever had the feeling you were being contacted by a spirit or the ghost of someone who died? What form did the communication take? Describe your experience.

Chinua Achebe

Things Fall Apart

Chinua Achebe was born in Ogidi, a village in eastern Nigeria, in 1930, the son of one of the first Igbo mission teachers. Igbo (previously spelled Igo) is his native tongue, but he learned English—the language in which he writes—at a young age. After taking a degree in English literature from University College, Ibadan in 1953, he worked as a producer and director of the Nigerian Broadcasting Service until the outbreak of the Nigerian civil war in 1967. Achebe actively supported the Biafran struggle for independence, but with the defeat of the Republic of Biafra he joined the University of Nigeria, Nsukka, as a senior research fellow and served as the editor of Okike, *a journal devoted to African literature. Although Achebe has written essays, poetry, children's literature, and short stories collected in* The Sacrificial Egg and Other Stories *(1962),* Girls at War *(1972) and* African Short Stories *(1985), it is as a novelist that he is best known. His first novel,* Things Fall Apart *(1958), from which the following chapter is drawn, is widely acclaimed as a classic of African literature. This work describes how a stable and traditional Nigerian society disintegrates as a result of contact with western Europeans who destroy its political, economic, and religious institutions. In it and succeeding works—*No Longer at Ease *(1960),* Arrow of God *(1964),* A Man of the People *(1966), and* Anthills of the Savannah *(1988)—Achebe continues to counteract European distortions of traditional African culture in his unique style, characterized by subtle irony and compassion. Much of Achebe's work explores the tragic consequences for tribal cultures and the individuals in them when they lose touch with the traditional values that have sustained them. When the protagonist of* Things Fall Apart, *Okonkwo, needlessly participates in slaughtering his adopted son rather than risk being perceived as unmanly, he sets in motion terrible consequences that destroy both him and his clan.*

1   For three years Ikemefuna lived in Okonkwo's household and the elders of Umuofia seemed to have forgotten about him. He grew rapidly like a yam tendril in the rainy season, and was full of the sap of life. He had become wholly absorbed into his new family. He was like an elder brother to Nwoye, and from the very first seemed to have kindled a new fire in the younger boy. He made him feel grown-up; and they no longer spent the evenings in mother's hut while she cooked, but now sat with Okonkwo in his *obi,*[1] or watched him as he tapped his palm tree for the evening wine. Nothing pleased Nwoye now more than to be sent for by his mother or another of his father's wives to do one of those difficult and masculine tasks in the home, like splitting wood, or

[1]*Obi,* the large living quarters of the head of the family.

pounding food. On receiving such a message through a younger brother or sister, Nwoye would feign annoyance and grumble aloud about women and their troubles.

Okonkwo was inwardly pleased at his son's development, and he knew it was due to Ikemefuna. He wanted Nwoye to grow into a tough young man capable of ruling his father's household when he was dead and gone to join the ancestors. He wanted him to be a prosperous man, having enough in his barn to feed the ancestors with regular sacrifices. And so he was always happy when he heard him grumbling about women. That showed that in time he would be able to control his women-folk. No matter how prosperous a man was, if he was unable to rule his women and his children (and especially his women) he was not really a man. He was like the man in the song who had ten and one wives and not enough soup for his foo-foo.[2]

So Okonkwo encouraged the boys to sit with him in his *obi*, and he told them stories of the land—masculine stories of violence and blood-shed. Nwoye knew that it was right to be masculine and to be violent, but somehow he still preferred the stories that his mother used to tell, and which she no doubt still told to her younger children—stories of the tortoise and his wily ways, and of the bird *encke-nti-oba*[3] who chal-lenged the whole world to a wrestling contest and was finally thrown by the cat. He remembered the story she often told of the quarrel be-tween Earth and Sky long ago, and how Sky withheld rain for seven years, until crops withered and the dead could not be buried because the hoes broke on the stony Earth. At last Vulture was sent to plead with Sky, and to soften his heart with a song of the suffering of the sons of men. Whenever Nwoye's mother sang this song he felt carried away to the distant scene in the sky where Vulture, Earth's emissary, sang for mercy. At last Sky was moved to pity, and he gave to Vulture rain wrapped in leaves of coco-yam. But as he flew home his long talon pierced the leaves and the rain fell as it had never fallen before. And so heavily did it rain on Vulture that he did not return to deliver his mes-sage but flew to a distant land, from where he had espied a fire. And when he got there he found it was a man making a sacrifice. He warmed himself in the fire and ate the entrails.

That was the kind of story that Nwoye loved. But he now knew that they were for foolish women and children, and he knew that his father wanted him to be a man. And so he feigned that he no longer cared for women's stories. And when he did this he saw that his father was pleased, and no longer rebuked him or beat him. So Nwoye and Ikemefuna would listen to Okonkwo's stories about tribal wars, or how, years ago, he had stalked his victim, overpowered him and ob-tained his first human head. And as he told them of the past they sat in darkness or the dim glow of logs, waiting for the women to finish their

---

[2]*foo-foo*, a mashed form of a starchy, edible root, also known as the coco-yam.
[3]*encke-nti-oba*, a kind of bird.

cooking. When they finished, each brought her bowl of foo-foo and bowl of soup to her husband. An oil lamp was lit and Okonkwo tasted from each bowl, and then passed two shares to Nwoye and Ikemefuna.

5   In this way the moons and the seasons passed. And then the locusts came. It had not happened for many a long year. The elders said locusts came once in a generation, reappeared every year for seven years and then disappeared for another lifetime. They went back to their caves in a distant land, where they were guarded by a race of stunted men. And then after another lifetime these men opened the caves again and the locusts came to Umuofia.

6   They came in the cold harmattan[4] season after the harvests had been gathered, and ate up all the wild grass in the fields.

7   Okonkwo and the two boys were working on the red outer walls of the compound. This was one of the lighter tasks of the after-harvest season. A new cover of thick palm branches and palm leaves was set on the walls to protect them from the next rainy season. Okonkwo worked on the outside of the wall and the boys worked from within. There were little holes from one side to the other in the upper levels of the wall, and through these Okonkwo passed the rope, or *tie-tie*,[5] to the boys and they passed it round the wooden stays and then back to him; and in his way the cover was strengthened on the wall.

8   The women had gone to the bush to collect firewood, and the little children to visit their playmates in the neighboring compounds. The harmattan was in the air and seemed to distill a hazy feeling of sleep on the world. Okonkwo and the boys worked in complete silence, which was only broken when a new palm frond was lifted on to the wall or when a busy hen moved dry leaves about in her ceaseless search for food.

9   And then quite suddenly a shadow fell on the world, and the sun seemed hidden behind a thick cloud. Okonkwo looked up from his work and wondered if it was going to rain at such an unlikely time of the year. But almost immediately a shout of joy broke out in all directions, and Umuofia, which had dozed in the noon-day haze, broke into life and activity.

10   "Locusts are descending," was joyfully chanted everywhere, and men, women and children left their work or their play and ran into the open to see the unfamiliar sight. The locusts had not come for many, many years, and only the old people had seen them before.

11   At first, a fairly small swarm came. They were the harbingers sent to survey the land. And then appeared on the horizon a slowly-moving mass like a boundless sheet of black cloud drifting towards Umuofia. Soon it covered half the sky, and the solid mass was now broken by tiny eyes of light like shining star dust. It was a tremendous sight, full of power and beauty.

12   Everyone was now about, talking excitedly and praying that the locusts should camp in Umuofia for the night. For although locusts had

---

[4]*harmattan*, a dry parching land-breeze charged with dust.
[5]*tie-tie*, a creeping vine used as rope.

not visited Umuofia for many years, everybody knew by instinct that they were very good to eat. And at last the locusts did descend. They settled on every tree and on every blade of grass; they settled on the roofs and covered the bare ground. Mighty tree branches broke away under them, and the whole country became the brown-earth color of the vast, hungry swarm.

Many people went out with baskets trying to catch them, but the elders counseled patience till nightfall. And they were right. The locusts settled in the bushes for the night and their wings became wet with dew. Then all Umuofia turned out in spite of the cold harmattan, and everyone filled his bags and pots with locusts. The next morning they were roasted in clay pots and then spread in the sun until they became dry and brittle. And for many days this rare food was eaten with solid palm-oil.

Okonkwo sat in his *obi* crunching happily with Ikemefuna and Nwoye, and drinking palm-wine[6] copiously, when Ogbuefi Ezeudu came in. Ezeudu was the oldest man in this quarter of Umuofia. He had been a great and fearless warrior in his time, and was now accorded great respect in all the clan. He refused to join in the meal, and asked Okonkwo to have a word with him outside. And so they walked out together, the old man supporting himself with his stick. When they were out of earshot, he said to Okonkwo:

"That boy calls you father. Do not bear a hand in his death." Okonkwo was surprised, and was about to say something when the old man continued:

"Yes, Umuofia has decided to kill him. The Oracle of the Hills and the Caves has pronounced it. They will take him outside Umuofia as is the custom, and kill him there. But I want you to have nothing to do with it. He calls you his father."

The next day a group of elders from all the nine villages of Umuofia came to Okonkwo's house early in the morning, and before they began to speak in low tones Nwoye and Ikemefuna were sent out. They did not stay very long, but when they went away Okonkwo sat still for a very long time supporting his chin in his palms. Later in the day he called Ikemefuna and told him that he was to be taken home the next day. Nwoye overheard it and burst into tears, whereupon his father beat him heavily. As for Ikemefuna, he was at a loss. His own home had gradually become very faint and distant. He still missed his mother and his sister and would be very glad to see them. But somehow he knew he was not going to see them. He remembered once when men had talked in low tones with his father; and it seemed now as if it was happening all over again.

Later, Nwoye went to his mother's hut and told her that Ikemefuna was going home. She immediately dropped her pestle with which she was grinding pepper, folded her arms across her breast and sighed, "Poor child."

[6]*palm-wine*, wine made with distilled, fermented palm-tree sap.

19   The next day, the men returned with a pot of wine. They were all fully dressed as if they were going to a big clan meeting or to pay a visit to a neighboring village. They passed their cloths under the right armpit, and hung their goatskin bags and sheathed machetes over their left shoulders. Okonkwo got ready quickly and the party set out with Ikemefuna carrying the pot of wine. A deathly silence descended on Okonkwo's compound. Even the very little children seemed to know. Throughout that day Nwoye sat in his mother's hut and tears stood in his eyes.

20   At the beginning of their journey the men of Umuofia talked and laughed about the locusts, about their women, and about some effeminate men who had refused to come with them. But as they drew near to the outskirts of Umuofia silence fell upon them too.

21   The sun rose slowly to the center of the sky, and the dry, sandy footway began to throw up the heat that lay buried in it. Some birds chirruped in the forests around. The men trod dry leaves on the sand. All else was silent. Then from the distance came the faint beating of the *ekwe*.[7] It rose and faded with the wind—a peaceful dance from a distant clan.

22   "It is an *ozo*[8] dance," the men said among themselves. But no one was sure where it was coming from. Some said Ezimili, others Abame or Aninta. They argued for a short while and fell into silence again, and the elusive dance rose and fell with the wind. Somewhere a man was taking one of the titles of his clan, with music and dancing and a great feast.

23   The footway had now become a narrow line in the heart of the forest. The short trees and sparse undergrowth which surrounded the men's village began to give way to giant trees and climbers which perhaps had stood from the beginning of things, untouched by the ax and the bush-fire. The sun breaking through their leaves and branches threw a pattern of light and shade on the sandy footway.

24   Ikemefuna heard a whisper close behind him and turned round sharply. The man who had whispered now called out aloud, urging the others to hurry up.

25   "We still have a long way to go," he said. Then he and another man went before Ikemefuna and set a faster pace.

26   Thus the men of Umuofia pursued their way, armed with sheathed machetes, and Ikemefuna, carrying a pot of palm-wine on his head, walked in their midst. Although he had felt uneasy at first, he was not afraid now. Okonkwo walked behind him. He could hardly imagine that Okonkwo was not his real father. He had never been fond of his real father, and at the end of three years he had become very distant indeed. But his mother and his three-year-old sister . . . . of course she would not be three now, but six. Would he recognize her now? She

---

[7]*ekwe*, a musical instrument; a type of drum made from wood.
[8]*ozo*, the name of one of the titles or rank men in the tribe sought to achieve.

must have grown quite big. How his mother would weep for joy, and thank Okonkwo for having looked after him so well and for bringing him back. She would want to hear everything that had happened to him in all these years. Could he remember them all? He would tell her about Nwoye and his mother, and about the locusts. . . . Then quite suddenly a thought came upon him. His mother might be dead. He tried in vain to force the thought out of his mind. Then he tried to settle the matter the way he used to settle such matters when he was a little boy. He still remembered the song:

> *Eze elina, elina!*
>> *Sala*
> *Eze ilikwa ya*
> *Ikwaba akwa oligholi*
> *Ebe Danda nechi eze*
> *Ebe Uzuzu nete egwu*
>> *Sala*[9]

He sang it in his mind, and walked to its beat. If the song ended on his right foot, his mother was alive. If it ended on his left, she was dead. No, not dead, but ill. It ended on the right. She was alive and well. He sang the song again, and it ended on the left. But the second time did not count. The first voice gets to Chukwu, or God's house. That was a favorite saying of children. Ikemefuna felt like a child once more. It must be the thought of going home to his mother.

One of the men behind him cleared his throat. Ikemefuna looked back, and the man growled at him to go on and not stand looking back. The way he said it sent cold fear down Ikemefuna's back. His hands trembled vaguely on the black pot he carried. Why had Okonkwo withdrawn to the rear? Ikemefuna felt his legs melting under him. And he was afraid to look back. 27

As the man who had cleared his throat drew up and raised his machete, Okonkwo looked away. He heard the blow. The pot fell and broke in the sand. He heard Ikemefuna cry, "My father, they have killed me!" as he ran towards him. Dazed with fear, Okonkwo drew his machete and cut him down. He was afraid of being thought weak. 28

As soon as his father walked in, that night, Nwoye knew that Ikemefuna had been killed, and something seemed to give way inside him, like the snapping of a tightened bow. He did not cry. He just hung limp. He had had the same kind of feeling not long ago, during the last harvest season. Every child loved the harvest season. Those who were big enough to carry even a few yams in a tiny basket went with grownups to the farm. And if they could not help in digging up the yams, they could gather firewood together for roasting the ones that would be eaten there on the farm. This roasted yam soaked in red palm-oil and 29

---

[9]A song Ikemefuna recites to allay his fears; the lyrics tell of a king whose uncontrolled hunger leads to his overthrow and to starvation for his people.

eaten in the open farm was sweeter than any meal at home. It was after such a day at the farm during the last harvest that Nwoye had felt for the first time a snapping inside him like the one he now felt. They were returning home with baskets of yams from a distant farm across the stream when they heard the voice of an infant crying in the thick forest. A sudden hush had fallen on the women, who had been talking, and they had quickened their steps. Nwoye had heard that twins were put in earthenware pots and thrown away in the forest, but he had never yet come across them.[10] A vague chill had descended on him and his head had seemed to swell, like a solitary walker at night who passes an evil spirit on the way. Then something had given way inside him. It descended on him again, this feeling, when his father walked in, that night after killing Ikemefuna.

Questions for Discussion and Writing

1. How are Okonkwo's aspirations for his son, Nwoye, reflected in the stories he tells him? By contrast, what values are expressed in the stories told to the children by his wife?
2. How might the vulture story, in which unexpected gifts from the gods must be paid for, explain why the elders required the sacrifice of Ikemefuna after the unexpected bounty of locusts?
3. How does hearing Ikemefuna call him "father" precipitate Okonkwo's participation in the murder, something he has been explicitly warned against by the elders of the tribe? How at this moment is his TRAGIC FLAW triggered?
4. How is the pathos of the murder increased by putting the reader in Ikemefuna's thoughts at the moment before his murder? To what extent does he suspect what is going to happen?
5. How do Okonkwo's actions transform him into an ARCHETYPAL tragic figure and change how others perceive him?
6. How does Nwoye react to learning of his step-brother's death and of his father's participation?
7. As in the Greek tragedies of *Oedipus Rex* by Sophocles and the *Oresteia* by Aeschylus, Achebe's story tells of a family cursed because of the wrongdoings of ancestors that will blight future generations. Describe the history of a family cursed because of the sin or wrongful act committed by an ancestor. When did they live and what act did they commit? What form does the curse take (insanity, suicides, and so forth)?

---

[10]For the Igbo, the birth of twins was perceived as splitting one soul between two bodies, and was considered to be an evil omen.

Leslie Marmon Silko

Language and Literature from a Pueblo Indian Perspective

Leslie Marmon Silko was born in 1948 in Albuquerque, New Mexico. Silko's writing draws on her heritage as a Native American of mixed ancestry (Laguna, Mexican, and white). She grew up on the Laguna Pueblo reservation in New Mexico and attended the University of New Mexico, graduating in 1969 with a B.A. in English. She then briefly attended law school, but decided to be a writer and teacher instead. Her first short story, "The Man to Send Rain Clouds," was published in New Mexico Quarterly *in 1969. She taught for two years at the Navajo Community College at Many Farms, Arizona, following which she spent two years in Ketchikan, Alaska. Her first novel,* Ceremony *(1977), about an Indian veteran of World War II and his search for sanity, is shaped by her innovative use of Pueblo oral storytelling techniques as are her later works* Laguna Woman *(1974),* Storyteller *(1981), a collection of poems and stories, and her second novel,* Almanac of the Dead *(1991). Her work has been widely praised. In 1981 she was the recipient of a MacArthur Foundation grant. In her 1991 essay,* Language and Literature from a Pueblo Indian Perspective, *Silko discusses and illustrates the relationship between Laguna Pueblo religious beliefs and the tradition of storytelling in Laguna society.*

Where I come from, the words most highly valued are those spoken from the heart, unpremeditated and unrehearsed. Among the Pueblo people, a written speech or statement is highly suspect because the true feelings of the speaker remain hidden as she reads words that are detached from the occasion and the audience. I have intentionally not written a formal paper because I want you to *hear* and to experience English in a structure that follows patterns from the oral tradition. For those of you accustomed to being taken from point A to point B to point C, this presentation may be somewhat difficult to follow. Pueblo expression resembles something like a spider's web—with many little threads radiating from the center, crisscrossing each other. As with the web, the structure emerges as it is made and you must simply listen and trust, as the Pueblo people do, that meaning will be made.

My task is a formidable one: I ask you to set aside a number of basic approaches that you have been using, and probably will continue to use, and instead, to approach language from the Pueblo perspective, one that embraces the whole of creation and the whole of history and time.

What changes would Pueblo writers make to English as a language for literature? I have some examples of stories in English that I will use to address this question. At the same time, I would like to explain the importance of storytelling and how it relates to a Pueblo theory of language.

4   So, I will begin, appropriately enough, with the Pueblo Creation story, an all-inclusive story of how life began. In this story, Tséitsínako, Thought Woman, by thinking of her sisters, and together with her sisters, thought of everything that is. In this way, the world was created. Everything in this world was a part of the original creation; the people at home understood that far away there were other human beings, also a part of this world. The Creation story even includes a prophecy, which describes the origin of European and African peoples and also refers to Asians.

5   This story, I think, suggests something about why the Pueblo people are more concerned with story and communication and less concerned with a particular language. There are at least six, possibly seven, distinct languages among the twenty pueblos of the southwestern United States, for example, Zuñi and Hopi. And from mesa to mesa there are subtle differences in language. But the particular language being spoken isn't as important as what a speaker is trying to say, and this emphasis on the story itself stems, I believe, from a view of narrative particular to the Pueblo and other Native American peoples—that is, that language *is* story.

6   I will try to clarify this statement. At Laguna Pueblo, for example, many individual words have their own stories. So when one is telling a story, and one is using words to tell the story, each word that one is speaking has a story of its own, too. Often the speakers or tellers will go into these word-stories, creating an elaborate structure of stories-within-stories. This structure, which becomes very apparent in the actual telling of a story, informs contemporary Pueblo writing and storytelling as well as the traditional narratives. This perspective on narrative—of story within story, the idea that one story is only the beginning of many stories, and the sense that stories never truly end—represents an important contribution of Native American cultures to the English language.

7   Many people think of storytelling as something that is done at bedtime, that it is something done for small children. But when I use the term *storytelling*, I'm talking about something much bigger than that. I'm talking about something that comes out of an experience and an understanding of that original view of creation—that we are all part of a whole; we do not differentiate or fragment stories and experiences. In the beginning, Tséitsínako, Thought Woman, thought of all things, and all of these things are held together as one holds many things together in a single thought.

8   So in the telling (and you will hear a few of the dimensions of this telling) first of all, as mentioned earlier, the storytelling always includes

the audience, the listeners. In fact, a great deal of the story is believed to be inside the listener; the storyteller's role is to draw the story out of the listeners. The storytelling continues from generation to generation.

Basically, the origin story constructs our identity—with this story, 9 we know who we are. We are the Lagunas. This is where we come from. We came this way. We came by this place. And so from the time we are very young, we hear these stories, so that when we go out into the world, when one asks who we are, or where we are from, we imme-diately know: we are the people who came from the north. We are the people of these stories.

In the Creation story, Antelope says that he will help knock a hole in 10 the earth so that the people can come up, out into the next world. Antelope tries and tries; he uses his hooves, but is unable to break through. It is then that Badger says, "Let me help you." And Badger very patiently uses his claws and digs a way through, bringing the peo-ple into the world. When the Badger clan people think of themselves, or when the Antelope people think of themselves, it is as people who are of *this* story, and this is *our* place, and we fit into the very beginning when the people first came, before we began our journey south.

Within the clans there are stories that identify the clan. One moves, 11 then, from the idea of one's identity as a tribal person into clan identity, then to one's identity as a member of an extended family. And it is the notion of "extended family" that has produced a kind of story that some distinguish from other Pueblo stories, though Pueblo people do not. Anthropologists and ethnologists have, for a long time, differenti-ated the types of stories the Pueblos tell. They tended to elevate the old, sacred, and traditional stories and to brush aside family stories, the family's account of itself. But in Pueblo culture, these family stories are given equal recognition. There is no definite, preset pattern for the way one will hear the stories of one's own family, but it is a very critical part of one's childhood, and the storytelling continues throughout one's life. One will hear stories of importance to the family—sometimes wonder-ful stories—stories about the time a maternal uncle got the biggest deer that was ever seen and brought it back from the mountains. And so an individual's identity will extend from the identity constructed around the family—"I am from the family of my uncle who brought in this wonderful deer and it was a wonderful hunt."

Family accounts include negative stories, too; perhaps an uncle did 12 something unacceptable. It is very important that one keep track of all these stories—both positive and not so positive—about one's own fam-ily and other families. Because even when there is no way around it—old Uncle Pete *did* do a terrible thing—by knowing the stories that orig-inate in other families, one is able to deal with terrible sorts of things that might happen within one's own family. If a member of the family does something that cannot be excused, one always knows stories about similarly inexcusable things done by a member of another family.

But this knowledge is not communicated for malicious reasons. It is very important to understand this. Keeping track of all the stories within the community gives us all a certain distance, a useful perspective, that brings incidents down to a level we can deal with. If others have done it before, it cannot be so terrible. If others have endured, so can we.

13   The stories are always bringing us together, keeping this whole together, keeping this family together, keeping this clan together. "Don't go away, don't isolate yourself, but come here, because we have all had these kinds of experiences." And so there is this constant pulling together to resist the tendency to run or hide or separate oneself during a traumatic emotional experience. This separation not only endangers the group but the individual as well—one does not recover by oneself.

14   Because storytelling lies at the heart of Pueblo culture, it is absurd to attempt to fix the stories in time. "When did they tell the stories?" or "What time of day does the storytelling take place?"—these questions are nonsensical from a Pueblo perspective, because our storytelling goes on constantly: as some old grandmother puts on the shoes of a child and tells her the story of a little girl who didn't wear her shoes, for instance, or someone comes into the house for coffee to talk with a teenage boy who has just been in a lot of trouble, to reassure him that someone else's son has been in that kind of trouble, too. Storytelling is an ongoing process, working on many different levels.

15   Here's one story that is often told at a time of individual crisis (and I want to remind you that we make no distinctions between types of story—historical, sacred, plain gossip—because these distinctions are not useful when discussing the Pueblo *experience* of language). There was a young man who, when he came back from the war in Vietnam, had saved up his army pay and bought a beautiful red Volkswagen. He was very proud of it. One night he drove up to a place called the King's Bar right across the reservation line. The bar is notorious for many reasons, particularly for the deep *arroyo* located behind it. The young man ran in to pick up a cold six-pack, but he forgot to put on his emergency brake. And his little red Volkswagen rolled back into the *arroyo* and was all smashed up. He felt very bad about it, but within a few days everybody had come to him with stories about other people who had lost cars and family members to that *arroyo*, for instance, George Day's station wagon, with his mother-in-law and kids inside. So everybody was saying, "Well, at least your mother-in-law and kids weren't in the car when it rolled in," and one can't argue with that kind of story. The story of the young man and his smashed-up Volkswagen was now joined with all the other stories of cars that fell into that *arroyo*.

16   Now I want to tell you a very beautiful little story. It is a very old story that is sometimes told to people who suffer great family or personal loss. This story was told by my Aunt Susie. She is one of the first generation of people at Laguna who began experimenting with

English—who began working to make English speak for us—that is, to speak from the heart. (I come from a family intent on getting the stories told.) As you read the story, I think you will hear that. And here and there, I think, you will also hear the influence of the Indian school at Carlisle, Pennsylvania, where my Aunt Susie was sent (like being sent to prison) for six years.

This scene is set partly in Acoma, partly in Laguna. Waithea was a little girl living in Acoma and one day she said, "Mother, I would like to have some *yashtoah* to eat." *Yashtoah* is the hardened crust of corn mush that curls up. *Yashtoah* literally means "curled up." She said, "I would like to have some *yashtoah*," and her mother said, "My dear little girl, I can't make you any *yashtoah* because we haven't any wood, but if you will go down off the mesa, down below, and pick up some pieces of wood and bring them home, I will make you some *yashtoah*." So Waithea was glad and ran down the precipitous cliff of Acoma mesa. Down below, just as her mother had told her, there were pieces of wood, some curled, some crooked in shape, that she was to pick up and take home. She found just such wood as these.

She brought them home in a little wicker basket. First she called to her mother as she got home, "*Nayah, deeni!* Mother, upstairs!" The Pueblo people always called "upstairs" because long ago their homes were two, three stories, and they entered from the top. She said, "*Deeni!* UPSTAIRS!" and her mother came. The little girl said, "I have brought the wood you wanted me to bring." And she opened her little wicker basket to lay out the pieces of wood but here they were snakes. They were snakes instead of the crooked sticks of wood. And her mother said, "Oh my dear child, you have brought snakes instead!" She said, "Go take them back and put them back just where you got them." And the little girl ran down the mesa again, down below to the flats. And she put those snakes back just where she got them. They were snakes instead and she was very hurt about this and so she said, "I'm not going home. I'm going to *Kawaik*, the beautiful lake place, *Kawaik*, and drown myself in that lake, *byn'yah'nah* [the "west lake"]. I will go there and drown myself."

So she started off, and as she passed by the Enchanted Mesa near Acoma she met an old man, very aged, and he saw her running, and he said, "My dear child, where are you going?" "I'm going to *Kawaik* and jump into the lake there." "Why?" "Well, because," she said, "my mother didn't want to make any *yashtoah* for me." The old man said, "Oh, no! You must not go my child. Come with me and I will take you home." He tried to catch her, but she was very light and skipped along. And every time he would try to grab her she would skip faster away from him.

The old man was coming home with some wood strapped to his back and tied with yucca. He just let that strap go and let the wood drop. He went as fast as he could up the cliff to the little girl's home.

When he got to the place where she lived, he called to her mother. "*Deeni!*" "Come on up!" And he said, "I can't. I just came to bring you a message. Your little daughter is running away. She is going to *Kawaik* to drown herself in the lake there." "Oh my dear little girl!" the mother said. So she busied herself with making the *yashtoah* her little girl liked so much. Corn mush curled at the top. (She must have found enough wood to boil the corn meal and make the *yashtoah*.)

21   While the mush was cooling off, she got the little girl's clothing, her *manta* dress and buckskin moccasins and all her other garments, and put them in a bundle—probably a yucca bag. And she started down as fast as she could on the east side of Acoma. (There used to be a trail there, you know. It's gone now, but it was accessible in those days.) She saw her daughter way at a distance and she kept calling: "Stsamaku! My daughter! Come back! I've got your *yashtoah* for you." But the little girl would not turn. She kept on ahead and she cried: "My mother, my mother, she didn't want me to have any *yashtoah*. So now I'm going to *Kawaik* and drown myself." Her mother heard her cry and said, "My little daughter, come back here!" "No," and she kept a distance away from her. And they came nearer and nearer to the lake. And she could see her daughter now, very plain. "Come back, my daughter! I have your *yashtoah*." But no, she kept on, and finally she reached the lake and she stood on the edge.

22   She had tied a little feather in her hair, which is traditional (in death they tie this feather on the head). She carried a feather, the little girl did, and she tied it in her hair with a piece of string, right on top of her head she put the feather. Just as her mother was about to reach her, she jumped into the lake. The little feather was whirling around and around in the depths below. Of course the mother was very sad. She went, grieved, back to Acoma and climbed her mesa home. She stood on the edge of the mesa and scattered her daughter's clothing, the little moccasins, the *yashtoah*. She scattered them to the east, to the west, to the north, to the south. And the pieces of clothing and the moccasins and *yashtoah*, all turned into butterflies. And today they say that Acoma has more beautiful butterflies: red ones, white ones, blue ones, yellow ones. They came from this little girl's clothing.[1]

23   Now this is a story anthropologists would consider very old. The version I have given you is just as Aunt Susie tells it. You can occasionally hear some English she picked up at Carlisle—words like "precipitous." You will also notice that there is a great deal of repetition, and a little reminder about *yashtoah*, and how it is made. There is a remark about the cliff trail at Acoma—that it was once there, but is there no longer. This story may be told at a time of sadness or loss, but within this story many other elements are brought together. Things are not separated out and categorized; all things are brought together. So that

[1] See Leslie Marmon Silko, *Storyteller* (1981).

the reminder about the *yashtoah* is valuable information that is repeated—a recipe, if you will. The information about the old trail at Acoma reveals that stories are, in a sense, maps, since even to this day there is little information or material about trails that is passed around with writing. In the structure of this story the repetitions are, of course, designed to help you remember. It is repeated again and again, and then it moves on.

The next story I would like to tell is by Simon Ortiz, from Acoma   24
Pueblo. He is a wonderful poet who also works in narrative. One of the things I find very interesting in this short story is that if you listen very closely, you begin to hear what I was talking about in terms of a story never beginning at the beginning, and certainly never ending. As the Hopis sometimes say, "Well, it has gone this far for a while." There is always that implication of a continuing. The other thing I want you to listen for is the many stories within one story. Listen to the kinds of stories contained within the main story—stories that give one a family identity and an individual identity, for example. This story is called "Home Country":

"Well, it's been a while. I think in 1947 was when I left. My husband had been   25
killed in Okinawa some years before. And so I had no more husband. And I had to make a living. O I guess I could have looked for another man but I didn't want to. It looked like the war had made some of them into a bad way anyway. I saw some of them come home like that. They either got drunk or just stayed around a while or couldn't seem to be satisfied anymore with what was there. I guess now that I think about it, that happened to me too although I wasn't in the war not in the Army or even much off the reservation just that several years at the Indian School. Well there was that feeling things were changing not only the men the boys, but things were changing.

"One day the home nurse the nurse that came from the Indian health ser-   26
vice was at my mother's home my mother was getting near the end real sick and she said that she had been meaning to ask me a question. I said what is the question. And the home nurse said well your mother is getting real sick and after she is no longer around for you to take care of, what will you be doing you and her are the only ones here. And I said I don't know. But I was thinking about it what she said made me think about it. And then the next time she came she said to me Eloise the government is hiring Indians now in the Indian schools to take care of the boys and girls I heard one of the supervisors saying that Indians are hard workers but you have to supervise them a lot and I thought of you well because you've been taking care of your mother real good and you follow all my instructions. She said I thought of you because you're a good Indian girl and you would be the kind of person for that job. I didn't say anything I had not ever really thought about a job but I kept thinking about it.

"Well my mother she died and we buried her up at the old place the ceme-   27
tery there it's real nice on the east side of the hill where the sun shines warm and the wind doesn't blow too much sand around right there. Well I was sad

we were all sad for a while but you know how things are. One of my aunties came over and she advised me and warned me about being too sorry about it and all that she wished me that I would not worry too much about it because old folks they go along pretty soon life is that way and then she said that maybe I ought to take in one of my aunties kids or two because there was a lot of them kids and I was all by myself now. But I was so young and I thought that I might do that you know take care of someone but I had been thinking too of what the home nurse said to me about working. Hardly anybody at our home was working at something like that no woman anyway. And I would have to move away.

28   "Well I did just that. I remember that day very well. I told my aunties and they were all crying and we all went up to the old highway where the bus to town passed by everyday. I was wearing an old kind of bluish sweater that was kind of big that one of my cousins who was older had got from a white person a tourist one summer in trade for something she had made a real pretty basket. She gave me that and I used to have a picture of me with it on it's kind of real ugly. Yeah that was the day I left wearing a baggy sweater and carrying a suitcase that someone gave me too I think or maybe it was the home nurse there wasn't much in it anyway either. I was scared and everybody seemed to be sad I was so young and skinny then. My aunties said one of them who was real fat you make sure you eat now make your own tortillas drink the milk and stuff like candies is no good she learned that from the nurse. Make sure you got your letter my auntie said. I had it folded into my purse. Yes I had one too a brown one that my husband when he was still alive one time on furlough he brought it on my birthday it was a nice purse and still looked new because I never used it.

29   "The letter said that I had a job at Keams Canyon the boarding school there but I would have to go to the Agency first for some papers to be filled and that's where I was going first. The Agency. And then they would send me out to Keams Canyon. I didn't even know where it was except that someone of our relatives said that it was near Hopi. My uncles teased me about watching out for the Hopi men and boys don't let them get too close they said well you know how they are and they were pretty strict too about those things and then they were joking and then they were not too and so I said aw they won't get near to me I'm too ugly and I promised I would be careful anyway.

30   "So we all gathered for a while at my last auntie's house and then the old man my grandfather brought his wagon and horses to the door and we all got in and sat there for a while until my auntie told her father okay father let's go and shook his elbow because the poor old man was old by then and kind of going to sleep all the time you had to talk to him real loud. I had about ten dollars I think that was a lot of money more than it is now you know and when we got to the highway where the Indian road which is just a dirt road goes off the pave road my grandfather reached into his blue jeans and pulled out a silver dollar and put it into my hand. I was so shocked. We were all so shocked. We all looked around at each other we didn't know where the old man had gotten it because we were real poor two of my uncles had to borrow on their accounts at

the trading store for the money I had in my purse but there it was a silver dollar so big and shining in my grandfather's hand and then in my hand.

"Well I was so shocked and everybody was so shocked that we all started crying right there at the junction of that Indian road and the pave highway I wanted to be a little girl again running after the old man when he hurried with his long legs to the cornfields or went for water down to the river. He was old then and his eye was turned gray and he didn't do much anymore except drive the wagon and chop a little bit of wood but I just held him and I just held him so tightly.

"Later on I don't know what happened to the silver dollar it had a date of 1907 on it but I kept it for a long time because I guess I wanted to have it to remember when I left my home country. What I did in between then and now is another story but that's the time I moved away," is what she said.[2]

There are a great many parallels between Pueblo experiences and those of African and Caribbean peoples—one is that we have all had the conqueror's language imposed on us. But our experience with English has been somewhat different in that the Bureau of Indian Affairs schools were not interested in teaching us the canon of Western classics. For instance, we never heard of Shakespeare. We were given Dick and Jane, and I can remember reading that the robins were heading south for the winter. It took me a long time to figure out what was going on. I worried for quite a while about our robins in Laguna because they didn't leave in the winter, until I finally realized that all the big textbook companies are up in Boston and *their* robins do go south in the winter. But in a way, this dreadful formal education freed us by encouraging us to maintain our narratives. Whatever literature we were exposed to at school (which was damn little), at home the storytelling, the special regard for telling and bringing together through the telling, was going on constantly.

And as the old people say, "If you can remember the stories, you will be all right. Just remember the stories." When I returned to Laguna Pueblo after attending college, I wondered how the storytelling was continuing (anthropologists say that Laguna Pueblo is one of the more acculturated pueblos), so I visited an English class at Laguna-Acoma High School. I knew the students had cassette tape recorders in their lockers and stereos at home, and that they listened to Kiss and Led Zeppelin and were well informed about popular culture in general. I had with me an anthology of short stories by Native American writers, *The Man to Send Rain Clouds.* One story in the book is about the killing of a state policeman in New Mexico by three Acoma Pueblo men in the early 1950s.[3] I asked the students how many had heard this story and

[2] In Simon J. Ortiz, *Howbah Indians* (Tucson: Blue Moon Press, 1978).

[3] See Simon J. Ortiz, "The Killing of a State Cop," in *The Man to Send Rain Clouds*, ed. Kenneth Rosen (New York: Viking Press, 1974), pp. 101–108.

steeled myself for the possibility that the anthropologists were right, that the old traditions were indeed dying out and the students would be ignorant of the story. But instead, all but one or two raised their hands—they had heard the story, just as I had heard it when I was young, some in English, some in Laguna.

35   One of the other advantages that we Pueblos have enjoyed is that we have always been able to stay with the land. Our stories cannot be separated from their geographical locations, from actual physical places on the land. We were not relocated like so many Native American groups who were torn away from their ancestral land. And our stories are so much a part of these places that it is almost impossible for future generations to lose them—there is a story connected with every place, every object in the landscape.

36   Dennis Brutus has talked about the "yet unborn" as well as "those from the past," and how we are still *all* in *this* place, and language—the storytelling—is our way of passing through or being with them, of being together again. When Aunt Susie told her stories, she would tell a younger child to go open the door so that our esteemed predecessors might bring in their gifts to us. "They are out there," Aunt Susie would say. "Let them come in. They're here, they're here with us *within* the stories."

37   A few years ago, when Aunt Susie was 106, I paid her a visit, and while I was there she said, "Well, I'll be leaving here soon. I think I'll be leaving here next week, and I will be going over to the Cliff House." She said, "It's going to be real good to get back over there." I was listening, and I was thinking that she must be talking about her house at Paguate Village, just north of Laguna. And she went on, "Well, my mother's sister (and she gave her Indian name) will be there. She has been living there. She will be there and we will be over there, and I will get a chance to write down these stories I've been telling you." Now you must understand, of course, that Aunt Susie's mother's sister, a great storyteller herself, has long since passed over into the land of the dead. But then I realized, too, that Aunt Susie wasn't talking about death the way most of us do. She was talking about "going over" as a journey, a journey that perhaps we can only begin to understand through an appreciation for the boundless capacity of language that, through storytelling, brings us together, despite great distances between cultures, despite great distances in time.

Questions for Discussion and Writing

1. How is the idea that a story is never self-contained, but is always connected to a network of related stories, illustrated in Silko's essay?
2. What peripheral stories can you discern radiating from the central story "Home Country" by Simon Ortiz? How does this story express the concept that no story is ever really self-contained?

3. How do "origin stories" function as myths in Laguna society? What questions do they answer? How do they provide a sense of identity and continuity?

4. Why is it significant that the Pueblo tradition of storytelling makes no distinction between types of stories, such as historical, sacred, or just plain gossip?

5. How is the function of storytelling illustrated in this essay by the story told by Aunt Susie? What moral values and ethical principles does the story express?

6. To some readers, Silko's account might seem unstructured. How does the very nature of her essay reflect the ideas discussed? How are different sections of her essay connected through the principle of emotional associations rather than through a logical order?

7. In a short essay, discuss the distinctive qualities that define the way stories are told in Native American cultures. How do these differ from what you might have thought of as a traditional story?

8. What legends or stories have come down from the past and have been told and retold in your family or community?

Jorge Luis Borges
Afterglow

Jorge Luis Borges (1899–1986), a master storyteller, poet, essayist, and man of letters, was born in Buenos Aires. His father, a professor of psychology, entertained him in childhood with intellectual and philosophical conundrums that remained a lifelong interest. Educated in Europe, at which time he learned French and German, he began to write as a member of the Spanish avant-garde literary movement called Ultraisme, a form of expressionism in which image and metaphor take precedence over plot, character, and theme. In later life, Borges remained an antirealist. When he returned to Buenos Aires in 1921, he worked in the National Library, and became its director before Juan Perón ousted him from his post because of political differences. In 1935 Borges had his collection of short narrative pieces published, under the title Universal History of Infamy. *His first major anthology of short stories,* The Garden of Forking Paths *(1941), introduced a collection whose imaginative world is an immense labyrinth of multidimensional reality; the stories are written in a playfully allusive literary and philosophical language in which the narrators seek to understand their own significance and that of the world. Borges developed these themes in a variety of styles in* Fictions *(1944),* The Aleph *(1949),* Labyrinths *(1962), and* Dr. Brody's Report *(1972). Borges lived in Buenos Aires until his death and had an enormous influence on contemporary Latin American writing. His dazzling sense of paradox and mystery can be seen in "Afterglow"—translated by Norman Thomas Di Giovanni, from Jorge Luis Borges's* Selected Poems 1923–1967 *(1972)—a poem that may reflect his increasing blindness as a result of the same hereditary eye disease that had blinded his father. Forced to dictate his work, he nevertheless continued to travel, teach, and lecture until his death in 1967.*

Sunset is always disturbing
whether theatrical or muted,
but still more disturbing is that last desperate glow
that turns the plain to rust
5   when on the horizon nothing is left
of the pomp and clamor of the setting sun.
How hard holding on to that light, so tautly drawn and different,
that hallucination which the human fear of the dark
imposes on space
10   and which ceases at once
the moment we realize its falsity,
the way a dream is broken
the moment the sleeper knows he is dreaming.

Questions for Discussion and Writing

1. What does the speaker's response to the fading sunset reveal about him? How does the way things are described suggest qualities about the perceiver?
2. How does the desire to hold onto the last light of the day produce the hallucination described in the title?
3. How does the poem suggest that the faculty of seeing things as they are without illusion is a great achievement?
4. What does the sunset and its afterglow seem to SYMBOLIZE for the speaker?
5. Describe the physical and psychological atmosphere of a place at night, emphasizing the feelings that are evoked, such as fear or enchantment.
6. Describe the figures, real (the operator of an all-night laundromat) or imagined (spirits, vampires) that you associate with the night world. Your description should start with sundown.

Ma Lihua

My Sun

Ma Lihua, born in China, 1955, lives in Lhasa, Tibet, and is one of the few writers in that country who enjoys a reputation throughout China. Quite versatile, she has published collections of her poetry as well as fiction and journalistic reports. Her work shows influences of Taoism, Buddhism, and Western modernism. The following selection of four poems constitutes a sequence entitled "My Sun," translated by Fang Dai, Dennis Ding, and Edward Morin (1990). In this sequence, Lihua attempts to recover and redefine the self by infusing the landscape with personal emotions, especially sentiments of awe.

Waiting for Sunrise

Let the eyes traverse the mountain
To meet the sunrise

He has framed the eastern pasture
In scarlet lace
Will the eternal lamp
That I share with the universe
    Come striding out on his vermilion carpet

5

For a long while   I stand on the grassy lowland
Knowing he is still too far away
10 Yet I believe it is possible to reach his brilliance and warmth
That is enough.   I allow
      My heart to feel exaltation or calm
      And my love for him to ascend and deepen

Let the eyes traverse the mountain
15 To meet the sunrise of the living

Injured hearts become more and more frail
So fragile they cannot continue resisting the temptation of
      disillusionment
When the small boat was led to an undertow in the cold spring
The strong sun's wind blew open the sail of destiny one more time
20 It is truly worthwhile to have one last overreaching desire
To sail toward that remote shore of gold
Sun O Sun
Let's not be on guard against each other
The sun has risen to a half circle
25 Like an eye or a brow on a smiling face
I belong to him and want to snuggle my back against him
Open both my arms high in an arc
Then take a gigantic picture against the light
Yes, there's the pasture—the sun—
30   And my own dark silhouette

The Sun Is Out

He comes sounding twelve thousand wind chimes
Saturating the universe with harmonious echoes of majesty
Flooding the watery pasture on which everything is visible at a
      glance
The sun raises vast tides

5 Sunlight combs my torrential thoughts
Extending them into a thick mane of cirrus
That moves parallel to the sun's track
In a wilderness where clumps of grass predominate
It's best to be a tall, straight sunflower.

10 Or could someone transform me into a cloud
So I could approach him on wings borrowed from the solicitous
      wind
I'd also be content as a rocky cliff standing erect since the world
      began

Eroded by wind into flying dust that settles back onto the great
   earth
Accepting the ceaseless caress of the sun
Or else could someone make me coextensive with Eros   15

Blades of grass flicker like swaying Buddhist streamers
Praying not for fortune but for love
The lives under the sun simply recite a magic word
I say secretly, Do you know
The creator made me for you alone   20
And designed me for your sake
Only I am able to decode
    The riddle of our destined relationship
I choose the pen of poetry only for the sun
Yes only for you the sun   25

The surging grassland suddenly becomes serene
Feeling a much deeper fresh state of turbulence
A host of sculls rises in seriousness and beauty
Their eyes all saluting in the same direction
Distant hymns pulsate faintly in chords   30
Where and from what century does that sound begin

Midday

penetrates me with brilliance and fills me to the brim
Heart purified to crystalline clarity
No trace of clouds in the sky
And hence no shadow beside me
The sun and I   5
Coincide vertically in the brightest of angles

Stay motionless in any relaxed posture
And for as long as you do not open your eyes
You melt into one being with the sunlight

The sun turns the heart's agitation into tranquility   10
And love becomes profound because of it, after sublimation.

The Sun at Dusk

Separated by huge expanses of time and space
I gaze ahead
Sight communicates in the language of the universe
I should probably laugh, sing a farewell song
And ask a gray swan to be my messenger, to carry the song in its   5
   beak

And to merge goldenly with the light at dusk
This may be the time for me to actualize my overreaching fantasies
Sail that small boat to the shore of gold
Experience the daily tides of love
10   Emotions transformed into a bountiful ocean

Beauty of tragic heroism
And tranquility
Farewell, my sun
A handkerchief of color-laden clouds waves at the setting sun
15   A treasury of good wishes to you all the way home
A treasury of good wishes

A pastoral tune sung at evening
I sigh for the silence in my heart
And so my mind closes a window and walks into our nightlong
        mutual yearning

20   Whoever indulges in fantasy and tires of waiting
Will inevitably misspend
The night and merely wait in silence, but the night
No longer chants about moonlight, and never chants
About that sliver of lunar ice so easily burst asunder
25   My sun is the one that never makes a promise
My sun is the one that never breaks an appointment

Questions for Discussion and Writing

1. What does the sun represent to the speaker in the first poem, "Waiting for Sunrise"? How would you characterize her mood as she waits for the sun to rise?

2. What effect does the sun's presence have on the speaker in the second poem, "The Sun Is Out"?

3. How does the sun's position in the third poem, "Midday," SYMBOLIZE the speaker's achievement of an inner equilibrium? How does the IMAGERY in which the speaker expresses this psychological state contrast with the IMAGERY in the two previous poems?

4. In the final poem, "The Sun at Dusk," how have the experiences of the day transformed the speaker? How would you characterize her attitude toward the sun in the last lines of the poem?

5. Have you ever observed changes in your feelings toward a natural phenomenon where the changes in your mood corresponded with how you perceived this phenomenon? For example, how did you perceive a thunderstorm, snowstorm, or beautiful sunset when you were happy or when you were sad?

Rita Dove

The Wake

Rita Dove was born in 1952 in Akron, Ohio. She went to Miami University in Ohio as a Presidential Scholar and graduated summa cum laude in English. She was awarded a Fulbright Fellowship to the University of Tubingen in Germany in 1974 where she studied modern European literature. She later received an M.F.A. in creative writing from the University of Iowa's Writer's Workshop. She is currently a professor of English at the University of Virginia. Her first collection of poems, The Yellow House on the Corner, *was published in 1980, followed by* Museum *(1983) and* Thomas and Beulah *(1986), a book of poetry about the history of blacks who migrated (as her own family did, from the South to the North) for which she was awarded the 1987 Pulitzer Prize. Dove became only the second black poet to win the Pulitzer Prize, after Gwendolyn Brooks. In 1993 she was appointed poet laureate of the United States by the Library of Congress. She is also the author of a collection of short stories,* Fifth Sunday *(1985). As a poet, Dove has the unique ability to explore the lyrical possibilities of events that take place over a long period of time by bringing them together into a single moment. "The Wake," drawn from* Grace Notes *(1989), presents a touching tribute to her mother. All the poems in this collection explore special events in ways that embellish the melody of daily life.*

Your absence distributed itself
like an invitation.
Friends and relatives
kept coming, trying   5
to fill up the house.
But the rooms still gaped—
the green hanger swang empty, and
the head of the table
demanded a plate.

                                                                10

When I sat down in the armchair
your warm breath fell
over my shoulder.
When I climbed to bed I walked
through your blind departure.   15
The others stayed downstairs,
trying to cover
the silence with weeping.

When I lay down between the sheets
I lay down in the cool waters
of my own womb   20

and became the child
inside, innocuous
as a button, helplessly growing.
I slept because it was the only
25   thing I could do. I even dreamed.
I couldn't stop myself.

Questions for Discussion and Writing

1. How do each of the three stanzas present responses from different angles to the circumstances described in the poem?
2. How would you characterize the VOICE you hear? What situation does the speaker confront and what mood does the poem communicate?
3. What details signal the increasingly personal nature of the speaker's response? For example, compare the number of times "I" appears in succeeding stanzas.
4. How does the IMAGERY of the poem present itself as a contrast between the images of waking and sleeping? How do different meanings of the word "wake" help explain the speaker's response to the death of her mother?
5. To what extent do the last lines ("I even dreamed./I couldn't stop myself") suggest that the speaker has regressed into a pre-natal state as a way of coping with the overwhelming sense of loss she is experiencing?
6. The ultimate loss of someone through death is but one of the ways we lose people. Describe an experience you have had involving the loss of a friend, a relative, parent through divorce, a teacher, coach, and explore your emotions, period of adjustment, and the extent to which someone new might have replaced that person. You might want to do this assignment for the loss of an object or a pet.
7. Have you ever reacted to the death of someone you loved in ways similar to those of the speaker in this poem? What insight did your own experience give you into the speaker's feelings? In the following poem by George L. De Victoria which first appeared in *Don't Hang Up: An Anthology About AIDS*, ed. by Andrew Miller (1992) to what extent are the speaker's reactions to the loss of someone he loved similar to those of the speaker in Dove's poem?

LARRY
Larry,

In the daytime my mind tells me that you are gone.
But at night I hear you call when the rooms are quiet
and the lights are out. I hear your footsteps next to mine.

Your breath whispers by my ear. And . . . just there . . . . in
the shadows . . . I can see your face.

At night I hear you call my name, beckoning, luring me to your
side.

Brushing my cheek with phantom fingers, whispering-urging-
tempting me to come with you.

I try not to listen. I try to endure—I try to continue alone.
O Larry how I miss you.

But again I hear you call and I know you're so close.
I want to succumb to your plea, to follow you, to spend
eternity by your side.

But I don't remember where you said you would be.

I love you.

Anna Kamieńska

Funny

Anna Kamieńska (1920–1986), a poet, translator, critic, essayist, and editor, was the author of numerous collections of original and translated poetry (from Russian and other Slavic languages) as well as of anthologies, books for children, and collections of interpretations of poems. She was a longtime editor of the book review section at the influential Warsaw monthly, Tworczosc. Initially a poet of peasant themes and moral concerns, she underwent a spiritual metamorphosis in the early 1970s, becoming an important poet of religious experience. "Funny," translated by Mieczyslaw Jastrun, offers a wryly thought-provoking view of the human condition.

What's it like to be a human
the bird asked

I myself don't know
it's being held prisoner by your skin
while reaching infinity   5
being a captive of your scrap of time
while touching eternity
being hopelessly uncertain
and helplessly hopeful
being a needle of frost   10
and a handful of heat
breathing in the air
and choking wordlessly
it's being on fire
with a nest made of ashes   15
eating bread
while filling up on hunger
it's dying without love
it's loving through death

20   That's funny said the bird
      and flew effortlessly up into the air

Questions for Discussion and Writing

1. How does Kamieńska use the differences in perception between the bird and its human respondent as an ALLEGORY for the gulf that makes it difficult for people in different life circumstances to understand each other?
2. What details suggest the difficulties, uncertainties, and precariousness of the human condition? How do these limitations SYMBOLIZE the human condition?
3. How does the fact that the bird is described as flying "effortlessly" help to explain its response—"That's funny"—to the answer given to its question "What's it like to be a human"?
4. How is the bird in this poem depicted in a way that links it with other ARCHETYPAL figures of birds (for example, the golden birds in William Butler Yeats's "Sailing to Byzantium" who tell the past, present, and future)?
5. Applying the insights of this poem, compose a dialogue that dramatizes one of the following: (a) the inability of the young to empathize with the old, or the reverse, (b) the gulf between the physically able and the disabled, (c) the gap between someone who is bright and someone who is a slow learner, or (d) any other difference in circumstances that would create a gap in understanding.
6. What ANALOGIES would you use to describe what possessing sight is like to someone who is blind, or what a particular color looks like to someone who is color blind?
7. Describe an object, animal, or natural force, using METAPHORS or SIMILES, but in the form of a riddle, without telling the reader what the answer is. Your description should use active verbs to help your readers imagine the answer to the riddle.
8. With another person, play the following game: One player writes down any question without letting the other player see it. The second player then writes down an answer to a question he or she doesn't know. After a series of these, put the answers and questions together as aphorisms and compare the result with "Funny."

Nelly Sachs

Chorus of the Dead

Nelly Sachs (1891–1970) was born in Berlin. Some of her poetry was published in the 1920s, but after Hitler came to power her work remained for the most part unknown. In 1940, she and her ailing mother were saved from being sent to a forced labor camp by the opportunity to emigrate to Sweden. At first, barely subsisting, she was able to earn a modest living by translating Swedish poetry into German; she published highly praised volumes of these translations. Her first published volume of poetry, Legends and Tales (1921) is rooted in the world of German mysticism in its exploration of the oppositions of good and evil, gentleness and violence, and love and hate. After 1933, she became intensely interested in her Jewish heritage and studied the Zohar, the book of splendor, a great cabalistic work of the thirteenth century. Under the influence of Martin Buber, she read the Old Testament, particularly the Psalms, and turned to Jewish mysticism, expecially Hasidism, for inspiration. While taking care of her mother, she learned of the existence of the Nazi death camps and devoted the rest of her life to giving voice to the millions consumed in the Holocaust. Of her work, she says "the terrible experiences which brought me to the verge of death and darkness were my teacher. My metaphors are my wounds; only in this way can my work be understood." Her poetry is mystical and visionary in quality, written in unrhymed freely flowing verse, replete with images drawn from Jewish mysticism. A frequent theme is the relationship between executioners and their victims, the murderers and the murdered. Collections of her work include Eli, a Dramatic Work Set in a Destroyed Polish Ghetto (1943), Signs in the Sand (1962), and The Seeker and Other Poems (1970), from which "A Chorus of the Dead" is taken. She won the Nobel Prize for literature in 1966. When the prize was awarded to her, Anders Osterling of the Swedish Academy said this of her work: "Miss Sachs has created a world of imagery which does not shun the terrible truth of the extermination camps and the corpse factories, but which at the same time arises above all hatred of the persecutors . . . revealing a genuine sorrow at man's debasement." "A Chorus of the Dead," translated by Ruth and Matthew Mead (1970), charts an emotional journey that affirms the unity of life in the midst of the infernos of the crematoria in the concentration camps.

We from the black sun of fear
Holed like sieves—
We dripped from the sweat of death's minute.
Withered on our bodies are the deaths done unto us
Like flowers of the field withered on a hill of sand.   5
O you who still greet the dust as friend
You who talking sand say to the sand:
I love you.
We say to you.
Torn are the cloaks of the mysterious dust   10
The air in which we were suffocated,
The fires in which we were burned,
The earth into which our remains were cast.
The water which was beaded with our sweat
Has broken forth with us and begins to gleam.   15
We are moving past one more star
Into our hidden God.

Questions for Discussion and Writing

1. How is the poem shaped as an ARCHETYPAL encounter between the dead and the living? What do the dead tell the living about the circumstances under which they died?
2. What details suggest that the VOICE we hear speaks for an entire group of people?
3. Where in the poem do elements of repetition and incantation communicate the transformation experienced by those who have died?
4. How do IMAGES of air, fire, earth, and water SYMBOLIZE the different conditions the dead have experienced?
5. What shift in emotional perspective takes place from the beginning to the end of the poem?
6. Are there any unusual inscriptions on the tombstones in your town cemetery? Elaborate on what any of them might mean.
7. If you could write your own epitaph what would it be?
8. In the following poem by Clifton Snider which first appeared in *Don't Hang Up: An Anthology of Poems About AIDS*, ed. by Andrew Miller (1992), how is the speaker's way of memorializing friends who have died and celebrating those who are still alive similar to the approach taken in "Chorus of the Dead"?

OUT OF THE PICTURE

Mostly I can't picture it at all—
the graphics in slick magazine color,
the hard-edged figures of T-cells,
proteins covers, viral invasions.
How to connect these pictures with
passion that happened 5–7–10
years ago?

This viral information,
like poisoned invisible glue
on an envelope, waits to be licked.

He said Charles died last week, too ill
to connect, and Randy's in a coma.
Ron went before him, then it was Doug.
Before Doug, Peter, Willis, Bill W., Paul G.,
Steve Y., John C., Chuck L., Bill Dry,
John's lover, Kevin, Jim and Larry—
they were among the first.

Travis and Tom
are splendidly alive. Don't know
what happened to Earl and now
Clay's moved back to Oklahoma.

My personal litany, undone,
reeling out numbers yet to come,

and I have no way of picturing
except to see a large circle, swirling,
blank, where the sun should be.

Zbigniew Herbert

Preliminary Investigation of an Angel

Born in Lwow, Poland, in 1924, Zbigniew Herbert wrote his first poetry during the devastating Nazi occupation of Poland and was a member of the Polish underground Resistance. When the war ended, he attended the University of Krakow and, later, the University of Torun, where he took a degree in civil law. During the oppressive years of Stalinism, his works went unpublished and he found work as a bank clerk and as a journalist. His first book of poems, The Cord of Light, *was not published until 1956. He was the co-editor of* Poezja, *a poetry journal, from 1965 to 1968, when he resigned in protest against anti-Semitic policies. He has been a professor of modern European literature at California State University at Los Angeles, and has received many awards for his poetry. The most distinctive quality of Herbert's poetry is its extraordinary fusion of biblical and mythological illusions, seen through a modern perspective. His work is collected in several volumes, including* Selected Poems *(1968) and* Pancogito *(1974). "Preliminary Investigation of an Angel," translated by Czeslaw Milosz and Peter Dale Scott (1968), depicts a trial of an angel who is judged guilty of crimes against the heavenly government. In this poem, Herbert uses myth to go beyond the specific historical events that might have prompted it—as some believe, the purge trials of Joseph Stalin during the 1930s—to look at the ultimate question of guilt and innocence.*

When he stands before them
in the shadow of a suspicion
he is still all
composed of light

the aeons of his hair   5
are pinned up in a bun
of innocence

after the first question
his cheeks flush with blood

10   the blood is helped on
with instruments and interrogations

with an iron ferrule
a slow fire
the limits of his body
15   are defined

a blow on his back
fixes his spine
between cloud and mudpuddle

after a few nights
20   the job is finished
the leather throat of the angel
is full of gluey agreement

how beautiful is the moment
when he falls on his knees
25   incarnate into guilt
saturated with contents

his tongue hesitates
between knocked-out teeth
and confession

30   they hang him head downwards

from the hair of the angel
drops of wax run down
and shape on the floor
a simple prophecy

Questions for Discussion and Writing

1. How would you characterize the speaker from whose POINT OF VIEW the events are described? Is this person horrified or satisfied with the ongoing inquisition? Whose side is the speaker on, the angel's or the inquisitor's?
2. Speculate on what you think the angel's "crime" might have been. To what extent does the angel embody characteristics of the scapegoat ARCHETYPE?
3. How is the change that takes place in the angel as a result of the inquisition depicted through images of heaviness, density, and subjection to suggest physical sensations of guilt and complicity?
4. Speculate on what the prophecy issuing from the angel at the end of the poem could have been.
5. In a short essay, discuss how the inquisition of the angel might be seen to symbolize any persecution of the innocent. For example, you might see it in

terms of the Spanish Inquisition, the Salem witch trials, the Stalin purge trials of the 1930s, the McCarthy hearings of the 1950s or any other political or social process of guilt by accusation.

6. Describe an impossible creature, other than an angel, like a minotaur or gnome.

Bella Akhmadulina

The Garden

Bella Akhmadulina was born in 1937 in Moscow. She attended the Gorky Institute of World Literature. Her first book of poetry, String *(1962), describes everyday sights and scenes with a whimsical perspective that transforms her descriptions into highly personal images that are celebrated for their original-ity, emotional intensity, and wit. Critics have called her poetry classical, point-ing out that her use of rhyme and meter recalls the poetry of Pushkin. Her grow-ing maturity as a poet can be seen in each new volume, including* Chills *(1968),* The Snowstorm *(1977),* Dreams of Georgia *(1977),* The Secret *(1983), and* Selected Poems *(1988). In recent poems she returns to familiar themes—such as evocation of the past—through visions of other Russian po-ets, including Pushkin, Akhmatova, and Pasternak. She finds consolation in the Russian forests, in walking in the snow, and in rural scenes set in the Georgian Republic. The growing reflective quality of her poems combined with her experimentation with form, complicated figures of speech, and always-present sense of wonder, can be seen in "The Garden," translated by F. D. Reeve (1988). For Akhmadulina, the world of the poem is an actual landscape in which she acts out the roles of naturalist, historian, and keeper of the language.*

I went out to the garden—but in *garden,*
    the word, lies lush luxuriance.
As gorgeous as a full-blown rose, it
    enriches sound and scent and glance.

The word is wider than what surrounds me: 5
    inside it all is well and free;
its rich black soil makes sons and daughters
    or orphaned and transplanted seeds.

Seedlings of dark innovations,
    O *garden,* word, you are the gardener,   10
who to the clippers' gleam and clatter
    increase and spread the fruits you bear.

Set within your free-and-easy
    space are an old estate and the fate
15 of a family long gone, and the faded
    whiteness of their garden bench.

You are more fertile than the earth:
    you feed the roots of others' crowns.
From oak to oakwood, Oakboy, you are
20   hearts' mail, and words'—the love, the blood.

Your shady grove is always darkened,
    but why did a lovelorn parasol
of lace look down in embarrassment
    in the face of hot weather coming on?

25 Perhaps I, who quest for a limp hand,
    redden my own knees on the stones?
A casual and impoverished gardener,
    what do I seek? Where do I tend?

If I had gone out, where would I really
30   have gone? It's May—and solid mud.
I went out to a ruined wasteland
    and in it read that life was dead.

Dead! Gone! Where had it hurried to?
    It merely tasted the dried-up agony
35 of speechless lips and then reported:
    all things forever; only a moment for me.

For a moment in which I could not manage
    to see either self or garden clearly.
"I went out to the garden" was what I wrote.
40   I did? Well, then, there must be

something to it? There is—and amazing
    how going to the garden takes no move.
I did not go out at all. I simply wrote the
    way I usually do,
45   "I went out to the garden . . ."

Questions for Discussion and Writing

1. How does the poem demonstrate that poetry, for the speaker, is capable of
   creating an imaginative reality more compelling than the reality of an actual
   garden?

2. How does stanza five use the image of the oak to illustrate how the imagination creates more fertile productive hybrids than can exist in material reality?

3. At what points did you become aware that the speaker was referring to the poet's power of image-making, storytelling, and ability to create SYMBOLS rather than an actual garden?

4. What details in the poem suggest that the speaker sees herself as a historian and caretaker of the language? To what extent does she feel adequate to her self-assigned mission?

5. In reading this poem, discuss the associations and experiences you have had that were triggered by images in "The Garden."

6. Describe a place, real or imagined, that you associate with your wishes coming true, or where the most amazing kinds of wonderful things grow.

7. Imagine what the interior landscape would be in any object around you, such as a light bulb, computer, pencil, and so on.

Vasko Popa

The Lost Red Boot

Vasko Popa was born in 1922 in Grebenats, Banat, in northern Yugoslavia. He studied at the universities of Belgrade, Vienna, and Bucharest and now lives in Belgrade where he is a member of the Serbian Academy of Sciences and an editor of the publishing house Nolit. Popa is one of a generation of east European poets, such as Zbigniew Herbert, whose poetry refuses to falsify experience through any hopeful efforts to change it. Popa's gift as a poet is to turn the most grisly confrontations into something playful. He draws on medieval literature, folk poetry, charms, riddles, games, and legends. He prefers older, native Slavonic words to terms drawn from international urban culture. Objects and beings in Popa's poetry are simultaneously earthy and spiritual. The image of the wolf that figures so prominently in Popa's work is both a four-footed beast and a metaphor that refers to St. Sava, the patron saint of Serbia. Popa is widely regarded as one of eastern Europe's foremost poets. Collections of his poetry include Bark *(1953),* Unrest-Field *(1956),* Secondary Heaven *(1968),* Earth Erect *(1972),* Wolf Salt *(1975),* Raw Flesh *(1975),* The House on the High Road *(1975),* Homage to the Lame Wolf: Selected Poems 1956–1975 *(1975), and* Collected Poems *(1978). "The Lost Red Boot," translated by Anne Pennington (1975), is typical of Popa's work in that it forces the reader to approach common things of everyday life with a new perspective. In this poem, he seeks to establish a new covenant between his family and himself as he begins a pilgrimage through his own Serbian past.*

My great-grandmother Sultana Uroshevitch
Used to sail the sky in a wooden trough
And catch rain-bearing clouds

With wolf-balms and others
5   She did many more
Great and small miracles

After her death
She went on meddling
In the business of the living

10   They dug her up
To teach her to behave
And to bury her better

She lay there rosy-cheeked
In her oaken coffin

15   On one foot she was wearing
A little red boot
With splashes of fresh mud

To the end of my life I'll search
For that other boot she lost

Questions for Discussion and Writing

1. What picture emerges of the speaker's great-grandmother? What details suggest that her free-spirited activities did not end with her death?
2. How does the antagonism of the staid, law-abiding townspeople to the
   great-grandmother's activities dramatize a choice between tradition and creativity?
3. How does the last image of "A little red boot/With splashes of fresh mud"
   SYMBOLIZE the values to which the speaker now commits himself?
4. To what extent does the poem embody the values the speaker admires? In
   your opinion, does the poem take risks, and make imaginative leaps? Is the
   speaker a worthy descendant of his great-grandmother?
5. Write about one of your grandparents or parents as seen through an object
   you connect with him or her. Under what circumstances did you first come
   across this object? What associations connect this object with your parent or
   grandparent?

William Butler Yeats

The Second Coming

William Butler Yeats (1865–1939), the distinguished Irish poet and play-wright, was the son of an artist, John Yeats. Although initially drawn toward painting, he soon turned to poetry and became fascinated by Irish sagas and folklore. The landscape of county Sligo, where he was born and lived as a child, and the exploits of Irish heroes such as Cuchulain frequently appear in his early poetry. An early long poem, The Wanderings of Oisin *(1889), shows an intense nationalism, a feeling strengthened by his hopeless passion for the Irish patriot Maude Gonne. In 1898, he helped found the Irish Literary Theatre and later the world-renowned Abbey Theatre. As he grew older, Yeats's poetry moved from transcendentalism to a more physical realism, and the tension between the physical and the spiritual are central to poems such as "Sailing to Byzantium" and the "Crazy Jane" sequence. Some of his best work came late in* The Tower *(1928),* The Winding Stair *(1933), and the work that was published posthumously in* Last Poems and Plays *(1940). Yeats received the Nobel Prize for literature in 1923 and is widely considered to be the greatest poet of the twentieth century. The prophetic quality of Yeats's poetry springs from his earlier interest in the occult, concerns that became tempered by his premonition that the political anarchy and materialism of the modern age would inevitably lead to its own destruction. This theme is most brilliantly realized in what is perhaps his signature poem, "The Second Coming" (1920).*

Turning and turning in the widening gyre
The falcon cannot hear the falconer;
Things fall apart; the centre cannot hold;
Mere anarchy is loosed upon the world,
The blood-dimmed tide is loosed, and everywhere   5
The ceremony of innocence is drowned;
The best lack all conviction, while the worst
Are full of passionate intensity.

Surely some revelation is at hand;
Surely the Second Coming is at hand.   10
The Second Coming! Hardly are those words out
When a vast image out of *Spiritus Mundi*
Troubles my sight: somewhere in sands of the desert
A shape with lion body and the head of a man,
A gaze blank and pitiless as the sun,   15
Is moving its slow thighs, while all about it
Reel shadows of the indignant desert birds.
The darkness drops again; but now I know

That twenty centuries of stony sleep
20   Were vexed to nightmare by a rocking cradle,
And what rough beast, its hour come round at last,
Slouches towards Bethlehem to be born?

Questions for Discussion and Writing

1. How is the poem shaped to contrast the speaker's expectations of the second coming of Christ with the hideous apparition that suggests qualities of inhuman cruelty?
2. How does the inability of the falconer to communicate with the falcon SYM-BOLIZE the loss of cohesion that the speaker sees as a defining characteristic of the twentieth century?
3. Why is it ironic that the landscape in which the "rough beast" appears is the same region with which Christ's birth and second coming are associated?
4. In what sense do you understand the speaker's statements that "Things fall apart; the centre cannot hold," or "The best lack all conviction, while the worst/Are full of passionate intensity"? Describe an event that has taken place in the twentieth century to which the speaker's insight applies.
5. What is the most interesting prophecy you ever heard? What conditions would have to be fulfilled for this prophecy to take place?
6. What form would your own dream monster take? Would it look like Freddy Kruger in "The Nightmare on Elm Street" films, Jason in the Halloween series, the "Doomsday" monster that destroys Superman, or would it assume a nonhuman form? Describe it in detail.

Christopher Durang

Sister Mary Ignatius Explains It All for You

Christopher Durang was born in Montclair, New Jersey, in 1949. Growing up in a small town and attending Catholic schools were major influences on his writing. He received a B.A. from Harvard and an M.F.A. from Yale in 1974, where he also taught playwriting. Durang wrote his first play while in the second grade at a school in Morristown, New Jersey, run by Benedictine priests. By the time he was in the eighth grade, one of his plays was produced at the school. In his senior year at Harvard he wrote The Nature and Purpose of the Universe *(1971), a satire on middle-class life that helped secure his acceptance at the Yale School of Drama. At Yale, Durang wrote and acted in many plays that formed the basis for works produced both on and off Broadway in the years that followed. These include* The Marriage of Bette and Boo *(1973),* The Idiot's Karamazov, *written with Albert Innaurato (1974), and* 'dentity Crisis *(1975). Success came with* Sister Mary Ignatius Explains It All for You *(1979), a play Durang wrote during a period when he was deeply depressed by his mother's hopeless fight against cancer. This play depicts the return of four students (an unwed mother, a homosexual, a suicidal alcoholic wife beater, and a rape victim) to visit their former teacher, a nun who victimized and terrified them. This work received the Off-Broadway (OBIE) Award in 1980. Other works that display Durang at his most iconoclastic are* Beyond Therapy *(1981),* The Actor's Nightmare *(1981),* Baby with the Bathwater *(1984), and* Laughing Wild *(1991).*

SCENE: *The stage is fairly simple. There should be a lectern, a potted palm, a few chairs. There is also an easel, or some sort of stand, on which are several drawings made on cardboard; the only one we can see at the top of the play is either blank or is a simple cross. Enter* SISTER MARY IGNATIUS, *dressed in an old-fashioned nun's habit.* SISTER *looks at the audience until she has their attention, then smiles, albeit somewhat wearily. She then begins her lecture, addressing the audience directly.*

SISTER (*Crossing herself*):   In the name of the Father, and of the Son, and of the Holy Ghost, Amen. (*Shows the next drawing on the easel, which is a neat if childlike picture of the planet earth, the sun, and moon.*) First there is the earth. Near the earth is the sun, and also nearby is the moon. (*Goes to next picture which, split in three, shows the gates of heaven amid clouds; some sort of murky area of paths, or some other image that might suggest waiting, wandering, and a third area of people burning up in flames, with little devils with little pitchforks, poking them.*) Outside the universe, where we go after death, is heaven, hell, and purgatory. Heaven is where we live in eternal bliss with our Lord Jesus Christ. (*Bows her head*) Hell is where we are eternally deprived of the presence of our Lord Jesus Christ (*Bows her head*), and are thus miserable. This is the greatest agony of hell, but there are also unspeakable physical torments, which we shall nonetheless speak of later. Purgatory is the middle area where we go after death to suffer if we have not been perfect in our lives and are thus not ready for heaven, or if we have not received the sacraments and made a good confession to a priest right before our death. Purgatory, depending on our sins, can go on for a very, *very* long time and is fairly unpleasant. Though we do not yet know whether there is any physical torment in purgatory, we do know that there is much psychological torment because we are being delayed from being in the presence of our Lord Jesus Christ. (*Bows her head*) For those non-Catholics present, I bow my head to show respect for our Savior when I say His Name. Our Lord Jesus Christ. (*Bows head*) Our Lord Jesus Christ. (*Bows head*) Our Lord Jesus Christ. (*Bows head*) You can expect to be in purgatory for anywhere from 300 years to 700 billion years. This may sound like forever, but don't forget in terms of eternity 700 billion years *does* come to an end. All things come to an end except our Lord Jesus Christ. (*Bows head. Points to the drawing again, reviewing her point*) Heaven, hell, purgatory. (*Smiles. Goes to the next drawing which, like that of purgatory, is of a murky area, perhaps with a prison-like fence, and which has unhappy baby-like creatures floating about in it*) There is also limbo, which is where unbaptized babies were sent for eternity before the Ecumenical Council and Pope John XXIII. The unbaptized babies sent to limbo never leave limbo and so never get to heaven. *Now* unbaptized babies are sent straight to purgatory where, presumably, someone baptizes them and *then* they are sent on to heaven. The unbaptized babies who died before the Ecumenical Council, however, remain in limbo and will never be admitted to heaven. Limbo is not all that unpleasant, it's just that it isn't heaven and you never leave there. I want to be very clear about the Immaculate Conception. It does not mean that the Blessed Mother gave birth to Christ without the prior unpleasantness of physical intimacy. That is true but is not called the Immaculate Conception; that is called the Virgin Birth. The Immaculate Conception means that the Blessed Mother was herself born without original sin. Everyone makes this error, it makes me lose my patience. That Mary's conception was immaculate is an infallible statement. A lot of fault-finding non-Catholics run around saying that Catholics believe that the Pope is infallible whenever he speaks. This is untrue. The Pope is infallible only on certain occasions, when he speaks "ex cathedra," which is Latin for "out of the cathedral." When he speaks ex cathedra, we must accept what he says at that moment as dogma, or risk hell fire; or, now that things are becoming more liberal, many, many years in purgatory. I would now like a glass of water. Thomas. (*Enter* THOMAS, *a parochial school boy wearing tie and blazer.*) This is Thomas, he is seven years old and in the second grade of Our Lady of Perpetual Sorrow School. Seven is the age of reason, so now that Thomas has turned seven he is capable of choosing to commit sin or not to commit sin, and God will hold him accountable for whatever he does. Isn't that so, Thomas?

THOMAS: Yes, Sister.

SISTER: Before we turn seven, God tends to pay no attention to the bad things we do because He knows we can know no better. Once we turn seven, He feels we are capable of knowing. Thomas, who made you?

THOMAS: God made me.

SISTER: Why did God make you?

THOMAS: God made me to show forth His goodness and share with us His happiness.

SISTER: What is the sixth commandment?

THOMAS: The sixth commandment is thou shalt not commit adultery.

SISTER: What is forbidden by the sixth commandment?

THOMAS: The sixth commandment forbids all impurities in thought, word or deed, whether alone or with others.

SISTER: That's correct, Thomas. (*Gives him a cookie*) Thomas has a lovely soprano voice which the Church used to preserve by creating castrati. Thomas unfortunately will lose his soprano voice in a few years and will receive facial hair and psychological difficulties in its place. To me, it is not a worthwhile exchange. You may go now, Thomas. What is the fourth commandment?

THOMAS: The fourth commandment is honor thy mother and thy father.

SISTER: Very good. (*Gives him a cookie. He exits.*) Sometimes in the mornings I look at all the children lining up in front of school, and

I'm overwhelmed by a sense of sadness and exhaustion thinking of all the pain and suffering and personal unhappiness they're going to face in their lives. (*Looks sad, eats a cookie*) But can their suffering compare with Christ's on the cross? Let us think of Christ on the cross for a moment. Try to feel the nails ripping through His hands and feet. Some experts say that the nails actually went through His wrists, which was better for keeping Him up on the cross, though of course most of the statues have the nails going right through His palms. Imagine those nails being driven through: pound, pound, pound, rip, rip, rip. Think of the crown of thorns eating into His skull, and the sense of infection that He must have felt in His brain and near His eyes. Imagine blood from His brain spurting forth through His eyes, imagine His vision squinting through a veil of red liquid. Imagine these things, and then just *dare* to feel sorry for the children lining up outside of school. We dare not; His suffering was greater than ours. He died for our sins! Yours and mine. We put Him up there, you did, all you people sitting out there. He loved us so much that He came all the way down to earth just so He could be nailed painfully to a cross and hang there for three hours. Who else has loved us as much as that? I come from a large family. My father was big and ugly, my mother had a nasty disposition and didn't like me. There were twenty-six of us. It took three hours just to wash the dishes, but Christ hung on that cross for three hours and *He* never complained. We lived in a small, ugly house, and I shared a room with all my sisters. My father would bring home drunken bums off the street, and let them stay in the same room as himself and my mother. "Whatever you do to the least of these, you do also to Me," Christ said. Sometimes these bums would make my mother hysterical, and we'd have to throw water on her. Thomas, could I have some more water please? And some chocolates? (*Enter* THOMAS) Who made you?

THOMAS: God made me.

SISTER: What is the ninth commandment?

THOMAS: The ninth commandment is thou shalt not covet thy neighbor's wife.

SISTER: What is forbidden by the ninth commandment?

THOMAS: The ninth commandment forbids all indecency in thought, word and deed, whether alone or with thy neighbor's wife.

SISTER: Thank you. Go away again. (*He exits.*) Bring the little children unto me, Our Lord said. I don't remember in reference to what. I have your questions here on some little file cards. (*Reads*) If God is all powerful, why does He allow evil in the world? (*Goes to next card with no reaction. Reads*) Tell us some more about your family. (*Smiles*) We said grace before every meal. My mother was a terrible cook. She used to boil chopped meat. She hated little children, but they couldn't use birth control. Let me explain this one more time. Birth control is wrong because God, whatever you may think about the wisdom involved, created sex for the purpose of procreation, *not* recreation. Everything in this world has a purpose. We eat food to feed our bodies. We don't eat and then make ourselves throw up immediately afterward, do we? So it should be with sex. Either it is done for its proper purpose, or it is just so much throwing up, morally speaking. Next question. (*Reads*) Do nuns go to the bathroom? Yes. (*Reads*) Was Jesus effeminate? Yes. (*Reads*) I have a brain tumor and am afraid of dying. What should I do? Now I thought I had explained what happens after death to you already. There is heaven, hell and purgatory. What's the problem? Oh ye of little faith, Christ said to someone. All right. As any seven-year-old knows, there are two kinds of sin: mortal sin and venial sin. Venial sin is the less serious kind, like if you tell a small lie to your parents, or when you take the Lord's name in vain when you break your thumb with a hammer, or when you kick a barking dog. If you die with any venial sins on your conscience, no matter how many of them there are, you can eventually work it all out in purgatory. However—mortal sin, on the other hand, is the most serious kind of sin you can do—murder, sex outside of marriage, hijacking a plane, masturbation—and if you die with any of these sins on your soul, even just one, you will go straight to hell and burn for all of eternity. Now to rid yourself of mortal sin, you must go make a good confession and vow never to do it again. If, as many of you know, you are on your way to confession to confess a mortal sin and you are struck by a car or bus before you get there, God may forgive you without confession if before you die you manage to say a good act of contrition. If you die instantaneously and are unable to say a good act of contrition, you will go straight to hell. Thomas, come read this partial list of those who are going to burn in hell. (*Enter* THOMAS)

THOMAS (*Reads*):   Christine Keeler, Roman Polanski, Zsa Zsa Gabor, the editors of *After Dark* magazine, Linda Lovelace, Georgina Spelvin, Big John Holmes, Brooke Shields, David Bowie, Mick Jagger, Patty Hearst, Betty Comden, Adolph Green.

SISTER: This is just a partial list. It is added to constantly. Thomas, how can we best keep from going to hell?

THOMAS: By not committing a mortal sin, by keeping close to the sacraments, especially going to confession and receiving communion, and by obeying our parents. (*She gives him a cookie.*)

SISTER: Good boy. Do you love our Lord, Thomas?

THOMAS: Yes, Sister.

SISTER: How much?

THOMAS: This much. (*Holds arms out wide*)

SISTER: Well, that's very nice, but Christ loves us an infinite amount. How do we know that, Thomas?

THOMAS: Because you tell us.

SISTER: That's right. And by His actions. He died on the cross for us to make up for our sins. Wasn't that nice of Him?

THOMAS: Very nice.

SISTER: And shouldn't we be grateful?

THOMAS: Yes we should.

SISTER: That's right, we should. (*Gives him a cookie*) How do you spell cookie?

THOMAS: C-o-o-k-i-e.

SISTER: Very good. (*Gives him a cookie*) Mary has had an argument with her parents and has shot and killed them. Is that a venial sin or a mortal sin?

THOMAS: That's a mortal sin.

SISTER: If she dies with this mortal sin on her soul, will she go to heaven or to hell?

THOMAS: She will go to hell.

SISTER: Very good. How do you spell ecumenical?

THOMAS (*Sounding it out*):   Eck—e-c-k; you—u; men—m-e-n; ical—i-c-k-l-e.

SISTER: Very good. (*Gives him a cookie*) What's two plus two?

THOMAS: Four.

SISTER: What's one and one and one and one and one and one and one and one and one?

THOMAS: Nine.

SISTER: Very good. (*Gives him a cookie*) Because she is afraid to show her parents her bad report card, Susan goes to the top of a tall building and jumps off. Is this a venial sin or a mortal sin?

THOMAS: Mortal sin.

SISTER: And where will she go?

THOMAS: Hell.

SISTER: Sit on my lap. (*He does*) Would you like to keep your pretty soprano voice forever?

THOMAS: Yes, Sister.

SISTER: Well, we'll see what we can do about it. (*Sings*)

> Cookies in the morning,
> Cookies in the evening,
> Cookies in the summertime,
> Be my little cookie,
> And love me all the time.

God, I've done so much talking, I've got to rest my voice some. Here, you take care of some of these questions, Thomas, while I rest, all right, dear? (*She hands him the file cards.*)

THOMAS: Yes, Sister. (*Reads*) How do we know there is a God? We know that there is a God because the Church tells us so. And also because everything has a primary cause. Dinner is put on the table because the primary cause, our mother, has put it in the oven and cooked it. (*Reads*) If God is all powerful, why does He allow evil? (*Skips that one; next one*) What does God look like? God looks like an old man, a young man, and a small white dove.

SISTER: I'll take the next one. (*Reads*) Are you ever sorry you became a nun? (*With deep sincerity and simplicity*) I am never sorry I became a nun. (*Reads*) It used to be a mortal sin to eat meat on Fridays, and now it isn't. Does that mean that people who ate meat on Fridays back when it was a sin are in hell? Or what? People who ate meat on Fridays back when it was a mortal sin are indeed in hell if they did not confess the sin before they died. If they confessed it, they are not in hell, unless they did not confess some other mortal sin they committed. People who would eat meat on Fridays back in the fifties tended to be the sort who would commit other mortal sins, so on a guess, I bet many of them *are* in hell for other sins, even if they did confess the eating of meat. (*Reads*) What exactly went on in Sodom? (*Irritated*) Who asked me this question? (*Reads*) I am an Aries. Is it a sin to follow your horoscope? It is a sin to follow your horoscope because only God knows the future and He won't tell us. Also, we can tell that horoscopes are false because according to astrology Christ would be a Capricorn, and Capricorn people are cold, ambitious and attracted to Scorpio and Virgo, and we know that Christ was warm, loving, and not attracted to anybody. Give *me* a cookie, Thomas. (*He does.*) I'm going to talk about Sodom a bit. (*Kisses the top of* THOMAS's *head*) Thomas, please leave the stage. (*He does.*) To answer your question, Sodom is where they committed acts of homosexuality and bestiality in the Old Testament, and God, infuriated by this, destroyed them all in one fell swoop. Modern-day Sodoms are New York City, San Francisco, Amsterdam, Los Angeles . . . well, basically anywhere where the population is over fifty thousand. The only reason that God has not destroyed these modern-day Sodoms is that Catholic nuns and priests live in these cities, and God does not wish to destroy them. He does, however, give these people body lice and hepatitis. It's so hard to know why God allows wickedness to flourish. I guess it's because God wants man to choose goodness freely of his own free will; sometimes one wonders if free will is worth all the trouble if there's going to be so much evil and unhappiness, but God knows best, presumably. If it were up to me, I might be tempted to wipe out cities and civilizations, but luckily for New York and Amsterdam, I'm not God. (*Reads*) Why is St. Christopher no longer a saint, and did anyone listen to the prayers I prayed to him before they decided he didn't exist? The name Christopher means Christ-bearer and we used to believe that he carried the Christ child across a river on his shoulders. Then sometime around Pope John XXIII, the Catholic Church decided that this was just a story and didn't really happen. I am not convinced that when we get to heaven we may not find that St. Christopher does indeed exist and that he dislikes Pope John XXIII; however, if he does not exist, then the prayers you prayed to him would have been picked up by St. Jude. St. Jude is the patron saint of hopeless causes. When you have a particularly terrible problem that has little hope of being solved, you pray to St. Jude. When you lose or misplace something, you pray to St. Anthony. (*Reads*) Tell us some more about your family. (*Smiles, pleased*) I had twenty-six brothers and sisters. From my family five became priests, seven became nuns, three became brothers, and the rest were institutionalized. My mother was also institutionalized shortly after she started thinking my father was Satan. Some days when we were little, we'd come home and not be able to find our mother so we'd pray to St. Anthony to help us find her. Then when we'd find her with her head in the oven, we would pray to St. Jude to make her sane again. (*Reads*) Are all our prayers answered? Yes, they are; what people who ask that question often don't realize is that sometimes the answer to our prayer is no. Dear God, please make my mother not be crazy. God's answer: no. Dear God, please let me recover from cancer. God's answer: no. Dear God, please take away this toothache. God's answer: alright, but you're going to be run over by a car. But every bad thing that happens to us, God has a special reason for. God is the good shepherd, we are His flock. And if God is grouchy or busy with more important matters His beloved mother Mary is always there to intercede for us. I shall now sing the Hail Mary in Latin. (SISTER *motions to the lighting booth, and the lights change to an apparently pre-arranged special spotlight for her, atmospheric with blue spill and back lighting; the rest of the stage becomes fairly dim. Sings*)

Ave Maria,
Gratia plena,
Maria, gratia plena,
Maria, gratia plena,
Ave, ave! . . . (etc.)

(*As* SISTER *sings, enter four people, ages twenty-eight to thirty. They are a woman dressed as the* BLESSED MOTHER, *a man dressed as* ST. JOSEPH, *and two people, a man and a woman, dressed as a camel. Because of the dim lighting, we don't see them too clearly at first.* SISTER, *either sensing something happening due to the audience or else just by turning her head, suddenly sees them and is terribly startled and confused.*)

ST. JOSEPH: We're sorry we're late.
SISTER: Oh dear God. (*Kneels*)

ST. JOSEPH: Sister, what are you doing?

SISTER: You look so real.

ST. JOSEPH: Sister, I'm Gary Sullavan, and (*Pointing to the* BLESSED MOTHER) this is Diane Symonds. We were in your fifth-grade class in 1959, and you asked us to come today. Don't you remember?

SISTER: 1959?

GARY: Don't you remember asking us?

SISTER: Not very distinctly. (*Louder, to lighting booth*) Could I have some lights please? (*Lights come back up to where they were before. To* GARY) What did I want you to do?

GARY: You wanted us to put on a pageant.

SISTER: That camel looks false to me.

PHILOMENA: Hello, Sister. (*She's the front of the camel.*)

SISTER: I thought so.

PHILOMENA: It's Philomena, Sister. Philomena Rostovitch.

ALOYSIUS: And Aloysius Benheim. (*He's the back of the camel.*)

SISTER: I don't really recognize any of you. Of course, you're not in your school uniforms.

DIANE: 1959.

SISTER: What?

DIANE: You taught us in 1959.

SISTER: I recognize you. Mary Jean Mahoney.

DIANE: I'm not Mary Jean Mahoney. I'm Diane Symonds.

SISTER: This is all so confusing.

GARY: Don't you want to see the pageant?

SISTER: What pageant is it?

GARY: We used to perform it at Christmas in your class; every class did. You said it was written in 1948 by Mary Jean Mahoney, who was your best student, you said.

DIANE: You said she was very elevated, and that when she was in the seventh grade she didn't have her first period, she had a stigmata.

SISTER: Oh yes. They discovered it in gym class. Mary Jean Mahoney. She entered a cloistered order of nuns upon her graduation from twelfth grade. Sometimes late at night I can hear her praying. Mary Jean Mahoney. Yes, let's see her pageant again. (*To audience*) She was such a bright student. (*Vague*) I remember asking them to come now, I think. I wanted to tell you about Mary Jean Mahoney, and the perfect faith of a child. Yes, the pageant, please. Thomas, come watch with me. (THOMAS *enters and sits on* SISTER's *lap.*)

GARY (*Announcing*):   The pageant of the birth and death of Our Beloved Savior Jesus Christ, by Mary Jean Mahoney as told to Mrs. Robert J. Mahoney. The setting: a desert near Bethlehem. St. Joseph and the Virgin Mary and their trusty camel must flee from the wicked King Herod.

DIANE (*Sings to tune of* "We Gather Together to Ask the Lord's Blessing"):

Hello, my name's Mary,
And his name is Joseph,
We're parents of Jesus,
Who's not been born yet.

We're fleeing from Herod,
And nobody knows if
We'll make it to the town,
But we'll try, you can bet.

And I'm still a virgin,
And he's not the father,
The father descended
From heaven above.

And this is our camel,
He's really not much bother,
We're off to Bethlehem,
Because God is love.

GARY: Here's an Inn, Mary. But there doesn't look like there's any room.

DIANE: Well ask them, Joseph.

GARY (*Knocks on imaginary door*): Excuse me, you don't have room at this Inn, do you? (*Listens*) He said they don't, Mary.

DIANE: Oh dear. Well let's try another Inn.

GARY (*Knocks*): Excuse me, you don't have room at this Inn, do you? (*Listens*) He says they don't allow camels.

DIANE: Let's try the third Inn.

GARY (*Knocks*): Excuse me, you don't have room at your Inn, do you? (*Listens*) I thought not . . . what? You would? Oh, Mary, this kind Innkeeper says that even though he has no room at the Inn, we can sleep in his stable.

DIANE: Oh, dear.

GARY: Mary, we really haven't any choice.

DIANE: Yes we do. Sister says we have choice over everything, because God gave us free will to decide between good and evil. And so I *choose* to stay in the stable.

GARY: Well here it is.

DIANE: Pew. It smells just like the zoo Mommy took me and Cynthia to visit last summer. We liked to look at the animals, but we didn't like to smell them.

GARY: I don't think there are any sheets.

DIANE: I don't need sheets, I'm so tired, I could sleep anywhere.

GARY: Well, that's good. Good night, Mary.

DIANE: But I do need pillows.

GARY: Mary, what can I do? We don't have any pillows.

DIANE: I can't sleep without pillows.

GARY: Let's pray to God then. If you just pray, He answers your prayers.

DIANE: Sometimes He says no, Joseph.

GARY: I know, but let's try. Dear God, we beseech Thee, hear our prayer.

DIANE: Pillows! Pillows! Pillows!

GARY: And behold God answered their prayers.

CAMEL (PHILOMENA):   We have an idea, Mary and Joseph. We have two humps, and you can use them as pillows.

DIANE: Thank you, God! Come on, Joseph. Let's go to sleep.

CAMEL (*As Mary and Joseph start to sleep,* CAMEL *sings a lullaby*):

Rockabye, and good night,
May God keep you and watch you,
Rockabye, and good night, (etc.)

(*They sleep.* ALOYSIUS *makes baby crying noises, tosses out a doll onto the floor*)

DIANE (*Seeing the doll*):   Joseph, He's born. Jesus is born.

GARY, DIANE, and CAMEL (*Sing*):

Joy to the world, the Savior's come,
Let earth receive her king,
La la la la la la la la,
La la la la la la la la,
Let heaven and nature sing,
Let heaven and nature sing,
Let heaven, and heaven, and nature sing!

GARY (*To doll*):   Can you say Poppa, Jesus? Can you say Momma?

DIANE: He's not that kind of child, Joseph. He was born without original sin like me. This is called my Immaculate Conception, which is not to be confused with my Virgin Birth. Everyone makes this error, it makes me lose my patience. *We* must learn from *Him,* Joseph.

GARY (*To audience*):   And so Jesus instructed His parents, and the priests in the Temple. And He performed many miracles.

DIANE: He turned water into wine.

GARY: He made cripples walk.

DIANE: He walked on the water.

GARY: And then came the time for His crucifixion. And His mother said to him:

DIANE (*To doll*):   But why, Jesus, why? Why must You be crucified?

GARY: And Jesus explained that because Adam and Eve, especially

Eve, had sinned that mankind was cursed until Jesus could redeem us by dying on the cross.

DIANE: But that sounds silly. Why can't God just forgive us?

GARY: But Jesus laughed at her and He said, "Yours is not to reason why, yours is but to do and die." And then He said, "But seriously, Mother, it is not up to God to justify His ways to man." And then Mary said:

DIANE: I understand. Or rather, I understand that I am not supposed to understand. Come, let us go to Golgotha and watch You be cruci-fied.

GARY: And Mary and the apostles and the faithful camel, whose name was Misty, followed Jesus to the rock of Golgotha and watched Him be nailed to a cross.

(GARY *has a hammer and nails, and nails the doll to a little cross; then stands it up that way.*)

And then He hung there for three hours in terrible agony.

DIANE: Imagine the agony. Try to feel the nails ripping through His hands and feet. Pound, pound, pound, rip, rip, rip. Washing the dishes for three hours is nothing compared to hanging on a cross.

GARY: And then He died. He's dead now, Mary.

DIANE (*Sad, lost*): Oh.

GARY: Let's go for a long walk.

DIANE: Oh, Joseph, I feel so alone.

GARY: So do I, Mary.

DIANE (*Truly wondering*): Do you think He was just a nut? Do you think maybe the Holy Ghost isn't His Father at all, that I made it all up? Maybe I'm not a virgin . . . Maybe . . .

GARY: But then Misty said . . .

CAMEL (PHILOMENA): Do not despair, Mary and Joseph. Of course, He is God, He'll rise again in three days.

DIANE: If only I could believe you. But why should I listen to a dumb animal?

CAMEL (PHILOMENA): O ye, of little faith.

DIANE (*Sad*): Oh, Joseph, I'm losing my mind.

GARY: And so Mary and Joseph and the camel hid for three days and three nights, and on Sunday morning they got up and went to the Tomb where Christ was buried. And when they got there, standing by the Tomb was an angel. And the angel spoke.

ALOYSIUS (*Back of camel*): Mary and Joseph, your son has risen from the dead, just like your dumb animal Misty told you He would.

DIANE: Thank you, Misty. You were right. (*Kisses Misty*)

GARY: And then Mary and Joseph, realizing their lack of faith, thanked Misty and made a good act of contrition. And then Jesus came out from behind the tree where He was hiding, they spent forty days on earth enjoying themselves and setting the ground-work for the Catholic Church, and then Jesus, Mary, Joseph and Misty ascended into heaven and lived happily ever after.

(DIANE *and* GARY, *holding the doll between them, stand in front of the camel. All sing the final jubilant phrase of* "Angels We Have Heard on High" *Christmas carol, as* DIANE *and* GARY *mime ascension by waving their arms in a flying motion.*)

ALL (*Singing*):   Glor-or-or-or-ia! In Excelsis Deo!

(*All four bow.* SISTER *applauds enthusiastically. After their bow, the four quickly get out of their costumes, continuing to do so during some of* SISTER's *next speech if necessary. Their "regular" clothes are indeed regular and not too noteworthy:* DIANE *might wear slacks or jeans but with an attractive sweater or blouse and with a blazer;* GARY *might wear chinos, a nice shirt with even a tie, or a vest—casual but neat, pleasant;* PHILOMENA *might wear a dress,* ALOYSIUS *a shirt and slacks [or, if played as a bit formal, even a suit].*)

SISTER: Oh, thank you, children. That was lovely. Thank you. (*To audience*) The old stories really are the best, aren't they? Mary Jean Mahoney. What a good child. And what a nice reunion *we're* having. What year did you say you were in my class again?
GARY: 1959.
SISTER: 1959. Oh, those were happy years. Eisenhower, Pope Pius still alive, then the first Catholic president. And so now you've all grown up. Let's do some of the old questions, shall we? (*To* ALOYSIUS) Who made you?
ALOYSIUS: God made me.
SISTER: Quite correct. What is the seventh commandment?
PHILOMENA: The seventh commandment is thou shalt not steal.
SISTER: Very good. (*To* DIANE) What is contrition? You.
DIANE: Uh . . . being sorry for sin?
SISTER (*Cheerfully chastising*):   That's not how we answer questions here, young lady. Thomas?
THOMAS: Contrition is sincere sorrow for having offended God, and hatred for the sins we have committed, with a firm purpose of sinning no more.
DIANE: Oh yes. Right.
SISTER (*Still kindly*):   For someone who's just played the Virgin, you don't know your catechism responses very well. What grade are you in?
DIANE: I'm not in a grade. I'm in life.
SISTER: Oh yes, right. Well, cookies anyone? Thomas, go bring our nice guests some cookies. (THOMAS *exits.*) It's so nice to see you all again.

You must all be married by now, I imagine. I hope you all have large families like we encouraged?

PHILOMENA: I have a little girl, age three.

SISTER: That's nice.

ALOYSIUS: I have two boys.

SISTER: I like boys. (*To* GARY) And you?

GARY: I'm not married.

SISTER: Well, a nice-looking boy like you, it won't be long before some pretty girl snatches you up. (*To* DIANE) And you?

DIANE: I don't have any children. But I've had two abortions.

(SISTER *is stunned. Enter* THOMAS *with cookies*)

SISTER: No cookies, Thomas. Take them away. (THOMAS *exits immediately. To* DIANE) You are in a state of mortal sin, young woman. What is the fifth commandment?

DIANE: Thou shalt not kill.

SISTER: You are a murderer.

DIANE (*Unemotional*):   The first one was when I was raped when I was eighteen.

SISTER: Well I am sorry to hear that. But only God has power over life and death. God might have had very special plans for your baby. Are you sure I taught you?

DIANE: Yes you taught me.

SISTER: Did I give you good grades?

DIANE: Yes. Very good.

SISTER: Have you told these sins in confession?

DIANE: What sins?

SISTER: You know very well what I mean.

DIANE: I don't go to confession.

SISTER: Well, it looks pretty clear to me, we'll just add you to the list of people going to hell. (*Calling*) Thomas! (*Enter* THOMAS) We'll put her name right after Comden and Green.

THOMAS: All right. (*Exits*)

SISTER: Now somebody change the subject. I don't want to hear any more about this.

GARY (*Trying to oblige*):   Ummmm . . . it certainly is strange being able to chew the communion wafer now, isn't it?

SISTER: What?

GARY: Well, you used to tell us that because the communion wafer was really the body of Christ, if we chewed it, it might bleed.

SISTER: I was speaking metaphorically.

GARY: Oh.

SISTER (*Pause*):   Well, I still feel shaken by that girl over there. Let's talk about something positive. (*Gestures to* PHILOMENA) You, with the little girl. Tell me about yourself.

PHILOMENA: Well my little girl is three, and her name is Wendy.

SISTER: There is no St. Wendy.

PHILOMENA: Her middle name is Mary.

SISTER: Wendy Mary. Too many y's. I'd change it. What does your husband do?

PHILOMENA: I don't have a husband. (*Long pause*)

SISTER: Did he die?

PHILOMENA: I don't think so. I didn't know him for very long.

SISTER: Do you sign your letters Mrs. or Miss?

PHILOMENA: I don't write letters.

SISTER: Did this person you lost track of *marry* you before he left?

PHILOMENA (*Quiet*): No.

SISTER: Children, you are making me very sad. (*To* PHILOMENA) Did you get good grades in my class?

PHILOMENA: No, Sister. You said I was stupid.

SISTER: Are you a prostitute?

PHILOMENA: Sister! Certainly not. I just get lonely.

SISTER: The Mother Superior of my own convent may get lonely, but does she have illegitimate children?

ALOYSIUS: There *was* that nun who stuffed her baby behind her dresser last year. (SISTER *stares at him.*) It was in the news.

SISTER: No one was addressing you, Aloysius. Philomena, my point is that loneliness does not excuse sin.

PHILOMENA: But there are worse sins. And I believe Jesus forgives me. After all, He didn't want them to stone the woman taken in adultery.

SISTER: That was merely a *political* gesture. In private Christ stoned *many* women taken in adultery.

DIANE: That's not in the Bible.

SISTER (*Suddenly very angry*): Not everything has to be in the Bible! (*To audience, trying to recoup*) There's oral tradition within the Church. One priest tells another priest something, it gets passed down through the years.

PHILOMENA (*Unhappy*): But don't you believe Jesus forgives people who sin?

SISTER: Yes, of course, He forgives sin, but He's *tricky*. You have to be *truly* sorry, and you have to *truly* resolve not to sin again, or else He'll send you straight to hell just like the thief He was crucified next to.

PHILOMENA: Well, I think Jesus forgives me.

SISTER: Well I think you're going to hell. (*To* ALOYSIUS) And what about you? Is there anything the matter with you?

ALOYSIUS: Nothing. I'm fine.

SISTER: But are you living properly?

ALOYSIUS: Yes.

SISTER: And you're married?

ALOYSIUS: Yes.

SISTER: And you don't use birth control?

ALOYSIUS: No.

SISTER: But you only have two children. Why is that? You're not spilling your seed like Onan, are you? That's a sin, you know.

ALOYSIUS: No. It's just chance that we haven't had more.

SISTER: And you go to Mass once a week, and communion at least once a year, and confession at least once a year? Right?

ALOYSIUS: Yes.

SISTER: Well I'm very pleased then.

ALOYSIUS (*Suddenly guilty, unhappy*): I am an alcoholic, and recently I've started to hit my wife, and I keep thinking about suicide.

SISTER: Within bounds, all those things are venial sins. At least one of my students turned out well. Of course, I don't know how hard you're hitting your wife; but with prayer and God's grace . . .

ALOYSIUS: My wife is very unhappy.

SISTER: Yes, but eventually there's death. And then everlasting happiness in heaven. Some days I long for heaven. (*To* GARY) And you? Have you turned out all right?

GARY: I'm okay.

SISTER: And you don't use birth control?

GARY: Definitely not.

SISTER: That's good. (*Looks at him*) What do you mean, "definitely not"?

GARY: I don't use it.

SISTER: And you're not married. Have you not found the right girl?

GARY (*Evasively*): In a manner of speaking.

SISTER (*Grim, not going to pursue it*): Okay. (*Walks away, but then knows she has to pursue it*) You do that thing that makes Jesus puke, don't you?

GARY: Pardon?

SISTER: Drop the polite boy manners, buster. When your mother looks at you, she turns into a pillar of salt, right?

GARY: What?

SISTER: Sodom and Gomorrah, stupid. You sleep with men, don't you?

GARY: Well . . . yes.

SISTER: Jesus, Mary, and Joseph! We have a regular cross section in here.

GARY: I got seduced when I was in the seminary. I mean, I guess I'd been denying it up to then.

SISTER: We don't want to hear about it.

GARY: And then when I left the seminary I was very upset, and then I went to New York and I slept with five hundred different people.

SISTER: Jesus is going to throw up.

GARY: But then I decided I was trashing my life, and so I only had sex with guys I had an emotional relationship with.

SISTER: That must have cut it down to about *three* hundred.

GARY: And now I'm living with this one guy who I'd gone to grade school with and only ran into again two years ago, and we're faithful with one another and stuff. He was in your class too. Jeff Hannigan.

SISTER: He was a bad boy. Some of them should be left on the side of a hill to die, and he was one.

GARY: You remember him?

SISTER: Not really. His type.

GARY: Anyway, when I met him again, he was still a practicing Catholic, and so now I am again too.

SISTER: I'd practice a little harder if I were you.

GARY: So I don't think I'm so bad.

SISTER (*Vomit sound*):   Blah. You make me want to blah. Didn't any of you listen to me when I was teaching you? What were you all doing? (*Mad, trying to set the record straight again*) There is the universe, created by God. Eve ate the apple, man got original sin, God sent down Jesus to redeem us. Jesus said to St. Peter, "Upon this rock," rock meaning Peter, "I build my Church," by which he meant that Peter was the first Pope and that he and the subsequent Popes would be infallible on matters of doctrine and morals. So your way is very clear: you have this infallible Church that tells you what is right and wrong, and you follow its teaching, and then you get to heaven. Didn't you all *hear* me say that? Did you all have wax in your ears? Did I speak in a foreign language? Or what? And you've all sinned against sex—(*To* ALOYSIUS) not you, you're just depressed, you probably need vitamins—but the rest of you. Why this obsession with sex? The Church has been very clear setting up the guidelines for you. (*To* PHILOMENA *and* DIANE) For you two girls, why can't you simply marry one Catholic man and have as many babies as chance and the good Lord allows you to? Simple, easy to follow directions. (*To* GARY) And for you, you can *force* yourself to marry and procreate with some nice Catholic girl—try it, it's not so hard— or you can be celibate for the rest of your life. Again, simple advice. (*Suddenly furious*) Those are your options! No others. They are your direct paths to heaven and salvation, to everlasting happiness! Why aren't you following these paths? Are you insane?

DIANE: You're insane.

SISTER: You know, you're my least favorite person here today. I mean, the great big effeminate one over there (*Points to* GARY) makes me want to blah, but I can tell he once was nice, and he might get better with shock treatments and aversion therapy. But I can tell shock treatments wouldn't help you. You're fresh as paint, and you're nasty. I can see it in your face.

DIANE: You shouldn't be teaching children. You should be locked up in a convent where you can't hurt anybody.

SISTER:　Me hurt someone. You're the one who runs around killing babies at the drop of a hat.

DIANE:　It's a medical procedure. And even the Church admits it can't pinpoint *when* life begins in the womb. Why should you decide that the minute the sperm touches the ovum that . . .

SISTER:　Don't talk filth to me, I don't want to hear it. (*Suddenly very suspicious*) Why did you all come here today? I don't remember asking you.

GARY:　It was Diane's idea.

SISTER:　What? What was?

PHILOMENA:　We wanted to embarrass you.

ALOYSIUS:　None of us ever liked you.

SISTER:　What do you mean? My students always loved me. I was the favorite.

ALOYSIUS:　No. We thought you were a bully.

SISTER:　I was the *favorite*.

ALOYSIUS:　You never let me go to the bathroom when I needed to.

SISTER:　All you had to do was raise your hand.

ALOYSIUS:　There were sixty children, and I sat in the back of the room; and I did raise my hand, but you never acknowledged me. Every afternoon my bladder became very full, and I always ended up wetting my pants.

SISTER:　Big deal.

ALOYSIUS:　I spoke to you about recognizing me sooner, and about my problem, but all you said then was "big deal."

SISTER:　I remember you. You used to make a puddle in the last row every day.

ALOYSIUS:　I have bladder problems to this day.

SISTER:　What a baby. You flunked. I was giving you a lesson in life, and you flunked. It was up to you to solve the problem: don't drink your little carton of milk at lunch; bring a little container with you and urinate behind your desk; or simply hold it in and offer the discomfort up to Christ. He suffered three hours of agony on the cross, surely a full bladder pales by comparison. I talk about the universe and original sin and heaven and hell, and you complain to me about bathroom privileges. You're a ridiculous crybaby. (*Cuffs him on the head*)

PHILOMENA:　You used to hit me too.

SISTER:　You probably said stupid things.

PHILOMENA:　I did. I told you I was stupid. That was no reason to hit me.

SISTER:　It seems a very good reason to hit you. Knock some sense into you.

PHILOMENA:　You used to take the point of your pencil and poke it up and down on my head when I didn't do my homework.

SISTER:　You should have done your homework.

PHILOMENA: And when I didn't know how to do long division, you slammed my head against the blackboard.

SISTER: Did I ever break a bone?

PHILOMENA: No.

SISTER: There, you see! (*To* GARY) And what about you?

GARY: You didn't do anything to me in particular. I just found you scary.

SISTER: Well I am scary.

GARY: But my lover Jeff doesn't like you 'cause you made him wet his pants too.

SISTER: All this obsession with the bladder. (*To* DIANE) And you, the nasty one, why did you want to embarrass me?

DIANE (*Said simply*):   Because I believed you. I believed how you said the world worked, and that God loved us, and the story of the Good Shepherd and the lost sheep; and I don't think you should lie to people.

SISTER: But that's how things are. I didn't lie.

DIANE: When I was sixteen, my mother got breast cancer, which spread. I prayed to God to let her suffering be small, but her suffering seemed to me quite extreme. She was in bad pain for half a year, and then terrible pain for much of a full year. The ulcerations on her body were horrifying to her and to me. Her last few weeks she slipped into a semi-conscious state, which allowed her, unfortunately, to wake up for a few minutes at a time and to have a full awareness of her pain and her fear of death. She was able to recognize me, and she would try to cry, but she was unable to; and to speak, but she was unable to. I think she wanted me to get her new doctors; she never really accepted that her disease was going to kill her, and she thought in her panic that her doctors must be incompetent and that new ones could magically cure her. Then, thank goodness, she went into a full coma. A nurse who I knew to be Catholic assured me that everything would be done to keep her alive—a dubious comfort. Happily, the doctor was not Catholic, or if he was, not doctrinaire, and they didn't use extraordinary means to keep her alive; and she finally died after several more weeks in her coma. Now there are, I'm sure, far worse deaths—terrible burnings, tortures, plague, pestilence, famine; Christ on the cross even, as Sister likes to say. But I thought my mother's death was bad enough, and I got confused as to why I had been praying and to whom. I mean, if prayer was really this sort of button you pressed—admit you need the Lord, then He stops your suffering—then why didn't it always work? Or ever work? And when it worked, so-called, and our prayers were supposedly answered, wasn't it as likely to be chance as God? God always answers our prayers, you said, He just sometimes says no. But why would He say no to stopping my mother's suffering? I wasn't even asking that she live, just that He end her suffering. And it can't be that He was letting her suffer because she'd been bad, because she hadn't been bad and besides suffering doesn't seem to work that way, considering the suffering of children who've obviously done nothing wrong. So why was He letting her suffer? Spite? Was the Lord God actually malicious? That seemed possible, but farfetched. Maybe He had no control over it, maybe He wasn't omnipotent as you taught us He was. Maybe He created the world sort of by accident by belching one morning or getting the hiccups, and maybe He had no idea how the whole thing worked. In which case, He wouldn't be malicious, just useless. Or, of course, more likely than that, He didn't exist at all, the universe was hiccupped or belched into existence all on its own, and my mother's suffering just existed like rain or wind or humidity. I became angry at myself, and by extension at you, for ever having expected anything beyond randomness from the world. And while I was thinking these things, the day that my mother died, I was raped. Now I know that's really too much, one really loses all sympathy for me because I sound like I'm making it up or something. But bad things sometimes happen all at once, and this particular day on my return from the hospital I was raped by some maniac who broke into the house. He had a knife and cut me up some. Anyway, I don't really want to go on about the experience, but I got very depressed for about five years. Somehow the utter randomness of things—my mother's suffering, my attack by a lunatic who was either born a lunatic or made one by cruel parents or perhaps by an imbalance of hormones or whatever, etc. etc.—*this randomness seemed intolerable*. I found I grew to hate you, Sister, for making me once expect everything to be ordered and to make sense. My psychiatrist said he thought my hatred of you was obsessive, that I just was looking for someone to blame. Then he seduced me, and he was the father of my second abortion.

SISTER: I think she's making all this up.

DIANE: He said I seduced him. And maybe that's so. But he could be lying just to make himself feel better. (*To* SISTER) And of course your idea that I should have had this baby, either baby, is preposterous. Have you any idea what a terrible mother I'd be? I'm a nervous wreck.

SISTER: God would have given you the strength.

DIANE: I suppose it is childish to look for blame, part of the randomness of things is that there is no one to blame; but basically I think everything is your fault, Sister.

SISTER: You have obviously never read the Book of Job.

DIANE: I have read it. And I think it's a nasty story.

SISTER: God explains in that story why He lets us suffer, and a very lovely explanation it is too. He likes to test us so that when we choose to love Him no matter what He does to us that proves how great and deep our love for Him is.

DIANE: That sounds like *The Story of O.*

SISTER: Well there's obviously no talking to you. You don't want help or knowledge or enlightenment, so there's nothing left for you but an unhappy life, sickness, death, and hell.

DIANE: Last evening I killed my psychiatrist and now I'm going to kill you. (*Takes out a gun*)

GARY: Oh dear. I thought we were just going to embarrass her.

SISTER (*Stalling for time*): And you have, very much so. So no need to kill me at all. Goodbye, Diane, Gary, Aloysius . . .

DIANE: You're insane. You shouldn't be allowed to teach children. I see that there's that little boy here today. You're going to make him crazy.

SISTER: Thomas, stay offstage with the cookies, dear.

DIANE: I want you to admit that everything's your fault, and then I'm going to kill you.

PHILOMENA: Maybe we should all wait outside.

SISTER: Stay here. Diane, look at me. I was wrong. I admit it. I'm sorry. I thought everything made sense, but I didn't understand things properly. There's nothing I can say to make it up to you but . . . (*Seeing something awful behind* DIANE's *head*) LOOK OUT! (DIANE *looks behind her,* SISTER *whips out her own gun and shoots* DIANE *dead.* SISTER *like a circus artist completing a stunt, hands up*) Ta-da! For those non-Catholics present, murder is allowable in self-defense, one doesn't even have to tell it in confession. Thomas, bring me some water.

GARY: We didn't know she was bringing a gun.

(THOMAS *brings water.*)

SISTER: I remember her now from class. (*Looks at her dead body*) She had no sense of humor.

ALOYSIUS: I have to go to the bathroom.

SISTER (*Aims gun at him*): Stay where you are. Raise your hand if you want to go to the bathroom, Aloysius, and wait until I have acknowledged you. (*She ignores him now, though keeps gun aimed at him most of the time.*) Thomas, bring me a cookie. (*He does.*) Most of my students turned out beautifully, these are the few exceptions. But we never give up on those who've turned out badly, do we, Thomas? What is the story of the Good Shepherd and the Lost Sheep?

THOMAS: The Good Shepherd was so concerned about his Lost Sheep that he left His flock to go find the Lost Sheep, and then He found it.

SISTER: That's right. And while he was gone, a great big wolf came and killed his entire flock. No, just kidding, I'm feeling lightheaded from all this excitement. No, by the story of the Lost Sheep, Christ tells us that when a sinner strays we mustn't give up on the sinner. (SISTER *indicates for* THOMAS *to exit; he does.*) So I don't totally despair for these people standing here. Gary, I hope that you will leave your friend Jeff, don't even tell him where you're going, just disappear, and then I hope you will live your life as a celibate. Like me. Celibate rhymes with celebrate. Our Lord loves celibate people. And you, Philomena, I hope you will get married to some nice Catholic man, or if you stay unmarried then you too will become a celibate. Rhymes with celebrate.

ALOYSIUS: Sister, I have my hand up.

SISTER: Keep it up. And you, Aloysius, I hope you'll remember not to kill yourself, which is a mortal sin. For if we live by God's laws even though we are having a miserable life, remember heaven and eternal happiness are our reward.

GARY: Should we help you with the body, Sister?

SISTER (*Confused for a moment, but then responds*) The janitor will help me later, thank you. You two may go now, so I can finish my lecture.

GARY: Why don't you let him go to the bathroom?

SISTER: Gary?

GARY: Yes, Sister?

SISTER: You still believe what you do with Jeff is wrong, don't you? I mean, you still confess it in confession, don't you?

GARY: Well I don't really think it's wrong, but I'm not sure, so I do still tell it in confession.

SISTER: When did you last go to confession?

GARY: This morning actually. I was going to be playing St. Joseph and all.

SISTER: And you haven't sinned since then, have you?

GARY: No, Sister.

(SISTER *shoots him dead.*)

SISTER (*Triumphantly*):   I've sent him to Heaven! (*To* PHILOMENA) Okay, you with the little girl, go home before I decide your little girl would be better off in a Catholic orphanage. (PHILOMENA *exits in terror. To audience*) I'm not really within the letter of the law shooting Gary like this, but really if he did make a good confession I have sent him straight to heaven and eternal, blissful happiness. And I'm afraid otherwise he would have ended up in hell. I think Christ will allow me this little dispensation from the letter of the law, but I'll go to confession later today, just to be sure.

ALOYSIUS: Sister, I have to go to the bathroom.

SISTER: Wait until I recognize you, Aloysius.

ALOYSIUS: I'm going to leave now.

SISTER (*Angry, emphasizing the gun*):   I've used this twice today, don't tempt me to use it again. Thomas! (*He enters.*) Who made you?

THOMAS: God made me.

SISTER: Why did God make you?

THOMAS: God made me to show forth His goodness and to share with us His happiness.

ALOYSIUS: If you don't let me go to the bathroom, I'm going to wet my pants.

SISTER: We all have free will, Aloysius. Thomas, explain about the primary cause again.

THOMAS: Everything has a primary cause. Dinner is put on the table because the primary cause . . .

SISTER: Thomas, I'm going to nap some, I'm exhausted. (*Hands him gun*) You keep that dangerous man over there covered, and if he moves shoot him; and also recite some nice catechism questions for us all while I rest. All right, dear?

THOMAS: Yes, Sister. (*He aims the gun at* ALOYSIUS. SISTER *sits on a chair, about to nap.*)

SISTER: Sit on my lap.

(THOMAS, *still aiming the gun at* ALOYSIUS, *sits on her lap, and begins to recite from memory.* ALOYSIUS *keeps his hand up.*)

THOMAS: "What must we do to gain the happiness of heaven?"
    To gain the happiness of heaven, we must know, love, and serve God in this world.

(*Lights start to dim.*)

"From whom do we learn to know, love and serve God?"
    We learn to know, love, and serve God from Jesus Christ, the Son of God, who teaches us through the Catholic Church.
"What are some of the perfections of God?"
    Some of the perfections of God are: God is eternal, all-good, all-knowing, all-present, and almighty.

(*Lights have dimmed to black.*)

Questions for Discussion and Writing

1. What factors in Sister Mary Ignatius's background might help explain her eccentric interpretation of traditional Catholic theology?
2. What function does the character of Thomas serve in the play?
3. When Sister Mary Ignatius reads cards containing questions supposedly submitted to her by the audience, why is it significant that she simply ignores questions about the existence of evil?
4. What motive prompts her former students—Diane, Gary, Philomena, and Aloysius—to visit Sister Mary Ignatius after twenty years?
5. For Sister Mary Ignatius, why does Mary Jean Mahoney represent the perfect student?

6. In performing the pageant, Diane says, "Everyone makes this error, it makes me lose my patience." Why is it significant that this is exactly the same phrase that Sister Mary Ignatius has used earlier in explaining points of theology?

7. What dramatic principle underlies the sequence in which the four students reveal their life experiences? How do Diane's experiences and her reactions to them pose the most direct challenge to Sister Mary Ignatius? In what way do Diane's experiences focus attention on the question Sister has ignored, that is, the existence of evil?

8. Why is it ironic that Sister Mary Ignatius says of Aloysius, "at least one of my students turned out well"?

9. How does Durang use certain props in the play to symbolize larger concepts? For example, what might the cookie or Sister Mary Ignatius's gun SYMBOLIZE?

10. Does your pastor, priest, rabbi, or other religious leader have a favorite sermon or speech that he or she likes to give?

11. If you had a religious upbringing, discuss the extent to which your experiences were similar to or different from those depicted in Durang's play.

WRITING ABOUT SYMBOLS AND MYTHS

Symbols in literary works refer to people, places, objects, or events that have their own meaning in the context of the work, but that also point beyond themselves to greater and more complex meanings. To determine whether any element in a literary work is symbolic, judge whether it consistently refers beyond itself to a significant idea, emotion, or quality.

Some symbols (cross, skull and crossbones) have universally recognized meanings that derive their significance from shared historical, cultural, or religious frameworks. For example, Inés Arredondo, in "The Shunammite," uses the desire to possess jewelry to symbolize greed for things of this world, and uses a rose that loses its freshness to symbolize the protagonist's loss of innocence. Other symbols that do not have universally recognized significance develop their symbolic meaning within the context of the specific work. These are often referred to as private, authorial, or contextual symbols. For example, in Abioseh Nicol's "Life Is Sweet at Kumansenu," the secret of opening the locket comes to symbolize unlocking the mystery of life after death.

Not every work of fiction uses symbols and not every character, incident, or object in a work has symbolic value. How do you know when the author intends something to serve as a symbol? The fact that an author chooses to write about particular people and their experiences means that they are seen as capable of revealing something meaningful. Symbols evolve within the context of the work when people, places, things, ideas, or events become so saturated with meaning that they begin to connect with more complex meanings beyond the confines of the story.

In preparing to write an essay on symbolism in a short story look for incidents, actions, objects, situations, or ideas that recur within the story in ways that suggest the author intends this feature to be taken symbolically. For example, the locket in Abioseh Nicol's story plays an important part in the events described and is mentioned repeatedly. Look for details that are placed in a conspicuous position, such as in the opening or closing of the story. Although the emphasis, repetition, and position of a detail may signal its symbolic status, care should be taken to establish that the symbol has its meaning in the context of the story. To be symbolic the detail or feature must suggest a meaning that transcends its literal function in the story. A good example of this is how the character known as the Cypriot man functions in Tayeb Salih's eerie story. He is mentioned repeatedly within the story and his name is used for the title. His importance is emphasized by his repeated, unexpected, and inexplicable appearances, wherever the narrator happens to be. On each of the occasions on which he appears someone dies, and his meaning as Death or the Devil incarnate is established in the context of the story. The way he presents himself in the story's conclusion suggests he represents a hidden possibility for acts of evil that are latent in everyone, including the narrator. The Cypriot man, in effect, compresses a range of qualities into a concrete symbol with great emotional power who suggests a range of complex and elusive meanings.

As you interpret the symbol in its context, discuss what it means without distorting the pattern in which the author has placed it. Don't impose your own interpretation, based on associations you may already have, because the author may have entirely different symbolic associations from yours. For example, you may think of a mime as a street-corner performer without imbuing him or her with the capacity to reflect universal truths in the way the Mime does in Peter Carey's story. This is especially true when the symbol is personal to the author and builds its meaning over the course of the story. Poets are more likely to use symbolism because of the concise nature of poetry that compresses meaning into relatively few words.

At first glance, symbols and metaphors would seem to be indistinguishable from each other. We can grasp the difference by realizing that a figurative term in a metaphor is meant to clarify the nature of an abstract idea or emotion by comparing it to something tangible and easily grasped. For example, Rita Dove in "The Wake" does this when she clarifies the difficult-to-grasp emotion she experienced following her mother's death:

> Your absence distributed itself
> like an invitation

The figurative term "like an invitation" clarifies the abstract idea "Your absence." By contrast, a symbol is an image that points beyond itself to an entire range of complex, not easily defined meanings, as we can see from the following famous lines from William Butler Yeats's "The Second Coming":

> And what rough beast, its hour come round at last,
> Slouches towards Bethlehem to be born?

We can certainly read this poem as an hallucinatory vision that overwhelms the speaker's consciousness. In other words, the image of the "rough beast" functions literally. But it also functions symbolically by suggesting possibilities that don't stop at the literal. Although we cannot say exactly what Yeats had in mind, the symbol suggests a range of qualities that refer to the destruction of what is normal, decent, traditional, innocent, and an ascendancy of an inhuman bestial power that will displace Christianity. The range of meaning extends outward from the symbol and adds another dimension to the poem. Symbols serve as a shorthand way to bridge the gap between the poet's vision of the world and that of the reader. As in fiction, symbols may take on unique private meanings or tap into preexisting cultural or religious meanings. Zbigniew Herbert does this in "Preliminary Investigation of an Angel" by using the angel as a symbol for innocence under siege.

An essay on symbolism in poetry should carefully examine the language used by the speaker. Try to identify recurrent references that invest a person, place, or thing with a special significance. Look at the diction, sentence rhythms, and imagery. Do these repeated references cumulatively throw light on a psychological truth that is at the center of the poem? Is there some charged or resonant image at the heart of the poem that clarifies the particular associations the imagery of the poem expresses?

In drama, as with fiction and poetry, characters, objects, actions, or situations can function as symbols. All dramas require the playwright and set designer to present the audience with certain stylized representations of the world beyond the theater that the audience is asked to accept as reality. Because the playwright must communicate the meaning of the play only through what the audience can see or hear on the stage, ordinary objects are more likely to be invested with special significance. In Durang's play, the repeated offering of a cookie to Thomas rewards him for providing correct answers to mainly theological questions asked him by Sister Mary Ignatius. The play furnishes clues that this detail is to be taken symbolically. It is emphasized by being repeated throughout the play, and is strongly emphasized by its position at the end of it. It accrues its meaning within the context of the play and suggests a cluster of related meanings that include the ideas of rote learning, blind acceptance of church doctrine, and a stimulus-response reinforcement schedule for providing correct answers. In effect, it comes to symbolize the kind of uncritical acceptance of Sister Mary Ignatius's teachings that Durang satirizes.

An essay on symbolism in drama should first determine if any characters, actions, objects, details of the setting, elements of dialogue, costumes, props, sounds, music, or lighting might serve as symbols. Do they convey generally recognized meanings or do the meanings evolve in the context of the play? To what extent does the symbolism shape the overall meaning of the play? For example, has the playwright assigned names to characters that suggest something about their nature or their roles? You are looking for any element that recurs from scene to scene that accrues an extraordinary significance as the play develops. Your essay should answer the question of how symbolism in the play directs the audience's attention to something beyond the drama that enhances the meaning and theatrical effect of the play.

When an entire story is symbolic, it is sometimes called a myth. Whereas a symbolic story may be personal or private, a myth relates to communal, cultural, or group experience. Myths are often stories of communal origin that aim at providing explanations or religious interpretations of nature, the universe, and humanity. Myths satisfy a basic human need to organize, explain, and humanize events or conditions that would otherwise remain mysterious and frightening. For this reason, myths are often associated with religion because they attempt to explain aspects of life that are too complex to be easily understood. Myths also embody the cultural and social values of the civilizations in which they are composed. Because myths usually are symbolic and extensive, they use plot or character elements that recur in the imaginative works of many civilizations, across cultures, from age to age. These recurrent cultural and communal figures or patterns are known as archetypes. Archetypes frequently present themselves as sets of opposing associations represented symbolically: if water represents creativity, rebirth, and life, then its opposite, drought and desertlike conditions, would represent sterility and death. For example, "The Shunammite" employs oppositions between the flesh and the spirit.

There are several ways to analyze the literary treatment of archetypes; you might identify and examine the presence of archetypal characters. Some frequently encountered archetypes include the hero, witch, scapegoat (the boy sacrificed in Achebe's work), virgin (the protagonist in Arrendondo's story), earth mother, femme fatale, star-crossed lovers, saint, martyr (the protagonist in Carey's story), or tyrant. The Cypriot man in Salih's story might be seen as representation of an archetype known in various cultures as the Devil. You might also examine the literary portrayal of archetypal situations, such as an extensive journey, examples of which include the quest for the Holy Grail, the rite of passage or initiation (an example of which might be seen in Mahfouz's "Half a Day"), an animal that serves as a guide (as the canary might be in Machado de Assis's "A Canary's Ideas"), death and rebirth (as in Paz's "Day of the Dead"), or completion of an arduous task (for example, the Mime in Carey's story that also taps into the archetype of the artist as martyr).

Your essay might investigate how the presence of any of these archetypal situations add an extra dimension of meaning to the work. For example, think of how the return of the ghost after death in Nicol's story, or the granting of the protagonist's wish for extraordinary powers in "The Man Who Stopped Trains," bring into each of these works situations that are recurrent universally in the literature of many civilizations.

Connections

1. What unusual attitudes toward time are expressed in the works by Paz and Mahfouz? How is time transcended, compressed, broken up, and with what results?

2. How do the poems "The Garden" and "The Lost Red Boot" explore the power of imagination to transfigure reality?

3. What similarities can you discover in the attitudes of the uncle in "The Shunammite" and the protagonist in "An Old Man" in confronting old age?

4. How does the use of the parable form enhance the effectiveness of the stories by Mahfouz and Carey?

5. How do both "The Cypriot Man" and "The Shunammite" dramatize a conflict between the spirit and the flesh?

6. Why do you think Achebe used the words "Things fall apart" from William Butler Yeats's "The Second Coming" as the title for his work? Compare how "things" fall apart in each.

7. What different perspectives on the human condition are offered in "A Canary's Ideas" and "Funny"? Why do you think the authors chose to express these perspectives through birds?

8. What similarities can you discover in attitudes toward spirits and the soul in "Life Is Sweet at Kumansenu" and Silko's essay?

9. How do the poems "Afterglow" and "The Wake" deal with the question of coming to terms with loss?

10. How do both Carey's and Barcelo's stories present possibilities of transcending the human condition with supernatural gifts?

11. What similarities can you discover in attitudes toward the sacredness of the natural world in the sequence entitled "My Sun" by Ma Lihua and the essay "Language and Literature from a Pueblo Indian Perspective," by Leslie Marmon Silko?

12. How do the protagonists in the poems by Herbert and Sachs reveal how it is possible for victims of religious persecution to transcend and forgive their tormentors?

13. How do the protagonists in Durang's play and in Carey's story illustrate people whose lives have been shaped by their attitudes toward religious belief?

Acknowledgments

TALAT ABBASI, "Facing the Light." Copyright © 1989 by Talat Abbasi. "Facing the Light" first appeared in *Sudden Fiction International*, W. W. Norton, 1989. Reprinted by permission of the author.

KŌBŌ ABE, *Friends* by Kōbō Abe, translated by Donald Keene. Copyright © 1969 by Grove Press, Inc. Originally published as *Tomodachi* by Kawade Shobo, Tokyo, © 1967. Used by permission of Grove Press, Inc.

CHINUA ACHEBE, "Things Fall Apart." Chapter seven from *Things Fall Apart* by Chinua Achebe, 1959. Reprinted by permission of William Heinemann, Limited.

JOHN AGARD, "Listen mr oxford don," from *Mangoes and Bullets*, published by Pluto Press, 1985. Reprinted by kind permission of John Agard c/o Caroline Sheldon Literary Agency.

BELLA AKHMADULINA, "The Garden," from *The Garden: New and Selected Poetry and Prose* by Bella Akhmadulina. Copyright © 1973, 1974, 1977, 1983, 1987, 1988, 1990 by Bella Akhmadulina. Translation copyright © 1990 by F. D. Reeve. Reprinted by permission of Henry Holt and Company, Inc.

ANNA AKHMATOVA, "Cinque," from *20th Century Russian Poetry*, Kozmik Press Ltd., 1985. Translated by Richard McKane. Distributed in the United States by Seven Hills, 49 Central Ave., Cincinnati, OH 45202. Reprinted by permission of Kozmik Press.

ROSANNE YAMAGIWA ALFARO, "Professor Nakashima and Tomiko Cat," from *Home to Stay*, 1990 (Footworks). *The Greenfield Review Press*. Reprinted by permission.

TEWFIK AL-HAKIM, *The Donkey Market*, translated by Denys Johnson-Davies. © 1981 by Denys Johnson-Davies. *Egyptian One-Act Plays*, 1981. Heinemann Educational Books, Ltd. and Three Continents Press. Reprinted by permission of Denys Johnson-Davies.

HANAN AL-SHAYKH, "The Persian Carpet," from *Modern Arabic Short Stories*, Three Continents Press, 1988. Edited and translated by Denys Johnson-Davies. Reprinted by permission of Quartet Books Limited.

YEHUDA AMICHAI, "An Arab Shepherd is Searching for his Goat on Mount Zion," from *Poems of Jerusalem* by Yehuda Amichai. Copyright © 1988 by Yehuda Amichai. Translation by Chana Bloch. Reprinted by permission of HarperCollins Publishers.

GLORIA ANZALDÚA, "Cervicide," from *Borderlands/La Frontera*. © 1987 by Gloria Anzaldúa. Reprinted by permission of aunt lute books (415) 558-8116.

INÉS ARREDONDO, "The Shunammite," translated by Alberto Manguel, from *Other Fires: Short Fiction by Latin American Women*, edited by Alberto Manguel, published by Clarkson N. Potter Inc., 1986.

JOAQUIM MARÍA MACHADO DE ASSIS, "A Canary's Ideas," from *The Devil's Church and Other Stories* by Joaquim María Machado de Assis, translated by Jack Schmitt and Lorie Ishimatsu. Copyright © 1977, by permission of the University of Texas Press.

JIMMY SANTIAGO BACA, "Spliced Wire," from *What's Happening*. © 1982 by Jimmy Santiago Baca. Curbstone Press. Reprinted by permission.

MURRAY BAIL, "The Drover's Wife," from *Contemporary Portraits* by Murray Bail published by University of Queensland Press, 1975. Reprinted with permission.

IMAMU AMIRI BARAKA, "An Agony. As Now," from *The Dead Lecturer*, 1964, published by Grove Press. Copyright © 1964 by Imamu Amiri Baraka. Reprinted by permission of Sterling Lord Literistic, Inc.

FRANÇOIS BARCELO, "The Man Who Stopped Trains," from *Intimate Strangers*, 1986. Penguin Books Canada Limited. English translation © by Matt Cohen, 1986. Reprinted by permission of the author and translator.

NEIL BISSOONDATH, "Insecurity," from *Digging Up the Mountain*, © 1984, Macmillan Canada, a division of Canada Publishing Corporation. Reprinted by permission.

EAVAN BOLAND, "Anorexic," from *Selected Poems, 1990*. Reprinted by permission of the author.

JORGE LUIS BORGES, "Afterglow," from *Jorge Luis Borges Selected Poems 1923–1967* by Jorge Luis Borges. Copyright © 1968, 1969, 1970, 1971, 1972 by Jorge Luis Borges. Emece Editores, S. A. and Norman Thomas Di Giovanni. Translated by Norman Thomas Di Giovanni. Used by permission of Delacorte Press/Seymour Lawrence, a division of Bantam Doubleday Dell Publishing Group, Inc.

GRACE CAROLINE BRIDGES, "Lisa's Ritual, Age 10," by Grace Caroline Bridges, was originally published in *Looking for Home: Women Writing about Exile* (Milkweed Editions, 1990). Reprinted by permission of the author.

JOSEPH BRODSKY, "A Halt in the Desert," from *Selected Poems* by Joseph Brodsky. Copyright © 1973 by Joseph Brodsky. Reprinted by permission of Farrar, Straus & Giroux, Inc.

DINO BUZZATI, "The Falling Girl." Excerpt from *Restless Nights* by Dino Buzzati, translation copyright © 1983 by Lawrence Venuti. Published by North Point Press and reprinted by permission of Lawrence Venuti.

ALBERT CAMUS, "The Guest." Excerpt from *Exile and the Kingdom* by Albert Camus, translated by J. O'Brien. Copyright © 1957, 1958 by Alfred A. Knopf, Inc. Reprinted by permission of the publisher.

ERNESTO CARDENAL, "The Swede." Copyright © 1965 Ernesto Cardenal. Translated by John Lyons. Copyright © 1992 John Lyons. Reprinted by permission.

PETER CAREY, "The Last Days of a Famous Mime," from *The Fat Man in History* by Peter Carey as published by Random House, 1981. Copyright © 1981 by Peter Carey. Used by permission of the author.

ROSARIO CASTELLANOS, "Chess," from A *Rosario Castellanos Reader,* edited and translated by Maureen Ahern. Fondo de Cultura Económica. Copyright © 1988. Reprinted by permission of the University of Texas Press.

ANA CASTILLO, "Napa, California," from *Women Are Not Roses.* Copyright © by Ana Castillo 1984. Originally published by Arte Publico Press. Reprinted by permission of Susan Bergholz Literary Services, New York.

RAHEL CHALFI, "Porcupine Fish," from *Contemporary Israeli Literature,* edited by Elliott Anderson. Translated by Robert Friend, 1977. Reprinted by permission of the author.

KIM CHI-WŎN, "A Certain Beginning," from *Words of Farewell: Stories by Korean Women Writers,* 1989. English translation copyright © 1989 by Bruce and Ju-Chan Fulton. Reprinted by permission of The Seal Press.

KATE CHOPIN, "Désirée's Baby," from *The Awakening and Other Stories* by Kate Chopin, edited by Lewis Leary. Holt, Rinehart & Winston, Inc., 1970. Reprinted with permission.

JUDITH ORTIZ COFER, "The Woman Who Was Left at the Altar," from *Reaching the Mainland,* included in *Triple Crown* (1987). Bilingual Press/Editorial Bilingüe (Arizona State University, Tempe, AZ). Reprinted by permission.

JULIO CORTÁZAR, "Letter to a Young Lady in Paris," from *End of the Game and Other Stories* by Julio Cortázar, translated by P. Blackburn. Copyright © 1967 by Random House, Inc. Reprinted by permission of Pantheon Books, a Division of Random House, Inc.

LÉON DAMAS, "Hiccup," from *Negritude: Black Poetry From Africa and The Caribbean,* edited and translated by Norman Shapiro. Copyright © 1970 by Norman R. Shapiro. Reprinted by permission of October House.

MAHASWETA DEVI, "Giribala," from *Of Women, Outcastes, Peasants, and Rebels: A Selection of Bengali Short Stories,* Bardhan, Kalpana, ed. Copyright © 1990. Reprinted by permission of the University of California Press.

RITA DOVE, "The Wake," from *Grace Notes, Poems by Rita Dove,* copyright © 1989 by Rita Dove. Reprinted by permission of W. W. Norton & Company, Inc.

SLAVENKA DRAKULIĆ, "Pizza in Warsaw, Torte in Prague," from *How We Survived Communism and Even Laughed* by Slavenka Drakulić . Reprinted by permission of W. W. Norton & Company, Inc. Copyright © 1991 by Slavenka Drakulić.

CHRISTOPHER DURANG, *Sister Mary Ignatius Explains It All For You.* © 1980, 1982 by Christopher Durang. Dramatists Play Service, Inc., 1982. Reprinted by permission of Helen Merrill, Ltd.

NAWAL EL-SAADAWI, "The Mutilated Half," from *The Hidden Face of Eve: Women in the Arab World,* Zed Books, 1980. Edited and translated by Dr. Sherif Hetata. Reprinted with permission of Beacon Press.

LOUISE ERDRICH, "The Bingo Van." Copyright © 1990 by Louise Erdrich. Originally published in *The New Yorker.* Reprinted by permission of the author, c/o Rembar and Curtis.

SANDRA MARÍA ESTEVES, "Weaver." "Weaver" first appeared in *Yerba Buena* by Sandra Mara Esteves; Chapbook #47. The Greenfield Review Press; Greenfield Center, New York 12833, 1980. Reprinted by permission of the author.

DARIO FO, *We Won't Pay! We Won't Pay!* © 1980, 1984 by Dario Fo and R. G. Davis. Translated by R. G. Davis. Samuel French, Inc. Reprinted by permission of Michael Imison Playwrights, Ltd.

ELENI FOURTOUNI, "Child's Memory," from *Greek Women Poets*, 1978. Reprinted by permission of the author and Thelphini Press.

XU GANG, "Red Azalea on the Cliff." From *Three Hundred Lyric Poems by Modern Young Poets* in *The Red Azalea: Chinese Poetry Since the Cultural Revolution*, edited by Edward Morin. Translated by Fang Dai, Dennis Ding, and Edward Morin. University of Hawaii Press, Honolulu, © 1990. Reprinted by permission of the University of Hawaii Press.

NABIL GORGY, "Cairo Is a Small City," from *Modern Arabic Short Stories*, Three Continents Press, 1983. Edited and translated by Denys Johnson-Davies. Reprinted by permission of Quartet Books Limited.

ALASDAIR GRAY, "The Crank That Made the Revolution," by Alasdair Gray, from *Unlikely Stories Mostly*, 1983. Reprinted with permission of Canongate Press PLC.

AMLIN GRAY, *How I Got That Story.* Nelson Doubleday "Fireside Theater Series." 1981. Reprinted by permission of the author.

WILLIAM HARRISON, "Roller Ball Murder," from *Roller Ball Murder and Other Stories*, 1974. Reprinted by permission of the author.

VÁCLAV HAVEL, *Protest*, from *The Vanck Plays*, Faber and Faber, Inc. 1990. © 1978 Václav Havel. Translated by Vera Blackwell. © 1984 by Vera Blackwell. Rowohlt Theater Verlag, Rheinbeck, Fed. Rep. of Germany. Reprinted by permission of Sanford J. Greenburger Associates and Robert Lantz-Joy Harris Literary Agency.

BESSIE HEAD, "Looking for a Rain God," from *The Collector of Treasures*. Copyright © 1977 by Bessie Head. Reprinted by permission of Heinemann Educational Books Ltd. and the author's agent, John Johnson, Ltd.

ZBIGNIEW HERBERT, "Preliminary Investigation of an Angel." © 1968 by Zbigniew Herbert. English translation © 1968 by Czeslaw Milosz and Peter Dale Scott. From *The Selected Poems* by Zbigniew Herbert, first published by The Ecco Press in 1986. Reprinted by permission.

LINDA HOGAN, "Workday," from *Harper's Anthology of 20th Century Native American Poetry*, edited by Duane Niatum, 1988. Harper & Row, Publishers, Inc. Reprinted by permission of the author.

LINDA HOGAN, "Hearing Voices," from *The Writer and Her Work: New Essays in New Territory, Volume II*, edited by Janet Sternburg, 1991. W. W. Norton & Co., Inc. Reprinted by permission of the author.

GARRETT HONGO, "Who Among You Knows the Essence of Garlic?" Reprinted from *Yellow Light*, © 1982 by Garrett Hongo. Wesleyan University Press. By permission of University Press of New England.

DIANA DER HOVANESSIAN, "Looking at Cambodian News Photos" from *Songs of Bread, Songs of Salt* © Diana Der-Hovanessian, 1991. Ashod Press, New York City. Reprinted by permission of the author.

CHENJERAI HOVE, "You Will Forget," from *Red Hills of Home* by Chenjerai Hove, 1990. Reprinted by permission of Mambo Press.

TED HUGHES, "Examination at the Womb-Door" from *Crow* by Ted Hughes. Copyright © 1971 by Ted Hughes. Reprinted by permission of HarperCollins Publishers.

KERI HULME, "Unnamed Island in the Unknown Sea," from *Contemporary New Zealand Short Stories*, Penguin Books, Ltd., 1989. Victoria University Press, Wellington. Reprinted by permission.

DAVID HENRY HWANG, *The Dance and the Railroad*. © 1982, 1983 David Henry Hwang. Dramatists Play Service. Reprinted by permission of Helen Merrill, Ltd.

PANOS IOANNIDES, "Gregory," from *The Charioteer, A Review of Modern Greek Literature*. Copyright © 1989 by Panos Ioannides. English language translation © 1989 by Marion Byron and Catherine Raizis. Copyright © Pella Publishing Co., Inc. Reprinted by permission.

ULFA IDELBI, "Seventy Years Later," from *Opening the Gates: A Century of Arab Feminist Writing*, 1990, Indiana University Press, edited by Margo Badran and Miriam Cooke. Translated by Simone Fattal. Reprinted with permission.

P'AN JEN-MU, "A Pair of Socks with Love," from *Bamboo Shoots After the Rain: Contemporary Stories by Women Writers of Taiwan*, 1985. Edited by Ann C. Carver and Sung-Sheng Yvonne Chang, 1990. Translated by Chen I-djen. The Feminist Press at The City University of New York. Reprinted with permission of The Taipei Chinese Center, International P.E.N.

CHARLES JOHNSON, "China," from *The Sorcerer's Apprentice* by Charles Johnson, copyright © 1986 by Charles Johnson. Reprinted with the permission of Atheneum Publishers, an imprint of Macmillan Publishing Company.

ANNA KAMIEŃSKA, "Funny," from *Polish Poetry of the Last Two Decades of Communist Rule: Spoiling Cannibals' Fun*, edited by Stanislaw Baranczak and Clare Cavanaugh, 1991. Translated by Mieczyslaw Jastrun. Reprinted by permission of Northwestern University Press.

DORIS KAREVA, "To make one life visible," from *Child of Europe: A New Anthology of East European Poetry*, edited Michael March. Penguin Books Ltd., © 1990 by Michael March. Translated by T. H. Ilves. Reprinted by permission of Michael March.

JULIA KASDORF, "Mennonites," by Julia Kasdorf was published in *Looking for Home: Women Writing about Exile*, Milkweed Editions, 1990. The poem first appeared in *West Branch* #24. Reprinted by permission of the author.

MAHDOKHT KASHKULI, "The Button," from *Stories by Iranian Women Since the Revolution*, translated by Soraya Sullivan, 1991. Center for Middle Eastern Studies, University of Texas. Reprinted by permission of the publisher.

MAURICE KENNY, "Sometimes . . . Injustice," from *The Mama Poems*, 1984, White Pine Press, copyright © 1984. Reprinted by permission of the publisher.

DANIEL KEYES, "Flowers for Algernon," (short story version), © 1979 by Mercury Press, Inc. Reprinted from *The Mazazine of Fantasy and Science Fiction*. © 1959, 1987, by Daniel Keyes. Reprinted by permission of the author.

ETHERIDGE KNIGHT, "Hard Rock Returns to Prison from the Hospital for the Criminal Insane" by Etheridge Knight, 1986. Reprinted with permission of Broadside Press.

CARMEN NARANJO, "And We Sold the Rain," from *And We Sold the Rain: Contemporary Fiction from Central America*, 1989, edited by Rosario Santos. Translated by Jo Anne Engelbert. © Translation copyright 1988 by Jo Anne Engelbert. Reprinted with permission of Four Walls Eight Windows.

PABLO NERUDA, "Goodbyes," from *Fully Empowered* by Pablo Neruda. Translation copyright © 1967, 1970, 1975 by Alastair Reid. Reprinted by permission of Farrar, Straus and Giroux, Inc.

ABIOSEH NICOL, "Life Is Sweet At Kumansenu," from *The Truly Married Woman and Other Stories*, 1965. Copyright © by Oxford University Press, 1965. Reprinted by permission of Harold Ober Associates, Incorporated.

ITABARI NJERI, "Hair Piece," from *Every Good-Bye Ain't Gone* by Itabari Njeri. Copyright © 1990 by Itabari Njeri. Reprinted by permission of Times Books, a Division of Random House, Inc.

YAMBO OUOLOGUEM, "When black men's teeth speak out" by Yambo Ouologuem, from *Negritude: Black Poetry From Africa and The Caribbean*, edited and translated by Norman Shapiro. Copyright © 1970 by Norman R. Shapiro. Reprinted by permission of October House.

SEMBENE OUSMANE, "Her Three Days," from *Tribal Scars* by Sembene Ousmane. Heinemann Educational Books, Portsmouth, NH, 1974. Translated by Len Ortzen. Reprinted by permission of the author.

OCTAVIO PAZ, "The Day of the Dead," from *Labyrinth of Solitude* by Octavio Paz, translated by Lysander Kemp. Copyright © 1962, 1990 by Grove Press, Inc. Used by permission of Grove Press, Inc.

OCTAVIO PAZ, "The Street," 1963. From *Spanish-American Literature in Translation*, published by Crossroad Publishing Company. Copyright © Crossroad/Continuum Publishing Company. Translated by Willis Knapp Jones. Reprinted with permission.

ELENA PONIATOWSKA, "The Night Visitor" translated by C. S. White-House. Originally appeared in *De noche vienes* (Stories), Grijalbo Press, 1979. From *Other Fires: Short Fiction by Latin American Women*, edited by A. Manguel, Clarkson N. Potter, 1986. English translation copyright © 1986 by Albert Manguel. Reprinted by permission of the author.

VASKO POPA, "The Lost Red Boot," from *Vasko Popa: Complete Poems*, translated by Anne Pennington, revised and expanded by Francis R. Jones, and published by Anvil Press Poetry in 1993. Reprinted by permission of the publisher.

JAN RABIE, "Drought," translated from the Afrikaans by the author, from *The Penguin Book of Southern African Stories*, edited by Stephen Gray. Penguin Books, Ltd. 1962. Reprinted by permission of the author.

SABINE REICHEL, "Learning What Was Never Taught." Excerpt from *What Did You Do in the War, Daddy?* by Sabine Reichel. Copyright © 1989 by Sabine Reichel. Reprinted by permission of Hill and Wang, a division of Farrar, Straus & Giroux, Inc.

ADRIENNE RICH, "Your Small Hands," Poem VI of "Twenty-One Love Poems," from *The Dream of a Common Language, Poems 1974–1977*, by Adrienne Rich, by permission of W. W. Norton & Company, Inc. Copyright © 1978 by W. W. Norton & Company, Inc.

YANNIS RITSOS, "Greek Carters," from *The Fourth Dimension*. Reprinted with permission of the American Friends of the Jewish Museum of Greece in memory of Rae Dalven.

SHEILA ROBERTS, "The Weekenders," from *A Land Apart*, edited by Andre Brink and J. M. Coetzee, Penguin, 1987. Reprinted by permission of the author.

MURIEL RUKEYSER, "Myth," from *Out of Silence*, 1992 Tri-Quarterly Press. © Muriel Rukeyser, by permission of William L. Rukeyser.

SHIRLEY SAAD, "Amina" from *Opening the Gates: A Century of Arab Feminist Writing*, 1990, Indiana University Press. Edited by Margot Badran and Miriam Cooke. Reprinted with permission.

NELLY SACHS, "Chorus of the Dead," from *The Seeker* by Nelly Sachs. Translated by Ruth and Matthew Mead. Copyright © 1970 by Farrar, Straus and Giroux, Inc. Reprinted by permission of Farrar, Straus & Giroux, Inc.

BHISHAM SAHNI, "We Have Arrived in Amritsar," from *The Penguin Book of Modern Indian Short Stories*, edited by Stephen Alter and Wimal Dissanayake. Translated by the author. Penguin Books India, 1989. Reprinted by permission of the author.

TAYEB SALIH, "The Cypriot Man," from *Modern Arabic Short Stories*, Three Continents Press, 1988. Edited and translated by Denys Johnson-Davies. Reprinted by permission of Quartet Books Limited.

MILCHA SANCHEZ-SCOTT, *The Cuban Swimmer*. © 1984 by Milcha Sanchez-Scott. Dramatists Play Service. Reprinted with permission of The William Morris Agency.

LEONARD SCHRADER, "Kiss of the Spider Woman: The Screenplay" by Leonard Schrader. © 1987 by Leonard Schrader, based on the novel *Kiss of the Spider Woman* by Manuel Puig, translated by Thomas Colchie. Reprinted by permission of Faber and Faber, Inc.

NTOZAKE SHANGE, "Betsey Brown," from the book *Betsey Brown*. Copyright © 1985 by Ntozake Shange. Reprinted with permission from St. Martin's Press, Inc., New York, N.Y.

LESLIE MARMON SILKO, "Language and Literature from a Pueblo Indian Perspective," from Fiedler and Baker (Eds.) *English Literature: Opening Up the Canon*, 1979. Copyright © 1979 by The Johns Hopkins University Press. Reprinted by permission of the publisher.

LENNART SJÖGREN, "The Roses," from *Four Swedish Poets*, 1990. Translated by Robin Fulton. Reprinted by permission of White Pine Press.

CATHY SONG, "'The Youngest Daughter," from *Picture Bride* by Cathy Song, 1983. Reprinted by permission of Yale University Press.

FERNANDO SORRENTINO, "The Life of the Party," from *Sanitary Centennial and Selected Short Stories*, by Fernando Sorrentino, translated by Thomas Meehan, Copyright © 1988 by the University of Texas Press. By permission of the author and the publisher.

JEAN-YVES SOUCY, "The Red Boots." Translated by Matt Cohen. English translation © 1986 by Matt Cohen, from *Intimate Strangers*, Penguin Books Canada Limited, 1986. Reprinted by permission of the author and translator.

WOLE SOYINKA, *The Lion and the Jewel*, © 1963 Wole Soyinka. Reprinted from

Wole Soyinka's *Collected Plays 2* (1974), by permission of Oxford University Press.

DAL STIVENS, "Warrigal." 1976. Reprinted by permission of Curtis Brown (Aust.) Pty. Ltd.

WISŁAWA SZYMBORSKA, "An Opinion on the Question of Pornography," from *Polish Poetry of the Last Two Decades of Communist Rule: Spoiling Cannibals' Fun*, edited and translated by Stanislaw Baranczak and Clare Cavanaugh, 1991. Reprinted by permission of Northwestern University Press.

NGUYEN CHI THIEN, "I Kept Silent." 1989. Translated by Nguyen Huu Hieu. Reprinted by permission of Index on Censorship.

VIKTORIA TOKAREVA, "Nothing Special," from *Balancing Acts: Contemporary Stories by Russian Women*. Edited and translated by Helena Goscilo. Indiana University Press, 1989. Reprinted by permission.

FADWA TUQAN, "I Found It," from *A Mountainous Journey: A Poet's Autobiography*. Arabic copyright by Fadwa Tuqan, 1985. Translated by Naomi Shihab Nye and Salma Khadra Jayyusi, 1990. Reprinted by the permission of Graywolf Press, Saint Paul, Minnesota.

LUISA VALENZUELA, "The Censors," translated by David Unger, from *Open Door* by Luisa Valenzuela, North Point Press. Copyright © 1988 by Luisa Valenzuela. Reprinted by permission of Harold Ober Associates, Inc.

LUISA VALENZUELA, "Writing with the Body," translated by Janet Sternburg and Cynthia Ventura, from *The Writer on Her Work, Volume II: New Essays in New Territory*, edited by Janet Sternburg, 1991. W. W. Norton & Co., Inc. Copyright © 1991 by Janet Sternburg. Reprinted by permission of Harold Ober Associates Inc.

KRISHNAN VARMA, "The Grass-Eaters," first published in *Wascana Review*. Copyright © 1985 by Krishnan Varma. Reprinted with permission.

DIANE WAKOSKI, "The Orange," from *Medea the Sorceress*, 1991. Reprinted by permission of Black Sparrow Press.

MITSUYE YAMADA, "I Learned to Sew," from *Desert Run: Poems and Stories*, Kitchen Table: Women of Color Press. Copyright © 1988 by Mitsuye Yamada. Used by permission of Kitchen Table: Women of Color Press, P. O. Box 908, Latham, N.Y. 12110 and the author.

WILLIAM BUTLER YEATS, "The Second Coming," from *The Poems of W. B. Yeats: A New Edition*, edited by Richard J. Finneran. Copyright 1924 by Macmillan Publishing Company, renewed 1952 by Bertha Georgie Yeats. Reprinted with permission of Macmillan Publishing Company.

EVGENY ZAMYATIN, "The Lion," from *The Penguin Book of Russian Short Stories*, translated by David Richards, 1939. Reprinted by permission of David Richards.

Glossary

ABSTRACT LANGUAGE   describes ideas, concepts, or qualities rather than specific persons, places, or things.

ACTION   the process by which characterization and plot develop, including physical and psychological events, that is, words and deeds as well as characters' expressed inner thoughts.

ALLEGORY   a type of narrative in which characters, events, and even the setting represent particular qualities, ideas, or concepts. (*See* Fable, Parable, and Symbol.)

ALLITERATION   the repetition of similar or identical sounds at the beginning of words or in accented syllables. Alliteration is used to underscore similarities and contrasts.

ALLUSION   a brief reference in a literary work to a real or fictional person, place, thing or event that the reader might be expected to recognize. (*See* Context and Reader Expectation.)

AMBIGUITY   a phrase, statement, or situation that may be understood in two or more ways.

ANALOGY   a comparison drawn between two basically different things that have some points in common, often used to explain a more complex idea in terms of a simpler and more familiar one. (*See* Metaphor and Symbol.)

ANTAGONIST   a character who opposes the protagonist's completion of his or her goal.

ARCHETYPES   themes, images, and narrative patterns that are universal and embody recurring features of human experience. Archetypal characters are, e.g., hero and scapegoat; an archetypal situation is, e.g., a quest. (*See* Myth and Symbol.)

ASSONANCE   the repetition of vowel sounds in a line, stanza, or sentence.

ASSUMPTIONS   the knowledge, values, and beliefs a reader brings to a text.

BIOGRAPHICAL CONTEXT   the facts and circumstances of the author's life that are relevant to the work.

BLANKS   (*See* Gaps.)

CAESURA   a pause introduced into the reading of a line of poetry unmarked by punctuation.

CHARACTERIZATION   technique a writer uses to create and reveal personalities of characters in a work of literature, usually by describing the characters' appearance, by directly ascribing character "traits," by presenting characters' actions, by revealing the characters' thoughts, or showing the reactions of other characters to them. In fiction, the *narrator* is a particular kind of character who relates events without necessarily having participated in them. In poetry, the *speaker* performs much the same function. (See Dynamic Characters, Flat Characters, Narrator, Round Characters, Speaker, Stock Characters, and Static Characters.)

CLIMAX   the high point of emotional intensity in a work of literature.

COMEDY   in drama, the representation of situations that are designed to be entertaining and in which humor is achieved by reversing what is expected.

COMMEDIA DELL'ARTE   broadly humorous farce developed in sixteenth-century Italy, featuring stock characters, humorous situations, and improvised dialogue.

COMPLICATION   the introduction of an obstacle that impedes the objectives of the protagonist.

CONFLICT   any of the various kinds of oppositions between a protagonist and an antagonist in a work of literature.

CONNOTATION   the emotional implications a word may suggest, as opposed to its literal meaning.

CONSONANCE   repetition of the final consonant sounds and stressed syllables. (*See* Assonance.)

CONTEXT   the surrounding situation that affects a literary work, including the writer's life and the political, historical, and social environment. (*See* Biographical Context, Historical Context, Literary Context, Psychological Context, Social Context.)

CONTEXTUAL SYMBOLS   a person, object, or event that acquires a more than literal meaning solely from the context of the work, also known as private, authorial, or personal symbols.

CONTROLLING IMAGE   an image or metaphor that determines the organization of an entire poem. (*See* Figurative Language and Metaphor.)

CRISIS   the point of highest tension in a work that precipitates an irrevocable outcome; often the result of a choice made by the protagonist. (*See* Climax.)

CULTURE   the totality of practices and institutions and the entire way of life of the people who produce them. In a narrow sense, specific aesthetic productions of literature, art, and music.

DENOTATION   the literal meaning of a word as found in the dictionary. (*See* Connotation.)

DESCRIPTIVE POETRY   poetry in which the external world is presented in visual terms of color, shape, form, and depth.

DIALOGUE   a conversation between characters. (*See* Monologue.)

DICTION   the choice of words in a work of literature and an element of style important to the work's effectiveness. (*See* Style and Tone.)

DRAMA   a literary work written to be acted on a stage.

DRAMATIC POETRY   poems that take the form of confrontations between characters, staged to suggest events are happening at the moment.

DRAMATIC POINT OF VIEW   action presented without a narrator commenting on the events or characters; also called the objective point of view.

DYNAMIC CHARACTERS   characters whose behavioral traits appear to change in response to events and experiences as opposed to static characters who change little, if at all.

EPIPHANY   an incident or event that evokes a sudden significant insight into the profound meanings of a situation.

ESSAY   a relatively brief prose discussion on a particular theme or subject.

EXPOSITION   the presentation of background material about the characters or the situation in a story, play, or poem, which supplies information necessary to understand events that follow: may appear either at the beginning or progressively throughout the work.

FABLE   a short tale that illustrates a moral whose characters are frequently animals who speak and act like human beings. (*See* Allegory.)

FAIRY TALE   a story frequently from the oral tradition that involves the help or hindrance of magical persons such as fairies, goblins, trolls, and witches.

FARCE   a type of comedy, usually satiric, that relies on exaggerated character types, slapstick, and other types of ridiculous behavior and situations that result from a contrived plot that makes use of surprises and coincidences.

FICTION   a mode of writing that constructs models of reality in the form of imaginative or mental experiences that are not literally true in the sense that they did not actually occur in the "real" world.

FIGURATIVE LANGUAGE   the use of words outside their literal or usual meanings, used to add freshness and suggest associations and comparisons that create effective images; includes figures of speech such as hyperbole, irony, metaphor, personification, and simile.

FIRST-PERSON NARRATOR   a narrator who is part of the story and refers to himself or herself as "I."

FLASHBACK   an interruption in the major action of a story, play or essay to show an episode that happened at an early time used to shed light on characters and events in the present by providing background information.

FLAT CHARACTERS   characters presented in terms of a single behavioral trait. (*See* Round Characters.)

FOLKTALE   a traditional story about common people from a culture's oral tradition.

FORESHADOWING   the technique of giving the reader, listener or viewer of a story or play a hint, clue or indication of what direction the plot will take in the work.

FREE VERSE   poetry that sets no set patterns of rhyme, meter or line length.

GAPS   absences of or missing information in a text that different readers will fill in or complete in different ways.

GENRE   a type of literary work defined by particular characteristics of form or technique—for example, the short story, novel, screenplay, poem, play, or essay.

HISTORICAL CONTEXT   applies to when the work was written and the time period in which it is set in terms of the applicable economic, social, political, and cultural values.

HYPERBOLE   a figure of speech involving great exaggeration used to emphasize strong feeling and to create a satiric or comic effect.

HYPOTHESIS (pl.: hypotheses)   the reader's provisional conjecture or anticipation of what will happen next; an essential element in the reader's interaction with the text. (*See* Reader Expectation.)

IMAGERY   in a basic sense, the use of language to convey sensory experience; most often refers to the creation of pictorial images through figurative language. (*See* Literal Imagery and Figurative Language.)

INFERENCE   a reasonable conclusion about the behavior of a character or the meaning of an event drawn from the details supplied by the author.

INTERTEXTUALITY   the influence of one literary text upon another, or reference to one text that occurs in another—for example, Rukeyser's "Myth" refers to *Oedipus Rex* by Sophocles.

IRONY, IRONIC   a contrast between appearance and reality, what is and what ought to be. *Dramatic irony* occurs when the reader or viewer can derive meaning from a character's words or actions that are unintended by the character. *Situational irony* occurs when circumstances turn out contrary to what is expected. *Verbal irony* is the contrast between what is said and what is actually meant, frequently used as a device in satire.

LIMITED OMNISCIENT POINT OF VIEW   narrative restricted to the perspective of a single major or minor character.

LITERAL IMAGERY   images that directly present the experience of the physical world through the senses.

LITERARY CONTEXTS   literary works by others that may have influenced the author; also includes the literary conventions prevailing at the time the work was composed that may have influenced the author's conceptions of plot, character, and other elements.

LITERATURE   a term that has come to stand for imaginative writing of high quality although it should be recognized that the term is an evaluative designation, not an absolute category.

LYRIC, LYRIC POETRY   a short poem expressing an intense, basic personal emotion, such as grief, happiness, or love; poetry in which we seem to overhear the thoughts and feelings of the speaker. Also called reflective poetry.

MAGICAL REALISM works in which mundane reality is displaced by fantastic, bizarre, or supernatural occurrences.

METAPHOR a figure of speech that implies comparison between two fundamentally different things without the use of "like" or "as." It works by ascribing the qualities of one to the other, linking different meanings together, such as abstract and concrete, and literal and figurative. (See Figurative Language.)

METER recurrent patterns in verse of accented and unaccented or stressed and unstressed syllables that create patterns of rhythm and emphasis. Meter is measured in units called feet of which the most typical types in English are *iambic* (in which an accented or stressed syllable is preceded by an unaccented or unstressed syllable); *trochaic* (a stressed syllable followed by an unaccented syllable); *anapestic* (two unstressed syllables followed by a stressed one); *dactylic* (a stressed syllable followed by two unstressed ones); *spondaic* (two accented syllables). A line of poetry with two feet is known as *dimeter*; with three feet, *trimeter*; with four feet, *tetrameter*; with five feet, *pentameter*. *Iambic pentameter* is the most common English metrical pattern. Poetry without a recognizable metrical pattern is called *free verse*.

MONOLOGUE a long speech by one character in a literary work.

MONTAGE a French term that means "mounting"; refers to the way a film is edited to create meaning by juxtaposing contrasting shots.

MOOD the atmosphere and feeling that a writer creates through the choice of setting, imagery, details, descriptions, and evocative words. (*See* Tone.)

MYTH ancient stories that set out a society's religious or social beliefs, that often embody and express a culture's assumptions and values as expressed through characters and images that are universal symbols. (*See* Archetypes.)

NARRATIVE an account of an actual or fictional event, or series of events, unique in that the time covered by the events in the narrative may or may not coincide with the time it takes to narrate them. (*See* Action and Plot.)

NARRATOR refers to the ostensible teller of a story, who may or may not have participated in the events he or she narrates.

OCTAVE an eight-line stanza that can stand alone or as the first eight lines of a fourteen-line sonnet.

OBJECTIVE POINT OF VIEW *See* Dramatic Point of View.

OMNISCIENT NARRATOR a narrator who knows everything about the characters and events and can move about in time and place as well as from character to character and enter the mind of any character.

ONE-DIMENSIONAL CHARACTERS (also known as Stereotyped or Flat Characters) characters whose personalities are centered around only one or two traits.

ONOMATOPOEIA   the use of words whose sounds suggest their sense.

PARABLE   a short, simple story that is designed to teach a moral.

PARADOX   a seemingly self-contradictory statement that may nevertheless be true.

PERSONA   a term that refers to the *voice*, and implied personality, the author chooses to adopt in order to tell the story in poetry or fiction. The persona may serve as a projection of views quite different from the author's. Persona literally means "actor's mask." (*See* Speaker and Voice.)

PERSONIFICATION   a figure of speech in which human characteristics are attributed to nonhuman things.

PLOT   a series of related events that present a conflict leading to a climax or point at which the conflict must be resolved. Conflicts may be external against characters, society, or the forces of nature, or internal between opposing emotions, such as between duty and conscience. (*See* Action, Complication, Conflict, Crisis, Exposition, Resolution, and Structure.)

POEM   a literary form that emphasizes rhythm and figurative language. Often used to express emotions. (*See* Lyric, Meter, and Rhyme.)

POINT OF VIEW   the perspective from which the events in a story are related; a story may be related in either the first-person ("I") or the third-person ("he," "she," or "they"). A first-person *narrator* is a character who tells the story he or she participated in or directly observed. The observations and inferences of such a narrator may be reliable, as far as they go, or unreliable. A third-person *omniscient narrator* stands outside the events of the story, but allows the reader unlimited access to the characters' thoughts and feelings and may comment on the story or characters; so too, the third-person *limited omniscient narrator* is not directly involved in the story and restricts the reader's access to the thoughts of one or two of the characters. The third-person *objective narrator* also stands outside the events of the story, but only reports, without comment, what the characters say and do without giving the reader access to any of the character's thoughts. (*See* Dramatic Point of View, First-Person Narrator, Limited Omniscient Point of View, Omniscient Narrator, and Third-Person Narrator.)

PROSODY   includes the theory and principles of the elements that make up poetry; refers to accent, rhythm, meter, rhyme, and stanza form.

PROTAGONIST   main character in a short story, play, or novel opposed by an adversary, or antagonist, who may be another character, the forces of fate, chance, nature, or any combination of these.

PSYCHOLOGICAL CONTEXT   the relevant conscious or unconscious motivations of the writer as these impulses, desires, and feelings influence the emotions and behavior of the characters.

READER EXPECTATION   the mental process by which readers form hypotheses and fill in gaps in the text. (*See* Assumption, Hypothesis, Inference.)

REALISM   a nineteenth-century literary movement that aims to depict life without artificiality or exaggeration. It uses ordinary language and focuses on ordinary people, events and settings, all of which are described in great detail.

REFLECTIVE POETRY   *See* Lyric Poetry.

RESOLUTION   the concluding events of the plot that bring the work to its conclusion.

RESPONSE STATEMENT   an essay that records the reader's reactions to a text, and explores the personal, literary, and cultural assumptions underlying those reactions.

RHYME   the repetition of similar or identical sounds to unify parts of a poem to emphasize important words or lines.

RHYTHM   the arrangement of stressed and unstressed sounds in speech and writing.

ROUND CHARACTERS   characters presented in terms of a complex variety of personality traits as opposed to a single behavioral trait. Rounded characters are psychologically complex in that they often embody conflicting impulses that make them seem more real.

SATIRE   a technique that ridicules both people and societal institutions, often in an effort to bring about social reform. Exaggeration, wit, and irony are frequent devices used by satirists.

SCENE   a division of an act in a play that may be long or short, serve as a transition or even have an inner dramatic structure of setting up and resolving a conflict comparable to the dramatic structure of the play itself.

SCREENPLAY   a motion picture script, the form of a play written as the basis for a film, which gives the sequence of actions making up the plot, dialogue, and description of camera angles, settings, music, and sound effects.

SCRIPT   the printed text of a play, including dialogue and stage directions.

SESTET   a six-line unit that can stand alone as a stanza or as the concluding six lines of a fourteen-line sonnet.

SETTING   the time and place in which the action of a story or play takes place. It may serve simply as a background or it may help create the atmosphere from which the story evolves and may even affect the plot's development.

SHORT STORY   a short work of narrative prose fiction that generally involves a small number of characters in a limited number of settings.

SIMILE   a figure of speech involving a direct comparison between two unlike things and using the words *like* or *as*.

SOCIAL CONTEXT   the relevant social conditions and the effect of social forces as they influence the depiction of characters and classes of people in literary works; it includes economic and political circumstances as well as the effects of culture, race, class, power, and gender.

SOLILOQUY   a long speech to the audience by one character in the absence of other characters, in which he or she shares private thoughts and feelings. (*See* Monologue.)

SONNET   a lyric poem of fourteen lines. In general, the sonnet establishes some issue in the first eight lines (octave) and then resolves it in the next six lines (sestet).

SPEAKER   the narrator of a poem; often a separate character created for the purpose of relating the events in a poem from a consistent point of view. (*See* Persona.)

STANZA   the grouping of a fixed number of verse lines in a recurring metrical and rhyme pattern.

STATIC CHARACTERS   Characters who change little if at all over the course of the work.

STEREOTYPE   a standardized conventional character, story line, or setting.

STOCK CHARACTERS   Conventional character types who appear through the ages in many different forms of literature; for example, the cruel stepmother, the servant-confidante, the court jester.

STRUCTURE   the fundamental organization or framework of a piece of writing, including both the principles underlying the form and the form itself. For example, in stories the plot is the structural element; in plays the divisions into acts and scenes express the inner dramatic structure; and in poetry the formal arrangement into stanzas that develop a specific sequence of images and ideas forms the structure.

STYLE   the author's characteristic manner of expression. Style includes the types of words used, their placement, as well as the distinctive features of tone, imagery, figurative language, sound, and rhythm.

SURREALISM   a movement in modern literature and art that emphasizes the expression of the imagination as manifested in dreams; stresses the subconscious, often through the unexpected juxtaposition of symbolic objects in mundane settings.

SUSPENSE   the feeling of psychological tension experienced by the reader or spectator in anticipation of learning the outcome of a developing sequence of events.

SYMBOL   something concrete, such as an object, person, place, or event, that stands for or represents something abstract, such as an idea, quality, concept, or condition. The symbol can be emphasized by repetition and position. (*See* Contextual Symbols, Archetypes.)

SYNTAX   the pattern or structure of the word order in a sentence or phrase; the study of grammatical structure.

TEXT   in the literal sense, the work itself, whether novel, poem, play, or story; can also include the work and its interpretations, which change from reader to reader or for the same reader over time.

THEATER OF THE ABSURD   a movement in the theater that dramatizes the contrast between humanity's desire for a sense of meaning and purpose and the incoherence, purposelessness, and illusion of everyday life; a kind of theater that challenges conventional assumptions underlying realistic drama.

THEME   an underlying important idea in a literary work. It may be stated or implied. Literary works commonly have more than one theme. The reader's reactions determine in large part which themes are perceived as important.

THESIS   the position taken by a writer, often expressed in a single sentence, that an essay develops or supports.

THIRD-PERSON NARRATOR   a narrator who is usually an anonymous objective observer who refers to characters as "he," "she," or "they." Also called the limited omniscient point of view.

TONE   the writer's attitude towards the subject or audience, which may or may not be identical with the work's emotional atmosphere. (*See* Mood.)

TRAGEDY   usually, a drama about a noble person whose character is flawed by a single weakness which inevitably leads to his or her downfall or destruction.

TRAGIC FLAW   in drama, the flaw in the character of the protagonist that leads to his or her downfall.

TURNING POINT   *See* Crisis.

UNDERSTATEMENT   a figure of speech that represents something as less important than it really is. Used as a form of irony. (*See* Irony.)

UNIVERSAL SYMBOLS   *See* Archetypes.

VOICE   an imagined projection of a speaker in a literary work (usually a poem), sometimes identified with the author. (*See* Persona and Speaker.)

Geographical Index

1085

CENTRAL AMERICA

EUROPE

MIDDLE EAST

NEW ZEALAND

NORTH AMERICA

Index of Authors and Titles

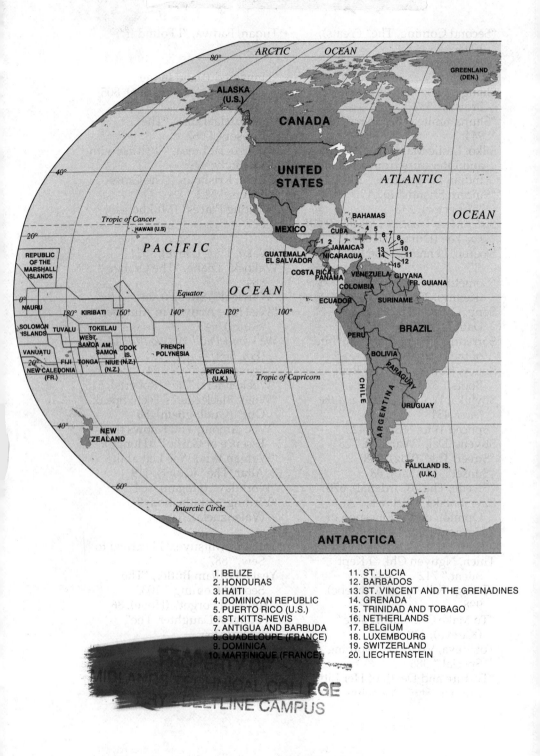

1. BELIZE
2. HONDURAS
3. HAITI
4. DOMINICAN REPUBLIC
5. PUERTO RICO (U.S.)
6. ST. KITTS-NEVIS
7. ANTIGUA AND BARBUDA
8. GUADELOUPE (FRANCE)
9. DOMINICA
10. MARTINIQUE (FRANCE)

11. ST. LUCIA
12. BARBADOS
13. ST. VINCENT AND THE GRENADINES
14. GRENADA
15. TRINIDAD AND TOBAGO
16. NETHERLANDS
17. BELGIUM
18. LUXEMBOURG
19. SWITZERLAND
20. LIECHTENSTEIN